CASES AND MATERIALS

FEDERAL WEALTH TRANSFER TAXATION

SIXTH EDITION

by

PAUL R. MCDANIEL
James J. Freeland Eminent Scholar in Taxation and Professor of Law
University of Florida Levin College of Law

JAMES R. REPETTI
William J. Kenealy, S.J. Professor of Law
Boston College Law School

Paul L. Caron
Associate Dean of Faculty and Charles Hartsock Professor of Law
University of Cincinnati College of Law

FOUNDATION PRESS
2009

THOMSON REUTERS

© 1977, 1982, 1987, 1999, 2003 FOUNDATION PRESS
© 2009 By THOMSON REUTERS/FOUNDATION PRESS

195 Broadway, 9th Floor
New York, NY 10007
Phone Toll Free 1–877–888–1330
Fax (212) 367–6799
foundation–press.com

Printed in the United States of America

ISBN 978–1–59941–044–9

 TEXT IS PRINTED ON 10% POST CONSUMER RECYCLED PAPER

*To: Susan, Jane, Tom, Caroline,
Cleo, and Memore*
J.R.R

*

PREFACE

The sixth edition of Federal Wealth Transfer Taxation, like its predecessors, is a coursebook designed to examine the structure—and the policies that undergird that structure—of the federal wealth transfer tax system. We believe it is important for the student to understand the role a particular rule does or should perform in a transfer tax system viewed as an integral whole. The emphasis, therefore, is not primarily on estate planning, which focuses on the uses to which the tax advisor may put the rule. On the other hand, the ingenuity of tax planners in exploring—or exploiting—existing tax rules may reveal structural problems, theretofore unnoticed or unappreciated by those concerned with formulating tax policy. Therefore tax planning materials have been included where they seemed helpful both in illustrating the estate planner's approach and in exposing areas requiring further attention by policymakers.

The present volume reflects case law, administrative developments, and legislative changes in the wealth transfer tax system through January 1, 2009.

This volume continues the prior format in discussing within each topic both the estate and gift tax provisions applicable to a particular type of transfer. This approach, we continue to believe, is sound because we feel that a fully unified transfer tax (in which transfers during life and at death are treated the same) is the norm against which existing law should be analyzed. Concurrent consideration of present estate and gift tax rules pertaining to a particular type of transfer facilitates consideration of the need for and the form of a completely unified transfer tax.

Any organizational format is, however, a matter of judgement. Therefore, we have attempted to present the materials in a manner that allows for individual preferences of teachers of taxation of wealth transfers. The materials can readily be used in rearranged form by those who prefer to treat the estate and gift taxes separately and by those who prefer to deal with the various provisions in the order set forth in the Code.

We recognize that there are almost as many techniques for teaching taxation of wealth transfers as there are teachers of the subject. An effort has been made, therefore, to present the materials in a form that can be readily adapted to different classroom approaches, whether that be the case method, the problem method, the clinical method or some combination thereof. And, just as teachers of transfer taxation employ differing pedagogical techniques, they approach the subject with different objectives in mind.

Some stress breadth of substantive coverage; others emphasize detailed technical analysis of the statutory, regulatory, and case materials; still others focus primarily on the social and economic policies that underlie the technical tax provisions. It is our hope that the arrangement and content of the present volume will permit the use of any, or a combination, of these approaches. But the editorial effort—as well as the constraints of the time allotted for the course—in turn places on the individual instructor the task of selecting the material that can be conveniently covered to achieve the course objectives.

This book is, of course, intended to be used in conjunction with the Internal Revenue Code of 1986 and Treasury Department Regulations issued thereunder.

As to editorial details, the statutory references throughout are to the 1986 Code. Accordingly, the references in the cases and materials to the 1954 Code or prior statutes generally have been edited to conform to the 1986 Code. Ordinarily, the change is to omit the 1954 Code or other citation and to refer to it in brackets as "the former version," "the predecessor of," or in some instances simply to give the 1986 Code section if there has been no significant change in the statutory language. Where a significant change has occurred, that fact is noted and the prior language is given. The statutory and regulatory references at the head of each topic are not intended to be exhaustive. Rather, they represent only the essential portions of the Code and Regulation which the student must understand to obtain the framework for the cases and materials under the particular topic. Footnotes in cases and materials very frequently have been omitted. Editorial footnotes for cases and materials are so designated and are generally starred.

We are indebted to Amelia Gray, Joshua Gutierrez, David Koonce, Brad Sagraves, Richard Segal, and Kevin Walker for research and editorial assistance. We also thank Jonathan Hixon for assistance in preparing the manuscript.

PAUL R. McDANIEL
JAMES R. REPETTI
PAUL L. CARON

January, 2009

ACKNOWLEDGMENTS

We gratefully acknowledge the permission extended by the following authors and publishers to reprint excerpts from the works listed (numbers in parenthesis indicate the pages on which the excerpts appear):

Matthew Bender & Company, Inc.: Browne, Effect of Elections by an Executor Upon the Estate and Upon the Beneficiaries (1965) (reprinted by permission from the New York University Proceedings of the Twenty–Third Annual Institute on Federal Taxation) (p. 797)

Frederic G. Corneel: The Duty of Loyalty in Estate Planning and Administration (unpublished paper, 1976) (p. 807)

Wojciech Kopczuk and Emmanuel Saez, Top Wealth Shares in the United States, 1916–2000: Evidence From Estate Tax Returns, NBER Working Paper No. 10399 (March 2004) (p. 38)

Michigan Law Review: Polasky, Marital Deduction Formula Clauses in Estate Planning–Estate and Income Tax Considerations (Copyright 1965 by The Michigan Law Review Association. Reprinted with permission) (p. 629)

Real Property, Probate and Trust Journal: Chason & Danford, The Proper Role of the Estate and Gift Taxation of Closely Held Businesses (1997) (p. 794); and Report of Committee on Tax Aspects of Decedents' Estates, Liability of Fiduciaries and Transferees for Federal Estate and Gift Taxes (1967) (p. 804)

Tax Law Review: Corneel, Ethical Guidelines for Tax Practice, (1972) (p. 757); and Repetti, Minority Discounts: The Alchemy in Estate and Gift Taxation (1995) (p. 776)

Tax Lawyer: Report of the Special Task Force on Formal Opinion 85–352 (1986) (p. 811)

Trust & Estates Magazine: Johnson & Rosenfeld, Factors Affecting Charitable Giving: Inferences from Estate Tax Returns (1991) (p. 583); and Casner, Estate and Gift Tax Changes (1964) (p. 707)

United Nations University–WIDER: Davies, Sandström, Shorrocks, and Wolff, The World Distribution of Household Wealth, Discussion Paper No. 2008/03 (Feb. 2008) (p. 40)

Virginia Law Review: Gutman, Reforming Federal Wealth Transfer Taxes After ERTA (1983) (pp. 787, 795)

*

SUMMARY OF CONTENTS

TABLE OF CONTENTS

TABLE OF CASES, REVENUE RULINGS AND PROCEDURES

Principal cases are in bold type. Non-principal cases are in roman type. References are to Pages.

*

FEDERAL WEALTH TRANSFER TAXATION

*

PART I

Overview of the Federal Wealth Transfer Tax System

CHAPTER 1

AN HISTORICAL REVIEW

SECTION A.   INTRODUCTION

Taxation of wealth transfers is only one element in our overall system of federal taxation. An examination of the revenue history of the United States discloses, however, that taxation of wealth transfers closely parallels the expansion or contraction of the federal taxing power into or out of other areas. The financial history of our nation is directly related to its political and social history. Economic, social, or political forces have dictated the revenue needs of the federal government.

Taxes must be collected. From whom and how are important questions that are resolved by Congress. The changing character of revenue sources and the degree to which any particular source is drawn upon are a part of our economic, political, and social history. Congress has had to decide to what extent, if any, the federal revenues should be derived from a tax on imports, on sales of real or personal property, on corporate income, on individual income, on transfers of property and the like. Whether transfers of property should be occasions for taxation at all, and if so, to what extent, is one of the choices which Congress has had to make. Resolution of that issue identified those on whom the federal tax burden was to fall and, to a certain degree, the standard of living of the classes affected by the Congressional decision. Groups developed to influence the legislative choice are fairly permanent in their composition. The final legislative choice inevitably is affected by the pressures that these groups are able to exert upon members of Congress. To that extent the federal tax system has reflected and today reflects the alignment of political strength among the various classes and forces of the country.

SECTION B.   FROM 1789 TO THE CIVIL WAR

During the pre-Civil War period the federal government relied almost entirely on customs receipts for its revenues. In 1789–91 total revenue receipts were $4,418,913, while $4,399,473 were from customs receipts. In 1862, total collections were $51,987,456, of which customs receipts comprised $49,056,398. Only once during this period did Congress levy any tax on the transfer of property—in 1798 a rudimentary death tax in the form of a stamp duty on receipts given for the payment of bequests of shares in intestate estates was imposed. This tax was in effect for only four years and was of no revenue significance. In 1815 further consideration was given to this form of federal taxation. As a result of increased expenditures prompted by the War of 1812, the Secretary of the Treasury recommended to

Congress in 1815 the enactment of an inheritance tax, but the war's end in that same year mooted the recommendation.

SECTION C.   THE CIVIL WAR PERIOD

The Civil War greatly expanded federal expenditures, which Congress sought to fund with a variety of taxes. In 1861 Secretary of the Treasury Chase recommended an inheritance tax to Congress. As a result, the inheritance tax made its initial appearance in our federal revenue system in the Act of 1862. The tax applied only to transfers of personal property; rates were graduated according to the relationship between beneficiary and decedent and were proportioned to the amount of the share. The inheritance tax was subsequently extended to transfers of real property, and the rates were increased to help meet rising war costs.

The first inheritance tax of this period produced rates ranging from 3/4 of 1% to 5%. The Revenue Act of 1864 raised rates slightly. Upon review, the Supreme Court determined that this levy was an excise tax and sustained its constitutionality. Scholey v. Rew, 90 U.S. (23 Wall.) 331 (1874). The federal inheritance tax was repealed in 1870 when no longer needed for large wartime revenues, but it was inevitable that, having once appeared, it would return in some form. During the next four decades, despite efforts to revive the inheritance tax, excise taxes on liquor and tobacco and customs receipts accounted for more than 90% of total federal revenue receipts. But groups representing classes and forces in our society were forming and exerting pressure on Congress to adopt other forms of taxation.

SECTION D.   1870–1916: FURTHER CONGRESSIONAL EXPERIMENTATION

Although the clamor for an income tax far outweighed any demand for an inheritance tax during the 1870's and 1880's, both taxes were gaining the backing of political forces whose power was increasing. Finally, in 1894, largely as a result of the Democratic coalition of the agrarian interests of the West and South and of the working and middle classes, which won ascendancy over the Democrats of the East and the Republicans, Congress reduced tariffs and enacted an income tax statute. The 1894 statute taxed income at a rate of 2%, with a $4,000 exemption; personal property received by gift or inheritance was treated as income subject to the tax. The Supreme Court in 1895 concluded that the tax was a direct tax and held it unconstitutional for lack of apportionment among the states. Pollock v. Farmers' Loan & Trust Co., 157 U.S. 429, rehearing, 158 U.S. 601 (1895). The decision swept away the income taxation of gifts and inheritances.

But the inheritance tax had gained a stronger foothold in the country's tax thinking. In 1898 Congress again enacted a death tax, which was a mixture of an estate tax and an inheritance tax.[1] The tax rate was progressive with respect to the size of the decedent's total estate, and was also graduated according to the relationship of the beneficiaries and heirs to the decedent. In 1900 the Supreme Court upheld the constitutionality of the statute, but construed it as applying rates based only on the shares of the individual beneficiaries and heirs and not on the size of the decedent's total estate. Knowlton v. Moore, 178 U.S. 41 (1900). The tax thus became only an ordinary inheritance tax. As was the case at the conclusion of the Civil War period, the end of the Spanish–American War and the lessening pressure on expenditures resulted in abolition of the inheritance tax in 1902.

Stronger groups continued to advocate resurrection of the federal income and inheritance taxes, but not just for the sake of raising revenue. They also wished to check the trend toward concentration of wealth through inheritance. Andrew Carnegie, in his essay, "The Gospel of Wealth," argued that parents left great fortunes to their children only because of misguided affection, and that the evils inherent in an institution of inheritance far outweighed its few benefits. President Theodore Roosevelt strongly supported a heavily progressive inheritance tax as a means of decreasing the concentration of wealth. The proponents of an income tax were at last successful in 1913 with the passage of the 16th Amendment and the enactment of the income tax. The opponents of the tax again took the issue to the courts, but this time they were defeated. Brushaber v. Union Pacific Railroad Co., 240 U.S. 1 (1916) (sustaining the statute).

Section E.   1916–1939: Development of a Basic Structure

The entry of the United States into World War I created revenue needs which made inevitable the return of some form of death taxation. Congress in 1916 enacted an estate tax based upon the value of the decedent's net estate rather than upon the values of the separate shares passing to heirs and distributees or devisees and legatees. The rates initially imposed ranged from 1% on the first $50,000 of a net estate to 10% on the net estate in excess of $5 million. The question of the constitutionality of the 1916 estate tax was settled by the Supreme Court in New York Trust Co. v. Eisner, 256 U.S. 345 (1921). Relying upon its decision in Knowlton v. Moore, the Court upheld the validity of the estate tax provisions of the 1916 Revenue Act as constituting an indirect tax not requiring apportionment among the states. The 1916 Act set the estate tax pattern which continued until 1976, although rates and exemptions varied and changes

---

1. In general, an estate tax is imposed on the transmission of wealth and the applicable rates are unaffected by the relationship between the transferor and transferee; an inheritance tax also is imposed on the transmission of wealth but the rates vary according to the relationship between the transferor and transferee.

were made from time to time to make the tax more effective in producing revenue and to achieve other nonfiscal purposes.

By 1916 most of the states had already enacted either an inheritance tax, an estate tax, or a tax embodying the principles of both. Despite the federal government's entrance into the death tax field immediately thereafter, state revenues from this source steadily increased. But the failure of some states to enact a death tax and the disparity in rates among the states that did resulted in a marked lack of uniformity. Wealthy persons often changed their domicile in their later years to states in which no death tax was imposed. To bring about uniformity among the states, Congress in the Revenue Act of 1924 allowed a credit against the federal estate tax for death taxes paid to the states. Originally, this credit was limited to 25% of the federal estate tax; it was increased to 80% by the Revenue Act of 1926. The credit device has promoted some uniformity in the total death tax burden of decedents irrespective of the state in which they die domiciled. Differences remain, however, because the death taxes of many states exceed the maximum allowable credit in varying degrees and other states have moved to impose only so-called "sponge" taxes designed to "soak up" an amount equal to the federal tax credit.

As soon as the estate tax became law, wealthy persons sought to avoid its provisions by transferring their property before death. Congress was at first unsuccessful in its attempts to apply the estate tax to these transfers, partly because of the then-prevailing attitude of the Supreme Court of the United States. Because of the difficulty of applying the estate tax to inter vivos transfers, and because the Republicans wished to reduce the surtax rates for the top income brackets, the gift tax entered our federal revenue system.

The tax on gifts imposed by the Revenue Act of 1924 applied to all gifts made after June 2, 1924. This gift tax was repealed, effective as of January 1, 1926, by the Revenue Act of 1926. Congress, however, added a provision to the estate tax that all gifts made within two years before death were presumed to be gifts made in contemplation of death, and therefore includible in the decedent's gross estate. On March 21, 1932, the Supreme Court held this two-year conclusive presumption unconstitutional. Heiner v. Donnan, 285 U.S. 312 (1932). In anticipation of this decision, the Ways and Means Committee of the House of Representatives had already recommended that the tax on gifts be restored. As a result, a gift tax, applicable to all gifts made after June 6, 1932, was imposed by the Revenue Act of 1932. This gift tax included a cumulative feature lacked by its 1924 predecessor: the tax on any gift by a donor was determined by adding the amount of the gift to prior taxable gifts and imposing the progressive gift tax rates.

By 1932 the country had entered into the depression years. Reduced tax yields from shrinking national income and increasing expenditures brought about deficits. Congress, in trying to stem the deficits, not only adopted the gift tax and increased the income tax rates, but also strengthened the estate tax by imposing an "additional estate tax," against which the credit for state death taxes did not apply. Clearly, 1932 was a watershed year: Congress decided that the transfer taxes should be an important source of revenue to the federal government.

Franklin D. Roosevelt's presidential message of 1935 gave further impetus to the then popular movement to effect a greater distribution of the national wealth by breaking up great fortunes. Reiterating the philosophy of Andrew Carnegie and Theodore Roosevelt, the President said:

"The desire to provide security for one's self and one's family is natural and wholesome, but it is adequately served by a reasonable inheritance. Great accumulations cannot be justified on the basis of personal and family security. In the last analysis such accumulations amount to the perpetuation of great and undesirable concentrations of control in a relatively few individuals over the employment and welfare of many, many others.

"Such inherited economic power is as inconsistent with the ideals of this generation as inherited political power was inconsistent with the ideals of the generation which established our government.

" * * * A tax upon inherited economic power is a tax upon static wealth, not upon that dynamic wealth which makes for the healthy diffusion of economic good.

"Those who argue for the benefits secured to society by great fortunes invested in great business should note that such a tax does not affect the essential benefits that remain after the death of the creator of such a business. The mechanism of production that he created remains. The benefits of corporate organization remain. The advantage of pooling many investments in one enterprise remains. Governmental privileges such as patents remain. All that is gone is the initiative, energy and genius of the creator—and death has taken these away."

The Revenue Act of 1935, enacted soon after the President's speech, imposed estate taxes at rates ranging from 2% to 70%.

Enactment of the Internal Revenue Code in 1939 represented a major structural improvement in the estate and gift tax provisions. This single Code contained all the then-current estate and gift tax provisions. Subsequent legislation was therefore to be in the form of amendments to the Code.

Section F.   1940–1947: World War II Period

This period was an era of great activity in federal revenue legislation. The withholding system converted the income tax into a mass tax. New excises were added to the revenue system, although most have since been repealed.

The estate and gift tax pattern, however, had already become fairly stabilized. With a few substantive changes, slight increases in the rates, and some decreases in the exemptions, this pattern continued throughout this period, except for the attempted equalization of the incidence of the transfer taxes between community property and common law states. The latter result was effected by the Revenue Act of 1942. When the husband died first in a community property state, his estate, instead of including only one-half the community property, was required to include all community property owned by husband and wife except that received by his surviving spouse as compensation for her individual services or traceable to such compensation or her separate property. When the wife died first, however, one-half the community property was made taxable to her estate, since under the law of community property states she had the right to dispose of one-half the community property by her will. A gift of community property was now also taxed in full to the donor-spouse with the same exception as noted with respect to the estate tax.

Section G. 1948–1976

In 1948 our federal revenue system adopted the "split income" principle, by means of which the combined income of married couples was taxed in an amount equal to twice the tax on one-half of their combined income. The Congressional representatives of the noncommunity property states were extremely anxious to have the split income provisions adopted. As part of the "package" enacted into law, of which split income was a part, marked changes in the estate and gift tax provisions were effected through introduction of the estate and gift tax marital deductions and the principle of split gifts as to married couples—that is, a married couple for gift tax purposes could treat any gift to a third person as being made one-half by each.

In general, the effect on estate and gift taxes was to restore the pre–1942 treatment of community property and to accord "community" treatment to noncommunity property. Thus, regarding community property, the surviving spouse's one-half share was exempt from taxation in the decedent spouse's estate; and as to noncommunity property, the surviving spouse could receive up to 50% of the decedent spouse's estate free of estate tax. Similarly, as to the gift tax on community property, each spouse owned one-half of the community property without any gift tax liability even though the services of only one spouse were the source of the community funds; as to noncommunity property, 50% of any outright gift to the other spouse was exempt from the gift tax.

Legislation affecting the estate and gift taxes during the five years following the 1948 Revenue Act was primarily of a technical nature. The rates of the estate and gift taxes during this period continued to remain stable. They ranged from 3% of the first $5,000 of a net estate to 77% of the net estate over $10 million, and from 2 1/4% of the first $5,000 of net gifts to 57 3/4% of net gifts over $10 million.

The Internal Revenue Code of 1954 made important changes throughout its predecessor Code of 1939. These reforms were most extensive as respects the income tax, although a number of estate and gift tax provisions also were affected. The two decades following enactment of the 1954 Code produced only minor technical revisions in the estate and gift tax provisions.

The 1960's, however, brought increasing interest in thorough-going reform of the wealth transfer tax system. The Treasury Department, in connection with its Tax Reform Studies and Proposals,[2] prepared in 1968 and released in early 1969, recommended a complete revision of the transfer tax system. The major proposals included a change from the then-dual estate and gift tax structure to a unified transfer tax system; revision of the rates to make them more uniformly progressive; redefinition of the taxable unit by providing a complete exemption for transfers between spouses; revision of the rules defining the tax base; taxation of transfers under which outright ownership skips generations (and thus avoids transfer taxation on the "skipped generation"); and liberalization of the tax payment rules for illiquid estates. The Treasury proposals reflected a parallel interest outside government in a major reform of existing estate and gift tax rules and were similar in significant respects to the recommendations of the American Law Institute's Federal Estate and Gift Tax Project.[3]

Section H.   1976 to 2001: Interstitial Reform

The Tax Reform Act of 1976 contained sweeping revisions of the estate and gift tax laws, although most of the reforms fell short of the 1969 Treasury Proposals.[4] The 1976 legislation did not adopt a completely unified transfer tax structure as recommended by the Treasury in 1969. Instead, the Act replaced the existing dual rate structure with a single, unified rate schedule, but retained separate estate and gift tax systems. Total lifetime gifts and transfers at death are cumulated and taxed in the decedent's estate under the unified rate schedule, with credit being given for the gift tax paid on lifetime transfers. The unified rate schedule began at 18% of the first $10,000 of taxable transfers, rising to 70% for taxable transfers above $5 million. A unified tax credit was adopted in lieu of the previous separate estate and gift tax exemptions. The credit, when fully phased in, was $47,000 (the equivalent of a $175,625 exemption). As a result, the first marginal tax rate normally applicable was 32% in the $150,000 to $200,000 bracket. The 1976 Act also provided a preferential

---

2. See U.S. Treasury Department, Tax Reform Studies and Proposals, House Ways and Means Comm. and Senate Finance Comm., 91st Cong., 1st Sess. 331–409 (Comm. Print, 1969).

3. See American Law Institute, Federal Estate and Gift Taxation—Recommendations of the American Law Institute and Reporters' Studies (1969).

4. For discussions of the legislation and the unusual legislative process which produced it, see Surrey, Reflections on the Tax Reform Act of 1976, 25 Clev.St.L.Rev. 303 (1976); McDaniel, The Interaction of Tax Planning and Tax Policy, 19 B.C.L.Rev. 387 (1978).

valuation method in which real property used in a farm or closely held business could be valued on the basis of its current use rather than at its "highest and best use." § 2032A.

The 1976 Act instituted a "generation-skipping" tax, which, in technical structure at least, was distinct from the estate and gift taxes. Under prior law, wealthy individuals could utilize trusts to skip transfer taxes on one or more intervening generations, even though the skipped generations derived substantial economic benefits from and exercised significant control over the trust. As enacted, the generation-skipping tax generally covered all trusts (or similar arrangements) for the benefit of persons two or more generations younger than the transferor. Exceptions were provided, however, for certain trusts for the benefit of children and grandchildren of the grantor and for outright gifts, not involving trusts or similar arrangements, regardless of the number of generations skipped by the transfer. In general, distributions from the principal of a trust that skipped a generation were taxed at the unified transfer tax rate that would have been applicable if the intervening generation (e.g., the parent of the transferor's grandchild) had actually made the transfer. However, the tax generally was to be paid only out of the trust property, not by the skipped generation. An extremely liberal transition rule exempted the principal of irrevocable trusts created on or before April 30, 1976.

The Revenue Act of 1978 included technical provisions correcting defects in the 1976 legislation and a few minor substantive changes in the wealth transfer tax rules.

The elections of 1980 produced a strongly conservative President and, as compared to its immediate predecessors, a much more conservative Congress. The shift in prevailing political philosophy was immediately translated by the Economic Recovery Tax Act of 1981 into sweeping changes in the role and structure of the wealth transfer tax system. Although President Reagan's initial tax program included only income tax proposals, Congress added transfer tax amendments which the President accepted.

The 1981 Act continued the dramatic reduction in the scope of the wealth transfer taxes by increasing, from $175,600 to $600,000, the level at which estates were exempt from tax. Technically, the higher exemption level was established by gradually raising the unified tax credit from $47,000 in 1981 to $192,800 in 1987. The complex marital deduction rules instituted in 1976 were replaced by an unlimited marital deduction that effectively permits deferral of the tax on property transferred to the surviving spouse until the death of that spouse. The increased exemption level, coupled with the step-up in basis rule for income tax purposes, meant that appreciation of up to $600,000 in value in property passing at death was subject neither to income tax nor wealth transfer tax; utilizing the marital deduction, a married couple could transfer $1.2 million of appreciated property as to which neither income nor estate tax is imposed. For property transfers beyond that level, the unlimited marital deduction and the § 1014 basis adjustment rules combine to permanently relieve from income tax all unrealized gains accruing before the death of the second spouse, at the cost at that time of an estate tax on the appreciation occurring between the deaths of the two spouses.

In other changes, the 1981 Act reduced the maximum transfer tax rate from 70% to 50%[5]; increased from $3,000 to $10,000 the amount of gifts that can be made annually to each donee under the present-interest exclusion; and excluded transfers in any amount for the payment of certain educational or medical expenses of a donee.

The Tax Equity and Fiscal Responsibility Act of 1982 (TEFRA) and the Tax Reform Act of 1984 made relatively minor technical changes in the transfer tax provisions. The most important of the substantive changes in the 1984 Act included deferral of the scheduled decrease in the maximum transfer tax rate until 1987, provision of wealth transfer tax rules for no-interest and below-market rate of interest loans, and repeal of the prior exclusion from the estate tax for qualified retirement plan benefits (which had already been limited by TEFRA to $100,000).

The Tax Reform Act of 1986 redesignated the 1954 Code as the Internal Revenue Code of 1986. Although the 1986 Act made sweeping revisions in the income tax structure, it changed the wealth transfer taxes relatively little. The most notable change retroactively replaced the system of taxing generation-skipping transfers introduced in the 1976 Act with a more simple and comprehensive version. Once again, extremely generous exceptions were provided for trusts that were irrevocable before September 26, 1985.

The Omnibus Budget Reconciliation Act of 1987 (OBRA) might be seen as a very modest retrenchment. OBRA again deferred the scheduled decrease to 50% in the maximum transfer tax rate, such that the top marginal rate of 55% remained in effect. Through a new phaseout provision, the very largest wealth transfers lost the benefit of both the unified credit and the "run up the brackets," such that cumulative gifts and death transfers in excess of $21,040,000 were taxed at a flat rate of 55% (in the phase-out range the top marginal rate in effect is increased to 60%). Of great significance, OBRA introduced the first statutory attempt to combat so-called "estate freeze" techniques, whereby an individual seeks to pass future appreciation with respect to property to succeeding generations without transfer tax cost, either present or future. Congress selected as its weapon a highly complex provision, the basic thrust of which was to hold open until death the valuation of property that has been subjected to a "freezing" arrangement and to include the property in the transferor's gross estate.

The Technical and Miscellaneous Revenue Act of 1988 (TAMRA) enacted a 15% excise tax on post-death "excess" distributions from qualified retirement plans; conformed the rates, exemptions and credits applicable to transfers by nonresident aliens to those of U.S. citizens; denied the marital deduction for transfers to a spouse who is not a U.S. citizen, except

---

5. The reduction was phased in ratably over a four-year period, beginning in 1982.

for transfers to a complex new statutory creature styled the "qualified domestic trust" (pronounced Q–DOT); and created a new $100,000 annual exclusion for gifts to a noncitizen spouse. The Revenue Reconciliation Act of 1989 wrought no major transfer tax changes.

Dissatisfaction with the 1987 approach to the "estate freeze" technique led to its retroactive repeal and replacement in the Revenue Reconciliation Act of 1990. The new provisions recognized the root problem as one of gift tax valuation rather than estate tax inclusion. Accordingly, special gift tax valuation rules are applied to the estate freeze and related situations to ensure that future appreciation cannot be transferred free of wealth transfer tax.

Subsequent "revenue reconciliation" acts made mostly minor changes in the estate and gift taxes during the early 1990s. In 1997, however, the Taxpayer Relief Act included several important wealth transfer tax provisions. The exemption equivalent of the unified credit was raised from $600,000 in 1997 to $1 million in 2006:

AMOUNT OF UNIFIED CREDIT AND EXEMPTION EQUIVALENT: 1997–2006		
Year	Amount of Unified Credit	Exemption Equivalent
1997	$192,800	$ 600,000
1998	$202,050	$ 625,000
1999	$211,300	$ 650,000
2000	$220,550	$ 675,000
2001	$220,550	$ 675,000
2002	$229,800	$ 700,000
2003	$229,800	$ 700,000
2004	$287,300	$ 850,000
2005	$326,300	$ 950,000
2006	$345,800	$1,000,000

The 1997 Act also provided two relief provisions for owners of closely-held business interests, effective for decedents dying after 1997. The first was an estate tax exclusion of up to $675,000 for "qualified family-owned business interests." However, after 1998 the maximum exclusion was gradually reduced: it could not exceed the excess of $1.3 million over the exemption equivalent of the unified credit. Thus, in 2006, the maximum estate tax exclusion for qualified family-owned business interests would be $300,000 ($1.3 million maximum less the $1 million exemption equivalent of the unified credit).

The second relief provision amended § 6166, which permits an executor to pay the estate tax attributable to a closely-held business interest in installments over a maximum period of 14 years. The 1997 Act provided a special 2% interest rate for the deferred estate tax attributable to the first $1 million in taxable value of the closely-held business (i.e., the first $1 million above the exemption equivalent of the unified credit). Thus, in

2006, the 2% interest rate would apply to the value of the closely-held business interest between $1 million and $2 million.

Beginning in 1998, various transfer tax provisions are indexed annually for inflation, including the $10,000 gift tax annual exclusion; the $750,000 ceiling on special-use valuations; the $1 million generation-skipping tax exemption;[6] and the $1 million ceiling on the value of a closely-held business eligible for the 2% interest rate on deferred installment payments. Interestingly, there was no provision for indexing the exemption equivalent of the unified credit after it reached $1 million in 2006.

The 1998 IRS Restructuring and Reform Act made "technical corrections" to several of the estate and gift tax provisions of the 1997 Act. The 1998 Act converted the qualified family-owned business exclusion into an elective deduction and redesignated § 2033A as § 2057.[7] Section 2057(a)(1) makes clear that the deduction only applies for estate tax purposes and is not available for gift tax or generation-skipping tax purposes. After the 1998 Act, the maximum § 2057 deduction remained at $675,000, while in this circumstance the exemption equivalent of the unified credit was reduced to $625,000. Thus, in 2006, the maximum § 2057 deduction would result in $62,500 of estate tax savings, after the required reduction in the exemption equivalent of the unified credit.[8]

SECTION I.   THE 2001 ACT: REPEAL (AND RESURRECTION) OF THE "DEATH TAX"

After years of sporadic attempts to repeal the wealth transfer taxes, Congressional Republicans, emboldened by the return of a Republican President to the White House, fortuitous federal budget surpluses, and political consultants who coined the epithet "death tax," succeeded in enacting the Economic Growth and Tax Relief Act of 2001. The 2001 Act gradually increases the amount exempt from estate tax and generation-skipping tax from $1 million in 2002 to $3.5 million in 2009, and reduces the highest tax rate in 1% increments from 50% in 2002 to 45% in 2009. In 2010, the estate tax and generation-skipping tax are repealed. Congress decoupled the gift tax from the estate tax, keeping the gift tax in force

---

6. The 1998 IRS Restructuring and Reform Act clarified the indexation of the GST exemption for different types of GST transfers. § 2631(c).

7. The legislative history explains that because it was unclear whether § 2033A "provides an exclusion of value or an exclusion of property from the estate, and thus it [was] unclear how [§ 2033A] interacts with other provisions in the Internal Revenue Code (e.g., §§ 1014 [step-up in basis for income tax purposes], 2032A [special use valuation], 2056 [marital deduction], 2612 [genera-

tion skipping tax], and 6166 [payment of estate tax in installments])." S. Rep. No. 174, 105th Cong., 2d Sess. 155 (1998).

8. The $375,000 increase in the amount eligible for the family-owned business deduction (from $300,000 under the 1997 Act to $675,000 under the 1998 Act) results in $206,250 of tax savings at the maximum 55% bracket, less the $143,750 increase in estate tax from the reduction in the exemption amount of the unified credit from $1 million to $625,000.

(with a $1 million exemption), ostensibly to prevent taxpayers from shifting assets to family members in lower income tax brackets.

Because Senate Republicans lacked the sixty votes necessary under arcane budget rules to implement tax cuts beyond a ten-year period, the 2001 Act is scheduled to "sunset" in 2010, with the pre–2001 Act tax law returning in force in 2011. As a result, the estate tax and generation-skipping tax are resurrected in 2011, at pre–2001 Act exemption levels and rates:

Exemptions & Rates After 2001 Act			
Year	Estate Tax Exemption	Gift Tax Exemption	GST Tax Exemption	Highest Tax Rate
2002	1,000,000	1,000,000	1,100,000	50%
2003	1,000,000	1,000,000	1,120,000	49%
2004	1,500,000	1,000,000	1,500,000	48%
2005	1,500,000	1,000,000	1,500,000	47%
2006	2,000,000	1,000,000	2,000,000	46%
2007	2,000,000	1,000,000	2,000,000	45%
2008	2,000,000	1,000,000	2,000,000	45%
2009	3,500,000	1,000,000	3,500,000	45%
2010	Tax Repealed	1,000,000	Tax Repealed	35% (Gift)
2011	1,000,000	1,000,000	1,350,000*	55%

* Based on CBO inflation projections.

Virtually no one expects the 2001 Act to unfold as scheduled, with the estate tax repealed in 2010 and resurrected in 2011 and beyond. But since 2001, a political logjam has existed on Capitol Hill, with Democrats and Republicans unable to agree on a course of action. As this edition goes to press, most observers expect President Obama and Congress to break the estate tax deadlock, with the likely reform encompassing a combination of an exemption and rates somewhere in the neighborhood of the 2009 levels. In the absence of a final legislative solution, families (and their counsel) face the formidable task of planning amidst this great uncertainty.[9]

In the unlikely event that estate tax repeal comes to pass, the 2001 Act provides for a modified carryover basis regime in its place. Under the general rule of new § 1022(a), those acquiring property from a decedent take as their basis the lesser of (1) the decedent's basis, or (2) the fair market value of the property at the date of death. Although this provision removes the incentive under existing law for decedents in certain situations to retain appreciated assets until their death in order to pass on a higher income tax basis in the assets to their heirs, Congress permitted a step-up in the basis of assets in two situations. First, § 1022(b) allows an increase of up to $1.3 million in the basis of assets received by any beneficiary.

---

9. The 2001 Act also repealed, as of 2004, the § 2057 qualified family-owned business deduction. In addition, the 2001 Act cynically shifted part of the cost of repeal of the estate tax onto the states by first reducing the current credit for state death taxes in 2002–04 and then replacing the credit with a deduction in 2005–09. § 2011.

Second, § 1022(c) allows an increase of up to $3 million in the basis of assets left to a surviving spouse either outright or as "qualified terminable interest property." As a result, a married couple has available a combined $5.6 million of basis increase in their estates. These amounts are adjusted for post–2009 inflation (§ 1022(d)(3)). However, any basis increase is capped at the fair market value of the asset at the date of death (§ 1022(d)(2)), and there are complex rules requiring that the decedent be treated as the owner of the property at death in order to be eligible for these basis increases (§ 1022(d)(1)). No basis increase is allowed if the decedent acquired the property within three years of death (§ 1022(d)(1)(C)). There are new informational reporting requirements to enforce these carryover basis rules (§ 6018).

The 2001 Act represented an outright rejection of the view espoused by President Franklin Roosevelt. Little concern was expressed in the congressional debates over the social and economic impact of large accumulations of wealth by relatively few families. Whether the present situation represents only a temporary swing in the pendulum of social, economic, and political attitudes in the United States, or whether it points to the permanent demise of the wealth transfer taxes as a revenue-significant element in the overall federal tax structure, remains to be seen. Some preliminary conclusions may be drawn from the materials below. In any event, as in the past, the direction of change in wealth transfer taxation continues to mirror the active socio-political currents in American life.[10]

10. For a vigorous defense of the wealth transfer taxes on economic and political grounds, see Repetti, Democracy, Taxes and Wealth, 76 N.Y.U.L.Rev. 825 (2001) (arguing that wealth transfer taxes decrease dynastic wealth concentration (and thereby contribute to long-term economic growth and to the health of our democratic institutions) and raise revenues without discouraging savings).

CHAPTER 2

THE LEGISLATIVE PROCESS

As history demonstrates, tax legislation is a dynamic process involving frequent revision. It is important to understand the process by which that revision takes place.[1]

Major tax legislation generally originates in response to Presidential recommendations. Sometimes, however, the initial impulse comes from Congress itself. The first Congressional step is generally the holding of a public hearing by the Committee on Ways and Means of the House of Representatives, since, under the Constitution, revenue legislation must originate in the House.[2] Usually the hearing is against a background of these general Presidential or Congressional proposals, but sometimes a particular bill is before the Committee. The first witness is generally the Secretary of the Treasury, who presents considerable tax data and, depending on the existing policy of the President and the Secretary, perhaps the recommendations of the Administration. The principal technical official of the Treasury Department who assists the Secretary in this regard and who is directly responsible for the supervision of tax legislation is the Assistant Secretary for Tax Policy.[3]

The Secretary of the Treasury may be followed by other Administration witnesses, such as the Chair of the Council of Economic Advisors or the Director of the Office of Management and Budget, depending on the nature of the proposals. Then appear representatives of various private interests or even taxpayers themselves who are concerned with the proposed legislation. Academic experts also may testify. This testimony before

1. The federal tax legislative process is discussed in Surrey, The Congress and the Tax Lobbyist—How Special Tax Provisions Get Enacted, 70 Harv.L.Rev. 1145 (1957); Surrey, The Federal Tax Legislative Process, 31 Rec.Bar Ass'n City N.Y. 515 (1976); McDaniel, Federal Income Tax Simplification: The Political Process, 34 Tax L.Rev. 27 (1978); Caron, Tax Myopia, Or Mamas Don't Let Your Babies Grow Up To Be Tax Lawyers, 13 Va.Tax Rev. 517 (1994).

2. Art. 1, Sec. 7, Cl. 1 provides "All Bills for raising Revenue shall originate in the House of Representatives; but the Senate may propose or concur with Amendments as on other Bills." The main body of the Tax Equity and Fiscal Responsibility Act of 1982 consisted of substantial Senate provisions added to a minor bill that had originated in the House. The legislation was attacked in a

declaratory judgment action in which the plaintiff asserted that the legislation violated the Origination Clause. The court held that it lacked jurisdiction to grant declaratory relief with respect to federal taxation and that the action was barred by the Anti–Injunction Act. Klingler v. The Executive Branch, 572 F.Supp. 589 (M.D.Ala.1983).

3. The Assistant Secretary is in charge of the Office of Tax Legislative Counsel and the Office of Tax Analysis. The various Tax Legislative Counsel's Offices consist of staffs of lawyers which continuously consider the policy and technical aspects of proposals for legislative changes, whether originating within or without the Treasury Department. The Office of Tax Analysis is composed of economists who consider the economic aspects of tax issues and furnish revenue estimates.

the Committee is published under the title of Hearings on Tax Reform, or some similar title.

After the public hearings, the Ways and Means Committee meets to make its decisions. All committee meetings are presumptively open to the public and a separate roll call vote is required to close any committee meeting. The Committee in these "mark-up" deliberations determines the main outlines of the bill it desires to report. Its policy decisions are then translated into statutory form by members of the Office of the House Legislative Counsel, which is responsible for drafting almost all important legislation originating in the House. To preserve continuity, the same representatives of this office generally work on tax legislation from year to year. They are assisted in the drafting process by technical representatives from the Treasury, including the Internal Revenue Service, the Staff of the Ways and Means Committee, and the Staff of the Joint Committee on Taxation. A report to accompany the bill, containing material explaining its policies and provisions, known as a Committee Report, is also prepared by this group. The bill and Committee Report are then considered by the Committee and, when approved, are both reported to the House. The bill is generally debated and voted on in the House under a "closed rule" procedure, which generally limits amendments to those offered by the Committee. As a result, the bill as reported by the Committee is generally the bill as passed by the House. The debate, which often touches on the interpretation of particular language in the bill in addition to the general policy, is contained verbatim in the Congressional Record.

A similar procedure then starts in the Senate Finance Committee. The cast of characters, with Senators replacing Representatives, is much the same. The hearings in the Senate proceed against the background of the House action. The Senate Finance Committee in turn makes its policy decisions, which may range from minor amendments of the House bill to a completely different bill.[4] It then reports the House bill, as amended by the Senate Committee, and with an accompanying Senate Finance Committee Report. The debate on the Senate floor is without restriction, and any Senator may propose an amendment dealing with any tax matter. Consequently, those interests seeking changes in the bill endeavor to secure the cooperation of a Senator or Senators in agreement with their objectives, to change the bill on the floor of the Senate.

The bill, with the Senate amendments, then generally goes to a Committee of Conference of the House and Senate composed of the ranking members, by parties, of the House Ways and Means Committee and the Senate Finance Committee.[5] The House and Senate conferees adjust the differences between the two bodies, mainly by compromising on the main issues. The Conference action is then set forth in a Conference Report which states the action on each Senate amendment and contains the

---

4. As in the House, meetings of the Senate Finance Committee are generally open to the public unless closed by a vote of the Committee to discuss specified matters.

5. In some cases, Conference Committee action is unnecessary as the Senate may accept the House bill or the House may accept the Senate amendments.

language of Conference changes. The Report also contains a Joint Explanatory Statement of the Conference Committee by the Managers on the part of the House and the Senate which explains the actions taken, thus performing the function of a Committee Report.[6] The House and Senate act on the Conference Report, and almost always approve it. The final legislation is then sent to the President for action. While revenue bills are usually approved, some have been vetoed with the veto in turn sometimes overridden, and others have become law without signature.

In recent years, the Senate has increasingly influenced this traditional process by involvement in the early stages of tax legislation. In practice, the Senate rarely waits for a completed House bill, but instead simultaneously holds hearings and drafts its own version of tax legislation. On occasion, the Senate begins drafting a bill before the House, in apparent defiance of the Constitution. The Conference Committee then selects among the provisions of the different bills. Recently, the Conference Committee itself has added provisions that appear in neither the House nor the Senate bills, and therefore may not have had critical examination in hearings and committee deliberations. The Constitutional requirement that revenue legislation originate in the House is satisfied by assigning the final bill the number of the original House bill, however different the two may be.

The deficit reduction process that began in 1990 produces only revenue-neutral tax bills. Any revenue-reducing amendment, whether offered on the floor or in Committee, is accompanied by changes increasing revenue by a like amount. This practice makes it increasingly difficult for the tax-writing Committees and the Treasury to draft tax legislation which embodies accepted tax policy principles. As a result, the complexity of tax legislation continues to increase.[7] The IRS Restructuring and Reform Act of 1998 sought to curb this complexity by formalizing the Service's role in the tax legislative process through a "sense of Congress" provision requiring that "during the legislative process, the tax writing committees of Congress should hear from front-line technical experts at the Internal Revenue Service with respect to the administrability of pending amendments to the Internal Revenue Code."

Major tax legislation commonly is followed by a "General Explanation," or "Blue Book,"[8] prepared by the Staff of the Joint Committee on Taxation of the Congress. The General Explanation is not official legislative history. It is, rather, a hindsighted consolidation of the material included in the official Committee Reports that often adds interpretations and positions not reflected in the Committee Reports or that sometimes even contradicts the Reports. Due to the great volume and complexity of recent

6. Committee Reports since 1939 and all tax legislation are reprinted in the Cumulative Bulletin, a semi-annual compilation of the weekly Internal Revenue Bulletins issued by the Internal Revenue Service.

7. For a discussion of the increasingly important role of revenue estimates and distributional tables in the tax legislative process, see Graetz, Paint–By–Numbers Tax Lawmaking, 95 Colum.L.Rev. 609 (1995).

8. The colloquial designation "Blue Book" apparently follows because the U.S. Government Printing Office typically binds the General Explanation within a blue cover.

tax legislation, promulgation of interpretative Treasury Regulations has fallen in arrears. The Joint Committee's General Explanation is in many cases taxpayers' sole source of guidance as to the likely position the government will take in interpreting and applying the new law.[9]

The legislative tools for the tax technician—the sources of legislative history—are evident from this procedure: Presidential messages, Committee hearings, the successive stages of the bill and its amendments, Committee and Conference Reports, the Congressional debates, a Presidential message accompanying action on the bill. Reports of Subcommittees, Treasury Department Statements, Summaries and other material prepared by the Staff of the Joint Committee on Taxation, and press conferences held by Committee Chairs, also provide interpretive material.[10]

In recent years, there has been much debate over the proper role of these legislative history materials in interpreting the Internal Revenue Code.[11] This debate has occurred in the context of differing perceptions of the tax legislative process. Some believe that Congress enacts tax legislation in furtherance of the general public interest.[12] Others adhere to a

---

9. For detailed discussion of the role of the "Blue Book," see Livingston, What's Blue and White and Not Quite as Good as a Committee Report: General Explanations and the Role of "Subsequent" Legislative History, 11 Am.J.Tax Pol'y 91 (1994); Note, The New Gray Area for the "Blue Book" After Robinson v. Commissioner: Twelve Factors to Keep in Mind When Using the Blue Book as a Tool of Statutory Interpretation, 57 Tax Law. 833 (2004).

10. The writers of Committee Reports are occasionally tempted to provide retroactive "clarification" of prior Congressional actions. In Hart v. United States, 585 F.2d 1025 (Ct.Cl.1978), the court held invalid a regulation based on a 1960 Committee Report which purported "to clarify" statutory language adopted in 1954, finding that the Committee Report statements contradicted the plain language of the statute. The court urged the use of corrective legislation to right perceived statutory errors, rather than the constitutionally problematic course of "legislating" by committee report, which the court considered an attempt to usurp the role of the judiciary in interpreting the intent of prior legislation.

11. See Zelenak, Thinking About Nonliteral Interpretations of the Internal Revenue Code, 64 N.C.L.Rev. 623 (1986); Livingston, Congress, the Courts, and the Code: Legislative History and the Interpretation of Tax Statutes, 69 Tex.L.Rev. 819 (1991); Geier, Commentary: Textualism and Tax Cases, 66

Temp.L.Rev. 445 (1993); Caron, Tax Myopia, Or Mamas Don't Let Your Babies Grow Up To Be Tax Lawyers, 13 Va.Tax Rev. 517 (1994); Geier, Interpreting Tax Legislation: The Role of Purpose, 2 Fla.Tax Rev. 492 (1995); Coverdale, Text as Limit: A Plea for a Decent Respect for the Tax Code, 71 Tul. L.Rev. 1501 (1997); Heen, Plain Meaning, the Tax Code, and Doctrinal Incoherence, 48 Hastings L.J. 771 (1997); Jensen, Respect for Statutory Text Versus "Blithe Unconcern": A Reply to Professor Coverdale, 72 Tul.L.Rev. 1749 (1998); Livingston, Practical Reason, "Purposivism," and the Interpretation of Tax Statutes, 52 Tax L.Rev. 677 (1998); Blatt, Interpretive Communities: The Missing Element in Statutory Interpretation, 95 Nw. U.L.Rev. 629 (2001); Schneider, Empirical Research on Judicial Reasoning: Statutory Interpretation in Federal Tax Cases, 31 N.M.L.Rev. 325 (2001); Madison, The Tension Between Textualism and Substance–Over–Form Doctrines in Tax Law, 43 Santa Clara L.Rev. 699 (2003); Cunningham & Repetti, Textualism and Tax Shelters, 24 Va. Tax Rev. 1 (2004); Lavoie, Subverting the Rule of Law: The Judiciary's Role in Fostering Unethical Behavior, 75 U.Colo.L.Rev. 114 (2004); Smith, The Deliberative Stylings of Leading Tax Scholars, 61 Tax Law. 1 (2007).

12. See Birnbaum & Murray, Showdown at Gucci Gulch: Lawmakers, Lobbyists, and the Unlikely Triumph of Tax Reform (1987).

public choice perspective in which Congress acts as a collection of rent-seekers, "selling" legislation to the highest bidders among varying interest groups.[13] Still others are critical of both the public interest and the public choice perspectives on the tax legislative process.[14]

---

13. See Doernberg & McChesney, Doing Good or Doing Well? Congress and the Tax Reform Act of 1986, 62 N.Y.U.L.Rev. 891 (1987); Doernberg & McChesney, On the Accelerating Rate and Decreasing Durability of Tax Reform, 71 Minn.L.Rev. 913 (1987); Roin, United They Stand, Divided They Fall: Public Choice Theory and the Tax Code, 74 Cornell L.Rev. 62 (1988); Holcombe, Tax Policy From a Public Choice Perspective, 51 Nat'lTax J. 359 (1998); Cavanaugh, On the Road to Incoherence: Congress, Economics, and Taxes, 49 UCLA L.Rev. 685 (2002).

14. See Shaviro, Beyond Public Choice and Public Interest: A Study of the Legislative Process as Illustrated by Tax Legislation in the 1980s, 139 U.Pa.L.Rev. 1 (1990); Zelinsky, James Madison and Public Choice at Gucci Gulch: A Procedural Defense of Tax Expenditures and Tax Institutions, 102 Yale L.J. 1165 (1993); McCaffery, Shakedown at Gucci Gulch: The New Logic of Collective Action, 84 N.C.L.Rev. 1159 (2006).

CHAPTER 3

THE ADMINISTRATIVE PROCESS

SECTION A. GENERAL ORGANIZATION OF THE INTERNAL REVENUE SERVICE

The Treasury tax staff is primarily concerned with the formulation of tax policy on behalf of the executive branch of the Government. The Commissioner of Internal Revenue and the officials and employees of the Internal Revenue Service are responsible for the administration of federal tax laws.[1] Prior to 1998, coordination was achieved in theory through the Service's position as an agency within the Treasury Department subject to the supervision of the Secretary. After a year-long study, the National Commission on Restructuring the IRS reported in 1997 that the Treasury in practice had generally provided little consistent strategic oversight or guidance to the Service. The Restructuring Commission recommended, and Congress created, a nine-member Oversight Board within the Treasury Department to oversee the Service in the administration, management, conduct, direction, and supervision of the execution and application of the tax laws. § 7802(c)(1)(A).[2] The Oversight Board does not have any responsibility or authority with respect to the development and formulation of federal tax policy. § 7802(c)(2)(A).

The Internal Revenue Service is divided into a central supervisory and planning organization known as the National Office located in Washington, D.C., and a much larger field organization located in the principal cities of the country.

The Office of Chief Counsel of the Internal Revenue Service is headed by the Chief Counsel, the legal advisor to the Commissioner, who is also appointed by the President, with the consent of the Senate. § 7803(b)(1). Each of its principal operating divisions is supervised by an Associate Chief Counsel. Each division is responsible for such matters as preparing regulations, analyzing legislative proposals, overseeing tax litigation, and preparing rulings on particular issues. The Office of Chief Counsel has a parallel field office structure, whose Regional Counsel are primarily responsible for Tax Court litigation.[3]

1. The Commissioner is appointed by the President, with the advice and consent of the Senate, and may be removed at will by the President. The Commissioner is appointed to a five-year term (§ 7803(a)(1)(A)) and may be reappointed to more than one five-year term (§ 7803(a)(1)(D)).

2. Six of the nine members must be individuals from the private section; the oth-

er three members are the Treasury Secretary (or Deputy Secretary), the Commissioner, and a federal employee (or union representative). § 7802(b).

3. The Justice Department represents the government in tax litigation in other federal courts.

The Service's operating field offices are organized largely on a state-wide basis. Each principal field office is headed by a District Director. Liaison between the operating field offices and the Washington headquarters is maintained through Regional Offices, headed by Regional Commissioners. Each Regional Commissioner supervises the District Directors in the region and has overall responsibility for the revenue activities within the region.

The District Director's offices are those with which the taxpayer and the taxpayer's attorney most frequently deal. There is one office for each state and several offices in the larger states. In addition, local branches of a District Director's office may be maintained in various parts of a state. The District Director is immediately responsible for the administration of the federal taxes. The IRS Restructuring and Reform Act of 1998 created the position of National Taxpayer Advocate, charged with assisting taxpayers in resolving problems with the Service and monitoring local offices of taxpayer advocates. § 7803(c).

The actual collection of taxes is generally the responsibility of the Regional Service Centers. Most taxpayers are required to file their returns with one of the Service Centers. They process tax returns and related documents through the use of data processing systems. Their activities are coordinated with those of the District Director.

SECTION B. ADMINISTRATIVE INTERPRETATION OF THE TAX LAWS

The administrative interpretation of the tax laws takes several forms, extending from general pronouncements to determinations bearing on a particular taxpayer's situation. The highest order of general pronouncement is in the form of a Treasury Regulation. Treasury Regulations are prepared for each of the taxes administered by the Service.[4] They are first made public as Proposed Regulations in accordance with the Administrative Procedure Act, so that interested parties may comment upon them and urge changes.[5] A public hearing may be held. The final Regulations are then issued over the signature of the Commissioner and the Assistant Secretary for Tax Policy and are known as Treasury Decisions. Amendments of Regulations follow the same procedure. Section 7805(b) bars retroactive regulations in most situations.

4. The Regulations appear in Title 26, Code of Federal Regulations, with the Income Tax Regulations designated as Part 1; the Estate Tax Regulations as Part 20; the Gift Tax Regulations as Part 25; the Generation–Skipping Tax Regulations as Part 26; and so on. Each Regulation has the same section number as the Code section to which it relates. Particular sections of the Regulations are cited in this book as "Reg. § ___".

5. Comments submitted in response to a notice of proposed rule-making are available to the public unless required to be kept confidential "under law." Reg. § 601.702(d)(7). A Temporary Regulation also must be issued as a Proposed Regulation and must expire within three years after it is issued. § 7805(e).

Some Regulations are issued pursuant to a specific grant of authority in the Code; these "legislative" Regulations generally are given binding effect by courts.[6] In contrast, most Regulations interpret specific statutory language under the general grant of authority under § 7805; these "interpretive" Regulations are given less deference by courts.[7] In practice, however, the distinction between legislative and interpretative Regulations often breaks down and the precise weight to be accorded Regulations typically will vary depending on the facts and circumstances in individual cases.[8]

The next level of interpretive pronouncement consists of the Service's published rulings. These are rulings on a stated set of facts which usually involve a problem common to a number of taxpayers and generally are issued in response to taxpayer requests for guidance. A reply to a request by a Regional or District office for technical advice on a substantive point may also be the subject of a published ruling. Published rulings issued by the Service are referred to as Revenue Rulings and are designated by two numbers, the first standing for the year of the ruling and the second for the ruling number for that year (e.g., Rev.Rul. 2009–1).[9] The designations "Commissioner Delegation Order No. ___" and "Rev.Proc. (for Revenue Procedure) 2009–1," etc., are used for public statements of internal practices and procedures. Delegation Orders deal with internal procedures. Revenue Procedures deal with procedural aspects of taxpayer contact with the Internal Revenue Service. Revenue Procedures also are used to announce "safe harbors"—circumstances under which the Service will not challenge the taxpayer's position concerning an income or deduction item. These administrative pronouncements are published on a current basis in the Internal Revenue Bulletin and are bound semiannually in Cumulative Bulletins (cited as "C.B." in this book).

Unlike Regulations, published rulings generally are not issued pursuant to the Administrative Procedure Act.[10] As a result, they do not receive the same judicial deference accorded Regulations when challenged by taxpayers.[11] The success of such challenges often depends upon the judicial

---

6. See United States v. Vogel Fertilizer Co., 455 U.S. 16 (1982); Krukowski v. Commissioner, 279 F.3d 547 (7th Cir.2002); Flynn v. Commissioner, 269 F.3d 1064 (D.C. Cir. 2001); UnionBancal Corp. v. Commissioner, 113 T.C. 309 (1999).

7. See Nichols v. United States, 260 F.3d 637 (6th Cir.2001); Tutor–Saliba Corp. v. Commissioner, 115 T.C. 1 (2000).

8. See ABA Section of Taxation Report of the Task Force on Judicial Deference, 57 Tax Law. 717 (2004); Polsky, Can Treasury Overrule the Supreme Court?, 84 B.U.L.Rev. 185 (2004); Hickman, The Need for Mead: Rejecting Tax Exceptionalism in Judicial Deference, 90 Minn.L.Rev. 1537 (2006); Berg, Judicial Deference to Tax Regulations: A Re-

consideration in Light of National Cable, Swallows Holding, and Other Developments, 61 Tax Law. 481 (2008).

9. Rev.Proc. 89–14, 1989–1 C.B. 814, sets forth the standards employed by the Internal Revenue Service for publication of Revenue Rulings and Revenue Procedures.

10. See Hickman, Coloring Outside the Lines: Examining Treasury's (Lack of) Compliance With Administrative Procedure Act Rulemaking Requirements, 82 Notre Dame L.Rev. 1727 (2007).

11. See Davis v. United States, 495 U.S. 472, 484 (1990) ("Although the Service's interpretative rulings do not have the force and effect of regulations * * * we give an

doctrines regarding the weight given to administrative interpretations.[12]

The Commissioner, by delegation from the Secretary of the Treasury, has the authority (§ 7805(b)(8)) to make any interpretive pronouncement of the Treasury nonretroactive. Changes in interpretive pronouncements are accordingly almost always made prospective in application, so as to preserve reliance by taxpayers upon the previous interpretation.[13]

Taxpayers may request an administrative interpretation on prospective transactions, or on completed transactions which are not involved in returns already filed. Generally rulings are issued in response to these requests. In some cases, because the particular issue is deemed too uncertain, or because the matter is regarded as primarily one of fact (e.g., fair market value), no ruling may be issued.[14] These "rulings," generally referred to as "private letter rulings," are issued by the National Office in Washington, D.C. The District Directors are authorized to issue "determination letters" in answer to a taxpayer inquiry if the inquiry relates to a situation governed by clearly established rules.[15] A procedure known as a closing agreement (under § 7121) is available whereby the taxpayer and the Treasury may formally bind themselves to observe a particular interpretation, represented by the result agreed to be accorded to a specified transaction. In some cases, the District Director will ask Washington for "technical advice" in a particular case,[16] in which event the taxpayer involved is afforded an opportunity to file a written statement and obtain a

agency's interpretations and practices considerable weight where they involve a contemporaneous construction of a statute and where they have been in long use.").

12. For example, in Stubbs, Overbeck & Associates, Inc. v. United States, 445 F.2d 1142, 1146–47 (5th Cir. 1971), the court stated: "A ruling is merely the opinion of a lawyer in the agency and must be accepted as such. It may be helpful in interpreting a statute, but is not binding on * * * the courts." In contrast, the court in Johnson City Medical Center v. United States, 999 F.2d 973 (6th Cir. 1993), announced that a revenue ruling is entitled to "some deference" unless it conflicts with the statute, legislative history, or is "otherwise unenforceable." For different views on the proper amount of deference to be afforded revenue rulings, see Galler, Judicial Deference to Revenue Rulings: Reconciling Divergent Standards, 56 Ohio St.L.J. 1037 (1995); Caron, Tax Myopia Meets Tax Hyperopia: The Unproven Case of Increased Judicial Deference to Revenue Rulings, 57 Ohio St.L.J. 637 (1996); Rubin, Private Letter and Revenue Rulings: Remedy or Ruse?, 28 N.Ky.L.Rev. 50 (2000); Gans, Deference and the End of Tax Practice, 36 Real Prop.,Prob. & Tr.J. 731

(2002); Coverdale, Chevron's Reduced Domain: Judicial Review of Treasury Regulations and Revenue Rulings After Mead, 55 Admin.L.Rev. 39 (2003); Pietruszkiewicz, Discarded Deference: Judicial Independence in Informal Agency Guidance, 74 Tenn.L.Rev. 1 (2006).

13. Rev.Proc. 89–14, 1989–1 C.B. 814, states: "When Revenue Rulings revoke or modify rulings previously published * * * the authority of § 7805(b) ordinarily is invoked to provide that the new rulings will not be applied retroactively to the extent that the new rulings have adverse tax consequences to taxpayers."

14. For a list of issues on which the Service ordinarily will not rule, see Rev.Proc. 2008–3, 2008–1 I.R.B. 110.

15. The procedures governing the issuance of private letter rulings and determination letters are described in a Revenue Procedure published as the first Revenue Procedure of each year. See, e.g., Rev.Proc. 2008–1, 2008–1 I.R.B. 1.

16. See Rev.Proc. 2008–2, 2008–1 I.R.B. 90. Changes to this Revenue Procedure are incorporated annually and published as the second Revenue Procedure of the year.

hearing.[17] The National Office also may respond to requests by the District Director for advice through field service advice and chief counsel advisories.

As in the case of other administrative materials, private letter rulings, technical advice memoranda, general counsel memoranda, chief counsel advice, field service advice, and legal advice issued by the associate chief counsel and by field attorneys are made available to the general public on www.irs.gov. Section 6110(j)(3) provides that such written determinations are to have no precedential status, except as otherwise provided by regulations. Another source of administrative interpretation is the Internal Revenue Manual issued by the National Office. The Manual provides guidelines to IRS auditing agents and is available to the public.

17. See Reg. § 601.105(b)(5).

CHAPTER 4

THE JUDICIAL PROCESS

SECTION A. ORIGINAL JURISDICTION

The most important court of original jurisdiction in tax cases is the United States Tax Court, formerly known as the Board of Tax Appeals. It has jurisdiction over taxpayers' appeals from income, estate, and gift tax deficiencies asserted by the Commissioner. All proceedings before it are suits by the taxpayer against the Commissioner, though the latter may assert additional deficiencies in the proceeding before the Court. The hearing is de novo. A taxpayer may file an action in the Tax Court only within the ninety day period following issuance of a statutory notice of deficiency by the Commissioner. The Tax Court has no jurisdiction over taxpayer attempts to obtain a refund of a tax claimed to have been paid erroneously, but once jurisdiction is obtained over a contested deficiency claim, the Tax Court may find that the proper result is a refund to the taxpayer.

Tax Court judges are appointed by the President for terms of fifteen years, and generally are reappointed to office. The court's headquarters is in Washington, D.C., but its judges hold hearings in principal cities. The Commissioner is represented before the Tax Court by the Office of Chief Counsel of the Internal Revenue Service.

Trials in the Tax Court are conducted in accordance with the federal rules of evidence by a single judge who prepares a decision consisting of findings of facts and an opinion.[1] The Chief Judge determines whether the decision is to be reviewed by the entire Court. Decisions reviewed by the entire Court carry greater weight than unreviewed decisions. Memorandum decisions usually, although not always, involve questions turning on factual issues or previously decided legal points and are not generally cited as authorities by the Tax Court or other courts. The decisions, whether or not reviewed, are issued as published decisions, later bound in volumes cited 1–47 B.T.A. and 1 T.C. et seq., or in Memorandum Decisions which are published only unofficially by commercial tax services[2] (and since January 1, 1999 on the Tax Court's web site).[3]

The Service responds to some Tax Court decisions with a notice of acquiescence or non-acquiescence. Acquiescence indicates acceptance of the legal interpretation and/or result of the decision, while non-acquiescence means that the Tax Court's interpretation will not be followed. Acquies-

---

1. Section 7463 provides special informal procedures for taxpayers to contest tax disputes involving $50,000 or less.

2. Citations in this book are to the Commerce Clearing House Tax Court Memorandum Decision reports.

3. http://www.ustaxcourt.gov.

cences and non-acquiescences are published in the Internal Revenue Bulletin.[4]

The other courts of original jurisdiction are the District Courts of the United States and the United States Court of Federal Claims (formerly the Claims Court). The cases in these courts are known as refund suits, in that the taxpayer is seeking to obtain a refund of tax previously paid.[5] The defendant in these courts is the United States. District Court suits generally must be brought in the district in which the taxpayer resides or, in the case of a corporation, in the district in which it has its principal place of business.[6] The District Courts have jurisdiction in any tax case against the United States seeking a refund of tax, regardless of the amount involved. A jury trial may be obtained in these suits. The Court of Federal Claims has jurisdiction over all tax suits against the United States, regardless of amount. There is no jury trial. The government is represented by the Tax Division of the Department of Justice, with advice and assistance from the Chief Counsel's office.

Section 7421(a) provides that no suit shall be maintained in any court for the purpose of restraining the assessment or collection of any tax. Although this section generally prevents such suits, injunctions are permitted under "exceptional circumstances" where the taxpayer proves that the collection of the tax would cause irreparable injury and that under no circumstances could the Government prevail on the underlying merits.[7] The declaratory judgment procedure generally is not available "with respect to federal taxes,"[8] although the Tax Court has been given the power to issue declaratory judgments in actions to determine the tax-exempt status of certain nonprofit organizations (§ 7428), retirement plans (§ 7478), and state and local obligations (§ 7476), and in actions to deter-

---

4. In Quinn v. Commissioner, 524 F.2d 617 (7th Cir.1975), the court held that an outstanding acquiescence in a case in point does not bar the Commissioner from taking a position contrary to the holding in the acquiesced case. The court indicated, however, that in appropriate circumstances it might be "unconscionable" for the Commissioner to take a position contrary to an acquiesced case. See also Cohen & Harrington, Is the Internal Revenue Service Bound By Its Own Regulations and Rulings?, 51 Tax Law. 675 (1998).

5. The District Courts and Court of Federal Claims have jurisdiction over tax refund suits only if the contested liability (including penalties) has been paid in full. Flora v. United States, 362 U.S. 145 (1960). Rocovich v. United States, 933 F.2d 991, 995 (Fed. Cir. 1991), held that where an executor elects under § 6166 to pay the estate tax relating to certain closely held business interests over a 14–year period, the *Flora* rule deprives these

courts of jurisdiction until the installments are paid in full: "While the *Flora* rule may result in economic hardship in some cases, it is Congress' responsibility to amend the law." Congress responded in the IRS Restructuring and Reform Act of 1998 by giving the District Courts and the Court of Federal Claims jurisdiction in this situation. § 7422(j).

6. 28 U.S.C. § 1402(a)(1)–(2).

7. See Enochs v. Williams Packing & Nav. Co., 370 U.S. 1 (1962) (collection of employer withholding taxes could not be enjoined where, on the basis of the record, the government claim was "not without foundation" despite the fact that enforcement of the tax would throw the taxpayer into bankruptcy); Hospital Resource Personnel, Inc. v. United States, 68 F.3d 421 (11th Cir. 1995) (injunction denied even though taxpayer ultimately prevailed in refund claim).

8. 28 U.S.C. § 2201.

mine an estate's eligibility to pay the estate tax in installments under § 6166 (§ 7479(a)).

SECTION B.   APPELLATE JURISDICTION

Appeals from the Tax Court are heard as a matter of right by the Courts of Appeals of the United States, jurisdiction going to the circuit in which the taxpayer resided at the time that the Tax Court petition was filed or, in the case of a corporation, in which it has its principal place of business.[9] The parties may also agree by stipulation to a particular court. If no return was filed, the case is heard by the Court of Appeals for the District of Columbia. Appellate jurisdiction is exercised in the same manner as that over civil actions in District Courts tried without a jury.[10] Appeals from the District Courts in tax cases also go to the Courts of Appeals. Appeals from the Court of Federal Claims go to the United States Court of Appeals for the Federal Circuit. The Government in all appeals is represented by the Tax Division of the Department of Justice.

Acquiescence or non-acquiescence announcements also are issued by the Service concerning District Court, Court of Federal Claims, or Court of Appeals decisions. The Service in some instances will announce by Revenue Ruling whether it agrees or disagrees with a particular decision of these courts.

The decisions of the Courts of Appeals are reviewed by the Supreme Court under the certiorari procedure. Review is generally granted only when an inter-circuit conflict exists or the issue is of unusual importance in the administration of the tax laws. The Supreme Court reviews only a few tax cases a year.[11] The Government is represented by the Office of the Solicitor General of the Department of Justice.

9. The Tax Court follows a decision which is squarely on point issued by the Court of Appeals to which the appeal from the Tax Court decision would go. Golsen v. Commissioner, 54 T.C. 742 (1970).

10. Section 7482(a) provides that Courts of Appeals shall review Tax Court decisions in the same manner as they review District Court decisions in civil actions without a jury. Rule 52(a) of the Federal Rules of Civil Procedure, applicable to review of a District Court's findings in a non-jury case, provides: "Findings of fact shall not be set aside unless clearly erroneous, and due regard shall be given to the opportunity of the trial court to judge the credibility of the witnesses."

The important problem of securing uniformity of tax decisions has periodically spurred recommendations for a single Court of Tax Appeals to review the tax decisions of the District Courts, the Tax Court and the Court of Federal Claims. See Griswold, The Need for a Court of Tax Appeals, 57 Harv. L.Rev. 1153 (1944); Popkin, Why a Court of Tax Appeals is So Elusive, 47 Tax Notes 1101 (1990); Geier, The Tax Court, Article III, and the Proposal Advanced by the Federal Courts Study Committee: A Study in Applied Constitutional Theory, 76 Cornell L.Rev. 985 (1991).

11. For a discussion of the Supreme Court's performance as the final arbiter in superintending the tax law, see Caron, Tax Stories: An In–Depth Look at the Leading Federal Income Tax Cases (2d ed. 2009).

CHAPTER 5

A BRIEF SUMMARY OF TRANSFER TAX PROCEDURE

SECTION A. FILING OF RETURN AND PAYMENT OF TAX

1. GIFT TAX

Taxable gifts are calculated on an annual basis. A taxable gift results once transfers to any donee during a calendar year exceed $13,000 (the 2009 figure, which is adjusted for inflation each year in $1,000 increments) or, in the case of a gift of a future interest, regardless of value. Certain transfers in payment of tuition or medical expenses of a donee are excluded from the tax base, regardless of amount, as are transfers in satisfaction of the transferor's legal obligation to support another. Specifically authorized deductions protect transfers to charity or a spouse against gift taxation.

Section 6019 requires any individual making a "transfer by gift" in any calendar year to file a gift tax return. However, a return is not required with respect to gifts within the inflation-adjusted $13,000 annual exclusion, gifts for tuition or medical expenses, and gifts eligible for the charitable deduction[1] or the marital deduction.[2] A gift tax return may be required even where there is no gift tax liability—e.g., gifts sheltered by the § 2010 unified credit and gifts split between husbands and wives under § 2513, even if each spouse's share is fully sheltered by the annual exclusion.

The return must be filed by April 15 of the year following the calendar year in which the gifts were made. § 6075(b)(1). An extension of time for filing the return may be obtained, but, unless the taxpayer is abroad, it is generally limited to six months. § 6081. Where a taxpayer is granted an extension of time for filing an income tax return, the time for filing the gift tax return is automatically extended for the same period. § 6075(b)(2). The returns must be filed with the Internal Revenue Service Center for the state in which the donor has his legal residence or principal place of business.

1. Prior to the 1997 Act, gift tax returns were required to be filed for gifts to charity in excess of the annual exclusion, even though no gift tax return was payable on the transfer. Current § 6019(3) exempts gifts to charity from the gift tax filing requirement if the entire value of the transferred property qualifies for the gift tax charitable deduction and the donor gave his entire interest in the property. Where the donor claims an itemized deduction with respect to the contribution for income tax purposes, the Service is afforded the opportunity to assess the validity of the charitable deduction.

2. Because the "qualified terminable interest property" form of marital deduction transfer is elective, Reg. § 25.2523(f)–1(b)(4)(i) requires that a gift tax return be filed to make the election.

The gift tax must be paid at the same time that the return is due. § 6151(a). Upon the showing of "undue hardship," the Service may extend the time for payment for a period not to exceed six months (or for longer if the taxpayer is abroad). The deadline for payment of a gift tax deficiency also may be extended for up to 30 months.

The primary liability for the payment of the gift tax falls upon the donor. § 2502(c). If the tax is not paid by the donor when due (taking into account any extensions), then the donee becomes personally liable to the extent of the value of the gift. § 6324(b). This rule applies even though no effort has been made to collect from the donor who may be solvent and able to pay.[3] However, the Service's current policy is that it "will not attempt to assert donee liability under § 6324(b) until all efforts to collect from the donor have been exhausted."[4] A donor who disposes of all or a part of a qualifying income interest (as defined in § 2523(f) or § 2056(b)(7)) may recover the gift tax attributable to the disposition from "the person receiving the property." The Code further facilitates collection of the tax by providing that the tax "shall be a lien upon all gifts made during the period for which the return was filed, for ten years from the time the gifts are made." § 6324(b). Where the property is sold by the donee to a bona fide purchaser, the lien is released from such property and transferred to all the property of the donee (including after-acquired property).

2.   ESTATE TAX

An estate tax return must be filed by the executor or administrator of the estate of every United States citizen or resident the value of whose gross estate, in general, exceeds a threshold amount—$3.5 million in 2009. § 6018 (as applicable in 2009, in 2011 the threshold amount returns to $1 million). This threshold is designed to require the filing of an estate tax return unless the unified credit eliminates any possibility of estate tax liability. The threshold amount is reduced by post–1976 taxable gifts because these gifts consume part of the unified credit. The return must be filed not later than nine months after the death of the decedent. § 6075(a). If the estate tax is repealed as scheduled in 2010, the executor or administrator of certain "large transfers" (those in excess of the inflation-adjusted $1.3 million figure set forth in § 1022(b)(2)(B)) must file an informational return under the new modified carryover basis regime § 6018 (as applicable in 2010).

Under the estate tax in effect through 2009, if the executor is unable to file a complete return within the prescribed time, he may apply for an extension of time. The application must be made in writing before the due date of the return and must state the reason why the extension is sought. Reg. § 20.6081–1(b). Such an extension will be granted "[i]n case it is

---

3. See Estate of O'Neal v. United States, 258 F.3d 1265 (11th Cir.2001); Estate of Sather v. Commissioner, 251 F.3d 1168 (8th Cir.2001); Mississippi Valley Trust v. Commissioner, 147 F.2d 186 (8th Cir.1945).

4. Chief Counsel Advisory 200018013 (Jan. 11, 2000). See also Internal Revenue Manual 4582.21.

impossible or impractical for the executor to file a reasonably complete return [by the due date of the return], * * * upon a showing of good and sufficient cause." Such an extension of time merely postpones the due date of the return but does not extend the time within which the tax must be paid. The extension of time for filing cannot exceed six months, unless the executor is abroad. § 6081(a). If a complete return cannot be made within that time, the executor must nevertheless file a return, including such information as is then available.

The return must be filed with the Internal Revenue Service Center for the state in which the decedent was domiciled at the time of death. § 6091(b)(3). That return, in the case of citizens or residents, is on Form 706 and must be accompanied by the documents and information required by that form. Estates of nonresident aliens file on Form 706NA, except that Form 706 must be used if deductions for charitable bequests or tax credits are claimed, or where powers of appointment or inter vivos transfers are involved. Returns for nonresidents are filed with the Internal Revenue Service Center in Philadelphia or the Director of International Operations, Washington, D.C., depending upon the place designated on the return form.

Payment of the estate tax is due nine months after the death of the decedent, regardless of when the return is filed. §§ 6075, 6151(a).[5] An extension for a period not to exceed ten years may be granted upon a written showing of "reasonable cause" filed with the District Director on or before the date the tax is due. § 6161(a)(2). Reg. § 20.6161–1(a)(1) defines and gives examples of "reasonable cause." The Service is authorized to require the estate to post a bond to secure payment in accordance with the extension in an amount up to twice the deferred amount. § 6165. An extension not to exceed four years to pay a deficiency in estate tax, should one result on audit, also may be granted if the request is made to the Commissioner on or before the date prescribed for payment thereof.

There are additional provisions for extensions of time to pay estate tax. Section 6163 permits the executor to postpone the payment of estate tax attributable to a remainder or reversionary interest until six months after the preceding interest terminates.[6] Section 6166 permits the executor to

---

5. Failure to pay the tax when due (taking into account any extensions which may have been granted) may result in the imposition of penalties under §§ 6651 and 6653. Under § 6651, a penalty is imposed for late filing of returns unless it is shown that the failure is due to "reasonable cause." A much litigated issue has been whether reliance on an accountant or attorney constitutes reasonable cause to excuse an executor from late filing of an estate tax return. In United States v. Boyle, 469 U.S. 241 (1985), the Court held that reliance on an agent did not constitute "reasonable cause" for a late filing under § 6651(a)(*l*). In a footnote, however, the Court recognized that a taxpayer who was incapable of meeting the criteria of "ordinary business care and prudence" under Reg. § 301.6651(c)(1) might be able to establish reasonable cause for the late filing. Courts generally conclude that an executor reasonably relied on an accountant or attorney's mistaken advice so long as the executor did not merely assign the nondelegable duty to file to the accountant or attorney. See, e.g., Young v. Commissioner, 110 T.C. 297 (1998).

6. Upon a showing of "reasonable cause," the Service can extend the time for payment for an additional three years. § 6163(b).

postpone the payment of estate tax attributable to closely-held business interests over a maximum period of 14 years. A special 2% interest rate applies to the deferred estate tax attributable to the first $1 million (as adjusted for inflation) in taxable value of a closely-held business (i.e., the first $1 million above the exemption equivalent of the unified credit). Thus, in 2009, the 2% rate will apply to the tax on a business interest valued between $4.5 million and $5.5 million. As a further relief for small business, the interest rate on the deferred estate tax attributable to the taxable value of a closely-held business interest in excess of $1 million is 45% of the rate applicable to underpayments of tax. The interest paid is not deductible for estate or income tax purposes.[7]

The estate tax is payable by the executor or administrator (§ 2002) but, if there is no executor or administrator appointed, qualified, and acting within the United States, the responsibility for payment of the tax shifts to any person in actual or constructive possession of any property of the decedent to the extent of the value of the property in her possession. § 6018(a). If the executor or, in her place, any other such person pays a debt of the decedent's estate or distributes any portion of the estate before all of the estate tax is paid, the executor or such other person is personally liable, to the extent of the payment or distribution, for so much of the estate tax as remains due and unpaid. Reg. § 20.2002–1. If the estate tax is not paid when due, § 6324(a)(2) imposes personal liability on persons who receive or are in possession of property included in the decedent's estate under §§ 2034–2042 to the extent of the value of the property at the time of the decedent's death.

3.   GENERATION–SKIPPING TAX

Sections 2601 and following impose a tax on certain generation-skipping transfers. In the case of a non-trust *direct skip* (an inter vivos gift to a "skip person"—a person in a generation which is two or more generations below the generation of the transferor), the tax must be paid by the transferor.[8] In the case of a *taxable distribution* (generally, a distribution from a trust to a skip person), tax must be paid by the transferee. In the case of a *taxable termination* (generally, the termination of an interest held in trust which occurs by reason of death, lapse of time, release of a power or otherwise) or in the case of a trust transfer which directly skips a generation, the tax must be paid by the trustee. § 2603(a). Unless otherwise directed by the governing instrument, the generation-skipping tax is charged to the property involved in the transfer. § 2603(b).

In general, the return-filing obligation is imposed on the person who is liable for payment of the tax. Reg. § 26.2662–1. In the case of a direct skip

---

7. The Tax Court is authorized to issue declaratory judgments regarding an estate's initial or continuing eligibility for deferral under § 6166. § 7479.

8. In the case of a direct skip made from a trust or a transfer of property that

continues to be held in trust, the tax must be paid by the trustee. However, § 2654(d) absolves a trustee from personal liability in certain situations.

(other than a direct skip made by distribution from a trust), the return is due at the same time as the estate or gift tax return is required to be filed with respect to the transfer. In all other cases, the return is due on the fifteenth day of the fourth month after the close of the taxable year of the person required to make the return.

SECTION B.   INVESTIGATION OF RETURNS AND SETTLEMENT PROCEDURES

The Regional Service Center makes a preliminary inspection of returns for mathematical errors. Any tax liability disclosed is billed at once and any excess payment refunded. The Examination Division of the District Director's Office then audits the returns. Many of the audits are either "correspondence examinations," carried on entirely by letter, or "office examinations," in which the taxpayer must appear at a local revenue office with the records and information requested. The remaining audits are "field examinations" in which the examining officer checks the taxpayer's books and records at her home or place of business.

The examining agent (usually a lawyer, accountant or auditor) investigating a case attempts to settle any dispute raised by the investigation. An agreement reached at this stage is considered in the District Director's Examination Division and, if approved, concludes the matter.

If no agreement is reached, the District Director will either drop the case or send a "thirty-day letter" to the taxpayer. This letter contains the report of the examining agent and gives the taxpayer thirty days in which to choose one of three courses of action: (1) file a formal protest, which is a written statement of the taxpayer's case, with the District Director and request a conference with an Appeals Office; (2) request (or receive through failure to respond) a statutory deficiency notice, a "90–day letter," from which an appeal may be taken to the Tax Court; or (3) concede liability by executing the agreement form accompanying the thirty-day letter, thereby closing the case.[9]

If the taxpayer elects to file a protest and requests a conference, the matter is transferred to the Appeals Office. Conferences with the Appeals Office are informal. No stenographic record is made. The taxpayer may bring witnesses to the hearing, but additional statements of fact to be added to the record must be submitted in affidavit form. Here also the effort is to settle the case, the IRS Practice Rules stating: "Appeals will ordinarily give serious consideration to an offer to settle a tax controversy on a basis which fairly reflects the relative merits of the opposing views in the light of the hazards which would exist if the case were litigated.

---

9. Under the "Taxpayer Bill of Rights" provisions of the 1988 Act, the 1996 Act, and the 1998 Act, the agent is required to begin the audit by providing the taxpayer with a pamphlet entitled "Your Rights as a Taxpayer." § 7521. It sets forth in nontechnical terms the rights of the taxpayer and the choice of procedures to be followed.

However, no settlement will be made based upon nuisance value of the case to either party."[10]

If the taxpayer elects not to pursue the Appeals procedure, or if agreement cannot be reached with the Appeals Officer, a statutory deficiency notice will be issued. The statutory deficiency notice, or 90–day letter, is a statement in the Commissioner's name that there is a deficiency in tax (additional tax is due) for the reasons stated in the notice. Assessment of tax, apart from agreement by the taxpayer on a Form 890 or other waiver, cannot be made unless this statutory deficiency notice is issued, except in the case of a jeopardy assessment where the Commissioner believes any delay will jeopardize collection of the tax. On the issuance of this letter, the taxpayer has 90 days after the date of mailing in which to petition the Tax Court for review. If this petition is not filed the tax must be paid and, if not paid, may be assessed and collected by appropriate procedures (including the use of liens or distraint). After payment, the taxpayer may still file a claim for refund and, if the claim is disallowed or not acted on within six months, bring suit in the District Court or Court of Federal Claims. The Tax Court procedure, by contrast, permits the taxpayer to obtain judicial consideration of the case without first paying the deficiency claimed by the Commissioner.

Section C. Tax Court Proceedings

Proceedings in the Tax Court are initiated by a petition filed by the taxpayer in accordance with the rules of the Tax Court. This is a formal document in which the taxpayer assigns the errors claimed to exist with respect to the asserted deficiency and states supporting facts. Prior to the IRS Restructuring and Reform Act of 1998, a rebuttable presumption of correctness attached to the Service's determination of tax liability. Welch v. Helvering, 290 U.S. 111, 115 (1933). As one court explained, "this presumption in favor of the Commissioner is a procedural device that requires the plaintiff to go forward with prima facie evidence to support a finding contrary to the Commissioner's determination. Once this procedural burden is satisfied, the taxpayer must still carry the ultimate burden of proof or persuasion on the merits. Thus, the plaintiff not only has the burden of proof of establishing that the Commissioner's determination was incorrect, but also of establishing the merit of its claims by a preponderance of the evidence." Danville Plywood Corp. v. United States, 90–1 U.S.T.C. ¶ 50,161 (Fed. Cir. 1990). Section 7491 shifts the burden of proof to the Service in any court proceeding with respect to any factual issues relevant to a taxpayer's income, gift, estate, or generation-skipping tax liability if the taxpayer (1) has complied with all substantiation and recordkeeping requirements; and (2) has cooperated with reasonable requests by the Service for witnesses, information, documents, meetings, and interviews.[11] It is too

---

10. 26 C.F.R. § 601.106(f)(2).

11. This shift in the burden of proof applies to taxpayers other than individuals

early to tell whether this shift in the burden of proof will have any measurable effect on the outcome of Tax Court litigation.[12] The Commissioner also bears the burden of proof where she claims an additional deficiency in her answer and raises affirmative issues.

Once a petition is filed, the Commissioner is barred from current administrative assessment of a further deficiency. The taxpayer may pay the asserted deficiency after filing a petition for its redetermination, thereby terminating accrual of interest on any deficiency ultimately found, without ousting the Tax Court of jurisdiction.

After filing the petition, the taxpayer may still attempt to settle the case through conferences conducted by the Appeals Office. Settlement is effected by stipulation filed with the Tax Court upon which it bases its final order.

The hearing in the Tax Court, if the case is not settled, is entirely *de novo* and is not restricted in any fashion by the material considered in the administrative stage. Under § 7453, evidence is presented under the federal rules applicable to non-jury trials. Briefs are filed after the hearing. If a deficiency is found by the Tax Court, the taxpayer must pay or appeal by posting bond. If he does not appeal, he may not relitigate the matter by way of a claim for refund.

Section 7463 permits the Tax Court to hear cases involving small amounts on an informal basis. Where the deficiency does not exceed $50,000 for any one taxable year, the taxpayer may elect to have the case heard under a procedure following less formal rules and decided with a brief summary opinion rather than a formal finding of facts. The small claims cases are not precedents for future cases and are not reviewable on an appeal.[13] The small claims procedures allow the taxpayer to present her claim to an impartial tribunal without the cost and delay of a full scale trial. Generally, the taxpayer appears on her own behalf, without an attorney.

SECTION D.   REFUND PROCEDURES

A taxpayer who believes she has overpaid her tax may file a claim for refund. An overpayment may result from payment of the original tax shown on the return as filed or from later payment of a deficiency asserted by the Service.[14] The claim must state the grounds and facts relied upon. It

---

only where they have a net worth of less than $7 million. § 7491(a)(2)(C).

12.   For an critical view of § 7491, see Johnson, The Dangers of Symbolic Legislation: Perceptions and Realities of the New Burden-of-Proof Rules, 84 Iowa L.Rev. 413 (1999)

13.   § 7463(b); Rogers v. Commissioner, 2001 WL 793703 (D.C. Cir. 2001); Cole v. Commissioner, 958 F.2d 288 (9th Cir.1992).

14.   The taxpayer must pay the entire amount of any deficiency before he may contest its correctness by a suit for refund. See Flora v. United States, 357 U.S. 63 (1958), on rehearing, 362 U.S. 145 (1960) (income tax); Miskovsky v. United States, 414 F.2d 954 (3d

may be denied in whole or in part by the Service. Refund claims are considered in a manner similar to that described above in deficiency cases. Any refund, or over-assessment, exceeding $1 million is reviewed by both the Chief Counsel's office and the Joint Committee on Taxation.

If the refund claim is denied, or not acted on within six months, the taxpayer may bring suit in the District Court or Court of Federal Claims. The suit must be brought within two years of the denial of the claim. § 6532(a).

Section E.   Statutes of Limitations, Interest, and Penalties

The Commissioner has three years from the later of the due date of the return or the date the return was actually filed within which to assess a tax deficiency. § 6501(a). In the case of the estate tax, the three-year period is extended to six years if the taxpayer omits from the gross estate items in excess of 25% of the gross estate stated in the return. An item is not considered omitted if it is "disclosed in the return, or in a statement attached to the return, in a manner adequate to apprise the Secretary of the nature and amount of such item." § 6501(e)(2). A similar extension applies to the gift tax return. The period is unlimited if no return is filed or if the return is false or fraudulent with intent to evade tax.

The gift tax statute of limitations runs only if the gift is disclosed on a gift tax return in a manner adequate to apprise the Service of the nature of the gift. §§ 2001(f), 6501(c)(9). The statute of limitations thus will not run on an inadequately disclosed gift regardless of whether a gift tax return was filed for transfers in that same year. The Tax Court has authority to issue declaratory judgments on the value of gifts disclosed on a return if there is a dispute with the Service and the donor has exhausted all administrative remedies. § 7477.

In estate tax cases, these periods of limitation upon assessment may not be extended. In gift tax cases, the periods may be extended by the taxpayer's written waiver prescribing a longer period. Generally, the taxpayer acquiesces in a request for such a waiver because the alternative is a deficiency notice that may be erroneous but is the only action the Service can take if it has not had time fully to consider the case.

The issuance of a statutory deficiency notice, the 90–day letter, suspends the running of the period of limitations on assessment for an additional 150 days (210 days for persons outside the United States). If, within the original 90–day period, the taxpayer files a petition in the Tax

Cir. 1969) (gift tax); Horne v. United States, 75–1 U.S.T.C. ¶ 13,055 (M.D.Ga. 1975), aff'd per curiam, 519 F.2d 51 (5th Cir. 1975) (estate tax). The *Flora* full payment rule is not satisfied until all of an estate's deferred installment payments under § 6166 are made. See Rocovich v. United States, 933 F.2d 991 (Fed.Cir. 1991).

Court, the period of limitations on assessment is further suspended until 60 days from the date the decision of the Tax Court becomes final.

The taxpayer has three years from the time the return was filed or two years from the time the tax was paid, whichever is later, to file a claim for refund. If, in gift tax cases, the period of limitations on assessment has been extended by waiver, the taxpayer may generally also file a refund claim within that extended period and six months thereafter.

Delinquent payments of tax and payments of deficiencies in tax bear interest at the rate under § 6621 from the time the tax should have been paid, normally the return filing date. Section 6621 sets the interest on deficiencies at the Federal short-term rate plus three percentage points. Interest on refunds is at the Federal short-term rate plus two percentage points. Interest rates are determined twice a year and announced by Revenue Ruling. Interest generally is compounded daily. Accrual of interest is not suspended by litigation in the Tax Court. The interest is assessed and collected as part of the tax. Refunds of tax carry interest from the date the refunded tax was overpaid by the taxpayer.

The tax laws provide civil and criminal penalties, the former being treated as additions to tax and collected as part of the tax through the deficiency procedure. The civil penalties comprise an accuracy-related penalty (§ 6662) and a fraud penalty (§ 6663). If any part of a deficiency is due to fraud with intent to evade tax, an additional 75% of the amount attributable to the fraud is recovered as a civil fraud penalty (whether or not a criminal penalty in the form of fine or imprisonment is also imposed).[15] If the Commissioner establishes that any portion of an underpayment is attributable to fraud, the entire underpayment is treated as so attributable unless the taxpayer is able to establish that some part is not due to fraud. Although the taxpayer has the burden of showing no deficiency exists, the Commissioner has the burden of showing fraud once a deficiency is found.

Absent fraud, three types of non-cumulative accuracy-related penalties relate to wealth transfer taxation, each of which costs the taxpayer 20% of the portion of the deficiency attributable to the proscribed behavior. First, a substantial valuation understatement triggers the penalty if the estate or gift tax return values an item of property at 50% or less of its correct value[16] and the resulting deficiency is more than $5,000. § 6662(g)(2).

---

15. Several cases have held taxpayers who pleaded guilty to criminal tax fraud or were convicted of such charges are subject to civil fraud penalties under § 6663(b) and are collaterally estopped from challenging the existence of fraud in the civil proceeding. See Blohm v. Commissioner, 994 F.2d 1542 (11th Cir. 1993); Gray v. Commissioner, 708 F.2d 243 (6th Cir. 1983). On the other hand, a failure to establish criminal fraud will not prevent a finding of civil fraud because the Government's burden of proof in a civil fraud case ("clear and convincing evidence") is lower than in a criminal fraud case ("guilt beyond a reasonable doubt"). See Traficant v. Commissioner, 884 F.2d 258 (6th Cir. 1989); Akland v. Commissioner, 767 F.2d 618 (9th Cir. 1985).

16. § 6662(g)(1). The penalty doubles to 40% of any deficiency attributable to a gross valuation understatement, which arises if the claimed value is 25% or less of the correct value. § 6662(h)(2)(C).

Second, a taxpayer also is penalized for negligence (including failure to make a reasonable attempt at compliance) or careless or intentional disregard of rules and regulations. § 6662(b)(1). Third, a taxpayer who overstates the value or basis of property by at least 50% is penalized if the resulting income tax deficiency is at least $5,000. § 6662(e)(1), (2).[17] When an accuracy-related penalty is asserted the taxpayer bears the burden of disproof.

Accuracy-related penalties do not apply to any part of a deficiency on which the fraud penalty is imposed. On the other hand, neither type of penalty applies to the extent that the deficiency stems from reasonable cause and the taxpayer acted in good faith. For example, a disagreement in good faith with an interpretation embodied in a rule or regulation may avoid a negligence penalty where the taxpayer makes a complete, item-specific disclosure of a non-frivolous position on his return which would tend to negate an intent to disregard rules or regulations.

In case of a failure to file a return on time, unless the failure is due to reasonable cause and not willful neglect, a civil penalty of 5% of the tax for each month's delay is imposed, up to a maximum of 25% of the tax. § 6651. This penalty is in addition to interest on the non-payment of tax.

The principal criminal penalties are the felony penalties for willfully attempting to evade tax (§ 7201) and making false returns (§ 7206), and the misdemeanor penalties for willfully failing to file a return or to pay tax (§ 7203) and making false statements (§ 7207).

---

17. Thus, if decedent's executor overvalues property by at least 100% for estate tax purposes, a legatee who claims the bloated value as his basis under § 1014 may suffer an accuracy-related penalty. Rev.Rul. 85–75, 1985–1 C.B. 376. This is a necessary result, lest property bequeathed to a surviving spouse be assigned an inflated value yielding bogus capital losses or cost recovery allowances without estate tax cost due to marital deduction qualification. The § 6662 penalty doubles to 40% if the claimed value is at least four times the correct value. § 6662(h)(2)(A).

CHAPTER 6

DATA ON U.S. WEALTH AND WEALTH TRANSFER TAXES

SECTION A.   DISTRIBUTION OF WEALTH IN THE UNITED STATES AND IN THE WORLD

Kopczuk & Saez, Top Wealth Shares in the United States, 1916–2000: Evidence From Estate Tax Returns

NBER Working Paper No. 10399 (March 2004).

This paper presents new homogeneous series on top wealth shares from 1916 to 2000 in the United States using estate tax return data. Top wealth shares were very high at the beginning of the period but have been hit sharply by the Great Depression, the New Deal, and World War II shocks. Those shocks have had permanent effects. Following a decline in the 1970s, top wealth shares recovered in the early 1980s, but they are still much lower in 2000 than in the early decades of the century. Most of the changes we document are concentrated among the very top wealth holders with much smaller movements for groups below the top 0.1%. Consistent with the Survey of Consumer Finances results, top wealth shares estimated from Estate Tax Returns display no significant increase since 1995. Evidence from the Forbes 400 richest Americans suggests that only the super-rich have experienced significant gains relative to the average over the last decade. Our results are consistent with the decreased importance of capital income at the top of the income distribution documented by Piketty and Saez (2003) and suggest that the rentier class of the early century is not yet reconstituted. The most plausible explanations for the facts are perhaps the development of progressive income and estate taxation which has dramatically impaired the ability of large wealth holders to maintain their fortunes, and the democratization of stock ownership which now spreads stock market gains and losses much more widely than in the past.

FIGURE 2

The Top 1% Wealth Share in the United States, 1916–2000

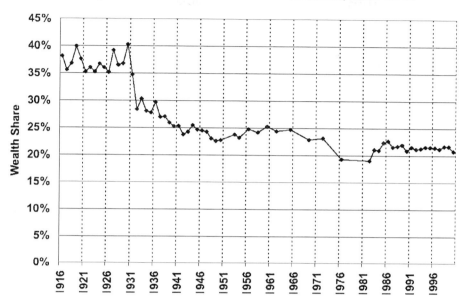

FIGURE 4

The Wealth Shares of Top 2–1%, 1–0.5%, and 0.5–0.1%, 1916–2000

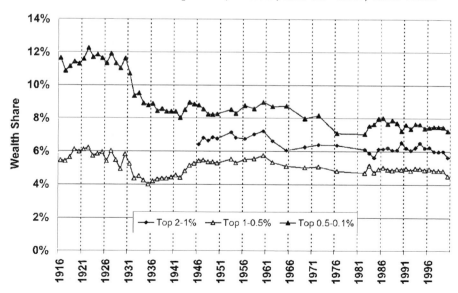

Davies, Sandström, Shorrocks & Wolff, The World Distribution of Household Wealth

United Nations University—WIDER Discussion Paper No. 2008/03 (Feb. 2008).

There has been much recent research on the world distribution of income, but also growing recognition of the importance of other contributions to well-being, including those of household wealth. Wealth is important in providing security and opportunity, particularly in poorer countries that lack full social safety nets and adequate facilities for borrowing and lending. We find, however, that it is precisely in the latter countries where household wealth is the lowest, both in absolute and relative terms. Globally, wealth is more concentrated than income both on an individual and national basis. Roughly thirty percent of world wealth is found in each of North America, Europe, and the rich Asian–Pacific countries. These areas account for virtually all of the world's top 1 per cent of wealth holders. On an official exchange rate basis India accounts for about a quarter of the adults in the bottom three global wealth deciles while China provides about a third of those in the fourth to eighth deciles. If current growth trends continue, India, China and the transition countries will move up in the global distribution, and the lower deciles will be increasingly dominated by countries in Africa, Latin American and poor parts of the Asian–Pacific region. Thus wealth may continue to be lowest in areas where it is needed the most. * * *

3.2   Geographic distribution of wealth

The world map in Figure 1 shows the per capita wealth of different countries. Western Europe, North America,13 and rich Asian–Pacific nations (principally Japan, South Korea, Taiwan, Australia and New Zealand) stand out as the richest areas, with per capita wealth exceeding $50,000 in the year 2000. Next come some prosperous developing and transition countries—for example Mexico, Chile, Argentina, Poland, the Czech Republic, and Ukraine—in the $10,000 to $50,000 band. The large transition countries, Russia and China, fall in the $2,000 to $10,000 range along with Turkey, Brazil, Egypt, Thailand, and South Africa. Finally, in the category below $2,000 are found India, Pakistan, Indonesia, and most of Central and West Africa.

FIGURE 1
World Wealth Levels in Year 2000

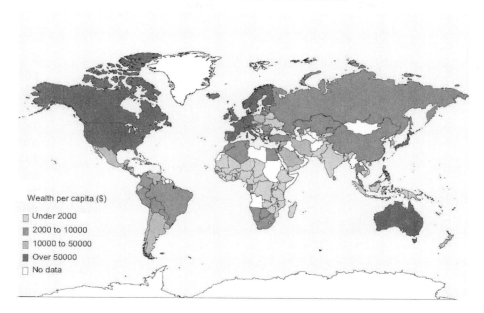

Regional wealth shares are interesting (see the last column of ...
[Figure] 2). North America owns about a third (34 per cent) of the world's
wealth. Europe has a fraction less (30 per cent) and rich Asia–Pacific is
close behind at 24 per cent. The rest of the world shares the remaining 12
per cent. Figure 2 shows how these wealth shares compare to population
shares. North America has the largest excess of wealth over its "fair share"
according to population, which is a mere 5 per cent. Europe has more than
double the population of North America, so that its large wealth share is
more aligned with its population. The case of rich Asia–Pacific is intermediate between Europe and North America.

FIGURE 2
Population and Wealth Shares by Region

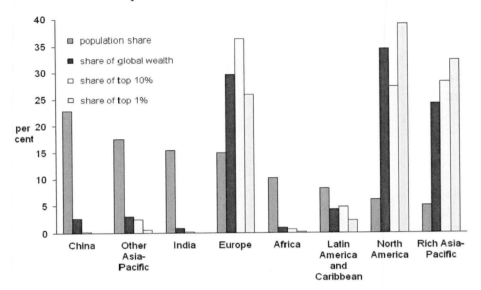

FIGURE 5
Percentage Membership of Wealthiest 10%

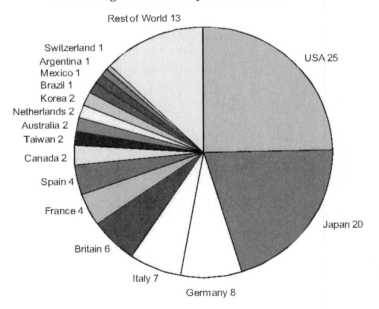

SECTION B.   WEALTH TRANSFER TAX DATA

Joint Committee on Taxation, History, Present Law, and Analysis of The Federal Wealth Transfer Tax System

(JCX–108–07) (Nov. 13, 2007).

Background and Analysis Relating to Estate and Gift Taxation

Background Data

Estates Subject to the Estate Tax

Table 3 details the percentage of decedents subject to the estate tax for selected years since 1935. The percentage of decedents liable for the estate tax grew throughout the postwar era reaching a peak in the mid–1970s. The substantial revision to the estate tax in the mid–1970s and subsequent further modifications in 1981 reduced the percentage of decedents liable for the estate tax to less than one percent in the late 1980s. The percentage of decedents liable for the estate tax gradually increased until 2001. The increases in the unified credit enacted in 2001 have reduced the percentage of decedents liable for the estate tax.

Table 3—Number of Taxable Estate Tax Returns Filed as a Percentage of Deaths, Selected Years, 1935–2004

| Year | Deaths | Taxable estate tax returns filed | |
		Number	Percent of deaths
1935	1,172,245	8,655	0.74
1940	1,237,186	12,907	1.04
1945	1,239,713	13,869	1.12
1950	1,304,343	17,411	1.33
1955	1,379,826	25,143	1.82
1961	1,548,665	45,439	2.93
1966	1,727,240	67,404	3.90
1970	1,796,940	93,424	5.20
1973	1,867,689	120,761	6.47
1977	1,819,107	139,115	7.65
1982	1,897,820	41,620	2.19
1984	1,968,128	31,507	1.60
1986	2,105,361	23,731	1.13
1988	2,167,999	18,948	0.87
1990	2,148,463	23,215	1.08
1992	2,175,613	27,187	1.25
1994	2,278,994	31,918	1.40
1996	2,314,690	37,711	1.63
1998	2,337,256	47,483	2.03
2000	2,403,351	51,159	2.12

| Year | Deaths | Taxable estate tax returns filed | |
		Number	Percent of deaths
2002	2,443,387	28,074	1.15
2004	2,397,615	19,294	0.80

* * *

The increasing percentage of decedents liable for estate tax in the period from 1940 through the mid–1970s and the similar increasing percentages from 1989 to 2000 are the result of the interaction of three factors: a fixed nominal exemption; the effect of price inflation on asset values; and real economic growth. * * *

Revenues from the Estate, Gift, and Generation–Skipping Taxes

Table 4 provides summary statistics of the estate and gift tax for selected years. Total estate and gift receipts include taxes paid for estate, gift, and generation-skipping taxes as well as payments made as the result of IRS audits.

Between 1990 and 1999, estate and gift tax receipts averaged double digit rates of growth. There are three possible reasons for the rapid growth in these receipts. First, because neither the amount of wealth exempt from the estate and gift taxes nor the tax rates were indexed, as explained above, an increasing number of persons became subject to estate and gift taxes. Second, the substantial increase in value in the stock market during the decade of the 1990s increased the value of estates that would have already been taxable, and increased the number of estates that became taxable. For example, the Dow Jones Industrial Average ended 1989 at approximately 2,750 and ended 1999 at approximately 11,000. On average, one-third of the wealth in taxable estates consists of publicly traded stocks. Because the value of this component of wealth more than tripled during the decade, one would expect brisk growth in estate tax receipts from this alone. Finally, the unlimited marital deduction included in the 1981 Act delayed the payment of estate tax, in most cases, until the surviving spouse died. On average, spouses survive their mates by about ten years. Therefore, during the decade of the 1990s, an increase in estate tax receipts is expected as the result of first-spouse deaths during the 1980s that used the unlimited marital deduction.

Table 4—Revenue from the Federal Estate, Gift, and Generation–Skipping Transfer Taxes, Selected Years, 1940–2006

Year	Revenue ($millions)	Percentage of total Federal receipts
1940	357	6.9
1945	638	1.4
1950	698	1.9
1955	924	1.4
1960	1,606	1.7
1965	2,716	2.3

Year	Revenue ($millions)	Percentage of total Federal receipts
1970	3,644	1.9
1975	4,611	1.7
1980	6,389	1.2
1985	6,422	0.9
1990	11,500	1.1
1995	15,087	1.1
1996	17,189	1.2
1997	19,845	1.3
1998	24,076	1.4
1999	27,782	1.5
2000	29,010	1.4
2001	28,400	1.4
2002	26,507	1.4
2003	21,959	1.2
2004	24,831	1.3
2005	24,764	1.1
2006	27,877	1.2

On the other hand, the 1997 Act and the 2001 Act included provisions that would be expected to reduce the number of estates subject to the estate tax. As explained in Part III.B, above, the exemption equivalent amount provided by the unified credit is to increase to $3.5 million in 2009. The average rate of increase in the exemption amount exceeds the rate of inflation. As explained above, increases in the real value of the unified credit generally would be expected to reduce the number of estates subject to tax. The 1997 Act also provided an additional exemption for certain qualified family-owned business interests and a partial exclusion from the estate tax of the value of land subject to certain conservation easements. While the exemption for qualified family-owned business is no longer operable, these changes reduced the number of estates that would be expected to be subject to tax between 1997 and the present.

Table 5 shows the Joint Committee on Taxation staff present-law estimate of revenues from the estate, gift, and generation-skipping taxes for fiscal years 2007–2016. These estimates are based on the January 2007 baseline forecast for estate, gift, and generation-skipping taxes supplied by the Congressional Budget Office. Table 5 also reports the Joint Committee on Taxation staff estimates of annual taxable estates and calculates the percentage of all deaths that taxable estates will represent.

Table 5—Projection of Taxable Estates and Receipts from Estate, Gift, and Generation–Skipping Transfer Taxes, 2007–2016

Year	Exemption Value Of Unified Credit	Number of Taxable Estates	Percent of Deaths	Receipts ($Billions)
2007	2,000,000	17,100	0.67	27.0
2008	2,000,000	18,600	0.76	27.1

Year	Exemption Value Of Unified Credit	Number of Taxable Estates	Percent of Deaths	Receipts ($Billions)
2009	3,500,000	9,600	0.39	21.8
2010	0	0	0.00	23.6
2011	1,000,000	61,900	2.48	50.7
2012	1,000,000	68,100	2.70	57.1
2013	1,000,000	72,600	2.85	62.9
2014	1,000,000	76,200	2.96	66.6
2015	1,000,000	82,700	3.18	72.6
2016	1,000,000	89,800	3.42	78.9

Comparison of Transfer Taxation in the United States and Other Countries

In 2003 the staff of the Joint Committee on Taxation ("JCT staff") surveyed the estate or inheritance tax and gift tax systems of 38 countries. The countries in this survey included most of the OECD countries, plus certain other countries. Among the countries surveyed, an inheritance tax is more common than an estate tax as is imposed in the United States. An inheritance tax generally is imposed on the transferee or donee rather than on the transferor or donor or the transferor's estate. That is, the heir who receives a bequest is liable for a tax imposed and the tax generally depends upon the size of the bequest received. The United States also imposes a generation-skipping tax in addition to any estate or gift tax liability on certain transfers to generations two or more younger than that of the transferee. This effectively raises the marginal tax rates on affected transfers. Countries that impose an inheritance tax do not have such a separate tax but may impose higher rates of inheritance tax on bequests that skip generations.

The survey generally reveals that the provisions of the U.S. estate and gift tax (1) exempting transfers between spouses, (2) providing an effective additional exemption of $1.0 million through the unified credit, and (3) providing an $11,000 annual gift tax exemption per donee, may result in a larger exemption (a larger zero-rate tax bracket) than many other developed countries. However, because most other countries have inheritance taxes, the total exemption depends upon the number and type of beneficiaries. While the effective exemption may be larger, with the exception of transfers to spouses which are untaxed, marginal tax rates on taxable transfers in the United States generally are greater than those in other countries. This is particularly the case when comparing transfers to close relatives, who under many inheritance taxes face lower marginal tax rates than do other beneficiaries. On the other hand, the highest marginal tax may be applied at a greater level of wealth transfer than in other countries. Again, it is often difficult to make comparisons between the U.S. estate tax and countries with inheritance taxes because the applicable marginal tax rate depends on the pattern of gifts and bequests.

What the survey cannot reveal is the extent to which the practice of any of the foreign transfer taxes is comparable to the practice of transfer taxation in the United States. For example, in the United States, transfers of real estate generally are valued at their full and fair market value. In Japan, real estate has been assessed at less than its fair market value. Also unclear in cross country comparisons based solely upon the legal requirements of various estate and inheritance taxes is the ability of transferors to exploit special tax breaks.

Table 6 compares total revenue collected by OECD countries from estate, inheritance, and gift taxes to total tax revenue and to gross domestic product ("GDP") to attempt to compare the economic significance of wealth transfer taxes in different countries. Among these selected OECD countries, in 2005, Belgium, Finland, France, Japan, the Netherlands, Spain, and the United Kingdom collected more such revenue as a percentage of GDP than did the United States. Denmark, Germany, Ireland, Korea, Luxembourg, and Switzerland collected modestly less revenue from such taxes as a percentage of GDP than did the United States. The remaining 16 countries in Table 6 collected less than half as much revenue as a percentage of GDP from such taxes as did the United States. As a percentage of tax revenue, Belgium, France, and Japan relied more heavily on their estate, inheritance, and gift taxes as a revenue source, although the Netherlands, Spain, and the United Kingdom each collected at least seven-tenths of one percent of total tax revenue from estate, inheritance, and gift taxes.

Table 6—Revenue from Estate, Inheritance and Gift Taxes as a Percentage of Total Tax Revenue and GDP in OECD Countries, 2005

Country	As a Percentage of Total Tax Revenue	As a Percentage of GDP
Australia	0.00	0.00
Austria	0.13	0.06
Belgium	1.30	0.59
Canada	0.00	0.00
Czech Republic	0.06	0.02
Denmark	0.40	0.20
Finland	0.70	0.31
France	1.19	0.52
Germany	0.53	0.18
Greece	0.41	0.11
Hungary	0.19	0.07
Iceland	0.20	0.08
Ireland	0.50	0.15
Italy	0.01	0.00
Japan	1.14	0.31
Korea	0.91	0.23
Luxembourg	0.38	0.15
Mexico	0.00	0.00
Netherlands	0.86	0.33
New Zealand	0.01	0.00
Norway	0.21	0.09
Poland	0.07	0.02

Country	As a Percentage of Total Tax Revenue	As a Percentage of GDP
Portugal	0.05	0.02
Slovak Republic	0.00	0.00
Spain	0.73	0.26
Sweden	0.08	0.04
Switzerland	0.67	0.20
Turkey	0.06	0.02
United Kingdom	0.70	0.26
United States	0.89	0.24

The United States is a wealthy country, with higher average household wealth than most of the OECD countries and the other countries in the JCT staff survey. While exemption levels are higher in the United States than most other countries, a significant amount of accumulated wealth still may be subject to estate and gift taxation as compared to the other countries. The data in Table 6 do not reveal the extent to which estate, inheritance, and gift taxes fall across different individuals within each country. In the United States, as reported in Table 3, above, of the 2.4 million deaths in 2004, only 19,294 or 0.8 percent of decedents, gave rise to any estate tax liability. Similar data were not available for the other countries in this survey.

Perhaps of particular note in light of present law in the United States for persons dying in 2010 is the taxation of decedents in Australia and Canada. For U.S. decedents dying in 2010 present law generally provides that the decedent's basis in capital assets is carried over to be the heir's basis in the assets. Both Australia and, to a lesser degree, Canada have carryover basis regimes for capital assets transferred at death.

CHAPTER 7

POLICY ASPECTS OF A TRANSFER TAX

SECTION A. INTRODUCTION

A government that decides to impose a tax on wealth may choose among several forms of taxation: a tax on the *transfer* of wealth (as in the case of an estate or gift tax); a tax on the *receipt* of wealth, either by focusing on receipts from a particular class of donors (as in an inheritance tax) or from all donors (as in an accessions tax); a tax on the *aggregate wealth* that an individual possesses at the end of each year (as in a wealth tax); and a tax on the *use* of wealth (as in a consumption tax). It also can treat receipts of gifts and bequests as income subject to the income tax.

In choosing among the available forms of taxation—which are not exclusive—the government may seek to achieve several goals:

- Raise revenue.
- Redistribute wealth.
- Tax accumulated wealth.
- Enhance progressivity of the federal tax system.
- Limit inheritance and thereby increase equality of opportunity and enhance incentive for each generation to produce its own economic resources.
- Assist in the formation and efficient deployment of capital.

In deciding which of these general forms of taxation to adopt, political leaders will seek advice from diverse constituencies as to the economic, political and social impact of each, the degree to which it can achieve the desired objectives, and the differences that would result if one form is adopted instead of another.

SECTION B. THE STRUCTURE OF A TRANSFER TAX

Once the political process has settled upon the form of wealth taxation, the structure of the tax must be fleshed out. The United States has decided to employ a transfer tax system, and structural judgments are required to implement that form. Some of these can be made by tax experts, responsible for making specific recommendations for governmental policy and pursuing the answers objectively. These experts, on the whole, are not likely to differ significantly in their decisions on issues such as:

- What types of wealth are to be included in the tax base and what is a "transfer" subject to the tax, e.g., will a transfer for consideration be taxed? Should gratuitous services performed for another be a taxable "transfer," or should only transfers of "property" in the traditional sense be covered?

- How is taxation of lifetime transfers to be integrated with taxation of transfers at death?

- How often is the tax to be imposed, e.g., once every generation?

- What administrative problems must be resolved, e.g., valuation techniques and de minimis transfers?

Other aspects of a transfer tax are recognized to depend more on society's view of the issues, and the decisions appropriately can differ from country to country. Such aspects relate to:

- What is the taxable unit, e.g., is a married couple a taxable unit, so that only transfers out of the unit are taxed, or is each individual spouse the basic tax unit so that transfers between spouses are subject to tax?

- What rate structure shall be applied? Should it be progressive, and if so, how progressive? At which point should tax rates commence (the exemption level)?

Most of the Internal Revenue Code's transfer tax provisions address these questions. The materials in Chapters 12 and 13 provide the statutory answer to the question, "What is the tax base"? Chapter 33 deals with those provisions that are involved in resolving the question of how often the tax is to be imposed. Chapters 26 and 34–37 consider those Code provisions that resolve administrative problems such as the treatment of small transfers and the valuation of assets. Chapter 32, dealing with the marital deduction, examines the statutory response to the question of what the taxable unit should be. The materials in Chapter 28 relate to the aspects of the rate structure.

As these materials are studied, it must be kept in mind that they involve responses to questions posed particularly by a *transfer* tax. A statutory provision appropriate to define the normative structure of a transfer tax is not necessarily appropriate to define the structure of some other form of taxation on the transmittal or accumulation of wealth. Different statutory responses might follow if the United States were to adopt a tax on receipts, accessions, or net wealth, or to include gifts and bequests in the income tax system.

SECTION C. SOME PARTICULAR ISSUES IN THE PRESENT TRANSFER TAX SYSTEM

Although the Internal Revenue Code's transfer tax provisions mainly deal with the structural matters listed above, they sometimes raise policy questions as to whether the rules depart from a normative transfer tax pattern, thereby creating tax preferences. Put another way, a normative transfer tax system is one that presumably will be regarded as "equitable" or "fair" by taxpayers. "Fairness" or "equity" in the context of a normative transfer tax requires that persons transferring like amounts of wealth by gift or at death be subject to the same amount of transfer tax. Provisions that depart from this standard are preferential. These tax preferences may be identified and should be analyzed as expenditure programs that the Government effects through the transfer tax system. The "tax expenditures" in the transfer tax system are explored in Chapter 31. Provisions that undermine the fairness of the present transfer tax system in the United States under the above standard—and which constitute tax expenditures—will be discussed in detail in later chapters. The major points are listed briefly now to facilitate recognition of the issues as the technical materials of the present system are considered.

Preferred Tax Treatment for Certain Lifetime Transfers. Although the Tax Reform Act of 1976 eliminated most of the features of the "dual" transfer tax system (i.e., one set of rates, rules and procedures applied to transfers made during lifetime; a separate and often different set applied to transfers made at death), the conversion to a "unified" transfer tax system (i.e., same set of rates, rules and procedures applied to all transfers of property, whether made by gift or at death) was not total. Thus, in technical structure, the 1976 Act retained separate estate and gift tax systems, with the rules governing some types of transfers varying depending on whether the transfer is effected by gift or bequest.

In addition, the gift tax base does not include the amount of the gift tax itself if the donor dies more than three years after making the gift, while the estate tax is imposed on the value of all property transferred at death, including the portion used to pay the estate tax. The failure to "gross up" lifetime transfers by the amount of the gift tax in effect gives the inter vivos donor a deduction for gift tax paid. But a similar deduction is not accorded deathtime transfers. This preference for lifetime giving is not required by the structural pattern necessary to a transfer tax. Instead, the preference appears to reflect economic and historical judgments about the desirability of offering financial inducements to lifetime as opposed to deathtime transfers.

The 2001 Act decoupled the gift tax from the estate tax, keeping the gift tax in force (with a $1 million exemption), ostensibly to prevent taxpayers from shifting assets to family members in lower income tax brackets. Thus, if the 2001 Act unfolds as scheduled, the estate tax will disappear in 2010 while the gift tax will remain in place (albeit at a top 35% rate). But the estate tax is scheduled to rejoin the gift tax in the transfer tax regime in 2011, and each will have a $1 million exemption with a return to the tax rate tables with a top 55% rate.

Exclusions From the Tax Base. Some transfers are excluded from the tax base because of the type of property that is transferred or the nature of the recipient. For example, life insurance proceeds may be excluded from estate taxation even though life insurance inherently involves a testamentary transfer. In such instances, the structural pattern of a transfer tax does not indicate exclusion from the tax base. The reasons for the exclusion must therefore be found in non-tax economic, social or historical judgments. When these reasons are identified, the policymaker can determine whether they are still valid and, if so, whether these non-tax objectives would be better achieved by non-tax programs.

The exclusion in § 2503(e) for certain transfers to pay tuition and medical expenses of another person contains elements that are structural in nature and also elements that are designed to achieve non-tax objectives. To the extent such payments satisfy a legal obligation of the transferor, they are properly excluded from the tax base. Moreover, because the definition of legal obligation varies from state to state (and in some states the extent and/or existence of the obligation is sometimes uncertain), the exclusion may be seen, in part, as providing a uniform federal transfer tax definition of support. To this extent, the exclusion may be viewed as a structural provision; its justification on that ground is seen most clearly, for example, in the payment of college tuition by a parent, whose legal obligation to pay might be uncertain under state law and, in any event, may differ from state to state. However, extension of the exclusion to transfers for the benefit of *any* person appears to be based on non-tax objectives, since the beneficiary need have no relationship to the transferor.

The inflation-adjusted annual $13,000 per donee present interest exclusion (in 2009) is available only for lifetime gifts, not for transfers at death. To some extent, the distinction may be justified on structural grounds. The need to report and monitor *all* lifetime gifts, no matter how small and regardless of occasion, ranging from traditional holiday observances to birthdays and anniversaries, would place intolerable burdens upon both the government and the citizenry. Without some exclusion, the gift tax surely would be met by widespread noncompliance. No such problem attends transfers at death, since all of a decedent's property is lumped in a single massive transfer. Therefore, § 2503(b) may be viewed as administratively necessary to the gift tax and normative in that respect. Still, at its current level, it creates a substantial bias in favor of lifetime giving. A married couple, for example, may transfer $156,000 per year to two children and four grandchildren without even filing a gift tax return and without generation-skipping tax consequences. The extent to which taxpayers embrace complex distortions in their dispositions simply for the sake of qualifying for the present interest exclusion can itself be viewed as a consumer judgment about the extent to which the exclusion is normative rather than preferential.

Charitable Contribution Deduction. As the material in Chapter 29 indicates, transfers to qualified charitable organizations are not subject to estate or gift taxes. Because charitable contributions are "transfers," the question must be asked why they are not taxed. If the reason for their exemption is not responsive to any of the structural questions raised by a decision to adopt a transfer tax, it must be analyzed quite differently from those provisions that respond to structural issues and provide the normative pattern. Such an analytical technique is considered at p. 561.

Credit for State Death Taxes. Section 2011 provides a limited credit against the federal estate tax for state death taxes. Is this provision a needed ingredient in the structure of a transfer tax in a country where the states and the federal government each have taxing power? Or is it a form of revenue sharing which should be examined as and compared to a federal revenue sharing system? See p. 559.

Generation–Skipping Transfers. The normal pattern of bequests in the United States is to pass property within the family from generation to generation. The transfer tax parallels this normal family behavior by imposing a tax, in general, at least once each generation. But the presence of the tax motivates families to create arrangements which provide the next generation with the economic benefits of the family wealth while "skipping" the transfer tax on that generation. As the materials in Chapter 33 indicate, despite the generation-skipping transfer tax, transfers of family wealth may still be structured so as to insulate intervening generations from transfer taxation.

Preferential Rules for Real Estate Used in a Family Farm or Business. Gifts and bequests normally are valued for transfer tax purposes at their fair market value. The Tax Reform Act of 1976, however, created an exception for real estate used in family farms or businesses. Special valuation rules enable qualifying real estate to be valued for transfer tax purposes at lower than fair market value. The avowed purpose was to provide financial aid to farmers and owners of small businesses to prevent a forced sale of such assets to pay federal estate taxes. The discussion at p. 787 considers whether this aid was needed and whether the technique adopted to provide it is equitable and efficient. Chapter 37 also considers the special estate tax exclusion and preferential interest rates available for family-owned businesses.

CHAPTER 8

CONSTITUTIONAL ASPECTS OF TRANSFER TAXES

SECTION A. POWER TO IMPOSE TRANSFER TAXES

ILLUSTRATIVE MATERIAL

A. FEDERAL ESTATE TAX

1. *Direct Tax*

Article I, Section 9 of the Constitution provides that a "direct" tax on property must be imposed "in proportion to the census." Knowlton v. Moore, 178 U.S. 41 (1900), held a federal inheritance tax constitutionally valid as an indirect tax. The Court reasoned that the inheritance tax was not a tax on property but rather was a tax on the passage or transmission of property by will or intestacy, similar to a duty or excise. For precisely the same reason, the Court in New York Trust Co. v. Eisner, 256 U.S. 345 (1921), upheld the constitutionality of the present federal estate tax, rejecting the taxpayer's attempt to distinguish Knowlton v. Moore on the ground that it had involved an inheritance tax. See also Estate of Jameson v. Commissioner, 267 F.3d 366, 374 (5th Cir.2001) (noting that "[t]he Supreme Court has repeatedly rejected attempts to portray the estate tax as an unconstitutional direct tax").

2. *"Uniform Throughout The United States"*

Knowlton v. Moore also addressed the taxpayer's assertion that the inheritance tax, as applied with progressive exemptions, violated the requirement imposed by Article I, Section 8 of the Constitution that tax be "uniform throughout the United States." The Court found that lack of uniformity in state law relating to intestate succession did not translate into impermissible lack of uniformity of a federal statute that depends on state law in its operation.

In Florida v. Mellon, 273 U.S. 12 (1927), the Court rejected the argument that the allowance of a credit computed with reference to state death taxes violated the uniformity requirement: "All that the Constitution * * * requires is that the law shall be uniform in the sense that by its provisions the rule of liability shall be alike in all parts of the United States."

3. *Specific Transfers of Property*

Taxpayers have raised constitutional objections to the inclusion of certain transfers of property within the decedent's gross estate. For example, in Heiner v. Donnan, 285 U.S. 312 (1932), the Court held unconstitutional on due process grounds an irrebuttable presumption that all transfers made within two years of death were made in contemplation of death and thus were includible in the decedent's estate. In contrast, the Seventh Circuit in Estate of Ekins v. Commissioner, 797 F.2d 481 (7th Cir. 1986), upheld the constitutionality of § 2035(a), which at the time included all transfers within three years of death in the decedent's estate. The court held that § 2035(a) did not create an irrebuttable presumption but instead simply made irrelevant the transferor's motive in making the transfer. The court observed that "it is questionable whether the 'irrebuttable presumption' doctrine has any continued vitality." Id. at 486. See Repetti, Minority Discounts: The Alchemy in Estate and Gift Taxation, 50 Tax L.Rev. 415, 484–85 (1995).

In Greiner v. Lewellyn, 258 U.S. 384 (1922), the Court upheld the inclusion of municipal bonds in the gross estate, rejecting the argument that this amounted to an unconstitutional tax on the bonds. The Court reasoned that because the estate tax is imposed on the transfer of the bonds and not on the interest they pay, it is not a constitutionally prohibited "direct tax." "The transfer upon death is taxable, whatsoever the character of the property transferred and to whomsoever the transfer is made." Id. at 387.

B. FEDERAL GIFT TAX

The Supreme Court upheld the constitutionality of the gift tax in Bromley v. McCaughn, 280 U.S. 124 (1929). The Court concluded that the gift tax was an indirect tax levied upon the use or exercise of power over property, not a direct tax upon general ownership of property. Neither the progressivity nor the exemptions of the gift tax structure violated the uniformity clause.

SECTION B.   POWER TO APPLY TRANSFER TAXES RETROACTIVELY

United States v. Carlton

512 U.S. 26 (1994).

■ JUSTICE BLACKMUN delivered the opinion of the Court.

[As adopted in October 1986, § 2057 granted an estate tax deduction for one-half of the proceeds of "any sale of employer securities by the executor of an estate" to "an employee stock ownership plan" (ESOP). In December 1986, Jerry W. Carlton, acting as the executor of the will of Willametta K. Day, purchased 1.5 million shares in MCI Communications Corp. for $11.2 million. Two days later, he sold them to MCI's ESOP for $10.6 million, and claimed a $5.3 million deduction under § 2057 on the estate tax return. In December 1987, § 2057 was amended to permit the deduction only where the securities sold to an ESOP were "directly owned" by the decedent "immediately before death." Because the amendment applied retroactively, as if it were incorporated in the original 1986 provision, the Service disallowed Carlton's claimed § 2057 deduction. The District Court entered summary judgment against the estate in its ensuing refund action, rejecting Carlton's contention that the amendment's retroactive application to his transaction violated the Due Process Clause of the Fifth Amendment. The Court of Appeals reversed, holding that such application was rendered unduly harsh and oppressive, and therefore unconstitutional, by Carlton's lack of notice that § 2057 would be retroactively amended and by his reasonable reliance to the estate's detriment on pre-amendment law. Section 2057 was repealed for estates of decedents who died after December 19, 1989.]

II

This Court repeatedly has upheld retroactive tax legislation against a due process challenge. Some of its decisions have stated that the validity of a retroactive tax provision under the Due Process Clause depends upon whether "retroactive application is so harsh and oppressive as to transgress the constitutional limitation." Welch v. Henry, [305 U.S. 134, 47 (1938)]. The "harsh and oppressive" formulation, however, "does not differ from the prohibition against arbitrary and irrational legislation" that applies generally to enactments in the sphere of economic policy. Pension Benefit Guaranty Corp. v. R.A. Gray & Co., 467 U.S. 717 (1984). The due process standard to be applied to tax statutes with retroactive effect, therefore, is the same as that generally applicable to retroactive economic legislation:

"Provided that the retroactive application of a statute is supported by a legitimate legislative purpose furthered by rational means, judgments about the wisdom of such legislation remain within the exclusive province of the legislative and executive branches. * * *

"To be sure, * * * retroactive legislation does have to meet a burden not faced by legislation that has only future effects. * * * 'The retroactive aspects of legislation, as well as the prospective aspects, must meet the test of due process, and the justifications for the latter may not suffice for the former.' * * * But that burden is met simply by showing that the retroactive application of the legislation is itself justified by a rational legislative purpose." Id., at 729–730.

There is little doubt that the 1987 amendment to § 2057 was adopted as a curative measure. As enacted in October 1986, § 2057 contained no requirement that the decedent have owned the stock in question to qualify for the ESOP proceeds deduction. As a result, any estate could claim the deduction simply by buying stock in the market and immediately reselling it to an ESOP, thereby obtaining a potentially dramatic reduction in (or even elimination of) the estate tax obligation.

It seems clear that Congress did not contemplate such broad applicability of the deduction when it originally adopted § 2057. That provision was intended to create an "incentive for stockholders to sell their companies to their employees who helped them build the company rather than liquidate, sell to outsiders or have the corporation redeem their shares on behalf of existing shareholders." Joint Committee on Taxation, Tax Reform Proposals: Tax Treatment of Employee Stock Ownership Plans (ESOPs), 99th Cong., 2d Sess., 37 (Joint Comm. Print 1985). When Congress initially enacted § 2057, it estimated a revenue loss from the deduction of approximately $300 million over a 5–year period. It became evident shortly after passage of the 1986 Act, however, that the expected revenue loss under § 2057 could be as much as $7 billion—over 20 times greater than anticipated—because the deduction was not limited to situations in which the decedent owned the securities immediately before death. In introducing the amendment in February 1987, Senator Bentsen observed: "Congress did not intend for estates to be able to claim the deduction by virtue of purchasing stock in the market and simply reselling the stock to an ESOP * * * and Congress certainly did not anticipate a $7 billion revenue loss." [133 Cong.Rec. 4294 (1987).] Without the amendment, Senator Bentsen stated, "taxpayers could qualify for the deductions by engaging in essentially sham transactions." Id.

We conclude that the 1987 amendment's retroactive application meets the requirements of due process. First, Congress' purpose in enacting the amendment was neither illegitimate nor arbitrary. Congress acted to correct what it reasonably viewed as a mistake in the original 1986 provision that would have created a significant and unanticipated revenue loss. There is no plausible contention that Congress acted with an improper motive, as by targeting estate representatives such as Carlton after deliberately inducing them to engage in ESOP transactions. Congress, of course, might have chosen to make up the unanticipated revenue loss through general prospective taxation, but that choice would have burdened equally "innocent" taxpayers. Instead, it decided to prevent the loss by denying the deduction to those who had made purely tax-motivated stock transfers. We cannot say that its decision was unreasonable.

Second, Congress acted promptly and established only a modest period of retroactivity. This Court noted in United States v. Darusmont, [449 U.S. 292, 296 (1981)], that Congress "almost without exception" has given general revenue statutes effective dates prior to the dates of actual enactment. This "customary congressional practice" generally has been "confined to short and limited periods required by the practicalities of producing national legislation." Id., at 296–297. In Welch v. Henry, 305 U.S. 134 (1938), the Court upheld a Wisconsin income tax adopted in 1935 on dividends received in 1933. The Court stated that the "recent transactions" to which a tax law may be retroactively applied "must be taken to include the receipt of income during the year of the legislative session preceding that of its enactment." Id., at 150. Here, the actual retroactive effect of the 1987 amendment extended for a period only slightly greater than one year. Moreover, the amendment was proposed by the IRS in January 1987 and by Congress in February 1987, within a few months of § 2057's original enactment.

Respondent Carlton argues that the 1987 amendment violates due process because he specifically and detrimentally relied on the pre-amendment version of § 2057 in engaging in the MCI stock transactions in December 1986. Although Carlton's reliance is uncontested—and the reading of the original statute on which he relied appears to have been correct—his reliance alone is insufficient to establish a constitutional violation. Tax legislation is not a promise, and a taxpayer has no vested right in the Internal Revenue Code. Justice Stone explained in Welch v. Henry, 305 U.S., at 146–147:

"Taxation is neither a penalty imposed on the taxpayer nor a liability which he assumes by contract. It is but a way of apportioning the cost of government among those who in some measure are privileged to enjoy its benefits and must bear its burdens. Since no citizen enjoys immunity from that burden, its retroactive imposition does not necessarily infringe due process * * *."

Moreover, the detrimental reliance principle is not limited to retroactive legislation. An entirely prospective change in the law may disturb the relied-upon expectations of individuals, but such a change would not be deemed therefore to be violative of due process.

Similarly, we do not consider respondent Carlton's lack of notice regarding the 1987 amendment to be dispositive. In Welch v. Henry, the Court upheld the retroactive imposition of a tax despite the absence of advance notice of the legislation. And in Milliken v. United States, the Court rejected a similar notice argument, declaring that a taxpayer "should be regarded as taking his chances of any increase in the tax burden which might result from carrying out the established policy of taxation." [283 U.S. 15, 23 (1931)].

In holding the 1987 amendment unconstitutional, the Court of Appeals relied on this Court's decisions in Nichols v. Coolidge, 274 U.S. 531 (1927), Blodgett v. Holden, 275 U.S. 142 (1927), and Untermyer v. Anderson, 276 U.S. 440 (1928). Those cases were decided during an era characterized by exacting review of economic legislation under an approach that "has long since been discarded." Ferguson v. Skrupa, 372 U.S. 726, 730 (1963). To the extent that their authority survives, they do not control here. *Blodgett* and *Untermyer*, which involved the Nation's first gift tax, essentially have been limited to situations involving "the creation of a wholly new tax," and their "authority is of limited value in assessing the constitutionality of subsequent amendments that bring about certain changes in operation of the tax laws." United States v. Hemme, [476 U.S. 558, 568 (1986)]. *Nichols* involved a novel development in the estate tax which embraced a transfer that occurred 12 years earlier. The amendment at issue here certainly is not properly characterized as a "wholly new tax," and its period of retroactive effect is limited. Nor do the above cases stand for the proposition that retroactivity is permitted with respect to income taxes, but prohibited with respect to gift and estate taxes. In *Hemme* and *Milliken*, this Court upheld retroactive features of gift and estate taxes.

III

In focusing exclusively on the taxpayer's notice and reliance, the Court of Appeals held the congressional enactment to an unduly strict standard. Because we conclude that retroactive application of the 1987 amendment to § 2057 is rationally related to a legitimate legislative purpose, we conclude that the amendment as applied to Carlton's 1986 transactions is consistent with the Due Process Clause. The judgment of the Court of Appeals is reversed.

■ JUSTICE O'CONNOR, concurring in the judgment. * * *

The Court finds it relevant that, according to prominent Members of the tax-writing committees of each House, the statute as originally enacted would have cost the Government too much money and would have allowed taxpayers to avoid tax by engaging in sham transactions. Thus, the Court reasons that the amendment to § 2057 served the legislative purpose of "correct[ing]" a "mistake" Congress made the first time. But this mode of analysis proves too much. Every law touching on an area in which Congress has previously legislated can be said to serve the legislative purpose of fixing a perceived problem with the prior state of affairs—there is no reason to pass a new law, after all, if the legislators are satisfied with the old one. Moreover, the subjective motivation of Members of Congress in passing a statute—to the extent it can even be known—is irrelevant in this context: it is sufficient for due process analysis if there exists some legitimate purpose underlying the retroactivity provision.

Retroactive application of revenue measures is rationally related to the legitimate governmental purpose of raising revenue. * * *

But "the Court has never intimated that Congress possesses unlimited power to 'readjust rights and burdens * * * and upset otherwise settled expectations.'" Connolly v. Pension Benefit Guaranty Corp., 475 U.S. 211, 229 (1986) (concurring opinion) (brackets omitted), quoting Usery v. Turner Elkhorn Mining Co., 428 U.S. 1, 16 (1976). The governmental interest in revising the tax laws must at some point give way to the taxpayer's interest in finality and repose. For example, a "wholly new tax" cannot be imposed retroactively, United States v. Hemme, 476 U.S. 558, 568 (1986), even though such a tax would surely serve to raise money. Because the tax consequences of commercial transactions are a relevant, and sometimes dispositive, consideration in a taxpayer's decisions regarding the use of his capital, it is arbitrary to tax transactions that were not subject to taxation at the time the taxpayer entered into them.

Although there is also an element of arbitrariness in retroactively changing the rate of tax to which a transaction is subject, or the availability of a deduction for engaging in that transaction, our cases have recognized that Congress must be able to make such adjustments in an attempt to equalize actual revenue and projected budgetary requirements. In every case in which we have upheld a retroactive federal tax statute against due process challenge, however, the law applied retroactively for only a relatively short period prior to enactment. * * * A period of retroactivity longer than the year preceding the legislative session in which the law was enacted would raise, in my view, serious constitutional questions. But in keeping with Congress' practice of limiting the retroactive effect of revenue measures (a practice that may reflect Congress' sensitivity to the due process problems that would be raised by overreaching), the December 1987 amendment to § 2057 was made retroactive only to October 1986. Given our precedents and the limited period of retroactivity, I concur in the judgment of the Court that applying the amended statute to respondent Carlton did not violate due process.

■ JUSTICE SCALIA, with whom JUSTICE THOMAS joins, concurring in the judgment.

If I thought that "substantive due process" were a constitutional right rather than an oxymoron, I would think it violated by bait-and-switch taxation. Although there is not much precision in the concept "harsh and oppressive," which is what the Court has adopted as its test of substantive due process unconstitutionality in the field of retroactive tax legislation, surely it would cover a retroactive amendment that cost a taxpayer who relied on the original statute's clear meaning over $600,000. * * *

The Court seeks to distinguish our precedents invalidating retroactive taxes by pointing out that they involved the imposition of new taxes rather than a change in tax rates. But eliminating the specifically promised reward for costly action after the action has been taken, and refusing to reimburse the cost, is even more harsh and oppressive, it seems to me, than merely imposing a new tax on past actions. The Court also attempts to soften the impact of the amendment by noting that it involved only a "modest period of retroactivity." But in the case of a tax-incentive provision, as opposed to a tax on a continuous activity (like the earning of income), the critical event is the taxpayer's reliance on the incentive, and the key timing issue is whether the change occurs after the reliance; that it occurs immediately after rather than long after renders it no less harsh.

The reasoning the Court applies to uphold the statute in this case guarantees that *all* retroactive tax laws will henceforth be valid. To pass constitutional muster the retroactive aspects of the statute need only be "rationally related to a legitimate legislative purpose." Revenue raising is certainly a legitimate legislative purpose, see U.S. Const., Art. I, § 8, cl. 1, and any law that retroactively adds a tax, removes a deduction, or increases a rate rationally furthers that goal. I welcome this recognition that the Due Process Clause does not prevent retroactive taxes, since I believe that the Due Process Clause guarantees no substantive rights, but only (as it says) process. * * *

NationsBank v. United States

269 F.3d 1332 (Fed. Cir. 2001).

■ RADER, CIRCUIT JUDGE.

*   *   *

I.

The federal estate tax law imposes a tax on the transfer of decedents' estates. The rate schedule at 26 U.S.C. § 2001(c) sets the amount of the tax. The Economic Recovery Tax Act of 1981 * * * contained a scheduled reduction in maximum estate tax rates from the then-current rate of seventy percent down to fifty percent over four years. When the top rate was fifty-five percent, the Deficit Reduction Act of 1984 * * *extended that rate through 1987. Later the Omnibus Budget Reconciliation Act of 1987 * * * further extended the top rate of fifty-five percent until January 1, 1993.

In late 1992, Congress passed legislation to extend the fifty-five percent rate again, but did not present it to the President within ten days of adjournment. President Bush did not sign it, instead using a "pocket veto" under Article I, Section 7, Clause 2 of the Constitution. Thus, the fifty-five percent rate lapsed on January 1, 1993. The highest rate defaulted to the previously scheduled fifty-percent rate.

When Ms. Ellen Clayton Garwood died in March 1993, with a gross estate of $28,108,968.72, the applicable estate tax rate was fifty percent. On August 10, 1993, President Clinton signed OBRA into law. Section 13208 of Title XIII of OBRA amended 26 U.S.C. § 2001(c), permanently increasing the estate tax rate for the transfer of taxable estates over $3,000,000 back to the fifty-five percent rate. OBRA also made the rate increase retroactive to include the estates of decedents who died on or after January 1, 1993. Under these provisions, Ms. Garwood's estate fell subject to the fifty-five percent rate.

NationsBank sought a refund of $1,320,190.07, the difference in tax paid under the retroactively applied fifty-five percent rate and the former fifty percent rate in effect on the date of Ms. Garwood's death. In its complaint filed in the Court of Federal Claims, NationsBank asserted that OBRA's retroactive rate increase violated several provisions of the Constitution, including the separation of powers doctrine, the apportionment clause, the *ex post facto* clause, the takings clause, the due process clause, and the equal protection clause. On the Government's summary judgment motion, the Court of Federal Claims addressed counts one through six of NationsBank's complaint and held that OBRA did not violate the Constitution. NationsBank, 44 Fed. Cl. at 664–69. The parties then stipulated to the dismissal of count seven, the only remaining count, and the Court of Federal Claims dismissed the complaint. NationsBank appeals. * * *

IV

The Constitution prohibits enactment of an *ex post facto* law. U.S. Const. art. I, § 9, cl. 3. This prohibition, however, applies solely to criminal enactments. Calder v. Bull, 3 U.S. 386, 390–91, 3 Dall. 386 (1798). * * * [T]he taxpayer in this case has timely paid the tax and seeks a refund. Thus, the taxpayer is not subject to any criminal penalty. * * *

Although the tax code does contain many provisions eventually subjecting recalcitrant taxpayers to criminal liability for refusing to pay taxes, the entire tax code is not criminal in nature. If the entire tax code were criminal, every retroactive tax law would become an unconstitutional *ex post facto* enactment. To the contrary, the Supreme Court has acknowledged Congress' constitutional authority to enact retroactive tax laws. See, e.g., United States v. Carlton, 512 U.S. 26 (1994). * * *

This court notes that the dissent in this case is not the only criticism of the limitations on *ex post facto* prohibitions acknowledged in *Calder.* However, the Supreme Court has not overruled *Calder.* Thus, this court must follow that rule. Because section 13208 of OBRA is not a criminal statute, it is not an *ex post facto* enactment. * * *

VI

Under the due process clause of the Fifth Amendment, "a rational legislative purpose" must justify a retroactive enactment. *Carlton,* 512 U.S. at 31. In other words, statutes "adjusting the burdens and benefits of economic life come to the Court with a presumption of constitutionality, and * * * the burden is on one complaining of a due process violation to establish that the legislature has acted in an arbitrary and irrational way." Usery v. Turner Elkhorn Mining Co., 428 U.S. 1 (1976).

In *Carlton,* the Supreme Court upheld the retroactive application of the estate tax to correct a mistake that had afforded an unjustified tax loophole. 512 U.S. at 32–33. *Carlton* does not stand for the proposition, however, that a retroactive enactment only has a rational legislative purpose when it corrects a mistake to close a loophole. Indeed all legislation in some sense corrects a perceived deficiency in past legal remedies and standards. The Supreme Court in *Carlton,* however, did not limit the retroactive application of revenue measures solely to enactments with a curative purpose. Rather the Supreme Court noted that timing was the essential purpose of making that enactment retroactive. The Supreme Court found the "rational legislative purpose" for the timing change in the procedural promptness of the enactment, accepting the reasoning of the Legislative Branch that the benefits of a "modest" retroactive application outweighed the burdens. Id. at 32. The Court noted that the prompt enactment only imposed a "modest" fourteen-month retroactive period. *Id.* at 32. Likewise, in this case, section 13208 promptly filled the temporal gap in the fifty-five percent rate. Imposition of a uniform fifty-five percent rate on estate tax transfers regardless of the particular month in which they occur suffices to supply the requisite rational purpose. Accordingly, NationsBank has not established that the "modest" eight-month retroactive period of section 13208 was arbitrary and irrational.

Another "rational legislative purpose" justifies this enactment. As noted below, this enactment achieves the purpose of treating similarly situated taxpayers similarly. Because this rational legislative purpose invokes an equal protection analysis, the next section of this discussion sets forth that purpose.

VII

Although the Equal Protection Clause of the Fourteenth Amendment applies only to the states, the Supreme Court has applied equal protection principles to the federal government under the Fifth Amendment's due process protections. Bolling v. Sharpe, 347 U.S. 497 (1954). "In areas of social and economic policy, a statutory classification that neither proceeds along suspect lines nor infringes fundamental constitutional rights must be upheld against equal protection challenge if there is any reasonably conceivable state of facts that could provide a rational basis for the classification." FCC v. Beach Communications, Inc., 508 U.S. 307 (1993). "This standard is especially deferential in the context of classifications made by complex tax laws." Nordlinger v. Hahn, 505 U.S. 1, 11 (1992). NationsBank argues that the retroactive effect of section 13208 discriminated against it by requiring it to pay higher taxes than the law required when the taxable event occurred. NationsBank also asserts that the need to raise revenue to reduce the budget deficit alone is not a legitimate governmental interest for retroactive application of section 13208.

Section 13208 did not discriminate against any narrow class of taxpayers because it did not treat any "other group" more advantageously. In fact, this legislation promoted tax equity and gave itself a further rational purpose by putting a first group of estates, those of decedents who died between January and August 1993, in parity with a second group of estates, those of decedents who died either during the nine years before 1993 or after August 1993. Were it not for section 13208's retroactive effect, the estate tax law would have applied a lower rate to the first group of estates, giving them more advantageous treatment than the second group of estates. Under section 13208, the estate tax law treats both groups equally. Accordingly, section 13208 not only complies with equal protection principles, it furthers those principles. Section 13208's retroactive effect does not violate equal protection principles because it is rationally related to the legitimate governmental purpose of raising revenue and fairly distributing the tax burden. * * *

■ Plager, Senior Circuit Judge, dissenting:

I cannot dispute that the weight of judicial opinion, though not the weight of either history or logic, currently argues for affirming the judgment of the trial court; the majority dutifully rounds up the usual judicial suspects. But there are times when the gap between law and justice is too stark to be ignored. This is one of them. It is simply unfair, and I believe it should be unconstitutional, in these circumstances to enact a statute that imposes a tax on a citizen based on an event that occurred before the tax was enacted. Retroactive legislation is inherently offensive to the natural law of decency, to the principles of the social compact set out in the Declaration of Independence, and to the underlying tenets of the Constitution. And from the viewpoint of the taxpayer, it is no help to say that the basic tax was already in place, only the amount has increased; it is the amount that counts.

Yes, the majority has the law on its side, if following what other courts have said is the law. Perhaps understandably, courts have been unwilling to confront Congress in an area that has been viewed as peculiarly the province of the legislature: the raising of revenue for the Government's purposes. In so doing, however, fundamental constitutional principles have had to be bent and distorted.

Plaintiff in this case cites a number of constitutional principles that could well dictate a result opposite to that reached. * * *

Congress is perfectly capable of raising all the revenue it needs without making its tax laws reach backward, taking property from citizens based on events that, at the time they occurred, were not subject to the new law. Congress has its role, but that role must be consonant with basic principles of law * * *, which include fundamental notions of fairness and fair-dealing. The Constitutional prohibition against *ex post facto* laws rests upon those notions. The preservation of individual freedom requires the protection of property rights as well as liberty interests.

The trial court observed that an interpretation of the Constitution such as this suggests would make every retroactive tax law *ipso facto* an unconstitutional *ex post facto* law. That is not necessarily so. There may be compelling circumstances in which it is necessary to the essential working of government—for example, when national security concerns are involved—that a law, perhaps even a tax law, be made retroactive. This is not such a case. Here, Congress attempted to make the increased tax rate effective at a time when it would have properly applied to this decedent. The President, pursuant to his Constitutional authority, prevented that law from taking effect. Now Congress seeks to attain the same result by subsequent legislation made retroactive. Congress should not be permitted to disregard an exercise of the President's Constitutional authority, and a citizen's property rights should not be subjected to such high-handed governmental action when there is no compelling reason to justify it.

The Supreme Court often has said that retroactivity is not favored. If Congress fails to heed that injunction, and to treat its citizens fairly, consistent with Constitutional principles, it is the duty of the courts to say so. The origin of the notion that *ex post facto* civil legislation is not precluded by Article I, Section 9, is attributed to *Calder v. Bull*, a 1798 Supreme Court decision in which several of the Justices opined on the subject. Neither history nor logic supports the proposition. Even those who attempt to find some reason for the distinction confess its shortcomings.

It is time for the Justices of the Supreme Court to make their views clearly understood, and to assign *Calder v. Bull* and its progeny to the historic dustbin where they belong. See, e.g., * * * Justices O'Connor and Scalia (with whom Justice Thomas joined), concurring separately in United States v. Carlton, 512 U.S. 26, 35–42 (1994). * * *

ILLUSTRATIVE MATERIAL

Other courts similarly have rejected constitutional challenges to the 1993 Act's retroactive application of the 55% rate. See Quarty v. United States, 170 F.3d 961 (9th Cir. 1999); Kane v. United States, 97–2 U.S.T.C. ¶ 60,280 (3d Cir.1997). See also Kitt v. United States, 277 F.3d 1330 (Fed.Cir.2002) (upholding retroactive application of § 72(t)'s 10% tax on premature withdrawals from Roth IRAs, citing rational legislative purpose to close unintended loophole and limited seven-month period of retroactivity).

CHAPTER 9

Basic Application of the Transfer Taxes

Section A. General Description of Gift Tax

Chapter 12 of the Code imposes a gift tax in terms that lack the thoroughness and detail of the income, estate, and generation-skipping transfer taxes. Sections 2501 and 2511 merely impose a tax upon "the transfer of property by gift * * * by any individual * * * whether the transfer is in trust or otherwise, whether the gift is direct or indirect * * *."

The legislative background of the gift tax proved to be a significant factor in retarding its independent development. The 1924 report of the House Ways and Means Committee explained that "the gift tax was passed not only to prevent estate tax avoidance, but also to prevent income tax avoidance through reducing yearly income and thereby escaping progressive surtax rates." Did this statement suggest that the gift tax must be coordinated in some way with the estate tax, and possibly the income tax as well? Or, should this background be disregarded and the clear language imposing the tax be given its full force and effect? Many gift tax cases have revolved around these questions, and the failure in 1976 and 1981 to integrate fully the gift and estate tax provisions into a single unified transfer tax system ensures that these questions will continue to arise. The 2001 Act made the problem more serious by decoupling the gift tax from the estate tax. Although the breach began in mild form in 2004 when for the first time the gift tax had a lower exemption amount ($1 million) than the estate tax ($1.5 million), it fully flowers in 2010 with the scheduled repeal of the estate tax and the continuation of the gift tax (with a $1 million exemption and 35% top rate).[1]

The gift tax is imposed at progressive rates upon all lifetime gifts made by individuals, resident or nonresident. §§ 2501(a)(1), 2511(a)(1). Only individuals make taxable gifts; nothing is said about transfers by corporations or other entities. In the case of nonresident aliens (other than certain expatriates), the tax base includes only tangible property situated in the United States. § 2501(a)(2). Thus, for example, a nonresident alien donor's gifts of stocks, bonds and money generally are not subject to the U.S. gift tax.

---

1. The statute in its current form "recouples" the gift tax with the estate tax in 2011, when both taxes return to the pre–2001 Act status with a unified $1 million credit and 55% top rate.

The tax is calculated on *taxable gifts*, defined as the *total gifts* during the calendar year minus allowable *exclusions* and *deductions*, such as (1) the inflation-adjusted $13,000 per donee annual exclusion (§ 2503(b)); (2) the unlimited exclusion for qualifying payments of tuition or medical expenses of another person (§ 2503(e)); (3) the charitable deduction (§ 2055); and (4) the marital deduction (§ 2056). Married couples may elect to treat gifts to third parties as though they had been made one-half by each spouse.

Although taxable gifts are determined on the basis of the calendar year, the gift tax is cumulatively progressive over the course of the donor's entire lifetime. To determine the tax for each calendar year for which a return is required, the donor follows three steps:

(1) She computes a tax at present rates (using the estate tax rates found in § 2001(c)) on the total of all taxable gifts made from June 6, 1932 (the date of enactment) to the end of the year under § 2502(a)(1).

(2) She subtracts a tax (computed at present rates) on the total of all taxable gifts made up to the beginning of the year under § 2502(a)(2). All pre–1977 taxable gifts are deemed to have been taxed at present rates even though the actual tax paid at the time was less due to a lower rate structure then in effect.

The difference is the tentative tax for the current year.

(3) She subtracts her remaining unified transfer tax credit under § 2505.

The balance, if any, is the gift tax payable for the current year.

Illustration of Federal Gift Tax Computation

Gift Tax on Initial Gift

Assume that a donor who has not previously made any taxable gifts made a gift of $1,112,000 in 2007 to her child. She incurs $41,000 of gift tax liability, computed as follows:

Taxable gifts prior to 2007 0
Total gifts in 2007 . . . . $1,112,000
Less: annual exclusion . . . . 12,000[2]
Taxable gifts in 2007 1,100,000
Total taxable gifts, present and prior years $1,100,000

Tax payable on $1,100,000 (gifts 1932 through 2007) $386,800
Less: gift tax at § 2001(c)(1) rates on $0 (gifts 1932 through 2006) . . . . (0)

Tentative tax on 2007 gifts $386,800

---

2. The inflation-adjusted annual exclusion was $12,000 in 2007.

Less:

    Unified credit against gift tax 345,800
    Less: Unified credit used in prior years 0
    Unified credit available 345,800
Tax due on 2007 gifts .... $41,000[3]

Gift Tax on Subsequent Gifts

Assume that the same donor makes another gift of $162,000 in 2008 to her child. She incurs $61,500 of gift tax liability, computed as follows:

Taxable gifts prior to 2008 .... $1,100,000
Total gifts in 2008................................... $162,000
Less: annual exclusion .... 12,000[4]
Taxable gifts in 2008 150,000
Total taxable gifts, present and prior years $1,250,000

Tax payable on $1,250,000 (gifts 1932 through 2008) $448,300
Less: gift tax at § 2001(c)(1) rates on $1,100,000 (gifts 1932 through 2008) .... (386,800)

Tentative tax on 2008 gifts $61,500
Less:
    Unified credit 345,800
    Less: unified credit used in prior years 345,800
    Unified credit available 0
Tax due on 2008 gifts $61,500

The combination of graduated rates and computational cumulation of all lifetime gifts effectively subjects gifts in succeeding years to higher and higher gift tax rate brackets. Thus, although the 2007 and 2008 gifts were taxed at the 41% marginal rate, future gifts may push the donor into higher marginal rates (although the maximum gift tax rate is scheduled to be 35% in 2010 when the estate tax is scheduled to be repealed), the maximum gift tax rate is scheduled to be 55% in 2011 and thereafter (when the estate tax is scheduled to be reinstituted). As a result, each succeeding taxable gift made during the donor's lifetime may be incrementally more costly.

SECTION B.   GENERAL DESCRIPTION OF ESTATE TAX

Chapter 11 of the Code, which imposes the present estate tax, contains a number of difficult and complex provisions, due in part to the piecemeal fashion in which the estate tax law has developed. The law starts out in

---

3. In effect, the $41,000 gift tax represents the 41% tax rate applied to the $100,000 of the gift in excess of the $1 million exemption.

4. The inflation-adjusted annual exclusion was $12,000 in 2008.

§ 2001 by imposing a tax at progressive rates on the transfer at death of the taxable estate of every citizen or resident of the United States. (Estates of nonresident aliens are covered in §§ 2101 through 2108.) The *taxable estate*, § 2051 declares, is equal to the gross estate less certain allowable deductions. Sections 2031 and 2033 indicate that the *gross estate* includes the value of all property interests owned by the decedent at the date of death, such as bank accounts, real estate, and securities. The gross estate is not limited, however, to the value of assets that are owned by the decedent as a matter of local law. It includes the value of other property in which the decedent had an interest at his death, such as general powers of appointment, as well as the value of certain transfers made by the decedent during his lifetime that the Code treats as substitutes for testamentary dispositions. The gross estate thus may greatly exceed the actual wealth which the decedent legally owned immediately before his death.

The executor then subtracts the deductions allowed by § 2053 through § 2056 from the value of the gross estate to determine the *taxable* estate. These deductions include funeral and administration expenses, claims against the estate, uncompensated casualty losses arising during settlement of the estate, charitable bequests, marital deduction bequests, and state death taxes (in 2005–09).

After the taxable estate has been determined, a tentative estate tax is computed by applying the rates set forth in § 2001 to the sum of the taxable estate plus the adjusted taxable gifts (taxable gifts made by the decedent after December 31, 1976, except those which are included in the gross estate), and subtracting from the amount thus determined the gift tax payable on the decedent's post–1976 gifts.

Sections 2010 through 2015 then allow five credits against the tax: (1) the unified credit; (2) the credit for state death taxes (in 2002–04); (3) the credit for estate tax paid on prior transfers of property to the decedent; (4) the credit for foreign death taxes; and (5) the credit for gift taxes paid with respect to property transferred prior to December 31, 1976 and included in the gross estate. Application of these credits is the final step in the determination of the estate tax payable.

Illustration of Federal Estate Tax Computation

Assume that the same donor as in the earlier gift tax computations dies in 2009 with a gross estate of $2,600,000 and her estate incurs $100,000 of funeral and administration expenses and has no other deductions. Her estate incurs $10,000 of estate tax liability, computed as follows:[5]

Gross estate	$2,600,000
Less: funeral and administration expenses	100,000
Taxable estate	$2,500,000

---

5. For ease of illustration, this example ignores the application of § 2035(b), discussed in Chapter 24(B)(3).

Plus: post–1976 taxable gifts .... <u>1,250,000</u>

Total transfers subject to tax $3,750,000

Tentative tax on total transfers subject to tax 1,568,300

Less: gift tax at § 2001(c)(1) rates on post–1976 gifts .... <u>(102,500)[6]</u>

Tentative tax on estate................................... $1,465,800

Less credits for:

    Unified credit............................. $1,455,800

Total credits against tax .... <u>1, 455,800</u>

Final estate tax payable .... $10,000[7]

Section C.   General Description of Generation-Skipping Transfer Tax

Chapter 13 of the Code imposes a third transfer tax, separate from the estate and gift tax systems, and introduces its own technical nomenclature. Section 2601 imposes the tax on specified types of transfers, denominated generation-skipping transfers, that usually are not otherwise subject to transfer tax in the skipped generation.[8] Generation-skipping transfers are *taxable distributions*, *taxable terminations*, and *direct skips*. Each of these taxable events is defined by reference to four other defined terms: *transferor*, *interest*, *skip person*, and *non-skip person*.

In general, the *transferor* of a testamentary transfer is the decedent and the transferor of an inter vivos transfer is the donor. If spouses elect gift-splitting, each is treated as a transferor as to one-half of the transfer.

A person has an *interest* in a trust if that person is currently eligible to receive, or has a present right to receive, income or corpus from the trust. A future interest is not an interest in the trust for purposes of the generation-skipping tax.

A *skip person* is one who is assigned to a generation that is two generations or more below that of the transferor. The assignment of beneficiaries to generations generally follows family lines, and rules are

---

6. To prevent the estate from receiving a double benefit from the unified credit, § 2001(b)(2) directs that the tentative estate tax be reduced by the gift tax "payable" on post–1976 gifts, which is the amount of the gift tax less the unified credit. Because the credit is thus subtracted out for purposes of computing the amount of gift tax which offsets the estate tax, the credit is allowed in computing the final estate tax payable.

7. In effect, the $10,000 estate tax reflects the 4% spread between the gift tax

marginal rate applied on the net $250,000 of taxable gifts in 2007 and 2008 (41%) and the estate tax rate applied to these net taxable gifts in the donor's estate (45%) [$250,000 x 4% = $10,000].

8. Generation-skipping transfers made from trusts that were irrevocable on September 25, 1985 are not subject to the tax, except to the extent that the transfer is made from corpus added to the trust after that date.

provided to determine the generation assignment of beneficiaries who are related neither to the transferor nor the transferor's spouse. A trust is a skip person if the only persons with an interest in the trust are skip persons or if no persons hold an interest in the trust and no distributions from the trust can be made to non-skip persons. Thus, a grandchild of a transferor is a skip person, as is a trust solely for the benefit of grandchildren of the transferor.

A *non-skip person* is any person, including a trust, that is not a skip person. Thus, a child of the transferor is a non-skip person, as is a trust for the benefit of issue of the transferor so long as a child of the transferor is alive.

A *taxable distribution* is a distribution, other than a taxable termination or a direct skip, from a trust to a skip person. Thus, a distribution of property from a discretionary trust to a grandchild of the transferor is a taxable distribution measured by the value received by the beneficiary. The tax is imposed on the beneficiary and, if paid by the trust, constitutes a further taxable distribution.

A *taxable termination* is the termination of the interest of any beneficiary if thereafter any of the beneficiaries is a skip person and none of them is a non-skip person. Thus, if a trust provides income to child A for life, remainder to grandchildren, the death of A is a taxable termination. On the other hand, if the trust provided for income to be paid to children A and B until the death of the survivor, remainder to grandchildren, the death of A before B would not be a taxable termination, because, at A's death, a non-skip person, B, possesses an interest in the trust. The amount of a taxable termination is the value of the property in which the terminated interest existed, reduced by amounts that would have been deductible (under principles similar to § 2053) had the transfer been subject to estate tax. The tax is payable from the trust assets.

A *direct skip* is any transfer to a skip person that is subject to estate or gift tax when made by the transferor. However, a transfer to or for the benefit of the transferor's grandchild after the grandchild's parent, who is the child of the transferor, is dead is not a direct skip. Thus, a bequest to a grandchild with living parents is a direct skip, as is an inter vivos transfer of property to a trust for the sole benefit of a grandchild with living parents. The amount of a direct skip is the value of the property received by the transferee. The tax is paid by the transferor, or, in the case of a transfer from a trust, the trustee. If an individual makes an inter vivos direct skip transfer, the amount of the generation-skipping tax is treated as a gift for gift tax purposes.

The amount of generation-skipping tax is the product of the taxable amount and the applicable rate. Every individual is allowed an exemption ($3.5 million in 2009, followed by the scheduled repeal of the tax in 2010 and its resurrection in 2011 with an inflation-adjusted $1 million exemption) to allocate among inter vivos and deathtime transfers. Allocation of the exemption to a particular transfer technically affects the computation of the applicable rate, but the practical effect of an allocation is to exempt from tax the fractional share of the transferred property to which the exemption has been allocated.

The applicable rate is the maximum federal estate tax rate (45% in 2009, followed by the scheduled repeal of the tax in 2010 and its resurrection in 2011 with a 55% rate), multiplied by an inclusion ratio of 1 minus the applicable fraction. The applicable fraction is, in general, the ratio of the amount of the generation-skipping tax exemption allocated to the transfer over the value of the property transferred.

Thus, if a transferor allocates her entire $3.5 million exemption to a generation-skipping transfer of $10.5 million made in 2009, the applicable fraction is 1/3, the inclusion ratio is 2/3, and the applicable rate is 30%. If no exemption amount is allocated to a transfer, the inclusion ratio is 1 and the applicable rate is 45%. Because the generation-skipping tax is imposed at an ungraduated flat rate set at the highest estate tax rate, it can be quite costly. Thus, if D leaves her estate in trust with income to her child C for life, remainder to C's children, a taxable termination triggered by C's death in 2004 subjects each dollar's worth of generation-skipping transfer to a tax rate of 45% (ignoring any initial allocation to the trust of D's $1.5 million exemption). But if the property were instead included in C's gross estate, the tax cost probably would be much less.

Illustration of Federal Generation–Skipping Tax Computation

A.   Taxable Distribution

Assume A created a trust in 1990 with a corpus of $500,000 and elected to allocate $200,000 of her generation-skipping tax exemption to the trust. The trustee had discretion to distribute income and principal to B, A's child, and C, A's grandchild, during B's life with remainder to C at B's death. In 2008 the trustee distributed $300,000 to C.

Taxable amount $300,000

Applicable fraction = $\dfrac{200,000}{500,000}$

Inclusion ratio = 1 − .4 = .6
Applicable rate = .6 × 45% = 27.0%
Generation-skipping tax payable by C (27.0% of $300,000) $81,000

B.   Taxable Termination

Assume D created a trust in 1990 with a corpus of $1,000,000 and elected to allocate $200,000 of his generation-skipping tax exemption to the trust. The trustee had discretion to distribute income or principal to E, D's child, for life, remainder to F, D's grandchild. At E's death in 2008, the trust corpus was $2,125,000. The trustee incurred $25,000 of expenses in terminating the trust.

Value of property in trust $2,125,000
Less: expenses attributable to termination $25,000
Taxable amount $2,100,000

Applicable fraction = $\dfrac{200,000}{1,000,000}$

Inclusion ratio = 1 − .2 = .8

Applicable rate = .8 × 45% = 36.0%

Generation-skipping tax payable by trustee (36.0% of $2,100,000) $756,000

C. *Direct Skip*

Assume G, with a remaining generation-skipping tax exemption of $300,000, transfers $1,013,000 outright to grandchild H in 2009.

Value of property received by H............................ $1,013,000

Less: Gift excluded by § 2503(b)   13,000

Taxable amount   1,000,000

Applicable fraction = $\dfrac{300,000*}{1,000,000}$

Inclusion ratio = 1 − .3 = .7

Applicable rate = .7 × 45% = 31.5%

Generation-skipping tax payable by G (31.5% of $1,000,000) ... $315,000**

* G's unused exemption amount of $300,000 is deemed allocated to the direct skip under § 2632(b)(1), unless G elects otherwise.

** The $1 million taxable gift gives rise to a gift tax as well as a generation-skipping tax. The generation-skipping tax payable by G is an additional taxable gift by G and generates additional gift tax. § 2515. G's total gifts as a result of this transfer are $1,315,000.

CHAPTER 10

COORDINATING THE COMPUTATION OF THE ESTATE AND GIFT TAXES

Internal Revenue Code: §§ 2001; 2010; 2035(b); 2504(c); 2505; 6501(c)(9)

House Ways and Means Committee Report, Revenue Reconciliation Bill of 1997[1]

H.R. Rep. No. 148, 105th Cong., 1st Sess. (1997).

[Pre–1997] Law

The Federal estate and gift taxes are unified so that a single progressive rate schedule is applied to an individual's cumulative gifts and bequests. The tax on gifts made in a particular year is computed by determining the tax on the sum of the taxable gifts made that year and all prior years and then subtracting the tax on the prior years' taxable gifts and the unified credit. Similarly, the estate tax is computed by determining the tax on the sum of the taxable estate and prior taxable gifts and then subtracting the tax on taxable gifts and the unified credit. Under a special rule applicable to the computation of the gift tax (§ 2504(c)), the value of gifts made in prior years is the value that was used to determine the prior year's gift tax. There is no comparable rule in the case of the computation of the estate tax.

Generally, any estate or gift tax must be assessed within three years after the filing of the return. No proceeding in a court for the collection of an estate or gift tax can be begun without an assessment within the three-year period. If no return is filed, the tax may be assessed, or a suit commenced to collect the tax without assessment, at any time. If an estate or gift tax return is filed, and the amount of unreported items exceeds 25 percent of the amount of the reported items, the tax may be assessed or a suit commenced to collect the tax without assessment, within six years after the return was filed (§ 6501).

Commencement of the statute of limitations generally does not require that a particular gift be disclosed. A special rule, however, applies to certain gifts that are valued under the special valuation rules of Chapter 14. The gift tax statute of limitations runs for such a gift only if it is disclosed on a gift tax return in a manner adequate to apprise the Secretary of the Treasury of the nature of the item.

Most courts have permitted the Commissioner to redetermine the value of a gift for which the statute of limitations period for the gift tax has

---

1. Upon passage, the Act was renamed the Taxpayer Relief Act of 1997.

expired in order to determine the appropriate tax rate bracket and unified credit for the estate tax. See, e.g., Evanson v. United States, 30 F.3d 960 (8th Cir. 1994); Stalcup v. United States, 792 F.Supp. 714 (W.D. Okla. 1991); Estate of Levin, 1991 T.C. Memo 1991–208, aff'd 986 F.2d 91 (4th Cir. 1993); Estate of Smith v. Commissioner, 94 T.C. 872 (1990). But see Boatmen's First National Bank v. United States, 705 F.Supp. 1407 (W.D. Mo. 1988) (Commissioner not permitted to revalue gifts).

Reasons for Change

Revaluation of lifetime gifts at the time of death requires the taxpayer to retain records for a potentially lengthy period. Rules that encourage a determination within the gift tax statute of limitations ease transfer tax administration by eliminating reliance on stale evidence and reducing the period for which retention of records is required.

Explanation of Provision

[Section 2001(f)] provides that a gift for which the limitations period has passed cannot be revalued for purposes of determining the applicable estate tax bracket and available unified credit. For gifts made in calendar years after the date of enactment, [§ 6501(c)(9)] also extends the special rule governing gifts valued under Chapter 14 to all gifts. Thus, the statute of limitations will not run on an inadequately disclosed transfer in calendar years after the date of enactment, regardless of whether a gift tax return was filed for other transfers in that same year.

It is intended that, in order to revalue a gift that has been adequately disclosed on a gift tax return, the IRS must issue a final notice of redetermination of value (a "final notice") within the statute of limitations applicable to the gift for gift tax purposes (generally, three years). This rule is applicable even where the value of the gift as shown on the return does not result in any gift tax being owed (e.g., through use of the unified credit). It is also anticipated that the IRS will develop an administrative appeals process whereby a taxpayer can challenge a redetermination of value by the IRS prior to issuance of a final notice.

A taxpayer who is mailed a final notice may challenge the redetermined value of the gift (as contained in the final notice) by filing a motion for a declaratory judgment with the Tax Court. The motion must be filed on or before 90 days from the date that the final notice was mailed. The statute of limitations is tolled during the pendency of the Tax Court proceeding.

ILLUSTRATIVE MATERIAL

A. COMPUTATION OF THE ESTATE TAX

Although formally separate, the gift and estate taxes prior to 2004 were in concept imposed at a single rate, prescribed by § 2001(c), on all of an individual's wealth transfers, whether made during life or at death. As the cumulative total of transfers grew, the marginal rates increased. A decedent's "taxable estate" represented the final transfer in a continuing process of wealth transmission that began during life. Lifetime gifts filled the bottom brackets of the rate structure. The transfer of the taxable estate was subject to estate tax beginning at that point within the rate schedule at which lifetime transfers left off.

While § 2505 provided a credit that may have relieved the donor of current gift tax liability, the form of that relief—a credit rather than a deduction or exemption—left the cumulative total of transfers unaffected for purposes of applying the § 2001(c) rates to cumulative transfers beyond the amount sheltered by the credit. That is, an exemption would have taken the amount exempted "off the top" of the taxable gifts, effectively delivering a benefit at the donor's highest marginal rate bracket. A credit, by contrast, delivered the same benefit to all donors, regardless of the size of their gifts, by sheltering the lowest regions of the base from tax. The credit of $345,800 in 2003 equaled the gift tax liability under § 2001(c) on cumulative taxable transfers of $1,000,000. Cumulative transfers of $1,000,000 in 2003 fell at the top of the $750,000 to $1,000,000 bracket band, to which a 39% marginal rate was applied; the 41% marginal rate was applied in the $1,000,000 to $1,250,000 bracket band. Thus, a donor who made lifetime taxable gifts of $1,000,000 incurred no actual gift tax liability, but the first $1 of taxable transfer beyond that point, whether during life or at death, prompted a gift or estate tax liability of 41 cents.

To ensure that the estate tax was imposed at rate levels beginning where lifetime gifts ended, § 2001(b) calculated the estate tax through a two-step process:

> (1) A hypothetical estate tax was calculated on the total of the taxable estate and the lifetime gifts, so called "adjusted taxable gifts." Inclusion of lifetime gifts swelled the hypothetical tax base, pushing the taxable estate into higher marginal bracket bands.

> (2) The gift tax payable on adjusted taxable gifts was then subtracted. This avoided taxing lifetime gifts twice and left as the balance of actual estate tax liability the product of exposing the taxable estate, the amount transferred at death, to the higher ranges of the rate bracket progression.[2]

In 2004, however, the gift tax became decoupled from the estate tax. The gift tax exemption remained at $1 million while the estate tax exemption rose to $1.5 million in 2004 (and 2005), with two additional increases to $2 million in 2006 (and 2007 and 2008) and $3.5 million in 2009, before the scheduled repeal of the estate tax in 2010. In the unlikely event that the 2001 Act's sunset provisions remain unaltered, the gift and estate become recoupled in 2011, with the return of the estate tax at the same $1 million exemption level afforded to gifts as well.

---

2. Section 2001(b)(2) provides a special rule to determine the subtraction for gift tax paid on post–1976 gifts in view of the reduction of the maximum rate of tax from 70% to 50% that was phased in between 1982 and 1993. The subtraction is computed by reference to the § 2001(c) rates in effect at the date of death, rather than the rates actually applicable to the gifts when made. As a result of § 2001(b)(2), the estate tax may not always be reduced by the full amount of gift tax paid on post–1976 gifts. For example, if an individual who made gifts in 1982 to which the 65% rate applied dies in 2003, the subtraction for gift tax payable would be computed on the basis of the 49% rate in effect in 2003.

B.   THE RELATIONSHIP BETWEEN LIFETIME GIFTS AND ESTATE TAX LIABILITY

1.   *Structural Relationships*

The definition of the term "adjusted taxable gifts" is critical, because it is the platform on which the taxable estate is placed in setting the starting point for the estate's run up the rate bracket schedule. Section 2001 defines "adjusted taxable gifts" as: (1) the "total amount of the gifts (within the meaning of section 2503)," (2) "made by the decedent after December 31, 1976," (3) "other than gifts which are includible in the gross estate of the decedent." Under the 1976 Act, a decedent's lifetime taxable gifts made on or before December 31, 1976 are ignored, thereby preventing retroactive application of the life-plus-death-cumulation technique.

As will be seen in Chapters 15–17, due to definitional differences in the estate and gift tax bases, certain transfers may be swept into the gross estate at death even if they were treated as completed lifetime gifts on which tax was paid. Transfers of this kind, obviously, should be counted only once. Single taxation is accomplished by leaving them within the "taxable estate" but excluding them from "adjusted taxable gifts." In effect, the date of death value of such a transfer is substituted for its date of gift value. If, after the gift, the property increases in value, the higher value will be reflected in the taxable estate on which the estate tax is imposed. Subtraction of the gift tax previously paid on the transfer's date-of-gift value ensures that this amount of tax is not doubled up. Even if a gift is later included in the gross estate, transfer tax thus is imposed only once, at death, on the date of death value, with the gift tax treated, in effect, as a prepayment.[3]

If a gift is later included in the gross estate but decreases in value after the gift, the lesser date-of-death value is used in calculating the hypothetical estate tax. The subtraction for gift tax payable, however, still uses the date of gift value. In that case, the amount subtracted may well exceed the amount of tax attributable to inclusion of the transfer in the taxable estate at its date of death value, thereby lowering the total transfer tax ultimately payable.

The subtraction mechanism serves an additional function. The hypothetical estate tax on the combined taxable estate and adjusted taxable gifts is determined after taking into account the estate tax unified credit allowed by § 2010. Gift taxes payable during life are also determined net of the credit under § 2505. On the face of it, then, a taxpayer who transfers wealth both during life and at death enjoys double use of the unified credit. But that is an illusion. A taxpayer who reduces her lifetime gift tax liability through use of the § 2505 credit also reduces the estate tax subtraction for gift taxes payable.

Assume, for example, that D made taxable gifts of $600,000 in 1999 and died in 2003 leaving a taxable estate of $675,000 more. In 2003 the unified credit was $345,800, which had the effect of exempting $1 million of transfers.

---

3. This subtraction mechanism eliminated the need for the specific credit under § 2012 for gift taxes paid. The credit does not apply to any gift made after December 31, 1976, § 2012(e), but it continues to be available to estates of decedents who paid tax on gifts made before 1977 that are included in the gross estate. As this population dies, the credit itself will expire. The complex calculations required to compute the credit are illustrated in Warren & Surrey, Federal Estate and Gift Taxation 252 (1961 ed.).

By applying her § 2505 credit, D avoided paying gift tax in 1999. Her hypothetical estate tax is computed on a base of $1,275,000 (taxable estate plus adjusted taxable gifts), yielding a gross hypothetical estate tax liability of $459,050, which is reduced to $113,250 through application of the § 2010 unified credit. The ultimate result is to tax D's total wealth transfers of $1,275,000 in a manner that relieves the first $1,000,000 of any liability but that exposes the remaining $275,000 to the unified rate schedule beginning in the 37% bracket. The method of computation automatically limits D to one application of the credit. Practically speaking, to the extent the credit is used during life, it is unavailable at death. In 2009, a taxpayer may fully use her gift tax credit during life and have additional credit to use in her estate due to the increased estate tax credit available during those years. If the 2001 Act unfolds as scheduled, after a one-year repeal of the estate tax in 2010, the gift tax and estate tax exemptions again will be equal ($1 million), and the taxpayer who fully uses up her gift tax credit during life in 2011 and beyond will not have any remaining credit at death.

Because "adjusted taxable gifts" under § 2001(b) are measured by a decedent's total post–1976 "taxable gifts (within the meaning of § 2503)," transfers that do not figure in the determination of taxable gifts are permanently excluded from the transfer tax base, at death as well as during life. Permanently excluded are the first $13,000 inflation adjusted present interest gifts made to any person in any year (§ 2503(b)); educational and medical expense payments described in § 2503(e)(2); payments in satisfaction of one's obligation under local law to support another; and consideration within the meaning of § 2512(b) received by the transferor. Thus, for example, even though the estate tax does not offer an exclusion, as such, of any kind, a donor might give $13,000 annually to each of 3 children and 7 grandchildren for each of the 5 years preceding her death, and the $650,000 total will not be subject either to the gift tax or the estate tax.[4]

A further incongruity is that the gift tax is "tax-exclusive," while the estate tax is "tax-inclusive." This means that the gift tax base does not include the amount of the gift tax itself, while the estate tax is imposed on the value of all property transferred at death, including the portion used to pay the estate tax. The failure to "gross up" lifetime transfers by the amount of the gift tax in effect gives the inter vivos donor a deduction for the gift tax paid. Thus, if D gives $100 and pays a gift tax of $40, D's adjusted taxable gift includes $100 at his death, but the $40 gift tax is permanently removed from the transfer tax base. If D instead made the transfer at death, the estate tax would be paid on a value of $140 (rather than on a value of $100 as during life), leaving a smaller net transfer to D's heirs. Consistency in determining the tax base requires that the gift tax be computed on the sum of the amount transferred to the donee and the gift tax liability itself. The 1976 Act partially redressed this distortion by requiring in § 2035(b) that gift tax paid by a decedent within three years prior to his death be included in the value of his gross estate.

---

4. Section 2642(c) would exonerate these outright (non-trust) transfers from the generation-skipping transfer tax as well.

2. *Valuation Relationships*

The greater the value of adjusted taxable gifts, the higher the marginal rates applicable to the taxable estate. The ultimate estate tax payable thus is a direct function of gift tax valuations. In enacting § 2001(f), the 1997 Act cured a nettlesome problem under prior law. Under Estate of Smith v. Commissioner, 94 T.C. 872 (1990), and the other cases cited in the House Report, the Service could revalue lifetime gifts for estate tax purposes many years after the statute of limitations had closed for gift tax purposes, creating potentially enormous record-keeping problems for donors, even though § 2504(c) prohibited such revaluation of such prior gifts for purposes of computing the gift tax payable on subsequent gifts.[5] Because the revalued gifts were included in computing the amount of gift tax payable on post–1976 gifts to be subtracted from the tentative estate tax liability, the net effect of the Service's revaluation was to put the estate into a higher marginal tax bracket. Revaluation of prior gifts for estate tax purposes could be a double-edged sword, however, because in other circumstances estates could *lower* the value of lifetime gifts in calculating their estate tax liability. See TAM 9718004 (Jan. 7, 1997). Section 2001(f) now prevents both the Service and taxpayers from revaluing gifts for estate tax purposes after the expiration of the statute of limitations for the year of the gift.

C. MOVEMENT TOWARD, AND THEN AWAY FROM, A UNIFIED TRANSFER TAX

Prior to the 1976 Act, the United States employed a dual transfer tax system consisting of separate estate and gift tax structures. Each of the taxes had its own set of rates, exemption levels and substantive rules, which combined to provide three significant tax advantages for lifetime transfers: (1) gift tax rates were only 75% of those applicable to transfers at death; (2) transfers during life were not cumulated with those at death, so that a donor could take advantage of two separate exemptions and two starts at the bottom of the separate progressive rate schedules; and (3) the gift tax base was tax-exclusive, while the estate tax base was tax-inclusive. These preferences for lifetime transfers provided substantial tax savings to wealthy donors who could afford to take advantage of them. In addition, the existence of dual transfer-tax structures created considerable complexity because detailed rules were needed to apply the higher estate tax rates to lifetime transfers that were really testamentary in nature.

These problems led the Treasury in 1969 to recommend the adoption of a completely unified transfer tax system with a single set of rates, a single exemption, and a single set of substantive rules for all transfers, whether made by gift or by bequest. The proposals ultimately led, in the 1976 and 1981 Acts, to adoption of a single cumulative rate schedule with a unified tax credit (in lieu of the prior separate exemptions) applicable both to lifetime and deathtime transfers. This measure eliminated the first two (but not the third) of the three ways in which lifetime transfers were preferred under pre–1977 law. Neither the tax base nor the substantive rules of the estate and gift taxes have been fully integrated, however, and the existing system falls short of the Treasury's

---

5. See Caron, Revaluation of Prior Gifts for Estate Tax Purposes After Expiration of   Statute of Limitations for Year of Gift, 67 Taxes 286 (1989).

1969 vision of complete unification. The 2001 Act reversed course, decoupling the gift tax from the estate tax, beginning in 2004 (with a lower gift tax exemption) and culminating in 2010 with the repeal of the estate tax and the continuation of the gift tax (subject to the "sunset" of the Act in 2011 and the return of the estate tax and its reunification with the gift tax).

As to the tax base, § 2035(b) is not a true gross-up measure, and in any case it only applies to gift tax paid on gifts made within three years before death. All earlier gifts in effect receive a deduction for the gift tax paid, a deduction that is not granted for transfers at death (or for taxable gifts made within three years of death). The failure to require that all gifts be grossed up by the gift tax paid perpetuates the tax preference for lifetime transfers.

Even for gifts made within three years of death, § 2035(b) does not achieve the result of a completely unified transfer tax that would gross up all gifts by the amount of the gift tax. This result occurs because § 2503(c) brings the gift tax paid back into the gross estate, but the amount of the gift tax is still understated due to failure to apply the gross-up rule to the gift itself. An example will illustrate the difference in result under § 2035(b) and a fully implemented gross-up system.

Assume A is in the 50% transfer tax bracket, has $200 of wealth, and wants to make a net after-tax transfer of $100 to B. Under a unified transfer tax with full gross-up, the amount of A's gift is $200, A pays a gift tax of $100 (50% of $200) and B receives the net $100. Because the gift is a completed transfer, A's estate is depleted by $200 and no further transfer tax consequences occur at A's death. Under § 2035(b), however, if A makes the $100 transfer within three years of death, A will pay a gift tax of only $50, because under present gift tax rules the rate is applied only to the net amount transferred and not to the tax itself. Upon A's death, the $50 gift tax paid is included in his estate plus the $50 that A did not have to pay due to the failure to gross up. A's taxable estate ($100) plus adjusted taxable gifts ($100) equals $200 and a $100 tentative estate tax is due. A's estate is credited with the $50 gift tax paid and owes $50 more in estate tax. The difference between a true gross-up rule and that in § 2035(b) is one of timing of the tax payment. In the former case, the full transfer tax is due at the time of the lifetime transfer; under § 2035(b), part of the tax is due at the time of the gift and the balance at death.

The § 2035(b) approach thus grants the benefit of deferral of part of the tax for a maximum of three years. Prior to the 1981 Act, the deferral benefit was roughly offset by the fact that § 2035(a) included in the transfer tax base any appreciation in value of a gift made during the same period (see Chapter 24). The 1981 Act generally eliminated the appreciation from the base, but did not correspondingly eliminate the deferral benefit by instituting a true gross-up rule. In a properly structured unified transfer tax, the full transfer tax would be due at the time of the gift, but future appreciation would be out of the donor's estate.

The failure of the 1976 Act to tax all gifts on the same basis as transfers at death was intended to retain an incentive for lifetime giving. The 1981 legislation continued this incentive (and provided an additional incentive through an increase in the amount of the annual exclusion). The 1969 Treasury Proposals had rejected this approach. Treasury proposals in 1984 also sought to eliminate the advantage accorded lifetime giving under current law by applying the gift tax on a tax-inclusive basis. The Treasury stated:

> "Such a rule hampers the overall fairness of the transfer tax system because the individuals it benefits are those who can afford to give away a significant portion of their property during life. Those individuals who are unable or unwilling to make lifetime gifts, and who therefore retain their property until death, are subject to tax at a higher effective rate * * *. In addition, the preferential treatment accorded lifetime gifts encourages individuals to make lifetime transfers solely to reduce their overall transfer tax burden. The transfer tax system should not treat an individual wishing to retain his or her property until death either more or less favorably than it treats an individual wishing to make lifetime gifts.

> "Finally, the preference given lifetime gifts has resulted in a complex and often arbitrary set of rules that attempt, with uneven results, to prevent taxpayers from taking unintended advantage of the preference. In some cases, these rules do not fully remove the preference given to lifetime gifts; in others, the rules are punitive and cause transfer tax consequences that are more severe than if the individual had not made a lifetime gift."

U.S. Dept. of the Treasury, 2 Tax Reform for Fairness, Simplicity and Economic Growth 376 (Nov. 1984).

In its analysis, Treasury stated that "application of the gift tax on a tax-inclusive basis would remove the primary tax incentive for lifetime gifts and therefore would make tax considerations a relatively neutral factor in the decision whether to dispose of property during one's lifetime or to retain it until death. Moreover, the proposal would provide greater fairness in the application of the transfer tax system because all persons paying the transfer tax would do so on the same tax-inclusive basis. Finally, by removing the major incentive for disguising testamentary transfers as lifetime gifts, the proposal would permit simplification of the rules governing when a transfer is complete for estate and gift tax purposes." Id. at 382. Congress did not adopt the Treasury proposals in the 1986 and 1997 Acts, and indeed reversed course with the 2001 Act.

The reverberations from the dis-unification of the gift tax from the estate tax, if indeed the 2001 Act unfolds as scripted, will be far-reaching. The ramifications were felt beginning in 2004–05 with the first differential between the gift tax and estate tax exemptions, and then become magnified as the differential increases in 2006–08 and 2009 until the estate tax is repealed in 2010. The scheduled return of the estate tax in 2011 and its shared exemption with the gift tax would return to the forefront problems inherent in the current imperfectly unified systems. At that point, the policy favoring lifetime transfers should be reconsidered.

For example, why should there be an incentive for lifetime gifts as compared to testamentary transfers? If the purpose is to move property into younger and, presumably, more venturesome hands, in a desire to produce economic benefits by supposedly increasing the mobility and risk-taking capacity of capital, analysis is then required as to whether this result in fact occurs. If the gifts are in trust, the economic effect is not likely to differ from continued ownership by the donor. If anything, the entrepreneurial enthusiasm of trustees is likely to be substantially muted by legal standards of accountability for prudent behavior to which donors are not subject in investing their own funds. Even if one favors the policy goal, closer analysis of the kinds of gifts that should be encouraged is required. Finally, it must be asked whether there is any justification for effecting the policy through the present inequitable and discriminatory system of encouraging lifetime transfers. Would Congress conceivably approve a direct federal subsidy program for lifetime gifts that provided the largest federal grant to the wealthiest donors and none at all to the least wealthy? It must be recognized that this is precisely the result produced when the present tax incentives for lifetime transfers are translated into a direct subsidy program.

The pre–2004 and post–2010 regimes also fail to maximize simplification that could result from complete unification of the substantive rules governing lifetime and deathtime transfers. Separate statutory structures are retained for the estate and gift taxes. In some instances, e.g., transfers incident to a divorce, the rules are actually different. Further, Congress left intact the present unsatisfactory state of the law as to when a gift is "complete" for transfer tax purposes, an issue discussed at p. 299. Additional legislation would be needed to complete the task of changing the United States' transfer tax structure from a dual to a unified system.

CHAPTER 11

THE ROLE OF STATE LAW

The wealth transfer tax statute is replete with instances in which Congress incorporates state law concepts rather than engrafting federal rules onto particular transfer tax issues. The cases excerpted in this chapter involve two of the many situations in which a determination of state law controls the federal wealth transfer tax result. In both cases, the federal tax question was whether an estate could claim a marital deduction with respect to transfers to a surviving spouse. In Commissioner v. Estate of Bosch, 387 U.S. 456 (1967), the federal tax result turned on whether the surviving spouse's release of a general power of appointment was valid under state law. In Estate of Goree v. Commissioner, 68 T.C.M. 123 (1994), the federal tax result turned on whether disclaimers executed by the decedent's three children were valid under state law.

The importance of *Bosch* and *Goree* at this point is not in their resolution of the technical marital deduction, general power of appointment, and disclaimer issues, which are discussed in detail later in Chapters 32, 22, and 25, respectively. Rather, the cases are included here because they raise a fundamental issue that cuts across the wealth transfer tax regime: Where the federal tax law incorporates state law as the rule of decision, how much weight must the Internal Revenue Service and the federal courts give to a lower state court's interpretation of state law in prior litigation involving the taxpayer?

Commissioner v. Estate of Bosch

387 U.S. 456 (1967).

■ MR. JUSTICE CLARK delivered the opinion of the Court.

These two federal estate tax cases present a common issue for our determination: Whether a federal court or agency in a federal estate tax controversy is conclusively bound by a state trial court adjudication of property rights or characterization of property interests when the United States is not made a party to such proceeding. * * *

I.

(a) No. 673, Commissioner v. Estate of Bosch.

In 1930, decedent, a resident of New York, created a revocable trust which, as amended in 1931, provided that the income from the corpus was to be paid to his wife during her lifetime. The instrument also gave her a general power of appointment, in default of which it provided that half of the corpus was to go to his heirs and the remaining half was to go to those of his wife. In 1951 the wife executed an instrument purporting to release the general power of appointment and convert it into a special power. Upon decedent's death in 1957, respondent, in paying federal estate taxes, claimed a marital deduction for the value of the widow's trust. The Commissioner determined, however, that the trust corpus did not qualify for the deduction under § 2056(b)(5) * * * and levied a deficiency.* Respondent then filed a petition for redetermination in the Tax Court. The ultimate outcome of the controversy hinged on whether the release executed by Mrs. Bosch in 1951 was invalid—as she claimed it to be—in which case she would have enjoyed a general power of appointment at her husband's death and the trust would therefore qualify for the marital deduction. While the Tax Court proceeding was pending, the respondent filed a petition in the * * * New York [state trial court] for settlement of the trustee's account; it also sought a determination as to the validity of the release under state law. The Tax Court, with the Commissioner's consent, abstained from making its decision pending the outcome of the state court action. The state court found the release to be a nullity; the Tax Court then accepted the state court judgment as being an "authoritative exposition of New York law and adjudication of the property rights involved," 43 T.C. 120, 124, and permitted the deduction. On appeal, a divided Court of Appeals affirmed. It held that "[t]he issue is * * * not whether the federal court is 'bound by' the decision of the state tribunal, but whether or not a state tribunal has authoritatively determined the rights under state law of a party to the federal action." 363 F.2d, at 1013. The court concluded that the "New York judgment, rendered by a court which had jurisdiction over parties and subject matter, authoritatively settled the rights of the parties, not only for New York, but also for purposes of the application to those rights of the relevant provisions of federal tax law." Id., at 1014. It declared that since the state court had held the wife to have a general power of appointment under its law, the corpus of the trust qualified for the marital deduction. We do not agree and reverse.**

III.

The problem of what effect must be given a state trial court decree where the matter decided there is determinative of federal estate tax

---

* [ED.: Section 2056(a) allows a deduction—the so-called marital deduction—from the gross estate for the value of an interest in property passing from a decedent to his surviving spouse. In the case of an interest in a trust, the deduction is allowed only if certain conditions are met. Among these conditions, § 2056(b)(5) requires that the surviving spouse hold a "general power of appointment" over the trust. A general power of appointment, in turn, is defined as a power that is exercisable in favor of the powerholder, her estate, her creditors, or the creditors of her estate. In general, property subject to a general power of appointment held by a decedent at death (but not property subject to other types of powers) is includible in the decedent's estate under § 2041. Mrs. Bosch apparently sought to avoid that result through a partial release of her general power that converted it into a lesser power that would not trigger any inclusion upon her death. If successful, however, that tactic would breach the requirement of § 2056(b)(5), resulting in a loss to Mr. Bosch's estate of the marital deduction for the value of the trust (as the Service claimed).]

** [ED.: In the companion case, Second National Bank of New Haven v. United States, No. 240, the Service was given notice of the state court proceeding but chose not to appear. 387 U.S. at 460–61.]

consequences has long burdened the Bar and the courts. This Court has not addressed itself to the problem for nearly a third of a century.[1] In Freuler v. Helvering, 291 U.S. 35 (1934), this Court, declining to find collusion between the parties on the record as presented there, held that a prior *in personam* judgment in the state court to which the United States was not made a party, "[o]bviously * * * had not the effect of *res judicata*, and could not furnish the basis for invocation of the full faith and credit clause * * *." At 43. In *Freuler's* wake, at least three positions have emerged among the circuits. The first of these holds that

> " * * * if the question at issue is fairly presented to the state court for its independent decision and is so decided by the court the resulting judgment if binding upon the parties under the state law is conclusive as to their property rights in the federal tax case * * *." Gallagher v. Smith, 223 F.2d 218, 225.

The opposite view is expressed in Faulkerson's Estate v. United States, 301 F.2d 231. This view seems to approach that of Erie R. Co. v. Tompkins, 304 U.S. 64 (1938), in that the federal court will consider itself bound by the state court decree only after independent examination of the state law as determined by the highest court of the State. The Government urges that an intermediate position be adopted; it suggests that a state trial court adjudication is binding in such cases only when the judgment is the result of an adversary proceeding in the state court. Pierpont v. C. I. R., 336 F.2d 277. Also see the dissent of Friendly, J., in *Bosch*, No. 673.

We look at the problem differently. First, the Commissioner was not made a party to either of the state proceedings here and neither had the effect of *res judicata*, Freuler v. Helvering; nor did the principle of collateral estoppel apply. It can hardly be denied that both state proceedings were brought for the purpose of directly affecting federal estate tax liability. Next, it must be remembered that it was a federal taxing statute that the Congress enacted and upon which we are here passing. Therefore, in construing it, we must look to the legislative history surrounding it. We find that the report of the Senate Finance Committee recommending enactment of the marital deduction used very guarded language in referring to the very question involved here. It said that "proper regard," not finality, "should be given to interpretations of the will" by state courts and then only when entered by a court "in a bona fide adversary proceeding." S. Rep. No. 1013, Pt. 2, 80th Cong., 2d Sess., 4. We cannot say that the authors of this directive intended that the decrees of state trial courts were to be conclusive and binding on the computation of the federal estate tax as levied by the Congress. If the Congress had intended state trial court determinations to have that effect on the federal actions, it certainly would have said so—which it did not do. On the contrary, we believe it intended the marital deduction to be strictly construed and applied. Not only did it indicate that only "proper regard" was to be accorded state decrees but it

---

1. It may be claimed that Blair v. Commissioner, 300 U.S. 5 (1937), dealt with the problem presently before us but that case involved the question of the effect of a property right determination by a state appellate court.

placed specific limitations on the allowance of the deduction as set out in §§ 2056(b), (c), and (d). These restrictive limitations clearly indicate the great care that Congress exercised in the drawing of the Act and indicate also a definite concern with the elimination of loopholes and escape hatches that might jeopardize the federal revenue. This also is in keeping with the long-established policy of the Congress, as expressed in the Rules of Decision Act, 28 U.S.C. § 1652. There it is provided that in the absence of federal requirements such as the Constitution or Acts of Congress, the "laws of the several states * * * shall be regarded as rules of decision in civil actions in the courts of the United States, in cases where they apply." This Court has held that judicial decisions are "laws of the * * * state" within the section. Erie R. Co. v. Tompkins * * *. Moreover, even in diversity cases this Court has further held that while the decrees of "lower state courts" should be "attributed some weight * * * the decision [is] not controlling * * * "where the highest court of the State has not spoken on the point * * * [and] that "an intermediate appellate state court * * * is a datum for ascertaining state law which is not to be disregarded by a federal court *unless it is convinced by other persuasive data that the highest court of the state would decide otherwise.*" * * * Thus, under some conditions, federal authority may not be bound even by an intermediate state appellate court ruling. It follows here then, that when the application of a federal statute is involved, the decision of a state trial court as to an underlying issue of state law should *a fortiori* not be controlling. This is but an application of the rule of Erie R. Co. v. Tompkins, supra, where state law as announced by the highest court of the State is to be followed. This is not a diversity case but the same principle may be applied for the same reasons, *viz.*, the underlying substantive rule involved is based on state law and the State's highest court is the best authority on its own law. If there be no decision by that court then federal authorities must apply what they find to be the state law after giving "proper regard" to relevant rulings of other courts of the State. In this respect, it may be said to be, in effect, sitting as a state court. * * *

We believe that this would avoid much of the uncertainty that would result from the "non-adversary" approach and at the same time would be fair to the taxpayer and protect the federal revenue as well. * * *

■ MR. JUSTICE DOUGLAS, dissenting.

As the Court says, the issue in these cases is not whether the Commissioner is "bound" by the state court decrees. He was not a party to the state court proceedings and therefore cannot be bound in the sense of *res judicata*. The question simply is whether, absent fraud or collusion, a federal court can ignore a state court judgment when federal taxation depends upon property rights and when property rights rest on state law, as they do here. * * *

I would adhere to Freuler v. Helvering, supra, and Blair v. Commissioner, supra. There was no indication in those cases that the state court decision would not be followed if it was not from the highest state court.

The idea that these state proceedings are not to be respected reflects the premise that such proceedings are brought solely to avoid federal taxes. But there are some instances in which an adversary proceeding is impossible * * * and many instances in which the parties desire a determination of their rights for other than tax reasons.

Not giving effect to a state court determination may be unfair to the taxpayer and is contrary to the congressional purpose of making federal tax consequences depend upon rights under state law. The result will be to tax the taxpayer or his estate for benefits which he does not have under state law. * * * [T]ake the case where a state court determines that X does not own a house. After X dies, a federal court determines that the state court was wrong and that X owned the house, and it must be included in his gross estate even though it does not pass to his heirs. I cannot believe that Congress intended such unjust results.

This is not to say that a federal court is bound by all state court decrees. A federal court might not be bound by a consent decree, for it does not purport to be a declaration of state law; it may be merely a judicial stamp placed upon the parties' contractual settlement. Nor need the federal court defer to a state court decree which has been obtained by fraud or collusion. But where, absent those considerations, a state court has reached a deliberate conclusion, where it has construed state law, the federal court should consider the decision to be an exposition of the controlling state law and give it effect as such.

■ MR. JUSTICE HARLAN, whom MR. JUSTICE FORTAS joins, dissenting. * * *

II.

The issue here, despite its importance in general, is essentially quite a narrow one. The questions of law upon which taxation turns in these cases are not among those for which federal definitions or standards have been provided * * *; it is, on the contrary, accepted that federal tax consequences have here been imposed by Congress on property rights as those rights have been defined and delimited by the pertinent state laws. The federal revenue interest thus consists entirely of the expectation that the absence or presence of the rights will be determined accurately in accordance with the prevailing state rules. The question here is, however, not how state law must in the context of federal taxation ordinarily be determined; it is instead the more narrow one of whether and under what conditions a lower state court adjudication of a taxpayer's property rights is conclusive when subsequently the federal tax consequences of those rights are at issue in federal court.

The problem may not, as the Court properly observes, be resolved by reference to the principles of *res judicata* or collateral estoppel * * *; the Revenue Service has not, and properly need not have, entered an appearance in * * * the state court proceedings in question here. Nor do the pertinent provisions of the revenue laws, or their legislative history, provide an adequate guide to the solution of the problem; the only direct reference in that lengthy history relevant to these questions is imprecise and equivocal.[2] The cases in this Court are scarcely more revealing; they are, as Judge Friendly remarked below, "cryptic" and "rather dated." 363 F.2d 1009, 1015.

It is, of course, plain that the Rules of Decision Act, 28 U.S.C. § 1652, is applicable here, as it is, by its terms, to any situation in which a federal court must ascertain and apply the law of the several States. Nor may it be doubted that the judgments of state courts must be accepted as a part of the state law to which the Act gives force in federal courts, Erie R. Co. v. Tompkins, 304 U.S. 64l; it is not, for that purpose, material whether the jurisdiction of the federal court in a particular case is founded upon diversity of citizenship or involves a question arising under the laws of the United States. This need not mean, however, that every state judgment must be accepted by federal courts as conclusive of state law. The Court has, for example, never held, even in diversity cases, where the federal interest consists at most in affording a "neutral" forum, that the judgments of state trial courts must in all cases be taken as conclusive statements of state law; * * * the Court has consistently acknowledged that the character both of the state proceeding and of the state court itself may be relevant in determining a judgment's conclusiveness as a statement of state law. The same result must surely follow *a fortiori* in cases in which the application of a federal statute is at issue.

Similarly, it is difficult to see why the formula now ordinarily employed to determine state law in diversity cases—essentially that, absent a recent judgment of the State's highest court, state cases are only data from which the law must be derived—is necessarily applicable without modification in all situations in which federal courts must ascertain state law. The relationship between the state and federal judicial systems is simply too delicate and important to be reduced to any single standard. * * * The inadequacy of this formula is particularly patent here, where, unlike the cases in which it was derived, the federal court is confronted by precisely the legal and factual circumstances upon which the state court has already passed.

Accordingly, although the Rules of Decision Act and the *Erie* doctrine plainly offer relevant guidance to the appropriate result here, they can scarcely be said to demand any single conclusion. * * *

III.

Given the inconclusiveness of these sources, it is essential to approach these questions in terms of the various state and federal interests fundamentally at stake. It suffices for present purposes simply to indicate the

2. A supplementary report of the Senate Finance Committee, concerned with the legislation which eventually became the Revenue Act of 1948, said simply that "proper regard should be given to interpretations of the will rendered by a court in a bona fide adversary proceeding." S. Rep. No. 1013, Pt. 2, 80th Cong., 2d Sess. 4. This language is doubtless broadly consistent with virtually any resolution of these issues, but it is difficult to see the pertinence of the sentence's last four words if, as the Court suggests, conclusiveness was intended to be given to the State's highest Court, but to none other.

pertinent factors. On one side are certain of the principles which ultimately are the wellsprings both of the Rules of Decision Act and of the Erie doctrine. First among those is the expectation that scrupulous adherence by federal courts to the provisions of state law, as reflected both in local statutes and in state court decisions, will promote an appropriate uniformity in the administration of law within each of the States. Uniformity will, in turn, assure proper regard in the federal courts for the areas of law left by the Constitution to state discretion and administration, and, in addition, will prevent the incongruity that stems from dissimilar treatment by state and federal courts of the same or similar factual situations. Finally, it must be acknowledged that state courts are unquestionably better positioned to measure the requirements of their own laws; even the lowest state court possesses the tangible advantage of a close familiarity with the meaning and purposes of its local rules of law.

On the other side are important obligations which spring from the practical exigencies of the administration of federal revenue statutes. It can scarcely be doubted that if conclusiveness for federal tax purposes were attributed to any lower state court decree, whether the product of genuinely adversary litigation or not, there would be many occasions on which taxpayers might readily obtain favorable, but entirely inaccurate, determinations of state law from unsuspecting state courts. One need not, to envision this hazard, assume either fraud by the parties or any lack of competence or disinterestedness among state judges; no more would be needed than a complex issue of law, a crowded calendar, and the presentation to a busy judge of but essentially a single viewpoint. The consequence of any such occurrence would be an explication of state law that would not necessarily be either a reasoned adjudication of the issues or a consistent application of the rules adopted by the State's appellate courts.

It is difficult to suppose that adherence by federal courts to such judgments would contribute materially to the uniformity of the administration of state law, or that the taxpayer would be unfairly treated if he were obliged to act, for purposes of federal taxation, as if he were governed by a more accurate statement of the requirements of state law. Certainly it would contribute nothing to the uniformity or accuracy of the administration of the federal revenue statutes if federal courts were compelled to adhere in all cases to such judgments.

IV.

The foregoing factors might, of course, be thought consistent with a variety of disparate resolutions of the questions these two cases present. If emphasis is placed principally upon the importance of uniformity in the application of law within each of the several States, and thereby upon the apparent unfairness to an individual taxpayer if an issue of state law were differently decided by state and federal courts, it might seem appropriate to accept, in all but the most exceptional of circumstances, the judgment of any state court that has addressed the question at issue. This is the viewpoint identified with the opinion of the Court of Appeals for the Third

Circuit in Gallagher v. Smith, 223 F.2d 218; it is, in addition, apparently the rule adopted today by my Brother Douglas. Conversely, if emphasis is placed principally upon the hazards to the federal fisc from dubious decisions of lower state courts, it might be thought necessary to require federal courts to examine for themselves, absent a judgment by the State's highest court, the content in each case of the pertinent state law. This, as I understand it, is the rule adopted by a majority of the Court today.

In my opinion, neither of these positions satisfactorily reconciles the relevant factors involved. The former would create excessive risks that federal taxation will be evaded through the acquisition of inadequately considered judgments from lower state courts, resulting from proceedings brought, in reality, not to resolve truly conflicting interests among the parties but rather as a predicate for gaining foreseeable tax advantages, and in which the point of view of the United States had never been presented or considered. The judgment resulting from such a proceeding might well differ only in form from a consent decree. The United States would be compelled either to accept as binding upon its interests such a judgment, or to participate in every state court proceeding, brought at the taxpayer's pleasure, which might establish state property rights with federal tax consequences.

The second position, on the other hand, would require federal intervention into the administration of state law far more frequently than the federal interests here demand; absent a judgment of the State's highest court, federal courts must under this rule re-examine and, if they deem it appropriate, disregard the previous judgment of a state court on precisely the identical question of state law. The result might be widely destructive both of the proper relationship between state and federal law and of the uniformity of the administration of law within a State.

The interests of the federal treasury are essentially narrow here; they are entirely satisfied if a considered judgment is obtained from either a state or a federal court, after consideration of the pertinent materials, of the requirements of state law. For this purpose, the Commissioner need not have, and does not now ask, an opportunity to relitigate in federal courts every issue of state law that may involve federal tax consequences; the federal interest requires only that the Commissioner be permitted to obtain from the federal courts a considered adjudication of the relevant state law issues in cases in which, for whatever reason, the state courts have not already provided such an adjudication. In turn, it may properly be assumed that the state court has had an opportunity to make, and has made, such an adjudication if, in a proceeding untainted by fraud, it has had the benefit of reasoned argument from parties holding genuinely inconsistent interests.

I would therefore hold that in cases in which state-adjudicated property rights are contended to have federal tax consequences, federal courts must attribute conclusiveness to the judgment of a state court, of whatever level in the state procedural system, unless the litigation from which the judgment resulted does not bear the indicia of a genuinely adversary proceeding. I need not undertake to define with any particularity the weight I should give to the various possible factors involved in such an assessment; it suffices to illustrate the more important of the questions which I believe to be pertinent. The principal distinguishing characteristic of a state proceeding to which, in my view, conclusiveness should be attributed is less the number of parties represented before the state court than it is the actual adversity of their financial and other interests. It would certainly be pertinent if it appeared that all the parties had instituted the state proceeding solely for the purpose of defeating the federal revenue. The taking of an appeal would be significant, although scarcely determinative. The burden would be upon the taxpayer, in any case brought either for a redetermination of a deficiency or for a refund, to overturn the presumption * * * that the Commissioner had correctly assessed the necessary tax by establishing that the state court had had an opportunity to make, and had made, a reasoned resolution of the state law issues, after a proceeding in which the pertinent viewpoints had been presented. Proceedings in which one or more of the parties had been guilty of fraud in the presentation of the issues to the state court would, of course, ordinarily be entitled to little or no weight in the federal court's determination of state law.

I recognize, of course, that this approach lacks the precision of both the contrasting yardsticks suggested by the Court and by my Brother Douglas. Yet I believe that it reflects more faithfully than either of those resolutions the demands of our federal system and of the competing interests involved.[3] * * *

■ MR. JUSTICE FORTAS, dissenting.

While I join the dissenting opinion of my brother Harlan, I believe it appropriate to add these few comments. As my Brother Harlan states, in a case in which federal tax consequences depend upon state property interests, a federal court should accept the final conclusions of a competent state court, assuming that such a conclusion is an adjudication of substance arrived at after adversary litigation and on the basis of the same careful consideration that state courts normally accord cases involving the determination of state property interests. The touchstone of whether the state proceeding was "adversary" is not alone entirely satisfactory. I think that this concept has been helpfully embellished by Judge Raum of the United States Tax Court in the *Bosch* case, 43 T.C. 120, 123–24. Judge Raum suggests that among the factors to be considered in determining whether the decision of the state court is to be accepted as final for federal tax purposes are the following: whether the state court had jurisdiction, and

---

3. It may be doubted, however, whether this approach would actually produce serious practical disadvantages. It is essentially the standard which has been embodied in the Treasury Regulations since 1919, see now Reg. §§ 20.2053–1(b)(2), 20.2056(c)–2(d)(2), and which was urged before this Court in these cases by counsel for the United States. It is, moreover, similar to the standards employed in various opinions by a number of the courts of appeals. * * * If any practical difficulties actually attend this standard, they have apparently not, despite its wide use, yet appeared.

whether its determination is fully binding on the parties; whether, in practice, the decisions of the state court have precedential value throughout the State; whether the Commissioner was aware of the state proceedings and had an opportunity to participate; whether the state court "rendered a reasoned opinion and reached a 'deliberate conclusion,' Blair v. Commissioner, 300 U.S. [5], at p. 10"; whether the state decision has potentially offsetting tax consequences in respect of the state court litigant's federal taxes; and, in general, whether the state court decision "authoritatively determined" future property rights, and thus, as Judge Raum stated, "provided more than a label for past events * * *."

ILLUSTRATIVE MATERIAL

A. FURTHER PROCEEDINGS IN *BOSCH*

On remand from the Supreme Court, in a one-paragraph per curiam opinion containing no reasoning and based solely on the briefs and arguments of the parties, the Second Circuit concluded that the highest court of New York State would not follow the lower state court decision and would uphold Mrs. Bosch's partial release of her general power of appointment. 382 F.2d 295 (2d Cir. 1967). Presumably, Mr. Bosch's estate lost the estate tax marital deduction.

B. SCOPE OF THE *BOSCH* "PROPER REGARD" TEST

What did the Supreme Court mean in *Bosch* when it said that the federal courts must give "proper regard" to lower state court decisions? As pointed out above, in the *Bosch* case itself, the Second Circuit on remand concluded that the lower state court had misapplied state law. A recent study examined the federal courts' application of the "proper regard" test since *Bosch* and found that they have held in over one-half of the cases that the lower state court had misapplied state law. See Caron, The Federal Tax Implications of *Bush v. Gore*, 79 Wash. U. L.Q. 749 (2001). The "proper regard" standard of review thus in practice has become a de novo standard. As the *Goree* case illustrates, there are other ways to implement the *Bosch* "proper regard" standard of review that do not convert it into a de novo standard.

Estate of Goree v. Commissioner

68 T.C.M. 123 (1994).

■ WELLS, JUDGE:

[Robert W. Goree Jr. died intestate in an airplane crash. He was survived by his wife and three minor children. The principal asset of his estate was $3.9 million of stock in Russell Corp. His father was appointed administrator of his estate and his wife was appointed as conservator of the estates of his children. Under Alabama's intestacy statute, one-half of his estate would be distributed to his wife and the other one-half would be divided among the three children, resulting in significant estate tax liability. To prevent these adverse tax consequences, the wife petitioned the state probate court to enter protective orders authorizing each child to execute partial disclaimers renouncing any interest in their father's estate in excess of $200,000. The plan thus was to defer the estate tax by having $600,000 pass to the three children to use up their father's unified credit, with the remaining assets passing to the wife under the state intestacy statute to qualify for the marital deduction. The probate court appointed the former head of the state trial lawyers association and family friend as guardian *ad litem* for the children. After a hearing, the probate court approved the disclaimers as being in the best interests of the children.] * * *

In the notice of deficiency, respondent determined that the disclaimers were not valid under Alabama law and disallowed the marital deduction for the property passing to Mrs. Goree as a result of the disclaimers.

The first issue we must decide is whether the disclaimers executed on behalf of decedent's children meet the requirements of § 2518(b). Petitioner contends that it is entitled to a marital deduction for the value of the property which passed to Mrs. Goree as a result of the disclaimers. Section 2056(a) allows a marital deduction from a decedent's gross estate for the value of property interests passing from a decedent to his or her surviving spouse. Reg. § 20.2056(d)–1(b) provides that, when property passes from a decedent to a person other than the surviving spouse, and that person makes a qualified disclaimer that results in the surviving spouse's being entitled to such property, the disclaimed interest is treated as passing directly from decedent to the surviving spouse. * * *

To satisfy the provision of § 2518(b)(4) requiring that the disclaimed interest pass without any direction from the disclaimant to either the surviving spouse or to a person other than the disclaimant, the disclaimer must result in a valid passing of the interest to such person by operation of State law. * * * In other words, as Federal law does not prescribe rules for the passing of disclaimed property interests, disclaimed property which does not pass in a manner that is provided by State law violates the "without any direction" requirement of § 2518(b)(4), because it therefore must pass by direction of the disclaimant. In the instant case, respondent concedes that if the Court finds that the disclaimers are valid under Alabama law, then they are qualified disclaimers within the meaning of § 2518(b). Consequently, we will focus our inquiry on whether the interests of decedent's children in decedent's estate were properly disclaimed under Alabama law. Petitioner bears the burden of proof. * * *

In the instant case, respondent contends that we are required, under the Supreme Court's holding in Commissioner v. Estate of Bosch, 387 U.S. 456 (1967), to review the Probate Court proceedings de novo to ascertain what is in the best interests of decedent's children, rather than applying the standard of review used by the Alabama appellate courts when reviewing findings of fact made by the lower courts. Respondent also contends that a de novo review of the Probate Court proceedings, based upon the testimony presented in the instant case, would show that the conservator's sole motive in seeking the protective orders authorizing the partial disclaimers was to minimize Federal estate taxes. Respondent contends that the disclaimers benefit only decedent's estate, through the reduction of Federal estate taxes, and, as a matter of Alabama law, are not in the best interests of decedent's children. In other words, respondent contends that the Probate Court judge misapplied Alabama law in deciding that the partial disclaimers were in the children's best interests, and that the disclaimers are therefore not valid under Alabama law. Accordingly, respondent argues that the disclaimers fail to qualify under § 2518(b) and that petitioner is therefore not entitled to a marital deduction for the value of the property interests passing to Mrs. Goree as a result of unqualified disclaimers.

In Estate of Bosch v. Commissioner, supra at 465, the Supreme Court held that Federal courts are not bound by a State trial court's adjudication of property rights under State law, but the State trial court's decision should be given due regard. The Supreme Court also stated that "state law as announced by the highest court of the State is to be followed." Id. The Supreme Court also stated that the State's intermediate appellate court decisions should be considered by Federal courts when deciding State law unless the Federal court is convinced that the highest court of the State would decide otherwise. Id.

To decide whether the highest court of Alabama would decide contrary to the Probate Court judge's decision in the instant case, we will consider the standard of review that the Alabama Supreme Court would use to review the Probate Court judge's decision. * * *

Under Alabama law, a reviewing court must affirm the trial court unless its findings are "plainly and palpably erroneous." * * * The standard of review applied by both the Alabama Supreme Court and the Alabama Civil Court of Appeals in reviewing a lower court judge's exercise of discretion when deciding what is in the best interests of the protected person before the court is whether the judge's decision is "plainly and palpably erroneous." * * *

In the instant case, petitioner has shown that the Probate Court judge's decision to enter protective orders permitting Mrs. Goree, as conservator, to partially disclaim her children's interests in their father's estate was not "plainly and palpably erroneous." All of the parties to the Probate Court proceedings, as well as the Probate Court judge, testified at the trial in the instant case.[4]

During the Probate Court hearing and during the trial of the instant case, Mrs. Goree testified that her primary motivation in executing the disclaimers was to preserve the capital of decedent's estate so that she would be better able to provide for her children. * * *

---

4. * * * [T]here was no record or transcript of the Probate Court proceedings. Unlike the Alabama Supreme Court or the Alabama Circuit Court, which would have to review the Probate Court proceedings without the benefit of a transcript, we had all of the parties, as well as the Probate Court judge, appear and testify before us in the instant case.

Decedent's father, Robert W. Goree, was not present at the Probate Court hearing but did testify in the instant case. Mr. Goree stated that he, along with the other members of his family, fully supported the execution of the disclaimers by Mrs. Goree. Moreover, Mr. Goree stated that he disclaimed any interest he might have been entitled to receive from his son's estate as a result of the children's disclaimers in order to insure that the disclaimed interests would pass to Mrs. Goree. Mr. Goree also testified that he believed that the disclaimers were in the children's best interests because it was the best way to preserve decedent's estate for the benefit of decedent's children. Additionally, Mr. Goree testified that decedent's grandfather was of the view that the family should not sell Russell Corp. stock as long as the company was doing well and that the grandfather's children had "inherited" their grandfather's philosophy. Mr. Goree stated that he believed that his son never sold any shares of Russell Corp. stock. Finally, Mr. Goree testified that upon his death, decedent's children would inherit 109,984 shares of Russell Corp. common stock from the estate of Julia Russell Goree.

The Probate Court judge testified that, during the Probate Court hearing, Mrs. Goree stated that she was seeking the disclaimers in order to preserve the capital of decedent's estate so that she could take better care of her children. Additionally, the Probate Court judge stated that he heard testimony regarding the inheritances decedent's children would be receiving in the future from other members of the Russell family and that all of such circumstances were factors in his decision to grant the protective orders authorizing the disclaimers.

Mr. Morris, the guardian ad litem who represented the children in the Probate Court proceedings, testified that he initially objected to the entering of the protective orders permitting the partial disclaimers. Upon hearing the evidence presented and Mrs. Goree's arguments as to why it was in the best interests of her children to execute the partial disclaimers, Mr. Morris withdrew his objection. He testified that he was persuaded that the proposed course of action was in the best interests of the children.

Respondent contends that the guardian ad litem and the Probate Court judge merely "rubber stamped" the conservator's petition for protective orders and that they did not actually consider the best interests of the children. Respondent contends that the guardian ad litem and the Probate Court judge only considered whether the disclaimers would reduce petitioner's Federal estate taxes. We do not agree with respondent's contention that tax considerations were the only reason for Mrs. Goree's decision to request the protective orders. Certainly, tax considerations were present: Decedent's children disclaimed only the amount of their inheritance that exceeded the amount equivalent to the unified credit that was available to decedent's estate. The mere fact that the parties to the Probate Court proceedings considered the Federal estate tax consequences of the partial disclaimers, however, does not alone convince us that the Probate Court judge abused his discretion, or in the terms of the standard of review under Alabama law, was "plainly and palpably erroneous" in finding that the disclaimers were in the best interests of decedent's children. * * * Based on the record of the instant case, the Probate Court, when deciding whether the disclaimers were in the best interest of decedent's children, considered the testimony that Mrs. Goree's ability to provide and care for her children would be greatly improved if decedent's Federal estate tax liability were minimized by making the partial disclaimers. The Probate Court judge also considered the testimony that both the Russell and the Goree families have a unique relationship to the Russell Corp. (including the families' long-held philosophy of retaining Russell Corp. stock for the benefit of their descendants which would inure to the benefit of decedent's children). The Probate Court judge also heard testimony that decedent's children are likely to receive large inheritances upon the deaths of other members of the Russell and Goree families. Consequently, there was support for the Probate Court judge's finding that the disclaimers served the best interests of decedent's minor children.

The only question we are asked to decide in the instant case is whether the interests in decedent's estate were properly disclaimed under Alabama law. Respondent argues that the interests were not properly disclaimed because the disclaimers were not in the best interests of decedent's children and that we must undertake a de novo review of the Probate Court disclaimer proceedings. We do not agree with respondent's contention that we are required to make such a review. Under Alabama law, the proper standard guiding our review of the Probate Court judge's decision is whether his decision was "plainly and palpably erroneous." Based on the record in the instant case, we hold that the Probate Court judge's decision as to the question of what was in the best interests of decedent's children was not "plainly and palpably erroneous" and that the partial disclaimers were therefore properly made under Alabama law. Consequently, the disclaimers qualify under § 2518(b), and petitioner is entitled to a marital deduction under § 2056(a) for the disclaimed interests. * * *

ILLUSTRATIVE MATERIAL

A.   FURTHER PROCEEDINGS IN GOREE

The Service issued a nonacquiescence in *Goree* and contended that the Tax Court erred in not conducting a de novo review of the Alabama probate court's ruling in light of the nonadversarial nature of the state proceeding:

"[T]he situation that prompted the rule in *Estate of Bosch* did not involve an adversarial 'main event,' but the opposite extreme of possible collusion between the parties. 387 U.S. at 462. Similarly, in this case there was doubt as to the adversarial nature of the state court proceeding, and as to the extent of the testimonial evidence available to the trier of fact. In addition, there was no factual record available for review; the Tax Court was required to make its own record, but then reviewed the state court conclusions of fact based upon this subsequently created record, using an appellate (palpably erroneous) standard. The utilization of the palpably erroneous standard for review of factual findings in a nonadversarial situation is inconsistent with the rationale for the palpably erroneous standard, which assumes a vigorously contested lower court hearing." A.O.D. 1996–001 (Mar. 4, 1996). The Service thus advocates a de novo standard where the lower state court proceeding lacks the requisite degree of nonadversariness, even though the *Bosch* majority adopted the "proper regard" standard as a way to "avoid much of the uncertainty that would result from the 'nonadversary' approach" urged by the dissent.

Despite the Service's apparent disagreement with the underpinnings of the *Bosch* decision, the Service did not recommend appeal of the Tax Court's decision in *Goree* because it was not convinced, even under a de minimis standard of review, that the Alabama probate court had erred in determining the best interests of the children. The Supreme Court previously granted a writ of certiorari to reconsider the *Bosch* "proper regard" standard but, after hearing oral argument, dismissed the writ on technical grounds. United States v. White, 853 F.2d 107 (2d Cir. 1988), cert. dismissed, 493 U.S. 5 (1989) (per curiam).

B. DEFERENCE TO STATE COURT DECISIONS IN "ADVERSARY" PROCEEDINGS

Other courts, like the Service in *Goree*, have embraced the adversariness approach despite its rejection in *Bosch*. See Brown v. United States, 890 F.2d 1329, 1342 (5th Cir. 1989) ("Federal courts have not looked favorably on taxpayer attempts to achieve post-death estate planning by employing nonadversary probate court proceedings that are essentially in the nature of consent decrees or advisory opinions."); Lemle v. United States, 579 F.2d 185, 187 (2d Cir. 1978) (probate court decision not followed where not "contested construction of state law").

In contrast, other courts have noted that *Bosch* rejected the use of the nonadversariness approach. See Keinath v. Commissioner, 480 F.2d 57, 62 n.7 (8th Cir. 1973) ("federal courts are not bound by a particular decision of a state court regardless of whether the adjudication was nonadversary, consensual or collusive"); Trent v. United States, 1990–1 U.S.T.C. ¶ 60,008, at 84,213 (S.D. Ohio 1987) (lower state court decision "need not be adversarial, as the government contends, in order to be binding" on federal court), rev'd, 893 F.2d 846 (6th Cir.), cert. denied, 498 U.S. 814 (1990).

Several commentators have argued that the result in *Bosch* seems questionable with regard to its impact on the administration of national tax laws. Applicable federal tax results turn on local law, to be sure, and a rule requiring federal relitigation of all questions involving state law obviously would be intolerable. On the other hand, the danger of a less than adversary adjudication in the state courts at the expense of the federal revenue and uniform administration of the tax laws is a serious one. From that perspective, the needs of the federal government could be best accommodated with those of the states by a rule such as that suggested by Justice Harlan, requiring federal deference to a truly adversary state proceeding, regardless of the level in the state judicial system at which the proceeding took place. If, under such a rule, a taxpayer decided to incur the expense of a non-adversary proceeding in a state court, he would do so in the knowledge that he might well have to relitigate the same issue in a federal tax action.

Under *Bosch*, a non-adversary proceeding that results in a judgment by the highest court in the state apparently precludes federal redetermination of the state law. Anecdotal evidence suggests that parties often seek and receive a determination of state law rights by the highest court in the state, notwithstanding the lack of material adverse interest between the litigants. Several commentators contend that the adversary proceeding rule would appear to achieve the desired tax uniformity without the possibility of duplicative or collusive litigation. Sometimes, it may be hard to determine whether the state proceeding was sufficiently "adversary," but this difficulty must be balanced against the difficulty and appropriateness of a federal court's determining the state law. See Wolfman, *Bosch*, Its Implications and Aftermath: The Effect of State Court Adjudications on Federal Tax Litigation, 3 U.Miami Inst.on Est. Plan 2–1 (1969); Bruce, *Bosch* and Other Dilemmas: Binding the Parties and the Tax Consequences in Trust Dispute Resolution, 18 U.Miami Inst.on Est. Plan. 9–1 (1984).

C. DEFERENCE TO STATE COURT DECISIONS THROUGH *ERIE* FRAMEWORK

Like the Tax Court in *Goree*, other courts, including the Second Circuit on remand from the Supreme Court in *Bosch*, have used the *Erie* framework to implement the *Bosch* "proper regard" standard by giving the same deference to the lower state court decision that it would have received on appeal in the state court system. See Commissioner v. Estate of Bosch, 382 F.2d 295, 295 (2d Cir. 1967) (per curiam) (highest state court "would not follow the decision of the [probate court]"); Estate of Salter v. Commissioner, 545 F.2d 494, 500–01 (5th Cir. 1977) ("best measure" of "proper regard" standard was to determine whether highest court of state "would have affirmed the [probate court's] decree had there been an appeal").

Several commentators argue that the *Erie* approach is preferable to the adversariness approach because it keeps the focus on the correctness of the state court decision rather than on the subsidiary issue of the adversariness of the state court proceeding. See Caron, Tax Court and Service Stake Out Positions in State Law Debate, 71 Tax Notes 229 (1996); Caron, *Bosch* and the Allure of Adversariness, 64 Tax Notes 674 (1994); Browne & Hinkle, Tax Effects of Non–Litigation: *Bosch* and Beyond, 27 N.Y.U. Inst. on Fed. Tax'n 1415 (1969).

*

PART II

COMPOSITION OF THE TAX BASE: GENERAL PRINCIPLES

CHAPTER 12

THE SCOPE OF THE ESTATE TAX: § 2033

Internal Revenue Code: §§ 2031(a); 2033; 2041

Regulations: §§ 20.2031–1(a); 20.2033–1

INTRODUCTORY MATERIAL

Current § 2033 originated in the Revenue Act of 1926. It brings into the gross estate "the value of all property to the extent of the interest therein of the decedent at the time of his death." The 1916 Act was phrased differently, including only property "[t]o the extent of the interest therein of the decedent at the time of his death *which* after his death is subject to the payment of the charges against his estate *and* the expenses of its administration *and* is subject to distribution as part of his estate." After interpreting the italicized conditions that qualify the word "interest" in the conjunctive, the Supreme Court in 1930 held that real estate which was not subject to the payment of administration expenses according to Missouri law was not part of the gross estate.[1] Anticipation of precisely that interpretation of the statute, and the resulting inequality of estate taxes among the states based solely on local law differences, prompted Congress to eliminate the qualifying conditions and adopt the wording of the 1926 Act.[2]

Since 1916, the statute has focused on the "interest" of the decedent in "property." When does the decedent have such an interest? Analytically, this question includes both state and federal law components: under state law, does the decedent possess an interest in property at death; if so, is that interest of a kind contemplated by the use in § 2033 of the words "interest" and "property"?

SECTION A. BENEFICIAL OWNERSHIP

Because the estate tax is an excise on the act of transferring wealth at death, the tax base must include the value of the property that most obviously is transferred: property directly owned by the decedent. That is the function of § 2033. Section 2033 applies to the decedent's securities, bank deposits, and real estate. Rights to income that accrued before death and are collectible by the estate, such as rents, interest, dividends, partnership profit shares, refunds, and vested rights to death benefits, are includa-

---

1. Crooks v. Harrelson, 282 U.S. 55 (1930).

2. See H.R.Rep. No. 1, 69th Cong., 1st Sess. 15 (1926).

ble in the gross estate. Also includable are promissory notes, whether matured or not, insurance policies owned by the decedent on the life of another, saleable leasehold interests, interests in property as tenant in common, and one-half of community property. Federal and state bonds are includable despite their exemption from other taxation either by their express terms or by law, since the estate tax is an excise tax imposed on the "transfer" only. See Greene v. United States, 171 F.Supp. 459 (Ct.Cl. 1959); Reg. § 20.2033–1. Of course, if the decedent holds only bare legal title to property, as in the case of a trustee under an enforceable oral or written trust agreement, she does not possess an interest taxable under § 2033. Reed v. Commissioner, 36 F.2d 867 (5th Cir. 1930).

The estate tax would be quickly marginalized were it concerned only with directly-owned property. Many property interests fall short of outright ownership, yet provide the decedent with a full measure of control or of economic enjoyment that passes to another at death. The evolution of sophisticated property law concepts and forms, particularly the common law institution of trusts and state statutory creations such as partnerships and limited liability companies, has challenged Congress to make difficult choices in the selection of the interests to be reflected in the tax base.

Principal reliance on judicial and administrative interpretation of § 2033's simple language potentially would yield overinclusion: on its face, the phrase "to the extent of the interest therein of the decedent" does not exclude much. Limits would have to be established; the definitional process would be unacceptably laborious. Congress has responded by specifically prescribing those property interests that are to be taxed, even though they lie beyond the reach of § 2033. The scope of § 2033 is best understood as a baseline, in contrast to other specific inclusion provisions, in particular, § 2041, relating to powers of appointment. The technicalities of § 2041 are explored in Chapter 22, but its general rules are described here because many of the materials that follow make that contrast.

Property law sees a power as an agency. In broad terms, a power of appointment is an authority created or reserved by a person (the "donor") having property subject to his disposition, enabling the powerholder (the "donee") to designate, within limits prescribed by the donor, who shall receive the property and in what shares or manner. As an agent, the donee does not own the appointive property directly. But he does hold one of the more significant attributes of an owner: the power to dispose. Despite its literal sweep, § 2033 has not been interpreted to reach that kind of power. Nonetheless, if a power to dispose of property is so broad as to permit the donee to appropriate the property to herself, the donee, economically speaking, has the functional equivalent of direct ownership. Section 2041, therefore, includes within the donee's gross estate property subject at her death to a *general* power of appointment: one that is exercisable in favor of the donee, her estate, her creditors, or the creditors of her estate. With some exceptions, property subject to lesser powers is not includable.

In most situations, there is no dispute over what property interests fall within § 2033. The types of property interests considered in the following materials represent items on the perimeter of § 2033, situations in which the Service has sought to extend the sweep of § 2033 to its outer limits. It should also be kept in mind that a court determination that a particular item is outside the scope of the estate tax may cause the Service to shift either to the gift tax or to the generation-skipping tax as the vehicle for imposition of a transfer tax.

Helvering v. Safe Deposit & Trust Co.

316 U.S. 56 (1942).

[Zachary Smith Reynolds ("D"), age 20, died on July 6, 1932. At the time, he was beneficiary of three trusts: one created by his father's will in 1918, one by deed executed by his mother in 1923, and one created by his mother's will in 1924. From his father's trust, D was to receive only a portion of the income prior to his 28th birthday, at which time, if living, he was to become the outright owner of the trust property, including all accumulated income. His mother's trusts directed that he enjoy the income for life, subject to certain restrictions before he reached the age of 28. Each of the trusts gave D a general testamentary power of appointment over the trust property; in default of exercise of the power the properties were to go to his descendants, or if he had none, to his brother and sisters and their issue per stirpes.

The Commissioner included all the trust property within D's gross estate for the purpose of computing the Federal estate tax. The Board of Tax Appeals and the Circuit Court of Appeals, however, held that none of the trust property should have been included.

On these facts the Government argued the following before the Supreme Court:

"The decedent had an 'interest' in the trust property within the meaning of [§ 2033] and the value of that property was therefore properly included by the Commissioner in decedent's gross estate.

"A. This Court has frequently ruled that one who has all the substantial attributes of ownership of property, although no title thereto, is to be treated as the owner of the property for tax purposes. This rule is based on the unassailable assumption that Congress, in enacting the revenue laws, intends tax consequences to depend upon the substance of things and not upon the 'niceties of the law of trusts and conveyances.' Helvering v. Clifford, 309 U.S. 331, 334. That rule is fully applicable to [§ 2033], for this Court has consistently recognized that the criterion for imposition of the estate tax is the transfer of the economic benefits of property at the decedent's death and not the mere passage of a technical legal or equitable title. * * *

"The court below disregarded these controlling principles. It held that Congress, in enacting [§ 2033], intended to tax only the devolution of property owned by the decedent and which passed at his death by will or intestacy, and that since, under state law, decedent had no legal or equitable title to the trust property and it therefore did not pass as part of his estate, it was not taxable to his estate under [§ 2033]. The court refused to consider whether the decedent's 'bundle of rights' in the trust property gave him the same rights of enjoyment and disposition as an owner; in the view of the court, it was decisive that, under state law, no single one of decedent's rights, considered separately, conferred upon decedent any technical, legal or equitable title.

"This construction of the statute accords neither with the literal language nor the legislative history of [§ 2033]. Had Congress intended to tax only the transfer of title to property which passes as part of the decedent's estate, it would scarcely have used the word 'interest' as the sole statutory test—a word completely inapt if intended to connote only legal or equitable titles. From 1916 until 1926, the statute was in fact confined to property interests of the decedent which were 'subject to distribution as part of his estate'; in the Revenue Act of 1926, however, Congress deleted this provision. To construe the statute as did the court below, therefore, is to read into it a limitation for which Congress not only failed to provide but which it saw fit specifically to eliminate. Furthermore, the construction of the statute adopted by the court below leaves unanswered the critical question of why Congress would have wanted to draw a distinction for tax purposes between an owner of property and a person having substantially the same rights of enjoyment and disposition as an owner, although not his legal title.

"B. At the time of his death, decedent did possess substantially all the attributes of ownership of the trust property:

"(1) He had an exclusive lifetime enjoyment of the property, subject only to a restraint on alienation and restrictions on the use of income until he reached the age of 28.

"(2) He had, in addition, an unrestricted power of testamentary disposition, including the power to appoint the property to his own estate or to his creditors. Such a power to bestow his property upon any person he chooses is the only attribute of ownership available even to an absolute fee owner 'at the time of his death'—the determinative time under the statute. This court has frequently stated that 'for purposes of taxation, a general power of appointment [is] equivalent to ownership of the property subject to the power' (Curry v. McCanless, 307 U.S. 357, 371 * * *), and has specifically pointed out that 'the nonexercise of the power may be as much a disposition of property testamentary in nature as would be its exercise at death.' Chase National Bank v. United States, 278 U.S. 327, 338.

"(3) Finally, decedent had the assurance that if he failed effectively to exercise his testamentary powers of appointment, the property would go to members of his immediate family who were the natural objects of his testamentary bounty, namely, his children, or, if none, his brother and sisters. Such a gift-over provision is comparable to the provision of law for the distribution of property in the event of the death of an absolute fee owner intestate.

"Because of this 'bundle of rights' possessed by the decedent, we think it plain that the attributes of ownership which he had at the time of his death were substantially the same as though he had been given a fee title to the trust property, subject to a restriction on alienation and limitations as to the use of the income, and that, therefore, under the rationale of the *Clifford* case, decedent was properly treated as the owner of the property for purposes of [§ 2033].

"C. There is nothing in the structure or legislative history of the estate tax law, or in the decisions construing it, which prevents application of the *Clifford* rule to the present case.

"(1) The legislative history of [§ 2033] refutes the view, expressed by the court below, that the specific provision of [§ 2041] for the taxation of property passing pursuant to the exercise of a power of appointment indicates that Congress did not intend to tax property subject to an unexercised power. To sustain the view of the court below in this respect, respondents must contend that Congress did not intend the combination of rights possessed by this decedent to constitute an 'interest' within [§ 2033] because when it amended [§ 2033] so as to broaden its scope and to make it susceptible of literal application to such a combination of rights, it failed at the same time to strike out the previously enacted provision of [§ 2041] which covered part of the same field. Such a contention does not accord with the realities of the lawmaking process.

"(2) United States v. Field, 255 U.S. 257, the principal authority relied upon by the court below, is distinguishable, for the statutory provision there under consideration was far narrower in scope than [§ 2033] as it appears at present.* Helvering v. Grinnell, 294 U.S. 153, and Morgan v. Commissioner, 309 U.S. 78, likewise relied upon by the court below, involved the interpretation of [the former version of § 2041]; no contention was made in either of those cases with respect to the proper construction of [§ 2033]."]

■ MR. JUSTICE BLACK delivered the opinion of the Court. * * *

The case presents two questions, the first of which is whether the decedent at the time of his death had by virtue of his general powers of appointment, even if never exercised, such an interest in the trust property as to require its inclusion in his gross estate under [§ 2033]. * * *

We find it unnecessary to decide between these [Government and taxpayer] conflicting contentions on the economic equivalence of the dece-

---

* [ED.: The Court in *Field* held that the value of property passing pursuant to the exercise of a testamentary general power of appointment was not includable in the powerholder's gross estate under the 1916 Act predecessor to § 2033, which at the time required as a condition of inclusion that property be "subject to distribution as part of the decedent's probate estate." The property subject to the power did not satisfy that condition and was not reached by the pre–1926 version of § 2033.]

dent's rights and complete ownership.[3] For even if we assume with the Government that the restrictions upon the decedent's use and enjoyment of the trust properties may be dismissed as negligible and that he had the capacity to exercise a testamentary power of appointment, the question still remains: Did the decedent have "at the time of his death" such an "interest" as Congress intended to be included in a decedent's gross estate under [§ 2033]? It is not contended that the benefits during life which the trusts provided for the decedent, terminating as they did at his death, made the trust properties part of his gross estate under the statute. And viewing [§ 2033] in its background of legislative, judicial, and administrative history, we cannot reach the conclusion that the words "interest * * * of the decedent at the time of his death" were intended by Congress to include property subject to a general testamentary power of appointment unexercised by the decedent.

The forerunner of [§ 2033] was section 202(a) of the Revenue Act of 1916, 39 Stat. 777. In United States v. Field, 255 U.S. 257, this Court held that property passing under a general power of appointment *exercised* by a decedent was not such an "interest" of the decedent as the 1916 Act brought within the decedent's gross estate. While the holding was limited to exercised powers of appointment, the approach of the Court, the authorities cited, and certain explicit statements in the opinion left little doubt that the Court regarded property subject to unexercised general powers of appointment as similarly beyond the scope of the statutory phrase "interest of the decedent."[4]

After the *Field* case, the provision it passed upon was reenacted without change in the Revenue Act of 1921 * * * and in the Revenue Act of 1924 * * *. If the implications of the *Field* opinion with respect to unexercised powers had been considered contrary to the intendment of the words "interest of the decedent," it is reasonable to suppose that Congress would have added some clarifying amendment.

If the counterparts in the earlier Acts of section 302(a) of the Revenue Act of 1926 did not require the inclusion of property subject to an unexercised general testamentary power of appointment within the decedent's gross estate, there is no basis for concluding that the amendment of 1926 changed the act in this respect. Prior to 1926 an "interest of the decedent" was to be included in his gross estate only if subject "after his death * * * to the payment of the charges against his estate and the

---

3. In declining to pass upon this issue, we do not reject the principle we have often recognized that the realities of the taxpayer's economic interest, rather than the niceties of the conveyancer's art, should determine the power to tax. See Curry v. McCanless, 307 U.S. 357, 371, and cases there cited. Nor do we deny the relevance of this principle as a guide to statutory interpretation where, unlike here, the language of a statute and its statutory history do not afford more specific indications of legislative intent. Helvering v. Clifford, 309 U.S. 331.

4. In Burnet v. Guggenheim, 288 U.S. 280, 288, this Court stated: "United States v. Field * * * holds that under the Revenue Act of 1916 * * * the subject of a power created by another is not a part of the estate of the decedent to whom the power was committed." It is to be noted that no distinction was recognized between exercised and unexercised powers under the rule of the *Field* case.

expenses of its administration and * * * subject to distribution as part of his estate." In the 1926 Act this qualification was abandoned. In the report accompanying the bill which embodied this change, the House Committee on Ways and Means stated only "[i]n the interest of certainty it is recommended that the limiting language * * * shall be eliminated in the proposed bill, so that the gross estate shall include the entire interest of the decedent at the time of his death in all the property."[5] Nothing in the report suggested that the change was intended to have any relevance to powers of appointment, and no such intention can reasonably be inferred from the amended section itself. * * *

When it was held in the *Field* case that property subject to an exercised general testamentary power of appointment was not to be included in the decedent's gross estate under the Revenue Act of 1916 [predecessor to § 2033], this Court referred to an amendment passed in 1919 [predecessor to § 2041] which specifically declared property passing under an exercised general testamentary power to be part of the decedent's gross estate. The passage of this amendment, said the Court, "indicates that Congress at least was doubtful whether the previous act included property passing by appointment." In the face of such doubts, which cannot reasonably be supposed to have been less than doubts with respect to *unexercised* powers, Congress nevertheless specified only that property subject to exercised powers should be included. From this deliberate singling out of *exercised* powers alone, without the corroboration of the other matters we have discussed, a Congressional intent to treat *unexercised* powers otherwise can be deduced. * * *

In no judicial opinion brought to our attention has it been held that the gross estate of a decedent includes, for purposes of the Federal Estate Tax, property subject to an unexercised general power. On the contrary, as the court below points out, "the courts have been at pains to consider whether property passed under a general power or not so as to be taxable under [§ 2041], a consideration which would have been absolutely unnecessary if the estate were taxable under [§ 2033] because of the mere existence of a general power whether exercised or not." 121 F.2d 307, 312. In addition, the uniform administrative practice until this case arose appears to have placed an interpretation upon the Federal Estate Tax contrary to that the Government now urges. No regulations issued under the several revenue acts, including those in effect at the time this suit was initiated, prescribe that property subject to an unexercised general testamentary power of appointment should be included in a decedent's gross estate. Because of the combined effect of all of these circumstances, we believe that a departure from the long-standing, generally accepted construction of [§ 2033], now contested for the first time by the Government, would override the best indications we have of Congressional intent. * * *

[The judgment of the Court of Appeals was reversed, however, on the ground that a part of the trust corpus passed under a general power of

---

5. House Report No. 1, 69th Cong., 1st Sess. 15.

appointment exercised by the decedent, and was therefore includable in his gross estate under § 2041.]

ILLUSTRATIVE MATERIAL

A.   ESTATE TAX TREATMENT OF PROPERTY SUBJECT TO POWER OF APPOINTMENT

The estate tax provisions applicable at the time of the *Safe Deposit & Trust Co.* case specifically included in the gross estate property passing pursuant to a general power of appointment exercised by the decedent, but were silent as to the effect of an unexercised power. The powers of appointment provisions were completely revised in 1942 and 1951, and property subject to a general power of appointment created after October 21, 1942 is includable in the gross estate under § 2041 regardless of whether it is exercised. See Chapter 22.

B.   THE RELATIONSHIP BETWEEN § 2033 AND OTHER PROVISIONS REQUIRING INCLUSION IN THE GROSS ESTATE

The *Safe Deposit & Trust Co.* decision continues to be important because it indicates that § 2033 is not to be read as broadly in the estate tax as is § 61 in the income tax. Thus, in the estate tax, §§ 2034–2044 generally expand the scope of § 2033. In contrast, §§ 71–138 generally limit the expansiveness of § 61 as interpreted by the courts.

Because the estate tax is an excise on the act of transfer, an "interest" in "property" is interpreted for purposes of § 2033 in terms of whether the decedent had at death something that she could transfer to a successor. If decedent's interest came into existence during her life and is not cut off by death, the value of the interest is includable in her gross estate. On the other hand, § 2033 does not reach an interest that is terminated by death.

For example, if A transfers property in trust to B for life, remainder to C, or if C predeceases B, remainder to D, nothing is included in B's estate at B's death because B's interest ends at her death. Remainder interests that are extinguished at death are excluded on the same ground, so nothing is includable in C's estate if C dies while B is still alive:

> "Where the interest retained by a decedent in transferred property is a possibility of reverter which is obliterated by his death, or, where the interest of a decedent in a trust created by another person is a contingent remainder which lapses at his death, such interest is not considered as an interest in property for the purposes of [§ 2033]."

Rev.Rul. 55–438, 1955–2 C.B. 601. Similarly, if D purchases a life annuity without refund or survivorship features, § 2033 includes nothing, because at D's death the annuity payments end. D possesses no interest that she can transfer to a successor (but § 2039, discussed in chapter 20, may be applicable if the annuity contract includes refund or survivorship elements).

Taxpayers have argued that § 2033 does not reach future interests possessed by a decedent because they are "contingent." Whether the interest is denominated by local law as "contingent," "vested," "vested subject to open," "vested subject to divestment," "future," "reversionary," "possibility of reverter,'' or anything else should not affect its includability under § 2033. Instead, if it is determined that D's interest survived him and could be transferred at death, only the question of valuation should remain. Estate of Henry v. Commissioner, 4 T.C. 423 (1944), aff'd on other grounds, 161 F.2d 574 (3d Cir. 1947) (D's possibility of reverter in a trust would have materialized only upon the failure of D's entire line of descent; the predecessor of § 2033 required inclusion of this interest, remoteness affected only the valuation of the reverter); Rev. Rul. 67–370, 1967–2 C.B. 324 (D's remainder interest in a trust, which could be revoked by grantor and was in fact revoked by grantor after D's death, was includible in D's gross estate because D held a transferable interest in the trust at death).

C. SECTION 2033 AND STATE PROPERTY LAW

Tangible and intangible property interests recognized by state law are covered by § 2033. See Reg. § 20.2033–1(a). In both cases, the application of § 2033 turns on whether the interest is covered by state law property concepts.

In most cases, the application of § 2033 to tangible property interests is straightforward. Occasionally, however, there may be a dispute over the scope of state property law. One example is Estate of Frazier v. Commissioner. A commercial tenant continued to occupy real estate owned by D after the expiration of a ten-year lease. The § 2033 question was whether certain improvements made by the tenant became D's property upon expiration of the lease. The Tax Court held that the value of the improvements was includible in D's estate on the ground that the tenant's right to remove its trade fixtures expired with the end of the lease under state property law. 77 T.C.M. 2197 (1999). The Ninth Circuit reversed, taking a different view of state property law in holding that a holdover tenant retained the right to remove its trade fixtures, but remanded the case back to the Tax Court to determine whether the improvements in question constituted trade fixtures under state property law. 12 Fed. Appx. 502 (9th Cir. 2001). On remand, the Tax Court surveyed state property law and concluded that certain improvements were not trade fixtures (those affixed to the ground) and thus were includible in D's estate under § 2033, while other improvements were trade fixtures (those not affixed to the ground) and thus not includible in D's gross estate. 83 T.C.M. 1636 (2002).

The same method of analysis applies to intangible property interests. For example, in Estate of Pascal v. Commissioner, 22 T.C.M. 1766 (1963), the Tax Court included in D's estate intangible property rights recognized under state law (the right to produce a musical based on George Bernard Shaw's play *Pygmalion*, released after D's death to widespread artistic and financial success as *My Fair Lady*). However, as state property law evolves to protect other types of intangible property interests, the reach of § 2033 also expands. For example, in Estate of Andrews v. United States, 850 F.Supp. 1279 (E.D.Va. 1994), the district court held that the value of the right of publicity embodied in a famous decedent's name was a property interest protected by state law and descendible to the heirs, and thus includable in D's estate under § 2033.

In these situations, it is state property law, rather than § 2033, that poses the more difficult interpretive issue. As noted in the previous chapter, the determination of state law in a federal tax proceeding can be a nettlesome issue. For example, in a 1980 diversity case, the Sixth Circuit held that Elvis Presley's right of publicity was not descendible under Tennessee law. Memphis Development Foundation v. Factors Etc., Inc., 616 F.2d 956 (6th Cir. 1980). In 1981, the Second Circuit deferred to the Sixth Circuit's view of Tennessee law. Factors Etc., Inc. v. Pro Arts, Inc., 652 F.2d 278 (2d Cir. 1981). The Second Circuit subsequently refused to recall its mandate after intermediate Tennessee appellate courts took conflicting positions on the descendibility of the right of publicity. Factors Etc., Inc. v. Pro Arts, Inc., 701 F.2d 11 (2d Cir. 1983). In 1987, an intermediate Tennessee appellate court concluded that these federal courts had misread Tennessee law. State ex rel. Elvis Presley v. Crowell, 733 S.W.2d 89 (Tenn. Ct. App. 1987). The Elvis Presley saga illustrates the difficult time the federal courts and the Service may face in determining whether a right of publicity otherwise includable in a decedent's estate under § 2033 is a recognized property interest under state law. See Caron, Estate Planning Implications of the Right of Publicity, 68 Tax Notes 95 (1995). For a recent discussion of this issue in the context of Marilyn Monroe's right of publicity, see Mitchell M. Gans, Bridget J. Crawford & Jonathan G. Blattmachr, Postmortem Rights of Publicity: The Federal Estate Tax Consequences of New State–Law Property Rights, 117 Yale L.J. Pocket Part 203 (2008); Joshua Tate, Marilyn Monroe's Legacy: Taxation of Postmortem Publicity Rights, 118 Yale L.J. Pocket Part 38 (2008); Mitchell M. Gans, Bridget J. Crawford & Jonathan G. Blattmachr, The Estate Tax Fundamentals of Celebrity and Control, 118 Yale L.J. Pocket Part 203 (2008).

SECTION B.   INTERESTS ARISING AT DEATH

Connecticut Bank & Trust Co. v. United States

465 F.2d 760 (2d Cir. 1972).

■ ROBERT P. ANDERSON, CIRCUIT JUDGE:

On June 14, 1965, Warren and Virginia Horton and Charles and Mary Ann Musk were killed when the car in which they were riding exploded after being struck by a tractor-trailer truck, owned by HMH Motor Service while traveling the Chesapeake Bay Bridge Tunnel in Virginia. The estate of Mrs. Horton is not involved in this litigation. Mr. and Mrs. Musk and Mr. Horton (the decedents) were domiciled in Connecticut at the time of their deaths and letters testamentary were issued to The Connecticut Bank and Trust Company as executor of their respective wills.

During 1966, the executor commenced wrongful death actions in the state courts of New York against HMH * * *. The suits were settled for $320,000 before going to trial. The recovery of this amount, which was made on the assumption of instantaneous deaths, included nothing for ante-mortem pain and suffering.

Although the proceeds were held by the executor for distribution in accordance with the terms of the wills, they were not included by the executor in the decedents' gross estates for the federal estate tax; the

Commissioner, however, determined that they should have been included and he accordingly assessed deficiencies against each of the estates. The deficiencies were paid and these suits were filed on the claims for refunds.

The district court * * * held that the wrongful death recoveries, and therefore the legal interests which the Commissioner sought to tax, * * * were ascertained and determined under Connecticut law, a conclusion, the correctness of which, is not questioned on these appeals; and it further held that all sums recovered under Connecticut's wrongful death statutes were properties held by the decedents at the time of their deaths and were therefore parts of their gross estates under § 2033 of the Internal Revenue Code. We are unable, however, to agree with this determination.

The crucial issue to be decided under § 2033 is whether or not the value of an action for wrongful death is "property * * * of the decedent at the time of his death." Much of the Government's argument and the opinion of the court below rest on the differences between the Connecticut statutory scheme for wrongful death recovery and the more common pattern of recovery in the majority of the states based upon "Lord Campbell's Act," which provides for a direct right of action on behalf of designated beneficiaries of the decedent to recover for his wrongful death, with damages to be measured by the loss to the survivors * * *. The Connecticut statutes, on the other hand, provide for a right of action in the executor or administrator, with damages to be measured on the basis of the loss of the decedent's ability to carry on life's activities * * *. In addition, by recent amendments, the wrongful death proceeds in Connecticut are distributed according to the terms of the decedent's will, if there is one, and are subject to the general claims of the estate. The differences in results under the two types of statutes may be more theoretical than real, * * * but in any event, these differences have little relevance concerning the question of whether or not the right of action for wrongful death was property owned at death.

Simple logic mandates the conclusion that an action for wrongful death cannot exist until the decedent has died, at which point, he is no longer a person capable of owning any property interests. The Government's reply to this is that at the very instant of death the right of action arose which the decedent was then capable of owning at death. The only authorities cited for this position, however, are cases where preexisting property interests were valued as of the instant of death, but valuation at time of death of prior existing interests is a far different concern from that in this case where the property interest itself has sprung from the fact that the death has taken place.

While it is true that Congress may constitutionally place an excise tax on property created by death, as well as upon property transferred by death, * * * § 2033 does not read so broadly. In a discussion of the estate tax the Supreme Court described the scope of § 2033: "What this law taxes is not the interest to which the legatees and devisees succeeded on death, but the interest which ceased by reason of the death," Y.M.C.A. of Columbus, Ohio v. Davis, 264 U.S. 47, 50 (1924) * * *. Where, as here, there was no property interest in the decedent which passed by virtue of his death, but rather one which arose after his death, such an interest is not property owned at death and not part of the gross estate under § 2033 * * *.

This construction of the relevant statutes is supported both by Connecticut law and Treasury Department Revenue Rulings. The Connecticut Supreme Court has stated that under Connecticut statutes "no person, during his lifetime, can possess an action or right of action embracing, as elements of damage, his own death or any of its direct consequences," * * *. Connecticut General Statute § 45–280 specifically states that wrongful death proceeds are not part of the gross estate for state succession tax purposes, and the Probate Court Administrator, a Connecticut Superior Court Judge, has ruled that wrongful death proceeds are not part of the gross estate for purposes of determining the probate court fee * * *.

The Treasury Department has issued three Revenue Rulings concerning the inclusion of wrongful death proceeds under § 2033, all of which hold that the proceeds are not part of the gross estate. In this case, the Government tries to distinguish them because they concerned rights of action arising under New Jersey and Virginia state law and the federal Death on the High Seas Act, 46 U.S.C. § 761; however, the rationale of those rulings is fully applicable here. In Rev.Rul. 54–19, 1954–1 C.B. 179, 180, the Department stated: "Inasmuch as the decedent had no right of action or interest in the proceeds at the time of his death, nothing 'passed' from the decedent to the beneficiaries. Accordingly, the amounts recovered by the beneficiaries would not be includable in the decedent's gross estate for Federal estate tax purposes."* It held that such proceeds were not part of the gross estate in Rev.Rul. 68–88, 1968–1 C.B. 397, 398, because "[t]he right of action for wrongful death does not accrue until death occurs," and in Rev.Rul. 69–8, 1969–1 C.B. 219, because "[t]he decedent in his lifetime never had an interest in either the right of action or the proceeds." See also Rev.Rul. 55–581, 1955–2 C.B. 381, holding that an allotment paid by the armed services to designated beneficiaries of servicemen who die in active duty is not part of the gross estate; and Rev.Rul. 55–87, 1955–1 C.B. 112, holding that a lump sum payment for funeral expenses to social security recipients is not taxable under § 2033. * * *

The judgments of the district court are reversed and the cases remanded for the determination of the amounts of the refunds due to the respective appellants and for their costs.

ILLUSTRATIVE MATERIAL

A. WRONGFUL DEATH STATUTES

After several losses in other cases, the Service conceded that the value of proceeds of settlement or recovery under a "survival" type of wrongful death

---

* [ED.: The wrongful death statute involved in Rev.Rul. 54–19 was that of New Jersey, which followed the "Lord Campbell's Act" model, to which the court referred earlier in the opinion, under which a wrongful death claim vests directly in a class of persons statutorily described by reference to their relationship to the victim.]

statute (e.g., Connecticut or Iowa) would not be includable under either § 2033 or § 2041. Rev.Rul. 75–127, 1975–1 C.B. 297. The holding under § 2041 followed from the same legal point that controlled the § 2033 outcome: because the wrongful death action cannot exist until D has died, there is no property over which D has a power of appointment at the time of his death. This result follows even if the amounts recovered in the wrongful death action are an asset of the estate subject to D's debts and liabilities under state law, Rev.Rul. 75–126, 1975–1 C.B. 296. If, however, the proceeds represent damages to which D became entitled during his lifetime (e.g., for pain and suffering or medical expenses), the Service will include their value under § 2033.

Assume that an individual whose death might occur in a state with a "survival" type of wrongful death statute could sell inter vivos the right to wrongful death proceeds in exchange for a promise to name the purchaser (e.g., a gambler) as beneficiary of the proceeds if any should arise from prosecution of a wrongful death claim. Does this possibility suggest that the court in *Connecticut Bank & Trust Co.* should have interpreted the current language of § 2033 to require inclusion of the cause of action in the gross estate, with valuation of the right the critical issue? Or does such a suggestion prove too much? It may be just as plausible that a member of the Rockefeller family might find a buyer for that member's share of his parent's estate under local law in case the parent dies intestate. Just because the mere possibility may have some exchangeable value does not alter its underlying character and does not raise the status of the possibility to that of an interest in property under § 2033 as currently interpreted. It would appear that the court in *Connecticut Bank & Trust Co.* was correct in concluding that the mechanism for determining who asserts and benefits from a wrongful death claim should not make a difference under the present statutory language.

More broadly, the wrongful death cases raise the issue whether § 2033 should be expanded to include: (1) property which passes at D's death from a third person (A) to a person designated by D where D has no control over A (e.g., A agrees to transfer $100,000 to any person designated in D's will if D dies in an airplane accident before reaching age 40); or (2) property which passes at D's death from A to a person designated by A where D had some control over the conditions of the transfer (e.g., A promises to transfer $100,000 to D's child at D's death, if D is then married to A's son).

B. OTHER STATUTORY DEATH BENEFITS

The refusal to include wrongful death benefits under § 2033 has been extended to other statutory recoveries where D lacks the power to designate the beneficiaries. See Rev.Rul. 82–5, 1982–1 C.B. 131 (survivors' benefits payable under compulsory no-fault automobile insurance policy); Rev.Rul. 76–102, 1976–1 C.B. 272 (annuity payable under federal mine health and safety act to surviving spouse of coal miner who died of black lung disease); Rev.Rul. 69–8, 1969–1 C.B. 219 (survivors' benefits payable under death on high seas act); Rev.Rul. 67–277, 1967–2 C.B. 322 (lump sum death benefit ($255 maximum) payable to D's surviving spouse under Social Security Act); Rev.Rul. 56–637, 1956–2 C.B. 600 (survivors' benefits payable under state workmen's compensation act for death due to occupational disease).

SECTION C.   "PROPERTY" VS. "EXPECTANCY"

Estate of Barr v. Commissioner

40 T.C. 227 (1963).

■ PIERCE, JUDGE: * * *

[Decedent's employer, the Eastman Kodak Co., had long paid employees on the payroll on the last day of the fiscal year "a wage dividend" in the following March if profits permitted.] To be eligible for a wage dividend, an Eastman employee had to be alive and employed by the company on the last day of the Kodak year. The company's policy with regard to payment of death benefits in lieu of a wage dividend to the survivors or the estate of an employee who died during the year, was stated in certain "Rules of Eligibility and Participation," and also in a pamphlet prepared by the company and distributed to its employees * * * as follows:

> *If before qualifying* an employee died in the Kodak year 1957 * * * and was not survived by a spouse, child or parent * * * *the company may, at its option, pay a wage dividend to the estate or other beneficiary that the officers may select.*

> The wage dividend should not be calculated until the officers of the company have approved the payment. * * * If an employee died after * * * 1957, *having qualified* for a wage dividend, but before receiving the wage dividend, a wage dividend is paid to the estate as a matter of right. (Emphasis supplied.)

The above-mentioned pamphlet for Eastman's employees, provided, so far as relevant to the issue here involved, as follows:

> ### Other Payments in Case of Death

> In addition to any group life insurance which may be payable, the immediate survivors of Kodak people *may expect* certain other payments made by the Company. These are (1) an amount equal to the wages or sickness allowance applicable to the balance of the pay period in which death occurred[4] and (2) an amount equal to the Wage Dividend that would have been paid in the year following death if the individual had lived to qualify under any of the rules which would have entitled him to a Wage Dividend. These payments are made to the husband or wife, if living; otherwise to the children in equal amounts; or to the surviving parent or parents if there are no children. In the event that none of the foregoing were living on payment date but were living at the end of the preceding year, the payment will be made to some other beneficiary. [Emphasis supplied.]

---

4. This amount is the so-called "salary" death benefit * * *.

The company's practice as reflected in the preceding quotation was adopted in 1932, and had in most cases been adhered to since that time. Before actual payment of a sum equivalent to a wage dividend to the survivor of a deceased employee, Eastman's board of directors caused an investigation into the circumstances of the deceased employee's family; and if the board was satisfied that the circumstances justified payment of a wage dividend death benefit, they would usually, but not always, approve payment of an amount equivalent to the wage dividend the employee would have received if he had lived and otherwise qualified therefor. * * *

The second death benefit amount involved in the instant case is the so-called salary death benefit. Decedent's death on March 30, 1957, occurred at the end of the first week of Eastman's fourth 4–week period in Kodak year 1957. Thereafter, on April 2, 1957, the company paid to the decedent's surviving spouse, Frances Barr, the sum of $1,742.31, which was equal to the amount that would have been paid to decedent as salary, if he had lived and continued to be employed by Eastman for the remaining 3 weeks of the pay period in which he died. The company charged the payment to an account on its books, designated "Death Benefit Expense."

Decedent's estate was paid in full by Eastman for the services which he had rendered to that company up to the date of his death.

As was the case with the wage dividend death benefit * * * a salary death benefit was not paid in the case of every employee who died. Such payments were made only after investigation by the company into the circumstances of the deceased employee's family. Also as has been found with respect to said wage dividend death benefit, the decedent made no contribution of his own funds for the salary death benefit; nor did the company insure against having to make such payment, or create any fund of its own from which to make such a payment. Moreover, no surviving spouse, or relative, executor, or administrator of any deceased employee has ever attempted to enforce a claim against Eastman for the payment of a salary death benefit; nor does the company consider that any such claim would be enforceable. * * *

I

The first issue relates to the so-called wage dividend death benefit which Eastman Kodak Co. paid to decedent's widow in March, 1958 (approximately 1 year after decedent's death). And the question presented with respect to this, is whether the amount of such payment is includable in the gross estate of the decedent for Federal estate purposes, under either § 2033 or § 2039 * * *.

It will be observed that [§ 2033] relates only to *interests in property* which the decedent had at the time of his death. And, as the Supreme Court pointed out in the leading case of Knowlton v. Moore, 178 U.S. 41, the justification for the Government's power to subject such interests to the Federal estate tax rests on the principle that such interests pass from the decedent at death, and that the estate tax is an excise tax on the

privilege of transmitting property at death to the survivors of the decedent.
* * *

It is our opinion that, in the present case, the decedent did not have at the time of his death any property interest, either in the "wage dividend" which Eastman's board of directors subsequently declared for the benefit of its living eligible employees (after it had declared a cash dividend for the benefit of its stockholders), or in the related death benefit which these directors then authorized to be paid to decedent's widow. Accordingly, there was no such interest which passed, or could have passed, from him to his widow; and hence no such interest upon which the excise tax on the privilege of transmitting property at death may be imposed under § 2033.

Both this Court and others have recognized that there is a distinction between *rights* of an employee to death benefits, and, on the other hand, mere hopes and expectancies on the part of an employee that death benefits may be paid. Thus, in the early case of Dimock v. Corwin, 19 F.Supp. 56 (E.D.N.Y.), affirmed on other issues 99 F.2d 799 (C.A.2), affd. 306 U.S. 363, it was shown that the Standard Oil Co. had adopted an annuity and insurance plan, subject to withdrawal or modification by Standard at its discretion, under which death benefits roughly equal to a year's salary of an employee might be paid to the widow of a deceased employee. The District Court concluded that the decedent had "only the right to render it possible for [his surviving spouse] to receive a grant from the Standard Oil Co., and that this did not constitute property of his" under * * * a statutory provision cognate to § 2033 of the 1954 Code. * * *

Authorities reaching differing results on the basis of the decedents having *enforceable vested* rights to have their employers pay death benefits to survivors, are typified by Estate of Charles B. Wolf, 29 T.C. 441, 447, in which case we stated:

> At the date of decedent's death he had *enforceable vested* rights in the three trusts [one profit-sharing trust, and two pension trusts], pro-cured by the rendition of services and by continuing in the employ of the respective corporations. He could be deprived of those rights only by deliberately terminating his employment or being discharged for cause. He had unlimited power to designate or change beneficiaries, and payments to his named beneficiaries were obligatory. The rights thus created were valuable property rights, capable of valuation, and in fact valued by the parties. The decedent's death was the decisive event that resulted in the passage of those rights to the beneficiary. It seems clear to us that they are includible in his gross estate either under the sweeping provisions of [§ 2033] or under the more specific provisions of [§ 2041] [dealing with powers of appointment]. * * *

> This case is to be sharply distinguished from cases such as Dimock v. Corwin, * * * where the employer retained the unfettered right to withdraw or modify the pension plan and where it was thought that the employee's interest could not rise above that of a mere expectancy.
> * * *

We are convinced that in the instant case, decedent had no more than a hope or expectancy that his surviving spouse might receive a wage dividend death benefit. There were so many events that had to occur before such hope could be realized that we find it impossible to conclude that, at the date of death, he had any property right which he could pass to her. Eastman had to realize earnings and profits for the year 1957; the directors, in the exercise of their discretion, had to declare a dividend to its stockholders; the directors, in further exercise of their discretion, had to declare a wage dividend payment to those employees who were alive and employed by the company on the last day of the Kodak year; and the directors, in the still further exercise of their discretion, had to approve a wage dividend death benefit to the widow of the instant decedent who had theretofore died. Moreover, the company, in its Rules of Eligibility and Participation and in the pamphlet distributed to its employees, made it clear that whether it might approve a wage dividend death benefit to the estate or beneficiary of a deceased employee was solely within its "option"; and that such situation would be distinguishable from that of an employee who had continued to live until after the close of the Kodak year for which the wage dividend was declared, and who thereby had acquired a "right" to the same. * * *

We hold that § 2033 is not here applicable.

[The court's discussion of the applicability of § 2039 is considered at p. 331. The same considerations that prevented § 2033 and § 2039 from reaching the wage dividend death benefit then were held to require exclusion of the salary death benefit.]

ILLUSTRATIVE MATERIAL

A.   VESTED RIGHTS TO BENEFITS

Benefits payable on account of death are includable in the gross estate of a deceased employee under § 2033 if, at the time of death, the employee had a legally enforceable right to receive the benefits had he remained alive.

1.   *Employer's Policy*

As illustrated by *Estate of Barr*, an employer's policy of paying death benefits, as evidenced by a consistent history of payment, coupled with actual payment, do not create an includable "interest," as long as the employer retains discretion over whether to make the payment. Although the policy may raise expectations on an employee's part, these fall short of the § 2033 "property" threshold of includability. Even death benefits paid as authorized by a pre-death corporate resolution were not included under § 2033 because the resolution did not give D a right that he could legally enforce during his lifetime. Estate of Bogley v. United States, 514 F.2d 1027 (Ct.Cl. 1975).

2.   *Contracts for Payment of Death Benefits*

If D contracts with her employer for the payment of death benefits directly to her husband or other irrevocably named beneficiaries on the sole condition that she remain employed by that employer at the time of her death, the value of the death benefits paid is not includable under § 2033 because D has no right to receive any benefits herself. Harris v. United States, 72–1 U.S.T.C. ¶ 12,845 (C.D.Cal. 1972); Hinze v. United States, 72–1 U.S.T.C. ¶ 12,842

(C.D.Cal. 1972). The same result was reached where the contract between D and her employer provided for the payment of retirement benefits to D, or, if D died before retirement, death benefits to named beneficiaries (who could be changed only if D and her employer agreed). D's death prior to retirement terminated her interest in the retirement benefits, and hence there was no taxable transfer as to these rights. The court held that the beneficiaries' right to the death benefits emanated from D's contract with her employer, not from a transfer by D. Estate of Wadewitz v. Commissioner, 39 T.C. 925 (1963), aff'd on other grounds, 339 F.2d 980 (7th Cir. 1964). See also Kramer v. United States, 406 F.2d 1363 (Ct.Cl.1969) (under employment contract, D entitled to receive fixed weekly amount during his lifetime, with surviving spouse entitled to receive substitute amount of $150 per week upon D's death; § 2033 not applicable because D's right to receive payment terminated at his death).

Should § 2033 be extended to cover these situations on the theory that (1) D has selected his death as the event upon which property will pass; (2) D has determined to whom it will pass; and (3) D has provided the consideration (performance of services) that gives rise to the post-death payments? Realistically, regardless of whether D explicitly or separately bargains for death benefit payments, they are an element of D's overall compensation package and displace current compensation that might otherwise have been paid directly to D, thereby enhancing the tax base.

3.   Benefits Paid From Funded Trusts

Employee death benefits may be includable under § 2033 when they are paid from separate trusts funded by the employee. For example, in Estate of Saxton v. Commissioner, 12 T.C. 569 (1949), an employer gratuitously created a funded trust to pay benefits to employees at a stated time, or, if an employee died before then, to his beneficiaries. The Tax Court held that the death benefits were not included under § 2033 because D did not have an enforceable right to receive the payments during his lifetime. On the other hand, § 2033 applies where the source of the death benefits was a qualified employee retirement trust to which the employee made contributions that were immediately credited to his account subject to defeasance only upon circumstances within his control. See Estate of Garber v. Commissioner, 271 F.2d 97 (3d Cir. 1959); Estate of Wolf v. Commissioner, 29 T.C. 441 (1957). Similarly, in Commissioner v. Albright, 356 F.2d 319 (2d Cir. 1966), D's wife received the amount of his contribution to a qualified pension plan as a death benefit upon D's death before reaching retirement age. The Second Circuit held that D's right to surrender his plan policies and recover his contribution at any time before he died caused the inclusion of the benefits in D's estate under § 2033.

B.   EFFECT OF ABILITY TO DESIGNATE BENEFICIARIES

The courts frequently refer to the decedent's ability to designate beneficiaries as a factor relevant to inclusion of death benefits under § 2033. Although this factor is relevant under § 2037, § 2039, and § 2041, it is of questionable importance under § 2033. For example, the Government's § 2033 argument in *Safe Deposit & Trust Co.* focused on D's dispositive control, but the Supreme Court refused to aggregate an unexercised general power of appointment with other economic benefits that D enjoyed during life. Under the Court's analysis, the question is whether the power to designate beneficiaries constitutes an enforceable right so that it can be said that D possessed a property interest to transfer at death. For example, would the results in *Harris*, *Hinze*, and *Wadewitz* have been different if D had the right unilaterally to change the designated beneficiary? In *Bogley*, the death benefits, if made at all, could be made to D's estate or to beneficiaries named by D; despite D's power to determine beneficiaries, the payments were not includable under § 2033 because D had no contractual right to them.

C. PAYMENTS IN THE NATURE OF DEFERRED COMPENSATION

As *Estate of Barr* and the preceding cases illustrate, the issue in employee death benefit cases is whether the decedent had an enforceable right to the benefits. Some cases have required inclusion of death benefits that were found to represent deferred compensation for decedent's services. As suggested previously, in a sense, every employee death benefit can be viewed as a form of "deferred compensation." The courts and the Service, however, appear to use that term to refer to the personal interest of the deceased employee, during her life, in the benefits payable under the contract. For example, in Beaver Trust Company v. United States, 184 F.Supp. 553 (W.D.Pa. 1960), D's employer, as an inducement to his continued employment, purchased an annuity contract providing D with monthly benefits during his life. The death benefits under the annuity were payable to the employer, but pursuant to the agreement, the employer assigned the annuity contract to D's estate. The court held that the death benefits were includable in D's estate on the alternative ground that the decedent possessed an interest in the annuity contract at death and that the benefits represented deferred compensation to the decedent. See also Goodman v. Granger, 243 F.2d 264 (3d Cir. 1957); Estate of King v. Commissioner, 20 T.C. 930 (1953); Rev.Rul. 65–217, 1965–2 C.B. 214. As noted above, other courts have included death benefits under § 2033 as deferred compensation where the source of the benefits was D's own contribution of salary that she otherwise would have been entitled to receive currently. See Estate of Garber v. Commissioner, 271 F.2d 97 (3d Cir. 1959).

D. EFFECT OF OTHER SECTIONS

Section 2039, enacted in 1954, would reach many of the employee death benefits described above. Section 2039, however, was not intended to be exclusive. S.Rep. No. 1622, 83d Cong., 2d Sess. 472 (1954). Section 2033 remains available as an alternative ground for inclusion, as asserted by the Government in *Estate of Barr*. Section 2039 is discussed in Chapter 20. The taxation of employee death benefits under §§ 2035–2038 is considered at p. 254, and application of the gift tax is discussed at p. 156.

Section D. Bank Deposits, Checks, and Notes

ILLUSTRATIVE MATERIAL

A. CHECKS

1. Estate of Belcher v. Commissioner

In Estate of Belcher v. Commissioner, 83 T.C. 227 (1984), D mailed 36 checks (totaling $94,960) to various charitable donees on December 21, 1973 (there were sufficient funds in her bank account to cover the checks). D died on December 31, 1973. The charities presented the checks for payment, and the checks cleared D's bank, during January 1974. The Tax Court held that even though D's bank account included the $94,960 at the date of her death, the funds were not includible in her estate under § 2033. The Tax Court applied the relation-back doctrine, which treats a charitable gift as having been made for income tax purposes when the checks were unconditionally delivered to the charitable donee where the checks thereafter are promptly presented to, and paid by, the donor's bank:

> "Respondent concedes the propriety of an income tax deduction in the year in which a check is unconditionally delivered, notwithstanding the fact that the issuer has died before the check is cashed, but argues that the income tax and the estate and gift tax are not to be construed in pari materia. * * * Petitioner states on brief that 'If it is a fact that payment of a charitable contribution has been made for income tax purposes, it must also be a fact that payment has been made for estate tax purposes.' (Emphasis in text.) We agree."

2. Post–Belcher Developments

The majority opinion in *Estate of Belcher* concludes by saying: "Similarly, we intend our holding in this case to apply only to charitable contributions for estate tax purposes. Sufficient unto another day the question of includibility of noncharitable gifts under similar circumstances." In its Action on Decision on *Belcher*, the Service indicated that it would not apply the relation-back doctrine in estate tax cases involving noncharitable donees:

> "In our view, and that of the dissenting judges in *Belcher*, the relation back doctrine should not be applied in the estate tax context, where the issue is not when payment occurred, but whether the decedent had a property interest in the funds at the moment of her death. Nevertheless, in view of the policy considerations identified by the court, the Service will read *Belcher* as creating a limited, equitable exception to the regulation for checks issued in good faith to charitable donees. We will continue to apply Reg. § 20.2031–5 in cases involving gift checks to noncharitable donees."

Action on Decision (Nov. 13, 1989). A series of cases has upheld the Service's position on noncharitable donees. For example, in Rosano v. United States, 245 F.3d 212 (2d Cir.2001), forty-five checks for slightly under $10,000 written to D's family members and friends shortly before D's death that were uncashed at the date of death were included in D's gross estate under § 2033. The Second Circuit held that D's gift of each check was incomplete when the check was written because under local law D could have stopped payment (since the check was issued without consideration), extinguishing her liability. The Second Circuit agreed with the Seventh Circuit's refusal to extend the "relation-back" doctrine to non-charitable donees in McCarthy v. United States, 806 F.2d 129 (7th Cir. 1986):

> "In *McCarthy,* the court offered two reasons for its refusal to extend the doctrine of relation-back. First, a rationale for applying the doctrine in the charitable context was not present in the non-charitable context. Checks delivered by the decedent to a charity but not paid until after the decedent's death, if included in the estate, would generate a deduction for

the estate. This deduction would result in a 'wash' for estate tax purposes, meaning that the estate would obtain the benefit of the charitable deduction whether or not the doctrine of relation-back was applied. For practical purposes, it makes more sense to consider the checks as outside the estate. 'No such practical consideration extends to noncharitable gifts. No offsetting deduction exists for gifts made to noncharitable donees.' *McCarthy*, 806 F.2d at 132. Second, the court thought that extending the doctrine would allow for improper tax avoidance: 'By issuing a check to a noncharitable donee with the understanding that it not be cashed until after his death, a decedent may effectively bequest up to $10,000 per donee, thus avoiding the estate tax consequences normally attending such transactions.' Id. * * *

"We agree with the policy concerns expressed by the *McCarthy* * * * court[]. Thus, we will not apply the doctrine where gifts are made to a noncharitable donee and the donor died prior to the date of payment."

In contrast, courts and the Service approve of a "limited extension" of the relation-back rule to year-end gifts to non-charitable donees for gift tax purposes where the donor is alive when the checks are paid. See Metzger v. Commissioner, 38 F.3d 118 (4th Cir.1994); Rev.Rul. 96–56, 1996–2 C.B. 161. For discussion of these gift tax rules, see p. 153.

In Newman v. Commissioner, 111 T.C. 81 (1998), the Tax Court refused to apply the relation-back rule where checks were drawn on D's checking account by her son acting under a power of attorney four days prior to her death but were not paid until after her death. As a result, the funds were included in D's estate under § 2033. The Tax Court emphasized that unlike the donor in *Metzger*, the decedent in *Newman* died before the checks were presented and paid by the drawee bank. Application of the relation-back rule in this situation would create "a very real danger of fostering estate tax avoidance." Id. at 90 (quoting *Metzger*, 38 F.3d at 122).

B. NOTES

A note held by a decedent is includable in the gross estate under § 2033 even though the note is cancelled by the decedent's will. Reg. § 20.2033–1(b). In this situation, the will's act of cancelling the note is tantamount to a bequest, thus triggering § 2033 inclusion. But what if the terms of the note itself cause cancellation upon the holder's death?

In Estate of Moss v. Commissioner, 74 T.C. 1239 (1980), D sold property to a corporation in exchange for notes. By their terms, the notes were extinguished at D's death. The parties stipulated that the sale of property (real estate plus all of D's shares of the corporate purchaser) for which the notes were issued was a bona fide sale for full and adequate consideration. Under these circumstances, the court rejected the Commissioner's contention that the self-cancellation provision was similar to a bequest. Analogizing the arrangement to an annuity or an estate limited to D's life, the court held that the notes were not includable in D's gross estate.

If, as a result of arm's length negotiations, the seller is adequately compensated—either through an increase in the principal of the note or an above-market interest rate—for assuming the actuarial risk of premature death, the transfer tax base is intact. In *Moss*, of course, the stipulation as to value placed the rabbit in the hat. Perhaps the government was lulled into the stipulation because all remaining shareholders were employees of the corporation unrelated to D. If an intra-family sale is involved, the government is certain to delve into valuation of the self-cancelling note. A seller who is shortchanged because the note does not reflect the actuarial value of the self-cancellation feature may be found to have made a gift or, depending on the facts, a retained-interest transfer (see p. 226) includable in the gross estate.

In Estate of Musgrove v. United States, 33 Fed.Cl. 657 (1995), one month before his death, D transferred over $250,000 to his son in exchange for a $300,000 interest-free demand note. The note by its terms was to be cancelled upon D's death if no prior demand for repayment had been made. The court held that the $250,000 was included in D's estate under § 2033. The court distinguished *Moss* on these grounds:

> "[I]n *Moss* the court made its finding, in large part, because the parties had stipulated that the sales of shares for the notes secured by the stock-pledge agreements were bona fide transactions for full and adequate consideration. The parties in *Moss* also had stipulated that there was no reason to believe that the decedent's life expectancy would have been shorter than the approximate ten years of life expectancy indicated by accepted mortality tables. Furthermore, the *Moss* transaction was not subjected to the heightened scrutiny surrounding an intrafamily transaction, and there was no other reason to suspect that the corporation would not repay the obligation in its entirety." Id. at 666.

SECTION E.   RIGHT TO ACCRUED PAYMENTS

Internal Revenue Code: § 691(a)(1), (c)

ILLUSTRATIVE MATERIAL

A.   INCLUDIBILITY OF RIGHT TO FUTURE PAYMENTS

1. Statutory Structure

Income earned but uncollected at death is property for purposes of § 2033, regardless of the nature of the income right. Compensation income—fees of a physician, for example, for services rendered prior to death but not paid by patients until after death—are of this variety. Similarly, accrued income rights attributable to D's status as an investor, such as interest and rents accrued at the date of death, are included in the gross estate, as are dividends payable to D or his estate if, on or before the date of death, D was a stockholder of record. Reg. § 20.2033–1(b). If D's income entitlements of this kind have matured prior to death, but have not been recognized in the technical income tax sense (for example, because D was a cash method taxpayer and received no cash, either actually or constructively), § 691(a) characterizes the amounts as income in respect of a decedent and includes them, upon receipt, in the gross income of the estate or other beneficiary who ultimately receives them. Lest the requirement of inclusion in gross income be neutralized by a § 1014(a) fair market value basis offset stemming from inclusion of the § 691 item in D's gross estate, § 1014(c) denies an adjustment to the income tax basis of the item. In effect, the recipient receives § 691 items with D's basis, which in most cases— compensation, dividends, interest, rents—is zero.

Section 691(c) provides an income tax deduction for federal estate taxes paid on an item of income in respect of a decedent. The allowable deduction equals the excess of the estate tax actually paid over the estate tax that would have been payable had the income in respect of a decedent not been included in the gross estate. In effect, this rule grants the deduction at the highest marginal rate achieved by the estate. Reg. § 1.691(c)–1(d) (Example 1); Estate of Kincaid v. Commissioner, 85 T.C. 25 (1985).

The § 691(c) deduction is premised on the assumption that an item of income which has economically accrued prior to D's death should bear the same combined income and estate tax, whether the income is received before or after death. For example, assume D and heir are both in the 25% income tax bracket and D's marginal estate tax rate is 45%. Before death, D had a right to an item of income having a basis of zero and value of $100. Were that item received before death, an income tax of $25 would be incurred. The net amount subject to estate tax would be $75 ($100 - $25 income tax liability), generating an estate tax liability of $33.75 (45% of $75). The combined income and estate taxes paid on the $100 income item would be $58.75 ($25 of income tax and $33.75 of estate tax). If, on the other hand, the item were held until death and were income in respect of a decedent included in D's gross estate at a value of $100, the estate tax attributable to its inclusion would be $45. Upon collection by D's heir, the $100 would be reduced for income tax purposes by the $45 in estate tax, leaving $55 subject to income tax at a 25% rate. An income tax of $13.75 would be due. The combined income and estate taxes again would be $58.75 ($45 of estate tax and $13.75 of income tax).

For a proposal to change the § 691(c) deduction to a basis adjustment, see American Law Institute, Federal Income Tax Project—Subchapter J 80 (1985).

B.   EFFECT OF CHARACTERIZATION AS INCOME IN RESPECT OF A DECEDENT

It is clear that an item may be treated for income tax purposes as income in respect of a decedent and yet not be includable in the estate of D for estate tax purposes. For example, a post-death bonus to which an employee had no enforceable right at the time of death might not be includable in the employee's estate for estate tax purposes, as in *Estate of Barr*. Nonetheless, such payments may be income in respect of a decedent. Rollert Residuary Trust v. Commissioner, 752 F.2d 1128 (6th Cir. 1985); Rev.Rul. 65–217, 1965–2 C.B. 214. If the item is not includable in the gross estate, there is no occasion for a § 691(c) deduction for federal estate taxes paid.

C.   REFORM PROPOSALS

The present tax treatment of income in respect of a decedent could be considerably simplified if the estate were required to include all such income in the final income tax return of the decedent and then deduct all income taxes paid from the gross estate. See U.S. Treasury Department, Tax Reform Studies and Proposals, House Ways and Means Comm. and Senate Finance Comm., 91st Cong., 1st Sess. 331–340 (Comm.Print, 1969), for a proposal to provide such treatment for accrued income items, in effect recommending return to the pre-§ 691 state of the law. Section 691 originally was enacted in part to eliminate the problem of bunching income in the final year of a deceased cash basis taxpayer. The 1969 Treasury proposal would have relied on the then income-averaging provisions to relieve the bunching problem, but those provisions have since been repealed. On the other hand, since the Treasury proposals were made, the top marginal income tax rates have been reduced from 50% to 35%, and the width of the 15%, 25%, 28%, and 33% bracket bands has been substantially narrowed. These changes mitigate the bunching problem.

CHAPTER 13

THE SCOPE OF THE GIFT TAX: §§ 2501 AND 2511

Internal Revenue Code: §§ 2501(a)(1); 2511(a)(1); 2512; 7872

Regulations: §§ 25.2501–1(a)(1); 25.2511–1(a), (c)–(h); 25.2512–8

INTRODUCTORY NOTE

The language of the gift tax is broad, and suggests a Congressional intent to leave extensive areas for administrative and judicial interpretation rather than resort to statutory detail. Section 2501(a) imposes the gift tax "on the transfer of property by gift," and § 2511(a) provides that the gift tax "shall apply whether the gift is in trust or otherwise, whether the gift is direct or indirect, and whether the property is real or personal, tangible or intangible." The committee reports accompanying enactment of the gift tax in 1932 explain that the terms "transfer," "property," "gift," and "indirect" are "used in the broadest and most comprehensive sense."[1]

Notice the difference in the statutory language that defines the respective bases of the estate and gift taxes: § 2033 refers to "property" in which the decedent had an "interest"; § 2501 refers to the "transfer" of "property" by "gift." Is there any substantive difference in the two transfer tax bases? Should there be? Is the answer to the latter question affected by whether a fully unified transfer tax has been adopted?

As the following materials indicate, the issues involved in determining the gift tax base in some instances have arisen in different contexts than in the estate tax. Presumably, the term "property" means the same in both. But the term "transfer" in the gift tax raises such questions as *when* did the transfer take place and *who* is the transferor? Further, the term "gift" must be given content. Does it imply that donative intent must be present in the transaction? What is the effect, if any, of the presence of a business or commercial element in the transaction? Is, or should there be, any difference in the estate and gift tax treatment of amounts expended for support of family members? Finally, some transfers are treated specifically in the gift tax for non-tax policy reasons (e.g., political contributions), or because the issue can arise only in a lifetime setting (e.g., the gratuitous rendition of personal services).

As the above issues are discussed in the following materials, consider whether the gift tax resolution is consistent with that of the estate tax. Or, to put the matter another way, are there any situations in which the tax

---

1. H.R. Rep. No. 708, 72d Cong., 1st Sess. 27 (1932); S. Rep. No. 665, 72d Cong., 1st Sess. 39 (1932).

result would be different if the transfer were effected at death rather than during lifetime? If there are differences, do they result from policy determinations, the nature of the transaction, or from structural differences inherent in the two bases?

SECTION A.   IS THERE A "TRANSFER" OF "PROPERTY"?

1.   COMPENSATION-FREE SERVICES

INTRODUCTORY NOTE

As the materials below indicate, the gift tax is not applied to the gratuitous performance of services by one individual for another. What is the reason for this result? Is there no "transfer," or alternatively, is the transfer not of "property"? Or does the result constitute a tax preference under the present transfer tax system, a preference that provides greater encouragement for gifts of services than for gifts of property? Or is the result simply a matter of administrability? Is the result consistent with § 7872, discussed at p. 141?

Commissioner v. Hogle

165 F.2d 352 (10th Cir. 1947).

[Parent (a successful stockbroker) set up irrevocable trusts with independent trustees for the benefit of his three children. The declarations of trust provided that Parent would maintain a trading account on margin for the benefit of the trusts. Profits from Parent's trading activities would be divided among the three children in set percentages; Parent agreed to reimburse the trusts for any losses, subject to reimbursement by the trusts from future profits.

In Hogle v. Commissioner, 132 F.2d 66 (10th Cir.1942) ("*Hogle I*"), the Tenth Circuit held that income from trading on margin was taxable to Parent rather than to the trusts because Parent controlled the amount of income through the exercise of his "personal skill and judgment" in trading the securities. The Service, in Commissioner v. Hogle, 165 F.2d 352 (10th Cir.1947) ("*Hogle II*"), then sought to impose a gift tax on the theory that the income from margin trading thus was earned by Parent and subsequently given to the trusts. Under this theory, § 2501(a) applied to this transfer of "property"—cash profits from the trading account—that both was removed from Parent's estate and taxed at the trusts' (or childrens') lower income tax rates.]

■ PHILLIPS, CIRCUIT JUDGE.

The Commissioner assessed gift taxes against Hogle for the years 1936 to 1941, inclusive. On review, the Tax Court held there were no deficiencies in gift taxes for those years.

The question presented is whether or not annual earnings of * * * trusts * * * from trading in securities and commodities carried on by the trusts under Hogle's direction, amounted to gifts by Hogle to the trusts. These trusts were before this court in [*Hogle I*] * * *.

In [*Hogle I*], we held, under the doctrine of Helvering v. Clifford, 309 U.S. 331,* that the net income resulting from trading on margin was taxable to Hogle. We do not think it follows, however, that the net income in each of the taxable years derived from trading constituted a gift thereof by Hogle to the trusts.

The net income derived from trading carried on in behalf of the trusts accrued immediately and directly to the trusts, and did not consist of income accruing to Hogle which he transferred by anticipatory gift to the trusts. Hogle never owned or held an economic interest in such income. Likewise, since the funds in the trusts were sufficient to provide the margins required to cover the trading carried on in the taxable years, any losses resulting from trading would have been suffered immediately and directly by the trusts. What, in fact and in reality, Hogle gave to the trusts in the taxable years was his expert services in carrying on the trading, personal services in the management of the trusts. Hogle could give or withhold his personal services in carrying on trading on margin for the trusts. He could not withhold from the trusts any of the income accruing from trading on margin. How could he give what he could not withhold? There was no transfer directly or indirectly from Hogle to the trusts of title to, or other economic interest in, the income from trading or margin, having the quality of a gift. In short, there was no transfer directly or indirectly by Hogle to the trusts of property or property rights.

The Commissioner places strong reliance upon [*Hogle I*] to sustain the contention that the income arising from the trading on margin represented personal earnings of Hogle; and that Hogle in substance gave to the trusts the profits derived from part of his individual efforts. Certain excerpts from the opinion are emphasized in support of the argument that the net income arising from the trading on margin for the benefit of the trusts represented earnings of Hogle, and that, upon the accrual of such income to the trusts, a transfer having the quality of a gift was effectuated within the meaning of [§ 2501(a)(1)]. But, we think a critical reading of the opinion in that case in its entirety will indicate that it does not support the Commissioner's contention. While the court drew a distinction between the income tax liability of Hogle on profits accruing to the trusts from trading on margin and gains accruing to the trusts from other sources, and held that he was liable for the tax on net income derived from such trading but not on gains accruing from other sources, his liability for tax on the net income derived from trading on margin was predicated upon his power to control indirectly

---

* [ED.: In *Clifford*, the grantor created a short-term trust for the benefit of his wife. After five years, the trust would terminate and the corpus would return to the grantor. The grantor appointed himself as sole trustee with the power to distribute trust income to his wife or to accumulate it for her benefit. The grantor was taxed on the trust income even though it was distributed to his wife.]

the extent of the profit derived from such trading by determining the extent and amount of such trading. Despite certain statements contained in the opinion on which the Commissioner relies, the basis of the holding that Hogle was liable for income tax on the net income resulting from trading on margin was his power to control the extent of such trading and therefore the extent of the income therefrom. It was predicated on his power to dominate the amount of income that would accrue from trading. That was the essence of our holding. We did not hold that such income accrued first to Hogle and was by him transferred by anticipatory gift to the trusts.

Our holding in [*Hogle I*] was an extreme application of the doctrine of the *Clifford* case, supra. To hold that the profits accruing from trading in margins constitute gifts from Hogle to the trusts, we think, would be an unjustified extension of the doctrine of the *Clifford* case.

Affirmed.

ILLUSTRATIVE MATERIAL

A.   THE PROPERTY v. SERVICES DISTINCTION

Subsequent cases and rulings rely on *Hogle II* for the proposition that the performance of gratuitous services is not subject to the gift tax. See Crown v. Commissioner, 585 F.2d 234, 236 n.6 (7th Cir.1978); Estate of Childers v. Commissioner, 10 T.C. 566, 579–80 (1948). The opinion in *Hogle II*, however, may not support this general proposition because the Government's position was that, based on *Hogle I*, the trading profits legally accrued to Parent as his property, which he then constructively transferred to the trusts. The opinion responded to this argument by focusing on the margin trading profits, not on the value of Parent's investment services. Indeed, the Tax Court opinion explicitly stated: "The question here is not whether Hogle may have made a gift to the trusts of personal services which might be valued independently of the profits derived from the marginal trading. The question is only whether he made a * * * [gift] to the trusts, consisting of the profits on the margin trading accounts." 7 T.C. 986, 989 (1946). As a result, the real basis for the court's holding may have been that there was no "transfer" subject to § 2501(a) because Parent did not have a legal right to the profits in the first place.

Nevertheless, *Hogle II* has been interpreted by *Crown, Estate of Childers*, and other cases to mean that the value of Parent's investment services was not subject to gift tax because there was no transfer of "property" for § 2501(a) purposes. This interpretation probably follows from the court's observation that "[w]hat, in fact and in reality, Hogle gave to the trusts in the taxable years was his expert services in carrying on the trading, personal services in the management of the trusts. Hogle could give or withhold his personal services in carrying on trading on margin for the trusts." The statutory rationale is that by referring only to gifts of "property," §§ 2501(a) and 2511(a) implicitly exempt gifts of services. This is so even though the gift tax typically is used to "backstop" the estate tax to reach inter vivos transfers that deplete the donor's estate. The Parent's estate in *Hogle II* was not actually depleted by his gratuitous performance of services as trustee. At most, the Government might have claimed that Parent's decision to serve as trustee for his children without compensation prevented augmentation of his estate by the compensation that Parent would have received had he performed the same services for a third party. The exclusion from the gift tax base of the value of gratuitous services, therefore, logically must rest on an unwillingness to assume that gratuitous services performed for the children necessarily displaced the performance of compensated services for others. Instead, Parent may have pursued other leisure activities that would not have augmented his estate. There also are other problems with applying the gift tax to the gift of services in the *Hogle II* context, such as determining how these services would be valued. See Repetti, The Alchemy in Estate and Gift Taxation, 50 Tax L.Rev. 416, 468 (1995) (arguing that imposition of gift tax "would represent too great a governmental intrusion on personal relationships").

Parents, of course, regularly provide their children with a range of opportunities that do not trigger the gift tax, presumably on the theory that they fall on the services side of the taxable property v. nontaxable services line. For example, in Estate of Blass v. Commissioner, 11 T.C.M. 622 (1952), parent was a financial consultant who, upon learning that one of his clients was selling an apple brandy business, retained a lawyer to conduct purchase negotiations on behalf of his wife and trusts for his children, and directed them to financing to fund the acquisition. The court held that, under *Hogle II*, the diversion of the business opportunity to his wife and the trusts was not a gift. However, the taxable property v. nontaxable services line becomes difficult to draw where the parent's services ultimately produce an item of "property," such as a book.

Revenue Ruling 66–167

1966–1 C.B. 20.

* * * In the instant case, the taxpayer served as the sole executor of his deceased wife's estate pursuant to the terms of a will under which he and his adult son were each given a half interest in the net proceeds thereof. The laws of the state in which the will was executed and probated impose no limitation on the use of either principal or income for the payment of compensation to an executor and do not purport to deal with whether a failure to withdraw any particular fee or commission may properly be considered as a waiver thereof.

The taxpayer's administration of his wife's estate continued for a period of approximately three full years during which time he filed two annual accountings as well as the usual final accounting with the probate court, all of which reported the collection and disposition of a substantial amount of estate assets.

At some point within a reasonable time after first entering upon the performance of his duties as executor, the taxpayer decided to make no charge for serving in such capacity, and each of the aforesaid accountings accordingly omitted any claim for statutory commissions and was so filed with the intention to waive the same. The taxpayer-executor likewise took no other action which was inconsistent with a fixed and continuing intention to serve on a gratuitous basis.

The specific questions presented are whether the amounts which the taxpayer-executor could have received as fees or commissions are includible in his gross income for Federal income tax purposes and whether his waiver of the right to receive these amounts results in a gift for Federal gift tax purposes.

In Revenue Ruling 56–472, the executor of an estate entered into an agreement to serve in such capacity for substantially less than all of the statutory commissions otherwise allowable to him and also formally waived his right to receive the remaining portion thereof. The basic agreement with respect to his acceptance of a reduced amount of compensation antedated the performance of any services and the related waiver of the disclaimed commissions was signed before he would otherwise have become entitled to receive them. Under these circumstances, the ruling held that the difference between the commissions which such executor could have otherwise acquired an unrestricted right to obtain and the lesser amount which he actually received was not includible in his income and that his disclaimer did not effect any gift thereof.

In Revenue Ruling 64–225, the trustees of a testamentary trust in the State of New York waived their rights to receive one particular class of statutory commissions. This waiver was effected by means of certain formal instruments that were not executed until long after the close of most of the years to which such commissions related. This circumstance, along with all the other facts described therein, indicated that such trustees had not intended to render their services on a gratuitous basis. The ruling accordingly held that such commissions were includible in the trustees' gross income for the taxable year when so waived and that their execution of the waivers also effected a taxable gift of these commissions.

The crucial test of whether the executor of an estate or any other fiduciary in a similar situation may waive his right to receive statutory commissions without thereby incurring any income or gift tax liability is whether the waiver involved will at least primarily constitute evidence of an intent to render a gratuitous service. If the timing, purpose, and effect of the waiver make it serve any other important objective, it may then be proper to conclude that the fiduciary has thereby enjoyed a realization of income by means of controlling the disposition thereof, and at the same time, has also effected a taxable gift by means of any resulting transfer to a third party of his contingent beneficial interest in a part of the assets under his fiduciary control. See the above cited revenue rulings and the authorities therein cited, as well as Reg. § 25.2511–1(c).

The requisite intention to serve on a gratuitous basis will ordinarily be deemed to have been adequately manifested if the executor or administrator of an estate supplies one or more of the decedent's principal legatees or devisees, or of those principally entitled to distribution of decedent's intestate estate, within six months after his initial appointment as such fiduciary, with a formal waiver of any right to compensation for his services. Such an intention to serve on a gratuitous basis may also be adequately manifested through an implied waiver, if the fiduciary fails to claim fees or commissions at the time of filing the usual accountings and if all the other attendant facts and circumstances are consistent with a fixed and continuing intention to serve gratuitously. If the executor or administrator of an estate claims his statutory fees or commissions as a deduction on one or more of the estate, inheritance, or income tax returns which are filed on behalf of the estate, such action will ordinarily be considered inconsistent with any fixed or definite intention to serve on a gratuitous basis. No such claim was made in the instant case.

Accordingly, the amounts which the present taxpayer-executor would have otherwise become entitled to receive as fees or commissions are not includible in his gross income for Federal income tax purposes, and are not gifts for Federal gift tax purposes. * * *

ILLUSTRATIVE MATERIAL

A. WAIVER BY FIDUCIARY OF RIGHT TO COMMISSIONS

Rev.Rul. 70–237, 1970–1 C.B. 13, held that the trustee of a testamentary trust did not make a taxable gift where, shortly after the passage of a law increasing the statutory commission, he waived the increase and continued to receive commissions at the prior rates.

B. POLICY ISSUES

Rev.Rul. 64–225, 1964–2 C.B. 15, and Rev.Rul. 66–167 state that a waiver (express or implied) of the compensation for services after it has been earned is insufficient to prevent the compensation from constituting income to the earner and hence the waiver constitutes a gift of that income. They thus appear to stand for the proposition that at least in a context where the individual is normally paid for his services, the free performance of those services is a taxable gift unless an effective waiver of payment is made within a reasonable time after the commencement of performance. Perhaps *Hogle* can be reconciled with these rulings by treating the Parent as having effectively waived any right to compensation prior to the performance of the services.

In the fiduciary commission cases, where the services have been performed prior to the waiver, the fiduciary by his waiver has produced the same economic result as if he had accepted the commission and then transferred the funds to the beneficiaries of the trust or estate. Suppose a lawyer normally would charge $400 to examine title and handle other aspects of the purchase of a home, but because the purchaser is also a lawyer, he charges only $200. Should a taxable gift result under Rev.Rul. 66–167?

2. INTEREST-FREE LOANS AND RENT-FREE USE OF OTHER ASSETS

Internal Revenue Code: § 7872

INTRODUCTORY NOTE

After *Hogle II*, several courts relied on the estate-depletion theory in refusing to subject interest-free loans from parents to their children to the gift tax. For example, in Johnson v. United States, 254 F.Supp. 73, 77 (N.D. Tex. 1966), the court stated that it was not necessary to subject the foregone interest to the gift tax in order to backstop the estate tax because "[t]he parents were under no duty to lend or otherwise invest their money. They had a right to keep it in cash." In dictum, the court went beyond the case of interest-free loans in suggesting that "[t]he time has not come when a parent must deal at arm's length with his children when they finish their education and start out in life." Id. The Service announced in Rev.Rul. 73–61, 1973–1 C.B. 408, that it would not follow *Johnson* and would continue to subject interest-free loans to the gift tax. The Service also stated more broadly that "[t]he right to use property * * * is itself an interest in property, the transfer of which is a gift within the purview of § 2501."

The tax-avoidance potential of interest-free loans is dramatically illustrated in Crown v. Commissioner, 67 T.C. 1060 (1977), aff'd, 585 F.2d 234 (7th Cir.1978), where Parent made over *$18 million* in interest-free loans to various family trusts. Both the Tax Court and the Seventh Circuit rejected the Service's attempt to impose the gift tax. The courts rejected the estate-depletion rationale,[2] were concerned about the practical ramifications of the Service's position,[3] and felt that Congress, rather than the courts, should change the tax treatment of interest-free loans. The Service announced that it would "continue to adhere to the position set forth in Rev.Rul. 73–61" and would "continue to litigate the *Crown* issue with the view towards another appellate test." A.O.D. 1979–197 (Nov. 23, 1979). The Service soon found such an opportunity.

Dickman v. Commissioner

465 U.S. 330 (1984).

■ CHIEF JUSTICE BURGER delivered the opinion of the Court.

We granted certiorari to resolve a conflict among the Circuits as to whether intrafamily, interest-free demand loans result in taxable gifts of the value of the use of the money lent.

2. "[A] taxpayer is not under any duty to cultivate the fruits of his capital (or labor) and will not be taxed as if he had when he hasn't." 585 F.2d at 236. The tax system does not impose on Parent "any obligation to continuously invest his money for a profit. The opportunity cost of either letting one's money remain idle or suffering a loss from an unwise investment is not taxable merely because a profit could have been made from a wise investment." 67 T.C. at 1063–64.

3. The Service's position would lead to finding taxable gifts not only where, as here, a parent loans $18 million to a child, but also where a parent loans $1,000 to a child graduating from college until he gets established;

an office worker loans $10 to a co-worker until the next payday; a homemaker loans a lawn mower to a neighbor; and a friend lets an out-of-town guest use a spare bedroom for one night. 585 F.2d at 241. The logic of the Service's position would extend beyond the interest-free use of money to "a multitude of situations involving gratuitous use or sharing of real or personal property among relatives. The application of the gift tax to common intrafamily sharing of use of property seems administratively unmanageable, and such situations point up the difficulty with the concept of gift taxation attaching to mere permissive use." 67 T.C. at 1065.

I

[Paul and Esther Dickman made over $1.3 million in interest-free demand loans over a five-year period to their son and to a family-owned corporation. The Tax Court followed *Crown* and refused to apply the gift tax to the value of the use of the loan proceeds. 41 T.C.M. 620 (1980). The Eleventh Circuit reversed, 690 F.2d 812 (11th Cir.1982), and the Supreme Court granted certiorari to resolve the conflict with the Seventh Circuit in *Crown*.]

II

A

The statutory language of the federal gift tax provisions purports to reach any gratuitous transfer of any interest in property. Section 2501(a)(1) of the Code imposes a tax upon "the transfer of property by gift." * * * Section 2511(a) highlights the broad sweep of the tax imposed by § 2501, providing in pertinent part:

> "Subject to the limitations contained in this chapter, the tax imposed by § 2501 shall apply whether the transfer is in trust or otherwise, whether the gift is direct or indirect, and whether the property is real or personal, tangible or intangible * * *."

The language of these statutes is clear and admits of but one reasonable interpretation: transfers of property by gift, by whatever means effected, are subject to the federal gift tax.

* * * The plain language of the statute reflects th[e] legislative history [of the gift tax]; the gift tax was designed to encompass all transfers of property and property *rights* having significant value.[4]

On several prior occasions, this Court has acknowledged the expansive sweep of the gift tax provisions. In Commissioner v. Wemyss, 324 U.S. 303, 306 (1945), the Court explained that:

> "Congress intended to use the term 'gifts' in its broadest and most comprehensive sense * * * [in order] to hit all the protean arrangements which the wit of man can devise that are not business transactions within the meaning of ordinary speech."

The Court has also noted that the language of the gift tax statute "is broad enough to include property, however conceptual or contingent," Smith v. Shaughnessy, 318 U.S. 176, 180 (1943), so as "to reach every kind and type of transfer by gift," Robinette v. Helvering, 318 U.S. 184, 187 (1943). Thus,

---

4. The comprehensive scope of the gift tax, reflected by its statutory language and legislative history, is analogous to that of § 61 of the Code, 26 U.S.C. § 61, which defines gross income as "all income from whatever source derived." Section 61 has long been interpreted to include all forms of income except those specifically excluded from its reach. See, e.g., Commissioner v. Glen- shaw Glass Co., 348 U.S. 426 (1955). Similarly, the gift tax applies to any "transfer of property by gift," Code § 2501(a)(1), "[s]ubject to the limitations contained in this chapter," Code § 2511(a). Accordingly, absent an express exclusion from its provisions, any transfer meeting the statutory requirements must be held subject to the gift tax.

the decisions of this Court reinforce the view that the gift tax should be applied broadly to effectuate the clear intent of Congress.

B

In asserting that interest-free demand loans give rise to taxable gifts, the Commissioner does not seek to impose the gift tax upon the principal amount of the loan, but only upon the reasonable value of the use of the money lent. The taxable gift that assertedly results from an interest-free demand loan is the value of receiving and using the money without incurring a corresponding obligation to pay interest along with the loan's repayment.[5] Is such a gratuitous transfer of the right to use money a "transfer of property" within the intendment of § 2501(a)(1)?

We have little difficulty accepting the theory that the use of valuable property—in this case money—is itself a legally protectible property interest. Of the aggregate rights associated with any property interest, the right of use of property is perhaps of the highest order. One court put it succinctly:

> " 'Property' is more than just the physical thing—the land, the bricks, the mortar—it is also the sum of all the rights and powers incident to ownership of the physical thing. Property is composed of constituent elements and of these elements the right to *use* the physical thing to the exclusion of others is the most essential and beneficial. Without this right all other elements would be of little value. * * * " Passailaigue v. United States, 224 F.Supp. 682, 686 (MD Ga. 1963) (emphasis in original).

What was transferred here was the use of a substantial amount of cash for an indefinite period of time. An analogous interest in real property, the use under a tenancy at will, has long been recognized as a property right. * * * For example, a parent who grants to a child the rent-free, indefinite use of commercial property having a reasonable rental value of $8000 a month has clearly transferred a valuable property right. The transfer of $100,000 in cash, interest-free and repayable on demand, is similarly a grant of the use of valuable property. Its uncertain tenure may reduce its value, but it does not undermine its status as property. In either instance, when the property owner transfers to another the right to use the object, an identifiable property interest has clearly changed hands.

The right to the use of $100,000 without charge is a valuable interest in the money lent, as much so as the rent-free use of property consisting of land and buildings. In either case, there is a measurable economic value associated with the use of the property transferred. The value of the use of money is found in what it can produce; the measure of that value is interest—"rent" for the use of the funds. We can assume that an interest-

---

5. The Commissioner's tax treatment of interest-free demand loans may perhaps be best understood as a two-step approach to such transactions. Under this theory, such a loan has two basic economic components: an arm's-length loan from the lender to the borrower, on which the borrower pays the lender a fair rate of interest, followed by a gift from the lender to the borrower in the amount of that interest. * * *

free loan for a fixed period, especially for a prolonged period, may have greater value than such a loan made payable on demand, but it would defy common human experience to say that an intrafamily loan payable on demand is not subject to accommodation; its value may be reduced by virtue of its demand status, but that value is surely not eliminated.

This Court has noted in another context that the making of an interest-free loan results in the transfer of a valuable economic right:

> "It is virtually self-evident that extending interest-free credit for a period of time is equivalent to giving a discount equal to the value of the use of the purchase price for that period of time." Catalano, Inc. v. Target Sales, Inc., 446 U.S. 643, 648 (1980) (per curiam).

Against this background, the gift tax statutes clearly encompass within their broad sweep the gratuitous transfer of the use of money. Just as a tenancy at will in real property is an estate or interest in land, so also is the right to use money a cognizable interest in personal property. The right to use money is plainly a valuable right, readily measurable by reference to current interest rates; the vast banking industry is positive evidence of this reality. Accordingly, we conclude that the interest-free loan of funds is a "transfer of property by gift" within the contemplation of the federal gift tax statutes.[6]

C

Our holding that an interest-free demand loan results in a taxable gift of the use of the transferred funds is fully consistent with one of the major purposes of the federal gift tax statute: protection of the estate tax and the income tax. The legislative history of the gift tax provisions reflects that Congress enacted a tax on gifts to supplement existing estate and income tax laws. * * * Failure to impose the gift tax on interest-free loans would seriously undermine this estate and income tax protection goal.

A substantial no-interest loan from parent to child creates significant tax benefits for the lender quite apart from the economic advantages to the

---

6. Petitioners argue that no gift tax consequences should attach to interest-free demand loans because no "transfer" of property occurs at the time the loan is made. Petitioners urge that the term "transfer" "connotes a discrete, affirmative act whereby a person conveys something to another person, not a continuous series of minute failures to require return of something loaned." Brief for Petitioners 22. We decline to adopt that construction of the statute.

In order to make a taxable gift, a transferor must relinquish dominion and control over the transferred property. Reg. § 25.2511–2(b), 26 CFR § 25.2511–2(b) (1983). At the moment an interest-free demand loan is made, the transferor has not given up all dominion and control; he could terminate the transferee's use of the funds by calling the loan. As time passes without a demand for repayment, however, the transferor allows the use of the principal to pass to the transferee, and the gift becomes complete. See ibid.; Rev.Rul. 69–347, 1969–1 C.B. 227; Rev.Rul. 69–346, 1969–1 C.B. 227. As the Court of Appeals realized, 690 F.2d, at 819, the fact that the transferor's dominion and control over the use of the principal is relinquished over time will become especially relevant in connection with the valuation of the gifts that result from such loans; it does not, however, alter the fact that the lender has made a gratuitous transfer of property subject to the federal gift tax.

borrower. This is especially so when an individual in a high income tax bracket transfers income-producing property to an individual in a lower income tax bracket, thereby reducing the taxable income of the high-bracket taxpayer at the expense, ultimately, of all other taxpayers and the government. Subjecting interest-free loans to gift taxation minimizes the potential loss to the federal fisc generated by the use of such loans as an income tax avoidance mechanism for the transferor. Gift taxation of interest-free loans also effectuates Congress' desire to supplement the estate tax provisions. A gratuitous transfer of income-producing property may enable the transferor to avoid the future estate tax liability that would result if the earnings generated by the property—rent, interest, or dividends—became a part of the transferor's estate. Imposing the gift tax upon interest-free loans bolsters the estate tax by preventing the diminution of the transferor's estate in this fashion.

III

Petitioners contend that administrative and equitable considerations require a holding that no gift tax consequences result from the making of interest-free demand loans. In support of this position, petitioners advance several policy arguments; none withstands studied analysis.

A

Petitioners first advance an argument accepted by the Tax Court in Crown v. Commissioner:

> "[O]ur income tax system does not recognize unrealized earnings or accumulations of wealth and no taxpayer is under any obligation to continuously invest his money for a profit. The opportunity cost of either letting one's money remain idle or suffering a loss from an unwise investment is not taxable merely because a profit *could have been made* from a wise investment." 67 T.C., at 1063–1064.

Thus, petitioners argue, an interest-free loan should not be made subject to the gift tax simply because of the possibility that the money lent *might* have enhanced the transferor's taxable income or gross estate had the loan never been made.

This contention misses the mark. It is certainly true that no law requires an individual to invest his property in an income-producing fashion, just as no law demands that a transferor charge interest or rent for the use of money or other property. An individual may, without incurring the gift tax, squander money, conceal it under a mattress, or otherwise waste its use value by failing to invest it. Such acts of consumption have nothing to do with lending money at no interest. The gift tax is an excise tax on *transfers* of property; allowing dollars to lie idle involves no transfer. If the taxpayer chooses not to waste the use value of money, however, but instead transfers the use to someone else, a taxable event has occurred. That the transferor himself could have consumed or wasted the use value of the money without incurring the gift tax does not change this result. Contrary to petitioners' assertion, a holding in favor of the taxability of interest-free loans does not impose upon the transferor a duty profitably to invest; rather, it merely recognizes that certain tax consequences inevitably flow from a decision to make a "transfer of property by gift." 26 U.S.C. § 2501(a)(1).

B

Petitioners next attack the breadth of the Commissioner's view that interest-free demand loans give rise to taxable gifts. Carried to its logical extreme, petitioners argue, the Commissioner's rationale would elevate to the status of taxable gifts such commonplace transactions as a loan of the proverbial cup of sugar to a neighbor or a loan of lunch money to a colleague. Petitioners urge that such a result is an untenable intrusion by the government into cherished zones of privacy, particularly where intra-family transactions are involved.

Our laws require parents to provide their minor offspring with the necessities and conveniences of life; questions under the tax law often arise, however, when parents provide more than the necessities, and in quantities significant enough to attract the attention of the taxing authorities. Generally, the legal obligation of support terminates when the offspring reach majority. Nonetheless, it is not uncommon for parents to provide their adult children with such things as the use of cars or vacation cottages, simply on the basis of the family relationship. We assume that the focus of the Internal Revenue Service is not on such traditional familial matters. When the government levies a gift tax on routine neighborly or familial gifts, there will be time enough to deal with such a case.

Moreover, the tax law provides liberally for gifts to both family members and others; within the limits of the prescribed statutory exemptions, even substantial gifts may be entirely tax free. First, under § 2503(e) of the Code, 26 U.S.C. § 2503(e), amounts paid on behalf of an individual for tuition at a qualified educational institution or for medical care are not considered "transfer[s] of property by gift" for purposes of the gift tax statutes. More significantly, § 2503(b) of the Code provides an annual exclusion from the computation of taxable gifts of $10,000 per year, per donee; this provision allows a taxpayer to give up to $10,000 annually to each of any number of persons, without incurring any gift tax liability. The "split gift" provision of Code § 2513(a), which effectively enables a husband and wife to give each object of their bounty $20,000 per year without liability for gift tax, further enhances the ability to transfer significant amounts of money and property free of gift tax consequences. Finally, should a taxpayer make gifts during one year that exceed the § 2503(b) annual gift tax exclusion, no gift tax liability will result until the unified credit of Code § 2505 has been exhausted. These generous exclusions, exceptions, and credits clearly absorb the sorts of *de minimis* gifts petitioners envision and render illusory the administrative problems that petitioners perceive in their "parade of horribles."

C

Finally, petitioners urge that the Commissioner should not be allowed to assert the gift taxability of interest-free demand loans because such a position represents a departure from prior Internal Revenue Service practice. This contention rests on the fact that, prior to 1966, the Commissioner had not construed the gift tax statutes and regulations to authorize the levying of a gift tax on the value of the use of money or property. See Crown v. Commissioner, 585 F.2d, at 241; Johnson v. United States, 254 F.Supp. 73 (ND Tex.1966). From this they argue that it is manifestly unfair to permit the Commissioner to impose the gift tax on the transactions challenged here.

Even accepting the notion that the Commissioner's present position represents a departure from prior administrative practice, which is by no means certain, it is well established that the Commissioner may change an earlier interpretation of the law, even if such a change is made retroactive in effect. * * *

IV

As we have noted, Congress has provided generous exclusions and credits designed to reduce the gift tax liability of the great majority of taxpayers. Congress clearly has the power to provide a similar exclusion for the gifts that result from interest-free demand loans. Any change in the gift tax consequences of such loans, however, is a legislative responsibility, not a judicial one. Until such a change occurs, we are bound to effectuate Congress' intent to protect the estate and income tax systems with a broad and comprehensive tax upon all "transfer[s] of property by gift." * * *

We hold, therefore, that the interest-free demand loans shown by this record resulted in taxable gifts of the reasonable value of the use of the money lent. Accordingly, the judgment of the United States Court of Appeals for the Eleventh Circuit is [a]ffirmed.

■ JUSTICE POWELL, with whom JUSTICE REHNQUIST joins, dissenting.

The Court's decision today rejects a longstanding principle of taxation, and creates in its stead a new and anomalous rule of law. Such action is best left to Congress.[7]

I

The Internal Revenue Service's attempts to assess gift taxes on interest-free demand loans is a relatively new development in the field of tax law. The gift tax provisions of the Internal Revenue Code were enacted in 1932. For 34 years—a third of a century—the IRS enforced these provisions

---

7. In United States v. Byrum, 408 U.S. 125 (1972), the Court stated:

"Courts properly have been reluctant to depart from an interpretation of tax law which has been generally accepted when the departure could have poten-

tially far-reaching consequences. When a principle of taxation requires re-examination, Congress is better equipped than a court to define precisely the type of conduct which results in tax consequences." Id., at 135.

without any intimation that an interest-free loan would have gift tax consequences. The IRS first pursued its present position in 1966 in Johnson v. United States, 254 F.Supp. 73 (N.D.Tex.). * * *

[U]ntil 1982, a long-standing principle of gift tax law, supported by IRS inaction and judicial opinion, was that interest-free demand loans had no gift tax significance. Relying on this principle, taxpayers made loans, tax commentators suggested making loans, and tax counselors used loans as integral parts of complex taxation minimization plans. In my view, petitioners' reliance also was justified.

Despite this justified reliance, the Court today subjects potentially all interest-free loans to gift taxation. The adverse effects of the Court's holding could be substantial. Many taxpayers may have used interest-free loans as an important part of a comprehensive plan to sell their business to a son, to send a daughter to medical school, or to provide for the support of an elderly parent. Such plans are not revamped easily. In addition, the recipients of the loans may not be in a position to help the taxpayers/lenders avoid future gift tax liability by making immediate repayment. The borrowed funds may have been invested in fixed assets or the borrowers simply may have spent the money. The result, in any event, is the assessment of gift taxes that might have been avoided lawfully if the taxpayer could have anticipated the Court's holding in this case. In light of the Commissioner's decision over a 34 year span to attach no significance to such loans, and his lack of success over the past 18 years in attempting to tax such loans, the Court of Appeals's decision is so fundamentally unfair that this Court should be unwilling to add its *imprimatur*.

II

There can be little doubt that the courts are not the best forum for consideration of the ramifications of the gift taxation of interest-free loans. * * *

The most troublesome issue generated by the Court's opinion is the scope of its new reading of the statute. The Court does not limit its holding to interest-free loans of money. The Court states: "We have little difficulty accepting the theory that the use of valuable property * * * is itself a legally protectible property interest." * * * Under this theory, potential tax liability may arise in a wide range of situations involving the unrecompensed use of property. Examples could include the rent-free use of a home by a child over the age of minority who lives with his parents, or by a parent over the age of self-support who lives with her child. Taken to its logical extreme, this theory would make the loan of a car for a brief period a potentially taxable event.

The possibility that the generous use by friends or family of property such as homes and even spare bedrooms could result in the imposition of gift tax liability highlights the valuation problems that certainly will result from the Court's holding. It is often difficult to place a value on outright ownership of items of real and personal property. Those difficulties multiply when the interest to be valued is the *use* of the property for varying lengths of time. Even in the simplest case—where the property that is borrowed is cash—valuation problems arise. In the three decided cases in which the Commissioner belatedly pursued the theory that the Court adopts today, the Service used three different methods for determining the interest rate that should be used to establish the use-value of the borrowed money.[8] Thus, it is clear that the Court's decision will generate substantial valuation problems.

The Court downplays the significance of its decision by "assum[ing] that the focus of the Internal Revenue Service is not on such traditional familial matters [as the use of cars or homes]." * * * The Court also concludes that the Tax Code's "generous exclusions, exceptions, and credits clearly absorb the sorts of *de minimis* gifts petitioners envision and render illusory the administrative problems that petitioners perceive." * * * In effect, the Court has chosen to turn its back on the ramifications of its decision.

The Court, aware of the potential for abuse of its new interpretation, "assume[s]" that the Internal Revenue Service will exercise the power conferred on it in a reasonable way. * * * This assumption is not likely to afford much comfort to taxpayers and the lawyers and accountants who advise them. The Commissioner, acting with utmost goodwill, is confronted with a dilemma. This Court today holds that the plain language of the statute mandates, and that Congress intended, the "gift tax statute to reach *all* gratuitous transfers of *any* valuable interest in property." * * * No discretion is given the Commissioner and the IRS to read "all" and "any" as meaning only such transfers and only such valuable interests in property that it seems reasonable to tax. The Court identifies no statutory basis for such discretion, and even if the Court itself undertook to confer it I am not aware that we have ever before "assumed" that *tax laws* would be enforced—not according to their letter—but reasonably.

III

The Court's answer to these concerns is that the exceptions and exemptions in the Tax Code will render most administrative problems "illusory." * * * Although the $10,000 annual per donee exclusion will shield many taxpayers from having to pay gift taxes on intra-family loans, the taxpayer cannot know whether he has exceeded the annual limit until

---

8. In *Johnson,* the Service apparently computed the amount of the gift using the interest rate specified in the regulations for valuing annuities, life estates, terms for years, remainders, and reversions. 254 F.Supp., at 76; see Reg. § 25.2512–5. In *Crown,* the Service used a rate that it considered reasonable under the circumstances. 67 T.C., at 1061. In this case, the rate was that specified in I.R.C. § 6621 for determining interest due on underpayments or refunds of taxes. 690 F.2d, at 814, n.4. The Service has urged yet another method in a recently docketed Tax Court case, LaRosa v. Commissioner, No. 29632–82. In *LaRosa,* the Service has arrived at a separate interest rate for each month the loan was outstanding. The monthly interest rates were provided by an "expert" who relied on estimated fair market interest rates considering the creditworthiness of the borrowers. On an annualized basis, the rates used in *LaRosa* range from 12.5% to 31.1%.

he has assigned a value to every "transfer" that falls within the Court's definition. In particular, a taxpayer who has made outright gifts during the year, approaching in dollar value the amount of the applicable annual exclusion, must be concerned with the value of intra-family loans. Once he has exceeded the exclusion, he must file a gift tax return, listing and describing each gift. I.R.C. § 6019(a)(1); Reg. § 25.6019–4.

Nor does it suffice to say that most taxpayers will be protected from payment of gift taxes by the Tax Code's "lifetime exemption." Regardless of the availability of an offsetting credit, all taxpayers who exceed the annual per donee exclusion must go through the uncertain process of valuing intra-family loans and filing a gift tax return. Moreover, if the taxpayer chooses to reduce his unified credit rather than pay the gift tax, he lessens the amount of credit that will be available to offset estate taxes at the time of his death. In short, the net result of the Court's decision will be to create potential tax liability for many taxpayers who have never been subject to it before, and create legal, tax accounting, and return filing nightmares for many others. * * *

None of the problems and anomalies I have outlined is insurmountable. They do involve, however, delicate issues of policy that should be addressed in the legislative forum. Instead of recognizing the long-standing practice of attaching no gift tax consequences to interest-free loans of money and property, and leaving these difficult issues to the body responsible for legislating tax policy, the Court now allows the Commissioner to decide these questions without guidance. That course is ill-advised and inequitable.

I dissent.

ILLUSTRATIVE MATERIAL

A. SCOPE OF *DICKMAN*

The majority in *Dickman* gave § 2501 an expansive scope, construing it more broadly than § 2033. See p. 107. Does the case indicate that a transfer of "property" by "gift" encompasses a broader category of wealth transfers than property in which the decedent possessed an "interest" at death, or is it simply complementary to § 2033 in the sense that transfers of property by gift may include certain types of transfers that can only arise during life?

As Justice Powell pointed out in dissent, the majority did not specifically limit its holding to interest-free loans of money. Thus, as he noted, "potential tax liability may arise in a wide range of situations involving the unrecompensed use of property." At least three issues are raised. First, does the gift tax reach the unrecompensed use of property, such as rent for use of a home by an adult who lives with his parents, or the loan of a car for a brief period? Second, if, in light of *Dickman* and general gift tax principles, these transactions do result in a transfer of property, is it appropriate for the Service to fail to enforce the statute with respect to such transactions? Third, how should the valuation issues to which Justice Powell refers be resolved? In connection with the last question, consider whether the problem is really valuation (i.e., lack of a market price for the rental of the item in question) or whether it is how the transfer tax system can deal with many small transactions? If the latter, is the inflation-adjusted $10,000 annual exclusion for gifts of present interests in property sufficient to deal with the problem? If Congress were to legislate, what should that legislation provide?

Dickman also undercuts the post-*Hogle II* rationale for excluding the performance of gratuitous services from the gift tax. Under this estate-depletion theory, gratuitous services are excluded from the gift tax because the tax law does not assume that the parent would have provided services to third parties for compensation if he did not provide the services to his children. Yet the majority in *Dickman* rejected the parent's argument that subjecting the transfer of the use of property to the gift tax imposed on them an affirmative legal duty to invest the property.

One co-author has examined the over one hundred subsequent cases and rulings that have applied *Dickman* and concluded that the majority's reliance on the Service's forbearance in not intruding on "traditional familial matters" has proven to have been misplaced. The Service has increasingly used the *Dickman* foregone earnings theory to reach various transfers of opportunity from parents to their children. See Caron, Taxing Opportunity, 14 Va.Tax Rev. 347 (1994).

For example, in Snyder v. Commissioner, 93 T.C. 529 (1989), D transferred shares of P Corp to a newly organized holding company, X Corp, in exchange for common stock and 7% noncumulative class A preferred stock of X. D transferred the X common stock to a trust for her great-grandchildren and retained the class A preferred stock. The class A preferred shares were redeemable at D's option and convertible into 7% cumulative class B preferred shares that also were redeemable at D's option at par plus accumulated dividends. The Tax Court refused to treat D's failure to exercise her redemption privilege as gift and held, under the *Dickman* rationale, that D's failure to convert her class A preferred shares into class B preferred shares constituted an ongoing gift to the X Corp common shareholders to the extent that dividends would have accumulated on the class B shares and the underlying X Corp assets increased sufficiently in value to pay the redemption price of the class B shares.

B.   LEGISLATIVE RESPONSE: § 7872

1.   *General*

In 1984, Congress recognized that "in many instances, the failure of the tax laws to treat [below-market loans] in accordance with their economic substance provided taxpayers with opportunities to circumvent well-established tax rules." Staff of Joint Committee on Taxation, General Explanation of the Revenue Provisions of the Deficit Reduction Act of 1984, 527 (Jt. Comm. Print Dec. 31, 1984). Although *Dickman* made the value of the foregone interest subject to the gift tax, the present interest exclusion and unified credit eliminated current gift tax in most situations. However, interest-free demand loans continued to present significant income shifting opportunities. In the family context, interest-free demand loans could be used to circumvent the grantor trust rules of §§ 671–678. An interest-free demand loan from A to B is substantively equivalent to a transfer of an equivalent amount by A to a trust for the benefit of B that is revocable by A. The trust transfer would not shift the income tax incidence of the transferred property to either the trust or B. Under the case law prior to 1984, the loan shifted the income tax incidence of the borrowed funds to the borrower. In the Tax Reform Act of 1984, Congress dealt with both the income and transfer tax aspects of below-market rate loans.

Adopting the two-step analysis set forth in a footnote in the *Dickman* opinion, Congress stated that a "below-market loan is the economic equivalent of a loan bearing a market rate of interest, and a payment by the lender to the borrower to fund the payment of interest by the borrower." Staff of Joint Committee on Taxation, General Explanation of the Revenue Provisions of the Deficit Reduction Act of 1984, 527 (Jt. Comm. Print Dec. 31, 1984). Accordingly, under § 7872 interest foregone on a below-market loan is treated as transferred from the lender to the borrower and then re-transferred by the borrower to the lender as interest. Broad classes of below-market rate loans are covered by § 7872, including gift loans, employer-employee loans, corporation-shareholder loans, loans in which tax avoidance is one of the principal purposes of the interest arrangements, and, to the extent provided in regulations, any below-market loan where the interest arrangements have a significant effect on the tax liability of either the lender or the borrower. § 7872(c).

2. Demand Loans

A demand loan is a below-market loan if interest is payable on the loan at a rate less than the applicable Federal rate. § 7872(e)(1)(A). A term loan is a below-market loan if the amount loaned exceeds the present value of all payments (interest and principal) due under the loan. § 7872(e)(1)(B). A "gift loan" is "any below-market loan where the foregoing of interest is in the nature of a gift." § 7872(f)(3). The effect of § 7872 on "gift loans" is to treat the amount of the foregone interest as a taxable gift from the lender to the borrower, create interest expense for the borrower in an amount equal to the foregone interest, and include in the lender's income an identical amount.

Foregone interest on a demand below-market gift loan is the difference between: (a) the interest determined at the applicable Federal rate for the period during the calendar year that the loan is outstanding, and (b) the interest payable on the loan and attributable to the same period. § 7872(e)(2). The applicable Federal rate is "the Federal short-term rate in effect under § 1274(d) for the period for which the amount of foregone interest is being determined." § 7872(f)(2)(B). In the case of a demand below-market loan, foregone interest is treated, for gift tax purposes, as having been transferred from the lender to the borrower on the last day of the calendar year. § 7872(a). To illustrate, assume that A makes a $100,000 interest-free demand loan to B on January 1, 2009 and the loan remains outstanding throughout 2009. Assume also that the applicable Federal rate for 2009 is 11%, compounded annually.[9] A has made a gift of .11 × $100,000 or $11,000 to B. If the loan had stated interest of 9% payable annually on December 31, the amount of the gift from A to B would be $2,000 ($11,000 - $9,000). For the computation of foregone interest in a variety of demand loan situations, see Prop. Reg. § 1.7872–13 (1985).

---

9. In most situations, the applicable Federal rate is compounded semi-annually. The text uses annual compounding to simplify the computation.

3. Term Loans

In the case of a term gift loan, the amount of the gift is determined at the time of the transfer and is equal to the excess of the amount loaned over the present value of all the payments that are required to be made under the terms of the loan. § 7872(d)(2), (b)(1). The present value of any payment to be made under the term loan is determined by using a discount rate equal to the § 1274(d) Federal rate applicable to an instrument of the same term as the term gift loan, compounded semi-annually. § 7872(f)(1), (2)(A). To illustrate, assume C makes a $200,000 interest-free three year term loan to D on July 1, 2009. The applicable Federal rate is 10%, compounded semi-annually. The present value of the right to receive $200,000 in three years on these assumptions is $149,243.08.* Thus, C makes a gift to D of $50,756.92 ($200,000 - $149,243.08) on July 1, 2009. For other examples of the calculation of present value, see Prop. Reg. § 1.7872–14 (1985).

4. Exceptions

Notwithstanding the foregoing, § 7872 does not apply to any day on which the aggregate outstanding amount of gift loans between individuals is not in excess of $10,000. § 7872(c)(2)(A). However, this *de minimis* exception does not apply to any gift loan directly attributable to the purchase or carrying of income-producing assets, § 7872(c)(2)(B), which is the case if "the loan proceeds are directly traceable to the purchase of the income-producing assets, the assets are used as collateral for the loan, or there is direct evidence that the loan was made to avoid disposition of the assets." Prop. Reg. § 1.7872–8(b)(3) (1985). An income-producing asset is an asset "of a type that generates ordinary income." However, "stock (whether or not dividends are paid)," is treated as "an income-producing asset." Prop. Reg. § 1.7872–8(b)(4) (1985). Moreover, the § 7872(b)(2) *de minimis* exception applies only to gift loans between natural persons. A loan between a parent and a guardian or custodian for a minor child is treated as a loan between natural persons, but a loan to a trust in which the child is the beneficiary does not qualify for the exception. Prop. Reg. § 1.7872–8(a)(2)(i) (1985).

SECTION B. WHEN IS THE TRANSFER "COMPLETED"?

1. EXECUTORY AGREEMENTS TO TRANSFER

Commissioner v. Estate of Copley

194 F.2d 364 (7th Cir. 1952).

■ MAJOR, CHIEF JUDGE: * * *

The decedent (* * * taxpayer) and his intended wife, Chloe Davidson–Worley, on April 18, 1931, while in Paris, France, in contemplation of

---

* Present Value $= \dfrac{\text{Future value}}{(1 + i)^n}$

i = interest rate

n = number of time periods

Therefore, in this example

present value $= \dfrac{200{,}000}{[1 + (.10/2)]^6}$

$= 149{,}243$

marriage and in consideration thereof entered into an antenuptial agreement by which "the said party of the first part [Copley] hereby agrees to pay to said party of the second part [the prospective wife], to be effective immediately after the solemnization of said marriage, the sum of one million dollars, the *said sum to become and to be her sole and separate property.*" The agreement continued, "In consideration of the payment to her of the said sum of one million dollars, the party of the second part agrees that she will accept and does accept the said sum in lieu of any and all rights, or claims of dower, inheritance and descent in and to the real property of the party of the first part now owned or that may hereafter be acquired by him, and in lieu of any and all other claims which might otherwise arise or accrue to her by reason of said marriage * * *." And it was provided that in the event of her death prior to his one-half of the said one million dollars should revert to him or, in the event of his death prior to hers, that said one-half should go to his estate.

The parties were married on April 27, 1931, after which they returned to the United States and took up their residence and domicile at Aurora, Illinois, which had long been the domicile and residence of Copley.

On January 1, 1936, Copley assigned and transferred to his wife notes of Southern California Associated Newspapers in the face amount of $500,000. On the following day, the wife entered into a revocable trust agreement with Copley as trustee, and assigned the notes to the trust, to terminate at the death of Copley or his wife, whichever should first occur, at which time the trust property was to go to the wife or her estate.

On November 20, 1944, Copley transferred to his wife cumulative preferred stock of the Copley Press, Inc., in the face amount of $500,000, under a trust agreement entered into between the parties. This agreement recited that "the said Chloe D. Copley does hereby agree and acknowledge that said Ira C. Copley, has, in all manners, performed the agreements on his part to be kept and performed as contemplated in said antenuptial agreement * * *."

The Commissioner determined a deficiency in the gift taxes of the taxpayer for the years 1936 and 1944, on the premise that the transactions in those years were transfers "of property by gift" under [the predecessor of § 2501]. The Tax Court decided in favor of the taxpayer, two members dissenting. * * *

The Commissioner poses the question for decision thus: "Were the gifts completed in the year when taxpayer promised to make the transfers * * *, or in the years when he actually made the transfers * * *?" On the other hand, respondents pose the question thus: "Did the discharge in 1936 and 1944 of the obligation created in 1931 by the antenuptial contract constitute a taxable gift within the meaning of the Revenue Act of 1932 * * *?"

We think the Commissioner in the question as posed, as well as in his brief, oversimplifies the situation. Typical of numerous statements in his brief are: "In this case taxpayer's agreement to transfer property remained wholly executory until after the gift tax statute was enacted * * *."

Copley in 1931 did not agree to transfer property to his wife in 1936 or 1944 or any other year. What he did was to obligate himself unconditionally to pay her "immediately after the solemnization of said marriage, the sum of one million dollars," which obligation became effective upon their marriage nine days later. And the nature of the transaction is not altered by the fact that Mrs. Copley at a subsequent time agreed to accept corporate stocks and notes in lieu of that which Copley had promised.

Under the law of Copley's residence and domicile (Illinois), there is no question but that the agreement of the parties, upon their marriage, became a binding and legally enforceable obligation. * * * Copley's obligation to pay his wife one million dollars the next day after their marriage was a debt and possessed all the indicia of a promissory note payable on demand. She could have assigned and conveyed good title to the instrument which evidenced his obligation to pay, and either Mrs. Copley or her assignee could have maintained an action against Copley and recovered a judgment. And it can hardly be questioned but that Copley by the obligation thus assumed depleted the net worth of his estate and that the net worth of his wife's estate was augmented, each to the extent of one million dollars.

Thus, the rights and obligations of Copley and his wife had become definitely fixed more than one year prior to the enactment of the gift tax act of 1932. True, at that time Copley had not discharged the contractual debt or obligation which he owed to his wife and, so far as the record discloses, she had made no effort to enforce payment. And any reason why discharge of the obligation was delayed we think immaterial. The point is that his wife in 1936 and 1944 agreed to and did accept on each occasion $500,000 in securities in discharge of Copley's obligation and in lieu of the money which he was obligated to pay her. It is contrary to reason and common sense to say that the delivery of such property by Copley in 1936 and 1944, and its acceptance by his wife, was other than a discharge of the 1931 obligation. However, unrealistic as it appears upon its face, the Commissioner contends that the transactions during the later years were transfers "of property by gift." * * *

The Commissioner places much reliance upon [Commissioner v. Wemyss, 324 U.S. 303,] and Merrill v. Fahs, 324 U.S. 308, decided by the Supreme Court on the same date. The Tax Court in the instant case distinguishes those cases on the ground that "These parties contracted when there was no gift tax law in effect. Gifts made in 1931 were not subject to any gift tax." In those cases the transfer of the property held to be "by gift" related to the performance of an antenuptial agreement but a study of the two opinions makes it plain that the court was considering the transaction as a whole, that is, the agreement and its performance, both of which took place simultaneously in the *Wemyss* case and within the same taxable year in the *Fahs* case.

The reasoning of both cases * * * is predicated solely upon the court's interpretation of [the predecessor of § 2512(b)] which reads as follows:

"Where property is transferred for less than an adequate and full consideration in money or money's worth, then the amount by which the value of the property exceeded the value of the consideration shall, for the purpose of the tax imposed by this title, be deemed a gift, and shall be included in computing the amount of gifts made during the calendar year."

The court in each case held that the receipt of property for the release of marital rights did not constitute "an adequate and full consideration in money or money's worth" under the section just quoted. In the absence of this provision, upon which the court bottomed its reasoning and its conclusion, there is no reason to think that the court would have held as it did; in fact, it is more reasonable to believe that it would not have done so. It is also interesting and perhaps pertinent to note that one member of the court dissented in the *Wemyss* case and four members in the *Fahs* case. In the former, the transfer of the property was made prior to and in contemplation of marriage, while in the latter an arrangement was made on the day prior to marriage and performance was had ninety days thereafter by the creation of a trust for the wife's benefit. This distinction in the factual situation, as we understand, increased the number of dissenters from one to four. As is pointed out in the dissenting opinion in the Fahs case, "Petitioner was obligated to create the trust upon consideration of the relinquishment of marital rights and did so, and hence this is not a case involving marriage alone as consideration."

In the instant situation, the facts are far more unfavorable to the Commissioner. Certainly, when the asserted transfers were made in 1936 and 1944, marriage had nothing to do with the consideration—that had been consummated in 1931—and it is equally certain that there was no relinquishment of marital rights because that also was consummated at the time of marriage, all of which emphasizes that the asserted transfers in 1936 and 1944 were none other than the discharge of a contractual obligation. Of more importance, however, is the fact that the gift tax statute of 1932, including of course [the predecessor of § 2512], upon which the decisions in *Wemyss* and *Fahs* rest, was enacted subsequent to the contract between Copley and his wife. To hold, as the Commissioner would have us do, that these decisions are controlling in the instant situation would require a retroactive application of [the predecessor of § 2512], which we think is not permissible. * * *

The Commissioner also professes to find support for his position in Taft v. Commissioner, 304 U.S. 351. It is significant that neither the majority members of the Tax Court nor the dissenters referred to this case. We suspect that the reason for this is that it was not considered to have any bearing upon the instant situation; in fact, we think if anything it militates against the Commissioner's contention. In that case, Mrs. Taft, the decedent, promised to make payments to certain charitable institutions which became binding obligations under the law of the State of Ohio. Such promises were not performed during her lifetime but the payments promised were made by her executors. They sought, in calculating the estate tax, to deduct such payments from the value of the gross estate under [the 1932 Act predecessors of §§ 2053 and 2055] * * *. The estate tax law of 1924 included for the first time a provision similar to that incorporated in the gift tax law of 1932 (to which we have previously referred), making such items of indebtedness deductible only where they were "incurred or contracted bona fide and for a fair consideration in money or money's worth" * * *. The court, referring to previous Acts, stated * * *: "Under these Acts the claims in question would have been deductible as enforceable by state law irrespective of the nature of the consideration. The Act of 1924 altered existing law and authorized the deduction of claims against an estate only to the extent that they were 'incurred or contracted bona fide and for a fair consideration in money or money's worth.'" It was for this reason that the court held the items non-deductible and it was for the same reasons, as heretofore shown, that the court held in the *Wemyss* and *Fahs* cases (heretofore discussed) that the transfers in those cases were not "by gift." By the same reasoning, the gift tax act of 1932 is not applicable to an obligation created prior to its enactment. * * *

The Commissioner, relying on *Taft* and other cases, states in his brief, "If taxpayer had died before carrying out the antenuptial agreement, the wife's contractual claim under that agreement to receive a part of his property clearly would not have been deductible from taxpayer's estate for estate tax purposes." That perhaps is correct but, if so, it is because of the provision in the estate tax law dating from 1924, which precluded the deduction unless it was in discharge of an obligation "for a fair consideration in money or money's worth." In the absence of such a provision, as we have shown from the *Taft* opinion, it would be deductible if enforceable by State law. In the instant situation, the Commissioner seeks to apply a similar provision in the gift tax law which was not enacted until after Copley's obligation became fixed.

The Commissioner also cites a number of cases * * * in which it has been stated that the gift tax was supplementary to the estate tax and that the two are *in pari materia* and must be construed together. As the court stated in the *Fahs* case, * * * "The phrase on the meaning of which decision must largely turn—that is, transfers for other than 'an adequate and full consideration in money or money's worth'—came into the gift tax by way of estate tax provisions." But certainly that principle can have no application between 1924, when the provision was inserted for the first time in the estate tax law, and 1932, when the gift tax law was enacted.

Neither do we agree with the Commissioner's theory that we must either hold that there was a transfer "by gift" in 1936 and 1944, when Copley discharged the obligation to his wife, or in 1931, when the obligation was created. All we are concerned with is whether the transactions in 1936 and 1944 were transfers "by gift." Certainly the contract between

Copley and his wife in 1931, whatever it be characterized, was not a transfer "by gift" as that term was defined in a law subsequently enacted. Whether it was a gift by State law, common law or in ordinary connotation is a question of no pertinency at the moment.

The taxpayer, as did the Tax Court, in our opinion places greater reliance upon Harris v. Commissioner, 178 F.2d 861, than it merits. It does, however, furnish some support for the taxpayer's contention. There, the taxpayer entered into an agreement with her husband to pay him $5,000 a year for a period of ten years as part of a settlement made preliminary to a divorce proceeding between the parties. The obligation thus incurred by the wife was conditioned upon the entry of a decree of divorce. The court held that the promises contained in the agreement survived the provisions of the divorce decree and that the promise to pay on the part of the wife constituted a transfer "by gift" and was, therefore, subject to a gift tax. The point pertinent to the instant situation was whether the gift was taxable for the year in which the promise was made or for the years in which the separate payments were made—more specifically, whether the gift was taxable in the year when the obligation was created or in the respective years when payments were made in discharge of the obligation. The court held that the gift was taxable in the year the obligation was created. Strangely enough, the position of both the taxpayer and the Commissioner in that case were just the opposite of what they are here. There, the taxpayer argued that the transaction constituted a series of independent gifts, each maturing when made—in other words, that the obligation did not constitute a gift but that it was only the separate payments as they were made which would fall into that category. On the other hand, the Commissioner argued that the obligation constituted intangible property and was effectively transferred to the donee in the year of its creation. The argument continued:

> "It was unquestionably fully assignable by him at and from that time and even in the event of his death was unqualifiedly payable to his assigns or his estate. Taxpayer's obligation was absolute and full, subject to no contingency, and expressly bound her estate in the event of her death; collectibility did not condition it, in view of her ample assets and the security assigned to him."

The Court of Appeals decision in the *Harris* case was reversed by the Supreme Court, 340 U.S. 106, which held that the transaction in question was not subject to a gift tax. The basis for the holding, as we understand it, is that the settlement agreement between the taxpayer and her husband became merged in the subsequently entered decree for divorce; that it was the decree and not the agreement which determined the rights and obligations of the parties and that the provision in the gift tax law relative to agreements for "an adequate and full consideration in money or money's worth" was not applicable. In view of the reasoning of and the conclusion reached by the Supreme Court, there was no occasion, of course, to consider or decide when the gift was made, that is, whether in the year the obligation was created or in the years when the obligation was discharged;

therefore, the decision and reasoning of the Court of Appeals on this point were left undisturbed.

We have examined other cases cited by the Commissioner, typical of which is Burnet v. Guggenheim, 288 U.S. 280, where the donor was under no binding legal obligation to make a transfer. In such cases it has been held that a completed gift is consummated only upon actual delivery since there is no enforceable right in the donee to receive. Such cases do not aid the Commissioner here where, as we have shown, the donor in 1931 created an obligation which he was without power to retract and which conferred upon the donee an enforceable right.

This case, unlike some cases, is untainted with any suspicion of fraud or an effort to evade taxation. A bona fide transaction took place between the parties, by which he became obligated to pay and she entitled to receive. By reason of a law subsequently enacted, it is now attempted to tax the transactions which in any fair appraisement were nothing more than a consummation of his obligation to pay and her right to receive. The question presented furnishes the premise for a first-class argument on both sides, but we reach the conclusion that it was correctly decided by the Tax Court. * * *

■ KERNER, CIRCUIT JUDGE, dissenting:

It is with regret that I find myself under the necessity of dissenting from my associates. The [predecessor of § 2501] is clear and unambiguous. It imposes a tax on transfers of property by gift, and since taxation is an intensely practical matter, the solution of our problem must be found in the statutory language.

The majority assume that the obligation to pay $1,000,000 was the equivalent of $1,000,000, having the immediate effect of depleting the net worth of the husband's estate and augmenting that of the wife by that precise amount. That I cannot understand. That the agreement was not self-executing is evidenced by the fact that thirteen years elapsed between the date of the promise and the date the wife actually came into possession of the full amount of the fund agreed to be turned over to her upon her marriage.

To me it is clear that the taxable event is the transfer of property. The essence of a transfer is the passage of control over the economic benefits of property rather than any technical changes in its title, Estate of Sanford v. Commissioner, 308 U.S. 39, and whatever may have been the equitable rights of the wife, until the Southern California notes and the preferred stock of the Copley Press were actually transferred in 1936 and 1944, the taxpayer remained and was the owner of the notes and stock. He had command over and enjoyed the economic benefits of the property.

As I construe the Act, the tax is to be imposed on the transfer of property, not on the promise to transfer, regardless of the enforceability of that promise under the Law of Contracts. It is the transfer of property which is taxable as a gift, not the promise to transfer; that is to say, the determinative factor is not the contract of 1931. And since the consideration for the promise, which we must construe in accordance with the statutory definition, is not adequate in money or money's worth, so that the transfer when actually made is, under the terms of that definition deemed a gift, then I think the transfers were not exempt—instead they were subject to the gift tax. I do not consider that this construction of the Act renders it retroactive. Retroactive effect would have been given if Congress had, by the Act, attempted to tax transfers previously made, as it did by the Act of 1924, held invalid or inoperative as to transfers by gift consummated before its enactment. See 2 Paul, Federal Estate and Gift Taxation (1942), p. 962. Here the actual "transfers by gift" were not consummated until after the enactment.

Revenue Ruling 98–21

1998–1 C.B. 975.

ISSUE

When is the transfer of a nonstatutory stock option (i.e., a compensatory stock option that is not subject to the provisions of § 421) by the optionee to a family member, for no consideration, a completed gift under § 2511?

FACTS

A is employed by Company. Company has one class of stock. Company has a stock option under which employees can be awarded nonstatutory stock options to purchase shares of Company's stock. These stock options are not traded on an established market. The shares acquired on the exercise of an option are freely transferable, subject only to generally applicable securities laws, and subject to no other restrictions or limitations.

Company grants to A, in consideration for services to be performed by A, a nonstatutory stock option to purchase shares of Company common stock. Company's stock option plan provides that the stock option is exercisable by A only after A performs additional services.

All options granted under Company's stock option plan expire 10 years from the grant date. The exercise price per share of A's option is the fair market value of one share of Company's common stock on the grant date. Company's stock option plan permits the transfer of nonstatutory stock options to a member of an optionee's immediate family or to a trust for the benefit of those individuals. The effect of such a transfer is that the transferee (after the required service is completed and before the option's expiration date) will determine whether and when to exercise the stock option and will also be obligated to pay the exercise price.

Before A performs the additional services necessary to allow A's option to be exercised, A transfers A's option to B, one of A's children, for no consideration.

LAW AND ANALYSIS

Section 2501 imposes a tax on the transfer of property by gift by any individual. The gift tax is not imposed upon the receipt of the property by the donee, is not necessarily determined by the measure of enrichment resulting to the donee from the transfer, and is not conditioned upon the ability to identify the donee at the time of the transfer. The tax is a primary and personal liability of the donor, is an excise upon the donor's act of making the transfer, is measured by the value of the property passing from the donor, and attaches regardless of the fact that the identity of the donee may not then be known or ascertainable. Reg. § 25.2511–2(a).

The gift tax applies to a transfer of property by way of gift, whether the transfer is in trust or otherwise, whether the gift is direct or indirect, and whether the property is real or personal, tangible or intangible. Reg. § 25.2511–1(a). For this purpose, the term property is used in its broadest and most comprehensive sense and reaches "every species of right or interest protected by law and having an exchangeable value." H.R.Rep. No. 708, 72d Cong., 1st Sess. 27 (1932); S.Rep. No. 665, 72d Cong., 1st Sess. 39, (1932); both reprinted in 1939–1 (Part 2) C.B. 476, 524. Some rights, however, are not property. See, e.g., Estate of Howell v. Commissioner, 15 T.C. 224 (1950) (nonvested pension rights were not property rights includible in gross estate under § 811(c) of the 1939 Code); Estate of Barr v. Commissioner, 40 T.C. 227 (1963), acq., 1964–1 C.B. 4 (death benefits payable at discretion of board of directors who usually but not always, agreed to payment, were in the nature of hope or expectancy and not property rights includible in gross estate for estate tax purposes).

Generally, a gift is complete when the donor has so parted with dominion and control over the property as to leave the donor no power to change its disposition, whether for the donor's own benefit or for the benefit of another. Reg. § 25.2511–2(b).

In Estate of Copley v. Commissioner, 15 T.C. 17 (1950), aff'd, 194 F.2d 364 (7th Cir.1952), acq., 1965–2 C.B. 4, the petitioner entered into an antenuptial agreement in which the petitioner promised to give the future spouse a sum of money in consideration of the marriage and in lieu of all the spouse's marital rights in the petitioner's property. The agreement became legally enforceable under state law on the date of the marriage in 1931. The petitioner transferred part of the sum of money in 1936 and the rest in 1944. The court concluded that a gift tax would have been due in 1931 if there had been a gift tax law in effect at that time.

In Rev. Rul. 79–384, 1979–2 C.B. 344, a parent promised to pay a child $10,000 if the child graduated from college. Rev. Rul. 79–384 holds that the parent made a gift on the day the child graduated from college, the date when the parent's promise became enforceable and determinable in value.

In Rev.Rul. 80–186, 1980–2 C.B. 280, a parent transferred to a child, for nominal consideration, an option to purchase real property for a specified period of time at a price below fair value. Rev.Rul. 80–186 holds that the transfer is a completed gift at the time the option is transferred provided the option is binding and enforceable under state law on the date of the transfer.

In the present case, Company grants to A a nonstatutory stock option conditioned on the performance of additional services by A. If A fails to perform the services, the option cannot be exercised. Therefore, before A performs the services, the rights that A possesses in the stock option have not acquired the character of enforceable property rights susceptible of transfer for federal gift tax purposes. A can make a gift of the stock option to B for federal gift tax purposes only after A has completed the additional required services because only upon completion of the services does the right to exercise the option become binding and enforceable. In the event the option were to become exercisable in stages, each portion of the option that becomes exercisable at a different time is treated as a separate option for the purpose of applying this analysis. * * *

HOLDING

On the facts stated above, the transfer to a family member, for no consideration, of a nonstatutory stock option, is a completed gift under § 2511 on the later of (i) the transfer [, or] (ii) the time when the donee's right to exercise the option is no longer conditioned on the performance of services by the transferor.

ILLUSTRATIVE MATERIAL

A. TIME OF COMPLETION IN GENERAL

Reg. § 25.2511–2(a) states the general rule that a gift is complete as to any property "of which the donor has so parted with dominion and control as to leave in him no power to change its disposition, whether for his own benefit or for the benefit of another." The rule in *Estate of Copley* is consistent with this standard: it looks past the property actually transferred in satisfaction of the obligation (of which the donor retained dominion and control until the actual transfer) and focuses on the contractual commitment binding the donor to transfer a specified sum in the future. See also Rosenthal v. Commissioner, 205 F.2d 505, 506 (2d Cir.1953) ("[A] binding promise to make a gift becomes subject to gift taxation in the year the obligation is undertaken and not when the discharging payments are made.").

After fifteen years of disagreement with the Tax Court decision in *Estate of Copley*, the Service finally acquiesced. 1965–2 C.B. 4. The Service thus accepts the view that a gift takes place, if at all, at the time a legally binding obligation is created, provided the gift is susceptible of valuation at that time. See Rev.Rul. 84–25, 1984–1 C.B. 191.

B. STOCK OPTIONS

Rev.Rul. 98–21 treats a transfer of a stock option as a completed gift when the option becomes binding and enforceable. On the facts of the ruling, that meant when the donor-employee performed additional future services for the employer. In other situations, the Service has treated transfers of options as completed gifts only when other conditions were satisfied that made the options binding and enforceable. See PLR 199952012 (Sept. 22, 1999) (one-year employment and stock price appreciation). Transfers of stock options also raise related income tax issues.[12]

C.   GIFTS INVOLVING PERIODIC PAYMENTS

Where the contract involves payments over time, the question is whether the gift occurs as each payment is made, or whether the present value of the future payments is taxed in the year the obligation is created. In a case involving a wife's agreement as part of a divorce settlement to pay an annuity to the husband, the court stated:

"There only remains the question whether it was proper to include the commuted actuarial value of the husband's annuity at the time when the decree passed. The taxpayer's argument is that the annuity was a series of independent gifts, each maturing when made, and not to be appraised as one. This misconceives the transaction; although the payments were subject to a gift tax, they were not gifts at all, the annuity was a contract made for a valid consideration, and it is classed as a gift only because the statute says so. Once it became a contract by entry of decree, since thereupon the taxpayer became bound to make all the payments, she did not make a new gift each month; indeed she never had any donative intent at the outset. In dealing with such a series of contractual payments, it has long been the accepted practice to appraise their present actuarial value as was done in the case at bar * * *."

Harris v. Commissioner, 178 F.2d 861, 865 (2d Cir.1949), rev'd on other grounds, 340 U.S. 106 (1950).

Gifts involving periodic payments also occur in other contexts. For example, assume Parent wins a state lottery and is to receive equal payments over 20 years. Parent agrees to make annual exclusion gifts to her children each year over the 20–year period. If the agreement is binding as a matter of state law, Parent will be treated as making completed gifts in the current year equal to the present value of the future payments. PLR 8940010 (Oct. 6, 1989). See also Aghdami, The Morning After: Tax Planning for Lottery Winners, 90 J. Tax'n 228 (1999). For a discussion of the estate tax consequences of lottery winnings, see p. 334.

D.   GIFTS OF NOTES AND CHECKS

Rev.Rul. 67–396, 1967–2 C.B. 351, provides:

"The question involved is when a completed gift was effected for purposes of the gift tax in the situations described below.

"Situation (1). On December 25, 1966, A, the donor, presented B with a check in excess of $3,000.00. A requested B not to deposit or cash the

---

12. The transferor-employee does not recognize income or gain on the transfer. If the donee-family member exercises the option and acquires the stock, the transferor-employee has compensation income under § 83, the employer receives a corresponding income tax deduction under § 162, and the donee-family member takes as her basis the fair market value of the stock on the date of exercise (which consists of the consideration paid by the donee-family member plus the income taxed to the donor-employee).

check for a few days, as he was not certain his bank balance was sufficient to cover the check. B held the check until January 2, 1967, when it was cashed by the drawee bank. The record shows that A's bank account was sufficient to cover the check from the date the check was presented to B until it was cashed by the bank.

"Situation (2). On August 29, 1965, C, the donor, transferred to a trustee an interest-bearing note executed by him on August 15, 1965. The note is payable within one year upon C's order, is endorsed by him in blank, and bears interest at the rate of six percent. The note was paid by C in 1966.

"A gift is complete as to any property of which the donor has so parted with dominion and control as to leave him no power to change its disposition, whether for his own benefit or for the benefit of another. Reg. § 25.2511–2. It is evident, therefore, that the effective date occurs at the time the donor can no longer revoke the gift, or revest the beneficial title to the property in himself or change the interest of the beneficiaries. A mere promise to make a gift is not a gift.

"A gift is not consummated by the mere delivery of the donor's own check or note. The gift of a check does not become complete until it is paid, certified, or accepted by the drawee, or is negotiated for value to a third person. Prior to payment, certification, or negotiation, a check is nothing more than an order on the drawee bank which may be revoked at any time by the drawer by stopping payment and is revoked ipso facto by the death of the drawer. * * * The gift of the donor's own note is not complete until the note is paid or transferred for value. * * *

"Accordingly, it is held that in the first situation the gift by A was completed on January 2, 1967, the date on which the check was cashed.

"In the second situation, the gift of the note by C was effected in 1966 when the note was paid. The amount of the gift is the amount of the principal and the interest thereon. * * * *"

The second situation of Rev.Rul. 67–396 was clarified in Rev.Rul. 84–25, 1984–1 C.B. 191, in which the Service explained that the earlier ruling applies only to the transfer of a legally unenforceable promissory note. In Rev.Rul. 84–25, A gratuitously transferred his own legally binding note payable to the transferee and died before the note was paid. The ruling held that A made a gift on the date the note became binding and the value of the gift was determinable. The amount of the gift was the fair market value of the note on that day. The ruling further held that as there was no consideration (in the transfer tax sense) for the promise to pay, the unsatisfied obligation was not deductible from A's gross estate. However, since the assets to be used to pay the unsatisfied portion of the obligation were included in A's gross estate, the earlier gift was not an adjusted taxable gift for purposes of determining the decedent's estate tax liability. Any portion of the note paid prior to death would be treated, for purposes of computing decedent's estate tax liability, as an adjusted taxable gift.

The first situation of Rev.Rul. 67–396 was modified in Rev.Rul. 96–56, 1996–2 C.B. 161:

" * * * In view of the Fourth Circuit's decision in Metzger v. Commissioner, 38 F.3d 118 (4th Cir.1994), the Internal Revenue Service has reconsidered the rationale for the holding in Situation 1 of Rev.Rul. 67–396, 1967–2 C.B. 351. In Situation 1, the donor transferred a gift check on December 25 to a noncharitable donee, but the donee held the check until January 2 of the following year when it was cashed by the drawee bank. Rev.Rul. 67–396 concludes that the gift was not complete for federal gift tax purposes until the check was paid by the drawee bank on January 2, because prior to the check's payment, certification, acceptance by the drawee, or negotiation, the donor had not relinquished dominion and control over the funds. Prior to the occurrence of one of these events, the donor could have stopped payment and revoked the gift.

"*Metzger* holds that if a check is delivered to a noncharitable donee, for federal gift tax purposes, completion of the gift relates back to the date the check was deposited by the donee, provided the check is paid by the drawee bank while the donor is alive and: (1) the donor intended to make a gift; (2) delivery of the check was unconditional; and (3) the donee presented the check for payment in the year for which completed gift treatment is sought and within a reasonable time of issuance. The Service will follow the *Metzger* decision. * * *

"Rev.Rul. 67–396 is modified to provide that the delivery of a check to a noncharitable donee will be deemed to be a completed gift for federal gift and estate tax purposes on the earlier of (i) the date on which the donor has so parted with dominion and control under local law as to leave in the donor no power to change its disposition, or (ii) the date on which the donee deposits the check (or cashes the check against available funds of the donee) or presents the check for payment, if it is established that: (1) the check was paid by the drawee bank when first presented to the drawee bank for payment; (2) the donor was alive when the check was paid by the drawee bank; (3) the donor intended to make a gift;[13] (4) delivery of the check by the donor was unconditional; and (5) the check was deposited, cashed, or presented in the calendar year for which completed gift treatment is sought and within a reasonable time of issuance. The result in Situation 1 of Rev.Rul. 67–396 remains the same for two reasons: the check was not delivered unconditionally (the donor requested that the donee not deposit or cash the check for a few days) and the check was not presented for payment in the same calendar year for which completed gift treatment was sought."

E. EFFECT OF CONDITION RELATING TO GIFT TAX LIABILITY

In Commissioner v. Procter, 142 F.2d 824, 827 (4th Cir.1944), a trust indenture provided that, to the extent a federal court of last resort held any portion of a transfer to the trust to be subject to the gift tax, the excess property transferred that gave rise to the gift tax liability would "automatically

---

13. [ED.: As explained at pp. 166–167, Reg. § 25.2511–1(g)(1) provides that "donative intent on the part of the transferor is not an essential element in the application of the gift tax," as the Supreme Court has repeatedly recognized. It is thus unclear why *Metzger* and Rev.Rul. 96–56 rely on the donor's intention as an essential element in the application of the relation-back rule.]

be deemed not to be included in the conveyance in trust * * * and shall remain the sole property of" the donor. The court treated the condition subsequent imposed on the transfer as a nullity and sustained a gift tax:

> "The condition is contrary to public policy for three reasons: * * * [First,] it has a tendency to discourage the collection of the tax by the public officials charged with its collection * * *. [Second,] the effect of the condition would be to obstruct the administration of justice by requiring the courts to pass upon a moot case. * * * [Third,] the condition is to the effect that the final judgment of a court is to be held for naught because of the provision of an indenture necessarily before the court when the judgment is rendered."

The Service, in Rev.Rul. 86–41, 1986–1 C.B. 300, examined two forms of savings clauses. The first provided that if the value of an undivided interest in property received by a donee exceeded $10,000, the donee's fractional interest in the property would be reduced so that its value did not exceed $10,000. The adjustment clause acted as a condition subsequent under local law (e.g., if the value exceeded $10,000, the effect of the adjustment clause would be to reconvey to the donor enough of the property to reduce the donee's interest to $10,000). The second clause provided that if the value of the donee's interest exceeded $10,000 the donee would transfer to the donor consideration equal to the excess. The ruling stated that the purpose of each clause was to recharacterize the nature of the transaction in the event of future adjustment by the Service and held that the Service will not give effect to such clauses. Gifts subject to such conditions subsequent "tend to discourage the enforcement of Federal gift tax provisions, because the operation of the provisions would either defeat the gift or otherwise render examination of the return ineffective." However, the ruling implied that if such a clause had been inserted to preserve or implement the original "bona fide intent of the parties, as in the case of a clause requiring a purchase price adjustment based on an appraisal by an independent third party retained for that purpose," the Service would give effect to the clause.

An adjustment clause of the first type described in Rev.Rul. 86–41 was held void as against public policy in Ward v. Commissioner, 87 T.C. 78 (1986). In particular, the court noted that if such an adjustment clause is given effect for gift tax purposes, "there is no incentive for the Commissioner to challenge the donor's valuation of the property transferred because no gift tax deficiency can result, and the Commissioner has no power to compel the donor to reclaim a portion of the property. * * * If valid, such condition would compel us to issue, in effect, a declaratory judgment as to the stock's value, while rendering the case moot as a consequence." The Service has refused to give effect to other formula clauses following Rev.Rul. 86–41 and *Ward*. See, e.g., TAM 200337012 (Sept. 12, 2003); TAM 200245053 (Nov. 8, 2002); FSA 200122011 (Feb. 20, 2001).

2.   TRANSFERRED INTEREST INCAPABLE OF VALUATION

Estate of DiMarco v. Commissioner
87 T.C. 653 (1986).

■ STERRETT, CHIEF JUDGE:

* * * [T]he only issue presented in this case is whether the present value of a survivors income benefit payable with respect to the decedent by

decedent's employer is an adjusted taxable gift within the meaning of § 2001. * * *

Anthony F. DiMarco (hereinafter referred to as the decedent) was born on August 31, 1925. He died on November 16, 1979, survived by his wife, Joan M. DiMarco, and five children. He had been employed continuously by the International Business Machines Corporation (IBM) as an active, regular, full-time permanent employee from January 9, 1950, until his death. On May 2, 1953, decedent and Joan M. DiMarco were married; he had not been previously married. Decedent's parents were not dependent upon him for their support at any time between the date when his employment with IBM began and the date of his marriage to Joan M. DiMarco. At the time of his death, decedent was employed as an electrical engineer at a salary of $5,250 per month. He was not an officer of the corporation and did not have a written employment contract.

On November 16, 1979, and at all other times relevant to this proceeding, IBM maintained a non-contributory Group Life Insurance and Survivors Income Benefit Plan (hereinafter referred to as the Plan) for the benefit of its regular employees. IBM established the Plan in September of 1934, and while the Plan has been amended on many occasions since that time, it has, since January of 1935, provided two basic benefits: (i) group term life insurance, and (ii) an uninsured and unfunded survivors income benefit. * * *

The Plan * * * provided a survivors income benefit on an uninsured and unfunded basis; that is, all survivors income benefits were paid out of IBM's general assets. With the exception of fewer than 30 top executives, all regular IBM employees, including decedent, were covered automatically by the survivors income benefit portion of the Plan. At the time of decedent's death, the amount of the survivors income benefit was equal to three times the employee's regular annual compensation. Under the terms of the Plan, the benefit was payable only to an employee's surviving spouse, certain minor and dependent children, and dependent parents. Payment was made semi-monthly, at the monthly rate of one-quarter of the employee's regular monthly compensation, and continued until the total benefit was paid. However, payments continued only so long as there remained at least one eligible survivor, and if the employee left no eligible survivor at death, no benefit was payable.

Decedent never had any power to alter, amend, revoke, or terminate the Plan in whole or in part. He had no power to select or change the beneficiaries of the survivors income benefit; no power to change the amount, form, or timing of the survivors income benefit payments; no power to substitute other benefits for the survivors income benefit; and, other than by resigning his employment with IBM, no power to terminate his coverage under the Plan. However, IBM expressly reserved the right, in its discretion, to modify the Plan if it determined that it was advisable to do so.

Joan M. DiMarco, as decedent's surviving spouse, was entitled under the Plan to receive a survivors income benefit, payable semi-monthly, in the amount of $656.25.[14] Decedent did not report the survivors income benefit as a gift on a gift tax return, and petitioner did not report it either as part of the gross estate or as an adjusted taxable gift on decedent's Federal estate tax return. However, the existence of the survivors income benefit was reported by petitioner on Schedule I of decedent's Federal estate tax return.

In his notice of deficiency, respondent "determined that an adjusted taxable gift of the present value of the IBM Survivor Annuity was made by the decedent on the date of death as it was not susceptible of valuation until the date of death." Respondent then determined that the present value of the survivors income benefit was $135,885.00, and he added this amount, as an adjusted taxable gift, to the taxable estate of decedent in computing the amount of the deficiency.

The only issue for decision in this case is whether the present value of the survivors income benefit that is payable by IBM to Joan M. DiMarco is an adjusted taxable gift within the meaning of § 2001. The term "adjusted taxable gifts" is defined by § 2001(b) as "the total amount of the taxable gifts (within the meaning of § 2503) made by the decedent after December 31, 1976, other than gifts which are includible in the gross estate of the decedent." Section 2503(a) in turn defines "taxable gifts" as the "total amount of gifts" made during the applicable period less certain statutory deductions. Thus, the survivors income benefit that is payable by IBM to Joan M. DiMarco is an adjusted taxable gift within the meaning of § 2001 only if it is also a taxable gift within the meaning of § 2503 that was made by decedent after December 31, 1976. * * *

After reviewing carefully respondent's briefs, the statutory notice of deficiency, and the stipulation of facts, it appears to us that respondent is making two arguments in this case. First, it appears that respondent argues that decedent made a completed transfer of a property interest in the survivors income benefit for gift tax purposes on January 9, 1950, but that because the interest could not be valued at that time, it was necessary to treat the transfer as an open transaction and to value the transferred property and impose the gift tax on the date of decedent's death, when the property interest finally became subject to valuation. In the alternative, respondent appears to argue that decedent made an incomplete transfer of a property interest in the survivors income benefit for gift tax purposes on January 9, 1950, because the property interest could not be valued at that time, but that the transfer became complete on November 16, 1979, when decedent died, because the transferred property could then and for the first time be valued.

---

14. Under the terms of the Plan, decedent's surviving spouse was entitled to receive these semi-monthly payments until her death, remarriage, or the exhaustion of the total amount of the survivors income benefit. If she died or remarried prior to the exhaustion of the fund, the semi-monthly payments would be continued to decedent's other eligible survivors.

Petitioner argues, for a variety of reasons, that decedent never made a taxable gift of the survivors income benefit. Petitioner argues that decedent never owned a property interest in the survivors income benefit that he was capable of transferring. Petitioner further contends that, even if decedent owned such an interest, he never transferred it, and if he did transfer it, he never did so voluntarily. Petitioner also asserts that transfers of property cannot become complete for gift tax purposes upon the death of the donor, and that decedent never made a completed transfer of any property interest he may have owned in the survivors income benefit before his death because he always had the power to revoke the transfer, if any was made, simply by resigning his employment with IBM. Petitioner finally argues that, if the decedent made a taxable gift of the survivors income benefit, he did so before December 31, 1976, and that such a gift does not qualify as an adjusted taxable gift within the meaning of § 2001. For the reasons set forth below, we find for petitioner. * * *

Respondent argues that decedent transferred a property interest in the survivors income benefit for gift tax purposes on January 9, 1950. This transfer was either complete or incomplete for gift tax purposes. If the transfer was complete, we have little difficulty in disposing of this case because a completed transfer would have been a taxable gift that was made by decedent before December 31, 1976, and § 2001 expressly defines an adjusted taxable gift as a taxable gift that was made after December 31, 1976. On the other hand, if the transfer was incomplete for gift tax purposes, we do not believe that it became complete or that we can deem that it became complete at the time of decedent's death.[15] Reg. § 25.2511–2(f) provides that—

> [t]he relinquishment or termination of a power to change the beneficiaries of transferred property, *occurring otherwise than by the death of the donor (the statute being confined to transfers by living donors),* is regarded as the event that completes the gift and causes the tax to apply. * * * [Emphasis added.]

We believe that this regulation precludes our finding in this case that the alleged transfer of property by decedent on January 9, 1950, became complete for gift tax purposes by reason of decedent's death.

We recognize, of course, that respondent does not assert in this case that the alleged transfer on January 9, 1950, became complete and subject to the gift tax because decedent's death terminated a power to change the beneficiaries of the transferred property. Even so, in view of the fact that a transfer of property that becomes complete because the donor's death terminates a power to change the beneficiaries of the transferred property is not subject to the gift tax, we decline to hold that a transfer of property that becomes complete because the donor's death makes it possible for the first time to value the transferred property is subject to the gift tax. We

---

15. Respondent does not assert that the transfer became complete for gift tax purposes at any time other than Jan. 9, 1950, or Nov. 16, 1979.

perceive nothing in the gift tax statute or the regulations that would justify such a result.

In addition, we believe that respondent has confused the issues of completion and valuation in this case. Respondent appears to argue that, because the value of the survivors income benefit could not be determined on January 9, 1950, when the alleged transfer occurred, the transfer should be treated as incomplete for gift tax purposes until the survivors income benefit became susceptible of valuation, when decedent died, at which time the transfer became complete and subject to the gift tax. For reasons stated above, we have already held that transfers of property do not become complete for gift tax purposes by reason of the death of the donor. We also question, however, whether the fact that the value of transferred property cannot be readily determined at the time of transfer is relevant in determining whether the transfer is complete for gift tax purposes. We have noted above that transfers of property are complete and subject to the gift tax at the time the donor relinquishes dominion and control over the transferred property. Nothing in the statute or the regulations suggests that, even if a donor relinquishes dominion and control over transferred property, the transfer is or can be considered to be incomplete for gift tax purposes if the value of the property is uncertain. To the contrary, in Smith v. Shaughnessy, 318 U.S. 176, 180 (1943), the Supreme Court appears to have considered and expressly rejected this argument in the following language:

> The government argues that for gift tax purposes the taxpayer had abandoned control of the remainder and that it is therefore taxable, while the taxpayer contends that no realistic value can be placed on the contingent remainder and that it therefore should not be classed as a gift.

> We cannot accept any suggestion that the complexity of a property interest * * * can serve to defeat a tax. * * * Even though these concepts of property and value may be slippery and elusive they can not escape taxation so long as they are used in the world of business. The language of the gift tax statute, "property * * * real or personal, tangible or intangible," is broad enough to include property, however conceptual or contingent. * * *

Accordingly, we reject any suggestion by respondent either that transfers of property are incomplete for gift tax purposes simply because "no realistic value can be placed" on the property at the time the transfer occurs, or that transfers of property become complete for gift tax purposes only when the value of the transferred property can be easily ascertained.

Respondent also argues that completed transfers of property for gift tax purposes can and should be treated as open transactions in those cases where the transferred property is difficult to value, and that valuation of the transferred property and the imposition of the gift tax should be postponed until the value of the property can be readily determined. We reject this contention. The clear language of the statute and the regulations requires that transferred property be valued for gift tax purposes at the time the transfer becomes complete. Section 2512(a) provides that, in the case of a gift, "the value thereof at the *date of the gift* shall be considered the amount of the gift." (Emphasis added.) In addition, § 25.2511–2(a), Gift Tax Regs., states as follows:

> The gift tax is not imposed upon the receipt of the property by the donee, nor is it necessarily determined by the measure of enrichment resulting to the donee from the transfer * * *. On the contrary, the tax is a primary and personal liability of the donor, is an excise upon his *act of making the transfer,* [and] *is measured by the value of the property passing from the donor* * * *. [Emphasis added.]

As a result, property must be valued and the gift tax imposed at the time a completed transfer of the property occurs.[16]

We also agree with petitioner that decedent never made a taxable gift of any property interest in the survivors income benefit because we find no act by decedent that qualifies as an act of "transfer" of an interest in property. His participation in the Plan was involuntary, he had no power to select or change the beneficiaries of the survivors income benefit, no power to alter the amount or timing of the payment of the benefit, and no power to substitute other benefits for those prescribed by the Plan. * * *

Respondent argues, however, that decedent's simple act of going to work for IBM on January 9, 1950, constituted an act of transfer by decedent for gift tax purposes. We disagree. None of the cases cited by respondent hold that, without more, the simple act of going to work for an employer that has an automatic, non-elective, company-wide survivors income benefit plan similar to the one at issue in this case constitutes a "transfer" of an interest in the benefit for either estate or gift tax purposes. Moreover, we doubt that it can be maintained seriously that decedent began his employment with IBM on January 9, 1950 (when he was 24, unmarried, and without dependents), for the purpose or with any intention of transferring property rights in the survivors income benefit. While we agree with respondent that a taxable event may occur without a volitional act by the donor, as in a case where an incomplete transfer of property becomes complete because of the occurrence of an event outside the donor's control, we do not believe that a taxable event can occur for gift tax purposes unless there is first and in fact an act of transfer by the donor; and there can be no act of transfer unless the act is voluntary and the transferor has some awareness that he is in fact making a transfer of property, that is, he must intend to do so. * * *[17] It is apparent to us that decedent never intended and never voluntarily acted to transfer any

---

16. Respondent relies heavily on Rev. Rul. 81–31, 1981–1 C.B. 475, and argues here that we should adopt its reasoning and holding. To the extent that this ruling can be read as holding either that a transfer of property can become complete for gift tax purposes by reason of the death of the donor, or that it is permissible to treat a completed transfer of property as an open transaction and to value the transferred property and impose the gift tax at some time other than when the completed transfer occurs, we regard the ruling as being inconsistent with the gift tax statute and the regulations.

17. The fact that there can be no taxable gift unless there is a voluntary act of transfer does not mean that the donor also must have donative intent when he makes

interest that he may have owned in the survivors income benefit. There being no act of transfer by decedent, there can be no transfer of property by gift.

Moreover, we question whether decedent ever owned a property interest in the survivors income benefit that he was capable of transferring during his lifetime. He had no voice in selecting the beneficiaries of the survivors income benefit and no ability to affect or determine the benefits payable to them. The categories of beneficiaries, the determination whether a claimant is an eligible beneficiary, and the amounts payable to the beneficiaries all were controlled directly by the provisions of the Plan and indirectly by IBM, and payments were made directly to the beneficiaries by IBM. Furthermore, the benefits were payable out of the general assets of IBM, not out of any fund in which decedent had a vested interest, and the benefits did not accrue until decedent's death. Most importantly, IBM had the power and the right to modify the Plan and the survivors income benefit at any time and in its sole discretion. Under these circumstances, we have little difficulty in concluding that decedent never acquired fixed and enforceable property rights in the survivors income benefit that he was capable of transferring during his lifetime. * * *

In our opinion, decedent never made a taxable gift of any interest in the survivors income benefit to his wife. It follows that the present value of the survivors income benefit is not an adjusted taxable gift within the meaning of § 2001.

ILLUSTRATIVE MATERIAL

A. OPEN TRANSACTION APPROACH

As noted in footnote 16 of its opinion, the Tax Court in *Estate of DiMarco* expressly rejected Rev.Rul. 81–31, 1981–1 C.B. 475, which held that a death benefit payable to a deceased employee's surviving spouse was a completed gift at the time of the employee's death, at which time the amount of the gift was first susceptible of valuation. In effect, the ruling applied an "open transaction" approach similar to the one adopted in the income tax context by Burnet v. Logan, 283 U.S. 404 (1931). The ruling accepted the proposition that the act of entering into the employment contract effected a "transfer" for gift tax purposes but, because the value of the interest was not ascertainable at the time of the transfer, the transaction would be kept "open" for tax purposes until valuation could be established.

Following the decision in *Estate of DiMarco*, the Service revoked Rev.Rul. 81–31. Rev.Rul. 92–68, 1992–2 C.B. 257. The Service acquiesced in *Estate of DiMarco* "where (1) decedent is automatically covered by the benefit plan and has no control over its terms; (2) decedent's employer retains the right to modify the plan; and (3) decedent's death is the event which first causes the value of the benefits to be ascertainable." 1990–2 C.B. 1. The Service's

the transfer. Reg. § 25.2511–1(g)(1); Commissioner v. Wemyss, 324 U.S. 303, 306 (1945). Any completed transfer of a beneficial interest in property for less than an adequate and full consideration in money or money's worth, unless made in the ordinary course of business, will be subject to the gift tax. Reg. § 25.2512–8.

acquiescence, however, is "in result" only, which signifies the Service's acceptance of the outcome in the case "but disagreement with some or all of the reasons assigned for the decision." 1990–2 C.B. 2.

The gift tax open transaction doctrine was articulated in Rev.Rul. 69–346, 1969–1 C.B. 227, involving a contract between H and W in which H agreed to transfer his share of the community property to a testamentary trust providing for W's "comfort," and W agreed that at H's death she would transfer her one-half share in the community property to the trust. The ruling relied on Rev.Rul. 69–347, 1969–1 C.B. 227, and held that a taxable gift did not result on the date the binding obligation was created because the gift was not susceptible of valuation at that time. Rev.Rul. 69–347, however, did not involve a gift which was incapable of valuation and thus did not establish the principle for which it was cited in Rev.Rul. 69–346. Moreover, it does not appear that Rev.Rul. 69–346 itself involved a completed transfer at the time of the contract. Each party in effect could have revoked the transfer, H by modifying his will and W by consuming or otherwise disposing of her share of the community property. Thus, there was no reason to value the interests at the time of the contract.

Estate of DiMarco might be analyzed in similar fashion, i.e., there was no gift when Mr. DiMarco began working for IBM because he could revoke the transfer by terminating his employment. Under this view, the transfer was completed only at Mr. DiMarco's death. The Tax Court, however, rejected this analysis of the transaction.

B.   POLICY ASPECTS

The Government's position in *Estate of DiMarco* represented its last clear chance of bringing a death benefit of the IBM-sort within the transfer tax base. Earlier attempts were unsuccessful under §§ 2033 (see p. 113), 2038 (see p. 260), and 2039 (see p. 320). Should the transfer tax system reach death benefits of this sort?

Mrs. DiMarco undeniably enjoyed the IBM payments only because of her late husband's employment with the company. But is that a sufficient nexus to treat the value of the payments as having been transferred by him to her either during his life or at his death? It is possible that the IBM plan was an important factor 30 years earlier when Mr. DiMarco decided to work for IBM rather than for another company. It is also possible that over the years Mr. DiMarco accepted less compensation than he would have in the absence of the plan. But these considerations cannot be taken into account because a tax base would be unadministrable if it sought to include every conceivable value that may be attributable in some fashion to a decedent.

3.   INDIRECT TRANSFERS

Heyen v. United States

945 F.2d 359 (10th Cir. 1991).

■ EBEL, CIRCUIT JUDGE.

* * * Decedent transferred 115 shares of stock in First National Bank and Trust of St. John to six persons. After receiving the stock certificates, all six signed the stock certificates in blank, and gave them to plaintiff or

the bank. Subsequently, the bank cancelled the certificates and the stock was reissued to members of decedent's family. Decedent also transferred 136 shares of stock in St. John National Bank to twenty-three other persons. All but two of the recipients endorsed the stock certificates in blank, resulting in a later reissuance of the stock to members of decedent's family. Based on the book value per share, each of the twenty-nine recipients received stock valued at slightly less than $10,000.00, the gift tax exclusion amount. The recipients either did not know they were receiving a gift of stock and believed they were merely participating in stock transfers or had agreed before receiving the stock that they would endorse the stock certificates in order that the stock could be reissued to decedent's family. It was decedent's wish in transferring the stock that gift taxes be avoided.

Decedent died nine months after the transfers. Plaintiff [the decedent's daughter and executrix of her estate] filed a gift tax return excluding the transfers of stock. * * *

Plaintiff argues that the stock transferred by decedent is not subject to gift tax liability. Plaintiff first contends that decedent did not make a gift of the stock to family members. Rather, plaintiff submits that decedent made separate gifts to the intermediate stock recipients, who voluntarily permitted retransfer of the stock to decedent's family members. Because decedent allegedly relinquished control over the stock to the intermediate recipients, plaintiff maintains the transfer to the decedent's family members was not subject to the gift tax.

A gift tax will be imposed on any transfers of property by gift. § 2501(a)(1). The tax applies to any transfer, whether direct or indirect, if the gift value is greater than the statutory exclusion amount of $10,000.00. §§ 2503(b), 2511(a). The language of the gift tax statutes clearly provides that "transfers of property by gift, by whatever means effected, are subject to the federal gift tax." Dickman v. Commissioner, 465 U.S. 330, 334 (1984) * * *.

* * * Decedent's initial transfer of stock to nonfamily members is not determinative. Reg. § 25.2511–1(g)(1) does not preclude consideration of decedent's actual intent to transfer the stock to family members, and § 2511(a) requires consideration of whether decedent made an indirect transfer. The evidence at trial indicated decedent intended to transfer the stock to her family rather than to the intermediate recipients. The intermediary recipients only received the stock certificates and signed them in blank so that the stock could be reissued to a member of decedent's family. Decedent merely used those recipients to create gift tax exclusions to avoid paying gift tax on indirect gifts to the actual family member beneficiaries. * * *

Plaintiff additionally contends that the transfers of the stock by decedent were not subject to gift tax because decedent relinquished control over the stock to the intermediate recipients * * *. To support her contention, plaintiff points to evidence establishing that two of such recipients kept the stock given to them without permitting retransfer to decedent's family, and she asserts that other recipients could have kept the stock as well had they decided to do so. * * *

Although the two transfers initially were the same as the other transfers, the end result was not the same. Despite the decision of two of the recipients to keep their stock, the decedent's intent with regard to all of the stock was apparently the same. The evidence at trial showed, and the jury properly found, that decedent intended her family to be the ultimate beneficiaries of the stock. Thus, the two recipients' decisions to keep their stock did not change the appropriate tax treatment for the other stock transfers. * * *

* * * The evidence amply showed that the stock transfers were indirect gifts to decedent's family which were subject to the gift tax.

[The court also upheld a civil fraud penalty imposed on plaintiff for the fraudulent evasion of gift tax in filing a gift tax return without including the 29 transfers of stock.]

ILLUSTRATIVE MATERIAL

A. OTHER INDIRECT GIFTS THROUGH INTERMEDIARIES

The regulations state that if in connection with a transfer by A of property to B there is imposed upon B the obligation of paying a commensurate annuity to C, the transaction is a gift from A to C. Reg. § 25.2511–1(h)(1). Similarly, the transfer of property from A to B in consideration of his rendering services to C is a gift to C, and also to B to the extent that the value of the services rendered C is less than what B receives. Reg. § 25.2511–1(h)(3).

In Estate of Cidulka v. Commissioner, 71 T.C.M. 2555 (1996), the donor purported to make gifts of stock to his daughter-in-law, who immediately retransferred them to her husband (the donor's son). The parties engaged in identical transactions in each of the three years before the Tax Court, as well as in a number of prior years. The Tax Court held that the gifts were to be treated as though made from donor to son because of an implied understanding that daughter-in-law would retransfer the stock to her husband. See also Estate of Bies v. Commissioner, 80 T.C.M. 628 (2000) (same result where parent made 27 annual exclusion gifts to her four children and nine grandchildren through two of the children and their spouses).

SECTION C. WHAT IS A "GIFT"?

1. DONATIVE INTENT AND "ADEQUATE AND FULL CONSIDERATION"

Internal Revenue Code: § 2512(b)

Regulations: § 25.2512–8

Commissioner v. Wemyss

324 U.S. 303 (1945).

■ MR. JUSTICE FRANKFURTER delivered the opinion of the Court.

In 1939 taxpayer proposed marriage to Mrs. More, a widow with one child. Her deceased husband had set up two trusts, one-half the income of which was for the benefit of Mrs. More and the other half for that of the child with provision that, in the event of Mrs. More's remarriage, her part of the income ceased and went to the child. The corpus of the two trusts consisted of stock which brought to Mrs. More from the death of her first husband to her remarriage, about five years later, an average income of $5,484 a year. On Mrs. More's unwillingness to suffer loss of her trust income through remarriage the parties on May 24, 1939, entered upon an agreement whereby taxpayer transferred to Mrs. More a block of shares of stock. Within a month they married. The Commissioner ruled that the transfer of this stock, the value of which, $149,456.13, taxpayer does not controvert, was subject to [§§ 2501, 2511, and 2512]. Accordingly, he assessed a deficiency which the Tax Court upheld, 2 T.C. 876, but the Circuit Court of Appeals reversed the Tax Court, 144 F.2d 78. We granted certiorari to settle uncertainties in tax administration engendered by seemingly conflicting decisions. 323 U.S. 703.

The answer to our problem turns on the proper application of [§§ 2501(a) and 2512(b)] to the immediate facts. * * *

* * * [W]hile recognizing that marriage was of course a valuable consideration to support a contract, the Tax Court did not deem marriage to satisfy the requirement of [§ 2512(b)] in that it was not a consideration reducible to money value. Accordingly, the Court found the whole value of the stock transferred to Mrs. More taxable under the statute and the relevant Reg. [§ 25.2512–8]: "A consideration not reducible to a money value, as love and affection, promise of marriage, etc., is to be wholly disregarded, and the entire value of the property transferred constitutes the amount of the gift." In the alternative, the Tax Court was of the view that if Mrs. More's loss of her trust income rather than the marriage was consideration for the taxpayer's transfer of his stock to her, he is not relieved from the tax because he did not receive any money's worth from Mrs. More's relinquishment of her trust income, and, in any event, the actual value of her interest in the trust, subject to fluctuations of its stock earnings, was not proved. One member of the Tax Court dissented, deeming that the gift tax legislation invoked ordinary contract conceptions of "consideration."

The Circuit Court of Appeals rejected this line of reasoning. It found in the marriage agreement an arm's length bargain and an absence of "donative intent" which it deemed essential: "A donative intent followed by a donative act is essential to constitute a gift; and no strained and artificial construction of a supplementary statute should be indulged to tax as a gift a transfer actually lacking donative intent." 144 F.2d 78, 82.

[Sections 2501(a) and 2512(b)] are not disparate provisions. Congress directed them to the same purpose, and they should not be separated in application. Had Congress taxed "gifts" *simpliciter*, it would be appropriate to assume that the term was used in its colloquial sense, and a search for "donative intent" would be indicated. But Congress intended to use the term "gifts" in its broadest and most comprehensive sense. * * * Congress chose not to require an ascertainment of what too often is an elusive state of mind. For purposes of the gift tax it not only dispensed with the test of "donative intent." It formulated a much more workable external test, that where "property is transferred for less than an adequate and full consideration in money or money's worth," the excess in such money value "shall, for the purpose of the tax imposed by this title, be deemed a gift * * *." And Treasury Regulations have emphasized that common law considerations were not embodied in the gift tax.

To reinforce the evident desire of Congress to hit all the protean arrangements which the wit of man can devise that are not business transactions within the meaning of ordinary speech, the Treasury Regulations make clear that no genuine business transaction comes within the purport of the gift tax by excluding "a sale, exchange, or other transfer of property made in the ordinary course of business (a transaction which is bona fide, at arm's length, and free from any donative intent)." Reg. § [25.2512–8]. Thus on finding that a transfer in the circumstances of a particular case is not made in the ordinary course of business, the transfer becomes subject to the gift tax to the extent that it is not made "for an adequate and full consideration in money or money's worth." * * *

The Tax Court in effect found the transfer of stock to Mrs. More was not made at arm's length in the ordinary course of business. It noted that the inducement was marriage, took account of the discrepancy between what she got and what she gave up, and also of the benefit that her marriage settlement brought to her son. These were considerations the Tax Court could justifiably heed, and heeding, decide as it did. Its conclusion on the issue before it was no less to be respected than were the issues which we deemed it was entitled to decide as it did in Dobson v. Commissioner, 320 U.S. 489 * * *.

If we are to isolate as an independently reviewable question of law the view of the Tax Court that money consideration must benefit the donor to relieve a transfer by him from being a gift, we think the Tax Court was correct. See Commissioner v. Bristol, 121 F.2d 129. To be sure, the Revenue Act of 1932 does not spell out a requirement of benefit to the transferor to afford relief from the gift tax. Its forerunner, [the 1924 Act], was more explicit in that it provided that the excess of the transfer over "the consideration received shall * * * be deemed a gift." It will hardly be suggested, however, that in reimposing the gift tax in 1932 Congress meant to exclude transfers that would have been taxed under the 1924 Act. The section [§ 2512(b)] taxing as gifts transfers that are not made for "adequate and full [money] consideration" aims to reach those transfers which are withdrawn from the donor's estate. To allow detriment to the donee to satisfy the requirement of "adequate and full consideration" would violate the purpose of the statute and open wide the door for evasion of the gift tax. * * *

Reversed.

Mr. Justice Roberts dissents * * *.

ILLUSTRATIVE MATERIAL

A.   BACKGROUND

1.   *Effect of Incorporation of Former § 1002 into Current § 2512*

Under the 1939 Code, § 1002 was a separate section, entitled "Transfers for Less Than Adequate and Full Consideration." In the 1954 Code (and continued in the 1986 Code), § 1002 was made a part of § 2512, "Valuation of Gifts." This reorganization did not signal a change in the prior interpretations of the "transfer for consideration" provisions. Thus, the courts have continued to treat § 2512(b) as a substantive measure and not simply as a provision dealing only with valuation problems in part-gift, part-sale situations.

The *Wemyss* result is consistent with § 2043, which provides that the release of marital rights does not constitute adequate consideration for estate tax purposes (p. 178), and § 2034, which requires inclusion in the decedent's estate of all dower or curtesy interests of a surviving spouse (p. 177). The marital rights area, in turn, is related to the § 2056 marital deduction (p. 572).

2.   *Concept of Gift for Income Tax Purposes*

Section 102(a) provides that gross income does not include the value of property "acquired by gift"; correspondingly, § 1015(a) provides that the basis for computing gain on the sale of property "acquired by gift" is the adjusted basis of the donor. If the concept of "gift" for income tax purposes and the concept of gift under the gift tax were defined in the same terms, the quoted language of the income tax provisions would pose no new problem in its application. However, no reference is made in the income tax or the gift tax provisions of the Code which would either require or preclude a correlation between the income tax concept of "gift" and the gift tax concept. The courts have consistently held that the concept of "gift" in the gift tax is not to be imported into the income tax. See, e.g., United States v. Davis, 370 U.S. 65 (1962); Farid–Es–Sultaneh v. Commissioner, 160 F.2d 812 (2d Cir.1947). See also Commissioner v. Estate of Beck, 129 F.2d 243, 246 (2d Cir.1942) ("Congress might use different symbols to describe the taxable conduct in the several statutes, calling it a 'gift' in the gift tax law, a 'gaft' in the income tax law, and a 'geft' in the estate tax law.").

3.   *Test of the Regulations in General*

The Regulations provide that "donative intent on the part of the transferor is not an essential element in the application of the gift tax to the transfer. The application of the tax is based on the objective fact of the transfer and the circumstances under which it is made, rather than on the subjective motives of the donor." Reg. § 25.2511–1(g)(1).

> "Transfers reached by the gift tax are not confined to those only which, being without a valuable consideration, accord with the common law concept of gifts but embrace as well sales, exchanges, and other dispositions of property for a consideration to the extent that the value of the property transferred by the donor exceeds the value in money or money's worth of the consideration given therefor. However, a sale, exchange, or other transaction of property made in the ordinary course of business (a transaction which is bona fide, at arm's length, and free from

any donative intent) will be considered as made for an adequate and full consideration in money or money's worth."

Reg. § 25.2512–8.

Are all transfers "made in the ordinary course of business" not taxable? Consider whether the case law in the following material establishes the broad proposition that the existence of a transaction in the ordinary course of business precludes the necessity of examining the adequacy of consideration. Does such a lack of examination result from (a) the difficulty of placing a money value on the consideration received in a bargaining context and/or (b) the presumption that what is acceptable to the parties in such a case should automatically be deemed adequate?

The following materials deal with the aspect of adequate consideration in intra-family, commercial and related situations. But the treatment of transfers for consideration arises in several contexts in the estate and gift tax area. Thus, marital transactions are considered at Chapter 14; the exception to §§ 2035–2038 is considered at Chapter 18; and problems in connection with claims against the estate under § 2053 are discussed at Chapter 27.

B.   INTRA–FAMILY TRANSFERS

1.   *In General*

Many transfers between family members—as, for example, the purchase of an airline ticket for a relative—constitute gifts for purposes of the gift tax, although it is likely that many persons do not understand this fact. On the other hand, the expenditure of funds by a parent in discharge of the legal obligation of support of a child is not a taxable gift. The doctrinal basis for the exclusion from the transfer tax base of transfers in discharge of a legal support obligation is somewhat uncertain. Arguably, the transferor receives consideration for the transfer and thus, under § 2512(b), there is no gift. The goods or services provided to the child might be seen as consideration running to the transferor in light of his legal obligation to procure them, or perhaps the consideration is the discharge itself. But in other situations, a payment in discharge of a legally binding obligation is not treated as made for consideration. Perhaps in the support context, the payments are more properly viewed as consumption by the transferor with the result that no "transfer" has occurred.

Whatever its doctrinal basis, the existence of an exclusion for payments in discharge of a support obligation is well established. The scope of the exclusion is difficult to ascertain, however, because local law, which varies among the states, determines the extent of the legal obligation of support. Thus, gift tax liability can vary from jurisdiction to jurisdiction. For example, one state may impose a legal obligation to provide a child with educational benefits only through the ninth grade while another might require the furnishing of a high school education.

This situation led the American Law Institute in 1969 to propose that "transfers for consumption" would be excluded from the gift tax whether or not a discharge of a legal obligation of support was involved. The ALI Recommendations would exclude from transfer taxation an expenditure for the benefit of any person residing in the transferor's household, or for the benefit of the transferor's child under 21 years of age, even if not residing in the transferor's household (provided that the expenditure did not result in the transferee acquiring property which can significantly appreciate in value over time). In addition, the ALI Recommendations would exempt any payment for current educational, medical or dental costs for the benefit of any person and current costs of food, clothing and maintenance of living accommodations for any person dependent upon the transferor. See American Law Institute, Federal Estate and Gift Taxation 19–21 (1969).

In 1981, Congress added § 2503(e), discussed in more detail at p. 488, to provide an unlimited exclusion for amounts paid by any person on behalf of an individual (1) as tuition to an educational organization or (2) to any person who provides medical care to an individual. Only direct payments to the provider of the educational or medical services qualify for the unlimited exclusion. Reimbursements of such expenses to the individual who receives the services do not qualify for the exclusion; nor do transfers to a trust, even if its sole purpose is to pay such expenses. Moreover, in the case of medical costs, the exclusion is not allowed to the extent the donee receives insurance reimbursements for those costs. The Committee Reports indicated that the purpose of § 2503(e) was to exclude "certain payments of tuition made on behalf of children who have attained their majority, and medical expenses on behalf of elderly relatives." H.R. Rep. No. 201, 97th Cong., 1st Sess. 193 (1981). Section 2503(e), however, is not confined to the categories of beneficiaries mentioned in the Committee Report.

What is the conceptual basis for § 2503(e) and for the ALI proposal that transfers for support and consumption (even if not in satisfaction of a legal obligation) be excluded from the gift tax base? If such transfers are made at death, they will be included in the estate tax base of the decedent. Administrative considerations may be involved, i.e., the difficulty the Service would encounter in learning about such lifetime transfers. But do difficulties in administration justify § 2503(e) or the broader exclusion proposed by the ALI?

2. Intra–Family Transfers Treated as Gifts

In many situations, courts treat intra-family transactions as gifts where the consideration received by the transferor is found to be inadequate. For example, in Estate of Cullison v. Commissioner, 221 F.3d 1347 (9th Cir.2000), an 81–year–old grandparent sold $1.9 million of land to her grandchildren in exchange for a nine-year private annuity that the Tax Court determined had a value of $1.4 million. The Ninth Circuit affirmed the Tax Court's treatment of the transaction as a gift under Reg. § 25.2512–8:

"A transfer between family members is presumed to be a gift. Appellant argues that the transfer was bona fide, at arm's length, and free of donative intent; therefore, it should not be considered a gift because it was made in the ordinary course of business. See Reg. § 25.2512–8. The record, however, clearly supports the Tax Court's finding of D's intent to give the land to her grandchildren as a gift. There is no evidence of arm's length negotiations or of a lack of donative intent."

3. Arm's Length Intra–Family Transactions

In other situations, courts respect intra-family transactions as arm's length situations in which the consideration received by the transferor is deemed to be equal to the value of the property transferred. For example, in Estate of Friedman v. Commissioner, 40 T.C. 714 (1963), the decedent had transferred certain property to her stepchildren within three years of her death in compromise of a dispute over title to the property; no taxable gift resulted since the court held that the release of the children's unliquidated claims "has a recognizable value in money or money's worth." Similarly, in Beveridge v. Commissioner, 10 T.C. 915 (1948), taxpayer's daughter in 1934 gratuitously transferred realty to the taxpayer. Following the daughter's marriage, taxpayer and daughter were completely estranged and in 1942 the daughter made demand for her property alleging duress in the transfer. After protracted negotiations the taxpayer obtained a full discharge of the daughter's claim for $120,000. The court held that the payment was not a gift as the taxpayer "was not actuated by love and affection or other motives which normally prompt the making of a gift, and further * * * the settlement to which she agreed on her attorneys' advice was that which they and she regarded as advantageous economically under the circumstances."

Haygood v. Commissioner, 42 T.C. 936 (1964), held that no taxable gift resulted where a mother transferred property to her two sons in exchange for vendor's lien notes payable $3,000 per year, even though the mother intended to and did make gifts to the sons by forgiving the $3,000 payments as they came due; the court concluded that at the time of the transfer the value of the notes was equal to the value of the property transferred. See also Estate of Kelley v. Commissioner, 63 T.C. 321 (1974) (taxpayers properly treated as gifts only the excess of value of property transferred to their children and grandchildren over the face amount of vendor's lien notes received, even though notes were extinguished without payment as they came due). The Service will not follow the decisions in *Haygood* and *Kelley*. Rev.Rul. 77–299, 1977–2 C.B. 343:

> "It should be noted that the intent to forgive notes is to be distinguished from donative intent, which, as indicated by Reg. § 25.2511–1(g)(1), is not relevant. A finding of an intent to forgive the note relates to whether valuable consideration was received and, thus, to whether the transaction was in reality a bona fide sale or a disguised gift. * * * Donative intent, on the other hand, rather than relating to whether a transaction was actually a sale or a gift, relates to whether the donor intended the transaction to be a sale or a gift. Although the same facts would be used in determining either type of intent, they relate to two entirely different inquiries."

Is the distinction drawn by the Service sustainable? Transactions within the ordinary course of business exception of Reg. § 25.2512–8 are *deemed* to be for full and adequate consideration in money or money's worth. The presence of donative intent removes the transaction from this rule and forces an inquiry into the quality and adequacy of the consideration. That, apparently, is the point of disagreement between the Service and the Tax Court. In both *Kelley* and *Haygood*, the deeds transferring real property recited that they were given in consideration of vendor's lien notes. The Tax Court found that under local law the notes created indebtedness enforceable against the transferees despite the transferor's intention to forgive the notes as they came due. As such they constituted consideration for the transfer. Consideration, in this view, depends solely on the objective circumstances. The Service, by contrast, appears to introduce a subjective element into the question whether the transfer is supported by consideration in the gift tax sense. In this view, the initial intent to forgive vitiates the quality of the notes as consideration for gift tax purposes even if, as an objective matter, the notes are regular and enforceable on their face. For example, assume Parent lends Child $65,000 and insists, despite an admitted intent to forgive the debt at the rate of $13,000 per year, that Child issue her an interest-bearing note to evidence the debt, payable in self-liquidating annual installments of $13,000 each. Does Parent's predisposition to piecemeal forgiveness prevent Child's note from qualifying as consideration at the outset, resulting in a $65,000 gift? Does the answer depend on hindsight on whether Parent eventually forgives the entire debt? What if Parent accepts some payments but forgives others? What if Parent forgives nothing, but gives Child $13,000 in cash each year, which Child uses to pay that year's installment on the note?

C.   USE OF BUSINESS ENTITIES TO EFFECT INTRA–FAMILY TRANSFERS

Reg. § 25.2511–1(h)(1) provides:

"A transfer of property by a corporation to B is a gift to B from the stockholders of the corporation. If B himself is a stockholder, the transfer is a gift to him from the other stockholders but only to the extent it exceeds B's own interest in such amount as a shareholder. A transfer of property by B to a corporation generally represents gifts by B to the other individual shareholders of the corporation to the extent of their proportionate interests in the corporation. However, there may be an exception to this rule, such as a transfer made by an individual to a charitable, public, political or similar organization which may constitute a gift to the organization as a single entity, depending upon the facts and circumstances in the particular case."

D.   COMMERCIAL TRANSACTIONS

The adequate consideration requirement raises the question whether non-familial, commercial transactions may be subject to the gift tax. For example, in Anderson v. Commissioner, 8 T.C. 706 (1947), two senior executives, Anderson and Clayton, made transfers of their common stock in a corporation to certain junior executives, in accordance with a plan for changing proportionate stockholdings among the management group from time to time as responsibilities were gradually shifted from the seniors to the juniors. The transfers were made at a price determined pursuant to written agreement among the common stockholders, all of whom were actively engaged in the business. Under the agreement no party could sell his stock without the consent of the holders of 75% of the common stock, and the holders of 75% could direct any party to sell all or any part of his stock. The court held that no taxable gifts resulted:

"At the threshold we are met with the question whether the sales of stock by Anderson and Clayton [petitioners] to the six individuals actively engaged in the Anderson–Clayton business enterprise are in any event subject to gift tax. Respondent concedes that these sales were bona fide and at arm's length; but he contends that they were not made in the ordinary course of business, that the value of the stock was greater than the value of the consideration received, and that the excess is therefore taxable as a gift under [§ 2512(b)]. He relies primarily upon Commissioner v. Wemyss, 324 U.S. 303, for the proposition that the absence of donative intent is immaterial. * * *

"The pertinent inquiry for gift tax purposes is whether the transaction is a *genuine business* transaction, as distinguished, for example, from the marital or family type of transaction involved in Wemyss and its companion case, Merrill v. Fahs, 324 U.S. 308. Surely it will not be said that there may not be a genuine business transaction not directly connected with the taxpayer's trade or business or even though the taxpayer be not engaged in 'carrying on any trade or business,' within the scope of that term as limited by Higgins v. Commissioner, 312 U.S. 212. Bad bargains, sales for less than market, sales for less than adequate consideration in money or money's worth are made every day in the business world, for one reason or another; but no one would think for a moment that any gift is involved, even in the broadest possible sense of the term 'gift.' * * *

"We have found that the sales of stock in issue were *bona fide* and made at arm's length in the ordinary course of business. Therefore, assuming, without deciding, that the value of the stock was greater than the value of the consideration, we hold that the transfers are not subject to gift tax."

Rev.Rul. 80–196, 1980–2 C.B. 32, adopted a similar approach where the shareholders of a corporation transferred stock to employees as bonuses for past services and to retain their services. The ruling concluded that the transfer was in the ordinary course of business and hence presumed to be for adequate consideration. No gift tax resulted (although the employees did realize taxable income under § 83).

In Weller v. Commissioner, 38 T.C. 790 (1962), the taxpayer sold a 2% interest in a partnership to an unrelated party in order to diversify his investments and to obtain cash for personal use. The Commissioner, because the sale price was less than fair market value, asserted that a taxable gift resulted. The court held that the transaction was one made in the "ordinary course of business," Reg. § 25.2511–1(g)(1), and therefore not subject to gift tax: "There is no evidence that [the purchaser] or anyone else would have given Carl [the taxpayer] more at that time for the 2–percent interest sold. Perhaps Carl was too anxious to sell, or simply made a bad bargain, but if he did, such a result—if it proceeds from a genuine business transaction—does not lead to a taxable gift." What is the conceptual basis for the "ordinary course of business" exception?

2.   POLITICAL CONTRIBUTIONS

Internal Revenue Code: § 2501(a)(4)

ILLUSTRATIVE MATERIAL

A.   THE SITUATION APART FROM § 2501(a)(4)

1.   Case Law

Prior to the enactment of § 2501(a)(4), courts split over the application of the gift tax to political contributions. In Stern v. United States, 436 F.2d 1327

(5th Cir.1971), the taxpayer was one of a group of Louisiana citizens who made political contributions to secure the election of a reform slate for statewide offices. She asserted that the contributions "were not gifts, but expenditures which I made to protect my property and personal interests by promoting efficiency in government." The court found for the taxpayer:

> "The transactions in controversy were permeated with commercial and economic factors. The contributions were motivated by appellee's desire to promote a slate of candidates that would protect and advance her personal and property interests. To assure that the funds would be spent in a manner consonant with the attainment of that goal, appellee and her group retained control over the disbursement of their contributions. In a very real sense, then, Mrs. Stern was making an economic investment that she believed would have a direct and favorable effect upon her property holdings and business interests in New Orleans and Louisiana. These factors, in conjunction with the undisputed findings of the lower court that the expenditures were bona fide, at arm's length and free from donative intent, lead us * * * to the conclusion that the expenditures satisfy the spirit of the Reg. [§ 25.2512–8] and are to be considered as made for an adequate and full consideration."

In contrast, DuPont v. United States, 97 F.Supp. 944 (D.Del. 1951), held that a retired executive's contributions to the National Economic Council, an organization whose purposes were "to preserve private enterprise, private property and private initiative and American independence," constituted taxable gifts:

> "Concededly, the plaintiff received no direct and personal consideration for the transfer which may be accurately reduced to a money value. It is true that the plaintiff considers that from improved economic conditions of the country he has profited to a much greater extent than the amount of the transfer. To what extent, if any, this improved economy is attributable to the activities or efforts of National Economic Council is impossible to determine. Nothing has been shown that may be attributable to it alone. Any consideration or benefit received by the plaintiff was not a benefit accruing to him alone, but one enjoyed by every citizen of the country, although the extent of benefit would have a direct relationship to the amount of property affected by improving economic conditions."

In Carson v. Commissioner, 71 T.C. 252 (1978), a closely-divided Tax Court split over the application of the gift tax to political contributions. The majority refused to apply the gift tax to campaign contributions because of the legislative history and purpose of the gift tax, and the Tenth Circuit affirmed. 641 F.2d 864 (10th Cir.1981).

2. The Service's Position

The Service historically took the position that gifts to political parties or candidates constituted transfers subject to the gift tax. Rev.Rul. 59–57, 1959–1 C.B. 626. In Rev.Rul. 72–583, 1972–2 C.B. 534, the Service announced that it would not follow *Stern*, except in the Fifth Circuit. The ruling stated that Reg. § 25.2512–8 applies only to "transactions characterized by negotiations or bargaining." The Service, however, has announced its acquiescence in the result of the *Carson* decision. 1982–2 C.B. 1.

3. *Political Contributions and the Concept of "Gift"*

By declining to follow the Fifth Circuit's approach in *Stern* to the gift tax treatment of political contributions, the majority of the Tax Court in *Carson* promulgated a novel approach to the concept of "gift" under the gift tax. The majority's suggestion that no gift is involved where an individual makes a transfer to an unrelated organization "to promote the social framework [the donor] considered most auspicious to the attainment of his objectives in life" and that thus the transfer is a "means to the ends of the contributor," if adopted in other situations, would introduce an inquiry into the donor's intent in making the transfer. The Supreme Court has repeatedly stated that such an inquiry is not appropriate in the gift tax context. Moreover, as the legislative history indicates, the gift tax does not have as its sole function the backstopping of the estate tax; thus the second ground on which the majority relied is dubious. Although the majority of the Tax Court seemed to believe that a testamentary transfer to a political organization was "unlikely" to occur, it is conceivable that an individual with strongly held political beliefs might make a bequest to a political organization which supports candidates of his or her political persuasion. As discussed below, in 1974 Congress acted to resolve the gift tax treatment of political contributions. However, the majority's approach to the question of what constitutes a "gift" under the gift tax, if pursued in cases other than political contributions, has the potential for creating considerable uncertainty and requiring an analysis of transferors' motives in situations in which such an inquiry has not been and should not be necessary. Rev.Rul. 82–216, 1982–2 C.B. 220, stated the Service's continuing position "that gratuitous transfers to persons other than organizations described in § 527(e) are subject to the gift tax absent any specific statute to the contrary, even though the transfers may be motivated by a desire to advance the donor's own social, political or charitable goals."

In Rev.Rul. 74–22, 1974–1 C.B. 16, a campaign committee for a candidate for public office turned over to the United States Treasury funds remaining unexpended after the election: held, since the transfer was "to carry out the purposes of the committee," it was not subject to gift tax. (The principal effect of the conclusion was to deny an income tax deduction for a charitable contribution, since for gift tax purposes § 2522 would have allowed a gift tax charitable contribution deduction even if the transfer had been held to constitute a gift.)

B. SECTION 2501(a)(4)

In 1974, Congress enacted § 2501(a)(4) to exempt from the gift tax transfers to political organizations as defined in § 527(e)(1).[18] However, transfers to political organizations are not exempted from the estate tax.

When originally approved by the House Ways and Means Committee, the exemption rested on the ground that it was "inappropriate to apply the gift tax

---

18. In 2000, Congress imposed new reporting and disclosure requirements on political organizations described in § 527. For questions and answers relating to these reporting and disclosure requirements, see Rev. Rul. 2003–49, 2003–1 C.B. 903. See generally Colvin, How Well Does the Tax Code Work in Regulating Politics?, 12 J.Tax'n Exempt Org. 66 (2000); Reis, Mr. Soros Goes to Washington: The Case for Reform of the Estate and Gift Tax Treatment of Political Contributions, 42 Real Prop.,Prob. & Tr.J. 299 (2007).

to political contributions because the tax system should not be used to reduce or restrict political contributions." H. Rep. No. 1502, 93d Cong., 2d Sess. 110 (1974). The justification offered during the House and Senate floor debates was somewhat different: "[The provision] also makes clear that campaign contributions in reality are not a gift, but rather constitute contributions to further the general political or good government objective of the donor." Statement of Chairman Ullman, 120 Cong.Rec. H12594 (daily ed., Dec. 20, 1974), and Statement of Chairman Long, 120 Cong.Rec. S21756 (daily ed., Dec. 17, 1974).

Does the exemption of political contributions from gift tax in effect constitute a program of federal financial assistance for such contributions? Or does the provision remove a tax penalty, thus correcting a potential structural defect? Neither of the above floor statements provides much assistance in answering these questions. However, under the basic principles of a transfer tax, since such transfers are normally without adequate consideration, it appears that the former interpretation is the correct one. In effect, the Government tells political donors, "Instead of paying federal gift taxes on political contributions, the Government will increase your after-tax contribution to the political organization of your choice in an amount equal to the gift tax that otherwise would have been due." As such, the exemption should be analyzed as a federal expenditure program. Several questions are pertinent: (1) Was federal financial support necessary to encourage lifetime giving to political organizations, or is the exemption simply a windfall? (2) If federal support is required, why is the greatest amount of federal benefit conferred on the wealthiest donors, i.e., those who by their other (perhaps nonpolitical) gifts have achieved a high gift tax bracket? (3) Why is the amount of federal benefit graduated by gift tax brackets, when the program of direct federal encouragement for political contributions allows each taxpayer to control only $1 of federal funds regardless of wealth? (4) Why is no federal benefit provided to taxpayers whose aggregate gifts (political and nonpolitical) are not in amounts sufficient to incur the gift tax liability? (5) Should there be limits on the amount of federal funds that a donor can control, as was the case of the credit for political contributions under § 24 before its repeal by the 1986 Act? There is, however, no evidence that Congress considered such questions before enacting § 2501(a)(4).

CHAPTER 14

TRANSFERS OF PROPERTY IN SATISFACTION OF MARITAL RIGHTS: ESTATE AND GIFT TAXES

This chapter considers the estate and gift tax implications of transfers of property in satisfaction of marital rights in three contexts: (1) the inclusion of a surviving spouse's dower or curtesy interest in his or her estate under § 2034; (2) the supporting rule in § 2043(b)(1) that refuses to treat the release of such dower or curtesy rights as adequate and full consideration; and (3) the treatment of transfers incident to separation and divorce under §§ 2053, 2043, and 2516.

SECTION A. DOWER AND CURTESY INTERESTS IN THE GROSS ESTATE

Internal Revenue Code: § 2034

Regulations: § 20.2034–1

INTRODUCTORY NOTE

The typical common law dower or curtesy interest of a surviving spouse is a life estate in the decedent spouse's property. Because the life estate expires at the death of the surviving spouse, nothing would be included in the spouse's estate. Therefore, unless the value of the dower and curtesy interest possessed by a surviving spouse is included in the estate of the decedent spouse, as is required by § 2034, there would be no estate taxation of that interest.

ILLUSTRATIVE MATERIAL

A. ASPECTS OF DOWER AND CURTESY INTERESTS

Although the Supreme Court has never directly passed on the issue, § 2034 should be held constitutional. Dower and curtesy are inchoate interests which do not have all the attributes of absolute ownership; thus, there is a shifting from the dead to the living of the economic benefit of use and enjoyment. Where a state statute creates an estate in lieu of dower or curtesy, the surviving spouse is in effect a forced heir; the same shifting of economic benefit occurs at death.

In Allen v. Henggeler, 32 F.2d 69 (8th Cir.1929), the taxpayer contended that the predecessor to § 2034 was an unconstitutional "direct" tax on the theory that because wife's dower interest arose as an incident of her marriage rather than from her husband's death, there was no "transfer" of property at the time of her husband's death properly reached by the estate tax. In rejecting this challenge, the Eighth Circuit emphasized that the husband had "very substantial rights" in the property during his life and that the wife "comes into" these right in the property only upon the husband's death. *Id.* at 72.

The impact of § 2034 has been modified in some cases by the enactment of § 2056(b)(7), which permits a marital deduction for the value of certain property in which a surviving spouse possesses a "qualified terminable interest." If a dower or curtesy interest satisfies the § 2056(b)(7) definition of a qualified terminable interest, the value of the property in which the interest exists is, upon election by the decedent's executor, deductible from the decedent's estate. This creates a larger deduction than would arise if only the value of the dower or curtesy interest were deducted or excluded. However, where a deduction has been claimed under § 2056(b)(7), § 2044 requires that the value of the property subject to the qualified terminable interest be included in the transfer tax base of the surviving spouse. Thus, although deferral of tax may be accomplished, the value of the interest itself does not escape tax. Sections 2056(b)(7) and 2044 are discussed beginning at p. 590.

B. ESTATES "IN LIEU OF DOWER OR CURTESY"

Section 2034 also reaches a surviving spouse's interest in property "by virtue of a statute creating an estate in lieu of dower or curtesy." Reg. § 20.2034–1 explains that "such other interest may differ in character from dower or curtesy." In Estate of Johnson v. Commissioner, 718 F.2d 1303 (5th Cir.1983), a surviving spouse's homestead interest under Texas law was treated as an estate in lieu of dower or curtesy under § 2034.

C. COMMUNITY PROPERTY

Community property laws do not themselves create estates in lieu of dower and curtesy (although, as illustrated by *Estate of Johnson*, these estates may exist in states that have community property laws); such laws make the right of each spouse in community property "present, existing, and equal." Section 2034 thus does not apply to community property interests, with the result that only one-half of the community property is included in the gross estate of the first spouse to die. Under the gift tax, the creation of community property through the sole efforts of one spouse does not constitute a transfer of one-half of such property to the other spouse. Gifts to third persons of community property after April 2, 1948, are considered as being one-half from each spouse.

SECTION B. MARITAL RIGHTS AS CONSIDERATION

Internal Revenue Code: §§ 2043; 2512

Regulations: §§ 20.2043–1(b); 25.2512–8

Merrill v. Fahs
324 U.S. 308 (1945).

■ MR. JUSTICE FRANKFURTER delivered the opinion of the Court. * * *

On March 7, 1939, taxpayer, the petitioner, made an antenuptial agreement with Kinta Desmare. Taxpayer, a resident of Florida, had been twice married and had three children and two grandchildren. He was a man of large resources, with cash and securities worth more than $5,000,000, and Florida real estate valued at $135,000. Miss Desmare's assets were negligible. By the arrangement entered into the day before their marriage, taxpayer agreed to set up within ninety days after marriage an irrevocable trust for $300,000, the provisions of which were to conform to Miss Desmare's wishes. The taxpayer was also to provide in his will for two additional trusts, one, likewise in the amount of $300,000, to contain the same limitations as the inter vivos trust, and the other, also in the amount of $300,000, for the benefit of their surviving children. In return Miss Desmare released all rights that she might acquire as wife or widow in taxpayer's property, both real and personal, excepting the right to maintenance and support. The inducements for this agreement were stated to be the contemplated marriage, desire to make fair requital for the release of marital rights, freedom for the taxpayer to make appropriate provisions for his children and other dependents, the uncertainty surrounding his financial future and marital tranquility. That such an antenuptial agreement is enforceable in Florida is not disputed, * * * nor that Florida gives a wife an inchoate interest in all the husband's property, contingent during his life but absolute upon death. * * * The parties married, and the agreement was fully carried out.

On their gift tax return for 1939, both reported the creation of the trust but claimed that no tax was due. The Commissioner, however, determined a deficiency of $99,000 in taxpayer's return in relation to the transfer of the $300,000. Upon the Commissioner's rejection of the taxpayer's claim for refund of the assessment paid by him, the present suit against the collector was filed. The District Court sustained the taxpayer, 51 F.Supp. 120, but was reversed by the Circuit Court of Appeals for the Fifth Circuit, one judge dissenting. 142 F.2d 651. We granted certiorari in connection with Commissioner v. Wemyss * * * and heard the two cases together. * * *

* * * [L]ike the *Wemyss* case, this case turns on the proper application of [§ 2512(b)]. * * * Taxpayer claims that Miss Desmare's relinquishment of her marital rights constituted "adequate and full consideration in money or money's worth." The Collector, relying on the construction of a like phrase in the estate tax, contends that release of marital rights does not furnish such "adequate and full consideration."

We put to one side the argument that in any event Miss Desmare's contingent interest in her husband's property had too many variables to be reducible to dollars and cents, and that any attempt to translate it into "money's worth" was "mere speculation bearing the delusive appearance of accuracy." Humes v. United States, 276 U.S. 487, 494. We shall go at once to the main issue.

The guiding light is what was said in Estate of Sanford v. Commissioner, 308 U.S. 39, 44: "The gift tax was supplementary to the estate tax. The two are *in pari materia* and must be construed together." The phrase on the meaning of which decision must largely turn—that is, transfers for other than "an adequate and full consideration in money or money's worth"—came into the gift tax by way of estate tax provisions. It first appeared in the Revenue Act of 1926. [The predecessor of § 2053(c)(1)(A)] allowed deductions from the value of the gross estate of claims against the estate to the extent that they were *bona fide* and incurred "for an adequate and full consideration in money or money's worth." It is important to note that the language of previous Acts which made the test "fair consideration" was thus changed after courts had given "fair consideration" an expansive construction.

The first modern estate tax law had included in the gross estate transfers in contemplation of, or intended to take effect in possession or enjoyment at, death, except "a bona fide sale for a fair consideration in money or money's worth." * * * Dower rights and other marital property rights were intended to be included in the gross estate, since they were considered merely an expectation, and in 1918 Congress specifically included them. * * * This provision was for the purpose of clarifying the existing law. * * * In 1924 Congress limited deductible claims against an estate to those supported by "a fair consideration in money or money's worth," * * * employing the same standard applied to transfers in contemplation of death. * * * Similar language was used in the gift tax, first imposed by the 1924 Act, by providing, "Where property is sold or exchanged for less than a fair consideration in money or money's worth" the excess shall be deemed a gift. * * *

The two types of tax thus followed a similar course, like problems and purposes being expressed in like language. In this situation, courts held that "fair consideration" included relinquishment of dower rights. * * * Congress was thus led, as we have indicated, to substitute in the 1926 Revenue Act, the words "adequate and full consideration" in order to narrow the scope of the exemptions. * * * When the gift tax was re-enacted in the 1932 Revenue Act, the restrictive phrase "adequate and full consideration" as found in the estate tax was taken over by the draftsman.

To be sure, in the 1932 Act Congress specifically provided that relinquishment of marital rights for purposes of the estate tax shall not constitute "consideration in money or money's worth." [§ 2043(b).] The Committees of Congress reported that if the value of relinquished marital interests "may, in whole or in part, constitute a consideration for an otherwise taxable transfer (as has been held to be so), or an otherwise unallowable deduction from the gross estate, the effect produced amounts to a subversion of the legislative intent. * * * " H.R. Rep. No. 708, 72d Cong., 1st Sess., p. 47; S. Rep. No. 665, 72d Cong., 1st Sess., p. 50. Plainly, the explicitness was one of cautious redundancy to prevent "subversion of the legislative intent." Without this specific provision, Congress undoubtedly intended the requirement of "adequate and full consideration" to exclude relinquishment of dower and other marital rights with respect to the estate tax. * * *

We believe that there is every reason for giving the same words in the gift tax the same reading. Correlation of the gift tax and the estate tax still requires legislative intervention. * * * But to interpret the same phrases in the two taxes concerning the same subject matter in different ways where obvious reasons do not compel divergent treatment is to introduce another and needless complexity into this already irksome situation. Here strong reasons urge identical construction. To hold otherwise would encourage tax avoidance. * * * And it would not fulfill the purpose of the gift tax in discouraging family settlements so as to avoid high income surtaxes. * * * There is thus every reason in this case to construe the provisions of both taxes harmoniously. * * *[1]

Affirmed.

■ Mr. Justice Reed, dissenting.

This case differs from Commissioner v. Wemyss. * * * Petitioner was obligated to create the trust upon consideration of the relinquishment of marital rights and did so, and hence this is not a case involving marriage alone as consideration. Through the tables of mortality, the value of a survivor's right in a fixed sum receivable at the death of a second party may be adequately calculated. * * *

The question of the taxability as gifts of transfers to spouses in consideration of the release of marital rights had been a matter of dispute in courts before the passage of the Revenue Act of 1932. * * * It seems to us clear that with the judicial history of the difficulties in estate and gift taxes as to the transfer of marital rights when Congress expressly provided [in 1932] that relinquishment of dower, curtesy or other statutory estate was not "consideration" for estate tax purposes and left the gift tax provision without such a limitation, it intended that these rights be accorded a different treatment under these sections. * * *

In our view this judgment should be reversed.

■ The Chief Justice and Mr. Justice Douglas join in this dissent.

ILLUSTRATIVE MATERIAL

A. THE ROLE OF THE "ADEQUATE AND FULL CONSIDERATION" RULE

To protect the integrity of § 2034, § 2043(b)(1) provides that the relinquishment of dower, curtesy or other marital rights is not adequate consideration in money or money's worth. This provision is necessary lest married couples enter into contractual arrangements that would avoid the result of § 2034. For example, a spouse could agree to leave property to the other in consideration for the release of dower or curtesy rights. Although the property would be included in the gross estate, there would presumably be an offsetting

---

1. [The predecessor of Reg. § 25.2512–8] is inapplicable. To find that the transaction was "made in the ordinary course of business" is to attribute to the Treasury a strange use of English.

deduction under § 2053 when the estate satisfied the contractual obligation. Similarly, in the absence of § 2043(b)(1), one spouse could create a trust reserving a life estate, with remainder to the other spouse, in consideration of a release of the dower or curtesy interest of that spouse. Although § 2036 includes in the gross estate the value of transferred property in which the transferor has retained a life estate, this transfer would escape estate tax if the release of the dower or curtesy rights were treated as adequate consideration under § 2043(a). The marital deduction (as discussed at Chapter 32) intersects with the issues raised in the interspousal transfers discussed in the following materials.

In Estate of Herrmann, 85 F.3d 1032 (2d Cir.1996), D agreed to give his fiancée a life interest in his apartment upon his death (provided they were still married when he died). In return, the fiancée gave up her rights to any of her future husband's property upon his death or their divorce. D died four years later, and his wife received the use of the apartment for life. D's executor deducted the value of the wife's life estate as a claim against the estate. The Second Circuit upheld the Tax Court's denial of the deduction because the wife's release of her marital rights was not "adequate and full consideration in money or money's worth" required by § 2053(c)(1)(A):

> "We hold that the estate tax prohibits a person from converting nondeductible claims against the estate into deductible claims through the simple device of a contract. In the current case, [wife] traded away only a contingent right to an equitable distribution of her husband's property in the event of a divorce that never occurred. In exchange, she received the right to a definite part of her husband's estate. What she gave up added nothing to her husband's estate; what she received depleted it. On these facts, [wife] did not give 'adequate and full consideration in money or money's worth' under § 2053(c)(1)(A). Her life interest in her husband's apartment must therefore be included in her husband's estate."

Merrill v. Fahs imported the rule of § 2043(b)(1) into the gift tax to insure that lifetime transfers of property in exchange for the release of marital rights do not escape gift tax. For example, in Rev.Rul. 79–312, 1979–2 C.B. 29, husband decided to sell real property held in his name. Under applicable local law, his estranged wife held an inchoate interest in the property similar to dower: if the parties were still married at his death, she was entitled to one-third of any real property owned by him during his life and conveyed without her participation. She refused to join in the conveyance unless he gave her one-half of the sale proceeds, which he did. The ruling held that the transfer of one-half of the proceeds by husband to wife was a taxable gift; her release of her inchoate right was not adequate and full consideration.

As a corollary to the rule that relinquishment of dower or other marital rights is not adequate and full consideration, transfers made in return for such relinquishment pursuant to antenuptial agreements may qualify for the marital deduction (discussed at p. 572). See Rev.Rul. 68–271, 1968–1 C.B. 409. Most of the litigation involving § 2043(b)(1) has arisen in the context of transfers incident to divorce or separation, discussed below.

B.   COMMUNITY PROPERTY

In a community property state, spouses may agree that upon the death of either spouse, the survivor will surrender his or her share of the community property in exchange for a life estate in the entire community property owned by the parties. Under such arrangements, the surviving spouse will have retained a life estate in the share of his or her own property transferred so that the property will be includible in the survivor's estate under § 2036(a)(1). The question is whether there is consideration for the transfer. In Estate of Gregory v. Commissioner, 39 T.C. 1012 (1963), husband died leaving his share of the community property in trust. Pursuant to husband's will, wife elected to have her share of the community property pass to the trust and in exchange received a life estate in the entire trust corpus. The court held that because wife had retained a life estate in her transferred share of the community property, that portion of the trust corpus was includible in her gross estate under § 2036. There was no consideration for this transfer, since a transfer of property already owned by the transferor in exchange for a life interest in that property did not give rise to consideration. However, the transfer also was in exchange for a life estate in the husband's share of the community property. This aspect of the transfer was for valuable consideration, and hence the portion of the trust corpus allocable thereto was not includible in her gross estate.

SECTION C. TRANSFERS INCIDENT TO SEPARATION AND DIVORCE

Internal Revenue Code: §§ 2053(c)(1)(A), (e); 2043; 2516

Regulations: §§ 20.2043–1(b); 25.2512–8; 25.2516–1(a), 2

INTRODUCTORY NOTE

Interests in property are commonly transferred when spouses obtain a divorce or legal separation. These property transfers may arise pursuant to a judicial decree, the agreement of the parties, or local law. Under the gift tax, in these situations, the issue is whether the transfer of the property is a gift or whether instead the transfer is for adequate consideration.

Estate tax problems arise in two areas. First, the form of the transfer of property incident to a divorce or legal separation may later cause the property to be included in the transferor's gross estate under §§ 2036–2038. Those sections provide for inclusion in the gross estate of the value of certain inter vivos transfers of property in which the decedent has retained an interest or which do not take effect until the death of the decedent. In each case, however, transfers for "adequate and full consideration" are excepted, subject to the limitations of § 2043.

Second, pursuant to a divorce or legal separation, the decedent may have incurred obligations that continue beyond or commence at death. Here the question is whether the value of the obligations is deductible from the decedent's gross estate under § 2053, which permits a deduction from the gross estate for claims against the estate to the extent that the claims are founded on an agreement and are for "adequate and full consideration." Section 2043(b) modifies this provision. Generally, the courts consider "adequate consideration" cases arising under §§ 2036–2038 to be authority for cases arising under § 2053, and vice versa.

Typically, in a divorce situation one spouse will transfer property to the other and the transferee spouse will release various rights which that spouse has in the marital property. The critical question is what is required in order for the release to constitute adequate and full consideration for gift and estate tax purposes. This is a question that involves both the nature of the released rights and the form of the release.

Harris v. Commissioner

340 U.S. 106 (1950).

■ MR. JUSTICE DOUGLAS delivered the opinion of the Court.

The federal estate tax and the federal gift tax, as held in a line of cases ending with Commissioner v. Wemyss, 324 U.S. 303, and Merrill v. Fahs, 324 U.S. 308, are construed *in pari materia*, since the purpose of the gift tax is to complement the estate tax by preventing tax-free depletion of the transferor's estate during his lifetime. Both the gift tax [§ 2512(b)] and the estate tax [§ 2053(c)(1)(A)] exclude transfers made for "an adequate and full consideration in money or money's worth." In the estate tax this requirement is limited to deductions for claims based upon "a promise or agreement"; but the consideration for the "promise or agreement" may not be the release of marital rights in the decedent's property [§ 2043(b)]. In the *Wemyss* and *Merrill* cases the question was whether the gift tax was applicable to premarital property settlements. If the standards of the estate tax were to be applied *ex proprio vigore* in gift tax cases, those transfers would be taxable because there was a "promise or agreement" touching marital rights in property. We sustained the tax, thus giving "adequate and full consideration in money or money's worth" the same meaning under both statutes insofar as premarital property settlements or agreements are concerned.

The present case raises the question whether *Wemyss* and *Merrill* require the imposition of the gift tax in the type of post-nuptial settlement of property rights involved here.

Petitioner divorced her husband, Reginald Wright, in Nevada in 1943. Both she and her husband had substantial property interests. They reached an understanding as respects the unscrambling of those interests, the settlement of all litigated claims to the separate properties, the assumption of obligations, and the transfer of properties.

Wright received from petitioner the creation of a trust for his lifetime of the income from her remainder interest in a then-existing trust; an assumption by her of an indebtedness of his of $47,650; and her promise to pay him $416.66 a month for ten years.

Petitioner received from Wright 21/90 of certain real property in controversy; a discontinuance of a partition suit then pending; an indemnification from and assumption by him of all liability on a bond and mortgage on certain real property in London, England; and an indemnification against liability in connection with certain real property in the agreement. It was found that the value of the property transferred to Wright exceeded that received by petitioner by $107,150. The Commissioner assessed a gift tax on the theory that any rights which Wright might have given up by entering into the agreement could not be adequate and full consideration.

If the parties had without more gone ahead and voluntarily unravelled their business interests on the basis of this compromise, there would be no question that the gift tax would be payable. For there would have been a "promise or agreement" that effected a relinquishment of marital rights in property. It therefore would fall under the ban of the provision of the estate tax which by judicial construction has been incorporated into the gift tax statute.

But the parties did not simply undertake a voluntary contractual division of their property interests. They were faced with the fact that Nevada law not only authorized but instructed the divorce court to decree a just and equitable disposition of both the community and the separate property of the parties. The agreement recited that it was executed in order to effect a settlement of the respective property rights of the parties "in the event a divorce should be decreed"; and it provided that the agreement should be submitted to the divorce court "for its approval." It went on to say, "It is of the essence of this agreement that the settlement herein provided for shall not become operative in any manner nor shall any of the Recitals or covenants herein become binding upon either party unless a decree of absolute divorce between the parties shall be entered in the pending Nevada action."

If the agreement had stopped there and were in fact submitted to the court, it is clear that the gift tax would not be applicable. That arrangement would not be a "promise or agreement" in the statutory sense. It would be wholly conditional upon the entry of the decree; the divorce court might or might not accept the provisions of the arrangement as the measure of the respective obligations; it might indeed add to or subtract from them. The decree, not the arrangement submitted to the court, would fix the rights and obligations of the parties. That was the theory of Commissioner v. Maresi, 156 F.2d 929, and we think it sound.

Even the Commissioner concedes that that result would be correct in case the property settlement was litigated in the divorce action. That was what happened in Commissioner v. Converse, 163 F.2d 131, where the divorce court decreed a lump-sum award in lieu of monthly payments provided by the separation agreement. Yet without the decree there would be no enforceable, existing agreement whether the settlement was litigated or unlitigated. Both require the approval of the court before an obligation arises. The happenstance that the divorce court might approve the entire settlement, or modify it in unsubstantial details, or work out material changes seems to us unimportant. In each case it is the decree that creates the rights and the duties; and a decree is not a "promise or agreement" in any sense—popular or statutory.

But the present case is distinguished by reason of a further provision in the undertaking and in the decree. The former provided that "the covenants in this agreement shall survive any decree of divorce which may be entered." And the decree stated "It is ordered that said agreement and said trust agreements forming a part thereof shall survive this decree." The Court of Appeals turned the case on those provisions. It concluded that since there were two sanctions for the payments and transfers—contempt under the divorce decree and execution under the contract—they were founded not only on the decree but upon both the decree and a "promise or agreement." It therefore held the excess of the value of the property which petitioner gave her husband over what he gave her to be taxable as a gift.

We, however, think that the gift tax statute is concerned with the source of rights, not with the manner in which rights at some distant time may be enforced. Remedies for enforcement will vary from state to state. It is "the transfer" of the property with which the gift tax statute is concerned, not the sanctions which the law supplies to enforce transfers. If "the transfer" of marital rights in property is effected by the parties, it is pursuant to a "promise or agreement" in the meaning of the statute. If "the transfer" is effected by court decree, no "promise or agreement" of the parties is the operative fact. In no realistic sense is a court decree a "promise or agreement" between the parties to a litigation. If finer, more legalistic lines are to be drawn, Congress must do it.

If, as we hold, the case is free from any "promise or agreement" concerning marital rights in property, it presents no remaining problems of difficulty. [Reg. § 25.2512–8] recognize[s] as tax free "a sale, exchange, or other transfer of property made in the ordinary course of business (a transaction which is bona fide, at arm's length, and free from any donative intent)." This transaction is not "in the ordinary course of business" in any conventional sense. Few transactions between husband and wife ever would be; and those under the aegis of a divorce court are not. But if two partners on dissolution of the firm entered into a transaction of this character or if chancery did it for them, there would seem to be no doubt that the unscrambling of the business interests would satisfy the spirit of the Regulations. No reason is apparent why husband and wife should be under a heavier handicap absent a statute which brings all marital property settlements under the gift tax. * * *

Reversed.

■ MR. JUSTICE FRANKFURTER, joined by MR. JUSTICE BLACK, MR. JUSTICE BURTON and MR. JUSTICE MINTON, dissenting.

* * * Unless we are now to say that a settlement of property in winding up, as it were, a marriage, smacks more of a business arrangement than an antenuptial agreement and therefore satisfies the requirement of "an adequate and full consideration in money or money's worth" which we found wanting in Merrill v. Fahs, and unless we are further to overrule Merrill v. Fahs insofar as it joined the gift tax and the estate tax of the Revenue Act of 1932, so as to infuse into the gift tax the explicitness of the estate tax in precluding the surrender of marital rights from being deemed

to any extent a consideration "in money or money's worth," we must hold that a settlement of property surrendering marital rights in anticipation of divorce is not made for "an adequate and full consideration in money or money's worth."

The same year that it enacted the gift tax Congress amended the estate tax by adding to the provision that "adequate and full consideration" was prerequisite to deduction of "claims against the estate" the phrase, "when founded upon a promise or agreement." [§ 2053(c)(1)(A).] Legislative history demonstrates that this amendment was intended not to change the law but to make clear that the requirement of consideration did not prevent "deduction of liabilities imposed by law or arising out of torts." H.R. Rep. No. 708, 72d Cong., 1st Sess. 48; S. Rep. No. 665, 72d Cong., 1st Sess. 51. A similar principle is implicit in the gift tax. By its statutory language and authoritative commentaries thereon Congress did not leave the incidence of the gift tax at large by entrusting its application to the play of subtleties necessary to finding a "donative intent." Commissioner v. Wemyss, 324 U.S. 303. But while by the gift tax Congress meant "to hit all the protean arrangements which the wit of man can devise that are not business transactions" to the common understanding, Commissioner v. Wemyss, a gift tax is an exaction which does presuppose the voluntary transfer of property and not a transfer in obedience to law. In Merrill v. Fahs, 324 U.S. at 313, we stated that "to interpret the same phrases in the two taxes concerning the same subject matter in different ways where obvious reasons do not compel divergent treatment is to introduce another and needless complexity into this already irksome situation." * * * Taxpayer contends (1) that the transfers in the situation now before us were or must be deemed to have been for an "adequate and full consideration in money or money's worth," and (2) that the Commissioner imposed a liability which was not "founded upon a promise or agreement." Her position was sustained by the Tax Court, 10 T.C. 741, but rejected by the Court of Appeals for the Second Circuit. 178 F.2d 861.

1. I would adhere to the views we expressed in the *Wemyss* and *Merrill* decisions as to the meaning to be given to the requirement of "adequate and full consideration" in the enforcement of the gift tax "in order to narrow the scope of tax exemptions." 324 U.S. at 312. Nor would I depart from the conclusion there reached that the relinquishment of marital rights is not to be deemed "money or money's worth" because that definition in the estate tax of 1932 is by implication to be read into the gift tax passed in the same year.

2. But was the transfer of the property here in controversy "founded upon a promise or agreement"? * * *

* * * The statute does not say founded "solely upon a promise or agreement." The statute does not say that the tax should not fall on "property transferred under the terms of a judgment or decree of the court." Nor is the phrase "founded upon agreement" a technical term having a well-known meaning either in law or in literature. The question is whether the transfer made by the taxpayer to her husband was, within the

fair meaning of the language, "founded" upon her agreement with her husband. Did the Nevada judge in decreeing the divorce describe what actually took place here when he said that on the "date of February 27, 1943, the plaintiff and defendant entered into an agreement and trust agreements forming a part thereof, under the terms of which the parties settled all obligations arising out of their marriage"?

The fact that the undertakings defined by this agreement would come into force only on the occurrence of a condition, to wit, the entering of a decree of divorce, is apparently regarded as decisive of taxability. But does this make any real difference? The terms of that decree might be different from the terms of the agreement; but "nevertheless the covenants in this agreement shall survive any decree of divorce which may be entered." If the divorce court had disapproved the agreement and had not decreed the transfer of any property of the wife to her husband, it is difficult to see how transfers which she made, solely because of the compulsion of the agreement, would be effected by court decree and for that reason not subject to tax. The condition on which an agreement comes into force does not supplant the agreement any more than a deed in escrow ceases to be a deed when it comes out of escrow. In the *Wemyss* and *Merrill* cases would the gifts have been any the less founded upon an agreement if, as a condition to the antenuptial arrangements in those cases, the consent of the parents of the fiancee had been made a condition of the marriage? Nor can excluding the transfers here involved from the gift tax be made tenable by resting decision on the narrower ground that to the extent the divorce decree "approved" the agreement or embodied its provisions so as to make them enforceable by contempt the transfers were not "founded upon" the agreement within the meaning of the statute.[2] If the taxpayer had been sued by her husband for the sums she was obligated to transfer to him could he not have brought the suit on the contract? Even though a promise for which inadequate consideration was given has been reduced to a judgment, a claim based upon it has been held not deductible from the gross estate and thus must have been deemed to be "founded upon a promise." If a transfer does not cease to be "founded upon a promise" when the promise is merged into a judgment, is not a transfer pursuant to an agreement which survives a ratifying decree a fortiori "founded upon" that agreement?

Judge Learned Hand's treatment of this matter is so hard-headed and convincing that it would be idle to paraphrase his views.

"In some jurisdictions contracts, made in anticipation of a divorce, are held to persist *ex proprio vigore* after the divorce decree has incorporat-

---

2. The ground adopted for reversal of the court below is important to the disposition of the case. On the broader ground apparently employed, no gift tax is due. But if the narrower basis be used, it is probable that some liability should be imposed. One of the transfers required by the agreement—the wife's assumption of a $47,650 indebtedness of her husband—was not incorporated into the divorce decree and therefore is presumably enforceable only under the contract. If enforceability under the decree is the criterion, a gift tax is due to the extent this indebtedness is reflected in the amount determined by the Commissioner to represent the value attributable to release of marital rights.

ed their terms, and has added its sanctions to those available in contract. That, for example, is the law of New York, where the contract remains obligatory even after the court has modified the allowances which it originally adopted; and where the promises will be thereafter enforced by execution and the like. Perhaps, that is also the law of Nevada, which the parties provided should govern 'all matters affecting the interpretation of this agreement or the rights of the parties.' Be that as it may, in the case at bar, the Nevada decree having declared that the agreement was 'entitled to be approved,' that included the provision that its 'covenants' should 'survive' as well as any of its other stipulations. Thus the payments made under it were 'founded' as much upon the 'promise or agreement' as upon the decree; indeed, they were 'founded' upon both; the parties chose to submit themselves to two sanctions—contempt under the divorce court and execution under the contract. The payments were therefore subject to the gift tax. 178 F.2d 861, 865.''

I would affirm the judgment.

ILLUSTRATIVE MATERIAL

A. GENERAL

Four separate grounds exist to supply adequate consideration for inter vivos transfers that would otherwise be subject to the gift tax. First, when applicable, § 2516 creates statutory consideration for the transfer. Second, the release of support rights is consideration to the extent of their value. Third, the release of marital rights constitutes adequate consideration in cases in which the divorce court has the power to declare the settlement of all property rights or to vary the terms of a prior settlement agreement and does approve the agreement. Fourth, a presently enforceable claim to an outright portion of the spouse's property upon divorce is not encompassed within the "other marital rights" language of § 2043(b)(1).

For estate tax purposes, statutory consideration for deductible transfers is provided by § 2043(b)(2) with respect to post-death transfers to a former spouse pursuant to agreements that satisfy § 2516. The remaining three categories also constitute consideration for estate tax purposes.

The scope of each of the foregoing categories is considered in the following material.

B. SECTION 2516

Section 2516(1) provides statutory consideration for purposes of the gift tax for transfers of property to either spouse incident to a written agreement where divorce occurs within the three-year period beginning on the date one year before the agreement is entered into (regardless of whether the agreement is incorporated in the divorce decree). Section 2516 embraces transfers in settlement of "marital or property rights." Therefore, if the conditions of § 2516 are met, interspousal transfers in exchange for the release of marital rights will not be subject to gift tax even if the property transferred exceeds the value of support rights surrendered.

It is necessary, however, that the surrendering spouse receive the transferred property. In Rev.Rul. 75–73, 1975–1 C.B. 313, a trust created pursuant to a separation agreement required all the income to be paid to wife for life but, if wife became "mentally or physically incompetent," the trustee had the discretion to pay any income not necessary for wife's proper maintenance and support either to wife or to the adult children of the marriage. The trust was funded with $400,000 and the present value of the wife's right to income for life was approximately $300,000; however, the present value of her right to a reduced amount if she became mentally or physically incompetent was only $186,000. The ruling held that the consideration supplied by § 2516 was limited to the present value of the smaller amount: "A transfer of property, in trust or otherwise, does not qualify under § 2516 if the ultimate beneficiary of the transfer cannot be presently identified as being within the class of persons specified in that section. Where a trustee's exercise of discretion must occur before any enforceable right to the transferred property vests in the donor's spouse, no transfer *to the spouse* has been accomplished at the time the trust is funded, and no exemption for gift taxation is available under § 2516. However, if it is possible to ascertain the limits on the trustee's exercise of discretionary power and thus predict with reasonable certainty that a given portion of the value of the transferred interest is necessarily payable to the spouse, such portion is deemed to be a transfer to the spouse for the purposes of § 2516 of the Code."

Section 2516(2) supplies consideration for transfers "to provide a reasonable allowance for support of issue of the marriage during minority" and thus allows the parties to estimate the value of support obligations for minor children without the risk of controversy with the Service. In addition, the drafters might have intended to provide protection for transfers made directly to the wife for the benefit of minor children. Where a transfer for the benefit of minor children falls outside § 2516, the "support exemption" and the *Harris* rule provide alternative grounds for finding consideration. In Rev.Rul. 79–363, 1979–2 C.B. 345, husband, pursuant to an agreement which met the conditions of § 2516, transferred $600,000 in trust to pay an annuity to wife for life, remainder to their adult child. In exchange, wife released all her marital rights. At the time of the transfer, wife's support rights were worth $200,000, and her other marital rights were valued at $400,000. The present value of her annuity and the present value of the remainder were each $300,000. The value of the annuity was not a taxable gift to wife because it was protected by § 2516. However, § 2516 was not applicable to the transfer of the remainder because the child was an adult. Absent proof that the wife "specifically and deliberately" released her support rights to induce the husband to make the transfer to the child, the transfer of the remainder was unsupported by consideration and was a gift to the full extent of its $300,000 value. See also Rev.Rul. 77–314, situation (2), p. 192.

Prior to 1984, § 2516 by its terms did not apply to the estate tax, and on several occasions the Tax Court refused to import § 2516 into the estate tax. See, e.g., Estate of Satz v. Commissioner, 78 T.C. 1172 (1982); Estate of Glen v. Commissioner, 45 T.C. 323 (1966). However, the Second Circuit took a contrary position in Natchez v. United States, 705 F.2d 671 (2d Cir.1983), and Congress in 1983 added § 2043(b)(2), expressly making § 2516 applicable for estate tax purposes. Section 2043(b)(2) supplies statutory consideration for purposes of § 2053 for post-death transfers to a former spouse pursuant to an agreement that satisfies the requirements of § 2516. Section 2043(b)(2) does not supply consideration for post-death transfers that provide a reasonable support allowance for minor children. Presumably the theory for limiting the application of § 2043(b)(2) is that the testator's obligation to support minor children disappears at death whereas a former spouse could have bargained for a deferred payment with respect to "marital and property rights."

The legislative history may indicate a narrow scope for § 2043(b)(2). It states that § 2043(b)(2) is intended to allow "an estate tax deduction for transfers pursuant to claims arising under a written agreement in settlement of marital or property rights where the agreement would have qualified those transfers as non-taxable for gift tax purposes (under § 2516). Thus, where the transferor dies prior to completing the transfers under the written agreement, no estate tax will be imposed with respect to the property transferred by the estate." H.R. Rep. No. 432, Pt. 2, 98th Cong., 2d Sess. 1504 (1984). This leaves a number of important issues unresolved. For example, suppose a transferor creates a revocable trust as required by a separation agreement that qualifies under § 2516. Under the terms of the trust, payments are to be made to the transferor's former spouse after the death of the transferor. The commuted value of the payments should be deductible from the transferor's gross estate. If the result were otherwise, an unwarranted distinction with respect to deductibility would arise based on whether the obligation was to be paid from the decedent's probate as opposed to non-probate assets.

C. SUPPORT RIGHTS

Section 2043(b)(1) provides that the release of dower, curtesy, or "other marital rights * * * shall not be considered to any extent a consideration 'in money or money's worth.'" In E.T. 19, 1946–2 C.B. 166, the Service concluded that, for both estate and gift tax purposes, transfers incident to a divorce or legal separation were supported by adequate and full consideration if in exchange for a release of *support* rights, but not for a release of *marital* rights. In Rev.Rul. 60–160, 1960–1 C.B. 374, the Service modified E.T. 19 in light of *Harris*:

> "[I]n a case in which the divorce court has power to decree a settlement of all property rights or to vary the terms of a prior settlement agreement, and does approve the agreement, any indebtedness arising out of such settlement is not considered to be founded upon a promise or agreement but, rather, it is considered to be founded upon such court decree and is, therefore, an allowable deduction from the gross estate in the amount of such indebtedness. If the court does not have the power to disregard the provisions of a previously existing property settlement agreement, a deduction is allowable only to the extent that the transfer does not exceed the reasonable value of the support rights of the wife."

Rev.Rul. 68–379, 1968–2 C.B. 414, explains that the transfer of property pursuant to a property settlement agreement will not result in a taxable gift to the extent that the value of the transferred property equals the value of the support rights surrendered by the transferee spouse. Rev.Rul. 77–314, 1977–2 C.B. 349, illustrates the gift tax consequences where the value of support rights surrendered differs from the value of the property transferred:

"Advice has been requested as to the application of the Federal gift tax where one spouse, A, who has created a trust pursuant to an agreement made with the other spouse, B, in contemplation of divorce, makes the transfers described below, and B surrenders B's support rights.

"In each of the following situations, A and B entered into a written agreement in contemplation of their obtaining a divorce. Except as specified below, each agreement contained a provision that, in exchange for the surrender by B of the right to support, A would transfer 100x dollars in cash to a trust upon issuance of a valid divorce decree. At the time of the agreement A and B had two adult children. In each case, the divorce occurred more than 2 years after the agreement was entered into, and the divorce decree was issued by a court that had no power to alter or invalidate the agreement.

"*Situation 1.* Under the terms of the trust to which A transferred 100x dollars, the income is payable to B for life, and at B's death the principal is payable to the children of the two spouses. The children are adults whom A and B have no legal obligation to support. The present value of the right of support surrendered by B is 50x dollars at the date of A's transfer. The present value of the right to trust income for B's lifetime is 60x dollars as of that date. The present value of the remainder is 40x dollars.

"*Situation 2.* The facts are the same as in *situation 1*, except the terms of the trust provide that one-third of the trust income is payable to an adult child of A and B, and two-thirds of the income is payable to B. At the death of B, all income payments cease and the remaining principal is payable to the children of the two spouses. The children are adults whom A and B have no legal obligation to support. The present values of the adult child's and B's rights to income for the life of B are, respectively, 20x dollars and 40x dollars. In the course of negotiating the settlement agreement, A agreed to provide the child with the one-third income interest after B asserted a preference to receive an income interest of lesser value than B might otherwise demand, in view of the value of B's support rights, in order to secure the income payments to their child.

"*Situation 3.* The facts are the same as those of *situation 1*, except the terms of the trust provide that upon the death of B (to whom all income is payable), the trust will terminate and the remaining principal is payable to a sibling of A. The present value of B's income interest is 60x dollars. The present value of the remainder interest is 40x dollars. The value of B's surrendered right to support in this situation is 70x dollars, thus exceeding the value of B's right to trust income by 10x dollars. B neither suggested nor was otherwise concerned with the naming of the person who would receive the remainder or the payment of trust principal after B's death. B's main concern was to avoid the possibility of any litigation or other delays; thus B settled for a monthly payment that was smaller than the amount B would have received if B had demanded and been paid the full value of support to which B was entitled. There is no indication that B agreed to receive the lesser amount in order to secure benefits to third parties. * * *

"Rev.Rul. 68–379, 1968–2 C.B. 414, holds that the surrender of a spouse's right to support constitutes a consideration in money or money's worth, and that a transfer of property in exchange for the surrender of support rights pursuant to a legal separation agreement results in a taxable gift to the extent of the excess of the value of transferred property over that of the support rights. * * *

"In the case of Estate of Harold Hartshorne, 48 T.C. 882 (1967), petition for review denied, 402 F.2d 592 (2d Cir.1968), an estate tax deduction was claimed for a 'debt' under § 2053 of the Code where the decedent was required by a prior divorce agreement to create a testamentary trust providing remainder interests for the decedent's children. The court, in holding that no valuable consideration had been shown for the creation of the debt, stated the following (p. 896):

> "With respect to the quid pro quo argument, case law indicates that merely because a husband, in his divorce settlement agreement, makes transfers to his adult children, that fact alone does not mean that such transfers are made for consideration. * * * Thus the taxpayer must show that such transfers to adult children are made at the insistence of the wife and for consideration in money or money's worth."

"In Spruance v. Commissioner, 60 T.C. 141, 154 (1973), aff'd, 505 F.2d 731 (3d Cir.1974), the court held that the taxpayer had not produced sufficient evidence that the taxpayer's former spouse had bargained away a portion of the spouse's rights in exchange for the taxpayer's designation of their adult children as persons to receive the remainder in a trust created pursuant to the divorce settlement. * * *

"Therefore, § 2512(b) of the Code is applicable in those situations where the donor has not only received a valuable transfer but has received it as an inducement for the donor's own transfer that would otherwise constitute a taxable gift in its full amount. Where a donor has made more than one transfer or created interests in trust for more than one person, each such transfer or interest created must be separately examined to determine whether any consideration in money or money's worth was received by the donor as inducement for that particular transfer.

"Accordingly, in the three situations described above, the following conclusions are reached:

"*Situation 1.* Since the value of the trust income interest transferred by *A* exceeds the value of *B*'s support rights surrendered by *B*, the amounts of *A*'s gifts, for Federal gift tax purposes, are: (1) 10x dollars, to *B*, the excess of the value of *B*'s income interest over that of the support rights; and (2) 40x dollars, to the children of the spouses, the full value of the remainder interest.

"*Situation 2.* In this situation, *B* bargained for a reduced income interest with the express purpose of securing an income interest in the trust for the adult child. Therefore, the excess (10x dollars) of the value of *B*'s support rights (50x dollars) over the value of the income interest received by *B* (40x dollars) is excludable from the value of the child's income interest (20x dollars) as consideration in money or money's worth under § 2512(b) of the Code. As a result, the amount of *A*'s gift to the child of the income interest is the excess of the value of the income interest transferred to the child over the value of consideration received by *A* for that transfer, or 10x dollars. It also follows that, since *B* transferred the excess value (10x dollars) of *B*'s support rights to secure the additional income interest to the child, *B* has made a taxable gift to the child of 10x dollars. The gift tax is also applicable to the full value, 40x dollars, of the remainder interest transferred by *A* to the child.

"*Situation 3*. In this situation, transfer of the income interest to *B* was adequately met by valuable consideration; so no gift was made to *B*. The amount of the gift of the remainder interest from *A* to the younger adult sibling, however, is its full present value as of the date of the gift, or 40x dollars. Although *A* obtained a release by *B* of support rights that exceeded the income interest transferred to *B*, such excess value was not paid and received in order to secure, even partially, the transfer of the remainder interest to the sibling. Therefore, no amount is excludable under § 2512(b) of the Code as consideration in money or money's worth from the value of the remainder interest transferred by A to the sibling.

"However, the value of the support rights *B* surrendered to *A* exceeded by 10x dollars the income interest *A* transferred to *B*. *B*'s motives for releasing the excess value of the support rights (to avoid litigation and delay) are not consideration for purposes of the gift tax. * * * Therefore, under § 2512(b) of the Code, *B* has made a taxable gift to *A* of 10x dollars."

Later courts have confirmed that the release of support rights can constitute "adequate and full consideration in money or money's worth" for purposes of §§ 2043(b) and 2053(c)(1)(A). See Estate of Hermann v. Commissioner, 85 F.3d 1032, 1038 (2d Cir.1996); Estate of Kosow v. Commissioner, 45 F.3d 1524, 1531 (11th Cir.1995). The principal difficulty is to determine the respective values of the support rights surrendered and the property rights received as of the date of the agreement or decree. For example, in Estate of Fenton v. Commissioner, 70 T.C. 263 (1978), a separation agreement incorporated in a subsequent Mexican divorce decree required that the decedent create a testamentary trust providing his wife an income interest for life in one-half of his net taxable estate and that he maintain certain life insurance policies with his wife as beneficiary. The decedent's executor sought to deduct the value of the life income interest and the insurance proceeds as claims against the decedent's estate under § 2053. After finding the wife's claims were founded on the separation agreement rather than on the divorce decree, the court determined that the value of the wife's future claims at the date the agreement was executed did not exceed the value, at that date, of the postponed support rights which she relinquished. Thus, the claims were supported by full and adequate consideration and the estate's deduction was allowed. See also Estate of Hundley v. Commissioner, 52 T.C. 495 (1969), aff'd, 435 F.2d 1311 (4th Cir.1971) (per curiam) (release by wife in immediately binding settlement agreement of then-existing right to support constituted consideration in money or money's worth); Estate of Iversen v. Commissioner, 552 F.2d 977 (3d Cir.1977) (estate tax value of trust created to secure payment of decedent's obligations under separation agreement not reduced under § 2043(a) because of lack of evidence that trust was created in consideration for release of support rights; commuted value of post-death payments to decedent's former wife from trust deductible under § 2053 because those payments were supported by adequate and full consideration resulting from wife's release of support rights).

D. TRANSFERS FOUNDED ON THE DIVORCE DECREE

Under *Harris*, the release of marital rights pursuant to a settlement agreement approved by a divorce court constitutes adequate and full consideration where the court has the power to vary the terms of the agreement. In Estate of Barrett v. Commissioner, 56 T.C. 1312 (1971), a property settlement agreement providing for payments by the husband to or for the benefit of the wife had been approved by the divorce court as a part of the divorce decree. However, the divorce court had no power to approve, disapprove, or modify the property settlement in the absence of fraud, compulsion or a violation of the confidential relation of the spouses. Accordingly, the Tax Court concluded that the obligation was not "founded on" the decree, so as to bring *Harris* into play, but instead was founded on the agreement. See also Rev.Rul. 79–118, 1979–1 C.B. 315 (separation agreement incorporated in divorce decree provided monthly alimony payments to wife in exchange for release of support rights; taxable gift resulted when husband voluntarily increased payments where divorce court had no power to modify alimony award).

Are all transfers in exchange for the release of marital property rights, if effectuated by a judicial decree from a court with authority to vary the terms of a settlement agreement, automatically free from tax under *Harris*? Or do the transfers have to relate to the spouse surrendering the marital rights or minor children? In Hooker v. Commissioner, 174 F.2d 863 (5th Cir.1949), the taxpayer established two trusts for his children pursuant to a divorce decree incorporating a separation agreement which was enforced by an action for specific performance. The Fifth Circuit held that the trust transfers were subject to the gift tax to the extent that the value of the transferred property exceeded the taxpayer's minimum support obligations, despite the involuntary nature of the transfer made under legal pressure. The Fifth Circuit affirmed the Tax Court, which had stated: "It may not be supposed that [Congress] intended to pass a law which could be circumvented by the clever process of entering into an agreement to make a transfer, supported by an inadequate money consideration, and then making the transfer to satisfy a judgment on the agreement." 10 T.C. 388, 392 (1948).

Rosenthal v. Commissioner, 205 F.2d 505 (2d Cir.1953), involved substantially the same arrangement as in *Hooker* case. In refusing to apply *Harris*, the Second Circuit stated:

> "The rationale of both the Harris and Converse decisions rests basically on the divorce court's power, if not duty, to settle property rights as between the parties, either by adopting their own agreement as in the Harris case, or by having the matter litigated as in [Commissioner v. Converse, 163 F.2d 131 (2d Cir.1948)]. We do not find this rationale applicable to a decree ordering payments to adult offspring of the parties or to minors beyond their needs for support—the only payments with which we are now concerned, since that part of the taxpayer's undertakings necessary for the support of his children during their minority is conceded-

ly not taxable. See Helvering v. U. S. Trust Co., 2 Cir., 111 F.2d 576.*
* * * While neither the Nevada statute * * * nor interpretive decisions
indicate the precise limits of the divorce court's authority in this area,
courts of other jurisdictions operating under similar statutes have been
restricted in their power to make awards of property to children to
amounts appropriate merely for the maintenance of minor children. * * *
Awards to children beyond their needs for support during minority have
been held enforceable where based upon a contractual agreement between
the parties to the divorce. * * * That is the situation here. But since such a
decree provision depends for its validity wholly upon the consent of the
party to be charged with the obligation and thus cannot be the product of
litigation in the divorce court, we do not consider the rationale of the
Harris decision applicable to the present case. We therefore conclude that
the arrangements here made for the taxpayer's daughters beyond their
support during minority do not obtain exemption from the federal gift tax
by simply receiving the court's imprimatur. The similar result reached in
Hooker * * * and Converse * * * appears to us a correct interpretation of
the law and not in conflict with the more recent decision in the Harris
case.''

The *Hooker* and *Rosenthal* cases were followed in Wiedemann v. Commissioner, 26 T.C. 565 (1956). See also Estate of Hartshorne v. Commissioner, 48
T.C. 882 (1967), where husband in his will created remainder interests for
three adult children in performance of his obligation under a settlement
agreement with his divorced wife. The children were minors at the time the
agreement was executed. The estate argued that *Harris* applied because the
settlement contract was confirmed in the divorce decree. However, following
Rosenthal, the court denied a § 2053 deduction for the value of the interests
created for the adult children. The Second Circuit affirmed, 402 F.2d 592 (2d
Cir.1968), but its opinion contained the following statement:

"The Commissioner takes the position that an agreement to make a
bequest to one's own children can never be a 'claim against the estate'
within the meaning of § 2053 because the decedent has simply agreed to
make a testamentary disposition to persons who are 'natural objects of his
bounty' and who would inherit anyway. According to the Commissioner,
these persons have 'an interest in the estate rather than a claim against it
for federal estate tax purposes.' * * *

"We agree that inheritance rights alone are not deductible claims
under § 2053. To hold the other way would be to open a large loophole in
the estate tax by encouraging taxpayers to contract with their wives and
children for whatever inheritance rights they would otherwise have in the
estate and thereby convert nondeductible claims into deductible contractual claims against the estate. * * * Under exceptional circumstances, however, it may be that a claim by someone who might otherwise inherit from
the decedent should be deductible under § 2053. If the claim is not simply
a subterfuge for a nondeductible legacy, if it is supported by 'adequate and

---

* [ED.: Judge Learned Hand, writing for
the majority, held that although wife's release of her own right to support did not
constitute consideration under the § 2043(b),
her promise to relieve the husband of his
obligation to support their child did constitute adequate consideration.]

full consideration', and if the consideration is a non-zero sum which augmented the decedent's estate, then it would seem that the deduction should be allowed. Whether or not a particular claim is deductible, then, will depend on the facts of each case." (402 F.2d at 594–95, n.2).

This "facts of each case" approach creates much uncertainty. See Estate of Nelson v. Commissioner, 47 T.C. 279 (1966), rev'd on other grounds, 396 F.2d 519 (2d Cir.1968) (interest in trust created for children includible in husband's estate because it had not been created in settlement of the support rights of wife); Rev.Rul. 78–379, 1978–2 C.B. 238 (insurance proceeds payable to decedent's minor children under policy maintained pursuant to divorce decree not deductible under § 2053 where decedent transferred to wife, pursuant to agreement, lump sum equal to the value of wife's support rights and in addition was required to pay monthly child support; Rev.Rul. 60–160 and *Harris* apply only to adjudications of rights between spouses and not to provisions requiring payments to children; because decedent's obligation to support children terminated at death, no consideration existed for post-death payments to minor children). Compare Estate of Glen v. Commissioner, 45 T.C. 323 (1966), where the court found that the transfer to a trust for the benefit of an adult child was supported by adequate consideration where wife specifically relinquished her support rights for the creation of the trust. Although the court noted that "transfers to third persons should be subject to close scrutiny, especially when the third person is an adult child or other natural object of the transferor's bounty," the taxpayer had established that the transfers "were not made with donative intent and were made at the insistence of the divorced spouse in full or partial satisfaction of her rights and that the transferor received money or money's worth consideration for them." Similarly, Leopold v. United States, 510 F.2d 617 (9th Cir.1975), allowed a § 2053 deduction for the payment of a bequest to a minor daughter pursuant to the terms of a separation agreement; there was evidence that the daughter, a child of the decedent's second wife, was not a natural object of decedent's bounty (because decedent's will favored the children of his first wife) and the second wife had accepted reduced payments for herself in order to obtain the promised bequest for her daughter.

E. RELEASE OF PRESENTLY ENFORCEABLE CLAIM TO A PORTION OF SPOUSE'S PROPERTY

In Estate of Glen v. Commissioner, 45 T.C. 323 (1966), the Service included in the decedent's estate under § 2036(a)(1) two trusts which had been created pursuant to a property settlement agreement in which wife had released all her rights against decedent and his estate. The Service argued that the released rights were "other marital rights" within the meaning of § 2043(b)(1) and that the transfers were not supported by adequate and full consideration. The Tax Court held that wife's release of a presently enforceable right (as contrasted to an inheritance right) against husband's property under applicable local (Scottish) law was not the release of an "other marital right":

" * * * If a wife has, under State law, a right to some portion of her husband's property immediately upon divorce, satisfaction of such a right in a property settlement agreement is no different from satisfaction of support rights pursuant to such an agreement. The husband is merely liquidating the obligation which he would have to his divorced wife *imme-*

diately upon divorce—not upon his death. The satisfaction of such an obligation is *not* 'a present transfer of what would otherwise constitute a major portion of the husband's estate on death,' and it 'does not have the effect of diminishing or depleting the husband's estate to any greater extent than the payment of other existing legal obligations.'

"[W]e conclude that § 2043(b)(1) should be limited in its application to the release of rights which accrue to a *surviving spouse* upon the decedent's death, i.e., dower, curtesy, or similar rights in the property or estate of a deceased spouse. Section [2043(b)(1)] is not applicable to the relinquishment of a presently enforceable claim to an outright portion of a spouse's property upon divorce."

The scope of the *Glen* case is unclear. The *Glen* rationale was applied in Estate of Carli v. Commissioner, 84 T.C. 649 (1985), which held that the release of a spouse's community property right to a share of the other spouse's earnings was not the release of a § 2043(b)(1) "other marital right." In a number of states, however, separately owned property acquired by joint efforts during marriage constitutes "jointly acquired property" in which the nontitle-holding spouse has a vested ownership interest. For income tax purposes, in these states, a transfer of such property to the nontitle-holding spouse in connection with a divorce has been treated as a non-taxable partition rather than as a transfer in exchange for the release of marital rights which would be treated as a realization event under United States v. Davis, 370 U.S. 65 (1962). See, e.g., Collins v. Commissioner, 412 F.2d 211 (10th Cir.1969) (Oklahoma); Imel v. United States, 523 F.2d 853 (10th Cir.1975) (Colorado). It is possible that the rationale of *Glen* could be extended to exclude such transfers from the transfer tax. Section 1041, enacted in 1984, provides a broad nonrecognition rule applicable to all transfers of property between spouses or, if incident to a divorce, between former spouses. Adoption of this income tax rule, however, does not alter the underlying nature of the "jointly acquired property" that might serve as the predicate for application of the *Glen* rationale.

F. TAX PLANNING CONSIDERATIONS

Many of the problems that have been considered in the foregoing material can be avoided by timely tax planning.

As to the gift tax, all pre-divorce outright transfers of property between spouses, as well as pre-divorce transfers to certain trusts, will qualify for the gift tax marital deduction, discussed p. 637, thereby avoiding the gift tax issue. Section 2516 eliminates most of the gift tax problems where either the property transfers follow the divorce or the pre-divorce transfers did not qualify for the marital deduction. There is an area of uncertainty in determining what constitutes a "reasonable" support allowance for minor children and what items constitute the legal obligation of support. Presumably these are matters to be determined under state law, and the scope of the obligation of support under state law may itself be difficult to determine.

If § 2516 cannot be satisfied, a properly drawn separation agreement would assign the maximum permissible amount as consideration for release of the transferee spouse's "support" rights rather than marital rights. Moreover, in light of Rev.Rul. 77–314 and Rev.Rul. 79–363, the parties should specify not only the value of the support rights released, but also the specific interests for which those rights were exchanged. Obviously, this approach may involve difficult valuation problems, but they are not insurmountable.

In the case of separation agreements, the tax advisor may want to include other provisions dealing with the gift tax. Thus, a provision may specifically state which of the spouses will be liable for any gift tax that may result from the transfer incident to the separation. In addition, it may be desirable to include a provision that details the extent of gift-splitting that the spouses have consented to in the past, so that both will be able to compute accurately their future gift tax liability. It also may be desirable for them to agree that each spouse will continue to consent to join in gifts by the other spouse to named donees, e.g., children, during the period that continued gift-splitting is available.

As to the estate tax, § 2043(b)(2) eliminates the § 2053 problems with respect to transfers made by estates of decedents dying after July 18, 1984, provided the transfer is made to a former spouse pursuant to an agreement that satisfies the requirements of § 2516. In addition, Rev.Rul. 60–160, p. 191, eliminates most of the similar problems where the agreement is incorporated into the divorce or separation decree and approved by a court with the power to modify the agreement. The value of a continuing obligation by the estate to make periodic alimony payments or to continue child support may be deducted by the estate under § 2053 to the extent that it is created in exchange for a release of support rights. Rev.Rul. 71–67, 1971–1 C.B. 271.

G. POLICY CONSIDERATIONS

The 1968 American Law Institute Federal Estate and Gift Taxation Recommendations provided that "any transfers of property made pursuant to a written agreement relative to the settlement of marital and property rights, if divorce occurs within two years thereafter, to provide a reasonable support for issue of the marriage during minority, shall be deemed to be transfers made for a full and adequate consideration in money or money's worth. Transfers to a spouse pursuant to such a written agreement in connection with a divorce are also for a full consideration in money or money's worth." (§ X27, pp. 157–158). The proposed change would appear to resolve the remaining problems in divorce situations. The 1969 U.S. Treasury Department Tax Reform Studies and Proposals apparently would have reached the same result. Both the American Law Institute Recommendations and the Treasury Proposals would continue the rule of § 2034, with respect to dower and curtesy interests.

*

PART III

COMPOSITION OF THE TAX BASE: SPECIFIC TRANSFERS

CHAPTER 15

TRANSFERS WITH RETAINED POWERS AND RIGHTS

Internal Revenue Code: §§ 2036, 2037, 2038

SECTION A. BACKGROUND AND STATUTORY FRAMEWORK OF §§ 2036–2038

Sections 2036–2038 seek to include in the gross estate inter vivos transfers that are essentially testamentary in nature. To illustrate the problem, consider a situation in which D, age 40, owns stock which is rapidly appreciating in value. If she holds the stock until her death, she will incur a large estate tax. If she makes an inter vivos gift of the stock, she loses the stock's dividend income. Suppose she makes an irrevocable transfer of the stock to a trust, retaining an income interest for life with remainder to C. If the form of this transaction is respected, D will have made a taxable gift of the remainder interest. (The valuation of remainder interests is discussed at pp. 723 to 727). She will also have excluded future appreciation of the stock from her gross estate, while retaining its benefits for her life.

Sections 2036, 2037 and 2038 include in the gross estate lifetime transfers in which the transferor has retained certain powers or rights with respect to the transferred property or has structured the transfer so that it is not complete until the transferor's death. In the above example, § 2036(a)(1) would require D's estate to include the stock's full value at death because she retained the right to its income. Recall from the discussion on p. 77, that inclusion of the full value of the stock in D's estate will not result in double taxation of the stock because gifts that are subsequently includible in the gross estate are not treated as "adjustable taxable gifts."

Several incentives may encourage wealthy donors to make inter vivos transfers while retaining significant economic benefit from or control over the transferred property. The tax exclusivity of the gift tax, the exclusion of the gift tax from the gross estate when the donor survives the gift by more than three years (see § 2035(b)), and the annual exclusion (see § 2503(b)) may motivate inter vivos gifts. These incentives will be reduced to the extent the unified credit exemption amount for the estate tax exceeds the exemption amount for gifts. Moreover, if a taxpayer believes that the repeal of the estate tax will occur as scheduled, she would prefer to avoid all taxable gifts.

Sections 2036, 2037 and 2038 represent three policy objectives:

(1) An estate tax should be imposed upon property transferred during life if the transferor still retains the economic benefit of the property. The transferor retains the economic benefit of the property when possession or enjoyment of the transferred property is held until death (§ 2036(a)(1)), or when the transferor retains the voting rights in transferred "controlled corporation" stock (§ 2036(b)).

(2) An estate tax should be imposed upon property transferred during life if the transfer is essentially testamentary. In addition to the situations in (a), a transfer is essentially testamentary when the death of the transferor is a precondition to the transferee's possession or enjoyment. (§§ 2036(a)(2), 2037 and 2038).

(3) An estate tax should be imposed upon property transferred during life if the transferor reserves significant powers over the possession or enjoyment of the property. Significant powers are reserved when the transferee is, by reason of the reserved powers, incapable of freely enjoying or disposing of his interest in the transferred property until the transferor's death (§§ 2036(a)(2) and 2038).

The adoption of these provisions occurred over many years in response to various ingenious and complex dispositive arrangements. The result is that the provisions are very complex and overlap one another. The adoption of a completely unified transfer tax structure would significantly reduce these complexities. Under the present estate and gift tax structure, transfers are subject to three forms of analysis: (1) those transfers that are subject to the estate tax only; (2) those transfers that are subject to the gift tax only; and (3) those transfers that are subject to both the estate tax and the gift tax. This complexity would decrease under a completely unified transfer tax that grossed-up all lifetime transfers by the amount of the gift tax and which contained a comprehensive set of rules for when a transfer is "complete" for transfer tax purposes so that a transfer is taxed only once.

In Section B of this Chapter, we consider situations governed by § 2036. Chapter 16 addresses the application of § 2038 to situations in which the transferor has retained the power to alter, amend, revoke or terminate a transfer. Chapter 17 discusses the application of § 2037 to situations in which the transferor has conditioned enjoyment of the property upon the transferee's surviving her. If a transfer described in Chapters 15–17 is for adequate consideration, then no avoidance of wealth transfer tax has occurred. Chapter 18 describes the rules applicable to such cases. Chapter 19 then explores the gift tax aspects of the transfers discussed in Chapters 15–17.

Section B.   Transfers with Retained Life Estates: § 2036

Internal Revenue Code: § 2036

Regulations: § 20.2036–1

INTRODUCTORY NOTE

Section 2036 includes in the gross estate of a decedent ("D") the value of *all* property as to which D has retained certain powers or rights. For example, if D transfers property in trust retaining the right to all income for life, the value of all the property at the time of her death is includible in her gross estate.

While tax lawyers customarily refer to § 2036 as the "retained life estate" provision, the statutory language of § 2036(a) distinguishes three different types of situations. Although there is some overlap among the three situations, it is useful to separate them for purposes of analysis. Section 2036(a) requires the inclusion of property in the gross estate where D has transferred property but retained:

    1.   the right to the income from the property transferred;

    2.   the possession or enjoyment of the property (including, as specified in § 2036(b), retention of voting rights in transferred shares of a controlled corporation); or

    3.   the right, either alone or in conjunction with any person, to designate the persons who shall possess or enjoy the property or the income therefrom.

Certain other statutory requirements must also be met before inclusion is required. D must have made a "transfer" of an "interest" in property; she must have "retained" one of the described interests; and the interest must be retained for life, for a period that is not ascertainable without reference to her death or for a period that does not in fact end before her death.

There are two exceptions to the application of § 2036:

    1.   a transfer for adequate and full consideration in money or money's worth;

    2.   a transfer before March 4, 1931.

The following materials first discuss the conditions that must be satisfied regardless of which type of interest is retained. Then cases under each of the various types of retained powers and rights are considered. The exception for transfers for adequate and full consideration, which also applies to §§ 2037 and 2038, is discussed in Chapter 18.

1.   TRANSFERS COVERED BY § 2036: IN GENERAL

a.   THE ELEMENTS OF § 2036

Estate of Nicol v. Commissioner

56 T.C. 179 (1971).

■ FEATHERSTON, JUDGE: [Decedent owned farm land which she leased to her daughter and son-in-law. Decedent agreed to pay all property taxes and one-third of the cost of raising grain crops. In return, decedent was entitled to receive one-third of all the grain crops grown on the property. The lease further provided that if decedent conveyed any part of the leased property to her daughter, decedent would continue to receive lease payments. A few days later, decedent did transfer one parcel of her farm land to her daughter. The Commissioner included the value of the farm land that decedent had transferred to her daughter in her estate under § 2036 "since the decedent, * * * [had] reserved to herself the rental income from the property for a period which did not, in fact, end before her death."]

OPINION

Under the terms of the 5–year lease of October 18, 1962, decedent was to be paid as rent the customary one-third of all grain crops grown on the farm, even if she should later convey the property to her daughter. Even though decedent, shortly after signing the lease, transferred the farm to her daughter by a deed, absolute on its face, decedent continued to receive the rent provided in the lease until she died on September 28, 1965. We think these facts are sufficient to require the inclusion of the value of the farm in her taxable estate under § 2036(a)(1) as a transfer of property under which decedent retained "the possession or enjoyment of, or the right to the income from, the property" for a period which did not in fact end before her death. McNichol's Estate v. Commissioner, 265 F.2d 667 (C.A. 3, 1959), affirming 29 T.C. 1179 (1958), certiorari denied 361 U.S. 829 (1959); Skinner's Estate v. United States, 316 F.2d 517 (C.A. 3, 1963).

Petitioner presents several arguments to support her view that § 2036(a)(1) does not apply. First, she contends that its heading, "TRANSFER WITH RETAINED LIFE ESTATE," shows that the section refers only to legal interests which constitute life estates under State law; under Montana law, according to the argument, decedent did not have a life estate in the farm and, indeed, had no legally enforceable interest therein. However, this heading of § 2036 was first adopted when the 1954 Code was enacted, and the committee reports declare that there was no intention to change the substance of the predecessor § 811(c)(1)(B) of the 1939 Code. H.Rept.No.1337, to accompany H.R. 8300 (Pub.L.No.591), 83d Cong., 2d Sess., p. A314; S.Rept.No.1622, to accompany H.R. 8300 (Pub.L.No.591), 83d Cong., 2d Sess., p. 469. While the language of the section heading may be used as an interpretative aid, it will not be so employed as to limit the meaning and purpose of the text. Maguire v. Commissioner, 313 U.S. 1 (1941) * * *

Quite clearly, the text of § 2036 is not limited to life estates under State law. It refers to any donative transfer under which the decedent has retained the enjoyment of property during his lifetime, and reflects a "legislative policy of subjecting to tax all property which has been the subject of an incomplete [donative] inter vivos transfer." United States v. O'Malley, 383 U.S. 627, 631 (1966). The section is designed to include in a decedent's taxable estate any property which has been transferred during the decedent's lifetime as a substitute for a testamentary disposition. Comm'r. v. Estate of Church, 335 U.S. 632 (1949).

In the present case, decedent continued to enjoy the fruits of owner-ship—the rental income from the property—for her lifetime; and her daughter, who was given legal title to the property, did not obtain the economic benefits of ownership until after decedent's death. Thus, as in the case of testamentary dispositions of property, the benefits of ownership did not pass from decedent until the time of her death. This is the kind of factual situation to which § 2036(a)(1) is intended to apply. See McNichol's Estate v. Commissioner, supra; Skinner's Estate v. United States, supra; * * *

While State law must be referred to for a definition of the legal interests of the parties, it does not limit the reach of § 2036(a)(1). The application of the section does not depend upon the retention of a legally enforceable interest in the property. In McNichol's Estate v. Commissioner, supra, the decedent transferred property to his children, but, by virtue of a contemporaneous oral agreement with them, continued to receive the rents therefrom until his death. Similarly, in Skinner's Estate v. United States, supra, the decedent transferred property to her children without any express agreement that she was to receive the rent therefrom; but such an agreement was inferred by the court from all the facts and circumstances, including decedent's continued receipt of the rents. In each of these cases, the decedent's taxable estate included the value of the property even though it had been transferred by a deed, complete and absolute on its face. As stated by the Court of Appeals in McNichol's Estate v. Commissioner, supra at 671, "Enjoyment as used in * * * [§ 2036(a)(1)] is not a term of art, but is synonymous with substantial present economic benefit." Dece-dent's retention of the right to the rent under the terms of the lease "for * * * [a] period which * * * [did] not in fact end before * * * [her] death" brings the farm within the broad sweep of § 2036(a).

The phrase "for any period which does not in fact end before his death," contained in § 2036(a), can be traced from the Joint Resolution of March 3, 1931, ch. 454, 46 Stat. 1516, when in response to May v. Heiner, 281 U.S. 238 (1930), Congress added a version of this language in an effort to insure that when a decedent transferred property, reserving its income for life, the value of the transferred property would be included in his taxable estate. The wording of this predecessor to § 2036(a), as modified by the Revenue Act of 1932, provided, in material part, that the value of the decedent's estate shall include the value of all property—

> To the extent of any interest therein of which the decedent has at any time made a transfer, by trust or otherwise, in contemplation of or intended to take effect in possession or enjoyment at or after his death, or of which he has at any time made a transfer, by trust or otherwise, under which he has retained for his life or for any period not ascertainable without reference to his death or for any period which does not in fact end before his death (1) the possession or enjoyment of, or the right to the income from, the property * * *. [Sec. 803, Revenue Act of 1932, 47 Stat. 169, 279.]

This language was adopted as § 811(c) of the 1939 Code, and was rearranged and modified in respects not material to this case by the Revenue Act of 1949. H.Rept.No.1412, 81st Cong., 1st Sess., 1949–2 C.B. 296–301. In this modification, the "for any period which does not in fact end before his death" provision was included in 1939 Code § 811(c)(1)(B), and the "intended to take effect in possession or enjoyment at or after his death" language became § 811(c)(1)(C). Section 811(c)(1)(B) of the 1939 Code was carried forward without substantive change into the 1954 Code as § 2036. H.Rept.No.1337, to accompany H.R. 8300 (Pub.L.No.591), 83d Cong., 2d Sess., p. A314; S.Rept.No.1622, to accompany H.R. 8300 (Pub. L.No. 591), 83d Cong., 2d Sess., p. 469.

Regulations promulgated under the 1939 Code provided that the "period which does not in fact end before his death" language contemplates a retention of income "for such a period as to evidence * * * [decedent's] intention that it should extend at least for the duration of his life." Sec. 81.18, Regs. 105. The regulations under the 1954 Code do not contain this limitation on the application of the statutory language, and such a limitation is not inherent in the text of § 2036. See Estate of Robert Manning McKeon, 25 T.C. 697, 703–705 (1956); * * * However, there is some authority for the proposition that, because of the legislative history of the language and the administrative construction given to the 1939 Code, the provision has obtained a gloss which requires that the period for which the income was retained must indicate an intention on the part of the decedent to retain the income for his life. National Bank of Commerce in Memphis v. Henslee, 179 F. Supp. 346 (M.D.Tenn. 1959).

Under either interpretation of the "for any period which does not in fact end before his death" language, the farm is includible in decedent's estate. Under the literal reading, the answer is obvious. Under the more flexible construction, we think decedent intended to retain enjoyment of the income for her life. The 5–year lease covered a period not much shorter than her life expectancy of 6 or 7 years, and the lease provided for a possible future renewal. Davis testified that decedent retained the rent from the transferred farm because "she had to have some income to live." From this evidence, we infer that the parties intended to renew the lease if decedent did not die within the 5–year term, and that there was, at the time of the transfer, at least an implicit understanding to that effect.

Referring to the fact that the rents were retained under the lease rather than the deed, petitioner contends that only the value of the leasehold interest is includible in the taxable estate. However, the lease and deed, executed within 11 days of each other, cannot be considered independently; the lease expressly referred to the possible subsequent execution of the deed. The net effect of the two instruments, read together, was to transfer the entire farm and to reserve all the rent therefrom for decedent for a period of at least 5 years. Section 20.2036–1(a), Estate Tax Regs., provides that if the decedent "reserved an interest or right with respect to all of the property transferred by him, the amount to be included in his gross estate under § 2036 is the value of the entire property." As stated in McNichol's Estate v. Commissioner, supra at 671, "one of the most valuable incidents of income-producing real estate is the rent which it yields. He who receives the rent in fact enjoys the property." See also Estate of Roy Barlow, 55 T.C. 666 (1971). Thus, the value of the entire farm must be included in decedent's taxable estate.

Petitioner next argues that, in any event, decedent retained the income from only part of the farm in that the lease called for rent of one-third of the grain crops grown on the land and provided for no rent for that part of the land used for grazing. We think this argument is without merit.

The lease signed by decedent calling for rental payments consisting of one-third of all grain crops grown on the premises covered the entire farm, including the pastureland. The parties have stipulated that "One-third (1/3) of all grain crops grown on leased premises delivered free of cost to the lessor is a standard landlord's portion of crop-share rent for farm land in Chouteau County, Montana," where the farm was located. While there is evidence that only 288 of the 640 acres were planted to crops, we think the lease agreement and the stipulation show that decedent received the customary rent for her entire farm as an economic unit, and that such rent represented compensation for both the cropland and the pastureland. Our interpretation of the lease and stipulation is confirmed by testimony that the grassland on the farm was not good pastureland and further testimony that no additional rent is usually paid for pastureland of poor quality included in a farming unit covered by a crop-share lease. In any event, in view of the terms of the lease and the stipulation, substantial evidence would be required to show that the rent which was paid covered only the cropland, and petitioner has not made such a showing.

We hold that the value of the farm is includible in decedent's taxable estate.

Decision will be entered * * *

ILLUSTRATIVE MATERIAL

A.   RETAINED INTERESTS

As the court in *Estate of Nicol* stated, it is not necessary that the interest retained be reserved in the legal instrument effecting the transfer. "The statute means only that the life interest must be retained in connection with or as an incident to the transfer. * * * [T]he reservation need not be expressed in the instrument of transfer * * *." Estate of McNichol v. Commissioner, 265 F.2d 667, 670 (3d Cir. 1959). Moreover, the reservation does not have to be in writing or enforceable for § 2036(a)(1) to apply. Estate of Paxton v. Commissioner, 86 T.C. 785, 809–810 (1986).

D bears the burden of proving that an implied agreement or understanding between decedent and his children did not exist when he transferred the property. See Estate of Skinner v. United States, 316 F.2d 517, 520 (3d Cir. 1963). In Estate of Reichardt v. Commissioner, 114 T.C. 144, 151 (2000), the court cautioned that this burden is "especially onerous for transactions involving family members."

B.   "TRANSFERS" UNDER § 2036

Section 2036 applies to transfers of property in which the transferor has retained an interest or power. The issue whether there is a "transfer" may arise in a variety of circumstances that are not always obvious. In Estate of Kinney v. Commissioner, 39 T.C. 728 (1963), D was the income beneficiary of a trust created by her husband. The trust received stock dividends to which D was entitled under state law. The stock dividends, however, were retained in the trust. The court held that D made a "transfer" of the stock dividends which required the inclusion in her estate of the value of that stock under § 2036. The court reasoned that the trust's retention of the stock dividends was the same as if D had received the stock and then transferred it to the trust, reserving the right to the income from the stock so transferred.

Similarly, where an income beneficiary was entitled to $500 per month plus any amount of trust income above that amount that she requested in writing, her failure to request the additional income constituted a "transfer" under § 2036 since any income that she did not request became a part of the principal of the trust under the trust terms. Horner v. United States, 485 F.2d 596 (Ct.Cl. 1973). See also Sexton v. United States, 300 F.2d 490 (7th Cir. 1962) (§ 2036 applied because the beneficiaries of 20–year trust, who agreed to extend the trust at the end of the term, effected a "transfer" by the relinquishment of the right to receive the trust corpus); Commissioner v. Estate of Vease, 314 F.2d 79 (9th Cir. 1963) (beneficiary of estate who agreed to abide by an unexecuted will of D which provided that D's share of the estate would be transferred to a trust under which she received income for life thereby effected a transfer with a retained income interest); Estate of Shafer v. Commissioner, 749 F.2d 1216 (6th Cir. 1984) (where D bought property and had seller make out a deed to him and his wife for life, then to their children; D made a "transfer" even though he never formally took title to the property).

In community property states, when D's will requires that the surviving spouse elect either to take her share of community property or let that share pass into D's testamentary trust in which she is granted a life estate, her election to take the life estate constitutes a "transfer" by her under § 2036. See, e.g., Estate of Gradow v. United States, 897 F.2d 516 (Fed. Cir. 1990); Estate of Gregory v. Commissioner, 39 T.C. 1012 (1963). Section 2036 will include in her gross estate her share of the community property that she allowed to pass to D's testamentary trust. See p. 194.

C.   "INCOME FROM" THE PROPERTY

"Income from" the property includes payments in kind. Following the approach in *Estate of Nicol*, Rev. Rul. 78–26, 1978–1 C.B. 286, held that where A conveyed forest land to B reserving the timber rights for ten years, and A died within the ten-year period, the entire value of the timber and the land was includible in A's estate because the timber rights represented the entire income-producing potential of the land.

D.   "INTEREST" IN THE PROPERTY

In order for § 2036 to be applicable, the transferor must have held a sufficient interest in the property she transferred. The IRS has ruled that a mere life estate does not constitute a sufficient interest in property for purposes of § 2036. This makes sense because § 2036 seeks to tax testamentary transfers. The holder of a life estate cannot make a testamentary transfer since it will terminate at the transferor's death. In Rev. Rul. 66–86, 1966–1 C.B. 216, the holder of a legal life estate transferred that life estate into a new trust created by her and by the holders of the remainder interest. The trust was to pay the income to her for life and then the corpus was to go to the remaindermen. The Ruling held that § 2036 did not apply to the life tenant's transfer because she possessed only a life estate.

E.   AMOUNT INCLUDIBLE

In general, a transferor's estate must include the proportion of property valued at the date of death or alternate valuation date with respect to which she reserved an interest or right. Reg. § 20.2036–1(a). In *Estate of Nicol*, the court required inclusion of the entire farm in D's estate after concluding that her income interest applied to the entire farm. Had D's income interest applied to only one-third of the property, her estate would have included the value of that one-third.

The regulations permit a reduction for the "value of any outstanding income interest which is not subject to decedent's interest or right and which is actually being enjoyed by another person at the time of the decedent's death." Reg. § 20.2036–1(a). As discussed at p. 211, this means that where D retained a secondary life estate in transferred property, his estate included the value of the property reduced by the value of the first life tenant's interest.

Computation of the includible amount may become difficult where the deceased income beneficiary was not the original settlor of the trust but made subsequent contributions to it. For example, suppose B created and funded a trust with $10,000 naming A as the income beneficiary. Subsequently, A contributed $45,000 of stock to the trust at a time when the originally transferred property was worth $15,000. At A's death, the entire trust corpus was valued at $400,000 and included A's contributed stock which was then worth $350,000. Rev. Rul. 78–74, 1978–1 C.B. 287, held that $350,000 was includible in A's estate because the stock was retained by the trust and could be directly traced to A's transfer. If the stock had been sold and the proceeds commingled with other trust assets so that A's transfer could not be traced, a ratio based upon the value of the property transferred by A to the total value of the trust (including the property transferred by A) at the date of the transfer would determine the includible amount. Thus A's estate would include $300,000 of the trust ($45,000/$60,000 x $400,000).

F.   RESERVATION OF A SECONDARY LIFE ESTATE

Where a grantor retains a secondary life estate, he need not actually come into the enjoyment of the income by surviving the first life tenant in order to make the transfer subject to § 2036. For example, suppose D transfers property to spouse S for life, then to D for life, remainder to children C. If D dies before S, the value of the property less the value of S's life estate is still includible in D's estate because the period for which D has retained an interest cannot be ascertained without reference to his death. Marks v. Higgins, 213 F.2d 884 (2d Cir. 1954); Commissioner v. Estate of Nathan, 159 F.2d 546 (7th Cir. 1947); Reg. § 20.2036–1(b)(1)(ii).

Consider a somewhat similar situation in which D's father set up a trust with income payable to A for life, and corpus payable to D if he survived A. While A was still alive, D made a gift of the remainder interest to B, reserving the income to himself for life for such period of time as he survived A. D survived A and received the income until his death. Section 2036 required the inclusion of the property in D's estate. Rev. Rul. 72–611, 1972–2 C.B. 526.

G.   TRANSFERS EXCEPTED

1.   *Transfers For Adequate and Full Consideration*

Cases arising under § 2036 involving the adequate and full consideration exception are considered in Chapter 18.

2.   *Transfers Prior to March 4, 1931*

Section 2036(c) exempts from § 2036 "transfers" made prior to March 4, 1931. The cases differ on whether the "transfer" referred to in § 2036(c) refers to an irrevocable transfer prior to March 4, 1931 or merely to the act of executing a valid and binding legal document. For example, Commissioner v. Estate of Talbott, 403 F.2d 851 (4th Cir. 1968), held that the word "transfer" in § 2036(c) means "became irrevocable". Thus, a trust in which the grantor retained the power to revoke the trust instrument during grantor's life with the consent of another person did not qualify for the § 2036(c) exception. See also Estate of Graves v. Commissioner, 92 T.C. 1294 (1989) (transfer occurred prior to 1931 where transferor could not revoke trust in her favor but could designate beneficiary other than herself.) On the other hand, several courts have held that the word "transfer" in § 2036(c) refers to the date of execution of the instrument effecting the transfer so that § 2036(c) was applicable to revocable transfers made prior to March 4, 1931. See, e.g., Commissioner v. Estate of Ridgway, 291 F.2d 257 (3d Cir. 1961); Commissioner v. Estate of Canfield, 306 F.2d 1 (2d Cir. 1962); Estate of Cuddihy v. Commissioner, 32 T.C. 1171 (1959).

Where § 2036 does not apply to pre-March 4, 1931 revocable transfers, § 2038 may nonetheless operate to tax the property in D's estate. See Florida National Bank of Jacksonville, Fla. v. United States, 336 F.2d 598 (3d Cir. 1964), discussed at p. 266.

H.   RELATION OF § 2036 TO OTHER SECTIONS

If a grantor terminates her retained interest within three years of death, § 2035(a) requires that § 2036 be applied as though the grantor had retained her interest until death. The result is that the date-of-death fair market value of the property in which she had retained an interest is included in her estate. See the discussion of § 2035 at p. 421.

Cases where the life estate is transferred for consideration are considered at p. 279.

See p. 348, for a discussion of the interaction between § 2036 and § 2040 where jointly owned property is transferred subject to the retention of an interest by the transferors.

See p. 409, for a discussion of the interaction between § 2036 and § 2042 where the property transferred constitutes life insurance.

b.   WHO IS THE TRANSFEROR?: RECIPROCAL TRUSTS

United States v. Estate of Grace

395 U.S. 316 (1969).

■ MR. JUSTICE MARSHALL delivered the opinion of the Court.

This case involved the application of [the predecessor of § 2036] to a so-called "reciprocal trust" situation. After Joseph P. Grace's death in 1950, the Commissioner of Internal Revenue determined that the value of a trust created by his wife was includible in his gross estate. A deficiency was assessed and paid, and, after denial of a claim for a refund, this refund suit was brought. The Court of Claims, with two judges dissenting, ruled that the value of the trust was not includible in decedent's estate under [the predecessor of § 2036] and entered judgment for respondent. * * * We granted certiorari because of an alleged conflict between the decision below and certain decisions in the courts of appeals and because of the importance of the issue presented to the administration of the federal estate tax laws. 393 U.S. 975 (1968). We reverse.

I.

Decedent was a very wealthy man at the time of his marriage to the late Janet Grace in 1908. Janet Grace had no wealth or property of her own, but, between 1908 and 1931, decedent transferred to her a large amount of personal and real property, including the family's Long Island estate. Decedent retained effective control over the family's business affairs, including the property transferred to his wife. She took no interest and no part in business affairs and relied upon her husband's judgment. Whenever some formal action was required regarding property in her name, decedent would have the appropriate instrument prepared and she would execute it.

On December 15, 1931, decedent executed a trust instrument, hereinafter called the Joseph Grace trust. Named as trustees were decedent, his nephew, and a third party. The trustees were directed to pay the income of the trust to Janet Grace during her lifetime, and to pay to her any part of the principal which a majority of the trustees might deem advisable. Janet was given the power to designate, by will or deed, the manner in which the trust estate remaining at her death was to be distributed among decedent and their children. The trust properties included securities and real estate interests.

On December 30, 1931, Janet Grace executed a trust instrument, hereinafter called the Janet Grace trust, which was virtually identical to the Joseph Grace trust [except that she designated Joseph as the life beneficiary]. The trust properties included the family estate and corporate securities, all of which had been transferred to her by decedent in preceding years.

The trust instruments were prepared by one of decedent's employees in accordance with a plan devised by decedent to create additional trusts before the advent of a new gift tax expected to be enacted the next year. Decedent selected the properties to be included in each trust. Janet Grace, acting in accordance with this plan, executed her trust instrument at decedent's request.

Janet Grace died in 1937. The Joseph Grace trust terminated at her death. Her estate's federal estate tax return disclosed the Janet Grace trust and reported it as a nontaxable transfer by Janet Grace. The Commissioner asserted that the Janet and Joseph Grace trusts were "reciprocal" and asserted a deficiency to the extent of mutual value. Compromises on unrelated issues resulted in 55% of the smaller of the two trusts, the Janet Grace trust, being included in her gross estate.

Joseph Grace died in 1950. The federal estate tax return disclosed both trusts. The Joseph Grace trust was reported as a nontaxable transfer and the Janet Grace trust was reported as a trust under which decedent held a limited power of appointment. Neither trust was included in decedent's gross estate.

The Commissioner determined that the Joseph and Janet Grace trusts were "reciprocal" and included the amount of the Janet Grace trust in decedent's gross estate. A deficiency in the amount of $363,500.97, plus interest, was assessed and paid.

II.

[The predecessor of § 2036] provided that certain transferred property in which a decedent retained a life interest was to be included in his gross estate. The general purpose of the statute was to include in a decedent's gross estate transfers that are essentially testamentary—i.e., transfers which leave the transferor a significant interest in or control over the property transferred during his lifetime. See Commissioner v. Estate of Church, 335 U.S. 632, 643–644 (1949).

The doctrine of reciprocal trusts was formulated in response to attempts to draft instruments which seemingly avoid the literal terms of [the predecessor of § 2036] while still leaving the decedent the lifetime enjoyment of his property.[1] The doctrine dates from Lehman v. Commissioner, 109 F.2d 99 (C.A.2d Cir.), cert. denied, 310 U.S. 637 (1940). In Lehman, decedent and his brother owned equal shares in certain stocks and bonds. Each brother placed his interest in trust for the other's benefit for life, with remainder to the life tenant's issue. Each brother also gave the other the right to withdraw $150,000 of the principal. If the brothers had each reserved the right to withdraw $150,000 from the trust that each had created, the trusts would have been includible in their gross estates as interests of which each had made a transfer with a power to revoke. When one of the brothers died, his estate argued that neither trust was includible because the decedent did not have a power over a trust which he had created.

The Second Circuit disagreed. That court ruled that the effect of the transfers was the same as if the decedent had transferred his stock in trust for himself, remainder to his issue, and had reserved the right to withdraw $150,000. The court reasoned:

> "The fact that the trusts were reciprocated or 'crossed' is a trifle, quite lacking in practical or legal significance. * * * The law searches out the reality and is not concerned with the form." 109 F.2d, at 100.

The court ruled that the decisive point was that each brother caused the other to make a transfer by establishing his own trust.

The doctrine of reciprocal trusts has been applied numerous times since the Lehman decision.[2] It received congressional approval in § 6 of the Technical Changes Act of 1949, 63 Stat. 893.[3] The present case is, however, this Court's first examination of the doctrine.

The Court of Claims was divided over the requirements for application of the doctrine to the situation of this case. Relying on some language in *Lehman* and certain other courts of appeals' decisions,[4] the majority held that the crucial factor was whether the decedent had established his trust as consideration for the establishment of the trust of which he was a beneficiary. The court ruled that decedent had not established his trust as a quid pro quo for the Janet Grace trust, and that Janet Grace had not established her trust in exchange for the Joseph Grace trust. Rather, the trusts were found to be part of an established pattern of family giving, with neither party desiring to obtain property from the other. Indeed, the court

---

1. See Colgan & Molloy, Converse Trusts—The Rise and Fall of a Tax Avoidance Device, 3 Tax. L.Rev. 271 (1948).

2. See, e.g., Glaser v. United States, 306 F.2d 57 (C.A.7th Cir. 1962); Estate of Moreno v. Commissioner, 260 F.2d 389 (C.A.8th Cir. 1958); Hanauer's Estate v. Commissioner, 149 F.2d 857 (C.A.2d Cir.), cert. denied, 326 U.S. 770 (1945); Cole's Estate v. Commissioner, 140 F.2d 636 (C.A.8th Cir. 1944).

3. See S.Rep. No. 831, 81st Cong., 1st Sess., 5–6 (1949); H.R. Rep. No. 920, 81st Cong., 1st Sess., 5 (1949).

4. See McLain v. Jarecki, 232 F.2d 211 (C.A.7th Cir. 1956); Newberry's Estate v. Commissioner, 201 F.2d 874 (C.A.3d Cir. 1953); In re Lueder's Estate, 164 F.2d 128 (C.A.3d Cir. 1947).

found that Janet Grace had created her trust because decedent requested that she do so. It therefore found the reciprocal trust doctrine inapplicable.

The court recognized that certain cases had established a slightly different test for reciprocity.[5] Those cases inferred consideration from the establishment of two similar trusts at about the same time. The court held that any inference of consideration was rebutted by the evidence in the case, particularly the lack of any evidence of an estate tax avoidance motive on the part of the Graces. In contrast, the dissent felt that the majority's approach placed entirely too much weight on subjective intent. Once it was established that the trusts were interrelated, the dissent felt that the subjective intent of the parties in establishing the trusts should become irrelevant. The relevant factor was whether the trusts created by the settlors placed each other in approximately the same objective economic position as they would have been in if each had created his own trust with himself, rather than the other, as life beneficiary.

We agree with the dissent that the approach of the Court of Claims majority places too much emphasis on the subjective intent of the parties in creating the trusts and for that reason hinders proper application of the federal estate tax laws. It is true that there is language in *Lehman* and other cases that would seem to support the majority's approach. It is also true that the results in some of those cases arguably support the decision below.[6] Nevertheless, we think that these cases are not in accord with this Court's prior decisions interpreting related provisions of the federal estate tax laws.

Emphasis on the subjective intent of the parties in creating the trusts, particularly when those parties are members of the same family unit, creates substantial obstacles to the proper application of the federal estate tax laws. As this Court said in Estate of Spiegel v. Commissioner, 335 U.S. 701, 705–706 (1949):

> "Any requirement * * * [of] a post-death attempt to probe the settlor's thoughts in regard to the transfer, would partially impair the effectiveness of * * * [§ 811(c)] as an instrument to frustrate estate tax evasions."

We agree that "the taxability of a trust corpus * * * does not hinge on a settlor's motives, but depends on the nature and operative effect of the trust transfer." *Id.* at 705. See also Commissioner v. Estate of Church, supra.

We think these observations have particular weight when applied to the reciprocal trust situation. First, inquiries into subjective intent, especially in intrafamily transfers, are particularly perilous. The present case illustrates that it is, practically speaking, impossible to determine after the death of the parties what they had in mind in creating trusts over 30 years earlier. Second, there is a high probability that such a trust arrangement

---

5. E.g., Orvis v. Higgins, 180 F.2d 537 (C.A.2d Cir.), cert. denied 340 U.S. 810 (1950).

6. See cases cited in n. 4, *supra*.

was indeed created for tax-avoidance purposes. And, even if there was no estate-tax-avoidance motive, the settlor in a very real and objective sense did retain an economic interest while purporting to give away his property.[7] Finally, it is unrealistic to assume that the settlors of the trusts, usually members of one family unit, will have created their trusts as a bargained-for exchange for the other trust. "Consideration," in the traditional legal sense, simply does not normally enter into such intra-family transfers.[8]

For these reasons, we hold that application of the reciprocal trust doctrine is not dependent upon a finding that each trust was created as a quid pro quo for the other. Such a "consideration" requirement necessarily involves a difficult inquiry into the subjective intent of the settlors. Nor do we think it necessary to prove the existence of a tax-avoidance motive. As we have said above, standards of this sort, which rely on subjective factors, are rarely workable under the federal estate tax laws. Rather, we hold that application of the reciprocal trust doctrine requires only that the trusts be interrelated, and that the arrangement, to the extent of mutual value, leaves the settlors in approximately the same economic position as they would have been in had they created trusts naming themselves as life beneficiaries.[9]

Applying this test to the present case, we think it clear that the value of the Janet Grace trust fund must be included in decedent's estate for federal estate tax purposes. It is undisputed that the two trusts are interrelated. They are substantially identical in terms and were created at approximately the same time. Indeed, they were part of a single transaction designed and carried out by decedent. It is also clear that the transfers in trust left each party, to the extent of mutual value, in the same objective economic position as before. Indeed, it appears, as would be expected in transfers between husband and wife, that the effective position of each party vis-à-vis the property did not change at all. It is no answer that the transferred properties were different in character. For purposes of the estate tax, we think that economic value is the only workable criterion. Joseph Grace's estate remained undiminished to the extent of the value of his wife's trust and the value of his estate must accordingly be increased by the value of that trust.

---

7.   For example, in the present case decedent ostensibly devised the trust plan to avoid an imminent federal gift tax. Instead of establishing trusts for the present benefit of his children, he chose an arrangement under which he and his wife retained present enjoyment of the property and under which the property would pass to their children without imposition of either estate or gift tax.

8.   The present case is probably typical in this regard. Janet Grace created her trust because decedent requested that she do so; it was in no real sense a bargained-for quid pro quo for his trust. See also Hanauer's Estate v. Commissioner, *supra*, n. * * * [2].

9.   We do not mean to say that the existence of "consideration," in the traditional legal sense of a bargained-for exchange, can never be relevant. In certain cases, inquiries into the settlor's reasons for creating the trusts may be helpful in establishing the requisite link between the two trusts. We only hold that a finding of a bargained-for consideration is not necessary to establish reciprocity.

The judgment of the Court of Claims is reversed and the case is remanded for further proceedings consistent with this opinion.

It is so ordered.

* * *

ILLUSTRATIVE MATERIAL

A. ASPECTS OF THE RECIPROCAL TRUST DOCTRINE

The Supreme Court in *Estate of Grace* created a two-part test for application of the reciprocal trust doctrine: (1) the trusts must be interrelated; and (2) the arrangement, to the extent of mutual value, must leave the settlors "in approximately the same economic position" as they would have been in had each created his or her own trust. The courts have continued to apply the reciprocal trust doctrine as a version of the well accepted tax doctrine that the substance of a transaction, not its form, controls its tax treatment. *Schuler v. Commissioner*, 282 F.3d 575, 578 (8th Cir. 2002).

Estate of Bischoff v. Commissioner, 69 T.C. 32 (1977) explored the significance of the second part of the test. A husband and wife each created four identical trusts for their grandchildren, each naming the other as trustee. As trustee, each had the discretionary power to accumulate income or to distribute income and principal to the beneficiaries of the trusts nominally created by the other spouse. The taxpayer argued that *Estate of Grace* did not apply since the spouses had no economic interest in any of the trusts. The Tax Court held that the reciprocal trust doctrine applies to crossed power situations as well as to crossed life-estate situations:

> "The purpose of the [reciprocal trust] doctrine is merely to identify the transferor of property. Standing alone, its application does not impose a tax; rather, the incidence of taxation depends upon the operation of a Code section when the shroud of form is lifted and the true transferor revealed. In other words, the doctrine's application is only part of a two-step process of taxation, i.e., it is not enough merely to 'uncross' the trusts, there must also exist a basis for their taxation. In Grace the two trusts were uncrossed because they were 'interrelated' and not, as petitioners urge, because the decedent therein held a direct economic interest in the property. The basis of taxation which led to the inclusion of the value of the trust corpus in the decedent's estate was crossed life estates under [the predecessor of § 2036(a)(1)]. Thus, in our opinion, the Court's reference to the 'same economic position * * * as life beneficiaries' was merely its formulation of the basis of taxation on the facts before it." (46).

Similarly, Exchange Bank and Trust Co. of Florida v. United States, 694 F.2d 1261 (Fed.Cir. 1982), held that the reciprocal trust doctrine applied where husband and wife transferred identical amounts of stock to each other as custodians under a Uniform Gift to Minors Act. The transfers were interrelated and the powers each possessed under the Act were sufficient to have caused the property to be included in the estate of each transferor under § 2036(a)(1) and § 2038(a)(1) if the transferor had named himself or herself as custodian.

In Estate of Green v. Commissioner, 68 F.3d 151 (6th Cir. 1995), however, the court rejected the reasoning of *Bischoff* and concluded that a prerequisite to the application of § 2036 to reciprocal trusts is that the settlors possess economic interests in the trusts.

When the reciprocal trust doctrine is applicable, the amount to be included in the estate of each transferor must be determined. Assume first that H and W create reciprocal trusts, H transferring $400,000 to his trust and W transferring $300,000 to her trust. If the values remain unchanged, $300,000 will be included in H's estate and $300,000 in W's estate under the reciprocal trust doctrine. But what if the values change? In Rev. Rul. 74–533, 1974–2 C.B. 293, H and W created reciprocal trusts. H transferred $400,000 to his trust and W transferred $300,000 to hers. H paid an $80,000 gift tax and W paid a gift tax of $70,000. At the date of H's death, the trust nominally created by W was worth $500,000; at the later death of W, the trust nominally created by H was worth $600,000. The Ruling held that the full $500,000 in value of the trust nominally created by W was includible in H's estate since W's trust was initially smaller than H's. Upon the death of W, 3/4 of the $600,000 value in the trust nominally created by H was includible in her estate (the ratio of the original value of W's transfer, $300,000, to the original value of H's transfer, $400,000). The Ruling further held that the credit for gift taxes available under § 2012, in effect prior to 1977, was available with respect to the property includible in the estate of each transferor, even though the gift taxes were actually paid by the other spouse. Thus, H's estate was entitled to a credit for the full $70,000 in gift taxes paid by W and the W's estate was entitled to a gift tax credit for 3/4 of the $80,000 in gift taxes paid by H. Although Rev. Rul. 74–533 applies to transfers prior to 1977, its principles appear equally applicable to determine under § 2001(b)(2) the amount of the reduction in estate tax for gift taxes previously paid by the other grantor.

B.   OTHER INDIRECT TRANSFERS

The question "Who is the actual transferor?" arises in other contexts. For example, in Estate of Marshall v. Commissioner, 51 T.C. 696 (1969), D had transferred shares of stock to her husband, H, in order to facilitate an acquisition by him. To pay D back, H created two trusts, which were divided into eighteen shares, and gave D six shares of the trusts. The court held that D had made a "transfer" to the trusts under § 2036. The net effect of the transaction was the same as if H had paid D the amount owed and she had transferred it to the trusts. H was merely D's agent in the transaction. Similarly, in Mahoney v. United States, 831 F.2d 641 (6th Cir. 1987), the court treated D as the transferor of stock to a trust, although his father had owned the shares and conveyed the stock to the trust naming D a life beneficiary, because D had contemporaneously delivered a note to his father. The court concluded that in effect D had purchased the stock from his father and conveyed it himself to the trust. Also, in Estate of Shafer v. Commissioner, 749 F.2d 1216 (6th Cir. 1984), D bought real estate and had the seller convey a life interest to him and his spouse and a remainder interest to his children. The court held that § 2036 applied to the real estate because in substance D had purchased the property and transferred the remainder interest to his children while retaining the life estate.

2.   RETENTION OF RIGHT TO INCOME FROM THE PROPERTY: § 2036(a)(1)

Cain v. Commissioner

37 T.C. 185 (1961).

■ FAY, JUDGE: [The majority shareholder in a corporation sold her stock to the corporation for $150,000, payable $6,000 down and $1,000 per month for 144 months. The payments, however, were to terminate at the death of the shareholder. The shareholder died prior to receiving all the payments and the Commissioner asserted that under § 2036(a)(1) the decedent's gross estate included the remaining unpaid installments.]

We feel respondent's contention that the decedent made a transfer of the purchase price to King's, Inc., and retained a right to a return of the purchase price is untenable. The record is devoid of evidence tending to show that the decedent at any time obtained possession or control over the entire purchase price of $150,000; that King's, Inc., tendered the entire purchase price to decedent; that the purchase price was, in fact, segregated by King's, Inc., from its other assets; that the books and records of King's, Inc., reflected the receipt of the purchase price from the decedent; or that the corporation as of December 20, 1948, actually possessed cash or liquid assets totaling $150,000. In the absence of such evidence, we are unable to conclude that the substance of the transaction was something other than what was evidenced by the form of the transaction.

This Court is also of the opinion that § 2036 has no application to the transfer of the stock itself as distinguished from the aforementioned transfer of the purchase price. The decedent agreed to sell her stock in King's, Inc., to the latter corporation in return for an immediate payment of $6,000 plus monthly payments of $1,000 to continue for 12 years or until decedent's death, whichever occurred first. It is clear that the decedent divested herself of all title to and control over the stock, and King's, Inc., entered into immediate and complete possession of the property. Furthermore, there is no evidence that the monthly installments were chargeable to the transferred stock or that the payments were in any way related to the potential or expected earnings of the 600 shares specifically or to the profits of King's, Inc., generally. To the contrary, the obligation to pay was fixed and dependent solely upon the singular obligation of King's, Inc.

In Fidelity–Phila. Trust Co. v. Smith, 356 U.S. 274, 280 (1958), the Supreme Court in discussing the scope of § 811(c)(1)(B) of the Internal Revenue Code of 1939, which is the predecessor to § 2036, said:

Where a decedent, not in contemplation of death, has transferred property to another in return for a promise to make periodic payments to the transferor for his lifetime, it has been held that these payments are not income from the transferred property so as to include the property in the estate of the decedent. E.g., Estate of Sarah A. Bergan, 1 T.C. 543, Acq., 1943 C.B. 2; * * * In these cases the promise is a personal obligation of the transferee, the obligation is usually not chargeable to the transferred property, and the size of the payments is not determined by the size of the actual income from the transferred property at the time the payments are made.

Since we can find no significant distinction between the case at hand and the cases cited by the Supreme Court, we conclude that the decedent retained neither possession, enjoyment, nor the right to income from the transferred stock. Accordingly, we hold that the unpaid balance of the purchase price is not includible in the decedent's gross estate.

Because of the uncontested adjustments,

Decision will be entered under Rule 50.

ILLUSTRATIVE MATERIAL

A.   RESERVATIONS OF INTERESTS SIMILAR TO LIFE ESTATES

If D transfers property in exchange for a series of payments, the issue arises whether the payments represent a retained interest in the property. In *Cain*, the court concluded that D had not retained an interest because the transfer was bona fide and payments were not dependent on income from the transferred property. As illustrated in the following material, the Commissioner has asserted that the transferor has retained the requisite life estate in a variety of other factual situations.

Interests Includible: In 1971, D created an irrevocable trust for the benefit of her grandchildren. She transferred bonds to the trust but retained interest coupons for the period 1971 to 1979. D died in 1974. Estate of Cooper v. Commissioner, 74 T.C. 1373 (1980), held that the value of the bonds was includible in D's estate under § 2036. The court concluded, contrary to the estate's contention, that the coupons and the bonds did not constitute separate property interests and, therefore, that D had retained an interest in the transferred property. Note that D's income was clearly dependent on the income from the transferred bonds.

In Estate of Fabric v. Commissioner, 83 T.C. 932 (1984), D transferred property to a foreign trust in exchange for an annuity. The Commissioner asserted that there was no exchange but only a transfer with a retained life estate. Many payments from the trust to D were late or were not made at all and some interest payments on property transferred to the trust were made directly to D rather than to the trust. The Tax Court refused to treat the annuity as a retained interest because an appeal would have gone to the Ninth Circuit which had upheld the annuity result in a similar transaction in the income tax context. But in Ray v. United States, 762 F.2d 1361 (9th Cir. 1985), the Ninth Circuit treated a purported annuity transaction as a retained life estate where D and his wife had created a trust as part of a divorce settlement. The trust provided that the husband was to receive $400 per month for life and the wife was to receive $300 per month for life. The court concluded that there was no intent to effect a sale or exchange, payments were set to approximate income very closely, and there was no personal obligation on the trustee to make payments if income and principal were exhausted.

Interests Not Includible: Rev. Rul. 77–193, 1977–1 C.B. 273, reached a result similar to *Cain*. The Ruling observed that the payments to D were "wholly independent of whether or not the transferred property * * * [produced] income for the transferee."

B. TRANSFERS IN DISCHARGE OF A LEGAL OBLIGATION

1. *In General*

Reg. § 20.2036–1(b)(2) provides that D will be considered to have retained or reserved the "use, possession, right to the income, or other enjoyment of the transferred property" to the extent that the income "is to be applied toward the discharge of a legal obligation of the decedent, or otherwise for his pecuniary benefit." A "legal obligation to support a dependent during the decedent's lifetime" constitutes a "legal obligation".

If D is the grantor-trustee of a trust, his retention of the power to use the trust corpus or income to discharge his legal obligations will trigger inclusion under § 2036(a)(1). In Estate of Pardee v. Commissioner, 49 T.C. 140 (1967), the value of a trust created by D was included in his estate where the trust provided for discretionary payouts of income and principal for the education, maintenance, medical expenses and other needs of D's children. Under the terms of a divorce, D was required to pay child support which he could satisfy through the trust. The court held that § 2036(a)(1) was applicable since D, as the trustee, retained the power to discharge his legal obligation of support. It was irrelevant whether that power actually was exercised. Similarly, in Estate of Sullivan v. Commissioner, 66 T.C.M. 1329 (1993), D's estate included the corpus of a trust he had established where he, as co-trustee, retained the power to use the corpus to discharge his legal obligation to support the trust beneficiary. The court rejected the estate's argument that D's status as co-trustee precluded § 2036(a)(1) from applying:

"While petitioner is correct that § 2036(a)(1), unlike §§ 2036(a)(2) and 2038(a), does not contain the 'in conjunction with any other person' language, this does not adequately address the question. The question of whether decedent retained the right to invade corpus [to satisfy his legal obligation] is a factual one. . . .

"The facts of this case demonstrate that decedent was for all intents and purposes the sole trustee." (1335–1336).

When the grantor is not the trustee, his estate will still include the trust property if the trustees are required to use it or its income to satisfy the grantor's obligations. In Richards v. Commissioner, 375 F.2d 997 (10th Cir. 1967), D created a trust for the "maintenance and support" of his wife under which the income was required to be paid to his wife for life at times determined by the trustees (who were D's sons and brother). Principal payments could also be made by the trustees for her "comfort and support". The assets of the trust consisted entirely of non-income producing stock and no amounts were ever paid to D's wife prior to his death. The court held that § 2036(a)(1) caused D's estate to include the trust property since the trust required the property to be used for his legal obligation, the support of his wife, and the trustees' discretion related solely to the time of payment. In Estate of Gokey v. Commissioner, 72 T.C. 721 (1979), trusts created for minor children were included in decedent-grantor's gross estate because the trust instrument provided that the trustee "shall use" part or all of the income for the "support, care, welfare and education" of the children. Under applicable state law, the quoted language created an ascertainable standard (see p. 248 for a discussion of ascertainable standards) which required the trustee (the grantor's wife) to use the income for the support of the children, a legal obligation of D.

The trust property is not included in the grantor's estate, however, if the grantor is not the trustee and the trustee has discretion to pay the grantor's obligations. In Rev. Rul. 2004–64, 2004–2 C.B. 7, the IRS ruled that D's gross estate did not include the assets of a trust he established where the trustee had the discretion, but not the obligation, to pay D's income tax liability. The IRS relied upon Estate of Mitchell v. Commissioner, 55 T.C. 576 (1970), where D transferred property to his son as trustee for the benefit of D's wife. The trustee had discretion to pay the income and principal to the wife for her "comfortable support and maintenance" in such amounts as the trustee in his unrestricted discretion should deem "necessary". Under applicable state law, the quoted language did not create an ascertainable standard which would require the trustee to expend funds to support the wife. No payments were ever made to D's wife prior to his death. The court held that the value of the trust was not includible in D's estate because Reg. § 20.2036–1(b)(2) does not apply where the discretionary power to apply trust income for the support of D's dependent is vested in an independent trustee. The court also refused to assume that the son would have disregarded his obligation to exercise his independent discretion as a fiduciary and pay over the funds to D's wife at the request of D. See also Commissioner v. Estate of Douglass, 143 F.2d 961 (3d Cir. 1944) (no inclusion required where the trustees had the power at their discretion to apply trust income to educate or support D's minor child).

See Chapter 18 for cases involving the question whether transfers in satisfaction of the decedent's obligation to support a dependent constitute transfers for adequate and full consideration.

2.   *Uniform Gifts to Minors Act and Uniform Transfer to Minors Act*

Several cases have arisen involving the applicability of Reg. § 20.2036–1(b)(2) to transactions in which the decedent holds property for the benefit of minor children as a custodian under a statute like the Uniform Gifts to Minors Act. Generally the various state Acts give the custodian the discretionary power to use the income for the support of the minor for whom the property is held. In Estate of Prudowsky v. Commissioner, 55 T.C. 890 (1971), aff'd per curiam, 465 F.2d 62 (7th Cir. 1972), the court held that if D has a support obligation and transfers property to himself as custodian under a Uniform Gifts to Minors Act which permits funds to be used to satisfy his support obligations, D has retained a power that requires inclusion of the property in his gross estate under § 2036(a)(1). The fact that other assets of D make it unlikely that the power will ever be exercised is irrelevant. D's ability to use the funds for support invokes § 2036, regardless of whether D ever intended to use the funds to satisfy his obligation. The analysis should be the same for the Uniform Transfers to Minor's Act. If D appoints someone other than herself as custodian, § 2036 should not apply to the transfer because the custodian has discretion to use or not use the transferred property for the minor's support. See *Estate of Mitchell*, p. 222.

C. FAMILY LIMITED PARTNERSHIPS

As discussed in more detail at p. 759, taxpayers use family limited partnerships to reduce the value of assets that will be included in their gross estates. Suppose, for example, that a taxpayer owns stock in a corporation that has a value of $1 million. A common strategy is to exchange that stock for an interest in a partnership that restricts the taxpayer's ability to withdraw the stock from the partnership and to participate in the management of the partnership. If the form of the transaction is respected, the value of the partnership interest will be included in the gross estate at a value much lower than the $1 million value of the transferred stock because any benefit that D may derive from the stock is dependent upon the partnership.

Recently the IRS has attempted to use § 2036(a)(1) to include in the taxpayer's gross estate the full value of the assets transferred to the partnership. The IRS has succeeded in situations where it has shown that the transferor retained an interest in the assets that were transferred to the partnership. For example, In Strangi v. Commissioner, 417 F.3d 468 (5th Cir. 2005), the court found an implied agreement for D to retain an interest in property he had transferred into a limited partnership where the partnership made distributions to D's estate after his death to pay his funeral expenses, estate administration expenses, specific bequests, and personal debts. For other cases where courts have applied § 2036(a)(1) because the transferor impliedly retained enjoyment of the assets transferred to the partnership, see, e.g., Estate of Thompson v. Commissioner, 382 F.3d 367 (3d Cir. 2004); Estate of Abraham v. Commissioner, 408 F.3d 26 (1st Cir. 2005); Estate of Bigelow v. Commissioner, 89 T.C.M. 954 (2005).

3. RETENTION OF POSSESSION OR ENJOYMENT OF THE PROPERTY: §§ 2036(a)(1) AND 2036(b)

a. IN GENERAL

Estate of Linderme v. Commissioner

52 T.C. 305 (1969).

■ TANNENWALD, JUDGE: * * *

The sole issue confronting us is whether the decedent retained the "possession or enjoyment" of his residence so as to bring its value within his gross estate for purposes of the Federal estate tax pursuant to § 2036(a)(1).

Petitioner insists that respondent's assertion of the applicability of § 2036(a)(1) constitutes an unwarranted attempt to create a statutory presumption of retention of "possession or enjoyment" from the mere fact of occupancy of the residence by the decedent from the time of the quitclaim deed in favor of his three sons in 1956 until his removal to a nursing home. We do not thus interpret respondent's position. Rather, we understand respondent to argue that, based upon an evaluation of all the facts and circumstances herein, there are adequate grounds for inferring an agreement or understanding on the part of decedent and his three sons sufficient to bring the transfer within the sweep of § 2036(a)(1). We agree with respondent.

The facts involved herein are clear. Decedent executed a quitclaim deed to the residence to his three sons in 1956. At that time, he delivered the deed to his son Emil. While the other two sons were not made aware of the delivery until after the father's death, we think it a reasonable assumption that Emil's actions in accepting the deed and in dealing with the decedent in respect of subsequent treatment of the property coincided with their views. Although the deed had been recorded prior to delivery, it was put into a file with decedent's other papers—a factor perhaps of more significance if there were an issue as to whether any gift was made, but also having some bearing on the existence, of an understanding with respect to decedent's interest in the property. Decedent continued in exclusive possession of the residence until he entered the nursing home. The residence was unoccupied from that time until his death about a year and a half later. There was neither consideration of any sale or rental of, nor any effort to sell or rent, the residence during that interval, thus indicating that the property was being held available for decedent's possible return. From the date of the quitclaim deed until his death, decedent's funds were used to pay all the expenses relating to the property, including real estate taxes, insurance premiums, and costs of maintenance. Even after the property was sold, part of the proceeds of sale were used to pay the obligations of decedent's estate. While this factor also would have greater bearing on the "any gift" issue * * *, it is a further indication, when taken into account with the other elements involved herein, of a retained interest in decedent.

Petitioner claims that the application of § 2036(a)(1) under the foregoing circumstances would unjustifiably extend the frontiers of that section contrary to the mandate of the decided cases and particularly our decision in Estate of Allen D. Gutchess, 46 T.C. 554 (1966), acq. 1967–1 C.B. 2. We disagree. Petitioner correctly concludes that it is neither necessary that the proscribed retained interest be expressed in the instrument of transfer nor necessary that the decedent have a legally enforceable right to possession or enjoyment. Petitioner, however, points out that, in all of the decided cases in which § 2036(a) was held applicable to situations similar to that involved herein, the property was income-producing (Estate of Daniel McNichol, 29 T.C. 1179 (1958), affd. 265 F.2d 667 (C.A. 3, 1959)); * * * and that, in all of the decided cases which refused to apply that section, the property involved was non-income-producing. Union Planters National Bank v. United States, 361 F.2d 662 (C.A. 6, 1966); * * * Estate of Allen D. Gutchess, supra; Estate of Robert W. Wier, 17 T.C. 409 (1951). Petitioner then seeks to parlay the foregoing decisions into the negative proposition that, unless income-producing property is involved, no agreement or understanding with respect to a decedent's retention of "possession or enjoyment" can be inferred.

To be sure, the factual distinction emphasized by petitioner does exist in these cases. But a more significant element seems to have been the fact that there was no withholding of occupancy from the donee. In the absence of such withholding, the continued co-occupancy of the property by the donor with the donee was considered, in and of itself, an insufficient basis for inferring an agreement as to retained possession or enjoyment. See Estate of Allen D. Gutchess, 46 T.C. at 556–557. The presence of income from the property was simply a useful ancillary tool for decision rather than a limiting principle imposed as a matter of law. The retention of income was thus only an example, albeit a very clear one, of "possession or enjoyment." Moreover, most of the cases decided in favor of the taxpayer involved a husband-wife relationship where the crosscurrent of § 2040 was at work. See concurring opinion in Estate of Allen D. Gutchess, 46 T.C. at 558.

In the instant case, the decedent continued to occupy the residence to the exclusion of the donees or anyone else whose status stemmed from their rights to the property. Surely that occupancy was as much an "economic benefit" as if decedent had rented the property and obtained the income therefrom. See Estate of Daniel McNichol, 29 T.C. at 1184. Additionally, such exclusive occupancy, while not necessarily determinative, should be accorded greater significance than co-occupancy in the process of evaluating the various facets of a particular situation in order to determine whether an understanding existed whereby a decedent would retain possession or enjoyment.

In Commissioner v. Estate of Church, 335 U.S. 632 (1949), the Supreme Court, in dealing with the predecessor of § 2036, in the context of transfers in trust, cut the shackles of earlier decisions and stated (335 U.S. at 645–646):

> an estate tax cannot be avoided by any trust transfer except by a bona fide transfer in which the settlor, absolutely, unequivocally, irrevocably, and without possible reservations, parts with all of his title and all of his possession and all of his enjoyment of the transferred property. After such a transfer has been made, the settlor must be left with no present legal title in the property, no possible reversionary interest in that title, and no right to possess or to enjoy the property then or thereafter. In other words such a transfer must be immediate and out and out, and must be unaffected by whether the grantor lives or dies.[10]

We take our cue from this mandate for a broad inclusion within the gross estate pursuant to § 2036(a)(1). The burden of proof is on the taxpayer and, in cases of this type, that burden may be a heavy one. Skinner's Estate v. United States, 316 F.2d 517, 520 (C.A. 3, 1963); cf. Estate of Henry Wilson, 2 T.C. 1059, 1091 (1943). But such difficulty does not justify exclusion from the operation of § 2036(a)(1). On the basis of the

---

10. The long judicial and legislative history involved in the Church doctrine is set forth in detail in McNichol's Estate v. Commissioner, 265 F.2d 667, 670–673 (C.A. 3, 1959).

entire record herein, we are satisfied as our ultimate finding of fact reflects that, beyond the mere existence of the family relationship and the mere occupancy of the premises, decedent did have an understanding whereby he retained the exclusive use of the residence until his death. The property in question is thus includible in decedent's gross estate under § 2036(a)(1).
* * *

ILLUSTRATIVE MATERIAL

A. RETENTION OF POSSESSION OR ENJOYMENT OF RESIDENCE

A number of cases involve D transferring title in a residence to a family member, but continuing to live in the residence until death without paying rent. The Commissioner has taken the position that the circumstances usually justify the inference of a prearrangement or agreement which would warrant inclusion of the value of the residence in D's gross estate. As the opinion in *Estate of Linderme* indicates, the courts have reached various results. Compare Estate of Trotter v. Commissioner, 82 T.C.M. 633 (2001) (same result as *Estate of Linderme*); Guynn v. United States, 437 F.2d 1148 (4th Cir. 1971) (value of residence includible where 81–year–old mother deeded residence to her daughter, but continued to live rent-free in the home until her death as both she and donee expected her to do); Union Planters National Bank v. United States, 361 F.2d 662 (6th Cir. 1966) (D transferred residence to his wife, but continued to live in the home until his death; the parties "assumed" that they would always live in the house, but there was no discussion or agreement to that effect; no inclusion under § 2036 since no agreement giving D the right to continued enjoyment could be inferred from mere continued occupancy).

Rev. Rul. 70–155, 1970–1 C.B. 189, accepted the distinction between exclusive occupancy cases and those in which D continues to occupy the residence with the donee when the donor and donee are husband and wife. The Ruling stated that continued co-tenancy does not alone support an inference of an understanding between the husband and wife as to retained possession or enjoyment of the property by the donor spouse. Where the donor and donee are not husband and wife, however, the Service asserts that continued co-tenancy does support the inference of an understanding between the parties. Rev. Rul. 78–409, 1978–2 C.B. 234.

D can avoid § 2036 by paying fair rental value for the continued occupancy of the transferred property. The payment of rent establishes that D has not retained an interest. Estate of Barlow v. Commissioner, 55 T.C. 666 (1971); Estate of du Pont v. Commissioner, 63 T.C. 746 (1975).

Sometimes taxpayers will attempt to disguise the retained interest by paying rent and then getting a refund in some way. In Estate of Maxwell v. Commissioner, 3 F.3d 591 (2d Cir. 1993), D, who was 82 years old and suffering from cancer, sold her home to her son for $270,000. She immediately forgave $20,000 of the purchase price as a gift and received a $250,000 mortgage note. D continued to live in her home and to pay rent to her son. The amount of rent D paid to her son the remaining 2 1/2 years of her life approximately equaled the amount of interest D's son paid to her. D forgave $20,000 of the mortgage principal each year, and at her death forgave the remaining balance. The court rejected the estate's argument that D's payment of the rent meant that she had not retained enjoyment of the residence. The matching of D's rental payments to her son with her son's interest payments back to her caused the rental payments to lack substance. The court also held that the exception in § 2036(a) for transfers for adequate and full consideration (see Chapter 18) did not apply because D and her son never intended the mortgage to be paid.

B. RETENTION OF POSSESSION OR ENJOYMENT OF INCOME PRODUCING PROPERTY

Where D transferred income producing real estate to his children pursuant to an oral agreement that he would retain for his lifetime the income therefrom, the predecessor of § 2036(a)(1) required inclusion of the property in D's gross estate: "The conclusion is irresistible that the petitioners' decedent 'enjoyed' the properties until he died. If, as was said in Commissioner v. Estate of Church, supra, 335 U.S. at page 645, * * * the most valuable property attribute of stocks is their income, it is no less true that one of the most valuable incidents of income-producing real estate is the rent which it yields. He who receives the rent in fact enjoys the property. Enjoyment as used in the death tax statute is not a term of art, but is synonymous with substantial present economic benefit. Commissioner v. Estate of Holmes, 1945, 326 U.S. 480, 486, * * *. Under this realistic point of view the enjoyment of the properties which the decedent conveyed to his children was continued in decedent by prearrangement and ended only when he died." Estate of McNichol v. Commissioner, 265 F.2d 667, 671 (3d Cir.1959).

In Estate of Paxton v. Commissioner, 86 T.C. 785 (1986), D transferred all his assets to a family trust of which his son was principal trustee in exchange for certificates of interest which entitled him and his spouse to receive discretionary distributions of income and principal. The court found an implied understanding between D and his son at the time the trust was created that D could get the income and principal upon demand based on the facts that D received several distributions, he was very wealthy and would hardly have parted with all his assets without some arrangement to get the income and principal if and when needed, upon his death his certificates of interest went to the natural objects of his bounty, and there was a close relationship between D and his son. In addition, D's creditors could have reached the certificates of interest under state law.

b. RETAINED VOTING RIGHTS

United States v. Byrum, Executrix
408 U.S. 125 (1972).

■ MR. JUSTICE POWELL delivered the opinion of the Court.

Decedent, Milliken C. Byrum, created in 1958 an irrevocable trust to which he transferred shares of stock in three closely held corporations. Prior to transfer, he owned at least 71% of the outstanding stock of each corporation. The beneficiaries were his children or, in the event of their death before the termination of the trust, their surviving children. The trust instrument specified that there be a corporate trustee. Byrum designated as sole trustee an independent corporation, Huntington National Bank. The trust agreement vested in the trustee broad and detailed powers with respect to the control and management of the trust property. These powers were exercisable in the trustee's sole discretion, subject to certain rights reserved by Byrum: (i) to vote the shares of unlisted stock held in the trust estate; (ii) to disapprove the sale or transfer of any trust assets, including the shares transferred to the trust; (iii) to approve investments and reinvestments; and (iv) to remove the trustee and "designate another corporate trustee to serve as successor." Until the youngest living child reached age 21, the trustee was authorized in its "absolute and sole discretion" to pay the income and principal of the trust to or for the benefit of the beneficiaries, "with due regard to their individual needs for education, care, maintenance and support." After the youngest child reached 21, the trust was to be divided into a separate trust for each child, to terminate when the beneficiaries reached 35. The trustee was authorized in its discretion to pay income and principal from these trusts to the beneficiaries for emergency or other "worthy need," including education.

When he died in 1964, Byrum owned less than 50% of the common stock in two of the corporations and 59% in the third. The trust had retained the shares transferred to it, with the result that Byrum had continued to have the right to vote not less than 71% of the common stock in each of the three corporations.[11] There were minority stockholders, unrelated to Byrum, in each corporation.

Following Byrum's death, the Commissioner of Internal Revenue determined that the transferred stock was properly included within Byrum's gross estate under § 2036(a) of the Internal Revenue Code * * * That section provides for the inclusion in a decedent's gross estate of all property which the decedent has transferred by *inter vivos* transaction, if he has retained for his lifetime "(1) the possession or enjoyment of, or the right to the income from, the property" transferred, or "(2) the right, either alone or in conjunction with any person, to designate the persons who shall possess or enjoy the property or the income therefrom." The Commissioner determined that the stock transferred into the trust should be included in Byrum's gross estate because of the rights reserved by him in the trust agreement. It was asserted that his right to vote the transferred shares and to veto any sale thereof by the trustee, together with the ownership of other shares, enable Byrum to retain the "enjoyment of * * * the proper-

---

11. The actual proportions were:

	Percentage Owned by Decedent	Percentage Owned by Trust	Total Percentage Owned by Decedent and Trust
Byrum Lithographing Co., Inc.	59	12	71
Graphic Realty, Inc.	35	48	83
Bychrome Co.	42	46	88

ty," and also allowed him to determine the flow of income to the trust and thereby "designate the persons who shall * * * enjoy * * * the income."

The executrix of Byrum's estate paid an additional tax of $13,202.45, and thereafter brought this refund action in District Court. The facts not being in dispute, the court ruled for the executrix on cross motions for summary judgment. 311 F. Supp. 892 (SD Ohio 1970). The Court of Appeals affirmed, one judge dissenting. 440 F.2d 949 (CA6 1971). We granted the Government's petition for certiorari. 404 U.S. 937 (1971).

[The Court's discussion of the applicability of § 2036(a)(2) to the trust is at p. 237]

II

The Government asserts an alternative ground for including the shares transferred to the trust within Byrum's gross estate. It argues that by retaining control, Byrum guaranteed himself continued employment and remuneration, as well as the right to determine whether and when the corporations would be liquidated or merged. Byrum is thus said to have retained "the * * * enjoyment of * * * the property" making it includible within his gross estate under § 2036(a)(1). The Government concedes that the retention of the voting rights of an "unimportant minority interest" would not require inclusion of the transferred shares under § 2036(a)(1). It argues, however, "where the cumulative effect of the retained powers and the rights flowing from the shares not placed in trust leaves the grantor in control of a close corporation, and assures that control for his lifetime, he has retained the 'enjoyment' of the transferred stock."[12] Brief for United States 23.

It is well settled that the terms "enjoy" and "enjoyment," as used in various estate tax statutes, "are not terms of art, but connote substantial present economic benefit rather than technical vesting of title or estates." Commissioner v. Estate of Holmes, 326 U.S. 480, 486 (1946).[13] For example, in Reinecke v. Northern Trust Co., 278 U.S. 339 (1929), in which the critical inquiry was whether the decedent had created a trust "intended

---

12.   At one point MR. JUSTICE WHITE seems to imply that Byrum also retained the enjoyment of the right to the income from the transferred shares:

"When Byrum closed the spigot by deferring dividends of the controlled corporations, *thereby perpetuating his own 'enjoyment' of these funds,* he also in effect transferred income from the life tenants to the remaindermen." (Emphasis added.) * * * But, of course, even if dividends were deferred, the funds remained in the corporation; Byrum could not use them himself.

13.   See 26 CFR § 20.2036–10(b)(1):

"The 'use, possession, right to the income, or other enjoyment of the transferred property' is considered as having been re-

tained by or reserved to the decedent to the extent that the use, possession, right to the income, or other enjoyment is to be applied toward the discharge of a legal obligation of the decedent, or otherwise for his pecuniary benefit."

Although MR. JUSTICE WHITE questions the Court's failure to interpret "possession or enjoyment" with "extreme literalness," * * *, apparently the Commissioner does not do so either. Reflection on the expansive nature of those words, particularly "enjoyment," will demonstrate why interpreting them with "extreme literalness" is an impossibility.

* * * 'to take effect in possession or enjoyment at or after his death,' '' id., at 348, the Court held that reserved powers of management of trust assets, similar to Byrum's power over the three corporations, did not subject an *inter vivos* trust to the federal estate tax. In determining whether the settlor had retained the enjoyment of the transferred property, the Court said:

> "Nor did the reserved powers of management of the trusts save to decedent any control over the economic benefits or the enjoyment of the property. He would equally have reserved all these powers and others had he made himself the trustee, but the transfer would not for that reason have been incomplete. The shifting of the economic interest in the trust property which was the subject of the tax was thus complete as soon as the trust was made. His power to recall the property and of control over it for his own benefit then ceased and as the trusts were not made in contemplation of death, the reserved powers do not serve to distinguish them from any other gift *inter vivos* not subject to the tax." 278 U.S., at 346–347.

The cases cited by the Government reveal that the terms "possession" and "enjoyment," used in § 2036(a)(1), were used to deal with situations in which the owner of property divested himself of title but retained an income interest, or, in the case of real property, the lifetime use of the property. Mr. Justice Black's opinion for the Court in Commissioner v. Estate of Church, 335 U.S. 632 (1949), traces the history of the concept. In none of the cases cited by the Government has a court held that a person has retained possession or enjoyment of the property if he has transferred title irrevocably, made complete delivery of the property and relinquished the right to income where the property is income producing.[14]

The Government cites only one case, Estate of Holland v. Commissioner, 1 T.C. 564 (1943), in which a decedent had retained the right to vote transferred shares of stock and in which the stock was included within the decedent's gross estate. In that case, it was not the mere power to vote the stock, giving the decedent control of the corporation, which caused the Tax Court to include the shares. The court held that " 'on an inclusive view of the whole arrangement, this withholding of the income until decedent's death, coupled with the retention of the certificates under the pledge and the reservation of the right to vote the stock and to designate the company officers' '' subjects the stock to inclusion within the gross estate. Id., at 565.

---

14. Helvering v. Hallock, 309 U.S. 106 (1940); Commissioner v. Estate of Church, 335 U.S. 632 (1949); Lober v. United States, 346 U.S. 335 (1953); United States v. Estate of Grace, 395 U.S. 316 (1969); Estate of McNichol v. Commissioner, 265 F.2d 667 (CA3), cert. denied 361 U.S. 829 (1959); Guynn v. United States, 437 F.2d 1148 (CA4 1971). In all of these cases, as in Church, the grantor retained either title or an income interest or the right to use real property for his lifetime.

Despite MR. JUSTICE WHITE'S suggestion, * * *, we have not "ignore[d] the plain language of the statute which proscribes 'enjoyment' as well as 'possession or * * * the right to income.' '' Rather, the cases we have cited clearly establish that the terms "possession" and "enjoyment" have never been used as the dissent argues.

The settlor in *Holland* retained a considerably greater interest than Byrum retained, including an income interest.[15]

As the Government concedes, the mere retention of the right-to-vote shares does not constitute the type of "enjoyment" in the property itself contemplated by § 2036(a)(1). In addition to being against the weight of precedent, the Government's argument that Byrum *retained* "enjoyment" within the meaning of § 2036(a)(1) is conceptually unsound. This argument implies, as it must under the express language of § 2036(a), that Byrum "retained for his life * * * (1) the possession or enjoyment" of the "*property*" transferred to the trust or the "*income*" therefrom. The only property he transferred was corporate stock. He did not transfer "control" (in the sense used by the Government) as the trust never owned as much as 50% of the stock of any corporation. Byrum never divested himself of control, as he was able to vote a majority of the shares by virtue of what he owned and the right to vote those placed in the trust. Indeed, at the time of his death he still owned a majority of the shares in the largest of the corporations and probably would have exercised control of the other two by virtue of being a large stockholder in each. The statutory language plainly contemplates retention of an attribute of the property transferred—such as a right to income, use of the property itself, or a power of appointment with respect either to income or principal.[16]

Even if Byrum had transferred a majority of the stock, but had retained voting control, he would not have retained "substantial present economic benefit," 326 U.S., at 486. The Government points to the retention of two "benefits." The first of these, the power to liquidate or merge, is not a *present* benefit; rather, it is a speculative and contingent benefit which may or may not be realized. Nor is the probability of continued employment and compensation the substantial "enjoyment of * * * [the transferred] property" within the meaning of the statute. The dominant stockholder in a closely held corporation, if he is active and productive, is likely to hold a senior position and to enjoy the advantage of a significant

---

15. A more analogous case is Yeazel v. Coyle, 68–1 U.S.T.C. ¶ 12,524 (ND Ill. 1968), in which a settlor-trustee, who transferred 60% of the shares of a wholly owned corporation to a trust, was found not to have retained the enjoyment of the property for her lifetime.

16. The interpretation given § 2036(a) by the Government and by MR. JUSTICE WHITE's dissenting opinion would seriously disadvantage settlors in a control posture. If the settlor remained a controlling stockholder, any transfer of stock would be taxable to his estate. * * * The typical closely held corporation is small, has a checkered earning record, and has no market for its shares. Yet its shares often have substantial asset value. To prevent the crippling liquidity problem that would result from the imposition of estate taxes on such shares, the controlling shareholder's estate planning often includes an irrevocable trust. The Government and the dissenting opinion would deny to controlling shareholders the privilege of using this generally acceptable method of estate planning without adverse tax consequences. Yet a settlor whose wealth consisted of listed securities of corporations he did not control would be permitted the tax advantage of the irrevocable trust even though his more marketable assets present a far less serious liquidity problem. The language of the statute does not support such a result and we cannot believe Congress intended it to have such discriminatory and far-reaching impact.

voice in his own compensation. These are inevitable facts of the free-enterprise system, but the influence and capability of a controlling stockholder to favor himself are not without constraints. Where there are minority stockholders, as in this case, directors may be held accountable if their employment, compensation, and retention of officers violate their duty to act reasonably in the best interest of the corporation and all of its stockholders. Moreover, this duty is policed, albeit indirectly, by the Internal Revenue Service, which disallows the deduction of unreasonable compensation paid to a corporate executive as a business expense. We conclude that Byrum's retention of voting control was not the retention of the enjoyment of the transferred property within the meaning of the statute.

For the reasons set forth above, we hold that this case was correctly decided by the Court of Appeals and accordingly the judgment is Affirmed.

* * *

ILLUSTRATIVE MATERIAL

A. RETENTION OF VOTING RIGHTS IN TRANSFERRED STOCK

The Tax Reform Act of 1976 amended § 2036 to overrule *Byrum* and require the transferor's gross estate to include the value of any stock in which the transferor retained the voting rights. The 1976 legislation went well beyond the situation in *Byrum* because it applied § 2036 to the retention of voting rights regardless of whether the donor was in control of the corporation.

The Revenue Act of 1978 changed § 2036 to its current form in § 2036(b), limiting its scope to the transfer of stock in a "controlled corporation" where the transferor retains the voting rights. A "controlled corporation" is one in which D owned, actually or constructively (under the rules of § 318), at least 20% of the total combined voting power of all classes of stock at any time after the transfer of the property and during the three-year period ending on the date of D's death. Even if the transferor did not own the requisite 20%, the definition applies if he had the right, either alone or in conjunction with any other person, to vote the required 20% amount of stock.

Although the current form of § 2036(b) is supposed to confine the anti-*Byrum* rule more closely to the facts presented in *Byrum*, it has its own peculiarities. For example, if donor A owns 20 out of the 100 outstanding voting shares of common stock of a corporation, the gift of 1 share in which voting rights are retained will invoke the provisions of § 2036(b). On the other hand, donor B, who owns 19 shares of the corporation, can give away all 19 shares, retaining the voting rights therein, and none of the shares will be included in B's gross estate. Thus, donor A comes under § 2036(b) by a transfer of only 5% of the shares A owned; donor B, however, is excluded from § 2036(b), even though 100% of the shares B owned were transferred subject to retained voting rights. See Prop. Reg. § 20.2036–2(d)(2) (1983) for rules concerning the computation of the requisite 20% voting power. Note that Prop. Reg. § 20.2036–2(d)(1) (1983) appears to apply the attribution rules of § 318 to the voting power test as well as to the ownership test, a questionable interpretation of § 2036(b).

Section 2036(b) requires inclusion of stock in D's gross estate even if the grantor can exercise the power to vote the stock only in a fiduciary capacity, such as trustee. The 1978 Committee Report stated:

"The rule requiring inclusion in the gross estate of stock of a controlled corporation applies where the decedent retained the voting rights of the stock which was directly or indirectly transferred by him. Thus, where the decedent within three years of his death, transfers cash or other property to a trust of which he is trustee and then the trust uses that cash or other property to purchase stock in a controlled corporation from himself, the value of the stock would be included in his gross estate. In addition, the indirect retention of voting rights in the case of reciprocal transfers of stock in trust would result in the inclusion of the stock with respect to which the decedent had voting rights as trustee. However, voting rights in stock transferred in trust by the decedent will not be considered to have been retained by the decedent merely because a relative was the trustee who voted the stock. In these cases, the voting rights would be considered to have been indirectly retained by the decedent if in substance the decedent had retained such voting rights, e.g., there had been an arrangement or agreement for the trustee to vote the stock in accordance with directions from the decedent." S.Rep. No. 745, 95th Cong., 2d Sess. 90–91 (1978).

Consider the effect of § 2036(b) on Estate of Gilman v. Commissioner, 65 T.C. 296 (1975), aff'd per curiam, 547 F.2d 32 (2d Cir. 1976), in which a majority of the Tax Court ruled that *Byrum* required exclusion from D's estate of stock he had transferred to a trust of which he, his son and his lawyer were trustees. The trustees' powers included the power to vote the stock, which represented control of a closely held corporation of which decedent was a director and chief executive officer. The decedent-trustee could only exercise the voting rights in the stock by casting one of three votes as a trustee. The 1976 House Ways and Means Committee Report indicates that Congress intended § 2036(b) to cover this situation. Prop. Reg. § 20.2036–2(c) (1983) states that "a fiduciary power exercisable as * * * co-trustee * * * is a right to vote stock within the meaning of this section" and, therefore, would change the result in *Gilman*.

It is not necessary that the transferor formally retain voting rights in the transferred stock. In Rev. Rul. 80–346, 1980–2, C.B. 271, D owned outright 19% of the shares of stock of a corporation and D's children owned the balance. The attribution rule in Prop. Reg. § 20.2036–2(d)(1) treated D as owning his children's shares as well. D transferred the shares into trusts for the benefit of the children, the trustee orally agreeing with D that the shares would be voted only with D's consent and, in fact, the trustee voted the shares only after obtaining D's approval. The Ruling concluded that the oral agreement satisfied the "indirect" retention of voting control requirement and § 2036(b) was applicable to the transfer.

Suppose in the *Byrum* situation, the controlling shareholder first effected a recapitalization of the corporation's stock by exchanging his shares of common stock for two new classes of stock, one voting and one non-voting. He then transferred the non-voting common to the trust. The practical result of the transaction is identical to that in *Byrum*, but can § 2036(b) be read to cover the situation? As another variation, suppose in the recapitalization the common stock is exchanged for voting preferred stock and non-voting common stock. If the non-voting common is then transferred to a trust, the donor has retained voting control and arguably has removed all future appreciation from his estate.[17] If § 2036(b) can be interpreted to cover these situations (because the transferor has indirectly made a transfer of stock in which he has retained the voting rights), will it then cover the situation where, at the time the corporation is created, for example, the voting stock is issued directly to the parent and the non-voting stock to the children (or trust)? It did not appear that Congress had these situations in mind in enacting the 1976 amendment to § 2036, and this was confirmed by the Committee Report to the 1978 amendment: "The rule [of § 2036(b)] would not apply to the transfer of stock in a controlled corporation where the decedent could not vote the transferred stock. For example, where a decedent transfers stock in a controlled corporation to his son and does not have the power to vote the stock any time during the three-year period before his death, the rule does not apply even where the decedent owned or could vote a majority of the stock. Similarly, where the decedent owned both voting and nonvoting stock and transferred the nonvoting stock to another person, the rule does not apply to the non-voting stock simply because of the decedent's ownership of the voting stock." S.Rep. No. 745, 95th Cong., 2d Sess. 91 (1978). See Prop. Reg. § 20.2036–2(a) (1983) and Rev. Rul. 81–15, 1981–1 C.B. 457, so applying § 2036(b).

B. CONTINUED VIABILITY OF BYRUM

Although Congress overruled *Byrum,* the case does have continuing importance. Lower courts frequently cite the Court's analysis of the "possession or enjoyment" aspect of § 2036(a)(1). In addition, the result itself might still apply in situations in which corporate stock is not involved. For example, what happens if a parent transfers a controlling partnership interest to a trust for the benefit of the parent's children, but the parent retains the voting rights with respect to the assigned partnership interest?

C. RELINQUISHMENT OF VOTING RIGHTS

If a donor retains the right to vote transferred stock in a controlled corporation and relinquishes those voting rights within three years of death, § 2035(a) treats the relinquishment as a transfer for purposes of § 2036. Presumably the full value of the shares at date of death will be included in the donor's estate by virtue of § 2035(a). See discussion of § 2035 at p. 418.

4. RETENTION OF POWER TO DESIGNATE WHO SHALL POSSESS OR ENJOY THE PROPERTY: § 2036(a)(2)

a. IN GENERAL

United States v. O'Malley

383 U.S. 627 (1966).

■ MR. JUSTICE WHITE delivered the opinion of the Court. * * *

Edward H. Fabrice, who died in 1949, created five irrevocable trusts in 1936 and 1937, two for each of two daughters and one for his wife. He was

---

17. Section 2701, which is discussed at p. 759, however, may treat donor as having transferred the value of all his stock, thereby imposing a large gift tax on his transfer of the non-voting common stock.

one of three trustees of the trusts, each of which provided that the trustees, in their sole discretion, could pay trust income to the beneficiary or accumulate the income, in which event it became part of the principal of the trust.[18] Basing his action on [the predecessor of § 2036(a)(2)], the Commissioner included in Fabrice's gross estate both the original principal of the trusts and the accumulated income added thereto. He accordingly assessed a deficiency, the payment of which prompted this refund action by the respondents, the executors of the estate. The District Court found the original corpus of the trusts includible in the estate, a holding not challenged in the Court of Appeals or here. It felt obliged, however, by Commissioner v. McDermott's Estate, 222 F.2d 665, to exclude from the taxable estate the portion of the trust principal representing accumulated income and to order an appropriate refund. 220 F. Supp. 30. The Court of Appeals affirmed, 340 F.2d 930, adhering to its own decision in McDermott's Estate and noting its disagreement with Round v. Commissioner, 332 F.2d 590, in which the Court of Appeals for the First Circuit declined to follow McDermott's Estate. Because of these conflicting decisions we granted certiorari. 382 U.S. 810. We now reverse the decision below.

The applicability of [the predecessor of § 2036(a)(2)] depends upon the answer to two inquiries relevant to the facts of this case: first, whether Fabrice retained a power "to designate the persons who shall possess or enjoy the property or the income therefrom"; and second, whether the property sought to be included, namely, the portions of trust principal representing accumulated income, was the subject of a previous transfer by Fabrice.

[The predecessor of § 2036(a)(2)], which originated in 1931, was an important part of the congressional response to May v. Heiner, 281 U.S. 238, and its offspring and of the legislative policy of subjecting to tax all property which has been the subject of an incomplete inter vivos transfer. Cf. Commissioner v. Estate of Church, 335 U.S. 632, 644–645; Helvering v. Hallock, 309 U.S. 106, 114. The section requires the property to be included not only when the grantor himself has the right to its income but also when he has the right to designate those who may possess and enjoy it. Here Fabrice was empowered, with the other trustees, to distribute the trust income to the income beneficiaries or to accumulate it and add it to the principal, thereby denying to the beneficiaries the privilege of immediate enjoyment and conditioning their eventual enjoyment upon surviving the termination of the trust. This is a significant power, see Commissioner v.

---

18. The following provision in the trust for Janet Fabrice is also contained in the other trusts:

"The net income from the Trust Estate shall be paid, in whole or in part, to my daughter, JANET FABRICE, in such proportions, amounts and at such times as the Trustees may, from time to time, in their sole discretion, determine, or said net income may be retained by the Trustees and credited to the account of said beneficiary, and any income not distributed in any calendar year shall become a part of the principal of the Trust Estate."

Estate of Holmes, 326 U.S. 480, 487, and of sufficient substance to be deemed the power to "designate" within the meaning of [the predecessor of § 2036(a)(2)]. This was the holding of the Tax Court and the Court of Appeals almost 20 years ago. Industrial Trust Co. v. Commissioner, 165 F.2d 142, affirming in this respect Estate of Budlong v. Commissioner, 7 T.C. 756. The District Court here followed Industrial Trust and affirmed the includibility of the original principal of each of the Fabrice trusts. That ruling is not now disputed. By the same token, the first condition to taxing accumulated income added to the principal is satisfied, for the income from these increments to principal was subject to the identical power in Fabrice to distribute or accumulate until the very moment of his death.

The dispute in this case relates to the second condition to the applicability of [the predecessor of § 2036(a)(2)]—whether Fabrice had ever "transferred" the income additions to the trust principal. Contrary to the judgment of the Court of Appeals, we are sure that he had. At the time Fabrice established these trusts, he owned all of the rights to the property transferred, a major aspect of which was his right to the present and future income produced by that property. Commissioner v. Estate of Church, 335 U.S. 632, 644. With the creation of the trusts, he relinquished all of his rights to income except the power to distribute that income to the income beneficiaries or to accumulate it and hold it for the remaindermen of the trusts. He no longer had, for example, the right to income for his own benefit or to have it distributed to any other than the trust beneficiaries. Moreover, with respect to the very additions to principal now at issue, he exercised his retained power to distribute or accumulate income, choosing to do the latter and thereby adding to the principal of the trusts. All income increments to trust principal are therefore traceable to Fabrice himself, by virtue of the original transfer and the exercise of the power to accumulate. Before the creation of the trusts, Fabrice owned all rights to the property and to its income. By the time of his death he had divested himself of all power and control over accumulated income which had been added to the principal, except the power to deal with the income from such additions. With respect to each addition to trust principal from accumulated income, Fabrice had clearly made a "transfer" as required by [the predecessor of § 2036(a)(2)]. Under that section, the power over income retained by Fabrice is sufficient to require the inclusion of the original corpus of the trust in his gross estate. The accumulated income added to principal is subject to the same power and is likewise includible. Round v. Commissioner, 332 F.2d 590; Estate of Yawkey v. Commissioner, 12 T.C. 1164.[19] * * *

Reversed.

---

19. This same result was reached, but without discussion, in Estate of Spiegel v. Commissioner, 335 U.S. 701, under the "take effect in possession or enjoyment" provision of [the predecessor of § 2037] and in Commissioner v. Estate of Holmes, 326 U.S. 480, under [the predecessor of § 2038]. Other cases reaching the same conclusion under [the predecessor of § 2038] or its predecessors are Commissioner v. Hager's Estate, 173 F.2d 613, petition for cert. dismissed, 337 U.S. 937; Estate of Showers v. Commissioner, 14 T.C. 902; Estate of Guggenheim v. Commissioner, 40 B.T.A. 181, aff'd, 117 F.2d 469, cert. denied, 314 U.S. 621.

United States v. Byrum, Executrix

408 U.S. 125 (1972).

[The facts of the case and the Court's resolution of the issues presented under § 2036(a)(1) are set forth above at p. 227.]

I.

The Government relies primarily on its claim, made under § 2036(a)(2) that Byrum retained the right to designate the persons who shall enjoy the income from the transferred property. The argument is a complicated one. By retaining voting control over the corporations whose stock was transferred, Byrum was in a position to select the corporate directors. He could retain this position by not selling the shares he owned and by vetoing any sale by the trustee of the transferred shares. These rights, it is said, gave him control over corporate dividend policy. By increasing, decreasing, or stopping dividends completely, it is argued that Byrum could "regulate the flow of income to the trust" and thereby shift or defer the beneficial enjoyment of trust income between the present beneficiaries and the remaindermen. The sum of this retained power is said to be tantamount to a grantor-trustee's power to accumulate income in the trust, which this Court has recognized constitutes the power to designate the persons who shall enjoy the income from transferred property.[20]

At the outset we observe that this Court has never held that trust property must be included in a settlor's gross estate solely because the settlor retained the power to manage trust assets. On the contrary, since our decision in Reinecke v. Northern Trust Co., 278 U.S. 339 (1929), it has been recognized that a settlor's retention of broad powers of management does not necessarily subject an *inter vivos* trust to the federal estate tax. Although there was no statutory analogue to § 2036 (a)(2) when *Northern Trust* was decided, several lower court decisions decided after the enactment of the predecessor of § 2036(a)(2) have upheld the settlor's right to exercise managerial powers without incurring estate-tax liability.[21] In Estate of King v. Commissioner, 37 T.C. 973 (1962), a settlor reserved the

---

20. United States v. O'Malley, 383 U.S. 627 (1966). It is irrelevant to this argument how many shares Byrum transferred to the trust. Had he retained in his own name more than 50% of the shares (as he did with one corporation), rather than retaining the right to vote the transferred shares, he would still have had the right to elect the board of directors and the same power to "control" the flow of dividends. Thus, the Government is arguing that a majority shareholder's estate must be taxed for stock transferred to a trust if he owned at least 50% of the voting stock after the transfer or if he retained the right to vote the transferred stock and could thus vote more than 50% of the stock. It would follow also that if a settlor controlled 50% of the voting stock and similarly transferred some other class of stock for which the payment of dividends had to be authorized by the directors, his estate would also be taxed. * * *

21. See, e.g., Old Colony Trust Co. v. United States, 423 F.2d 601 (CA1 1970); United States v. Powell, 307 F.2d 821 (CA10 1962); Estate of Ford v. Commissioner, 53 T.C. 114 (1969), aff'd, 450 F.2d 878 (CA2 1971); Estate of Wilson v. Commissioner, 13 T.C. 869 (1949) (en banc), aff'd, 187 F.2d 145 (CA3 1951); Estate of Budd v. Commissioner, 49 T.C. 468 (1968); Estate of Pardee v. Commissioner, 49 T.C. 140 (1967); Estate of King v. Commissioner, 37 T.C. 973 (1962).

power to direct the trustee in the management and investment of trust assets. The Government argued that the settlor was thereby empowered to cause investments to be made in such a manner as to control significantly the flow of income into the trust. The Tax Court rejected this argument, and held for the taxpayer. Although the court recognized that the settlor had reserved "wide latitude in the exercise of his discretion as to the types of investments to be made," *id.*, at 980, it did not find this control over the flow of income to be equivalent to the power to designate who shall enjoy the income from the transferred property.

Essentially the power retained by Byrum is the same managerial power retained by the settlors in *Northern Trust* and in *King*. Although neither case controls this one—*Northern Trust*, because it was not decided under § 2036(a)(2) or a predecessor; and *King*, because it is a lower court opinion—the existence of such precedents carries weight.[22] The holding of *Northern Trust*, that the settlor of a trust may retain broad powers of management without adverse estate-tax consequences, may have been relied upon in the drafting of hundreds of *inter vivos* trusts.[23] The modification of this principle now sought by the Government could have a seriously adverse impact, especially upon settlors (and their estates) who happen to have been "controlling" stockholders of a closely held corporation. Courts properly have been reluctant to depart from an interpretation of tax law which has been generally accepted when the departure could have potentially far-reaching consequences. When a principle of taxation requires reexamination, Congress is better equipped than a court to define precisely the type of conduct which results in tax consequences. When courts readily undertake such tasks, taxpayers may not rely with assurance on what appear to be established rules lest they be subsequently overturned. Legislative enactments, on the other hand, although not always free from ambiguity, at least afford the taxpayers advance warning.

The Government argues, however, that our opinion in United States v. O'Malley, 383 U.S. 627 (1966), compels the inclusion in Byrum's estate of the stock owned by the trust. * * *

22. The dissenting opinion attempts to distinguish the cases, holding that a settlor-trustee's retained powers of management do not bring adverse estate-tax consequences, on the ground that management of trust assets is not the same as the power retained by Byrum because a settlor-trustee is bound by a fiduciary duty to treat the life tenant beneficiaries and remaindermen as the trust instrument specifies. But the argument that in the reserved-power-of-management cases there was "a judicially enforceable strict standard capable of invocation by the trust beneficiaries by reference to the terms of the trust agreement," * * *, ignores the fact that trust agreements may and often do provide for the widest investment discretion.

23. Assuming, *arguendo,* that MR. JUSTICE WHITE is correct in suggesting that in 1958, when this trust instrument was drawn, the estate-tax consequences of the settlor's retained powers of management were less certain than they are now, this Court's failure to overrule *Northern Trust*, plus the existence of recent cases such as *King* and the cases cited in n. [28], have undoubtedly been relied on by the draftsmen of more recent trusts with considerable justification. Our concern as to this point is not so much with whether Byrum properly relied on the precedents, but with the probability that others did rely thereon in good faith.

In our view, and for the purposes of this case, *O'Malley* adds nothing to the statute itself. The facts in that case were clearly within the ambit of what is now § 2036(a). That section requires that the settlor must have "retained for his life * * * (2) the *right* * * * to designate the persons who shall possess or enjoy the property or the income therefrom." O'Malley was covered precisely by the statute for two reasons: (1) there the settlor had reserved a legal right, set forth in the trust instrument; and (2) this right expressly authorized the settlor, "in conjunction" with others, to accumulate income and thereby "to designate" the persons to enjoy it.

It must be conceded that Byrum reserved no such "right" in the trust instrument or otherwise. The term "right," certainly when used in a tax statute, must be given its normal and customary meaning. It connotes an ascertainable and legally enforceable power, such as that involved in *O'Malley*.[24] Here, the right ascribed to Byrum was the power to use his majority position and influence over the corporate directors to "regulate the flow of dividends" to the trust. That "right" was neither ascertainable nor legally enforceable and hence was not a right in any normal sense of that term.[25]

Byrum did retain the legal right to vote shares held by the trust and to veto investments and reinvestments. But the corporate trustee alone, not Byrum, had the right to pay out or withhold income and thereby to designate who among the beneficiaries enjoyed such income. Whatever power Byrum may have possessed with respect to the flow of income into the trust was derived not from an enforceable legal right specified in the trust instrument, but from the fact that he could elect a majority of the directors of the three corporations. The power to elect the directors conferred no legal right to command them to pay or not to pay dividends. A majority shareholder has a fiduciary duty not to misuse his power by promoting his personal interests at the expense of corporate interests.[26] Moreover, the directors also have a fiduciary duty to promote the interests of the corporation. However great Byrum's influence may have been with the corporate directors, their responsibilities were to all stockholders and were enforceable according to legal standards entirely unrelated to the needs of the trust or to Byrum's desires with respect thereto.

---

24. Although MR. JUSTICE WHITE's dissent argues that the use of the word "power" in *O'Malley* implies that the Court's concern was with practical reality rather than legal form, an examination of that opinion does not indicate that the term was used other than in the sense of *legally* empowered. At any rate, the "power" was a right reserved to the settlor in the trust instrument itself.

25. The "control" rationale, urged by the Government and adopted by the dissenting opinion, would create a standard—not specified in the statute—so vague and amorphous as to be impossible of ascertainment in many instances. See n. [34], *infra.* Neither the Government nor the dissent sheds light on the absence of an ascertainable standard. The Government speaks vaguely of drawing the line between "an unimportant minority interest" (whatever that may be) and "voting control." The dissenting opinion does not address this problem at all. See Comment, Sale of Control Stock and the Brokers' Transaction Exemption—Before and After the Wheat Report, 49 Tex.L.Rev. 475, 479–481 (1971).

26. Such a fiduciary relationship would exist in almost every, if not every, State. * * *

The Government seeks to equate the *de facto* position of a controlling stockholder with the legally enforceable "right" specified by the statute. Retention of corporate control (through the right to vote the shares) is said to be "tantamount to the power to accumulate income" in the trust which resulted in estate-tax consequences in *O'Malley*. The Government goes on to assert that "[t]hrough exercise of that retained power, [Byrum] could increase or decrease corporate dividends * * * and thereby shift or defer the beneficial enjoyment of trust income."[27] This approach seems to us not only to depart from the specific statutory language, but also to misconceive the realities of corporate life.

There is no reason to suppose that the three corporations controlled by Byrum were other than typical small businesses. The customary vicissitudes of such enterprises—bad years; product obsolescence; new competition; disastrous litigation; new, inhibiting Government regulations; even bankruptcy—prevent any certainty or predictability as to earnings or dividends. There is no assurance that a small corporation will have a flow of net earnings or that income earned will in fact be available for dividends. Thus, Byrum's alleged *de facto* "power to control the flow of dividends" to the trust was subject to business and economic variables over which he had little or no control.

Even where there are corporate earnings, the legal power to declare dividends is vested solely in the corporate board. In making decisions with respect to dividends, the board must consider a number of factors. It must balance the expectation of stockholders to reasonable dividends when earned against corporate needs for retention of earnings. The first responsibility of the board is to safeguard corporate financial viability for the long term. This means, among other things, the retention of sufficient earnings to assure adequate working capital as well as resources for retirement of debt, for replacement and modernization of plant and equipment, and for growth and expansion. The nature of a corporation's business, as well as the policies and long-range plans of management, are also relevant to dividend payment decisions. Directors of a closely held, small corporation must bear in mind the relatively limited access of such an enterprise to capital markets. This may require a more conservative policy with respect

---

27. The Government uses the terms "control" and "controlling stockholder" as if they were words of art with a fixed and ascertainable meaning. In fact, the concept of "control" is a nebulous one. Although in this case Byrum possessed "voting control" of the three corporations (in view of his being able to vote more than 50% of the stock in each), the concept is too variable and imprecise to constitute the basis *per se* for imposing tax liability under § 2036(a). Under most circumstances, a stockholder who has the right to vote more than 50% of the voting shares of a corporation "controls it" in the sense that he may elect the board of directors. But such a stockholder would not control, under the laws of most States, certain corporate transactions such as mergers and sales of assets. Moreover, control—in terms of effective power to elect the board under normal circumstances—may exist where there is a right to vote far less than 50% of the shares. This will vary with the size of the corporation, the number of shareholders, and the concentration (or lack of it) of ownership. See generally 2 L.Loss, Securities Regulation 770–783 (1961). Securities law practitioners recognize that possessing 10% or more of voting power is a factor on which the Securities and Exchange Commission relies as one of the indicia of control. SEC, Disclosure to Investors—The Wheat Report 245–247 (1969).

to dividends than would be expected of an established corporation with securities listed on national exchanges.

Nor do small corporations have the flexibility or the opportunity available to national concerns in the utilization of retained earnings. When earnings are substantial, a decision not to pay dividends may result only in the accumulation of surplus rather than growth through internal or external expansion. The accumulated earnings may result in the imposition of a penalty tax.

These various economic considerations are ignored at the directors' peril. Although vested with broad discretion in determining whether, when, and what amount of dividends shall be paid, that discretion is subject to legal restraints. If, in obedience to the will of the majority stockholder, corporate directors disregard the interests of shareholders by accumulating earnings to an unreasonable extent, they are vulnerable to a derivative suit. They are similarly vulnerable if they make an unlawful payment of dividends in the absence of net earnings or available surplus, or if they fail to exercise the requisite degree of care in discharging their duty to act only in the best interest of the corporation and its stockholders.

Byrum was similarly inhibited by a fiduciary duty from abusing his position as majority shareholder for personal or family advantage to the detriment of the corporation or other stockholders. There were a substantial number of minority stockholders in these corporations who were unrelated to Byrum.[28] Had Byrum and the directors violated their duties, the minority shareholders would have had a cause of action under Ohio law. The Huntington National Bank, as trustee, was one of the minority stockholders, and it had both the right and the duty to hold Byrum responsible for any wrongful or negligent action as a controlling stockholder or as a director of the corporations. Although Byrum had reserved the right to remove the trustee, he would have been imprudent to do this when confronted by the trustee's complaint against his conduct. A successor trustee would succeed to the rights of the one removed.

We conclude that Byrum did not have an unconstrained *de facto* power to regulate the flow of dividends to the trust, much less the "right" to designate who was to enjoy the income from trust property. His ability to affect, but not control, trust income, was a qualitatively different power from that of the settlor in *O'Malley,* who had a specific and enforceable right to control the income paid to the beneficiaries.[29] Even had Byrum managed to flood the trust with income, he had no way of compelling the trustee to pay it out rather than accumulate it. Nor could he prevent the

28. App. 30–32. In Byrum Lithographing Co., Inc., none of the other 11 stockholders appears to be related by name to Byrum. In Bychrome Co. five of the eight stockholders appear to be unrelated to the Byrums; and in Graphic Realty Co. 11 of the 14 stockholders appear to be unrelated.

29. The Government cites two other opinions of this Court, in addition to *O'Mal-*

ley, to support its argument. In both Commissioner v. Estate of Holmes, 326 U.S. 480 (1946), and Lober v. United States, 346 U.S. 335 (1953), the grantor reserved to himself the power to distribute to the beneficiaries the entire principal and accumulated income of the trust at any time. This power to terminate the trust and thereby designate the beneficiaries at a time selected by the settlor, is

trustee from making payments from other trust assets,[30] although admittedly there were few of these at the time of Byrum's death. We cannot assume, however, that no other assets would come into the trust from reinvestments or other gifts.[31]

We find no merit to the Government's contention that Byrum's *de facto* "control," subject as it was to the economic and legal constraints set forth above, was tantamount to the right to designate the persons who shall enjoy trust income, specified by § 2036(a)(2).[32] * * *

* * *

Jennings v. Smith

161 F.2d 74 (2d Cir. 1947).

■ SWAN, CIRCUIT JUDGE.

This is an action by the executors of the will of Oliver Gould Jennings, a resident of Connecticut whose death occurred on October 13, 1936, to

not comparable to the powers reserved by Byrum in this case.

30. While the trustee could not acquire or dispose of investments without Byrum's approval, he was not subject to Byrum's orders. Byrum could prevent the acquisition of an asset, but he could not require the trustee to acquire any investment. Nor could he compel a sale, although he could prevent one. Thus, if there were other income-producing assets in the trust, Byrum could not compel the trustee to dispose of them.

31. In purporting to summarize the basis of our distinction of *O'Malley,* the dissenting opinion states:

"Now the majority would have us accept the incompatible position that a settlor seeking tax exemption may keep the power of income allocation by rendering the trust dependent on an income flow he controls because the general fiduciary obligations of a director are sufficient to eliminate the power to designate within the meaning of § 2036(a)(2)." Post, at 157.

This statement, which assumes the critical and ultimate conclusion, incorrectly states the position of the Court. We do not hold that a settlor "may keep the power of income allocation" in the way MR. JUSTICE WHITE sets out; we hold, for the reasons stated in this opinion, that this settlor did not retain the power to allocate income within the meaning of the statute.

32. The dissenting opinion's view of the business world will come as a surprise to many. The dissent states:

"Thus, by instructing the directors he elected in the controlled corporations that he thought dividends should or should not be declared Byrum was able to open or close the spigot through which the income flowed to the trust's life tenants." Post, at 152.

This appears to assume that all corporations, including the small family type involved in this case, have a regular and dependable flow of earnings available for dividends, and that if there is a controlling stockholder he simply turns the "spigot" on or off as dividends may be desired. For the reasons set forth in this opinion, no such dream world exists in the life of many corporations. But whatever the situation may be generally, the fallacy in the dissenting opinion's position here is that the record simply does not support it. This case was decided on a motion for summary judgment. The record does not disclose anything with respect to the earnings or financial conditions of these corporations. We simply do not know whether there were any earnings for the years in question, whether there was an earned surplus in any of the corporations, or whether—if some earnings be assumed—they were adequate in light of other corporate needs to justify dividend payments. Nor can we infer from the increase in dividend payments in the year following Byrum's death that higher dividends could have been paid previously. The increase could be explained as easily by insurance held by the corporations on Byrum's life.

recover such part of the estate tax paid by them to the defendant collector as had been illegally collected. Their right to a refund of the amount claimed is clear under Maass v. Higgins, 312 U.S. 443 and was not disputed; but the defendant set up in defense an additional estate tax liability (greater than the alleged overpayment) based on the failure to include in the decedent's gross estate the value of certain property which he had transferred in trust in 1934 and 1935. Although assessment of an additional estate tax was barred by the statute of limitations, the plaintiffs do not contend that they are entitled to a refund unless the tax legally due was overpaid. See Lewis v. Reynolds, 284 U.S. 281. Hence the question presented at the trial, and renewed here, is whether the value of the trust property should have been included in the gross estate. The district court held it includible under [the predecessor of § 2038]. Accordingly judgment was given for the defendant, and the plaintiffs have appealed.

In December 1934 the decedent set up two trusts: one for the family of his elder son, B. Brewster Jennings, the other for the family of his younger son, Lawrence K. Jennings. The trust instruments were identical, except for the names of the beneficiaries and the property transferred. In discussing the terms of the trusts it will suffice to refer to the one set up for the elder son's family. The trust was irrevocable and in so far as legally permissible its provisions were to be interpreted and enforced according to Connecticut law. It reserved no beneficial interest to the settlor. He and his two sons were named as the trustees; in case a vacancy should occur provision was made for the appointment of a successor trustee having like powers; there were always to be three trustees and they were authorized to act by majority vote. At the end of each year during the life of the son, the trustees were to accumulate the net income by adding it to the capital of the trust but they were given power, "in their absolute discretion" at any time during the year and prior to the amalgamation of that year's net income into capital, to use all or any part of it for the benefit of the son or his issue provided "the trustees shall determine that such disbursement is reasonably necessary to enable the beneficiary in question to maintain himself and his family, if any, in comfort and in accordance with the station in life to which he belongs." Upon the death of the son the capital of the trust was to be divided into separate equal trust funds, one for each of his surviving children and one for each deceased child who left issue surviving at the death of the son. The trustees also had power to invade the capital [for extraordinary medical expenses, financial misfortune or to provide a residence]. In the Lawrence K. Jennings trust all current net income for the years 1935 and 1936 was paid to him, the trustees, of whom the decedent was one, having unanimously determined that such payments were necessary to enable Lawrence to maintain himself and his family in comfort and in accordance with his station in life. No payment or application of income of the B. Brewster Jennings trust, and none of capital of either trust, was made or requested during the life of the decedent.

Gift tax returns covering the transfers in trust were duly filed and taxes paid thereon. The trusts were not created in contemplation of death, nor to reduce estate taxes on the settlor's estate.

[The predecessor of § 2038(a)(2)] provides for inclusion in the gross estate of all property "To the extent of any interest therein of which the decedent has at any time made a transfer, by trust or otherwise, where the enjoyment thereof was subject at the date of his death to any change through the exercise of a power, either by the decedent alone or in conjunction with any person, to alter, amend, or revoke, * * *".

The appellants contend that this section embraces only powers exercisable by the settlor in his individual capacity and does not include powers exercisable by him in a fiduciary capacity, either alone or as one of several trustees. Under [the predecessor of § 2038(a)(1)] the existence of a power to alter, amend or revoke "(in whatever capacity exercisable)" is sufficient. Whether the quoted parenthetical phrase was intended to effect a change or was declaratory of existing law was left open in Commissioner v. Estate of Holmes, 326 U.S. 480, at page 490. But in Commissioner v. Newbold's Estate, 2 Cir., 158 F.2d 694, this court recently held, following the first and third circuits, that the phrase was merely declaratory and its absence from [§ 2038(a)(2)] is consequently not significant. Despite the appellants' able argument to the contrary, we adhere to [the] view [that § 2038(a)(2) applies to powers exercisable in a fiduciary capacity.]

The next question is whether the powers conferred upon the trustees in the case at bar are powers of the character described in [the predecessor of § 2038(a)(2)], which requires that enjoyment of the trust property must be subject at the date of the decedent's death to change through the exercise of a power. The trustees' power to invade the capital of the trust property was exercisable only if the son or his issue "should suffer prolonged illness or be overtaken by financial misfortune which the trustees deem extraordinary." Neither of these contingencies had occurred before the decedent's death; hence enjoyment of the capital was not "subject at the date of his death to any change through the exercise of a power." In Commissioner v. Flanders, 2 Cir., 111 F.2d 117, although decision was rested on another ground, this court expressed the opinion that a power conditioned upon an event which had not occurred before the settlor's death was not within the section. In support of this view we cited Tait v. Safe Deposit & Trust Co., 4 Cir., 74 F.2d 851, 858; Day v. Commissioner, 3 Cir., 92 F.2d 179; Patterson v. Commissioner, 36 B.T.A. 407. The question has recently been explored by the Tax Court in Estate of Budlong v. Commissioner, 7 T.C. 758. There it was held in a convincing opinion that the power of trustees to invade corpus in case of "sickness or other emergency," which had not occurred before the decedent's death, was not a power to "alter, amend or revoke" within the meaning of the statute. The court reasoned that the trustees had not unlimited discretion to act or withhold action under the power, since the trust instrument provided an external standard which a court of equity would apply to compel compliance by the trustees on the happening of the specified contingency or to restrain threatened action if the condition were not fulfilled. In the case at bar the district judge was of the opinion that even if the trustees found that the stated conditions had been fulfilled, "their finding created no enforceable rights in any of the beneficiaries." 63 F. Supp. 834, at page 837. In this view we are unable to concur. The condition upon which the power to invade capital might arise is sufficiently definite to be capable of determination by a court of equity. As Judge L. Hand said in Stix v. Commissioner, 2 Cir., 152 F.2d 562, 563, "no language, however strong, will entirely remove any power held in trust from the reach of a court of equity." * * * Since the trustees were not free to exercise untrammeled discretion but were to be governed by determinable standards, their power to invade capital, conditioned on contingencies which had not happened, did not in our opinion bring the trust property within the reach of [the predecessor of § 2038(a)(2)].

Similar reasoning leads to the same conclusion with respect to the trustees' power over net income. At the end of each calendar year they were to accumulate the net income of that year unless prior to its amalgamation into capital they exercised their power to disburse it to, or for the benefit of, the son or his issue. The power the trustees had with respect to disbursing income was exercisable year by year; and at the date of the decedent's death the only income of which the enjoyment was subject to change through exercise of a power was the income of the B. Brewster Jennings trust for the year 1936. But the exercise of this power was conditioned on the trustees' determination that disbursement of the income was necessary to enable the beneficiary to whom it might be allotted to maintain himself and his family "in comfort and in accordance with the station in life to which he belongs." The contingency which would justify exercise of the power had not happened before the decedent's death; consequently the 1936 net income of the B. Brewster Jennings trust was not subject at the date of the decedent's death "to any change through the exercise of a power." Hence it was not includible in the gross estate of the decedent under [the predecessor of § 2038(a)]. This conclusion is not inconsistent with Commissioner v. Newbold's Estate, 2 Cir., 158 F.2d 694, for there the trustees had unlimited discretion, the trust instrument expressly providing that no beneficiary should have any vested right to receive any payment from income.

There remains for consideration the question whether the value of the trust property is includible in the decedent's estate under [the predecessor of § 2036(a)] upon which the appellee also relies. This section, derived from § 302(c) of the Revenue Act of 1926 as amended by the Joint Resolution of March 3, 1931 and § 803 of the Revenue Act of 1932, provides for inclusion within the gross estate of all property "To the extent of any interest therein of which the decedent has at any time made a transfer, by trust or otherwise, in contemplation of or intended to take effect in possession or enjoyment at or after his death, or of which he has at any time made a transfer by trust or otherwise, under which he has retained for his life or for any period not ascertainable without reference to his death or for any period which does not in fact end before his death (1) the possession or enjoyment of, or the right to the income from, the property, or (2) the right, either alone or in conjunction with any person, to designate the persons who shall possess or enjoy the property or the income therefrom; * * *".

Section 302(c) of the Revenue Act of 1926 was supposed to reach transfers made in contemplation of death or intended to take effect in possession or enjoyment at or after the settlor's death. The amendments, as the legislative history discloses, were intended to avoid the effect of the decision in May v. Heiner, 281 U.S. 238, where the settlor reserved a life estate, and to reach transfers closely akin to testamentary dispositions. See Report No. 708, 32d Cong., 1st Sess. at page 46; Beach v. Busey, 6 Cir., 156 F.2d 496, 497. The possession or enjoyment referred to in clause (1) is plainly that of the settlor. The "right," referred to in clause (2), to designate the persons who shall possess or enjoy the property or the income therefrom, is not so limited and apparently overlaps the powers mentioned in § 302(d), as amended, [by the predecessor of § 2038]. At first glance it might seem that clause (2) covers the present case, because the decedent, for a period that did not in fact end before his death, "retained the right," in conjunction with another of the trustees, to designate the persons who should enjoy the trust property or the income therefrom. But for the reasons that moved us when considering the applicability of [the predecessor of § 2038], we think the decedent effectively put that "right" beyond his own control or retention by imposing conditions upon the exercise of it. A "right" so qualified that it becomes a duty enforceable in a court of equity on petition by the beneficiaries does not circumvent the obvious purpose of [the predecessor of § 2036(a)] to prevent transfers akin to testamentary dispositions from escaping taxation. In this respect the case at bar differs from the trust involved in Budlong's Estate, 7 T.C. 758, where the court held that [the predecessor of § 2036(a)(2)] was applicable to the unlimited power of the decedent, as sole trustee, to distribute the trust income or to accumulate and add it to the principal. In the Jennings trusts the rights of the beneficiaries were no more affected by the settlor's death in October 1936 than they would have been had he resigned as a trustee in January 1936. In either event the contingent power of the trustees to invade corpus or to disburse the net income of 1936 or any subsequent year would remain the same as before his death or resignation. Only when the interest of some beneficiary is enlarged or matured by the decedent's death, is [the predecessor of § 2036(a)(2)] applicable, in our opinion. In the case at bar the decedent's death had no such effect.

The judgment is reversed and the cause remanded with directions to enter judgment for the plaintiffs.

ILLUSTRATIVE MATERIAL

A. POWERS RETAINED BY GRANTOR–TRUSTEE

In cases under § 2036(a)(2), wealthy individuals have on the one hand sought to avoid the estate tax by transferring property irrevocably in trust, but on the other to retain sufficient "strings" on the property to enable them to control its ultimate disposition. The history of the litigation in this area largely reflects the addition or subtraction of various kinds of "strings" by taxpayers and their advisors in attempts to keep family arrangements outside the scope of § 2036(a)(2), while allowing the grantor to retain practical control over the trust property.

1.   Discretionary Power Over Income and Principal

One of the "strings" that grantors would most like to retain is the discretionary power to accumulate or pay out the income and/or principal of the trust at such times, to such persons, and in such amounts as the grantor-trustee might determine. Where the exercise of such a power is in the discretion of the grantor-trustee, either alone or in conjunction with other persons, the courts have held § 2036(a)(2) applicable. It does not matter that the power is shared with an adverse party. Reg. § 20.2036–1(b)(3).

Courts have applied *O'Malley* to include property in the estate of the grantor-trustee in a number of situations. For example, in Estate of Bowgren v. Commissioner, 105 F.3d 1156 (7th Cir. 1997), the court applied § 2036(a)(2) to a trust in which D had retained the unrestrained right to change beneficiaries.

Section 2036(a)(2) also applies where D retained the power to distribute income currently to a sole beneficiary or instead to retain the income until the beneficiary reached age 21. In Estate of O'Connor v. Commissioner, 54 T.C. 969 (1970), the grantor-trustee retained the discretionary power to expend or accumulate the principal and income for the trust's sole beneficiary. All principal and accumulated income were payable to the beneficiary upon reaching age 21. The grantor-trustee died before the trust beneficiary reached 21. The estate argued that § 2036(a)(2) was not applicable because the trust instrument provided that no part of the principal or income of the trust could revert to the grantor, be used directly or indirectly for the grantor's benefit, or be used to satisfy his legal obligation of support. It asserted these restrictions neutralized the discretionary powers over income and principal and rendered *O'Malley* inapplicable. The court held that these provisions did not restrict the trustee's powers over income and principal and the trust assets were therefore includible in the grantor-trustee's estate under § 2036(a)(2). A similar result was reached in Estate of Skifter v. Commissioner, 56 T.C. 1190 (1971), where the grantor-trustee had the power to accumulate income until the trust beneficiaries (his grandchildren) reached age 21. Joy v. United States, 404 F.2d 419 (6th Cir. 1968), held that 80 percent of the corpus and all of the undistributed income were includible in the grantor-trustee's estate where the trust provisions required that 20 percent of trust income be added to corpus each year, but the other 80 percent could be paid out or accumulated at the trustee's discretion. In Estate of Alexander, 81 T.C. 757 (1983), the grantor-trustee had the power to accumulate the income for the beneficiary of the trust until she reached age twenty-one, after which she was to receive distributions of $5,000 every five years until she reached age sixty-six. At that time, she was to receive all the accumulated income and principal of the trust. The court held § 2036(a)(2) applicable because the power to accumulate income is sufficient to invoke that section even if the income beneficiary is entitled to the entire remainder interest in the trust.

If a discretionary power over trust income and principal is effectively released by the grantor-trustee under state law more than three years before death, then § 2036(a)(2) is not applicable. Estate of Ware v. Commissioner, 480 F.2d 444 (7th Cir. 1973). But a taxable gift would result, see p. 313.

2.   Powers Limited by Ascertainable Standard

As illustrated by Jennings v. Smith, if an "ascertainable standard" limits the grantor-trustee's discretionary power to distribute or accumulate income, the trust property will not be includible in his estate under § 2036(a)(2). A standard is "ascertainable" if it is sufficiently definite such that a court with equitable powers will compel the trustee to comply with the trust provision. The theory for noninclusion is that the ascertainable standard limits the grantor-trustee's discretion to such an extent that she does not have a right to designate possession or enjoyment. If the standard is not definite, a court of equity will not restrict the trustee's discretion with the result that inclusion in the estate is required. Considerable litigation has occurred as grantor-trustees seek to give themselves the widest possible discretionary powers but still try to fit within the ascertainable standard exception.

Ascertainable Standard Absent:

In Old Colony Trust Co. v. United States, 423 F.2d 601 (1st Cir. 1970), D was the grantor-trustee of a trust which provided that 80% of the income was payable to D's son and the balance of the income was to be added to principal. D retained the discretionary power, exercisable with other trustees to increase the income payments in excess of the 80% figure "in case of sickness or [if] desirable in view of changed circumstances." Furthermore, D, with the other trustees, had the discretionary power to cease paying any income to D's son and to add all of such accumulated income to principal if the trustees decided that this was in the son's "best interests". The court held D's powers over trust income were not limited by an ascertainable standard and hence the value of the trust property was includible in his estate:

> "Under [the distribution powers] the trustee can, expressly, prefer one beneficiary over another. Furthermore, his freedom of choice may vary greatly, depending upon the terms of the individual trust. If there is an ascertainable standard, the trustee can be compelled to follow it.[33] If there is not, even though he is a fiduciary, it is not unreasonable to say that his retention of an unmeasurable freedom of choice is equivalent to retaining some of the incidents of ownership. Hence, under the cases, if there is an ascertainable standard, the settlor-trustee's estate is not taxed; * * * Estate of Budd, 1968, 49 T.C. 468; * * * but if there is not, it is taxed. Henslee v. Union Planters Nat'l Bank & Trust Co., 1949, 335 U.S. 595, * * *.

> "The trust provision which is uniformly held to provide an ascertainable standard is one which, though variously expressed, authorizes such distributions as may be needed to continue the beneficiary's accustomed way of life. * * * On the other hand, if the trustee may go further, and has

---

33. See, e.g., Old Colony Trust Co. v. Rodd, 1970 Mass.A.S. 25, 254 N.E.2d 886, trustee of trust to provide "comfortable support and maintenance," rebuked for "parsimonious" exercise of judgment.

power to provide for the beneficiary's 'happiness,' * * * or 'pleasure,' * * *, or 'use and benefit,' * * * or 'reasonable requirement[s],' * * *, the standard is so loose that the trustee is in effect uncontrolled.

"In the case at bar the trustees could increase the life tenant's income 'in case of sickness, or [if] desirable in view of changed circumstances.' Alternatively, they could reduce it 'for his best interests.' 'Sickness' presents no problem. Conceivably, providing for 'changed circumstances' is roughly equivalent to maintaining the son's present standard of living. * * * The unavoidable stumbling block is the trustees' right to accumulate income and add it to capital (which the son would never receive) when it is to the 'best interests' of the son to do so. Additional payments to a beneficiary whenever in his 'best interests' might seem to be too broad a standard in any event. * * * [S]ee Estate of Yawkey, 1949, 12 T.C. 1164, where the court said, at p. 1170,

> 'We can not regard the language involved ["best interest"] as limiting the usual scope of a trustee's discretion. It must always be anticipated that trustees will act for the best interests of a trust beneficiary, and an exhortation to act "in the interests and for the welfare" of the beneficiary does not establish an external standard.'

"Power, however, to decrease or cut off a beneficiary's income when in his 'best interests,' is even more troublesome. When the beneficiary is the son, and the trustee the father, a particular purpose comes to mind, parental control through holding the purse strings. The father decides what conduct is to the 'best interests' of the son, and if the son does not agree, he loses his allowance. Such a power has the plain indicia of ownership control. The alternative, that the son, because of other means, might not need this income, and would prefer to have it accumulate for his widow and children after his death is no better. If the trustee has power to confer 'happiness' on the son by generosity to someone else, this seems clearly an unascertainable standard. Cf. Merchants Nat'l Bank v. Com'r of Internal Revenue, 320 U.S. at 261–263, 64 S.Ct. 108.

"The case of Hays' Estate v. Com'r of Internal Revenue, 5 Cir., 1950, 181 F.2d 169, is contrary to our decision. The opinion is unsupported by either reasoning or authority, and we will not follow it. With the present settlor-trustee free to determine the standard himself, a finding of ownership control was warranted. To put it another way, the cost of holding onto the strings may prove to be a rope burn. State Street Bank & Trust Co. v. United States, 313 F.2d 29 (1st Cir. 1963)." (603–605).

In Estate of Cutter v. Commissioner, 62 T.C. 351 (1974), D was the grantor-trustee of eight trusts for the benefit of his children. Although the trust provided that D was required to accumulate income until each child reached a designated age, at which time the trust was to terminate, D had the discretionary power to distribute income "necessary for the benefit of" a beneficiary and to distribute principal for the "support and education" of a beneficiary. The court held that D's power to distribute principal was limited by an ascertainable standard, but the power over income was not so limited and the trust property was includible in D's estate. See also Estate of Yawkey v. Commissioner, 12 T.C. 1164 (1949) (no ascertainable standard where the grantor-trustee had the power to invade corpus for the "best interests" of the beneficiary);

Leopold v. United States, 510 F.2d 617 (9th Cir. 1975) (where the trustees, including the grantor-trustee, had the power to distribute trust principal as they deemed "necessary and proper", the value of the corpus of each of two trusts was includible in the estate of the grantor, reduced, however, by the present value of the income that the trustees were to pay to the beneficiaries for their "support, education, maintenance and general welfare"; an ascertainable standard limited the trustees' power over the income).

Ascertainable Standard Present:

The court in Estate of Budd v. Commissioner, 49 T.C. 468 (1968), held the power of the grantor-trustee to invade corpus for the "care, support and medical attention" and "for the support, education and maintenance" of the trust beneficiaries was limited by an ascertainable standard. In Estate of Ford v. Commissioner, 53 T.C. 114 (1969) the court found an ascertainable standard where the grantor-trustee had the power to invade corpus for sickness and the "support, maintenance, education, welfare and happiness" of the beneficiary. The court held that the term "happiness" was limited by the general direction in the trust instrument to consider the "need" of the beneficiary. See also Estate of Wier v. Commissioner, 17 T.C. 409 (1951) (ascertainable standard existed where income and corpus were payable at the discretion of the grantor-trustee for the "support, maintenance and education" of the grantor-trustee's daughter in such amounts as the trustees in their sole discretion considered to be for her "interest and advantage").

3. Retention of Broad Administrative Powers

Several cases have involved the question whether the retention by the grantor-trustee of broad powers over the administration of the trust, such as the power to manage trust investments, requires inclusion of the trust property in the estate of the grantor-trustee under § 2036(a)(2). The Government has generally been unsuccessful in contending that the retention of broad administrative powers over trust property is sufficient to invoke § 2036(a)(2). The courts have reasoned that administrative powers are exercisable as fiduciaries and trustees are subject to control by the courts. In Old Colony Trust Co. v. United States, 423 F.2d 601 (1st Cir. 1970), the grantor-trustee had broad administrative powers over trust investments, the power to allocate receipts and expenditures between income and principal, and the power to do "all things in relation to the Trust Fund which the Donor could do if living and this Trust had not been executed." The court held that § 2036(a)(2) did not require inclusion of the trust property in the estate of the grantor-trustee solely because of the retention of these broad administrative powers:[34]

> "It is common ground that a settlor will not find the corpus of the trust included in his estate merely because he named himself a trustee. Jennings v. Smith, 2 Cir., 1947, 161 F.2d 74. He must have reserved a power to himself that is inconsistent with the full termination of ownership. The government's brief defines this as 'sufficient dominion and

34. This holding overruled the court's earlier decision in State Street Trust Co. v. United States, 263 F.2d 635 (1st Cir. 1959), in which it had held that the aggregation of broad administrative powers could justify inclusion of the trust property in the estate of the grantor-trustee.

control until his death.' Trustee powers given for the administration or management of the trust must be equitably exercised, however, for the benefit of the trust as a whole. * * * [W]e find it difficult to see how a power can be subject to control by the probate court, and exercisable only in what the trustee fairly concludes is in the interests of the trust and its beneficiaries as a whole, and at the same time be an ownership power.

"The government's position, to be sound, must be that the trustee's powers are beyond the court's control. Under Massachusetts law, however, no amount of administrative discretion prevents judicial supervision of the trustee. * * *

"We do not believe that trustee powers are to be more broadly construed for tax purposes than the probate court would construe them for administrative purposes. More basically, we agree with Judge Magruder's observation that nothing is 'gained by lumping them together.' State Street Trust Co. v. United States, * * *, 263 F.2d at 642. We hold that no aggregation of purely administrative powers can meet the government's amorphous test of 'sufficient dominion and control' so as to be equated with ownership." (602–603).

Similarly, in Estate of Budd v. Commissioner, 49 T.C. 468 (1968), administrative powers to retain or invest in property that did not constitute a proper trust investment under state law, to determine what is income and what is principal, and to permit the grantor to buy or sell from the trust, did not require inclusion of the trust property in the grantor-trustee's estate.

B. RETENTION OF CONTROLS OVER TRUST BY GRANTOR WHO IS NOT A TRUSTEE

1. *Power in Grantor to Remove Trustee and Appoint Self as Trustee*

If the grantor of a trust is not a trustee, but retains the power to remove the trustee and appoint himself as a successor trustee, the above rules are applied as if the grantor were a trustee. See Rev. Rul. 73–21, 1973–1 C.B. 405 (D reserved the power to appoint a successor trustee upon the death, resignation, or inability of the original trustee to serve; Reg. § 20.2036–1(b)(3) required inclusion of the trust in the grantor's estate even though the grantor could only appoint himself trustee upon the happening of a contingency beyond his control); Estate of Farrel v. United States, 553 F.2d 637 (Ct.Cl.1977) (same result; Reg. § 20.2036–1(b)(3) held valid); Estate of Gilchrist v. Commissioner, 630 F.2d 340 (5th Cir. 1980) (same result even though grantor of trust was adjudicated an incompetent and remained so until death). Durst v. United States, 559 F.2d 910 (3d Cir. 1977) (although the power of the grantor of a trust to appoint himself as trustee was not specifically withheld in the trust instrument, under applicable local law the trust instrument as a whole evidenced an intent on the part of the grantor to withhold that power and hence § 2036(a)(2) was not applicable); Rev. Rul. 73–142, 1973–1 C.B. 405 (court decree, binding on D, that D was not empowered under a trust created by him to appoint himself as a successor trustee precluded the application of § 2036(a)(2)).

In Rev. Rul. 79–353, 1979–2 C.B. 325, the IRS initially extended the above principles to hold § 2036(a)(2) applicable where D could remove the original corporate trustee without cause and substitute another corporate trustee, even though the grantor could not appoint himself as a successor trustee. The Ruling concluded that the power to remove a trustee was equivalent to the retention of the trustee's powers. However, in Estate of Wall v. Commissioner, 101 T.C. 300 (1993), the Tax Court explicitly rejected the holding of Rev. Rul. 79–353 and assessed attorney fees against the IRS.[35] The IRS subsequently revoked Rev. Rul. 79–353 and issued Rev. Rul. 95–58, 1995–2 C.B. 191, holding that a grantor has not retained trustee powers where the grantor has the power to remove a trustee and appoint a successor trustee that is not related or subordinate to the grantor within the meaning of § 672(c). Note that a similar power was involved in *Byrum*, although there was little discussion of the effect of that power in the Supreme Court or lower court opinions.

2. *Discretionary Power to Direct Distribution of Income and Principal*

In Estate of Thomson v. Commissioner, 495 F.2d 246 (2d Cir. 1974), D in 1928 created a trust for the benefit of his children with a bank as trustee. The trust provided for mandatory accumulation of income, but D, who was not a trustee, reserved the power to direct the trustee to distribute income to a beneficiary. The power was never exercised and all accumulated income was added to principal. The court held that post–1931 accumulations of income constituted "transfers" under *O'Malley*, and hence were includible in D's estate under § 2036(a)(2). Section 2036(c) precluded the application of § 2036(a)(2) to the 1928 transfer. A similar result was reached in Estate of Craft v. Commissioner, 68 T.C. 249 (1977), aff'd per curiam, 608 F.2d 240 (5th Cir. 1979).

Compare Rev. Rul. 80–255, 1980–2 C.B. 272, where a parent created a trust which provided that the income was payable in equal shares to the children and, upon termination, the trust would be divided equally among the children. The trust instrument also provided that after-born or adopted children were to be treated as additional beneficiaries of the trust. The Ruling held that the value of the trust was not included in the parent's estate since the parent's act of having or adopting additional children represented an act of "independent significance" and not a power to change beneficial interests under the terms of the trust itself.

3. *Power to Direct and Substitute Trust Investments*

D's retention of the power to direct trust investments after transferring assets in trust and designating another person as trustee does not trigger application of § 2036. See e.g. United States v. Byrum, p. 237; Estate of King v. Commissioner, 37 T.C. 973 (1962) (D created a trust for each of his three children, with a bank as sole trustee; D's retention of power to direct investment of trust assets did not trigger application of § 2036 (a) (2) because D's exercise of the power would be subject to the control of a court of equity).

Similarly, in Rev. Rul. 2008–22, 2008–16 I.R.B. 796 (2008), the IRS ruled that D's retained power to substitute trust property does not trigger application of § 2036 where D transferred property in trust, naming a third party as trustee, and retained the right to substitute the trust property with property of equal value. The Ruling reasoned that the trustee had a fiduciary obligation

---

35. The fees were assessed in Estate of Wall v. Commissioner, 102 T.C. 391 (1994).

(under local law or the trust instrument) to ensure that the property substituted by D was equal in value to the original property and did not shift benefits among the trust beneficiaries.

C.   CONTINGENT POWERS

Section 2036(a)(2) applies even if the transferor's right to designate who shall possess or enjoy the property is subject to a contingency beyond her control which did not occur prior to her death. Reg. § 20.2036–1(b)(3). This approach is consistent with the treatment of secondary life estates under 2036(a)(1) discussed at p. 211. D, who retains a secondary life estate and dies before the first life tenant, must include in his gross estate under § 2036(a)(1) the value of the property (reduced by the value of the first life estate) even though the contingency necessary to D's enjoyment—the death of the first life tenant—has not occurred prior to his death.

D.   OTHER SITUATIONS

1.   *Control Over Remainder Interests*

As discussed at p. 246, the transferor's ability to delay payment of income to a sole beneficiary will cause inclusion under § 2036(a)(2). Suppose that D transfers property to trust, income to her son for life, but she retains the power in her discretion to terminate the trust and pay the corpus to her son. Will D's ability to accelerate payment of the corpus be treated the same as the ability to delay payment of income? Note that accelerating payment of the corpus has no effect on son's income interest. When son receives the corpus, he will still be receiving all income from the corpus. Reg. § 20.2036–1(b)(3) states that the scope of § 2036(a)(2) "does not include a power over the transferred property itself which does not affect the enjoyment of the income received or earned during the decedent's life." Based on this regulation, Rev. Rul. 70–513, 1970–2 C.B. 194 held on the above facts that § 2036(a)(2) did not apply to D's power to terminate the trust and vest the corpus in her son. However, as discussed at p. 257, the Ruling also held that § 2038 does apply to require inclusion of the remainder interest in the transferor's gross estate.

2.   *President of Charitable Corporation*

Section 2036 by its terms applies to transfers "by trust or otherwise". In Rev. Rul. 72–552, 1972–2 C.B. 525, D transferred property to a charitable corporation of which he was one of the organizing members, a director, and its president. The board of directors authorized D as president to determine who would receive charitable distributions from the corporation. The Ruling held that the property transferred to the corporation was includible in D's estate under § 2036(a)(2) since D's position as a member of the corporation gave him the power to designate the persons who would possess or enjoy the property. Although D's gross estate would be entitled to an offsetting charitable deduction (see Chapter 29), inclusion in the gross estate could preclude benefits that depend upon the relative size of the gross estate. For example, the 10 year period for paying estate taxes is available in § 6166 (see p. 782) if the value of D's interest in a closely held business exceeds 35% of her adjusted gross estate. Similarly special valuation rules in § 2032A for real property used by D in a trade or business apply only if such property comprises at least 25% of the adjusted value of his gross estate (see p. 786).

3. *Employee Benefit Plan*

Kramer v. United States, 406 F.2d 1363 (Ct.Cl. 1969), involved the applicability of § 2036(a)(2) to payments made under an employee benefit plan. D had been the president and a director of a corporation owned by his family but in which he owned no stock. In 1956 he entered into a contract with the corporation to serve as general manager for a salary of $12,000 per year. The contract provided that in the event of illness or other inability to serve as general manager, D would remain as a consultant for life at $12,000 per year. In the event of death, D's wife would be paid $150 per month for her life. The board of directors that approved the contract was composed of D, his son, and his son-in-law. The court assumed that there was a present transfer by virtue of D's promise of future employment in consideration for the post-death benefits (see discussion of transfers at p. 209), but D had no right to change the beneficial enjoyment or otherwise designate beneficiaries under the contract. The court held that § 2036(a)(2) was inapplicable, rejecting the IRS argument that D's position with the corporation in effect gave him the power to renegotiate the agreement and thus change the beneficial enjoyment under the annuity contract. (The court also rejected § 2039 as a basis for inclusion. See p. 324).

CHAPTER 16

TRANSFERS WITH RETAINED POWERS TO ALTER, AMEND, REVOKE, OR TERMINATE: § 2038

Internal Revenue Code: § 2038

Regulations: § 20.2038–1(a), (b)

Section 2038(a)(1) includes in the gross estate the value of all property transferred by the decedent ("D") where the enjoyment of the property was subject at the date of death to any change through D's exercise of a power to "alter, amend, revoke, or terminate." The power to change the enjoyment of property through the exercise of a power specified in § 2038(a)(1) is very similar to a power under § 2036(a)(2) to designate the persons who shall possess or enjoy the property or the income therefrom. Many of the cases considered in the following materials were also discussed in connection with § 2036(a)(2). Usually, the courts reach the same conclusion with respect to includibility under both sections. Nonetheless, it is useful to consider the issues raised by each section separately because the sections are neither coextensive nor mutually exclusive. The differences between § 2038(a)(1) and § 2036(a)(2) are summarized at p. 266.

The major exception to § 2038 is transfers for "adequate and full consideration" which is discussed in Chapter 18.

Lober v. United States

346 U.S. 335 (1953).

■ MR. JUSTICE BLACK delivered the opinion of the Court.

This is an action for an estate tax refund brought by the executors of the estate of Morris Lober. In 1924 he signed an instrument conveying to himself as trustee money and stocks for the benefit of his young son. In 1929 he executed two other instruments, one for the benefit of a daughter, the other for a second son. The terms of these three instruments were the same. Lober was to handle the funds, invest and reinvest them as he deemed proper. He could accumulate and reinvest the income with the same freedom until his children reached twenty-one years of age. When twenty-one they were to be paid the accumulated income. Lober could hold the principal of each trust until the beneficiary reached twenty-five. In case he died his wife was to be trustee with the same broad powers Lober had conveyed to himself. The trusts were declared to be irrevocable, and as the case reaches us we may assume that the trust instruments gave Lober's children a "vested interest" under state law, so that if they had died after creation of the trusts their interests would have passed to their estates. A crucial term of the trust instruments was that Lober could at any time he saw fit turn all or any part of the principal of the trusts over to his children. Thus he could at will reduce the principal or pay it all to the beneficiaries, thereby terminating any trusteeship over it.

Lober died in 1942. By that time the trust property was valued at more than $125,000. The Internal Revenue Commissioner treated this as Lober's property and included it in his gross estate. That inclusion brought this lawsuit. The Commissioner relied on [the predecessor of § 2038(a)(2)]. That section, so far as material here, required inclusion in a decedent's gross estate of the value of all property that the decedent had previously transferred by trust "where the enjoyment thereof was subject at the date of his death to any change through the exercise of a power * * * to alter, amend, or revoke. * * * "In Commissioner v. Holmes, 326 U.S. 480, we held that power to terminate was the equivalent of power to "alter, amend, or revoke" it, and we approved taxation of the Holmes estate on that basis. Relying on the Holmes case, the Court of Claims upheld inclusion of these trust properties in Lober's estate. 108 F. Supp. 731. This was done despite the assumption that the trust conveyances gave the Lober children an indefeasible "vested interest" in the properties conveyed. The Fifth Circuit Court of Appeals had reached a contrary result where the circumstances were substantially the same, in Hayes' Estate v. Commissioner, 5 Cir., 181 F.2d 169, 172–174 [1950]. Because of this conflict, we granted certiorari. 345 U.S. 969.

Petitioners stress a factual difference between this and the Holmes case. The Holmes trust instrument provided that if a beneficiary died before expiration of the trust his children succeeded to his interest, but if he died without children, his interest would pass to his brothers or their children. Thus the trustee had power to eliminate a contingency that might have prevented passage of a beneficiary's interest to his heirs. Here we assume that upon death of the Lober beneficiaries their part in the trust estate would, under New York law, pass to their heirs. But we cannot agree that this difference should change the Holmes result.

We pointed out in the Holmes case that [the predecessor of § 2038(a)(2)] was more concerned with "present economic benefit" than with "technical vesting of title or estates." And the Lober beneficiaries, like the Holmes beneficiaries, were granted no "present right to immediate enjoyment of either income or principal." The trust instrument here gave none of Lober's children full "enjoyment" of the trust property, whether it "vested" in them or not. To get this full enjoyment they had to wait until they reached the age of twenty-five unless their father sooner gave them the money and stocks by terminating the trust under the power of change he kept to the very date of his death. This father could have given property to his children without reserving in himself any power to change the terms as to the date his gift would be wholly effective, but he did not. What we said in the Holmes case fits this situation too: "A donor who keeps so strong a hold over the actual and immediate enjoyment of what he puts beyond his own power to retake has not divested himself of that degree of control which [the predecessor of § 2038(a)(2)] requires in order to avoid the tax." Commissioner v. Holmes, supra, 326 U.S. at p. 487.

Affirmed.

■ MR. JUSTICE DOUGLAS and MR. JUSTICE JACKSON, dissent.

ILLUSTRATIVE MATERIAL

A. PRIOR CASE LAW

Lober refers to Commissioner v. Estate of Holmes, 326 U.S. 480 (1946). There, D created three trusts, income payable to each of his three sons respectively, each son to receive the corpus at the end of fifteen years. D, as trustee, had the right to withhold and accumulate income and invade the principal for the benefit of the beneficiaries. He also had the right to terminate the trust and distribute the entire corpus to the beneficiaries. Upon the death of any son his interest was to pass to his issue, or if none, to his surviving brothers. The Court held that D's powers caused the full value of the trust property to be includible in his estate.

B. POWERS INCLUDED UNDER § 2038

1. *Discretionary Power to Distribute Income and Principal*

As *Lober* indicates, the grantor's retention of the unrestricted power to distribute trust principal to the beneficiaries is equivalent to the retention of a power to terminate the trust under § 2038. In Estate of Varian v. Commissioner, 47 T.C. 34 (1966), aff'd per curiam, 396 F.2d 753 (9th Cir. 1968), a husband and wife created trusts for the benefit of their three children, naming themselves as trustees. Each trust was to terminate as the beneficiary reached age 21, but the trustees had discretionary power to pay out income and principal to a beneficiary before age 21. If a beneficiary died before attaining age 21, the trust principal would pass to the beneficiary's estate or pursuant to the beneficiary's exercise of a general power of appointment. Following *Lober*, the court held that § 2038 required the trusts to be included in the husband's estate where he died before any of the children reached age 21. That the husband's other financial resources were sufficient to enable him to provide for the children, thus rendering it unlikely that the retained power would be exercised, was irrelevant.

Rev. Rul. 70–513, 1970–2 C.B. 194, involved a trust in which the income was payable to D's son for life. The trustees, none of whom was D, had discretionary power to terminate the trust and to pay over the trust corpus to D's son. However, this power could only be exercised during D's life with his written consent. The Ruling held that § 2038 applied even though D only held a veto power rather than a power to initiate termination of the trust.

2. *Powers Limited by Ascertainable Standard*

As in the case of § 2036(a)(2) (see p. 248), if D's power to invade corpus is limited by an ascertainable standard (i.e., a standard which is sufficiently definite such that a court in equity will enforce it), § 2038 does not apply. The theory of this exception in § 2038, as in § 2036, is that D does not have any "power" with an ascertainable standard, but only an obligation to carry out the terms of the transfer. Litigation under § 2038 has centered, therefore, on whether D's ability to "alter, amend, revoke, or terminate" is limited by an ascertainable standard.

Ascertainable Standard Absent:

The following decisions found no ascertainable standard because the standard lacked definiteness. See, e.g., Old Colony Trust Co. v. United States, 423 F.2d 601 (1st Cir. 1970), p. 248 (an ascertainable standard was not present for purposes of § 2038); Leopold v. United States, 510 F.2d 617 (9th Cir. 1975) (grantor-trustee had power to distribute income and principal for his daughter's "benefit" until she reached age 21, at which time the trust terminated; the term "benefit" was too indefinite); Rev. Rul. 73–143, 1973–1 C.B. 407 (grantor-trustee's retained power to invade corpus for the "special need" of his son was too indefinite); Estate of Bell v. Commissioner, 66 T.C. 729 (1976) (power in grantor-trustee to invade principal to provide a beneficiary-daughter with funds "for a home, business, or any other purpose believed by the trustees to be for her benefit" was too broad).

Ascertainable Standard Present:

Jennings v. Smith, 161 F.2d 74 (2d Cir. 1947), p. 242, is the leading case establishing the proposition that the retention of a power subject to an ascertainable standard is not within the scope of § 2038. See also, e.g., Commissioner v. Estate of Wilson, 187 F.2d 145 (3d Cir. 1951) (power to invade corpus "in case of need for educational purposes or because of illness or for any other good reason" was sufficiently definite); Estate of Wier v. Commissioner, 17 T.C. 409 (1951) (income and corpus payable at the discretion of the grantor-trustee for the "support, maintenance and education" of the grantor-trustee's daughter in such sums as the trustees in their sole discretion considered to her "interest and advantage" qualified as sufficiently definite); Estate of Budd v. Commissioner, 49 T.C. 468 (1968) (power in grantor-trustee to invade corpus in the event of "sickness, accident, misfortune or other emergency" satisfied definiteness requirement); Estate of Pardee v. Commissioner, 49 T.C. 140 (1967) (power in grantor-trustee to invade principal for the "education, maintenance, medical expenses, or other needs of the Beneficiaries occasioned by emergency" qualified).

3.   Power in Grantor to Remove Trustee and Appoint Self as Trustee

Under Reg. § 20.2038–1(a)(3), if D has the unrestricted power to remove or discharge a trustee and appoint herself trustee, she is considered as having the powers of the original trustee. Thus, if the powers of the original trustee are not limited by an ascertainable standard, the power to remove the original trustee and appoint herself as trustee requires the inclusion of the property in D's gross estate under § 2038. Conversely, if the power of the original trustee is limited by an ascertainable standard, the property is not included merely because D might have appointed herself as successor trustee.

In Mathey v. United States, 491 F.2d 481 (3d Cir. 1974), D created thirteen trusts for the benefit of her grandchildren, naming a bank as trustee. She had the power to change the trustee and the trust instrument did not preclude her from appointing herself as successor trustee. Since the original trustee had the power to pay out income and corpus before the final date of distribution of the trust estate, § 2038 was held applicable to require inclusion of the value of all the trusts in D's estate. The court rejected as irrelevant the argument that D did not intend to appoint herself as trustee. The estate could not establish that a state court would have precluded D from appointing herself as successor trustee. To the same effect is Estate of Edmonds v. Commissioner, 72 T.C. 970 (1979). See p. 251, for a discussion of similar issues under § 2036(a)(2).

In United States v. Winchell, 289 F.2d 212 (9th Cir. 1961), D had the power to appoint a successor trustee, including herself, if the original trustee resigned. The court held that § 2038 did not apply because D did not have any power to remove the original trustee.

As discussed at p. 252, Rev. Rul. 95–58, 1995–2 C.B. 191, holds that a grantor has not retained powers over trust corpus or income because she has the power to remove a trustee and appoint a successor trustee that is not related or subordinate to her within the meaning of § 672(c).

4. Possession of Broad Administrative Powers

In several cases, the IRS has asserted that D's possession of broad administrative powers to control the composition of trust investments, to allocate receipts and expenditures between income and principal, to invest in "non-legals" (investments not authorized for trustees by state law), and the like require inclusion of the trust property in D's estate under § 2038. Courts rejecting that argument under § 2036(a)(2) also rejected the argument under § 2038 because the administrative powers are subject to fiduciary standards and to review by courts. See e.g., Old Colony Trust Co. v. United States, p. 268.

In United States v. Powell, 307 F.2d 821 (10th Cir. 1962), the Commissioner asserted that the power in a grantor-trustee to invest in life insurance or annuities gave him the power either to deprive the income beneficiaries of income (by investing in life insurance) or to deprive the remaindermen of benefits (by investing in annuities). The court held that this power did not require inclusion of the trust property under § 2038 since it had to be exercised in a fiduciary capacity for the benefit of both income beneficiaries and remaindermen. See also Estate of Graves v. Commissioner, 92 T.C. 1294 (1989) (D's powers to appoint a successor trustee, approve the trustee's designation of trust receipts as principal or income, and to approve trust investments were not governed by § 2038); Estate of Jordahl v. Commissioner, 65 T.C. 92 (1975) (power of grantor to substitute property for that initially transferred in trust did not constitute a power to alter, amend, or revoke under § 2038(a)(2)). If a retained power to vote controlled corporation stock were involved in the above cases, § 2036(b) would require inclusion of the stock in the grantor's gross estate.

The discussion, at p. 246, concerning the treatment under § 2036(a)(2) of retained powers by grantors and by grantor-trustees is equally applicable to § 2038.

5. *Uniform Gifts to Minors Act and Uniform Transfers to Minors Act*

Section 2038, like § 2036 (see p. 222), applies where D transfers property to herself as custodian under the Uniform Gifts to Minors Act ("UGMA") for the benefit of minor children. In Rev. Rul. 57–366, 1957–2 C.B. 618, the applicable version of UGMA authorized the custodian to apply, in her sole discretion, as much of the income and principal as she deemed advisable for the support, maintenance, general use and benefit of the minor, without regard to another's duty of support or the availability of other funds for such purposes. Unused principal and income were to be paid to the minor upon attaining age 21 or to the minor's estate if death occurred prior to age 21. The ruling held, relying on *Holmes* and *Lober*, that the entire amount of the custodial property was includible in the estate of a donor-custodian. This result has been uniformly reached by the courts under the various state custodial acts. See, e.g., Estate of Prudowsky v. Commissioner, 55 T.C. 890 (1971), aff'd per curiam, 465 F.2d 62 (7th Cir. 1972). The analysis should be the same for the Uniform Transfers to Minors Act.

6. *Employee Death Benefits*

In Kramer v. United States, 406 F.2d 1363 (Ct.Cl. 1969), discussed at p. 254, D was the general manager of a family corporation, but owned no stock in the corporation himself. He signed an employment contract which provided for a death benefit payable to his wife for life if he died while in the employ of the corporation. The contract did not permit D to change beneficiaries. The court held that § 2038 was not applicable, rejecting the Government's argument that D could have bargained for a change in beneficiaries or payment amounts because of his position in the company. The court found that the possibility of such bargaining was too speculative to constitute a power.

Estate of Tully v. United States, 528 F.2d 1401 (Ct.Cl. 1976) involved a similar situation. There, death benefits were paid to D's widow pursuant to a contract entered into between D and a corporation. The contract did not permit D to change the beneficiary. The court rejected the Government's argument that D's 50% stock ownership of the corporation "gave him unfettered power to change the death benefit plan to suit his own tastes." D's attempt to effect such a change could have been blocked by the other 50% shareholder and therefore he did not possess a § 2038(a)(1) power, which "must be demonstrable, real, apparent and evident, not speculative." The fact that D might have altered the plan by persuading the other 50% shareholder to agree to a change also did not constitute a § 2038 power, since that section does not encompass "powers of persuasion." Moreover, although the amount of the widow's death benefit was determined by D's compensation from the corporation, D's ability to affect the amount of the death benefit by accepting lesser compensation or terminating his employment was a "remote possibility" which did not rise to the level of a § 2038 power. Finally, D's ability to revoke or terminate the transfer to his wife by divorcing her was not a § 2038 power. The court also rejected the Government's argument that the value of the death benefits were includible in D's estate under § 2033, and commented about the relationship between § 2038 and § 2033:

> "Within this context, the two estate tax sections involved in the instant case, 2038(a)(1) and 2033, both impose a tax on property trans-

ferred at death. However, they are directed at two different situations. Section 2038(a)(1) is specific in its terms. It taxes property which an individual has given away while retaining enough 'strings' to change or revoke the gift. Section 2033 is more general in its approach, and taxes property which has never really been given away at all.

"Certain of defendant's arguments misconstrue this basic difference between § 2038(a)(1) and § 2033. By suggesting that the same 'controls' over property which might represent a § 2038(a)(1) 'power' can also be viewed as a § 2033 'interest,' the government attempts to turn § 2033 into an estate tax 'catch all.' This was not the intent of Congress in enacting § 2033. Congress has provided a 'catch all' in the income tax statutes. It has not done so in the estate tax area. * * * Therefore, defendant's efforts to treat the two sections as virtually identical by the 'catch all' method are misplaced.

"In accordance with this analysis, our inquiry takes two avenues. First, did Tully transfer the death benefits but keep a power to change or revoke them until the time of his death? If so, § 2038(a)(1) applies. Second, did Tully have an 'interest' in the benefits at his death? If he had an 'interest,' § 2033 applies.

"We find that Tully effectively transferred his interests in the death benefits before his death, determine that he did not keep any significant powers to 'alter, amend, revoke or terminate' the transfer and conclude that he had no 'interest' in the benefits at the time of his death. We, therefore, hold that the death benefits at issue here were not includible in Tully's gross estate. * * *

"Defendant would use § 2033 as a 'catch all.' The simple answer to this is that § 2033 is not a 'catch all,' but applies to situations where decedent kept so much control over an item of property that in substance he still owns the property. 'Interest' as used in § 2033 connotes a stronger control than 'power' as used in § 2038(a)(1). If controls over property cannot rise to the dignity of § 2038(a)(1) 'powers' they equally cannot create § 2033 'interests'. In the instant case, having failed to establish that corporate stock ownership, 'pegging' the benefits to Tully's salary and naming the 'widow' as beneficiary created § 2038(a)(1) 'powers,' defendant equally fails to demonstrate that the same facts create § 2033 'interests.'" (1403, 1406).

If D possessed the power to change the beneficiary of a death benefit, § 2038(a)(1) requires its inclusion. In Rev. Rul. 76–304, 1976–2 C.B. 269, the IRS reiterated its view that the "transfer" requirement of § 2038 is satisfied where an employee agrees to perform services in exchange for the employer's agreement to pay a death benefit to the employee's designated beneficiary. In addition, the Ruling stated that the power in the employee to change the beneficiary constituted a power to "alter," thus requiring inclusion of the amount of the decedent's benefit in the employee's estate under § 2038(a)(1). Similarly, where an employee entered into an employment contract which provided for death benefits payable to the employee's children and the contract specifically provided that the agreement could be modified by the "mutual consent" of the employee and employer, the value of the death benefit was includible in the employee's estate under § 2038. Estate of Siegel v. Commissioner, 74 T.C. 613 (1980). The Tax Court distinguished the decisions in *Tully* and *Kramer* on the basis that the contracts in those cases contained no express provision reserving the power to modify the rights of the beneficiaries.

See also the cases under § 2037 and § 2039, discussed at p. 269 and p. 320, respectively.

7. *Powers of Attorney*

Disputes often arise about the effects of gifts made on behalf of D by her representative pursuant to a power of attorney granted by D. If such gifts are voidable under state law because the representative lacked authority to make gifts, § 2038 will include them in D's gross estate since D possessed the power to revoke the gift. See e.g. Estate of Swanson v. United States, 46 Fed. Cl. 388 (2000), aff'd in unpublished opinion, 2001–1 USTC ¶ 60,408 (Fed. Cir. 2001)

8. *Contingent Powers and Powers Exercisable Only By Will*

As a condition precedent to taxability under § 2038(a)(1) or (2), the power must exist at the date of D's death. Section 2038(b) provides that this requirement is satisfied even though the exercise of the power is subject to a precedent giving of notice or the transfer can take effect only upon the expiration of a stated period after the exercise of the power. It is of no consequence that such notice had not been given, or that the power had not been exercised, at the time of death.

A negative inference from the language of § 2038(b) would appear to be that the existence of more remotely contingent powers (i.e., those whose very exercise depend upon the happening of an event which is beyond D's control) at the time of D's death would not be sufficient to bring the trust corpus within his taxable estate. Reg. § 20.2038–1(b) adopts this view and provides that § 2038 is not applicable where the exercise of the power is subject to a contingency which did not occur before D's death and is beyond D's control, such as the death of another person during D's life.

This approach differs from that of § 2036(a)(2). Reg. § 20.2036–1(b)(3) states that for § 2036 it is immaterial whether the exercise of the power was subject to a contingency beyond D's control. The court in Estate of Farrel v. United States, 553 F.2d 637 (Ct.Cl. 1977), discussed at p. 265, justified the different approaches under § 2036(a)(2) and § 2038(a) as follows:

> "The two separate provisions appear to diverge sharply in their perspective—the point from which the pertinent powers and rights are to be seen. Section 2038(a) looks at the problem from the decedent's death— what he can and cannot do at that specific moment. Excluded are contingent rights and powers (beyond the decedent's control) which are not exercisable at that moment because the designated contingency does not exist at that time. Section 2036(a), on the other hand, looks forward from the time the decedent made the transfer to see whether he has retained any of the specified rights 'for his life or for any period not ascertainable without reference to his death or for any period which does not in fact end before his death.' This language makes the transferor's death one pole of the specified time-span but the whole of the time-span is also significant. Because of the statute's reference to the time-span, differences of interpretation are quite conceivable. It is possible for instance, to hold the words to

mean that the retained right has to exist at all times throughout one of the periods, but it is also possible to see the language as covering contingencies which could realistically occur at some separate point or points during the designated periods—always including the moment of decedent's death. * * *

"There is nothing unreasonable about this latter construction, which accords with Congress' over-all purpose to gather into the estate tax all transfers which remain significantly incomplete—on which the transferor still holds a string—during his lifetime." (640).

Occasionally a transferor will reserve the right to change the beneficiaries of her trust but only in her will. Section 2038 applies to such testamentary powers. See Adriance v. Higgins, 113 F.2d 1013 (2d Cir. 1940).

9.   *Joint Powers*

Sections 2038(a)(1) and (2) apply to powers to "alter, amend or revoke" held by the decedent either "alone or . . . in conjunction with any other person . . ." The regulations interpret the phrase "any other person" to include powers shared jointly with one or more other persons. Reg. § 20.2038(1)(a). It is irrelevant under § 2038 that the transferor shares the power with an adverse party. Reg. § 20.2038–1(a).

Suppose that the transferor reserves the power to terminate a trust and distribute corpus to the beneficiaries only with the consent of all beneficiaries. Does § 2038 apply? In Swain v. United States, 147 F.3d 564 (7th Cir. 1998), the court held that § 2038 applies if the consent of less than all the beneficiaries is required, but reserved for future consideration whether § 2038 would apply if the consent of *all* beneficiaries is required.

Reg. § 20.2038–1(a)(2) applies to unanimous-consent situations. It provides that a § 2038 power does not exist if D's power can only be exercised with the consent of all parties having an interest (vested or contingent) in the transferred property and such power adds nothing to the rights of the parties under local law. The *Swain* court's reservation of the effect of unanimous consent may be attributable to the need to determine whether local law permitted alteration of the trust with the consent of all parties.

C.   NECESSITY OF A "TRANSFER BY DECEDENT" AND THE RESERVATION OF THE POWER IN THAT TRANSFER

1.   *"Transfer"*

The significance of the "transfer by decedent" requirement of § 2038 arose in Estate of Reed v. Commissioner, 171 F.2d 685 (8th Cir. 1948). D had claimed an absolute one-third interest in the estate of her husband under a statute which was subsequently declared unconstitutional. The other legatees claimed that she was lawfully entitled only to a life interest in one-third as provided by the husband's will. A compromise settlement was made in which D received $100,000 outright from one-third of the estate. The value of one-third of the estate in excess of $100,000 was placed in trust with D receiving the income for life plus a restricted testamentary power to change the trust's remaindermen (which she never exercised). Although the D's testamentary power to change beneficiaries qualifies as a § 2038 power, the court held that a "transfer by the decedent" had not occurred because her claim was based upon an unconstitutional statute and, therefore, she never had absolute ownership in one-third which she could transfer.

In Rev. Rul. 74–556, 1974–2 C.B. 300, a husband transferred property to himself as custodian under a Uniform Gifts to Minors Act. He became incapacitated, resigned, and his wife was appointed as successor custodian. At the time of the original transfer, she had consented to the gifts and, under § 2513, was treated as having made a gift of one-half of the property for gift tax purposes. The wife died while still a custodian. The Ruling held that § 2038 did not apply to include the custodial property in her estate. She did not make a transfer for purposes of § 2038 even though, for gift tax purposes, she was considered to be the donor of one-half of the custodial property. If the wife had been deemed to have made a transfer, then as discussed in Rev. Rul. 70–348, immediately below, § 2038 would have applied.

2. Reservation of Power

Section 2038(a)(1) requires inclusion of property subject to a power to alter, amend, revoke or terminate "... without regard to when or from what source the decedent acquired such power...."[1] This contrasts starkly with § 2036(a) which applies only to powers actually retained by the transferor. In Rev. Rul. 70–348, 1970–2 C.B. 193, D transferred property to his wife as custodian for their child under the Uniform Gift to Minors Act. After she resigned, D became the successor custodian. As successor custodian, D had the power under the Act to accumulate or distribute corpus to the child. Note that § 2036 could not apply because D had not retained the power at the time of the transfer. The Ruling held that § 2038 did apply and in sweeping language stated: " * * * it is not necessary that the power to alter, amend, revoke, or terminate the enjoyment of the beneficial interests be retained by the donor at the time of the transfer. The mere possession thereof by the donor at the time of death is the factor that results in the inclusion of the value of the transferred property in his gross estate."

In Rev. Rul. 70–348, D had initially created the power that returned to him. The courts have not applied § 2038, however, where the transferor did not create the powers that she subsequently acquires. In Estate of Skifter v. Commissioner, 468 F.2d 699 (2d Cir. 1972), D transferred all the incidents of ownership in nine insurance policies on his life to his wife. The wife then died and left the policies in trust for the benefit of their daughter for life and then to certain remaindermen. D was named as trustee and, under the trust, had the power to terminate the trust by distributing all the property to the income beneficiary. The Commissioner included the value of the life insurance policies in D's estate on the ground that he possessed the incidents of ownership in the policy by virtue of his powers as trustee. (Under § 2042, discussed at p. 381, possession of incidents of ownership with respect to life insurance policies requires inclusion of the policies in the estate of the deceased insured.) The court, in resolving the issue under § 2042, looked to whether the trustee's

---

1. Section 2038(a)(2), which applies to transfers on or before June 22, 1936, does not contain this language. Such transfers are governed by the rule articulated in White v. Poor, 296 U.S. 98 (1935), which held that the predecessor of § 2038 does not apply to powers acquired after the original transfer. See Reg. § 20.2038–1(c).

powers would have required inclusion of the property under § 2038. The court concluded that § 2038 would not have required inclusion because D did not create the powers. A similar result was reached in Estate of Reed v. United States, 75–1 U.S.T.C. ¶ 13,073 (M.D.Fla. 1975), where a husband transferred stock in a family corporation to his wife as custodian for their daughter under a Uniform Gifts to Minors Act. When the daughter reached age 21 the shares were issued to her outright. Nineteen months later, as she was about to be married, the daughter transferred the stock to a trust naming her parents as trustees. The husband then died and the court held that § 2038 did not apply to include the trust property in his estate:

> "Section 2038(a)(1) does not seem to be intended to reach the value of a property interest of which the decedent, prior to his death, made a complete, absolute disposition simply because, at the time of his death, by a totally unrelated and fortuitous reconveyance, he had some degree of fiduciary power or control over the interest."

D.   AMOUNT INCLUDIBLE

Recall that § 2036 includes in D's estate all the property subject to a retained power. For example, if D transfers property in trust, all income payable to A and B in such proportions as D in her discretion may determine, remainder to C, § 2036 includes the value of all the property in D's estate, although D's reserved power only affects the income interests. In contrast, § 2038 only includes in D's estate the property affected by the § 2038 power, i.e., the value of the income interests. The method for valuing income interests is discussed at p. 723.

In Rev. Rul. 70–513, 1970–2 C.B. 194, the trust income was required to be paid to the grantor's son for life. The trustees had the discretionary power with the written consent of the grantor to terminate the trust by paying over the corpus to the son. As discussed at p. 253, § 2036 does not apply to this power. Section 2038 required that only the value of the remainder interest be included in the grantor's estate because the son's life interest was not subject to change through the exercise of the grantor's retained power. After exercise of the power, the son would still be entitled to all income since he would then own the corpus. The method for valuing remainder interests is discussed at p. 723.

Frequently, § 2038 and § 2036(a)(2) will apply to the same power. For example, suppose D transfers property in trust, all income payable to A and B for 30 years in such proportions as D in her discretion may determine, remainder to C. If D dies holding this power, § 2038 requires D's estate to include only the value of A and B's life interests since her power applied only to those interests. She could not affect the remainder interest. In contrast, since D's power applied to all the income of the trust, § 2036(a)(2) would require D's gross estate to include the value of the entire trust corpus. Sections 2036 and 2038 are not mutually exclusive. Where they overlap, the courts apply the section resulting in the largest inclusion. See, e.g., Estate of Farrel v. United States, 553 F.2d 637 (Ct.Cl. 1977).

E.   OTHER ASPECTS OF § 2038

1.   *Release of § 2038 Powers*

A release of a § 2038 power precludes the inclusion of the value of property subject to the power under § 2038. Estate of Ware v. Commissioner, 480 F.2d

444 (7th Cir. 1973). However, if the release occurs within three years of the transferor's death, § 2035(a) requires such inclusion. See discussion of § 2035(a) at p. 418. Also, in many instances the release itself would effect a completed gift for gift tax purposes. See p. 313.

2.   Interaction with § 2036(c)

As discussed, at p. 211, § 2036(c) excepts from the reach of § 2036 certain transfers made prior to March 4, 1931. Section 2038 does not have a comparable exception that applies to reach transfers excluded from § 2036. The Florida National Bank of Jacksonville, Fla. v. United States, 336 F.2d 598 (3d Cir. 1964); Estate of Cohn v. United States, 371 F.2d 642 (2d Cir. 1967).

F.   SUMMARY OF DIFFERENCES BETWEEN § 2036(a)(2) AND § 2038

Although the analysis for § 2038 is similar to § 2036(a)(2), important differences exist:

1.   Section 2038 only includes in D's gross estate the specific property interest subject to D's power. For example, § 2036(a)(2) would require D's gross estate to include the entire trust corpus where D has retained the right to revoke all income interests in the trust. In contrast, § 2038 would only require inclusion of the value of the income interests. See p. 265. Where §§ 2036 and 2038 overlap, courts apply the section resulting in the largest inclusion. See p. 265.

2.   Section 2036(a)(2) only applies to powers that affect income interests. See p. 253. In contrast, § 2038 applies to powers over both income and corpus.

3.   Section 2036 requires that D have retained the power at the time of transfer. See p. 204. Section 2038 does not have such a requirement. It applies regardless of "when or from what source decedent acquired such power."

4.   Although § 2036(a)(2) does not apply to the acceleration of a remainder interest, § 2038 does. Thus, when D transfers property in trust, income to A for ten years and then remainder to A, and D possesses the power to transfer the corpus to A prior to the expiration of ten years, § 2038 applies.

5.   Unlike § 2036, § 2038 does not apply to powers subject to contingencies beyond D's control. See p. 262.

G.   THE ADEQUATE AND FULL CONSIDERATION EXCEPTION

The "adequate and full consideration" exception to § 2038 is considered in Chapter 18.

H.   ESTATE PLANNING AND THE REVOCABLE TRUST

The revocable living trust, although subject to inclusion in D's estate, has become a familiar device for estate planning. Following are some of the advantages of a trust in which the grantor retains the power to alter, amend or revoke, the full right of enjoyment of income or principal, or both:

1.   Establishment of Managerial Committee. The trustees of the revocable trust constitute an active managerial committee, established by the grantor during life to carry on the administration of his affairs after his death. Thus, an

advisory management service is created which continues uninterrupted by the grantor's death or incompetency.

2.   Avoidance of Publicity. The requirements of inventory and accounting in probate proceedings are generally avoided at the death of the grantor. Complete privacy may be maintained in connection with the value and the disposition of property. This may be an extremely important consideration in the case of a wealthy person, particularly from the standpoint of business competitors who might be able to secure valuable information unobtainable otherwise than from the probate accounting and administration.

3.   Avoidance of Attacks on Probate Proceeding. The property transferred to the revocable trust is not subject to the perils of testamentary proof as in the case of the last will and testament. Only rarely is an inter vivos transfer upset because of unsound mind or undue influence.

4.   Choice of Governing State Law. The grantor has the option of selecting the particular jurisdiction under the laws of which he wants the revocable trust to be interpreted. This may be possible to some extent in the case of estate administration, insofar as the grantor may have volition in selecting his residence and domicile. But selection of residence and domicile is fraught with pitfalls, and is not necessary in the case of a revocable trust. The grantor may be domiciled in California and prefer to have the revocable trust administered under New York law. In such case the grantor may establish such a trust with a New York trustee and provide in the trust instrument that it be interpreted and administered under the laws of the State of New York. Whether this is an advantage will depend, of course, upon the state in which the grantor is domiciled.

5.   Costs. The expenses involved in establishing a revocable trust are comparatively small. The property held in trust will not be included in the grantor's probate estate, so that the greater expense and delay which are characteristic of Probate Court procedure are entirely avoided.

6.   Alternative to Power of Attorney. The revocable trust may also present an alternative to a power of attorney or agency arrangement. An agent not knowing whether he can exercise the power of attorney because of his inability to determine whether his principal is still alive can cause difficulty. Legislation has been adopted in some states to allow the exercise of the power of attorney after the death of the principal but before notice of death has reached the agent, but not all jurisdictions have enacted such legislation. The revocable living trust arrangement, by its very nature, survives the death of the grantor. The administration of the grantor's property continues uninterrupted after the grantor's death and there is never any question whether the persons entrusted with the management have the power to act. The revocable trust is also advantageous if the grantor later suffers legal incompetency or the practical incapacity to handle his own affairs. The law is not always clear as to the powers, duties and responsibilities of an agent or attorney in such circumstances; a freely alterable and revocable living trust can be drawn and administered to provide for these situations.

7.   Increased Charitable Dispositions. Some states limit the value of property that can be given to charity by will. The revocable living trust may be used

to provide for the subsequent distribution of property to charity beyond these limits.

8. Receptacle for Non-trust Assets. The revocable trust may be made the receptacle for later additions, such as life insurance proceeds, payments under employee benefit plans, and probate assets payable to the trust under a "pour-over" provision in the grantor's will.

9. Flexibility. The revocable trust possesses the great virtue that the grantor does not lose control of her property until her death. She may fashion her trust to suit her particular needs or desires. She may retain the right to designate the persons who shall enjoy the income, the right to alter, amend, revoke or terminate, or any combination of these rights. The tax savings that some people weigh in determining whether to create a revocable or an irrevocable trust may be more than offset by the value or advantage to the grantor of retaining these rights. The widespread use of revocable living trusts, despite the estate tax treatment, is evidence of their utility.

Transfers to a revocable living trust will not be subject to gift taxes, but the corpus of the trust will be included in the grantor's gross estate at her death under §§ 2038 and 2036. Careful planning may provide that such property will be used to take advantage of the marital deduction and other possible tax saving techniques, with the result that the federal estate taxes are not significantly increased.

CHAPTER 17

TRANSFERS WITH RETAINED REVERSIONARY INTERESTS: § 2037

Internal Revenue Code: § 2037

Regulations: § 20.2037–1

INTRODUCTION

Section 2037 requires the gross estate to include the value at the date of death (or the alternate valuation date under § 2032) of any interest in property that can be obtained only by surviving the decedent ("D"). Section 2037 applies where:

(1) D has transferred property;

(2) the possession or enjoyment of the property is conditioned upon surviving her;

(3) she has retained a reversionary interest that may bring the property to her or her estate, or becomes subject to her power of disposition; and

(4) the value of such reversionary interest immediately before her death exceeds 5% of the value of the transferred property.

The second requirement can be confusing since it can be interpreted in two ways. First, it could mean that the transferee literally must live longer than D. Second, it could mean that the death of D is a precondition to possession by the transferee or the transferee's estate. The regulations adopt the latter interpretation, as illustrated by Example 3 of Reg. § 20.237–1(e). In Example 3, D irrevocably transfers property in trust, income to S, D's spouse, for life, and upon S's death, corpus to D if living, and if not, to D's child C or C's estate. If immediately prior to D's death, the value of the possibility that the property would revert to D upon S's death exceeds 5% of the value of the transferred property, § 2037 will apply. D's death is a precondition to possession by C or C's estate. Under § 2037 the value of all interests in the property that are dependent on surviving D, here the value of C's remainder interest, will be includible in D's gross estate.

SECTION A. OPERATION OF § 2037

Estate of Thacher v. Commissioner

20 T.C. 474 (1953).

Respondent has determined a deficiency in estate tax in the amount of $511,345. The issues presented are: * * *

(4) Whether respondent erred in including in the taxable value of the corpus of the wife's trust, under [the predecessor of § 2037] of the Internal Revenue Code, the value of the widow's life interest. * * *

The petitioners are the duly qualified executors of the estate of Frank W. Thacher, who died testate on September 2, 1943, a resident of New Jersey. * * *

On May 10, 1922, the decedent created five trusts by five separate deeds designating in each instance the Provident Trust Company of Philadelphia as trustee. Four of these trusts were for the benefit of decedent's four minor children. The fifth trust was for the benefit of decedent's wife, Catharine L. Thacher.

* * *

The corpus of each trust consisted of $100,000 in insurance upon the life of the decedent which he had taken out in prior years and approximately $95,000 in railway, utility, and industrial bonds or other securities. Each trust was by its terms made irrevocable and the trustee was granted specifically the right to sell and dispose of all or any part of the investments, securities, real estate and property which may from time to time or at any time comprise the capital or principal of said trust. The decedent retained no right to participate in the management of any one of the trusts or to direct the trustee in the exercise of the powers conferred upon it. * * * [Income from each trust was to be distributed to the beneficiary for life and then the remainder to the beneficiary's issue.]

With respect to the trust for the benefit of decedent's wife, the provisions were the same * * *. However, in * * * [wife's] trust instrument the decedent retained a specific reversion by a provision that in case of divorce or legal separation or in case his wife predeceased him, the corpus of the trust was to be paid over to him by the trustee. This trust further provided that in case his wife survived him and remarried, the trust would terminate and the corpus be paid over to the trusts created in 1922 for his then four children. * * *

■ BRUCE, JUDGE. Respondent has included in the gross estate of the decedent the value of the corpora of all of the trusts here involved, including that for the benefit of the widow. * * *

This brings us to consideration of the trust created for decedent's wife. * * * Petitioners concede * * * that [the predecessor of § 2037] applies to the remainder interest [of wife's trust] * * *. There remains for consideration the issue whether the respondent erred in including in the taxable value of the * * * [life estate] of the wife's trust, under [the predecessor of § 2037] of the Internal Revenue Code, the value of the wife's life interest.

With respect to the reversionary interest based upon "divorce or legal separation" petitioners argue that the value of the life estate of the wife may not be included in the gross estate under [the predecessor of § 2037] inasmuch as the wife's possession and enjoyment of her life estate commenced as soon as the trust was created and did not take effect at or after decedent's death. * * *

It becomes necessary, therefore, to consider whether, in view of the reversionary interest retained by decedent based upon divorce or legal separation, in connection with the trust created for his wife, decedent made a transfer of an interest in property "intended to take effect in possession or enjoyment at or after his death," within the meaning of [the predecessor of § 2037].

Petitioners argue that the wife's possession and enjoyment of her life estate commenced as soon as the trust was created, that it was at all times completely beyond the control and dominion of the decedent who retained no power to terminate it by any act of his own, and that it rested entirely within the control of his wife as to whether or not there would ever be a divorce or legal separation. On the other hand respondent contends that the decedent's transfer in trust for the benefit of his wife did not create a life estate which may be excluded from the gross estate since the life estate was intended to take effect at decedent's death, that the wife's right to income during decedent's life was contingent upon the absence of a legal separation or divorce and only at the husband's death was the possibility of separation or divorce eliminated.

It cannot be questioned that the wife became entitled to income from the trust estate immediately upon the transfer in question and that this was a positive, substantial and present beneficial interest which could have been enforced against the trustee and could not have been cut off or diminished by action of the decedent. It likewise cannot be questioned, however, that by express terms of the trust instrument the decedent retained the right to have the entire corpus of the trust estate returned to him in the event they were divorced or legally separated. This was a condition which affected the life estate of the wife and might terminate it at any time while the parties were alive. Only upon the death of the decedent was this possible termination of the wife's life estate removed. Only then did the wife's interest in the income of the trust estate ripen into an absolute, unconditional life estate, subject only to termination in event of remarriage.

* * * [T]he question whether the wife's life estate was intended to take effect in possession or enjoyment at or after decedent's death, is controlled by the Supreme Court's decision in Helvering v. Hallock, 309

U.S. 106, which held that any expressly reserved possibility of reverter would render the entire value of the transfer taxable. As stated in the Conference Report accompanying the Technical Changes Act, "The existing rule that a transfer of a property interest is not intended to take effect in possession or enjoyment at or after the decedent's death unless the beneficiaries must survive the decedent to obtain possession or enjoyment is not disturbed."

Here, although the wife acquired an interest in the income from the trust estate, immediately upon its transfer, this interest was subject to being cut off in the event she and decedent were divorced or legally separated. She only acquired a life estate, absolute and unconditional, except in event of remarriage, upon her survival of decedent. We therefore hold that the wife's life estate was a transfer "intended to take effect in possession or enjoyment at or after the decedent's death," within the meaning of [the predecessor of § 2037], and that the value of such life estate is includible in the gross estate of the decedent. Cf. Commissioner v. Estate of C. D. Marshall, 203 F.2d 534 (C.A. 3, 1953), affirming 16 T.C. 918.

* * *

Reviewed by the Court.

Decision will be entered under [Rule 155].

ILLUSTRATIVE MATERIAL

A.   THE TRANSFER REQUIREMENT

Consistent with its approach under § 2038 (see p. 260), the IRS held in Rev. Rul. 78–15, 1978–1 C.B. 289, that the transfer requirement of § 2037 is satisfied by the employee's performance of services. In Rev. Rul. 78–15, D entered into an employment contract with a corporation. The contract provided that, in consideration of D's performance of services, the corporation would pay a death benefit to D's spouse, S, provided D was employed by the Corporation at his death. If S predeceased D, the death benefit was to be paid to D's estate. The Ruling held that by entering into the employment contract, D had effected a transfer under § 2037. Since S had to survive D, in order to receive the payment that was the subject of the transfer, D retained a reversionary interest in the death benefit payment. Section 2037 required inclusion of the value of the death benefit in D's gross estate because the value of the reversionary interest immediately before D's death exceeded 5 percent of the payment.

To the same effect are Worthen v. United States, 192 F.Supp. 727 (D.Mass. 1961) (death benefits paid to wife of deceased shareholder-officer of corporation were includible under the predecessor of § 2037; the "transfer" requirement was satisfied because D had promised to continue to work for the corporation so that in effect the funds were transferred by him); Estate of Bogley v. United States, 514 F.2d 1027 (Ct.Cl. 1975); Rev. Rul. 78–15, 1978–1 C.B. 289. But compare McCobb v. All, 206 F.Supp. 901 (D.Conn. 1962), rev'd on other issues, 321 F.2d 633 (2d Cir. 1963) (payments to D's wife pursuant to an unfunded employee death benefit plan held not covered by § 2037, the court concluding that D was not the transferor).

B.   THE SURVIVORSHIP REQUIREMENT

In *Thacher,* the wife's life estate was secure only if she remained married to D until his death. Sometimes, however, a person holding an interest contingent upon surviving the transferor may be able to sever the contingency. In Smith v. United States, 158 F.Supp. 344 (D.Colo. 1957), certain income certificates (presumably taken out by D) provided that the income be paid to D's wife if living, and otherwise to D. The wife, however, could withdraw the entire principal on 3 months notice. If she failed to exercise her withdrawal rights and predeceased D, withdrawal rights and rights to interest reverted to D. The court held that nothing was includible in D's estate under the predecessor of § 2037 because "possession or enjoyment could be had not only by surviving decedent, but also by [his wife's] exercise of the conferred power of termination." The last sentence of § 2037(b) now makes clear that the section is inapplicable "if possession or enjoyment * * * could have been obtained by any beneficiary during the decedent's life through the exercise of a general power of appointment (as defined in § 2041) which in fact was exercisable immediately before decedent's death." The wife's ability to withdraw the entire principal in *Smith* was a general power of appointment since such a power includes the right to assign property to oneself. See p. 356.

The regulations also make clear that § 2037 does not apply where a beneficiary could receive property either by surviving D or through the occurrence of some other event that is not "unreal." Reg. § 20.2037–1(b). In Example 5 of Reg. § 20.2037–1(e), D transferred property in trust with the income to be accumulated for a period of 20 years or until D's prior death, at which time the corpus and accumulated income was to be paid to D's son if then surviving. If D's son were not living at D's death, the corpus and income would revert to D's estate by operation of law. D died before the expiration of the 20–year period. The Example states that, if, at the time of the transfer, the decedent was 30 years old and in good health, the son will be considered able to possess or enjoy the property without surviving D, since D would be likely to collect at the end of the twenty year period. If, on the other hand, D was 70 years old at the time of the transfer, the son will not be considered able to possess or enjoy the property without surviving D, since the son would likely be collecting as a result of D's death, not the expiration of the twenty year period. In this latter case, if the value of D's reversionary interest immediately before his death exceeded 5 percent of the value of the property, the value of the property would be includible in the D's gross estate.

C.   REVERSIONARY INTEREST

Section 2037(b)(1) defines reversionary interest to include the *possibility* that D's transferred property may return to D or D's estate. In *Thacher,* D possessed a reversionary interest under § 2037 because his wife's life interest would revert to him if a divorce occurred. It was irrelevant that a divorce never occurred; the possibility of a divorce which would trigger the reversion was sufficient for § 2037 to apply.

Section 2037(b)(2) expands the scope of "reversionary interest" beyond the possibility of the property returning to D or D's estate. It includes property that "is subject to a power of disposition" by D. In Estate of Tarver v. Commissioner, 255 F.2d 913 (4th Cir. 1958), the court concluded that D had a reversionary interest in a trust he had created where the trust instrument stated that, if certain events did not occur during his life, it would terminate and its corpus go to whomever D designated as a residual legatee in his will. The court stated: "Since the decedent retained the power during his lifetime to change the provisions of his will relating to the disposition of the residuary estate, it is obvious that there was a possibility that the property transferred . . . [in trust] might be 'subject to a power of disposition by him.' "

D. VALUATION OF THE REVERSIONARY INTEREST

Section 7520(a)(1), which applies for estates with valuation dates after April 30, 1989, states that the values of reversionary interests shall be determined under actuarial tables prescribed by the IRS. The value of a reversionary interest equals the product of the probability that D will survive the measuring life (determined immediately before D's death) times the value of the interest D would have received if D had survived. See p. 725. To illustrate, suppose D transfers property in trust with income payable to S for life and with remainder payable to D, or if D is not living, to C or C's estate. The value of D's reversionary interest equals the probability that D would survive S immediately before D's death multiplied by the value of the remainder interest.

Does the state of D's health immediately prior to D's death affect this calculation? Reg. § 20.7520–3(b)(3)(ii) (last sentence) states that D's health prior to death is irrelevant for purposes of valuing D's reversionary interest under § 2037. In a case decided prior to the adoption of § 7520, however, a court considered D's health immediately prior to death in valuing her reversionary interest. Hall v. United States, 353 F.2d 500 (7th Cir. 1965). Based on medical testimony that D was a pathological alcoholic, under constant psychiatric care, and suffered from hypertension, hepatic insufficiency, gall bladder difficulty and diabetes, the court found that the value of D's reversionary interest was less than 5%. Other cases, also decided prior to § 7520, however, have rejected this approach, noting that a "drastically foreshortened actual life expectancy would bring any retained reversion below the 5 percent level" with the result that § 2037 would apply "only in cases of sudden death." Estate of Roy v. Commissioner, 54 T.C. 1317, 1322–23 (1970). The express grant of authority in § 7520 to the IRS to prescribe valuation tables and the statement in Reg. § 20.7520–3(b)(3)(ii) that D's state of health immediately prior to death is irrelevant now seems to resolve this issue.

E. AMOUNT INCLUDIBLE

Once D's reversionary interest has been valued for purposes of the 5% requirement, the amount includible in D's estate under § 2037 must be determined. If the 5% test is not satisfied, then the actual value of the reversionary interest should be included in D's estate under § 2033 unless the interest is terminated by D's death. See p. 723. But if the 5% requirement is met, then the entire value of the interest subject to the reversion is included in D's gross estate. That is to say, the amount subject to estate taxation includes the value at the applicable estate tax valuation date of all those interests which are dependent upon surviving the decedent. See Rev. Rul. 76–178, 1976–1 C.B. 273.

For example, suppose D transfers property in trust, income payable to W for life, and the remainder payable to S or, if S is not living at W's death, to D or, if D is not then living to X or X's estate. Assume that D is survived by W, S and X. Only X's interest is dependent on surviving D. Thus, if the value of D's reversionary interest immediately before D's death exceeds 5% of the value of the transferred property, the value of X's remainder interest is includible in D's estate. Reg. § 20.2037–1(e) Ex. (4).

F.   EXCEPTION FOR ADEQUATE AND FULL CONSIDERATION

Section 2037(a)(1) states that § 2037 does not apply to a transfer which is "a bona fide sale for an adequate and full consideration in money or money's worth." This exception also applies to § 2036 and § 2038 and is discussed in Chapter 18.

G.   RELATIONSHIP OF *THACHER* TO SECTION 2036

It is possible that, in addition to § 2037, § 2036(a)(2) would also require inclusion of the entire corpus of the wife's trust in facts similar to *Thacher*. The issue is whether D's ability to initiate a divorce proceeding, which would result in the return of the trust corpus to him, is a "power" subject to § 2036(a)(2). Reg. § 20.2036–1(b)(3) says that a power reserved by D to designate who will enjoy the property causes inclusion of the property in the gross estate regardless of whether the power is "exercisable alone or only in conjunction with another person" and regardless of whether the power is "subject to a contingency beyond decedent's control." (see p. 204). This broad language suggests that the requirement that a divorce be granted or approved by a court may not preclude the application of § 2036(a)(2). On the other hand, the requirement that a court approve a divorce may cause D's retained power to be viewed as too speculative. See generally Rev. Rul. 77–460, 1977–2 C.B. 323 (parent's right under the Uniform Gift To Minors Act to petition court to require assets held under the Act to be used for the child's support did not constitute a general power of appointment).

SECTION B.   POLICY CONSIDERATIONS FOR §§ 2036–2038

Given the complexity of §§ 2036, 2037 and 2038, it is appropriate to consider a proposal to simplify the current statutory scheme advanced in 1984 by the Treasury Department.

U.S. Treasury Department, Tax Reform for Fairness, Simplicity, and Economic Growth

Volume 2, pp. 378–380 (Nov. 1984).

Simplification of Rules Pertaining to Completed Gifts and Testamentary Strings

Application of the gift tax on a tax-inclusive basis would eliminate the major disparity between the transfer tax treatment of lifetime gifts and transfers at death. * * * The complex retained interest rules would be replaced with a simpler set of rules determining when a transfer of less than an entire interest constitutes a completed gift for Federal transfer tax purposes. These new rules would ensure that a transfer is subject to gift or estate tax, but not to both taxes. In addition, the rules would assure a more accurate valuation and provide greater consistency between the transfer tax rules and the rules governing when trust income is taxed at the grantor's rate.

Retained beneficial enjoyment. The proposal would simplify present law by providing that a transfer tax would be imposed only once, when the beneficial enjoyment retained by the donor terminates. Thus, if a donor makes a gift of a remainder interest in property, but retains the intervening income interest, no gift would occur until the termination of the donor's income interest. At that time, the property would be subject to gift or estate tax at its full fair market value. Because the transferor would be treated as the owner of the property during the interim, any distributions made to beneficiaries other than the transferor would be treated as transfers when made.

The transferor would continue to be treated as owner of the property for all transfer tax purposes. Such treatment would foreclose any opportunity for tax avoidance through the transferor's repurchase of the remainder interest free of gift tax.

The proposal would also apply to the creation of inter vivos charitable lead trusts. The creator of such a trust would be treated as owning the property for transfer tax purposes until the vesting of the noncharitable interest or his or her death, if sooner. (Testamentary charitable lead trusts would be taxed as under present law.)

Revocable transfers. The rules of present law would continue with respect to any transfer where the transferor retains the right to regain possession or enjoyment of the property. Such a transfer would be treated as incomplete for gift and estate tax purposes, and would be treated as complete only when the transferor's retained right or power to revoke terminates. Distributions from the property to beneficiaries other than the donor would be treated as gifts when made, thereby providing consistency with the rules governing the income taxation of trusts as well as the rules governing the income and gift tax treatment of demand loans.

Retained powers. In determining whether a gift is complete for transfer tax purposes, the proposal would treat a retained power to control the beneficial enjoyment of the transferred property as irrelevant where the power could not be used to distribute income or principal to the donor. Thus, the fact that the transferor as trustee or custodian can exercise control over the identity of the distributee of the property or over the amount or timing of a distribution would be irrelevant in determining whether a gift is complete (although such factors may be relevant in determining whether the transfer qualifies for the annual gift tax exclusion). Under this rule, a transfer would be complete for gift tax purposes where the grantor creates an irrevocable trust but retains the absolute right to determine who (other than himself) will receive the trust income or principal.

Reversionary interests. Current rules regarding retained reversionary interests would be replaced by a rule that disregards reversionary interests retained by the grantor in valuing transferred property for Federal gift tax purposes. The existence of the reversionary interest would be relevant only for purposes of determining the timing of the transfer for estate and gift tax purposes.

If the donor makes a gift of property for a term of years or for the life of one or more beneficiaries, and if the donor retains a reversionary interest that is more likely than not to return the property to the donor or his or her estate, the transfer would be treated as incomplete. Interim distributions of income or principal (or the value of the use of the property) would be treated as gifts by the donor on an annual basis. On the other hand, if it is more likely than not that the reversionary interest will not return the property to the donor or his or her estate, the transfer will be treated as complete and the full fair market value of the property will be subject to gift tax, without reduction for the actuarial value of the reversionary interest. If the donor dies with the reversion outstanding, the value of the reversionary interest will be excluded from the donor's estate, whether or not the reversion terminates at that time. If the property reverts to the donor prior to his or her death, the donor would have the right to retransfer the property at any time free from additional gift tax liability. If not retransferred during the donor's lifetime, the property would be excluded from the donor's estate. In order to prevent disputes arising from the reversion and subsequent retransfer of fungible assets, however, the proposal would require the donor to place the reverted property in a segregated account in order to benefit from the exclusion.

The determination of whether a reversionary interest is more likely than not to return property to the donor during his lifetime generally would depend on the life expectancy of the donor and the anticipated duration of the intervening interest. For example, a reversion following a term of years less than the donor's life expectancy or following the life of a beneficiary older than the donor would be more likely than not to return the property to the donor. Similar actuarial determinations would be made for multiple intervening income beneficiaries. * * *

ILLUSTRATIVE MATERIAL

A.   "EASY–TO–COMPLETE" VERSUS "HARD–TO–COMPLETE" GIFT APPROACH

Present law rules with respect to retained powers and interests reflects a "hard-to-complete" gift approach in that numerous inter vivos transfers are brought back into the transferor's gross estate. The Treasury in 1984 proposed to move in the direction of an "easy-to-complete" gift approach in which more inter vivos transfers would be completed for transfer tax purposes despite the existence of retained powers or interests. The Treasury proposals stopped short of a comprehensive easy-to-complete gift approach in which, for example, a transfer by A in trust to A for life, remainder to B would constitute a completed transfer for transfer tax purposes.

Whether adoption of a completely unified transfer tax should be accompanied by a shift to an "easy-to-complete" gift approach is not entirely clear even though considerable simplification would be achieved by such a change. An "easy-to-complete" gift approach permits the transferor to exclude future appreciation of the transferred property from her transfer tax base. On the other hand, the transfer tax is paid earlier under an "easy-to-complete" gift approach and any subsequent gifts may be subject to tax in higher brackets. The "easy-to-complete" gift approach places great stress on proper valuation.

CHAPTER 18

THE "ADEQUATE AND FULL CONSIDERATION" EXCEPTION FOR §§ 2036–2038

When a person transfers property in which she retains an interest or power, §§ 2036, 2037 and 2038 do not include such property in her gross estate if the transfer was a "bona fide sale for an adequate and full consideration in money or money's worth." Suppose decedent ("D") transferred property to A for cash but retained a life interest in the property. For the "adequate and full consideration" exception to apply, must D have received an amount of cash equal to the entire value of the property or just the remainder interest? As illustrated in the principal case in Section A, the matter is not settled.

Estate of D'Ambrosio v. Commissioner

101 F.3d 309 (3d Cir. 1996).

■ NYGAARD, CIRCUIT JUDGE.

Vita D'Ambrosio, executrix of the estate of Rose D'Ambrosio, appeals from a judgment of the United States Tax Court upholding a statutory notice of deficiency filed against the estate by the Commissioner of Internal Revenue. The tax court held that, even though the decedent had sold her remainder interest in closely held stock for its fair market value, § 2036(a)(1) brought its entire fee simple value back into her gross estate. We will reverse and remand with the direction that the tax court enter judgment in favor of appellant.

I.

The facts in this case have been stipulated by the parties. Decedent owned * * * one half of the preferred stock of Vaparo, Inc.; these 470 shares had a fair market value of $2,350,000. In 1987, at the age of 80, decedent transferred her remainder interest in her shares to Vaparo in exchange for an annuity which was to pay her $296,039 per year and retained her income interest in the shares. There is no evidence in the record to indicate that she made this transfer in contemplation of death or with testamentary motivation. According to the actuarial tables set forth in the Treasury Regulations, the annuity had a fair market value of $1,324,014. The parties stipulate that this was also the fair market value of the remainder interest.

Decedent died in 1990, after receiving only $592,078 in annuity payments and $23,500 in dividends. Her executrix did not include any interest in the Vaparo stock when she computed decedent's gross estate. The Commissioner disagreed, issuing a notice of deficiency in which she asserted that the gross estate included the full, fee simple value of the Vaparo shares at the date of death, still worth an estimated $2,350,000, less the amount of annuity payments decedent received during life.[1] The estate then petitioned the tax court for redetermination of the alleged tax deficiency.

The tax court, relying largely on Gradow v. United States, 11 Cl.Ct. 808 (1987), aff'd, 897 F.2d 516 (Fed. Cir. 1990), and Estate of Gregory v. Commissioner, 39 T.C. 1012 (1963), ruled in favor of the Commissioner. Eschewing any attempt to construe the language of either the Code or the applicable Treasury Regulations, the tax court reasoned that the transfer of the remainder interest in the Vaparo stock was an abusive tax avoidance scheme that should not be permitted:

> In the instant case, we conclude that Decedent's transfer of the remainder interest in her preferred stock does not fall within the bona fide sale exception of § 2036(a). Decedent's gross estate would be depleted if the value of the preferred stock, in which she had retained a life interest, was excluded therefrom. Decedent's transfer of the remainder interest was of a testamentary nature, made when she was 80 years old to a family-owned corporation in return for an annuity worth more than $1 million less than the stock itself. Given our conclusion that Decedent did not receive adequate and full consideration under § 2036(a) for her 470 shares of Vaparo preferred stock, we hold that her gross estate includes the date of death value of that stock, less the value of the annuity.

Estate of D'Ambrosio v. Commissioner, 105 T.C. 252, 260 (1995). The executrix now appeals; we have jurisdiction under § 7482. Both parties agree that our standard of review for this issue of law is plenary.

II.

Our nation's tax laws have, for several generations, imposed a tax upon decedents' estates. Under § 2033, a decedent's gross estate includes "[t]he value of all property to the extent of any interest therein of the decedent at the time of his death." In addition the Code contains, among other provisions, § 2036(a), which provides, in pertinent part:

> The value of the gross estate shall include the value of all property to the extent of any interest therein of which the decedent has at any time made a transfer (except in case of a bona fide sale for adequate and full consideration in money or money's worth), by trust or otherwise, under which he has retained for his life or for any period not ascertainable without reference to his death or for any period which does not in fact end before his death—
>
> (1) the possession or enjoyment of, or the right to the income from the property [.]

---

1. The Commissioner now concedes that the estate must be credited for the fair market value of that annuity rather than the lifetime payments received under it.

Section 2036(a) effectively discourages manipulative transfers of remainder interests which are really testamentary in character by "pulling back" the full, fee simple value of the transferred property into the gross estate, except when the transfer was "a bona fide sale for adequate and full consideration."

There is no dispute that Rose D'Ambrosio retained a life interest in the Vaparo stock and sold the remainder back to the company. The issue is whether the sale of a remainder interest for its fair market value constitutes "adequate and full consideration" within the meaning of § 2036(a). Appellant argues that it does. The Commissioner takes the position that only consideration equal to the fee simple value of the property is sufficient. Appellant has the better argument.

A.

The tax court and the Commissioner rely principally on four cases, Gradow v. United States, 11 Cl.Ct. 808 (1987), aff'd for the reasons set forth by the claims court, 897 F.2d 516 (Fed. Cir. 1990); United States v. Past, 347 F.2d 7 (9th Cir. 1965); Estate of Gregory v. Commissioner, 39 T.C. 1012 (1963); United States v. Allen, 293 F.2d 916 (10th Cir. 1961). We find these cases either inapposite or unpersuasive; we will discuss them in chronological order.

In *Allen*, the decedent set up an irrevocable inter vivos trust in which she retained a partial life estate and gave the remainder (as well as the remaining portion of the income) to her children. Apparently realizing the tax liability she had created for her estate under the predecessor of § 2036, she later attempted to sell her retained life interest to her son for an amount slightly in excess of its fair market value. After she died, the estate took the position that, because decedent had divested herself of her retained life interest for fair market value, none of the trust property was includible in her gross estate. The Court of Appeals disagreed, holding that consideration is only "adequate" if it equals or exceeds the value of the interest that would otherwise be included in the gross estate absent the transfer. See 293 F.2d at 917. Although acknowledging that the decedent owned only a life estate, which she could not realistically hope to sell for its fee simple value, the court nevertheless rejected the estate's argument, opining:

> It does not seem plausible, however, that Congress intended to allow such an easy avoidance of the taxable incidence befalling reserved life estates. This result would allow a taxpayer to reap the benefits of property for his lifetime and, in contemplation of death, sell only the interest entitling him to the income, thereby removing all of the property which he has enjoyed from his gross estate. Giving the statute a reasonable interpretation, we cannot believe this to be its intendment. It seems certain that in a situation like this, Congress meant the estate to include the corpus of the trust or, in its stead, an amount equal in value.

Id. at 918 (citations omitted).

Allen, however, is inapposite, as the Commissioner now concedes, because it involved the sale of a life estate after the remainder had already been disposed of by gift, a testamentary transaction with a palpable tax evasion motive. This case, in contrast, involves the sale of a remainder for its stipulated fair market value. Nevertheless, we agree with its rationale that consideration should be measured against the value that would have been drawn into the gross estate absent the transfer. As the tax court persuasively reasoned in a later case:

> Where the transferred property is replaced by other property of equal value received in exchange, there is no reason to impose an estate tax in respect of the transferred property, for it is reasonable to assume that the property acquired in exchange will find its way into the decedent's gross estate at his death unless consumed or otherwise disposed of in a nontestamentary transaction in much the same manner as would the transferred property itself had the transfer not taken place. . . .

> In short, unless replaced by property of equal value that could be *exposed to inclusion* in the decedent's gross estate, the property transferred in a testamentary transaction of the type described in the statute must be included in his gross estate.

Estate of Frothingham v. Commissioner, 60 T.C. 211, 215–16 (1973) (emphasis added).

Gregory presents a closer factual analogy to D'Ambrosio's situation. *Gregory* was a "widow's election" case involving the testamentary disposition of community property. Typically in such cases, the husband wishes to pass the remainder interest in all of the marital property to his children, while providing for the lifetime needs of his surviving spouse. In a community property state, however, half of the marital property belongs to the wife as a matter of law, so he cannot pass it by his own will. To circumvent this problem, the will is drafted to give the widow a choice: take her one-half share in fee simple, according to law, or trust over her half of the community property in exchange for a life estate in the whole. Put another way, she trades the remainder interest in her half of the community property in exchange for a life estate in her husband's half.

In *Gregory*, the widow exchanged property worth approximately $66,000 for a life estate with an actuarial value of only around $12,000; by the time she died eight years later, the property she gave up had appreciated to approximately $102,000. The tax court compared the $102,000 outflow to the $12,000 consideration and concluded that the widow's election did not constitute a bona fide sale for an adequate and full consideration. 39 T.C. at 1015–16. It also stated that "the statute excepts only those bona fide sales where the consideration received was of a comparable *value which would be includable in the transferor's gross estate*." Id. at 1016 (emphasis added).

We believe that the *Gregory* court erred in its analysis, although it reached the correct result on the particular facts of that case. There is no way to know ex ante what the value of an asset will be at the death of a testator; although the date of death can be estimated through the use of actuarial tables, the actual appreciation of the property is unknowable, as are the prevailing interest, inflation and tax rates. Consequently, there is no way to ever be certain in advance whether the consideration is adequate and thus no way to know what tax treatment a transfer will receive. This level of uncertainty all but destroys any economic incentive to ever sell a remainder interest; yet, Congress never said in § 2036 that all transfers of such interests will be taxed at their fee simple value or that those transfers are illegal. Instead, it clearly contemplated situations in which a sale of a remainder would not cause the full value of the property to fall into the gross estate. Without some express indication from Congress, we will not presume it intended to eliminate wholesale the transfers of remainder interests. Therefore, rather than evaluate the adequacy of the consideration at the time the decedent dies, we will compare the value of the remainder transferred to the value of the consideration received, measured as of the date of the transfer. Here, we need not address that valuation issue, because it is stipulated that the fair market value of the stock was the same on the date of transfer as it was on the date of death.

In *Gregory*, however, the $12,000 the decedent received was grossly inadequate against the value of the property she transferred, regardless of the valuation date. The court was therefore correct that the transfer was not for adequate and full consideration. Because of that gross inadequacy, however, the holding of *Gregory* does not extend to the issue now before us: whether, when a remainder is sold for its stipulated fair market value, the consideration received is inadequate because it is less than the fee simple value of the property.

The *Past* case was factually somewhat different, in that it involved a divorce settlement, but the substance of the transaction was the same as in *Gregory*: the sale of a remainder in one-half of the marital property in exchange for a life estate in the whole. In that case, however, the court valued the property the divorcing spouse gave up at about $244,000 and the life estate she received at about $143,000; as a result, it held that the consideration was inadequate. 347 F.2d at 13–14. In making these valuations, however, the court took the fee simple value of the trust property and divided it in half. This was analytically incorrect, however, because the divorcing wife never gave up the life estate in her half of the marital property. She contributed only her remainder interest in that half, and that is the value that should have been used in the court's analysis. Alternatively, the *Past* court could have used the fee simple value of the wife's share, but it would then have needed to measure that against the value of the life estate in both halves of the property. Had the court employed this latter methodology, it would have seen that the $287,000 value of the life estate exceeded the $244,000 she contributed and would have found adequate consideration. Instead, it compared "apples and oranges" and, we believe, reached the wrong result.

B.

The facts in *Gradow* were similar to those in *Gregory*; both are "widow's election" cases. That case is particularly significant, however, because the court focused on the statutory language of § 2036. The court began its analysis, however, with a discussion of *Gregory*, *Past* and *Allen*. While acknowledging that it was not bound by those three cases, the *Gradow* court found them persuasive, for two reasons: 1) "the most natural reading of § 2036(a) leads to the same result[;]" and 2) their holding is "most consistent with the purposes of § 2036(a)." 11 Cl.Ct. at 813. We will discuss these rationales in turn

1.

We examine first the *Gradow* court's construction of the statute. It opined that

> there is no question that the term "property" in the phrase "The gross estate shall include ... all property ... of which the decedent has at any time made a transfer" means that part of the trust corpus attributable to plaintiff. If § 2036(a) applies, all of Betty's former community property is brought into her gross estate. Fundamental principles of grammar dictate that the parenthetical exception which then follows—"(except in case of a bona fide sale ...)"—refers to a transfer of that same property, i.e. the one-half of the community property she placed into the trust.

Id. (ellipses in original). We disagree; although the *Gradow* court's rational appears plausible, we note that the court, in quoting the statute, left out significant portions of its language. Below is the text of § 2036, with the omitted words emphasized:

> The *value of the* gross estate shall include *the value of* all property *to the extent of any interest therein* of which the decedent has at any time made a transfer (except in case of a bona fide sale for an adequate and full consideration in money or money's worth), by trust or otherwise, under which he has retained for his life * * * (1) the possession or enjoyment of, or the right to the income from, the property * * *

After parsing this language, we cannot agree with the *Gradow* court's conclusions that "property" refers to the fee simple interest and that adequate consideration must be measured against that value. Rather, we believe that the clear import of the phrase "to the extent of any interest therein" is that the gross estate shall include the value of the remainder interest, unless it was sold for adequate and fair consideration.

In addition to § 2036, Treas. Reg. § 20.2036–1 also addresses this issue. It provides, in pertinent part (emphases added):

> (a) In general. A decedent's gross estate includes under § 2036 the value of any *interest* in property *transferred* by the decedent ... except to the extent that the transfer was for an adequate and full consideration in money or money's worth if the decedent retained or reserved (1) for his life ...

(i) the use, possession, right to the income, or other enjoyment of *the transferred property*, . . .

Appellant refers us to the emphasized words "interest" and "transferred" in § 20.2036–1(a) and argues that "adequate and full consideration" must be measured against the interest transferred. The Commissioner, on the other hand, looks at the phrase "of the transferred property" in § 20.2036–1(a)(i) and concludes that, because one cannot retain any lifetime interest in a remainder, "property" must refer to the fee simple interest.

The regulation, unfortunately, is not exactingly drafted and does not parse "cleanly" under either party's interpretation. The Commissioner is of course correct that one cannot enjoy any sort of life interest in a remainder. On the other hand, appellant validly asks why, if the drafters of the regulation meant to include the full value of the property, they referred to the value of any "interest in property transferred." On balance, we believe that, if some words of the regulation must be construed as surplusage, it is more reasonable and faithful to the statutory text to render inoperative the word "transferred" in § 20.2036–1(a)(i) than it would be to strike "interest" in the first part of the section. We think it is likely that, although the choice of verbiage was less than precise, the drafters meant merely to refer to the "transferred" property so as to distinguish it from other property owned by the estate. It strains the judicial imagination, however, to conclude that the drafters used the term of art "interest in property" when they meant simply "property."

2.

The *Gradow* court also believed that its construction of § 2036 was "most consistent" with its purposes. 11 Cl.Ct. at 813. The tax court in this case, although recognizing that the issue has spawned considerable legal commentary and that scholars dispute its resolution, 105 T.C. at 254, was persuaded that decedent's sale of her remainder interest was testamentary in character and designed to avoid the payment of estate tax that otherwise would have been due. Id. at 260. It noted particularly that the transfer was made when decedent was eighty years old and that the value of the annuity she received was over $1 million less than the fee simple value of the stock she gave up. Id. Again, we disagree.

We too are cognizant that techniques for attempting to reduce estate taxes are limited only by the imagination of estate planners, and that new devices appear regularly. There is, to be sure, a role for the federal courts to play in properly limiting these techniques in accordance with the expressed intent of Congress. Under long-standing precedent, for example, we measure "consideration" in real economic terms, not as it might be evaluated under the common law of contract or property. E.g., Commissioner v. Wemyss, 324 U.S. 303 (1945) (promise of marriage insufficient consideration, for gift tax purposes, for tax-free transfer of property); Merrill v. Fahs, 324 U.S. 308 (1945) (same). Likewise, when the transfer of the remainder interest is essentially gratuitous and testamentary in character, we focus on substance rather than form and require that the full value of trust property be included in the gross estate, unless "the settlor absolutely, unequivocally, irrevocably, and without possible reservations, parts with all of his title and all of his possession and all of his enjoyment of the transferred property." See Commissioner v. Estate of Church, 335 U.S. 632, 645 (1949) (gratuitous transfer of remainder in trust for family members with possibility of reverter to estate); accord Helvering v. Hallock, 309 U.S. 106, 110 (1940) (consolidation of three cases involving "dispositions of property by way of trust in which the settlement provides for return or reversion of the corpus to the donor upon a contingency terminable at his death").

On the other hand, it is not our role to police the techniques of estate planning by determining, based on our own policy views and perceptions, which transfers are abusive and which are not. That is properly the role of Congress, whose statutory enactments we are bound to interpret.[2] As stated supra, we think the statutory text better supports appellant's argument.

Even looking at this case in policy terms, however, it is difficult to fathom either the tax court's or the Commissioner's concerns about the "abusiveness" of this transaction. A hypothetical example will illustrate the point.

A fee simple interest is comprised of a life estate and a remainder. Returning to the widow's election cases, assume that the surviving spouse's share of the community property is valued at $2,000,000. Assuming that she decides not to accept the settlement and to keep that property, its whole value will be available for inclusion in the gross estate at death, but only as long as the widow lives entirely on the income from the property. If she invades principal and sells some of the property in order to meet living expenses or purchase luxury items, then at least some of that value will not be included in the gross estate. Tax law, of course (with the exception of the gift tax), imposes no burdens on how a person spends her money during life.

Next, assume that same widow decides to sell her remainder and keep a life estate. As long as she sells the remainder for its fair market value, it makes no difference whether she receives cash, other property, or an annuity. All can be discounted to their respective present values and quantified. If she continues to support herself from the income from her life estate, the consideration she received in exchange for the remainder, if properly invested, will still be available for inclusion in the gross estate when she dies, as *Frothingham* and *Gregory* require. On the other hand, if her life estate is insufficient to meet her living expenses, the widow will have to invade the consideration she received in exchange for her remainder, but to no different an extent than she would under the previous hypothetical in which she retained the fee simple interest. In sum, there is

---

2. Indeed, subsequent to the transfer at issue here, Congress did enact legislation dealing with abusive transfers of remainder interests. See *26 U.S.C. §§ 2036*(c) (repealed), 2701.

simply no change in the date-of-death value of the final estate, regardless of which option she selects, at any given standard of living.

On the other hand, if the full, fee simple value of the property at the time of death is pulled back into the gross estate under § 2036(a), subject only to an offset for the consideration received, then the post-sale appreciation of the transferred asset will be taxed at death. Indeed, it will be double-taxed, because, all things being equal, the consideration she received will also have appreciated and will be subject to tax on its increased value. In addition, it would appear virtually impossible, under the tax court's reasoning, ever to sell a remainder interest; if the adequacy of the consideration must be measured against the fee simple value of the property at the time of the transfer, the transferor will have to find an arms-length buyer willing to pay a fee simple price for a future interest. Unless a buyer is willing to speculate that the future value of the asset will skyrocket, few if any such sales will take place.

Another potential concern, expressed by the *Gradow* court, is that, under appellant's theory, "[a] young person could sell a remainder interest for a fraction of the property's [current, fee simple] worth, enjoy the property for life, and then pass it along without estate or gift tax consequences." 11 Cl.Ct. at 815. This reasoning is problematic, however, because it ignores the time value of money. Assume that a decedent sells his son a remainder interest in that much-debated and often-sold parcel of land called Blackacre, which is worth $1 million in fee simple, for its actuarial fair market value of $100,000 (an amount which implicitly includes the market value of Blackacre's expected appreciation). Decedent then invests the proceeds of the sale. If the rates of return for both assets are equal and decedent lives exactly as long as the actuarial tables predict, the consideration that decedent received for his remainder will equal the value of Blackacre on the date of his death. The equivalent value will, accordingly, still be included in the gross estate. Moreover, decedent's son will have only a $100,000 basis in Blackacre, because that is all he paid for it. He will then be subject to capital gains taxes on its appreciated value if he decides to ever sell the property. Had Blackacre been passed by decedent's will and included in the gross estate, the son would have received a stepped-up basis at the time of his father's death or the alternate valuation date. We therefore have great difficulty understanding how this transaction could be abusive.

On this appeal, the Commissioner likewise argues for the *Gradow* rule on the rationale that "the retained life interest is in closely held stock whose dividend treatment is subject to the control of decedent and her family. In such circumstances, the amount of the dividend income that decedent was to receive from her life income interest in the Vaparo preferred stock was susceptible of manipulation[.]" Commissioner's Brief at 33. There is no evidence, however, that the Vaparo dividends were manipulated, and the Commissioner directs us to no authority that we should presume so. In addition, implicit in her argument is the proposition that the life estate was overvalued by the executor and the remainder correspondingly undervalued. Such a position, however, is directly contrary to the Commissioner's own stipulation regarding the values of those interests.

The Commissioner also asserts that the D'Ambrosio estate plan is "calculated to deplete decedent's estate in the event that she should not survive as long as her actuarially projected life expectancy." Commissioner's Brief at 34–35. We note first that the Commissioner does not argue that decedent transferred her remainder in contemplation of imminent death under such circumstances that the tables should not be applied. Leaving aside the untimely death of Rose D'Ambrosio, any given transferor of a remainder is equally likely to outlive the tables, in which case she would collect more from her annuity, the gross estate would be correspondingly larger and the Commissioner would collect more tax revenue than if the remainder had never been transferred.

3.

Several courts have followed the holding in *Gradow*, but none of their opinions provides any cogent analysis that persuade us it is sound. See Pittman v. United States, 878 F. Supp. 833, 835 (E.D.N.C. 1994) (applying *Gradow* without analysis); Wheeler v. United States, No. SA–94–CA–964, 77 A.F.T.R. 2d 96–1405, 96–1411 (W.D. Tex. Jan. 26, 1996) (similar). Two other courts have questioned the soundness of *Gradow*, but have either applied it reluctantly or decided the case on other grounds. See Parker v. United States, 894 F. Supp. 445, 447 (N.D. Ga. 1995); Estate of McLendon v. Commissioner, Nos. 20324–90, 20325–90, 66 T.C.M. 946 n.24 and accompanying text (Tax Ct. Sept. 30, 1993), rev'd on other grounds, 77 F.3d 477 (5th Cir. 1995).

The holdings of *Gradow* and the earlier cases such as *Gregory* have inspired considerable legal commentary, most of it critical. See Jacques T. Schlenger et al., Cases Addressing Sale of Remainder Wrongly Decided, 22 Estate Planning 305 (1995) (reproducing Professor Pennell's remarks criticizing Pittman as a "mindless" decision); 2 A. James Casner, Estate Planning § 6.15.2, at 6–146–50, 6–158 (Supp. 1995) (Professor Casner, criticizing *Gradow* court as lacking understanding of future interests, economics and time value of money); Jacques T. Schlenger et al., Property Included in Estate Despite Sale of Remainder Interest, 23 Estate Planning 132 (1996) (criticizing reasoning of tax court in D'Ambrosio); Richard B. Stephens et al., Federal Estate and Gift Taxation P 4.08[1], at 4–138 (6th ed. 1991) (stating that payment of full consideration for remainder interest alone is sufficient under § 2036, but noting *Gregory*, *Past* and *Gradow* in a footnote); Peter M. Weinbaum, Are Sales of Remainder Interests Still Available in Light of a New Decision?, 14 Estate Planning 258 (1987) (criticizing *Gradow* for quoting and analyzing § 2036(a) out of context and for ignoring the value of the life estate in the wife's community property as consideration received in the transfer).[3] As discussed supra, we find this criticism to be well-taken.

---

3. But see Joseph M. Dodge, Tax Management A–67, A–87 (1992); Stanley M. Johanson, Revocable Trusts, Widow's Election Wills, and Community Property: The Tax

III.

Because we conclude that the tax court erred as a matter of law when it determined that the consideration received by Rose D'Ambrosio for her remainder interest was not adequate and full, we will reverse and remand for it to enter judgment in favor of the estate.

■ Cowen, Circuit Judge, dissenting.

Today the majority holds that a tax-avoidance approach previously considered "too good to be true"[4] can, at least in limited circumstances, actually be true. I respectfully dissent. The tax court's opinion is supported by well-established case law and the plain language of the Internal Revenue Code. It should be affirmed.

I.

The value of a gross estate includes the value of all property held by the decedent on the date of death. I.R.C. § 2033. Pursuant to § 2036(a), for federal estate tax purposes the gross estate also includes any property that is the subject of an inter vivos transfer and in which the taxpayer reserves an income interest in that property until death. The sole exception authorized by § 2036(a) is a "bona fide sale" in which the transferor receives "adequate and full consideration" in exchange for the transferred property. I.R.C. § 2036(a). The majority holds that under § 2036(a), "adequate and full consideration" must be provided merely for that portion of the taxpayer's property interest actually transferred, rather than for the full value of the property that is the basis for the ongoing income interest.

The majority excludes from the computation of "full and adequate consideration" the value of decedent's life interest in the transferred stock, on the grounds that D'Ambrosio retained that interest. The intended purpose of § 2036 is to prevent decedents from avoiding estate taxes by selling their property to a third party but retaining the benefits of ownership during their lives. It includes in a decedent's gross estate the date-of-death value of

> all property to the extent of any interest therein of which the decedent has at any time made a transfer (except in the case of a bona fide sale for an adequate and full consideration in money or money's worth), by trust or otherwise, under which he has retained for his life * * * the possession or enjoyment of, or the right to the income from, the property.

I.R.C. § 2036(a). When a taxpayer makes a transfer with a retained life interest, the powerful arm of § 2036(a) pulls into the gross estate the full

Problems, 47 Tex. L. Rev. 1247 (1969); Charles L.B. Lowndes, Consideration and the Federal Estate and Gift Taxes: Transfers for Partial Consideration, Relinquishment of Marital Rights, Family Annuities, the Widow's Election, and Reciprocal Trusts, 35 Geo. Wash. L. Rev. 50 (1966). We have reviewed these sources and find them unpersuasive, largely for the reasons already discussed.

4. Stock Included in Estate Despite FMV Sale of Remainder, 24 Tax'n for Law. 248 (1996).

value of the transferred property, not merely the value of the remainder interest.

The majority accepts the view of the estate that the decedent "sold" only the remainder interest to Vaparo. This view of § 2036 sanctions tax evasion: It enables strategic segmentation of the property into multiple interests, with "adequate and full consideration" now required only for a specific transferred segment, rather than the indivisible whole. Such an interpretation of § 2036(a) thwarts its very purpose, enabling taxpayers to avoid paying estate taxes on property while retaining the income benefits of ownership. I would affirm the tax court's holding that "adequate and full consideration" assesses whether the consideration received is equal to the value of the property that would have remained in the estate but for the transfer, not whether it is commensurate with the value of the artfully separated portion of the property technically transferred.

II.

The well-reasoned case law construing § 2036(a) supports the ruling of the tax court. That law correctly tests the adequacy of the consideration received by a taxpayer against the amount that otherwise would be included in that taxpayer's gross estate. The majority distinguishes these cases by focusing on irrelevant distinctions, and overlooks the commanding principle that a taxpayer who fails to convey all interests in an asset, continuing to derive some benefit from the asset until death, must include the entire asset in the taxpayer's estate.

In Gradow v. United States, 11 Cl.Ct. 808 (1987), aff'd, 897 F.2d 516 (Fed. Cir. 1990), the surviving spouse transferred her full community property interest into a trust that held all of the couple's community property. Thereafter, the trust paid her all of the trust income during her life, and distributed the entire corpus of the trust to her son upon her death. Gradow's executor asserted that decedent's retained life interest was received in exchange for adequate and full consideration, so that none of the trust's assets were includable in her gross estate. The court disagreed, holding that the consideration paid by the decedent had to cover not only the remainder interest that was left to her son in the trust, but also her half of the underlying community property.

Other courts have acknowledged and followed this rule. See United States v. Past, 347 F.2d 7 (9th Cir. 1965) (consideration decedent received from trust had to be measured against the total value of the property she contributed to the trust, not only against the remainder interest in the property); United States v. Allen, 293 F.2d 916 (10th Cir. 1961) (decedent who received most of trust's income for life but before death sold her remainder interest to her children had to include the value of the trust assets corresponding to the percentage of the trust's income that she received); Estate of Gregory v. Commissioner, 39 T.C. 1012, 1016 (1963) (decedent who received a life estate in exchange for transferring property to a trust failed to qualify for exception because "the statute excepts only those bona fide sales where the consideration received was of a comparable value which would be includable in the transferor's gross estate").

The paramount purpose of § 2036(a) is to prevent the depletion of estate assets when individuals retain the use and enjoyment of those assets until death. In Commissioner v. Estate of Church, 335 U.S. 632 (1949), the Supreme Court emphatically noted that

> an estate tax cannot be avoided by any trust transfer except by a bona fide transfer in which the settlor, absolutely, unequivocally, irrevocably, and without possible reservations, parts with all of his title and all of his possession and all of his enjoyment of the transferred property.

Id. at 645. D'Ambrosio clearly fails this requirement that all title, enjoyment, and possession of the transferred property be unequivocally halted. Commenting on the forerunner to § 2036(a) more than a half century ago, the Supreme Court state that the law

> taxes not merely those interests which are deemed to pass at death according to refined technicalities of the law of property. It also taxes inter vivos transfers that are too much akin to testamentary dispositions not to be subjected to the same excise.

Helvering v. Hallock, 309 U.S. 106, 112 (1940).

These cases clearly demonstrate that the concept of "adequate and full consideration," as use in §§ 2035 through 2038, must be construed with reference to the special problems posed by trying to prevent testamentary-type transfers from evading estate tax. The bona fide sale analysis, which exempts property from inclusion in the gross estate pursuant to § 2036(a), cannot focus merely on the value of the limited property interest that is sold. It must also consider the property that would otherwise be included in the decedent's gross estate.

III.

The estate asserts that the tax court erred because it misunderstood or disregarded the "economic reality" of a sale of a remainder interest. To the contrary, it was precisely the tax court's awareness of the economic realities of a retained interest transaction that led it to follow well-established law. Executrix D'Ambrosio alleges that *Gradow* is inapposite and, in any event, was erroneously decided. She states that

> if the Decedent had retained and invested the dividends from the Vaparo Stock and from the annuity payments received during her life, the potential value of her gross estate as a result of the sale would be worth no less on the date of her death, than if she had never sold the remainder interest in the Vaparo Stock or if she had sold the entire interest in the Vaparo Stock and invested the proceeds therefrom for the rest of her life.

Appellant's brief at 11.

This view ignores the very reason for § 2036(a). Its purpose is precisely to prevent taxpayers from retaining the practical benefits of asset ownership during their lifetime while divesting themselves for estate tax purposes of a portion of that property. As the court in *Gradow* correctly explained:

> [The "economic reality" argument] flies squarely in the face of the Supreme Court's analysis as to the assumptions and purposes behind [§] 2036(a). The Court has taught that while tax limitation is perfectly legitimate, § 2036(a) is a reflection of Congress' judgment that transfers with retained life estates are generally testamentary transactions and should be treated as such for estate tax purposes. The fond hope that a surviving spouse would take pains to invest, compound, and preserve inviolate all life income from half of a trust, knowing that it would thereupon be taxed without his having received any lifetime benefit, is a slim basis for putting a different construction on § 2036(a) than the one heretofore consistently adopted.

11 Cl.Ct. at 815–816.

Even if the annuity decedent received were not an attempt to deplete her property for estate tax purposes, courts have consistently held that § 2036(a) does not exempt transfers of property in which the taxpayer retains an income interest in his or her underlying assets. As the Tenth Circuit concluded in *Allen*:

> It does not seem plausible ... that Congress intended to allow such an easy avoidance of the taxable incidence befalling reserved life estates. This result would allow a taxpayer to reap the benefits of property for his lifetime and, in contemplation of death, sell only the interest entitling him to the income, thereby removing all of the property which he has enjoyed from his gross estate ... In a situation like this, Congress meant the estate to include the corpus of the trust or, in its stead, an amount equal in value.

293 F.2d at 918 (citations omitted).

IV.

I would affirm the decision of the tax court. I respectfully dissent.

ILLUSTRATIVE MATERIAL

A. SUBSEQUENT COURT DECISIONS

Two other courts of appeal have followed the *D'Ambrosio* majority. In Wheeler v. United States, 116 F.3d 749, 762 (5th Cir. 1997), the court adopted the *D'Ambrosio* holding and explained why D's estate had not been depleted as follows:

> "The sale of a remainder interest for its actuarial value does not deplete the seller's estate. 'The actuarial value of the remainder interest equals the amount that will grow to a principal sum equal to the value of the property that passes to the remainderman at termination of the retained interest. To reach this conclusion, the tables assume that both the consideration received for the remainder interest and the underlying

property are invested at the table rate of interest, compounded annually.' Jordan, Sales of Remainder Interests, at 692–93 (citing Keith E. Morrison, The Widow's Election: The Issue of Consideration, 44 Tex. L. Rev. 223, 237–38 (1965)). In other words, the actuarial tables are premised on the recognition that, at the end of the actuarial period, there is no discernible difference between (1) an estate holder retaining the full fee interest in the estate and (2) an estate holder retaining income from the life estate and selling the remainder interest for its actuarial value—in either case, the estate is not depleted. This is so because both interests, the life estate and the remainder interest, are capable of valuation. Recognizing this truism, the accumulated value of a decedent's estate is precisely the same whether she retains the fee interest or receives the actuarial value of the remainder interest outright by a sale prior to her actual death. Id. at 691–92; Morrison, The Issue of Consideration, at 237–38."

Subsequently, the Court of Appeals for the Ninth Circuit also adopted the *D'Ambrosio* approach. Estate of Magnin v. Commissioner, 184 F.3d 1074 (9th Cir. 1999).

B. ESTATE FREEZE ASPECTS OF *D'AMBROSIO*

If the property in fact appreciates at a rate greater than the interest rate used to calculate the value of the remainder interest, D will have successfully avoided transfer tax on the excess appreciation.

Section 2702, however, which is discussed in Chapter 37, significantly reduces the desirability of using the sale of remainder interests as an estate planning device. Where D transfers a remainder interest to "family members" while retaining a life interest, § 2702 treats the retained life interest as having a zero value. The result is that D is deemed to have made a taxable gift to the extent the value of her interest in the entire property exceeds the consideration received for the remainder interest. Congress adopted § 2702 because it was concerned that the actuarial and interest rate assumptions used to value remainder interests could be manipulated in the family context where the transferor and transferee might know that the assumptions underestimated the remainder interest's actual value. Section 2702 does not, however, eliminate the usefulness of the sale of remainder interests. The term "family members" does not include nephews, nieces and same-sex spouses.

C. THE *ALLEN* "PALPABLE TAX EVASION MOTIVE"

Why did the *D'Ambrosio* court distinguish the *Allen* case as involving a "palpable tax evasion motive?" Consider a situation where D, age 95, gives away the remainder interest in his property, retaining a life interest. Suppose that subsequently in the same year, he sells his life interest for its actuarial value. If D invests the amount he receives for a period equal to his remaining life expectancy, the amount he will possess at death will not equal the value of his entire interest in the property prior to the transfer. In contrast, as noted in *D'Ambrosio*, where D sells his remainder interest and retains a life interest, the amount in D's estate will equal the value of the entire property at the time of transfer if he lives for the period of his life expectancy and invests the sale proceeds.

D.   PARTIAL CONSIDERATION AND § 2043(a)

1.   *In General*

Section 2043(a) states that where a transferor receives consideration that does not qualify as adequate and full consideration, the transferor's gross estate shall include only the excess of the fair market value of the property at the time of death over the value of the consideration. For example, suppose D retains a life interest, transfers a remainder interest worth $100,000 to A, and receives $40,000 of consideration from A. If at D's death the remainder interest is worth $150,000, $110,000 will be included in D's gross estate. See Reg. § 20.2043–1(a).

Suppose that the consideration of $40,000 received by D in the above example appreciated to $60,000 on the date of D's death. Should the amount includable in D's estate be determined by valuing the consideration at the date of receipt ($40,000) or at the date of death ($60,000)? The courts have concluded that the value at the time of receipt governs. United States v. Righter, 400 F.2d 344 (8th Cir. 1968); Gregory Estate v. Commissioner, 39 T.C. 1012 (1963). The correctness of this result is debatable. If the purpose of § 2043(a) is to restore D's estate to the position he would have been in had the transfer not occurred, the value of the consideration at the date of death should be used. In the above example, had D retained the property, $150,000 would be includable in his estate. Since the consideration D received is included in his estate at a value of $60,000, only $90,000 of the retained interest ($150,000 minus the value at death of $60,000) should be included to achieve parity. On the other hand, using the value of the consideration at the date of death creates difficult tracing problems which are avoided by using the date-of-receipt value.

2.   *"Approximate" Adequate and Full Consideration*

How close in value does the consideration for a transferred interest have to be to constitute "adequate and full consideration"? The courts have suggested that "adequate and full consideration" need only be of "approximately equal value." Estate of Davis v. Commissioner, 440 F.2d 896, 900 (3d Cir. 1971); Estate of Magnin v. Commissioner, 184 F.3d 1074, 1081 (9th Cir. 1999). In Estate of Magnin v. Commissioner, 81 T.C.M. 1126 (2001), on remand from, 184 F.3d 1074 (9th Cir. 1999), the Tax Court determined that where the actual value of the transferred interest exceeded the consideration received by more than 100 percent, the consideration was not "approximately equal" to the transferred interest.

Family limited partnerships have provided an opportunity for the courts to expand on the application of the adequate and full consideration requirement where the taxpayer transfers property to a limited partnership in exchange for an interest in that partnership. As discussed at p. 223, taxpayers use family limited partnerships to reduce the value of assets that will be included in their gross estates. Suppose for example that a taxpayer owns an asset that has a value of $1 million. A common strategy is to exchange that asset for an interest in a partnership that restricts the taxpayer's ability to withdraw the asset from the partnership and to participate in the management of the partnership. If the form of the transaction is respected, the value of the partnership interest will be included in the gross estate at a value much lower than $1 million. This strategy means the interest received in the partnership has a much lower fair market value than the property transferred to the partnership.

The Tax Court has confirmed that the value of the property transferred by a taxpayer to a family limited partnership need not equal the value of the partnership interest received in order for the adequate and full consideration exception to apply. In Estate of Stone v. Commissioner, 86 T.C.M. 551 (2003), the Tax Court reasoned that requiring the value of the interest received in an entity, such as a partnership or corporation, to equal the value of the property transferred to it would have the unintended effect of eliminating applicability of the adequate and full consideration exception to all transfers of property to partnerships and corporations. The court in Kimbell v. United States, 371 F.3d 257, 266 (5th Cir. 2004), elaborated:

> "We would only add to the Tax Court's rejection of the government's * * * argument that it is a classic mixing of apples and oranges: The government is attempting to equate the venerable 'willing buyer-willing seller' test of fair market value (which applies when calculating gift or estate tax) with the proper test for adequate and full consideration under § 2036(a). This conflation misses the mark: The business decision to exchange cash or other assets for a transfer-restricted, non-managerial interest in a limited partnership involves financial considerations other than the purchaser's ability to turn right around and sell the newly acquired limited partnership interest for 100 cents on the dollar. Investors who acquire such interests do so with the expectation of realizing benefits such as management expertise, security and preservation of assets, capital appreciation and avoidance of personal liability. Thus there is nothing inconsistent in acknowledging, on the one hand, that the investor's dollars have acquired a limited partnership interest at arm's length for adequate and full consideration and, on the other hand, that the asset thus acquired has a present fair market value, i.e., immediate sale potential, of substantially less than the dollars just paid * * *.

> "As this principle applies to wholly unrelated buyers and sellers of interests in limited partnerships, it must be equally true of buyers and sellers of such interests who happen to be related by blood or affinity, unless * * * the evidence demonstrates the absence of good faith, i.e., a sham transaction motivated solely by tax avoidance * * *. Certainly, close scrutiny must be applied when the parties are related, but close scrutiny is not synonymous with automatic proscription or impossibility * * *."

The courts have cautioned, however, that the taxpayer's willingness to receive an interest in the partnership that is worth less than the value of the property transferred to it must be based on an expectation of deriving benefits from pooling resources with other partners in the partnership's conduct of a business. In Estate of Harper v. Commissioner, 83 T.C.M. 1641, 1654 (2002), the court said that "a genuine pooling for business purposes injects something different into the adequate and full consideration calculus" and "there is at least a potential that intangibles stemming from a pooling for joint enterprise might support a ruling of adequate and full consideration." In the case before it, the *Harper* court found no such pooling where one partner, the decedent, had contributed all the assets to the partnership. The court stated:

"In actuality, all the decedent did was to change the form in which he held his beneficial interest in the contributed property. . . . without any change whatsoever in the underlying pool of assets or prospect for profit, as, for example, where others make contributions of property or services in the interest of true joint ownership, or enterprise, there exists nothing but a circuitous 'recycling' of value. We are satisfied that such instances of pure recycling do not rise to the level of a payment of consideration. To hold otherwise would open section 2036 to a myriad of abuses engendered by unilateral paper transformations."

Similarly, in Estate of Strangi v. Commissioner, 85 T.C.M. 1331, 1344 (2003), the court ruled that decedent's receipt of a limited partnership interest did not constitute adequate and full consideration where decedent had contributed over 99 percent of the partnership's assets and the partnership was not a "functioning business enterprise."

3.   *"Bona Fide Sale"*

The exception for adequate and full consideration requires that such consideration be received in a "bona fide sale." In the context of family limited partnerships, the courts have required that there be a legitimate non-tax business reason for the transfer of property to the partnership in order for the transfer to qualify as a "bona fide sale."

In Estate of Thompson v. Commissioner, 382 F.3d 367, 382 (3d Cir. 2004), the court said that a bona fide sale does not "necessarily require an arms-length transaction between the transferor and an unrelated third party." However, the court observed that a bona fide sale does require that the sale be made in good faith. The court determined that the contribution of assets to a family limited partnership in exchange for partnership interests was not in good faith where the partnership did not conduct an active trade or business. The court stated:

"We similarly believe a 'bona fide sale' does not necessarily require an 'arm's length transaction' between the transferor and an unrelated third-party. Of course, evidence of an 'arm's length transaction' or 'bargained-for exchange' is highly probative to the § 2036 inquiry. But we see no statutory basis for adopting an interpretation of 'bona fide sale' that would automatically defeat the § 2036 exception for all intrafamily transfers.

"We are mindful of the mischief that may arise in the family estate planning context. As the Supreme Court observed, 'the family relationship often makes it possible for one to shift tax incidence by surface changes of ownership without disturbing in the least his dominion and control over the subject of the gift or the purposes for which the income from the property is used.' Comm'r v. Culbertson, 337 U.S. 733, 746 (1949). But such mischief can be adequately monitored by heightened scrutiny of intrafamily transfers, and does not require a uniform prohibition on transfers to family limited partnerships. See id. ('[The] existence of the family relationship does not create a status which itself determines tax questions, but is simply a warning that things may not be what they seem.'); Kimbell, 371 F.3d at 265 ('[W]hen the transaction is between family members, it is subject to heightened scrutiny.'). * * *

"However, while a 'bona fide sale' does not necessarily require an 'arm's length transaction,' it still must be made in good faith. See 26 C.F.R. § 20.2043–1(a). A 'good faith' transfer to a family limited partnership must provide the transferor some potential for benefit other than the potential estate tax advantages that might result.... Even when all the 'i's are dotted and t's are crossed,' a transaction motivated solely by tax planning and with 'no business or corporate purpose ... is nothing more than a contrivance.' Gregory v. Helvering, 293 U.S. 465, 469 (1935) * * * [O]bjective indicia that the partnership operates a legitimate business may provide a sufficient factual basis for finding a good faith transfer. But if there is no discernable purpose or benefit for the transfer other than estate tax savings, the sale is not 'bona fide' within the meaning of § 2036. * * *

"After a thorough review of the record, we agree with the Tax Court that decedent's inter vivos transfers do not qualify for the § 2036(a) exception because neither * * * [family partnership] conducted any legitimate business operations, nor provided decedent with any potential non-tax benefit from the transfers."

Estate of Bigelow v. Commissioner, 503 F.3d 955 (9th Cir. 2007) reached a similar result. For a contrary result, see Kimbell v. United States, 371 F.3d 257, 267 (5th Cir. 2004), where the court concluded that a bona fide sale had occurred because the decedent had non-tax business reasons for creating the partnership and had contributed active business assets along with other non-business assets to the partnership.

Courts have also refused to find a bona fide sale where the taxpayer who transferred assets to the partnership stood on both sides of the transaction. In Estate of Harper v. Commissioner, 83 T.C.M. 1641, 1653 (2002), the court refused to find a bona fide sale where there was no independent party involved in the formation and transfer of assets to the partnership. Similarly, in Estate of Strangi v. Commissioner, 85 T.C.M. 1331, 1343 (2003), the court held that the sale was not bona fide where decedent's attorney-in-fact had organized the partnership and determined the interest of other partner without any meaningful negotiation with other partners.

E.   MARITAL RIGHTS AS ADEQUATE CONSIDERATION

Although § 2043(b)(2) specifically imports the consideration rule of § 2516 (see p. 189) into the estate tax with regard to § 2053, §§ 2036–2038 are not mentioned. This omission can create anomalous results.

For example, assume that, pursuant to a written agreement that satisfies the requirements of § 2516, A creates an irrevocable trust under which the income is to be paid to A for life, with the remainder to B, A's former spouse. Assume further that § 2516 is the sole source of consideration for the inter vivos transfer which, by virtue of that section, is not a taxable transfer. Under the literal language of § 2043(b), this consideration is not adequate for purposes of § 2036(a)(1) with the result that A's estate includes the trust corpus.

Could A's estate deduct the value of the trust corpus under § 2053? The legislative history of § 2043(b)(2) states that it is intended to allow "an estate tax deduction for transfers pursuant to claims arising under a written agreement in settlement of marital or property rights where the agreement would have qualified those transfers as non-taxable for gift tax purposes (under § 2516). Thus, where the transferor dies prior to completing the transfers under this written agreement, no estate tax will be imposed with respect to the property transferred by the estate." H.R. Rep. No. 432, Pt. 2, 98th Cong., 2d Sess. 1504 (1984). Here, the transfer of the remainder interest to B was completed prior to A's death, but the actual transfer of assets to B will not occur until after A's death. It is not clear whether this latter transfer is the type of transfer referred to in the legislative history as being incomplete at the transferor's death.

Compare the foregoing situation with one in which A creates a revocable trust pursuant to a written agreement that satisfies § 2516. Under the terms of the trust, payments are to be made to B, after A's death. At A's death, § 2038 will require A's estate to include the trust corpus since § 2043(b) precludes the written agreement from constituting adequate consideration. Should A's estate be allowed a deduction under § 2053 since the transfer will only be completed upon A's death? Again it is not clear whether this is the type of incomplete transfer mentioned in the above quoted legislative history. A stronger argument for deductibility exists compared to the preceding situation because the transfer was in fact incomplete for gift tax purposes prior to A's death. Moreover, to conclude otherwise would cause deductibility to depend upon whether A's obligation was to be paid from A's probate as opposed to non-probate assets.

It seems inappropriate that a deduction should be allowed for § 2038 transfers but not for § 2036(a)(1) transfers. Consequently, the deduction should be permitted in both situations.

CHAPTER 19

GIFT TAX EFFECTS OF TRANSFERS WITH RETAINED INTERESTS OR POWERS

INTRODUCTION

The application of the estate tax to an inter vivos transfer because of a retained interest or power does not necessarily relieve the inter vivos transfer of gift tax consequences. It is possible for a transfer to be subject to a gift tax and subsequently to be included in the transferor's gross estate.

For example, suppose that A irrevocably transfers property in trust, retaining an income interest for herself, remainder to B. A is treated as having made a completed gift of the value of B's remainder interest which will be subject to gift tax at the time of the transfer in trust. At A's death, the entire value of the trust corpus will also be included in A's estate under § 2036.

Two mechanisms exist for avoiding double taxation of the same transfer. First, § 2012 avoids double taxation of gifts made prior to 1977 which are included in the decedent's gross estate by providing a credit for the gift taxes paid against the estate tax. See p. 68. Second, the gifts made after 1976 which are included in the gross estate avoid double taxation due to the method of calculating the estate tax in § 2001(b). Recall that § 2001(b)(1) calculates a tentative tax (see p. 68) based upon the sum of the taxable estate and "adjusted taxable gifts," as defined in the last sentence of § 2001(b). The tentative tax is then reduced in § 2001(b)(2) by the gift tax payable with respect to post–1976 gifts. Since the "adjusted taxable gifts" do not include post–1976 gifts which are included in the decedent's gross estate and since the tentative tax is reduced by the gift tax payable on all post–1976 gifts (including post–1976 gifts included in the decedent's gross estate), the post–1976 gifts are not taxed twice.

SECTION A.   TRANSFERS WITH RETAINED POWERS

Internal Revenue Code: §§ 2501; 2511(a)

Regulations: § 25.2511–2

Estate of Sanford v. Commissioner

308 U.S. 39 (1939).

■ MR. JUSTICE STONE delivered the opinion of the Court.

This and its companion case, Rasquin v. Humphreys [308 U.S. 54], present the single question of statutory construction whether in the case of an inter vivos transfer of property in trust, by a donor reserving to himself the power to designate new beneficiaries other than himself, the gift becomes complete and subject to the gift tax imposed by the federal revenue laws at the time of the relinquishment of the power. Correlative questions, important only if a negative answer is given to the first one, are whether the gift becomes complete and taxable when the trust is created or, in the case where the donor has reserved a power of revocation for his own benefit and has relinquished it before relinquishing the power to change beneficiaries, whether the gift first becomes complete and taxable at the time of relinquishing the power of revocation.

In 1913, before the enactment of the first gift tax statute of 1924, decedent created a trust of personal property for the benefit of named beneficiaries, reserving to himself the power to terminate the trust in whole or in part, or to modify it (by changing beneficiaries). In 1919 he surrendered the power to revoke the trust by an appropriate writing in which he reserved "the right to modify any or all of the trusts" but provided that this right "shall in no way be deemed or construed to include any right or privilege" in the donor "to withdraw principal or income from any trust." In August, 1924, after the effective date of the gift tax statute, decedent renounced his remaining power to modify the trust. After his death in 1928, the Commissioner following the decision in Hesslein v. Hoey, 91 F.2d 954, in 1937, ruled that the gift became complete and taxable only upon decedent's final renunciation of his power to modify the trusts and gave notice of a tax deficiency accordingly.

The order of the Board of Tax Appeals sustaining the tax was affirmed by the Court of Appeals for the Third Circuit, 103 F.2d 81, which followed the decision of the Court of Appeals for the Second Circuit in Hesslein v. Hoey, supra, in which we had denied certiorari, 302 U.S. 756. In the Hesslein case, as in the Humphreys case now before us, a gift in trust with the reservation of a power in the donor to alter the disposition of the property in any way not beneficial to himself, was held to be incomplete and not subject to the gift tax under the 1932 Act so long as the donor retained that power.

We granted certiorari in this case, 307 U.S. 618, and in the Humphreys case, id. 619, upon the representation of the Government that it has taken inconsistent positions with respect to the question involved in the two cases and that because of this fact and of the doubt of the correctness of the decision in the Hesslein case, decision of the question by this Court is desirable in order to remove the resultant confusion in the administration of the revenue laws.

It has continued to take these inconsistent positions here, stating that it is unable to determine which construction of the statute will be most advantageous to the Government in point of revenue collected. It argues in this case that the gift did not become complete and taxable until surrender by the donor of his reserved power to designate new beneficiaries of the trusts. In the Humphreys case it argues that the gift upon trust with power reserved to the donor, not afterward relinquished, to change the beneficiaries was complete and taxable when the trust was created. It concedes by its brief that "a decision favorable to the government in either case will necessarily preclude a favorable decision in the other." * * *

There is nothing in the language of the statute, and our attention has not been directed to anything in its legislative history to suggest that Congress had any purpose to tax gifts before the donor had fully parted with his interest in the property given, or that the test of the completeness of the taxed gift was to be any different from that to be applied in determining whether the donor has retained an interest such that it becomes subject to the estate tax upon its extinguishment at death. The gift tax was supplementary to the estate tax. The two are in pari materia and must be construed together. Burnet v. Guggenheim, [288 U.S. 280], 286. An important, if not the main, purpose of the gift tax was to prevent or compensate for avoidance of death taxes by taxing the gifts of property inter vivos which, but for the gifts, would be subject in its original or converted form to the tax laid upon transfers at death.[1]

[The predecessor of § 2012(a)][2] provides that when a tax has been imposed by [the predecessor of § 2502] upon a gift, the value of which is required by any provision of the statute taxing the estate to be included in the gross estate, the gift tax is to be credited on the estate tax. The two taxes are thus not always mutually exclusive * * *. But [the predecessor of § 2012(a)] is without application unless there is a gift inter vivos which is taxable independently of any requirement that it shall be included in the gross estate. Property transferred in trust subject to a power of control over its disposition reserved to the donor is likewise required by [the predecessor of § 2038] to be included in the gross estate. But it does not follow that the transfer in trust is also taxable as a gift. The point was decided in the Guggenheim case where it was held that a gift upon trust, with power in

---

1. The gift provisions of the Revenue Act of 1924 were added by amendments to the revenue bill introduced on the floor of the House and the Senate. Cong.Rec., Vol. 65, Part 3, pp. 3118–3119; Part 4, pp. 3170, 3171; Part 8, p. 8094. The sponsor of the amendment in both houses urged the adoption of the bill as a "corollary" or as "supplemental" to the estate tax. Cong.Rec., Vol. 65, Part 3, pp. 3119–3120, 3122; Part 4, p. 3172; Cong. Rec., Vol. 65, Part 8, pp. 8095, 8096.

The gift tax of 1924 was repealed when Congress, concurrently with the enactment of § 302(c) of the Revenue Act of 1926, 44 Stat. 70, 125, 126, establishing a conclusive presumption that gifts within two years of death were made in contemplation of death and therefore subject to the estate tax. A gift tax was reenacted by § 501 of the Revenue Act of 1932, 47 Stat. 169, shortly after it was decided in Heiner v. Donnan, 285 U.S. 312, that the legislative enactment of such a presumption violated the Fifth Amendment.

Section 501(c) of the 1932 Act added a new provision that transfers in trust, with power of revocation in the donor, should be taxed on relinquishment of the power. This was repealed by § 511 of the Act of 1934, 48 Stat. 680, because Burnet v. Guggenheim, 288 U.S. 280, had declared that such was the law without specific legislation. H.R.No. 704, 73rd Cong., 2d Sess., p. 40; Sen.Rep. No. 558, 73rd Cong. 2d Sess., p. 50.

2. [ED.: See p. 75, for the current treatment of a prior gift tax paid on the transfer of property which is includible in the transferor's gross estate.]

the donor to revoke it is not taxable as a gift because the transfer is incomplete, and that the transfer whether inter vivos or at death becomes complete and taxable only when the power of control is relinquished.[3] We think, as was pointed out in the Guggenheim case, supra, 285, that the gift tax statute does not contemplate two taxes upon gifts * * *, one upon the gift when a trust is created or when the power of revocation, if any, is relinquished, and another on the transfer of the same property at death because the gift previously made was incomplete.

It is plain that the contention of the taxpayer in this case that the gift becomes complete and taxable upon the relinquishment of the donor's power to revoke the trust cannot be sustained unless we are to hold, contrary to the policy of the statute and the reasoning in the Guggenheim case, that a second tax will be incurred upon the donor's relinquishment at death of his power to select new beneficiaries, or unless as an alternative we are to abandon our ruling in the Porter case. The Government does not suggest, even in its argument in the Humphreys case, that we should depart from our earlier rulings, and we think it clear that we should not do so both because we are satisfied with the reasoning upon which they rest and because departure from either would produce inconsistencies in the law as serious and confusing as the inconsistencies in administrative practice from which the Government now seeks relief.

There are other persuasive reasons why the taxpayer's contention cannot be sustained. By [the predecessor of §§ 6324(a)(2) and 2502], and more specifically by [the predecessor of § 6324(b)], the donee of any gift is made personally liable for the tax to the extent of the value of the gift if the tax is not paid by the donor. It can hardly be supposed that Congress intended to impose personal liability upon the donee of a gift of property, so incomplete that he might be deprived of it by the donor the day after he had paid the tax. Further, [the predecessor of § 2522(a)(2)] exempts from the tax, gifts to religious, charitable, and educational corporations and the like. A gift would seem not to be complete, for purposes of the tax, where the donor has reserved the power to determine whether the donees ultimately entitled to receive and enjoy the property are of such a class as to exempt the gift from taxation. Apart from other considerations we should hesitate to accept as correct a construction under which it could plausibly be maintained that a gift in trust for the benefit of charitable corporations is then complete so that the taxing statute becomes operative and the gift escapes the tax even though the donor should later change the beneficiaries

---

3. [ED.: In Burnet v. Guggenheim, 288 U.S. 280 (1933), the taxpayer created two trusts in 1917, before the enactment of the first gift tax statute, reserving to himself an unqualified power to modify, alter or revoke, except as to income already received or accrued. In 1925, while the 1924 gift tax was in effect, the taxpayer relinquished this power, and the Commissioner assessed a gift tax on the value of the securities constituting the corpus of the two trusts. The taxpayer contended that the transfers became complete in 1917 when the title passed, not in 1925 when his control was extinguished. Rejecting this argument, the Court stated that while the power of revocation stood uncancelled, the gifts remained "inchoate and imperfect", and became subject to the gift tax when the transfers became absolute through the cancellation of the power.]

to the non-exempt class through exercise of a power to modify the trust in any way not beneficial to himself.

The argument of petitioner that the construction which the Government supports here, but assails in the Humphreys case, affords a ready means of evasion of the gift tax is not impressive. It is true, of course, that under it gift taxes will not be imposed on transactions which fall short of being completed gifts. But if for that reason they are not taxed as gifts they remain subject to death taxes assessed at higher rates, and the Government gets its due, which was precisely the end sought by the enactment of the gift tax. * * *

Affirmed.

■ MR. JUSTICE BUTLER took no part in the consideration or decision of this case.

Camp v. Commissioner

195 F.2d 999 (1st Cir. 1952).

■ MAGRUDER, CHIEF JUDGE: Frederic E. Camp petitions for review of a decision of the Tax Court entered November 7, 1950, holding that petitioner was deficient in his gift tax for the year 1937 in the amount of $55,737.08 * * *.

The dispute centers about the effect of a transfer in trust made by the taxpayer in 1932, prior to the enactment of the [predecessor of § 2501(a)] which imposed a tax on gifts. * * * Petitioner insists that this transfer in trust was a completed gift of the whole corpus, so that the transaction in its entirety was outside the incidence of the gift tax subsequently enacted. The Tax Court has held, however, that there was no completed gift at all in 1932, because the donor reserved in the deed of trust full power to alter, amend or revoke, in conjunction with his half brother, who, the court concluded, had no "substantial adverse interest" in the trust property; and that there was a completed gift of the whole of the corpus of the trust in 1937, when the trust instrument was amended so as to vest the power of further amendment or revocation in the donor in sole conjunction with the donor's wife, who had a life interest in the trust income.

We are unable to accept altogether either the taxpayer's argument or the conclusion of the Tax Court. This segment of tax law, as to when a transfer in trust is to be deemed a completed gift for purposes of the gift tax, has been in a somewhat cloudy state, as perhaps is evident from the fact that in the present case the Commissioner has taken several successive positions, each asserting a larger deficiency for the years in question.

The case was tried in the Tax Court upon a stipulation of facts, supplemented by a deposition by petitioner which was read into evidence.

On October 30, 1931, the taxpayer married Alida Donnell Milliken. No children have issued from this marriage; but at various dates within the period January 19, 1937, to October 3, 1942, taxpayer and his wife have adopted four children.

On February 1, 1932, taxpayer executed a trust indenture naming Bankers Trust Company of New York as trustee, and transferred to said trustee, as corpus of the trust, securities then having a fair market value of $416,131.72.

The trust instrument provided that the income should be payable to taxpayer's wife Alida during her life, and that upon her death the principal of the trust should be paid to the then living issue of the donor per stirpes; and in default of such issue, that the trustee should continue to hold the principal in trust, paying the income therefrom to Johanna R. Bullock, mother of the donor, during her life, and upon her death, that the trustee should pay the principal of the trust fund onto H. Ridgely Bullock, half brother of the donor, or if he be then dead, unto the then living issue of said H. Ridgely Bullock per stirpes, or if there be none, to the trustees of Princeton University.

The tenth article of the trust indenture provided:

"This indenture shall not be subject to revocation, alteration or modification by the Donor, alone, but nevertheless, he may, in conjunction with either H. Ridgely Bullock or Johanna R. Bullock, beneficiaries hereunder, during the continuance of this trust, by instrument, in writing, executed and acknowledged by the Donor and either the said H. Ridgely Bullock or the said Johanna R. Bullock, * * * modify or alter in any manner, or revoke in whole or in part, this indenture and the trusts then existing, and the estates and interests in property hereby created. * * * "

When the trust was thus created in February, 1932, taxpayer's wife Alida was 23 years of age, his mother Johanna R. Bullock was 63, and his half brother H. Ridgely Bullock was 22.

On August 30, 1934, the taxpayer, in conjunction with Ridgely, exercised the power to alter or amend by inserting a provision that Alida, wife of the donor, should receive the income of the trust only so long as she, during the donor's lifetime, should continue to be his wife and to reside with him.

On December 11, 1937, the taxpayer, in conjunction with Ridgely, exercised the amendatory power so as to provide that the term "issue of the Donor", as used in the trust instrument, should be deemed to include any child or children then or thereafter legally adopted by the donor and his said wife, and their issue. At the same time the trust instrument was further modified so as to strike out the above-quoted provision in the tenth article with reference to the power to alter, amend or revoke, and to substitute in lieu thereof a provision containing the same words except that the name of Alida Donnell Milliken Camp was substituted for the names of H. Ridgely Bullock and Johanna R. Bullock. Thus, on and after December 11, 1937, taxpayer reserved the power to alter, amend or revoke the trust in sole conjunction with his wife Alida, who was entitled to all the income from the trust during her lifetime, with the qualification previously stated.

The fair market value of the corpus of the trust, as of December 11, 1937, was $518,089.76.

On June 6, 1946, the taxpayer, in conjunction with his wife Alida, further modified the trust instrument by striking out in its entirety the provision of the tenth article, as amended, dealing with the power to alter, amend or revoke, and substituting in lieu thereof an unqualified provision that the trust indenture "shall not be subject to revocation, alteration or modification."

Section 501(c) of the Revenue Act of 1932 [the substance of this section is now contained in Reg. § 25.2511–2] contained the following specific provision:

> "The tax shall not apply to a transfer of property in trust where the power to revest in the donor title to such property is vested in the donor, either alone or in conjunction with any person not having a substantial adverse interest in the disposition of such property or the income therefrom, but the relinquishment or termination of such power (other than by the donor's death) shall be considered to be a transfer by the donor by gift of the property subject to such power, and any payment of the income therefrom to a beneficiary other than the donor shall be considered to be a transfer by the donor of such income by gift."

This subsection was repealed in 1934, 48 Stat. 758, for the reason, as explained in the committee reports, that "the principle expressed in that section is now a fundamental part of the law by virtue of the Supreme Court's decision in the Guggenheim case, * * *." H.Rep. 704, 73d Cong., 2d Sess. (1934) p. 40; Sen. Rep. 558, 73d Cong., 2d Sess., p. 50. The reference was to Burnet v. Guggenheim, 1933, 288 U.S. 280, which involved the tax upon transfers by gift imposed by [the predecessor of § 2501(a)]. The Court held, without the aid of any specific language in the statute comparable to § 501(c) of the Revenue Act of 1932, that a deed of trust made in 1917, with a reservation to the grantor alone of the power of revocation, became subject to the gift tax when, in 1925, there was a change of the deed by the cancellation of the power.

It is to be noted that the facts of the Guggenheim case were narrower than the situations specifically covered in § 501(c), in that the Supreme Court was not passing upon the case where the donor did not reserve to himself alone the power of revocation, but vested such power in himself in conjunction with some other person who might or might not have had a substantial adverse interest in the disposition of the property or the income therefrom. However, the committee reports in 1934 expressed the view that this latter situation was covered in principle by the Supreme Court's decision in the Guggenheim case, and therefore recommended the repeal of § 501(c) because it had become unnecessary and superfluous.

What, then, was this "principle" recognized in the Guggenheim case? We think it is to be found in the Court's opinion, 288 U.S. at 286, that the gift tax was not aimed at every transfer of the legal title without consideration, which would include a transfer to trustees to hold for the use of the grantor, but was aimed, rather, "at transfers of the title that have the quality of a gift, and a gift is not consummate until put beyond recall."

Subsequent cases have elaborated upon this concept of a "gift", and have settled that a transfer in trust is incomplete as a gift, not only where the donor reserves the power to revest the trust property in himself, but also where he reserves the power to alter the disposition of the property or the income therefrom in some way not beneficial to himself. Estate of Sanford v. Commissioner, 1939, 308 U.S. 39; Rasquin v. Humphreys, 1939, 308 U.S. 54. See the discussion in Higgins v. Commissioner, 1 Cir., 1942, 129 F.2d 237.

[The predecessor of Reg. § 25.2511–2 contained] the following provisions, which we take to be declaratory of the intent of the Act and of the gloss which later cases have put upon the concept of a "gift" as expressed in Burnet v. Guggenheim:

"[§ 25.2511–2] Cessation of donor's dominion and control. * * *

"As to any property, or part thereof or interest therein, of which the donor has so parted with dominion and control as to leave in him no power to change the disposition thereof, whether for his own benefit or for the benefit of another, the gift is complete. But if upon a transfer of property (whether in trust or otherwise) the donor reserves any power over the disposition thereof, the gift may be wholly incomplete, or may be partially incomplete, depending upon all the facts in the particular case. Accordingly, in every case of a transfer of property subject to a reserved power, the terms of the power must be examined and its scope determined.

"A gift is incomplete in every instance where a donor reserves the power to revest the beneficial title to the property in himself. A gift is also incomplete where and to the extent that a reserved power gives the donor the right to name new beneficiaries or to change the interests of the beneficiaries as between themselves. * * *

"A donor shall be considered as himself having the power where it is exercisable by him in conjunction with any person not having a substantial adverse interest in the disposition of the transferred property or the income therefrom. A trustee, as such, is not a person having an adverse interest in the disposition of the trust property or its income.

"The relinquishment or termination of a power to change the disposition of the transferred property, occurring otherwise than by the death of the donor (the statute being confined to transfers by living donors), is regarded as the event which completes the gift and causes the tax to apply. * * *"

Where a donor makes a transfer in trust for numerous beneficiaries, it is obvious that there may be several distinct gifts or potential gifts. For purposes of the gift tax, some of the interests created may be completed gifts, and others may not be, depending upon the facts of the particular case—as is stated in the first paragraph of the above quotation from [the predecessor of Reg. § 25.2511–2].

From the foregoing, we think the following propositions are reasonably clear:

(1) If the trust instrument gives a designated beneficiary any interest in the corpus of the trust property or of the income therefrom, which is capable of monetary valuation, and the donor reserves no power to withdraw that interest, in whole or in part, except with the consent of such designated beneficiary, then the gift of that particular interest will be deemed to be complete, for the purposes of the gift tax. See * * * Commissioner v. Prouty, 1 Cir., 1940, 115 F.2d 331, 334 * * *. This is true, though at the time of the creation of the trust there might be extraneous considerations, whether of a pecuniary or sentimental nature, which would give the donor every confidence that such designated beneficiary would acquiesce in any future desire of the donor to withdraw the gift, in whole or in part. See Commissioner v. Prouty, supra at 335–36. In that respect the donor is taken at his word; he has legally given away something which he cannot take back except with the consent of the donee. The transfer fulfills the concept of a completed gift, quite as much as if a husband makes an outright gift of securities to his wife, being confident that his wife would reconvey the securities to him if he ever asked for them. If there was an advance agreement between the donor and the donee, prior to the transfer in trust, to the effect that the donee would acquiesce in any future exercise of the power of modification proposed by the donor, then the situation would be different. The trust instrument would not express the true intention of the parties. A real gift is not intended, where the purported donee has agreed ahead of time to hold the "gift" subject to the call and disposition of the purported donor.[4]

(2) If the only power reserved by the donor is a power to revoke the entire trust instrument (not a power to modify the trust in any particular), and this power may be exercised only in conjunction with a designated beneficiary who is given a substantial adverse interest in the disposition of the trust property or the income therefrom, then the transfer in trust will be deemed to be a present gift of the entire corpus of the trust, for purposes of the gift tax. In such cases, the gift of the entire corpus will be deemed to have been "put beyond recall" by the donor himself.

---

4. In the present case, the Tax Court inferred from petitioner's deposition, which was read in evidence, that there was such an advance agreement here between petitioner and his half brother Ridgely. In the view we take, it is unnecessary for us to determine whether such an inference of fact was warranted.

(3) If the trust instrument reserves to the donor a general power to alter, amend or revoke, in whole or in part, and this power is to be exercised only in conjunction with a designated beneficiary who has received an interest in the corpus or income capable of monetary valuation, then the transfer in trust will be deemed to be a completed gift, for purposes of the gift tax, only as to the interest of such designated beneficiary having a veto over the exercise of the power.[5] As to the interests of the other beneficiaries, the gifts will be deemed to be incomplete, for as to such interests the donor reserves the power to take them away in conjunction with a person who has no interest in the trust adverse to such withdrawal. The gifts to the other beneficiaries have not been "put beyond recall" by the donor; in such cases the regulation recognizes realistically that when the donor has reserved the power to withdraw any of the donated interests with the concurrence of some third person who has no interest in the trust adverse to such withdrawal, it is in substance the same as if the donor had reserved such power in himself alone. In further support of this proposition, see the discussion in Estate of Sanford v. Commissioner, 1939, 308 U.S. 39, 46–47.

Coming back, then, to the terms of the trust which petitioner created in February, 1932: It is clear that there was not at that time a completed gift of the life income to petitioner's wife Alida. Under the original provisions of the trust indenture, this life estate was subject to revocation by the donor in conjunction either with the donor's half brother Ridgely or his mother Johnanna, neither of whose interests in the trust were adverse to the withdrawal of the life estate from Alida.

When the trust instrument was amended on December 11, 1937, so as to transfer to Alida alone the veto power over any further proposals by the donor for amendment of the trust, there was on that date a completed gift to Alida of the interest which she then held in the trust. It is stipulated that the value on December 11, 1937, of the income of a trust having a principal value of $518,089.76, payable during the life of a woman of 29 (Alida's age), was $356,492.38. However, it is to be noted that Alida did not at this time hold an absolutely unqualified life interest in the income. By prior amendment, the indenture provided that the income of the trust was to be payable to Alida, wife of the donor, only "as long as she, during his lifetime, shall continue to be his wife and to reside with him". Whether, in the valuation of the gift to Alida on December 11, 1937, some allowance should be made for this qualification upon the life estate we do not now

---

5. This proposition is subject to qualification in the rather unusual situation like that presented by Trust No. 1 in Commissioner v. Prouty, C.A. 1, 115 F.2d 331. There under the terms of the trust instrument, the grantor reserved a power to revoke or amend, with the written consent of her husband. Although the husband was not given the entire beneficial interest in the trust property, nevertheless he did have substantial interests, both in the disposition of the income and in the disposition of the corpus, which were adverse to any modification of the trust other than by way of augmenting the husband's interests. In these circumstances we held that there had been a completed gift of the entire corpus.

undertake to say. Cf. Robinette v. Helvering, 1943, 318 U.S. 184, 188. The Tax Court was in error, we think, in ruling that upon the execution of the amendment of December 11, 1937, petitioner made a taxable gift of the whole corpus of the trust, valued then at $518,089.76. There were at that time no completed gifts to the succeeding income beneficiaries and beneficiaries in remainder, for Alida's interest in the trust was not adverse to the donor's revocation of those succeeding interests by an exercise of the reserved power.

By the amendment of June 6, 1946, whereby all power to revoke, alter or modify the trust was eliminated, there resulted a taxable gift of the then value of the corpus, minus the sum determined to be the value of the gift to Alida on December 11, 1937, and minus also the values of any completed gifts which may be deemed to have been made at the time of the creation of the trust on February 1, 1932. This latter point we do not have to determine in the present case, because petitioner's liability for the year 1946 is not before us. In passing, we simply allude to a possible difficulty, in that the donor originally reserved a power to revoke or modify the trust in conjunction with either Ridgely or Johnanna. Ridgely's contingent remainder interest might have been revoked by the donor, in conjunction with Johnanna, whose interest in the trust was not adverse to such revocation. Johnanna's contingent life estate could have been revoked by the donor in conjunction with Ridgely, whose interest in the trust was not adverse to such revocation. Where the veto power is thus lodged in the alternative, it may be that, for purposes of the gift tax, there is not a completed gift to either of such beneficiaries. But cf. Estate of Leon N. Gillette, 7 T.C. 219 (1946); Commissioner v. Betts, 7 Cir., 1941, 123 F.2d 534.

The decision of the Tax Court is vacated, and the case is remanded to that court for further proceedings not inconsistent with this opinion.

ILLUSTRATIVE MATERIAL

A.   GENERAL

In determining whether powers retained by the grantor are sufficient to render the gift incomplete for gift tax purposes (and hence not subject to gift tax), it is useful to distinguish three situations: (1) where the grantor has retained the power to revoke the transfer or change beneficiaries; (2) where a trustee other than the grantor holds powers which may be exercised for the benefit of the grantor; and (3) where the grantor has retained powers that may be exercisable only with the consent of another person, who may or may not have a substantial adverse interest in the disposition of the property transferred. The following materials consider situations that have arisen in these categories.

B.   POWER IN GRANTOR TO REVOKE TRANSFER

Reg. § 25.2511–2(c) states that a gift is incomplete where the donor reserves the power to revest the transferred property in herself. Although the reservation of the power to revoke or alter beneficial interests causes the transfer to the trust to be incomplete, subsequent transfers from the trust to beneficiaries will constitute taxable gifts by the grantor in the year of the distribution. Reg. § 25.2511–2(f); Commissioner v. Warner, 127 F.2d 913 (9th Cir. 1942).

Sometimes the grantor will not explicitly retain the power to revoke, but will retain such extensive control over the transferred property that the court will treat the transfer as revocable. In Merritt v. Commissioner, 29 T.C. 149 (1957), stockholders of a family corporation entered into an agreement reserving to each a life interest in the stock owned by each, with provisions for ultimate devolution of the remainder interests to their children. The purpose of the agreement was to restrict ownership of the stock to members of the family. The stockholders reserved the right to vote the stock and to receive all dividends in money whether paid out of earnings or capital. The court held that because the donors retained the right literally to strip the shares of value by causing distributions of capital to themselves, no completed gifts were made. See also Mandels v. Commissioner, 64 T.C. 61 (1975) (court treated transfer into trust as revocable because retention by transferor of the rights to receive all dividends and distributions from any redemption or liquidation of the stock, coupled with a prohibition preventing the trustee from selling the stock during the transferor's lifetime, provided "no assurances whatsoever ... that any of the beneficiaries ... would receive anything under the trust.")

Transfers will also be treated as incomplete where the transferor has the right to revoke by operation of law. In Commissioner v. Allen, 108 F.2d 961 (3d Cir. 1939), cert. den., 309 U.S. 680 (1940) a minor transferred property to a trust prior to the effective date of the Gift Tax Act of 1932. Under state law, the minor had the legal right to disaffirm the transfer during minority and for a reasonable period thereafter. The Court of Appeals, reversing the Board of Tax Appeals, held that there was no completed gift until such time as the minor reached the age of majority, at which time his power to revoke the trust terminated. A similar situation occurs where gifts are made on behalf of a donor by her representative pursuant to a power of attorney. If such gifts are voidable under state law because the representative lacked authority to make gifts, the gift will be incomplete. See, e.g., T.A.M. 9403004 (Oct. 8, 1993).

C.   POWER IN THIRD PARTY TRUSTEE TO BENEFIT GRANTOR

Rev. Rul. 77–378, 1977–2 C.B. 347, holds that a completed gift results when a grantor transfers property in trust and gives the trustee broad administrative powers to distribute income and principal to the grantor in the trustee's sole discretion. However, if the exercise of the trustee's power in favor of the grantor is governed by a fixed or ascertainable standard which is enforceable by or on behalf of the grantor, the gift is incomplete to the extent of the value of the grantor's enforceable right to receive distributions. Reg. § 25.2511–2(b) (last sentence).

In Estate of Holtz v. Commissioner, 38 T.C. 37 (1962), the settlor created a trust, naming a bank as trustee. The trust required income to be paid to the settlor and empowered the trustee to distribute principal for "the welfare, comfort and support of settlor, or for his hospitalization or other emergency needs." Upon the settlor's death, the trust was to continue for his wife if living.

The trust terminated upon the death of the survivor of the settlor and his wife, at which time the remainder was to pass to the estate of the survivor. The Commissioner treated the transfer as a taxable gift, reducing the amount of the gift by the actuarial value of the settlor's life estate and reversionary interest. The court held that there was no completed gift because the above-quoted language would require the trustee to pay the entire principal in the described circumstances to the settlor:

> "A number of cases decided by this and other courts have held that the placing of discretionary power in the trustee to invade corpus makes the gift of corpus incomplete under certain circumstances. The rule ... generally accepted seems to be that if the trustee is free to exercise this unfettered discretion and there is nothing to impel or compel him to invade corpus, the settlor retains a mere expectancy which does not make the gift of corpus incomplete. Herzog v. Commissioner, 116 F.2d 591 (C.A. 2, 1941), affirming 41 B.T.A. 509 (1940). But if the exercise of the trustee's discretion is governed by some external standard which a court may apply in compelling compliance with the conditions of the trust agreement, and the trustee's power to invade is unlimited, then the gift of corpus is incomplete, Commissioner v. Irving Trust Co., 147 F.2d 946 (C.A. 2, 1945), affirming 2 T.C. 1052 (1943), and this is true even though such words as 'absolute' and 'uncontrolled' are used in connection with the trustee's discretion, provided the external standards are clearly for the guidance of the trustee in exercising his discretion. Estate of John J. Toeller, 6 T.C. 832 (1946), affd. 165 F.2d 665 (C.A. 7, 1948); Estate of Lelia E. Coulter, 7 T.C. 1280 (1946).

> "The theory behind this rule seems to be that by placing such standards for guidance of the trustee's discretion in the trust agreement itself, the settlor has not actually lost all dominion and control of the trust corpus or put it completely beyond recall because to ignore the implications and purpose for writing the standards into the invasion clause would be an abuse of discretion on the part of the trustee which the trustee would neither desire to do nor be likely to risk doing under State laws; see Estate of Christianna K. Gramm, 17 T.C. 1063 (1951); Estate of John J. Toeller, supra; or because by borrowing money and relegating his creditors to the trustee for satisfaction of their debts the settlor could have effective use of the corpus for his own benefit, see Alice Spaulding Paolozzi, 23 T.C. 182 (1954); Sarah Gilkey Vander Weele, 27 T.C. 340 (1956), affd. 254 F.2d 895 (C.A. 6, 1958)." (42–43).

D.   POWER IN GRANTOR TO CHANGE INTERESTS OF BENEFICIARIES

Reg. § 25.2511–2(d) states that a gift is not considered incomplete "merely because the donor reserves the power to change the manner or time of enjoyment" thereof. For example, suppose D transfers property to trust, income to A for 10 years and then remainder to A, but D reserves the right to require that income be accumulated and distributed with the remainder. Reg. § 25.2511–2(d) treats such a transfer as a completed gift.

On the other hand, Reg. § 25.2511–2(c) provides that a gift is incomplete if the reserved power gives the donor the power "to name new beneficiaries or to change the interests of the beneficiaries as between themselves unless the power is a fiduciary power limited by a fixed or ascertainable standard." In Estate of Goelet v. Commissioner, 51 T.C. 352 (1968), the grantor was a co-trustee of a trust under which the trustees had the power to pay out income and principal to the trust beneficiaries as the trustees "in their absolute discretion" determined. The Commissioner argued that this was merely a power to change the manner or time of enjoyment, and hence there was a completed gift. The court held, however, that the gift was incomplete because the power enabled the grantor-trustee to change the interests of the beneficiaries among themselves and it was not limited by an ascertainable standard.

E. GRANTOR'S POWER EXERCISABLE WITH CONSENT OF ANOTHER PARTY

1. *Application of* Camp *Case*

Latta v. Commissioner, 212 F.2d 164 (3d Cir. 1954), involved a situation similar to that in Camp v. Commissioner, discussed at p. 303. In *Latta*, the settlor created a trust in 1930 for the benefit of herself for life, with the remainder to her two children. The settlor could rescind or change the trust at any time, but only with the unanimous consent of the trustees. In 1947 this provision was deleted from the instrument. The Commissioner asserted that the gift did not become complete until 1947 and that a gift tax was due in that year. The court, following *Camp*, upheld the validity of the predecessor of Reg. § 25.2511–2(e), and concluded that the gift became complete in 1947. The trustees, whose consent was required, did not have the requisite adverse interest. They were the estranged husband of the settlor, her lawyer, and another lawyer who was one of her friends. Although admittedly the two lawyers were not parties with adverse interests, the taxpayer contended that the estranged husband had an adverse interest. The court conceded that the settlor and her husband may well have been adverse parties, but concluded that he had no substantial adverse interest in the trust property.

In Rev. Rul. 58–395, 1958–2 C.B. 398, five grantors created a trust which was divided into five separate trust funds, each for the benefit of one of the grantors for life, remainder to his spouse and issue. The trust was revocable in whole or as to any one of the respective trust funds upon the unanimous consent of all of the living grantor-beneficiaries. It was held that since no grantor-beneficiary had a beneficial interest in any trust fund other than his own, none had an adverse interest in the disposition of the property or income of any other grantor-beneficiary's trust fund. Accordingly, since each grantor retained the right to revoke together with a non-adverse party, the gift was not complete.

2. *Family Beneficiaries*

Is the approach of *Camp* that a grantor's powers are restricted by the consent of a party with an adverse interest realistic where the parties are related? In Commissioner v. Prouty, 115 F.2d 331 (1st Cir. 1940), the court said:

"Examining these intimate family trusts, one must recognize an element of unreality in the inquiry whether a beneficiary's interest is substantially adverse to the grantor. The supposition is that, given a sufficient stake in the trust, the beneficiary is not likely to yield to a wish of the grantor to revoke the trust. In many cases the grantor may have full confidence in the compliant disposition of the member of the family he selects to share his power of revocation, even though such member is named as beneficiary of a handsome interest in the trust. The very fact that the grantor reserved a power to revoke indicates a mental reservation on his part as to the finality of the gift; and if the grantor wishes to hold on to a power of recapture, it stands to reason he will vest the veto power in someone whose acquiescence he can count on. * * * However, we cannot read into the gift tax * * * the proposition that a member of the grantor's immediate family can never be deemed to have 'a substantial adverse interest.' * * * [As] the law now stands * * * we must give weight to the formal rights conferred in the trust instrument in determining whether a given beneficiary has a substantial adverse interest, bearing in mind the admonition of Helvering v. Clifford, 309 U.S. 331, 335, that 'where the grantor is the trustee and the beneficiaries are members of his family group, special scrutiny of the arrangement is necessary * * *.' " (335–336).

3. Contingent Beneficiaries

In Estate of Gillette v. Commissioner, 7 T.C. 219 (1946), the decedent had reserved a power in conjunction with contingent remaindermen to invade corpus for the benefit of the current income beneficiaries. The decedent later relinquished his power and the Commissioner sought to impose a gift tax on the ground that the gifts were not completed until the relinquishment. The Tax Court rejected the Commissioner's position:

"Neither the family relationship of decedent to his wife and son nor the remoteness of their contingent remainders suffice to persuade us that their respective interests in the trust fail to be both substantial and adverse. This is the sole question, respondent's determination of gift tax deficiencies being based upon the incompleteness of the original gifts, which in turn arises from the claim that petitioner's right of revocation was not limited by the required concurrence of a person possessing a substantial adverse interest. Burnet v. Guggenheim, 288 U.S. 280 * * *.

"It is true that the wife's interest in the son's trust was contingent upon outliving both decedent and their son, and that the son's interest in the other trust was limited by his required survival of his mother, father, and younger sister, and the sister's death without issue. But the trusts were substantial in amount. See Commissioner v. Prouty (C.C.A., 1st Cir.), 115 F.2d 331. And in Meyer Katz, 46 B.T.A. 187; aff'd (C.C.A., 7th Cir.), 139 F.2d 107, a wife's interest who 'would benefit from the trust only if the minor beneficiary should predecease her and the grantor leaving no issue' was held to be a substantial adverse interest. Clair R. Savage, 4 T.C. 286, 293. Manifestly, the life expectancy of decedent's wife was not as great as that of her son, but a similar situation existed in the Katz case. And the son's chances of surviving his father and mother were so great that his contingency was virtually confined to survival of his nearly contemporary sister. We are not persuaded that in either instance the prospects of succession are sufficiently different from those in the Katz case to call for the opposite result." (222).

F. RELINQUISHMENT OF POWER

As several of the cases discussed in the preceding materials have indicated, a gift which is incomplete because of the retention of powers by the grantor becomes complete at the time those powers are relinquished. See, e.g., Rev. Rul. 72–571, 1972–2 C.B. 533; Rev. Rul. 79–421, 1979–2 C.B. 347.

Suppose that the grantor of a trust retains a power which is exercisable only with the consent of a beneficiary of the trust who has a substantial adverse interest in the property. For example, assume that A transfers property in trust, income payable to B for life, remainder to C. During C's life, the grantor retains the power to add additional income beneficiaries with the consent of B. Assume that B consents to the addition of D, E and F as income beneficiaries. Has B made a gift to D, E and F as the result of consenting to the exercise of the power by A, since, in effect, B has joined in the transfer of a part of the income to which B is otherwise entitled? Cerf v. Commissioner, 141 F.2d 564 (3d Cir. 1944), indicates that the holder of the consent power does in fact make a gift in such a situation. In that case, the settlor in 1928 created four trusts, each of which was for the benefit of his wife and one of their four children. The husband and wife, along with a bank, were the trustees. The corpus of each trust consisted of the right to receive certain renewal commissions as they became payable to the husband under an agency contract with an insurance company. The trust agreements provided that the trustees were to pay the net income to the wife during her lifetime "if she shall accept it". Income not accepted by the wife was to be added to the corpus of each trust. Upon the death of the survivor of the husband and the wife, the trust income and corpus were to be distributed to the particular child who was the beneficiary of each trust. The husband reserved the right to amend or revoke the trusts only with the written consent of the wife in her capacity as beneficiary. In June, 1932, the husband, with the written consent of the wife, amended all four trust instruments to provide that all the net income from each of the trusts would thereafter be paid to the husband. In August, 1932, a second set of amendments executed by the husband with the written consent of his wife gave to the husband the right to amend or revoke any of the trusts without the wife's consent. The court held that, by virtue of the amendments in 1932, the wife made taxable gifts to her husband. The court concluded that the wife had a vested interest in the trust which had been given to her by means of a completed gift by her husband in 1928. By abandoning her control over her income rights, the wife in June, 1932, made a completed gift of the value of the income rights. Similarly, the August, 1932 amendments constituted a transfer of the wife's remaining rights in the trusts, and a gift tax was due.

SECTION B.   TRANSFERS WITH RETAINED INTERESTS

Internal Revenue Code: §§ 2501(a); 2511(a); 2512

Regulations: Reg. §§ 25.2511–1(e), (f); 25.2511–2

Smith v. Shaughnessy

318 U.S. 176 (1943).

■ MR. JUSTICE BLACK delivered the opinion of the Court.

The question here is the extent of the petitioner's liability for a tax under [the 1932 Act predecessor of §§ 2501(a), 2511(a) and 2512], which

[Act] imposes a tax upon every transfer of property by gift, "whether the transfer is in trust or otherwise, whether the gift is direct or indirect, and whether the property is real or personal, tangible or intangible; * * *."

The petitioner, age 72, made an irrevocable transfer in trust of 3,000 shares of stock worth $571,000. The trust income was payable to his wife, age 44, for life; upon her death, the stock was to be returned to the petitioner, if he was living; if he was not living, it was to go to such persons as his wife might designate by will, or in default of a will by her, to her intestate successors under applicable New York law. The petitioner, under protest, paid a gift tax of $71,674.22, assessed on the total value of the trust principal, and brought suit for refund in the district court. Holding that the petitioner had, within the meaning of the Act, executed a completed gift of a life estate to his wife, the court sustained the Commissioner's assessment on $322,423, the determined value of her life interest; but the remainder was held not to be completely transferred and hence not subject to the gift tax. 40 F. Supp. 19. The government appealed and the Circuit Court of Appeals reversed, ordering dismissal of the petitioner's complaint on the authority of its previous decision in Herzog v. Commissioner, 116 F.2d 591. We granted certiorari because of alleged conflict with our decisions in Helvering v. Hallock, 309 U.S. 106, and Sanford v. Commissioner, 308 U.S. 39. In these decisions, and in Burnet v. Guggenheim, 288 U.S. 280, we have considered the problems raised here in some detail, and it will therefore be unnecessary to make any elaborate re-survey of the law.

Three interests are involved here: the life estate, the remainder, and the reversion. The taxpayer concedes that the life estate is subject to the gift tax. The government concedes that the right of reversion to the donor in case he outlives his wife is an interest having value which can be calculated by an actuarial device, and that it is immune from the gift tax. The controversy, then, reduces itself to the question of the taxability of the remainder.

The taxpayer's principal argument here is that under our decision in the Hallock case, the value of the remainder will be included in the grantor's gross estate for estate tax purposes; and that in the Sanford case we intimated a general policy against allowing the same property to be taxed both as an estate and as a gift.

This view, we think, misunderstands our position in the Sanford case. As we said there, the gift and estate tax laws are closely related and the gift tax serves to supplement the estate tax.[6] We said that the taxes are not "always mutually exclusive," and called attention to [the predecessor of § 2012] which charts the course for granting credits on estate taxes by

---

6. The gift tax was passed not only to prevent estate tax avoidance, but also to prevent income tax avoidance through reducing yearly income and thereby escaping the effect of progressive surtax rates. House Report No. 708, 72d Cong., 1st Sess. p. 28; Brandeis, J., dissenting in Untermyer v. Anderson, 276 U.S. 440, 450; Stone, J., dissenting in Heiner v. Donnan, 285 U.S. 312, 333.

reason of previous payment of gift taxes on the same property. The scope of that provision we need not now determine. It is sufficient to note here that Congress plainly pointed out that "some" of the "total gifts subject to gift taxes * * * may be included for estate tax purposes and some not." H.Rep. No. 708, 72d Cong., 1st Sess., p. 45. Under the statute the gift tax amounts in some instances to a security, a form of down-payment on the estate tax which secures the eventual payment of the latter; it is in no sense double taxation as the taxpayer suggests.

We conclude that under the present statute, Congress has provided as its plan for integrating the estate and gift taxes this system of secured payment on gifts which will later be subject to the estate tax.[7]

Unencumbered by any notion of policy against subjecting this transaction to both estate and gift taxes, we turn to the basic question of whether there was a gift of the remainder. The government argues that for gift tax purposes the taxpayer has abandoned control of the remainder and that it is therefore taxable, while the taxpayer contends that no realistic value can be placed on the contingent remainder and that it therefore should not be classed as a gift.

We cannot accept any suggestion that the complexity of a property interest created by a trust can serve to defeat a tax. For many years Congress has sought vigorously to close tax loopholes against ingenious trust instruments.[8] Even though these concepts of property and value may be slippery and elusive they cannot escape taxation so long as they are used in the world of business. The language of the gift tax statute, "property * * * real or personal, tangible or intangible," is broad enough to include property, however conceptual or contingent. And lest there by any doubt as to the amplitude of their purpose, the Senate and House Committees, reporting the bill, spelled out their meaning as follows:

"The terms 'property,' 'transfer,' 'gift,' and 'indirectly' [in the predecessor of § 2511(a)] are used in the broadest and most comprehensive

---

7. It has been suggested that the congressional plan relating the estate and gift taxes may still be incomplete. See e.g., Griswold, A Plan for the Coordination of the Income, Estate, and Gift Tax Provisions etc., 56 Harv. L. Rev. 337; Magill, The Federal Gift Tax, 40 Col. L. Rev. 773, 792; Kauper, The Revenue Act of 1942: Estate and Gift Tax Amendments, 41 Mich. L. Rev. 369, 388; and see Commissioner v. Prouty, 115 F.2d 331, 337; Higgins v. Commissioner, 129 F.2d 237, 239. [ED.: The Tax Reform Act of 1976 eliminated the credit for gift taxes paid previously contained in section 2012:

"Transfers included in the tax base as lifetime transfers (described as 'adjusted taxable gifts' by § 2001(b)]) are not to include transfers which are also included in the decedent's gross estate (i.e., transfers made

within three years of the date of death and lifetime transfers where the decedent had retained certain interests, rights or powers in the property). This is to preclude having the same lifetime transfers taken into account more than once for transfer tax purposes. The gift tax payable on these transfers is to be subtracted in determining the estate tax imposed." H.Rep. No. 94–1380, 94th Cong., 2d Sess. 13 (1976).]

8. 2 Paul, Federal Estate & Gift Taxation, Chap. 17; Schuyler, Powers of Appointment and Especially Special Powers: The Estate Taxpayer's Last Stand, 33 Ill. L. Rev. 771; Leaphart, The Use of the Trust to Escape the Imposition of Federal Income & Estate Taxes, 15 Corn. L. Q. 587.

sense; the term 'property' reaching every species of right or interest protected by law and having an exchangeable value."[9]

The Treasury regulations, which we think carry out the Act's purpose, made specific provisions for application of the tax to, and determination of the value of, "a remainder * * * subject to an outstanding life estate."[10]

The essence of a gift by trust is the abandonment of control over the property put in trust. The separable interests transferred are not gifts to the extent that power remains to revoke the trust or recapture the property represented by any of them, Burnet v. Guggenheim, supra, or to modify the terms of the arrangement so as to make other disposition of the property, Sanford v. Commissioner, supra. In the Sanford case the grantor could, by modification of the trust, extinguish the donee's interest at any instant he chose. In cases such as this, where the grantor has neither the form nor substance of control and never will have unless he outlives his wife, we must conclude that he has lost all "economic control" and that the gift is complete except for the value of his reversionary interest.[11]

The judgment of the Circuit Court of Appeals is affirmed with leave to the petitioner to apply for modification of its mandate in order that the value of the petitioner's reversionary interest may be determined and excluded.

It is so ordered.

ILLUSTRATIVE MATERIAL

A.   COMPLETED GIFTS

As illustrated in *Smith*, a completed gift occurs for the portion of an irrevocable transfer in trust in which the transferor has not retained an interest. Taxable gifts occur for completed transfers of future interests as well as current interests. Robinette v. Helvering, 318 U.S. 184 (1943). Thus, in *Smith*, the transferor was treated as having made a completed gift of the life estate and remainder interest. Only the portion of the transfer in which the grantor had retained a reversionary interest was not treated as a completed gift.

B.   REVERSIONS INCAPABLE OF BEING VALUED

The donor who has retained a reversionary interest must establish its value. In the companion case to *Smith*, Robinette v. Helvering, 318 U.S. 184 (1943), the taxpayer had transferred property in trust reserving a life estate in

---

9. S.Rep. No. 665, 72d Cong., 1st Sess., p. 39; H.Rep. No. 708, supra, p. 27.

10. [The predecessor of Reg. § 25.2511–1(e) and (f), 25.2512–9(a), (d).] Cf. Commissioner v. Marshall, 125 F.2d 943, 945 (1942).

11. The conclusion reached here is in accord with that of the several Circuit Courts

of Appeals which have considered the problem: Commissioner v. Marshall, 125 F.2d 943 (C.C.A.2d); Commissioner v. Beck's Estate, 129 F.2d 243 (C.C.A.2d); Commissioner v. McLean, 127 F.2d 942 (C.C.A.5th); Helvering v. Robinette, 129 F.2d 832 (C.C.A.3d), affirmed, post, p. 184; Hughes v. Commissioner, 104 F.2d 144 (C.C.A.9th); * * *.

the income for herself, with a second life estate for her mother and stepfather if she should predecease them. The remainder was to go to her issue upon their reaching the age of 21, or if no issue existed, as directed by the will of the last surviving life tenant. In resisting the Commissioner's attempt to assess a gift tax on the remainder interests, the taxpayer advanced arguments which had not been made in the *Smith* case. First, she argued that the gifts were not complete because at the date of the creation of the trust there were no donees in existence to accept the remainders. In reply, the Court, speaking through Mr. Justice Black, pointed out that under the gift tax "the effort of Congress was to reach every kind and type of transfer by gift. * * * The instruments created by these grantors purported on their face wholly to divest the grantors of all dominion over the property; it could not be returned to them except because of contingencies beyond their control. Gifts of future interests are taxable under [the predecessor of § 2503(b)], and they do not lose this quality merely because of the indefiniteness of the eventual recipient. The petitioners purported to give the property to someone whose identity could be later ascertained and this was enough." (187).

Second, she argued that, in computing the value of the gift, allowance should be made for the value of the grantor's reversionary interest. The Court said:

"Here, unlike the Smith case, the government does not concede that the reversionary interest of the petitioner should be deducted from the total value. In the Smith case, the grantor had a reversionary interest which depended only upon his surviving his wife, and the government conceded that the value was therefore capable of ascertainment by recognized actuarial methods. In this case, however, the reversionary interest of the grantor depends not alone upon the possibility of survivorship but also upon the death of the daughter without issue who should reach the age of 21 years. The petitioner does not refer us to any recognized method by which it would be possible to determine the value of such a contingent reversionary remainder. It may be true, as the petitioners argue, that trust instruments such as these before us frequently create 'a complex aggregate of rights, privileges, powers and immunities and that in certain instances all these rights, privileges, powers and immunities are not transferred or released simultaneously.' But before one who gives his property away by this method is entitled to deduction from his gift tax on the basis that he had retained some of these complex strands it is necessary that he at least establish the possibility of approximating what value he holds. Factors to be considered in fixing the value of this contingent reservation as of the date of the gift would have included consideration of whether or not the daughter would marry; whether she would have children; whether they would reach the age of 21; etc. Actuarial science may have made great strides in appraising the value of that which seems to be unappraisable, but we have no reason to believe from this record that even the actuarial art could do more than guess at the value here in question." (188–189).

The *Robinette* case was followed in Lockard v. Commissioner, 166 F.2d 409 (1st Cir. 1948). In *Lockard*, the donor created a trust the income of which was payable to her husband for life, with remainder to the donor. Corpus could be invaded up to $3,000 a year if necessary for the husband's comfort, maintenance and support. The taxpayer argued that only the life estate was subject to gift tax, and that further gifts would be made when and if corpus was invaded. The gift was held to be equal to a $3,000 annuity plus the value of the income from the diminishing corpus for the husband's life. Actuarial science was held to be insufficient to measure the possibility of the donor's receiving back the corpus.

Would *Lockard* have been decided differently if it could be proven that the husband's outside sources of support made the likelihood of corpus invasion remote? In McHugh v. United States, 142 F.Supp. 927 (Ct.Cl. 1956), the taxpayer created a short-term trust for the benefit of her sister-in-law, and directed the trustee to apply so much of the principal as it found necessary, in its sole discretion, to meet the essential needs of the income beneficiary. The court, finding that the trustee's discretion to invade corpus was limited by a definite standard, held that the taxpayer was entitled to show the likelihood of invasion for purposes of valuing the gift. Cf. Clement v. Smith, 167 F.Supp. 369 (E.D.Pa. 1958), where the taxpayer created a trust for his father's life, corpus to himself or to his estate if he predeceased his father. The income was to be accumulated during his father's lifetime and was to be paid to the father by the trustees when necessary for his maintenance and support. The court, relying on the father's net worth of $700,000 and outside annual income of $30,000, held that the probability of the father's receiving the income was "at the nil point of speculative thought," and that no completed gift had been made.

C.   RELEASE OF RETAINED OR REVERSIONARY INTERESTS

If the grantor releases her retained or reversionary interest, a completed gift occurs with respect to that interest. See Rev.Rul. 79–421, 1979–2 C.B. 347. The value of the gift is the value of the released interest at the time of the release.

CHAPTER 20

ANNUITIES AND EMPLOYEE BENEFITS

Internal Revenue Code: § 2039

Regulations: § 20.2039–1

INTRODUCTION

Section 2039 includes in the gross estate of a decedent ("D") the value of annuity payments paid to D's survivor if D was entitled to receive, or had actually received such payments, while alive. D's gross estate will include the value of the portion of the annuity payable to the survivor equal to the portion of consideration that D provided for the annuity. § 2039(b). For example, if D paid one-third of the purchase price for the annuity, then D's gross estate will include one-third of the value of the payments to be made to D's survivor.

Practitioners encounter three types of annuities that are covered by § 2039: the commercial annuity, the private annuity and the employer survival annuity. The treatment of the commercial annuity is straightforward. Suppose D transfers $100,000 to an insurance company for a contract that pays $10,000 per year to D for life and thereafter to S for life. D dies shortly after he begins to receive the annuity payments. The value of the annuity for S is included in D's estate under § 2039(a). If S had contributed $50,000 of the initial purchase price, only one-half the value of the annuity would be includible in D's estate. § 2039(b). A private annuity is similar to a commercial annuity except that the annuity is provided to D by an individual, rather than an insurance company, in exchange for D's payment.

Annuities provided by employers for employees and their beneficiaries are much more common than commercial and private annuities and have been the source of considerable litigation and legislation. Usually, D's employer, in consideration of D's services, agrees to make contributions to a survivor annuity plan on D's behalf. The typical annuity is payable to D after retirement, and upon D's death to a designated surviving beneficiary for life. However, several variations can exist. An employee entitled to certain retirement benefits may be allowed to elect a lesser benefit in favor of an annuity payable to her spouse or other beneficiary after her death. Or the employee, though not entitled to any retirement benefits, may have the right to designate a beneficiary to whom an annuity will become payable on death. In some cases, the beneficiaries entitled to the survivorship annuity may be designated only by the employer. The employee's or the survivor's rights to the annuity may, at the time of death, be either vested or forfeitable.

Prior to the enactment of the § 2039, the Commissioner attempted to tax survivor annuities purchased or provided by employers under the predecessors of §§ 2033, 2035, 2038, and 2041 by arguing that the annuities were property which D had transferred. But, while the policy considerations in favor of taxing survivorship annuities may seem clear, the government was occasionally unsuccessful.

Section 2039 was enacted to resolve the uncertainties of previous law. It requires the inclusion in the gross estate of the value of any annuity or other payment receivable by any beneficiary by reason of surviving D under any form of contract or agreement (other than insurance) if, under such contract or agreement (1) an annuity or other payment was payable to D, or (2) D possessed the right to receive such annuity or payment, either alone or in conjunction with another for his life or for any period not ascertainable without reference to his death or for any period which does not in fact end before his death.

The following materials first consider the scope of and issues that arise under § 2039. Section 2039 is not, however, exclusive. The materials then turn to the potential application of other Code provisions to employee annuities.

It is important to consider that in many employee benefit cases, the payments to the surviving beneficiary will constitute income in respect of a decedent, with the results described at p. 122.

SECTION A.   THE SCOPE OF § 2039

Estate of Schelberg v. Commissioner

612 F.2d 25 (2d Cir. 1979).

■ FRIENDLY, CIRCUIT JUDGE.

This appeal by a taxpayer from a decision of the Tax Court, 70 T.C. 690 (1978), raises a serious question with respect to the interpretation of § 2039, which was added to the Internal Revenue Code in 1954.

I.

Decedent William V. Schelberg was born on March 14, 1914 and died on January 6, 1974 from lung cancer after a week's illness. He was survived by his wife, Sarah, and two daughters, one aged 23 and the other 19. He had been employed by International Business Machines Corp. (IBM) since 1952. At his death he was serving as assistant director of international patent operations at a salary of $4,250 per month.

IBM maintained a variety of employee benefit plans, each adopted at a different time and separately administered. Those here relevant are the Group Life Insurance Plan, the Retirement Plan, the Sickness and Accident

Income Plan, and the Total and Permanent Disability Plan. Schelberg was entitled to participate in each.

The Group Life Insurance Plan provided two basic benefits—a group term life insurance, which is not here at issue, and an uninsured and unfunded survivors income benefit, which is. This benefit, determined on the basis of the employee's compensation at the time of death and the amount of the aforementioned life insurance, was payable to a decedent's "eligible" survivors in an order of preference stated in the plan. Payment was to be made monthly, at the rate of one-quarter of the decedent's regular monthly compensation, until the total benefit was exhausted. Payments continued only so long as at least one eligible survivor remained.

The Retirement Plan was a qualified pension plan under I.R.C. § 401. Under IBM's general employment policy, Schelberg would have been required to retire at age 65 and would have been entitled to the retirement benefits provided in the plan.

Under the Sickness and Accident Plan all regular IBM employees were entitled to receive full salary (reduced by any workmen's compensation payments) while absent from work on account of sickness or accident for up to 52 weeks in any 24–month period. Benefits could be continued for more than 52 weeks at IBM's discretion in individual cases; these were known as "individual consideration" benefits.

The Disability Plan covered all IBM employees with more than five years' service. Eligibility was based on determination of "total and permanent disability" by a corporate panel on the basis of medical evidence. The quoted phrase was defined to mean that the employee was unable to perform any employment for pay or profit and had no reasonable expectation of becoming able to do so. Benefits were calculated on the basis of the employee's regular compensation prior to disability, taking account of eligibility for Social Security payments and workmen's compensation. They began on the expiration of the 52–week period of Sickness and Accident benefits plus any period of individual consideration benefits and continued until normal retirement date, at which time the employee became eligible for benefits under the Retirement Plan.[1] During the period of disability an employee remained covered by a variety of other IBM employee plans[2] and could, under certain conditions, accrue further credits under the Retirement Plan.[3] If, contrary to expectation, the employee became able to work

---

1. Disability benefits began at 75% of regular compensation and continued at that rate for the first 18 months less any period during which the employee had received "individual consideration" benefits under the Sickness and Accident Plan. Thereafter the benefits were the greater of 40% of regular compensation at the time of disability or accrued retirement income under the Retirement Plan based on actual service and imputed earnings during the receipt of payments under the Sickness and Accident Plan, with

an upward adjustment for employees, disabled before attaining age 55. See note 5, infra.

2. These included the Family Hospitalization Plan, the Major Medical Plan, the Dental Plan, the Medical Plans with Medicare, the Special Care for Children Assistance Plan, the Adoption Assistance Plan and various educational benefit plans.

3. The Tax Court stated in its findings that "[t]he period of disability payments was not considered service with IBM for purposes

again, he was entitled to return, but few did so. As of January 1, 1974, a total of 393 IBM employees out of 150,000 were receiving benefits under the Disability Plan.

At the time of his death Schelberg was not receiving benefits under any of these plans. By virtue of his decease his widow became entitled under the Group Life Insurance Plan to a death benefit of $23,666.67 under the group life insurance policy, and to a survivors benefit of $1,062.50 per month. The value of the latter amount was not included in decedent's gross estate in his federal estate tax return, although its existence was reported. The Commissioner of Internal Revenue entered a notice of deficiency on the sole ground that the present value of the survivors annuity, which is stipulated to have been $94,708.83, was includible in the estate pursuant to I.R.C. § 2039, * * *. The Tax Court upheld the Commissioner * * *.

II.

The estate does not dispute that the survivors benefit constituted "an annuity or other payment receivable by any beneficiary by reason of surviving the decedent under any form of contract or agreement entered into after March 3, 1931 (other than as insurance under policies on the life of the decedent)" within the opening clause of § 2039(a). It is likewise indisputable that this alone would not suffice to make the survivors benefit includible in the gross estate. The Commissioner must also satisfy the condition that "under such contract or agreement, an annuity or other payment was payable to the decedent, or the decedent possessed the right to receive such annuity or payment, either alone or in conjunction with another for his life or for any period not ascertainable without reference to his death or for any period which does not in fact end before his death."

Not contending that he can satisfy this requirement within the four corners of the Group Life Insurance Plan, the Commissioner asserts that, as provided by the Treasury Regulations, 26 C.F.R. § 20.2039–1(b), he is entitled to consider "any arrangement, understanding or plan, or any combination of arrangements or plans arising by reason of the decedent's employment". Although this is a rather sharp departure from the letter of the statute, see Pincus, Estate Taxation of Annuities and Other Payments, 44 Va.L.Rev. 857, 868–69 (1958), we accept it with the caveat that while the Commissioner is entitled to "consider" such arrangements, this does not mean that the mere possibility of an employee's receiving some benefit under an arrangement other than that giving rise to the survivors benefit necessarily satisfies the condition of § 2039(a). The Commissioner does not rely on either the Retirement Plan or the Sickness and Accident Plan to

---

of the Retirement Plan." 70 T.C. at 695. It relied at least in part on this finding in linking the Disability Plan with the Retirement Plan as a post-employment benefit, rather than linking it with the Sickness and Accident Plan, under which service credits continue to accrue, as a wage continuation benefit. See id. at 701–02. The Retirement Plan specifically provides in Article 11(E), however, that employees receiving benefits under the Disability Plan would continue to accrue service credits until age fifty-five. There is a provision to the same effect in the Disability Plan.

satisfy the condition that "an annuity or other payment" was payable to Schelberg. Apart from other considerations, any such reliance is precluded by previous revenue rulings.[4] Revenue Ruling 76–380, 1976–2 C.B. 270, concluded that qualified plans, like the Retirement Plan, and non-qualified plans, like the Survivors Income Benefit Plan, were not to be considered together in determining the applicability of § 2039(a) and (b). See also Estate of Brooks v. C. I. R., 50 T.C. 585, 594–95 (1968).[5] Revenue Ruling 77–183, 1977–1 C.B. 274, held that benefits such as those Schelberg might have been entitled to under the Sickness and Accident Plan had he lived longer "were in the nature of compensation" and thus no more meet the test set out in the condition than would compensation payments themselves, Estate of Fusz v. C. I. R., 46 T.C. 214 (1966), acq. 1967–2 C.B. 2; see also Kramer v. United States, 406 F.2d 1363, 186 Ct.Cl. 684 (1969). This left as the Commissioner's sole reed the fact that, at the time of his death, Schelberg possessed the right that after 52 weeks (or more if he qualified for "individual consideration") under the Sickness and Accident Plan, he might become entitled to payments under the Disability Plan. The estate contends that Schelberg's rights under the Disability Plan were too dissimilar in nature from an "annuity or other payment" and too contingent to meet the condition of § 2039(a). We agree.

It is worth repeating that the Commissioner's position here would apply to every IBM employee having more than five years' service who dies before attaining age 64 (or taking early retirement) although he neither received nor had any reasonable expectation of receiving anything under the Disability Plan. On the other hand, if he died after attaining age 64 but before taking retirement, the survivors benefit would not be includible since the first twelve months away from work would be covered by the Sickness and Accident Plan and he could never become eligible for the Disability Plan. And, of course, if he died after actually taking retirement, the most common case, the survivors benefit would not be includible by virtue of Revenue Ruling 76–380, 1976–2 C.B. 270. We find nothing in the language of § 2039, in its legislative history, or in the Treasury Regulations sufficient to justify a conclusion that the action of an employer in creating a plan whereby a handful of employees can receive disability benefits because of a rare health or accident syndrome should bring the survivors of all within § 2039.

As recognized by a learned commentator shortly after § 2039 was enacted, the statute was aimed at "annuity contracts under which the purchaser (alone or with a joint annuitant) was entitled to payments for his life, with payments to continue after his death, at either the same or a

---

4. Both of the Revenue Rulings clearly cover the IBM plans in question; indeed, it appears that the rulings were based on the IBM plans themselves.

5. The Commissioner reached this result primarily in reliance on the parenthetical language in Regs. § 20.2039–1(b)(2), example (6), quoted infra. The language of § 2039(c) itself, providing that annuities or payments receivable by a beneficiary pursuant to qualified plans were excludable from the gross estate, does not seem to lead inexorably to such a conclusion. [ED.: § 2039(c) was repealed in 1984.]

reduced rate, to a survivor." Bittker, Estate and Gift Taxation under the 1954 Code: The Principal Changes, 29 Tul.L.Rev. 453, 469 (1955). While inclusion of the survivor's rights in the estate had been generally sustained, courts had differed as to the reason. Some courts had proceeded on the theory that purchase of the contract was in effect a transfer of property with the reservation of a life estate and thus taxable under the predecessors of I.R.C. § 2036. Others had proceeded on the theory that the transfer was intended to take effect at death. Id. A fundamental purpose of § 2039 was to supply an affirmative answer to the question of inclusion in such cases without further need to debate the theory.

A further purpose, as revealed by the relevant House and Senate Committee reports on what became § 2039 of the revised I.R.C. of 1954, * * * was to settle the question of includibility of a joint and survivor annuity where the annuity was purchased by the decedent's employer or both the decedent and the employer made contributions. Congress decided that such an annuity should be included except when the employer's contributions were made pursuant to "an approved trust, pension or retirement plan."

Both text and context show that § 2039 was conceived as dealing only with the problem of what in substance was a joint annuity, although to be sure in all its various ramifications, not with the whole gamut of arrangements under which an employee, his employer or both may create benefits for the employee's survivors. The new section applied only "if, under such contract or agreement, an annuity or other payment was payable to the decedent, or the decedent possessed the right to receive such annuity or payment, either alone or in conjunction with another for his life or for any period not ascertainable without reference to his death or for any period which does not in fact end before his death." If Congress had wished to legislate more broadly, it would have eliminated this clause or chosen more general language for it. The intended sphere of application is made quite clear by the illustrations given in the House and Senate reports "as examples of contracts, but * * * not necessarily the only forms of contracts to which this section applies."[6] Under all of these the decedent was

---

6. (1) A contract under which the decedent immediately before his death was receiving or was entitled to receive for the duration of his life an annuity, or other stipulated payment, with payments thereunder to continue after his death to a designated beneficiary if surviving the decedent.

(2) A contract under which the decedent immediately before his death was receiving or was entitled to receive, together with another person, an annuity, or other stipulated payment payable to the decedent and such other person for their joint lives, with payments thereunder to continue to the survivor following the death of either.

(3) A contract or agreement entered into by the decedent and his employer under which the decedent immediately before his death and following retirement was receiving or was entitled to receive an annuity or other stipulated payment, payable to the decedent for the duration of his life and thereafter to a designated beneficiary, if surviving the decedent, whether the payments after the decedent's death are fixed by the contract or subject to an option or election exercised or exercisable by the decedent.

(4) A contract or agreement entered into by the decedent and his employer under which at decedent's death, prior to retirement or prior to the expiration of a stated

receiving or entitled to receive at death what anyone would consider an "annuity or other payment" for the duration of his life or for a stipulated term.[7] Furthermore, in each case the beneficiary succeeded to the interest of the decedent, as in the classic instance of a joint and survivor annuity, quite unlike the present case. Although the term "other payment" is literally broad, Congress was clearly thinking of payments in the nature of annuities—the same types of payments which, if made to the survivor, would be includible in the estate. See *Estate of Fusz*, supra, 46 T.C. at 217. None of the examples is even close to payments receivable only if the deceased employee might have become totally and permanently disabled had he lived.

We do not consider the case to be altered in the Government's favor by the Treasury Regulations. While these contain some broad language, there is nothing to indicate that their framers addressed the problem here presented. The closest of the illustrations is example (6).[8] While we have no quarrel with this, it is inapposite since the payments both to the employee and to the beneficiary were life annuities. Without endeavoring to be too precise, we deem it plain that, in framing the condition on § 2039(a), Congress was not going beyond benefits the employee was sure to get as a result of his prior employment if he lived long enough. Even more plainly Congress was not thinking of disability payments which an employee would have had only a remote chance of ever collecting had he lived. Not only are the disability payments in this case extremely hypothetical, they are also

period of time, annuity or other payment was payable to a designated beneficiary if surviving the decedent.

(5) A contract or agreement under which the decedent immediately before his death was receiving or was entitled to receive an annuity for a stated period of time, with the annuity or other payment to continue to a designated beneficiary, upon the decedent's death prior to the expiration of such period, if surviving the decedent.

H.R.Rep.No.1337, supra, at A314–16; S.Rep.No.1622, supra, at 469–72, U.S. Code Cong. & Admin. News 1954, pp. 4458, 5114.

7. The sole exception is example (4) which omits any requirement of annuity or other payment to the decedent. However, it has been recognized that this example simply cannot be correct unless amplified. See Estate of Bahen v. United States, 305 F.2d 827, 834 n. 14, 158 Ct.Cl. 141 (1962), citing Bittker, supra, 29 Tul.L.Rev. at 469–70 n. 58 and Pincus, supra, 44 Va.L.Rev. at 866–67 (1958). As the Tax Court concluded in Estate of Fusz, supra, 46 T.C. at 218, "example 4 in the report of the Senate Finance Committee, in juxtaposition with other statements in the report and the other five [sic] examples, nec-

essarily implies that post-employment benefits payable to decedent during his lifetime were also involved."

8. *Example (6).* The employer made contributions to two different funds set up under two different plans. One plan was to provide the employee, upon his retirement at age 60, with an annuity for life, and the other plan was to provide the employee's designated beneficiary, upon the employee's death, with a similar annuity for life. Each plan was established at a different time and each plan was administered separately in every respect. Neither plan at any time met the requirements of § 401(a) (relating to qualified plans). The value of the designated beneficiary's annuity is includible in the employee's gross estate. All rights and benefits accruing to an employee and to others by reason of the employment (except rights and benefits accruing under certain plans meeting the requirements of § 401(a) (see § 20.2039–2)) are considered together in determining whether or not § 2039(a) and (b) apply. The scope of § 2039(a) and (b) cannot be limited by indirection.

far from the "annuity or other payment" contemplated by Congress. Courts have, consistent with basic principles of statutory construction, recognized that "annuity or other payment" does not mean "annuity or any payment," but that the phrase is qualitatively limited by the context in which it appears. See Estate of Fusz, supra, 46 T.C. at 217–18. The Service itself has acquiesced in and furthered this view. See Rev. Rul. 77–183, supra. Thus, it seems clear to us that Congress did not intend the phrase to embrace wages, *Estate of Fusz*, supra, 46 T.C. at 217; Kramer v. United States, supra, 406 F.2d 1363, 186 Ct.Cl. 684; Eichstedt v. United States, 354 F. Supp. 484, 491 (N.D.Cal. 1972); possible sickness and accident payments, which were a substitute for wages, Rev. Rul. 77–183, supra; or the disability payments involved in this case, which likewise were a partial continuation of wages when an employee's physical health deteriorated even further. The disability payments theoretically achievable here by the decedent in his lifetime are closer to the sickness benefits which he would have received at an early stage of his illness than they are to post-retirement benefits. The Tax Court's treatment of possible disability benefits as presupposing a post-retirement status linked to the widow's ultimate succession thereto seems to us to be unsupported in fact. And see footnote [3] * * *.

III.

* * * The most influential decision on what the decedent must receive or be entitled to receive in order to trigger application of § 2039 is Estate of Bahen v. United States, 305 F.2d 827, 158 Ct.Cl. 141 (1962) (Davis, J.). The opinion is indeed a virtuoso performance which has tended to dominate the field to the extent that * * * courts seem to look to the *Bahen* opinion rather than to the statute and the committee reports as indicative of the legislative intent. Beyond all this it is of peculiar importance here since it involved a sum payable only in the event of disability, and the Commissioner quite properly relies heavily upon it.

The case involved payments by the Chesapeake & Ohio Ry. to Mr. Bahen's widow under two benefit plans. Under the more significant, a non-qualified Deferred Compensation Plan applicable only to 40 officers and executives, on Mr. Bahen's death the C. & O. would pay $100,000 to his widow or surviving children in 60 equal monthly installments; if, prior to retirement, he became totally incapacitated, the payments would be made to him so long as he survived, any amounts unpaid at the time of his death to go to his widow or minor children. Another plan provided that if an employee with more than 10 years service died while in the company's employ and before becoming eligible for retirement, the company would pay a sum equal to three months salary to his widow or minor children. Mr. Bahen died suddenly while in the railway's employ and before becoming eligible for retirement. The court held that payments to Mrs. Bahen under both plans were includible in the estate since "[e]very requirement [of § 2039] is squarely met, not only in literal terms but in harmony with the legislative aim." 305 F.2d at 829, 158 Ct.Cl. at [146]. Most relevantly for our purposes, the court held that the provision for payments to Mr. Bahen under the Deferred Compensation Plan in the event of his disability prior to retirement satisfied the condition of § 2039(a), for the purposes of both payments to Mrs. Bahen, since at the time of his death he possessed the right to receive such payments.

While, as indicated, the case bears some resemblance to ours, there is a different flavor about it, at least so far as concerns the payments under the Deferred Compensation Plan. There was in fact a unitary right to receive deferred compensation of $100,000 in 60 equal monthly payments, this to be paid to Mrs. Bahen if Bahen died or to him if he became totally disabled prior to retirement. There was no question of grouping separate plans together, since both Mr. and Mrs. Bahen's rights were pursuant to the same Deferred Compensation Plan. Even more to the point, if payments were being made to Mr. Bahen due to his disability and he died prior to exhausting the fund, the remaining payments would be made to Mrs. Bahen. In this respect the Deferred Compensation Plan was much like the joint and survivor annuity at which § 2039 was aimed. Here, of course, Mrs. Schelberg had no rights to any payments under the Disability Plan. The possible payments to Mr. Bahen were not, as under IBM's Disability Plan, true disability payments intended to cover a portion of previous salary; they were deferred compensation, as the plan's title indicates, payable by the railway in any event, to be made available to Mr. Bahen at a date earlier than death if his needs so required. They thus met the test laid down in *Estate of Fusz*, supra, 46 T.C. at 217–18, as IBM's disability benefits do not, of being of the same nature as the payments to the beneficiary. We are not sure that the distinction is sufficient or—what is more or less the same thing—that we would have decided *Bahen* as the Court of Claims did.[9] For the moment we shall leave the matter that way.[10]

The other cases cited by the Tax Court do not require so much discussion. In re Estate of Wadewitz, 339 F.2d 980 (7 Cir. 1964), concerned an employment contract under which Wadewitz, the president of a company, was entitled to certain annual sums for a fifteen year period starting with his retirement or the termination of his employment; if he died before the end of the 15 years, remaining payments were to be made to designated beneficiaries. He died in the company's employ before retiring and all payments were made to the beneficiaries. The court nevertheless sustained the Tax Court's holding, 39 T.C. 925 (1963), that Wadewitz had an enforceable right to receive payments, on the ground that he could have accelerated his rights by retiring, as he was free to do at any time. The beneficiary in *Wadewitz*, as in *Bahen* but not the present case, succeeded to the decedent's interest in the same set of payments pursuant to a single, unitary plan. In Gray v. United States, 410 F.2d 1094 (3 Cir. 1969), the majority found the condition to § 2039(a) satisfied by the decedent's

---

9. This is especially so in regard to "the more difficult question", 305 F.2d at 834, 158 Ct.Cl. 141, in regard to the small amounts payable to Mrs. Bahen under the Death Benefit Plan.

10. The suggested distinction of *Bahen* would not cover Gaffney v. United States, 200 Ct.Cl. 744 (1972), but this was simply an order which is not entitled to great precedential weight.

participation in a retirement plan, taken by the court to be non-qualified, id. at 1111–12, under which he had a vested right to annuity payments commencing at age 65, an age he had not reached, or at earlier dates, which were available to him, see id. at 1098 n. 4. The decedent's rights to payments were thus not conditional upon such unlikely events as total disability, but merely survival until retirement age; and in any event decedent was actually in a position to receive payments under early retirement options if he had so desired. Hetson v. United States, 209 Ct.Cl. 691 (1976), adopted a recommended decision of a trial judge, 75–2 U.S.T.C. ¶ 13,098 (1975), that the decedent's entitlement to and receipt of a "salary" which was payable regardless of the amount of time he devoted to a family company's business and of his ability to do so satisfied the condition in § 2039(a). Silberman v. United States, 333 F. Supp. 1120 (W.D.Pa.1971), had been much to the same effect. Finally, Estate of Beal, 47 T.C. 269 (1966), seems quite irrelevant. The same plan provided for a provision after retirement and a survivor's death benefit, the decedent had retired and received pension payments, and the case was a paradigm for application of § 2039(a). The upshot is that the decisions in the cases reviewed in this paragraph, as distinguished from their frequent approving citation of and quotation from *Bahen*, supra, furnish no support to the extreme position taken by the Commissioner in this case.

We here decide only that to consider a deceased employee's potential ability to have qualified at some future time for payments under a plan protecting against total and permanent disability—a disagreeable feat that had been accomplished as of January 1, 1974, by only a quarter of one percent of IBM's employees—as meeting the condition in § 2039(a) that there must be a contract or agreement under which the decedent received or be entitled to receive "an annuity or other payment", is such a departure from the language used by Congress, read in the light of the problem with which it was intending to deal, as to be at war with common sense. Cf. United States v. American Trucking Associations, Inc., 310 U.S. 534 (1940). * * * Of the * * * decisions cited to us, there are clear grounds of distinguishing all with the possible exception of the leading one, *Estate of Bahen*, supra, 305 F.2d 827, 158 Ct.Cl. 141, and the certain exception of *Gaffney*, supra, 200 Ct.Cl. 744. Although we have been able to distinguish the cases other than *Gaffney* and possibly *Bahen* on grounds that seem to us sufficient, we would not wish to be understood as necessarily agreeing with all of them or with the general approach taken in *Bahen*, see 305 F.2d at 833, 158 Ct.Cl. 141. Some other case may require complete rethinking whether courts, under the influence of the *Bahen* opinion, have not unduly eroded the condition in § 2039(a), as is pointedly suggested by Judge Aldisert's dissent in Gray v. United States, supra, 410 F.2d at 1112–14; on the other hand, Congress might decide to cast its net more widely and eliminate or broaden the condition, as it could have done in 1954. We simply decline to carry the erosion of the condition to the extent here urged by the Commissioner.

The judgment is reversed and the cause remanded with instructions to annul the determination of a deficiency.

ILLUSTRATIVE MATERIAL

A. ANNUITY OR OTHER PAYMENT

Section 2039 includes in the gross estate "the value of an *annuity or other payment* receivable by any beneficiary by reason of surviving the decedent . . ., if . . . *an annuity or other payment* were payable to the decedent, or the decedent possessed the right to receive such annuity or payment. . . ." Reg. § 20.2039–1(b)(1)(ii) provides: "The term 'annuity or other payment' as used with respect to both the decedent and the beneficiary has reference to one or more payments extending over any period of time. The payments may be equal or unequal, conditional or unconditional, periodic or sporadic." As *Estate of Bahen* and *Estate of Schelberg* indicate, the scope of the phrase "other payment" as applied to the deceased employee is not clear. The difficulty arises because the drafters of § 2039 had considered an annuity plan different from the employee benefit plans in the principal case. The statutory model was a commercial joint and survivor annuity purchased by an employer for an employee which provided payments to the employee and then to the employee's survivor. See footnote 6 in *Estate of Schelberg*. In such a case, the application of § 2039(a) is clear. But where the employer, itself, provides payments instead of purchasing a commercial annuity, the question arises whether the payments to the employee are within the scope of the statutory terms "annuity or other payment."

At one time, the Commissioner asserted that salary payments and payments under wage continuation plans (i.e. payments where the employee was expected to return to work) could constitute the requisite "other payment" to the employee, but the courts disagreed. Estate of Fusz v. Commissioner, 46 T.C. 214 (1966) (the term "other payment" is "qualitatively limited to post-employment benefits" paid or payable during the employee's lifetime). The Commissioner accepted this limitation on the definition "other payment" in Rev. Rul. 77–183, 1977–1 C.B. 274 (payments under a wage continuation plan during a period of illness or temporary incapacity are not an "other payment" within the meaning of § 2039(a)). Moreover, payments from qualified pension plans which satisfy § 401(a) and which pay benefits to D while living are not treated as "other payments" for purposes of determining whether benefits payable to D's survivor under a nonqualified survivor's benefit plan are includible in D's estate. See Reg. § 20.2039–1(b)(2), Ex. (6); Rev. Rul. 76–380, 1976–2 C.B. 270.[11]

As the opinion in *Estate of Schelberg* indicates, the omission of wage continuation payments from the term "other payment" has put greater pressure on the characterization of the nature of benefits under employee benefit

---

11. Some doubt exists on the conclusion with respect to qualified plans. The cited Regulation and Rev. Rul. 76–380 were issued at a time when qualified plans were exempt from estate tax under § 2039(c)–(g). The provisions granting the exemption were generally repealed in 1984. Subsequently, the Service issued Rev. Rul. 88–85, 1988–2 C.B. 333, in which it declared several rulings, including Rev. Rul. 76–380, obsolete "to the extent" that they referred to § 2039(c)–(g). Rev. Rul. 76–380 has no such reference; it dealt only with § 2039(a) and (b). Moreover, the cited Regulation has not been changed. The issue is whether the Regulation and Rev. Rul. 76–380 were premised on the policies behind the then existing exclusions in § 2039(c)–(g) for qualified plans or whether they are based on policies unrelated to those exclusions. The lack of developments in the area suggests that the IRS has adopted the latter view.

plans. See Estate of Siegel v. Commissioner, 74 T.C. 613 (1980), where the court meticulously examined D's employment contract which provided both disability and post-death benefits and determined that, if disabled, D was obligated to continue to render services to the extent possible and to return to work as soon as recovery permitted. The court concluded that § 2039 was inapplicable because the disability payments, if made, would be wages or payments in a wage continuation plan and, therefore not "other payments." (However, the court also concluded that § 2038(a) would require inclusion of the death benefits, see p. 261.)

B. PAYMENTS RECEIVABLE BY A "BENEFICIARY"

The courts have also addressed the significance of the term "beneficiary" in § 2039. Estate of Allen v. Commissioner, 39 T.C. 817 (1963), involved a contract purchased by a company plan providing for survivorship benefits to the surviving spouse of a deceased employee in the form of an annuity for life with 120 payments certain and the balance, if any, to the employer. The court held that only the value of the benefits to the wife was includible in the deceased employee's gross estate. Since the employer was not a "beneficiary" under § 2039, the value of the employer's share of D's annuity contract was not includible in D's estate under § 2039.

C. CONTRACT OR AGREEMENT

1. *Private Employment Arrangements*

Section 2039 requires that the annuity or other payments be payable to D's survivor "under any form of contract or agreement...." Reg. § 20.2039–1(b)(1) defines the term "contract or agreement" to include "any arrangement, understanding or plan, or any combination of arrangements, understandings or plans arising by reason of the decedent's employment."

There was no question in *Estate of Schelberg* that the "contract or agreement" test in § 2039(a) was met. The decision turned solely on whether the "annuities or other payment" requirement was satisfied. A number of the following authorities were distinguished by Judge Friendly for the point at issue but they also interpret the "contract or agreement" language of § 2039(a).

Estate of Beal v. Commissioner, 47 T.C. 269 (1966), involved a single non-qualified plan providing both retirement and death benefits. The death benefit was equal to the employee's salary at the time of retirement diminished by 10 percent for each full year of retirement. The court viewed the two portions of the benefit plan together and found that the "contract or agreement" requirement was met because, although a retirement committee was required to act to determine if there was a qualified beneficiary, once that determination was made the payment of death benefits was mandatory.

In Estate of Barr v. Commissioner, 40 T.C. 227 (1963), the court found that there was no "contract or other agreement" where the company had a "wage dividend" plan under which "at its option" it might "pay a wage dividend to the estate or other beneficiaries as the officers may select." The company, generally, although not always, paid the wage dividend benefit to the beneficiary of a deceased employee. The court held that there was no "contract or agreement" within the meaning of § 2039:

> "The repeated reference (in both sub-sections (a) and (b)) to the requirement for some form of contract or agreement, indicates that the rights of both the decedent and the survivor must be enforceable rights; and that voluntary and gratuitous payments by the employer are not taxable under § 2039. This is expressly recognized in example (4) of [Reg. § 20.2039–1(b)(2)]. However, this same example does state that where the terms of an enforceable retirement plan have been modified by consistent practice of the employer, the annuity received pursuant to such modification will be considered to have been paid under a 'contract or agreement'. We do not think that the latter statement was intended to mean that where there was no enforceable arrangement, contract or agreement whatever, the mere consistency of an employer in making voluntary or gratuitous payments would be sufficient to supply the essential 'contract or agreement'." (235–236).

In Estate of Neely v. United States, 613 F.2d 802 (Ct.Cl. 1980), D, who owned 50 percent of a corporation, retired and the Board of Directors voted him a pension, payable $1,000 a month to him for life and then to his wife for her life if she survived him. D's wife owned 20 percent of the corporation, D's will left his 50 percent stock interest to her, and the balance was owned by family members. D died after receiving three payments. No annuity contract was purchased nor was any separate fund created by the corporation. D's estate argued that § 2039(a) was inapplicable because the agreement to pay the pension was not an enforceable contract under local law. The court stated that the words "any arrangement, understanding or plan" in Reg. § 20.2039–1(b)(1) clearly encompass more than enforceable contracts, and without defining the outer scope of the language, held that the resolution in question was covered by the Regulations language. The court characterized the above quotation from *Estate of Barr* as dictum and noted that any requirement of enforceability with respect to the payments at issue would be an empty formality because D's widow controlled the corporation. Allowing the annuity to escape taxation would "seriously erode § 2039(a) with respect to pensions and death benefits paid by a closely held corporation with any knowledgeable tax planning."

2. Government Benefit Payments

Social security benefits are often paid to an employee and to the employee's surviving spouse after the employee's death. In Rev. Rul. 81–182, 1981–2 C.B. 179, the IRS held that § 2039 did not apply to the benefits paid to the employee's surviving spouse because no "contract or agreement" existed within the meaning of § 2039. The ruling reasoned that the payments arose from the Social Security Act, not from any agreement or contract. For similar rulings involving other types of governmental benefits, see, Rev. Rul. 60–70, 1960–1 C.B. 372 (Railroad Retirement Act); Rev. Rul. 76–102, 1976–1 C.B. 272 (Federal Coal Mine Health and Safety Act of 1969); Rev. Rul. 2002–39, 2002–2 C.B. 33 (accidental death benefits payable by state statute to spouses of deceased firefighters).

D.   NECESSITY THAT ANNUITY BE PAYABLE TO DECEDENT

D entered into a contract providing for non-qualified retirement benefits for a period of sixteen years. If he died prior to the expiration of the period, the payments were made to his beneficiary. The contract contained a clause prohibiting D from engaging in activity competitive with the company. D died prior to retirement. The court in Estate of Wadewitz v. Commissioner, 339 F.2d 980 (7th Cir. 1964), held that § 2039 should include in D's estate the value of the benefits payable to his beneficiary, rejecting the estate's argument that D's rights were forfeitable. While the receipt of the retirement benefits was contingent upon D satisfying the specified conditions, the employer could not stop the payments or refuse to make them. The court observed that only events that were wholly within D's control could cause a cessation of the payments. The court likewise rejected the argument that § 2039 required that D actually have received the retirement benefit before his death. It was sufficient that D possessed the requisite right to the retirement benefits throughout his employment:

> "It is, of course, true that under the statute a 'right to possess' in the future must be nonforfeitable insofar as the obligator of the contract is concerned; that is, the promise to make payments must be a continually enforceable one possessed by the obligatee. If [the employer] could have stopped payments at its discretion, [D] would not have possessed a 'right to receive' but a mere expectancy; thus, the statutory requirement would not be satisfied. The promise of [the employer], however, to make payments if [D] retired constituted a nonforfeitable right which [D] possessed since [the employer] was unable to revoke its promise unless there was activity that could be initiated only by [D]. Just as [the employer] had no discretion over the start of payments, it had no discretion over their being stopped. [D's] right to payments (if he retired and refrained from the proscribed acts listed in the contract) was entirely within his control. Hence, he possessed an enforceable, nonforfeitable right to future payments. * * *

> "Petitioner's argument, when analyzed, would limit the [application of § 2039] to a situation where a contingent right to receive has ripened upon the occurrence of the contingency into an immediate right to receive. This interpretation cannot be justified. The statute clearly covers a period during which there exists a right to receive payments in the future upon the happening of a contingency as well as for a period during which the decedent has a right to receive immediate payments." (983–984)

Suppose that D's rights are forfeitable but that he is receiving payments at death? Reg. § 20.2039–1(b)(2) Ex. (2) states that where D was receiving an annuity at the time of his death, it is immaterial that his rights are forfeitable.

E.   ANNUITIES UNDER QUALIFIED EMPLOYEE RETIREMENT PLANS AND INDIVIDUAL RETIREMENT ACCOUNTS

Prior to 1985, up to $100,000 of benefits payable to D's survivor pursuant to certain qualified retirement plans were excluded from the decedent-employee's gross estate. Former § 2039(c)–(g). The Tax Reform Act of 1984 generally repealed this exclusion for the estates of decedents dying after 1984. Thus, the value of all annuities payable to D's survivors under employee retirement plans that satisfy § 401, and under Individual Retirement Accounts, are, in general, includible in the gross estate under § 2039. However, since the surviving spouse typically is the beneficiary of death benefits paid under such qualified plans, the marital deduction, discussed in Chapter 32, usually shelters the plan assets from taxation at the death of the employee spouse.

F.   PRIVATE ANNUITIES

When D transfers property to a trust or an individual in exchange for a series of payments, a threshold issue is whether the annuity constitutes a retained interest in the transferred property that will trigger application of § 2036. In Cain v. Commissioner, p. 219, the court concluded that D had not retained an interest to which § 2036 applied because the transfer was bona fide and payments to D were not dependent on income from the transferred property.

Assuming that § 2036 does not apply and that annuity payments to D's estate will continue after D's death, D's gross estate will include the value of those payments under § 2033. See p. 107. If the payments are instead made to D's survivor, D's gross estate will include the value of such payments under § 2039. If, alternatively, the annuity payments terminate at D's death pursuant to the terms of the annuity, nothing will be included in D's gross estate so long as the initial transfer was bona fide. See p. 320.

Both § 2036 and § 2039 may apply where D has transferred property to a trust or individual and has retained the right to that property's income that will then become payable to D's survivor after D's death. The overlap could present a problem because § 2036 would require inclusion of the value of the *transferred property* while § 2039 would require inclusion of the value of the *payments* to D's survivor. Proposed regulations resolve this dilemma with respect to transfers in trust by holding that § 2036, not § 2039, will apply where D's transfers were in trust. Prop. Reg. § 20.2039–1(e)(1) (2007). There is no authority resolving the potential overlap with respect to transfers to individuals.

G.   LOTTERY PRIZES AND SECTION 2039

Many state lotteries pay the prize to the winner over a period of years. Usually, the annual payments will be made to the heirs of the lottery winner in the event the winner dies. Since the amounts payable to the heirs were contractually "payable to the decedent . . . for any period which does not in fact end before his death," § 2039 will require the value of the payments to the winner's heirs be included in the winner's gross estate. In Estate of Shackleford v. United States, 98–2 U.S.T.C. ¶ 60,320 (E.D. Cal. 1998), aff'd, 262 F.3d 1028 (9th Cir. 2001), the winner's estate argued that § 2039(b) should limit the amount includible because D's payment of one dollar was only a small portion of the millions of dollars paid by other participants for lottery tickets in that lottery. The court rejected that argument, stating that Congress had adopted § 2039(b) because it felt that the portion of an annuity that had been purchased by someone else did "not represent the accumulated wealth of the decedent which should be subject to the estate tax." *Estate of Shackleford*, quoting Neely v. United States, 613 F.2d 802, 809 n.5 (Ct. Cl. 1980). The court concluded that the winner's award was attributable to his purchase of the winning ticket, not the purchase of tickets by others.

The courts have split about the proper method for valuing the payments to be included in the lottery winner's gross estate. See p. 727 for a discussion of the valuation issues.

H.   THE LIFE INSURANCE EXCEPTION

Section 2039 does not apply to life insurance payments received by D's survivor. In All v. McCobb, 321 F.2d 633 (2d Cir. 1963), the taxpayer asserted that the death benefits were "functionally insurance" and § 2039, therefore, did not apply. The court held that merely providing the deceased employee's beneficiary with protection as a result of the employee's death did not qualify the benefits as insurance. There were no premium payments and no shifting or spreading of the risk of a premature death which normally occurs with real insurance. Thus, the death benefits constituted an annuity within § 2039. For further discussion as to what constitutes "life insurance", see p. 379.

I.   GIFT TAX ASPECTS OF ANNUITIES

Under Reg. § 25.2511–1(h)(10), an individual who has an unqualified right to an annuity makes a taxable gift when he accepts a reduced annuity so that an annuity may be paid after his death to his spouse. The value of the gift is computed pursuant to the rules set forth in the Regulations under § 7520, discussed in Chapter 35.

SECTION B.   THE TREATMENT OF EMPLOYEE BENEFITS UNDER OTHER CODE PROVISIONS

ILLUSTRATIVE MATERIAL

A.   INCLUSION UNDER § 2033

As previously noted, § 2039 is not the exclusive method for the IRS to seek to include the value of employee death benefits in the employee's gross estate. At one time, § 2033 was the favored alternative route. But the courts generally rejected the applicability of § 2033 on many grounds. In Estate of Barr v. Commissioner, 40 T.C. 227 (1963), discussed at p. 113, the Commissioner sought to bring the value of deferred compensation arrangements into the deceased employee's gross estate under either § 2033 or § 2039. The court held for the taxpayer with respect to § 2033 since the employee at the time of his death had no "enforceable rights" (which would constitute a property interest under § 2033), but merely a "hope or expectancy" that his employer would pay his surviving spouse death benefits under the company's deferred compensation plan. The ability of the employee to designate the beneficiary of the death benefits did not render § 2033 applicable. Even if the employee contracts with her employer to provide death benefits directly to her surviving spouse or other beneficiaries on the sole condition that she remains employed at the time of death, inclusion does not result under § 2033 because the employee has no enforceable right to receive the benefits during her lifetime. See, e.g., Kramer v. United States, 406 F.2d 1363 (Ct.Cl. 1969). See p. 204.

The IRS has been more successful in applying § 2033 to annuities outside the death-benefit area. For example, in Estate of Gribauskas v. Commissioner, 116 T.C. 142 (2001), the Tax Court applied § 2033 to a state lottery prize that was payable to the winner over a twenty year period. When the winner died during the period, payments were made to the winner's estate. With no analysis, the court stated that it concurred with the estate's concession that the value of the remaining payments was includible in the winner's gross estate under § 2033. This is correct since D had the right to receive payments while alive. See p. 116.

B. INCLUSION UNDER §§ 2036–2038

The Commissioner has had greater success in invoking §§ 2036–2038 in employee death benefits cases where neither §§ 2039 nor 2033 was applicable.

Under §§ 2036–2038, the threshold question is whether the deceased employee has made a "transfer" by entering into an agreement with the employer to continue to provide services in return for the transfer of property to a beneficiary designated by the employee. See, e.g., Estate of Fried v. Commissioner, 445 F.2d 979 (2d Cir. 1971) (agreement satisfied the "transfer" requirement under § 2037; reversionary interest created by provision that benefits were payable to the employee's estate if the named beneficiary predeceased the employee); Kramer v. United States, 406 F.2d 1363 (Ct.Cl. 1969) (similar provision assumed to satisfy "transfer" requirement of § 2036(a)(2) but the employee had no right to change the beneficial enjoyment or otherwise designate beneficiaries under the contract).

Estate of Levin v. Commissioner, 90 T.C. 723 (1988), aff'd in unpublished opinion, 891 F.2d 281 (3d Cir. 1989), involved the applicability of § 2038(a)(1) to an employee death benefit agreement. D was the owner of over 83% of the voting stock of a corporation. The corporation adopted a plan to pay an annuity to the surviving spouses of its officers who met certain eligibility requirements. At the time of adoption of the plan, only D satisfied those requirements. D's two sons and a trusted employee were officers in the corporation and managed its day-to-day affairs. The IRS asserted that the value of the death benefits payable under the plan was includible in D's estate under § 2038(a)(1). Relying on cases such as those discussed above, the court concluded that the "transfer" requirement was satisfied by D's agreement to continue in the employ of the corporation as consideration of the payment of the annuity to his surviving spouse. Moreover, D retained the power to alter, amend, revoke or terminate the transfer because he could do so "as a member of the board of directors in conjunction with the other members," and that "by virtue of his control of [the corporation], [D] was able to structure and amend the plan to suit his needs."

Where the employee's control over the corporation is not as complete as in *Estate of Levin*, the courts have been less willing to find the requisite § 2038 power. See, e.g., Kramer v. United States, 406 F.2d 1363 (Ct.Cl. 1969) (D was the general manager of a family corporation but owned no stock in it); Estate of Tully v. United States, 528 F.2d 1401 (Ct.Cl. 1976) (the deceased employee owned exactly 50% of the stock of the corporation; a § 2038(a)(1) power "must be *demonstrable, real, apparent* and *evident*, not speculative" and the standard was not met where the other 50% shareholder could have blocked any attempt to alter or amend the decedent's death benefit agreement with the corporation).

In a case where the employee death benefit agreement itself stated that it could be amended by "mutual agreement" of the employer and employee, the value of the death benefit was includible in the employee's estate under § 2038. Estate of Siegel v. Commissioner, 74 T.C. 613 (1980). The court distinguished *Kramer* and *Tully* on the basis that the agreements in those cases had contained no express provision reserving the power to modify the rights of the beneficiaries.

C.   OTHER APPROACHES

As discussed at p. 370, the IRS may seek to invoke § 2041, dealing with powers of appointment, to require benefits payable under employee death benefit agreements to be included in the gross estate.

A novel approach to the employee death benefit cases was advanced by the IRS in Rev. Rul. 81–31, 1981–1 C.B. 475. The Service ruled that when an employee entered into a death benefit agreement, the employee made a transfer for gift tax purposes. However, because the interest could not be valued at that time, the transaction would be kept "open" until the value could be established. The Ruling concluded that the survivor's benefit could be valued immediately before the employee's death and a completed gift was made at that time. This "open transaction" approach was rejected in Estate of DiMarco v. Commissioner, 87 T.C. 653 (1986), p. 156, in a case involving an employee death benefit plan unilaterally adopted by IBM. Merely going to work for IBM did not constitute a "transfer" for gift tax purposes and the employee had no property interest to transfer because he had no rights at all with respect to naming of beneficiaries, determining the level of benefits or amending the IBM plan. Moreover, Reg. § 25.2511–2(f) specifically provides that a gift does not become complete by reason of the death of a donor. The Service subsequently revoked Rev. Rul. 81–31. Rev. Rul. 92–68, 1992–2 C.B. 257. However, in acquiescing in the result in *DiMarco*, the Service stated that it did so in situations in which the employee is automatically covered by the employer plan and has no control over the plan's terms, the employer can modify the plan, and the value of the benefit becomes determinable only upon the employee's death. 1990–2 C.B. 1. If these conditions are not satisfied, however, the Service appears on stronger ground in requiring inclusion of the value of employee death benefits under § 2038(a)(1), as discussed at p. 261.

CHAPTER 21

JOINT INTERESTS IN PROPERTY

INTRODUCTION

The common characteristic of property held in joint tenancy, tenancy by the entirety, or in a joint and survivor bank account—which contrasts with other forms of ownership—is the right of *survivorship*. When one of several joint tenants dies, her interest in property subject to the tenancy passes automatically to the surviving joint tenants. The interest of the decedent ("D") in the joint tenancy does not become part of her probate estate, and her personal representatives, heirs, creditors, and devisees have no interest in the tenancy. Similarly, when a tenant by the entirety or a depositor in a joint and survivor bank account dies, the existence of the right of survivorship causes D's interest to pass automatically to the surviving tenant or to the surviving depositors.

Aside from the common factor of survivorship, however, the characteristics of joint tenancies, tenancies by the entirety, and joint and survivor bank accounts vary substantially.

A *joint tenancy* may exist among any number of people, who need not be related to one another. Each joint tenant is considered to own all of the property, subject to the rights of the other joint tenants. Each joint tenant has equal rights and obligations with respect to the property, including, in most cases, an equal right to the property's income. A joint tenant may at any time terminate the right of survivorship of the remaining joint tenants, either by effecting a partition of the property or by selling her interest in the property. See Powell on Real Property, § 51.04 (Michael A. Wolf ed, 2007). Joint tenancies exist in a majority of American jurisdictions with respect to both personal and real property and are a common form of ownership, although a majority of jurisdictions have statutorily reversed the common law presumption favoring their creation. See id. at §§ 50.02[2], 51.01[3] (2007).

A *tenancy by the entirety* can exist only between a husband and wife. In general, neither tenant can terminate the other's right of survivorship during marriage and, many jurisdictions restrict the right of either spouse, acting alone, to alienate any interest in the property. In general, tenants by the entirety are equally entitled to the income and use of the property.

Joint and survivor bank accounts are a widely used form of property interest. The specific rights of the depositors in these accounts vary depending upon applicable state law, upon the intention of the parties, and upon the rules of the particular banking institution. In general, each depositor has the right during his life to withdraw all funds on deposit in the account, although his right to dispose of these funds for his own benefit after withdrawal will depend on state law and on the parties' intent.

Eight states—Arizona, California, Idaho, Louisiana, Nevada, New Mexico, Texas, and Washington—employ the traditional community property system. See id. at § 53.02[2][a] n.6 (2007). Unless the spouses agree otherwise, these jurisdictions generally treat property acquired by husband and wife during marriage, other than by gift, descent, or devise, as community property.[1] Upon death, the decedent spouse has the right to dispose of one-half of the community property as she wishes. Some traditional community property states provide, however, that property conveyed to spouses as joint tenants will be characterized as a joint tenancy unless the spouses agree to treat it as community property. See Estate of Young v. Commissioner, 110 T.C. 297, 300–301 (1998) (discussing California law).

SECTION A. ESTATE TAX

If the joint tenants are not husband and wife or include persons in addition to a husband and wife, § 2040(a) determines the amount includible in the deceased tenant's estate. It requires the estate to include the full value of the jointly held property, less the value attributable to contributions made by the surviving tenant. The property rights of the joint tenants under local law are irrelevant. Thus, if A pays $100 for securities, taking title in joint tenancy with B, and A predeceases B, the entire value of the securities is includible in A's estate. It is irrelevant that the creation of the joint tenancy was a completed gift to B and that B has a determinable legal interest in the securities under the applicable state law.

If the only joint tenants are a husband and wife, § 2040(b) requires one-half of the value of property held in joint tenancy to be includible in the estate of the first joint tenant to die, regardless of the respective contributions by husband and wife to the acquisition of the property.

Section 2040 is not applicable to community property or tenancies in common because there is no right of survivorship. The absence of the right of survivorship distinguishes the tenancy in common and community property from joint tenancies and tenancies by the entirety. Each tenant's fractional interest in a tenancy in common or community property, as determined under state law, is includible in his gross estate under § 2033. The relative contributions of the tenants or spouses are only relevant to the extent considered by state law in determining the fractional interests.

---

1. In contrast to the traditional community property system described above, which automatically treats most property acquired during marriage as community property, Wisconsin has a community property law that treats property received by spouses as not being community property unless the spouses elect otherwise. Powell on Real Property, § 53.02[1] (Michael A. Wolf ed, 2007).

1.   NON-SPOUSAL JOINT TENANCIES

Internal Revenue Code: § 2040(a)

Regulations: § 20.2040–1

GENERAL

Under § 2040(a), D's gross estate includes the value of all property jointly owned at his death except to the extent that (1) a portion of the property may be shown to have been acquired by contributions from the surviving joint tenant(s) which did not have as their source gifts from D, or (2) the jointly owned property was acquired by gift, devise, bequest or inheritance from a third party, in which event the includible portion is D's fractional share of the property. The executor of D's estate has the burden of establishing that some portion of the consideration for the property was contributed by the surviving joint tenant(s) or that the property was acquired by gift, devise, bequest or inheritance from a third party.

The cases and Rulings in the following materials address the method for determining the extent to which the surviving joint tenant contributed to the acquisition of property. Some arose under § 2040 prior to the addition of § 2040(b), which addresses joint tenancies held by spouses. The results in such cases would be changed if spouses were the only joint tenants, but the issues raised and principles established continue for a joint tenancy involving persons other than spouses.

ILLUSTRATIVE MATERIAL

A.   WHEN IS PROPERTY JOINTLY HELD

A question which recurs throughout the analysis of § 2040(a) is whether the mere retention of title in a joint tenancy will invoke § 2040(a). Is the retention of property in joint names sufficient to invoke § 2040(a) even if D's estate is able to demonstrate that under state law she has made a completed gift of the property?

In order to exclude a joint tenancy from D's estate, taxpayers have sometimes argued that the joint tenancy should be ignored because it was merely a convenience and that D intended to convey all ownership rights to her co-owner at the time of the tenancy's creation. For example, in Wilson v. Commissioner, 56 T.C. 579 (1971), D created joint savings accounts and purchased time certificates of deposit in her name and that of her children jointly, thereafter giving the passbooks to the children and telling them the money was theirs. The court rejected the estate's contention that the joint tenancy was a convenience and that D had made a completed gift of all her interests. In concluding that the amounts were includible in D's estate under § 2040, the court observed that there was no evidence of any intent to complete the gift, the money was still in the joint accounts at the time of D's death, the donees never reported interest income, no gift tax return had been filed, and the jointly held funds represented a substantial portion of the D's assets.

Similar results were reached in Estate of Avery v. Commissioner, 40 T.C. 392 (1963), and Estate of Stimson v. Commissioner, 63 T.C.M. 2855 (1992).

However, in Estate of Chrysler v. Commissioner, 361 F.2d 508 (2d Cir. 1966), D's interest in the property was held to be purely nominal and no portion was includible in his estate under § 2040(a) where D, as a device for making completed gifts without creating guardianships or trusts, transferred to joint accounts with his minor children property for which he had supplied all the consideration. The court found that D had intended to give up his survivorship interest, kept separate ledgers accounting for each joint account in the name of each child, reported each transfer as a separate gift, filed income tax returns reporting the income as that of the children and never used any of the funds for his own benefit. Limiting its holding to the special facts involved, the court stated that had the joint tenants been other than minor children, the estate would have had difficulty sustaining its contention that the joint owner-ship was nominal rather than beneficial.

The *Chrysler* decision seems incorrect. D had retained the right under state law to withdraw all the funds and, therefore, had retained beneficial ownership as a joint tenant. In United States v. Chandler, 410 U.S. 257 (1973) (per curiam), the Court ruled that although D had transferred jointly owned savings bonds to the other joint tenant, the bonds were includible in D's gross estate under § 2040(a) for two reasons. First, federal non-tax regulations provided that the form of savings bonds registration "will be considered as conclusive of such ownership and interest." This meant that D, who had not changed the form of registration, still held title in the bonds as a joint tenant. Second, D still held beneficial interest as a joint tenant because under such regulations D retained the right to redeem the bonds at any time.

2.   DETERMINING THE TENANT'S CONTRIBUTIONS

Many of the cases arising under § 2040(a) illustrate the difficulty encountered by an executor in sustaining the burden of tracing the source of contributions to jointly held property or joint bank accounts. The difficulty of the task is compounded where jointly held funds are invested and reinvested and amounts are withdrawn by one of the joint tenants for individual use.

Section 2040(a) and the cases place two heavy burdens on the estate seeking to prove that any part of the jointly held property was contributed by a surviving joint owner. First, § 2040(a) assumes that D contributed all the joint property and requires the estate to prove that part of the joint property "originally belonged" to the surviving joint owner. A presumption of state law that in the absence of proof one-half the amount of a joint bank account was contributed by each depositor will not be given effect in determining the value of the surviving depositor's contribution to the account for purposes of § 2040(a). Robinson v. Commissioner, 63 F.2d 652 (6th Cir. 1933). Second, § 2040(a) requires the estate to prove that the surviving joint owner's contribution to the tenancy had not been received from D for less than adequate consideration in money or money's worth.

Estate of Goldsborough v. Commissioner

70 T.C. 1077 (1978).

■ Featherston, Judge.

Respondent determined a deficiency in the amount of $51,790.20 in the Federal estate taxes of the Estate of Marcia P. Goldsborough. In these consolidated cases, the issues for decision are as follows:

> (1) To what extent, if any, are the values of certain stocks and securities jointly held by the decedent Marcia P. Goldsborough on the date of her death excludable from the gross estate under § 2040[a].

* * *

Section 2040[a] provides in general that the decedent's gross estate includes the entire value of jointly held property but that section "except[s] such part thereof as may be shown to have originally belonged to * * * [the surviving joint tenant(s)] and never to have been received or acquired by the latter from the decedent for less than an adequate and full consideration in money or money's worth." Section 2040[a] further provides that if the decedent owned property jointly with another, the amount to be excluded from the decedent's gross estate is "only such part of the value of such property as is proportionate to the consideration furnished by * * * [the surviving joint tenant(s)]." Mathematically this "consideration furnished" exclusion can be expressed as follows:

$$\text{Amount excluded} = \begin{pmatrix} \text{Entire value of property} \\ \text{(on the date of death or} \\ \text{alternate valuation date)} \end{pmatrix} \times \frac{\text{Survivor's consideration}}{\text{Entire consideration paid}}$$

In the instant case, the decedent (Goldsborough) acquired on May 12, 1937, real property (St. Dunstans) in her individual name. On April 4, 1946, decedent transferred St. Dunstans, valued at $25,000 on that date, to her two daughters (Eppler and O'Donoghue) as a gift. On July 17, 1949, the daughters sold St. Dunstans to H. W. Ford and his wife for $32,500. Sometime in that same year, each daughter invested her share of the proceeds from the sale of St. Dunstans in various stocks and securities; each daughter took title to her respective stocks and securities in joint tenancy with decedent. These stocks and securities remained in joint tenancy until December 21, 1972, the date of decedent's death, and during the period of joint tenancy the stocks and securities appreciated in value to $160,383.19, the value on the alternate valuation date.

Thus, the § 2040[a] exclusion depends on the amount, if any, of the consideration Eppler and O'Donoghue, the surviving joint tenants, furnished toward the $32,500 purchase price of the jointly held stocks and securities.

Respondent contends that all the funds used to purchase the stocks and securities in question were derived from decedent and thus the entire value of the jointly held property ($160,383.19) is includible in her gross estate.

Petitioners * * * argue that only the value of St. Dunstans at the time the gift was made to decedent's two daughters (i.e., $25,000) is includible in decedent's gross estate. In the alternative, petitioner Eppler contends that the gain of $7,500, measured by the appreciation in value from the time St. Dunstans was given to the two daughters in 1946 until that property was sold by them in 1949, constitutes consideration furnished by the daughters toward the $32,500 purchase price of the jointly held stocks and securities. Thus Eppler argues that $37,011.50 ($7,500/$32,500 of $160,383.19), the value of the jointly held property on the alternate valuation date, should be excluded from decedent's gross estate. We agree with this alternative argument.

To be sure, § 2040[a] is not a paragon of clarity, and the courts and Internal Revenue Service have wrestled with the question of whether a contribution made out of gain representing appreciation in value of property received gratuitously from decedent is attributable to the decedent or, instead, is to be treated as income from the property and thus separate funds of the surviving tenant. [T]he law, as we perceive it, recognizes two distinct situations and treats the two differently. In one situation, the surviving joint tenant receives property gratuitously from the decedent; the property thereafter appreciates, and the property itself is contributed in an exchange for jointly held property. In this circumstance § 20.2040–1(c)(4), Estate Tax Regs., treats all the property as having been paid for by the decedent, and the entire value of the property is included in the decedent's gross estate. See Estate of Kelley v. Commissioner, 22 B.T.A. 421, 425 (1931).

In the second situation, the surviving joint tenant receives property gratuitously from the decedent; the property thereafter appreciates or produces income and is sold, and the income or the sales proceeds are used as consideration for the acquisition of the jointly held property. In this situation, the income or the gain, measured by the appreciation from the time of receipt of the gift to the time of sale, has been held to be the surviving joint tenant's income and a part of that joint tenant's contribution to the purchase price. Harvey v. United States, 185 F.2d 463, 467 (7th Cir. 1950); * * *. Thus, in the words of the statute, "such part of the value of such property as is proportionate to the consideration furnished by [the surviving joint tenant]" is excluded. * * *

The facts of the instant case fall precisely within this second situation. In Harvey v. United States, supra at 465, the court characterized the facts and framed the issue as follows:

> The jointly held property is not the gift property itself, in either its original or transmuted form, but property traceable to (1) the profits made through sales of the original gift property and successive reinvestments of the proceeds of such sales or (2) the rents, interest and dividends produced by such property in its original or converted form, while title thereto was in the wife. The question presented by this appeal, then, is whether such profits and income, realized from property originally received by the wife as a gift from her husband and

traceable into property which was held by them as joint tenants at the time of the husband's death, came within the exception to the requirement of * * * [the predecessor to § 2040(a)] that the entire value of property held in joint tenancy shall be included in the decedent's gross estate.

The Government in *Harvey* argued that the full value of the jointly held property should be included in the decedent's gross estate, and the court dealt with that argument in the following manner (185 F.2d at 467):

> It seems clear that none of the cases cited contains any support for the novel proposition that income produced by gift property, after the gift has been completed, belongs to the donor and is property received or acquired from him by the donee; nor is there, in these cases, anything to impeach the conclusion of the trial court, or that of the Tax Court in the *Howard* case, that the income produced by property of any kind belongs to the person who owns the property at the time it produces such income and does not originate with a donor who has made a completed gift of that property prior to its production of the income. * * *
>
> * * * Moreover, no reason is suggested for holding that one form of income, i.e., "profit gained through a sale or conversion of capital assets," * * * is outside the exception, whereas other forms of income, such as dividends, rentals and interest, fall within its terms. It follows that the government's contention that the full value of the property held in joint tenancy by decedent and his wife at the time of his death should have been included in decedent's gross estate must be rejected. [Citations omitted.]

Thus we conclude that Eppler and O'Donoghue furnished $7,500 toward the $32,500 purchase price paid for the stocks and securities they held in joint tenancy with decedent until her death on December 21, 1972. Under the terms of the statute, such part of the value of the property, i.e., $160,383.19 on the alternate valuation date, as is proportionate to the $7,500 of consideration Eppler and O'Donoghue furnished is excluded from decedent's gross estate. Under the mathematical formula, set out above, the amount of the exclusion is $37,011.50.

* * *

ILLUSTRATIVE MATERIAL

A. DECEDENT'S FUNDS AS ORIGINAL SOURCE OF CONTRIBUTION MADE BY SURVIVING TENANT

The IRS accepted the *Goldsborough* analysis in Rev. Rul. 79–372, 1979–2 C.B. 330: "When the transfer to the joint tenancy consists of proceeds realized by the survivor upon a sale of property acquired with monies transferred from the decedent, the sale proceeds attributable to appreciation in value during the survivor's ownership of the acquired property are considered the survivor's individual contribution to the joint tenancy for purposes of section 2040[a]."

In Endicott Trust Co. v. United States, 305 F.Supp. 943 (N.D.N.Y. 1969), D supplied all the consideration for jointly owned securities. The securities were subsequently sold, the proceeds deposited in a joint bank account and then used to purchase other jointly owned securities. The entire value of the securities jointly owned at D's death was held includible under § 2040(a). The court found that changing the character of the property where there was no change in the character of the joint ownership "should not permit an escape from taxation as joint property." The court interpreted the *Harvey* case discussed in the *Goldsborough* opinion as limited to situations in which D had, prior to the acquisition of the jointly owned property, given property outright to the survivor who subsequently sold that property and used the proceeds to invest in the newly acquired jointly owned property.

The estate in *Endicott Trust* tried to analogize to *Harvey* by arguing that the transfer of property into joint names was a completed gift under state law, with the donee entitled to one-half of the income from that property. It asserted that one-half of the appreciation from the time of the gift up to the sale of that property should be treated as separate property of the surviving joint owner for purposes of determining the amount contributed by that donee. (The estate said that the intermediary step of depositing the sales proceeds in a joint bank account should be ignored because the creation of a joint account does not constitute a gift and the joint tenants had the same interests in the subsequently acquired property as they had in the bank account. See p. 352.) The court, quoting *Estate of Peters*, p. 347, rejected the estate's argument:

> "The obvious scheme of [§ 2040(a)] is to recapture the entire value of jointly-held property into a decedent's gross estate, notwithstanding the fact that the decedent may have made a gift under local law of one-half of the property. Section [2040(a)] looks to the source of the consideration represented by the property and disregards legal title." (945)

The holding in *Endicott Trust* is correct. Frequently, transfers which are completed gifts for state law and gift tax purposes may still be included in the donor's gross estate where he has retained some degree of control over the property. See, e.g., the discussion of § 2036 and § 2038, at pp. 202 and 255. Indeed, the creation of most joint tenancies is a completed gift for state law and gift tax purposes, yet neither fact is a bar to includibility under § 2040(a). The reach of that section should not be avoided where jointly held property which is otherwise includible in the donor's estate is merely transferred to a different form of joint ownership. If, however, the jointly owned securities in *Endicott Trust* had been partitioned and then sold with the proceeds deposited in a joint account or reinvested in jointly owned securities, the *Goldsborough* result should follow if the transactions were in fact independent and not part of a plan.

B. APPORTIONMENT PROBLEMS WHERE BOTH JOINT OWNERS MAKE CONTRIBUTIONS

The includible portion of jointly held property is determined by the original source of the property. If the property was originally economically attributable to D, then the entire property will be includible in his gross estate. Conversely, any portion of the property which can be shown to have originally belonged to the surviving co-owner is excluded. Reg. § 20.2040–1(a)(2) provides that the portion of the property to be excluded in such a case is calculated by multiplying the fraction of the total consideration supplied by the surviving co-owner by the value of the jointly owned property at the time of D's death. Thus, where D and another person jointly acquire property for a price of $100, D paying $80 and the other person $20, $800 is includible in D's estate if the property is worth $1,000 at D's death.

Similar rules apply where jointly owned property is acquired subject to a mortgage on which both joint tenants are jointly and severally liable and the liability of the deceased joint tenant continues as a liability of his estate. Each mortgage payment is treated as a contribution by the payor. At death, one-half of the outstanding mortgage balance, for which D's estate remains liable, is also treated as a contribution by D. Thus, assume E and F purchase property as joint tenants for $1000, each pays $100, and takes the property subject to a mortgage of $800. If E, prior to death, pays $200 in mortgage principal payments and F pays zero, 60% of the date of death value of the property is includible in E's estate. F's initial contribution of $100 plus F's $300 share of the mortgage balance at E's death equals $400 of the $1000 consideration paid to acquire the property. Rev. Rul. 79–302, 1979–2 C.B. 328.

It is more difficult to apply this statutory scheme to a situation where both D and the surviving joint owner have, at different times, made contributions to property, the value of which has appreciated between the contributions. For example, suppose A supplies the entire purchase price of $100 for the acquisition of a parcel of real property owned jointly with B. When the value of the property is $200, B contributes $50 to construct a building. A dies when the property is worth $300. How much is included in A's estate? Reg. § 20.2040–1(a)(2) appears to require that the includible portion be determined solely on the basis of the relative cash contributions of A and B. Thus, 100/150 x 300 or $200 is included.

Rev. Rul. 81–183, 1981–2 C.B. 180, confirms this conclusion. In that Ruling, two individuals each contributed $10,000 toward the acquisition of a $100,000 house, purchasing the house subject to a mortgage of $80,000. Five years later they took out a second mortgage of $50,000 and constructed a $50,000 addition to the house. At the time of his death, the first joint tenant had made $20,000 of payments on the first mortgage and the other joint tenant had paid $10,000 on the second mortgage. The house, at that time, was worth $200,000. The surviving joint tenant's contribution was held to be the initial payment ($10,000), plus the payment on the second mortgage ($10,000), plus one-half of the first mortgage balance ($30,000), plus one-half of the second mortgage balance ($20,000), or a total of $70,000. The survivor's contribution to the total acquisition of the property was $70,000 divided by $150,000 (the total contributions of both parties) or .467. Thus, the product of .467 multiplied by $200,000, or $93,340, was excluded from D's estate. The Ruling also stated that if the proceeds from the second mortgage had not been reinvested in the real property, the second mortgage would not have been considered in determining the amount of the survivor's contribution. In such a case, the survivor's contribution would be equal to $10,000 (initial contribution) plus $30,000 (one-half of the first mortgage balance) for a total of $40,000. The applicable portion would then be $40,000 divided by $100,000 (total contributions) or .4.

While the solution adopted by the Regulations and Rev. Rul. 81–183 is relatively easy to apply, in many cases it will not accord with economic reality. Returning to the above example of A and B, suppose A died just before B contributed the funds to construct the building; $200 would be includible in his estate. If A died immediately after the building was completed and the Regulation's solution is applied, $166.67 (100/150 x 250) would be included in A's estate. The result does not accord with the economic fact that the appreciation prior to B's contribution is directly attributable to A's investment and never "originally belonged to" B.

To resolve this problem, post-contribution appreciation could be viewed as additional consideration supplied by the joint owner who supplied the last contribution. Thus, the appreciation of $100 from the date of acquisition to the date of B's contribution could be viewed as further consideration supplied by A. The allocation of the appreciation subsequent to B's contribution is more difficult, but it would seem that unless that appreciation can be traced specifically to the investment made by B, it would be appropriate to allocate it in proportion to the relative contributions (including the appreciation specifically attributable to such contributions) made by each joint owner, i.e., 200/250 x 250 to A and the balance to B. (The same result occurs if appreciation which is not specifically attributable to any particular contribution is ignored.) The foregoing solution is essentially that adopted by Reg. § 25.2515–1(c) to solve a similar problem under § 2515 of the gift tax prior to its repeal. See Surrey, Warren, McDaniel & Gutman, Federal Wealth Transfer Taxation 505 (1977).

Alternatively the $50 addition by B could be treated as the acquisition of a separate jointly owned property. Thus, at A's death, the entire value attributable to the original parcel would be included in A's estate and no portion of the value of the addition would be included. This solution was adopted in 1978 by the addition of § 2040(d) which then was repealed by the Economic Recovery Tax Act of 1981. Temp. Reg. § 23.1 supplied rules to allocate mortgage payments between the separate interests thus created. While the separate property rule was specifically mandated by § 2040(d)(6), it would seem within the Commissioner's authority to provide a similar rule under § 2040(a). Either of the foregoing solutions would be more complex, but would reflect economic reality more accurately than that adopted in Rev. Rul. 81–183.

In Estate of Peters v. Commissioner, 386 F.2d 404 (4th Cir. 1967), the only case in which the issue was raised, the taxpayer failed to introduce any evidence of post-contribution appreciation so that the issues discussed above were not resolved. The Tax Court noted, however, that had such evidence been introduced, "it might have been necessary * * * to devise a formula or ratio of [its] own." Estate of Graham v. Commissioner, 46 T.C. at 415.

3. JOINT TENANCIES BETWEEN SPOUSES

Internal Revenue Code: § 2040(b)

Senate Finance Committee Report, Economic Recovery Tax Act of 1981

S. Rep. No. 97–144, 97th Cong., 1st Sess. 126–128 (1981).

* * *

Reasons for Change

[T]he committee believes that the taxation of jointly held property between spouses is complicated unnecessarily. Often such assets are purchased with joint funds making it difficult to trace individual contributions. In light of the unlimited marital deduction adopted by the committee bill, the taxation of jointly held property between spouses is only relevant for determining the basis of property to the survivor (under § 1014) and the qualification for certain provisions (such as current use valuation under § 2032A, deferred payment of estate taxes [under § 6166] and for income taxation of redemptions to pay death taxes and administration expenses under § 303). Accordingly, the committee believes it appropriate to adopt an easily administered rule under which each spouse would be considered to own one-half of jointly held property regardless of which spouse furnished the consideration for the property.

Explanation of [§ 2040(b)]

[T]he bill provides special rules for determining ownership of property held by spouses in joint tenancy with a right of survivorship. Under [§ 2040(b)], each spouse will be deemed to own one-half of the value of the property regardless of which spouse furnished the consideration. * * *

ILLUSTRATIVE MATERIAL

A.   ASPECTS OF PRE–1982 LAW

Controversy has surrounded the effective date of § 2040(b). The IRS contends that the 1981 revision of § 2040(b) applies to all Ds dying after 1981 and to Ds dying after 1976 whose joint tenancy interests were created by gift after 1976. However, in Gallenstein v. United States, 975 F.2d 286 (6th Cir. 1992), the court ruled that § 2040(b) only applies to joint interests created after 1976. See also Patten v. United States, 116 F.3d 1029 (4th Cir. 1997) and Hahn v. Commissioner, 110 T.C. 140 (1998) (same result). The effect of *Gallenstein* is that spousal joint interests created prior to 1977 will be included in a decedent-spouse's estate to the extent of his contribution. If the decedent-spouse provided all the consideration, the full value of the property will be included in his estate. The result will normally be a full step-up in basis for the surviving spouse under § 1014 with no estate tax liability, since the transfer to that spouse will usually qualify for the marital deduction.

B.   REQUIREMENTS

Section 2040(b) applies only where the spouses are the sole joint tenants and D and his spouse were married at the time of D's death. It generally does not apply where the surviving spouse is not a U.S. citizen. See Chapter 41 which discusses the special rules applicable to non-citizen spouses.

4.   Relationship of § 2040 to Other Sections

ILLUSTRATIVE MATERIAL

A.   TRANSFERS OF JOINTLY OWNED PROPERTY IN EXCHANGE FOR A LIFE ESTATE

Suppose that D supplies all the consideration for property held jointly with her son, B. Under § 2040(a), all the property will be included in D's estate upon her death. Can D avoid this result if she and B transfer the property to C, retaining a joint and survivor life income interest in the property?

In Glaser v. United States, 306 F.2d 57 (7th Cir. 1962), D purchased property, taking title as tenants by the entirety with his wife. Under applicable state law, each tenant had a 50% interest in the property. D and the wife later conveyed the properties outright to their children and reserved a joint and survivor life estate. The Government argued that §§ 2040(a) and 2036(a)(1) should be read together to include the entire value of the previously jointly owned property in D's estate. It contended that had D died prior to the transfer, § 2040(a) would have included all the property in his estate (§ 2040(b) had not yet been enacted). Although the conveyance to the children destroyed the tenancy by the entirety and left D with a joint life interest, in substance D retained the same interest he had before the conveyance. The court disagreed, holding that § 2040(a) applies only to property held jointly "at the time of decedent's death." At the time of D's death there was no joint interest to which § 2040(a) could apply since the conveyance to the children destroyed the tenancy by the entirety under state law. The court also concluded that at the time of the transfer, each tenant conveyed a 50% interest to which § 2036(a)(1) applied.[2] Thus, one half of the property was includible in D's gross estate. A similar result was reached in United States v. Heasty, 370 F.2d 525 (10th Cir. 1966). The Commissioner conceded this issue in Rev. Rul. 69–577, 1969–2 C.B. 173, in situations where it is clear under state law that each tenant was entitled to one-half of the income from the property prior to the transfer so that in effect each tenant is only conveying a one-half interest.

Rev. Rul. 69–577 creates a significant opportunity for avoiding transfer tax. Where § 2040(a) applies, D can reduce the size of her estate by engaging in a transaction similar to *Glaser*. D's transfer with a retained life interest must be irrevocable, however. In Estate of Hornor v. Commissioner, 305 F.2d 769 (3d Cir. 1962), a husband bought property with his own funds which was placed in a tenancy by the entirety. He and his wife then transferred the property to a revocable inter vivos trust retaining the income for the life of each and the survivor, the trust to become irrevocable upon the death of the first spouse to die. The court held that the value of all the property was includible in the husband's estate under the predecessor of § 2040(a) and that upon the wife's subsequent death, a portion of the trust was includible in her estate under the predecessor of § 2036. The court reasoned that upon the husband's death, two events took place: there was a testamentary disposition of all the property by the husband and a transfer by the wife with a retained life estate. (If § 2040(b) applied, only one-half the property would be includible in the husband's estate.)

B. TRANSFERS OF JOINT INTERESTS WITHIN THREE YEARS OF DEATH

A transfer within three years of death of an interest in jointly-owned property is not included in the decedent's gross estate. The transferred interest is treated as an adjusted taxable gift and is not returned to the gross estate under § 2035(a).

---

2. The other half of the property might have been included under § 2038 or § 2036(a)(2) if D had retained sufficient powers to require applicability of those sections.

5.   Community Property

ILLUSTRATIVE MATERIAL

A.   AMOUNT INCLUDIBLE

Tenancies in community property states which are treated under state law as a tenancy with a right to survivorship are governed by § 2040. In contrast, ownership rights which are characterized as community property under state law result in one-half of the property being included in the deceased spouse's estate since his interest under state law is one-half. T.D. 2450, 19 Treas. Dec. Int. Rev. 38 (1919).

Section B.   Gift Tax

Internal Revenue Code: § 2511(a)

Regulations: §§ 25.2511–1(h)(4), (5)

ILLUSTRATIVE MATERIAL

A.   CREATION OF JOINT TENANCY

The creation of a joint tenancy in any type of property (other than in certain intangibles discussed below) among any number of joint tenants is a taxable transfer to the extent the value of the interest received by any tenant exceeds the amount he contributed. However, to the extent the creation of the joint tenancy results in a transfer from one spouse to another, the value of the interest received by the transferee spouse is eligible for the gift tax marital deduction. See p. 637.

Where, under applicable state law, any of the joint tenants may defeat the survivorship right of the other, the value of the interest received by each is proportional to the number of joint owners because each tenant may, at any time, partition the property and receive a proportionate share in sole possession. See Reg. § 25.2511–1(h)(5). Thus, if A supplies $40,000 and B supplies $10,000 for the purchase of securities to which title is taken as joint tenants, A has made a gift of $15,000 to B, regardless of the ages of A and B. But if neither joint tenant unilaterally can defeat the survivorship rights of the other, the actual value of the interest received by each depends upon their relative ages and is computed by reference to actuarial tables in IRS Publication 1457, "Actuarial Values, Book Aleph." See Reg. § 25.2515–2(b)–(d).[3] If A and B own property jointly and the property is subject to a mortgage for which they are jointly and severally liable, A's payment of the mortgage is a taxable gift to B to the extent of B's interest in the property if, at the time of the payment, A releases her right to contribution from B for the mortgage payment. Rev. Rul. 78–362, 1978–2 C.B. 248.

---

3. Although § 2515 was repealed effective for post–1981 gifts, the regulations thereunder still provide helpful guidance for the appropriate treatment of gifts.

An issue may arise with regard to the value of the consideration furnished when a joint tenancy is created. For example, suppose that A creates a joint tenancy with B in exchange for B's promise to render services to A or as the result of an agreement to hold jointly any property earned or accumulated by the joint efforts of A and B. In Estate of Trafton v. Commissioner, 27 T.C. 610 (1956), a husband and wife orally agreed that property earned and accumulated through their joint efforts was to be owned jointly. The husband's transfer of securities into joint names to effectuate the agreement was held not a taxable gift because the wife's joint efforts constituted full consideration for her share.

The release of marital rights, other than support rights, is not consideration for gift tax purposes. See Chapter 18. Thus, except in divorce situations where either § 2516 or the *Harris* rule applies, p. 189, the creation of a joint tenancy in exchange for the release of marital rights is a gift. However, if the parties are married at the time of the creation of the joint tenancy, the unlimited gift tax marital deduction eliminates gift tax consequences.

The creation of joint tenancies in certain intangibles is not a taxable gift if the donor can withdraw the full amount of the transfer. See Reg. 25.2511–2(e). Thus, deposits to a joint bank account from which the contributor can withdraw funds without the consent of the joint owner under local law is not a gift until the non-contributing owner withdraws funds from the account. Where both joint owners contribute funds, no gift occurs until one has withdrawn more than he has contributed. Similarly, if A purchases United States savings bonds registered as payable to "A or B", there is no gift until B redeems the bonds without an obligation to account to A for the proceeds. Rev. Rul. 68–269, 1968–1 C.B. 399. In addition, the creation of a joint brokerage account by one individual where securities are registered in the name of a nominee of the brokerage firm is not a gift until the other joint owner draws on the account for his own benefit. Rev. Rul. 69–148, 1969–1 C.B. 226 (securities held in the described manner more closely resemble a joint bank account than specific jointly owned securities).

As under § 2040, taxpayers may argue that the creation of a joint tenancy under state law should be ignored for gift tax purposes. In extraordinary circumstances taxpayers succeed. In Bouchard v. Commissioner, 285 F.2d 556 (1st Cir. 1961), D, to insure that certain securities would pass to his wife at death, caused the certificates to be reissued in their names as joint tenants. He put the certificates in a safe to which his wife did not have access, never told her of the transfer, and the wife never saw the certificates until after his death. The court held that no joint tenancy was ever created because D had no intention to make a present gift. More commonly, legal title under state law will govern notwithstanding the donor's intention at the time the tenancy is created or the donor's action thereafter with regard to the jointly held property. See, e.g., Estate of Young v. Commissioner, 110 T.C. 297 (1998).

B.   TERMINATION OF JOINT TENANCY

The termination of a joint tenancy between husband and wife may constitute a gift but no gift tax will be payable because of the gift tax marital deduction. However, the termination of a joint tenancy in which someone other than a husband and wife is a joint tenant may have gift tax consequences. If the creation of such a non-spousal joint tenancy constituted a gift and, on termination, each joint tenant receives his proportionate share of the property, there is no further gift. For example, assume A supplied all the consideration for the acquisition of $50,000 of securities owned jointly with B and either can defeat the survivorship right of the other, A has made a $25,000 gift to B. When the securities are worth $100,000, A and B partition the property each taking $50,000. There is no additional gift of the $25,000 in increased value received by B. However, to the extent one of the joint owners receives more property than his proportionate share as determined by the original gift, the joint owner receiving less is considered to have made a gift in that amount to the one who receives more. Thus, in the above example, if B received all the property upon termination, A has made an additional gift to B of $50,000.

A similar rule applies where the joint tenancy is one in which neither tenant has the right to defeat the survivorship interest of the other without consent. A gift will occur to the extent a tenant receives more than the actuarial value of her tenancy at the termination date. See Reg. § 25.2515–4(b).

Where the creation of the joint tenancy was not a completed gift, the termination will result in a gift to the extent any joint owner receives an amount in excess of his contribution.

C. JOINT INTERESTS CREATED BETWEEN SPOUSES: PRE–1982 LAW

The unlimited gift tax marital deduction eliminates any gift tax consequences to the post–1981 creation and termination of joint interests in property between spouses. However, the pre–1982 creation and termination of joint interests between spouses did have gift tax consequences under certain circumstances. Therefore, pre–1982 law remains relevant in determining the amount of an individual's cumulative and adjusted taxable gifts. In this regard, it is necessary not only to apply the rules relating to the gift tax consequences of the creation and termination of joint interests, but also the applicable gift tax marital deduction. These rules are discussed in Surrey, McDaniel and Gutman, Federal Wealth Transfer Taxation 483–485 (1987).

D. COMMUNITY PROPERTY

A gift of community property by either spouse to a third person is taxed one-half to each. Similarly, division of community property between spouses, each to hold separately, does not constitute a gift. Rev. Rul. 75–551, 1975–2 C.B. 378.

E. POLICY OPTIONS

Under current law, there is a dichotomy between the gift and estate tax rules governing jointly owned property. For gift tax purposes, the amount of the gift depends upon whether the joint owners have the right to partition. At death, however, it is the relationship between or among the joint owners that is crucial; one set of rules applies to joint tenancies between spouses and a different set of rules applies to property in which a non-spouse owns an interest. This situation unnecessarily complicates the treatment of jointly owned property.

In its 1969 tax reform proposals, the Treasury Department recommended that a uniform set of rules apply to jointly owned property. In situations in which the joint owners have a right to partition, if a person transferred property into a joint tenancy, there would be a taxable gift measured by each owner's interest in the property; the ages of the co-owners would be irrelevant. The balance of the transfer would be subject to estate tax upon the death of the transferor. Regardless of the type of property involved, if the form of ownership permitted any of the joint owners to take the entire property during the joint lives of the co-owners, the current rules governing joint bank accounts (p. 352) would be applicable. In each case, the relationship between the co-owners would be irrelevant although the marital deduction (discussed at p. 572) would be available for qualifying transfers between spouses. U.S. Treasury Department Tax Reform Studies and Proposals, House Ways and Means Committee and Senate Finance Committee, 91st Cong., 1st Sess. 375–376, Part 3 (Comm. Print 1969). Since under current law all property can be transferred free of tax between spouses, special rules for property jointly owned by spouses are unnecessary.

Section C.   Estate Planning Aspects of Jointly Owned Property

Estate planning for property jointly owned by spouses is intertwined with marital deduction planning and is generally discussed in conjunction with the marital deduction at p. 572. It is important to note that the *Gallenstein* decision, p. 348, provides the opportunity for an executor to employ § 2040(a) to include the entire value of jointly held property acquired prior to 1977 in the deceased spouse's estate if that spouse provided all the consideration for the property. Where the property has appreciated, this will provide the surviving spouse with a stepped-up basis and will normally not increase the estate tax since the transfer to the surviving spouse will usually qualify for the marital deduction.

Where an executor can determine that there are tax advantages to having the entire value of jointly owned property included in the estate of the first to die (e.g., a stepped-up basis for the property), may she take advantage of the statutory presumption of § 2040(a) and include the full value of the property on the estate tax return of the first to die? Or is she under an obligation to ascertain the amount contributed by the survivor and include only that amount which is not attributable to such contributions? See Madden v. Commissioner, 52 T.C. 845 (1969), aff'd per curiam, 440 F.2d 784 (7th Cir. 1971) (taxpayer relying on step-up in basis to decrease gain on sale of stock has burden of proving that stock was required to be included in D's estate).

Different estate planning issues arise with respect to nonspousal jointly owned property. If, after determining the estate tax consequences of retention of property in joint names, it is concluded that some or all of the joint tenancies should be terminated, the parties will desire to terminate at the least tax cost. There are several possibilities. If no gift was made at the time the property was placed in joint names, the return of the property to each of the owners in proportion to the consideration supplied by each will terminate the tenancy with no gift tax cost. If, however, the gift was complete at the time the tenancy was created, the termination of the tenancy, in a way different from their fractional interests will result in a second gift. Alternatively, the property may be given to a third party, or sold or exchanged with the proceeds distributed so as to minimize the gift tax payable.

Glaser offers some tax planning opportunities where property, if held jointly at death, would be fully includible under § 2040(a). By disposing of such property to a trust or third party with the reservation of life estate, the donor may avoid the inclusion in his estate of one-half the value of the jointly owned property.

Jointly owned property subject to estate tax under § 2040(a) may cause administrative difficulties for an executor. Notwithstanding payment of a gift tax on the creation of the tenancy, the property will be included in the estate of the first to die to the extent the survivor did not contribute to its acquisition. The problems of tracing contributions are often very difficult and may result in the inclusion of property in D's estate solely because of the executor's inability to meet the burden of proof with regard to establishing the surviving joint tenant's contributions.

CHAPTER 22

POWERS OF APPOINTMENT

SECTION A. AN OVERVIEW OF POWERS OF APPOINTMENT

Suppose that donor transfers property in trust, income to A, and that donor also gives A a testamentary power to appoint the trust corpus to anyone he chooses. The trust instrument states that if A fails to exercise his testamentary power of appointment, the corpus will pass to C. Although A's right to the income and his testamentary power to appoint the corpus approximate outright ownership, the Supreme Court held in Helvering v. Safe Dep. & Trust Co., 316 U.S. 56 (1942), that the predecessor of § 2033 did not require the property's inclusion in A's gross estate. The Court reasoned that A possessed no property interest at death because his income interest terminated and A's power of appointment was not an interest in property.

The Supreme Court's refusal to treat a power of appointment as an interest in property is attributable to the failure of common law to recognize a power as a property interest. 5 Casner, American Law of Property § 23.4 (1952). Common law generally treats powers of appointments as agency relationships between the grantor of the power and the holder of the power. The exercise of the power by the holder is treated as a completion of a transfer by the grantor of the power. Powell on Real Property § 33.03[1] (Michael A. Wolf ed., 2007).

As discussed in Section B, § 2041 currently treats the holder of a certain type of powers of appointment at death as though she is the property owner and requires inclusion of the property in her gross estate. As discussed in Section C, § 2514 adopts a similar approach for gift tax purposes and imposes a gift tax on the inter vivos exercise, release or lapse of certain types of powers of appointments.

Powers of appointment are popular today because they provide the grantor of the power great flexibility in dealing with future contingencies. The Restatement of Property, Ch. 25, Introductory Note (1936–1944) explained:

> "Owners often wish to control the devolution of their property through two or more generations; and the rule against perpetuities does not prevent an owner who is competently advised from exercising such control for about a century. Plainly no human foresight is adequate to frame in advance dispositions which will meet the exigencies of the maximum period of control or even of the comparatively small fraction thereof commonly utilized by testators and settlors. Births and deaths in varying combinations, the commercial success of some family members and the failure of others, the varying capacities

of individuals as to the husbanding of resources, fluctuation in income returns and the value of the monetary unit, legislative action and constitutional amendment reflecting social and political change—all these are factors whose unpredictability indicates the folly of rigid pre-determined future limitations and the desirability of gifts containing a substantial element of flexibility. The power of appointment . . . is the most efficient device yet contrived by which an owner may obtain such flexibility while still controlling the general purposes to which his property shall be devoted. When A leaves his property in trust for his son, B, for life and then in trust for such children of B as B shall by will appoint, he makes it possible for the manner of distribution among B's children to be determined in accordance with the changes which may occur during the rest of B's life while at the same time ensuring that the remainder interest will not be diverted from the children. In a sense the power of appointment extends the personality of A through the balance of the life of B.''

The validity of a holder's power to appoint property is determined under state law. Morgan v. Commissioner, 309 U.S. 78 (1940). If a donor's grant of the power to the holder is ineffective under state law, §§ 2041 and 2514 will not apply. Rev. Rul. 54–153, 1954–1 C.B. 185. Most states have adopted statutes which augment the common law of powers of appointment. See, e.g. Mass. G.L. ch. 204 §§ 27–37 (stating the method for releasing a power of appointment). After the rights of the power holder under state law are determined, federal law then applies to decide whether those rights are subject to taxation under §§ 2041 and 2514.

SECTION B.   ESTATE TAXATION OF POWERS OF APPOINTMENT

Internal Revenue Code: § 2041

Reg. §§ 20.2041–1, 3

1.   INTRODUCTION

Section 2041 distinguishes between general powers of appointment created on or before October 21, 1942 and powers created thereafter. Section 2041(a)(1), which applies to general powers of appointment created on or before October 21, 1942, includes property subject to a general power of appointment in decedent's gross estate if the decedent exercised the power in her will or, alternatively, exercised the power while alive and retained at death an interest in the appointive property. In contrast, § 2041(a)(2), which applies to general powers of appointment created after October 21, 1942, generally includes in a decedent's gross estate property subject to a general power of appointment that decedent held at death regardless of whether decedent exercised it. Section 2041(a)(2) in effect, continues the approaches of §§ 2036(a)(2) and 2038 that property subject to decedent's control should be included in the gross estate.

To understand § 2041 it is necessary to master the terms used in the statute and by attorneys in estate planning.

General Power of Appointment. A general power of appointment is defined in § 2041(b)(1) as "a power which is exercisable in favor of the decedent, his estate, his creditors or the creditors of his estate." Note the disjunctive: property subject to such a power is includible in the powerholder's gross estate if it is exercisable in favor of any one of the four specified classes. For example, if A transfers property in trust for B and the trust instrument provides that B may withdraw the principal from the trust, B has a general power of appointment over the trust corpus because she holds a power which is exercisable in her favor.

Special Power of Appointment. Powers that are not general powers of appointment are known by estate planners (though not in the Code) as special powers of appointment. Thus a power that is not in favor of the holder, his estate, his creditors or the creditors of his estate is a special power of appointment. For example, if A creates a trust with income to B for life, remainder to such of B's issue as B shall designate by will, otherwise to C, B does not have a general power of appointment because neither she, her estate, her creditors, nor creditors of her estate may receive corpus. Special powers of appointment are not includible in the powerholder's gross estate.

Other Powers That Are Not General Powers. In addition, powers falling within the exceptions set forth in § 2041(b)(1)(A) through (C) are not general powers. One exception refers to powers involving an ascertainable standard. If A transfers property in trust for the benefit of B and B may withdraw corpus solely for her health, education, support or maintenance, B's withdrawal right is limited by an ascertainable standard and is not a general power. § 2041(b)(1)(A).

Another exception covers a joint power involving adverse interests. If a power created after October 21, 1942 may be exercised only in conjunction with the donor or with a person having a substantial adverse interest in the property subject to the power, the power is not a general power. § 2041(b)(1)(C). For example, if A created a trust for the benefit of B and C and the trust provided that B could withdraw corpus only with the approval of C, the power held by B is not a general power.

Another exception relates to a pre-existing joint power. If the power of appointment was created on or before October 21, 1942 and the holder of the power may exercise it only in conjunction with another person (whether or not that person possesses an adverse interest in the appointive property), the power is not a general power. § 2041(b)(1)(B). For example, if A created an irrevocable trust in 1930 for the benefit of B and the trust provided that B could withdraw corpus only with the consent of X, a corporate trustee, B's right to withdraw corpus is not a general power.

Exercise. The terms exercise and exercised as used in § 2041(a) relate to whether the holder of a power utilized the rights granted by the power. The concept of "exercise" is relevant to § 2041 in two situations. First, the estate tax only applies to property subject to a general power of appointment created on or before October 21, 1942 that is held by the decedent at death if the decedent exercised that power in his will.

Second, if a decedent exercised either a pre- or post-October 21, 1942 power while alive, and retained an interest in the appointive property that is described in §§ 2035–2038, § 2041(a)(1) and (a)(2) include that property in the decedent's gross estate. Section 2041(a)(1) and (2) accomplish this by asking whether §§ 2035–2038 would have applied had the decedent actually owned the appointive property and transferred it herself. For example, assume A creates a trust for the benefit of B, granting B the power to amend the trust. Since B is not precluded from exercising her power to amend the trust to permit transfer of the corpus to herself, she possesses a general power of appointment. B subsequently exercises her power by amending the trust to provide an income interest to herself for life, remainder to C. Had B actually owned the corpus, transferred it in trust, and retained an income interest, § 2036(a)(1) would have required inclusion of the corpus in B's gross estate. Consequently, the property subject to the power is included in B's gross estate under § 2041(a)(1)(B) in the case of a pre-October 21, 1942 power or under the second part of the first sentence of § 2041(a)(2) in the case of a post-October 21, 1942 power. On the other hand, if B had amended the trust to make C the sole beneficiary of the trust, no part of the property which had been subject to the power would be included in B's gross estate under § 2041 because B's transfer, had she owned the appointive property outright, would not trigger inclusion under §§ 2035 through 2038 and B did not hold the power at death.[1]

Release. A release of a power occurs when the powerholder relinquishes all or a part of the power over the property.[2] The release of a power created after October 21, 1942 is deemed to be an exercise of the power under § 2041(b)(2). Thus, the rules applicable to powers that have been exercised determine whether the property subject to the released power is includible in the power holder's gross estate. To illustrate, suppose A creates a trust for the benefit of B, granting B a life income interest and the right to withdraw principal during life. B's power to withdraw principal is a general power of appointment. The release by B of her right to principal during life is deemed to be an exercise of the power. The trust corpus will be included in B's estate because B is treated as though she appointed the principal to herself and then transferred it to the trust while retaining an income interest. § 2041(b)(2); Reg. § 20.2041–3(d)(1).

Lapse. A general power of appointment may by its terms expire if not exercised within a specified time. Such an expiration is a lapse. A lapse is treated as a release of the power under § 2041(b)(2) to the extent that, in any calendar year, the value of the property which could have been appointed exceeds the greater of $5,000 or 5% of the value, at the time of the lapse, of the assets out of which the power could have been satisfied.

---

1. B's exercise of the power is a taxable gift, however, under § 2514. See p. 372.

2. A qualified disclaimer of a general power of appointment, however, is not considered a release of the power. See p. 434.

For example, donor transfers $400,000 in trust with income payable to B and gives B the right in the year of transfer to withdraw $30,000 from the trust corpus. B fails to exercise the power and dies in a subsequent year. A lapse of B's power to withdraw $30,000 has occurred, but only $10,000 will be treated as a release (the excess of $30,000 over 5% of $400,000). Because a release is treated as an exercise, $10,000 is includible in B's estate as a transfer that would have resulted in includibility under § 2036 had B owned that property outright.

2.   SECTION 2041(a)(2): POST-OCTOBER 21, 1942 POWERS

Estate of Kurz v. Commissioner

68 F.3d 1027 (7th Cir. 1995).

■ EASTERBROOK, CIRCUIT JUDGE.

Between her husband's death, in 1971, and her own, in 1986, Ethel H. Kurz was the beneficiary of two trusts. Kurz received the income from each. She was entitled to as much of the principal of one (which we call the Marital Trust) as she wanted; all she had to do was notify the trustee in writing. She could take only 5% of the other (which we call the Family Trust) in any year, and then only if the Marital Trust was exhausted. When Kurz died, the Marital Trust contained assets worth some $3.5 million, and the Family Trust was worth about $3.4 million. The estate tax return included in the gross estate the whole value of the Marital Trust and none of the value of the Family Trust. The Tax Court held that Kurz held a general power of appointment over 5% of the Family Trust, requiring the inclusion of another $170,000 under 26 U.S.C. § 2041(a)(2). 101 T.C. 44 (1993) * * *.

Section 2041(b)(1) defines a general power of appointment as "a power which is exercisable in favor of the decedent, his estate, his creditors, or the creditors of his estate". Kurz had the power to consume or appoint the corpus of the Marital Trust to anyone she pleased whenever she wanted, and the Estate therefore concedes that it belongs in the gross estate [under § 2041(a)(2)]. For her part, the Commissioner of Internal Revenue concedes that the 95% of the Family Trust that was beyond Kurz's reach even if the Marital Trust had been empty was not subject to a general power of appointment. What of the other 5%? None of the Family Trust could be reached while the Marital Trust contained 1 cent, and the Estate submits that, until the exhaustion condition was satisfied (which it never was), the power to appoint 5% in a given year was not "exercisable", keeping the Family Trust outside the gross estate. To this the Commissioner replies that a power is "exercisable" if a beneficiary has the ability to remove the blocking condition. Suppose, for example, that the Family Trust could not have been touched until Ethel Kurz said "Boo!" Her power to utter the magic word would have been no different from her power, under the Marital Trust, to send written instructions to the trustee.

The Tax Court was troubled by an implication of the Commissioner's argument. Suppose the Family Trust had provided that Kurz could reach 5% of the principal if and only if she lost 20 pounds, or achieved a chess rating of 1600, or survived all of her children. She could have gone on a crash diet, or studied the games of Gary Kasparov, or even murdered her children. These are not financial decisions, however, and it would be absurd to have taxes measured by one's ability to lose weight, or lack of moral scruples. Imagine the trial, five years after a person's death, at which friends and relatives troop to the stand to debate whether the decedent was ruthless enough to kill her children, had enough willpower to lay off chocolates, or was smart enough to succeed at chess. The Tax Court accordingly rejected the Commissioner's principal argument, ruling that raw ability to satisfy a condition is insufficient to make a power of appointment "exercisable".

If not the Commissioner's position, then what? The Estate's position, 180 [degrees] opposed, is that the condition must be actually satisfied before a power can be deemed "exercisable". The Tax Court came down in the middle, writing that a condition may be disregarded when it is "illusory" and lacks any "significant non-tax consequence independent of the decedent's ability to exercise the power." Of course, illusions are in the eye of the beholder, and we are hesitant to adopt a legal rule that incorporates a standard well suited to stage magicians (though some legal drafters can give prestidigitators a run for their money). No one doubts that the Kurz family had good, non-tax reasons for the structure of the trust funds. The only question we need resolve is whether a sequence of withdrawal rights prevents a power of appointment from being "exercisable". Despite the large number of trusts in the United States, many of them arranged as the Kurz trusts were, this appears to be an unresolved issue. Neither side could find another case dealing with stacked trusts, and we came up empty handed after independent research.

For a question of first principles, this one seems remarkably simple. Section 2041 is designed to include in the taxable estate all assets that the decedent possessed or effectively controlled. If only a lever must be pulled to dispense money, then the power is exercisable. The funds are effectively under the control of the beneficiary, which is enough to put them into the gross estate. Whether the lever is a single-clutch or double-clutch mechanism can't matter. Imagine a trust divided into 1,000 equal funds numbered 1 to 1,000, Fund 1 of which may be invaded at any time, and Fund n of which may be reached if and only if Fund n−1 has been exhausted. Suppose the beneficiary depletes Funds 1 through 9 and dies when $10 remains in Fund 10. Under the Kurz Estate's view, only $10 is included in the gross estate, because Funds 11 through 1,000 could not have been touched until that $10 had been withdrawn. But that would be a ridiculously artificial way of looking at things. Tax often is all about form * * *, but § 2041 is an anti-formal rule. It looks through the trust to ask how much wealth the decedent actually controlled at death. The decedent's real wealth in our hypothetical is $10 plus the balance of Funds 11 through 1,000; the decedent could have withdrawn and spent the entire amount in a trice. Whether this series of trusts has spend-thrift features (as the Kurz trusts did) or is invested in illiquid instruments (as the Kurz trusts were) would not matter. The Estate does not deny that Kurz had a general power of appointment over the entire Martial Trust, despite these features. If the costs of removing wealth from the trust do not prevent including in the gross estate the entire corpus of the first trust in a sequence (they don't), then the rest of the sequence also is includible.

Wait!, the Estate exclaims. How did first principles get into a tax case? After consulting the statute, a court turns next to the regulations. 26 C.F.R. § 20.2041–3(b) provides:

> For purposes of section 2041(a)(2), a power of appointment is considered to exist on the date of a decedent's death even though the exercise of the power is subject to the precedent of giving of notice, or even though the exercise of the power takes effect only on the expiration of a stated period after its death notice has been given or the power has been exercised. However, a power which by its terms is exercisable only upon the occurrence during the decedent's lifetime of an event or a contingency which did not in fact take place or occur during such time is not a power in existence on the date of the decedent's death. For example, if a decedent was given a general power of appointment exercisable only after he reached a certain age, only if he survived another person, or only if he died without descendants, the power would not be in existence on the date of the decedent's death if the condition precedent to its exercise had not occurred.

The Kurz Estate takes heart from the provision that "a power which by its terms is exercisable only upon the occurrence during the decedent's lifetime of an event or a contingency which did not in fact take place or occur during such time is not a power in existence on the date of the decedent's death." Like the Tax Court, however, we do not find in this language the strict sequencing principle the Estate needs.

This is the Commissioner's language, and the Commissioner thinks that it refers only to conditions that could not have been satisfied. Regulation-writers have substantial leeway in their interpretation * * * because the delegation of the power to make substantive regulations is the delegation of a law-creation power, and interpretation is a vital part of the law-creation process. * * * A reading must of course be reasonable—must be an interpretation—else the rulemaker is revising the law without the requisite notice and opportunity for comment. * * * The Commissioner's understanding of the regulation tracks its third sentence, which is designed to illustrate the second. It says: "For example, if a decedent was given a general power of appointment exercisable only after he reached a certain age, only if he survived another person, or only if he died without descendants, the power would not be in existence on the date of the decedent's death if the condition precedent to its exercise had not occurred." All three examples in the third sentence deal with conditions the decedent could not have controlled, at least not in the short run, or lawfully. The rate of chronological aging is outside anyone's control, whether one person survives another does not present an option that may be exercised lawfully, and whether a person has descendants on the date of death is something that depends on the course of an entire life, rather than a single choice made in the administration of one's wealth.

By contrast, the sequence in which a beneficiary withdraws the principal of a series of trusts barely comes within the common understanding of "event or ... contingency". No one could say of a single account: "You cannot withdraw the second dollar from this account until you have withdrawn the first." The existence of this sequence is tautological, but a check for $2 removes that sum without satisfying a contingency in ordinary, or legal, parlance. Zeno's paradox does not apply to financial transactions. Breaking one account into two or more does not make a sequence of withdrawal more of a "contingency"—at least not in the sense that § 20.2041–3(b) uses that term.

No matter how the second sentence of § 20.2041–3(b) should be applied to a contingency like losing 20 pounds or achieving a chess rating of 1600, the regulation does not permit the beneficiary of multiple trusts to exclude all but the first from the estate by the expedient of arranging the trusts in a sequence. No matter how long the sequence, the beneficiary exercises economic dominion over all funds that can be withdrawn at any given moment. The estate tax is a wealth tax, and dominion over property is wealth. Until her death, Ethel Kurz could have withdrawn all of the Marital Trust and 5% of the Family Trust by notifying the Trustee of her wish to do so. This case is nicely covered by the first sentence of § 20.2041–3(b), the notice provision, and the judgment of the Tax Court is therefore.

AFFIRMED.

ILLUSTRATIVE MATERIAL

A.   EXISTENCE OF GENERAL POWER OF APPOINTMENT

As illustrated in *Estate of Kurz,* a general power of appointment exists regardless of how the power is named so long as that power contains the requisite rights.

Estate of Kurz also illustrates the treatment of contingent powers. If the contingency is beyond the holder's control, Reg. § 20.2041–3(b) will treat the power as not existing. However, if the contingency can be controlled by the holder, the power is treated as existing.

B.   TIME OF EXERCISE

Another issue pertaining to the application of § 2041 is when must the power be exercisable? Section 2041(a)(2) requires that decedent possess a general power of appointment "at the time of death." Suppose that the holder can exercise the general power during her life but that the power terminates at her death. In Jenkins v. United States, 428 F.2d 538 (5th Cir.), the wills of each of two sisters gave all her property to the other for life "with full and unlimited power and authority to dispose of the same in fee simple by gift or otherwise at any time *during her life* without accountability to anyone." (emphasis added).

If the power was not exercised, the property passed to a named remainder interest. The court held that the holder of an unlimited inter vivos power to dispose of or consume property possesses a general power of appointment "at the time of death" and that § 2041(a)(2) requires inclusion. Similarly, Estate of Edelman v. Commissioner, 38 T.C. 972 (1962), held that a power, exercisable by will only, to appoint corpus of a trust to a powerholder's estate is a general power under § 2041.

C. SPECIAL POWERS OF APPOINTMENT

A power that is not exercisable in favor of the powerholder, her creditors, her estate or creditors of her estate is not a general power of appointment, Reg. § 20.2041–1(c)(1)(*a*) and (*b*) but instead is called a special power of appointment. Thus if A's will creates a trust, the income of which is to be paid to S for life and, upon the death of S, the trust principal is to be appointed among such of A's issue as S may determine, S does not hold a general power of appointment and the trust principal is not included in S's gross estate.

Suppose that A transfers property to trust, income to B for life and, upon B's death the trust principal is to be appointed among such of B's issue as B may determine. B does not hold a general power of appointment because she cannot appoint the property to herself, her estate, her creditors or her estate's creditors. Maryland National Bank v. United States, 236 F.Supp. 532 (D. Md. 1964). B's ability to appoint the property to her issue is not equivalent to an appointment to her estate. An appointment to her estate would occur if her estate could thereafter use the property to pay its expenses or debts. See Reg. § 20.2041–1(c)(1).

D. POWERS SUBJECT TO AN ASCERTAINABLE STANDARD

A power which is "limited by an ascertainable standard relating to the health, education, support, or maintenance of the decedent" is not a general power of appointment. § 2041(b)(1)(A). Reg. § 20.2041–1(c)(2) states that a "power is limited by such a standard if the extent of the holder's duty to exercise and not to exercise the power is reasonably measurable in terms of his needs for health, education, or support (or any combination of them)." The regulations state that language which satisfies this requirement includes, "support in reasonable comfort," "maintenance in health and reasonable comfort," "support in his accustomed manner of living," "education, including college and professional education" and "medical, dental, hospital and nursing expenses and expenses of invalidism." *Id*.

The Tax Court has interpreted § 2041(b)(1)(A) to create two requirements: (1) the standard used in the governing instrument must be ascertainable, i.e. enforceable by a court of equity, and (2) the standard must relate to the decedent's health, education, support or maintenance. Estate of Little v. Commissioner, 87 T.C. 599, 601 (1986). Where the governing instruments use language other than the "health, education, support or maintenance" standards, the federal courts have looked to state law to determine whether state law interprets the language used to mean "health, education, support or maintenance." As illustrated by the cases described below, resorting to state law often results in similar language being treated differently depending upon the state source.

Ascertainable Standard Present:

Estate of Brantingham v. United States, 631 F.2d 542 (7th Cir. 1980), involved a provision permitting distributions for the decedent-beneficiary's "maintenance, comfort and happiness." State law permitted the court to examine the settlor's intent. Finding that the settlor intended the trust to be administered to preserve principal, the court interpreted the governing instrument to permit only distributions which satisfied the statutory ascertainable standard limitation. Rev. Rul. 82–63, 1982–1 C.B. 135, stated that *Brantingham* was incorrectly decided and the IRS will not follow it because the trust language did not impose an ascertainable standard under applicable local law. Estate of Sowell v. Commissioner, 708 F.2d 1564 (10th Cir. 1983), ruled that the power to invade corpus of a trust in case of "emergency or illness" qualified as an ascertainable standard since the term "emergency" did not expand upon the statutory standards of "health, education, support or maintenance." See also Finlay v. United States, 752 F.2d 246 (6th Cir. 1985) (trustee-beneficiary had the right to "encroach" on trust principal "if she so desires;" the court held that under applicable state law the language would be construed to limit the decedent's right to invade to "support and maintenance").

Ascertainable Standard Not Present:

In Peoples Trust Company of Bergen County v. United States, 412 F.2d 1156 (3d Cir. 1969), a surviving wife was the beneficiary of a trust under which the trustee was empowered to distribute "such amounts out of the principal as my said wife from time to time may require; she to be the sole judge as to the amounts and frequency of such principal payments." The wife never requested any principal. Her estate argued that under New Jersey law the word "require" should be read as "needs" and that the power to consume was thus limited under local law to amounts necessary for the statutorily approved standards of maintenance and support. The court rejected this argument, concluding that her husband's will evidenced no such intent. See also Independence Bank Waukesha (N.A.) v. United States, 761 F.2d 442 (7th Cir. 1985) (decedent was given the discretion under testamentary trust "as to how much of my property she will use for her own maintenance during her lifetime and I specifically direct that she may use so much of my property as she desires for her own use and for whatever purpose she desires to use the same;" since the only restriction on the decedent's powers was that she exercise them in good faith, no ascertainable standard was present); Estate of Little v. Commissioner, 87 T.C. 599 (1986) (ascertainable standard not satisfied where power held by decedent as sole beneficiary and trustee of a testamentary trust to pay income or principal to himself "for his proper support, maintenance, welfare, health and general happiness in the manner to which he is accustomed" at the time of the death of the creator of the trust). Forsee v. United States, 76 F. Supp. 2d 1135 (D.KS 1999) (trustee's ability to invade corpus for his "happiness, health, support and maintenance" constituted a general power of appointment).

The issue whether a § 2041 ascertainable standard exists also arises in connection with powers held by life tenants. For example, in First Virginia Bank v. United States, 490 F.2d 532 (4th Cir. 1974), decedent received stock from her husband "for her comfort and care" with an inter vivos power to "dispose, sell, trade or use such holdings." At her death the remaining stock was to go to their daughter. The court held that under state law the wife's inter vivos power was not limited by a § 2041 ascertainable standard.

As discussed in Chapters 15 and 16, the "ascertainable standard" concept is relevant under §§ 2036 and 2038, but its role as developed under those sections has no necessary relationship to the concept as employed in § 2041. See Steinkamp, Estate and Gift Taxation of Powers of Appointment Limited by Ascertainable Standards, 79 Marq. L. Rev. 195, 243–244 (1995). In a § 2041 situation, if the standard in the governing instrument does not parallel the requirement in § 2041(b)(1)(A) of "health, education, support or maintenance," the courts must decide whether the powers granted are limited by local law to such a standard. On the other hand, in § 2036 and § 2038 situations, the ascertainable standard is not limited to such terms. It may be measured by terms other than the "health, education, support or maintenance" powers permitted by § 2041(b)(1)(A). See Strite v. McGinnes, 330 F.2d 234 (3d Cir. 1964).

E. JOINTLY HELD POWERS

A power is not a general power of appointment if the holder may exercise it only in conjunction either with the creator of the power or with a person who has a substantial adverse interest in the property subject to the power. § 2041(b)(1)(C). In the latter case, the requirement that the co-holder have an "interest in the property was intended at the very least to require that the co-holder have a present or future chance to obtain a personal benefit from the property itself." Estate of Towle v. Commissioner, 54 T.C. 368, 372 (1970).

In *Estate of Towle*, decedent had the right to withdraw all the principal of certain life insurance proceeds with the consent of a bank acting as trustee of a residuary trust created by the will of her father. At her death, any remaining proceeds were payable to the bank to administer under the terms of the residuary trust. The estate argued (1) that the bank, as trustee, had an interest in the insurance proceeds and (2) its interest was substantial and adverse to that of the decedent because it had a duty to protect the interests of the trust. The court disagreed, holding that the bank was not a beneficiary of the proceeds in its own right but was simply an entity administering property for the benefit of the trust beneficiaries and remaindermen.

Rev. Rul. 79–63, 1979–1 C.B. 302, involved a decedent who was the trustee and life income beneficiary of a trust in which the remainder was payable to the decedent's children equally or to any of his children whom he might designate. The trust also provided that during life the decedent could distribute corpus to anyone, including the decedent, but only with the consent of one of the decedent's children. The Ruling held that the decedent possessed a general power of appointment over the trust corpus. The consent right held by the decedent's child was not an adverse interest with respect to the decedent's lifetime power to appoint the corpus. The child would not necessarily be better off by failing to consent to a lifetime exercise of the power because the decedent acting alone could appoint the property at death to one or more of the child's siblings. The child would have possessed a substantial adverse interest only if the child was the taker in default of exercise of the lifetime power. Thus, if the child had been the decedent's only child, a substantial adverse interest would have existed.

In Estate of Witkowski v. United States, 451 F.2d 1249 (5th Cir. 1971), the court, in dictum, stated that it was probable that the adverse interest required by the statute must be created simultaneously with the power and by the same instrument; a powerholder cannot create an adverse interest by a later action.

Section 2041(b)(1)(C)(ii) provides that if a person, "X", possesses a power of appointment (with respect to property subject to the decedent's power) which may be exercised in X's favor after decedent's death, X is deemed to have an interest in the property adverse to the exercise of the decedent's power. Accordingly the decedent does not possess a general power of appointment, if the decedent must obtain X's consent before exercising the power. See Rev. Rul. 75–145, 1975–1 C.B. 298.

F.   AMOUNT INCLUDIBLE FOR GENERAL POWERS HELD AT DEATH

Only the property subject to the general power of appointment is includible under § 2041. Thus, if a power exists over only a limited interest (e.g., one-half of remainder interest), only that partial interest is includible in the holder's estate. Reg. § 20.2041–1(b)(3).

Where a general power is held jointly, the includible amount is determined by dividing the value of the property subject to the power by the total number of joint powerholders who are also permissible appointees of the property. Reg. § 20.2041–3(c)(3).

G.   CAPACITY TO EXERCISE POWER

Section 2041(a)(2) requires inclusion "of any property with respect to which the decedent has at the time of his death a general power of appointment." This language has generally been construed to treat as irrelevant whether the decedent is capable of exercising that power. This result follows whether the powerholder has been adjudicated incompetent, Williams v. United States, 634 F.2d 894 (5th Cir. 1981), the powerholder has at all times after the creation of the power been incompetent to exercise it, Boeving v. United States, 650 F.2d 493 (8th Cir. 1981), or if a guardian has been appointed, Estate of Gilchrist v. Commissioner, 630 F.2d 340 (5th Cir. 1980). Rev. Rul. 75–351, 1975–2 C.B. 368, involved a decedent who was the beneficiary of a § 2503(c) trust. (As discussed at p. 446, transfers to such trusts qualify for the present interest exclusion from the gift tax under § 2503(b); but in order to qualify, either the corpus must be payable to the estate of the beneficiary if the beneficiary dies before attaining age 21 or the trust beneficiary must possess a general power of appointment as defined in § 2514(c).) The decedent possessed a testamentary general power of appointment and died at age 16 without having exercised it. Under local law an individual had to be 21 years old to make a valid will. Although the decedent was legally incompetent to execute a will at the time of his death, the corpus of the trust was included in the decedent's gross estate under § 2041. The Ruling held that the trust did not "by its terms" set forth "an event or contingency" (legal capacity to make a will) upon which the power was dependent as required by Reg. § 20.2041–3(b) and, therefore, the power was in existence at the date of decedent's death. See also Estate of Rosenblatt v. Commissioner, 633 F.2d 176 (10th Cir. 1980) (property held in trust for 16–year–old decedent was includible even though under state law decedent was incapable of exercising the power).

Comparable to cases involving powers of revocation under § 2038, the critical factor under § 2041 is possession of the power of appointment, not its probability of exercise. In Estate of Bagley v. United States, 443 F.2d 1266 (5th Cir. 1971), a husband and wife died simultaneously. Under the wills of both, the wife was presumed to be the survivor. The husband's will created a trust for the benefit of his wife, giving her a general power of appointment. The court held that the property subject to the power was includible in her estate. Under applicable state law the power of appointment was inchoate pending probate but dated back to the date of death of the testator upon probate. Thus, the husband's will became effective at his death, and if the wife had attempted to exercise the power in her will, the exercise would have been valid.

Similarly, where A devised property in trust for the benefit of B with B holding a general power of appointment over that property and B died before A's estate was distributed, B's estate included the property subject to the power even though the property passed directly from A's estate to the remaindermen of the trust. Rev. Rul. 69–616, 1969–2 C.B. 45.

Section 2013, discussed at p. 552, provides a credit for taxes paid where decedents die within a relatively short time of each other and mitigates the seemingly harsh results in situations like those in *Bagley* and Rev. Rul. 69–616.

H.   LAPSE OF GENERAL POWER OF APPOINTMENT

Section 2041(b)(2) provides that the "lapse of a power of appointment * * * during the life of the individual possessing the power shall be considered a release of such power." However, the applicability of this rule is limited to the excess of the value of the property which could have been appointed over the higher of (a) $5,000 or (b) 5% of the assets subject to the power valued at the time of the lapse. Thus, if in 2008 A creates a trust of $300,000, the income payable to B for life, remainder to C, and gives B the non-cumulative power to withdraw $45,000 of principal annually, B's failure to exercise that power in each year will result in a lapse of the power for that year and a release of the power as to $30,000 of the trust assets ($45,000 minus $15,000, 5% of the trust assets, assuming no change in the value of the trust assets). The value of the corpus released ($30,000) is a taxable gift by B under § 2514. See p. 373.

Section 2041(a)(2) in turn requires the inclusion of amounts attributable to releases of the power in prior years if such releases had the effect of transfers which would have been included in the decedent's gross estate under §§ 2035–2038 had the property been owned outright by the decedent. To illustrate, assume that B in the above example allowed his power to withdraw $45,000 to lapse in the years 2008 through 2011 and that he died on December 31, 2012 without exercising his power for 2012 At all times the trust assets had a value of $300,000. In each of the years 2008 through 20011, since § 2036 would have applied if B had owned the property outright, B is treated under § 2041(a)(2) as if he had withdrawn $30,000 per year and transferred it back to the trust, retaining the income therefrom for life by virtue of his original income interest. Such a transfer would have required inclusion of the property in B's gross estate under § 2036. Therefore, § 2041(a)(2) would require inclusion in B's estate of the total value of the 2008–2011 imputed transfers, i.e., (4 x $30,000) or $120,000. Moreover, in the year of a powerholder's death, the entire value of the property subject to a power which is unexercised at death is includible under section 2041(a)(2). The "$5,000 or 5%" exclusion is not available because the power has not lapsed at the time of death. Thus, in the year B dies, 2012, the full $45,000 subject to withdrawal is also includible. As a result, B's estate would include $165,000 ($120,000 plus $45,000).

To avoid estate tax inclusion of any property subject to a lapsed power (except in the year of the powerholder's death), instruments creating powers of appointment often limit the annual power to the greater of $5,000 or 5% of the assets subject to the power.

I.   POWERS IN A TRUST CONTEXT

1.   *Power Held by Trustee–Beneficiary*

An individual may hold a general power of appointment in his capacity as a trustee of a trust of which he is also a beneficiary by virtue of a power to make distributions to himself, his creditors, his estate or creditors of his estate. In Maytag v. United States, 493 F.2d 995 (10th Cir. 1974), the decedent, in conjunction with two other non-adverse trustees, had the power to terminate a trust of which he was beneficiary. The court held that the trust corpus was includible in his estate under § 2041(a)(2). It reasoned that the settlor of the trust could under local law participate in any decision to terminate the trust, which would result in a distribution to him. That the power was unexercised at the decedent's death and was shared with non-adverse co-trustees did not change the result. Compare Rev. Rul. 54–153, 1954–1 C.B. 185 (where a trustee-beneficiary was prevented by state law from participating in a decision to distribute corpus to himself, his estate, his creditors or the creditors of his estate, no part of the corpus was includible in his estate under § 2041).

2.   *Powers Held by Trust Beneficiary*

In Ewing v. Rountree, 346 F.2d 471 (6th Cir. 1965) the court held that where a trust beneficiary possessed the right to request a trustee to sell trust assets and distribute the proceeds to the beneficiary, the beneficiary held a general power of appointment over the trust assets. In *Ewing*, the beneficiary could compel a distribution without an allegation of abuse of trustee discretion because the trust instrument did not permit discretion as to distributions requested by the beneficiary. A contrary holding resulted, however, where the trustee was authorized to pay principal to the beneficiary in the trustee's sole discretion with a direction to be liberal "to promote the health, comfort, maintenance or welfare of beneficiary." The court found that under state law the trustee alone had discretion to distribute, which discretion had to be exercised reasonably for the benefit of all beneficiaries. Thus, the beneficiary did not have the power to transfer or appropriate the trust corpus to herself and did not possess a general power of appointment. Security–Peoples Trust Company v. United States, 238 F.Supp. 40 (W.D. Pa. 1965). To the same effect see Rev. Rul. 76–368, 1976–2 C.B. 271.

Reg. § 20.2041–1(b)(1) provides:

"A power in a donee to remove or discharge a trustee and appoint himself may be a power of appointment. For example, if under the terms of a trust instrument, the trustee or his successor has the power to appoint the principal of the trust for the benefit of individuals including himself, and the decedent has the unrestricted power to remove or discharge the trustee at any time and appoint any other person including himself, the decedent is considered as having a power of appointment."

This language is virtually identical to that of Reg. § 20.2036–1(b)(3), last sentence. In Rev. Rul. 95–58, 1995–2 C.B. 191, (see p. 252) the Service held that a decedent-grantor's reservation of an unqualified power to remove a trustee and appoint an individual or corporate successor as trustee that is not related or subordinate to the decedent within the meaning of § 672(c) is not considered a reserved power within the scope of § 2036. Such a power should also not be a power of appointment. See, e.g. PLR 9831005 (April 28, 1998) (so holding).

3. *Uniform Gift to Minors Act and Uniform Transfer to Minors Act*

A parent who is the custodian of an account established for her child under the Uniform Gift To Minors Act has the right to use the account for the support of her child. Since this is her legal obligation, she will be deemed to have a general power of appointment. Under Reg. § 20.2041–1(c)(1), her power to appoint property to satisfy her legal obligations is tantamount to a power to appoint the property to herself or creditors.

If someone other than the parent is custodian of the account, however, § 2041 should not apply. In Rev. Rul. 77–460, 1977–2 C.B. 323, the Service ruled that the ability of a parent to petition a court to use the account for the child's support is not a general power of appointment because it is not "... an absolute unfettered right in a parent to force a custodian to make such payments."

Similar analysis should apply to accounts established under the Uniform Transfer to Minors Act.

J. POWERS UNDER INSURANCE POLICIES

There is a conflict among the Courts of Appeals over the includibility of insurance proceeds where the insured elected a settlement option which provided that the decedent-beneficiary was to receive interest on the insurance proceeds for life and at death the proceeds were to be paid to the "executors or administrators of the decedent." Payment to the decedent-beneficiary's executor or administrator means that the insurance proceeds would be distributed in accordance with the decedent-beneficiary's testamentary wishes.

In Second National Bank of Danville v. Dallman, 209 F.2d 321 (7th Cir. 1954), the court, focusing solely on the fact that the proceeds passed to the decedent-beneficiary's executor pursuant to the insurance contract between the insured and the insurance company without any action by the decedent-beneficiary, held that the right to have the proceeds paid to decedent-beneficiary's executors was not a general power of appointment held by the decedent-beneficiary. In Rev. Rul. 55–277, 1955–1 C.B. 456, the Internal Revenue Service announced it would not follow *Second National Bank of Danville*. The Service's position was upheld in Keeter v. United States, 461 F.2d 714 (5th Cir. 1972). There, the court, finding "no substantive difference between directly granting the power to dispose of property and placing the same property in such a position that the donee is able to dispose of it to her benefit by means of some power that existed prior to or separate from the settlor's grant" (719), held that the decedent's right to direct the payment of the proceeds from her estate constituted a general power of appointment which was exercised by the provision in her will devising the residue of her estate to her daughter. The *Keeter* court correctly noted that "the critical question is whether the decedent directed her property after her death, not how that property got into the position from which she could direct it." (720)

In Rev. Rul. 79–154, 1979–1 C.B. 301, the decedent had a life income interest in an insurance fund coupled with a power to appoint the remainder for the health, education, support and maintenance of adult children whom the decedent was not obligated to support. The Ruling stated that the principles of § 2041 "apply to the taxation of a life insurance fund subject to powers of appointment in the same manner that the principles are applied to determine the taxability of other forms of property subject to powers of appointment." Because the fund could be appointed only to persons whom the decedent was not obligated to support, the power was a special power of appointment. However, if the decedent had been under a legal duty to support the potential appointees, the power would have been a general power to the extent it could be exercised to satisfy those obligations.

K.   POWERS UNDER EMPLOYEE DEATH BENEFIT PLANS

As discussed at p. 116, the IRS has been largely unsuccessful in applying § 2033 to employee death benefits that an employee was not entitled to receive while alive but that are instead paid to the employee's survivor. If the employee is able to designate any person to receive the death benefits, however, § 2041 will include the benefits in his gross estate because he had the power to name his estate or the creditors of his estate. The IRS employed § 2041 to include nonqualified pension benefits in a decedent's gross estate prior to the enactment of § 2039 where the employee could assign the benefits at death to whomever she wished. For example, in Estate of Wolf v. Commissioner, 29 T.C. 441 (1957), the court held that an employee's ability to name the beneficiaries of employee benefits would cause those benefits to be included in his estate as property subject to a general power of appointment. Estate of Wolf v. Commissioner, 29 T.C. 441 (1957). However, the right of a decedent to appoint benefits at his death to such of his widow and issue as were living at that time was not a general power of appointment because the decedent did not possess the power to appoint in favor of himself, his estate, his creditors or the creditors of his estate. Hanner v. Glenn, 111 F.Supp. 52 (W.D.Ky. 1953).

L.   PROPERTY SUBJECT TO POWER

Occasionally, questions arise about the property subject to a general power of appointment. In Estate of Margrave v. Commissioner, 618 F.2d 34 (8th Cir. 1980), the decedent's surviving spouse had purchased an insurance policy on his life, naming a revocable trust created by him as beneficiary. At all times she possessed the right to revoke the beneficiary designation. The Commissioner argued that the insurance proceeds should be included in the decedent's gross estate under § 2041 on the ground that the insurance proceeds passed pursuant to the direction of the decedent. The court acknowledged that the decedent possessed a general power of appointment over property which was in his revocable trust at death. However, the insurance proceeds were not in existence until the decedent's death. See Connecticut National Bank and Trust Co. v. United States, p. 109. Consequently, at the moment of death, the decedent possessed a power of appointment over an expectancy, not over property in existence at his death, and the insurance proceeds were not includible in his estate. The result appears incorrect and inconsistent with the approach in Keeter v. United States, p. 369.

Similarly the power of a decedent to direct the disposition of wrongful death proceeds through his will is not a general power because, *at the time of death*, the decedent had no interest in the proceeds which he could direct to himself, his creditors, his estate, or creditors of his estate. Maxwell Trust v. Commissioner, 58 T.C. 444 (1972).

M. SUCCESSIVE POWERS

The exercise of a power is considered taxable if it is exercised by will to create another power which under applicable local law can be validly exercised (1) so as to postpone the vesting of any interest in the property or (2) suspend the absolute ownership or power of alienation of the property for a period ascertainable without regard to the date of creation of the first power. § 2041(a)(3).[3] This provision, which applies to special as well as general powers, is designed to prevent the perpetual avoidance of Federal transfer taxes in states that begin the period for the rule against perpetuities by reference to the creation date of the new power, not the creation date of the first power. Since the statutory language is in the alternative, the result of a given case can vary depending on the type of rule against perpetuities adopted by a given state. For an extensive discussion of the function and scope of § 2041(a)(3), see Estate of Murphy v. Commissioner, 71 T.C. 671 (1979).

N. RELATIONSHIP WITH OTHER SECTIONS

Reg. § 20.2041–1(b)(2) provides that "[n]o provision of § 2041 * * * is to be construed as in any way limiting the application of any other section of the Internal Revenue Code." Moreover, interests which are otherwise included in the gross estate under other estate tax sections are to be included under those sections and not § 2041. For example, retained powers or interests includible under §§ 2036 through 2038 are not includible under § 2041. Similarly the power of a property owner to consume or dispose of the property is an interest includible under § 2033, notwithstanding the applicability under § 2041.

This can affect the amount includible in the gross estate of an individual holding powers which could be includible under § 2041 or some other estate tax section. For example, if the holder of a general power of appointment over the income interest in a trust is also the grantor and life income beneficiary of the trust, the total value of the trust corpus is includible under § 2036 but only the value of the income interest is includible under § 2041. Pursuant to the Regulation, § 2036 controls.

Section 2043(a) applies to § 2041. Unlike §§ 2035 to 2038, however, § 2041 contains no provision that the value of the interest includible in the estate is to be reduced by consideration received at the time of the transfer creating the power. Thus, only consideration received at the time of the exercise or relinquishment will reduce the amount includible in the powerholder's estate. Estate of Frothingham v. Commissioner, 60 T.C. 211 (1973). In Estate of Steinman v. Commissioner, 69 T.C. 804 (1978), the decedent resided

---

3. Section 2041(a)(3) also applies in these circumstances if the power is exercised during life in such a way that had powerhold-er transferred the appointive property, §§ 2035–2038 would have applied.

in a community property state and elected to take under her husband's will rather than taking her share of their community property. Under the will, she had received a life estate in a trust and a general power of appointment over the trust corpus, which she exercised in her will. At her death, the trust was included in her gross estate under § 2041. The estate argued that pursuant to *Estate of Gregory*, p. 183, the value of the trust should be reduced by the value of the interest the wife received as the result of her election. While that would have been the result had § 2036 been applicable, under § 2041 the full value of the trust was included in her estate because the decedent did not receive any consideration for the testamentary exercise of her power.

Section 2518, dealing with disclaimers, applies to § 2041. See p. 443.

The relationship between § 2041 and the marital deduction is discussed at p. 587.

3.   Section 2041(a)(1): Pre–October 21, 1942 Powers

Property subject to a general power of appointment created on or before October 21, 1942 is taxable under § 2041(a)(1) only if the power is exercised by the holder, either by will or by the kind of inter vivos disposition which would have caused the property subject to the power to be includible in the powerholder's estate under §§ 2035 through 2038 if the property transferred had been owned outright by the holder.

Pre–October 21, 1942 powers are not taxed if they are not exercised or if they have been completely released by the holder prior to death. The complete release of a pre-October 21, 1942 power is not taxable at any time. Moreover, if a pre-October 21, 1942 power was partially released by the powerholder before November 1, 1951 and the release had the effect of reducing the general power to a special power, the subsequent exercise of that special power is not treated as the exercise of a general power and the property subject to the power is not included in the powerholder's estate.

Finally, a pre-October 21, 1942 power of appointment exercisable by the decedent only in conjunction with another person is not a general power of appointment. Where a decedent, prior to November 1, 1951, entered into an enforceable agreement not to exercise a pre-October 21, 1942 general power of appointment without the consent of her siblings, the power fell within the § 2041(d)(1)(B) exception to the definition of a general power of appointment. Estate of Drake v. Commissioner, 67 T.C. 844 (1977).

Section C.   Gift Taxation of Powers of Appointment

Internal Revenue Code: § 2514

Regulations: § 25.2514–1, 3

1.   Creation of Powers of Appointment

As discussed below, § 2514 addresses the gift tax effect of the exercise, release or lapse of a general power of appointment. It does not address the treatment of the creation of a general power. Usually, the appropriate treatment of the grant of the power of appointment is not an issue because the grantor has transferred all his interest in the appointive property at the time he also transfers the power. For example, the grantor might irrevocably transfer property in trust, income to A, who is also the trustee, remainder to B, and also grant to A a general power of appointment to distribute corpus to herself as well. In this situation, the grantor will have made a taxable gift of his entire interest in the property. It is not necessary to consider separately the gift tax impact of transferring the general power.

But suppose that, instead of creating a trust, the grantor merely gives A a power to appoint the property to herself whenever she wishes. Until A exercises the power, grantor will retain the property. Assuming that such a grant is valid under state law, has grantor made a taxable gift? The answer is yes, although some explanation is required in light of the Supreme Court's holding in Helvering v. Safe Dep. & Trust Co., 316 U.S. 56 (1942), that a general power is not an interest in property for purposes of § 2033. A taxable gift has occurred because the grant of a valid general power shifts complete dominion and control over the appointive property to the power holder. Moreover, since an enforceable promise to make a gift is a taxable gift, see p. 161, the grant of a valid general power of appointment is also a taxable gift. The grant of a valid power is equivalent to an enforceable promise to make a gift to the holder since the holder can seek to enforce the power for her own benefit.

Like the grant of a general power, the gift tax treatment of the grant of a special power is usually not an issue because the grant normally accompanies a taxable gift of the appointive property. For example, a donor may irrevocably transfer property in trust, income to A and remainder to any issue of A that she may select, otherwise to B. Since the donor's transfer is a taxable gift of the appointive property, it is not necessary to consider separately the effect of the special power on the gift. Suppose, however, that grantor retained the property, but granted a power valid under state law to A to transfer the property to any of A's issue that A may select during her life. If the special power is not exercised, grantor retains ownership. Has grantor made a taxable gift? No taxable gift has occurred. The grant of the special power is not equivalent to the grantor entering into an enforceable promise to make a gift because none of the potential appointees could force an appointment of the property to herself or himself. Moreover, there has been no shift of complete dominion and control over the property to the power holder since she cannot appoint the property to herself.

2.   GIFT TAX EFFECT OF EXERCISE, RELEASE OR LAPSE OF GENERAL POWERS OF APPOINTMENT

The terms used in §§ 2041 and 2514 are defined identically and the court decisions and administrative interpretations under § 2041 apply equally to § 2514. Rev. Rul. 76–547, 1976–2 C.B. 302.

The inter vivos exercise of a post-October 21, 1942 general power is treated as a taxable transfer of the appointed property by the powerholder for gift tax purposes. The complete release of such a general power after May 31, 1951 is likewise a gift tax transfer. A lapse is treated as a release by § 2514(g), but only to the extent that the property which could have been appointed by exercise of such lapsed power exceeds the greater of $5,000 or 5% of the assets subject to appointment.

The partial release of a post-October 21, 1942 general power is not a completed gift where the power holder may still appoint property among a limited class of persons not including herself. Since the powerholder has retained the right to designate the ultimate beneficiaries of the appointive property, "only the termination of such control * * * completes a gift." Reg. § 25.2514–3(c)(1). The effect of the subsequent exercise of the reduced power depends upon the chronology of events. Where a post-October 21, 1942 general power was partially released prior to June 1, 1951 so that it no longer constituted a general power, a subsequent exercise of the reduced power is not a taxable gift. Regs. § 25.2514–3(c)(2). However, if such a power was partially released after May 31, 1951, the subsequent exercise of the reduced power is a taxable gift. Reg. § 25.2514–3(c)(3).

ILLUSTRATIVE MATERIAL

A.   EXERCISE OF GENERAL POWER

Sometimes transferors will be unaware that they have made a gift by exercising a general power. In Estate of Campbell v. Commissioner, 59 T.C. 133 (1972), decedent's husband had transferred a partnership interest to her, giving her unfettered use and control during her life, with any amount unexpended at her death to go to their three children. Under local law, decedent possessed every incident of outright ownership over the partnership interest other than the right to dispose of it by will. The court held that these rights constituted a general power of appointment under Reg. § 25.2514–1(b) because she could consume the entire value of the partnership interest. Decedent's transfer of the interest to one of the children for less than adequate consideration was held to be a taxable exercise of a general power of appointment under § 2514 to the extent of the excess of the value of the partnership interest over the consideration received.

B.   RELEASE OF POWER

In Rev. Rul. 79–421, 1979–2 C.B. 347, A was appointed trustee of a trust created by his parents. As trustee he could accumulate income or to distribute it to himself. Upon A's death, principal and any accumulated income was to be paid to A's children. However, under the trust instrument, if A appointed three additional trustees, A could not make decisions with respect to distributions of income to himself. A appointed two individuals and a bank as additional trustees. The Ruling held that A's power to make payments of income to himself constituted a general power of appointment which was released when he appointed three additional trustees. The release of the general power of appointment constituted a taxable gift.

Sometimes the occurrence of a release will be less apparent. A decedent's will created two trusts. Trust A gave the surviving spouse the income for life with a general power of appointment over the trust corpus. Trust A was funded with the shares of closely held stock worth $120x. Trust B provided the surviving spouse with a life income interest with the remainder to decedent's child. Trust B was funded with $80x shares of the same stock. Independent third parties served as trustees of both trusts. Two years later, the corporation was recapitalized with voting common and nonvoting preferred stock. Preferred stock worth $50x was allocated to Trust A and common stock worth $150x to Trust B in exchange for the previous stock held by the Trusts. The surviving spouse released the trustees from any challenge to their action in agreeing to the recapitalization. At the time of the surviving spouse's death, Trust A was worth $55x and Trust B was worth $225x. Rev. Rul. 86–39, 1986–1 C.B. 301, held that the consent by the surviving spouse to the recapitalization constituted a release of the general power of appointment over $70x and therefore there was a gift to the child of the present value of the remainder interest in the $70x. The same property was also included in the surviving spouse's gross estate under § 2041(a)(2) since it would have been includible under § 2036 by virtue of the surviving spouse's retention of an income interest for life in the property which in effect was transferred to Trust B.

Rev. Rul. 85–88, 1985–2 C.B. 201 held that where a beneficiary of multiple trusts created by the same grantor has a "$5,000 or 5%" power with respect to each trust, only one "$5,000 or 5%" exemption is available in each year. The exempt amount is determined by aggregating the maximum amount in each trust which would be subject to the powerholder's withdrawal powers. Any amount in excess of the "$5,000 or 5%" amount so determined constitutes a gift by the powerholder with a retained life interest if the powerholder is an income beneficiary of the trust. The Ruling similarly held that where a series of gifts to a trust are made during a single year, and the income beneficiary allows his withdrawal rights to lapse with respect to each contribution, only one "$5,000 or 5%" exemption is available.

C.   RELATIONSHIP OF SECTION 2514 TO OTHER SECTIONS

Reg. § 25.2514–1(b)(2) parallels Reg. § 20.2041–1(b)(2) in providing that § 2514 does not limit the applicability of any other section of the Code. Disclaimers of general powers of appointment are covered by § 2518, discussed at p. 443.

D.   SECTION 2514(a): PRE–OCTOBER 21, 1942 POWERS

The exercise of a pre-October 21, 1942 general power is subject to gift tax, but failure to exercise the power or the complete release of the power is not taxable. A partial release, before November 1, 1951, cutting down a general power to a special power, was free of gift tax; in addition the subsequent exercise of the reduced power has no gift or estate tax consequences.

A partial release of a pre-October 21, 1942 general power after November 1, 1951 occasions no gift tax at the time of release, but the subsequent exercise of the reduced power gives rise to either a gift or estate tax, whichever is appropriate. § 2514(a).

3. GIFT TAX EFFECT OF EXERCISE OF SPECIAL POWERS OF APPOINTMENT

In general, the exercise of a special power of appointment is not a taxable gift by the holder. However, several exceptions may apply.

First, § 2514(d) will tax the exercise of a special power or a general power if it is exercised during life to create a new power of appointment that can be exercised under local law without reference to the date of creation of the first power. The purpose is to prevent the perpetual avoidance of transfer taxes in states that begin the period for the rule against perpetuities by reference to the creation date of the new power, not the creation date of the first power.

Second, if a power holder has both a special and general power in the same property, the exercise of the special power is treated as the exercise of the general power, triggering application of § 2514. Reg. § 25.2514–1(d).

To consider the third exception, suppose A holds a life estate in Trust X with a special power to appoint corpus to his issue. During his lifetime, A partially exercises his special power and creates a separate trust for the benefit of his issue with a portion of the assets of Trust X. Has A made a taxable gift of the actuarially determined value of his income interest in the portion of the corpus he transferred or is the entire transfer exempt from gift tax as the exercise of a special power? Reg. § 25.2514–1(b)(2) takes the position that A has made a gift of the income interest. The result in Monroe v. United States, 301 F.Supp. 762 (E.D. Wash. 1969), aff'd per curiam, 454 F.2d 1169 (9th Cir. 1972), supports this view. But in Self v. United States, 142 F.Supp. 939 (Ct.Cl. 1956), the described transaction was held to constitute solely a tax-exempt exercise of a special power of appointment on the ground that when the holder of a special power of appointment over income-producing property exercises that power, the income from the property automatically follows the legal title and cannot be separated from the property subject to the power. While it may be true that the income from the transferred property will follow the title to the property, that conclusion alone does not compel the result reached in *Self*. Apparently, the court chose to ignore the existence of A's separate income interest in the corpus of Trust X and, contrary to the intent of the regulations, held that any part of a transfer pursuant to the exercise of an exempt power is protected by the exempt transfer. The Internal Revenue Service will not follow the *Self* decision. See Rev. Rul. 79–327, 1979–2 C.B. 342. Subsequently, the Tax Court also disagreed with Self in Estate of Regester v. Commissioner, 83 T.C. 1 (1984). There a life income beneficiary of a testamentary trust also had a special power of appointment over the trust corpus exercisable during her life. She exercised the special power to transfer all the trust property to three other trusts. The court held that where the taxpayer had an unrestricted right to dispose of the income interest as she saw fit, the exercise of a special power of appointment over the trust corpus necessarily effected a gift of the income interest. Reg. § 25.2514–1(b)(2), was sustained against the taxpayer's challenge of invalidity.

CHAPTER 23

LIFE INSURANCE

SECTION A. ESTATE TAX TREATMENT OF LIFE INSURANCE

Internal Revenue Code: § 2042

Regulations: § 20.2042–1

INTRODUCTION

Life insurance often comprises a significant portion of a decedent's ("D's") estate. Its prevalence is partly attributable to the benefits it receives under the income tax law. Employers frequently provide group term life insurance as a tax-free fringe benefit to employees. Life insurance also represents an attractive investment to high-income individuals because it enables them to earn and accumulate income on a tax-free basis. Life insurance may be a helpful estate planning tool as well. Insurance proceeds payable to D's estate help pay the estate's debts, including taxes, and, therefore, allow the estate to avoid selling other assets that D may wish to transfer to legatees.

The purchaser of life insurance makes premium payments to a life insurance company. In its pure form, life insurance represents a promise by the insurer to pay a certain amount to the purchaser or a beneficiary designated by the purchaser upon the death of the insured person. The insured person may be the purchaser or someone else in whom the purchaser has an "insurable interest." Usually the purchaser will have an "insurable interest" in a close relative or business associate.

Pure insurance is sold as "term" insurance pursuant to which the insurer promises to pay a fixed amount if the insured dies during a specified term. For example, the purchaser may acquire annual term insurance for $300 that will pay a designated beneficiary $100,000 if the insured dies during a one year period. If the insured does not die during the year, the insurance provider will keep the premium. If the insured dies during the year, the insurance provider will pay $100,000. The premium charged for annual term insurance usually increases as the insured becomes older or the insured's actuarial risk of death increases.

In addition to term insurance, insurance companies offer another type of insurance called "whole" (or "ordinary") life insurance. In contrast to the premium costs of term insurance that increase periodically, whole life insurance contracts normally provide for a fixed premium cost over the period of the policy. The premium costs of whole life insurance exceed the costs for term life insurance in the early years of the policy, but are less than the costs of term insurance in later years. The excess premium payments in the early years are invested by the insurance provider and help to defray the costs in later years. The owner of the policy does not pay income tax on this investment income as it is earned. In the event the owner cancels the policy, she is entitled to receive the "cash surrender value" (or "net surrender value"), which is any remaining excess premium payments and investment income, reduced by a "load charge" that accounts for the insurer's profit and expenses. The owner in general will recognize taxable income only to the extent that the net surrender value exceeds the *total* amount of premiums paid. § 72(e)(5) and (6). Moreover, § 101 permits the policy owner in most circumstances to receive both the insurance proceeds and the investment income upon the death of the insured free of income tax. Thus, ordinary life insurance provides both pure life insurance and a method for generating investment income.

Section 2042 includes in D's gross estate the proceeds of life insurance on her life (1) if the proceeds are receivable by her executor or (2) if the proceeds are receivable by other beneficiaries and she possessed any incident of ownership over the policy. Note that § 2042 concerns the proceeds of life insurance *"on the life of the decedent."* D may also possess an interest in an insurance policy on the life of another person. The value of D's interests in such other policies would be includible in her gross estate as property in which she had an interest at the time of her death under § 2033 or other relevant provisions, as discussed at p. 407. The process of valuing such an interest is discussed at p. 415.

The language of § 2042 raises several issues which are addressed in this Section A. Since § 2042 applies to "insurance under policies on the life of the decedent," the first issue considered is the definition of insurance. Next, the standards for determining whether the insurance proceeds are "receivable by the executor" within the meaning of § 2042(1) are explored. The most difficult issue under § 2042 concerns whether D has possessed "any of the incidents of ownership" within the meaning of § 2042(2) for insurance that paid its proceeds to beneficiaries other than her executor. Incidents of ownership possessed by D in her individual capacity, as a fiduciary and through her controlled corporation are discussed. Section A will also discuss the special problems of applying § 2042 in community property states. The Section concludes with a consideration of the estate taxation of life insurance proceeds under provisions other than § 2042. Section B then explores the gift tax treatment of life insurance.

1. "Insurance Under Policies on the Life of the Decedent"

Section 2042 applies to "insurance under policies on the life of the decedent." Section 2042(a)(1) and (2). As discussed below in the *Illustrative Material*, resolving the issue what constitutes insurance on the life of D involves analysis under the tax "common law" as well as statutes. It is important to determine whether certain proceeds arise from life insurance because § 2042 can cast a much broader net than § 2033 to cause inclusion in the gross estate.

ILLUSTRATIVE MATERIAL

A. THE NONSTATUTORY DEFINITION OF "INSURANCE" CRAFTED BY THE COURTS

1. General

The courts have held that for an arrangement to constitute "life insurance", there must be (1) a shifting of the risk of a premature death from the insured to the insurance provider and (2) a spreading of that risk by the insurance provider among several insureds. Helvering v. Le Gierse, 312 U.S. 531 (1941). In Commissioner v. Treganowan, 183 F.2d 288 (2d Cir. 1950), the court held that a fund established by members of the New York Stock Exchange which would pay a benefit to the survivors of a deceased member qualified as "life insurance" under the predecessor of § 2042(2). Observing that, if a member died prematurely, the fund would pay to the member's survivors a greater amount than the member had contributed, the court stated that "the risk of loss is effectively shifted from the individual to the group of other members of the Exchange." The court also found an adequate spreading of risk because "the risk of premature death . . . [was] borne by the 1373 other members of the Exchange."

Rev. Rul. 65–222, 1965–2 C.B. 374, followed *Treganowan* in holding that death benefits paid to members of the Federal Special Agents Insurance Fund qualified as life insurance under § 2042, although the benefits were funded by payments the surviving members made at D's death, rather than through fixed periodic payments.

In Commissioner v. Estate of Noel, p. 381, the Supreme Court held that flight accident death policies were insurance within the meaning of § 2042(2). The lower court had reasoned that § 2042 applies to insurance under a contract where the insurer "agrees to pay a specified sum upon the occurrence of an inevitable event" and that flight insurance only covers the risk of a fatal plane crash "which is evitable and not likely to occur." The Supreme Court disagreed, concluding that in either case the "risk assumed by the insurer is the loss of the insured's life", which is the essence of insurance. See also All v. McCobb, p. 335 (employee death benefits paid pursuant to employer's Death Benefit Plan were not insurance because employee did not shift any risk of premature death to employer).

B. THE STATUTORY DEFINITION OF INSURANCE

The judicial definition of life insurance is supplemented by statutory provisions. The deferral or avoidance of an income tax on investment income generated by insurance policies under § 101 encouraged insurance providers to market policies, sometimes called "flexible premium" or "universal life" policies, that provided only nominal life insurance protection but substantial tax-deferred investment income potential. Congress responded by adopting § 7702 in the Tax Reform Act of 1984, which defines the term "life insurance contract" for all purposes of the Internal Revenue Code. The provision distinguishes between contracts which are primarily investment rather than protection oriented. S.Rep. No. 97–494, 97th Cong., 2d Sess. 352 (1982). If an insurance contract meets the judicially created nonstatutory tests discussed above, and also satisfies the § 7702 definition, the entire contract qualifies as "life insurance" under § 2042. On the other hand, if a contract fails to meet the definitional standards of § 7702, even if it is an insurance contract under the nonstatutory rules, only the excess of the amount paid under the contract over the net surrender value of the contract will be treated as "life insurance" for transfer tax purposes. § 7702(g)(2).[1] Presumably, the remaining net surrender value will be included in D's gross estate under § 2033 if she owned it at death since, in effect, that aspect of the contract is treated as an investment account of the insured. The statute, however, is not explicit on this point.

C.   PAYMENTS BY INSURANCE COMPANY ON ACCOUNT OF LIABILITY INSURANCE POLICIES

Automobile owner's liability policies frequently contain, in addition to the standard liability clause, provisions for payments to the estate of any passenger killed as the result of an accident. These payments are made without regard to the insured's legal liability for damages to the passenger, provided that his estate executes a full release of all claims for damages against the insured arising out of the accident. Rev. Rul. 57-54, 1957-1 C.B. 298, held that the amount received under a similar clause in an airplane owner's liability policy did not qualify as life insurance proceeds because the estate "could not, after accepting the payment, prosecute a claim for damages under any statute imposing a liability for wrongful death." In effect, the payment was settlement of a potential wrongful death action, not the payment of life insurance. If, however, the insurance company had remained unconditionally liable to the deceased passenger's estate, the Ruling stated that the amount received by the estate would have been "insurance" proceeds under § 2042.

The principles of Rev. Rul. 57-54 have been extended to mandatory no-fault insurance which provide death benefits to the driver and any passenger of a vehicle killed in an automobile collision. Rev. Rul. 83-44, 1983-1 C.B. 228, concluded that the no-fault insurance was a life insurance policy because the death benefits were not substitutes for wrongful death actions. Receipt of the benefits did not preclude the recipient's estate from pursuing additional tort damages arising out of the accident. The insurance policy also satisfied the requirements of *LeGierse* that the risk of premature death shift to the insurer and that the insurer distribute that risk among those participating in the no-fault insurance program.

2.   PROCEEDS "RECEIVABLE BY THE EXECUTOR"

Section 2042(1) requires inclusion of "the amount receivable by the executor as insurance under policies on the life of D, whether or not" she possessed any incidents of ownership at death. It has been held that only proceeds received by the estate for administration and distributable as an asset thereof are "receivable by the executor."[2] State law is controlling. If,

---

1. In 1988 Congress further restricted the favorable income tax treatment of certain life insurance policies by adopting § 7702A. Section 7702A does not affect the definition of life insurance for purposes of the estate tax.

2. See, e.g., Estate of Margrave v. Commissioner, 618 F.2d 34 (8th Cir. 1980). See also First Kentucky Trust Co. v. United States, 737 F.2d 557 (6th Cir. 1984), where the D was murdered by her husband who had purchased four life insurance policies on the

under state law, policies payable to D's estate are deemed to inure to the sole benefit of D's surviving spouse and children, free of claims of the D's creditors, the proceeds are not includible under § 2042(1).[3]

Insurance payable to beneficiaries other than D's estate will also be included under § 2042(1) to the extent proceeds are received by such a beneficiary "subject to an obligation, legally binding * * * to pay taxes, debts or other charges" of D's estate.[4]

Finally, if the insurance is procured by D and made payable to the lender as collateral security for a loan to D, it is considered to be receivable for the benefit of the estate.[5] Similarly, if the policies have been assigned as security, and the creditor uses the proceeds to satisfy D's debt, the amount used is deemed receivable by the estate.[6]

3. PROCEEDS RECEIVABLE BY BENEFICIARIES OTHER THAN THE EXECUTOR OF THE DECEDENT

a. INCIDENTS OF OWNERSHIP POSSESSED BY A DECEDENT

Where insurance proceeds are payable to someone other than D's estate, the proceeds may still be included in D's estate if she possessed "any of the incidents of ownership." § 2042(2).

Commissioner v. Estate of Noel

380 U.S. 678 (1965).

◼ MR. JUSTICE BLACK delivered the opinion of the Court.

This is a federal estate tax case, raising questions under § 2042(2) * * *, which requires inclusion in the gross estate of a decedent of amounts received by beneficiaries other than the executor from "insurance under policies on the life of the decedent" if the decedent "possessed at his death any of the incidents of ownership, exercisable either alone or in conjunction with any other person . . . ." The questions presented in this case are whether certain flight insurance policies payable upon the accidental death of the insured were policies "on the life of the D" and whether at his death he had reserved any of the "incidents of ownership" in the policies.

These issues emerge from the following facts. Respondent Ruth M. Noel drove her husband from their home to New York International Airport where he was to take an airplane to Venezuela. Just before taking

---

D's life, all payable to him. Under applicable state law, a convicted murderer forfeited all interest in insurance policies on the life of the victim. Accordingly, the policy proceeds were payable to the executor of the D's estate and the court held that they were includible in her estate under § 2042(1).

3. Id.

4. Reg. § 20.2042–1(b). Compare Estate of Mason v. Commissioner, 43 B.T.A. 813

(1941), with Cowles v. United States, 152 F.2d 212 (2d Cir. 1945), as to whether insurance purchased to satisfy marital rights is used to meet "charges enforceable against the estate" under the predecessor of § 2042(1).

5. Reg. § 20.2042–1(b).

6. See, e.g., Bintliff v. United States, 462 F.2d 403 (5th Cir. 1972).

off, Mr. Noel signed applications for two round-trip flight insurance policies, aggregating $125,000 and naming his wife as beneficiary. Mrs. Noel testified that she paid the premiums of $2.50 each on the policies and that her husband then instructed the sales clerk to "give them to my wife. They are hers now, I no longer have anything to do with them." The clerk gave her the policies, which she kept. Less than three hours later Mr. Noel's plane crashed into the Atlantic Ocean and he and all others aboard were killed. Thereafter, the companies paid Mrs. Noel the $125,000 face value of the policies, which was not included in the estate tax return filed by his executors. The Commissioner of Internal Revenue determined that the proceeds of the policies should have been included and the Tax Court sustained that determination, holding that the flight accident policies were insurance "on the life of the decedent"; that Mr. Noel had possessed exercisable "incidents of ownership" in the policies at his death; and that the $125,000 paid to Mrs. Noel as beneficiary was therefore includible in the gross estate. 39 T.C. 466. Although agreeing that decedent's reserved right to assign the policies and to change the beneficiary amounted to "exercisable incidents of ownership within the meaning of the statute," the Court of Appeals nevertheless reversed, holding that given "its ordinary, plain and generally accepted meaning," the statutory phrase "policies on the life of the decedent" does not apply to insurance paid on account of accidental death under policies like those here. 332 F.2d 950. The court's reason for drawing the distinction was that under a life insurance contract an insurer "agrees to pay a specified sum upon the occurrence of an *inevitable* event," whereas accident insurance covers a risk "which is *evitable* and not likely to occur." (Emphasis supplied.) 332 F.2d at 952. Because of the importance of an authoritative answer to these questions in the administration of the estate tax laws, we granted certiorari to decide them. 379 U.S. 927.

[The Court's discussion of the issue whether flight accident insurance is "insurance" within the meaning of § 2042 is summarized at p. 379.]

II.

The executors' second contention is that even if these were policies "on the life of the decedent," Mrs. Noel owned them completely, and the decedent therefore possessed no exercisable incident of ownership in them at the time of his death so as to make the proceeds includible in his estate. While not clearly spelled out, the contention that the decedent reserved no incident of ownership in the policies rests on three alternative claims: (a) that Mrs. Noel purchased the policies and therefore owned them; (b) that even if her husband owned the policies, he gave them to her, thereby depriving himself of power to assign the policies or to change the beneficiary; and (c) even assuming he had contractual power to assign the policies or make a beneficiary change, this power was illusory as he could not possibly have exercised it in the interval between take-off and the fatal crash in the Atlantic.

(a) The contention that Mrs. Noel bought the policies and therefore owned them rests solely on her testimony that she furnished the money for their purchase, intending thereby to preserve her right to continue as beneficiary. Accepting her claim that she supplied the money to buy the policies for her own benefit (which the Tax Court did not decide), what she bought nonetheless were policy contracts containing agreements between her husband and the companies. The contracts themselves granted to Mr. Noel the right either to assign the policies or to change the beneficiary without her consent. Therefore the contracts she bought by their very terms rebut her claim that she became a complete, unconditional owner of the policies with an irrevocable right to remain the beneficiary.

(b) The contention that Mr. Noel gave or assigned the policies to her and therefore was without power thereafter to assign them or to change the beneficiary stands no better under these facts. The contract terms provided that these policies could not be assigned nor could the beneficiary be changed without a written endorsement on the policies. No such assignment or change of beneficiary was endorsed on these policies, and consequently the power to assign the policies or change the beneficiary remained in the decedent at the time of his death.

(c) Obviously, there was no practical opportunity for the decedent to assign the policies or change the beneficiary between the time he boarded the plane and the time he died. That time was too short and his wife had the policies in her possession at home. These circumstances disabled him for the moment from exercising those "incidents of ownership" over the policies which were undoubtedly his. Death intervened before this temporary disability was removed. But the same could be said about a man owning an ordinary life insurance policy who boarded the plane at the same time or for that matter about any man's exercise of ownership over his property while aboard an airplane in the three hours before a fatal crash. It would stretch the imagination to think that Congress intended to measure estate tax liability by an individual's fluctuating, day-by-day, hour-by-hour capacity to dispose of property which he owns. We hold that estate tax liability for policies "with respect to which the decedent possessed at his death any of the incidents of ownership" depends on a general, legal power to exercise ownership, without regard to the owner's ability to exercise it at a particular moment. Nothing we have said is to be taken as meaning that a policyholder is without power to divest himself of all incidents of ownership over his insurance policies by a proper gift or assignment, so as to bar its inclusion in his gross estate under § 2042(2). What we do hold is that no such transfer was made of the policies here involved. The judgment of the Court of Appeals is reversed and the judgment of the Tax Court is affirmed.

It is so ordered.

■ MR. JUSTICE DOUGLAS dissents.

ILLUSTRATIVE MATERIAL

A. "ANY OF THE INCIDENTS OF OWNERSHIP, EXERCISABLE EITHER ALONE OR IN CONJUNCTION WITH ANY OTHER PERSON"

Where insurance proceeds are payable to someone other than D's estate, the proceeds may still be included in D's estate if she possessed "any of the incidents of ownership". § 2042(2). Reg. § 20.2042–1(c)(2), which provides examples of powers constituting incidents of ownership, states that in general "the term has reference to the *right* of the insured or his estate to the *economic benefits* of the policy." The regulations further state that incidents of ownership include "the power to change the beneficiary, to surrender or cancel the policy, to assign the policy...." Reg. § 20.2042–1 (c)(2). (Emphasis added).

The following illustrates the types of situations involved in determining whether D had a right to an economic benefit and, therefore, possessed an incident of ownership.

1.   Cases Finding the "Right" and the "Economic Benefit"

The right to change beneficiaries only with consent of the existing beneficiaries is an incident of ownership. Nance v. United States, 430 F.2d 662 (9th Cir. 1970). Moreover, the term "incidents of ownership" is not confined to rights which enable the possessor to initiate changes. In Schwager v. Commissioner, 64 T.C. 781 (1975), D's wife was the beneficiary of an insurance policy owned by his employer. The designation of D's wife as beneficiary could only be changed by the employer with D's consent. The court concluded that the requirement that D consent to the beneficiary change was an incident of ownership. The court saw no difference between the power to initiate a change and the power to bar a change. See also Commissioner v. Estate of Karagheusian, 233 F.2d 197 (2d Cir. 1956) (proceeds includible where D's consent as trustee was required before grantor of trust owning insurance policies on D's life could change or modify such policies).

Rev. Rul. 79–46, 1979–1 C.B. 303, extended the rationale of *Schwager* and *Estate of Karagheusian* to a split-dollar policy owned by D's employer but which D had the right to purchase for its cash surrender value if the employer decided to terminate the policy. See p. 403 for a discussion of a split-dollar insurance policies. The Ruling held that D's contractual right to purchase the policy circumscribed the employer's power to discontinue premium payments or surrender the policy and was, therefore, an incident of ownership. A power to veto the exercise of an incident of ownership is the same as an affirmative incident of ownership. Although D's rights over the policy depended upon initiation of action by the employer, the existence of an incident of ownership does not depend upon D's practical ability to exercise the power. Rather, the IRS said, its mere existence is sufficient. The Tax Court rejected Rev. Rul. 79–46 in Estate of Smith v. Commissioner, 73 T.C. 307, 311 (1979)(A): "At his death, [D] could neither have initiated changes in the * * * policies nor consented to them; the company alone maintained full control over the policies." Can *Estate of Smith* be reconciled with *Schwager* and *Estate of Karagheusian*? How is the power to veto termination of the policy by purchasing it from the owner different from the power to veto beneficiary changes?

Courts have disagreed about whether D must be able to designate herself in order for the power to change beneficiaries to constitute an incident of ownership. In Estate of Lumpkin v. Commissioner, 474 F.2d 1092 (5th Cir. 1973), D, under the provisions of a group term policy on his life, had no powers except the right to elect different modes of payment under optional settlement provisions. By exercising this right, D could not benefit himself or his estate nor could he designate beneficiaries. The court held that the power to alter the time of enjoyment is a power of substantial control over the policy and an incident of ownership. The court's holding was based on an analysis of the relationship between § 2042 and §§ 2036 and 2038. For § 2038 purposes, the timing of enjoyment is a power to "alter, amend, revoke or terminate" (see *Lober*, p. 255); under § 2036, a right which alters the time and manner of enjoyment is a right to designate who will enjoy the property (see *O'Malley*, p. 234). The court determined that since the power to alter the time and manner of payment is sufficient to cause includibility under §§ 2036 and 2038, it should result in includibility under § 2042 as well. The only difference between the sections is that the former requires an incomplete transfer, while no transfer is required under § 2042 so long as the decedent at death possesses an incident of ownership. This distinction, in the court's view, did not "suggest that there is a further difference among these sections * * * as to the degree of power a decedent must hold [to cause the property to be includible]." Estate of Connelly v. United States, 551 F.2d 545 (3d Cir. 1977), involved the same group term policy as that considered in *Lumpkin*. That decision rejected *Lumpkin* and held § 2042(2) "inapplicable on the ground that the retention of the right to elect different settlement options conferred no economic benefit on the decedent or his estate." The IRS will not follow *Estate of Connelly*. Rev. Rul. 81–128, 1981–1 C.B. 469.

2.   Cases Finding No "Right"

The Regulations in effect prior to the passage of the Revenue Act of 1942 referred to "any of the legal incidents of ownership." See Regulation 80, Article 27 (1934). The requirement that the incident of ownership be a "legal" one was dropped by the 1942 Act. Thus, the Committee Reports state: "Incidents of ownership are not confined to those possessed by the decedent in a technical legal sense." H.Rep. No. 2333, 77th Cong., 2d Sess. 163 (1942); S.Rep. No. 1631, 77th Cong., 2d Sess. 235 (1942).

Despite the Committee Report's statement, the courts have refused to find a right to an economic benefit where the exercise of the "right" constitutes an illegal act. In Estate of O'Daniel v. United States, 6 F.3d 321 (5th Cir. 1993), D transferred life insurance policies for which he was the insured to an irrevocable trust. Subsequently, he illegally withdrew the cash value of the policies from the trust. In rejecting the government's argument that the withdrawal was an incident of ownership, which should cause the policies to be included in his estate under § 2042(2), the court stated:

> "Incidents of ownership connote the legal power to exercise ownership, not the decedents practical ability to do so. * * *
>
> "Even though * * * [D] possessed and exercised the practical ability to withdraw the cash value of the insurance policies, he did not possess a legal incident of ownership over the policies * * *. Therefore, the proceeds for the * * * life insurance policies should have been excluded from his estate." (328)

3.   Cases Finding No "Economic Benefit"

Not every economic benefit received by D and attributable to an insurance policy on his life constitutes an incident of ownership. The Tax Court has held, for example, that a right to the dividends on a policy of insurance on D's life owned by another was not an incident of ownership. The court considered the right to the dividends "nothing more than a reduction in the amount of premiums paid." Estate of Bowers v. Commissioner, 23 T.C. 911 (1955); Estate of Carlton v. Commissioner, 34 T.C. 988 (1960), rev'd on another issue, 298 F.2d 415 (2d Cir. 1962).

The Tax Court has also held that D's right to substitute other insurance policies on his life with equal value for existing policies on his life owned by another was not an incident of ownership. The "[d]ecedent's power to reacquire was, in effect, a power to exchange at arm's length. * * * [S]uch power, in effect to purchase the policies, cannot be considered an 'incident of ownership.' * * * [T]he possession of such a right to substitute cannot be seen as a right to the 'economic benefits of the policy'." Estate of Jordahl v. Commissioner, 65 T.C. 92 (1975).

A mere expectancy will also not qualify as an "economic benefit." In Estate of Margrave v. Commissioner, 618 F.2d 34 (8th Cir. 1980), discussed at p. 370, D created a revocable trust which became irrevocable at his death. Following creation of the trust, D's wife purchased a term life insurance policy on his life, naming D's revocable trust as beneficiary under the policy. D's wife retained all rights to modify or terminate the policy. The court ruled that in these circumstances, D's power to alter or revoke his trust and thereby designate the beneficiary of the insurance policy did *not* constitute an "incident of ownership." The court reasoned that D never possessed more than a mere expectancy in the insurance proceeds since his trust's interest in the policy was subject to the absolute control of the policy by his wife. The IRS acquiesced to *Margrave* in Rev. Rul. 81–166, 1981–1 C.B. 477. As discussed at p. 412, Rev. Rul. 81–166 also concluded that D's wife made a taxable gift at D's death when the policy proceeds were payable to his trust, and that the transfer was subject to inclusion in her gross estate under § 2036 because she had an income interest in the trust.

4. *Cases Involving the Use of Insurance Policies as Collateral*

Cases involving the use of insurance policies as collateral appear to fall into two categories. First, where D uses an insurance policy as collateral for a personal loan, his continued use of the policy as collateral after he transfers the policy to a third party constitutes an incident of ownership. In Estate of Krischer v. Commissioner, 32 T.C.M. 821 (1973), the court held that "the decedent possessed a valuable economic benefit in the life insurance policies since he reserved the right to have the policies continued as collateral security for loans secured prior to [transferring the policies to his children], and, in addition, possessed the right to utilize the policies as collateral security for future loans." Similarly, in Prichard v. United States, 397 F.2d 60 (5th Cir. 1968), the proceeds of an insurance policy obtained by D but owned by his wife and assigned by her as collateral for a mortgage loan made to both of them were included in his estate on the ground that the assigned policy stood between his estate and the possible liability of his property for the debt. The court found that the acquisition of the insurance policy was an integral part of the mortgage loan transaction.

On the other hand, it appears that where D had not used the policy as collateral for a personal loan prior to transfer of all rights in the policy to a third party, his subsequent use of the policy as collateral after the transfer will not constitute an incident of ownership. In Estate of Goodwyn v. Commissioner, 32 T.C.M. 740 (1973), D absolutely assigned ownership of three policies to third parties but later the third parties assigned the policies to a bank as collateral for a loan to decedent and the third parties. The court held that D did not acquire an incident of ownership as a result of the use of the policies as collateral where he possessed no other rights or privileges. Rather, the court characterized the arrangement as an "accommodation" from the third parties. It is difficult to reconcile the disparate treatment in the two factual categories.

B.   INCIDENTS OF OWNERSHIP AS DETERMINED BY THE "POLICY FACTS"

As a result of *Noel*, D's outright retention, as described by the insurance policy itself, of any incident of ownership will result in includibility, even if it is improbable that D would actually exercise the power. In United States v. Rhode Island Hospital Trust Co., 355 F.2d 7 (1st Cir. 1966), the court noted that two types of facts are potentially relevant to the determination whether D possessed incidents of ownership: (1) "policy facts" which are powers D possesses under the express terms of the insurance contract and (2) "intent facts" which relate to D's intent to exercise any of these powers. The court interpreted the legislative history of the predecessor of § 2042 and the *Noel* case as requiring that policy facts, not intent facts, control the determination. The court recognized one exception, however, to the rule that the "policy facts" control whether D possessed incidents of ownership. Where D can demonstrate that the policy facts did not reflect the parties' instructions to the insurance company, the true intention of the parties will prevail. Thus, in Estate of Fuchs v. Commissioner, 47 T.C. 199 (1966), proof of an insurance agent's failure to effectuate explicit instructions of the insured that insurance policies be owned by the beneficiaries and not by the insured was sufficient to remove the proceeds from D's estate despite D's retention of incidents of ownership under the policies.

C.   EFFECTIVE ASSIGNMENT OF INSURANCE POLICIES

The question may arise whether an assignment of an insurance policy has effectively divested the insured of all incidents of ownership because the assignor did not comply technically with all the insurance company requirements regarding assignment. In Estate of Bartlett v. Commissioner, 54 T.C. 1590 (1970), the IRS contended an assignment of insurance policies to a trust was not complete because D had not provided the insurance company with copies of the assignment form. The policies provided that no assignment was binding on the company until it had received copies. The court rejected the IRS' argument on the ground that the policy provision existed solely to protect the company. While D could retain the right to cash in the policies by failing to notify the company, such an action would constitute a breach of the trust agreement and a fraud against the trustees. Although D had the ability to cash in the policies, he did not have the "legal power" to do so; the ability without the legal power did not constitute retention of an incident of ownership.

D.   AMOUNT INCLUDIBLE

Where an individual possesses an incident of ownership in an insurance policy, that is, the right to an economic benefit of the policy, the entire policy proceeds will be includible in the estate. In Rev. Rul. 79–129, 1979–1 C.B. 306, D assigned the ownership of a $150,000 life insurance policy on his life to an irrevocable insurance trust and retained the right to borrow against the cash surrender value. His estate was the designated beneficiary under the policy to the extent of the cash surrender value; the trust was the beneficiary of the balance. D paid premiums to the extent of the annual increase in cash surrender value. The balance of the annual premium was paid by the trust. At his death the cash surrender value of the policy was $12,000. Accordingly, $12,000 was paid to D's estate and $138,000 to the trust. The Ruling held that the entire $150,000 was includible in D's gross estate, $12,000 under § 2042(1) and the balance under § 2042(2): "If the decedent possessed an incident of ownership * * * then the entire policy proceeds * * * are includible * * * regardless of the fact that a portion of the proceeds subject to inclusion could not be affected by the exercise of the incident of ownership."

E. INCIDENTS OF OWNERSHIP IN GROUP TERM INSURANCE

Employees insured under group term plans generally have the right to designate a beneficiary and upon termination of employment to convert the coverage into individual insurance without a medical examination. Initially, Rev. Rul. 69–54, 1969–1 C.B. 221, held that where an employee assigns to a third party the certificate under a group term insurance policy, including the conversion right, he no longer retains any incidents of ownership in the certificate. The same Ruling, however, held that a transfer of the insurance benefits only, the employee retaining the conversion right, would not exclude the proceeds from the employee's estate. Subsequently, however, Estate of Smead v. Commissioner, 78 T.C. 43 (1982), held that a retained conversion privilege was not an incident of ownership because it was unlikely that D would terminate employment in order to convert the policy: "We conclude that the conversion privilege that decedent could exercise or control only by quitting his job was entirely too contingent and too remote to be considered an incident of ownership possessed by the decedent at the time of his death." (52). The Commissioner acquiesced in *Estate of Smead* in Rev. Rul. 84–130, 1984–2 C.B. 194.

The estate tax consequences of the assignment of a group term certificate where neither the master policy nor state law gives the employee a conversion right was addressed in Rev. Rul. 72–307, 1972–1 C.B. 307. It held that the power to terminate insurance by terminating employment is merely a collateral consequence of the power every employee has to terminate his employment and not an incident of ownership in the group term certificate. The Service distinguished the examples in Reg. § 20.2042–1(c), on the ground that they concern powers that directly affect the insurance policy or the payment of its proceeds without potentially costly related consequences.

An assignment of a group term certificate is ineffective if the master policy itself does not permit assignment. Estate of Bartlett v. Commissioner, 54 T.C. 1590 (1970). However, an assignment was held valid where the master policy permitted assignments but the individual policy certificates did not. Estate of Gorby v. Commissioner, 53 T.C. 80 (1969).

F.   REVERSIONARY INTERESTS AS "INCIDENTS OF OWNERSHIP"

Section 2042(2) provides that "the term 'incident of ownership' includes a reversionary interest (whether arising by the express terms of the policy or other instrument or by operation of law) only if the value of such reversionary interest exceeded 5% of the value of the policy immediately before the death of the decedent."

Usually, application of this rule is straightforward. For example, Rev. Rul. 76–113, 1976–1 C.B. 276, held that D's gross estate included insurance policies which a divorce decree had required him to transfer to his former wife and to continue paying premiums because the policies would revert to D if the former wife died or remarried before D's death. However, the breadth of the reversionary rule in § 2042(2) is unclear.

The Committee Reports state: "The bill retains the present rule including life-insurance proceeds in decedent's estate if the policy is owned by him or payable to his executor, * * *. To place life-insurance policies in an analogous position to other property, * * * it is necessary to make the 5% reversionary interest rule, applicable to other property, also applicable to life insurance." See H.Rep. No. 1337, 83d Cong., 2d Sess. 91 (1954); S.Rep. No. 1622, 83d Cong., 2d Sess. 124 (1954). The Reports elaborate that the "5% reversionary interest rule applicable to other property" is the rule of § 2037 that "property previously transferred by a decedent will be includible in his estate only if he still had (either expressly or by operation of law) immediately before his death a reversionary interest in the property exceeding 5% of its value, that is, if he, prior to his death, had one chance in twenty that the property would be returned to him." H.Rep., supra, p. 90; S.Rep., supra, p. 123. Although the Reports state that Congress intended to make the 5% reversionary interest rule of § 2037 applicable to life insurance, § 2042 differs from § 2037. Section 2042 refers to incidents of ownership and therefore reversionary interests "which the decedent possessed at his death * * *," while § 2037 refers to reversionary interests "retained" by the decedent.

If this difference was intentional, does it mean that Congress intended § 2042 to reach the case in which D merely possessed, rather than retained a reversionary interest? Suppose that D's wife, took out insurance on D's life and she owned the policy, but the policy contained a provision stating "if there be no beneficiary living at the death of the insured, the amount of insurance shall be payable to the executors, administrators, or assigns of the insured." Ford v. Kavanaugh, 108 F.Supp. 463 (E.D. Mich. 1952), held in this situation that D possessed a reversionary interest. Reg. § 20.2042–1(c)(3) also states that "the term 'reversionary interest' includes a possibility * * * that the policy or its proceeds may become subject to a power of disposition by him." However, if D never owned the policy, how could his potential possession of it or its proceeds be a "reversion"?

The broad language of § 2042 that "the term 'incident of ownership' includes a reversionary interest (whether arising by the express terms of the policy or other instrument or by operation of law)" and that a reversionary interest includes "a possibility that the policy, or the proceeds of the policy, may return to the decedent or his estate" had occasioned speculation as to whether an insured who transfers a policy of insurance on his life and who may inherit from the transferee of the policy has a reversionary interest. Reg.

§ 20.2042–1(c)(3), however, provides that the term " 'reversionary interest' [does] not include the possibility that the decedent might receive a policy or its proceeds by inheritance through the estate of another person or as a surviving spouse under a statutory right of election or a similar right." Actuarial tables must be used to value the reversionary interest notwithstanding any known facts surrounding D's death. See the discussion of the valuation of reversionary interests, p. 725. However, where D's reversionary interest may, at the time of death, be revoked by another, the value of the interest is deemed to be less than 5% of the value of the policy notwithstanding the fact that valuation of the interest using the actuarial tables might result in a value in excess of 5% of the value of the policy. Rev. Rul. 79–117, 1979–1 C.B. 305.

It should also be noted that § 2042 does not contain a provision analogous to that of § 2037 which disregards a reversionary interest if "possession or enjoyment of the property could have been obtained by any beneficiary during the decedent's life through the exercise of a general power of appointment * * * which in fact was exercisable immediately before the decedent's death." Reg. § 20.2042–1(c)(3), however, does provide that: "[T]here must be specifically taken into consideration any incidents of ownership held by others immediately before the decedent's death which would affect the value of the reversionary interest. For example, the decedent would not be considered to have a reversionary interest in the policy of a value in excess of 5% if the power to obtain the cash surrender value existed in some other person immediately before the decedent's death and was exercisable by such other person alone and in all events."

G.   SECTION 2206

If the proceeds of insurance on D's life are includible in his gross estate but are payable to beneficiaries other than his estate, § 2206 requires that the federal estate tax resulting from the inclusion be apportioned among the beneficiaries "unless the decedent directs otherwise in his will." D's executor can recover the relevant estate tax from the life insurance beneficiaries. An important exception exists, however, for insurance proceeds payable to D's surviving spouse. The executor may only recover estate taxes from D's surviving spouse that are attributable to the proceeds she received in excess of the marital deduction.

b.   INCIDENTS OF OWNERSHIP POSSESSED BY A DECEDENT IN A FIDUCIARY CAPACITY

Regulation: § 20.2042–1(c)(4)

Rev. Rul. 84–179

1984–2 C.B. 195.

FACTS

In 1960, D, purchased an insurance policy on D's life and transferred all incidents of ownership to D's spouse. The spouse designated their adult child as the policy beneficiary.

The spouse died in 1978 and, by will, established a residuary trust for the benefit of the child. D was assigned as trustee. The insurance policy on D's life was included in the spouse's residuary estate and was transferred to the testamentary trust. The drafting of the spouse's will to provide for the residuary trust and the appointment of D as a trustee were unrelated to D's transfer of the policy to the spouse.

As trustee, D had broad discretionary powers in the management of the trust property and the power to distribute or accumulate income. Under the terms of the policy, the owner could elect to have the proceeds made payable according to various plans, use the loan value to pay the premiums, borrow on the policy, assign or pledge the policy, and elect to receive annual dividends. The terms of the will did not preclude D from exercising these rights, although D could not do so for D's own benefit. D paid the premiums on the policy out of other trust property.

D was still serving as trustee when D died in 1984.

LAW AND ANALYSIS

Section 2042(2) of the Code provides that the value of the gross estate includes the value of all property to the extent of the amount receivable as insurance under policies on the life of the decedent by beneficiaries (other than the executor), with respect to which the decedent possessed at date of death any of the incidents of ownership in the policies, exercisable either alone or in conjunction with any other person.

Section 20.2042–1(c)(2) of the Estate Tax Regulations provides that the meaning of the term "incidents of ownership" is not confined to ownership of the policy in the technical legal sense. The term includes the power to change the beneficiary, to surrender or cancel the policy for a loan, or to obtain from the insurer a loan against the surrender value of the policy, etc.

Section 20.2042–1(c)(4) of the regulations provides that a decedent is considered to have an incident of ownership in a policy held in trust if under the terms of the policy the decedent (either alone or in conjunction with another person) has the power (as trustee or otherwise) to change the beneficial ownership in the policy or its proceeds, or the time or manner of enjoyment thereof, even though the decedent has no beneficial interest in the trust.

The legislative history of § 2042 indicates that Congress intended § 2042 to parallel the statutory scheme governing those powers that would cause other types of property to be included in a decedent's gross estate under other Code sections, particularly §§ 2036 and 2038. S.Rep. No. 1622, 83rd Cong., 2d Sess. 124 (1954). See Estate of Skifter v. Commissioner, 468 F.2d 699 (2d Cir. 1972).

Sections 2036(a)(2) and 2038(a)(1) concern lifetime transfers made by D. Under these sections, it is the decedent's powers to affect the beneficial interests in, or enjoyment of, the transferred property that required inclusion of the property in the gross estate. Section 2036 is directed at those powers retained by the decedent in connection with the transfer. See, for example, United States v. O'Malley, 383 U.S. 627 (1966) * * *. Section 2038(a)(1) is directed at situations where the transferor-decedent sets the machinery in motion that purposefully allows fiduciary powers over the property interest to subsequently return to the transferor-decedent, such as by an incomplete transfer. See Estate of Reed v. United States, Civil Commissioner No. 74–543 (M.D. Fla., May 7, 1975); Estate of Skifter v. Commissioner, above cited, at 703–05.

In accordance with the legislative history of § 2042(2), a decedent will not be deemed to have incidents of ownership over an insurance policy on decedent's life where decedent's powers are held in a fiduciary capacity, and are not exercisable for decedent's personal benefit, where decedent did not transfer the policy or any of the consideration for purchasing or maintaining the policy to the trust from personal assets, and the devolution of the powers on decedent was not part of a prearranged plan involving the participation of decedent. This position is consistent with decisions by several courts of appeal. See *Estate of Skifter*; Estate of Fruehauf v. Commissioner, 427 F.2d 80 (6th Cir. 1970); Hunter v. U.S., 624 F.2d 833 (8th Cir. 1980). But see Terriberry v. United States, 517 F.2d 286 (5th Cir. 1975), cert. denied, 424 U.S. 977 (1976); Rose v. United States, 511 F.2d 259 (5th Cir. 1975), which are to the contrary. Section 20.2042–1(c)(4) will be read in accordance with the position adopted herein.

The decedent will be deemed to have incidents of ownership over an insurance policy on the decedent's life where decedent's powers are held in a fiduciary capacity and the decedent has transferred the policy or any of the consideration for purchasing and maintaining the policy to the trust. Also, where the decedent's powers could have been exercised for decedent's benefit, they will constitute incidents of ownership in the policy, without regard to how those powers were acquired and without consideration of whether the decedent transferred to property to the trust. *Estate of Fruehauf*; *Estate of Skifter*, * * *. Thus, if the decedent reacquires powers over insurance policies in an individual capacity, the powers will constitute incidents of ownership even though decedent is a transferee.

In the present situation, D completely relinquished all interests in the insurance policy on D's life. The powers over the policy devolved on D as a fiduciary, through an independent transaction, and were not exercisable for D's own benefit. Also, D did not transfer property to the trust. Thus, D did not possess incidents of ownership over the policy for purposes of § 2042(2) of the Code.

HOLDING

An insured decedent who transferred all incidents of ownership in a policy to another person, who in an unrelated transaction transferred powers over the policy in trust to the decedent, will not be considered to possess incidents of ownership in the policy for purposes of § 2042(2) of the Code, provided that the decedent did not furnish consideration for maintaining the policy and could not exercise the powers for personal benefit.

The result is the same where the decedent, as trustee, purchased the policy with trust assets, did not contribute assets to the trust or maintain the policy with personal assets, and could not exercise the powers for personal benefit.

ILLUSTRATIVE MATERIAL

A. GENERAL

Rev. Rul. 84–179 holds that a trustee possesses incidents of ownership in an insurance policy for which she is the insured if (1) she can exercise her powers for her personal benefit, (2) she transferred the policy into the trust, or (3) she transferred any consideration for purchasing or maintaining the policy.

B. TRUSTEE'S POWER EXERCISABLE FOR PERSONAL BENEFIT

Although the following cases precede Rev. Rul. 84–179, they provide examples of where the trustee will have powers exercisable for her personal benefit.

In Commissioner v. Karagheusian, 233 F.2d 197 (2d Cir. 1956), D's wife purchased an insurance policy on the life of D and transferred ownership of the policy to a trust, the trustees of which were D, D's wife and their daughter. The trust instrument provided for the income to be paid to the wife during her life and to the daughter thereafter, with the remainder to the husband if living at the death of the income beneficiaries. The trust also provided that the wife could modify the trust in any manner with the written consent of the other trustees. D died while a trustee of the trust and the insurance proceeds were held includible in his estate because he, together with his wife and daughter, could modify the trust in any way and thereby affect the ultimate recipient (including himself) of the economic benefits of the policy. In Estate of Fruehauf v. Commissioner, 427 F.2d 80 (6th Cir. 1970), D's wife was the beneficiary of policies she had purchased on her husband's life and at her death the policies passed to a trust under her will for the benefit of her husband. The husband was co-executor of the will and co-trustee of the trust. The trust indenture gave the trustees wide powers to deal with the insurance policies, specifically the power to sell the policies to the insured or to surrender them for their cash surrender value. The husband died before the trust was actually funded, but the court held the proceeds includible because he possessed the right to receive the cash surrender value in his capacity as trustee. Despite the fact that he possessed this incident in a fiduciary capacity, it could be exercised in conjunction with a co-trustee for his economic benefit as a beneficiary of the trust. Gesner v. United States, 600 F.2d 1349 (Ct.Cl. 1979), reached the same result on similar facts.

C. TRANSFEROR ACTING AS TRUSTEE

Where D is the transferor of the policy, but has no power exercisable for her personal benefit, she will still possess incidents of ownership where she "has the power ... to change the beneficial ownership of the policy or its proceeds, or the time or manner of enjoyment thereof ..." Reg. § 20.2042–1(c)(4). Rev. Rul. 84–179 takes this one step further by treating the transferor as having incidents of ownership where she has no power to change beneficial owners, but merely has the normal administrative powers of a trustee. Cases under §§ 2036 and 2038 establish that the power to administer a trust, when exercisable in a fiduciary capacity, does not cause the trust property to be includible in the grantor-trustee's gross estate. See p. 259. Thus, this aspect of Rev. Rul. 84–179 does not parallel §§ 2036 and 2038 and appears to be incorrect.

D. TRUSTEE'S PAYMENT OF PREMIUMS

Prior to the enactment of § 2042(2), the Code included insurance proceeds in decedent's estate if the insurance had been "purchased with premiums ... paid directly or indirectly by the decedent" or the decedent possessed incidents of ownership. When Congress adopted § 2042(2) it intended to eliminate the payment of premium test as a criterion for determining whether proceeds from life insurance should be includible. S.Rep. 1622, to accompany H.R. 8300 (Pub. L. 591), 83d Cong., 2d Sess. 124, 472–473 (1954). It is, therefore, questionable whether Rev. Rul. 84–179 is correct in using D's payment of premiums as a trigger for the applicability of Reg. § 20.2042–1(c)(4).

E. TRANSFEROR RETAINING RIGHT TO REMOVE TRUSTEE

Suppose that the transferor of an insurance policy in trust does not serve as trustee but retains the power to remove the trustee. Is this retained power an incident of ownership? In Rev. Rul. 95–58, 1995–2 C.B. 191, discussed at p. 252, the Service ruled that the grantor of a trust had not retained powers under § 2036 where the grantor had the power to remove the trustee and appoint a successor trustee that is not related or subordinate to him within the meaning of § 672(c). The same analysis should apply to § 2042 so that the grantor's power is not an incident of ownership.

F. COMPARISON OF REG. § 20.2042–1(c)(4) TO REG. § 20.2042–1(c)(2)

Reg. § 20.2042–1(c)(2) provides that, in general, the term " 'incidents of ownership' * * * has reference to the right of the insured or his estate to the economic benefits of the policy." Reg. § 20.2042–1(c)(4) provides that a "decedent is considered to have an 'incident of ownership' in an insurance policy on his life held in trust if, under the terms of the policy, the decedent (either alone or in conjunction with any other person or persons) has the power (as trustee or otherwise) to change the beneficial ownership of the policy or its proceeds, or the time or manner of enjoyment thereof, even though the decedent has no beneficial interest in the trust." This regulatory structure implies that the "right to * * * the economic benefit of a policy" refers not just to the ability to obtain the policy proceeds or cash value, but also to the power to control the disposition of the policy or its benefits.[7] The latter "economic benefits" are obviously different from a beneficial interest in the policy itself. For example, if A transfers a policy on his life to B, retaining only the power to change beneficiaries among a group consisting of B's issue, the policy proceeds will be

---

7. But see Estate of Rockwell v. Commissioner, 779 F.2d 931 (3d Cir. 1985) (D's retention of right to veto designation of beneficiaries of life insurance policy held in trust was not an incident of ownership because D could not use the veto power for his own economic benefit.)

included in A's estate even though he has no "beneficial interest" in the policy. The Regulations adopt the same position when A holds the power as trustee.

In *Estate of Connelly*, p. 385, the court held that the insured's power to elect a settlement option was not an incident of ownership under Reg. § 20.2042–1(c)(2). Reg. § 20.2042–1(c)(4), however, classifies a trustee's power to change the time and manner of enjoyment (where the trustee has transferred the policy or paid premiums) as an "incident of ownership," a power that is not enumerated in the examples of "incidents of ownership" set forth in Reg. § 20.2042–1(c)(2). Although the illustrative examples given in each subparagraph of the Regulations differ, neither is exhaustive nor exclusive. If the power involved in *Connelly* had been held by the insured as a trustee, it would seem to fall within the language of Reg. § 20.2042–1(c)(4). See *Estate of Lumpkin*, p. 384. It is difficult to justify a different result when D holds the power as an individual. Thus, the *Connelly* decision appears incorrect.

c. INCIDENTS OF OWNERSHIP POSSESSED BY A DECEDENT THROUGH A CONTROLLED CORPORATION

Estate of Levy v. Commissioner

70 T.C. 873 (1978).

■ GOFFE, JUDGE.

The Commissioner determined a deficiency in petitioner's Federal estate tax in the amount of $42,042.90.

Due to concessions by petitioner, the issues for our decision are:

(1) Whether § 20.2042–1(c)(6), Estate Tax Regs., is valid;

(2) If valid, whether § 20.2042–1(c)(6), Estate Tax Regs., as amended in 1974, applies retroactively to petitioner estate; and, if so—

(3) Whether the proceeds of life insurance policies owned by Levy Bros. (80.4% of the voting stock of which was owned by decedent) and payable to decedent's widow, are includible in decedent's estate pursuant to § 2042, I.R.C. 1954.

* * *

Mr. Milton L. Levy (D) died on November 11, 1970 * * *.

At the time of his death decedent owned 80.4% of the issued and outstanding voting stock and 100% of the issued and outstanding nonvoting stock of Levy Bros. of Elizabeth, New Jersey, Inc. (Levy Bros.). He was never the sole stockholder of the corporation. Levy Bros. owned the following two life insurance policies on the life of decedent:

	Policy A	Policy B
Insurance company	New York Life Insurance Co.	New York Life Insurance Co.
Policy number	27,701,728	27,499,704
Face amount of policy	$128,500.00	$128,500.00

	Policy A	**Policy B**
Principal of indebtedness	32,220.36	32,242.19
Interest of indebtedness	692.96	693.43
Amount of accumulated dividends	5,416.86	5,416.86
Amount of postmortem dividends	921.08	921.08
Premiums adjustment mortuary	2,300.18	2,300.18
Amount of proceeds payable	104,224.80	104,302.50
Amount of proceeds payable to Iris Levy, widow	103,350.50	103,350.50
Amount of proceeds payable to Levy Bros., owner	874.18	851.88

The life insurance policies were characterized as "split-dollar" policies[8] whereby Levy Bros. owned the policies and were entitled to the net * * * [surrender] cash value as set forth above ($1,726.06). In addition, Levy Bros. held the right to change the beneficiary of the cash value, the right of assignment, the right of borrowing against the policies, and the right to modify the policies. The decedent, apart from his stock ownership of Levy Bros., had no incidents of ownership in either life insurance policy at the time of his death. Mrs. Levy, decedent's widow, as beneficiary, was entitled to and was paid proceeds from the policies in the amount of $206,701 [the pure life insurance component of the policy] as set forth above. The beneficiary of the death benefits under the policies could not be changed without the approval of Mrs. Levy.

The proceeds of the policies paid to Mrs. Levy were not included in the estate tax return of decedent's estate. The Commissioner, in his statutory notice of deficiency, determined that the proceeds of the policies paid to Mrs. Levy were includible in decedent's estate pursuant to § 2042.

The issues involved in the instant case deal not only with new regulations adopted under § 2042(2) during 1974 but also with the language of § 2042(2) of the Code, the legislative history relating back to the Revenue Act of 1942, and the original regulations adopted in 1958 under § 2042. For these reasons we feel it appropriate to describe the background which leads up to the adoption of the new regulations in 1974 which constitute the focal point of our decision.

The general rule set forth in § 2042(2) is that if an insured, at the time of his death, possesses any incidents of ownership in life insurance policies, the proceeds from such policies are includible in his gross estate. The predecessor to § 2042(2), § 811(g), I.R.C. 1939, provided for the inclusion of life insurance proceeds in a decedent's gross estate if such policy were taken out by the decedent on his own life. As we stated in Estate of Lumpkin v. Commissioner, 56 T.C. 815, 822 (1971), vacated and remanded 474 F.2d 1092 (5th Cir. 1973), "The statutory language providing for this inclusion [referring to the test of whether a decedent took out a policy on his own life] often presented difficult problems of interpretation and

8. [ED.: See p. 403 for a description of split-dollar life insurance.]

through judicial decisions two tests evolved: 'payment of premium' and possession of 'incidents of ownership.' " In an effort to eliminate these problems of interpretation, the Revenue Act of 1942 adopted the tests which evolved from judicial criteria. The House and Senate Committee Reports of the Act set forth an explanation relating to the criteria utilized in determining inclusion of insurance proceeds in the gross estate of a decedent, in pertinent part as follows:

> The inclusion in the gross estate of proceeds which are payable to beneficiaries other than the executor is to be determined for the purposes of this section by criteria set forth therein. These criteria are (1) the payment of premiums or other consideration by the decedent for the insurance, and (2) incidents of ownership possessed by the decedent at death. If either of these criteria is satisfied the proceeds are includible in the gross estate. * * *

> There is no specific enumeration of incidents of ownership, the possession of which at death forms the basis for inclusion of insurance proceeds in the gross estate, as it is impossible to include an exhaustive list. Examples of such incidents are the right of the insured or his estate to the economic benefits of the insurance, the power to change the beneficiary, the power to surrender or cancel the policy, the power to assign it, the power to revoke an assignment, the power to pledge the policy for a loan, or the power to obtain from the insurer a loan against the surrender value of the policy. *Incidents of ownership are not confined to those possessed by the decedent in a technical legal sense. For example, a power to change the beneficiary reserved to a corporation of which the decedent is sole stockholder is an incident of ownership in the decedent.* [H.Rep. 2333, 77th Cong., 2d Sess. (1942), 1942–2 C.B. 372, 491; S.Rep. 1631, 77th Cong., 2d Sess. (1942), 1942–2 C.B. 504, 676–677; emphasis added.]

The adoption of § 2042(2) saw the elimination of the "payment of premium" test thereby leaving the "incidents of ownership" test as the sole criterion for determining whether the proceeds from life insurance should be includible in a decedent's gross estate. S.Rep. 1622, to accompany H.R. 8300 (Pub.L. 591), 83d Cong., 2d Sess. 124, 472–473 (1954). While § 2042(2) applies the incidents of ownership test it does not set forth a definitive list of what constitutes an incident of ownership. Regulations were promulgated in 1958 which, in many respects, incorporated the language of the committee reports accompanying the Revenue Act of 1942. The pertinent part of the 1958 Estate Tax Regulations stated:

> Sec. 20.2042–1(c). *Receivable by other beneficiaries.* (1) Section 2042 requires the inclusion in the gross estate of the proceeds of insurance on decedent's life not receivable by or for the benefit of the estate if decedent possessed at the date of his death any of the incidents of ownership in the policy, exercisable either alone or in conjunction with any other person.

* * *

(2) For purposes of this paragraph, the term "incidents of ownership" is not limited in its meaning to ownership of the policy in the technical legal sense. Generally speaking, the term has reference to the right of the insured or his estate to the economic benefits of the policy. Thus, it includes the power to change the beneficiary, to surrender or cancel the policy, to assign the policy, to revoke an assignment, to pledge the policy for a loan, or to obtain from the insurer a loan against the surrender value of the policy, etc. Similarly, the term includes a power to change the beneficiary reserved to a corporation of which the decedent is sole stockholder.

This language is consistent with the legislative history of the Revenue Act of 1942, and the provisions of § 2042(2), in that the test for inclusion of proceeds depends upon who possesses the incidents of ownership. More specifically, if the incidents of ownership are possessed by a corporation owned by the decedent, the incidents of ownership are attributed to decedent, requiring inclusion of the insurance proceeds in the gross estate.

In April 1974, new regulations were adopted with respect to the attribution of corporate incidents of ownership to a stockholder. T.D. 7312, 1974–1 C.B. 277. See Estate of Huntsman v. Commissioner, 66 T.C. 861, 873 (1976). These new regulations expand the attribution of corporate incidents of ownership to sole *and* controlling stockholders. § 20.2042–1(c)(6), Estate Tax Regs. (1974). In addition, the new regulations limit the amount which is includible in a decedent's gross estate. Section 20.2042–1(c)(6), Estate Tax Regs., in pertinent part provides:

In the case of economic benefits of a life insurance policy on decedent's life that are reserved to a corporation of which the decedent is the sole or controlling stockholder, the corporation's incidents of ownership will not be attributed to the decedent through his stock ownership to the extent the proceeds of the policy are payable to the corporation. * * * If any part of the proceeds of the policy are not payable to or for the benefit of the corporation, and thus are not taken into account in valuing the decedent's stock holdings in the corporation [see § 20.2031–2(f), Estate Tax Regs.] for purposes of § 2031, any incidents of ownership held by the corporation as to that part of the proceeds will be attributed to the decedent through his stock ownership where the decedent is the sole or controlling stockholder. Thus, for example, if the decedent is the controlling stockholder in a corporation, and the corporation owns a life insurance policy on his life, the proceeds of which are payable to the decedent's spouse, the incidents of ownership held by the corporation will be attributed to the decedent through his stock ownership and the proceeds will be included in his gross estate under § 2042. If in this example the policy proceeds had been payable 40% to decedent's spouse and 60% to the corporation, only 40% of the proceeds would be included in decedent's gross estate under § 2042. * * *

* * * Petitioner contends that § 20.2042–1(c)(6), Estate Tax Regs., promulgated in 1974, is invalid for a variety of reasons. It argues that the

new regulation is inconsistent and out of harmony with the incidents of ownership test set forth in § 2042(2). Petitioner argues that the new regulation ignores the incidents of ownership test in determining the amount of proceeds includible in a decedent's gross estate. Respondent takes the position that the amendment to § 20.2042–1(c), Estate Tax Regs., in 1974, merely expanded the concept in the original regulations by attributing corporate held incidents of ownership to a controlling stockholder, as well as to a sole stockholder, to the extent that the life insurance proceeds are not payable to the corporation or for its benefit. For these reasons respondent urges that this represents an amplification of the prior interpretation rather than a radical departure from it.

In his statutory notice of deficiency, the Commissioner determined that only the portion of the insurance proceeds payable to decedent's widow are includible in the gross estate. That determination is consistent with the regulations as amended in 1974. The other adjustments to the estate tax liability were conceded by petitioner and respondent has not claimed an increased deficiency. If we held that the regulations were invalid and the entire proceeds of the policies were includible, a decision would be entered for respondent but we would be unable to enter a decision for a deficiency large enough to include all of the insurance proceeds in the gross estate. Cf. H.F. Campbell Co. v. Commissioner, 54 T.C. 1021 (1970), a supplemental opinion to 53 T.C. 439 (1969), aff'd. 443 F.2d 965 (6th Cir. 1971); § 6214(a), I.R.C. 1954.

* * * The legislative history and the regulations both before and after the 1974 amendment support the Commissioner's determination that the insurance proceeds payable to the widow of decedent are includible although decedent did not own all of the outstanding stock of the corporation. Although the 1974 amendment to the regulations specifically makes them applicable to a controlling shareholder and the regulations prior to the amendment do not specifically apply to controlling shareholders, we conclude that the legislative history supports applicability to controlling shareholders before and after the regulations were amended in 1974.

* * *

While § 2042(2) does not specifically provide an exhaustive list of what constitutes an incident of ownership, it clearly stands for the proposition that if a decedent possesses any incident of ownership, at the time of his death, relating to a policy on his life, the entire amount of the proceeds from such policy will be includible in his gross estate. Moreover, the origin of the "incidents of ownership test" is founded in the Revenue Act of 1942 and was later incorporated in the 1954 Code as the exclusive test for determining the includibility of proceeds in a decedent's gross estate.

Petitioner contends that the committee reports of the Revenue Act of 1942, the language of which was adopted in the original regulations of § 2042(2), preclude the attribution of corporate incidents of ownership to any stockholder other than a sole stockholder and that § 20.2042–1(c)(6), Estate Tax Regs., is invalid. Based on this contention, petitioner argues that if Congress intended that attributions apply to a controlling stockholder it could have included a broader declaration in the committee reports of the Revenue Act of 1942. We do not agree. As discussed above, the committee reports stated that it was impossible to formulate an exhaustive list of incidents of ownership. However, the reports further stated that incidents of ownership are not confined to those possessed by the decedent in a technical legal sense. The reports stated by way of an example that incidents of ownership possessed by a corporation were attributable to the sole stockholder.

The example in the committee reports and the original regulations are an illustration of incidents of ownership not held by a decedent directly in the technical legal sense just as the power to change a beneficiary, used in the same example, described an example of an incident of ownership. Moreover, the original regulations adopted under § 2042(2), as indicated above, do not set forth a rule that attribution of corporate incidents of ownership applies only to a sole shareholder but, instead, these regulations adopt the example used in the committee reports.

Therefore, the ultimate question for our decision on this final issue is whether a controlling stockholder (80.4% of all voting stock in the instant case) is to be treated in the same manner as a sole stockholder for purposes of attribution. We see no distinction between a sole or controlling stockholder with regard to the application of the provisions of § 2042. In either situation the stockholder possesses the power over the activities of the corporation so as to affect the disposition of the insurance proceeds. Clearly, Congress did not intend to attribute corporate incidents of ownership to a sole stockholder while excluding a stockholder owning 99% of the voting stock of a corporation, or 80.4% in the instant case. Petitioner relies upon Casale v. Commissioner, 247 F.2d 440 (2d Cir. 1957), revg. 26 T.C. 1020 (1956), for the proposition that the application of the "sole stockholder example" to a controlling stockholder is inconsistent with the separate entity approach to corporations. However, the holding in *Casale* is inapposite to the facts in the instant case because our focus is limited to the application of § 2042(2). In *Casale*, a corporation purchased a combined life and annuity contract insuring a taxpayer who was the president and majority stockholder (98%) of the corporation. Under the provisions of the insurance policy, the corporation was the designated owner of the policy and held the rights to assign the policy, to change its beneficiary, to receive dividends as declared by the insurer, and to borrow on the policy in an amount not exceeding its loan value. The president and majority stockholder had the right under a compensation agreement to designate a beneficiary in the event he died only after he became entitled to annual annuity payments. We held that the premium payments (made by the corporation) were equivalent to a dividend distribution to taxpayer. On appeal, the Second Circuit Court of Appeals reversed and held that the taxpayer received no immediate benefit from the premium payments and that any rights possessed by the taxpayer were subject to termination prior to his receiving annuity payments in the future. In addition, the court, taking the position that the corporation was not a sham operating as a conduit on behalf of the taxpayer merely because the taxpayer was a controlling stockholder, stated: "We have been cited to no case or legislative proposition which supports the proposition that the entity of a corporation which is actually engaged in a commercial enterprise may be disregarded for tax purposes merely because it is wholly owned or controlled by a single person."

Levy Bros. possessed the right to change the beneficiary of the cash value, the right of assignment, the right to borrow against the policies, and the right to modify the policies. Although the parties did not stipulate the specific terms of the policies, it is apparent that the corporation, by the exercise of its rights in the policies, had the power to realize all or at least the greater portion of the proceeds of the policies prior to decedent's death and thus prevent decedent's widow from receiving much of the insurance proceeds. By his stock ownership, decedent had the power to elect the board of directors who, in turn, had the power to elect corporate officers who would be amenable to decedent's wishes as to the exercise of the incidents of ownership held by the corporation. United States v. Rhode Island Hospital Trust Co., 355 F.2d 7 (1st Cir. 1966). Decedent could indirectly exercise such power with ownership of less than all of the voting stock.

Petitioner further argues that any incidents of ownership held by a corporation controlled by the decedent are restricted by a fiduciary capacity, citing Estate of Fruehauf v. Commissioner, 427 F.2d 80 (6th Cir. 1970), affg. 50 T.C. 915 (1968). In that case, the decedent held the incidents of ownership as co-trustee of a testamentary trust created in his wife's will. We held that merely because decedent could exercise the incidents of ownership in a fiduciary capacity, nevertheless such capacity was no bar to inclusion by reason of possession of incidents of ownership. The Court of Appeals affirmed but rejected the broad rule we adopted and held that under the special facts of the case the incidents of ownership were attributable to decedent. In the instant case, decedent did not possess the incidents of ownership as a fiduciary. The record is silent as to whether petitioner was an officer or director of Levy Bros., in either event of which he would be in a fiduciary capacity. But it is not contended by either party that the incidents of ownership are attributable to decedent in such a capacity but, instead, by reason of his controlling stock ownership. Even if decedent, as a shareholder, were considered in a fiduciary capacity, it is difficult to see how the corporation or minority shareholders could be injured by exercising the incidents of ownership to defeat the widow. Numerous situations are apparent where it would be in the best interests of the corporation to exercise its incidents of ownership and deprive decedent's widow of the proceeds, i.e., e.g., borrowing against the insurance policies at a lower rate of interest than borrowing from other sources, especially if the loan could be deducted from the proceeds and repayment by the corporation never be required.

Includibility of the proceeds under § 2042(2) is based upon stock ownership as demonstrated in its legislative history and not upon retention of control or enjoyment as in § 2036(a)(1). Estate of Gilman v. Commissioner, 65 T.C. 296 (1975), aff'd. 547 F.2d 32 (2d Cir. 1976).

Accordingly, we hold that proceeds of the two life insurance policies on the life of decedent payable to his widow are includible in decedent's gross estate.

Decision will be entered for the respondent.

ILLUSTRATIVE MATERIAL

A. BACKGROUND

As discussed in *Estate of Levy*, prior to 1974, Reg. § 20.2042–1(c)(2) provided that the term "incidents of ownership" includes "a power to change the beneficiary reserved to a corporation of which the decedent is the sole stockholder." Subsequently, the Regulations at issue in *Estate of Levy* were promulgated, deleting the above-quoted sentence in Reg. § 20.2042–1(c)(2) and adding subparagraph (6) to Reg. § 20.2042–1(c). Reg. § 20.2031–2(f) was also amended to provide that the life insurance proceeds excluded under the amended Regulations would be taken into account in valuing the shares of stock owned by D.

Reg. § 20.2042–1(c)(6) defines control as ownership of more than 50% of the total combined voting power of the corporation. The Regulation provides that the corporation's incidents of ownership will not be attributable to D to the extent the proceeds of the policy are payable to the corporation or to a third party for a valid business purpose of the corporation. If either test is met, the value of the proceeds will be reflected only in the value of D's shares.

To illustrate, consider a company in which Jane owns 51% and Caroline 49% of the stock. Suppose that the company has purchased and owns the following four policies in which neither Jane nor Caroline has a direct incident of ownership:

1. $100,000 on Jane's life, payable to the company.
2. $100,000 on Caroline's life, payable to the company.
3. $100,000 on Jane's life, payable to Jane's spouse.
4. $100,000 on Caroline's life, payable to Caroline's spouse.

The proceeds of policy (3) will be included in Jane's estate even though she possesses no direct incident of ownership because she is a controlling stockholder. In contrast, the proceeds of policy (4) will not be included in Caroline's estate because she is not a controlling stockholder and possesses no direct incidents of ownership. The proceeds of policies (1) and (2) will not be included in Caroline's or Jane's estate but will affect the valuation of Jane's and Caroline's stock ownership in the Company.

Sometimes a company will use the insurance proceeds it has received on the life of a stockholder to redeem D's stock. In Rev. Rul. 82–85, 1982–1 C.B. 137, the sole shareholder of a corporation caused it to obtain and pay the premiums on a life insurance policy on the shareholder's life. The corporation and the shareholder agreed that the insurance proceeds would be used by the corporation to redeem that portion of his stock equal in value to the insurance proceeds. The Ruling concluded that under Reg. § 20.2042–1(c)(6), the incidents of ownership were not attributable to the shareholder because the corporation was the beneficiary of the policy. Accordingly, the proceeds of the life insurance policy were to be reflected in the value of D's stock and the insurance proceeds were not separately included in D's gross estate under § 2042.

B. SPLIT–DOLLAR LIFE INSURANCE

A split-dollar life insurance arrangement often involves a corporation and a controlling stockholder "splitting" ownership of a life insurance policy. The corporation pays a portion of the premium for a life insurance policy for which the corporation's controlling stockholder is the insured. The portion of the premium paid by the corporation often equals the increase in the cash surrender value of the policy. The controlling stockholder or the beneficiary of the policy pays the other portion of the premium. The corporation is entitled to the cash surrender value of the policy upon the death of the insured or termination of the policy. The beneficiary of the policy is entitled to the pure insurance (i.e., the amount payable in excess of the cash surrender value upon the insured's death). In Rev. Rul. 76–274, 1976–2 C.B. 278, amplified by Rev. Rul. 82–145, 1982–2 C.B. 213, the Service ruled that where the corporation's only interest is in the cash surrender value of the policy, the corporation will not be deemed to possess incidents of ownership in the pure insurance payable to the beneficiary. Thus, if the controlling stockholder does not directly possess any incidents of ownership and the pure insurance proceeds are payable to a third party, the pure insurance proceeds will not be includible in the controlling stockholder's estate.

Care is required to insure that the corporation's only interest in the policy is the cash surrender value. In Rev. Rul. 82–145, 1982–2 C.B. 213, amplifying Rev. Rul. 76–274, the Service ruled that where D's controlled corporation possessed the right to borrow against the cash surrender value of a life insurance policy on D's life, any policy proceeds payable other than to or for the benefit of the corporation are includible in D's gross estate under Reg. § 20.2042–1(c)(6). In Estate of Dimen v. Commissioner, 72 T.C. 198 (1979), aff'd without opinion, 333 F.2d 203 (2d Cir. 1980), the court applied Reg. § 20.2042–1(c)(6) to include in the estate of the sole shareholder of a corporation the portion of the proceeds of a split-dollar life insurance policy which was owned by the corporation and paid to his daughter. The corporation had retained the right to exercise all incidents of ownership of the policy, although the written concurrence of the beneficiary was required in some circumstances. The beneficiary also had the right to purchase the policy if the corporation decided to let it lapse. The court rejected the taxpayer's argument that the beneficiary's right so substantially restricted the corporation's ownership rights that it should be deemed not to possess incidents of ownership over the portion of the policy paid to the beneficiary.

C. PARTNERSHIPS

The Internal Revenue Service has also applied the principles of Reg. § 20.2042–1(c)(6) in partnership situations. Thus, in Rev. Rul. 83–147, 1983–2 C.B. 158, a three-person partnership obtained a life insurance policy on the life of one of the partners, whose child was named as the beneficiary. The partner possessed no incident of ownership in the policy at death. The Ruling concluded that for purposes of § 2042(2) a partnership is regarded as an aggregate of its individual partners and, as a result, any incident of ownership held by the partnership is held by the partners as individuals. Thus, the value of the insurance proceeds was includible in the deceased partner's estate. The Ruling also noted that had the policy proceeds been payable to or for the benefit of the partnership, the proportionate share of the policy proceeds would be included in the value of the decedent's partnership interest rather than in the gross estate directly.

In Rev. Rul. 83–148, 1983–2 C.B. 157, the Service also applied to partnerships the statement in Reg. § 20.2042–1(c)(6) that the corporation's power to surrender or cancel a group term life insurance should not be attributed to the stockholder. There, D was a partner in a large law firm that obtained a group term life insurance policy covering the lives of the partners and the partnership employees. One of the partners created an irrevocable trust for the benefit of that partner's children and assigned to the trust all interest in the group term life insurance policy insuring the partner's life. The partnership, however, retained the right to surrender or cancel the group term policy. By analogy to the group-term cancellation rule in Reg. § 20.2042–1(c)(6), the Ruling concluded that the partnership's power to surrender or cancel its group term policy should not be attributed to any of individual partners and thus D did not possess any incident of ownership in the master term policy at death.

D.   GROUP TERM LIFE INSURANCE

Reg. § 20.2042–1(c)(6) also states that the power to surrender or cancel a group term life insurance policy held by a corporation will not be attributable to any D through his stock ownership.

E.   POLICY CRITIQUE

Is Reg. § 20.2042–1(c)(6) conceptually correct in determining the includibility of life insurance proceeds by looking to the nature of the recipient of the proceeds or the use to which the proceeds are put? Since the estate tax is assessed on the transfer of property, the nature or identity of the recipient is usually irrelevant. However, the approach is defensible when one considers that those inquiries are directed to a determination whether the corporation is serving as a conduit for D. Where the corporation is merely directing insurance proceeds on behalf of the controlling stockholder, it is appropriate to impute the proceeds to the stockholder.

F.   COMMUNITY PROPERTY

1.   *Life Insurance as Community Property*

a.   *§ 2042(1)*

Reg. § 20.2042–1(b)(2) addresses the interaction of § 2042(1) with life insurance which is community property. It provides that where the proceeds of an insurance policy made payable to D's estate are community assets under state law, such that one-half of the proceeds belong to D's spouse, "then only one-half of such proceeds is considered to be receivable by or for the benefit of" D's estate under § 2042(1).

Estate of Street v. Commissioner, 152 F.3d 482 (5th Cir. 1998), is an unusual case involving the application of this provision to Texas community property. D named his estate as the beneficiary of life insurance policies he had purchased. In a state court challenge by D's wife, the court upheld D's designation of his estate, holding that although the insurance proceeds were community property, they were subject to D's exclusive management and control.[9] D's estate then argued in federal court that, as community property, only one-half of the proceeds should be included in his gross estate under Reg. § 20.2042–1(b)(2). The estate asserted that D, acting as agent for the marital community, had made a "gift" of his wife's one-half interest to his estate and, therefore, that she had made a taxable gift of her one-half. To support its argument, the estate cited Reg. § 25.2511–1(h)(9) which provides that "where property held by a husband and wife as community property is used to purchase insurance upon the husband's life and a third person is . . . designated as beneficiary . . ., there is a gift by the wife at the time of the husband's death of half the amount of proceeds." The Court of Appeals rejected this argument:

> " * * * I.R.C. § 2042(1) provides that 'the value of the gross estate shall include the value of all property . . . to the extent of the amount receivable by the executor as insurance under policies on the life of the decedent.' Whatever receivable might mean as a general matter, and whatever nuances Treas. Reg. § 20.2042–1(b)(2) might add to that analysis, we find it impossible that insurance proceeds that were designated as payable to a decedent's estate, and that were, in fact, paid to his estate, and that further were allowed to remain in the estate's hands following a state court challenge regarding their ownership, could somehow be characterized as not 'receivable by the executor' for purposes of I.R.C. § 2042(1). Cf. Commissioner of Internal Revenue v. Estate of Hubert, 520 U.S. 93 (1997) (noting that interpretive regulations must 'implement the congressional mandate in some reasonable manner' to receive court deference)."

b. § 2042(2)

The scope of D's incidents of ownership under § 2042(2) in community property states is determined by examining the relevant community property law. Lang v. Commissioner, 304 U.S. 264 (1938). In many community property states, if life insurance is acquired during marriage by a spouse and the premiums are paid from community funds, the life insurance policy and proceeds are treated as community property. Freedman v. United States, 382 F.2d 742 (5th Cir. 1967); Davis v. Prudential Insurance Co. of America, 331 F.2d 346 (5th Cir. 1964). As a result, only one-half of the insurance proceeds are includible in D's estate. Reg. § 20.2042–1(c)(5); Rev. Rul. 94–69, 1994–2 C.B. 241. This rule applies even though D possessed incidents of ownership that effect the entire policy e.g., the right to terminate the policy or to change beneficiaries. Reg. § 20.2042–1(c)(5) states that where D purchased life insurance on his life with community funds, naming his son as beneficiary, but retaining the rights to surrender the policy, only one-half of the insurance proceeds are includible in his estate. Noting that under local law, any proceeds upon surrender of the policy would have inured to the marital community, the

---

9. Street v. Skipper, 887 S.W.2d 78 (Tex. App.–Ft. Worth 1994).

Regulation concludes that "the power of surrender possessed by the decedent as agent for his wife with respect to one-half of the policy is not, for purposes of this section, an 'incident of ownership'. . . ." Id. The Regulation also states that if wife had predeceased husband, one-half of the value of the policy would have been included in her estate as an interest in a community asset.

2.   Separate Ownership of Life Insurance in Community Property States

Where D owns life insurance policies that were purchased while he was a resident of a common law state or prior to marriage, all proceeds are included in his estate subject to a right of reimbursement in the community for premiums subsequently paid with community funds. Therefore, the amount included is the face amount of the policies less one-half of the premiums paid with community funds. Parson v. United States, 460 F.2d 228 (5th Cir. 1972); Estate of Wildenthal v. Commissioner, 29 T.C.M. 519 (1970); Rev. Rul. 74–312, 1974–2 C.B. 320.

If a policy on the life of one spouse has been assigned to the other and the premiums have been paid with community funds, the Commissioner has sought—unsuccessfully where an effective assignment was made—to include one-half of the proceeds in the estate of the assignor. See, e.g., Kern v. United States, 491 F.2d 436 (9th Cir. 1974) (Washington); Estate of Meyer v. Commissioner, 66 T.C. 41 (1976), aff'd without opinion, 566 F.2d 1182 (9th Cir. 1977) (Washington); but cf. Estate of Madsen v. Commissioner, 659 F.2d 897 (9th Cir. 1981) (Washington); Kroloff v. United States, 487 F.2d 334 (9th Cir. 1973) (Arizona). The important issue is whether the uninsured spouse actually owns the policies. In Louisiana, if a husband acquires an insurance policy on his life and assigns it irrevocably to his wife, the policy is her separate property and her interest in it is not affected by the husband's payment of premiums from community funds. Catalano v. United States, 429 F.2d 1058 (5th Cir. 1969); Estate of Saia v. Commissioner, 61 T.C. 515 (1974); Bergman v. Commissioner, 66 T.C. 887 (1976); Rev. Rul. 94–69, 1994–2 C.B. 241. In Texas, a policy may become the separate property of one spouse if the other takes an affirmative act to transfer ownership of the policy. In Bintliff v. United States, 462 F.2d 403 (5th Cir. 1972), D's husband had executed a special control clause at the time of issuance of the policies providing that all powers over the policies belonged to the beneficiary, his wife. This action constituted an affirmative act as required under Texas law and, therefore, no portion of the proceeds was includible in the husband's estate despite payment of premiums with community funds. Parson v. United States, 460 F.2d 228 (5th Cir. 1972), holds similarly when in connection with an insurance application the husband completed the space on the application form indicating that his wife was to own the policy.

A special situation may arise where identical policies are purchased simultaneously with community funds by a husband and his wife, each naming the other as owner and beneficiary. The presumption that the policies are community property will prevail unless it can be shown that the transfers were not reciprocal and that gifts were intended. Rev. Rul. 67–228, 1967–2 C.B. 331; cf. Estate of Wilmot v. Commissioner, 29 T.C.M. 1055 (1970) (the purchase of a policy by each spouse on the life of the other with community funds pursuant to a plan amounted to a conversion of those funds to separate property; upon the death of the wife, no portion of the proceeds of the insurance on her life owned by the husband was includible in her estate); Estate of Marks v. Commissioner, 94 T.C. 720 (1990) (without addressing Rev. Rul. 67–228, court held that under Louisiana law policies purchased by each spouse on the life of the other with community funds constituted separate property).

4. TAXATION OF LIFE INSURANCE PROCEEDS UNDER PROVISIONS OTHER THAN § 2042

ILLUSTRATIVE MATERIAL

A. TRANSFERS WITHIN THREE YEARS OF DEATH

1. Introduction

Section 2035(a)(2) applies to insurance proceeds if, within three years of death, the transferor transferred an interest in the policy which, had it been retained, would have caused the policy to be included in the transferor's gross estate under § 2042. Since the payment of premiums is not an incident of ownership, see p. 394, § 2035(a)(2) does not apply to the transferor's payment of premiums within three years of his death for policies he transferred more than three years before his death. Premium payments on a policy transferred more than three years before death, to the extent they exceed or fail to qualify for the present interest exclusion, are treated as taxable gifts when made.

In Rev. Rul. 82–141, 1982–2 C.B. 209, amplified by Rev. Rul. 90–21, 1990–1 C.B. 172, D owned 80% of the voting stock of a corporation which possessed all incidents of ownership in a life insurance policy on D's life. For no valid business purpose, the corporation assigned all of its incidents of ownership in the policy to a third person. D filed a gift tax return and died one year after the transfer of the policy. The Ruling concluded that since D owned more than 50% of the voting stock in the corporation at the time the policy was transferred, the attribution principles underlying Reg. § 20.2042–1(c)(6) required that the incidents of ownership possessed by the corporation be attributed to D for purpose of § 2035. Because those incidents were transferred within three years of death, the policy proceeds were fully included in D's estate under § 2035(a)(2). Rev. Rul. 90–21, 1990–1 C.B. 172, extended the logic of Rev. Rul. 82–141 to situations where the controlling stockholder transfers her stock. In Rev. Rul. 90–21, D's corporation owned an insurance policy on her life, payable to her child. D transferred her stock for less than full and adequate consideration. The Service ruled that since Reg. § 20.2042–1(c)(6) treats D as owning the corporation's insurance policy by virtue of her stock ownership, transfer of D's stock within three years of her death for less than full and adequate consideration was tantamount to transfer of the insurance policy.

2. Constructive or "Beamed" Transfers

The focus of § 2035 on whether the transferor possessed incidents of ownership creates significant planning opportunities. Consider the following situations. (1) D obtains and pays the premiums on an insurance policy which, from its inception, is owned by B. D dies within three years of the date the policy was purchased. (2) D transfers to an irrevocable trust for the benefit of B an amount equal to the premiums on a policy on D's life which had been purchased within three years of D's death by the trustee and in which the trustee was named as the beneficiary. (3) B at D's request purchases an insurance policy on D's life. D transfers to B cash equal to the premiums and dies within three years of the purchase of the policy.

Under pre–1982 law each of these transfers resulted in the inclusion of the policy proceeds in D's estate. See Bel v. United States, 452 F.2d 683 (5th Cir. 1971); Detroit Bank & Trust Co. v. United States, 467 F.2d 964 (6th Cir. 1972); First National Bank of Oregon v. United States, 488 F.2d 575 (9th Cir. 1973); Estate of Kurihara v. Commissioner, 82 T.C. 51 (1984); Estate of Schnack v. Commissioner, 848 F.2d 933 (9th Cir. 1988); Knisley v. United States, 901 F.2d 793 (9th Cir. 1990). In those cases, however, the theory of inclusion was not that the decedent-insured had transferred incidents of ownership in the policy within three years of death. In *Bel*, the court stated:

> "[Section] 2042 and the incidents of ownership test are totally irrelevant to a proper application of § 2035. We think our focus should be on the control beam of the word 'transfer.' The decedent, and the decedent alone, beamed the accidental death policy at his children, for by paying the premium he designated ownership of the policy and created in his children all of the contractual rights to the insurance benefits. These were acts of transfer. * * * Had the decedent, within three years of his death, procured the policy in his own name and immediately thereafter assigned all ownership rights to his children, there is no question but that the policy proceeds would have been included in his estate. In our opinion the decedent's mode of execution is functionally indistinguishable. Therefore, we hold that the action of the decedent constituted a 'transfer' of the accidental death policy within the meaning of § 2035 * * *." (691–692)

In the cases applying pre–1982 law, the courts were not required to focus on whether incidents of ownership in the policies had been transferred because, under the pre–1982 version of § 2035, the intent "to reach substitutes for testamentary dispositions" was broad enough to cause includibility. But the 1981 amendment to § 2035 creates a loophole of considerable magnitude. Since § 2035(a)(2) only requires that D had possessed incidents of ownership within the three-year period preceding death, D can avoid inclusion of the insurance policy or proceeds in her estate by carefully avoiding the possession of any incidents of ownership during the three-year period. As discussed at p. 394, paying premiums does not constitute an incident of ownership. Thus, the courts in applying the post–1981 version of § 2035 have concluded that D's instigation of the insurance plan and payment of the premiums within three years of death is insufficient to cause inclusion of the policy in D's estate. Estate of Perry v. Commissioner, 927 F.2d 209 (5th Cir. 1991) (policy for which D signed applications, paid premiums, and designated sons as owners and beneficiaries within three years of death was excluded from estate); Headrick v. Commissioner, 918 F.2d 1263 (6th Cir. 1990) (policy excluded where D established irrevocable trust, trustee purchased insurance policy on D's life and D gave cash to trust to pay premiums); Estate of Leder v. Commissioner, 893 F.2d 237 (10th Cir. 1989) (policy excluded where within three years of death, D's wife signed policy application as owner, D signed as insured and D's corporation paid the premiums).

In AOD 1991–012, the Service stated that in light of the foregoing three decisions it would no longer litigate the issue "[w]hether the proceeds ... are includible in a decedent's gross estate where, even though the decedent was never listed as owner of the policy, the policy was procured at his instance, he paid the insurance premiums and he died within three years of taking out the policy...."

3. *Amount Includible*

For those who die after 1981, if all incidents of ownership in a life insurance policy were transferred more than three years before death, no portion of the proceeds is included under § 2035. Moreover, if D continued to pay premiums on the transferred policy until death, none of those payments is included in D's gross estate and only that portion of the premiums in excess of the present interest exclusion is included in D's adjusted taxable gifts.

Where D transferred incidents of ownership in the policy within three years of death, the policy proceeds are includible in D's gross estate pursuant to § 2035(a)(2) and § 2035(a). Do premiums paid by D within this three year period constitute adjusted taxable gifts to the extent they exceed the present interest exclusion, thus including both the premiums and the proceeds in the decedent's transfer tax base? In Peters v. United States, 572 F.2d 851 (Ct.Cl. 1978), a case of first impression, post-transfer premiums paid by D on a life insurance policy, which was included in D's estate under the pre–1977 version of § 2035, were not included in D's gross estate. The court stated:

> "[I]t would be incongruous to include in the estate both the proceeds of the policy and the premiums paid. * * * Had [the decedent] not made a gift of the policy, the amount of premiums paid from her assets would of course not be includible in her gross estate. The gift of the policy is now held to be ineffectual to keep the proceeds of the policy from inclusion in the estate. The gift should not inconsistently be given effect to make the premiums includible as well. * * * As such the premiums are not to be included in her estate." (856)

Suppose D transfers the incidents of ownership in an insurance policy within three years of death and the donee pays the post-transfer premiums on the policy. Are the entire policy proceeds includible in D's gross estate or does the payment of premiums by the donee reduce the includible amount? In Estate of Silverman v. Commissioner, 61 T.C. 338 (1973), aff'd, 521 F.2d 574 (2d Cir. 1975), six months before his death a father transferred to his son ownership of a life insurance policy which the father had owned more than three years. The son paid the post-transfer premiums. The court limited the includible amount to "that portion of the face value of the life insurance policy which the decedent's premium payments bore to all premium payments." (343) In Estate of Friedberg v. Commissioner, 63 T.C.M. 3080 (1992), the Tax Court applied this proportionate approach in a situation where D died after 1981.

B. TAXATION UNDER § 2036

In Goodnow v. United States, 302 F.2d 516 (Ct.Cl. 1962), D transferred policies on his life to an unfunded revocable life insurance trust. The trust became irrevocable upon his death, the income payable to his wife for life and the remainder to their children. D retained the incidents of ownership in the policies, and the policy proceeds were included in his estate under the predecessor of § 2042. The wife, however, paid all of the premiums out of her separate funds. The IRS argued that the trust should be included in the wife's estate upon her subsequent death because she was the real settlor of the trust by virtue of paying the premiums and hence had retained a life estate. The court held that the wife was not the transferor of the policies but only of the premiums and she retained no life interest in these funds. Her right to the income was given by the terms of the trust instrument created by her husband and the insurance proceeds were not to be equated with the premium payments.

C.   TAXATION UNDER § 2039

Annuity-type payments otherwise includible under § 2039 escape that section if the source of such payment is an insurance policy on the life of D. See p. 335.

D.   INCIDENTS OF OWNERSHIP COMPARED TO POWERS OF APPOINTMENT

The phrase "any of the incidents of ownership" covers more powers than a general power of appointment as defined in § 2041(b)(1). (See p. 356 for a discussion of general powers of appointment.) It includes special powers of appointment, such as a power to name the beneficiary, even if limited to choosing as beneficiary only one or more of a named person's children. Moreover, the fact that an incident of ownership possessed by D is exercisable "in conjunction with any other person," including a person with a substantial interest adverse to the exercise of the power, does not shield the insurance proceeds from inclusion in the decedent's gross estate. In contrast, under § 2041(b)(1)(C)(ii), see p. 365, if the donee of a power of appointment can exercise that power only in conjunction with a person having a substantial interest adverse to the exercise of the power, the appointive property is not includible in the donee's gross estate.

SECTION B.   GIFT TAX TREATMENT OF LIFE INSURANCE

Internal Revenue Code: §§ 2501(a); 2511(a)

Regulations: § 25.2511–1(h)(8)

1.   GIFTS OF INSURANCE ON THE LIFE OF THE DONOR

A transfer by gift of a policy of insurance on the life of the donor or payment of premiums on such a policy is subject to gift tax. By making an inter vivos transfer of insurance on her own life, the donor can—unless the transfer is taxable under a provision of the Code other than § 2042—remove the proceeds of the insurance from her gross estate.

Reg. § 25.2511–1(h)(8) provides:

"If the insured purchases a life insurance policy, or pays a premium on a previously issued policy, the proceeds of which are payable to a beneficiary or beneficiaries other than his estate, and with respect to which the insured retains no reversionary interest in himself or his estate and no power to revest the economic benefits in himself or his estate or to change the beneficiaries or their proportionate benefits (or if the insured relinquishes by assignment, by designation of a new beneficiary or otherwise, every such power that was retained in a previously issued policy), the insured has made a gift of the value of the policy, or to the extent of the premiums paid, even though the right of the assignee or beneficiary to receive the benefits is conditioned upon his surviving the insured."

Under this rule, gift tax would not be imposed even though all the incidents of ownership except the power to name the beneficiary were transferred. Presumably, there would be a gift tax if and when the donee surrendered the policy for its cash surrender value. Is that an opportune time to impose the tax? The donor may not know that the donee surrendered the policy or may not be able financially to pay the tax at that time. The Regulation apparently attempts to correlate the estate tax and gift tax treatment of the transfer of incidents of ownership. Presumably, gift tax is not payable where the right to name a beneficiary is retained, because that right will require the proceeds to be included in the insured's gross estate under § 2042. Of course, if the policy were cashed in, there would be no estate tax liability.

ILLUSTRATIVE MATERIAL

A. PREMIUM PAYMENTS AS GIFTS

Reg. § 25.2511–1(h)(8) was applied in Bolton v. Commissioner, 1 T.C. 717 (1943), in which a taxpayer who owned insurance policies on the life of her husband transferred them to an irrevocable trust for the benefit of her sons. Her subsequent payment of premiums constituted taxable gifts.

In general, the entire amount of premiums paid on policies irrevocably assigned for the benefit of another measures the taxable gift. Thus, in Commissioner v. Estate of Beck, 129 F.2d 243 (2d Cir. 1942), the taxpayer transferred insurance policies and securities to an irrevocable trust which provided that the income from the securities would be used to pay the insurance premiums. In determining the amount of the taxable gift upon creation of the trust, the taxpayer subtracted the present value of the expected premiums on the ground that he would be taxed on the income used to pay the premiums and, therefore, could not have made a gift of that amount. The court rejected taxpayer's approach, stating the income tax treatment did not control gift tax valuation.

Where group term life insurance has been assigned, the amount of each premium payment made by the assignor's employer (whether or not it constitutes taxable income to the assignor) is a taxable gift from the assignor to the assignee. The economic benefit of the assignor's additional compensation has been conferred upon the assignee. Rev. Rul. 76–490, 1976–2 C.B. 300. Rev. Rul. 84–147, 1984–2 C.B. 201, provides rules for determining the amount of the gift.

The assignment by the employee of his interest in the split-dollar policy constitutes a taxable gift. Rev. Rul. 78–420, 1978–2 C.B. 67. Rev. Rul. 81–198, 1981–2 C.B. 188, held similarly with respect to a "private" split-dollar arrangement in which D assigned the pure insurance component in a split-dollar policy to a trust for the benefit of his child while remaining liable for annual premiums to the extent of the annual increase in the cash surrender value of the policy.

B.   PREMIUM PAYMENTS BY BENEFICIARIES OF INSURANCE POLICIES

Insurance premiums may be paid by beneficiaries of policies on the lives of others. The question then arises whether the premium payments constitute taxable gifts. Where the payment of a premium by a beneficiary is made to protect a direct, unconditional and non-contingent interest in the proceeds of the policy, the portion of the premiums attributable to the beneficiary's interest will not be a gift. In Pleet v. Commissioner, 17 T.C. 77 (1951), the taxpayer's father transferred to an irrevocable trust ten insurance policies on his life. If the grantor predeceased his sons (the taxpayer and his brother), the income from the trust was payable to the grantor's wife for life, thereafter to his sons, with the remainder to his sons' issue. The trust provided that the trustee, for any reason it deemed sufficient, could pay corpus to any beneficiary. The trustee was also directed to borrow at any time such amount on the policies as directed by the taxpayer and his brother and to pay the proceeds of the loan to them. The court held that premium payments made by the taxpayer were not gifts, primarily on the ground that the power to compel distribution of loans on the policies constituted a present pecuniary interest in the policies which was protected by the payment of premiums. In Commissioner v. Berger, 201 F.2d 171 (2d Cir. 1953), a husband created an irrevocable life insurance trust which provided that after his death his mother would receive $3,000 income per year and his wife the balance of the income. At the death of the taxpayer's mother, income was to be paid to the taxpayer's wife for life but at no time did she have the right to dispose of the corpus. The wife paid the premiums on the policies. The court held that the portion of the payments attributable to her actuarially determinable income interest was not a gift; the balance of the premium payments was a gift.

Premium payments by a person who does not possess a direct and unconditional interest in the proceeds are taxable gifts. Thus, in Harris v. Commissioner, 10 T.C. 741 (1948), aff'd on other issues, 340 U.S. 106 (1950), premium payments made by a wife on policies owned by her husband were gifts to her husband because her possible receipt of insurance proceeds on her husband's death as a beneficiary of his estate did not constitute an interest in the policies. She did not acquire an interest by paying premiums because her husband, as owner, could let the policies lapse or otherwise dispose of them at any time.

The question whether the payment of premiums qualifies for the § 2503(b) present interest exclusion is discussed at p. 453.

C.   TRANSFER OF POLICY PROCEEDS AS GIFT

Rev. Rul. 81–166, 1981–1 C.B. 477, dealt with the gift tax aspects of the transaction described in *Estate of Margrave*, p. 370. D created an unfunded revocable trust which provided that after D's death the income was to be paid to D's wife for life, remainder to his children. D's wife purchased a life insurance policy on D's life, named the revocable trust as beneficiary, and retained the right to change the beneficiary. After D died survived by his wife, the insurance proceeds were paid to the trust. The ruling held that the wife made a gift at D's death equal to the value of the remainder interest in the trust. The transfer was also subject to inclusion in her gross estate under § 2036 because the wife retained a life estate in the insurance proceeds which she was transferring to the trust.

D. COMMUNITY PROPERTY

Reg. § 25.2511–1(h)(9) provides that where community funds are used to purchase insurance on the husband's life and a third party is designated as beneficiary, if, under the applicable state law, "the husband's death is considered to make absolute the transfer by the wife, there is a gift by the wife at the time of the husband's death of half the amount of the proceeds of such insurance."

Issues may arise about the amount of the surviving spouse's gift. Suppose the community property fund of the spouses consists of $300,000 in securities and $100,000 of life insurance proceeds. At the death of the husband, the wife receives $200,000 of securities and the children receive $100,000 of securities plus $100,000 of insurance proceeds. Two approaches are possible. First, since the wife received no insurance proceeds, she could be treated as having made a gift of $50,000, her share of the insurance proceeds. But this would ignore her receipt of $200,000, an amount equal to one-half of her interest in the total marital assets. The second approach would be that she made no taxable gift since she received an amount equal to her interest in the total marital property. In Kaufman v. United States, 462 F.2d 439 (5th Cir. 1972), the Court adopted this second approach, stating that "we hold that the rule * * * attributing one-half of any bequest to others as a gift by a surviving spouse in a community property state must be limited to situations in which the surviving spouse receives less than his or her community share." Under this second approach, if the wife received only $100,000 of securities plus $50,000 of insurance proceeds, she would have made a gift of $50,000.

2. THE VALUATION OF LIFE INSURANCE POLICIES

United States v. Ryerson

312 U.S. 260 (1941).

■ Mr. Justice Douglas delivered the opinion of the Court.

The question here is the same as that in Guggenheim v. Rasquin [312 U.S. 254]. Consequently, the decision of the Circuit Court of Appeals holding that cash-surrender value on the dates of the gifts was the proper method of valuing single-premium life insurance policies for gift-tax purposes (114 F.2d 150) must be reversed, unless the elapse of time between the issuance of the policies and the making of the gifts calls for a different result. The single-premium policies here involved were taken out by the insured in 1928 and 1929. They were assigned as gifts in December, 1934, when the insured was 79 years old. The cost of the policies was less than their cash-surrender value at the dates of the gifts. But the cost of replacing the policies at the then age of the insured would have been in excess of their cash-surrender value. We think that such cost of replacement, as held by the District Court, is the best available criterion of the value of the policies for the purposes of the gift tax. The elapse of time between issuance and assignment of the policies does not justify the substitution of cash-surrender value for replacement cost as the criterion of value. We cannot assume with respondents that at the dates of the gifts the policies presumably had no insurance, as distinguished from investment, value to the donor. Here, as in the case where the issuance of the policies and their assignment as gifts are simultaneous, cash-surrender value reflects only a part of the value of the contracts. The cost of duplicating the policies at the dates of the gifts is, in absence of more cogent evidence, the one criterion which reflects both their insurance and investment value to the owner at that time. Cf. Vance on Insurance (2d ed.) pp. 332–333; Speer v. Phoenix Mutual Life Ins. Co., 36 Hun 322. The fact that the then condition of an insured's health might make him uninsurable emphasizes the conclusion that the use of that criterion will result in placing a minimum value upon such a gift.

Reversed.

ILLUSTRATIVE MATERIAL

A.   GIFT TAX VALUE

Consistent with *Ryerson*, Guggenheim v. Rasquin, 312 U.S. 254 (1941), held that when the purchase and assignment of a single premium life insurance policy occurred at "substantially the same time" the value of the policy for gift tax purposes was its cost rather than its cash surrender value. See also Reg. § 25.2512–6(a) Ex. (1) (where donor purchases insurance policy for the benefit of another, value of gift is the cost of the policy).

The rule of the *Ryerson* and *Guggenheim* cases also applies to the valuation of paid-up policies that are not single premium policies. For gift tax purposes the value of such policies is their replacement cost. Reg. § 25.2512–6(a) Ex. (3). See, e.g., Houston v. Commissioner, 124 F.2d 518 (3d Cir. 1941).

The value for gift tax purposes of a life insurance policy in force for some time on which all the premiums have not yet been paid is the interpolated terminal reserve[10] on the date of the transfer plus the unearned portion of the last premium paid on the policy. This amount is adjusted to reflect the amount of any dividends to the credit of the policy and the amount of any indebtedness that is outstanding against it. See Reg. § 25.2512–6. This relatively simple method of valuation, rather than the replacement value method, presumably is used to facilitate administration of the Code.

---

10. The "terminal reserve" is the reserve maintained by the insurer to cover its liability under the policy.

The following example taken from Reg. § 25.2512–6(a), Ex. 4 illustrates the operation of the interpolated terminal reserve method of valuation:

"A gift is made four months after the last premium due date of an ordinary life insurance policy issued nine years and four months prior to the gift thereof by the insured, who was 35 years of age at the date of issue. The gross annual premium is $2,811. The computation follows:

Terminal reserve at end of tenth year	$14,601.00
Terminal reserve at end of ninth year	12,965.00
Increase	$ 1,636.00
One-third of such increase (the gift having been made four months following the last preceding premium due date), is	$ 545.33
Terminal reserve at end of ninth year	$12,965.00
Interpolated terminal reserve at date of gift	$13,510.33
Two-thirds of gross premium ($2,811)	1,874.00
Value of the gift	$15,384.33"

B.   ESTATE TAX VALUE

When insurance on the life of D is includible in his gross estate and the proceeds are payable at death, the total amount receivable by the beneficiaries is included in his gross estate. If, at the option either of the insured during his lifetime or of the beneficiaries, the proceeds are payable on an installment basis, the lump sum which could have been elected by the insured or the beneficiaries is includible. If no such option was available, the principal sum used by the insurer in determining the amount of periodic payments is includible. Reg. § 20.2042–1(a)(3).

The value of a life insurance policy owned by D on the life of another is its replacement cost and not the cash surrender value. Estate of Du Pont v. Commissioner, 233 F.2d 210 (3d Cir. 1956). See also Reg. § 20.2031–8(a)(1), applying the replacement cost theory where the issuing company is regularly engaged in selling "comparable contracts." A "comparable contract" is a policy which provides the same economic benefits as the policy owned by the dece-dent. For example, where the cash surrender value of a replacement policy was less than the cash surrender value of a policy owned by D, the policies were not comparable because the differing values demonstrated that the replacement policy did not reflect all the economic benefits of the policy actually owned by D. Rev. Rul. 78–137, 1978–1 C.B. 280.

Where a comparable contract cannot be found or where the valuation through sale of comparable contracts is not readily ascertainable, as when "the contract has been in force for some time and further premium payments are to be made, the value may be approximated by adding to the interpolated terminal reserve at the date of the decedent's death the proportionate part of the gross premium last paid before the decedent's death which covers the period extend-ing beyond that date." Reg. § 20.2031–8(a)(2). Rev. Rul. 79–429, 1979–2 C.B. 321, illustrates the application of the Regulations to a split-dollar policy the pure insurance component of which was owned by the deceased spouse of the employee-insured.

If a spouse owns life insurance policies on the life of the other spouse and both die simultaneously in a state where applicable law provides that the insured survives the beneficiary, the value of the policy to be included in the estate of the beneficiary spouse is determined by the interpolated terminal reserve method of Reg. § 20.2031–8(a)(2). Estate of Chown v. Commissioner, 428 F.2d 1395 (9th Cir. 1970); Estate of Wien v. Commissioner, 441 F.2d 32 (5th Cir. 1971); Estate of Goldstone v. Commissioner, 78 T.C. 1143 (1982).

3.   LIFE INSURANCE AND ESTATE PLANNING

Life insurance has long been an important estate planning tool. Under § 2042 an insured can remove the proceeds of existing policies of insurance on her life from her gross estate by making the proceeds payable to someone other than her executor and by relinquishing all the incidents of ownership. Similarly, with respect to new policies, she can structure her payment of premiums so that they will qualify for the gift tax present interest exclusion (p. 478) and that the proceeds of such policies will not be included in her gross estate (by having the proceeds not be payable to her executor and not possessing any incidents of ownership).

An estate plan attempting to utilize insurance in the above fashion must be carefully drawn to achieve the desired tax savings. For example, care must be taken to assure that the insured does not possess a reversionary interest that is valued at more than 5% of the value of the policy immediately before her death. But uncontrollable circumstances can change the anticipated transfer tax results. First, the insured may inherit the policy if the named beneficiary dies before the insured. If this happens, the gifts of policies or premiums made by the insured will have been to no avail, the value of the policy will be includible in the donee's gross estate, and the insured will have to make a gift of the policy to another if she still wishes to remove its proceeds from her gross estate. Second, if the insured makes a gift of a policy on her life within three years of death, § 2035 may be invoked as discussed at p. 407. It is the lawyer's responsibilities to inform her client of these dangers so that the client can make an informed decision.

Insurance, like other estate planning tools, cannot be used indiscriminately. The ends of any estate plan are to achieve the client's wishes in providing for her family after her death without adversely affecting her familial relationships or interfering with her financial security during life. Many persons, for example, prefer paying estate taxes to giving their children control over substantial amounts of property at a time when, in their opinion, the children are not "ready" to control the property. Others prefer paying estate taxes to surrendering control over property that may be of use to them in the future. These persons, despite the possibility of tax savings, may be unwilling irrevocably to give others the incidents of ownership on policies of insurance on their lives for which they have paid or are paying the premiums.

If an insured person wishes his surviving spouse and children to benefit from the life insurance policy, he may wish to transfer the policy to an irrevocable inter vivos trust. A properly structured life insurance trust will allow the insured's surviving spouse to benefit from the insurance proceeds but, at the same time, exclude the proceeds from the surviving spouse's estate. If properly drafted, the life insurance trust could also qualify as a "spendthrift" trust which would not be subject to the claims of creditors of surviving spouse or children under state law. See Restatement (Second) of Trusts §§ 149, 162.

To exclude the insurance proceeds from the surviving spouse's estate, it is important to carefully delineate the powers of the trustees to avoid application of §§ 2041 and 2035–2038. The power of a trustee, other than the surviving spouse, to spray the insurance proceeds or income thereon to the surviving spouse or children as trust beneficiaries will not cause such proceeds or income to be includible in the surviving spouse's estate. Moreover, if a trustee, other than the surviving spouse, has the power to distribute income or principal to the children of the surviving spouse, such distributions will not be treated as gifts by the surviving spouse. Also, surviving spouse's right to direct distributions to herself as a beneficiary will not cause the proceeds to be includible in her estate so long as such right is determined under an "ascertainable standard." Reg. § 20.2041–1(c)(2).

CHAPTER 24

TRANSFERS MADE WITHIN THREE YEARS OF DEATH

Internal Revenue Code: § 2035

INTRODUCTORY NOTE

Section 2035 historically played an important and much-litigated role in the Federal estate tax structure. The Economic Recovery Tax Act of 1981, however, reduced the scope of the section so that it performs only two relatively minor functions. First, it serves as a backstop to §§ 2036–2038 and 2042 to forestall attempts made shortly before death to remove interests from the transferor's gross estate which otherwise would be includible under one or more of those sections. Second, it provides a limited "gross-up" rule, requiring that gift tax paid on transfers within three years of death be included in the decedent's gross estate. Aside from these two aspects, transfers completed within three years of death are treated the same for estate tax purposes as any other lifetime transfer. Thus, post-transfer appreciation in, and income from, the property will not be brought back into the transferor's gross estate. The Taxpayer Relief Act of 1997 made various technical changes to § 2035 but did not alter its basic scope.

SECTION A. HISTORICAL BACKGROUND

The forerunner of § 2035 initially appeared in the Revenue Act of 1916 as a provision including the value of transfers made in contemplation of death as part of the gross estate. From the outset, the provision was a constant source of strife. Its purpose was to prevent estate tax avoidance by reaching substitutes for testamentary dispositions. United States v. Wells, 283 U.S. 102 (1931). Realizing the difficulties involved in the proof of contemplation of death, Congress at first coupled the rule with a rebuttable presumption that gifts made within two years of death were in contemplation of death. The presumption, however, proved ineffective in practical administration. In view of the imminent repeal of the gift tax, Congress in 1926 instead made the presumption irrebuttable, reasoning that this was the only way to block avoidance of estate taxes. See H.R. Rep. No. 1, 69th Cong., 1st Sess. 15 (1926). The Supreme Court, however, found that this provision, whether interpreted as a gift tax or as an estate tax, violated the due process clause of the Fifth Amendment. Heiner v. Donnan, 285 U.S. 312, 325 (1932) ("[A] statute which imposes a tax upon an assumption of fact which the taxpayer is forbidden to controvert is so arbitrary and unreasonable that it cannot stand under the [Fifth] Amendment.").

As a result of *Donnan*, Congress in 1932 restored the rebuttable presumption and also enacted a tax on gifts made by individuals. But because the Service had been singularly unsuccessful in establishing the taxability, as part of the gross estate, of transfers made several years before death, Congress in 1950 sought to eliminate such unproductive litigation by establishing a conclusive presumption that transfers of property (or relinquishments of powers, or releases or exercises of powers of appointment) made more than three years before death were not made in contemplation of death. This provision also increased from two to three years the period before death during which a transfer was deemed to have been made in contemplation of death unless shown to the contrary.

Despite the 1950 changes, litigation continued as decedents' estates marshalled voluminous and ingenious factual assemblages portraying a decedent during the three years prior to death as full of exuberance and motivated only by a zest for life, with nary a thought of death. No action of the decedent was too small to bring to the court's attention, from an 87 year old's habit of gamboling in the Atlantic ocean at dawn to an 89 year old's jumping in the air and clicking his heels together. The incentive for litigation was, of course, the much lower tax burden imposed on gifts as compared to transfers at death under the pre–1977 rules. Even if the taxpayer lost the case, a gift in contemplation of death generally produced a tax saving because gifts were not grossed-up by the gift tax paid (see p. 51).

Congress, in the Tax Reform Act of 1976, sought to bring an end to the litigation engendered by the contemplation of death test. Section 2035 was amended to provide that the decedent's gross estate would include all gifts made during the three-year period ending on the date of death. The included amount was the value of the property transferred on the applicable estate tax valuation date. The House Ways and Means Committee Report distinguished the 1976 provision from that held unconstitutional in *Donnan*:

> "First, [amended § 2035] does not provide a presumption as to whether a transfer is in contemplation of death. The theory underlying the provision does not depend on whether the transfer was in contemplation of death as a substitute for a testamentary disposition. The donor's motive is immaterial. Second, the 1932 decision dealt with the impact of the contemplation of death rules under a taxing statute where substantial differences in tax liability would have arisen, depending upon whether or not a lifetime transfer was included in a decedent's gross estate because no gift tax was imposed at that time." H.R. Rep. No. 94–1380, 94th Cong., 2d Sess. 14 (1976).

The 1976 amendments required that tax paid by the decedent or his estate on a gift made by the decedent or his spouse during the three years before death also be included in the decedent's gross estate. On the other hand, the 1976 Act liberalized prior law, under which a gift in contemplation of death was includible in a decedent's estate even if it was not subject to gift tax by reason of the then–$3,000 annual exclusion (discussed in

Chapter 26). The 1976 legislation excluded from § 2035 any transfers (other than transfers with respect to a life insurance policy) aggregating less than $3,000 per donee in any year. Inclusion in the gross estate of transfers made within three years of death carried two important tax consequences: for transfer tax purposes, post-transfer appreciation was included in the transferor's gross estate; for income tax purposes, the property transferred received a step-up in basis under § 1014. The Economic Recovery Tax Act of 1981 changed both of these results, as explained in the following excerpt from the House Ways and Means Committee Report:

"Under the unified transfer tax system adopted in the Tax Reform Act of 1976, the inclusion in the gross estate of gifts made within 3 years of death generally has the effect of including only the property's post-gift appreciation in the gross estate (because the gift tax paid with respect to the transfer is allowed as a credit against the decedent's estate tax). The committee believes that inclusion of such appreciation generally is unnecessary except for gifts of life insurance and certain property included in the gross estate pursuant to certain of the so-called transfer sections (§§ 2036, 2037, 2038, * * * and 2042). However, gifts made within 3 years of death should be included in a decedent's gross estate to determine the estate's eligibility for favorable redemption, valuation, and deferral provisions (under §§ 303, 2032A, and 6166) to preclude deathbed transfers designed to qualify that estate for such favorable treatment. * * *

"In general, * * * gifts made within 3 years of death will not be included in the decedent's gross estate, and the post-gift appreciation will not be subject to transfer taxes. Accordingly, such property will not be considered to pass from the decedent and the step-up basis rules of § 1014 will not apply.

"[However, under § 2035(a), if the decedent made a transfer of an interest in property, or relinquished a power with respect to any property, within 3 years of the decedent's death, and the value of such property would have been included in the decedent's gross estate under §§ 2036, 2037, 2038, and 2042 if the decedent had retained such interest or power on the date of death, then the value of the property is included in the decedent's gross estate.]

"In addition, [under § 2035(c)(1) & (2),] all transfers within 3 years of death (other than gifts eligible for the annual gift tax exclusion) will be included for purposes of determining the estate's qualification for special redemption, valuation, and deferral purposes (under §§ 303, 2032A, and 6166) and for purposes of determining property subject to the estate tax liens (under subchapter C of Chapter 64).

"Section [2035(b)], requiring the inclusion of all gift taxes paid by the decedent or his estate on any gift made by the decedent or his spouse after December 31, 1976, and within 3 years of death, will continue to apply to all estates."

H.R. Rep. No. 201, 97th Cong., 1st Sess. 186–87 (1981).

The Taxpayer Relief Act of 1997 made various technical changes to § 2035 "to improve its clarity," but did not alter its basic scope. See H.R. Conf. Rep. No. 220, 105th Cong., 1st Sess. 436 (1997).

SECTION B.   TECHNICAL ASPECTS OF § 2035

1.   SECTION 2035(a)

The three-year rule applies to include in the decedent's estate the value of any interest in property if (i) the decedent made a transfer of the interest, or relinquished a power with respect to the property, within three years of the decedent's death, and (ii) the value of such property would have been included in the decedent's gross estate under §§ 2036, 2037, 2038, or 2042 if the decedent had retained such interest or power on the date of death. For example, assume Parent in 2004 transfers all incidents of ownership in a policy on her life to daughter. Upon Parent's death in 2006, the life insurance proceeds are included in Parent's estate under § 2035(a) because she (i) transferred the incidents of ownership in the policy within three years of her death, and (ii) the proceeds would have been included in her estate under § 2042 had she retained the incidents of ownership in the policy until her death.

Similarly, if X, more than three years before death, creates a trust in which X retains a life income interest and, within three years of death, transfers the life income interest to Y, no amount would be included in X's estate under § 2036. However, § 2035(a) requires that the entire trust corpus be included in X's estate. See also Rev.Rul. 79–62, 1979–1 C.B. 295 (decedent, within three years of death, transferred retained reversionary interest valued at more than 5% of corpus at time of transfer, but at less than 5% of corpus at date of death; § 2035 not applicable because interest would not have been included in decedent's estate under § 2037 had decedent held interest at date of death).

2.   AMOUNT INCLUDIBLE

The value of an interest in property transferred to a donee during life but included in a decedent's gross estate under § 2035 is determined as of the applicable estate tax valuation date. In Rev.Rul. 81–14, 1981–1 C.B. 456, D, within three years of death, transferred an insurance policy on the life of a third party who died after the transfer but before D. The Service ruled that the face amount of the policy, rather than the value of the policy at the time of transfer, was included in D's estate. This result is consistent with § 2035(a)'s purpose to produce the same estate tax result that would have obtained had the decedent never transferred the property during her lifetime. Where the inter vivos transfer occurs through a trust, the following case holds that the value of the trust at the date of death is included in the decedent's estate under § 2035(a), rather than the value of the property originally transferred into trust.

Estate of DeWitt v. Commissioner

68 T.C.M. 1136 (1994).

■ WRIGHT, J.:

The issue before us for partial summary judgment is whether under § 2035(a), a transfer in trust, originally funded with cash, is includable in decedent's gross estate at the value of the trust res at the date of decedent's death, or at the value of the cash with which the trust was funded. * * *

On January 30, 1981, decedent created an irrevocable trust for the income benefit of her son, petitioner John H. DeWitt, for life, with the remainder to his children, subject to a special testamentary power of appointment. The trust was funded with $250,000 cash. Decedent and petitioner John H. DeWitt were appointed as trustees. Decedent filed a Federal gift tax return with respect to the gift in trust, and paid the gift tax thereon.

The trustees invested the trust funds in an income-producing note of an unrelated business partnership (note). On September 10, 1982, the date of decedent's death, the trust consisted entirely of the note, which the executors valued at $187,500. The executors timely filed a Federal estate tax return and * * * included the amount of $187,500 in decedent's gross estate [under § 2035(a)]. Respondent determined that the amount includable in the gross estate is $250,000, the value of the cash with which the trust was funded. * * *

Reg. § 20.2035–1(e) provides:

Valuation. The value of an interest in transferred property includible in a decedent's gross estate under this section is the value of the interest as of the applicable valuation date. * * * However, if the transferee has made improvements or additions to the property, any resulting enhancement in the value of the property is not considered in ascertaining the value of the gross estate. Similarly, neither income received subsequent to the transfer nor property purchased with such income is considered.

The purpose of § 2035 is to prevent the avoidance of estate tax through the use of gifts as a substitute for testamentary disposition of what would otherwise be included in the gross estate. * * *

Simply stated, respondent's position is that the interest in property to be valued and included in decedent's gross estate is the cash transferred by decedent at the inception of the trust. The value of cash does not fluctuate; therefore $250,000 should be included in the gross estate. The executors argue that decedent transferred an interest in a trust; therefore the trust interest is the property which is to be included in decedent's gross estate. The value of the trust interest was $187,500 on the date of death.

Respondent bases her position on a plain reading of § 2035 and Reg. § 20.2035–1(e), and Humphrey's Estate v. Commissioner, 162 F.2d 1 (5th Cir. 1947), affg. a Memorandum Opinion of this Court. We do not believe that a plain reading of the statute resolves the dispute in the instant case. Further, respondent's reliance on *Humphrey's Estate* is misplaced.

The decedent in *Humphrey's Estate* * * * transferred $40,000 outright to each of his two sons within 2 years of his death. The sons subsequently invested the funds, and at the date of the decedent's death, the investment declined by 50 percent. The Tax Court held that the transfers by the decedent were made in contemplation of death and therefore were includable in the gross estate. We did not, however, address the valuation issue. The U.S. Court of Appeals for the Fifth Circuit held that the property originally transferred is the property to be valued, i.e., $40,000 cash, not the substituted property. The Court of Appeals stated:

> What is to be valued at the time of decedent's death is the very property which the decedent transferred. He transferred $40,000 [to each son], and its money value was the same [at the date of transfer as at the date of death] * * *. That the transferees may have lost some of it does not diminish the sum that was transferred. * * *

In the present case, unlike *Humphrey's Estate*, the transfer was made into trust. The applicable precedent in this Court, with respect to the valuation of property for estate tax purposes, in a case where the trust has disposed of the transferred property and at the date of death holds substituted property, is Estate of Kroger v. Commissioner, a Memorandum Opinion of this Court dated Aug. 17, 1943, affd. 145 F.2d 901 (6th Cir. 1944). In *Estate of Kroger*, the decedent established two trusts prior to his death. The first trust was funded with $2,000,000 par value U.S. Treasury notes and the second was funded with $10,000,000 par value U.S. Treasury notes. On the date of the decedent's death, the values of the trusts were $1,736,414 and $10,461,490, respectively. We held that the value to be included in the gross estate was the value of the trust corpora at the decedent's date of death, not the value of the amounts used to fund the trusts. The Tax Court stated:

> The estate tax is imposed upon the value of the net estate as it exists at the date of the death of the decedent. If the decedent had made an inter vivos gift of property in contemplation of death that property would have to be valued as of the date of death whether that value be more or less than at the date of the gift; and if property has been converted into other property the value of such other property at the date of death is the measure of the tax. The same rule applies where property is transferred to a trust in contemplation of death. * * *

We follow the holding in Estate of Kroger v. Commissioner, supra. Accordingly, we hold that the value of the trust res at the date of decedent's death, $187,500, is includable in the gross estate under § 2035(a). * * *

3.   SECTION 2035(b)

Section 2035(b), which requires inclusion in the gross estate of any gift tax paid by the decedent or his estate on any gift made by the decedent or his spouse during the three-year period ending on the date of the decedent's death, applies whether or not the gift is included in the gross estate under § 2035(a). See Rev.Rul. 81–229, 1981–2 C.B. 176. The computation of the three-year period is different under § 2035(b) than the computation of other periods in the tax law. For general tax purposes, the clock starts running the day *after* a specified date or event. For example, § 6501(a) requires that tax be assessed "within 3 years after the return was filed"— the statute of limitations on an income tax return filed on April 15, 2009 thus begins running on April 16, 2009, and the tax can be assessed up to and including April 15, 2012. In contrast, the § 2035(b) clock starts running *on* the specified date or event: § 2035(b) requires that gift taxes be included in the estate on any gifts made by the decedent or his or her spouse "during the 3–year period ending on the date of the decedent's death." The § 2035(b) clock thus begins running on April 15, 2009 with respect to a gift made on that date, and the gift tax is included in the estate of a decedent who dies up to and including April 14, 2012. See Tech.Adv. Mem. 200432016 (Mar. 10, 2004).

The purpose of this gross-up rule is to eliminate "any incentive to make death-bed transfers to remove an amount equal to the gift taxes from the transfer tax base." Staff of Joint Comm. on Tax'n, 94th Cong., 2d Sess., General Explanation of the Tax Reform Act of 1976, at 529. This incentive otherwise would exist because the gift tax is imposed on a tax-exclusive basis while the estate tax is imposed on a tax-inclusive basis. See p. 51.

The simplest application of this gross-up rule occurs in the case of an unmarried decedent who uses her own funds both to make the gift and to pay the gift tax within three years of death. For example, assume A has a terminal illness, is in the 50% estate and gift tax bracket, and has $1,200 she would like to use to fund a gift to B. Absent § 2035(b), prior to her death A could give away $800 to B and use the remaining $400 to pay the gift tax. In contrast, if A keeps the $1,200 until her death, the estate would pay $600 in estate tax, leaving only $600 to pass to B ($200 less than in the non–§ 2035(b) gift example). Section 2035(b) puts the gift scenario on a par with the bequest scenario. Thus, if A dies within three years of making the $800 gift, the $400 of gift tax paid is included in her estate, resulting in a $200 estate tax. The aggregate transfer tax in this § 2035(b) scenario is $600 ($400 gift tax plus $200 estate tax), the same as in the bequest scenario.

The gross-up rule also applies to gift tax paid by a married decedent (or the decedent's estate) on gifts made within three years of death, regardless of whether the gifts were made by the decedent or by the decedent's spouse. Where spouses split gifts under § 2513 (see p. 638), and thus each spouse is jointly and severally liable for the entire gift tax, the deceased spouse's payment of gift tax is subject to § 2035(b). But where the surviving spouse makes a gift which is not split, is the decedent-spouse's payment of the gift tax subject to the gross-up rule, or is it instead treated as a gift to the surviving spouse not subject to § 2035(b)?

Technical Advice Memorandum 9729005

(Apr. 9, 1997).

ISSUE:

For purposes of § 2035([b]) of the Internal Revenue Code, did the Decedent pay gift taxes on transfers made by the Decedent or his Spouse during the three-year period ending on the date of his death?

CONCLUSION:

For purposes of § 2035([b]), the Decedent paid gift taxes in the amount of $1,415,732 on transfers made by the Decedent and his Spouse during the three-year period ending on the date of his death.

FACTS:

The Decedent and the Spouse lived in a community property state. On September 2, 1992, the Decedent and the Spouse created an irrevocable trust (Trust) for the benefit of four individuals. Three of the individuals are children of the Decedent from a prior marriage, and one of the individuals is the child of the Decedent and the Spouse. Article FIRST states: "Trustors hereby declare that they have transferred and delivered to the Trustee, in trust, the sum of * * * $3,102,000 * * *." On the following day, the Decedent gave the Spouse a check for $3,102,000. The check was drawn against funds held in an account that was separate property of the Decedent. The Spouse deposited the check in her personal account. Two days after creating Trust, on September 4, 1992, the Spouse wrote a check for the same amount ($3,102,000) and delivered the check to the trustees. During 1992, the Decedent also made gifts of separate property to two of his children in the amount of $1,311,000.

The September 3, 1992, transfer was treated by the Decedent, although not reflected on the Decedent's gift tax return, as a gift to Spouse. The Spouse characterized the September 4, 1992, transfer as a gift to the Trust by the Spouse. The Decedent and the Spouse elected to split the Decedent's $1,311,000 gift and the Spouse's $3,102,000 gift. As a consequence of the elections, each owed $707,866 in gift taxes; and the combined liability was $1,415,732.

On April 13, 1993, the Decedent gave the Spouse two checks that totaled $1,415,732. The checks were again drawn from an account that was the Decedent's separate property. The Spouse deposited the checks in her personal account. On April 14, 1993, the Spouse wrote two separate checks for $707,866 (total amount $1,415,732) payable to the Internal Revenue Service. Decedent died six months later on October 14, 1993.

Prior to receiving the checks from the Decedent on April 13, 1993, the Spouse owned insufficient assets to pay her gift tax liability. Despite living in a community property state, nearly all of the marital assets were owned by the Decedent as separate property.

LAW AND ANALYSIS:

* * * The estate argues that each transfer from the Decedent to the Spouse was a completed gift when the checks were honored by the Decedent's bank. The Spouse had complete freedom to do what she wanted with the money but chose to use the cash from the first transfer to fund the trust and the cash from the second transfer to pay the gift taxes. Because the gift taxes were paid with checks drawn on the Spouse's account, the estate argues that the Decedent did not pay any gift tax within the meaning of § 2035([b]). We do not agree.

The provisions of § 2035([b]) were added to the Code when the single unified rate schedule for gift and estate taxes was adopted as part of the Tax Reform Act of 1976. The unified rate schedule is a progressive schedule that is based on an individual's cumulative lifetime and deathtime transfers. The unified rate schedule thus eliminated the preferential rates provided under prior law for lifetime transfers so that lifetime and deathtime transfers would be taxed comparably.

As part of this unified approach to gift and estate taxes, § 2035([b]) was added to provide that the amount of gift tax paid with respect to transfers made within three years of a decedent's death is includible in the decedent's gross estate. According to the legislative history of this provision:

> This "gross-up" rule for gift taxes eliminates any incentive to make deathbed transfers to remove an amount equal to the gift taxes from the transfer tax base. The amount of gift tax subject to this rule would include tax paid by the decedent or his estate on any gift made by the decedent or his spouse after December 31, 1976. It would not, however, include any gift tax paid by the spouse on a gift made by the decedent within 3 years of death which is treated as made one-half by the spouse, since the spouse's payment of such tax would not reduce the decedent's estate at the time of death.

H.R. Rep. No. 1380, 94th Cong., 2d Sess. 14 (1976) * * *.

In the present situation, there is no dispute that the cash used to pay the gift taxes was originally derived from the Decedent's separate property. Thus, if the Decedent had written the checks directly to the Internal Revenue Service for the gift taxes, the amount of those checks would have been includible in his gross estate under § 2035([b]) because he died six months later. The only question is whether the Decedent could avoid the application of § 2035([b]) by running the payment through the Spouse's separate checking account.

It is a well established legal principle that the form of a transaction will be recognized for federal tax purposes only if it comports with the substance of the transaction. * * *

On September 2, 1992, the Decedent and the Spouse executed the trust agreement which stated in the First Article that they had transferred $3,102,000 to the Trust. The Trust was for the benefit of the Decedent's three children from his prior marriage and the one child of the Decedent and the Spouse. Based on the facts, it is clear that the Decedent transferred $3,102,000 to the Spouse on September 3, 1992, with the understanding that she would use that money to fund the Trust that they had created and purportedly funded the previous day. The Spouse in fact used all the money for that purpose by transferring it to the Trust the next day, September 4, 1992.

Similar transactions took place the following April when it came time to pay the gift taxes due on the gifts made during the previous year. On April 13, 1993, the Decedent wrote two checks payable to the Spouse in the exact amount necessary to pay his and her federal gift tax liabilities assuming that they agreed to split all the gifts made the previous year. On April 14, 1993, the Decedent and the Spouse filed gift tax returns agreeing to split the gifts, and the Spouse wrote two checks to the Internal Revenue Service using the funds the Decedent had transferred to her the day before. Apart from the money transferred to her by the Decedent, the Spouse had no other resources with which to pay her gift tax liability. Based on the facts, it is clear that the Decedent transferred the money to the Spouse with the understanding that the Spouse would use it to pay their gift tax liabilities.

In the present situation, the Decedent transferred to the Spouse the exact amount of cash needed to pay the gift taxes due on the Decedent's and the Spouse's returns. The only discernable purpose for this transaction was to reduce the Decedent's gross estate by the amount of the gift taxes paid. Thus, by running the payment through the Spouse's bank account, the Decedent attempted to do indirectly what he could not do directly. In substance, the Decedent paid gift taxes in the amount of $1,415,732 on gifts made by the Decedent and the Spouse during the three-year period ending on the date of the Decedent's death. The Decedent's gross estate, therefore, is increased by the amount of these gift taxes under § 2035([b]). * * *

ILLUSTRATIVE MATERIAL

A. NET GIFTS

Consider the application of § 2035(b) to a net gift made within three years of death. Assume A transfers to B property worth $100 with the requirement that B pay the gift tax of $30. Under the net gift rule, A has received consideration of $30 for the transfer and therefore has made a gift of $70. Is any amount brought back into A's estate if the transfer is made within three years of A's death? Does the phrase "tax paid * * * by the decedent" include "tax payable by the decedent"? In the following case, gift tax paid by the donee was included in the donor's gross estate under the predecessor to § 2035(b) on the ground that the donee of a net gift is a mere conduit for payment of the donor's gift tax liability.

Estate of Sachs v. Commissioner

88 T.C. 769 (1987).

■ COHEN, J. * * * Decedent gave 14,000 shares of Sachs Holding Company to each of three irrevocable trusts established for the benefit of his grandchildren (the trusts). Article Ninth of the Trust Instrument provided, in relevant part, that decedent's gift was "made subject to and upon the conditions * * * that the Trustees shall promptly pay, or cause to be paid, any and all gift taxes which may be found to be due to the United States because of the making of such gifts * * *."

Decedent and his wife reported the gifts as split, net gifts on gift tax returns * * *.

Pursuant to § 2035, the shares transferred to the trusts were included in decedent's gross estate at date of death value ($2,196,180) reduced by the amount of gift tax ($612,700) paid by the donee trusts. Although the gift tax paid by the trusts was not included in the gross estate, in the computation of estate tax it was deducted under § 2001(b)(2) from the tentative estate tax computed under § 2001(b)(1). In his notice of deficiency, respondent determined that the gift tax paid by the trusts is included in decedent's gross estate pursuant to § 2035([b]). * * *

Petitioners contend that § 2035([b]) does not "gross up" decedent's estate to include gift tax paid by the donee on a net gift made within 3 years of decedent's death. Petitioners maintain that gift tax paid by the donee trusts is not tax paid by "the decedent or his estate" and argue that the "concise and unambiguous" language of the statute thus dictates our decision.

Respondent contends that § 2035([b]) reaches gift tax paid by the donee of any gift included in decedent's gross estate pursuant to § 2035(a). Respondent argues that the legislative history of § 2035([b]) supports this construction of the statute.

* * * The Supreme Court has recently reaffirmed th[e] "familiar rule, that a thing may be within the letter of the statute and yet not within the statute, because not within its spirit, nor within the intention of its makers." * * *

Thus, although we are not "free * * * to twist [the Code] beyond the contours of its plain and unambiguous language in order to comport with good policy," * * * we may go beyond the literal language of the Code if reliance on that language would defeat the plain purpose of Congress. * * * Because "words do not have an immutable meaning," we have interpreted the Code in a manner contrary to its literal wording where necessary to implement clearly expressed congressional intent. Carson v. Commissioner, 71 T.C. 252, 262 (1978), affd. 641 F.2d 864 (10th Cir. 1979) * * *.

Application of the literal language of § 2035([b]) would dictate a result inconsistent with the architecture of the transfer tax system. This case thus presents circumstances "plainly at variance with the policy of the legislation as a whole" that warrant our search for unequivocal evidence of the purpose of § 2035([b]). * * *

The 1976 Tax Reform Act * * * did much to reduce the disparity of treatment between lifetime gifts and transfers at death. The Act established a unified cumulative rate schedule and a unified credit to replace the separate rate schedules and exemptions of prior law. * * *

The 1976 Act also sharpened the distinction between lifetime gifts and "deathbed" gifts, i.e., gifts made within 3 years of the taxpayer's demise. * * *

Congress carefully distinguished "deathbed" gifts from other lifetime gifts because, although the 1976 Act reduced the disparity of treatment between gifts and transfers at death, the Act retained several provisions favoring lifetime gifts. * * * The annual gift tax exclusion of $3,000 per donee was retained. Donors of lifetime gifts continued to avoid tax on appreciation that might accrue between the date of a gift and the date of the taxpayer's death. The 1976 Act also left undisturbed prior law under which funds used to pay gift tax are not included in the transfer tax base. * * *

The provisions that favor other lifetime gifts are not generally applicable to gifts made within 3 years of death. Although the annual gift tax exclusion of $3,000 per donee is available to the taxpayer in the year of gift, the benefit of the exclusion is in many cases eliminated by § 2035, which can bring the ENTIRE amount of the taxable deathbed gift into the estate tax base. Section 2035(a) also eliminates the possibility of avoiding tax on appreciation that might accrue between the date of gift and the date of death; gifts are included in the gross estate at date of death value. Section 2035([b]) includes in the tax base funds used by the donor or his estate to pay the gift tax.

Insistence on the literal language of § 2035([b]) would distort the framework erected by the Tax Reform Act of 1976. The Act retained some of the prior law's preferences for lifetime gifts; however, these preferences were not made available to deathbed gifts. Petitioners' construction of § 2035([b]) extends the benefit of one such preference to deathbed net gifts. Mechanical application of § 2035([b]) would completely remove from the transfer tax base all funds used to pay gift tax on such gifts. This interpretation of the statute is wholly inconsistent with Congress' goal of sharply distinguishing deathbed gifts from other gifts and eliminating the disparity of treatment between deathbed gifts and transfers at death.

The legislative history of § 2035([b]) confirms our analysis. The House Committee on Ways and Means stated:

> Since the gift tax paid on a lifetime transfer which is included in a decedent's gross estate is taken into account both as a credit against the estate tax and also as a reduction in the estate tax base, substantial

tax savings can be derived under present law by making so-called "deathbed gifts" even though the transfer is subject to both taxes. To eliminate this tax avoidance technique, the committee believes that the gift tax paid on transfers made within 3 years of death SHOULD IN ALL CASES be included in the decedent's gross estate. This "gross-up" rule will eliminate any incentive to make deathbed transfers to remove an amount equal to the gift taxes from the transfer tax base. * * *

Our analysis is also consistent with the Supreme Court's holding in Diedrich v. Commissioner, 457 U.S. 191 (1982). In *Diedrich*, the Court held that a donor's gross income includes the excess of gift tax paid by the donee over the donor's basis in the given property. The Court noted that the donor is liable for payment of gift tax and held that * * * relief of the donor's liability to the Government must be treated as indirect income. * * * In this case, as in *Diedrich*, * * * the substance of decedent's transaction dictates our decision. Decedent was primarily liable for payment of the gift tax. As donor of a net gift, he may be deemed to have paid the tax by ordering the donee to pay it over to the Internal Revenue Service on his behalf in satisfaction of his gift tax liability. Decedent gave property worth $2,399,044 to the trusts. Because the trusts paid gift tax in the amount of $612,700, decedent and his wife reported the three net gifts at an aggregate value of $1,786,340 (sic). The funds used to pay the gift tax were thus excluded from the transfer tax base pursuant to § 2512(a). When decedent died, the shares transferred to the trusts were included in his estate at date of death value reduced by the amount of gift tax paid by the donee trusts. But for § 2035([b]), $612,700 transferred within 3 years of decedent's death would escape the transfer tax system altogether.

Section 2035([b]) speaks of gift taxes "paid * * * by the decedent or his estate" rather than gift taxes "paid" without modification because payment of tax on gifts described in § 2035(a) does not always remove funds from the transfer tax base. * * * Although the language selected for this purpose does not, in isolation, describe net deathbed gifts, our analysis of § 2035([b]), its legislative history, and the framework erected by the 1976 Act persuades us that Congress did not intend to distinguish net deathbed gifts from other deathbed gifts. * * *

■ HAMBLEN, J., concurring: I concur with the majority opinion and think it appropriate to respond to Judge Chabot's concurring and dissenting opinion as to the § 2035 issue in that it fails to recognize that a net gift is merely a conduit for the payment of the donor-decedent's tax liability. The net gift concept is a gift made on condition that the donee or a third party pay the tax imposed on the donor of the gift. Consequently, when the donee or other party pays the tax, it simply is an indirect payment by the donor which was reserved as a condition of the gift. As such, the tax paid should be included in the gross-up. Overall Congressional intent reflected in the structure of the estate tax provisions of the Revenue Act of 1976 would be frustrated otherwise and a loophole would be created. * * *

Indeed, if the majority opinion has a fault it is in devoting too much attention to the charge that our rationale departs from the statute. I believe we are simply adhering to the elementary principle of not exalting form over substance. In any realistic view, the gift tax at issue was paid by the donor and, therefore, falls squarely within the statutory language of § 2035([b]). * * *

■ CHABOT, J., concurring and dissenting: * * * I would hold for petitioner that the statute provides the answer—no gross-up since the gift tax was not paid by decedent or petitioner. The statute should control over the Congress' unclear intent. * * *

ILLUSTRATIVE MATERIAL

A.   SUBSEQUENT DEVELOPMENTS

On appeal, the Eighth Circuit affirmed, holding that the distinction between tax payments made by donees of net gifts and tax payments made directly by decedent-donors "has little force" after *Diedrich*: "Just as the donee's tax payment must be included in the donor's taxable income, a donee's tax payment (on a gift made within three years of the donor's death) is an includable part of the donor's gross estate under § 2035([b])." Estate of Sachs v. Commissioner, 856 F.2d 1158, 1164 (8th Cir.1988). The Eighth Circuit agreed with the Tax Court that "the donor of a net gift uses the donee as a conduit for the payment of his tax liability." *Id.* See also Estate of Armstrong v. United States, 277 F.3d 490 (4th Cir.2002) (refusing to apply net gift principles to reduce value of gift made within three years of death where donee's obligation to pay resulting estate tax was "highly conjectural").

B.   SECTION 2035(e)

The House Report accompanying the 1997 Act explains the impetus behind § 2035(e):

"Present Law * * *

"The value of the gross estate includes the value of any previously transferred property if the decedent retained the power to revoke the transfer (§ 2038). The gross estate also includes the value of any property with respect to which such power is relinquished during the three years before death (§ 2035). There has been significant litigation as to whether these rules require that certain transfers made from a revocable trust within three years of death be includible in the gross estate. See, e.g., Estate of Jalkut v. Commissioner, 96 T.C. 675 (1991) (transfers from revocable trust included in gross estate); McNeely v. Commissioner, 16 F.3d 303 (8th Cir. 1994) (transfers from revocable trust not includible in gross estate); Kisling v. Commissioner, 32 F.3d 1222 (8th Cir. 1994) (transfers from revocable trust not includible in gross estate).

"Reasons for Change

"The inclusion of certain property transferred during the three years before death is directed at transfers that would otherwise reduce the amount subject to estate tax by more than the amount subject to gift tax, disregarding appreciation between the times of gift and death. Because all amounts transferred from a revocable trust are subject to the gift tax, the Committee believes that inclusion of such amounts is unnecessary where the transferor has retained no power over the property transferred out of the trust. The Committee believes that clarifying these rules statutorily will lend certainty to these rules.

"Explanation of Provision

"[Section 2035(e)] codifies the rule set forth in the *McNeely* and *Kisling* cases to provide that a transfer from a revocable trust (i.e., a trust described under § 676) is treated as if made directly by the grantor. Thus, an annual exclusion gift from such a trust is not included in the gross estate. * * *

H.R. Rep. No. 148, 105th Cong., 1st Sess. 384 (1997).

C. SECTION 2035(c)(1) AND (2)

The three-year rule also applies in determining the availability of the following three statutory relief provisions, which depend on the size and composition of the gross estate: § 303, relating to redemptions of stock to pay death taxes (§ 2035(c)(1)(A)); § 2032A, relating to special valuation rules applicable to qualified real property used for farming or in some other trade or business (§ 2035(c)(1)(B)); and § 6166, granting an extension of time for the payment of estate tax attributable to certain closely-held businesses (§ 2035(c)(2)). Congress applies the three-year rule in these situations to prevent a decedent from making deathbed transfers of nonqualifying property to make her estate eligible for these special rules. See H.R. Rep. No. 201, 97th Cong., 1st Sess. 187 (1981). In addition, the family-owned business exclusion expressly applies the three-year rule. § 2033A(c)(2).

D. SECTION 2035(c)(3)

Prior to 1981, when § 2035 included in the gross estate all gifts made within three years of death, an exception protected gifts which were not required to be reported on gift tax returns (i.e., gifts to spouses sheltered by the marital deduction and gifts to other donees sheltered by the annual exclusion). Keying the exception to return filing requirements, however, created some curious results. For example, a married couple who took advantage of the gift-splitting provisions of § 2513 to transfer $26,000 tax-free to a donee was subject to former § 2035 if a spouse died within three years, even though the gift was fully excludable in computing taxable gifts, because gift-splitting must be elected on a gift tax return. See S. Rep. No. 745, 95th Cong., 2d Sess. 87 (1978). In addition, the reliance on return filing requirements produced a "cliff effect" whereby annual gifts to a donee totalling $13,000 or less were wholly excluded from the decedent's estate while gifts totalling $13,001 or more were wholly included. This principle could combine with the time-of-completion rules to yield dramatic results.

For example, in Bacchus v. United States, 86–1 U.S.T.C. ¶ 13,669 (D. N.J. 1985), when the annual exclusion was $3,000, D wrote three $3,000 checks on December 31, 1976 and three $3,000 checks to the same donees in 1977. D died in 1979. If the checks delivered in 1976 were deemed completed transfers in 1977 when presented and honored, $18,000 would be included in D's gross estate under former § 2035. On the other hand, if the 1976 checks were deemed completed gifts in 1976, nothing would be included in D's gross estate.

The District Court applied the "relation-back" doctrine adopted by the Tax Court in *Estate of Belcher*, p. 118, and held that the 1976 checks were completed gifts in that year and thus did not trigger former § 2035.

After the 1981 tax legislation, however, the exception for marital deduction and annual exclusion gifts now plays a more limited role because § 2035(c)(3) applies only for purposes of § 2035(c)(1). Yet the increase in the annual exclusion in both 1981 and 1997 raises the stakes on the completed gift issue for § 2033 purposes rather than for § 2035 purposes: a gift of a check completed before death is removed from the transfer tax base to the extent of the $13,000 inflation-adjusted annual exclusion; but if the gift is completed after death, the amount that otherwise would have qualified for the annual exclusion is included in the estate tax base under § 2033 (not § 2035). Thus, assume D writes ten checks in the amount of the annual exclusion but dies before the checks clear her bank. If these checks are deemed to be gifts completed prior to D's death, nothing is included in his estate; if the checks are deemed completed after death, $130,000 is included in D's estate. Compare Rosano v. United States, 245 F.3d 212 (2d Cir.2001) (refusing to apply "relation-back" doctrine in holding that gifts were incomplete at date of delivery of checks where donor not alive when checks paid), cert. denied, 534 U.S. 1135, 122 S.Ct. 1080 (2002) and McCarthy v. United States, 806 F.2d 129 (7th Cir. 1986) (same), with Metzger v. Commissioner, 38 F.3d 118 (4th Cir.1994) (applying "relation-back" doctrine to year-end gifts where donor alive when checks paid) and Rev.Rul. 96–56, 1996–2 C.B. 161 (same).

E.   MISCELLANEOUS PROVISIONS

Property transferred within three years of death remains subject to tax liens created by §§ 6321 through 6324B. § 2035(c)(1)(C). In addition, the three-year rule does not apply to any bona fide sale for adequate and full consideration in money or money's worth. § 2035(d).

CHAPTER 25

Disclaimers

INTRODUCTION

Section 2518 states that if a person makes a qualified disclaimer of an interest in property, the wealth transfer tax rules shall apply as though the interest "had never been transferred" to the disclaimant. The use of qualified disclaimers provides a powerful tool for engaging in post-mortem estate planning.

Qualified disclaimers may be used to account for circumstances that change after the decedent's death without incurring two transfer tax liabilities. For example, suppose that decedent's will bequeaths income-producing property to A. A disclaims the property, so that it will pass under the will's residuary clause to B, who needs more income. Without a gift tax provision for qualified disclaimers, the property would be subject to the estate tax in decedent's estate and then to the gift tax upon A's disclaimer. A would be treated as though she had received the property and then made a taxable gift to B. With a qualified disclaimer, only the estate tax applies because the property is treated as passing directly from decedent to B.

Disclaimers may also be used to reduce estate taxes. For example, decedent's children may disclaim interests in property without incurring a gift tax that will then pass to the surviving spouse and qualify for the marital deduction. See p. 572.

The following materials consider first the general scope of qualified disclaimers under § 2518. Qualified disclaimers are then considered in the context of joint tenancies and powers of appointment.

Section A. Disclaimers in General

Internal Revenue Code: § 2518

Reg. §§ 20.2518–1; 20.2518–2; 20.2518–3(a),(b) and (d).

House Ways and Means Committee Report Estate and Gift Tax Reform Act of 1976

H.Rep. 1380, 94th Cong., 2d Sess. 65–68 (1976).

Explanation of [§ 2518]

[Section 2518] provides definitive rules relating to disclaimers for purposes of the estate, gift and generation-skipping transfer taxes. If the requirements of the provision are satisfied, a refusal to accept property is to be given effect for Federal estate and gift tax purposes even if the applicable local law does not technically characterize the refusal as a "disclaimer" or if the person refusing the property was considered to have been the owner of the legal title to the property before refusing acceptance of the property. If a qualified disclaimer is made, the Federal estate, gift and generation-skipping transfer tax provisions are to apply with respect to the property interest disclaimed as if the interest had never been transferred to the person making the disclaimer.

A person making a qualified disclaimer is not to be treated as having made a gift to the person to whom the interest passes by reason of the disclaimer. In addition, the disclaimer is to be taken into account for purposes of the estate tax, charitable and marital deduction * * *. A qualified disclaimer of a general power of appointment is not to be treated as a release of the power.

Under [§ 2518] a "qualified disclaimer" means an irrevocable and unqualified refusal to accept an interest in property that satisfies four conditions. First, the refusal must be in writing. Second, the written refusal must be received by the transferor of the interest, his legal representative, or the holder of the legal title to the property not later than 9 months after the day on which the transfer creating the interest is made. However, if later, the period for making the disclaimer is not to expire in any case until 9 months after the day on which the person making the disclaimer has attained age 21. For purposes of this requirement, a transfer is considered to be made when it is treated as a completed transfer for gift tax purposes with respect to inter vivos transfers or upon the date of the decedent's death with respect to testamentary transfers.[1] Third, the person must not have accepted the interest or any of its benefits before making the disclaimer. For purposes of this requirement, the exercise of a power of appointment to any extent by the donee of the power is to be treated as an acceptance of its benefits. In addition, the acceptance of any consideration in return for making the disclaimer is to be treated as an acceptance of the benefits of the interest disclaimed. Fourth, the interest must pass [either to

---

1. [ED.: The Conference Committee Report, S. Rep. No. 94–1236. 94th Cong., 2d Sess. 623–624 (1976), explained the operation of the rule as follows:

"The conferees intend to make it clear that the 9–month period for making a disclaimer is to be determined in reference to each taxable transfer. For example, in the case of a general power of appointment where the other requirements are satisfied, the person who would be the holder of the power will have a 9–month period after the creation of the power in which to disclaim and the person to whom the property would pass by reason of the exercise or lapse of the power would have a 9–month period after a taxable exercise, etc., by the holder of the power in which to disclaim. Similarly, in the case where a lifetime transfer is included in the transferor's gross estate because he had retained an interest in the property (e.g., § 2038), the person who would receive an interest in the property during the lifetime of the grantor will have a 9–month period after the original transfer in which to disclaim and a person who would receive an interest in the property on or after the grantor's death would have a 9–month period after the grantor's death in which to disclaim if the other requirements of the provision are satisfied (e.g., that person had not accepted the interest or any of the benefits attributable to the interest before making the disclaimer)."]

the spouse of the decedent[2] or] to a person other than the person making the disclaimer as a result of the refusal to accept the property. For purposes of this requirement, the person making the disclaimer cannot ... direct the redistribution or transfer of the property to another person....[3]

Under [§ 2518], a disclaimer with respect to an undivided portion of an interest is to be treated as a qualified disclaimer of the portion of the interest if the requirements are satisfied as to the undivided portion of an interest. Also, a power with respect to property is to be treated as an interest in the property for purposes of the provisions.

ILLUSTRATIVE MATERIAL

A.   SECTION 2518

1.   "Transfers Creating the Interest"

Section 2518 applies to "transfers creating the interest" that occur after December 31, 1976. Section 2518(b) requires that the disclaimant provide a written disclaimer of a property interest to the transferor of the interest, her legal representative (the executor of the estate) or the holder of legal title to the property to which the interest relates (the trustee) within nine months of the date of the "transfer creating the interest."

In general, Reg. § 25.2518–2(c)(3) states that an inter vivos transfer qualifies as a "transfer creating the interest" when there is a completed gift for federal gift tax purposes regardless of whether a gift tax is imposed. Thus, a completed gift which is not taxable because it qualifies for the annual gift exclusion under § 2503(b) (see p. 446) constitutes a "transfer creating the interest." Similarly, Reg. § 25.2518–2(c)(3) states that a "transfer creating the interest" occurs at death when the transfer becomes irrevocable at death even if no estate tax is imposed.

There is some controversy about the treatment of a completed inter vivos transfer which is subsequently included in the donor's estate. Reg. § 25.2518–2(c)(3) states that the date of the "transfer creating the interest" is the date of the completed inter vivos gift even if the gift is subsequently included in the donor's estate. For example, if S transfers property to an irrevocable trust on January 1, 2009, income to S for life, remainder to A, the date of the transfer creating the interest in A is January 1, 2009 even though the property will be

---

2. [ED.: The Revenue Act of 1978 amended § 2518(b)(4) to provide that a qualified disclaimer may result where a surviving spouse refuses to accept all or a portion of an interest in property passing from the deceased spouse and, as a result of that refusal, the property passes, for example, to a trust in which the spouse has an income or other interest. The principal effect of the 1978 amendment is to permit a post-mortem adjustment to the amount of a marital bequest that qualifies for the marital deduction, as discussed at pages 643–44.]

3. [ED.: The Economic Recovery Tax Act of 1981 added § 2518(c)(3) to allow a disclaimant to transfer property herself where her disclaimer was ineffective under local law to transfer the property. Section 2518(c)(3) permits a disclaimant, whose disclaimer failed to result in a transfer, to transfer the property to the person who would have received it had the disclaimer resulted in an effective transfer under local law. See p. 437]

includable in the gross estate of S under § 2036. This position in the Regulation contradicts the Conference Report quoted in footnote 1 at p. 435 which states that if the original lifetime transfer was included in the donor's estate, the interest that passes on or after the donor's death is deemed created at the date of the donor's death.

2. Relation Back

When a person makes a qualified disclaimer, the disclaimed property interest is treated as though it had never been transferred to that person for purposes of the estate, gift and generation-skipping transfer tax provisions. Reg. § 25.2518–1(b). For example, if decedent bequeaths property to husband, husband disclaims, and the property then passes to children, the property will be treated as though it had passed directly from the decedent to the children.

3. Requirement That Disclaimed Property Pass "Without Any Direction" by the Disclaimant

Although § 2518 greatly reduced the role of local law in determining federal tax consequences of disclaimers, it did not eliminate it. Section 2518(b)(4) requires that a disclaimed property interest pass "without any direction" by the disclaimant to a person other than the disclaimant. This requirement means that there must be an effective passing under local law without any participation in the transfer by the disclaimant. Estate of Bennett v. Commissioner, 100 T.C. 42 (1993); Rev. Rul. 90–110, 1990–2 C.B. 209. Any action by the disclaimant, other than making the disclaimer, to help transfer the property will disqualify the disclaimer. For example, if the disclaimant has to execute a deed to transfer the disclaimed property, the execution of the deed will disqualify the disclaimer and result in two transfer taxes—an estate tax with respect to the bequest and a gift tax with respect to the subsequent transfer.

Congress enacted § 2518(c)(3) to ameliorate the adverse impact of local law on § 2518(b)(4). H. Rep. No. 201, 97th Congress 1st Session 190–191 (1981). Section 2518(c)(3) applies to disclaimers of interests created after 1981. Where local law does not automatically transfer property to a new beneficiary upon a disclaimer, § 2518(c)(3) allows the disclaimant to transfer the property to the person who would have received it had the disclaimer been effective under local law. It is important that the disclaimant make a transfer that is, itself, effective under local law within the requisite nine-month period. See *Estate of Bennett* (§ 2518(c)(3) did not apply where the disclaimants failed to make a transfer of the disclaimed property that was effective under local law); Rev. Rul. 90–110 (§ 2518(c)(3) did not apply to trustee's disclaimer of a beneficial interest on behalf of beneficiary where, under local law, the trustee, acting alone, could not make an effective transfer).

Sometimes, a state or federal statute will invalidate disclaimers in order to protect the creditors of the disclaimant. Reg. § 25.2518–1(c)(2) states that the fact that a disclaimer is voidable under creditor law by the disclaimant's creditors "has no effect" on the disclaimant's status as a qualified disclaimer. However, if the transfer is void ab initio or is in fact voided by the disclaimant's creditors, the Regulation states that the disclaimer will not be qualified.

4. Acceptance of an Interest or Any of Its Benefits

Reg. § 25.2518–2(d)(1) provides that a disclaimer is ineffective for "an interest in property if the disclaimant has accepted the interest or any of its benefits, expressly or impliedly, prior to making the disclaimer." Whether a disclaimant has accepted an interest is a matter of federal tax law. Reg. § 25.2518–2(d)(1) states that "acts indicative of acceptance include using the property or the interest in property, accepting dividends, interest, or rents from the property and directing others to act with respect to the property or interest in property."

A qualified disclaimer can be made even if under local law legal title to the property vested in the disclaiming party before the execution of a written disclaimer. Reg. § 25.2518–2(d)(1). For example, if a donor delivered 1000 shares of corporate stock to her donee on February 1, 2009, causing the shares to be registered in the donee's name on that date, the donee can subsequently disclaim the stock so long as he has not engaged in any act indicating acceptance, such as pledging the shares or accepting dividends. Reg. § 25.2518–2(d)(4) Ex. (6).

The election by a spouse to take a statutory share in decedent's estate does not constitute acceptance of benefits. The spouse may make a qualified disclaimer with respect to property in the statutory share if the election to disclaim is made within nine months of decedent's death. Rev. Rul. 90–45, 1990–1 C.B. 175.

The acceptance of any consideration in exchange for making a disclaimer is treated as an acceptance of the benefits of the entire disclaimed interest. Rev. Rul 90–45, supra. In Estate of Thompson v. Commissioner, 89 T.C. 619 (1987), rev'd on other grounds, 864 F.2d 1128 (4th Cir. 1989), the Tax Court held that a life tenant's disclaimer of her interest in farm land was not qualified when she had been paid the actuarial value of her interest by holders of the remainder interests. In Estate of Monroe v. Commissioner, 124 F.3d 699 (5th Cir. 1997), the court held that a "mere expectation" or an "implied promise" that a disclaimant will be better off executing a disclaimer does not violate the requirement that the disclaimer be unqualified. The court said that a disclaimer will be upheld despite future gifts to a disclaimant unless there was "actual bargained-for consideration for the disclaimer." The dissent argued that the majority's bargained-for consideration requirement was not supported by the Regulation and created "ample possibilities for tax evasion."

5. Disclaiming Partial Interests

A disclaimant may wish to disclaim only a portion of property. The issue is whether that disclaimed portion constitutes "an interest in property" separate from the retained portion so that the act of retaining a portion is not an acceptance of the disclaimed interest. Section 2518(c)(4) states that a "disclaimer with respect to an undivided portion of an interest . . . shall be treated as a qualified disclaimer of such portion of the interest." This language is intended to allow qualified disclaimers of a portion of the disclaimant's interest for the entire term of that interest. Treas. Reg. § 25.2518–3(b). For example, if D bequeaths 500 acres to A, A may validly disclaim 300 acres while retaining 200 acres. Reg. § 25.2518–3(d) Ex (3). A may not, however, attempt to carve out a term for which he will retain the property and disclaim the rest. For example, A cannot retain a life interest while disclaiming a remainder interest.

The regulations state that "in general each interest in property that is separately created by the transferor is treated as a separate interest." Treas. Reg. § 25.2518–3(a)(1). Thus, if D bequeaths an income interest in securities to A for life, then to B for life, with the remainder to A's estate, A can make a qualified disclaimer of the income interest or the remainder. A can also make a qualified disclaimer of an undivided portion of either interest (such as 50 percent of the life income interest). Id. A could not, however, make a qualified disclaimer of the income interest for a certain number of years since that carved-out interest had not been transferred by D and was not an undivided portion of the income interest. Consistent with this approach, the court in Walshire v. United States, 288 F.3d 342 (8th Cir. 2002), held that a disclaimer was not qualified where decedent had bequeathed a fee simple interest in property and the transferee sought to disclaim a remainder interest in the property while retaining an income interest.

It is important to ascertain that the disclaimant's separate interests have not merged under local law. Where local law merges the interests, a qualified disclaimer may be made only if there is a disclaimer of all or an undivided portion of the merged interests. For example, suppose that D makes a specific bequest of a life estate in 100 acres of real estate to A and that the remainder interest in the same real estate also passes to A under the residuary clause. Suppose further that under local law, A's interests merge to give A a fee simple interest in the real estate. A can validly disclaim an undivided portion of the 100 acres. For example, A may retain 70 acres while disclaiming 30 acres. Reg. § 25.2518–3(d) Ex. (12). A cannot, however, make a valid disclaimer of a life interest or remainder interest in the 70 acres.

As discussed at p. 437, Congress intended that § 2518(c)(3) would permit qualified disclaimers even if the disclaimer was ineffective under local law to transfer the property to the person then entitled to receive it. However, it is not clear that § 2518(c)(3) achieves parity with § 2518(b) because § 2518(c)(3) by its terms applies only to disclaimers of the transferor's "entire interest in the property." It is not clear whether this means that for § 2518(c)(3) to apply a disclaimant must disclaim all her separate interests in the property or merely all of one of her separate interests in the property.

6. Requirement That Disclaimed Property Pass to a Person Other Than Disclaimant

The requirement of § 2518(b)(4)(B) that disclaimed property pass "to a person other than the person making the disclaimer" can present significant unanticipated problems. The disclaimant has to be sure that she does not have a "right to receive such property as an heir at law, residuary beneficiary, or by any other means...." Treas. Reg. § 25.2518.2(e)(3). In Hamilton v. Commissioner, 130 T.C. 1 (2008), decedent's daughter attempted to disclaim a fee simple interest in over $6 million of property that was then transferred to a trust pursuant decedent's will. The trust would pay an annuity of 7% of the corpus' net fair market value to a charity for 20 years. At the end of 20 years, any remaining trust property would pass to daughter if she were still alive. The court held that daughter's contingent remainder interest in decedent's trust violated the requirement of § 2518(b)(4) that the disclaimed property pass to a person other than the disclaimant. The court rejected the estate's argument that daughter's disclaimer was valid for interests in the property other than the value of her contingent remainder interest. It reasoned that the contingent remainder interest was not a separate interest possessed by the daughter in the property. (See p. 438 for a discussion of disclaiming partial interests.) As a result, the court held that daughter's disclaimer of her entire interest in $6 million property was invalid.

7. Disclaimers by Persons Lacking Legal Capacity

A minor will not be deemed to have accepted an interest in property that he seeks to disclaim at age 21, if, during minority, income from that property was used by a guardian or trustee for his benefit. Reg. § 25.2518–2(d)(3) and (4) Ex. (9)–(11). Under § 2518(b)(1), a written refusal to accept an interest in property may be executed by the guardian of a person lacking capacity or the executor of the estate of an individual who was entitled while alive to receive the interest sought to be disclaimed. Reg. § 25.2518–2(b)(1).

8. Disclaimers by a Fiduciary

Where the beneficiary of a trust who is also a trustee seeks to disclaim her beneficial interest, her disclaimer will qualify so long as her prior actions with respect to the beneficial interest were solely in a fiduciary capacity and her power to make discretionary distributions to other beneficiaries of the disclaimed interest is limited by an ascertainable standard after the disclaimer. Reg. §§ 25.2518–2(d)(2) and 25.2518–2(e)(5) Ex. (12).

A trustee also may disclaim a fiduciary power if state law permits such a disclaimer to be effective. In Rev. Rul. 90–110, see p. 437, the decedent's will created a trust which permitted the trustee to invade the principal of the trust for the benefit of a grandchild. In order to qualify the bequest for the marital deduction (see p. 578), the trustee sought to disclaim this power. The IRS ruled that the disclaimer was ineffective because, under state law, the trustee could not disclaim the power without authorization in the trust instrument or court approval. See also *Estate of Bennett*, supra (trustee's disclaimer of powers did not qualify under § 2518(b) because the disclaimer was ineffective under local law).

B.   ESTATE PLANNING ASPECTS OF DISCLAIMERS

Disclaimers are frequently used in post-mortem estate planning to reduce estate taxes. Disclaimers may be very valuable in taking advantage of the alternative valuation date, (see p. 680), the special use valuation provisions (see p. 786), the marital deduction (see p. 572), the charitable contribution deduction (see p. 532) and in minimizing the generation-skipping transfer tax (see p. 669). For example, in DePaoli v. Commissioner, 62 F.3d 1259 (10th Cir. 1995), a disclaimer by decedent's child enabled property to pass to the surviving spouse and thereby qualify for the marital deduction.

Section 2518(b)(4)(A) allows a decedent's spouse to make a qualified disclaimer of property although an interest in the property will return to her without her direction. As discussed in note 2 on p. 436, this provision is intended to allow for post-mortem adjustments of marital bequests, which will in turn affect the amount of the marital deduction. The regulations limit the scope of § 2518(b)(4)(A), stating that a disclaimer is not qualified if the surviving spouse has the right after the disclaimer to direct the beneficial enjoyment of the disclaimed property in a transfer that is not subject to estate or gift tax. Treas. Reg. 25.2518–2(e)(2). The implications of this rule for post-mortem planning with respect to the marital deduction are discussed at pages 643–644.

SECTION B. DISCLAIMERS IN SITUATIONS INVOLVING JOINT TENANCIES AND POWERS OF APPOINTMENT

Notice of Proposed Rulemaking
Disclaimer of Interests and Powers

1996–2 C.B. 491.

Background

... The current regulations provide, in general, that in order to be a qualified disclaimer under section 2518, a surviving joint tenant's disclaimer of *both* an interest passing to the joint tenant on the creation of the tenancy, and the survivorship interest in the joint tenancy or tenancy by the entirety [that will pass to the survivor upon the death of the other joint tenant], must be made within 9 months after the transfer creating the tenancy....

The validity of the current regulations with respect to joint interests that are unilaterally severable has been the subject of repeated litigation. In *Kennedy v. Commissioner,* 804 F.2d 1332 (7th Cir. 1986), the court held that the surviving spouse's survivorship interest in the decedent's one-half interest in jointly held real property was created on the decedent's death since, prior to that time, the decedent could have unilaterally severed the interest and defeated the spouse's survivorship right in that interest. Accordingly, the court held that the survivorship interest could be disclaimed within 9 months of the decedent's death. The court concluded that the current regulations are invalid to the extent that they require a survivorship interest in a severable joint tenancy to be disclaimed within 9 months of the creation of the tenancy. In *Estate of Dancy v. Commissioner,* 872 F.2d 84 (4th Cir. 1989) (involving personal property), and *McDonald v. Commissioner,* 853 F.2d 1494 (8th Cir. 1988) (involving real property), the courts also held the regulations invalid....

The proposed amendments would revise the regulations to provide that, in general, if a joint tenancy may be unilaterally severed by either party, then a surviving joint tenant may disclaim the one-half survivorship interest in property held in joint tenancy with right of survivorship within 9 months of the death of the first joint tenant to die, even if the surviving joint tenant provided some or all of the consideration for the creation of the tenancy.

Treasury Decision 8744
Disclaimer of Interests and Powers

1998–1 C.B. 537.

Background

... Under the proposed regulations, the one-half survivorship interest in jointly held property that was unilaterally severable could be disclaimed within 9 months of the date of death of the first joint tenant to die. The proposed regulations did not extend the same treatment to joint interests that are not unilaterally severable (e.g., tenancies by the entirety), but the preamble invited comments on this subject.

The comments received unanimously suggested that a surviving joint tenant should be allowed to disclaim, within 9 months of the date of death of the first joint tenant to die, his or her survivorship interest in a tenancy, whether or not that tenancy is unilaterally severable. The comments noted that parties purchasing a residence often do not make an informed decision regarding whether the residence should be held as joint tenants or tenants by the entirety, and generally are not aware that the decision to take title to the property as either joint tenants with right of survivorship or tenants by the entirety will affect the ability to disclaim their interest in the property after the death of the first joint tenant to die.

Accordingly, the final regulations allow the disclaimer of jointly-held property that is not unilaterally severable on the same basis as joint property that is unilaterally severable. Thus, a surviving joint tenant may disclaim the one-half survivorship interest in property that the joint tenant held either in joint tenancy with right of survivorship or in tenancy by the entirety, within 9 months of the death of the first joint tenant to die....

ILLUSTRATIVE MATERIAL

A.   DISCLAIMERS OF JOINT TENANCIES

As discussed in the background to the Notice of Proposed Rulemaking and in Treasury Decision ("T.D.") 8744, which adopted the current regulation, the courts invalidated a prior regulation to the extent it suggested that an interest in a severable joint tenancy received by the surviving tenant as the result of the death of the deceased tenant could only be validly disclaimed within 9 months of the joint tenancy's creation. Treasury issued the existing regulation, Reg. § 25.2518–2(c)(4)(i), in T.D. 8744. It states that a surviving tenant in a joint tenancy is permitted to make a qualified disclaimer within 9 months of the deceased joint tenant's death with respect to the survivorship interest regardless of whether the tenancy could have been severed unilaterally by either owner. Reg. § 25.2518–2(c)(4)(i). Note that the Regulation draws no distinction between a severable tenancy and one which may not be severed. The Background in T.D. 8744, quoted above, explains that "parties purchasing a residence * * * generally are not aware that the decision to take title to the property as either joint tenants with right of survivorship or tenants by the entirety will affect the ability to disclaim their interest in the property after the death of the first joint tenant to die.'' T.D. 8744 (Dec. 30, 1997).

B.   COMMUNITY PROPERTY

The Regulations treat the transfer of a decreased spouse's community property interest to the surviving spouse as occurring at the date of death. Reg. § 25.2518–2(c)(5) Ex. 11.

C.   ACCEPTANCE BY JOINT TENANTS

As discussed at p. 438, the acceptance of any benefits associated with a property interest precludes a qualified disclaimer. § 2518(b)(3). Suppose that two persons live in the same home which they hold as joint tenants. One person dies and the surviving joint tenant continues to live in the residence prior to her disclaimer. Reg. § 25.2518–2(d)(1) states that her continued occupancy of the residence prior to her disclaimer will not disqualify her disclaimer. Similarly, in Delaune v. United States, 143 F.3d 995, 1005 (5th Cir. 1998), the court held that taxpayer's use of her share of funds held in a joint community property account with her husband did not constitute acceptance of her husband's share, which she had disclaimed.

D.   POWERS OF APPOINTMENT

Although the release of a general power of appointment is deemed to be the exercise of the power, a qualified disclaimer of a general power of appointment is not considered a release of the power for purposes of §§ 2041 and 2514. Reg. § 20.2041–3(d)(6). See § 2518(a) and (c)(2). A person who is given a general power of appointment has nine months to disclaim it. Thus, for example, if A gives B a general power of appointment over property, B may validly disclaim that general power within nine months and B's qualified disclaimer will not constitute a release of the power.

A person obtaining a property interest as the result of the exercise or lapse of a general power may disclaim such property interest within a nine-month period of such exercise or lapse. Reg. § 25.2518–2(c)(3).

The holder of a special power of appointment also has a nine-month period after creation of the power to disclaim the power. However, in contrast to the situation involving the exercise or lapse of a general power, persons receiving property as a result of the exercise or lapse of a special power must disclaim the property within nine-months of the creation of the special power. Id. This rule for special powers is a trap for the unwary and suggests the importance of having the special power holder consult the transferee before exercising the power.

SECTION C.   POLICY ASPECTS OF DISCLAIMERS

The American Law Institute, in its 1968 estate and gift tax recommendations, proposed a somewhat broader disclaimer rule than was adopted by Congress in § 2518. Under the ALI recommendations, a disclaiming party would have been permitted to direct the disclaimed property to a recipient of his own choice if the dispositive instrument failed to provide directions as to where a disclaimed interest would go. Section 2518(b)(4), except where § 2518(c)(3) is applicable, imposes a gift tax on the disclaiming party in such a case. In other respects the ALI recommendations generally paralleled the approach adopted in § 2518.

From a tax policy standpoint, did Congress move in the proper direction by liberalizing the disclaimer rules, or instead should the existing rules have been tightened or eliminated? Compare the following cases. *Case 1*: A by will leaves nothing to B and $200,000 to C, B and C each having $100,000 estates prior to A's death. *Case 2*: Before his death A asked B whether he desired $100,000, and B responded, "No, leave all your estate to C." *Case 3*: A by will leaves $100,000 to B and $100,000 to C; after five years, B decides he does not need his $100,000 bequest and makes a gift in that amount to C. *Case 4*: The same as Case 3 except that immediately after A's death, B effectively disclaims his $100,000 bequest and, pursuant to A's will, the $100,000 goes to C. There plainly is no gift by B in Cases 1 or 2; equally clearly B made a gift in Case 3. The disclaimer rules assume that Case 4 is more like Cases 1 and 2 than Case 3, but is it clear that this is so? In Case 1, B's estate remains at $100,000 and no action on his part affects that fact. But in Case 3 B's action has transferred $100,000 to C, thus invoking the gift tax. In Cases 2 and 4, B's action in conjunction with A's effected a $100,000 transfer to C, yet no gift tax results. If one assumes that no gift should result in Case 2, what weight should be given to the fact B in Case 4 is given a second chance?

The ALI justified broader disclaimer rules on the basis that its recommendations would permit more flexible estate planning. Others assert that the disclaimer situation should not be subject to gift tax because the disclaiming party has not transferred the property, but instead has simply refused to accept it. The first justification does not answer the question whether the disclaimer is a "transfer"; indeed it suggests that there is a transfer, but for estate planning reasons, preferential treatment should be given to this particular form of transfer. The second justification appears merely to state the problem. Thus in Case 4 above, B can be regarded as having received the $100,000 and then transferred it back to A's estate, knowing that the funds will in fact go to C who is the object of B's bounty (as in Case 3). The only expressed Congressional purpose in enacting § 2518 was to provide "uniform" disclaimer rules. But obviously this objective could have been achieved by moving to a more restrictive rule. It appears that a case can be made for the proposition that the proper direction for tax policy to move is toward elimination of the present disclaimer exception. Further study on this issue is warranted.

PART IV

Exclusions, Deductions, and Credits Necessary to Define the Tax Base

CHAPTER 26

THE GIFT TAX ANNUAL EXCLUSION: RESOLUTION OF ADMINISTRATIVE PROBLEMS OF TAXING SMALL TRANSFERS

INTRODUCTORY NOTE

Section 2501(a) imposes a tax on "the transfer of property by gift." The tax is imposed on the "taxable gifts" made during the relevant reporting period. § 2502. Section 2503(a) defines the term "taxable gifts" as the total amount of gifts made during the calendar year, minus certain specified deductions. However, § 2503(b)(1) excludes from "taxable gifts" the first $10,000 of gifts (other than gifts of future interests) made to any one person during the calendar year.[1] Beginning in 1999, the $10,000 figure is to be adjusted for inflation in $1,000 increments. § 2503(b)(2). The inflation adjustment first took effect in 2002, when the annual exclusion increased to $11,000 and continued at that level through 2005. The annual exclusion increased to $12,000 in 2006–2008, and to $13,000 in 2009.

The annual exclusion was introduced in the gift tax as an administrative measure intended to "obviate the necessity of keeping an account of and reporting numerous small gifts and * * * to fix the amount sufficiently large to cover in most cases wedding and Christmas gifts and occasional gifts of relatively small amounts." H.R. Rep. No. 708, 72d Cong., 1st Sess. 29 (1932).[2] The annual exclusion was $5,000 from 1932–38, reduced to $4,000 for 1939–42 and to $3,000 in 1943–81, and increased to $10,000 in the Economic Recovery Tax Act of 1981 "in view of the substantial increases in price levels." H.R. Rep. No. 201, 97th Cong., 1st Sess. 193 (1981).

---

1. The exclusion is measured on an annual basis, with no carryover of unused amounts to succeeding years.

The gift tax is cumulative in its application. To determine the tax for a reporting period, the total taxable gifts made from June 6, 1932 (the date of enactment of the gift tax) to the end of the current reporting period are aggregated and a tax computed at present rates. From this is deducted the tax (computed at present rates) on the total taxable gifts made prior to the beginning of the current reporting period. The resulting amount is the gift tax for the current reporting period. For the purpose of determining the aggregate amount of taxable gifts, the annual exclusion is computed on the basis of the amount allowable in the year the gifts were made. Therefore, the amount of exclusion allowed in prior years is still important under the present tax structure.

2. The House Ways and Means Committee Report on the Estate and Gift Tax Reform Act of 1976, however, appeared to view the annual exclusion as an incentive for making lifetime transfers. H.R. Rep. No. 1380, 94th Cong., 2d Sess. 12 (1976).

The effect of the gift splitting allowed by § 2513 (discussed p. 638) is to double the value of the exclusion. Married persons in 2009 thus may exclude $26,000 of gifts annually per donee. The annual exclusion is an important estate planning tool in that it can be used, in conjunction with the gift-splitting provisions, sophisticated trusts, and deathbed transfers, to avoid transfer taxation. Moreover, as the following materials indicate, the limitation of the annual exclusion to gifts of a "present interest" has given rise to a substantial amount of litigation. This raises the question whether the annual exclusion is fulfilling its intended function of providing an administratively convenient method of dealing with small gifts.

Many of the disputes under § 2503 have dealt with the meaning of the term *"future interests"* in § 2503(b)(1). The question whether a particular transfer is a gift of a *future interest* is relevant solely to the applicability of the annual exclusion. Since the Revenue Act of 1932, the annual exclusion has been denied to gifts of future interests. The Committee Reports explained that the exclusion should be "available only insofar as the donees are ascertainable at the time of transfer, and that the exclusion must be denied in the case of future interests because of the apprehended difficulty, in many instances, of determining the number of eventual donees and the values of their respective gifts." S. Rep. No. 66B, 72d Cong., 1st Sess. 41 (1932); H.R. Rep. No. 708, 72d Cong., 1st Sess. 29 (1932). Thus, only gifts of *present interests* qualify for the annual exclusion.

The Supreme Court laid the foundation for the exclusion problem in relation to gifts in trust in Helvering v. Hutchings, 312 U.S. 393 (1941), where it held that the individual beneficiary, and not the trustee, is the donee to whom the exclusion applies. Thus, as indicated in United States v. Pelzer, 312 U.S. 399 (1941), although the donor divests herself of ownership entirely, she is not entitled to the exclusion unless the beneficiary can receive some present enjoyment from the transferred property. The Court further explained the concept of "future interests" in Fondren v. Commissioner, 324 U.S. 18 (1945):

> "These terms are not words of art, * * * but connote the right to substantial present economic benefit. The question is of time, not when title vests, but when enjoyment begins. Whatever puts a barrier of a substantial period between the will of the beneficiary or donee now to enjoy what has been given him and that enjoyment makes the gift one of a future interest within the meaning of the regulation."

Despite the Court's attempt to settle the definition of "future interest" for tax purposes, its application continued to remain uncertain.

The 1954 Code added two new provisions designed to narrow the scope of the future interest exception and to overcome in part the formalism of prior court decisions. The first provision, § 2503(b)(1), is applicable to all gifts and to all donees. The second provision, § 2503(c), applies chiefly to gifts in trust and only where the donee beneficiary is a minor. The following materials first consider the general scope of the future interest concept under § 2503(b)(1). The materials then turn to gifts for the benefit of minors, both under § 2503(b)(1) and § 2503(c), where its application has proven to be especially difficult.

SECTION A.   PRESENT INTERESTS VERSUS FUTURE INTERESTS—IN GENERAL

Internal Revenue Code: § 2503(b)(1)

Regulations: § 25.2503–3

Maryland National Bank v. United States

609 F.2d 1078 (4th Cir. 1979).

■ BUTZNER, CIRCUIT JUDGE:

Maryland National Bank, executor of the estate of Katherine L. N. Willis, deceased, appeals the district court's denial of claims for refund of gift taxes based on the disallowance of seventeen $3,000 exclusions in both 1971 and 1972. Before her death, Mrs. Willis contended that her transfers into an inter vivos trust were in part gifts to the beneficiaries of income qualifying for the annual $3,000 per donee exclusion from taxation under § 2503(b), and she sought to value the worth of the income interests by reference to the actuarial tables of Reg. § 25.2512–9(f).[3] The district court ruled that the gifts did not qualify for exclusion, and it held that use of the actuarial tables was impermissible.[4] We affirm.

The relevant, historical facts are not in dispute. By successive assignments in 1971 and 1972, Mrs. Willis transferred her one-half interest in a partnership owning real estate into an inter vivos trust for the benefit of seventeen members of her family. The other one-half of the partnership was held in trust under the will of E. Paul Norris. The partnership property had been owned by members of these two families, Norris and Willis (descendants of a common ancestor), for over 70 years. One tract was a farm; the other was waterfront property which contained recreational facilities, including a tennis court and swimming pool. Both tracts contained rental housing. Mrs. Willis had rented one of the houses on the waterfront property for a number of years before and after placing her interest in trust. The Norris family owned and occupied rent free another dwelling on this piece of land. Despite gross receipts from rents and farming, between 1968 and 1976 the partnership produced a net income of only $774.91 in 1971. That income was not distributed to the partners. All other years showed net losses, which aggregated $42,000 for the years 1963 through 1972 and $13,000 during the period 1973–76.

---

3. [ED.: These tables have been replaced and are now published in Reg. § 20.2031–7(d)(6)]

4. The district court's opinion is reported in Willis v. United States, 450 F.Supp. 52 (D.Md. 1978).

Under the partnership agreement the partners held options on portions of the land. They also held rights of first refusal on any resale to third parties of land purchased under the options. A large portion of the waterfront property, approximately 45 acres including the recreational facilities, could not be partitioned for sale.

The Willis trust named as trustees three of the seventeen beneficiaries and directed them to disburse "the entire net income of the trust estate" at least annually among the beneficiaries in set proportions. The trustees were given broad powers, without incurring liability, to invest in or retain nonproductive assets. They were required to disburse within three years rather than reinvest the net proceeds received from any sale of the partnership's land unless the proceeds were "used to purchase an additional or increased interest in [the original holdings], whether the purchase is of the real estate directly or indirectly by purchase of an interest in a partnership or other entity holding said real estate." Thus, the trustees could not convert the unproductive real estate into other holdings. The trustees had no explicit duty to make the property generate income.

Although the parties phrase the issues somewhat differently, they agree that the district court's judgment raises two questions on appeal: (1) Did Mrs. Willis give her beneficiaries present income interests that qualify for the $3,000 exclusion from gift tax? and (2) Can the income value of the gifts be computed by use of the actuarial tables?

Only gifts of "present interests" are eligible for exclusion under § 2503(b). The parties agree that the corpus of the trust was a gift of a future interest that cannot be excluded. Therefore, the unqualified right to receive profits from the operation of the partnership's business presents the only arguable circumstance for holding that the beneficiaries received an excludable present income interest.

Mrs. Willis' executor contends that the provisions of the trust agreement are controlling. The executor insists that Mrs. Willis was entitled to the $3,000 exclusions under the statute and regulations because the trustees absolutely must disburse annually to the beneficiaries all the income from the partnership interest. In response, the government says one must probe deeper: that before the executor can rely on the disbursal clause of the trust, the executor must prove that income will be available for distribution. Lacking such proof, the government continues, the beneficiaries have only a future interest, not a present interest qualifying for exclusion within the meaning of the statute and regulations.

The Internal Revenue Code does not define either future or present interest. The Service, however, has stated that " '[f]uture interest' is a legal term, and includes reversions, remainders, and other interests or estates, whether vested or contingent, and whether or not supported by a particular interest or estate, which are limited to commence in use, possession, or enjoyment at some future date or time." Reg. § 25.2503–3(a). In contrast, a present interest is "[a]n unrestricted right to the immediate use, possession, or enjoyment of property or the income from property * * *." Reg. § 25.2503–3(b). The Supreme Court in Fondren v.

Commissioner, 324 U.S. 18, 20–21 (1945), construing these definitions, held that the distinction turns on whether the donor conferred a real and immediate benefit upon the donee:

> "[I]t is not enough to bring the exclusion into force that the donee has vested rights. In addition he must have the right presently to use, possess or enjoy the property. These terms are not words of art, like 'fee' in the law of seizin, * * * but connote the right to substantial present economic benefit. The question is of time, not when title vests, but when enjoyment begins. Whatever puts the barrier of a substantial period between the will of the beneficiary or donee now to enjoy what has been given him and that enjoyment makes the gift one of a future interest within the meaning of the regulation."

The Internal Revenue Code's "present interest" differs from the technical concept of a present estate for life or a term of years, because even a vested interest may be considered a "future interest" for gift tax purposes if the donee gets no immediate use, possession, or enjoyment of the property. The donor is entitled to the exclusion only if he has conferred on the donee "the right to substantial present economic benefit." 324 U.S. at 20.

These principles are exemplified by Commissioner v. Disston, 325 U.S. 442 (1945). There the trust had income, but it placed such limitations on disbursement that the Court concluded that only a future interest was created. It was in that context that the Court explained:

> In the absence of some indication from the face of the trust or surrounding circumstances that a steady flow of some ascertainable portion of income to the [beneficiary] would be required, there is no basis for a conclusion that there is a gift of anything other than for the future. The taxpayer claiming the exclusion must assume the burden of showing that the value of what he claims is other than a future interest. 325 U.S. at 449.

The absence of a steady flow of ascertainable income to the beneficiary can result just as surely from a lack of any prospect of income as it can from restrictions on the trustees' power to disburse income. In either event the result is the same, and the exclusion should be denied because no present interest was conveyed. *Disston* places a dual burden on the taxpayer—the first is implicit, the second explicit. The taxpayer must show that the trust will receive income, and, second, that some ascertainable portion of the income will flow steadily to the beneficiary.

Application of these principles to the facts of this case presents little difficulty. The executor has failed to prove that the partnership has produced any income for distribution to the beneficiaries, that steps have been taken to eliminate the losses it has sustained annually, or that there will be any income in the foreseeable future. Moreover, the trust authorizes the trustees to hold this unproductive property, and it bars them from reinvesting for more than three years the proceeds from the sale of partnership real estate, which is the trust's only significant asset, into stocks, bonds, or other real estate to generate income. In sum, neither the circumstances of the case nor the provisions of the trust realistically establish that the beneficiaries actually will receive a steady flow of income.

The executor, however, urges that this hiatus in the proof can be filled by use of the actuarial tables, which calculate the present value of an estate for a term of years by assuming a prescribed rate of return on the corpus. * * * It is undisputed that if use of the tables is permissible, the present worth of each beneficiary's interest would exceed $3,000.

The tables are appropriate only when there is proof that some income will be received by the trust beneficiaries. "Where the property may yield no income at all * * * the tables are not applicable." Elise McK. Morgan, 42 T.C. 1080, 1088 (1964), aff'd, 353 F.2d 209 (4th Cir. 1965). The tables are designed to calculate the value of a present interest, not create it. Indeed, even if it is assumed that the disbursal clause of the trust standing alone is facially sufficient to create a present interest, the uncertainty that the beneficiaries will receive income precludes exclusion, whether or not resort is had to the tables. * * * Although the Willis trust gave the beneficiaries an unconditional right to receive income, bestowing this right did not of itself create a present interest. Without any prospect of income, the bare right to receive income was illusory, and all that characterized the gift was the future enjoyment of the corpus.

Rosen v. Commissioner, 397 F.2d 245 (4th Cir.1968), upon which the executor primarily relies, is readily distinguishable. In that case, the evidence disclosed, and the government acknowledged, that a gift in trust of publicly traded corporate stock conferred a present interest, even though the stock had never paid dividends. The corporation was a profitable enterprise, and it had retained its earnings for growth. The trustees intended to hold the stock, although they had authority to sell, because they anticipated that dividends would be paid in the future and the stock would enhance in value. The income component of the gift was currently reflected by the stock's growth. Pointing out that the present income interest had value, we concluded that use of the tables would not "result in an 'unrealistic and unreasonable' valuation." 397 F.2d at 247.

Unlike the corporation in *Rosen*, the Willis partnership was not a profitable enterprise. It consistently operated at a loss. The executor's use of the tables if allowed, would create an income value from assets that have never shown any capacity to produce income for the trust. Use of the tables under these circumstances would convert a portion of the future interest into a present interest by a simple computation. This legerdemain would surely transgress the statutory ban on the exclusion of future interests.

Accordingly, we conclude that Mrs. Willis' gift did not create a present interest that qualified for exclusion from the gift tax. We also conclude that even if a present interest were created by the bare language of the trust agreement, the executor's inability to prove the probability of income forecloses reliance on the actuarial tables.

Affirmed.

■ K. K. HALL CIRCUIT JUDGE, dissenting:

I respectfully dissent. The only issue in this appeal is whether a gift of the present right to receive all income produced from valuable trust property, which historically has produced no income, can qualify the donor taxpayer for a per donee gift tax exclusion under § 2503(b). The majority holds it does not, absent some undefined proof by taxpayer that money will flow to the donees in the future, where none would have flowed in the past.

This holding is contrary to the rule of Rosen v. Commissioner, 397 F.2d 245 (4th Cir.1968), where we held that a bona fide right of income from valuable property qualifies for the exclusion regardless of its past earnings. Here, the right is given, the underlying asset is very valuable and we should apply the actuarial value set forth in the Commissioner's tables. Reg. § 25.2512–9.[5]

The gift here of family-controlled assets is similar to the gift of dividends in a family-controlled corporation which we considered in *Rosen*. There, no dividends had ever been voted, and the corporation's income was accumulated for investment by the family directors, to increase the value of its stock. As in the case of the proverbial "ugly widow" who "everybody knows" will never remarry, the Commissioner argued that no dividend would ever be voted in the future since the corporation would continue to be family-controlled and ever directed toward the investment rather than distribution of income.

In this case the trust asset is valuable real property which steadily appreciates in value each year it is held without sale. It is valuable for multiple dwelling residential development; however, at the time of the gift, it was used as a family rental estate and farming operation which together did not produce enough income to meet expenses. The property produced income year after year, unlike in *Rosen*, but it never produced a distributable profit. If the business use of the property by the trustees were to change, its profit potential would change. If a higher yielding asset were substituted for the real property, the income potential would change.

Rosen teaches that we should not second-guess how trustees will elect to manage valuable trust assets, nor should we attempt to predict the future income of those assets on a case-by-case basis. Instead, we should turn to the actuarial valuation tables promulgated by the Commissioner.

These tables are structured to set a present worth on rights of income, the amount of which will be determined in the future. The tables index these present rights to the fair market sale value of the assets rather than to their profit histories. Implicit in such an approach is that the present value of all gifts of income should be set by the use and value of the asset to

---

5. The tables apply where "the interest to be valued is the *right to receive income of property or to use nonincome-producing property*." (Emphasis added) Reg. § 25.2512–9(c). Here, the Commissioner's argument turns on a technicality since the legal basis of the gift was only a right of trust income in a partnership which owned the real estate. If the beneficiaries had been given a right of personal possession, the tables would apply by the express terms of the regulations.

any willing purchaser. Such a theoretical user would put it to its most valuable *potential* use in the marketplace.

Despite the "bright line" of this policy, the Commissioner asks us to reject it in this case. As in *Rosen*, the Commissioner argues that the value of the donee's gift as a whole is the gift of corpus, not the income from it. And since "everybody knows" the trustees will never decide to change the *use* or *kind* of trust assets to create income, we should consider the negative profit history of the asset as the "true" measure of its present worth—not its vast income potential. This analysis assumes that the present income-producing worth of the underlying asset will never change, either with changing economic conditions or from any decision of the trustees to change the asset's present use or to exchange it for one with a higher yield. *Rosen* rejected such an approach, the policy of the tables reject it, and we should reject it.

Of course, under the *Rosen* analysis, our rejection of such argument by the Commissioner does not end the case since *Rosen* allows an exception for "extraordinary circumstances," where the tables are not applicable. 397 F.2d at 248. This exception was not explained. Contrary to the majority's broad-ranging analytical undertaking, I think only in "extraordinary circumstances" can we hold the tables inapplicable—if we are to follow *Rosen*.

Because he seeks an exception to the *Rosen* rule, the Commissioner bears the burden of persuasion on the issue. On the facts before us, I think the Commissioner has not carried it because neither the restrictions of the trust nor the relationship of the trustees and beneficiaries to the trust assets are so "extraordinary" that we can hold there is absolutely *no potential for distributable income* by the trust.

Therefore, just as I would give the proverbial widow credit for her inherent value to all possible suitors, I would reverse the district court to allow the gift tax exclusion.

ILLUSTRATIVE MATERIAL

A.   PRESENT INTEREST IN NON–INCOME PRODUCING PROPERTY

For purposes of § 2503(b)(1), transfers in trust can be divided into their component parts, income and principal, and either part may constitute a present interest. As *Maryland National Bank* indicates, trust instruments often provide that all income is to be paid annually to a beneficiary or that the beneficiary may withdraw current income. In form, such trust instruments create a present interest in the beneficiary equal to the present value of the right to the current income. Nonetheless, a § 2503(b)(1) present interest exclusion may be denied upon the transfer of property to such a trust because: (1) the type of property transferred and/or the powers of the trustee over the trust corpus indicate no present benefit was intended to be created; and/or (2) even though a present interest is nominally created, the characteristics of the property transferred, when combined with the trustee's powers, render the interest incapable of valuation.

For example, in Hackl v. Commissioner, 118 T.C. 279 (2002), aff'd, 335 F.3d 664 (7th Cir.2003), husband and wife gave 16% voting and nonvoting interests in a limited liability company (LLC) to their eight children, their children's spouses, and to a trust for their twenty-five grandchildren. The Tax Court held that the gifts of the LLC units themselves, along with the right to income from the LLC units, did not constitute gifts of present interests because they did not "render[]n economic benefit presently reachable by the donees." *Id.* at 294.

The Tax Court rejected the taxpayer's contention "that when a gift takes the form of an outright transfer of an equity interest in a business or property, '[n]o further analysis is needed or justified.' To do so would be to sanction exclusions for gifts based purely on conveyancing form without probing whether the donees in fact received rights differing in any meaningful way from those that would have flowed from a traditional trust arrangement." *Id.* at 292. Because the husband, as manager of the LLC, controlled distributions and the transfers of the LLC units, the donees lacked the current use, possession, or enjoyment of the units for § 2503(b) purposes.

The Tax Court employed its "three-part test for ascertaining whether rights to income satisfy the criteria for a present interest under § 2503(b). Calder v. Commissioner, 85 T.C. [713,] 727–728 [(1985)]. The taxpayer must prove, based on surrounding circumstances and the trust agreement: '(1) That the trust will receive income, (2) that some portion of that income will flow steadily to the beneficiary, and (3) that the portion of income flowing out to the beneficiary can be ascertained.' " *Id.*; see also Maryland Natl. Bank v. United States, 609 F.2d 1078, 1080–1081 (4th Cir.1979). *Hackl*, 118 T.C. at 298. The taxpayer failed to meet this test because (1) the primary business purpose of the LLC was to acquire and manage timberland for long-term income and appreciation, not to produce immediate income—indeed, the LLC operated at a loss and did not make any distributions in the previous seven years; and (2) even if the taxpayer had shown that the LLC would generate income, the record failed to establish that any ascertainable portion of the income would flow out to the donees because distributions would be made only in the discretion of the manager-husband. As a result, the Tax Court concluded that "any economic benefit the donees may ultimately obtain from their receipt of the [LLC] units is future, not present. In other words, the economic benefit has been postponed in a manner contrary to the regulatory and judicial pronouncements establishing the meaning of a present interest gift for purposes of § 2503(b)." *Id.* at 299.

The Seventh Circuit affirmed:

"The crux of the Hackls' appeal is that the gift tax doesn't apply to a transfer if the donors give up all of their legal rights. In other words, the future interest exception to the gift tax exclusion only comes into play if the donee has gotten something less than the full bundle of legal property rights. Because the Hackls gave up all of their property rights to the shares, they think that the shares were excludable gifts within the plain meaning of § 2503(b)(1). The government, on the other hand, interprets the gift tax exclusion more narrowly. It argues that any transfer without a substantial present economic benefit is a future interest and ineligible for the gift tax exclusion.

"The Hackls' initial argument is that § 2503(b)(1) automatically allows the gift tax exclusion for their transfers. The Hackls argue that their position reflects the plain—and only—meaning of 'future interest' as used in the statute, and that the Tax Court's reliance on materials outside the statute (such as the Treasury regulation definition of future interest and case law) was not only unnecessary, it was wrong. We disagree. Calling any tax law 'plain' is a hard row to hoe, and a number of cases * * * have looked beyond the language of § 2503(b)(1) for guidance. * * * The Hackls do not cite any cases that actually characterize § 2503(b)(1) as plain, and the term 'future interest' is not defined in the statute itself. Furthermore, the fact that both the government and the Hackls have proposed different—yet reasonable—interpretations of the statute shows that it is ambiguous. Under these circumstances, it was appropriate for the Tax Court to look to the Treasury regulation and case law for guidance. * * *

"We previously addressed the issue of future interests for purposes of the gift tax exclusion in Stinson Estate [v. United States, 214 F.3d 846 (7th Cir.2000)]. * * * We said that the 'sole statutory distinction between present and future interests lies in the question of whether there is postponement of enjoyment of specific rights, powers or privileges which would be forthwith existent if the interest were present.' Id. at 848–49 (quoting Howe v. United States, 142 F.2d 310, 312 (7th Cir.1944)). In other words, the phrase 'present interest' connotes the right to substantial present economic benefit.

"In this case, [the LLC's] operating agreement clearly foreclosed the donees' ability to realize any substantial present economic benefit. Although the voting shares that the Hackls gave away had the same legal rights as those that they retained, [the LLC's] restrictions on the transferability of the shares meant that they were essentially without immediate value to the donees. Granted, [the] operating agreement did address the possibility that a shareholder might violate the agreement and sell his or her shares without the manager's approval. But, as the Tax Court found, the possibility that a shareholder might violate the operating agreement and sell his or her shares to a transferee who would then not have any membership or voting rights can hardly be called a substantial economic benefit. Thus, the Hackls' gifts—while outright—were not gifts of present interests.

"The Hackls protest that [the LLC] is set up like any other limited liability corporation and that its restrictions on the alienability of its shares are common in closely held companies. While that may be true, the fact that other companies operate this way does not mean that shares in such companies should automatically be considered present interests for purposes of the gift tax exclusion. * * * The onus is on the taxpayers to show that their transfers qualify for the gift tax exclusion, a burden the Hackls have not met." (666–667).

See also PLR 199905010 (Oct. 30, 1998) (gifts of limited partnership interests qualified for annual exclusion even though distributions were in sole discretion of general partners, where limited partnership interests could be assigned); TAM 9751003 (Aug. 28, 1997) (gifts of limited partnership interests did not qualify for annual exclusion where distributions were in sole discretion of general partners and limited partnership interests could not be assigned); Kalinka, Should Gifts of Limited Partnership Interests Constitute Future Interests?, 76 Taxes 12 (April 1998).

B.   TRUSTEE'S ADMINISTRATIVE POWERS

Even though a present interest exists, that interest may be rendered incapable of valuation because of the existence of powers in the trustee which render uncertain the actual receipt by the beneficiary of an ascertainable present benefit from the trust. In Fischer v. Commissioner, 288 F.2d 574 (3d Cir.1961), the settlor created a trust for his three adult daughters, transferring two parcels of real estate to the trust. The "net income" of the trust was payable quarterly in equal shares to the daughters for life, and thereafter to their issue. The term "net income" was defined in the trust instrument to mean receipts in excess of disbursements and operating expenses and amounts paid for amortization of any mortgages. The trustees were given broad powers to sell, invest in non-income producing assets, charge expenses to income or principal, borrow, and pledge the property. The real estate transferred to the trust was subject to a large mortgage and substantial operating expenses were required to be incurred. There was no evidence that the rental income from the property would in fact exceed the operating expenses plus the amounts necessary to amortize the mortgage. The court therefore held that no present interest exclusion was available for the daughters' income interests because this uncertainty rendered the income interest incapable of valuation. In addition, the powers granted to the trustee constituted powers to divert income from the beneficiaries and hence also prevented valuation with reasonable certainty.

Similarly, Rev.Rul. 77–358, 1977–2 C.B. 342, involved a trust instrument which provided annual income payments to a beneficiary for life, but required that all capital gains and losses be credited or charged to income. This direction in effect required the trustee to allocate trust income to principal to offset any capital losses and therefore rendered the income interest incapable of accurate determination.

On the other hand, normal trustee powers do not run afoul of the present interest requirement even if the donee must go through various minor hurdles to obtain access to the income from the transferred property. See, e.g., Mercantile–Safe Deposit & Trust Co. v. United States, 311 F.Supp. 670 (D.Md. 1970) (trustee's discretionary power over investments and power to apportion receipts and expenses between principal and income).

C.   TRUSTEE'S POWER TO INVADE PRINCIPAL

The second sentence in § 2503(b)(1) provides that the possibility that a present interest may be diminished by the exercise of a power is of no consequence unless the interest will pass to someone other than the donee. Thus, if A creates a trust to pay the income to B annually, with the power in the trustee to invade corpus for the benefit of B, B's income interest will constitute a present interest under § 2503(b)(1). The rationale is that invasion merely accelerates B's enjoyment of the principal as well as the income. On the other hand, if the trustee can invade the principal for the benefit of persons in addition to B, then B's income interest will not constitute a present interest under § 2503(b)(1). The rationale is that there is no assurance that B will receive any of the income. See Funkhouser's Trusts v. Commissioner, 275 F.2d 245 (4th Cir.), cert. denied, 363 U.S. 804 (1960).

Suppose that the trustee's power over corpus is exercisable in favor of someone other than the income beneficiary, but the power is limited by an ascertainable standard and/or the possibility of invasion is remote. *Mercantile–Safe Deposit and Trust Co.* may indicate that the existence of an ascertainable standard will protect the status of the income interest as a present interest because it renders the income interest capable of valuation by accepted actuarial methods. See Jones v. Commissioner, 29 T.C. 200 (1957) (power to invade disregarded and annual exclusion allowed where only negligible possibility that power would be exercised).

Suppose a trust is created to pay the income to B for life, remainder to C, with the trustee empowered to invade up to one-half of the corpus for the benefit of D. Because one-half of B's income interest may be obliterated, is B's entire income interest a future interest or only one-half? Kniep v. Commissioner, 172 F.2d 755 (8th Cir.1949), indicates that the present interest exclusion is allowable as to the one-half of the corpus which may not be invaded.

D.   GIFTS TO CLASS INCLUDING AFTER–BORN CHILDREN

The annual exclusion is threatened by class gifts because the possibility of later-born members joining the class can render the gift to current members of the class incapable of valuation. For example, in Rev.Rul. 55–678, 1955–2 C.B. 389, the settlor transferred property to a trust, with income to a class of beneficiaries consisting of the settlor's children and grandchildren during his lifetime, provided that after-born members of each class would share in the trust income to the same extent as if they were living at the time the trust was created. Upon the death of the settlor, the trust would terminate with the corpus distributed to members of the class then entitled to share in trust income. The gifts of the right to share in the trust corpus constituted gifts of future interests. But the gifts of the right to share in the income during the settlor's life did constitute gifts of present interests to the members of the class living at the time the trust was created (to the extent that the present interests were capable of valuation based on sound actuarial principles). Compare Rev.Rul. 75–506, 1975–2 C.B. 375, where the grantor created a trust the income of which was to be paid in separate shares to A and B equally for life. Upon the death of either A or B, the separate shares were to be combined and all income was to be paid to the survivor. The rights of A and B to income for life constituted gifts of present interests, but the right to receive the income upon surviving the other beneficiary constituted gifts of future interests.

E.   EFFECT OF SPENDTHRIFT CLAUSE

A gift of an income interest in a trust will not constitute a future interest solely because the trust contains a "spendthrift clause" prohibiting the income beneficiary from alienating or assigning the income. See, e.g., Rev.Rul. 54–344, 1954–2 C.B. 319. In contrast, a gift of stock may constitute a future interest if there are restrictions on the sale of the stock. See, e.g., Hutchinson v. Commissioner, 47 T.C. 680 (1967) (stock subject to ten-year restriction on sale, transfer, or pledge); Rev.Rul. 76–360, 1976–2 C.B 298 (stock subject to two-year restriction on sale, with no restriction on ability to pledge stock or give it to family members).

F.   REMAINDER INTERESTS

Reg. § 25.2503–3(a) provides that " '[f]uture interests' is a legal term, and includes reversions, remainders, and other interests or estates, whether vested or contingent, and whether or not supported by a particular interest or estate, which are limited to commence in use, possession or enjoyment at some future date or time." Thus, the transfer by a remainderman of his vested remainder interest is a gift of a future interest. Rev.Rul. 54–401, 1954–2 C.B. 320. However, the gift of a remainder interest to an income beneficiary constitutes a gift of a present interest where the income and remainder interests are merged into a single fee under state law. Rev.Rul. 78–168, 1978–1 C.B. 298. However, a gift of a remainder to an income beneficiary is not treated as a gift of a present interest where either state law or the trust instrument requires the trust to terminate before the income beneficiary can obtain title to trust property. Rev.Rul. 78–272, 1978–2 C.B. 247.

G.   CONTRACTUAL RIGHTS TO FUTURE PAYMENTS

Despite the requirement that a present interest give the donee "an unrestricted right to the immediate use, possession, or enjoyment of property or the income from property," the regulations permit "such contractual rights as exist in a bond, note (though bearing no interest until maturity), or in a policy of life insurance, the obligations of which are to be discharged by payments in the future." Reg. § 25.2503–3(a). See Rev.Rul. 55–408, 1955–1 C.B. 113 ("[W]here a policy of insurance, which grants to the owner the usual incidents of ownership, including the right to change the beneficiary and the right to surrender the policy for its cash value, if any, is transferred or assigned to a donee as absolute owner, and the donee, or his guardian, is not restricted in any manner from exercising all legal incidents of ownership in the policy, by prior endorsement or otherwise, a gift of the policy and subsequent payment of premiums thereon by the donor will constitute gifts of present interests for the purpose of determining the gift tax exclusion authorized by § 2503(b) * * *."). Previously, Nashville Trust Co. v. Commissioner, 2 T.C.M. 992 (1943), had held that gifts of insurance policies having no cash values did not constitute gifts of present interests because the donor, prior to the transfer, had executed settlement options which limited the interests of the donees to future interests. Rev.Rul. 55–408 made clear that the presence or absence of a cash value is not determinative of the present interest question; it is the presence or absence of restrictions that is controlling. Why is a gift of a vested remainder interest a future interest, but the payment of premiums on a term life insurance policy (with no present realizable cash value) a gift of a present interest? Moreover, even in the case of a life insurance policy with a cash value, it would appear that only the portion of the premium attributable to the cash value itself should be a gift of a present interest with the portion of the premium attributable to the protection element of the policy treated as a gift of a future interest.

H.   GIFTS TO CORPORATIONS

Reg. § 25.2511–1(h) (Example 1) provides that "[a] transfer of property by B to a corporation generally represents gifts by B to the other individual shareholders of the corporation to the extent of their proportionate interests in the corporation." Such gifts are gifts of future interests because the donee shareholders "could possess or enjoy the [capital contribution] or income derived therefrom only upon declaration of dividends, an act which required the joint action of members of the competent corporate body and which no single shareholder could perform." Heringer v. Commissioner, 235 F.2d 149, 152 (9th Cir.1956). See also Shepherd v. Commissioner, 283 F.3d 1258 (11th Cir.2002) (gifts to general partnership constituted gifts to individual partners); Estate of Stinson v. United States, 214 F.3d 846 (7th Cir.2000) (decedent's cancellation of indebtedness owed to decedent by corporation constituted gifts to individual shareholders); Estate of Bosca v. Commissioner, 76 T.C.M. 62 (1998) (gifts to corporation constituted gifts to individual shareholders); TAM 200212006 (Nov. 20, 2001) (gifts to limited partnership constituted gifts to individual partners); FSA 200143004 (July 5, 2001) (gifts to corporation constituted gifts to individual shareholders).

Reg. § 25.2511–1(h)(1) provides an exception to this general rule under which transfers to charitable, public, or political organizations are treated as a gift to the organization as a single entity eligible for the annual exclusion. See PLR 9818042 (Jan. 18, 1998) (cash contribution to § 501(c)(7) social club qualified for annual exclusion).

I.   POWER TO DEMAND ALL OR A PORTION OF ANNUAL TRANSFERS

A trust instrument may contain a provision which grants a beneficiary the right to demand all or some portion of a donor's annual transfers to the trust. The availability of the present interest exclusion in such a situation is considered at p. 463.

J.   LEVERAGING THE ANNUAL EXCLUSION

As discussed at p. 164, taxpayers seek to maximize the number of annual exclusion gifts in a variety of ways. Courts often use substance-over-form and other doctrines to defeat attempts to manipulate the number of annual exclusion gifts. For example, in Sather v. Commissioner, 251 F.3d 1168 (8th Cir.2001), three brothers and their wives made a series of $10,000 gifts of stock in a family corporation to their three children as well as to their six nieces and nephews. Applying the reciprocal gift transfer doctrine discussed at p. 212, the Eighth Circuit held that "[t]he transfers of stock to each donor's nieces and nephews were reciprocal transfers, or cross-gifts, made in exchange for identical transfers from the nieces and nephew's parents to the donor's own children. As such, the transfers must be uncrossed and the tax code applied to the substance of the transactions. The IRS correctly determined that each donor was entitled to three $10,000 exclusions." Id. at 1176.

K.   SECTION 529 PLANS

Section 529(c)(2)(B) permits a taxpayer to take up to five years' worth of annual exclusion gifts ($65,000 at current rates) for a single-year's contribution to a qualified state-sponsored college-savings plan. These plans consist of both a pre-paid tuition plan (which permits a taxpayer to purchase tuition credits on behalf of a designated beneficiary) and a savings account plan (which permits a taxpayer to contribute to an investment account on behalf of a designated beneficiary). In both cases, earnings in the plan grow tax-free and there is no tax upon withdrawal of the funds if they are used to pay qualified higher education expenses.

SECTION B. GIFTS TO MINORS

INTRODUCTORY NOTE

The future interest problem is particularly complex in the area of gifts for the benefit of minors. This is primarily due to the question whether minors can "presently" enjoy their ownership in property despite legal disabilities that may be imposed on them by state law.

As the following materials indicate, substantial litigation has resulted from attempts by donors to qualify gifts to minor donees as present interests under § 2503(b)(1). In response to this problem, Congress in 1954 enacted § 2503(c) to provide a set of "safe harbor" rules which, if complied with, will ensure that a gift to a minor will be treated as a present interest qualifying for the annual exclusion under § 2503(b)(1). Section 2503(c) is not exclusive, however, and a gift that fails to meet its conditions nonetheless may qualify as a present interest under § 2503(b)(1). Accordingly, these materials first consider the cases and administrative decisions involving gifts to minors under § 2503(b)(1) before taking up the problems arising under the special rule of § 2503(c).

1. SECTION 2503(b)(1)

a. NON–TRUST GIFTS TO MINORS

Revenue Ruling 54–400

1954–2 C.B. 319.

Advice is requested whether a gift of shares of stock to a minor is a gift of a present or a future interest where the shares are issued in the name of a minor (1) before the appointment of a legal guardian, (2) after the appointment of a legal guardian, or (3) if no legal guardian is appointed. [The predecessor of Reg. § 25.2503–3] provides that no part of the value of a gift of a future interest may be excluded in determining the total amount of gifts made during the calendar year. "Future interests" is a legal term, and includes reversions, remainders, and other interests or estates, whether vested or contingent, and whether or not supported by a particular interest or estate, which are limited to commence in use, possession, or enjoyment at some future date or time.

An unqualified and unrestricted gift to a minor, with or without the appointment of a legal guardian, is a gift of a present interest; and disabilities placed upon minors by State statutes should not be considered decisive in determining whether such donees have the immediate enjoyment of the property or the income therefrom within the purport of the

Federal gift tax law. * * * In the case of an outright and unrestricted gift to a minor, the mere existence or non-existence of a legal guardianship does not of itself raise the question whether the gift is of a future interest. * * * It is only where delivery of the property to the guardian of a minor is accompanied by limitations upon the present use and enjoyment of the property by the donee, by way of a trust or otherwise, that the question of a future interest arises. * * *

In view of the foregoing, it is held that a gift of the type involved herein to a minor is a gift of a present interest unless the use and enjoyment of the property is in some manner limited or restricted by the terms of the donor's conveyance. The exclusion authorized by [the predecessor of § 2503(b)(1)] may be applied against such gift.

ILLUSTRATIVE MATERIAL

A. PROBLEMS IN MANAGEMENT OF GIFTS TO MINORS

Following Rev.Rul. 50–400, outright gifts of any type of property to minors will not be disqualified from present interest classification under § 2503(b)(1) simply because the donee is a minor. Gifts of certain types of property can be easily adapted to ownership by minors: e.g., United States Savings Bonds (which may be purchased and registered in the sole name of a minor and may be redeemed at the option of the minor (or the minor's parent)), cash (which may be kept in savings accounts by the parent in trust for the child), and securities (requiring no managerial control where there is no intent to dispose of them prior to majority). However, gifts of property requiring close supervision may create complications.

For example, stock brokers are reluctant to deal in gifts of stocks to minors. If the donor trades the stock originally given, which later rises in value, for one which later declines in value, the broker fears a successful suit for the difference because the minor may disavow transactions entered into during minority. The broker therefore often insists that the donor or another adult who will manage the investment become a legal guardian. Although there is usually little difficulty in securing the appointment by the state court, the guardian's investment powers are subject to state law fiduciary standards, which vary from state to state. The guardian generally must post a performance bond, secure court certification for the sale of guardianship property, and present annual or periodic accounts to the court for approval. In some states, the guardian must limit investments in securities to those contained in a statutory "legal list." The sureties on the bond also will exercise some supervisory control. Where the scrutiny of the court is less stringent, the guardian nevertheless is responsible to the minor for any loss caused by the failure to adhere to fiduciary duties.

These restrictions and limitations do not prevent the transfer to a guardian from qualifying as a § 2503(b)(1) present interest under Rev.Rul. 54–400 because they are imposed by state law and not by the terms of the donor's conveyance. In other contexts, however, the Service has noted the restrictions imposed by state law on a minor's ability to exercise ownership of property. See FSA 200220026 (Mar. 28, 2002) (Service will not enter into § 7122 closing agreement because of minor's state law disabilities in enjoying attributes of property ownership). In any event, these restrictions and limitations can be avoided by placing physical possession of property in the hands of a party designated as "custodian" of the minor. This custodianship arrangement has the effect of creating an principal-agent relationship, which is legally valid despite the minor-principal's incapacity and despite the minor's power to revoke the custodianship at any time.

A donor thus might open a bank or brokerage account for a minor in the name of a third party, transfer the pass book or other evidence of ownership to the custodian, and then clearly evidence her intention of making a present gift to the minor through a letter to him and to one of his parents, or through some other identifiable and unequivocal act. Because there would be no stated qualifications or restrictions upon the gift, and the minor, as principal, would have the present right to use, possess, or enjoy the property through his unlimited right to terminate the agency and exercise dominion over the property, the arrangement would seem to qualify for the annual exclusion under Rev.Rul. 54–400. However, the imposition of conditions on the transfer may disqualify the custodial arrangement as a present interest gift. See, e.g., Downey v. Commissioner, 11 T.C.M. 203 (1952) (opening of bank account "in trust" for minor created future interest).

B.   TRANSFERS UNDER UNIFORM GIFTS TO MINORS ACTS

To eliminate the expense, inflexibility, and impracticability of a court-created guardianship and the uncertainties of the common law custodianship arrangement, all states and the District of Columbia have enacted statutes providing for simplified ways to make gifts of certain property or securities to minor children. Under the Uniform Gifts To Minors Act and the Uniform Transfer to Minors Act, donors transfer property to a custodian (typically the donor, the donor's spouse, or a bank) with authority to use the property and the income for the minor's benefit with only minimum legal supervision. Any unexpended income and principal is payable to the minor at age 21 (or, if the minor dies before attaining age 21, to the minor's estate). The Service has ruled that these gifts qualify as gifts of present interests. Rev.Rul. 59–357, 1959–2 C.B. 212. See also Rev.Rul. 73–287, 1973–2 C.B. 321 (such gifts continue to qualify as gifts of present interests where state reduces age of majority from 21 to 18). It is important to remember, however, that where a parent acts as custodian, the gift may be includible in the parent's gross estate under § 2036, p. 222, § 2038, p. 260, or § 2041, p. 369.

b.   GIFTS IN TRUST FOR MINORS

Crummey v. Commissioner

397 F.2d 82 (9th Cir. 1968).

■ Byrne, District Judge:

[In 1962, petitioners Mr. and Mrs. Crummey created an irrevocable trust for the benefit of their four children. Two of the children were minors under California law. The trust was initially funded with $50, and petitioners each made additional contributions of approximately $54,000 in 1962 and $13,000 in 1963. Petitioners each claimed the benefit of the then–$3,000 annual exclusion for gifts of present interests.] * * *

The Commissioner of Internal Revenue determined that each of the petitioners was entitled to only one $3,000 exclusion for each year. This determination was based upon the Commissioner's belief that the portion of the gifts in trust for the children under the age of 21 were "future interests" which are disallowed under § 2503(b). The taxpayers contested the determination of a deficiency in the Tax Court. [The Tax Court upheld the annual exclusion for the gifts to the adult children (Janet and John), but disallowed the exclusion for gifts to the minor children (David and Mark)]. * * *

The key provision of the trust agreement is the "demand" provision which states:

> " * * * With respect to such additions, each child * * * may demand at any time (up to and including December 31 of the year in which a transfer to his or her Trust has been made) the sum of Four Thousand Dollars ($4,000.00) or the amount of the transfer from each donor, whichever is less, payable in cash immediately upon receipt by the Trustee of the demand in writing and in any event, not later than December 31 in the year in which such transfer was made. Such payment shall be made from the gift of that donor for that year. If a child is a minor at the time of such gift of that donor for that year, or fails in legal capacity for any reason, the child's guardian may make such demand on behalf of the child. The property received pursuant to the demand shall be held by the guardian for the benefit and use of the child. (emphasis supplied)"

The whole question on this appeal is whether or not a present interest was given by the petitioners to their minor children so as to qualify as an exclusion under § 2503(b). * * *

It was stipulated before the Tax Court in regard to the trust and the parties thereto that at all times relevant all the minor children lived with the petitioners and no legal guardian had been appointed for them. In addition, it was agreed that all the *children* were supported by petitioners and none of them had made a demand against the trust funds or received any distribution from them.

The tax regulations define a "future interest" for the purposes of § 2503(b) as follows:

> " 'Future interests' is a legal term, and includes reversions, remainders, and other interests or estates, whether vested or contingent, and whether or not supported by a particular interest or estate, which are limited to commence in use, possession or enjoyment at some future date or time." Reg. § 25.2503–3.

This definition has been adopted by the Supreme Court. Fondren v. Commissioner, 324 U.S. 18 (1945); Commissioner v. Disston, 325 U.S. 442 (1945). In *Fondren*, the court stated that the important question is when enjoyment begins. There the court held that gifts to an irrevocable trust for the grantor's minor grandchildren were "future interests" where income was not to be paid until designated times commencing with each grandchild's 25th birthday. The trustee was authorized to spend the income or invade the corpus during the minority of the beneficiaries only if need was shown. The facts demonstrated that need had not occurred and was not likely to occur.

Neither of the parties nor the Tax Court has any disagreement with the above summarization of the basic tests. The dispute comes in attempting to narrow the definition of a future interest down to a more specific and useful form.

The Commissioner and the Tax Court both placed primary reliance on the case of Stifel v. Commissioner, 197 F.2d 107 (2d Cir.1952). In that case an irrevocable trust was involved which provided that the beneficiary, a minor, could demand any part of the funds not expended by the Trustee and, subject to such demand, the Trustee was to accumulate. The trust also provided that it could be terminated by the beneficiary or by her guardian during minority. The court held that gifts to this trust were gifts of "future interests." They relied upon *Fondren* for the proposition that they could look at circumstances as well as the trust agreement and under such circumstances it was clear that the minor could not make the demand and that no guardian had ever been appointed who could make such a demand.

The leading case relied upon by the petitioners is Kieckhefer v. Commissioner, 189 F.2d 118 (7th Cir.1951). In that case the donor set up a trust with his newly born grandson as the beneficiary. The trustee was to hold the funds unless the beneficiary or his legally appointed guardian demanded that the trust be terminated. The Commissioner urged that the grandson could not effectively make such a demand and that no guardian had been appointed. The court disregarded these factors and held that where any restrictions on use were caused by disabilities of a minor rather than by the terms of the trust, the gift was a "present interest." The court further stated that the important thing was the right to enjoy rather than the actual enjoyment of the property. * * *

Although there are certainly factual distinctions between the *Stifel* and *Kieckhefer* cases, it seems clear that the two courts took opposing positions on the way the problem of defining "future interests" should be resolved. As we read the *Stifel* case, it says that the court should look at the trust instrument, the law as to minors, and the financial and other circumstances of the parties. From this examination it is up to the court to determine whether it is likely that the minor beneficiary is to receive any present enjoyment of the property. If it is not likely, then the gift is a "future interest." At the other extreme is the holding in *Kieckhefer* which says that a gift to a minor is not a "future interest" if the only reason for a delay in enjoyment is the minority status of the donee and his consequent disabilities. The *Kieckhefer* court noted that under the terms there present, a gift to an adult would have qualified for the exclusion and they refused to discriminate against a minor. The court equated a present interest with a present right to possess, use or enjoy. The facts of the case and the court's reasoning, however, indicate that it was really equating a present interest with a present right to possess, use or enjoy except for the fact that the beneficiary was a minor. In between these two positions there is a third possibility. That possibility is that the court should determine whether the donee is legally and technically capable of immediately enjoying the property. Basically this is the test relied on by the petitioners. Under this theory, the question would be whether the donee could possibly gain immediate enjoyment and the emphasis would be on the trust instrument and the laws of the jurisdiction as to minors. It was primarily on this basis that the Tax Court decided the present case, although some examination of surrounding circumstances was apparently made. * * *

Under the provisions of this trust the income is to be accumulated and added to the corpus until each minor reaches the age of 21, unless the trustee feels in his discretion that distributions should be made to a needy beneficiary. From 21 to 35 all income is distributed to the beneficiary. After 35 the trustee again has discretion as to both income and corpus, and may distribute whatever is necessary up to the whole thereof. Aside from the actions of the trustee, the only way any beneficiary may get at the property is through the "demand" provision, quoted above.

One question raised in these proceedings is whether or not the trust prohibits a minor child from making a demand on the yearly additions to the trust. The key language from paragraph three is as follows: "If the child is a minor at the time of such gift of that donor for that year, or fails in legal capacity for any reason, the child's guardian may make such demand on behalf of the child." The Tax Court interpreted this provision in favor of the taxpayers by saying that "may" is permissive and thus that the minor child can make the demand if allowed by law, or, if not permitted by law, the guardian may do it. Although, as the Commissioner suggests, this strains the language somewhat, it does seem consistent with the obvious intent in drafting this provision. Surely, this provision was intended to give the minor beneficiary the broadest demand power available so that the gift tax exclusion would be applicable.

There is very little dispute between the parties as to the rights and disabilities of a minor accorded by the California statutes and cases. The problem comes in attempting to ascertain from these rights and disabilities the answer to the question of whether a minor may make a demand upon the trustee for a portion of the trust as provided in the trust instrument.

It is agreed that a minor in California may own property. * * * He may receive a gift. * * * A minor may demand his own funds from a bank * * *, a savings institution * * *, or a corporation * * *. A minor of the age of 14 or over has the right to secure the appointment of a guardian and one will be appointed if the court finds it "necessary or convenient." Cal.Prob.Code, § 1406 * * *.

It is further agreed that a minor cannot sue in his own name * * * and cannot appoint an agent. * * * With certain exceptions a minor can disaffirm contracts made by him during his minority. * * * A minor under the age of 18 cannot make contracts relating to real property or personal property not in his possession or control. * * *

The parent of a child may be its natural guardian, but such a guardianship is of the person of the child and not of his estate. * * *

After examining the same rights and disabilities, the petitioners, the Commissioner, and the Tax Court each arrived at a different solution to our problem. The Tax Court concentrated on the disabilities and concluded that David and Mark could not make an effective demand because they could not sue in their own name, nor appoint an agent and could disaffirm contracts. The court, however, concluded that Janet could make an effective demand because [the state statute] indirectly states that she could make contracts with regard to real and personal property.

The Commissioner concentrated on the inability to sue or appoint an agent and concluded that none of the minors had anything more than paper rights because he or she lacked the capacity to enforce the demand.

The petitioners urge that the right to acquire and hold property is the key. In the alternative they argue that the parent as a natural guardian could make the demand although it would be necessary to appoint a legal guardian to receive the property. Finally, they urge that all the minors over 14 could make a demand since they could request the appointment of a legal guardian.

The position taken by the Tax Court seems clearly untenable. The distinction drawn between David and Mark on the one hand, and Janet on the other, makes no sense. The mere fact that Janet can make certain additional contracts does not have any relevance to the question of whether she is capable of making an effective demand upon the trustee. We cannot agree with the position of the Commissioner because we do not feel that a lawsuit or the appointment of an agent is a necessary prelude to the making of a demand upon the trustee. As we visualize the hypothetical situation, the child would inform the trustee that he demanded his share of the additions up to $4,000. The trustee would petition the court for the appointment of a legal guardian and then turn the funds over to the guardian. It would also seem possible for the parent to make the demand as natural guardian. This would involve the acquisition of property for the child rather than the management of the property. It would then be necessary for a legal guardian to be appointed to take charge of the funds. The only time when the disability to sue would come into play, would be if the trustee disregarded the demand and committed a breach of trust. That would not, however, vitiate the demand.

All this is admittedly speculative since it is highly unlikely that a demand will ever be made or that if one is made, it would be made in this fashion. However, as a technical matter, we think a minor could make the demand.

Given the trust, the California law, and the circumstances in our case, it can be seen that very different results may well be achieved, depending upon the test used. Under a strict interpretation of the *Stifel* test of examining everything and determining whether there is any likelihood of present enjoyment, the gifts to minors in our case would seem to be "future interests." Although under our interpretation neither the trust nor the law technically forbid a demand by the minor, the practical difficulties of a child going through the procedures seem substantial. In addition, the surrounding facts indicate the children were well cared for and the obvious intention of the trusters was to create a long term trust. No guardian had been appointed and, except for the tax difficulties, probably never would be appointed. As a practical matter, it is likely that some, if not all, of the beneficiaries did not even know that they had any right to demand funds from the trust. They probably did not know when contributions were made to the trust or in what amounts. Even had they known, the substantial contributions were made toward the end of the year so that the time to make a demand was severely limited. Nobody had made a demand under the provision, and no distributions had been made. We think it unlikely that any demand ever would have been made. * * *

Under the general language of *Kieckhefer* which talked of the "right to enjoy," all exclusions in our case would seem to be allowable. The broader *Kieckhefer* rule which we have discussed is inapplicable on the facts of this case. That rule, as we interpret it, is that postponed enjoyment is not equivalent to a "future interest" if the postponement is solely caused by the minority of the beneficiary. In *Kieckhefer*, the income was accumulated and added to the corpus until the beneficiary reached the age of 21. At that time everything was to be turned over to him. This is all that happened unless a demand was made. In our case, on the contrary, if no demand is made in any particular year, the additions are forever removed from the uncontrolled reach of the beneficiary since, with the exception of the yearly demand provision, the only way the corpus can ever be tapped by a beneficiary, is through a distribution at the discretion of the trustee.

We decline to follow a strict reading of the *Stifel* case in our situation because we feel that the solution suggested by that case is inconsistent and unfair. It becomes arbitrary for the I.R.S. to step in and decide who is likely to make an effective demand. Under the circumstances suggested in our case, it is doubtful that any demands will be made against the trust—yet the Commissioner always allowed the exclusion as to adult beneficiaries. There is nothing to indicate that it is any more likely that John will demand funds than that any other beneficiary will do so. The only distinction is that it might be easier for him to make such a demand. Since we conclude that the demand can be made by the others, it follows that the exclusion should also apply to them. In another case we might follow the broader *Kieckhefer* rule, since it seems least arbitrary and establishes a clear standard. However, if the minors have no way of making the demand in our case, then there is more than just a postponement involved, since John could demand his share of yearly additions while the others would never have the opportunity at their shares of those additions but would be limited to taking part of any additions added subsequent to their 21st birthdays. * * *

The decision of the Tax Court denying the taxpayers' exclusions on the gifts to David and Mark Crummey is reversed. The decision of the Tax Court allowing the taxpayers' exclusions on the 1962 gift to Janet Crummey is affirmed.

Estate of Cristofani v. Commissioner

97 T.C. 74 (1991).

■ RUWE, JUDGE:

* * * The sole issue for decision is whether transfers of property to a trust, where the beneficiaries possessed the right to withdraw an amount not in excess of the § 2503(b) exclusion within 15 days of such transfers, constitute gifts of a present interest in property within the meaning of § 2503(b). * * *

[Decedent during her lifetime created a trust, with income to her two children for life, and remainder to them at her death. Decedent's five minor grandchildren had contingent remainders in the trust (they would receive the remainder only if their parent predeceased their grandparent).

Each child and grandchild was given a *Crummey* demand power exercisable within fifteen days of a contribution to the trust. The trustees (decedent's two children) could invade corpus for the benefit of the children as necessary for their "support, health, maintenance, and education." In exercising this discretion, the trustees were directed to take several factors into account, including decedent's desire to treat the "children as primary beneficiaries and the other beneficiaries of secondary importance." The trustees were required to give notice of a contribution to each trust beneficiary. Decedent funded the trust in 1984 and 1985 by conveying each year an undivided interest in rental real estate worth $70,000. Decedent did not report any gifts, claiming instead seven $10,000 annual exclusions.

The Service allowed the annual exclusion for the gifts to the children but disallowed the exclusion with respect to gifts to the grandchildren.]

In the instant case, petitioner argues that the right of decedent's grandchildren to withdraw an amount equal to the annual exclusion within 15 days after decedent's contribution of property to the Children's Trust constitutes a gift of a present interest in property, thus qualifying for a $10,000 annual exclusion for each grandchild for the years 1984 and 1985. Petitioner relies upon Crummey v. Commissioner, 397 F.2d 82 (9th Cir. 1968), revg. on this issue T.C. Memo. 1966–144. * * *

In deciding whether the minor beneficiaries received a present interest, the Ninth Circuit specifically rejected any test based upon the likelihood that the minor beneficiaries would actually receive present enjoyment of the property.[6] Instead, the court focused on the legal right of the minor

---

6. The Ninth Circuit stated:

Although under our interpretation neither the trust nor the law technically forbid a demand by the minor, the practical difficulties of a child going through

beneficiaries to demand payment from the trustee. * * * The court found that the minor beneficiaries had a legal right to make a demand upon the trustee, and allowed the settlors to claim annual exclusions, under § 2503(b), with respect to the minor trust beneficiaries.

The Ninth Circuit recognized that there was language in a prior case, Stifel v. Commissioner, 197 F.2d 107 (2d Cir.1952), affg. 17 T.C. 647 (1951), that seemed to support a different test.

> As we read the *Stifel* case, it says that the court should look at the trust instrument, the law as to minors, and the financial and other circumstances of the parties. From this examination it is up to the court to determine whether it is likely that the minor beneficiary is to receive any present enjoyment of the property. If it is not likely, then the gift is a "future interest."

As previously stated, the Ninth Circuit rejected a test based on the likelihood that an actual demand would be made. Respondent does not rely on or cite *Stifel* in his brief. We believe that the test set forth in *Crummey* * * * is the correct test.

Subsequent to the opinion in *Crummey*, respondent's revenue rulings have recognized that when a trust instrument gives a beneficiary the legal power to demand immediate possession of corpus, that power qualifies as a present interest in property. See Rev.Rul. 85–24, 1985–1 C.B. 329 * * *; Rev.Rul. 81–7, 1981–1 C.B. 474 * * *. While we recognize that revenue rulings do not constitute authority for deciding a case in this Court, * * * we mention them to show respondent's recognition that a trust beneficiary's legal right to demand immediate possession and enjoyment of trust corpus or income constitutes a present interest in property for purposes of the annual exclusion under § 2503(b). * * * We also note that respondent allowed the annual exclusions with respect to decedent's two children who possessed the same right of withdrawal as decedent's grandchildren.

In the instant case, respondent has not argued that decedent's grandchildren did not possess a legal right to withdraw corpus from the Children's Trust within 15 days following any contribution, or that such demand could have been legally resisted by the trustees. In fact, the parties have stipulated that "following a contribution to the Children's Trust, each of the grandchildren possessed the *same right of withdrawal* as * * * the withdrawal rights of Frank Cristofani and Lillian Dawson." (Emphasis

the procedures seem substantial. In addition, the surrounding facts indicate the children were well cared for and the obvious intention of the trustors was to create a long term trust. * * * As a practical matter, it is likely that some, if not all, of the beneficiaries did not even know that they had any right to demand funds from the trust. They probably did not know when contributions were made to the trust or in what amounts. Even had they known, the substantial contributions were made toward the end of the year so that the time to make a demand was severely limited. * * * We think it unlikely that any demand ever would have been made. [Crummey v. Commissioner, 397 F.2d 82, 87–88 (9th Cir. 1968).]

added.) The legal right of decedent's grandchildren to withdraw specified amounts from the trust corpus within 15 days following any contribution of property constitutes a gift of a present interest. * * *

On brief, respondent attempts to distinguish *Crummey* from the instant case. Respondent argues that in *Crummey* the trust beneficiaries not only possessed an immediate right of withdrawal, but also possessed "substantial, future economic benefits" in the trust corpus and income. Respondent emphasizes that the Children's Trust identified decedent's children as "primary beneficiaries," and that decedent's grandchildren were to be considered as "beneficiaries of secondary importance."

Generally, the beneficiaries of the trust in *Crummey* were entitled to distributions of income. Trust corpus was to be distributed to the issue of each beneficiary sometime following the beneficiary's death. * * * Aside from the discretionary actions of the trustee, the only way any beneficiary in *Crummey* could receive trust corpus was through the demand provision which allowed each beneficiary to demand up to $4,000 in the year in which a transfer to the trust was made. The Ninth Circuit observed:

> In our case * * * if no demand is made in any particular year, the additions are forever removed from the uncontrolled reach of the beneficiary since, with exception of the yearly demand provision, the only way the corpus can ever be tapped by a beneficiary, is through a distribution at the discretion of the trustee. * * *

In the instant case, the primary beneficiaries of the Children's Trust were decedent's children. Decedent's grandchildren held contingent remainder interests in the Children's Trust. Decedent's grandchildren's interests vested only in the event that their respective parent (decedent's child) predeceased decedent or failed to survive decedent by more than 120 days. We do not believe, however, that *Crummey* requires that the beneficiaries of a trust must have a vested present interest or vested remainder interest in the trust corpus or income, in order to qualify for the § 2503(b) exclusion.

As discussed in *Crummey*, the likelihood that the beneficiary will actually receive present enjoyment of the property is not the test for determining whether a present interest was received. Rather, we must examine the ability of the beneficiaries, in a legal sense, to exercise their right to withdraw trust corpus, and the trustee's right to legally resist a beneficiary's demand for payment. * * * Based upon the language of the trust instrument and stipulations of the parties, we believe that each grandchild possessed the legal right to withdraw trust corpus and that the trustees would be unable to legally resist a grandchild's withdrawal demand. We note that there was no agreement or understanding between decedent, the trustees, and the beneficiaries that the grandchildren would not exercise their withdrawal rights following a contribution to the Children's Trust.

Respondent also argues that since the grandchildren possessed only a contingent remainder interest in the Children's Trust, decedent never intended to benefit her grandchildren. Respondent contends that the only reason decedent gave her grandchildren the right to withdraw trust corpus was to obtain the benefit of the annual exclusion.

We disagree. Based upon the provisions of the Children's Trust, we believe that decedent intended to benefit her grandchildren. Their benefits, as remaindermen, were contingent upon a child of decedent's dying before decedent or failing to survive decedent by more than 120 days. We recognize that at the time decedent executed the Children's Trust, decedent's children were in good health, but this does not remove the possibility that decedent's children could have predeceased decedent.

In addition, decedent's grandchildren possessed the power to withdraw up to an amount equal to the amount allowable for the § 2503(b) exclusion. Although decedent's grandchildren never exercised their respective withdrawal rights, this does not vitiate the fact that they had the legal right to do so, within 15 days following a contribution to the Children's Trust. Events might have occurred to prompt decedent's children and grandchildren (through their guardians) to exercise their withdrawal rights. For example, either or both of decedent's children and their respective families might have suddenly and unexpectedly been faced with economic hardship; or, in the event of the insolvency of one of decedent's children, the rights of the grandchildren might have been exercised to safeguard their interest in the trust assets from their parents' creditors. In light of the provisions in decedent's trust, we fail to see how respondent can argue that decedent did not intend to benefit her grandchildren.[7]

Finally, the fact that the trust provisions were intended to obtain the benefit of the annual gift tax exclusion does not change the result. As we stated in Perkins v. Commissioner * * *,

> regardless of the petitioners' motives, or why they did what they in fact did, the legal rights in question were created by the trust instruments and could at any time thereafter be exercised. Petitioners having done what they purported to do, their tax-saving motive is irrelevant. [Perkins v. Commissioner, 27 T.C. 601, 606 (1956)]

Based upon the foregoing, we find that the grandchildren's right to withdraw an amount not to exceed the § 2503(b) exclusion, represents a present interest for purposes of § 2503(b). Accordingly, petitioner is entitled to claim annual exclusions with respect to decedent's grandchildren as

---

7. We note that the facts of the instant case are very similar to the facts that respondent was presented with in PLR 9030005 (Apr. 19, 1990), wherein A created a trust for the benefit of B, in which B was entitled to receive trust income during A's lifetime. Upon A's death, trust corpus was to be distributed to B. If B predeceased A, one-half of the corpus was to be distributed to B's children and the other one-half was to be distributed to A's children. Within 30 days of receiving notice of a contribution to corpus, both B and B's children had the power to withdraw from corpus a proportionate amount of the contribution not to exceed the § 2503(b) exclusion. Citing *Crummey*, respondent allowed A to claim annual gift exclusions for both B and B's children. Although private letter rulings are not precedent, § 6110(j)(3), they "do reveal the interpretation put upon the statute by the agency charged with the responsibility of administering the revenue laws." Hanover Bank v. Commissioner, 369 U.S. 672, 686 (1962) * * *.

a result of decedent's transfers of property to the Children's Trust in 1984 and 1985. * * *

ILLUSTRATIVE MATERIAL

A. POST–*CRISTOFANI* DEVELOPMENTS

The Service announced that it would acquiesce only in the result in *Cristofani* and that it would continue to litigate cases raising similar issues:

> "The Service does not contest annual gift tax exclusions for *Crummey* powers held by current income beneficiaries and persons with vested remainder interests. However, the Service will deny exclusions for powers held by individuals who either have no property interests in the trust except for *Crummey* powers, or hold only contingent remainder interests. To extend the gift tax benefit of *Crummey* powers to beneficiaries with interests more remote than current income or vested remainders would undermine significantly the unified system of estate and gift taxation which Congress intended, and would invite flagrant abuse in the future.

> "Although the Service will not recommend appeal of this case, we disagree with the Tax Court's sweeping interpretation of *Crummey*. Accordingly, we shall litigate other cases whose facts indicate a greater abuse of the *Crummey* power than those of *Cristofani*, preferably outside the Ninth Circuit."

A.O.D. 1992–09 (Mar. 23, 1992).

In 1996, the Service issued a harsher condemnation of the practice of giving *Crummey* demand powers to contingent beneficiaries:

> "The Service does not contest annual gift tax exclusions for *Crummey* powers where the trust instrument gives the power holders a bona fide unrestricted legal right to demand immediate possession and enjoyment of trust income or corpus. * * * Current income beneficiaries and persons with vested remainder interests have a continuing economic interest in the trust and must weigh the benefit of a present withdrawal against their long term interests. Generally, the Service will not contest annual gift tax exclusions for *Crummey* powers held by these beneficiaries.

> "In *Cristofani*, the court followed *Crummey* and held that *Crummey* does not require a trust beneficiary to have a vested present interest or vested remainder interest in order to qualify for the annual gift tax exclusion; rather, it is the legal right to withdraw that is significant. However, the Service will deny the exclusions for *Crummey* powers, regardless of the power holders' other interests in the trust, where the withdrawal rights are not in substance what they purport to be in form. * * * If the facts and circumstances of a particular case show that there was a prearranged understanding that the withdrawal right would not be exercised or that doing so would result in adverse consequences to its holder (e.g., losing other rights or gifts under the instant trust instrument or other beneficial arrangement), the creation of the withdrawal right is not a bona fide gift of a present interest in property. * * *

"Although the Service did not appeal this case, the Service disagrees with the Tax Court's sweeping interpretation of *Crummey*. To extend the benefit of the annual exclusion to illusory gifts of present interests would undermine significantly the unified system of estate and gift taxation and invite flagrant abuse of the benefit which Congress intended in enacting § 2503(b). Accordingly, the Service will continue to litigate cases whose facts indicate that the substance of the transfers was merely to obtain annual exclusions and that no bona fide gift of a present interest was intended."

A.O.D. 1996–010 (July 15, 1996).

In recent years, the Service has aggressively applied this "prearranged understanding" concept to deny annual exclusions to *Crummey* demand powers held by contingent beneficiaries. For example, TAM 9731004 (Apr. 21, 1997) denied annual exclusions for 16 *Crummey* beneficiaries who held either "a contingent interest, a remotely contingent interest, or no possible interest in any property left in the trust upon the expiration of the withdrawal rights." According to the Service:

"The fact that none of the withdrawal rights was ever exercised, even by those who had no other interests in the trusts, leads to the conclusion that as part of a prearranged understanding, all of the individuals (other than the primary beneficiary) knew their rights were paper rights only, or that exercising them would result in unfavorable consequences. There is no other logical reason why these individuals would choose not to withdraw the amount specified in each trust as a gift which would neither be includible in their income nor subject the Donor to the gift tax."

Estate of Kohlsaat v. Commissioner

73 T.C.M. 2732 (1997).

■ SWIFT, JUDGE:

* * * [T]he issue for decision is whether, in the computation of petitioner's Federal estate tax, decedent's inter vivos transfer of property to an irrevocable trust is eligible under § 2503(b) for the annual gift tax exclusion with respect to each of 16 contingent beneficiaries of the trust. * * *

On March 27, 1990, decedent formed the Lieselotte Kohlsaat Family Trust as an irrevocable trust (the trust) and transferred to the trust a commercial building owned by decedent and managed for many years by various Kohlsaat family members. At the time of decedent's transfer of the building to the trust, the building was valued at $155,000. Thereafter, no other transfers were made to the trust.

Under provisions of the trust, Beatrice Reinecke (Beatrice) and Peter Kohlsaat (Peter), decedent's two adult children, were designated as cotrustees and primary beneficiaries of the trust. Beatrice and Peter each received an interest in one-half of the corpus and income of the trust, and each received a special power to appoint the corpus of his or her one-half share of the trust to his or her children or grandchildren.

Under the trust provisions, 16 contingent remainder beneficiaries were designated. Beatrice's three children and eight grandchildren were designated as contingent remainder beneficiaries in Beatrice's one-half share of the trust, and Peter's spouse and four sons were designated as contingent remainder beneficiaries in Peter's one-half share of the trust.

Beatrice and Peter, as well as the 16 contingent beneficiaries, were each given the right—following each transfer of property to the trust—to demand from the trust an immediate distribution to them of property in an amount not to exceed the $10,000 annual gift tax exclusion under § 2503(b) that was considered to be available to each beneficiary. Each beneficiary's right to demand a distribution lapsed 30 days after a transfer of property to the trust. The guardian of any minor beneficiary was authorized to exercise the minor beneficiary's right to demand a distribution of property from the trust.

On April 2, 1990, within 6 days of decedent's transfer of the commercial building to the trust, the beneficiaries of the trust were timely notified of their rights to demand distributions of trust property of up to $10,000 each. None of the beneficiaries exercised his or her right to demand a distribution from the trust, and none of the beneficiaries requested notification of future transfers of property to the trust. * * *

On petitioner's Federal estate tax return, petitioner treated the interests of the 16 contingent beneficiaries as qualifying for 16 annual gift tax exclusions under § 2503(b) with regard to decedent's 1990 transfer of the commercial building to the trust.

On audit of petitioner's Federal estate tax return, respondent denied the above 16 annual gift tax exclusions claimed by petitioner on the grounds that the contingent beneficiaries did not hold present interests in the trust. * * *

Where trust beneficiaries, including minor and contingent beneficiaries, are given unrestricted rights to demand immediate distributions of trust property, the beneficiaries generally are treated, under § 2503(b), as possessing present interests in property. Estate of Cristofani v. Commissioner, 97 T.C. 74, 84–85 (1991); see also Crummey v. Commissioner, 397 F.2d 82, 88 (9th Cir.1968) * * *.

Respondent argues that understandings existed between decedent and the 16 contingent beneficiaries of decedent's trust to the effect that the beneficiaries would not exercise their rights to demand distributions of trust property, that these understandings negate decedent's donative intent, and that the substance-over-form doctrine should apply to deny the annual gift tax exclusions with regard to the interests held by the 16 contingent beneficiaries.

We disagree.

Pursuant to the provisions of the trust, for a 30–day period following a transfer of property to the trust, the contingent beneficiaries were given unrestricted rights to legally demand immediate distribution to them of trust property. The evidence does not establish that any understandings existed between decedent and the beneficiaries that the contingent beneficiaries would not exercise those rights following a transfer of property to the trust. At trial, several credible reasons were offered by the trust beneficiaries as to why they did not exercise their rights to demand a distribution of trust property. The fact that none of the beneficiaries exercised their rights or that none of the beneficiaries requested notification of future transfers of property to the trust does not imply to us that the beneficiaries had agreed with decedent not to do so, and we refuse to infer any understanding.

The evidence does not support respondent's contention that the contingent beneficiaries believed they would be penalized for exercising their rights to demand distributions of trust property or that the trustees purposefully withheld information from the beneficiaries.

Further, the contingent beneficiaries received actual notice from the trustees with regard to their rights. Decedent intended to benefit the contingent beneficiaries by giving them interests in the trust. The contingent beneficiaries were decedent's relatives.

For the reasons stated above, the contingent beneficiaries' unrestricted rights to demand immediate distributions of trust property are to be treated as present interests in property. Decedent's transfer of the commercial building to the trust qualifies for 16 annual gift tax exclusions under § 2503(b) with regard to the present interests of the 16 contingent beneficiaries therein. * * *

ILLUSTRATIVE MATERIAL

A.   IMPLIED AGREEMENT NOT TO EXERCISE *CRUMMEY* DEMAND POWER

The Service has been unsuccessful in other cases where it has tried to deny the annual exclusion on grounds that there was an implicit understanding between the donor and donee that the *Crummey* demand power would not be exercised. For example, in Estate of Holland v. Commissioner, 73 T.C.M. 3236 (1997), decedent made $10,000 annual gifts to her three children, to her daughter-in-law, and to *Crummey* trusts established for her eight grandchildren, some of whom were minors. Decedent did not have sufficient available cash, so each year she borrowed $120,000 from a bank to fund the gifts. Her son Jack guaranteed the loans, both personally and as agent for decedent. Jack then purchased a $120,000 certificate of deposit ("CD") for the donees and pledged the CD as security for his guarantee of the loan as decedent's agent.

"Decedent [and her three children] discussed how the gifts were to be used prior to decedent's taking out the loan or making the gifts. * * * The donees unanimously agreed to pool their gifts in order to realize a greater return on their investments.

"Pooling the gifts to purchase the CD and pledging it to secure Jack's guarantee of the note benefited both the donees and the donor. The interest rate paid on a $120,000 CD was higher than the interest rate paid on a CD in an amount less than $100,000. Thus, by pooling their gifts, the donees were able to receive a greater rate of interest than if they had each bought a CD in the amount of the individual gifts.

"Pledging the CDs as security for Jack's guarantee benefited decedent by lowering her cost of borrowing. * * * [T]he bank regarded the Holland family as a valuable account * * * [and] accepted Jack's strategy to make the loan 'self-funding' by accepting his pledge of the CD as security for his guarantee. The interest rate on a self-funded loan was only [slightly] above the interest rate paid on the $120,000 CD. [The bank] did not require the CD to be pledged for it to make the loan; however, without the pledge the interest rate on the loan would have been higher. Therefore, the purpose of pledging the CD as security for Jack's guarantee of decedent's unsecured loan was to reduce decedent's cost of borrowing. * * *

"[W]e agree with respondent that if the beneficiaries, trustees, and donor had an agreement or understanding that limited the ability, in a legal sense, of the beneficiaries to exercise their right to withdraw trust corpus, then the beneficiaries may not have received gifts of a present interest.

"Respondent contends that there was an agreement between the decedent, the trustees, and the beneficiaries that denied the trust beneficiaries a present interest in the transfers. In respondent's view, the fact that the family discussed how the children would use the gifts prior to decedent's making the transfers, and then pooled the gifts to buy a CD that Jack pledged as security for his guarantee, is evidence of this agreement. We disagree.

"There is no evidence to support a finding that the donees' legal ability to demand payment from the trustees was limited by their informal agreement to purchase a CD after the gifts were made. Nor is there any evidence that decedent would not have made the gifts to any donee who did not agree to invest rather than spend the gift.

"To the contrary, the facts of this case support a finding that the family was investment orientated, that they discussed various investment choices, and they agreed that the best choice was to pool their gifts to purchase a larger CD that paid a higher rate of interest than the rate they would have received if they had each bought a smaller CD in the amount of the individual gifts. The fact that Jack was able to pledge the CD after the donees purchased it to lower decedent's cost of borrowing in no way limited the donees' legal ability to demand payment from the trustees before the CD was purchased.

"We hold, therefore, that the $10,000 annual transfers decedent made to each of the eight [family trusts] in 1985, 1986, 1987, and 1988, were transfers of present interests."

In issuing rulings approving annual exclusions in the *Crummey* context, the Service often conditions its ruling on the assumption that "there is no understanding, express or implied, that the withdrawal right will not be exercised." PLR 200123034 (Mar. 8, 2001); PLR 199912016 (Dec. 21, 1998). But no annual exclusion will be allowed where there is a legal impediment to the beneficiaries' exercise of the *Crummey* power. TAM 200341002 (June 5, 2003).

B.   TECHNICAL ASPECTS OF *CRUMMEY* DEMAND POWERS

The Service takes the position that a present interest exclusion will be allowed only where the holder of a *Crummey* power is granted a meaningful opportunity to exercise the power. For example, Rev.Rul. 81–7, 1981–1 C.B. 474, involved a discretionary trust which gave an adult beneficiary the noncumulative right to withdraw $3,000 from contributions made to the trust in that year. The right could be exercised up to and including December 31 of any year in which a contribution was made to the trust. The trust was created on December 29. Neither the grantor nor the trustee informed the beneficiary of his demand right before it lapsed. The ruling denied a present interest exclusion:

> "When the delivery of property to a trust is accompanied by limitations upon the donee's present enjoyment of the property in the form of conditions, contingencies, or the will of another, either under the terms of the trust or other circumstances, the interest is a future interest even if the enjoyment is deferred only for a short time.

> "[T]he donor's intent, as gleaned from the circumstances of the transfer, is a relevant consideration in determining when the rights actually conferred are meant to be enjoyed. * * * Where the facts and circumstances of a particular case show that the donor did not intend to give the donee a present interest, no annual exclusion under § 2503(b) is allowable.

> " * * * In failing to communicate the existence of the demand right and in narrowly restricting the time for its exercise, [the grantor] did not give [the beneficiary] a reasonable opportunity to learn of and to exercise the demand right before it lapsed. [The grantor's conduct made the demand right illusory and effectively deprived [the beneficiary] of the power."

On the other hand, in Rev.Rul. 83–108, 1983–2 C.B. 167, the trustee was required to give written notice of a beneficiary's *Crummey* withdrawal power within 10 days of a transfer to the trust. The beneficiary's right to exercise the withdrawal right terminated 45 days after receipt of the notice. The trust was created on December 29, 1981; the beneficiary received the notice on January 6, 1982 and did not have any prior knowledge of the withdrawal right. The ruling concluded that the 1981 gift was of a present interest because, unlike the situation in Rev.Rul. 81–7, the notice provision was intended to give the beneficiary a reasonable opportunity to exercise the withdrawal right rather than to preclude that opportunity. In contrast, the Service denied an annual exclusion where the *Crummey* beneficiary had only four days to exercise the withdrawal power. TAM 9628004 (July 12, 1996). See also PLR 200130030 (April 30, 2001) (thirty days *Crummey* notice is sufficient); TAM 9809008 (Nov. 6, 1997) (same).

The Service in technical advice denied an annual exclusion where the *Crummey* beneficiaries waived their right to notice: "[W]ithout the current notice that a gift is being transferred, it is not possible for a donee to have the real and immediate benefit of the gift. The immediate use, possession, or enjoyment of property is clearly restricted if the donee does not know of its existence. Accordingly, a donee must have current notice of any gift in order for that gift to be a transfer of a present interest. Because of the waiver by the grandchildren of their right to receive notice regarding their right of withdrawal as to future gifts as well as the lack of proof that any current notice was given to the grandchildren regarding any gifts after the initial gift, all transfers to the trust after the initial transfer were transfers of a future interest." TAM 9532001 (Apr. 12, 1995). The Service also has denied an annual exclusion in the case of "haphazard execution of the notification procedure" (the trustee often sent the *Crummey* notice after the expiration of the withdrawal period). TAM 200341002 (June 5, 2003).

In Estate of Holland v. Commissioner, 73 T.C.M. 3236 (1997), however, the court held that the trustee's failure to give written notice to *Crummey* beneficiaries of their withdrawal rights did not preclude the annual exclusion:

> "The sufficiency of the notice given the beneficiaries is a factor in the likelihood that the right of withdrawal will be exercised; it is not a factor in the legal right to demand payment from the trustee. * * * Furthermore, during the years of the transfers, the only minor beneficiaries of the [family trusts] were the children of the trustees. We do not think that the failure of a trustee to give written notice to himself should require a finding that notice was not given.

> "Finally, convincing testimony was heard at trial that the adult beneficiaries were given actual notice of the gifts and their right to immediately withdraw the money."

C. PLANNING IMPLICATIONS

In *Crummey* and *Cristofani*, a beneficiary's demand was to be satisfied in cash from the donor's gift for that year. Must a demand be satisfied by a distribution of some or all of the actual contribution to the trust in any particular year or may it be satisfied by the distribution of an amount equal to the value of the donee's demand right in that year? Suppose a trust instrument grants a beneficiary the right to withdraw the lesser of $13,000 or the amount contributed to the trust by the donor in that year. The donor transfers to the trust real property with a value of $130,000. The trustee may satisfy a demand by borrowing against the security of the real property and need not distribute to the beneficiary a 1/10th undivided interest in the property.

The foregoing questions are particularly important with respect to trusts funded solely with insurance policies on the life of the donor. Rev.Proc. 2008–3, 2008–1 I.R.B. 110, stated that the Service will not rule on whether a present interest exclusion is allowable with respect to transfers to a trust where (1) the trust corpus consists substantially of insurance policies on the life of the grantor or the grantor's spouse, (2) the trustee or any other person has the power to apply the trust income or corpus to premium payments on insurance on the life of the grantor or the grantor's spouse, (3) the trustee or any other person has a power to use the trust's assets to make loans to the grantor's estate or purchase assets from it, (4) the trust beneficiaries have a *Crummey* power and (5) there is a right or power that would cause the grantor to be treated as the owner of all or a portion of the trust under §§ 673–677.

A *Crummey* power is a general power of appointment. The lapse of a *Crummey* power constitutes a taxable transfer by the power holder to the extent that the power exceeds the "$5,000 or 5%" exception of § 2514(e). See p.

374. In addition, if the power holder is an income beneficiary of the trust, the lapse of a *Crummey* power also constitutes a § 2036 transfer to the extent that the power exceeds the "$5,000 or 5%" exception of § 2041(b)(2). See p. 367. To avoid these results, many *Crummey* powers are limited to the lesser of the amount contributed to the trust or $5,000 or 5% of the trust corpus. This drafting technique continues to be used even though the amount of the present interest exclusion has been increased to an inflation-adjusted $13,000 in order to avoid the adverse estate and gift tax consequences of a lapse of a general power in excess of the $5,000 or 5% exception. However, this approach forfeits some of the leverage from the annual exclusion and has led to the popularity of other techniques to maximize the annual exclusion without any adverse estate and gift tax problems resulting from the lapse of the *Crummey* power. For example, the *Crummey* trust can be funded with at least $260,000, thereby sheltering the lapse under the 5% exception. Alternatively, separate *Crummey* trusts can be established for each beneficiary, thereby preventing the lapse from constituting a gift to a third party. Finally, the *Crummey* trust can incorporate a "hanging power," permitting a beneficiary to withdraw $13,000 but tying the lapse to the $5,000 or 5% exception, with any excess amount carrying over (or "hanging") to the subsequent year. A further planning problem with *Crummey* trusts is that the Service treats the holder of a lapsed withdrawal right as the owner of the trust for income tax purposes under the grantor trust rules. See, e.g., PLR 200011058 (Dec. 15, 1999); PLR 200011056 (Dec. 15, 19999); PLR 200011055 (Dec. 15, 1999); PLR 200011054 (Dec. 15, 1999); PLR 9812006 (Nov. 6, 1997); PLR 9810008 (Nov. 6, 1997); PLR 9809004 (Nov. 6, 1997).

2. SECTION 2503(c)

Internal Revenue Code: § 2503(c)

Regulations: § 25.2503–4

INTRODUCTORY NOTE

Section 2503(c) provides a safe haven rule for those donors who are willing to meet its conditions. Thus, gifts of interests which might or might not otherwise qualify as present interests under § 2503(b)(1) will qualify for the annual exclusion if: (1) the property and income can be expended only by or for the donee before the donee reaches age 21; and (2) to the extent not so expended, the property and income passes to the donee at age 21 or, if the donee dies before that time, to the donee's estate or appointees, pursuant to a general power of appointment in the donee's hands.

For example, Parent creates a trust for Child, who is two years of age, to last for a period of 19 years. Corpus and accumulated income are payable to Child at age 21 or to Child's estate in the event of death before reaching that age. The trustee is given the power, in its discretion, to accumulate income and to invade corpus for Child's benefit. Each year, Parent transfers $13,000 in cash to the trust. These annual gifts would qualify for the gift tax exclusion under § 2503(c) even though Child might receive no income during minority if the trustee exercises its discretion to accumulate the income. The property and income *can* be expended for Child; whether such expenditures *are* made is immaterial. Moreover, to the extent not so expended, property and income *must* pass to Child upon reaching age 21, or to Child's estate upon death prior to that time.

Commissioner v. Herr

303 F.2d 780 (3d Cir. 1962).

■ GOODRICH, CIRCUIT JUDGE.

This case involves the question of what is a present interest in a trust for a minor under § 2503(c). The issue arises in connection with the gift tax return of the settlor of a trust. The settlor in 1954 set up four trusts, all the same except for the identity of the beneficiaries, who were his grandchildren. He made additions to each trust in 1955. As to each of the trusts, the trustee was to pay over the income to the beneficiary until his arrival at age thirty and then to pay over the principal. By Article Third of the trust the trustee was to retain the income payable to any minor, reinvesting it and paying over so much of the income and principal as he deemed necessary for the maintenance and support of the minor. All unexpended sums of accumulated income were to be paid to the minor at his majority.

The Commissioner disallowed the annual exclusions on the gift tax return for 1956 on the ground that the transfers were gifts of future interests. The Tax Court held, in a very able opinion by Judge Raum, that those parts of the gifts which were of income during minority were present interests entitling the taxpayers to the claimed deductions. 35 T.C. 732 (1961). The Commissioner has appealed and we are told that this is the first case to reach an appellate court under this provision of the 1954 Code. There is no dispute on the facts and the question is a very narrow one.

* * * The question in this case is limited to the tax-free nature of the trust income to the minor during minority. There is no claim that the income following majority up to age thirty and the right to the principal at age thirty are present interests. The Government's argument turns upon the phrase "if the property and the income therefrom." It argues strenuously that "property" is equivalent to "corpus," and therefore both the corpus and the income must meet both statutory conditions in order not to be treated as a future interest.

The problem comes in the use of the term "property." The introductory note to the Restatement of Property discusses its use of the word "property":

> "The word 'property' is used in this Restatement to denote legal relations between persons with respect to a thing. The thing may be an object having physical existence or it may be any kind of an intangible such as a patent right or a [chose] in action. The broader meanings of the word 'property,' which include any relationship having an exchange value, are not used."

It is apparent that when the thing in question is a piece of land the term "property" may include several different interests. One may lease the land for a term of years and have a lessee's interest which is certainly an interest in property. Then there may be an estate for life, an estate per autre vie, a contingent remainder and a vested remainder. The Supreme Court in Fondren v. Commissioner, 324 U.S. 18, 21 (1945), recognizes that there can be a present interest and a future interest in the same thing.

To bring out our problem here, let us suppose this case: A settlor creates a trust, the income of which is to go to M, a minor, until M is twenty-one. When M is twenty-one the corpus of the trust is to be given to X. Can there be any doubt that in this case the income of the trust is a "present interest" to M as he receives the payments year after year? If we add an additional provision that the minor is to receive, until he is twenty-one, so much of the income as is necessary for his support and that any undistributed income and interest thereon is to go to him at twenty-one, does he not still have a present interest?

If this is right, does it change the situation, if instead of the corpus going to X when M is twenty-one, it is to go to M when he is thirty? That is this case. We think the Tax Court was right in looking at this problem in the light of division of interest in the thing (corpus) in the way it did. The right to income during minority is a present interest; the right to income and principal after minority are future interests.

If that conclusion is not correct we have a very incongruous set of results in the distinction between the right of a stranger to receive the future interest and the right to receive the future interest when it is to go to the one entitled to the income during his minority.

The decisions of the Tax Court will be affirmed.

ILLUSTRATIVE MATERIAL

A.   DEFINITION OF "PROPERTY AND THE INCOME THEREFROM"

The courts have uniformly rejected the view that the reference to "property and the income therefrom" in § 2503(c) encompasses the entire gift. As in *Herr*, income interests can be separated from remainder interests, with the income interests qualifying as present interests while the remainder interests do not qualify. See Rollman v. United States, 342 F.2d 62 (Ct.Cl. 1965); Weller v. Commissioner, 38 T.C. 790 (1962). In Commissioner v. Thebaut, 361 F.2d 428 (5th Cir.1966), the Service conceded the correctness of *Herr* and *Rollman*, and in Rev.Rul. 68–670, 1968-2 C.B. 413, the Service formally announced that it would follow the decisions in *Herr* and *Thebaut* to the effect that an income interest itself can constitute the "property" under § 2503(c).

However, what about other ways to parse the phrase "property and the income therefrom"? Can a qualifying remainder interest be separated from a nonqualifying income interest? What about an income interest that has both qualifying and nonqualifying components?

Commissioner v. Estate of Levine

526 F.2d 717 (2d Cir. 1975).

■ KAUFMAN, CHIEF JUDGE:

One suspects that because the Internal Revenue Code * * * piles exceptions upon exclusions, it invites efforts to outwit the tax collector. The case before us is an example of adroit taxpayers seizing upon words in the Code which, if interpreted as they urge, would distort congressional intent and violate well-established rules of statutory construction. We therefore reverse the decision of the Tax Court favoring the taxpayers, 63 T.C. 136 (1974).

I

The facts in this case have been stipulated. On December 30, 1968 David H. Levine, a Connecticut resident, established identical irrevocable trusts for five grandchildren whose ages then ranged from 2 to 15 years. The corpus of each trust consisted of common stock of New Haven Moving Equipment Corporation. The shares were valued at $3,750. Unless a designated "Independent Trustee" saw fit in his discretion to direct otherwise, the trustees were to retain all income generated until the grandchild-beneficiary reached age 21. At that time, the accumulated income would be distributed *in toto*. Thereafter, the beneficiary would receive payments at least annually of all income earned by the trust. If the grandchild died before his or her twenty-first birthday, all accumulated income would go to the estate of the grandchild.

During the lifetime of the beneficiary, control over the trust corpus was vested exclusively in the "absolute and uncontrolled discretion" of the Independent Trustee. He could permit the principal to stand untouched or he could pay out any portion directly to, or for the benefit of, the beneficiary. In addition, the trustee could terminate the trust at any time by distributing the entire corpus. The trust also provided the beneficiary with a limited power of appointment in the event that any of the principal remained in the trust upon his or her death. The corpus, or any part of it, could be designated to pass to some or all of David H. Levine's lineal descendents. The original beneficiary could not elect to leave corpus to his or her own estate, his or her creditors, or the creditors of the original beneficiary's estate. * * *

II

The dispute focuses on the interpretation and interrelation of §§ 2503(b) and (c) * * *. Section 2503(b) permits a donor to escape gift tax on the first $3,000 of gifts to each donee yearly, so long as the gift is not "of future interests in property." Although the term "future interests" is nowhere defined in the Code, the Supreme Court has instructed that "the question is * * * when enjoyment [of the property] begins." Fondren v. CIR, 324 U.S. 18, 20 (1945). The gift is of a future interest if "limited to commence in use, possession, or enjoyment at some future date or time." Id.; Reg. § 25.2503–3(a). The gift of a remainder interest in a trust has thus been considered a future interest. CIR v. Disston, 325 U.S. 442, 447 (1945). An income interest for life, however, is a present interest if payments commence immediately. *Fondren*, supra, at 21.

Despite the attractions of the § 2503(b) gift tax exclusion, donors hesitate to make outright gifts of principal or income to minors. In response to such understandable concerns, and the existence of many state statutory prohibitions against minors accepting and exercising dominion over property, * * * Congress in 1954 added § 2503(c) to the Code. * * *

At first blush, it might seem that the Levine trusts clearly fail to satisfy the requirements of § 2503(c)(2). The "property"—if defined as the corpus—would not pass to the donee when the beneficiary turned 21. Nor would it be payable to the donee's estate if death occurred before the age of 21 years. The power of appointment established by each trust over the corpus also fails the test set forth in § 2514(c).

The problem, however, is somewhat more complex. The Supreme Court in *Disston* and *Fondren*, supra, recognized that a gift may be divided into component parts for tax purposes. One or more of those elements may qualify as present interests even if others do not. The Tax Court applied these principles in a 1961 decision involving a trust similar to Levine's. Herr v. CIR, 35 T.C. 732 (1961). Treating the income to be accumulated to age 21 (the "pre–21 income interest") as a separate element of "property," id. at 737, the Tax Court held that this segment satisfied the requirements of § 2503(c) and the taxpayer could therefore benefit from the § 2503(b) exclusion.[8] The Third Circuit affirmed the Tax Court, 303 F.2d 780 (3d Cir.1962). The Commissioner has acquiesced in the *Herr* decision, 1968–2 C.B. 2, and accordingly concedes in the present case that the pre–21 income interest is eligible for the gift tax exclusion.

The pre–21 income interests in the Levine trusts do not, however, exhaust the $3,000 per donee annual exclusion.[9] Knowing that the remainder interests cannot qualify as present interests under either § 2503(b) or § 2503(c), the Levines have concentrated their attention on the post–21 income interests. Although the taxpayer in *Herr* did not suggest that the post–21 segment could properly be considered a present interest, the Tax Court explicitly spoke to the issue: "[I]ncome [after] 21 * * * [is a] future interest." 35 T.C. at 736. And the Court of Appeals commented similarly: "[T]he right[s] to income and principal after minority are future interests." 303 F.2d at 782. The taxpayers ask us to disregard these views and to extend the holding of *Herr* so that the post–21 income interests will be treated as present interests. We decline to do so.

III

If the post–21 income interests are looked upon as separate gifts, they cannot be considered present interests under § 2503(b). As in the case of

---

8. The Tax Court correctly observed that this pre–21 income interest would have been considered a future interest ineligible for the § 2503(b) exclusion if § 2503(c) had never been enacted. The ability of the trustee to accumulate income during the beneficiary's minority would have been fatal.

9. Using actuarial tables, the value of each gift is allocated between the present values of the pre–21 income interest, post–21 income interest, and remainder interest. See Reg. § 25.2512–5.

the remainder interests, initial enjoyment is delayed until a time in the future. Moreover, the requirements of § 2503(c)(2) are not satisfied.

The taxpayers urge that we are required to treat the post–21 income interests as one with the pre–21 income interests, but that the remainder interests should be considered a separate gift. The taxpayers recognize that the combined pre– and post–21 income interests do not qualify as a present interest when viewed solely in the light of § 2503(b). This is so because the accumulation of income before age 21 works as a postponement of immediate enjoyment. In addition, the combined income interests fail to meet the criteria of § 2503(c)(2).

The Levines seek to overcome these obstacles by means of an ingenious argument. The combination of pre–21 and post–21 income interests resembles a unitary life estate, they argue. The only reason it cannot qualify as a § 2503(b) present interest, they urge, is the accumulation provision that permits enjoyment to be delayed until age 21. But, they say, § 2503(c) as interpreted by *Herr* permits the future interest characteristic of the pre–21 income interests to be disregarded for the purpose of receiving the § 2503(b) exclusion. In other words, they assert that *Herr* and § 2503(c) in effect transform the pre–21 income interests into present interests. Then, by a giant leap, the taxpayers conclude that a single, lifetime present interest is produced by linking the pre–21 constructive present interests with the post–21 income interests.

A study of the statutory language, however, convinces us that Congress did not contemplate such an "off-again, on-again" elusive treatment of the pre–21 segment of the transfers in trust. Moreover, we cannot be unmindful of the rule of construction that Congress permits exclusions only as a matter of grace, and the exclusions sections are to be strictly construed against the taxpayer. * * * Nor does the legislative history prove more helpful to the taxpayers. The House Report, H.R. Rep. No. 1337, 83d Cong., 2d Sess. A322, 3 U.S. Code Cong. & Admin. News 4465 (1954), explained that § 2503(c):

> "*partially* relaxes the 'future interest' restriction contained in [§ 2503(b)], in the case of gifts to minors by providing a *specific type of gift* for which the exclusion will be allowed. If *the gift* may be expended by, or for the benefit of, the minor donee prior to his attaining the age of 21 years, and, to the extent not so expended, will pass to the donee at that time, but if the donee dies prior to that time, will pass to the donee's estate or as he may appoint by will under a general power of appointment, *the gift* will not be treated as a future interest." [emphasis added]

See also 3 U.S. Code Cong. & Admin. News at 5123 (Senate Report, refers to a "*certain type* of gift to a minor which will not be treated as a gift of a future interest" [emphasis added]). The special treatment of pre–21 income interests in *Herr* could be justified as not *penalizing* the taxpayer for linking pre–21 income interests with other interests. But, the Levines would have us *reward* such a combination, since the post–21 income interest clearly could not, by itself, qualify for the annual exclusion.

There is one additional factor that we cannot ignore. The *Herr* opinions rejecting the contention that a post–21 income interest can be a § 2503 present interest were rendered more than a decade ago. Extensive attention has been paid by the treatises, commentators, and tax services to the *Herr* decisions, and "no other field of legislation receives as much continuous, sustained and detailed attention" from Congress as does tax law. 3 Sutherland on Statutory Construction § 66.02 at 184 (4th ed. 1974). Congress has had ample opportunity to amend the Code if it disagreed with the interpretation of §§ 2503(b) and (c) set forth in *Herr.* * * *

Accordingly, we reverse the decision of the Tax Court and remand.

ILLUSTRATIVE MATERIAL

A.   DEFINITION OF "PROPERTY AND THE INCOME THEREFROM"

Rev.Rul. 76–179, 1976–1 C.B. 290, followed *Estate of Levine* in disallowing a present interest exclusion for a 10–year extension of an income interest in a trust that followed a 5–year income interest that had qualified under § 2503(c).

B.   EXPENDITURE OF INCOME OR PROPERTY BY OR FOR DONEE BEFORE AGE 21

Reg. § 25.2503–4(b)(1) provides that a transfer otherwise meeting the requirements of § 2503(c) will not be disqualified merely because the trustee has the discretion to determine the amount of income or property to be expended for the benefit of the minor, or the purpose for which the distribution is to be made, provided that the governing instrument does not place "substantial restrictions" on the exercise of the trustee's discretion. Predictably, the meaning of "substantial restrictions" has given rise to controversy.

In Ross v. United States, 348 F.2d 577 (5th Cir.1965), the grantors created a trust for their grandchildren under which the trustees had the power to use trust income for the "support, maintenance and education" of the beneficiaries. In addition, the trust could hold and dispose of the income "to the same extent as if [the trustees] were the guardian" of the beneficiaries and as if the payments had been made by the trustees in that capacity. The trust instrument also authorized the trustees to exercise all powers of guardians under applicable state law. The court held that the trust qualified under § 2503(c): "The words 'may be expended' in the statute mean '*may be expended within the limitations imposed on guardians by state law.*'" The state law restrictions imposed on a guardian's expenditure of corpus were not fatal to qualification under § 2503(c). See also Williams v. United States, 378 F.2d 693 (Ct.Cl. 1967) (no substantial restriction where trustee had discretionary power to distribute income and principal if beneficiary were "in need of additional funds for maintenance, education, medical care, support and general welfare * * * if the costs and expenses incident thereto are not otherwise adequately provided for").

The Tax Court in Pettus v. Commissioner, 54 T.C. 112 (1970), upheld the validity of Reg. § 25.2503–4(b)(1), concluding that the phrase "may be expended" appeared to have been taken from the law relating to guardians. The Tax Court read *Ross* as holding that the phrase meant may be expended *within* the limitations imposed on guardians by state law. The Tax Court did not read *Williams* as implicitly overruling the Regulations; in the court's view, *Williams* merely held that § 2503(c) was satisfied if the restrictions imposed on the trustee were no greater than restrictions imposed on guardians under state law. Thus, the annual exclusion was not available with respect to the corpus of the trust which could be distributed only for the "illness, infirmity or disability" of the minor beneficiary. Limiting the trustee's discretion to distribute principal only for medical care is a more severe restriction than is imposed on guardians: "Since there is no evidence that any beneficiary was in special need of medical care when the gifts herein were made, there existed at those times only a bare technical possibility that any part of the principal would benefit the donee before he reached age 21." 54 T.C. at 121–22. On the other hand, income rights in the trust qualified under § 2503(c) even though the trust instrument gave the trustees the power to add accumulated income to principal "at such time or times as the trustee determined." The court held that this provision did not require the addition of accumulated income to principal (which would have thus disqualified the income interest because of the substantial restrictions imposed on principal distributions); the trustee had discretion only as to the timing of additions of accumulated income to principal. In addition, broad administrative powers granted to the trustee over trust investments (e.g., to invest in life insurance policies, to buy and sell assets, to allocate receipts between income and principal) did not prevent valuation of the income interest by utilizing the tables in the regulations.

C.   PROPERTY AND INCOME PASS TO DONEES AT AGE 21

Although § 2053(c) requires that the property and income therefrom, to the extent not expended by or for the benefit of the donee, must pass to the donee at age 21, the Service has ruled that this sets "maximum restrictions" and permits the property and income to pass to the donee at a younger age (such as age 18 if that is the age of adulthood under state law). Rev.Rul. 73–287, 1973–2 C.B. 321.

Reg. § 25.2503–4(b) permits the donee, upon reaching age 21, to extend the life of the trust. In Heidrich v. Commissioner, 55 T.C. 746 (1971), the Tax Court held that a trust, consistent with § 2503(c), could last until the donee reached age 25, if the donee had a continuing power to terminate the trust at age 21. In Rev.Rul. 74–43, 1974–1 C.B. 285, the Service went further in approving a trust giving the donee the right to compel distribution during a limited period after reaching age 21. See also TAM 200634007 (Aug. 25, 2006) (donee has sixty days after turning age 21 to terminate trust); TAM 200633017 (May 12, 2006) (same). In these situations, of course, the donee has made a transfer which will cause the property to be included in her estate under § 2036 or § 2038.

D.   DISPOSITION IF DONEE DIES BEFORE AGE 21

Section 2503(c)(2)(B) requires that if the donee dies before age 21, the unspent property and income must be payable to the donee's estate or to the persons designated by the donee under a general power of appointment. This is a disjunctive test; under either alternative, the property will be included in the donee's estate for estate tax purposes.

To satisfy the first test, "payment [must] be directly to the donee's estate without prior possible transfers." Ross v. Commissioner, 652 F.2d 1365, 1367 (9th Cir.1981). Provisions that direct payment to the donee's heirs rather than to the donee's estate do not satisfy this requirement.

To satisfy the second test, the donee must have a general power of appointment. Reg. § 25.2503–4(b) permits the general power to be either an inter vivos power or a testamentary power. Moreover, a minor's disability to exercise the power under local law will not of itself disqualify the transfer. A provision in the trust instrument designating a gift over of unexpended corpus or income in the event of the minor's failure to exercise the general power of appointment will not cause disqualification of the trust under § 2503(c). However, a power that is not exercisable until the donee reached age 19 does not qualify where state law permits powers to be exercised by married persons over age 18. Gall v. United States, 521 F.2d 878 (5th Cir.1975), cert. denied, 425 U.S. 972 (1976).

E. ESTATE TAX CONSEQUENCES OF TRANSFERS QUALIFYING UNDER § 2503(c)

Although a gift may qualify as a gift of a "present interest" under § 2503(c), the property nonetheless may be included in the grantor's gross estate for estate tax purposes under §§ 2036–2038.

SECTION C.   POLICY ISSUES

A normative transfer tax could properly employ some mechanism to eliminate small gifts from the tax base on the ground of administrative convenience. As previously noted, this was the original justification for the annual per donee exclusion in the present gift tax. However, as the preceding materials have indicated, the annual per donee exclusion (even at a level of $3,000) has been utilized by estate planners for significant avoidance of gift taxes by wealthy donors in highly sophisticated transactions. For example, the trust instrument in *Estate of Levine*, p. 481, represents a marked departure from the image of the small Christmas gift that Congress originally had in mind in enacting the gift tax annual per donee exclusion. Similarly, the use of sixteen contingent beneficiaries in *Kohlsaat*, p. 473, illustrates the availability of multiple annual exclusions.

As a result of the utilization of the annual per donee exclusion for purposes other than elimination of record keeping requirements for small gifts, significant modification of the provision appears appropriate. Thus, it would appear desirable to return to the rule that prevailed during the 1939–1942 period under which gifts in trust could not qualify for the annual exclusion.

Moreover, the present annual exclusion could also be improved whether or not it is continued for gifts in trust. $13,000—or any other number— is arbitrary to the extent it does not reflect administrative efficiencies. Conceptually, one would not expect to find a per-donee exclusion in a tax levelled on the donor. In any event, administrative efficiencies ideally would require quantification of the savings. But these savings disappear once the gift exceeds the exemption amount. Thus, the exclusion should be phased-out, for example, on a dollar-for-dollar basis, so that once gifts to an individual donee during the year exceeded $13,000 no gift tax exclusion would be available. If the justification for an annual per donee exclusion is the elimination of the record keeping requirements for small gifts, this justification disappears once gifts to a donee in a given year exceed the annual exclusion amount and a gift tax return is required to be filed in any event. In addition, with an unlimited marital deduction, only one annual per donee exclusion should be available to the marital unit. The present rule which permits a married couple to have the benefit of two annual per donee exclusions should be eliminated because the theory of an unlimited marital deduction is that the marital unit should be considered a single donor for transfer tax purposes.

On the other hand, if Congress now views the annual exclusion as an "incentive" to donors to make lifetime transfers, then the provision must be evaluated under tests applied to other government financial incentive programs: Is there a need for the incentive; do the benefits of the incentive equal its costs; are the benefits of the incentive program distributed equitably among families according to wealth?

SECTION D.   TRANSFERS FOR TUITION OR MEDICAL EXPENSES

Internal Revenue Code: § 2503(e)

Regulations: § 25.2503–6

House Ways and Means Committee Report, Tax Incentive Bill of 1981[10]

H.R. Rep. No. 201, 97th Cong., 1st Sess (1981).

Reasons for Change

 * * * [T]he committee is concerned that certain payments of tuition made on behalf of children who have attained their majority, and medical expenses on behalf of elderly relatives are technically considered gifts under present law. The committee believes such payments should be exempt from gift taxes without regard to the amount paid for such purposes.

Explanation of Provision

 * * * [Section 2503(e)] provides that any amount paid on behalf of any individual (1) as tuition to certain educational organizations for the education or training of such individual, or (2) as payment for medical care to

---

10. This is the title of the House Ways and Means Committee version of the Eco-   nomic Recovery Tax Act of 1981.

any person who provides medical care (as defined in § 213(e)) with respect to such individual, will not be considered as transfers by gift. This exclusion for medical expenses and tuition would be in addition to the $10,000 annual gift tax exclusion and would be permitted without regard to the relationship between the donor and the donee.

The exclusion for medical expenses (including medical insurance) applies only with respect to direct payments made by the donor to the individual or organization providing medical services (i.e., no reimbursement to the donee, as intermediary, will be excludable). Qualifying medical expenses are limited to those defined in § 213 (i.e., those incurred essentially for the diagnosis, cure, mitigation, treatment, or prevention of disease, or for the purpose of affecting any structure or function of the body). However, medical expenses are excludable from gift tax without regard to the percentage limitation contained in § 213.

However, the unlimited exclusion is not permitted for amounts that are reimbursed by insurance. Thus, if a donor pays a qualifying medical expense and the donee also receives insurance reimbursement, the donor's payment, to the extent of the reimbursement, is not eligible for the unlimited exclusion whether or not such reimbursement is paid in the same or subsequent taxable year.

With respect to educational expenses, an unlimited exclusion is permitted with respect to any tuition paid on behalf of an individual directly to the qualifying educational institution providing such service. A qualifying organization is an educational organization described in § 170(b)(1)(A)(ii), i.e., an institution which normally maintains a regular faculty and curriculum and normally has a regularly enrolled body of pupils or students in attendance at the place where its educational activities are regularly carried on. The exclusion is permitted with respect to both full- and part-time students, but is limited to direct tuition costs (i.e., no exclusion is provided for books, supplies, dormitory fees, etc.).

In providing an unlimited exclusion for certain medical expenses and tuition, the committee does not intend to change the law that there is no gift if the person paying the medical expenses or tuition is under an obligation under local law to provide such items to the recipient. In addition, the committee bill does not change the income tax consequences otherwise applicable to such payments.

ILLUSTRATIVE MATERIAL

A. TECHNICAL ASPECTS OF § 2503(e)

Section 2503(e) redefines the term "transfer by gift" to exclude from the gift tax base the "qualified transfers" specified in § 2503(e)(2). "Qualified transfers" do not affect the otherwise allowable present interest exclusion.

Under pre–1982 law, the payment of medical expenses for an individual whom the payor was legally obligated to support did not constitute a gift because the discharge of the support obligation constituted consideration for the transfer. Similarly, the payment of tuition expenses, if encompassed within the payor's obligation of support, did not constitute a gift. Payments which were not in discharge of the payor's support obligation were gifts. The determinations of those to whom an individual owed an obligation of support and of what payments were encompassed within each obligation were made under state law. Thus, whether a particular payment constituted a gift depended upon varying, and often imprecisely defined, state law rules.

To the extent that tuition payments made on behalf of children of the donor or medical expenses paid on behalf of elderly relatives of the donor are not, under state law, considered to be made in discharge of the donor's support obligation, § 2503(e) may be viewed as creating a federal support obligation, the discharge of which constitutes consideration for the transfer. This creation of a federal support obligation may be justified for reasons of administrative convenience and uniform application of the wealth transfer tax.

Nevertheless, § 2503(e) is both too broad and too narrow. It is too broad because it is not limited to qualified payments made on behalf of children, elderly relatives, or even dependents of the donor. See Reg. § 25.2503–6(a) ("an exclusion for a qualified transfer is permitted without regard to the relationship between the donor and the donee"); Reg. § 25.2503–6(c) (Example 2) (grandfather paid grandchild's tuition expenses indirectly through trust); Reg. § 25.2503–6(c) (Example 3) (individual paid hospital bills of unrelated person injured in automobile accident); TAM 200602002 (Sept. 6, 2005) (grandparent made pre-paid tuition payments directly to grandchildren's school). Congress instead could have chosen to limit the exclusion to payment on behalf of a member of the donor's family and used one of the existing statutory rules to define family.

On the other hand, § 2503(e) is too narrow because it is limited to direct payment of tuition or medical bills to the organization or person providing the educational or medical services. Although the legislative history does not explain the policy behind this direct payment requirement, presumably it was a matter of administrative convenience to avoid tracing problems. Thus, tuition payments indeed are an easily identifiable component of educational expenses, and § 2503(e) eliminates the need to inquire whether ancillary payments for lodging, board, books, etc. are reasonable in amount and are actually related to the donee's education. However, such ancillary payments would not constitute gifts if encompassed within the donor's support obligation.

No exclusion is permitted for medical expenses that are reimbursed by insurance. This limitation introduces some complexity into the administration of § 2503(e). An insurance reimbursement occurring in a year subsequent to that in which the donor made the payment will require that a late or amended gift tax return be filed if the payment exceeded the otherwise available annual exclusion with respect to the donee.

CHAPTER 27

ESTATE TAX DEDUCTIONS NECESSARY TO DEFINE THE NET TRANSFER

Internal Revenue Code: §§ 2053; 2054; 642(g)

Regulations: §§ 20.2053; 20.2054; 1.642(g)–1, 2

INTRODUCTORY NOTE

The estate tax is imposed on the "net transfer" from the decedent to her heirs or beneficiaries. Accordingly, the deductions allowable under §§ 2053 and 2054 reduce the gross estate to ensure that the estate tax is imposed on "what of value passes from the dead to the living." Jacobs v. Commissioner, 34 B.T.A. 594, 597 (1936).

The deductions enumerated in § 2053(a) are amounts:

"(1) for funeral expenses,

(2) for administration expenses,

(3) for claims against the estate, and

(4) for unpaid mortgages on, or any indebtedness in respect of, property where the value of the decedent's interest therein, undiminished by such mortgage or indebtedness, is included in the value of the gross estate."

Section 2053(b) allows as a deduction from the gross estate amounts representing expenses incurred in administering "property not subject to claims" which is included in the gross estate. Although the meaning of "property not subject to claims" is not apparent on the face of the statute, it was intended to refer to property not included in the decedent's probate estate under state law. See S. Rep. No. 1622, 83d Cong., 2d Sess. 474 (1954). Congress apparently thought that expenses for administering non-probate property that was includible in the gross estate for federal estate tax purposes would not be deductible without specific statutory authority. Section 2053(b) thus allows the estate to deduct administration expenses for property included in the gross estate under §§ 2033–2042 but not includible in the state probate estate.

Section 2053(a) and (b) can cover the same types of expenditures, and the tests for deductibility are the same for each. Accordingly, in the following materials, cases arising under both provisions are included in the discussion of each type of estate expenditure.

Section 2054 allows a deduction for "losses incurred during the settlement of estates arising from fires, storms, shipwrecks, or other casualties,

491

or from theft, when such losses are not compensated for by insurance or otherwise."

Section A.   The Role of State Law

Deductions under § 2053 are limited to those "allowable by the laws of the jurisdiction, whether within or without the United States, under which the estate is being administered." Does a state probate court's approval of an expense for state probate purposes also control for federal estate tax purposes? Reg. § 20.2053–1(b)(2) provides that although the "decision of a local court as to the amount and allowability under local law of a claim or administration expense will ordinarily be accepted if the court passes upon the facts upon which deductibility depends, * * * [i]t must appear that the court actually passed upon the merits of the claim."

Estate of Millikin v. Commissioner
106 F.3d 1263 (6th Cir.1997).

■ Moore, Circuit Judge. * * *

I.   FACTS AND PROCEDURAL HISTORY

* * * Marguerite S. Millikin, a resident of Ohio, died testate on June 18, 1989. Marguerite's spouse, Severance A. Millikin, had predeceased her, leaving three trusts that he had established during his lifetime: (1) Trust A, "Endowment Fund," a charitable trust for the benefit of three Cleveland-area non-profit organizations (Cleveland Museum of Art, Case Western Reserve University, and University Hospitals of Cleveland); (2) Trust B, "Marital Trust," a marital deduction trust with general power of appointment in Marguerite under which, if not exercised at her death, any unappointed portion of the Trust B corpus would transfer to Trust C; and (3) Trust C, "Family Trust," a residuary trust for twenty-eight family beneficiaries. Society National Bank is the acting trustee of all three trusts, with Quentin Alexander serving as the sole advisory trustee after Marguerite's death. The trustee is empowered to sell any trust property with approval of the advisory trustee.

Marguerite executed a Last Will and Testament on November 19, 1987, in which she designated Quentin Alexander as executor of her estate. Alexander's wife was the Millikins' niece. Marguerite's will was probated in the Probate Court of Cuyahoga County, Ohio. Marguerite's gross estate included the property held by Trust B because it was subject to her general power of appointment. See § 2041(a). The Trust B assets, however, were not probate assets and were not subject to claims against the decedent's estate.

Marguerite's gross estate was reported in the estate tax return as $22,851,356.30, including a 150–acre estate in Gates Mills, Ohio called Ripplestone, consisting of a main house, a detached garage, various cottages, a barn, a stable, a swimming pool, and a tennis court. The main house contained a climate-controlled gallery to display the Millikins' extensive art collection (estimated at $1.5 million). In accordance with Severance's will, title to Ripplestone was transferred to Trust B on May 7, 1986, where ownership remained at all times pertinent to this action. Trust B paid the expenses to maintain Ripplestone prior to and after Marguerite's death. Even though the expenses to maintain Ripplestone were technically not part of the probate estate, Alexander elected to report the expenses to the probate court in his periodic accountings.

Marguerite's will authorized her executor to sell any of her estate as he deemed necessary without obtaining the approval of any person or court. She left the residue of her estate to an inter vivos trust she had previously established ("Marguerite Trust"). With respect to personal property, she granted the Cleveland Museum of Art a right to select and retain any objects of art, including paintings, books, porcelains, furniture, and silver. Marguerite also partially exercised her power of appointment over Trust B by appointing $2 million to be allocated to Trust A and distributed to the identified charitable organizations. Marguerite further designated in her will that all federal and state estate and death taxes owed as a result of Trust B assets being included in her gross estate for tax purposes were to be paid from Trust B itself. At the date of Marguerite's death, Trust B held assets which were worth $9,026,540.75, not including Ripplestone.

When Marguerite died, Alexander and the trustee assumed control of Ripplestone and decided to sell the property as soon as possible, but not before they distributed the art collection and other items of personal property inside Ripplestone. Alexander reduced Ripplestone's staff, keeping enough people to maintain the house and grounds while the Cleveland Museum of Art selected the items it wanted. Several times during 1989 and 1990 various museum staff members went to Ripplestone to analyze the collection. By March of 1990, the museum had finished its selection process and the remaining personal property was sold. On March 20, 1990, Ripplestone was offered for sale. Because of the premium asking price (initially $4.2 million), necessary environmental remediation efforts (six underground fuel storage tanks had leaked and contaminated nearby soil, a situation which came to light only after the estate tax return was filed), and certain zoning laws that precluded subdivision of the property, Ripplestone proved difficult to sell. Ripplestone was eventually sold on April 20, 1994, for $2,301,750. Selling expenses were $142,079.70.

The estate filed its federal estate tax return on March 16, 1990, asserting $3,892,355.31 total federal estate tax liability and $1,379,745.66 federal generation-skipping transfer tax liability, and claiming a credit of $1,071,656.26 for state death taxes paid. The executor deducted $555,409.20 in funeral and administration expenses, including $150,000 estimated costs for selling Ripplestone. In total, charitable organizations received over $12 million of Marguerite's gross estate.

The Internal Revenue Service ("IRS") audited the estate and on February 25, 1993, issued notices of deficiency * * * arising from discrepancies in the valuation of Ripplestone. * * *

The estate challenged the deficiency notices by filing a petition in the Tax Court on May 17, 1993, seeking redetermination of the deficiencies. In light of the environmental remediation and other selling obstacles, the parties eventually stipulated that the fair market value of Ripplestone at the time of Marguerite's death was only $2.4 million, thereby mooting the valuation dispute.

In the meantime, however, Alexander notified the IRS of additional administration expenses for maintaining and selling Ripplestone incurred after the 1990 filing of the estate tax return. This is where the present dispute arose, for the IRS claimed that the estate was not entitled to deduct such expenses.

The issue of deductibility of these additional administration expenses went to trial before the Tax Court on February 10, 1994. The Tax Court determined that deductibility was governed by Ohio law and that an Ohio probate court would allow an estate to pay administration expenses only to the extent that those expenses were necessary, reasonable, and just. The Tax Court decided that the executor could deduct administration expenses incurred to maintain and sell Ripplestone prior to March 16, 1990, but not after that date. According to the Tax Court, the sale of Ripplestone was not "necessary" to insure that sufficient assets were in reserve for contingent tax and other liabilities, as Ripplestone had been intended for sale long before the notices of deficiency, and Trust B held over $9 million in liquid assets that could have been used to pay any deficiencies. * * *

II. ADMINISTRATION EXPENSES * * *

A. Federal Law

The estate seeks to deduct as administration expenses under § 2053 amounts expended by the executor with respect to the maintenance and sale of decedent's residence incurred after the estate tax return's filing date of March 16, 1990.

For federal estate tax purposes, expenses of administering the probate estate, deductible under § 2053(a), are distinguished from expenses incurred in administering nonprobate assets, deductible under § 2053(b). Because Ripplestone was actually owned by Trust B and was only included in Marguerite's gross estate because of her general power of appointment over Trust B property, see § 2041, Ripplestone is properly considered nonprobate property. Section 2053(b) provides that an estate may deduct expenses to administer nonprobate property if: (1) the nonprobate property is included in the gross estate (undisputed here); (2) the expenses are paid before the period of limitation for assessment expires (conceded by the IRS * * *); and (3) the expenses would be allowable under § 2053(a) if the property were probate property. See § 2053(b); Reg. § 20.2053–8. Thus, under the present circumstances, the distinction between probate and nonprobate assets loses its significance. The question before us is whether the expenses to maintain and sell Ripplestone after the estate tax return filing date would be deductible if Ripplestone was a probate asset.

Section 2053(a) provides that the taxable estate is to be determined by deducting from the gross estate such amounts for funeral expenses, administration expenses, claims against the estate, and certain indebtedness with respect to estate property "as are allowable by the laws of the jurisdiction ... under which the estate is being administered." § 2053(a). Reg. § 20.2053–1(b)(2) addresses the effect of a state court decree:

> "The decision of a local court as to the amount and allowability under local law of a claim or administration expense will ordinarily be accepted if the court passes upon the facts upon which deductibility depends. * * * It must appear that the court actually passed upon the merits of the claim. This will be presumed in all cases of an active and genuine contest. * * * The decree will not be accepted if it is at variance with the law of the State[.]"

Thus, the decree of a local court ordinarily controls the federal estate tax deductibility only where the requisite foundation has been established.

Federal regulations under § 2053 provide the federal standard for deductibility of administration expenses. Reg. § 20.2053–3(a) states that amounts deductible as "administration expenses" are limited to expenses "actually and necessarily incurred in the administration of the decedent's estate." That regulation further elucidates that "actually and necessarily incurred" in estate administration means:

> "[I]n the collection of assets, payment of debts, and distribution of property to the persons entitled to it. The expenses contemplated in the law are such only as attend the settlement of an estate and the transfer of the property of the estate to individual beneficiaries or to a trustee. * * * Expenditures not essential to the proper settlement of the estate, but incurred for the individual benefit of the heirs, legatees, or devisees, may not be taken as deductions."

The regulations then consider the application of these general principles to specific types of administration expenses. Expenses with respect to preserving and distributing estate property are classified as miscellaneous administration expenses by Reg. § 20.2053–3(d). As to the expenses to maintain property, that regulation provides:

> "Expenses necessarily incurred in preserving and distributing the estate are deductible, including the cost of storing or maintaining property of the estate, if it is impossible to effect immediate distribution to the beneficiaries. Expenses for preserving and caring for the property may not include outlays for additions or improvements; nor will such expenses be allowed for a longer period than the executor is reasonably required to retain the property."

Reg. § 20.2053–3(d)(1). Likewise, the regulation provides that expenses for selling estate property are deductible only "if the sale is necessary in order to pay the decedent's debts, expenses of administration, or taxes, to preserve the estate, or to effect distribution." Reg. § 20.2053–3(d)(2).

B. Estate of Park v. Commissioner

Petitioners rely upon Estate of Park v. Commissioner, 475 F.2d 673 (6th Cir.1973), as controlling authority for their contention that the expenses at issue are deductible. In that case, this court reversed the Tax Court's denial of deductibility and allowed the estate to deduct real estate selling expenses that had been approved by a Michigan probate court applying state law, even though it was not shown that those expenses were necessary to the administration of the estate as required by the applicable federal regulations. Id. at 676–77. According to *Park's* literal reading of the statute, Congress intended the deductibility of administration expenses to be governed exclusively by state law * * *

Park illustrates two difficulties that have arisen from the interpretation of § 2053(a). First, in terms of interplay between the federal statute and its corresponding regulations, it has been argued that for over seventy years the regulations have imposed an additional requirement beyond what is stated in the statute. See Paul L. Caron, The Estate Tax Deduction for Administration Expenses: Reformulating Complementary Roles for Federal and State Law under I.R.C. § 2053(a)(2), 67 Cornell L. Rev. 981 (1982). The statutory language broadly allows all administration expenses as deductions subject only to the limitation that such expenses be allowable under state law. See § 2053(a). The regulations interpreting § 2053 convey a further "necessity" requirement, that deductible administration expenses be "actually and necessarily, incurred in the administration of the decedent's estate." Reg. § 20.2053–3(a). Thus, the "necessity" requirement contained in the regulations conditions deduction on an independent evaluation of necessity beyond the statute's only expressed restriction (i.e., state law allowability). * * * [I]t can be argued that to the extent that the regulations extend beyond the plain language of the statute, the regulations are subject to further judicial evaluation and possible invalidation. See generally Chevron, U.S.A., Inc. v. Natural Resources Defense Council, Inc., 467 U.S. 837 (1984). Because of this circuit's decision in *Park*, as explained *infra*, we need not resolve this issue.

The second related difficulty with interpreting § 2053(a) is the relationship between federal and state law. The circuits are divided regarding the proper level of deference to state probate law when determining federal estate tax deductibility. It is clear that in this circuit *Park* controls; the deductibility of administration expenses under I.R.C. § 2053(a) is governed by state law alone. * * * Although *Park's* approach has not been widely acclaimed, the Seventh Circuit has similarly concluded that state law is conclusive. Estate of Jenner v. Commissioner, 577 F.2d 1100, 1106 (7th Cir.1978) * * *. Thus, because deductibility is exclusively governed by state law, the federal "necessity" standard plays no role in jurisdictions, such as ours, that adhere to this position.[1]

---

1. We note that in the instant case the application of state law is not necessarily in conflict with the federal regulations. While the latter require that deductible administra-

The majority of circuits faced with the determination of which sovereign's law governs federal deductibility of administration expenses have acknowledged the importance of state law, but have held that federal regulations are controlling. These circuits take the position that the phrase "as are allowable" establishes merely a threshold; administration expenses must meet the federal necessity standard, and, in addition, not be foreclosed by local law. Put another way, because federal law governs the meaning of a term in the Internal Revenue Code, see Lyeth v. Hoey, 305 U.S. 188, 193 (1938), an initial inquiry into whether an expense is an "administration expense" is determined by federal law as guided by the applicable Treasury Regulations. Only then should a court look to state law to ensure that the expense is not thereunder precluded. If the expense satisfies the two-step inquiry it will be deductible. Courts advancing this threshold inquiry generally support their position with three arguments: first, that the language of the Code and its legislative history do not declare that state law alone governs deductibility; second, that because the "necessity" requirement has been in effect in substantially similar form since 1919, Congress has essentially approved the requirement by regularly reenacting § 2053 without material changes; and third, that for important policy reasons federal interests underpinning estate taxation should not receive disparate local treatment, particularly given the importance of protecting estates from depletion by expenses incurred on behalf of the beneficiaries rather than the estate as a whole. Caron, The Estate Tax Deduction for Administration Expenses: Reformulating Complementary Roles for Federal and State Law under I.R.C. § 2053(a)(2), *supra*. The Tax Court has adopted the position of these circuits, reasoning that Congress did not intend "to allow the integrity of the Federal estate tax to be undermined by the vagaries of State law." Estate of Posen v. Commissioner, 75 T.C. 355, 367–68 (1980). Thus, according to the predominant view, the question of deductibility for federal estate tax liability is a federal question governed by the applicable federal regulations.

Respondent urges that *Park* was incorrectly decided and should be reversed. It is well established that a panel of this court cannot overrule the decision of another panel. * * * The Supreme Court has yet to resolve the conflict. In 1989, the Court first granted but later dismissed certiorari in a case which could have shed light upon the validity of the federal regulations, United States v. White, 853 F.2d 107 (2d Cir.1988), cert. granted, 489 U.S. 1051 (1989), cert. dismissed, 493 U.S. 5 (1989). See

tion expenses be "actually and necessarily incurred in the administration of the decedent's estate," Reg. § 20.2053–3(a), the state law counterpart provides that "[a]llowances * * * which the probate court considers just and reasonable shall be made for actual and necessary expenses." Ohio Rev. Code Ann. § 2113.36 (Banks–Baldwin West 1996). Therefore, in the sense that both Ohio law and the federal regulations employ the term

"necessary," they are not in conflict. In view of our holding that petitioners failed to establish that the expenses at issue were necessary under Ohio law, we do not determine whether the "necessary" mandate in the state statute means the same as its counterpart in the federal regulations. As long as *Park* remains the law of this circuit, such consideration will always be rendered superfluous.

generally Paul L. Caron, Must an Administration Expense Allowed by State Law also Meet a Federal Necessity Test?, 70 J. Tax'n 352 (1989). * * *

Without further instruction from the Supreme Court, this circuit remains bound by *Park*, and the deductibility of administration expenses is governed solely by allowability under state law. To the extent that Treasury Regulations require anything more, they are inapplicable in this circuit because of the prior holding in *Park*.

In view of *Park's* binding precedent, petitioners make two primary arguments why we should conclude that the expenses at issue are deductible. First, according to petitioners, *Park* dictates that approval by the Ohio probate court of the expenses at issue is conclusive for federal estate tax deductibility. Second, petitioners argue that as a matter of Ohio law the expenses to maintain and sell the decedent's residence beyond the filing date of the estate tax return were necessary and otherwise allowable. As developed below, we need only resolve the latter issue.

C. State Court Approval

Not only have the circuits expressed differing opinions on the conclusiveness of state law, but variances also exist concerning the appropriate degree of federal court deference under § 2053 to lower state courts' interpretations of state probate law. Pursuant to *Park*, petitioners insist that in this circuit the plain meaning of § 2053 precludes federal court review of the deductibility of administration expenses that have been approved by the proper probate court * * *.

[R]espondent argues that *Park* is factually distinguishable because in *Park* the Commissioner conceded that the expenses at issue were allowable under the state's applicable law. No such concession occurred here. Therefore, according to respondent, this circuit has never indicated how a federal court passing on the deductibility of an administration expense should determine whether that expense would, in fact, be allowable under applicable state law. Because *Park* simply maintained the status quo with respect to the degree of deference, respondent argues that the rule announced in Commissioner v. Estate of Bosch, 387 U.S. 456 (1967), is apposite.

In *Bosch*, the Supreme Court considered the effect of a state trial court decree in a subsequent federal tax proceeding in the context of characterizing property interests for purposes of the marital deduction under § 2056. While federal authorities are bound to apply state law as explained by the state's highest court, the Court declared that Congress had only intended that federal courts give "proper regard" to the interpretation of state law by lower state courts. * * * Respondent suggests that because *Park* was decided on the heels of *Bosch*, *Park* should be read consistently with the preceding Supreme Court directive. A probate court is not the highest state court, and its approval of administration expenses would be persuasive, but not conclusive, proof of deductibility under state law. * * *

* * * [I]n the present action there is nothing in the record before us to establish that the local probate court actually reviewed and approved the

disputed expenses. * * * Petitioners' counsel admitted at oral argument that there was never a hearing conducted with respect to these accountings.

Moreover, the jurisdiction of an Ohio probate court to approve expenses to administer nonprobate assets is controvertible. Because Ripplestone was never part of the decedent's probate estate, respondent maintains that an Ohio probate court, a court of limited jurisdiction, is without jurisdiction to approve the expenses at issue here. Petitioners have not countered with a showing of sound authority for the probate court's jurisdiction to approve expenses to administer nonprobate property. * * *

In view of the controverted nature of the probate court's jurisdiction, combined with a record that falls far short of demonstrating probate court approval, it is clear that the situation here in no way parallels the situation described in *Park*, where confirmed approval by a state probate court definitively determined the federal deductibility question. Therefore, we need not further address petitioners' first argument.

D. Necessity of Expenses

Since we are bound by *Park's* directive exclusively to apply state law, petitioners must demonstrate that the expenses at issue in the present case qualify for deductibility under Ohio law. Ohio probate law specifies that "[A]llowances * * * which the probate court considers just and reasonable shall be made for actual and necessary expenses." Ohio Rev. Code Ann. § 2113.36 (Banks–Baldwin West 1996). Thus, despite *Park's* rejection of using the "necessity" standard contained in the federal regulations, the estate still must show that the expenses it incurred with respect to the maintenance and sale of the residence after March 16, 1990, were actual, necessary, just, and reasonable under Ohio law.

The Tax Court concluded that expenses to maintain Ripplestone until March 16, 1990, were necessary, but maintenance and selling expenses beyond that point were not necessary. As the Tax Court explained, the estate preserved Ripplestone until March 16, 1990, in order to effectuate the provision in decedent's will granting the Cleveland Museum of Art a right of selection of personal property. After the distribution of all personal property and the filing of the estate tax return, the estate had no reason not to distribute Ripplestone according to the trust agreement. Following the appointment of $2 million of Trust B's assets to Trust A and payment by Trust B of the taxes attributable to Trust B's inclusion in decedent's gross estate, at that point Trust B had no further reason to exist and the remaining assets should have been transferred to Trust C, whereupon Trust C would bear the maintenance burden and decide whether to sell the property. Therefore, the estate's retention of Ripplestone until it could be sold benefitted Trust C's beneficiaries at the expense of the overall estate. * * *

Insofar as the Cleveland Museum of Art had yet to finish its selection process, the maintenance of Ripplestone through March 16, 1990, was directly related to the distribution of the personal property of the decedent in accordance with her will. Thus, the estate properly deducted Ripple-stone's maintenance costs incurred through March 16, 1990. In contrast, we hold that the expenses incurred in selling the property and maintaining it beyond March 16, 1990, do not constitute deductible administration expenses under Ohio law. Because there is no reason why the residence was not transferred to the designated Trust C after distribution of the personal property and the filing of the estate tax return (even if Ripplestone is considered a probate asset), and because Trust B maintained sufficient liquid assets to cover the tax burden (which was likely only to diminish in the future), the further expenses of maintaining and selling the property beyond March 16, 1990, were not incurred by the estate out of necessity.[2]

* * *

Estate of Millikin v. Commissioner

125 F.3d 339 (6th Cir.1997) (en banc).

■ Merritt, Circuit Judge. * * *

II.   ANALYSIS

A.   The Standard for Determining Deductibility of Administration Expenses

* * * The estate argues that the costs of maintaining Ripplestone are administration expenses allowed under Ohio law. Therefore, the estate claims, they are deductible under §§ 2053(a)(2) & 2053(b). The Commissioner, however, claims that state law alone should not be determinative. The Commissioner relies on Reg. § 20.2053–3(a), which provides, in part: "The amounts deductible from a decedent's gross estate as 'administration expenses' * * * are limited to such expenses as are actually and necessarily incurred in the administration of the decedent's estate; that is, in the collection of assets, payment of debts, and distribution of property to the persons entitled to it." The Commissioner asserts that this regulation imposes a separate, federal requirement that expenses must be "actually and necessarily incurred" in order to be deductible, and claims that this requirement is in addition to the statutory requirement that the expenses must be "allowable by the laws of the jurisdiction." The Commissioner argues that this additional requirement does not conflict with the statutory standard. Instead, the regulation merely defines the allegedly ambiguous term "administration expenses" in the statute.

Over twenty years ago, a panel of this Court considered a similar question in Estate of Park v. Commissioner, 475 F.2d 673 (6th Cir.1973), and ruled that deductibility of administration expenses is determined solely under state probate law. The Tax Court properly considered itself bound by Estate of Park, as did the panel of our Court that heard the estate's initial

---

2. No party has asked us to review the deductions that were actually included in the estate tax return, including the $150,000 esti-mated selling expenses; therefore, we do not address the propriety of that deduction.

appeal. In this en banc review, however, the Commissioner has asked us to reconsider *Estate of Park*. In light of developments in the law since *Estate of Park* was decided—particularly the Supreme Court's decision in Chevron U.S.A. Inc. v. Natural Resources Defense Council, Inc., 467 U.S. 837 (1984), and opinions from other circuits—we find that *Estate of Park* is no longer good law, and we therefore overturn that decision.

The *Estate of Park* panel held that "[b]y the literal language of § 2053(a), Congress has left the deductibility of administrative expenses to be governed by their chargeability against the assets of the estate under state law." *Estate of Park*, 475 F.2d at 676. The panel did not provide any analysis for its conclusion that the Commissioner's definition of deductible expenses should be ignored. * * *

The Commissioner argues that the statutory phrase "administration expenses" is not self-defining, and that the treasury regulation in question provides a permissible construction of the statute to which we must defer. We agree. In Chevron U.S.A. Inc. v. Natural Resources Defense Council, Inc., the Supreme Court held:

> "When a court reviews an agency's construction of the statute which it administers, it is confronted with two questions. First, always, is the question whether Congress has directly spoken to the precise question at issue. If the intent of Congress is clear, that is the end of the matter; for the court, as well as the agency, must give effect to the unambiguously expressed intent of Congress. If, however, the court determines Congress has not directly addressed the precise question at issue, the court does not simply impose its own construction on the statute, as would be necessary in the absence of an administrative interpretation. Rather, if the statute is silent or ambiguous with respect to the specific issue, the question for the court is whether the agency's answer is based on a permissible construction of the statute."

467 U.S. 837, 842–43 (1984) (citations omitted).

The structure of § 2053(a) compels a two-part test for deductibility of expenses under that statute. First, an expense must be one of the four types of expenses specifically enumerated in the statute. If an expense qualifies as one of those four types, it must further be "allowable by the laws of the jurisdiction * * * under which the estate is being administered." § 2053(a). We agree with the Commissioner that the phrase "administration expenses" is neither self-defining nor unambiguous. Moreover we find that the Treasury Regulation's construction of that phrase to include only those expenses "actually and necessarily[ ] incurred in the administration of the decedent's estate; that is, in the collection of assets, payment of debts, and distribution of property to the persons entitled to it," Reg. § 20.2053–3(a), is a permissible construction of the statute. We are therefore bound by that construction.

Our decision is consistent with the decisions of all the other circuits, with one possible exception,[3] that have considered this issue. * * *

B. Necessity of the Claimed Administration Expenses

The Tax Court held that the costs of maintaining Ripplestone after March 16, 1990, were not allowable administration expenses under Ohio law. Our decision today imposes an additional requirement that expenses must meet in order to be deductible as administration expenses, but does not alter the statutory requirement that such expenses must be allowable under applicable state probate law. Therefore, affirmance would be required if the Tax Court's analysis of this issue were correct. Unfortunately, we find that the factual record is not sufficiently clear for us to determine this issue. Therefore, we must remand the case to the Tax Court for further factual development and application of the correct standard as set forth above.

The Tax Court * * * found that Ohio law allows only those administrative expenses that are necessary, reasonable, and just. * * * The Tax Court held that maintenance of Ripplestone was not necessary because Trust B held assets other than Ripplestone worth $9,026,540.75 at the time of Marguerite Millikin's death. The Tax Court held that Ripplestone should have been transferred to Trust C, rather than being maintained by the executor and Trust B's trustee.

The estate does not challenge the Tax Court's holding that Ohio law allows only necessary administration expenses. The estate argues, however, that maintenance of Ripplestone and the resulting costs were necessary to administer the estate properly. In particular, the estate claims that it was necessary for it to delay the final distribution of Trust B's assets pending an audit of the estate that it reasonably believed to be inevitable. The estate contends that an audit was nearly certain in light of the large size of the gross estate (just under $23 million) and the uncertainty inherent in valuing Ripplestone. It argues that Ripplestone, in particular, had to be maintained in Trust B because that trust contained only $220,822 in other assets immediately after the estate filed its estate tax return. That amount, the estate claims, was an insufficient reserve against the possibility of a tax deficiency assessment.

The estate's theory, if supported by the facts concerning the amount of available resources and the uncertainty of the tax situation, may be meritorious. Several state probate courts have approved the reservation of assets against the possibility of a tax audit and a deficiency assessment. * * *

We express no opinion on the necessity of the estate's retention of Ripplestone, however, because the factual record is not sufficiently developed to allow us to resolve that issue. The Commissioner disputes the

---

3. Estate of Jenner v. Commissioner, 577 F.2d 1100 (7th Cir.1978), can be read to hold that deductibility of administration expenses is governed solely by state law. Indeed, at least one other circuit appears to have read Estate of Jenner in that manner. See Estate of Love v. Commissioner, 923 F.2d 335, 337 n.6 (4th Cir.1991). That is not the only possible reading of that case, however. * * *

estate's claim that Trust B contained only $220,822 in assets other than Ripplestone after the estate filed its tax return. We are unable to resolve this dispute on the record before us. In addition, the estate conceded at oral argument that Trust B's trustee disbursed income from its securities to Trust C. The current record is inadequate to determine the number and amount of those disbursements, or whether they were required under Trust B's terms. All of these factors are relevant to proper resolution of the estate's claim that it was necessary to reserve Ripplestone against potential tax liability. Remand is therefore required. * * *

ILLUSTRATIVE MATERIAL

A. THE ROLE OF STATE LAW UNDER § 2053

Although the issue of the role of state law pervades the deduction of all of the items listed in § 2053(a), much of the litigation, as *Estate of Millikin* illustrates, has focused on the deductibility of administration expenses under § 2053(a)(2). With the Sixth Circuit's en banc overruling of its prior *Estate of Park* decision, the Seventh Circuit now is the only Circuit to give state law controlling weight. In 1989, the Supreme Court granted certiorari in a case involving the impact of state law in the deduction of attorneys' fees as administration expenses under § 2053(a)(2) but, after hearing oral arguments, dismissed the case on technical grounds. United States v. White, 853 F.2d 107 (2d Cir.1988), cert. granted, 489 U.S. 1051, cert. dismissed, 493 U.S. 5 (1989) (per curiam).

B. OTHER ISSUES UNDER § 2053

1. *Estimated Expenses*

Reg. § 20.2053–1(b)(3) provides that an expense may be deducted under § 2053 even though "its exact amount is not then known, provided it is ascertainable with reasonable accuracy." However, "[n]o deduction may be taken upon the basis of a vague or uncertain estimate." Finally, if the amount cannot be ascertained at the time of final audit of the return, the executor may seek relief if the amount becomes fixed before expiration of the period allowed for filing a petition in the Tax Court or a claim for refund.

2. *Amounts Deductible Under Both the Estate Tax and the Income Tax*

Section 642(g) provides that amounts deductible under §§ 2053 or 2054 for estate tax purposes cannot be claimed by the estate as income tax deductions (or utilized to offset the sales price of property for purposes of determining gain or loss) unless the estate files (1) a statement that the amounts have not been allowed as deductions under §§ 2053 or 2054, and (2) a waiver of the right to have such amounts allowed at any time as deductions for estate tax purposes. Although the language of § 642(g) applies to any amount deductible under § 2053, Reg. § 1.642(g)–1 limits the application of § 642(g) to amounts deductible under § 2053(a)(2). Because amounts paid in satisfaction of claims against the estate are deductible under § 2053(a)(3), not § 2053(a)(2), payments made during administration for claims against the estate can be deducted for both estate and income tax purposes.

Although no double tax benefit is permitted with respect to § 2053(a)(2) and § 2054 items, the election gives the executor or administrator the opportunity to utilize the expenditure either against the gross estate or against estate income, depending upon which tax bracket is higher. Of course, given that income tax rates are lower than estate tax rates, the election typically will be made to use such expenses as estate tax deductions. In making the election, however, the executor or administrator must take into account the respective interests of the beneficiaries of the income and of the corpus of the estate.

It is not necessary that administration expenses subject to the election be taken in their entirety either on the estate tax or the income tax return. Thus, for example, where an estate paid administration expenses in two separate years, it was entitled to take the expenses incurred in the first year as an estate tax deduction and those incurred in the second year as an income tax deduction, assuming that the proper waiver was filed under § 642(g). Rev.Rul. 70–361, 1970–2 C.B. 133. The same rule applies to deductions within a single year. Reg. § 1.642(g)–2.

Care must be taken in exercising the election because the waiver required by § 642(g) is irrevocable once it is filed. For example, in Estate of Darby v. Wiseman, 323 F.2d 792 (10th Cir.1963), the executors filed income tax returns claiming certain administration expenses as income tax deductions and also filed the requisite waivers. Later it was discovered that the deductions did not provide an income tax benefit to the estate. While the statute of limitations was still open both for the estate and the income tax returns, the executors filed a statement changing their election and claimed the right to take the deductions on the estate tax return. The court upheld the Service's determination that, under the predecessor of Reg. § 1.642(g)–1, the waivers filed with the income tax returns constituted an irrevocable relinquishment of the right to claim the expenses as estate tax deductions. The court noted that although the Regulations are generous in deferring the time for filing the required waiver, the waiver once filed becomes final. As a result, the typical practice either is to defer filing the waiver until audit of the estate tax return or to deduct the expense on both the estate and the income tax returns (with appropriate disclosure) and to subsequently abandon the deduction on one of the returns (by filing or failing to file the requisite waiver) when the facts reveal the more desirable option.

SECTION B.   SPECIFIC DEDUCTIONS

1.   FUNERAL EXPENSES

Generally, expenses incurred by the estate for the burial of the decedent are deductible. The Regulations provide that reasonable expenditures incurred "for a tombstone, monument, mausoleum, or for a burial lot, either for the decedent or his family, including a reasonable expenditure for its future care, may be deducted [as funeral expenses] provided such an expenditure is allowable by the local law. Includible in funeral expenses is the cost of transportation of the person bringing the body to the place of burial." Reg. § 20.2053–2.

ILLUSTRATIVE MATERIAL

A.   SCOPE OF "FUNERAL EXPENSES"

In sanctioning expenses "for the decedent or his family," the regulations permit the deduction for a bequest to a cemetery association for the perpetual care of a family burial lot in which the decedent was interred. Rev.Rul. 57–530, 1957–2 C.B. 621. This avoids difficult allocation issues, but the decedent cannot unreasonably provide for the burial expenses of his family. For example, Rev.Rul. 57–530 disallowed a deduction for a bequest for the perpetual care of family burial lots other than that in which the decedent was buried, even though the lots were located in the same cemetery.

In Estate of Davenport v. Commissioner, 92 T.C.M. 324 (2006), the Tax Court disallowed a claimed $3,639 deduction for a "funeral luncheon":

> "[T]he record is likewise insufficient to establish the requisite necessity in connection with decedent's funeral. From the testimony at trial, it is to be inferred that the focus of the luncheon was on recognizing and thanking third parties for their support both during decedent's life and after her passing. That represents a shift from the traditional focus of a funeral in eulogizing and laying to rest the deceased. The evidence, consisting only of broad and generalized statements about the intent of the luncheon, deprives the Court of any ability to compare what may in fact have transpired there with activities typically associated with funeral services."

B.   EFFECT OF REIMBURSEMENT OF FUNERAL EXPENSES

The Service has ruled that the deduction for funeral expenses must be reduced by amounts paid by the Veteran's Administration or the Social Security Administration for funeral expenses. Rev.Rul. 66–234, 1966–2 C.B. 436. This same principle applies if the funeral expenses are later recovered by the executor in a wrongful death action. Rev.Rul. 77–274, 1977–2 C.B. 326.

2.   ADMINISTRATION EXPENSES

As explained in *Estate of Millikin*, Reg. § 20.2053–3(a) provides that the amounts deductible as administration expenses "are limited to such expenses as are actually and necessarily incurred in the administration of the decedent's estate; that is, in the collection of assets, payments of debts, and distribution of property to the persons entitled to it. * * * Expenditures not essential to the proper settlement of the estate, but incurred for the individual benefit of the heirs, legatees, or devisees, may not be taken as deductions. Administration expenses include (1) executor's commissions; (2) attorney's fees; and (3) miscellaneous expenses."

ILLUSTRATIVE MATERIAL

A.   VALIDITY OF THE "NECESSITY" REQUIREMENT

With the Sixth Circuit's en banc overruling of its prior *Estate of Park* decision in *Estate of Millikin*, the Seventh Circuit now is the only remaining Circuit to hold that the necessity requirement of the regulations is invalid on the ground that § 2053(a)(2) requires that a state probate court's allowance of an administration expense is controlling for estate tax purposes. See Ballance v. United States, 347 F.2d 419, 423 (7th Cir.1965). The Second, Fourth, Fifth, Ninth, and Eleventh Circuits have held that the necessity requirement of the regulations is valid because federal law is properly invoked to define the term "administration expenses" in the statute. See Estate of Love v. Commissioner, 923 F.2d 335, 337–38 (4th Cir.1991); United States v. White, 853 F.2d 107, 112–15 (2d Cir.1988), cert. granted, 489 U.S. 1051, cert. dismissed, 493 U.S. 5 (1989) (per curiam); Marcus v. DeWitt, 704 F.2d 1227, 1229–30 (11th Cir.1983); Hibernia Bank v. United States, 581 F.2d 741, 744 (9th Cir.1978); Pitner v. United States, 388 F.2d 651, 658 (5th Cir.1968). See also Estate of Posen v. Commissioner, 75 T.C. 355, 366–68 (1980). For an argument that both of these approaches are flawed, see Caron, Confusion Reigns Over State Law and Administration Expenses, 74 Tax Notes 1314 (1997).

B. EXECUTOR'S COMMISSIONS

The regulations permit an executor or administrator to deduct her commissions if they are paid or fixed by a probate court decree. Reg. § 20.2053–3(b)(1). Absent such a decree, the Service will approve the commissions in its final audit if the Service is satisfied that the commissions will be paid and are within the amounts allowed by state law and customarily allowed for estates of similar size and character. See Estate of Tehan v. Commissioner, 89 T.C.M. 1374 (2005) (disallowing portion of executor's commission allowed by probate court in excess of maximum amount allowed by state statute). Although Reg. § 20.2053–3(b)(2) precludes a deduction for a bequest or devise to the executor in lieu of commissions, a deduction is allowed where the will sets the compensation payable to the executor and this amount does not exceed the compensation allowable by the local law or practice.

C. ATTORNEY'S FEES

Reg. § 20.2053–3(c) provides that "[t]he executor or administrator, in filing the estate tax return, may deduct such an amount of attorney's fees as has actually been paid, or an amount which at the time of filing may reasonably be expected to be paid." If the audit of the estate's tax return is completed before the fee is approved by the probate court and paid, the Service will allow the claimed deduction upon a showing that "the amount claimed will be paid and that it does not exceed a reasonable renumeration for the services rendered, taking into account the size and character of the estate and the local law and practice." Factors considered in determining the reasonableness of attorney's fees under § 2053 include the size and the nature of the estate, the amount of work involved, actual and contemplated litigation, and the length of time the estate was under administration. Estate of Prell v. Commissioner, 48 T.C. 67, 74 (1967).

As in the case of administration expenses generally, attorney's fees incurred by beneficiaries and reimbursed by the estate are not deductible if they are incident to litigation that "is not essential to the proper settlement of the estate." Reg. § 20.2053–3(c)(3). Thus, attorney's fees incurred by beneficiaries in will contests generally are deductible under this standard. See, e.g., Pitner v. United States, 388 F.2d 651 (5th Cir.1967) (litigation to establish decedent's agreement to execute joint and mutual wills deductible under § 2053(a)(2)). But attorney's fees incurred by beneficiaries in other situations are not deductible where the litigation is not essential to the settlement of the estate. See, e.g, LeFever v. Commissioner, 100 F.3d 778 (10th Cir.1996) (litigation to contest § 2032A recapture tax imposed when special use property no longer put to qualified use not deductible under § 2053(a)(2) because tax imposed on heirs rather than estate).

Several recent cases discuss the role of state law in deducting attorney's fees under § 2053(a)(2). In United States v. White, 650 F.Supp. 904 (W.D.N.Y. 1987), rev'd, 853 F.2d 107 (2d Cir.1988), cert. granted, 489 U.S. 1051, cert. dismissed, 493 U.S. 5 (1989) (per curiam), the decedent left a gross estate of $455,000. Her will named a local attorney as executor of her estate. The executor appointed himself as attorney for the estate. The estate deducted executor's commissions of $17,500 and attorney's fees of $16,500 on the federal estate tax return. The probate court approved these expenses in its final accounting under applicable state statutes that set the allowable executor's commission as a percentage of the estate and the allowable attorney's fee as a "just and reasonable" amount. Under New York law, attorney's fees are fixed either by an adversary proceeding or a judicial settlement in which releases are obtained from all legatees. In *White*, the executor followed the latter route and obtained releases from the nine residuary legatees.

On the audit of the estate tax return, the Service requested that the estate provide "justification for the legal fees claimed" as an administration expense deduction. The Service noted that the allowance of attorneys' fees as an administration expense depended on the facts and circumstances of each case, including (1) the amount involved; (2) the time and effort of the attorney; (3) the seriousness of problems; (4) the results obtained; (5) the experience and ability of the attorney; and (6) the length of administration. The Service sought either the attorney's time records or an itemized list of legal work performed for the estate, the time expended for each service, and the hourly rate charged. The attorney refused to supply the requested information and instead forwarded to the Service a letter he had obtained from the probate court. The letter stated that upon "re-review" of the case, the probate court was convinced that the attorney's fees were properly allowed under state law.

The Service was not satisfied with this response and issued two summonses demanding "any and all records and documents relating to the administration of the estate," including records of the activities as both executor and attorney. The attorney refused to comply with the summonses, and the Service disallowed the administration expense deduction for the attorney's fees (but not the executor's commissions). The Service then instituted a summons enforcement proceeding.

The district court refused to enforce the summonses for two reasons. First, the district court did not want to "second guess" the probate court's decision where the probate court had applied the appropriate state law criteria for determining the allowance of attorney's fees as announced by the highest court of the state. Second, the district court held that the Service had not produced evidence of fraud or overreaching by the attorney or the probate court indicating that the probate court had not passed on the factors upon which deductibility depended. As a result, the district court concluded that the Service had failed to satisfy the first requirement for judicial enforcement of a summons: because the Service was bound under § 2053(a)(2) to accept the probate court's application of state law in allowing the attorney's fee, the Service failed to make the necessary showing that its investigation would be conducted for a "legitimate purpose."

The Second Circuit reversed and ordered the enforcement of the summonses. The Second Circuit ruled that Congress had not intended to make probate court decrees controlling on the federal courts and the Service in determining the deductibility of administration expenses. Instead, under Commissioner v. Estate of Bosch, 387 U.S. 456 (1967), the federal courts and the Service could reexamine the application of state law by the probate court, after giving "proper regard" to the probate court's decision. The Second Circuit held that although the federal courts and the Service are bound by the factors established by the highest court of the state for awarding attorney's fees, they are not bound by the probate court's application of those factors. The Second Circuit noted that at the summons enforcement stage of the proceedings, the validity of the probate court's decree was not at issue. Although the Second Circuit questioned whether the Service was "allocating wisely the time and effort of its limited staff" in pursuing this matter, it concluded that the Service had a "legitimate purpose" for issuing the summonses to investigate the circumstances of the expenses.

The Supreme Court granted a writ of certiorari but, two weeks after hearing oral argument, the Court dismissed the writ as having been "improvidently granted." 493 U.S. 5 (1989). Although the Court did not explain further its reasons for dismissing the case, the likeliest ground is that it was moot because the attorney's time records would be disclosed in the estate's pending refund case in district court. The refund case was settled one year later when the Government agreed to refund the entire amount of estate tax attributable to the disputed attorney's fees deduction. Consent to Judgment, White v. United States, No. 88–0725T (W.D.N.Y. Sept. 18, 1990). See also O'Neal v. United States, 258 F.3d 1265 (11th Cir.2001) (upholding denial of deduction of $75,000 attorney's fee in $5.3 million estate because estate refused to turn over time records supporting amount of fee claimed); Estate of Baird v. Commissioner, 73 T.C.M. 1883 (1997) (upholding deduction of $368,000 attorney's fee in $17.2 million estate as consistent with reasonableness standard of New York law, but denying portion of fee attributable to two activities not necessary to administration of estate: (1) sale of decedent's residence that was specifically devised to one of her children; and (2) obtaining advance payment of executor's commissions to decedent's two children); TAM 200532049 (Mar. 23, 2005) (upholding deduction of attorney's fee in successful malpractice action against former attorney for estate).

D.   MISCELLANEOUS EXPENSES

1.   General

In addition to executor's commissions and attorney's fees, the regulations include a variety of other "miscellaneous" administration expenses, including court costs, surrogates' fees, accountants' fees, appraisers' fees, clerk hire, costs of preserving and distributing the estate, and costs of storing or maintaining property of the estate, if it is impossible to effect immediate distribution to the beneficiaries. Reg. § 20.2053–3(d). The regulations also explain that expenses for preserving and caring for property are not deductible under § 2053(a)(2) if they include capital outlays for additions or improvements. See Estate of Love v. Commissioner, 923 F.2d 335 (4th Cir.1991) (estate's payment to owner of stallion treated as nondeductible purchase of asset rather than as deductible administration expense).

The two categories of miscellaneous administration expenses that have generated the most litigation are interest and selling expenses.

2. *Interest*

Interest on money borrowed to pay death taxes generally is deductible under § 2053(a)(2) where the estate lacks sufficient liquidity and otherwise would be forced to sell estate assets to pay the tax. See Estate of Knepp v. United States, 358 F.Supp.2d 421 (M.D.Pa.2004); Estate of McKee v. Commissioner, 72 T.C.M. 324 (1996); Estate of Todd v. Commissioner, 57 T.C. 288 (1971); Rev.Rul. 84–75, 1984–1 C.B. 193. Interest on late payment of estate taxes is deductible, even absent such liquidity problems. See Estate of Bahr v. Commissioner, 68 T.C. 74 (1977); Rev.Rul. 78–125, 1978–1 C.B. 292. See also Rev.Rul. 83–24, 1983-1 C.B. 229 (interest on late payment of foreign death taxes); Rev.Rul. 81–256, 1981–2 C.B. 183 (interest on deferred, late payment, or deficiency assessment of state death taxes); Rev.Rul. 79–252, 1979–2 C.B. 333 (interest on federal estate tax deficiency); cf. Rev.Rul. 81–154, 1981–1 C.B. 470 (§ 6651 penalty for willful failure to file timely returns and to make timely payment not deductible administration expense).[4] However, interest on additional estate tax imposed on an heir because the heir disposed of property subject to special use valuation under § 2032A is not deductible under § 2053(a)(2) because the liability for the tax is imposed on the heir rather than on the estate. Rev.Rul. 90–8, 1990–1 C.B. 173.[5]

Where the decedent had taken out a loan during life, interest accrued to the date of death is deductible as a claim against the estate under Reg. § 20.2053–4. However, the courts have held that the post-death interest on such obligations is deductible under § 2053(a)(2), assuming that payment of the interest was allowable under local law and was necessary to avoid a forced sale of assets of the estate. See Estate of Wheless v. Commissioner, 72 T.C. 470 (1979); Estate of Webster v. Commissioner, 65 T.C. 968 (1976); Ballance v. United States, 347 F.2d 419 (7th Cir.1965). Rev.Rul. 77–461, 1977–2 C.B. 324, is to the contrary, holding that only post-death interest on debt incurred by the estate to preserve estate assets is a deductible administration expense.[6]

---

4. In Estate of O'Daniel v. United States, 6 F.3d 321 (5th Cir.1993), the court denied a deduction for interest paid on an estate tax liability that eventually was refunded to the taxpayer.

5. Prior to 1997, interest on estate tax deferred under § 6166 (see p. 782) was deductible without regard to the reasons for the election (although the interest was deductible only as it accrued (Estate of Bailly v. Commissioner, 81 T.C. 246 (1983); Rev. Rul. 80–250, 1980–2 C.B. 278)). Section 7481(d), enacted in 1988, permitted the Tax Court to reopen a case to allow a § 2053(a)(2) deduc-

tion for such interest in determining estate tax liability. The 1997 Act added § 2053(c)(1)(D) to deny a deduction for interest paid on estate taxes deferred under § 6166. The legislative history explains that this change was made to eliminate "the need to file annual supplemental estate tax returns and make complex iterative computations to claim an estate tax deduction for interest paid." S. Rep. No. 949, 105th Cong., 1st Sess. 48 (1997).

6. Rev.Rul. 69–402, 1969–2 C.B. 176, allowed as deductible administration expenses the post-death interest on federal and

3. Selling Expenses

Reg. § 20.2053–3(d)(2) provides that expenses incurred in selling estate assets are deductible under § 2053(a)(2) "if the sale is necessary in order to pay the decedent's debts, expenses of administration, or taxes, to preserve the estate, or to effect distribution." Examples of such selling expenses include brokerage commissions and appraisal fees. As *Estate of Millikin* illustrates, much of the litigation involving the deductibility of selling expenses turns on the factual necessity for the sale of estate property.

For example, in Estate of Smith v. Commissioner, 57 T.C. 650 (1972), aff'd, 510 F.2d 479 (2d Cir.), cert. denied, 423 U.S. 827 (1975), the estate incurred commission expenses to sell sculpture created by the decedent. The sales resulted in proceeds in excess of those required to pay debts of the decedent, taxes, and expenses of administration. The Tax Court held that only the commissions on the sales necessary to raise the cash to pay the administration expenses were deductible under § 2053(a)(2). The Second Circuit affirmed. Subsequently, Estate of Vatter v. Commissioner, 65 T.C. 633 (1975), aff'd, 556 F.2d 563 (2d Cir.1976) (per curiam), allowed a deduction for certain expenses incurred in disposing of property for amounts in excess of the cash needs of the estate. The executor sold three pieces of real estate and distributed the proceeds in excess of the cash required by the estate to the trustee of a residuary trust who did not desire to have the real estate in the trust. The Tax Court upheld the deductibility of the selling expenses for all three pieces of real estate. The court distinguished *Estate of Smith* on the ground that the will involved in that case had contemplated a distribution in kind of the sculptures to the testamentary trustee and therefore the sales were for the benefit of the trust. Additionally, in *Estate of Smith* there was doubt whether the expenses were allowable under state law; in *Estate of Vatter* the Tax Court concluded that state law allowed the expenses and also relied on the fact that both the executor and the trustee were given the power to sell the property, so that there was no express or implied intention that the property pass in kind to the testamentary trustee. The Tax Court declined to rule on the validity of the Regulations because it found that the expenses were allowable both under state law and under the Regulations. Similarly, in Estate of Papson v. Commissioner, 73 T.C. 290 (1979), a deduction was allowed for brokers' commissions incurred by an executor-testamentary trustee to replace a primary tenant in a shopping center held by the estate; the court rejected the Commissioner's argument that the cost was incurred for the benefit of the testamentary trust rather than the estate.

Although anticipated costs of disposing of property may affect the valuation of property, several courts have permitted the deduction of such selling

---

state income tax deficiencies originally asserted against the decedent but incurred by the executor as a result of contesting the imposition of the taxes. Rev.Rul. 71–422, 1971–2 C.B. 255, held that interest on an income tax deficiency of the decedent paid after death, but allocable to a period prior to death, is a § 691(b) deduction for estate income tax purposes in the year paid and is also a § 2053(a)(3) deduction; for the period after death, interest could be deducted either as a § 2053 deduction or as a § 642(g) deduction, but not both. Estate of Webster v. Commissioner, 65 T.C. 968 (1976), held that post-death interest on decedent's gift tax liability constituted a deductible administration expense.

expenses under § 2053(a)(2). See Estate of Jenner v. Commissioner, 577 F.2d 1100 (7th Cir.1978) (underwriter's discount); Estate of Joslyn v. Commissioner, 566 F.2d 677 (9th Cir.1977) (underwriter's discount); Estate of Joslyn v. Commissioner, 500 F.2d 382 (9th Cir.1974) (underwriter's fee). However, in Rev.Rul. 83–30, 1983–1 C.B. 224, the Service ruled that although underwriting fees were deductible under § 2053(a)(2), they would not be taken into account in determining the blockage discount (see p. 697) in valuing the stock. See also Gillespie v. United States, 94–1 U.S.T.C. ¶ 60,166 (2d Cir.1994) (following Rev.Rul. 83–30).

E. EXPENSES OF PROTRACTED ADMINISTRATION AND EXPENSES THAT BENEFIT BENEFICIARIES RATHER THAN THE ESTATE

The regulations and case law distinguish deductible administration expenses from nondeductible expenses in two related contexts. First, although "[e]xpenses necessarily incurred in preserving and distributing the estate are deductible, including the cost of storing or maintaining property of the estate, if it is impossible to effect immediate distribution to the beneficiaries," these expenses are not allowed "for a longer period than the executor is reasonably required to retain the property." Reg. § 20.2053–3(d)(1). Second, even if the estate's administration is not unduly protracted, expenses are not deductible if they are incurred for the benefit of the beneficiaries rather than for the benefit of the estate: "Expenditures not essential to the proper settlement of the estate, but incurred for the individual benefit of the heirs, legatees, or devisees, may not be taken as deductions." Reg. § 20.2053–3(a).

For example, in Estate of Posen v. Commissioner, 75 T.C. 355, 367–68 (1980), the Tax Court stated that "a distinction can and should be drawn between expenses necessary to the estate and those incurred solely for the benefit of the beneficiaries. While we acknowledge that any expense which serves to preserve the estate also benefits the beneficiaries, it does not follow that any expenditure which benefits the beneficiaries can properly be considered an expense of the estate." Similarly, in Hibernia Bank v. United States, 581 F.2d 741 (9th Cir.1978), the court held that where an executor borrowed money to maintain a mansion owned by the decedent until it could be sold, interest payments were not deductible administration expenses because the mansion was not sold for seven years and the estate was kept open because the heirs wanted cash instead of the property. In Estate of Peckham v. Commissioner, 19 B.T.A. 1020 (1930), a provision in a will requiring that an estate be kept intact for six years constituted an unreasonable prolongation of the estate, and the court allowed deductions only for those expenses incurred in the first three years. See also Marcus v. DeWitt, 704 F.2d 1227 (11th Cir.1983); Estate of Streeter v. Commissioner, 491 F.2d 375 (3d Cir.1974).

Expenses incurred in connection with will contests frequently involve the question whether such expenses are incurred on behalf of the estate or on behalf of the actual or claimed beneficiaries of the estate. Pitner v. United States, 388 F.2d 651 (5th Cir.1967), drew a distinction between expenses incurred as a result of beneficiaries suing to determine their share of an estate as against other beneficiaries (which generally would not be deductible) and expenses incurred to determine which one of two groups had an interest in the estate (which would be deductible). See also Estate of Heckscher v. Commissioner, 63 T.C. 485 (1975) (applying this distinction).

3. CLAIMS AGAINST THE ESTATE

Estate of McMorris v. Commissioner

243 F.3d 1254 (10th Cir.2001).

■ BRISCOE, CIRCUIT JUDGE: * * *

I.

The facts are undisputed. Donn McMorris, Evelyn's husband, died in 1990, and Evelyn received 13.4[] shares of stock in NW Transport Service, Inc., from his estate. The stock was reported in Donn's estate tax return at an appraised value of $1,726,562.50 per share as of the date of his death and that value became Evelyn's basis in the stock. Evelyn, through her conservator Jerry McMorris, entered into an agreement with NW Transport to redeem the stock for $29,500,000 (approximately $2,200,000 per share), payable over 120 months at ten percent interest.

Evelyn died in 1991, a resident of Colorado. In her federal estate tax return, her estate claimed deductions of $3,960,525 and $641,222, respectively, for her 1991 federal and state income tax liabilities. * * * A large part of the income reported on Evelyn's income tax returns resulted from the gain on redemption of the NW Transport stock.

In January 1994, the Commissioner issued a deficiency notice to Donn's estate disputing, among other things, the value of the NW Transport stock. Specifically, the Commissioner valued the stock at $3,618,040 per share. Donn's estate contested the Commissioner's determinations and, after lengthy negotiations, the parties reached a settlement in January 1996 for an increased value of the NW Transport stock at $2,500,000 per share as of Donn's death. This value became the new basis for the NW Transport stock redeemed by Evelyn. As a result of her increased basis, the taxable gain from Evelyn's redemption of the stock was eliminated and she realized a loss.

Evelyn's estate filed an amended 1991 federal individual income tax return seeking a refund of $3,332,443. The amended return reflected a loss from redemption of the NW Transport stock and eliminated certain dividend income reported on the original return. Meanwhile, Evelyn's estate was challenging a deficiency notice received in November 1994 concerning an unrelated gift deduction in the amount of $140,000.00 in her estate tax return. The estate contested the deficiency in tax court and that litigation was ongoing when Evelyn's amended 1991 federal income tax return was filed in January 1996.

In March 1996, the Commissioner filed an amended answer in Evelyn's estate tax litigation, asserting an increased deficiency in estate taxes. According to the Commissioner, the estate was no longer entitled to deduct

Evelyn's 1991 federal and state individual income taxes because those liabilities were subject to refunds. * * *

* * * [T]he estate refused to accept the Commissioner's view that the estate's deduction for Evelyn's income tax liabilities should be limited to the amount ultimately found to be due and owing by Evelyn. The estate instead took the position that post-death events may not be considered in determining the amount of its deduction for Evelyn's individual income tax liabilities because those liabilities were valid and enforceable claims against the estate at the time of Evelyn's death. Unable to resolve their differences, the parties submitted the case to the tax court on a fully stipulated basis.

The tax court held that the estate's deduction for Evelyn's 1991 federal income tax liability must be reduced by the amount actually refunded in 1997. According to the tax court, it was proper for the Commissioner to consider events occurring after Evelyn's death in calculating this deduction because the estate challenged Evelyn's individual income tax liability through her amended return. The tax court also held that the estate's deduction for Evelyn's 1991 Colorado income tax liability should be reduced to reflect the proper amount of tax after being adjusted downward as a result of her decreased federal taxable income. Although the record revealed that Evelyn's estate had not filed an amended Colorado income tax return and Evelyn had not received a refund of any 1991 state income taxes, the tax court reasoned that nothing prevented the estate from seeking such a refund on Evelyn's behalf. * * * The estate appeals * * *.

III.

Section 2053(a)(3) authorizes a deduction for "claims against the estate" in calculating the value of a decedent's taxable estate. There is no dispute in this case that unpaid income taxes incurred by a decedent prior to death may be deducted as a claim against the estate. *See* Treas. Reg. § 20.2053–6(f). Rather, the disagreement centers on whether events occurring after a decedent's death may be considered in calculating that deduction. In particular, the parties debate the effect of the 1996 settlement between Donn's estate and the Commissioner on the value of the § 2053(a)(3) deduction taken by Evelyn's estate for her 1991 income taxes. The estate argues the settlement is not relevant because the value of its deduction should be determined as of Evelyn's death. The Commissioner counters that the settlement was properly considered because the deduction is limited to the actual amount of taxes Evelyn ultimately owed.

This is an issue of first impression in our circuit * * *

* * * Neither § 2053(a)(3) nor the tax regulations clearly indicate whether events that occur after a decedent's death are relevant in calculating a deduction for a claim against the estate. The statute is silent on this issue. The regulations, on the other hand, contain language which arguably supports the positions of both parties. For instance, one regulation cited by the estate provides: "The amounts that may be deducted as claims against a decedent's estate are such only as represent personal obligations of the decedent existing at the time of his death." Treas. Reg. § 20.2053–4. But,

another regulation relied upon by the Commissioner permits estates to deduct a decedent's tax liabilities as a claim against the estate even if the exact amount is not known, as long as the deduction "is ascertainable with reasonable certainty, and will be paid." Treas. Reg. § 20.2053–1(b)(3). In light of these apparent inconsistencies, the most we can discern "from these Regulations is that the situation we now face is not expressly contemplated." Estate of Smith v. Comm'r, 198 F.3d 515, 521 (5th Cir. 1999).

We therefore begin our analysis with the leading case on this issue, Ithaca Trust Co. v. United States, 279 U.S. 151 (1929). In *Ithaca Trust,* the decedent left the residue of his estate to his wife for life, with the remainder to certain charities. To ascertain the amount of the charitable deduction for estate tax purposes, the wife's residual was calculated with a mortality table and subtracted from the principal of the estate. However, the wife died much sooner than expected. The question for the Court was whether the value of the estate's deduction should be calculated according to the wife's life expectancy as of the date of the testator's death or by applying the wife's actual date of death. In a unanimous opinion, the Court adopted a date-of-death valuation rule: "The estate so far as may be is settled as of the date of the testator's death." *Id.* at 155. The Court acknowledged that "[t]he first impression is that it is absurd to resort to statistical probabilities when you know the fact," but it stated that "the value of the thing to be taxed must be estimated as of the time when the act is done," *i.e.,* the passing of the decedent's estate at death. *Id.* The Court therefore concluded by stating that, as "[t]empting as it is to correct uncertain probabilities by the now certain fact, we are of opinion that it cannot be done." *Id.*

Several courts have relied on the date-of-death valuation rule announced in *Ithaca Trust* to hold that events occurring after a decedent's death are irrelevant in valuing an estate's deduction under § 2053(a)(3). See *Estate of Smith*, 198 F.3d at 520–26 (allowing estate to deduct date-of-death value of claim against it even though estate later settled for lesser amount); Propstra v. United States, 680 F.2d 1248, 1253–56 (9th Cir.1982) (same); Estate of Van Horne v. Comm'r, 78 T.C. 728, 732–39 (1982) (same), aff'd, 720 F.2d 1114 (9th Cir.1983); Greene v. United States, 447 F.Supp. 885, 892–95 (N.D. Ill.1978) (declining to consider creditor's failure to comply with statute of limitations for filing claim after decedent's death in allowing estate's deduction for claim); * * * While most of these courts acknowledged that *Ithaca Trust* involved a different section of the federal estate tax statute, i.e., charitable bequest deductions under the precursor to § 2055, they interpreted the opinion as announcing a broad principle that the value of a taxable estate should be determined as closely as possible to the date of the decedent's death.

Other courts, however, have refused to extend the principle of *Ithaca Trust* beyond charitable bequest deductions, holding that postmortem events may properly be considered in calculating the value of a claim against the estate deduction. See Estate of Sachs v. Comm'r, 856 F.2d 1158,

1160–63 (8th Cir.1988) (holding that Commissioner could rely on retroactive tax forgiveness legislation enacted four years after decedent's death in disallowing estate deduction for paying those taxes); Comm'r v. Estate of Shively, 276 F.2d 372, 373–75 (2d Cir.1960) (holding that decedent's estate could not deduct full date-of-death value of spousal support obligations because ex-wife re-married before estate filed return); *Jacobs,* 34 F.2d at 235–36 (holding that husband's estate could not deduct amount of claim against it arising from antenuptial agreement as a result of wife's waiver of claim after husband's death); Estate of Kyle v. Comm'r, 94 T.C. 829, 848–51 (1990) (disallowing estate's deduction for date-of-death value of litigation claim against it because case was resolved in estate's favor six years after decedent's death); Estate of Hagmann v. Comm'r, 60 T.C. 465, 466–69 (1973) (refusing to allow estate to deduct valid claims against it because creditors never filed those claims after decedent's death), aff'd per curiam, 492 F.2d 796 (5th Cir.1974). Although these courts have offered a variety of reasons why *Ithaca Trust* should be limited to charitable bequests, three recurring themes emerge.

One explanation for not extending *Ithaca Trust* to claims against the estate is that the congressional purpose underlying that deduction is different from that of deductions for charitable bequests. According to this rationale, the date-of-death valuation rule does not apply to § 2053(a)(3) because the purpose of that deduction is to appraise the decedent's actual net worth at death, while the purpose of § 2055 is to encourage charitable bequests by ensuring that if a testator makes a charitable gift in a prescribed form, a deduction will be allowed in a specified amount. * * *

Another justification for not applying *Ithaca Trust* to § 2053(a)(3) is based on the other deductions in the section. This approach places heavy reliance on the fact that § 2053(a) allows a deduction not only for claims against the estate but also for funeral and estate administration expenses. Under this view, since these expenses are calculated after death, Congress must also have intended that claims against the estate be ascertained by post-mortem events. * * *

The third reason these courts reject a date-of-death valuation approach is they do not consider it sensible to allow an estate to deduct a claim it does not ultimately owe or pay. * * *

We do not find any of these explanations particularly persuasive. Even assuming Congress had different motives for allowing deductions under § 2053 than it did for deductions under § 2055, this distinction "fails to explain why deductions for claims against the estate should be computed [any] differently from charitable bequests." *Propstra,* 680 F.2d at 1255 n.11. Further, we find it insignificant that Congress placed funeral and estate administration expenses, which are calculated after death, with claims against the estate in § 2053(a), because that section also contains a deduction for unpaid mortgages, which may be calculated without reference to post-death events. Finally, we note that the emphasis on actuality in valuing claims against the estate is at odds with the Supreme Court's admonition that as "[t]empting as it is to correct uncertain probabilities by the now certain fact, we are of opinion that it cannot be done." *Ithaca Trust*, 279 U.S. at 155. Thus, instead of facing compelling arguments why we should reject date-of-death valuation for claims against the estate, we are left with ambiguous interpretations of the appropriate method for calculating § 2053(a)(3) deductions.

These ambiguities, of course, do not automatically lead to the conclusion that events occurring after a decedent's death may never be considered in valuing a claim against the estate. But neither do they provide us license to ignore the Supreme Court's pronouncement that "[t]he estate so far as may be is settled as of the date of the testator's death." *Ithaca Trust*, 279 U.S. at 155. We therefore agree with the Fifth Circuit that a "narrow reading of *Ithaca Trust*, a reading that limits its application to charitable bequests, is unwarranted." *Smith*, 198 F.3d at 524. Accordingly, we hold that the date-of-death valuation rule announced in *Ithaca Trust* applies to a deduction for a claim against the estate under § 2053(a)(3). As a result, in this circuit, events which occur after the decedent's death may not be considered in valuing that deduction.

Sound policy reasons support our adoption of the date-of-death valuation principle for § 2053(a)(3) deductions. Specifically, this principle provides a bright line rule which alleviates the uncertainty and delay in estate administration which may result if events occurring months or even years after a decedent's death could be considered in valuing a claim against the estate. * * * Our holding resolves these problems by bringing more certainty to estate administration, an ideal which has long been promoted by judge and commentator alike. * * *

Although our holding ultimately benefits the estate in this case, application of the rule we announce today just as easily can favor the Commissioner. As one commentator has observed, when it serves his interests the Commissioner "has not been loathe to employ the principle that deductible claims against the estate become fixed at death." Craig S. Palmquist, The Estate Tax Deductibility of Unenforced Claims Against a Decedent's Estate, 11 Gonz. L.Rev. 707, 712 (1976). For example, in Estate of Lester v. Commissioner, 57 T.C. 503 (1972), the estate was obligated by a divorce decree to pay $1,000 per month to the decedent's ex-wife. The estate made twenty-four payments and then settled with the ex-wife by purchasing an annuity policy for her benefit for $78,700. The estate argued it was entitled to deduct at least $102,700, the total of its payments and the annuity policy, as a claim against the estate. Invoking *Ithaca Trust,* the Commissioner insisted the deduction was limited to $92,456, the actuarial value of the ex-wife's life expectancy as of the decedent's death. The tax court agreed with this position:

> We think there is no reason in this case to go beyond the principle of *Ithaca Trust Co.*—that the value of the judgment in the divorce proceedings is to be determined as of the date of the husband's death by the use of the tables employed here by the Commissioner, which take into consideration the contingency of the wife's death prior to final payment of the installments to become due. There is no need to

go into the effect of events subsequent to the husband's death, *i.e.,* how the estate finally freed itself of a continuing and admitted liability.

Id. at 507. Thus, as the facts of *Lester* demonstrate, whether our holding benefits the government or the taxpayer depends on the particular circumstances of each case.

In this case, the tax court concluded it was appropriate to consider post-mortem events because the estate later sought a refund of Evelyn's 1991 federal income tax and could have done the same with regard to her state income tax. Emphasizing that "a claim that is valid and enforceable at the date of a decedent's death must remain enforceable in order for the estate to deduct the claim," McMorris v. Commissioner, 77 T.C.M. (CCH) 1552, 1554 (1999), the tax court reasoned that once the estate challenged Evelyn's tax liabilities, they were "no longer a valid and enforceable claim against the estate," id. at 1555. As support, the tax court cited its prior holding in Estate of Smith v. Commissioner, 108 T.C. 412 (1997), rev'd and vacated, *Smith,* 198 F.3d 515, which distinguished cases involving the *valuation* of claims that are certain and enforceable on the date of a decedent's death from cases where the *enforceability* of the claims were unknown at death because they were disputed or contingent. Under this approach, the former claims are calculated as of the date of death, while the latter claims are calculated by considering post-death events. * * *

In examining the "enforceable" nature of the estate's claims in this case, the tax court did not have the benefit of the Fifth Circuit's subsequent decision in *Smith,* which concluded that "this dichotomy, which distinguishes between enforceability on the one hand and valuation on the other, * * * is not a sound basis for distinguishing claims in this context." 198 F.3d at 525. As the Fifth Circuit explained:

> There is only a semantic difference between a claim that may prove to be invalid and a valid claim that may prove to have a value of zero. For example, if given the choice between being the obligor of (1) a claim known to be worth $1 million with a 50 percent chance of being adjudged unenforceable, or (2) a claim known to be enforceable with a value equally likely to be $1 million or zero, a rational person would discern no difference in choosing between the claims, as both have an expected value $500,000.

Id. Because the tax court in *Smith* improperly relied on the "contingent" nature of the estate's claim to consider post-death events, the Fifth Circuit remanded the case with instructions that the tax court "neither * * * admit nor consider evidence of post-death occurrences when determining the date-of-death value of [the] claim." Id. at 526.

In this case, instead of focusing on whether the estate's § 2053(a)(3) deduction for Evelyn's income tax liabilities "remained enforceable" for an infinite period of time, the tax court should have examined whether the estate properly calculated that deduction as of the date of Evelyn's death. Had the tax court done so, it would have recognized that the increased deficiency at issue in this appeal was not premised on a date-of-death miscalculation. The increased deficiency was based solely on the fact that the federal and state income taxes incurred by Evelyn in 1991 became subject to a refund as a result of a settlement between another estate and the Commissioner in 1996. Therefore, the tax court erred when it considered that settlement in calculating the total tax deficiency for Evelyn's estate. * * *

ILLUSTRATIVE MATERIAL

A. GENERAL

The deductions allowed under § 2053(a)(3) are for payment of legally enforceable obligations of the decedent existing at the time of death. Thus, for example, only interest accrued at the date of the decedent's death is allowable even though the executor elects to use the alternate valuation date for computing the value of the gross estate. Reg. § 20.2053–4. For discussion of the deductibility, under § 2053(a)(2), of interest accrued after the decedent's death to pay estate taxes, see p. 509.

There must exist a *claim*. In Estate of Hester v. United States, 2007–1 U.S.T.C. ¶ 60,537 (W.D.Va.2007), aff'd, 2008 WL 4660189 (4th Cir.2008), wife established a testamentary trust and named husband as trustee. After husband misappropriated trust funds for his own use in violation of his fiduciary duty and commingled them with his own assets, he died and his executor included the commingled funds in his estate. The executor then sought a refund on the ground that the funds wrongly appropriated from wife's trust were deductible under § 2053(a)(3). The district court denied the refund because "nothing remotely suggests that the trust's beneficiaries ever made a *claim* against [husband] or his estate or that [husband] or his estate ever expected such a claim to be made or paid, a requirement of § 2053(a)(3)":

> "[I]in the present case the estate does not contend that the trust beneficiaries ever asserted any right against Wendell or his estate or that the estate ever anticipated a claim to be made. To accept the estate's arguments here, where there is no actual or expected claimant, for all intents and purposes, would be to replace the statutory language, 'claims against the estate' with 'theoretical liabilities of the estate.' Accordingly, the court concludes that the estate is not entitled to a deduction under § 2053(a)(3) because there has never been an actual or expected claim against Wendell or the estate."

There must exist a claim *against* the estate. In Estate of Lazar v. Commissioner, 58 T.C. 543 (1972), a husband and wife had entered into an agreement that in return for his maintaining her as the sole beneficiary under his will, she in her will would leave three-fourths of her estate to five of the husband's nieces and nephews. However, the wife later executed a will leaving her property to her own nephew. The husband's nephews and nieces then brought an action to set aside the will, which the estate settled by paying them $150,000. The court held that the payment was not deductible under § 2053(a)(3) because the claim was for a "share in" the estate, not a claim "against" the estate. The $150,000 payment thus was an estate distribution, not a payment of a claim.

The claim must be *enforceable* against the estate. For example, Estate of Lewis v. Commissioner, 49 T.C. 684 (1968), held that a claim barred by the state statute of limitations was not deductible, even though the probate court had allowed the claim with the consent of the parties. See also Rev.Rul. 66–300, 1966–2 C.B. 437 (surviving spouse's claim under loan made 25 years earlier to deceased spouse enforceable where statute of limitations tolled during marriage because deceased spouse had never denied the debt); Rev.Rul. 75–24, 1975–1 C.B. 306 (claim not deductible if executor had been liable to surcharge for paying claim because estate would not have suffered economic harm); Rev.Rul. 83–54, 1983–1 C.B. 229 (claim by decedent's child, upheld in state court judgment against decedent, not deductible because it was mere "cloak" for gift by decedent to child).

B.   POST–DEATH EVENTS

The Eleventh Circuit has followed *McMorris* and *Smith* in refusing to consider post-death events in valuing claims against the estate. O'Neal v. United States, 258 F.3d 1265 (11th Cir.2001) (post-death $560,000 settlement ignored in valuing $9.4 million claim against estate for reimbursement of gift tax paid by donees on pre-death gifts be decedent). The Service continues to insist that *Ithaca Trust Co.* is not controlling for § 2053 purposes and that post-death events can be considered where the claim is contested, contingent, or unenforceable at the date of death. A.O.D. 2004–04 (Estate of Smith) (May 8, 2000). See also FSA 200217022 (Jan. 17, 2002) (post-death settlement of wrongful death lawsuit taken into account in valuing claim against estate). For a critical view of the courts of appeals' approach in these cases, see Wendy C. Gerzog, Ithaca Trust and Section 2053: *Smith, McMorris,* and *O'Neal,* 95 Tax Notes 570 (2002).

C.   THE ADEQUATE AND FULL CONSIDERATION REQUIREMENT

Section 2053(c)(1)(A) provides that "claims against the estate, unpaid mortgages, or any indebtedness shall, when founded on a promise or agreement," be deductible only "to the extent that they were contracted bona fide and for an adequate and full consideration in money or money's worth."[7] The purpose of this rule is to prevent voluntary transfers that deplete the estate from being disguised as deductible claims or debts. For example, one court has noted that in enacting § 2053(c)(1)(A), Congress sought "to permit the deduction of claims only to the extent that such claims were contracted for a consideration which at the time either augmented the estate of the decedent, granted to him some right or privilege he did not possess before, or operated to discharge a then existing claim, as for breach of contract or personal injury." Latty v. Commissioner, 62 F.2d 952, 954 (6th Cir.1933).

For example, in Estate of Stern v. Dep't of Treasury, 98–1 U.S.T.C. ¶ 60,299 (D.C. Ind. 1998), D died after a lengthy illness and left his entire $1 million estate to the friend of his deceased sister who let D live in her home and cared for him for the last 1,825 days of his life. Although there was no written

---

7. Enforceable pledges and subscriptions to charitable organizations are explicitly exempted from this requirement. If the charity is of the type defined in § 2055, the deduction only will be "limited to the extent that it would be allowable as a deduction under § 2055 if such promise or agreement constituted a bequest."

contract requiring that D pay for the services, the state probate court approved payment of $182,500 ($100 per day) on the ground that D had promised to pay for the services and that this promise constituted an enforceable implied promise under state law. The district court permitted the estate to deduct the payment as a claim against the estate under § 2053(c)(1)(A) because the caregiver's services constituted adequate and full consideration. See also Estate of Huntington v. Commissioner, 16 F.3d 462 (1st Cir.1994) (no deduction for payment to decedent's step-children in settlement of claim that decedent breached agreement to make reciprocal wills with spouse because no evidence presented that "agreement was other than a collaborative effort to pass on the family's assets"). The adequate and full consideration requirement was considered at p. 178 (marital rights), p. 279 (§§ 2036–2038 transfers), and p. 165 (gift tax).

4.   TAXES

Taxes are deductible for estate tax purposes if they qualify as claims against the estate or as administration expenses. See Reg. § 20.2053–6(a). However, § 2053(c)(1)(B) provides that "income taxes on income received after the death of the decedent, or property taxes not accrued before his death, or any estate, succession, legacy or inheritance taxes" may not be taken as deductions.

Taxes that were due and payable when the decedent died are deductible as claims against the estate under § 2053(a)(3). This rule applies to gift tax and income tax liabilities, including such liabilities for the year of death, even though the returns are filed by the executor. See Reg. § 20.2053–6(d) (gift tax), –6(f) (income tax). In Rev.Rul. 70–600, 1970–2 C.B. 194, the decedent's spouse made a gift prior to his death. The decedent's executor consented to have the gift treated as made one-half by the decedent under § 2513 and paid the gift tax. The Ruling held that the estate was not entitled to a § 2053 deduction because claims are deductible only if they were in existence at the date of death. The executor's consent after the husband's death did not create a liability retroactive to the date of death. On the other hand, if the husband had consented to the gift before his death, a deduction would have been allowable under Reg. § 20.2053–6(d). See also Proesel v. United States, 585 F.2d 295 (7th Cir.1978) (same result). However, the amount of any gift tax paid by the husband's estate would be required to be included in the gross estate under § 2035(b). For rules on the allocation of income taxes on a joint return, see Reg. § 20.2053–6(f).

Taxes accruing after the decedent's death thus are not deductible under § 2053(a)(3) as claims against the estate. However, such taxes may be deductible as administration expenses under § 2053(a)(2). For example, Reg. § 20.2053–6(e) provides that excise taxes incurred in selling the decedent's property are deductible as administration expenses if the sale is necessary to pay the estate's debts, preserve the estate, or effect distribution of estate property.

With respect to the exclusion for certain income taxes, Reg. § 20.2053–6(f) clarifies that although taxes paid on income received after the decedent's death are not deductible, unpaid income taxes are deductible "if they are on income properly includible in an income tax return of the decedent for a period before his death." Estate of McClure v. United States, 288 F.2d 190 (Ct.Cl. 1961), upheld the validity of Reg. § 20.2053–6(f). The Regulation requires apportionment of income tax liability between the estate and a surviving spouse in a situation where a joint return was filed for the year in which the decedent's death occurred. The theory of the Regulations is that the estate has a right of contribution from the surviving spouse with respect to income taxes the estate pays that are attributable to the income of the surviving spouse.

Reg. § 20.2053–6(b) states that property taxes are deductible if they constitute an "enforceable obligation" of the decedent at the time of his death. However, because property taxes typically are enforceable only against the underlying property, property taxes can be treated in one of two ways. First, property taxes may reduce the underlying value of the property, as with the case of nonrecourse mortgages. Reg. § 20.2053–7. Second, if the underlying property is included in the estate at its unencumbered value, the case law permits a § 2053(a)(3) deduction for property taxes accruing before death, notwithstanding the decedent's absence of personal liability. See Estate of Pardee v. Commissioner, 49 T.C. 140 (1967).

With respect to the exclusion of estate, succession, legacy, or inheritance taxes, Rev.Rul. 82–82, 1982–1 C.B. 127 stated that the common element in these taxes "is that they are all taxes imposed on the value of the property transferred from a decedent to an heir." In First National Bank & Trust Company of Tulsa v. United States, 787 F.2d 1393 (10th Cir.1986), the decedent made a gift that was subject to state gift tax and died within one year thereafter. The property was included in her gross estate for both state and federal estate tax purposes. The estate paid the state gift tax, but the state tax commission treated it as an advance payment of state death taxes. The estate claimed a § 2011 credit based on the amount of the state death taxes paid (including the "gift" tax)[8] and also a deduction for the gift tax under § 2053. The court disallowed the deduction. The court concluded that, under applicable state law, if death occurs within one year, the state gift tax obligation was extinguished and replaced by the state death tax on the gifted property. Because there was no obligation on the decedent at the date of death to pay the state gift tax, no § 2053(a) deduction was allowable and § 2053(c)(1)(B) was applicable. The Tenth Circuit believed that prior cases that had taken a contrary position (Estate of Lang v. Commissioner, 613 F.2d 770 (9th Cir.1980), and Horton v. United States, 79–2 U.S.T.C. ¶ 13,316 (M.D.N.C. 1979)) were incorrect because they did not understand that all state gift taxes are either defeasible (if owing) or contingent (if paid) if a decedent dies within the specified period after making the gift.

---

8. The Service apparently allowed the § 2011 credit even though it had ruled in Rev.Rul. 81–302, 1981–2 C.B. 170, that the credit was not available in a similar situation.

5. UNPAID MORTGAGES OR OTHER INDEBTEDNESS

In order for an unpaid mortgage or indebtedness to qualify for deduction under § 2053(a)(4), the value of the property against which the mortgage or indebtedness lies must be included in the gross estate. Reg. § 20.2053–7. See Estate of Parrott v. Commissioner, 30 F.2d 792 (9th Cir.1929) (decedent owned only one-half of mortgaged property, but he was jointly and severally liable on mortgage; his estate could deduct only one-half of the mortgage debt even though the executors paid the entire amount). On the other hand, the value of the property included in the gross estate does not limit the amount of the mortgage indebtedness deduction. The estate can deduct the full amount of the mortgage even where the amount of the decedent's liability exceeds the value of the property. Estate of Crail v. Commissioner, B.T.A. memo. op. CCH dec. 12,579–E (1942). Thus, for example, if the value of a decedent's one-half interest in real estate is $10,000, but her one-half share of the mortgage on the real estate is $15,000, the latter amount is deductible. In Rev.Rul. 83–81, 1983–1 C.B. 230, the estate made a § 2032A special use election with respect to a farm includible in the decedent's gross estate (see p. 786. The § 2032A value was $600x, but the fair market value of the farm was $1,000x. The farm was subject to a $700x mortgage for which the decedent was personally liable. The Ruling held that because § 2032A does not diminish the quantum of a decedent's interest included in the gross estate, but rather simply affects its value, the estate could deduct the mortgage in full because 100% of the mortgaged property was included in the decedent's gross estate.

If the decedent was personally liable for the debt ("recourse debt"), the debt is deductible either as a claim against the estate under § 2053(a)(3) or as an unpaid mortgage under § 2053(a)(4). See Rev.Rul. 81–183, 1981–2 C.B. 180; Rev.Rul. 79–302, 1979–2 C.B. 328. In contrast, if the decedent was not personally liable for the debt ("nonrecourse debt"), § 2053(a)(3) does not apply because there is no claim against the estate. As a result, the nonrecourse debt is deductible solely under § 2053(a)(4), although the same net result is reached without regard to § 2053(a)(4) by including only the decedent's equity in the property in the decedent's gross estate. See Reg. § 20.2053–7. See also TAM 200104008 (Jan. 26, 2001) (where husband and wife owned property subject to recourse mortgage as tenants-by-the-entirety and one-half of property included in husband's estate under § 2040(b), one-half of mortgage balance deductible under § 2053(a)(3) or (4)).

In some situations, treatment of a debt as nonrecourse (and thus including in the estate only the net amount of the decedent's equity in the property) is preferable to treatment of the debt as recourse (and thus including the fair market value of the property in the estate, with a deduction for the mortgage as a claim against the estate). See Estate of Fung v. Commissioner, 117 T.C. 247 (2001) (where decedent was non-resident alien taxable only on property located in the United States, classification of mortgage as recourse under state law increased decedent's estate tax liability because debt prorated between United States and foreign assets).

Where property of the decedent has been pledged for the debt of another, the entire value of the pledged property is includible in her estate, and the value of the property actually used to satisfy the debt is allowed as a deduction. Estate of Borland v. Commissioner, 38 B.T.A. 598 (1938). However, § 2053(a)(4) does not apply where the decedent is only secondarily liable or is merely an accommodation party for another. Rev.Rul. 84–42, 1984–1 C.B. 194. Section 2054(a)(4) also does not apply to funds misappropriated by the testamentary trustee in violation of his fiduciary duty. Estate of Hester v. United States, 2007–1 U.S.T.C. ¶ 60,537 (W.D.Va.2007).

6. DEDUCTIONS IN COMMUNITY PROPERTY STATES

In community property states, only those claims and expenses which are the obligation of the decedent personally or of his estate may be deducted in full. An obligation which is attributable to the marital estate, of which only one-half is included in the decedent's estate, is deductible from the latter only to the extent of one-half of its amount. The attribution of particular claims and expenses to either estate is a matter of local law in each state.

In most community property states, the entire marital estate comes into the hands of the executor or administrator for administration even though only one-half of it is included in the decedent's estate. Although commissions and expenses of administration (including attorney's fees) are computed upon and incurred on behalf of the entire community property, only one-half of such amounts are deductible from the decedent's estate. United States v. Stapf, 375 U.S. 118 (1963) (even though decedent's will provided that such expenses were to be paid out of his share of community property; the Court concluded that this provision simply constituted additional bequest to surviving spouse). Where, however, particular items of administration expense can be attributed specifically to the decedent's estate (e.g., attorney's fees and expenses incurred in settlement of the estate tax), they will be fully deductible. Estate of Lang v. Commissioner, 97 F.2d 867 (9th Cir.1938). To the extent that such expenses are not deductible by the estate under § 2053, they will frequently be deductible by the surviving spouse for income tax purposes under § 212 as expenses paid for the production or collection of income, or for the management, conservation, or maintenance of property held for the production of income. Rev.Rul. 55–524, 1955–2 C.B. 535.

In those community property states where funeral expenses are attributable to the decedent's estate alone, the entire amount of such expenses is deductible. Estate of Lee v. Commissioner, 11 T.C. 141 (1948); Rev.Rul. 71–168, 1971–1 C.B. 271. Where, however, local law characterizes such costs as expenditures on behalf of the community property, only one-half of the amount expended is deductible. Estate of Lang v. Commissioner, 97 F.2d 867 (9th Cir.1938).

Claims against the estate are fully deductible where they represent the personal debts of the decedent. Estate of Fulmer v. Commissioner, 83 T.C. 302 (1984) (estate paid damages for torts committed by decedent prior to death pursuant to state court order that damages be paid from decedent's separate property). Where, however, they are debts of the community, only one-half of the amount is deductible from the decedent's estate, *Estate of Lang*, regardless of whether the debt was contracted by the decedent or by the survivor, Estate of Lucey v. Commissioner, 13 T.C. 1010 (1949). Unpaid mortgages on community property, generally, fall into this category.

Whether a claim may be characterized as a community obligation or a personal obligation of the decedent depends on local law, Sweeney v. Commissioner, 15 B.T.A. 1287 (1929), which varies considerably from one community property state to the other.

CHAPTER 28

THE UNIFIED TRANSFER TAX CREDIT

Internal Revenue Code: §§ 2001(a)–(c); 2010; 2502(a); 2505(a), (c).

House–Senate Conference Committee, Economic Growth and Tax Relief Reconciliation Act of 2001

H.R. Conf. Rep. No. 84. 107th Cong., 1st Sess. (2001).

* * * Overview * * *

Under the conference agreement, the estate, gift, and generation-skipping transfer taxes are reduced between 2002 and 2009, and the estate and generation-skipping transfer taxes are repealed in 2010.

Phaseout and repeal of estate and generation-skipping transfer taxes

In general

Under the conference agreement, in 2002, the 5–percent surtax (which phases out the benefit of the graduated rates) and the rates in excess of 50 percent are repealed. In addition, in 2002, the unified credit effective exemption amount (for both estate and gift tax purposes) is increased to $1 million. In 2003, the estate and gift tax rates in excess of 49 percent are repealed. In 2004, the estate and gift tax rates in excess of 48 percent are repealed, and the unified credit effective exemption amount for estate tax purposes is increased to $1.5 million. (The unified credit effective exemption amount for gift tax purposes remains at $1 million as increased in 2002.) In addition, in 2004, the family-owned business deduction is repealed. In 2005, the estate and gift tax rates in excess of 47 percent are repealed. In 2006, the estate and gift tax rates in excess of 46 percent are repealed, and the unified credit effective exemption amount for estate tax purposes is increased to $2 million. In 2007, the estate and gift tax rates in excess of 45 percent are repealed. In 2009, the unified credit effective exemption amount is increased to $3.5 million. In 2010, the estate and generation-skipping transfer taxes are repealed. From 2002 through 2009, the estate and gift tax rates and unified credit effective exemption amount for estate tax purposes are as follows:

Calendar Year	Estate and GST tax death-time transfer exemption	Highest estate and gift tax rates
2002	$1 million	50%
2003	$1 million	49%

Calendar Year	Estate and GST tax death-time transfer exemption	Highest estate and gift tax rates
2004	$1.5 million	48%
2005	$1.5 million	47%
2006	$2 million	46%
2007	$2 million	45%
2008	$2 million	45%
2009	$3.5 million	45%
2010	N/A (taxes repealed)	top individual rate under bill (gift tax only)

The generation-skipping transfer tax exemption for a given year (prior to repeal) is equal to the unified credit effective exemption amount for estate tax purposes. In addition, as under present law, the generation-skipping transfer tax rate for a given year will be the highest estate and gift tax rate in effect for such year.

Repeal of estate and generation-skipping transfer taxes; modifications to gift tax

In 2010, the estate and generation-skipping transfer taxes are repealed. Also beginning in 2010, the top gift tax rate will be the top individual income tax rate as provided under the bill, and, except as provided in regulations, a transfer to a trust will be treated as a taxable gift, unless the trust is treated as wholly owned by the donor or the donor's spouse under the grantor trust provisions of the Code. * * *

ILLUSTRATIVE MATERIAL

A.   TECHNICAL ASPECTS OF THE UNIFIED CREDIT

Prior to 2004, the credit continued to be "unified" in the sense that it was available against gift taxes incurred on lifetime transfers (§ 2505), as well as against estate taxes incurred on testamentary transfers (§ 2010). Under this regime, a decedent who had made lifetime gifts did not get the benefit of two credits; the credit was used only once to eliminate transfer tax on the first $1,000,000 (in 2002–03) of taxable gifts and bequests. The unified credit was mandatory—a taxpayer is required to use it to reduce gift taxes and cannot preserve it to be used entirely against estate tax. Rev.Rul. 79–398, 1979–2 C.B. 338.[1]

Beginning in 2004, the credit for gift tax purposes is only partially unified with the credit for estate tax purposes, as the gift tax exemption remains $1 million while the estate tax exemption increases in stages from $1.5 million in 2004–2005, to $2 million in 2006–2008, to $3.5 million in 2009, until the estate

---

1. A transferor could obtain a greater tax benefit by foregoing the unified credit and paying gift tax on inter vivos transfers and using the credit against the estate tax on testamentary transfers because the gift tax is tax-*exclusive* (meaning that the amount paid as gift tax is not itself subject to transfer tax) while the estate tax is tax-*inclusive* (meaning that the amount paid as estate tax is a part of the estate against which the tax is computed).

tax is repealed in 2010. But as currently structured, the credits become unified again in 2011 and thereafter when the estate tax returns with a $1 million exemption to match that of the gift tax.

B.   THE LEVEL OF TRANSFER TAXATION

1.   *In General*

Setting the appropriate transfer tax exemption—or credit level—amount raises fundamental issues about the overall level of transfer taxation. On what transfers should the tax fall? What should the burden be on the transfers that are subject to tax? If estate tax repeal sticks beyond 2010 while the gift tax remains, what is the appropriate gift tax exemption level?

It is easy to lose perspective in considering the transfer taxes. In one aspect they resemble the income tax, for they exempt a basic amount from tax (through the unified credit) and then apply a progressive rate scale. As a consequence, one is apt to approach these taxes with individual income tax attitudes, such as be careful about making the exempt level too low, be careful about the height of the starting rates, be careful about the pace of progression. But such income tax attitudes derive from the fact that our present income tax has a wide coverage of the population. These income tax attitudes have real meaning and force under such circumstances.

But the starting point of "wealth," the distribution of wealth, and consequently the universe occupied by the transfer taxes, are far different. In such a universe, income tax attitudes can easily lead one astray. Thus, in 2009 the estate tax will be imposed on the estates of decedents with net worth of over $3,500,000. Yet, far less than 1% of adult decedents leave taxable estates of over this amount. Everything that takes place in the estate tax thus concerns no far less than 1% of adult decedents, while everything that takes place in our individual income tax concerns most of the adult population.

There is a vast difference between speaking of the "little person" under the individual income tax and the "small estate" under the estate tax. Yet Congress and others often carry over to the "small estate" the protectionist attitudes involved in the reference to the "little person." The "small estate," it is true, is less than a dwarf in the scale of large estates, but viewed from the perspective of almost all of our population the "small estate" represents wealth beyond the realities of most everyone. That perspective must be kept constantly in mind in evaluating the effectiveness of the present system in taxing the transfer of wealth in the United States.

The level of transfer taxation, and the resulting burden it imposes, are determined by the point at which estates become subject to tax and the positive rate structure applied to the transfer tax base (assuming that the base has been established on sound and fair principles).

Essentially, the determinants of the starting point and the rate levels to be used for a tax on the transfer of wealth will be the views held on the social desirability—or undesirability—of inheritances and on the overall degree of progressivity in the federal tax system. The transfer tax is the principal factor—the only direct factor—operating to control the size of inheritances. It combines with the individual income tax in shaping directly the progressivity of the federal tax system. Views on these matters seem more directly relevant to the level of rates than the matter of absolute revenue needs. It should be observed, though, that revenue raised by a transfer tax on wealth makes it unnecessary to raise that same amount through other taxes and, in the catalogue of taxes to be utilized by a government, a transfer tax on wealth has a high rating. Dollar for dollar, the funds it raises will provide fewer problems than those created by placing a similar revenue load on other types of taxes. This being so, those holding strong views on the desirability of limiting inheritances or on strengthening the progressivity of the tax system, and thus urging a high level of rates, will thereby be producing a revenue yield that also would be viewed by some as a useful purpose in itself.

2.   Setting the Level Below Which Transfers Should be Exempt from Tax

The 2001 Act's increase in the effective exemption of the estate tax credit from $1 million 2003 to $3.5 million in 2009 reflects Congress's desire to encourage saving, promote capital formation and entrepreneurial activity, and help preserve existing family-owned farms and businesses. Indeed, the credit initially was set at an effective exemption amount of $120,667 in 1977, and its growth over the subsequent thirty years has exceeded the actual and expected inflation rate over this period:[2]

EXEMPTION EQUIVALENT OF THE ESTATE TAX CREDIT: 1977–2011	
Year	Exemption Equivalent
1977	$ 120,667
1978	$ 134,000
1979	$ 147,333
1980	$ 161,563
1981	$ 175,625
1982	$ 225,000
1983	$ 275,000
1984	$ 325,000
1985	$ 400,000
1986	$ 500,000
1987–1997	$ 600,000
1998	$ 625,000
1999	$ 650,000
2000–2001	$ 675,000
2002–2003	$1,000,000
2004–2005	$1,500,000
2006–2008	$2,000,000
2009	$3,500,000
2010	Tax Repealed
2011–	$1,000,000

Other commentators have proposed a different tack, arguing that a lowering of the exemption level, even a significant lowering, would still keep the

2. For example, $120,667 in 1977 is the equivalent of approximately $358,000 in 2002 and $451,000 in 2009 (assuming a 3.5% annual inflation rate for 2009).

transfer tax a rather exclusive levy. What exemption level is required to keep most small or average estates outside the scope of the tax? One possible figure is approximately $135,000.[3]

The next question is whether there are persons receiving property from a decedent who are entitled to claim that a higher figure should be used. Thus, what about the interests of a surviving spouse? But here the marital deduction (discussed p. 572) provides the answer. An unlimited marital deduction protects the interests of a surviving spouse in full. So, given the unlimited marital deduction, the interests of a surviving spouse do not require an exemption higher than $100,000.

What about surviving children? Professor Boris Bittker has pointed out that in all probability the surviving children of decedents possessing more than $100,000 of wealth are likely themselves to be adults and even adults well along in life. Although adult children may welcome inheritances, their claims usually are not founded on the need or hardship that can arise when the provision of support is suddenly removed, as would be the case for a minor child. The inquiry therefore can be shifted to minor children. Where there is a surviving parent, the marital deduction would ensure that surviving minor children have the benefit of the full amount of the decedent's estate unburdened by transfer taxes. The issue thus is narrowed to minor orphan children who would be left with inadequate financial resources to replace the loss of support provided by the deceased parents. The straight-forward response to this problem is a program of direct financial aid to such children (or, less desirably, a special tax credit or deduction for transfers to such children). In any event, the existence of a relatively few needy orphans cannot justify a high exemption level for the estate of every decedent.

What about liquidity problems, allegedly encountered by decedents who die owning farms or small businesses? Although Congress in the 2001 Act cited these concerns in first raising the credit amount and then repealing the estate tax effective in 2010, the data indicate that the vast majority of assets owned by decedents consists of highly liquid forms of property, such as stocks, bonds, life insurance, and cash. Thus, only a very small part of the revenue loss actually benefits decedents owning farms and small businesses. And the Code contains several special measures designed to meet the liquidity needs of these estates at relatively small revenue cost, including §§ 2033A and 6166. Owners of farms and small businesses thus do not have strong claims to a higher exemption level.

This discussion leads to the conclusion that the only consideration for establishing the point at which positive tax rates are begun should be determining the level below which administrative costs (both to the government and to taxpayers) are excessive in relation to the amount of tax collected. This figure

---

3. Bittker, Federal Estate Tax Reform: Exemptions and Rates, 57 A.B.A. J. 236 (1971), suggested a figure of $25,000. The text figure reflects an adjustment for inflation between 1971 and 2008. Others propose lower amounts (e.g., Westfall, Revitalizing the Federal Estate and Gift Taxes, 83 Harv. L.Rev. 986 (1970) ($20,000, or approximately $112,000 in 2008 dollars)); others suggest higher amounts (e.g., Ascher, Curtailing Inherited Wealth, 89 Mich. L. Rev. 69 (1990) ($250,000, or approximately $418,000 in 2008 dollars)). In order to eliminate minor current gifts for administrative reasons, there could be a small annual per donee exclusion. See p. 446.

could be adjusted annually for inflation (as is the case with the gift tax annual exclusion). Relying on periodic Congressional increases in the exemption amount is problematic; as seen with the 2001 Act, Congress often increases the exemption amount by far more than would have been justified by inflation.

3. *The Setting of Transfer Tax Rates*

Once the exemption level is established, attention then shifts to the rate structure to be employed. Several questions must be faced, including the degree of progressivity desired, which may be affected both by the rates themselves and the width of the brackets to which the rates apply, and the top rate which should be employed. There is no single rate and bracket structure that all would agree is appropriate. Indeed, both rates and brackets have been adapted from time to time as Congress has reflected changes in societal attitudes on issues such as the distribution (or concentration) of wealth in the country, the impact of inflation on asset values, and the like.

There have been numerous suggestions concerning the appropriate rate structure for the transfer tax, ranging from suggestions for reductions in existing rates to imposition of a 100% marginal rate for estates above a given value. Present law falls between these positions by adopting a very high exemption level but employing a relatively high starting rate for transfers above the exemption level. Although § 2001(c)(1) appears to establish 18% as the first positive tax rate, application of the estate tax credit means that the first positive tax rate actually is 45% in 2009. Many commentators view the jump from a 0% rate to a 45% as excessive. Reducing the exemption level would permit Congress to set a much lower initial positive rate and smooth the tax progressivity in a way that § 2001(c)(1) nominally suggests.

Consensus on the appropriate level of transfer taxation is difficult to discern. But it is important for those considering revision of the transfer taxes to understand that the burden of a transfer tax raises questions independent of the structure of such a tax. These questions in turn require detailed research involving quantitative aspects of the distribution of wealth, qualitative studies on the uses of wealth, and consideration of the value judgments of the American people on the appropriateness of transfers of wealth and inherited wealth.

PART V

OTHER DEDUCTIONS AND CREDITS

CHAPTER 29

THE DEDUCTION FOR CHARITABLE CONTRIBUTIONS

INTRODUCTION

The exclusions from the tax base considered previously in Part IV represent legislative responses to structural issues involved in a transfer tax system. Sections 2053 and 2054 are required to determine the net transfer which is the object of the estate tax. The gift tax annual exclusion in § 2503(b) is concerned with the problems of eliminating numerous small transfers from the scope of the tax, although the provision appears defective as a means of dealing with such problems. A basic exemption (or unified credit) for transfer tax purposes is also consistent with the structure of a normative transfer tax.

There are other provisions in the transfer taxes, however, which achieve non-tax objectives. Some of those provisions have been encountered previously. For example, gifts to political organizations and payments of certain educational and medical expenses where the donor has no legal obligation to support the donee constitute transfers properly subject to tax. These items are excluded from the transfer tax base under § 2501(a)(5) and § 2503(e) to achieve non-tax policy objectives. Chapters 29 considers the deduction for charitable contributions, which encourages contributions. This objective may be thought of as a spending objective or "tax expenditure" because the Federal government foregoes revenue in order to encourage charitable transfers. The method for analyzing such tax expenditures is described in Chapter 31.

SECTION A. OUTRIGHT TRANSFERS TO CHARITY

Internal Revenue Code: § 2055; 2522

Regulations: § 20.2055–1, 2, 3, 4; 25.2522(a), (c)–1

Rev. Rul. 67–325

1967–2 C.B. 113.

Advice has been requested whether contributions to an organization which provides recreational facilities without charge to residents of the township of Y are deductible * * * where the organization restricts the use of its facilities to less than the entire community on the basis of race.

The organization is a nonprofit corporation organized for the purpose of providing community recreational facilities including a swimming pool, an athletic field, and a pavilion suitable for picnics and other activities. The facilities are available without charge to residents of the community without regard to age, physical condition, or social or economic circumstances. However, the corporation restricts the use of the facilities to persons of a particular race.

Section 170 of the Code provides a deduction for income tax purposes, subject to limitations which are not material for present purposes, for contributions made to or for the use of a corporation, trust, or community chest, fund, or foundation—

> * * * organized and operated exclusively for religious, charitable, scientific, literary, or educational purposes or for the prevention of cruelty to children or animals * * *.

(Section 170(c)(2)(B).)

Similar provisions allowing deductions for charitable contributions for estate and gift tax purposes are contained in §§ 2055, 2106, and 2522 of the Code. Corporations, and any community chest, fund, or foundation, organized and operated exclusively for similar purposes, are also exempted from Federal income taxes, subject to limitations not here material, by § 501(a) and (c)(3) of the Code.

Prior to 1959 the Internal Revenue Service did not generally recognize that contributions to organizations providing community recreational facilities were deductible for income tax purposes even though the facilities were provided free of charge for use by all the residents of the particular community. In 1959, however, the previously published nonacquiescence in the decision of the Tax Court of the United States in Isabel Peters v. Commissioner, 21 T.C. 55 (1953), nonacquiescence, C.B. 1955–1, 8 was withdrawn and an acquiescence was substituted therefor * * *.

The *Peters* case involved an issue as to the deductibility under [the predecessor of § 170] * * * of a contribution by an individual to a nonprofit corporation formed to operate a public beach, playground, and bathing facilities for the residents of a particular geographical area. No charge was made for the use of the beach. The operations of the corporation were supported solely from contributions, but contributions were not a condition to use of the beach. The Tax Court specifically found as a fact that there was "no restriction or discrimination" in the use of the beach other than its restriction to the residents of the defined community. The corporation was otherwise organized and operated in accordance with the requirements of [the predecessor of § 170]. * * *.

The majority opinion of the Tax Court, after discussing the general meaning of the word "charitable," went on to hold that the taxpayer's contribution had been made to a corporation organized and operated exclusively for charitable purposes within the meaning of [the predecessor of § 170(c)(2)]. The opinion stated (at page 59):

> * * * The evidence clearly shows that the dominant purpose in establishing and maintaining the Foundation was to provide convenient swimming and recreation facilities for all persons residing in

Cold Spring Harbor School district of the Town of Huntington and especially those who could not afford individually to acquire and maintain such facilities. A contribution was not a prescribed condition to the use of * * * [the community beach and recreation facilities] by any resident of Cold Spring Harbor. It was open to contributors and noncontributors alike. No fees were charged. See James Irvine, 46 B.T.A. 246.

In our opinion the Foundation, a nonprofit organization dedicated solely to the promotion of social welfare, should be classified as charitable as that term is used in the statute relied upon. * * *

The conclusions reached in the *Peters* case * * * are in accord with the general law of charity, that is, that community recreational facilities may be classified as charitable if they are provided for the use of the general public of the community. If that condition is satisfied, a sufficient public purpose is deemed to be served to justify treatment of the dedication of the facility as charitable for purposes of the law of charitable trusts, the main branch of the general law of charity (apart from laws pertaining to taxation) in which questions as to whether particular purpose are charitable have arisen.

In that general body of law, certain purposes have been deemed to be beneficial to the community as a whole even though the class or classes of possible beneficiaries eligible to receive a direct benefit from the dedication of property to the particular purposes do not include all the members of the community. See in that regard Restatement (Second) Trusts § 368, comment b, and §§ 369–373 (1959); IV Scott on Trusts (2d ed. 1956), § 368.

Providing a community recreational facility is in the general class of purposes which are recognized as charitable only where all the members of the community are eligible for direct benefits. As was stated in the concurring opinion of Mr. Justice White in Evans v. Newton, 382 U.S. 296, at 308–309 (1966):

> Otherwise a trust to establish a country club for the use of the residents of the wealthiest part of town would be charitable. Professor Scott states this principle as follows:

> "As we have seen, a trust to promote the happiness or well-being of members of the community is charitable, although it is not a trust to relieve poverty, advance education, promote religion, or protect health. In such a case, however, *the trust must be for the benefit of the members of the community generally* and not merely for the benefit of a class of persons." IV Scott on Trusts § 375.2, at 2715 (2d ed. 1956). [Emphasis added.]

* * *

In this body of general law pertaining to purposes considered charitable only where all the members of the community are eligible to receive a direct benefit, no sound basis has been found for concluding that there would be an adequate charitable purpose if some part of the whole community is excluded from benefiting except where the exclusion is required by the nature or size of the facility. Exclusion of a part of the entire community on the basis of race, religion, nationality, belief, occupation, or other classification having no relationship to the nature or the size of the facility, would prevent the purpose from being recognized as a sufficient public purpose to justify its being held charitable under this general body of law.

The favored treatment of charitable organizations for Federal tax purposes in the income, estate, and gift tax legislation enacted in the current century has not provided a comprehensive definition of charitable purposes in the various statutory provisions that have been enacted. It is clear for this and other reasons that those statutory provisions do not reflect any novel or specialized tax concept of charitable purposes, and that the income, estate, and gift tax provisions of the Code here in question should be interpreted as favoring only those purposes which are recognized as charitable in the generally accepted legal sense.

That the Congress has legislated in this area with reference to organizations generally recognized as charitable is demonstrated by the legislative history of the Corporation Tax Law of 1909 (§ 38 of the Act of August 5, 1909, 36 Stat. 112), which specifically exempted from that tax, among others, "any corporation or association organized and operated exclusively for religious, charitable, or educational purposes, no part of the net income of which inures to the benefit of any private stockholder or individual." That provision, which was the forerunner of all the statutory provisions here in question, originated in a Senate amendment, the debate on which indicates that the provision was intended to favor organizations which were generally recognized as organized and operated for exclusively charitable purposes. See in that regard 44 Cong. Rec. 4148–4151, 4154–4157.

The legislative history of that provision and the absence of other revealing indications of congressional intent in relation to the many subsequent provisions of the internal revenue laws providing favored tax treatment for charitable organizations tend strongly to support the position taken in the only comprehensive definition of the term "charitable" provided in the regulations concerning the income, estate, and gift tax provisions of the Code. Section 1.501(c)(3)–1(d)(2) of the Income Tax Regulations provides:

> *Charitable defined.* The term "charitable" is used in § 501(c)(3) in its generally accepted legal sense and is, therefore, not to be construed as limited by the separate enumeration in § 501(c)(3) of other tax-exempt purposes which may fall within the broad outlines of "charity" as developed by judicial decisions.

For the foregoing reasons it is concluded that §§ 170, 2055, 2106, and 2522 of the Code, to the extent that they provide deductions for contributions or other transfers to or for the use of organizations organized and operated exclusively for charitable purposes, or to be used for exclusively charitable purposes, do not apply to contributions or transfers to any organization whose purposes are not charitable in the generally accepted legal sense or to any contribution for any purpose that is not charitable in the generally accepted legal sense. For the same reasons, § 501(c)(3) of the Code does not apply to any such organization.

Accordingly, contributions to the organization described in the instant case are not deductible under § 170 of the Code. Transfers to such an organization are not deductible for estate or gift tax purposes under §§ 2055, 2106, and 2522 of the Code.

Furthermore, this organization is not exempt from income taxes under § 501(a) of the Code as an organization described in § 501(c)(3).

ILLUSTRATIVE MATERIAL

A.   GENERAL LIMITATIONS

1.   The Definition of "Charitable"

Courts have struggled with the meaning of the word "charitable" for centuries. The Statute of Elizabeth enumerated twenty-one distinct charities. Stat. 43 Eliz., C. 4 (1601). A modern list would be far more extensive. The Board of Tax Appeals offered the following definition: "In its widest sense, charity denotes all the good affections which men should bear to each other, and in that sense embraces what is generally understood as benevolence, philanthropy, and good will." Turnure v. Commissioner, 9 B.T.A. 871, 873 (1927).

Although a "charitable" organization is only one of the types of organizations enumerated in § 2055(a)(2) and § 2522(a)(2), the courts and the IRS have imposed a general gloss requiring that all enumerated organizations conform to generally accepted concepts of "charitable" even though they may be exclusively devoted to one of the other qualifying activities, such as education. Rev. Rul. 71–447, 1971–2 C.B. 230, held that segregated private schools did not constitute "charitable organizations" under §§ 170, 501(c)(3), and "other relevant federal statutes." Bequests or gifts to such organizations, accordingly, will not qualify for the charitable contribution deduction under § 2055 or § 2522. See Green v. Connally, 330 F.Supp. 1150 (D.D.C.1971), aff'd without opinion sub nom., Coit v. Green, 404 U.S. 997 (1971). Also, the Supreme Court has upheld the revocation of the tax exempt status of segregated private schools, rejecting assertions that the revocation violated their First Amendment freedom of religion rights. Bob Jones University v. Simon, 416 U.S. 725 (1974).

2.   "To or For the Use of" Qualifying Organizations

Only transfers "to or for the use of" organizations specifically described in § 2055 or to entities described in § 2512 qualify for the deduction.[1] The "to or for the use of" language requires that the transfers be directly to a qualifying

---

1. The statutory requirements for the charitable gift tax deduction are substantially the same as the estate tax deduction, but differences do exist. Compare § 2055(a) to § 2522(b). For example, § 2055(a)(4) allows a deduction for bequests to "any veterans' or- ganizations incorporated by Act of Congress" while § 2522(a)(4) is more expansive. It allows a deduction for gifts to veterans' organizations "organized in the United States or any of its possessions. . . ."

charity or in trust for a qualifying charity. If the transfer is in trust and the trustee has discretion to spray income or corpus among a group of charities, all such charities must be qualified organizations. Rev. Rul. 71–200, 1971–1 C.B. 272, held that a bequest in trust giving the trustees the power to distribute the trust corpus to any organization to which gifts were deductible under the income, estate or gift tax laws of the United States, or for the use of any state having jurisdiction over the trust, did not qualify for the deduction because the bequest was not confined to entities that satisfied § 2055. Compare Rev. Rul. 69–285, 1969–1 C.B. 222 (where the decedent bequeathed property to an individual "to be distributed to whatever charities she may deem worthy," a charitable contribution deduction was allowed because state law required her to distribute the funds to the types of charitable organizations defined in § 2055).

Sections 2055(a)(1) and § 2522(a)(1) allow a deduction for property transferred to or for the use of the United States, any state, territory, or political subdivision thereof, or the District of Columbia, for exclusively public purposes. Edwards v. Phillips, 373 F.2d 616 (10th Cir. 1967), held broadly that any bequest to a foreign government or political subdivision thereof, here the Denmark public school system, could not qualify for the charitable contribution deduction under § 2055. In contrast, several other cases held that contributions to foreign governments or their political subdivisions could qualify under § 2055(a)(2) or (a)(3) if the bequest was restricted to charitable purposes listed in § 2055(a)(3) instead of for general governmental use. Kaplun v. United States, 436 F.2d 799 (2d Cir. 1971) (bequest of coin collection to State of Israel on condition that it be exhibited in a museum qualified under § 2055(a)(2)); Old Colony Trust Co. v. United States, 438 F.2d 684 (1st Cir. 1971) (bequest to hospital owned by a Canadian county and city qualified); National Savings and Trust Co. v. United States, 436 F.2d 458 (Ct.Cl.1971) (bequest to German city to construct home for the aged qualified). The Internal Revenue Service announced in Rev. Rul. 74–523, 1974–2 C.B. 304, that it would follow *Kaplun* and *Old Colony Trust Co.,* and would no longer rely on Edwards v. Phillips.

Bequests and gifts to certain private foundations for which a deduction would otherwise be allowable are disallowed because of concerns about the extent to which such foundations serve charitable purposes. See §§ 2055(e)(1), 2522(e)(1) and 508(d). Contributions to employee welfare or retirement benefit funds are also generally nondeductible because such funds are not organized and operated exclusively for charitable purposes, e.g., their purpose is to provide additional compensation to employees. Estate of Leeds v. Commissioner, 54 T.C. 781 (1970); Watson v. United States, 355 F.2d 269 (3d Cir. 1965). However, § 2055(a)(5) permits an estate tax deduction for the bequest of stock to an employee stock ownership plan in certain narrow circumstances.

To provide assurance that contributions to a given organization will qualify for deduction, the IRS annually issues its Cumulative List, Publication No. 78, which contains the names of all organizations which qualify for deductible contributions. Prospective donors may rely on an organization's inclusion in the list until IRS removes it because it no longer meets the requirements for exempt charitable status. The Service publishes notices of revocations in the weekly Internal Revenue Bulletin in the period between the publication dates of the Cumulative List. Rev. Proc. 82–39, 1982–1 C.B. 759. See also, Estate of Clopton v. Commissioner, 93 T.C. 275 (1989) (once an organization has also been removed from the Cumulative List there is no assurance that transfers to an organization will qualify for a charitable deduction).

B. THE "PRIVATE INUREMENT" RESTRICTIONS

Sections 2055(a)(2) and (4), and 2522(a)(2) and (4) provide that contributions to the organizations described therein qualify for the deduction only if "no part of the net earnings of [the organization] inures to the benefit of any private stockholder or individual." Sections 2055(a)(3) and 2522(a)(3) reflect similar limitations in the requirement that transferred property be used "exclusively" for charitable purposes.

These provisions reflect a determination that the deduction should not be allowed if the contribution is made for the benefit of a private person or if a private person receives any part of the net earnings of the donee organization. It is not necessary that earnings actually be distributed to the private individual. Thus, Rev. Rul. 57–574, 1957–2 C.B. 161, held that bequests and gifts to a communal religious organization that operated a commercial enterprise, the proceeds of which were used to support the members and their families, did not qualify for the deduction. See also Better Business Bureau v. United States, 326 U.S. 279 (1945) (holding nondeductible contributions to an organization having as its primary purpose the promotion of "not only an ethical but also a profitable business community"); First National Bank of Omaha v. United States, 681 F.2d 534 (8th Cir. 1982) (bequest to cemetery association which was directed to use the funds first to maintain the decedent's family plot and then for the maintenance of the entire cemetery did not qualify since the noncharitable beneficiaries were given precedence and local law imposed no restrictions on the use of the funds for the private purpose).

C. ATTEMPTS TO INFLUENCE LEGISLATION OR POLITICAL CAMPAIGNS

A contribution is not deductible if the charity's activities in attempting to influence legislation or elections disqualify it from being tax exempt under § 501 (c)(3). Sections 2055(a)(2) and 2522(a)(2) provide that a charitable deduction is allowed for a contribution to or for the use of an organization "which is not disqualified for tax exemption under § 501(c)(3) by reason of attempting to influence legislation, and which does not participate in, or intervene in (including the publishing or distributing of statements), any political campaign on behalf (or in opposition to) of any candidate for public office." Buder v. United States, 7 F.3d 1382 (8th Cir. 1993), held that, where the governing instrument of a testamentary trust satisfied the "exclusively" requirement of § 2055(a)(2) because it required the trustee to distribute corpus and income to qualifying charities, there was no further requirement that the trust instrument also include a provision specifically prohibiting the trustees from engaging in lobbying or participation in a political campaign. Estate planners typically do include such a provision in the governing instruments of qualifying charitable organizations but not, as *Buder* illustrates, in the governing instruments of trusts which hold assets for the use of qualifying charitable organizations.

D.   CONDITIONAL BEQUESTS

Since Reg. § 20.2055–2(a) requires that the value of an interest given to charity be presently ascertainable at the death of the decedent ("D"), no deduction is allowed when the bequest to charity is contingent. Reg. § 20.2055–2(b) provides that if the transfer to charity depends on the occurrence of an event, the deduction will be allowed only if the nonoccurence of the event is "so remote as to be negligible." Rev. Rul. 70–452, 1970–2 C.B. 199, held that for purposes of Reg. § 2055–2(b), any possibility in excess of 5% that the contingency will occur is not so remote as to be negligible. Compare Estate of Gooel v. Commissioner, 68 T.C. 504 (1977) (a 22% chance that a 60–year–old woman would live 27 years, at which point the corpus designated for the charity would be exhausted, was not so remote as to be negligible); Rev. Rul. 77–374, 1977–2 C.B. 329 (same result where probability of exhaustion by life beneficiary was 63%); United States v. Dean, 224 F.2d 26 (1st Cir. 1955) (same result where probability of exhaustion by life beneficiary was 9%); Rev. Rul. 78–255, 1978–1 C.B. 294 (where probability of exhaustion by the life beneficiary was less than 1%, the deduction was allowed).

The Tax Court applied Reg. § 20.2055–2(a) to deny a charitable contribution deduction in Estate of Woodworth v. Commissioner, 47 T.C. 193 (1966), where D made a bequest to trustees for the purpose of assisting in the establishment or maintenance of a Catholic hospital in Spartanburg County, South Carolina. At the date of death there was no Catholic hospital in the county, nor was there any evidence that one would be built. As there was no cy pres doctrine in South Carolina, the court concluded that the possibility that the charitable transfer would become effective was so remote as to be negligible. The court stated:

> "The phrase 'so remote as to be negligible' contained in § 20.2555–2(b) of the regulations has been defined as 'a chance which persons generally would disregard as so improbable that it might be ignored with reasonable safety in undertaking a serious business transaction.' United States v. Dean, 224 F.2d 26 (C.A.l, 1955). It is likewise a chance which every dictate of reason and common sense would justify an intelligent person in disregarding as so highly improbable and remote as to be lacking in reason and substance. United States v. Provident Trust Co., 291 U.S. 272 (1934). Applying these criteria to the facts of this case, it is apparent that the possibility that a Catholic hospital would not be built in Spartanburg could not be ignored with reasonable safety if this were connected with a serious business transaction. There is nothing absolute or certain with respect to the fact that a Catholic hospital might or might not come into existence and, therefore, is not so remote as to be negligible." (197)

Rev. Rul. 72–442, 1972–2 C.B. 527, subsequently held in a situation similar to that in *Estate of Woodworth*, that the charitable deduction would be allowable if the applicable state law included a cy pres doctrine.

There are many other circumstances that raise the issue whether the bequest is contingent. See United States v. Fourth National Bank in Wichita, 83 F.2d 85 (10th Cir. 1936) (bequest to a charity conditioned on similar contributions by other persons held to be too contingent to qualify for a deduction; the court examined the relative contingency of the bequest as of D's death; satisfaction of the condition precedent after D's death but prior to suit was given no weight); Rev. Rul. 64–129, 1964–1 C.B. 329 (no deduction for bequest to charity conditioned on approval by D's sister); Rev. Rul. 67–229, 1967–2 C.B. 335 (bequest to a corporation so long as it was maintained in a specific county and operated as an association for the care and maintenance of orphans qualified for the deduction since the occurrence of either disqualifying event was highly improbable at the date of death). In Marine v. Commissioner, 990 F.2d 136 (4th Cir. 1993), D's will transferred the residue of his estate to qualified charities. A codicil, however, provided that his executors had the absolute discretion to compensate persons who had contributed to D's "well being" or had been "otherwise helpful" to him during his lifetime. The court held that the codicil provision caused the charitable bequest to be too contingent.

Bequests to charity contingent on death without issue have also been the subject of much litigation. See United States v. Provident Trust Co., 291 U.S. 272 (1934), where the gift to charity was contingent on the death without issue of the life tenant, a woman fifty years of age who had no children. Upon proof that the woman had undergone surgery which made her incapable of bearing children, the court allowed the deduction. The holding of *Provident Trust* has not been limited to cases in which surgery has made childbearing impossible. See Rev. Rul. 59–143, 1959–1 C.B. 247; Commissioner v. Estate of Sternberger, 348 U.S. 187 (1955); Humes v. United States, 276 U.S. 487 (1928).

The ability of heirs to defeat a charitable bequest in a will contest or pursuant to a forced heir statute is not a contingency. In Longue Vue Foundation v. Commissioner, 90 T.C. 150 (1988), a charitable bequest was effective as of the date of death but was voidable under a state forced heir statute. The heirs did not exercise their rights and the charity received the bequest. Under these circumstances the Tax Court concluded that voidability did not cause the bequest to fail. Reg. § 20.2055–2(b).

E.   TRANSFER FROM THE DECEDENT

To qualify for the estate tax charitable contribution deduction, the property must pass directly from D to a qualifying charitable organization or a trust for a qualifying organization by will or by some other testamentary disposition. Senft v. United States, 319 F.2d 642 (3d Cir. 1963) (property passing to a state by escheat did not qualify for the deduction). Estate of Lamson v. United States, 338 F.2d 376 (Ct.Cl. 1964), is one of numerous authorities holding that no estate tax charitable deduction is allowed for a bequest to D's son, a priest bound by religious vows of absolute poverty to turn over any property acquired by him to his Order. The court concluded property did not pass from D to the charity, rejecting the argument that D's son received the property as constructive trustee for the religious order. See also Davis v. United States, 495 U.S. 472 (1990) (income tax charitable deduction denied for transfers to taxpayers' sons who were serving as full-time unpaid missionaries). Similarly, in Pickard v. Commissioner, 60 T.C. 618 (1973), aff'd mem. order, 503 F.2d 1404 (6th Cir. 1974), no charitable deduction was allowed where D left property to her stepfather who had predeceased her and whose will left the residue of his estate to charity. The court held that property did not pass from D to the charitable organization as the result of her testamentary disposition, but rather as a result of the "operation of an external force."

Section 2055(b) provides that where A grants B a general power of appointment but, in the event of default in the exercise of the power, the property passes to a qualified charity, B's estate will be allowed a charitable deduction. In the absence of the provision, the property would not have passed from B by bequest or otherwise, even though § 2041 would require the value of the property to be included in B's gross estate for federal estate tax purposes. See Reg. § 20.2055–1(b).

F.   DISCLAIMERS

If a beneficiary of an estate makes a qualified disclaimer of his interest pursuant to § 2518, p. 434, and as a result the interest passes to charity, D's estate is allowed a deduction under § 2055 since under § 2518 the interest is treated as though it had never passed to the disclaimant.

Section 2055(a) creates another opportunity for disclaimer in addition to the qualified disclaimer rules of § 2518. It provides that the complete termination of a power to consume, invade or appropriate property for the benefit of an individual, before the estate tax return due date and before the exercise of that power, will be deemed a qualified disclaimer sufficient to qualify the property for the estate tax charitable deduction if it passes to or for the use of charitable organizations. For examples of disclaimers that preserved a charitable contribution deduction, see Jaecker v. Commissioner, 58 T.C. 166 (1972); Rev. Rul. 71–483, 1971–2 337. But compare Rev. Rul. 76–546, 1976–2 C.B. 290 (death of life beneficiary before due date of estate tax return did not effect a disclaimer under § 2055(a) because a life beneficiary does not possess the power to consume, invade or appropriate property as required by § 2055(a)).

G.   AMOUNT OF DEDUCTION

Under § 2055(d), the amount of the charitable deduction for estate tax purposes cannot exceed the value at which the transferred property is included in the gross estate. Sometimes, the amount of the deduction will be less than the gross estate value. In Ahmanson Foundation v. United States, 674 F.2d 761 (9th Cir. 1981), D owned all the voting and nonvoting stock of a corporation. He bequeathed the voting stock to his son and the nonvoting stock to a charity. The court held that the nonvoting shares had a higher value for purposes of calculating the gross estate than for calculating the charitable deduction. For calculating the gross estate, the nonvoting shares would have to be valued together with the voting shares because the focus of the estate tax is on what is owned at death. (See p. 712 for further discussion of this issue.) This resulted in a higher valuation because the holder of both the voting and nonvoting shares could recapitalize the corporation and grant voting rights to the nonvoting shares, thereby increasing their value. In contrast, for purposes of valuing the charitable deduction, the court determined that the value of the nonvoting shares should be measured separate from the voting shares since only the nonvoting shares were transferred to charity. This approach resulted in a smaller charitable deduction. See Repetti, "Minority Discounts: The Alchemy In Estate And Gift Taxation", 50 Tax Law Review 416, 422–423 (1995) for a discussion of *Ahmanson* and related cases.

As discussed below, the estate tax deduction is also reduced by state and federal taxes and administration expenses paid out of the charitable bequest.

The charitable deduction for gift tax purposes equals the value of the qualifying transfers less the amounts excludable from gift tax under § 2503(b). § 2524. See Reg. §§ 25.2522(a)–1(a); 25.2503–1; and 25.2524–1.

H.   REDUCTION OF CHARITABLE CONTRIBUTION BY TAXES AND ADMINISTRATION EXPENSES

1.   Taxes

Under § 2055(c), any state or federal taxes payable out of the charitable bequest, either under state law or the provisions of the will, reduce the bequest in computing the charitable deduction. Therefore, when the residue is left to charity and state law directs that estate taxes be paid out of the residue, the taxes must first be deducted before the charitable deduction can be computed. If the state has an apportionment statute prescribing how much of the estate tax liability is allocable to the charitable bequest, the statute controls. Frequently, however, state apportionment statutes provide that the will of the testator may apportion state or federal taxes in a manner different from that specified by the statute. In such situations, the courts must interpret the will to see if the charitable bequest is burdened with its share of federal or state taxes. See, e.g., First National Bank of Omaha v. United States, 490 F.2d 1054 (8th Cir. 1974) (specific charitable bequests were not reduced by estate taxes on general principle that gifts to charity do not generate estate taxes but rather benefit the recipients by lowering the total taxable amount; "equity as well as state * * * legislative intent require that such charitable gifts be relieved from sharing the burden of estate taxes assessed against the estates").

If the charitable bequest bears a portion of the taxes imposed, the decrease in the amount passing to charity will further reduce the allowable deduction and in turn increase the taxable estate. In such a case, the amount of the charitable deduction can be obtained only by a series of trial-and-error computations or by formulae. Reg. § 20.2055–3(b); Estate of Bush v. United States, 618 F.2d 741 (Ct. Cl. 1980); Dulles v. Johnson, 273 F.2d 362 (2d Cir. 1959); Edwards v. Slocum, 264 U.S. 61 (1924). Rev. Rul. 76–358, 1976–2 C.B. 291, and Rev. Rul. 76–359, 1976–2 C.B. 293, provide examples of computations to determine the allowable charitable contribution deduction where taxes must be apportioned between charitable and non-charitable bequests.

Where the taxes payable out of the charitable bequest are sizable, the resultant increase in the taxable estate often causes the estate to move into succeedingly higher estate tax brackets. This jump into higher brackets increases the complexity of the computation, and also pyramids the tax. If state or foreign death taxes are also payable, the pyramid effect is somewhat alleviated by § 2053(d). Although state and foreign death taxes are normally not deductible, § 2053(d) allows the estate to deduct such taxes imposed on or payable out of a charitable bequest provided (1) the decrease in federal estate tax resulting from the deduction inures solely to the benefit of the charity, or (2) the federal estate tax is equitably apportioned among all transferees of property included in D's gross estate. See Reg. § 20.2053–9(a) and (b). Thus, if § 2053(d) applies, there will be no tax pyramiding on account of state death taxes borne by the charity, since the initial reduction in the charitable deduction occasioned by the state death tax will be offset by the additional deduction allowed under § 2053(d). Since § 2053(d) does not provide a deduction for federal estate tax payable out of charitable bequests, the pyramiding problem still exists for the federal estate tax.

2.   Administration Expenses

Regulations specify the treatment of administration expenses paid from the charitable bequest. Reg. § 20.2055–3(b)(1). The regulations distinguish between "management expenses" and "transmission expenses". "Management expenses" are expenses incurred in connection with the investment of estate assets or with their preservation or maintenance. Reg. § 20.2055–3(b)(1). They include investment advisory fees, stock brokerage commissions, custodial fees, and interest. "Transmission expenses" are expenses that would not have been incurred but for the decedent's death and the consequent necessity of collecting the decedent's assets, paying the decedent's debts and death taxes, and distributing the property to those who are entitled to receive it. They include executor commissions and probate fees.

The charitable deduction is reduced by transmission expenses paid from the portion of the estate designated for the charity. Reg. § 20.2055–3(b)(2). It is also reduced by management expenses that are attributable to managing assets not in the charity's share of the estate but that are paid from the charity's share. Reg. § 20.2055–3(b)(4). The charitable deduction is not reduced by management expenses paid from the charity's share that are attributable to managing that share unless the estate deducts such expense under § 2053. Reg. § 20.2055–3(b)(3).

SECTION B.   SPLIT-INTEREST TRANSFERS TO CHARITY

Internal revenue Code: §§ 2055(e); 2522(c); 664(a)–(d); 642(c)(5)

Regulations: §§ 20.2055–2(a)–(b)

ILLUSTRATIVE MATERIAL

A.   BACKGROUND

Prior to the Tax Reform Act of 1969, a transferor could create a trust with the income payable to a member of her family and the remainder to charity at a designated time. Under these circumstances, the transferor (or her estate) received a charitable contribution deduction for the present value of the remainder interest to charity. But the amount of that deduction might bear little relation to the amount that the charity ultimately received. There was an incentive on the part of the creator of the trust to have the trust follow investment policies that would favor the income beneficiary at the expense of the charity. Similarly, a transferor might create a trust with the income payable to charity for a designated period of years, with the remainder then payable to some member of the donor's family. If properly structured the transfer would qualify for the charitable contribution deduction. Here, however, the trustee had an incentive to invest in low-yield, high-appreciation assets to the detriment of charity, since the amount of the donor's deduction was not dependent on the amount that charity in fact received.

These problems caused the Treasury to recommend and the Congress to adopt in 1969 substantial restrictions on the use of split-interest trusts to insure that the amount ultimately received by charity bore some reasonable relationship to the amount claimed as gift or estate tax charitable deductions by the creator of the split-interests. See U.S. Treasury Department, Tax Reform Studies and Proposals, House Ways and Means Comm. and Senate Finance Comm., 91st Cong., 1st Sess. 182–85 (Comm. Print 1969); S. Rep. No. 91–552, 91st Cong., 1st Sess. 86–93 (1969).

B. THE TAX TREATMENT OF SPLIT–INTEREST TRUSTS

1. Charitable Remainder Trusts in General

In general, the grantor of an inter vivos qualified charitable remainder trust which satisfies all the requirements is entitled to a charitable deduction for income taxes under § 170 equal to the value of the charity's remainder interest. The grantor is also entitled to charitable deduction under § 2522 which will offset the gift tax attributable to the transfer of the charity's remainder interest. Of course, no deduction will apply to the transfer of the income interest to the noncharitable beneficiary. If the donor retains the income interest for himself, the entire trust corpus is includible in his gross estate but will be offset by an estate tax charitable deduction under § 2055 equal to the value of the charity's interest.

Sections 2055(e)(2)(A) and 2522(c)(2)(A) require that if the transferor desires to create a split-interest trust with the income payable to a non-charitable beneficiary and the remainder to charity, one of the three specified forms must be used to obtain a charitable deduction for the present value of the remainder interest. The approved devices are the charitable remainder annuity trust as defined in § 664(d)(1), the charitable remainder unitrust as defined in § 664(d)(2) and the pooled income fund as defined in § 642(c)(5).

The qualified charitable remainder trust rules do not replace the requirements of § 2055(a) or § 2522(a). Thus, if any of the requirements in § 2055(a) or § 2522(a) for a charitable contribution deduction are not satisfied, no deduction will be allowed, even if the charitable remainder trust satisfies the conditions of § 2055(e) or § 2522(c)(2)(A). Rev. Rul. 78–255, 1978–1 C.B. 294; Rev. Rul. 77–374, 1977–2 C.B. 329; Rev. Rul. 85–23, 1985–1 C.B. 327.

2. Charitable Remainder Annuity Trust

In general, a charitable remainder annuity trust ("CRAT") is one in which the non-charitable income beneficiary is entitled to receive annually a specified dollar amount or a fixed percentage (that is not less than 5%) of the fair market value of the trust corpus at the time it is created. This requirement is intended to prevent taxpayers from using charitable remainder trusts as private foundations without being subject to all the restrictions applicable to private foundations. The term of the income beneficiary's interest may be measured by her life or, if a life term is not used, a term not exceeding 20 years.

Two additional payment requirements are intended to prevent taxpayers from exploiting the tax exempt status of the trust by contributing appreciated assets to the trust, causing the trust to sell the assets without incurring an income tax and then quickly distributing most of the proceeds to beneficiaries in such a way that will minimize the taxable income the beneficiaries recognize. First, the trust cannot pay an annuity in any year that is greater than 50% of the initial fair market value of the trust property. § 664(d)(1)(A). Second, the present value of the charity's remainder interest must equal 10% of the initial fair market value of the trust property. § 664(d)(1)(D).[2] This value is determined under § 7520. See p. 723. Reg. § 1.664–1(a) and 2 provides additional rules that must be complied with if the gift in trust is to qualify for the charitable deduction.

Since the specified percentage for the non-charitable annuity is based on the value of the trust principal at the time of the creation of the trust, any gain or loss due to changes in value inures to the charitable remainder.

Sample forms of charitable remainder annuity trusts are contained in Rev. Proc. 2003–53, 2003–2 C.B. 230; Rev. Proc. 2003–54, 2003–2 C.B. 236; Rev. Proc. 2003–55, 2003–2 C.B. 242; Rev. Proc. 2003–56, 2003–2 C.B. 249; Rev. Proc. 2003–57, 2003–2 C.B. 257; Rev. Proc. 2003–58, 2003–2 C.B. 262; Rev. Proc. 2003–59, 2003–2 C.B. 268; and Rev. Proc. 2003–60, 2003–2 C.B. 274.

3. *Charitable Remainder Unitrust*

A charitable remainder unitrust ("CRUT") is one in which the non-charitable income beneficiary is entitled to receive an annual payment equal to a specified percentage of the trust corpus valued annually. The income interest must not be less than 5% of the fair market value of the trust assets as determined annually. § 664(d)(2). Also, similar to the rules described above for charitable remainder annuity trusts, the trust cannot pay income that exceeds 50% of the fair market value of its assets, valued annually. § 664 (d)(2)(A).[3] Moreover, the present value of the charity's remainder interest must equal 10% of the initial fair market value of the trust property. § 664(d)(2)(D).[4] As with the annuity interest, the term of an individual's income interest may be the individual's life, but if her life is not used as the measure, may not exceed 20 years. Reg. § 1.664–1(a) and 3 describes additional rules that must be complied with in order for a trust to qualify as a charitable remainder unitrust.

Since the payment to the non-charitable and the charitable remainder interest is determined annually in the case of a unitrust, the non-charitable beneficiary and the charitable remainder interest share equally in the increases or decreases in value of the trust corpus.

One major advantage of the unitrust is that the trust instrument can limit the payment to the lesser of the net income of the trust or the percentage amount. § 664(d)(3). This permits the trust to avoid invading principal in order to pay the income beneficiary and, thereby, to avoid reducing the charitable remainder interest. In the event the trust pays income which is less than the percentage amount, the trust instrument may (but is not required to) contain a

---

2. There is an exception for certain testamentary trusts of settlors dying before January 1, 1999. P.L. 105–34, § 1089(b)(6)(A).

3. This rule applies to transfers in trust after June 18, 1997. P.L. 105–34, § 1089(a)(2).

4. This rule generally applies to transfers occurring after July 28, 1997. There is an exception for certain testamentary of settlors dying before January 1, 1999. P.L. 105–34, § 1089(b)(6)(A).

make-up provision which in subsequent years permits it to pay out net income in excess of the percentage amount to the extent of the shortfall.

Sample forms for charitable remainder unitrusts are presented in Rev. Proc. 2005–52, 2005–2 C.B. 326; Rev. Proc. 2005–53, 2005–2 C.B. 339; Rev. Proc. 2005–54, 2005–2 C.B. 353; Rev. Proc. 2005–55, 2005–2 C.B. 367; Rev. Proc. 2005–56, 2005–2 C.B. 383; Rev. Proc. 2005–57, 2005–2 C.B. 392; Rev. Proc. 2005–58, 2005–2 C.B. 402; and Rev. Proc. 2005–59, 2005–2 C.B. 412.

4. Pooled Income Funds

The pooled income fund, as defined in § 642(c)(5), constitutes another vehicle by which donors or testators can make split-interest transfers with remainder interests to charity. Generally, a pooled income fund is a trust or other fund maintained by a charitable organization to which donors transfer property. Under the terms of the transfers the remainder interest in the property is irrevocably assigned to the charity and each donor retains the life income for himself (or others). The charitable institution invests the funds and pays out a proportionate share of the total income earned by the fund to each of the donors to the fund. As each life income interest terminates, the remainder interest is separated from the pooled income fund and goes to the charity for its unrestricted use.

If the charitable institution maintains a pooled income fund that qualifies under section 642(c)(5) and Reg. § 1.642(c)–5, the transferor can obtain the benefit of a gift or estate tax charitable contribution deduction for the charitable interest. Rev. Rul. 72–196, 1972–1 C.B. 194 and Rev. Rul. 82–38, 1982–1 C.B. 96 set forth sample provisions for the governing instruments of pooled income funds that will qualify for the charitable contributions deductions under § 2055 and § 2522.

5. Relation to Private Foundation Rules

In general, § 4947(a)(2) and § 508(e) require that the governing instrument for charitable remainder and pooled income trusts contain provisions which satisfy certain rules applicable to private foundations. For example, the instruments should prohibit the trust from engaging in "self-dealing" transactions with persons who transferred property to the trust. Self-dealing includes borrowing from the trust or selling property to or buying property from the trust. § 4941(d). Moreover the governing instrument should prevent the trust from making disqualifying expenditures such as payments for unreasonable compensation. Reg. § 53.4945–6(b)(2).

C. CHARITABLE LEAD TRUSTS

The charitable lead trust reverses the order of payments compared to the charitable remainder trust. A lead trust pays the income interest (sometimes called the "lead" interest) to the charity while the remainder interest either reverts to the grantor or to another person selected by the grantor. There is no limit imposed by the transfer tax on the duration of the lead interest.

An inter vivos transfer into trust will be a taxable gift to the extent the grantor does not retain a reversionary interest. The value of the charity's income interest, however, is deductible for gift tax purposes if the requirements of § 2522(c)(2)(B) are satisfied. Similarly, property transferred into a charitable lead trust at death will be includible in the transferor's gross estate but the estate may deduct the value of the charity's interest subject to § 2055(e)(2)(B).

Sections 2522(c)(2)(B) and 2055(e)(2)(B) require that the charity's income interest either be a "guaranteed annuity" or unitrust amount. In general, a guaranteed annuity is a fixed dollar amount to be paid at least annually. Reg. § 20.2055–2(e)(2)(vi). The unitrust amount is a fixed percentage of the value of the trust property determined annually. § 2055(e)(2)(B).

Unlike the charitable remainder trust, no minimum percentage is set for the income payout. The grantor of an inter vivos charitable lead trust may also qualify for an income deduction under § 170 for the value of the charity's income interest if trust income is taxable to the grantor under the grantor trust rules of §§ 671–679. See § 170(f)(2)(B). The grantor's retention of a reversionary interest having a value greater than 5 percent of the trust's corpus will normally cause trust income to be taxable to the grantor under § 673(a).

Since a charitable lead trust is a split interest trust, it is generally subject to the private foundation rules described above for remainder trusts. See §§ 508(e) and 4947(a)(2).

D. NON–TRUST LEGAL INTERESTS

Estate and gift tax charitable contribution deductions will be allowed for certain partial interests transferred to charity in non-trust form. A charitable deduction is generally allowed for the transfer of an undivided portion of the decedent's entire interest in property, Reg. § 20.2055.–2(e)(2)(i)[5]; for a remainder interest in a personal residence or a farm, Reg. § 20.2055–2(e)(2)(ii),(iii); for certain partial interests transferred for conservation purposes, Reg. § 20.2055–2(e)(2)(iv); for certain transfers of works of art, even though the copyright on the work is retained by the transferor, if the transfer is to a publicly supported charitable organization other than a private foundation and is used in a manner that is related to the exempt purpose of the organization, § 2055(e)(4); for a "guaranteed annuity interest" as defined in Reg. § 20.2055–2(e)(2)(vi); and for transfers in the form of a "unitrust interest" as defined in Reg. § 20.2055–2(e)(vii). The purpose of the last two exceptions is to permit, in general, deductions for split-interest transfers in non-trust form only if the value of the remainder interest would have been allowable as a deduction had the property been transferred in trust.

It is important to note that if the bequest or gift of a partial interest is in trust, the trust must satisfy the qualified charitable remainder or lead trust rules in order for the transfer to be deductible. Even though a non-trust gift of the partial interest would have qualified under the rules discussed above for partial interest, the transfer in trust is not deductible if the trust fails as a qualified charitable remainder or lead trust. See Estate of Burgess v. Commissioner, 622 F.2d 700 (4th Cir. 1980). Ellis First National Bank v. United States, 550 F.2d 9 (Ct. Cl. 1977); Rev. Rul. 76–357, 1976–2 C.B. 285.

---

5. Section 2055(e) carves out a special rule for inter vivos charitable contributions of personal tangible property. In general, a deduction is allowed only if the donor, either alone or in conjunction with the charitable donee, holds all interests in the property immediately prior to the contribution.

E. CONSERVATION EASEMENT EXCLUSION

Congress has provided another tax expenditure to encourage the dedication of land for conservation purposes in the form of an estate tax exclusion. Under § 2031(c), an exclusion is allowed for a portion of the value of land that is subject to a "qualified conservation easement." The amount of the exclusion is based on the "applicable percentage" of the value of land subject to a conservation easement, less any estate tax charitable deduction with respect to the land. § 2031(c)(1). The applicable percentage is 40%, reduced by 2 percentage points for each percentage point by which the value of the qualified conservation easement is less than 30% of the value of the land unencumbered by the easement. § 2031(c)(2). The exclusion is capped at $500,000 for decedents dying in 2002 and beyond. § 2031(c)(3).

SECTION C. POLICY ISSUES

Factors Affecting Charitable Giving: Inferences from Estate Tax Returns, 1986

by Barry W. Johnson and Jeffrey P. Rosenfeld, Ph.D.

COMPENDIUM OF FEDERAL ESTATE TAX AND PERSONAL WEALTH STUDIES

INTERNAL REVENUE SERVICE, STATISTICS OF INCOME (MARCH, 1994)

Introduction

Analysis of Federal Estate Tax Returns (Forms 706) filed for 1986 decedents shows the interplay of social and economic factors on bequest decisions. Data from 706 returns show that marital status, gender and social class are important predictors of charitable giving. These factors, coupled with individual values and beliefs, predispose a person to make a charitable bequest. Tax incentives can also affect the amount given, as well as the timing and form of such bequests.

Total giving to charities in 1986 was nearly $92 billion, or about 2 percent of the Gross National Product * * *. The majority of these gifts were given by individuals, both directly (82.2%) and through bequests (6.7%). Total bequests to charities amounted to $6.2 billion in 1986. These bequests can have a significant impact on recipient organizations.

Data on the charitable bequests of wealthy decedents dying in 1986 [show that, as] a group, these "top wealthholders" gave $4.1 billion, and accounted for about 71 percent of all such bequests made by U.S. decedents * * *. Nine percent of the estate tax decedents made gifts of $1 million or more. These large gifts totaled nearly $3 billion, or about 72 percent of the charitable bequests made by top wealthholders. The majority of the remaining decedents * * * made bequests of less than $250,000. Even so, the sum of these "small" bequests was over $200 million. It is no wonder that organizations expend considerable fund raising effort to garner bequests.

1986 DECEDENTS

* * * This article presents data from returns filed in 1986–1988, focusing on 1986 as the year of death. A Federal estate tax return was required for all 1986 decedents with at least $500,000 in total gross estate at the time of their death; the top tax rate was 55%.

There were an estimated 45,800 U.S. citizens who died in 1986 with gross estates above the $500,000 filing requirement, representing only about 2.2 percent of the U.S. decedent population. These decedents had a combined gross estate of over $66 billion. Over 56% of them were male, most of whom were married; most of the female decedents were widowed. The average age at death for males and females was 73.8 and 79.5, respectively.

Almost 20% of these 1986 decedents made bequests to charitable organizations. These bequests accounted for slightly over 24% of their net estates. (Net estate, or net worth, is defined as total assets, including life insurance owned by the decedent and certain lifetime transfers, minus debts.) The average (mean) bequest amount was $461,000. The minimum bequest value was $100 and the maximum, well over $150 million. Gender and net worth are the two most important variables for predicting the value of bequests.

Female decedents were almost twice as likely as males to make bequests to charitable organizations. * * * [T]heir rate of charitable giving exceeds the rate for men and also exceeds the aggregate rate for all decedents. [Analysis] also illustrates that, regardless of sex, the likelihood of making a charitable bequest increases significantly as net worth rises. Almost half the women and 35% of the men in the highest net worth group made bequests to charities. This may be due to the ability of larger estates to adequately provide for family members and make a significant gift, or to the lower cost of charitable giving incurred at the higher tax rates.

* * *

THE CHARITABLE DEDUCTION

There has been much debate over the effectiveness of the charitable deduction allowed for both the Federal income and estate tax. Economists argue that a significant amount of charitable behavior depends on these deductions. According to this line of reasoning, the tax and the deduction have two opposing effects. First, the tax reduces the estate available for division between potential heirs and charities. This is known as the wealth effect and should have a negative effect on gifts to charity. Second, the deduction reduces the price of giving to charity relative to giving to a non-charity which should encourage charitable giving. This is called the price effect because the price of each additional dollar given to charity relative to a non-charity, is only $1—the marginal tax rate (the amount of tax savings attributable to the deduction) * * *. Thus, in the highest tax bracket, the cost of a dollar given to charity, rather than a non-charity, is only $.45 ($1 minus .55). The progressive structure of the tax rates suggests that both the wealth and price effects increase with the size of the taxable estate. The magnitude of these effects determines the effect of changes in the tax system on charitable giving * * *.

Survey research * * * indicates that tax consequences are not a major consideration when people decide to make charitable gifts. Ninety percent of respondents surveyed in 1986 said they would not change their charitable giving patterns in 1987 in response to the limits placed on both the valuation of assets given to charity and on the relative size of the charitable deduction as a part of the Tax Reform Act of 1986. Only 2% of the respondents in the sample attributed their charitable giving to tax incentives, while 37% said they gave because of strong feelings toward a particular charity.

A series of focus groups with estate-planning professionals confirm that taxes affect the level and timing of a gift, but not the decision to make a gift. In 1986 and 1989, the Statistics of Income Division of IRS conducted focus groups with estate-planning professionals to discuss a wide range of issues associated with charitable giving. Estate planners, accountants, and bank trust officers who work with affluent clients say that these clients come to them with pre-existing goals concerning charitable bequests. They rarely suggest charitable giving as a tax savings option. This finding is consistent with the survey research mentioned earlier, and helps put taxes, as incentives or constraints on charitable giving, in perspective. They affect timing and level of charitable giving. By examining price elasticities, it is possible to measure this effect.

Empirical Studies

In order to examine the effects of taxes on charitable bequests, a measure of the change in giving associated with a change in the tax rate is needed. This measure is known as the price elasticity of charitable giving. An elasticity greater than one (in absolute terms) means that a change in the tax rate stimulates a relatively larger change in the amount bequeathed. In that case, the tax is said to be an efficient means of stimulating behavior. If, on the other hand, the elasticity is less than one, it can be argued that the deduction is inefficient, as the loss in revenue is not made up by gifts to charity; in this case, charities would fare better if the deduction were abolished, and instead, the government were to distribute tax revenue directly to them.

Several economists have used both Federal estate tax returns and state probate records to quantify the effects of taxes on giving * * *. Two separate studies using 1957–59, 1969, and 1976 Federal estate tax data showed a price elasticity of charitable bequests greater than one for small and moderate size estates * * *. Elasticities very close to one were calculated for the very largest estates, leading to the conclusion that the tax deduction was efficient for all but the very wealthy. Both concluded that eliminating the deduction would sharply curtail charitable bequests and increase bequests to heirs. A reduction in tax rates would have a similar, although less severe, effect. (135–139)

ILLUSTRATIVE MATERIAL

A. TAX EXPENDITURE ANALYSIS

The estate and gift tax deductions for transfers to charitable organizations are not necessary to determine a normative wealth transfer tax base. From its inception, the deduction has been justified as an incentive or reward for the socially desirable activity of supporting charity.[6] However, a different analytic technique which is discussed in Chapter 31 would view the deduction as the equivalent of a government matching grant program.

B. EMPIRICAL STUDIES

Consistent with the empirical studies referred to above, studies using data for decedents dying in 1992 and 1995 suggest that charitable bequests would fall by approximately 12 percent in the event the estate tax is repealed. Joulfaian, *Taxing Wealth Transfers and Its Behavioral Consequences*, 53 Nat'l Tax J. 933, 951–952 (2000).

---

6. See, e.g., Paul, Federal Estate and Gift Taxation 645 (1942); House Ways and Means Committee, Hearings on Federal Estate and Gift Taxes, 94th Cong., 2d Sess. 1090 (1976) (Statement of American Association of Presidents of Independent Colleges and Universities et. al.).

CHAPTER 30

OTHER TAX CREDITS

SECTION A.   THE CREDIT FOR TAX ON PRIOR TRANSFERS

Internal Revenue Code: Section 2013

Regulations: Section 20.2013–1, 2, 3

The purpose of the credit for estate taxes on previously taxed transfers of property is to prevent the depletion of a family's wealth by the estate taxation that could result from the circumstance of successive deaths within a relatively short period of time.[1] Suppose, for example, that a parent dies in 2008 with an estate that is large enough to incur an estate tax and leaves all his property to a child, who dies in 2009. If there were no relief for previously taxed transfers of property comparable to that provided by § 2013, the transfer of the same assets by the child at her death in 2009 would be subject to a second estate tax, even though she died soon after her parent. Congress has decided that in this and other situations involving the closely spaced deaths of a transferor and a decedent, the estate tax otherwise payable by the decedent, in this case the child, should be reduced through a credit device.

ILLUSTRATIVE MATERIAL

A.   GENERAL OPERATION

An estate is entitled to a credit for estate taxes paid on prior transfers if the property was transferred to the decedent by a person whose death occurs within ten years before or within two years after the death of the decedent. The amount of the credit depends on the amount of the estate tax paid by the person who transferred property to the decedent, and the length of time that elapsed between the death of the transferor and that of the decedent. The larger the estate tax of the transferor, the larger the credit allowed to the decedent is apt to be, and vice versa. Moreover, the shorter the interval between the death of the transferor and the decedent, the larger the credit.

The credit may not exceed the lower of (1) the estate tax paid by the transferor's estate with respect to the value of the assets transferred to the decedent,[2] or (2) the amount by which the decedent's estate tax is increased if the value of the transferred assets are included in his gross estate compared to the estate tax without such inclusion, computed of course without the § 2013

---

1. See S.Rep.No.1622, 83rd Cong., 2d Sess. 122 (1954); H.Rep. No.767, 65th., 2d Sess. 22–23 (1918).

2. This is the "first limitation" of Reg. § 20.2013–2.

credit.[3] Because of these limitations the credit is not "refundable." In addition, if the transferor died more than two years before the decedent, the figure obtained as the lower of (1) or (2) must be reduced by 20 percent for each two-year period by which the transferor's death preceded that of the decedent. Thus, if the interval between the deaths of the transferor and the decedent exceeds ten years, no credit is allowable.

Section 2013(c)(1), by limiting the credit to the amount of Federal estate tax attributable to the transferred property in the decedent's estate, provides for a comparison between the estate tax payable (without the credit) on the actual taxable estate, and an estate tax computed by reducing the gross estate by the value of the transferred assets. The transferred assets do not actually have to be included in the decedent's gross estate. For example, in Rev. Rul. 59–9, 1959–1 C.B. 232, the credit was allowed where decedent received a life estate in a testamentary trust from his father and died within 10 years of his father's death, even though the value of the life estate was not included in decedent's gross estate. Moreover, it is not even necessary that an estate tax on the property transferred actually have been paid by the transferor's estate. This is because the credit allowed is on a proportion of the transferor's estate tax before reduction by credits for gift tax or previously taxed transfers. Conceivably, no net tax may have been due because of the allowance of such credits against the transferor's gross estate tax. § 2013(b). On the other hand, the transferor must have had a *taxable estate* before the § 2013 credit is allowable to the decedent. The fact that the transferor's estate would have been entitled to a § 2012 or § 2013 credit if it had been subject to tax apart from the credits is irrelevant. United States v. Denison, 318 F.2d 819 (5th Cir. 1963); Estate of La Sala v. Commissioner, 71 T.C. 752 (1979).

The value of the transferred assets subtracted from decedent's gross estate is the value at which they were included in the *transferor's* gross estate (to the extent of the decedent's interest) less any taxes, encumbrances, or obligations imposed by the transferor and incurred by the decedent with respect to such property upon the transfer to the decedent.[4] § 2013(d). If the interest received by the decedent from the transferor is a limited one, for example a life estate or a term of years, the value of that interest is determined as of the date of the transferor's death utilizing recognized valuation principles. Reg. § 20.2013–4(a). Moreover, if the decedent was the transferor's spouse, the value of the interest is also reduced by any marital deduction allowed to the transferor's estate. Reg. § 20.2013–4(b)(2).[5] Thus, if the transferor spouse transfers property to the surviving spouse in a form that allows the entire value of the property to qualify for the marital deduction, the surviving spouse's estate will not be entitled to a credit under § 2013. Since those assets were not subject to estate tax at the time of transfer, they are properly excluded from the determination of the credit for tax on prior transfers.

---

3. The is the "second limitation" of Reg. § 20.2013–3.

4. For purposes of determining the value of property transferred to the decedent, all encumbrances and taxes relating to the transferred property must be deducted, even though a marital deduction was claimed in the transferor's estate with respect to some of the transferred property. Reed v. United States, 743 F.2d 481 (7th Cir. 1984).

5. See Rev. Rul. 90–2, 1990–1 C.B. 169, and Rev. Rul. 61–208, 1961–2 C.B. 148, for illustrations of computations involving the marital deduction and charitable deduction.

Where the estate of a decedent is entitled to § 2013 credits with respect to property received from more than one transferor, the § 2013 credit is calculated separately with respect to the property received from each transferor. The estate of the decedent is entitled to an aggregate credit equal to the sum of the separately computed credits. Estate of Meyer v. Commissioner, 778 F.2d 125 (2d Cir. 1985).

B.   ESTATES ELIGIBLE FOR THE CREDIT

Generally, the estates of all persons are eligible for the credit for estate tax on prior transfers. Thus, the provisions of § 2013 which apply to estates of citizens or residents are made applicable by § 2102 to the estates of nonresident decedents who are not citizens of the United States.

B.   TYPES OF TRANSFERS FOR WHICH CREDIT IS ALLOWED

1.   Gifts by Transferor

The credit allowed by § 2013 is available only with regard to estate taxes paid on transfers that were included in the transferor's estate. Therefore no credit is allowed for any gift tax paid by a transferor with respect to gifts received by a decedent, even though the gift may have been made the day before the decedent's death.[6]

2.   Successive Relief

A decedent's estate can take advantage of the credit for estate tax on prior transfers even though the decedent received the transferred assets from an estate which had taken advantage of the credit. This result occurs because § 2013(b) defines the estate tax paid by the decedent's transferor, which is the basis of the credit, to include any credits for tax on prior transfers allowed the estate of the transferor *if the transfer to the transferor was from a person who died within ten years before the decedent's death.*

The operation of this provision is illustrated by the following example: Parent died on December 15, 2008, leaving all his assets to his child. His estate is subject to a $50,000 tax. Child died on December 1, 2009, leaving the same assets to grandchild. Under § 2013, the child's estate will receive a credit equal to 100 percent of the tax paid by the parent's estate and therefore will pay no tax. If the grandchild dies on December 1, 2018, his estate will be entitled to a credit of 20 percent of the tax paid by the child's estate (because the transferor child received the property from a person—her parent—who died within ten years before the decedent grandchild's death). Since the tax paid by the child's estate is defined to include the $50,000 credit allowed the child's estate for the tax paid by the parent's estate, the grandchild's estate will be entitled to a credit of $10,000, i.e., 20 percent x ($0 + $50,000). But if the grandchild dies on January 1, 2019, the $50,000 credit allowed the child's estate will not be

---

6. For gifts made prior to 1977, a credit against estate taxes is allowed for certain gift taxes previously paid by the decedent. See Rev. Rul. 67–110, 1967–1 C.B. 262, for an illustration of the computation required where the decedent's estate is entitled both to a credit under § 2012 and to a credit under § 2013.

For gifts made after December 31, 1976, § 2012 is inapplicable since the estate tax is reduced by the gift tax previously paid by the decedent. § 2001(b)(2).

considered part of the tax paid by the child's estate, because the parent died more than ten years before the grandchild's death. Under these circumstances, since the child's estate actually paid no tax, the grandchild's estate would not be entitled to any credit for prior estate tax paid.[7]

The percentage of credit granted to the grandchild's estate is determined according to the length of time between the grandchild's death and the child's death, and not the period between the grandchild's death and that of the parent. If the grandchild dies on December 16, 2010—or at any other time that is more than two years after the death of the parent, but less than two years after the child's death—the grandchild's credit will be based upon the period between his and the child's deaths and would be 100 percent of the tax deemed paid by the child's estate, namely $50,000. This result does not appear to be warranted, since the idea of the declining scale provision is to reduce proportionately the credit after any interval between successive deaths that extends beyond two years. The occurrence of the child's death should not preclude this reduction, since the parent died more than two years before the grandchild's death.

3. *Subsequently Taxed Transfers*

Under § 2013(a) a decedent's estate is entitled to a credit for tax paid on transfers that are subjected to tax in the estate of a transferor who dies within two years after the decedent's death. The credit amounts to 100 percent of the lower of (1) the tax paid by the estate of the transferor, or (2) the amount by which the decedent's estate tax is increased by virtue of including the value of the transferred assets in his gross estate and not applying the § 2013 credit. Such situations arise where inter vivos gifts are subject to tax in the estate of a donor who dies after the decedent. For example, where the corpus of an inter vivos trust is included in the estate of the grantor because of a retained life estate, a credit for the estate tax may be obtained by the estate of a beneficiary having a general power of appointment requiring the same corpus to be included in his estate, provided the grantor dies within two years after the beneficiary having the power of appointment. The net result is to treat the grantor as if he had died before the grantee.[8]

---

7. See Rev. Rul. 71–480, 1971–2 C.B. 327, for an example of a similar situation. See also Estate of La Sala v. Commissioner, 71 T.C. 752 (1979) (decedent's daughter predeceased him by two years and two months and one-half of her estate went to decedent's spouse and the other one-half to decedent; the decedent's spouse then predeceased him by approximately two months and left her entire estate to the decedent, utilizing the marital deduction; the § 2013 credit for the tax incurred by the daughter's estate on property that passed ultimately to the decedent through the decedent's spouse was limited to the credit actually used by the wife's estate which, because of the use of the mari-

tal deduction in her estate, was less than the tax actually paid by the daughter's estate on the property).

8. Since the statute of limitations for filing a refund is generally three years from the date the estate tax return is filed, the executor or administrator of the decedent's estate must be alert to the possibility that the statute of limitations may bar the filing of a claim for refund resulting from the credit created by the subsequent death of the transferor. The executor may want to file a protective claim for refund after the transferor's death.

4.   Computation of Credit

The following example will help illustrate the operation of section 2013: Husband died on December 1, 2008. His gross estate was $4,740,000 with administration expenses of $240,000.[9] He bequeathed $2,000,000 to his wife, of which only $1,000,000 qualified for the marital deduction, and the remainder of his estate after payment of estate taxes to his son. The wife dies on December 10, 2009. She has a gross estate of $4,200,000, administration expenses of $200,000 and she bequeathed her entire estate to the son. All parties are citizens of the United States, no state death taxes were payable and the unified credit in 2008 is $780,800 and in 2009 is $1,455,800.

Wife's credit for tax paid by husband's estate
  a.   Estate tax paid by husband's estate

Gross Estate		$4,740,000
Expenses		−240,000
Adjusted Gross Estate		4,500,000
Marital deduction		−1,000,000
Taxable estate		3,500,000
Tentative estate tax (§ 2001)	$1,455,800	
Unified credit (§ 2010)	−780,800	
Estate tax		$675,000

  b.   Credit under § 2013(b)

Tax paid by husband's estate		$ 675,000
Value of property transferred to wife per § 2013(d)		
Value	$2,000,000	
Marital deduction	1,000,000	1,000,000
Husband's taxable estate		3,500,000
Death taxes paid by husband's estate		$ 675,000

$$\frac{\text{Property transferred to decedent}}{\text{Taxable estate of } - \text{ Death taxes on}} \quad \text{x} \quad \begin{array}{c} \text{Estate tax on} \\ \text{transferor's estate} \end{array} \quad = \quad \begin{array}{c} \text{Credit} \\ \text{Base} \end{array}$$

transferor   transferor's estate

Accordingly, $\dfrac{1,000,000}{3,500,000 - 675,000}$ x 675,000 = $238,938.05 credit base under § 2013(b)

---

9. For purposes of computing the limitations under § 2013(c), the value of the property received by the decedent must be reduced by the administration expenses of the transferor's estate *allowable* as deductions under § 2053, even if the transferor's estate actually exercised its election to take such expenses as income tax deductions. Rev. Rul. 66–233, 1966–2 C.B. 428, modified by, Rev. Rul. 93–48, 1993–2 C.B. 270. Estate of Gilruth v. Commissioner, 50 T.C. 850 (1968). However, such expenses, if taken as income tax deductions, do not reduce the transferor's taxable estate for purposes of computing the limitations. Estate of Wood v. Commissioner, 54 T.C. 1180 (1970).

c. Limitation on credit per § 2013(c)

(1) Estate tax payable by wife's estate
if § 2013 were not law:

Gross estate		$4,200,000
Expenses		−200,000
Taxable estate		4,000,000
Tentative estate tax	$1,680,800	
Unified credit	−1,455,800	
Estate tax		225,000

(2) Estate tax payable by wife's
estate if wife's gross estate
did not include value of
property transferred to her
by husband:

Gross estate	$4,200,000
Value of property transferred to wife (§ 2013(d))	−1,000,000
Gross estate for purpose of limitation on credit	$3,200,000
Expenses	−200,000
Taxable estate	3,000,000

Tentative estate tax	$1,230,800	
Unified credit	−1,455,800	
Estate tax		$0

(3) Credit to wife's estate under § 2013(c):

Tax payable under (1)	$ 225,000
Tax payable under (2)	−0
Credit may not exceed	225,000

d. Credit allowed

The credit base under § 2013(b) is larger than the limitation computed under § 2013(c). Consequently, since the wife died within 2 years of the husband, her estate is entitled to a credit for the prior estate tax paid by the husband's estate in an amount equal to 100 percent of $225,000.

5. *Generation–Skipping Transfers*

Section 2013 does not apply to generation-skipping taxes.

6. *Availability of § 2013 Credit Where Payment of Estate Tax Has Been Deferred*

Rev. Rul. 83–15, 1983–1 C.B. 224, held that when the federal estate tax of a transferor decedent is being paid in installments under § 6166, or is deferred under § 6161 or § 6163, only the amount of estate tax actually paid may be used in computing the "first limitation" on the § 2013 credit. Subsequent tax payments by the transferor's estate increase the first limitation and the amount of the § 2013 credit. The Ruling permits a decedent's estate to file a protective claim for the deferred credit and to collect a refund of the proportionate amount of the credit when each tax payment is made.

7.   *Special Valuation Rules for Family Farms and Real Estate Used in Family Businesses*

Section 2013(f) integrates the credit for prior transfers with the additional tax that can be incurred upon the occurrence of an event that triggers an additional estate tax under § 2032A(c).

C.   POLICY ISSUES

The 1969 Treasury Department Proposals eliminated the credit for prior transfers contained in § 2013 and included an unlimited marital deduction so that transfers between spouses would not be subject to transfer tax. In the view of the Treasury the situation in which spouses die within a relatively brief period of time is the one that gives the "most concern" and the unlimited marital deduction proposal eliminated this problem. "The remaining situations in which two transfer taxes will be levied on successive deaths occurring within a brief period of time do not involve patterns of disposition which warrant special relief." U.S. Treasury Department, Tax Reform Studies and Proposals, House Ways and Means Comm. and Senate Finance Comm., 91st Cong., 1st Sess. 371 (Comm. Print 1969). Although Congress did adopt an unlimited marital deduction in 1981, it retained the credit for prior transfers in § 2013.

The 1969 Treasury proposal to eliminate the credit for prior transfers was consistent with its basic view of the proper structure of a transfer tax. That is, a tax should be imposed upon each transfer from the taxable unit, with one generation constituting the maximum period of time for which the tax can be deferred. The situation, for example, of two parents dying leaving their property to a child who dies shortly thereafter does not warrant special relief. The transfer tax should be imposed once each generation and the fact that the duration of a generation is shorter for some families than for others does not warrant special relief from the basic tax rule.

The 1984 Treasury Proposals recommended an expansion of § 2013 to permit an estate tax credit that would not phase out over time with respect to property included in a decedent's estate that had been inherited from a member of the same generation or a lower generation. By failing to recommend the repeal of the § 2013 credit for transfers to subsequent generations, the 1984 Proposals implicitly rejected the view that the length of time a person in a lower generation enjoys property is not relevant with respect to relief from the basic tax rule.

The 1984 proposal was justified on the basis that current section 2013 "is inconsistent with the rationale underlying the * * * tax on generation-skipping transfers, i.e. that the transfer tax ought to be imposed once per generation. * * * [I]f A leaves property to his brother, B, and B dies more than two years after A, the property will be subject to more than one full estate tax in the generation of A and B. If B dies more than ten years after A, the property will be subject to two full estate taxes in that generation. A could avoid the second estate tax at B's death by leaving the property in trust for the benefit of B during his lifetime or by giving B a life estate in the property. As it is possible to avoid the second tax through a trust disposition, expansion of the credit results in a neutral result for outright transfers." See U.S. Department of the Treasury, 2 Tax Reform for Fairness, Simplicity and Economic Growth 393 (1984).

SECTION B.   THE STATE DEATH TAX CREDIT

ILLUSTRATIVE MATERIAL

A.   THE PRE–2005 CREDIT

Prior to 2005, § 2011(a) allows a credit against the federal estate tax for "estate, inheritance, legacy, or succession taxes actually paid to any State or the District of Columbia, in respect of any property included in the gross estate."

Beginning in 2005, the § 2011 state death tax credit was replaced by the § 2058 deduction. This change from a credit to a deduction reduces the federal estate tax benefits of state death tax payments. A credit is subtracted from the tax itself, resulting in a dollar-for-dollar reduction in tax liability (up to the statutory maximum). A deduction, in contrast, is subtracted from the gross estate, resulting in tax savings tied to the marginal tax rate. As a result, federal estate tax savings from the state death tax deduction will be less than 50% of what they would have been under a credit.[10] As was the case with the credit, the deduction is allowed only for taxes actually paid to a state, and only if a claim for credit is filed within four years after the filing of the estate tax return.[11]

B.   STATE EFFECTS

Because the 2001 Act did not repeal the estate tax until 2009 but phased-out the state death tax credit in 2002–2004 and replaced the credit with a deduction in 2005–2009, Congress shifted part of the cost of repeal onto the thirty-seven states with "sponge" or "pick-up" taxes (designed to impose no more state death tax from a decedent's estate than is allowed under the § 2011 credit). These decreased state death tax revenues will be felt particularly in those states such as Florida, New Hampshire, New Jersey, New York, Pennsylvania, and Vermont which derive more than 2% of their tax revenue from death taxes.[12] The states will need to decide whether to enact other forms of estate, inheritance, or succession taxes to make up for the state revenue lost due to the reduction and later repeal of the federal credit.

C.   POLICY ASPECTS

It would appear that in a normative wealth transfer tax, a deduction should be allowed for lower governmental-level wealth taxes imposed on the

---

10. The maximum federal estate tax marginal rate is 45% in 2008–2009.

11. The four-year period is extended in the case of (1) a Tax Court proceeding involving a federal estate tax deficiency; (2) a claim for refund of federal estate tax; (3) an extension of time for payment of estate tax under §§ 6161 and 6166; and (4) an extension of time for assessing a federal estate tax deficiency. § 2058(b).

12. See Citizens for Tax Justice, The Effects of the Bush Tax Cuts on State Tax Revenues (2001), http://www.ctj.org/html/statefx.htm.

same transfers. Thus, state death taxes would seem to be as much a charge against the decedent's estate as are funeral expenses, probate costs, and the like. The object of the tax is the net amount which at death passes from the deceased person to the living. Unless one adopts the somewhat strained view that payment of state death taxes stands on the same qualitative level as payment of a legacy to the natural object of one's bounty, such taxes should be excluded from the federal wealth transfer tax base.

The credit for state death taxes was instituted in 1924 and enlarged in 1926. Originally, the purpose of the credit was to eliminate the incentive for some states to try to attract residents by low or no state death taxes. Thus, in 1924 and 1925, Florida and Nevada repealed their state death taxes, hoping to attract wealthy individuals to establish domicile in their respective states. The federal estate tax credit alleviated these problems. The tax advantages sought by Florida and Nevada were substantially mitigated because decedents in those states would pay the full federal estate tax, whereas decedents in other states would divide their estate tax burden between the state and federal governments. As noted above, thirty-seven states now limit their death taxes to an amount necessary to "soak up" the federal credit.

The state death tax credit in force until 2005 constitutes a tax preference if the amount of the credit exceeds the net after-tax benefit that the estate would have received had the full amount of the state death taxes been deductible; a tax penalty is involved if the amount of the allowable federal credit is less than the after-tax benefit the estate would have received from full deductibility of state death taxes. Where a tax preference is involved, the tax credit provides a form of federal revenue sharing. Where the amount of state death tax is not sufficient to absorb the full amount of the credit allowable under § 2011, many states impose an additional estate tax which is sufficient to absorb the balance of the credit. The excess of the allowable state death tax credit over the amount of the state death taxes that would have been imposed in the absence of the "sponge" provision also constitutes a form of revenue sharing.

The revenue sharing that is effected through the state death tax credit may be compared to the federal government's former direct revenue sharing program. That comparison reveals significant differences between the two methods of delivering the revenue sharing benefits. For example, the direct revenue sharing program provided funds not only to state governments, but to local government units as well. The state death tax credit confines its revenue sharing benefits to the state level. The amount of revenue sharing benefit that a particular state derived via the estate tax credit is a function of the wealth of the decedents dying within its borders in a given year and its own basic death tax structure. On the other hand, general revenue sharing applied much more sophisticated formulae to determine the level of revenue sharing funds that would be obtained by a state or local government in a given year. Congress' decision in the 2001 Act to replace the § 2011 state death tax credit with the § 2058 deduction in 2005 thus may be desirable from a tax policy perspective.

CHAPTER 31

TAX EXPENDITURES IN THE WEALTH TRANSFER TAXES

SECTION A. THE TAX EXPENDITURE CONCEPT

The tax expenditure concept was initially developed in the United States in the context of the income tax system.[1] As applied to an income tax, the concept views the tax as composed of two elements. The first element contains the structural provisions necessary for a normative income tax, such as the determination of net income, the use of annual accounting periods, the determination of the entity subject to tax, and the rate schedule and exemption levels. These provisions compose the revenue raising aspects of the tax. The second element consists of the special preferences, often called tax incentives or tax subsidies, that constitute departures from the normative tax structure and are designed to favor a particular industry, activity or class of persons. The special provisions may take the form of exclusions, deductions, deferrals, credits or special rates. Those financial assistance programs which the government has decided to effect through the tax system have been given the name "tax expenditures."

As stated by the Senate Budget Committee:[2] "Tax expenditures are revenue losses that occur as a result of Federal tax provisions that grant special tax relief to encourage certain kinds of activities by taxpayers or to aid taxpayers in special circumstances. The net result of these provisions is equivalent to a simultaneous collection of revenue and a direct budget outlay of an equal amount."

Tax expenditures thus represent government spending for the benefit of activities or groups that is effected through the tax system rather than through direct government assistance. Consequently, whenever government decides to provide financial assistance or support to an activity or group, it has the choice whether to provide that assistance directly through various forms of financial programs such as grants, loans, loan guarantees, etc., or through the tax system by means of a special exclusion, deduction, credit or the like.

The legislative recognition by Congress in the Budget Reform Act of 1974 of the role played by tax expenditures has induced considerable study

1. For discussions of the tax expenditure concept, see Surrey, Pathways To Tax Reform (1973); Surrey and McDaniel, Tax Expenditures (1985).

2. Report of the Senate Budget Committee, First Concurrent Resolution on The Budget—Fiscal Year 1977, S. Rep. No. 94–731, 94th Cong., 2d Sess. 8 (1976).

of tax expenditures in the income tax system.[3] The concept is equally valid when applied to the transfer tax system, a fact which, prior to the fiscal year 2003 Budget, led the Congressional Budget Office to include a list of tax expenditures in the wealth transfer tax system in its publication of tax expenditure estimates in the annual U.S. Budget.

SECTION B.   DEFINITION OF "TAX EXPENDITURE"

Section 3(a)(3) of the Budget Reform Act of 1974 defined tax expenditures in terms of the income tax as follows:

> "[T]hose revenue losses attributable to provisions of the Federal tax laws which allow a special exclusion, exemption, or deduction from gross income or which provide a special credit, a preferential rate of tax, or a deferral of tax liability."

The legislative history of the Act indicates that the term "special" refers to a "deviation from the normal tax structure for individuals and corporations."[4] The term "special" stands in contradistinction to a "normal" (or normative) income tax. This distinction was derived from criteria utilized by the Treasury Department which, in developing a tax expenditure list for the income tax, relied on "widely accepted definitions of income," the "generally accepted structure of an income tax," and widely accepted "standards of business accounting" used to determine income and expenses for financial reports.[5]

The definition of tax expenditures developed in the income tax context and the methodology utilized in determining the current list of tax expenditures in the income tax system are equally applicable to the wealth transfer taxes.[6] Just as the income tax has a "global" or overall reach designed to encompass all items of "net income," a normative transfer tax has a similar global reach since it is designed to cover all net wealth transferred for less than adequate and full consideration by the donor or decedent.

In the wealth transfer tax context, the Budget Reform Act definition could be modified to read:

> "The revenue losses attributable to provisions of the Federal tax laws which allow a special exclusion, exemption, or deduction from the gross estate or which provide a special credit, a preferential rate of tax, or a deferral of tax liability."

---

3.   See Surrey and McDaniel, note 1, at 233.

4.   The quoted language is from the Senate version of the Budget Reform Act, Section 3, S.1541, 93rd Cong., 2d Sess. (1974).

5.   Annual Report of the Secretary of the Treasury on the State of the Finances for Fiscal Year 1968, 326–340.

6.   See the following statement by Senator Muskie, later Chairman of the Senate Budget Committee, during the floor consideration on the Budget Reform Act of 1974: "The use of the words 'income tax' in the definition [of tax expenditures] should not preclude consideration of tax expenditures in the gift and estate tax systems." 120 Cong. Reg. 7935 (1974).

Here again, the term "special" refers to a deviation from a normal (or normative) transfer tax structure.

As discussed at p. 50, a normative wealth transfer tax seeks to tax all transfers of wealth for less than adequate and full consideration. Thus, normal transfer tax structure requires the application of the tax to a net transfer tax base, ascertained by including all items transferred and allowing as deductions those items necessary to determine the *net* transfers which the decedent had the power to make. In addition a taxable unit must be determined, and an appropriate rate schedule and exemption level must then be applied to the tax base.

The first task, then, in establishing a tax expenditure list for the wealth transfer tax system is to identify those provisions that are present not because they help define some part of the normal transfer tax structure, but instead are intended to effect government spending through the transfer tax system. The enumeration of these tax expenditures does not reflect a judgment as to the wisdom of the items included. Rather, the goals are the identification of the tax expenditure items, their quantification, and examination of the relationship of particular tax expenditures to comparable outlays in the direct budget.

SECTION C. WEALTH TRANSFER TAX EXPENDITURES BY BUDGET FUNCTION

BUDGET OF THE U.S. GOVERNMENT FOR FISCAL YEAR 2002, ANALYTICAL PERSPECTIVES, TAX EXPENDITURES*

TAX EXPENDITURES IN THE UNIFIED TRANSFER TAX

Exceptions to the general terms of the Federal unified transfer tax favor particular transferees or dispositions of transferors, similar to Federal direct expenditure or loan programs. The transfer tax provisions identified as tax expenditures satisfy the reference law criteria for inclusion in the tax expenditure budget that were described above. There is no generally accepted normal tax baseline for transfers.

Unified Transfer Tax Reference Rules

The reference tax rules** for the unified transfer tax from which departures Represent Tax expenditures include:

---

* [ED.: The following discussion and revenue estimates do not reflect changes made by the 2001 Act.]

** [ED.: With respect to the income tax, the "reference tax rules (or baseline)" are described as "patterned on a comprehensive income tax, but [are] closer to existing law. While tax expenditures under the reference law baseline are generally tax expenditures under the normal tax baseline, the reverse is not always true." The items in the tax expenditure list constitute tax expenditures under the normal tax structure described at p. 564.]

- *Definition of the taxpaying unit.* The payment of the tax is the liability of the transferor whether the transfer of cash or property was made by gift or bequest.

- *Definition of the tax base.* The base for the tax is the transferor's cumulative, taxable lifetime gifts made plus the net estate at death. Gifts in the tax base are all annual transfers in excess of $10,000 (indexed for inflation) to any donee except the donor's spouse. Excluded are, however, payments on behalf of family members' educational and medical expenses, as well as the cost of ceremonial gatherings and celebrations that are not in honor of the donor.

- *Property valuation.* In general, property is valued at its fair market value at the time it is transferred. This is not necessarily the case in the valuation of property for transfer tax purposes. Executors of estates are provided the option to value assets at the time of the testator's death or up to six months later.

- *Tax rate schedule.* A single graduated tax rate schedule applies to all taxable transfers. This is reflected in the name of the "unified transfer tax" that has replaced the former separate gift and estate taxes.

- *Time when tax is due and payable.* Donors are required to pay the tax annually as gifts are made. The generation-skipping transfer tax is payable by the donees whenever they accede to the gift. The net estate tax liability is due and payable within nine months after the decedent's death. The Internal Revenue Service may grant an extension of up to 10 years for a reasonable cause. Interest is charged on the unpaid tax liability at a rate equal to the cost of Federal short-term borrowing, plus three percentage points.

Tax Expenditures by Function

The estimates of tax expenditures in the Federal unified transfer tax for fiscal years 2000–2006 are displayed by functional category in table 5–6
* * *

Table 5–6. Revenue Loss Estimates for Tax Expenditures in the Federal Unified Transfer Tax

(In millions of dollars)

	Description	2001	2001	2002	2003	2004	2005	2006	2002–2006
1	**Natural Resources and Environment:** Donations of conservation easements ----	----	----	----	10	10	10	20	50
	Agriculture:								
2	Special use valuation of farm real property	110	110	120	120	130	130	130	630
3	Tax deferral of closely held farms	----	----	10	10	20	20	30	90
4	**Commerce:** Special Use valuation of real property used in closely held businesses	10	10	10	10	10	10	10	50
5	Tax deferral of closely held business ----	–20	30	60	80	100	130	140	510
6	Exclusion for family owned businesses	130	140	150	160	170	170	170	820

Description	2001	2001	2002	2003	2004	2005	2006	2002–2006
Education, training, employment, and social services:								
7 Deduction for charitable contributions (education)	780	880	960	990	1,030	1,060	1,100	5,140
8 Deduction for charitable contributions (other than education and health)	2,300	2,600	2,830	2,930	3,050	3,120	3,260	15,190
Health:								
9 Deduction for charitable contributions (health)	700	800	870	900	930	960	1,000	4,660
General government:								
10 Credit for State death taxes	6,420	6,720	7,030	7,340	7,660	8,000	8,350	38,380

ILLUSTRATIVE MATERIAL

A. CONCEPTUAL ISSUES

There are some items not listed as tax expenditures in the Congressional Budget Office (CBO) list that should be classified as tax expenditures under either the normal or reference tax baseline. These include failure to gross-up gifts by the gift tax for gifts made more than three years prior to death (Income Security), the exclusion from gift tax for tuition payments for the benefit of non-dependents (Education) and for medical payments for non-dependents (Health), and the exclusion for gifts to political organizations (General Government). No explanation is given for the omission of these items from the CBO list.

The CBO list also does not include the various exclusions from the generation-skipping tax discussed at pages 658–660. This omission reflects more complex issues than those listed in the preceding paragraph. Some would assert that a transfer tax system contains an inherent requirement of periodicity as the measuring device of the appropriate tax period. Others, however, would argue that a transfer tax system does not contain such an inherent requirement of periodicity. They would assert that the object of the tax is a "transfer," and if that transfer is taxed it is irrelevant whether the transferee is in a preceding, parallel, or succeeding generation. These, obviously, are structural rather than incentive- or subsidy-type arguments.

On the other hand, others argue that the taxation of generation-skipping transfers under the normal pattern of generation to generation devolution of property would interfere with valuable estate planning tools which are necessary to provide needed flexibility for family financial planning. This does not appear to be an argument for a proper structural provision in the transfer tax system, but for a form of federal subsidy to provide financial security for the decedent's family through a particular type of estate planning mechanism. As such, the exclusion for some generation-skipping transfers constitutes a tax expenditure.

Congress, in the Tax Reform Act of 1976 and the Tax Reform Act of 1986, appeared to accept that the equity and structural considerations inhering in the concept of taxing wealth through a transfer tax mechanism require the imposition of the transfer tax at least once each generation so as not to differentiate in the tax burden between families simply because they have different financial planning objectives. Congress, however, failed to adopt the rules necessary to effectuate this policy in full. See p. 671. But the legislative history does lead to the conclusion that the present failure to tax all generation-skipping transfers is more than just a defective structural component of the transfer tax system but instead contains elements of incentives to certain trust and family planning devices. Therefore, that failure should be included in the tax expenditure budget.

B.   THE FISCAL YEAR 2003 BUDGET

The Analytic Perspectives chapter of the 2003 Budget and subsequent budgets have not included estimates of tax expenditures in the wealth transfer taxes. The reasons stated in the 2003 Budget were:

"Tax expenditure estimates under the unified transfer (i.e., estate and gift) tax have been eliminated from the presentation because there is no generally accepted normal baseline for transfer taxes and this tax has been repealed under the Economic Growth and Tax Relief Reconciliation Act of 2001 (EGTRRA)."

The stated reasons are both specious and wrong. First, as the material quoted from the 2002 Analytic Perspectives stated, the estimates were not made on a "normal tax baseline" but rather on a "reference tax baseline." There actually is a normal tax baseline, as described at p. 562, but nothing in the 2001 Act prevented CBO from continuing to show estimates derived from using the reference tax baseline. Second, the 2001 Act did not repeal the wealth transfer taxes (except for the year 2010).

The omission from the 2001 Act seems more likely attributable to the Bush Administration's aversion to the wealth transfer taxes than to any technical problems in continuing to publish tax expenditure lists for the wealth transfer taxes. That omission deprives policy makers and the public of important information in the coming fiscal years.

C.   ASPECTS OF TAX EXPENDITURE ANALYSIS

Overall Consideration of Wealth Transfer Tax Revision and Tax Reform. An understanding that the wealth transfer tax system consists of two structures serving different functions makes a difference in the approach to "tax revision" or "tax reform." Tax reform is one thing if it means looking at a part of the tax structure that is not working well and asking where the tax experts went wrong in shaping that part. The issues posed and the answers to be explored are considered within the premises of a wealth transfer tax and can be judged accordingly. But "tax reform" is quite another matter if it means examining a program of financial assistance to a particular group to decide whether that assistance should be given, in what amount and on what terms. The latter process really is not tax reform but "expenditure reform," and the issues and answers to be explored involve different premises and require different expertise.

Effective Tax Rate Analysis. A traditional method of making interpersonal comparisons of the tax burden is "effective tax rate analysis." Under this method of analysis, the actual tax check remitted to the government is divided by the taxpayer's economic estate and the resulting percentage figure is treated as the effective tax rate. Where two taxpayers with the same economic wealth are shown to have different effective tax rates under this analysis, it is asserted that horizontal equity has been violated and that the provisions causing the differences in effective tax rates are therefore objects of tax reform.

Tax expenditure analysis indicates that this traditional method of using effective rate analysis is seriously defective. Under the tax expenditure analytic technique, the taxpayer is deemed to have paid the tax on the total economic wealth transferred (the taxpayer's "economic tax check"). The taxpayer in turn receives a check from the Treasury equal to the total of the tax expenditures for which the taxpayer has qualified (the taxpayer's "tax subsidy check"). Of course, these two checks are not actually exchanged. Instead, in the computation of tax liability on the tax return, the taxpayer in effect nets the economic tax check with the tax subsidy check and remits the balance to the Treasury. Although this check has traditionally been referred to as the taxpayer's "tax liability," and is so used in effective rate analysis, the number is in fact simply the mathematical netting of the two checks. The effective tax rate ratio derived is defective because the fraction involves two quite different numbers. The denominator of the fraction includes total economic wealth transferred; but the numerator is not the taxpayer's total economic "tax." As a result, effective tax rates can give seriously misleading information about the impact of the normal tax structure on taxpayers. To illustrate this point most dramatically, if all wealth transfer tax expenditures were repealed and were replaced by identical direct expenditure programs, every taxpayer's effective tax rate would immediately rise yet the taxpayer's economic transfers would be unchanged. In short, traditional effective rate analysis really tells policymakers very little. A low effective rate is simply an indication that the taxpayer is in receipt of a significant amount of tax expenditures.

This is not to say that there is no role for a properly structured effective rate analysis. The correct determination of taxpayers' effective tax rates can be obtained by comparing the economic tax to economic wealth. If differing effective rates occur at the same wealth level, that difference will result from defects within the normal structure of the tax itself and can be addressed.

For a discussion of these issues, see McDaniel, "Identification of the 'Tax' in 'Effective Tax Rates,' 'Tax Reform' and 'Tax Equity,'" 38 Nat'l Tax J. 273 (1985); Bittker, Effective Tax Rates: Fact or Fancy, 122 U. Pa. L. Rev. 780 (1974).

Tax Simplification and Tax Complexity. In much the same way, the tax expenditure concept permits one to consider the matter of tax simplification—or tax complexity—in a different way from that usually followed. The perennial desire for tax simplification always makes that goal one of the objectives of tax revision and tax reform campaigners. The efforts at tax simplification are rarely preceded by a consideration of what factors are inherent in a wealth tax or instead are the result of faulty policies or faulty techniques. But tax expenditure analysis indicates that one significant source of complexity is the presence of the tax expenditure apparatus within the wealth transfer tax system. One is thus led to inquire how much of the complexity of the present tax systems stems from that apparatus and how much follows just from having a wealth transfer tax itself. A wealth transfer tax contains some inherent complexity, but it should not be faulted as a tax because of the additional complexities forced on it when it is required also to carry out a number of expenditure programs.

Tax Administration. Problems of tax administration are complicated by the presence of tax expenditures. In effect, the Commissioner of Internal Revenue is required to administer programs that are within the province of other executive branch departments and agencies. For each tax expenditure program, regulations must be prepared, rulings issued, agents trained, audits conducted, and litigation pursued. In turn, the Commissioner inevitably becomes involved in issues that have nothing to do with the collection of revenue, but rather with the administration of spending programs.

International Aspects. A number of other countries publish official tax expenditure budgets.[8] One study provides a comparative analysis of the uses made of tax expenditures by selected industrialized countries, and the possible utility of the concept in working out international tax relationships.[9]

Evaluation of Tax Expenditure Programs. The tax expenditure concept enables one to look at special wealth transfer tax provisions in a different light. Once it is seen that expenditure programs rather than technical tax provisions are being evaluated, one can ask the traditional questions and use the analytical tools that make up the intellectual apparatus of direct expenditure experts:

Is There a Need for Federal Financial Aid? Tax expenditures involve spending federal money. If a tax expenditure is adopted or continued, reduced revenues will be available for tax reductions or other spending programs. This is precisely the effect of a decision to continue or adopt new direct spending programs.

What is the Optimal Form of Federal Assistance? If a need for federal aid is established, the appropriate form of federal assistance must be determined. In general, Congress can choose among such techniques as direct grants, loans, interest subsidies, and loan guarantees. Each technique can be implemented in direct or tax expenditure programs. Thus, the following steps are required to analyze an existing or proposed tax expenditure.

—First, determine the optimal form of a federal expenditure program to meet the identified need.

—Second, reconstruct the tax expenditure under review as a direct expenditure program.

—Third, compare the restructured tax expenditure to the optimal direct program and to existing direct programs.

—Fourth, identify the points at which differences exist in the tax and direct expenditure programs, and to ask whether these differences produce results that are rational and desirable.

The translation and consequent restatement of a tax expenditure program in direct expenditure terms generally show an upside-down result at variance with usual expenditure policies. This upside-down effect is produced because the value of a tax expenditure is a function of the marginal tax bracket of the taxpayer who utilizes the special provision. Thus, for example, for those whose wealth is below the exemption level and whose marginal tax bracket is therefore zero, tax expenditures provide no benefit at all. As the transferor's wealth increases the amount of the tax expenditure rises.

---

8. See Organization for Economic Development and Cooperation, Tax Expenditures: Recent Experiences (1996).

9. See, McDaniel and Surrey (eds.), International Aspects of Tax Expenditures: A Comparative Study (1985).

Consider the deduction for charitable contributions discussed at p. 532. Under a normative wealth transfer tax system, the amount of the contribution would be included in the transferor's taxable transfers. The deduction in effect means that the government is paying a portion of the contribution to charity. If the tax expenditure program were translated into a direct expenditure program, the program (using 2009 rates) would look as follows:

—For a transferor with more than $2.5 million of transfers subject to tax, the Government would, for each $100 of contributions, pay $45 to the charity, leaving the transferor to pay $55 from his own funds.

—For a transferor with $1 million in taxable transfers, the Government would pay the charity $41 for each $100 of contribution, with the transferor paying $59.

—For a transferor with less than $600,000 of wealth to transfer, the Government would pay nothing to the charity, leaving the transferor to pay the entire $100 contribution herself.

One can assume that no Government official would ever present to Congress a direct program to support charity with this upside-down effect. The tax expenditure for charitable contributions also involves efficiency and equity issues, although these concepts are those applied to spending programs rather than to tax systems (as discussed at p. 570). As the excerpt at p. 548 discussed, there is an income and a price effect associated with contributions to charity. Tax expenditure analysis casts these effects in a somewhat different light. For example, a price elasticity of 1.0 means that for every $100 the government provides via the charitable contributions deduction, the charity receives $100. Thus, this situation is described as "efficient" in the sense that federal funds are not being wasted. Another way to look at the situation is to observe that, for the wealthiest donors, charity in effect receives a $55 check out of the donor's own funds and a $45 check from the government. If the charitable contributions deduction were repealed the "efficiency" argument also means that the wealthiest donors would only give $48 to charity and would not increase their giving to make up for the lost government subsidy. This result in turn leads to an equity question: why do those who give to charity, but who are not subject to transfer taxes because they are not wealthy enough to exceed the existing exemption level, not allowed to transfer any federal funds to the charities of their choice, even though, as a percentage of their total estates, they may be giving relatively more of their wealth then their higher-wealth counterparts?

Analyzing special tax provisions in the wealth transfer tax system can thus provide policy-makers and the public with different kinds of information than traditional tax analysis:

—Impacts on the total U.S. Budget and interactions with direct programs in that budget.

—Economic and equity analyses that parallel those of comparable direct spending programs.

—Insights into the differing political processes applicable to tax and direct spending programs.

—Better understanding of what actually is involved in many debates that come under the rubric of "tax" simplification, reform and equity.

*

PART VI

THE TAXABLE UNIT

CHAPTER 32   The Marital Deduction

CHAPTER 32

THE MARITAL DEDUCTION

SECTION A. INTRODUCTION

A central structural issue that must be resolved in any transfer tax system is the definition of the taxable unit. The marital deduction and split-gift provisions perform this function in the transfer tax structure.

The estate tax marital deduction, found in § 2056, permits a deduction from the gross estate of an amount equal to the value of the property "passing" from the decedent to the surviving spouse,[1] but only to the extent that this property is not treated as a "nondeductible terminable interest."[2] "Passing" and "nondeductible terminable interest" are technical terms which are defined in § 2056 and have been the subject of extensive litigation.

The parallel gift tax marital deduction, found in § 2523, allows a deduction for the full value of gifts to a spouse, subject basically to the same qualifications as the estate tax deduction.[3]

Section 2513 provides for the splitting of gifts made to third parties by a husband and wife. Upon the consent of both spouses given for any year, one-half of any gift made by one spouse to a person other than the donor's spouse during that year is taxed as if it were made by the other spouse. Thus, if a husband gives $106,000 to his child, and his wife consents to gift-splitting, each spouse is treated as having made a $40,000 gift ($53,000 less an inflation-adjusted $13,000 annual exclusion) to the child.

From a tax planning standpoint, the marital deduction and split gifts, properly utilized, can reduce the tax cost of transferring wealth. Especially in the case of the marital deduction, however, this result can be achieved

---

1. Prior to 1988, the marital deduction was not allowed unless the decedent was a U.S. citizen or resident at the time of death. However, the marital deduction was allowed to the estate of such a decedent even where the surviving spouse was not a U.S. citizen or resident. Both rules were changed in 1988. See pp. 846, 853.

2. The amount of the allowable estate tax marital deduction has changed over time. Prior to 1977, the deduction was limited to 50% of the decedent's adjusted gross estate. For decedents dying after 1976 and before 1982, the deduction was limited to the greater of $250,000 or 50% of the decedent's adjusted gross estate, reduced in either case by

the excess, if any, of the amount of the gift tax marital deduction claimed for post–1976 inter-spousal transfers over 50% of the value of such transfers. There has been an unlimited estate tax marital deduction since 1982.

3. The amount of the allowable gift tax marital deduction also has changed over time. Prior to 1977, the deduction was limited to 50% of the value of the property given. For inter-spousal gifts made after 1976 but prior to 1982, § 2523 allowed a full deduction for the first $100,000 in value of post–1976 gifts, no deduction for the next $100,000, and a 50% deduction for gifts in excess of $200,000. There has been an unlimited gift tax marital deduction since 1982.

only by careful attention to the precise limitations laid down by the Code and the Regulations. A large portion of the following discussion contains technical material with which estate planners must be familiar to achieve the desired marital deduction result. The sheer volume of litigation and number of issues litigated attest to the complexity of the marital deduction provisions. The cases noted in the illustrative material are representative, but far from exhaustive, of the litigation in each area covered.

ILLUSTRATIVE MATERIAL

A. HISTORICAL BACKGROUND

Some familiarity with the genealogy of the present marital deduction and split-gift provisions is necessary to their understanding. Under the decision in Poe v. Seaborn, 282 U.S. 101 (1930), only one-half the income earned by the personal efforts of a married person living in a community property state is taxed to that person for income tax purposes, the other half being taxed to the spouse. Similarly, one-half of the income from community property is taxed to each spouse. Prior to 1948, this "splitting" of income gave spouses in community property states a considerable advantage under the progressive rate structure of the Federal income tax over those spouses living in common law states, where, at that time, all or most of the family's income typically was taxed in the hands of the wage-earning spouse. In addition, because one-half the family's community property generally was considered as owned by each spouse, only one-half the property which had been accumulated for the family by the efforts of the income earner was subject to estate tax at that person's death. Similarly, a gift of community property was generally considered a gift of one-half the property by each spouse. Again, this provided families in community property states with a substantial tax advantage over those in common law states.

In 1942, Congress eliminated the estate and gift tax advantages enjoyed by spouses in community property states. However, Congress did not eliminate the income tax advantages enjoyed by spouses in community property states, and five states and the Territory of Hawaii substituted the community property system for the common law system during 1945–48 to obtain these tax advantages for their residents. In 1948, Congress responded by enacting the present joint return and split-income provisions of the Code to equalize the income tax treatment of spouses in common law states and community property states.

At the same time, Congress repealed the 1942 estate and gift tax amendments in order to provide a measure of estate and gift tax equality of treatment between common law and community property states comparable to that provided by the split-income provisions. In place of the 1942 amendments, the pre–1977 marital deduction and split-gift provisions were hastily enacted, with little public scrutiny before they became law. The change restored to spouses in community property states the transfer tax status they had before 1942 and also created generally comparable treatment to spouses in common law states.

The rationale underlying the pre–1977 50% marital deduction provisions was to permit one spouse to pass non-community property to the other spouse and receive the same transfer tax treatment as if the property had passed pursuant to a community property system, but only if the recipient spouse had or received substantially the same property rights that a surviving spouse had or received in community property. In essence, in order for property to qualify for the deduction, the surviving spouse must have received an interest with respect to the property that would result in its inclusion in that spouse's gross estate, or in taxable gifts if the recipient spouse disposed of the interest. Thus, the pre–1977 transfer tax system adopted the community property concept as its fundamental model for defining the taxable unit.

The Tax Reform Act of 1976 modified the quantitative limits on the estate and gift tax marital deductions. The 1976 Act amended the estate tax marital deduction to provide that the maximum deduction would be the greater of $250,000 or 50% of the decedent's "adjusted gross estate," reduced in either case by the excess, if any, of the amount of the gift tax marital deduction claimed for post–1976 inter-spousal transfers over 50% of the value of such transfers. Lifetime inter-spousal gifts were deductible in full up to the first $100,000 in value of post–1976 gifts, nondeductible for the next $100,000, and a 50% deduction for gifts in excess of $200,000. The changes effected by the 1976 Act appeared to reflect a movement away from the community property model. Under the 1976 amendments the proper combination of lifetime and deathtime transfers permitted one spouse to transfer to the other property worth $601,250 without incurring any transfer tax liability. As to that $601,250 the taxable unit was, in effect, the marital unit. Tax liability then phased in for estates up to $851,250.[4] The community property model was retained only for amounts in excess of those figures.

The Economic Recovery Tax Act of 1981 removed all quantitative limits on the allowable marital deduction for both inter vivos and testamentary transfers between spouses in community and common law states alike. The move to unlimited deductibility thus abandoned the community property model and treated the marital unit as the taxable unit for estate and gift tax purposes for transfers between spouses, much like the joint return treats a husband and a wife as a single economic unit for income tax purposes. The marital deduction thus operates to postpone the estate and gift tax until the property leaves the marital unit such as through a gift or bequest to a child or grandchild. Congress continued gift-splitting of inter vivos transfers, thus eliminating the need for a transfer of property by one spouse to the other, followed by another transfer of the same property from the donee spouse to the ultimate donee.

SECTION B.   THE ESTATE TAX MARITAL DEDUCTION

1.   THE STATUTORY STRUCTURE

Internal Revenue Code: § 2056

Regulations: § 20.2056

Section 2056(a) permits a deduction for "the value of [1] any interest in property [2] which passes or has passed from the decedent to his

---

4.   Computation of the amounts specified is illustrated in Surrey, Warren, McDaniel & Gutman, Federal Wealth Transfer Taxation 800 (1977 ed.).

surviving spouse, but only to the extent that such interest is included in determining the value of the gross estate." It is useful to examine briefly each of these elements before beginning to study the detailed technical exposition to which each has been subjected by the courts and by the Internal Revenue Service.

Interest in property. The Senate Finance Committee Report on the Revenue Act of 1948 stated that the definition of such interests "is broad enough to cover all the interests included in determining the value of the decedent's gross estate under the [predecessors of §§ 2031, 2033–2038 and 2040–2043] of the Code." S. Rep. No. 1013 (Part 2), 80th Cong., 2d Sess. 3 (1948).

This broad definition is, however, subject to several exceptions. The major exception is § 2056(b)(1), which disallows a marital deduction for an interest in property that is a "nondeductible terminable interest" (the "terminable interest rule"). In general, § 2056(b)(1) defines a "nondeductible terminable interest" as one that will terminate or fail "on the lapse of time, on the occurrence of an event or contingency, or on the failure of an event or contingency to occur," but only if upon such termination or failure an interest in the same property passes for less than full and adequate consideration from the decedent to a third party other than the surviving spouse and, by reason of such passing, the third party may possess or enjoy any part of the property.

The function of the terminable interest rule is to assure that the deduction is allowed only for the property which, if not taxable in the estate of the first spouse to die, will be subject to transfer tax if disposed of inter vivos or at death by the surviving spouse. This objective could not be met if, for example, the value of the property in which the surviving spouse was granted a life estate and an inter vivos special power of appointment was allowed as part of the marital deduction because the exercise of the inter vivos power of appointment would not be subject to gift tax. The terminable interest rule would operate to disallow the marital deduction, thereby treating the property as if it were transferred directly by the decedent to the appointee.

However, not all interests that terminate are nondeductible terminable interests. For example, the bequest of a patent outright to a surviving spouse qualifies for the marital deduction because, although the property interest will terminate upon the lapse of time, no part of that property interest can pass from the decedent to a third party. The fact that the surviving spouse may die before the interest terminates does not affect this result since the remaining rights in the interest will, due to the surviving spouse's outright ownership, pass to the next taker from the surviving spouse and not from the decedent.

The terminable interest rule is itself subject to exceptions set forth in §§ 2056(b)(3), (5), (6), (7) and (8). If the requirements of these sections are met, an interest in property which falls within the terminable interest rule will nonetheless be eligible for the marital deduction. The terminable interest rule and its exceptions are discussed in detail at p. 579.

Prior to the Economic Recovery Tax Act of 1981, the bequest of a life estate to a surviving spouse with a remainder over at death to a third party was a nondeductible terminable interest. Upon the death of the surviving spouse, no part of the property would be included in the gross estate of that spouse and the property subject to the interest passed to a third party pursuant to the decedent's direction. Section 2056(b)(7), however, permits, at the election of the decedent's executor, deduction of the value of the property to which the income interest relates if certain conditions are met. If such a deduction has been allowed, the value of the property to which the income interest relates must then be included in the transfer tax base of the surviving spouse. In the materials that follow, marital bequests that were treated as nondeductible under the terminable interest rule might be deductible under § 2056(b)(7) if the executor made the requisite election.

Interest which "passes or has passed" from the decedent to the "surviving spouse." "Passing" is defined in § 2056(c) to include all of those methods by which property may be transmitted at death as well as any transfer "by the decedent at any time." Furthermore, except where the surviving spouse has elected to take against the decedent's will, or a person other than the surviving spouse has disclaimed an interest, the statute contemplates that only those interests qualify which the decedent intends the surviving spouse to take, whether under the will or other instrument or under the laws of intestacy, and which the surviving spouse in fact accepts. The purpose of the "passing" requirement is to disqualify property that the surviving spouse gets from persons other than the decedent, even if the decedent's estate was the original source of the property.

In determining whether property passes to the decedent's "surviving spouse," the executor has the burden of proving both marital status and survivorship. "The status of an individual as the decedent's surviving spouse is determined at the time of the decedent's death." S. Rep. No. 1013, p. 6.

2. INTEREST PASSING TO THE SURVIVING SPOUSE

Internal Revenue Code: § 2056(a)

Regulations: § 20.2056(c)(1)–(3)

ILLUSTRATIVE MATERIAL

A. STATUS AS SURVIVING "SPOUSE"

Status as a surviving "spouse" turns on the validity of the decedent's marriage at the date of death. In many cases, the issue arises because of questions concerning the validity of the decedent's prior divorce. For example, in Estate of Steffke v. Commissioner, 538 F.2d 730 (7th Cir.1976), a couple who thought they were married were Wisconsin residents at the time of the man's death. The woman previously had obtained a Mexican divorce on grounds not recognized in Wisconsin. In a state inheritance tax proceeding, the Wisconsin Supreme Court held that the Mexican divorce was not recognized in Wisconsin and thus the woman was not the decedent's wife under Wisconsin law. The Seventh Circuit relied on this Wisconsin ruling in denying a marital deduction claimed by the decedent's estate: "When there are conflicting judicial decrees regarding the validity of a divorce, the decision should be followed for federal estate taxation purposes that would be followed by the state which has primary jurisdiction over the administration of a decedent's estate, i.e., the jurisdiction in which the decedent was domiciled at the time of his death." Id. at 734.

In other situations, the validity of a decedent's marriage is called into question on other grounds. For example, Rev.Rul. 76–155, 1976–1 C.B. 286, denied a claimed marital deduction where there was insufficient evidence that the decedent's relationship constituted a common law marriage under state law. But spouses who are legally separated or subject to an interlocutory divorce which does not terminate their rights in each other's estate would be considered spouses for purposes of § 2056. See Eccles v. Commissioner, 19 T.C. 1049 (1953), aff'd, 208 F.2d 796 (4th Cir.1953) (per curiam); Rev.Rul. 57–368, 1957–2 C.B. 896.

As this book goes the press, same-sex couples are permitted to marry as a matter of state law in Connecticut and Massachusetts. Under the Defense of Marriage Act, Pub. L. No. 104–199, 110 Stat. 2419 (1996) (codified at 1 U.S.C. § 7 and 28 U.S.C. § 1738C), such marriages are not recognized for purposes of federal law. As a result, such couples are not eligible for the marital deduction (and other federal tax provisions applicable to married heterosexual couples).

B.   STATUS AS "SURVIVING" SPOUSE

Reg. § 20.2056(e)–2(e) provides that, where it is otherwise impossible to determine the order of death, a presumption established by law or by the decedent's will that his or her spouse survived will be recognized as to property passing under the will, but only to the extent that it results in giving the surviving spouse an interest in property that is includable in his or her gross estate. It has become common practice to include in wills a clause creating a presumption as to order of death to take full advantage of the marital deduction. Where the decedent's estate seeks to take advantage of such a presumption, the estate has the burden of establishing that the order of deaths cannot be determined. Where the will of a decedent does not contain an order-of-death clause, the estate is administered in a jurisdiction that has adopted the Uniform Simultaneous Death Act (USDA), and a determination cannot be made as to which spouse has survived, each spouse is deemed to have survived the other for purposes of distributing that spouse's estate. Thus, H's estate is distributed as though he survived W (and thus his property goes to his beneficiaries), and W's estate is distributed as though she survived H (and thus her property goes to her beneficiaries). In many cases, however, the operation of the USDA may defeat the parties' marital deduction planning objectives. See p. 640.

C.   ANY "INTEREST" IN PROPERTY WHICH "PASSES OR HAS PASSED FROM THE DECEDENT TO HIS SURVIVING SPOUSE"

1.   An "Interest in Property"

In Estate of Critchfield v. Commissioner, 32 T.C. 844 (1959), D's widow, pursuant to an option granted her under state law, purchased, at the appraised value for probate inventory purposes of $58 a share, stock which was included in D's gross estate at its fair market value on the alternate valuation date at $65 a share. The court held that the difference between the purchase price and the fair market value of the purchased shares did not qualify for the marital deduction on the ground that the "right of a surviving spouse, under a statute to purchase property from the estate is not an interest in property which passes from the decedent to his surviving spouse * * *."

2. The "Passing" Requirement

The purpose of this requirement is to deny the marital deduction where the surviving spouse receives the property from sources other than the decedent.

a. Election to Take Against the Will

Where the surviving spouse elects to take against the will, the resulting amounts received as a dower or statutory forced share are deemed to have passed to the surviving spouse from the decedent. Reg. § 20.2056(e)–2(c). However, the courts require strict compliance with local procedural requirements regarding the widow's election.

b. Settlement of Will Controversy

The Code and Regulations contain a number of safeguards to insure that property does not qualify for the marital deduction unless it passes to the recipient spouse from the decedent, and not as the result of an arrangement by the heirs. Thus, a property interest assigned or surrendered to a surviving spouse as a result of a will contest "will be regarded as having 'passed from the decedent to his surviving spouse' only if the assignment or surrender was a bona fide recognition of enforceable rights of the surviving spouse in the decedent's estate." Reg. § 20.2056(e)–2(d)(2). A recognition is presumed bona fide under the Regulations if it is "pursuant to a decision of a local court upon the merits in an adversary proceeding following a genuine and active contest."

A court order, however, is not a necessary prerequisite to a determination that a particular settlement was "a bona fide recognition of enforceable rights". The Service has ruled that "a valid claim to a share in decedent's estate made in good faith and settled as a result of arm's-length negotiations without any court contest will qualify as a bona fide claim within the meaning of [Reg. § 20.2056(e)–2(d)(2)]." Rev.Rul. 66–139, 1966–1 C.B. 225. Despite this good faith standard, the Service and the federal courts may look behind a settlement and inquire into the validity of a claim under state law.

D. DISCLAIMERS

On the one hand, the marital deduction is not available if a surviving spouse effectively disclaims, under § 2518, discussed at p. 434, an interest that would have been considered as passing to such spouse from the decedent because the disclaimed interest is considered as passing to the persons who are entitled to receive it as a result of the disclaimer. On the other hand, the marital deduction is available if a valid disclaimer is made by any person other than the surviving spouse and, as a result of the disclaimer, the surviving spouse is entitled to receive the disclaimed interest because the interest is considered as having passed from the decedent to the surviving spouse.

Disclaimers are frequently used to "fine tune" the amount of a marital bequest to achieve tax minimization with respect to the aggregate estates of the two spouses. The use of the disclaimer as a post-mortem estate planning tool is discussed at p. 643.

3. THE TERMINABLE INTEREST RULE

Internal Revenue Code: § 2056(b)

Regulations: § 20.2056(b)

a. THE STATUTORY SCHEME

The terminable interest rule and its various exceptions are, for the tax advisor, probably the most important part of the marital deduction provisions. Its requirements must be adhered to precisely if a gift or bequest is to qualify for the deduction. Much of the litigation about the marital deduction has arisen in connection with these requirements.

The basic policy underlying the marital deduction provisions is that property qualifying for the deduction be includible in the surviving spouse's transfer tax base. No marital deduction is allowed where an interest in the property bequeathed to the surviving spouse could pass to other persons, after the termination of the surviving spouse's interest, without the inclusion of such interest in the surviving spouse's transfer tax base. Such disqualified terminable interests have their own built-in transfer tax avoidance because the interests passing to third parties from the decedent would automatically escape estate tax at the death of the first legatee—the surviving spouse—to enjoy the property.

The basic terminable interest rule found in § 2056(b)(1) attempts to incorporate this policy objective in specific statutory language. The objective also is reflected in §§ 2044 and 2519, which require inclusion of certain qualified terminable interest property (§ 2056(b)(7)) in the transfer tax base of the transferee spouse even though the property would not have been included under general transfer tax rules.

The general rule (§ 2056(b)(1)) prevents an interest in property from qualifying for the marital deduction where all of the following conditions exist: (1) an interest in the property passes from the decedent to both the surviving spouse and a third person; (2) the surviving spouse's interest will terminate or fail upon the lapse of time or the occurrence or nonoccurrence of an event or contingency; and (3) the third person may possess or enjoy the property upon the termination or failure of the surviving spouse's interest. For example, the following types of interest would be disqualified under this general terminable interest rule: "to my wife for life" or for "10 years"; "to my husband until he remarries"; or "to my wife, but if she fails to survive my brother, then to my children."

Mere termination of the surviving spouse's interest, or the mere passing of an interest to a third party, however, will not, by itself, disqualify the bequest. For example, a remainder interest to a surviving spouse may qualify even though an interest has passed to the life beneficiary because the interest passing to the third party does not take effect *after* the surviving spouse's interest. Moreover, a joint and survivor annuity payable to the surviving spouse for life and included in the decedent's gross estate under § 2039, will qualify for the marital deduction because no interest has passed to a third party. Reg. § 20.2056(b)–1(g) (Example (3)); Rev.Rul. 76–404, 1976–2 C.B. 294.

The terminable interest rule is expressly deactivated in five situations to which it would otherwise apply, but for special statutory provisions that have the effect of treating the entire interest in the property as passing to the surviving spouse and not to any other person:

(1) Under § 2056(b)(3), if the only condition under which the surviving spouse's interest can terminate is death in a common disaster or within six months of the decedent's death, and such death does not occur.

(2) Under § 2056(b)(5), if the surviving spouse is entitled for life to all the income from an interest in property, or to the income from a specific portion of that interest, payable at least annually in either case, and if the surviving spouse has a general power of appointment with respect to the interest in property or that specific portion. The property subject to the income interest and power of appointment may or may not be held in trust. The surviving spouse's power may be exercisable during life or by will, or both, but in any case it must be exercisable alone and in all events. The typical situation in which § 2056(b)(5) will rescue an interest that would otherwise be considered "terminable" is that in which the testator leaves property in trust "to pay income to my wife for life, and at her death, to pay the corpus to such persons, including her estate, as she may appoint by will, but, in default of such appointment, to pay the corpus to my issue then living." The deduction is allowed in these cases because the surviving spouse's rights with respect to the property are the practical equivalent of outright ownership and the property is included in that spouse's gross estate under § 2041 by virtue of the general power of appointment.

(3) Under § 2056(b)(6), if the interest passing to the surviving spouse consists of the proceeds of a life insurance, endowment, or annuity contract payable in installments or held by an insurance company under an agreement to pay interest thereon and the surviving spouse has rights under the contract analogous to those under § 2056(b)(5). The annuity presupposes a survivorship feature whereby an interest in corpus or a survivorship annuity will pass to a third person on the termination of the spouse's interest, in the absence of appointment. Otherwise, it would qualify despite the termination because no interest would have passed to a third person. The policy

behind the § 2056(b)(6) exception to the terminable interest rule is the same as the policy underlying the § 2056(b)(5) exception.

(4) Under § 2056(b)(7), if a decedent's executor elects to deduct the value of "qualified terminable interest property" ("QTIP"), defined as property from which all of the income is payable at least annually to the surviving spouse for life and over which no person has a power of appointment exercisable in favor of any person other than the surviving spouse during the life of the surviving spouse. The surviving spouse's interest in property meeting this description is called a "qualifying income interest." The property subject to the interest may or may not be held in trust. If QTIP status is elected, the value of the property subject to the income interest is included in the transfer tax base of the surviving spouse. Under § 2519, the inter vivos disposition by the surviving spouse of all or a part of the qualifying income interest is treated as a taxable transfer of the property to which the interest relates. If the qualifying income interest is retained until death, § 2044 includes the value of the property subject to the interest in the surviving spouse's gross estate. Thus, a decedent may leave property for the benefit of the surviving spouse for life, specify who will receive the property upon the death of the surviving spouse, and no transfer tax will be incurred with respect to the property on the decedent's death. Because the value of the property in which the surviving spouse has a qualifying income interest is included in the transfer tax base of that spouse, the QTIP provisions maintain the basic principle that any transfer outside the marital unit is subject to transfer tax.

(5) Under § 2056(b)(8), if the value of the surviving spouse's current income interest in a qualified charitable remainder trust is the only non-charitable income interest. Absent § 2056(b)(8), the current interest would be a nondeductible terminable interest because an interest in the same property to which the surviving spouse's current interest relates will pass to a third party at the decedent's direction upon the death of the life tenant.[5] Where § 2056(b)(8) applies, the decedent's estate receives a marital deduction equal to the value of the surviving spouse's current interest and a charitable contribution deduction for the value of the remainder. In contrast to § 2056(b)(7), § 2056(b)(8) is not elective. Moreover, upon the death of the surviving spouse, the value of the property in which the spouse had an interest is not included in that spouse's estate. Inclusion under such circumstances would be superfluous because the spouse presumably would be entitled to an offsetting charitable contribution deduction.

Unlike the above five statutory exceptions to the terminable interest rule, an "estate trust" qualifies for the marital deduction because it is not technically a terminable interest. In an estate trust, the surviving spouse is

---

5. The surviving spouse's interest in a charitable remainder trust is required to be in the form of an annuity or unitrust, which run afoul of the qualifying income interest rules and thus would render the trust ineligible for QTIP treatment.

the only income beneficiary, and any accumulated income and corpus are payable to the estate of the surviving spouse. The surviving spouse's interest thus is not a terminable interest because it cannot terminate or fail with the lapse of time or the occurrence of an event.

b.   DISQUALIFICATION UNDER THE "TERMINABLE INTEREST" RULE

Regulations: § 20.2056(b)–1(c)

Jackson v. United States

376 U.S. 503 (1964).

■ MR. JUSTICE WHITE delivered the opinion of the Court.

Since 1948 [§ 2056(a) has] allowed a "marital deduction" from a decedent's gross taxable estate for the value of interests in property passing from the decedent to his surviving spouse. [Section 2056(b)(1)] adds the qualification, however, that interests defined therein as "terminable" shall not qualify as an interest in property to which the marital deduction applies. The question raised by this case is whether the allowance provided by California law for the support of a widow during the settlement of her husband's estate is a terminable interest.

Petitioners are the widow-executrix and testamentary trustee under the will of George Richards who died a resident of California on May 27, 1951. Acting under the Probate Code of California, the state court, on June 30, 1952, allowed Mrs. Richards the sum of $3,000 per month from the corpus of the estate for her support and maintenance, beginning as of May 27, 1951, and continuing for a period of 24 months from that date. Under the terms of the order, an allowance of $42,000 had accrued during the 14 months since her husband's death. This amount, plus an additional $3,000 per month for the remainder of the two-year period, making a total of $72,000, was in fact paid to Mrs. Richards as widow's allowance.

On the federal estate tax return filed on behalf of the estate, the full $72,000 was claimed as a marital deduction under [§ 2056]. The deduction was disallowed, as was a claim for refund after payment of the deficiency, and the present suit for refund was then brought in the District Court. The District Court granted summary judgment for the United States, holding * * * that the allowance to the widow was a terminable interest and not deductible * * *. The Court of Appeals affirmed * * *. For the reasons given below, we affirm the decision of the Court of Appeals.

In enacting the Revenue Act of 1948, * * * with its provision for the marital deduction, Congress left undisturbed § 812(b)(5) of the 1939 Code, which allowed an estate tax deduction, as an expense of administration, for amounts "reasonably required and actually expended for the support during the settlement of the estate of those dependent upon the decedent." * * * As the legislative history shows, support payments under § 812(b)(5) were not to be treated as part of the marital deduction allowed by [§ 2056(a)]. The Revenue Act of 1950, * * * however, repealed § 812(b)(5) because, among other reasons, Congress believed the section resulted in discriminations in favor of States having liberal family allowances. Thereafter allowances paid for the support of a widow during the settlement of an estate "heretofore deductible under § 812(b) will be allowable as a marital deduction subject to the conditions and limitations of [§ 2056]." S. Rep. No. 2375, 81st Cong., 2d Sess., p. 130.

The "conditions and limitations" of the marital deduction under [§ 2056] are several but we need concern ourselves with only one aspect of [§ 2056(b)(1)], which disallows the deduction of "terminable" interests passing to the surviving spouse. It was conceded in the Court of Appeals that the right to the widow's allowance here involved is an interest in property passing from the decedent within the meaning of [§ 2056(d)], that it is an interest to which the terminable-interest rule of [§ 2056(b)(1)] is applicable, and that the conditions set forth in [(A) and (B) of § 2056(b)(1)] were satisfied under the decedent's will and codicils thereto. The issue, therefore, is whether the interest in property passing to Mrs. Richards as widow's allowance would "terminate or fail" upon the "lapse of time, upon the occurrence of an event or contingency, or upon the failure of an event or contingency to occur."

We accept the Court of Appeals' description of the nature and characteristics of the widow's allowance under California law. In that State, the right to a widow's allowance is not a vested right and nothing accrues before the order granting it. The right to an allowance is lost when the one for whom it is asked has lost the status upon which the right depends. If a widow dies or remarries prior to securing an order for a widow's allowance, the right does not survive such death or remarriage. The amount of the widow's allowance which has accrued and is unpaid at the date of death of the widow is payable to her estate but the right to future payments abates upon her death. The remarriage of a widow subsequent to an order for an allowance likewise abates her right to future payments. * * *

In light of these characteristics of the California widow's allowance, Mrs. Richards did not have an indefeasible interest in property at the moment of her husband's death since either her death or remarriage would defeat it. If the order for support allowance had been entered on the day of her husband's death, her death or remarriage at any time within two years thereafter would terminate that portion of the interest allocable to the remainder of the two-year period. As of the date of Mr. Richards' death, therefore, the allowance was subject to failure or termination "upon the occurrence of an event or contingency." That the support order was entered in this case 14 months later does not, in our opinion, change the defeasible nature of the interest.

Petitioners ask us to judge the terminability of the widow's interest in property represented by her allowance as of the date of the Probate Court's order rather than as of the date of her husband's death. The court's order, they argue, unconditionally entitled the widow to $42,000 in accrued allowance of which she could not be deprived by either her death or remarriage. It is true that some courts have followed this path, but it is difficult to accept an approach which would allow a deduction of $42,000 on the facts of this case, a deduction of $72,000 if the order had been entered at the end of two years from Mr. Richards' death and none at all if the order had been entered immediately upon his death. Moreover, judging deductibility as of the date of the Probate Court's order ignores the Senate Committee's admonition that in considering terminability of an interest for purposes of a marital deduction "the situation is viewed as at the date of the decedent's death." S. Rep. No. 1013, Part 2, 80th Cong., 2d Sess., p. 10. We prefer the course followed by both the Court of Appeals for the Ninth Circuit * * * and by the Court of Appeals for the Eighth Circuit * * *. Both courts have held the date of death of the testator to be the correct point of time from which to judge the nature of a widow's allowance for the purpose of deciding terminability and deductibility under [§ 2056]. This is in accord with the rule uniformly followed with regard to interests other than the widow's allowance, that qualification for the marital deduction must be determined as of the time of death.

Our conclusion is confirmed by [§ 2056(b)(3)], which saves from the operation of the terminable-interest rule interests which by their terms may (but do not in fact) terminate only upon failure of the widow to survive her husband for a period not in excess of six months. The premise of this provision is that an interest passing to a widow is normally to be judged as of the time of the testator's death rather than at a later time when the condition imposed may be satisfied; hence the necessity to provide an exception to the rule in the case of a six months' survivorship contingency in a will. A gift conditioned upon eight months' survivorship, rather than six, is a nondeductible terminable interest for reasons which also disqualify the statutory widow's allowance in California where the widow must survive and remain unmarried at least to the date of an allowance order to become indefeasibly entitled to any widow's allowance at all.

Petitioners contend, however, that the sole purpose of the terminable-interest provisions of the Code is to assure that interests deducted from the estate of the deceased spouse will not also escape taxation in the estate of the survivor. This argument leads to the conclusion that since it is now clear that unless consumed or given away during Mrs. Richards' life, the entire $72,000 will be taxed to her estate, it should not be included in her husband's. But as we have already seen, there is no provision in the Code for deducting all terminable interests which become nonterminable at a later date and therefore taxable in the estate of the surviving spouse if not consumed or transferred. The examples cited in the legislative history make it clear that the determinative factor is not taxability to the surviving spouse but terminability as defined by the statute. Under the view advanced by petitioners all cash allowances actually paid would fall outside [§ 2056(b)(1)]; on two different occasions the Senate has refused to give its approval to House-passed amendments to the 1954 Code which would have made the terminable-interest rule inapplicable to all widow's allowances actually paid within specified periods of time.

We are mindful that the general goal of the marital deduction provisions was to achieve uniformity of federal estate tax impact between those States with community property laws and those without them. But the device of the marital deduction which Congress chose to achieve uniformity was knowingly hedged with limitations, including the terminable-interest rule. These provisions may be imperfect devices to achieve the desired end, but they are the means which Congress chose. To the extent it was thought desirable to modify the rigors of the terminable-interest rule, exceptions to the rule were written into the Code. Courts should hesitate to provide still another exception by straying so far from the statutory language as to allow a marital deduction for the widow's allowance provided by the California statute. The achievement of the purposes of the marital deduction is dependent to a great degree upon the careful drafting of wills; we have no fear that our decision today will prevent either the full realization of the marital deduction or the proper support of widows during the pendency of an estate proceeding.

Affirmed.

■ MR. JUSTICE DOUGLAS dissents.

ILLUSTRATIVE MATERIAL

A.   EVENTS OR CONTINGENCIES THAT TERMINATE THE SURVIVING SPOUSE'S INTEREST

1.   In General

"Terminable interests" are interests "which will terminate or fail on the lapse of time or on the occurrence or the failure to occur of some contingency." Reg. § 20.2056(b)–1(b). A terminable interest is nondeductible, however, only if an interest in the property which has passed from the decedent to the surviving spouse may pass from the decedent to any third party for less than full and adequate consideration. Reg. § 20.2056(b)–1(c). Thus, the holding in *Jackson* that the contingent widow's allowance was a terminable interest did not, by itself, make the interest nondeductible. But the taxpayer conceded that their child would inherit any amount not paid to the surviving spouse as a widow's allowance.

As the *Jackson* case states, the determination whether a terminable interest is nondeductible must be made at the moment of the decedent's death. If, at that time, it is possible that any portion of the interest passing to the surviving spouse may pass to a third party from the *decedent*, the bequest will constitute a nondeductible terminable interest unless excepted by § 2056(b)(3), (5), (6), (7) or (8).

The following material illustrates the application of these rules in various factual contexts.

2. The Contingency of Death or Remarriage: The Widow's Allowance Cases

The widow's allowance in *Jackson* was a terminable interest because it would terminate or fail under California law if the widow died or remarried within two years after D's death. Other cases have similarly held that the widow's allowances in other states were nondeductible terminable interests because they do not vest on the death of the first spouse. See Estate of Abely v. Commissioner, 489 F.2d 1327 (1st Cir.1974) (Massachusetts law); Hamilton National Bank of Knoxville v. United States, 353 F.2d 930 (6th Cir.1965) (Tennessee law); Estate of Snider v. Commissioner, 84 T.C. 75 (1985) (Texas law); Rev.Rul. 72–153, 1972–1 C.B. 309 (Washington law). In other states, however, the widow's allowance creates an unconditional right that vests in the surviving spouse immediately upon D's death that is not defeated by the surviving spouse's death or remarriage. The widow's allowance in these states thus is not treated as a terminable interest, even though the widow must petition the local probate court for the allowance and the amount must be fixed by the court. See Estate of Green v. United States, 441 F.2d 303 (6th Cir.1971) (Michigan law); Estate of Watson v. Commissioner, 94 T.C. 262 (1990) (Mississippi law); Estate of Radel v. Commissioner, 88 T.C. 1143 (1987) (Minnesota law).

3. The Contingency of Death: The Widow's Election Cases

Reg. § 20.2056(e)–2(c) provides that if a surviving spouse elects to take against the decedent's will, the interest received is considered as having passed from the decedent to the surviving spouse. However, where, under local law, the surviving spouse is required to take some affirmative action to exercise such election, the question arises whether the possibility of death of the surviving spouse before exercise is a "contingency" which renders the interest terminable. The Service at one time took this position (Rev.Rul. 279, 1953–2 C.B. 275), but the courts rejected it, holding that marital deduction qualification is not governed by the procedure required to claim statutory rights but, rather, by the nature of the interest granted. See Hawaiian Trust Company, Ltd. v. United States, 412 F.2d 1313 (Ct.Cl. 1969). The Service subsequently accepted this position. See Rev.Rul. 83–107, 1983–2 C.B. 159; Rev.Rul. 72–8, 1972–1 C.B. 309; Rev.Rul. 72–7, 1972–1 C.B. 308.

4. Contingency Created by Conditional Bequests

An issue similar to a surviving spouse's election against a decedent's will arises when a surviving spouse makes an election between alternative bequests. In a series of cases, the courts have held that the marital deduction is available where the surviving spouse chooses a non-terminable interest (such as cash) rather than a terminable interest (such as a life estate).

c. EXCEPTIONS

(1) Common Disaster and Six–Month Survivorship

Internal Revenue Code: § 2056(b)(3)

Regulations: § 20.2056(b)–3

Ordinarily, a bequest to a surviving spouse that is conditioned on surviving the decedent by a specified period is a nondeductible terminable interest if the property passes to someone other than the surviving spouse's estate upon failure to satisfy the condition. Section 2056(b)(3), however, provides that such a bequest is not a nondeductible terminable interest if it is conditioned upon the survival of the surviving spouse for a period not greater than six months after the decedent's death and such spouse does live that long. The requirement that the spouse survive for six months prevents qualification for the marital deduction if the surviving spouse dies within that time and the property passes to someone other than the surviving spouse's estate. The exception also applies to interests that will terminate or fail if the surviving spouse and the decedent die as a result of a common disaster. Reg. § 20.2056(b)–3(b) states that if the contingency contained in the bequest "(unless it relates to death as a result of a common disaster) is one which may occur either within the 6–month period or thereafter, the exception provided by § 2056(b)(3) will not apply."

(2) Life Estate with Power of Appointment in Surviving Spouse

Internal Revenue Code: § 2056(b)(5)

Regulations: § 20.2056(b)–5

Section 2056(b)(5) provides a significant exception to the terminable interest rule. It permits the use of a wide number of dispositive devices which could not otherwise be used in connection with property for which the decedent sought the marital deduction qualification. The manner in which § 2056(b)(5) functions can be seen by the following example: Assume A leaves Blackacre in trust "to pay income to my spouse, B, for life, with power in B to appoint corpus by will to whomsoever B directs, remainder over to my son, C, if B should fail to appoint". B's power of appointment is not eligible for the marital deduction, since it is not an "interest in property which passes * * * from the decedent to his surviving spouse." Even if B's power of appointment were treated as in effect giving B ownership of the underlying remainder, that interest would also be terminable, since, if B died without exercising the power, the remainder would pass to C in possession or enjoyment pursuant to an interest which passed to him from A. The life interest which passed to B would also be terminable and hence would not qualify for the deduction, since, if B failed to exercise the power, C might come into possession and enjoyment of the property as a result of the contingent remainder interest passing to him from A. In sum, A's estate would not receive a marital deduction for the value of Blackacre, even though the entire property would be included in B's gross estate under § 2041 by virtue of B's general power of appointment.

However, if the requirements of § 2056(b)(5) are met, the entire value of the property subject to B's life interest and power of appointment is considered to have passed from A to B for purposes of § 2056(a) and no interest in the property is considered to have passed to any person other than B for purposes of the terminable interest rule. The property thus becomes qualified for the marital deduction.

In general the requirements of § 2056(b)(5) break down into three groups: (1) requirements as to the disposition of the income from the interest in the property; (2) requirements as to the surviving spouse's power of appointment over the interest in the property; and (3) requirements as to whether the income interest and power of appointment relate either to the entire interest passing from the decedent or to a "specific portion" thereof.

Income requirements. Section 2056(b)(5) requires that the surviving spouse be "entitled for life to all the income from the entire interest, or all the income from a specific portion thereof." In addition, Reg. § 20.2056(b)–5(a)(1) allows the deduction where the surviving spouse is entitled "to a specific portion of all the income from the entire interest," even though a given portion of the entire income may not be equivalent to the entire income from the same portion of corpus.

The income must also be payable to the surviving spouse at annual or more frequent intervals. The Regulations discuss this requirement at great length. Reg. § 20.2056(b)–5(f). On the whole, the Regulations permit the grantor or testator a substantial degree of latitude in establishing a trust so long as the basic intent to provide the surviving spouse with a reasonable income from the property qualifying for the deduction is indicated.

Power of appointment requirements. In addition to assuring the surviving spouse of the income of the property qualifying for the marital deduction under § 2056(b)(5), the testator must give the surviving spouse a power, exercisable either by will or at any time during life, to appoint the entire interest in property or "such specific portion" thereof to the surviving spouse, or to the surviving spouse's estate, or to either one of them. This power must be exercisable alone and in all events. Moreover, no one other than the surviving spouse may have the power to appoint any part of the property or of the "specific portion" thereof qualifying for the deduction to any person other than the surviving spouse.

A power satisfying these requirements is a general power of appointment within the meaning of §§ 2041 and 2514(c). The legislative history states that § 2056(b)(5) "is designed to allow the marital deduction for such cases where the value of the property over which the surviving spouse has a power of appointment will (if not consumed) be subject to either the estate tax or the gift tax in the case of such surviving spouse." See S. Rep. No. 1013 (pt. 2), 80th Cong., 2d Sess. 16 (1948).

Entire interest/specific portion requirements. The surviving spouse's right to income and power of appointment can relate either to the "entire interest" in property or to a "specific portion thereof." Reg. § 20.2056(b)–5(c) defines the term "specific portion" as "a fractional or percentage share" of the underlying property interest. Until the enactment of § 2056(b)(10) in 1992, there was much controversy over whether the right to receive a fixed dollar amount of trust income, or a power of appointment over a fixed dollar amount of trust assets, would qualify under § 2056(b)(5).

(3) Estate Trust

ILLUSTRATIVE MATERIAL

An "estate trust" is a trust all or a part of the income of which is to be accumulated during the surviving spouse's life and added to corpus, with the accumulated income and corpus being paid to the estate of the surviving spouse at death. As a result, the income and corpus will pass to the persons named in the surviving spouse's will; if the surviving spouse dies without a will, the income and corpus will pass under the state's intestacy laws. The estate trust qualifies for the marital deduction without compliance with § 2056(b)(5) because the surviving spouse's interest in the trust is not "terminable". No interest which may take effect on the occurrence or non-occurrence of any contingency has passed from the decedent to any person other than the spouse or the spouse's estate.

Although the estate trust resembles a § 2056(b)(5) trust with a testamentary power of appointment, it has some unique advantages. The testator may make an estate trust the receptacle for unproductive or speculative property which will not produce income during the lifetime of the surviving spouse. Rev.Rul. 68–554, 1968–2 C.B. 412. Moreover, if the trust assets produce income, the testator may give the trustees the power to withhold income and to pay it to the surviving spouse at intervals of more than a year, or only as the surviving spouse has need of it. Id. The estate trust offers obvious advantages when the testator feels that the surviving spouse may squander the income of the trust if all of it has to be paid out annually. Prior to the Tax Reform Act of 1986, an estate trust offered income tax advantages by permitting a trustee to accumulate trust income at trust income tax rates lower than those applicable to distributions to the surviving spouse. The rate structure applicable to trust income after the 1986 Act eliminated much of this income tax advantage.

The estate trust device, however, is not without its limitations. The grantor or testator can only utilize a trust of this kind if the governing local law permits an accumulation of income during the surviving spouse's life. Furthermore, the testator who establishes an estate trust also runs the risk of the surviving spouse's dying intestate with a new spouse taking a share that the testator otherwise would have preferred go to the children of the first marriage. This danger is avoided in the § 2056(b)(5) trust by specifying the persons who are to take if the surviving spouse fails to exercise a testamentary power of appointment. The estate trust also subjects the property to claims of the surviving spouse's creditors.

(4) Life Insurance, Annuity, and Endowment Proceeds with Power of Appointment in Surviving Spouse

Internal Revenue Code: § 2056(b)(6)

Regulations: § 20.2056(b)–6

Section 2056(b)(6) performs a function analogous to that of § 2056(b)(5) in cases where the proceeds of a life insurance, annuity, or endowment policy are held by the insurer after the decedent's death.[6] Interests with respect to such proceeds that otherwise would be treated as nondeductible terminable interests qualify for the marital deduction under § 2056(b)(6) if the surviving spouse receives rights substantially equivalent to outright ownership with respect to such proceeds.

---

6.   The provision applies only so long as an insurance company holds the proceeds. If the proceeds of a policy are paid over to a trustee,   § 2056(b)(5),   rather   than § 2056(b)(6), controls.

To qualify for the deduction under § 2056(b)(6), the interest in property must be the proceeds ("or a specific portion thereof") of a life insurance, annuity, or endowment policy held by an insurance company under an agreement to pay the proceeds in installments, or to pay interest thereon. The installments or interest payments must commence no more than thirteen months after the decedent's death and must be payable annually or more frequently. All such payments payable during the surviving spouse's life must be payable only to the spouse. The contract may provide for a combination of methods of payment. For example, it may provide for payment of interest on the proceeds to the spouse for a number of years and for the payment of annual installments of proceeds after that time. Reg. § 20.2056(b)–6(a)(1). Again, corresponding to § 2056(b)(5), the surviving spouse must have a power to appoint all amounts payable under the contract or from "such specific portion thereof" and it must be exercisable in favor of such spouse, or such spouse's estate, or either of them. The surviving spouse's power may be exercisable during life or by will, but in either case it must be exercisable "alone and in all events". Moreover, no person other than the surviving spouse may have a power to appoint the proceeds in question to anyone other than the surviving spouse.

As under § 2056(b)(5), where the contract places formal limitations, such as a requirement of proof of death, on the commencement of payment of installments or interest, no deduction will be allowed if the surviving spouse cannot make an effective exercise of the power of appointment until proof of death is presented, unless the proceeds subject to the power would be included in the gross estate under § 2041 if the surviving spouse's death occurs before presentation of proof. Reg. § 20.2056(b)–6(e)(2).

The features of § 2056(b)(6) that differ from § 2056(b)(5) arise principally as a result of the special characteristics of insurance contracts. For example, § 2056(b)(6) permits the proceeds of an insurance contract to be paid to a surviving spouse in installments or to be held for the payment of interest; § 2056(b)(5), in contrast, requires that all income generated by the property to be paid to the surviving spouse. In addition, § 2056(b)(6) expressly permits a thirteen-month grace period for commencement of the installment or interest payments; § 2056(b)(5) does not prescribe a starting date for payment of income to the surviving spouse.

(5) Qualified Terminable Interest Property

Internal Revenue Code: §§ 2056(b)(7); 2044; 2207A; 2519

Regulations: §§ 20.2056(b)–7; 20.2044–1

INTRODUCTORY NOTE

Under § 2056(b)(7), the value of property passing from a decedent in which a surviving spouse has a "qualifying income interest" for life is, at the election of the decedent's executor, deductible from the gross estate. A qualifying income interest exists if the surviving spouse is entitled to all of the income from property (or a specific portion of the property) and the property may not be appointed to anyone other than the surviving spouse during that spouse's life.

Without § 2056(b)(7), the life income interest of the surviving spouse would be a nondeductible terminable interest because, upon the death of the surviving spouse, the underlying property passes to a third party. Section 2056(b)(7), therefore, represented a significant change in the structure of the qualitative limitations on marital deduction bequests. Allowance of the marital deduction for a terminable interest, however, required the enactment of other statutory provisions to ensure that the value of the property for which a deduction was allowed is subject to transfer tax if unconsumed by the surviving spouse. Accordingly, under § 2519, the inter vivos disposition of all or a portion of a qualifying income interest by the surviving spouse is treated as a transfer of the property to which that interest relates. Absent such an inter vivos disposition, the value of the property to which the qualifying income interest relates is included in the gross estate of the surviving spouse under § 2044.

Consider the underlying premise of the QTIP rules—that decedents should be able to protect their children from disinheritance by surviving spouses. On the one hand, because no one can have the power to appoint the property to the children during the surviving spouse's lifetime, the children's enjoyment of their inheritance may be controlled by the surviving spouse for decades. On the other hand, because, statistically, most surviving spouses are women, others argue that the QTIP rules are degrading to women. See Gerzog, The Marital Deduction QTIP Provisions: Illogical and Degrading to Women, 5 UCLA Women's L.J. 301 (1995); Gerzog, The Illogical and Sexist QTIP Provisions: I Just Can't Say It Ain't So, 76 N.C.L.Rev. 1597 (1998). For a contrary view, see Zelenak, Taking Critical Tax Theory Seriously, 76 N.C.L.Rev. 1521 (1998).

House Ways and Means Committee Report, Tax Incentive Act of 1981[7]

H.R. Rep. No. 201, 97th Cong., 1st Sess. (1981).

[Pre–1982] Law

* * * Under [pre–1982 law], transfers of * * * terminable interests do not qualify for either the gift or estate tax marital deductions. Terminable interests generally are created where an interest in property passes to the spouse and another interest in the same property passes from the donor or decedent to some other person for less than adequate consideration.[8]

---

7. The House Ways and Means Committee title for its version of the Economic Recovery Tax Act of 1981.

8. For example, the gift of an income interest by a donor to his spouse would not qualify for the marital deduction where the remainder interest is transferred by the donor to a third party.

Reasons for Change

* * * [T]he committee believes that the present limitations on the nature of interests qualifying for the marital deduction should be liberalized to permit certain transfers of terminable interests to qualify for the marital deduction. Under [pre–1982] law, the marital deduction is available only with respect to property passing outright to the spouse or in specified forms which give the spouse control over the transferred property. Because the surviving spouse must be given control over the property, the decedent cannot insure that the spouse will subsequently pass the property to his children. * * * [U]nless certain interests which do not grant the spouse total control are eligible for the unlimited marital deduction, a decedent would be forced to choose between surrendering control of the entire estate to avoid imposition of estate tax at his death or reducing his tax benefits at his death to insure inheritance by the children. The committee believes that the tax laws should be neutral and that tax consequences should not control an individual's disposition of property. Accordingly, the committee believes that a deduction should be permitted for certain terminable interests.

Nevertheless, the committee believes that property subject to terminable interests qualifying for the marital deduction should be taxable, as under present law, upon the death of the second spouse (or, if earlier, when the spouse disposes of the terminable interest in such property). Though the committee believes that property subject to the qualifying income interest should be aggregated with the spouse's cumulative gifts to determine the amount of the transfer tax, it does not believe that the spouse's heirs should bear the burden of this tax. Accordingly, the committee believes it appropriate to provide an apportionment rule * * * to insure that the transfer taxes imposed on property subject to certain terminable interests are borne by that property. * * *

Explanation of Provision

* * * Under [§ 2056(b)(7)], if certain conditions are met, a life interest granted to a surviving spouse will not be treated as a terminable interest. The entire property subject to such interest will be treated as passing to such spouse and no interest in such property will be considered to pass to any person other than the spouse. Accordingly, the entire interest will qualify for a marital deduction.

In general, transfers of terminable interests may be considered qualified terminable interests if the decedent's executor (or donor) so elects and the spouse receives a qualifying income interest for life. A qualifying income interest must meet several conditions. First, the spouse must be entitled for a period measured solely by the spouse's life to all the income from the entire interest, or all the income from a specific portion thereof, payable annually or at more frequent intervals. Thus, income interests granted for a term of years or life estates subject to termination upon remarriage or the occurrence of a specified event will not qualify under [§ 2056(b)(7)]. [Section 2056(b)(7)] does not limit qualifying income interests to those placed in trust. However, a qualifying life income interest in any other property must provide the spouse with rights to income which are sufficient to satisfy the rules applicable to marital deduction trusts under present law (Reg. § 20.2056(b)–(f)).

Second, there must be no power in any person (including the spouse) to appoint any part of the property subject to the qualifying income interest to any person other than the spouse during the spouse's life. This rule will permit the existence of powers in the trustee to invade corpus for the benefit of the spouse but will insure that the value of the property not consumed by the spouse is subject to tax upon the spouse's death (or earlier disposition). However, [§ 2056(b)(7)] permits the creation or retention of any powers over all or a portion of the corpus, provided all such powers are exercisable only at or after the death of the spouse.

[Sections 2519 and 2044] provide that property subject to an election to be treated as a qualified terminable interest will be subject to transfer taxes at the earlier of (1) the date on which the spouse disposes (either by gift, sale, or otherwise) of all or part of the qualifying income interest, or (2) upon the spouse's death.

If the property is subject to tax as a result of the spouse's lifetime transfer of the qualifying income interest, the entire value of the property, less amounts received by the spouse upon disposition, will be treated as a taxable gift by the spouse under new § 2519. In general, no annual gift tax exclusion will be permitted with respect to the imputed transfer of the remainder interest (to a person other than the income beneficiary) because the remainder is a future interest. However, if the spouse makes a gift of the qualifying income interest, the gift of the income interest will be considered a gift to the donee, eligible for the annual exclusion and marital deduction, if applicable.

If the property subject to the qualifying income interest is not disposed of prior to the death of the surviving spouse, the fair market value of the property subject to the qualifying income interest determined as of the date of the spouse's death (or the alternate valuation date, if so elected) will be included in the spouse's gross estate pursuant to a new § 2044.

[Section 2207A] also provides apportionment provisions under which the additional estate taxes attributable to the taxation of the qualified terminable interest property (other than the spouse's life estate) are borne by that property. Unless the spouse directs otherwise, the spouse (or the spouse's estate) is granted a right to recover the gift tax paid on the remainder interest as a result of a lifetime transfer of the qualifying income interest, or the estate tax paid as a result of including such property in the spouse's estate. Under [§ 2207A(d)], the spouse is also entitled to recover any penalties or interest paid which are attributable to the additional gift or estate tax. If, however, as a result of a lifetime disposition of the qualifying income interest, the inclusion of the entire property as a taxable transfer uses up some or all of the spouse's unified credit, the bill does not permit the spouse to recover the credit amount from the remaindermen.

Similar rules may apply with respect to lifetime transfers to a spouse which are qualifying terminable interests if the donor makes an irrevocable election at the time of gift.

(A) INCOME REQUIREMENTS

Estate of Shelfer v. Commissioner

86 F.3d 1045 (11th Cir.1996).

■ KRAVITCH, CIRCUIT JUDGE.

The Commissioner of the Internal Revenue Service ("Commissioner") appeals the Tax Court's decision in favor of the estate of Lucille Shelfer. The court held that Lucille's estate was not liable for a tax deficiency assessed on the value of a trust from which she had received income during her lifetime. The estate of Lucille Shelfer's husband, Elbert, previously had taken a marital deduction for these trust assets, claiming that the trust met the definition of a qualified terminable interest property trust ("QTIP") pursuant to § 2056(b)(7).

This case presents an issue of first impression for this circuit: whether a QTIP trust is established when, under the terms of the trust, the surviving spouse is neither entitled to, nor given the power of appointment over, the trust income accumulating between the date of the last distribution and her death, otherwise known as the "stub income." The Commissioner interprets the QTIP statutory provisions to allow such trusts to qualify for the marital deduction in the decedent's estate; accordingly, the value of the trust assets must be included in the surviving spouse's estate. We agree with the Commissioner and REVERSE the Tax Court.

I.

Elbert Shelfer died on September 13, 1986 and was survived by his wife, Lucille. Elbert's will provided that his estate was to be divided into two shares, that were to be held in separate trusts. The income from each trust was to be paid to Lucille in quarterly installments during her lifetime. The first trust was a standard marital deduction trust consisting of one-third of the estate. It is not at issue in this case. The second trust, comprising the remaining two-thirds of the estate, terminated upon Lucille's death. The principal and all undistributed income was payable to Elbert's niece, Betty Ann Shelfer.

Elbert's will designated Quincy State Bank as the personal representative for his estate, and on June 16, 1987, the bank filed a tax return on behalf of the estate. The bank elected to claim a deduction for approximately half of the assets of the second trust under the QTIP trust provisions of § 2056(b)(7). The IRS examined the return, allowed the QTIP deduction, and issued Quincy Bank a closing letter on May 10, 1989. The statute of limitations for an assessment of deficiency with respect to Elbert's return expired on June 16, 1990.

On January 18, 1989, Lucille died; Quincy State Bank served as personal representative for her estate. The bank filed an estate tax return on October 18, 1989 and did not include the value of the assets in the trust, even though the assets previously had been deducted on her husband's estate tax return. The IRS audited the return and assessed a tax deficiency for the trust assets on the ground that the trust was a QTIP trust subject to taxation. Quincy State Bank commenced a proceeding in tax court on behalf of Lucille's estate, claiming that the trust did not meet the definition of a QTIP trust because Lucille did not control the stub income; therefore, the Bank argued, the estate was not liable for tax on the trust assets under § 2044. The Tax Court agreed. The Commissioner appeals this decision.

II.

* * * Lucille's estate contends, and the Tax Court held, that the phrase "all of the income" [in §§ 2056(b)(7) and 2044] includes income that has accrued between the last distribution and the date of the spouse's death, or the stub income. They argue that "all" refers to every type of income. Stub income is a kind of income, and thus the surviving spouse must be entitled to stub income in order for the trust to qualify as a QTIP trust. They conclude that because Elbert's will did not grant Lucille control over the stub income, the QTIP election fails.

In contrast, the Commissioner and amicus argue that the statute is satisfied if the surviving spouse controls "all of the income" that has been distributed. They contend that the requirement that income be, "payable annually or at more frequent intervals," limits "all of the income" to distributed income, namely those payments that have been made to the surviving spouse during her life. See Estate of Howard v. Commissioner, 910 F.2d 633, 635 (9th Cir.1990) (concluding that "if [the surviving spouse] has been entitled to regular distributions at least annually, she has had an income interest for life").

The estate replies that the phrase "payable annually or at more frequent intervals" is separated from the preceding clause by commas, and thus is a parenthetical clause. Because parenthetical clauses are non-restrictive, it contends that the clause is merely a description of the distribution process and does not in any way limit the preceding requirement that the spouse must be entitled to "all of the income."

Both parties insist that their reading of the statute is "plain." We do not agree. Although the use of commas around the clause "payable annually or at more frequent intervals" does indicate a parenthetical clause, we refuse to place inordinate weight on punctuation and ignore the remainder of the sentence. It is equally plausible that the next clause is designed to provide a context from which to define "all of the income." Nothing in this statutory provision on its face allows us to choose between these interpretations. Accordingly, we must look to other sources for guidance. * * *

Our conclusion is further supported by the lack of consensus among jurists as to the clear meaning of this statute. In this case, the Tax Court split on the issue, with ten judges joining the majority and six judges dissenting. Moreover, in a Ninth Circuit case involving this same provision, the majority reversed the Tax Court and concluded that the statute plainly allowed the trust to qualify. *Howard.* The dissent, however, agreed with the Tax Court's reading of the statute. Accordingly, we must look beyond the "plain language" of the statute for guidance. When faced with a similarly ambiguous tax code provision, the Supreme Court thoroughly examined the history and purpose of the tax provision at issue, past practices, and the practical implications of its ruling. Commissioner v. Engle, 464 U.S. 206 (1984).[9] We follow suit, beginning with the history and purpose of the marital deduction.

III.

* * * An essential goal of the marital deduction statutory scheme "from its very beginning, however, was that any property of the first spouse to die that passed untaxed to the surviving spouse should be taxed in the estate of the surviving spouse." Estate of Clayton v. Commissioner, 976 F.2d 1486, 1491 (5th Cir.1992). * * *

The original statute allowed three exceptions to the terminable property rule for interests that would not escape taxation in the spouse's estate. Property interests would qualify for the marital deduction under any of the following conditions: 1) the interest of the spouse was conditional on survival for a limited period and the spouse survived that period [§ 2056(b)(3)]; 2) the spouse had a life estate in the property with the power of appointment over the corpus [§ 2056(b)(5)]; or 3) the spouse received all life insurance or annuity payments during her lifetime with the power to appoint all payments under the contract [§ 2056(b)(6)]. To take advantage of these exceptions, however, the decedent had to relinquish all control over the marital property to the surviving spouse.

As divorce and remarriage rates rose, Congress became increasingly concerned with the difficult choice facing those in second marriages, who could either provide for their spouse to the possible detriment of the children of a prior marriage or risk under-endowing their spouse to provide directly for the children. In the Economic Recovery Act of 1981, Congress addressed this problem by creating the QTIP exception to the terminable property interest rule. According to the House of Representatives Report, the QTIP trust was designed to prevent a decedent from being "forced to choose between surrendering control of the entire estate to avoid imposition of estate tax at his death or reducing his tax benefits at his death to insure inheritance by the children." H.R. Rep. No. 201, 97th Cong., 1st Sess. 160 (1981). Thus, the purpose of the QTIP trust provisions was to

9. In both *Engle* and the case before us, the Commissioner's interpretation was set forth in a proposed regulation. * * * Because we conclude that the history, purpose, and practical implications of the statute support the Commissioner's reading of the statute, we need not decide the appropriate degree of deference to accord her position.

liberalize the marital deduction to cover trust instruments that provide ongoing income support for the surviving spouse while retaining the corpus for the children or other beneficiaries.

In addition to creating the QTIP trust provisions, the 1981 Act also substantially changed the marital deduction by lifting the limitations on the amount of the deduction. The Senate Report for the 1981 Act states the reason for the change: "The committee believes that a husband and wife should be treated as one economic unit for purposes of estate and gift taxes, as they generally are for income tax purposes. Accordingly, no tax should be imposed on transfers between a husband and wife." S. Rep. No. 144, 97th Cong., 1st Sess. 127 (1981), reprinted in 1981 U.S.C.C.A.N. 105, 228.

Although the legislative history of the 1981 Act sets forth Congress's reasons for enacting the statute, it does not directly address the stub income issue. * * * Accordingly, we must decide which interpretation of the statute best comports with the two general goals discussed above: expanding the marital deduction to provide for the spouse while granting the decedent more control over the ultimate disposition of the property, and treating a husband and wife as one economic entity for the purposes of estate taxation.

Under the Commissioner's interpretation of the statute, the decedent would gain the tax benefit, retain control of the trust corpus, and provide the spouse with all of the periodic payments for her personal support. The stub income, which accrues after her death and is thus not used for her maintenance, could be appointed to someone else. This result is consistent with the statutory goals of expanding the deduction while providing for the spouse's support. In contrast, the Tax Court's reading of the statute would condition the tax benefit for the entire trust corpus on ceding control over a much smaller amount that is not needed for the spouse's support.

The statute's second goal, treating a married couple as one economic entity, was effected in a comprehensive statutory scheme. In addition to the QTIP provisions of § 2056(b)(7), Congress added § 2044, which requires the estate of the surviving spouse to include all property for which a marital deduction was previously allowed, and § 2056(b)(7)(B)(v), which states that a QTIP "election, once made, shall be irrevocable." Taken together, these sections of the code provide that assets can pass between spouses without being subject to taxation. Upon the death of the surviving spouse, the spouse's estate will be required to pay tax on all of the previously deducted marital assets. The Commissioner's position comports with the statutory scheme because it compels the surviving spouse to abide by the irrevocable election of a QTIP trust and to pay taxes on property that had previously been subject to a deduction. * * *

Following the logic of the regulations, the person with the power to appoint the property in the trust corpus should be permitted to have the power to appoint the stub income; the stub income will then be subject to taxation along with the corpus property. Under the QTIP provisions, that person is the decedent. The trust corpus and the stub income would be taxable pursuant to § 2044, which requires the spouse to include all previously deducted property in which she has a qualifying interest for life.[10] This comprehensive scheme, like that of the power of appointment trust, allows an initial deduction and later taxation of the property.[11] * * *

Examining the legislative history of the 1981 Act, we conclude that Congress intended to liberalize the marital deduction, to treat a husband and wife as one economic unit, and to allow the stub income to be treated in the same manner as the trust corpus for taxation purposes. These goals favor a broad interpretation of the statute that would allow the QTIP election in this case. Having assessed the legislative history and purpose of the statute, we turn to the practical implications of this interpretation.

IV.

Our construction of the statute has several practical advantages over the Tax Court's position. First, it would assure certainty in estate planning. The status of trust instruments that were set up in accordance with the Commissioner's advice will not be in question and the validity of the Commissioner's final regulation on this matter will be affirmed.

Second, our result comports with standard trust practices. Under the Tax Court's approach, a trust fund that made daily payments to the surviving spouse would qualify for the deduction because there would be no undistributed income; in contrast, one that made quarterly payments would be ineligible. * * *

Finally, a broad reading of the marital deduction provisions benefits the federal Treasury and furthers Congressional intent to ensure taxation of all previously deducted property. * * *

10. We acknowledge that § 2044 does not expressly apply to stub income because it provides that the surviving spouse's estate must include all property over which the spouse had a qualifying income interest for life. Although we have already shown that the trust property can be a qualifying income interest for life even if the surviving spouse is not given control of the stub income, we have not determined whether the stub income can be part of the qualifying income interest for life. The Commissioner's regulation, now finalized at [Reg. § 20.2044–1(d)(2)], clarifies the issue by specifically including the stub income in the spouse's gross estate. We note that although the regulation was not finalized at the time of this action, it is the most consistent interpretation of the statute for the same reason that the regulations for the power of appointment trust are reasonable. Both regulations ensure that previously deducted property is taxed at the death of the surviving spouse. Moreover, both regulations are faithful to the statutory scheme. In the power of appointment regulations, the stub income is rendered subject to the power of appointment and becomes taxable. In the QTIP provisions, the stub income is included in the spouse's estate along with the trust corpus, both of which are not controlled by the spouse.

11. Our reading of the regulation does not disqualify a trust instrument that provides for the surviving spouse to have the power of appointment over the stub income or to receive the stub income as part of her estate. Under those circumstances, congressional goals will be served because the stub income will clearly be taxable and the couple will be considered one economic unit. We merely hold that the estate planning document at issue here also qualifies for the deduction because Congress provided a statutory scheme which will require taxation of the stub income if it reverts to the trust remainderman.

For all of these reasons, we conclude that our interpretation of the statute will better serve the practical realities of trust administration and estate taxation.

V.

After determining that the statutory language is ambiguous, we looked beyond the statute to additional sources of information, such as the legislative history. Careful consideration of these documents leads us to discern two purposes for the 1981 Act: treating the married couple as one economic unit, and expanding the deduction to include arrangements that divest the surviving spouse of control over property. These congressional goals are best served by allowing the deduction in the decedent's estate and requiring subsequent inclusion in the surviving spouse's estate when trust documents do not grant control over the stub income to the surviving spouse. Accordingly, we REVERSE the Tax Court.

ILLUSTRATIVE MATERIAL

A.   SURVIVING SPOUSE'S RIGHT TO INCOME

Section 2056(b)(7)(B)(ii)(I), in defining a qualifying income interest, states that the surviving spouse must be entitled for life "to all of the income from the property, payable annually or at more frequent intervals." This requirement is the same as that of § 2056(b)(5), and Reg. § 20.2056(b)–7(d)(2) provides that the principles outlined in Reg. § 20.2056(b)–5(f) apply in determining whether the § 2056(b)(7)(B)(ii)(I) requirement is met. Thus, like § 2056(b)(5), § 2056(b)(7) does not permit the trustee to accumulate trust income for beneficiaries other than the surviving spouse. Similarly, § 2056(b)(7), like § 2056(b)(5), does not allow the surviving spouse's income interest to be cut off upon remarriage. Reg. § 20.2056(b)–7(h) (Example 5).

An annuity included in the decedent's estate under § 2039 is treated as a qualifying income interest for life under § 2056(b)(7)(C) if all of the annuity payments during the surviving spouse's lifetime are payable to the surviving spouse. As a result, an individual retirement account (IRA) is included in the decedent's estate under § 2039 where it is payable to the surviving spouse, either directly or indirectly through a trust. Reg. § 20.2056(b)–7(h) (Example 10); Rev.Rul. 89–89, 1989–2 C.B. 231. Section 2056(b)(7)(C)(ii) reverses the usual election presumption: the annuity is treated as QTIP "unless the executor otherwise elects."

B.   "STUB" INCOME

The issue addressed in both *Estate of Howard* and *Estate of Shelfer* is whether income earned between the date of the last distribution to the surviving spouse and the surviving spouse's death can be paid to a beneficiary other than the surviving spouse's estate without violating § 2056(b)(7)(B)(ii)(I). The parties' usual positions were reversed because both cases involved the tax consequences to the estate of a surviving spouse who died soon after her husband. In both cases, the wife's estate argued, and the Tax Court agreed, that the payment of stub income to someone other than the wife invalidated husband's QTIP election and thus the property was not taxable in wife's estate. The Service took the opposite position and prevailed in the court of appeals in both cases, and the regulations now confirm that the payment of stub income to someone other than the surviving spouse does not invalidate a QTIP election, with the result that the property is eventually taxed in the surviving spouse's estate under § 2044. Reg. §§ 20.2044–1(d)(2), 20.2056(b)–7(d)(4). Careful drafting nonetheless usually specifically provides for "stub" income with language that ensures QTIP qualification.

(B) POWERS OF APPOINTMENT

Estate of Clack v. Commissioner

106 T.C. 131 (1996).

■ WELLS, JUDGE:

Respondent determined a deficiency of $2,284,008 in the Federal estate tax of the Estate of Willis Edward Clack (estate). * * * The issue to be decided in this Opinion is whether the interest of decedent's surviving spouse in certain marital trust property is "qualified terminable interest property" (QTIP) within the meaning of § 2056(b)(7), where the passage to the surviving spouse of the interest in the property is contingent upon the coexecutors' QTIP election as to the property. * * *

Decedent was survived by his wife, Alice Clack, his sons, Richard E. Clack and Robert A. Clack, and his daughter, Ann Clack Klimnowicz. During his lifetime, decedent was the owner and operator of a successful plastic extrusion company, Clack Corp., located in Winsor, Wisconsin. At the time decedent executed his will, his sons were active in the company. Richard E. Clack was "the number two person in the company." Robert A. Clack had just started working in the business.

Decedent consulted an attorney in Wisconsin about preparing a will. Decedent was concerned about keeping the control of Clack Corp. in the family. Although decedent wanted his son Robert A. Clack to remain with the company, he wanted his other son Richard E. Clack to have control of the company. Decedent also wanted to minimize his estate taxes and to provide for his wife.

Decedent executed his will on August 27, 1986. The will names decedent's son Richard E. Clack and the Marshall & Ilsley Trust Co. of Milwaukee, Wisconsin, as co-personal representatives of his estate and cotrustees of the trusts created by the will. * * *

Article IV, paragraph C of the will states:

It is my intention that this bequest shall qualify for the federal estate tax marital deduction to the extent that my Personal Representative elects that any part or all of any amount passing under this Article IV be treated as qualified terminable interest property, and the terms of this Will shall be construed in accordance with such intent. * * *

Article IV, paragraph F of the will provides for an election as follows:

My Personal Representative may elect that any part or all of any amount passing under this Article IV be treated as qualified terminable interest property for the purpose of qualifying for the marital deduction allowable in determining the federal estate tax upon my estate. While I anticipate that the election will be made for all of such property, my Personal Representative shall have the authority not to make the election should no election or a partial election be advantageous for some reason I have not foreseen. Any part of any amount passing under this Article IV with respect to which my Personal Representative does not so elect to be treated as qualified terminable interest property shall continue to be held by my Trustee and administered and distributed pursuant to the terms of the Family Trust hereunder.

Article V of the will provides for "Family Trust Administration," in which the trustee is to receive the residue of decedent's estate in order to fund the family trust. Decedent's wife, children, and the issue of any deceased children constitute the beneficiaries of the family trust. * * *

The facts in the instant case fall within this Court's holding in Estate of Clayton v. Commissioner, 97 T.C. 327 (1991), revd. 976 F.2d 1486 (5th Cir.1992). After our opinion in *Estate of Clayton* was issued, but before it was reversed by the Fifth Circuit, we decided Estate of Robertson v. Commissioner, 98 T.C. 678 (1992), revved. 15 F.3d 779 (8th Cir.1994), and Estate of Spencer v. Commissioner, 64 T.C.M. 937 (1992), revved. 43 F.3d 226 (6th Cir.1995), in both of which we followed our holding in *Estate of Clayton*. Subsequently, those decisions were reversed, first by the Fifth Circuit, which reversed our decision in Estate of Clayton v. Commissioner, supra, then by the Eighth Circuit, which, following the Fifth Circuit, reversed our decision in Estate of Robertson v. Commissioner, supra, and finally by the Sixth Circuit, which reversed our decision in Estate of Spencer v. Commissioner, supra. * * *

The Tax Court, in those opinions, held that the surviving spouse did not have a qualifying income interest for life because the passage of an income interest in the property to the surviving spouse was contingent upon the executor's QTIP election as to such property and was therefore subject to the executor's power to appoint the property to someone other than the surviving spouse. Accordingly, the Tax Court concluded that the property did not meet the requirements of § 2056(b)(7)(B)(ii)(II), that the surviving spouse did not have a "qualifying income interest for life," and that the property therefore was not QTIP. * * *

In Estate of Clayton v. Commissioner, supra, the taxpayer argued that, by definition, an interest in property is QTIP only if the election is made, and that, once the election is made, the surviving spouse has a qualifying income interest for life, effective as of the date of the decedent's death. In response, we stated:

An election, by definition, is necessary to insure that the property is qualified terminable interest property. The essence of § 2056(b)(7)(B)(i), however, is that a terminable interest is deductible only if it is an interest in property "in which the surviving spouse has a qualifying income interest for life"; if so, then an applicable election may be made with respect to such property. Whether the surviving spouse has an income interest for life in the property is independent of, and not dependent upon, the requirement that an election be made with respect to that property. If the surviving spouse does not have an income interest for life in the trust, then the election to treat the trust as a QTIP trust is ineffective. * * *

Suffice it to say that, in light of the reversals of this Court's decisions by three different circuits, we now decide that we will accede to the result in those appellate decisions and will no longer disallow the marital deduction for interests that are contingent upon the executor's election under § 2056(b)(7)(B)(v), where the election is actually made under facts similar to those in the instant case. Accordingly, we hold that the marital trust property in the instant case qualifies as QTIP under § 2056(b)(7).

One caveat to our holding is in order. Reg. § 20.2056(b)–7(d)(3) provides that the marital deduction is not available under the circumstances of the instant case. Because the regulation is effective for estates of decedents dying after March 1, 1994 * * *, it is not applicable to the instant case. Consequently, we leave for another day the issue of the validity of that regulation. Obviously, if the regulation were held to be valid, there might be a different result for estates of decedents dying after March 1, 1994.

ILLUSTRATIVE MATERIAL

A. POWERS OF APPOINTMENT

Section 2056(b)(7)(B)(ii)(II) states that no person may have a power to appoint any part of the property subject to the surviving spouse's income interest to any person other than the surviving spouse during the lifetime of the surviving spouse. Reg. § 20.2056(b)–7(h) (Example 4) makes clear that this prohibition includes powers held by the surviving spouse. For example, in Estate of Manscill v. Commissioner, 98 T.C. 413 (1992), the Tax Court held that a trust violated § 2056(b)(7)(B)(ii)(II) where the trustee, with the surviving spouse's consent, could invade corpus for the support of her child. See also Estate of Bowling v. Commissioner, 93 T.C. 286 (1989) (same result where trustee authorized to invade corpus for support of decedent's brother and disabled child). This provision is intended to ensure that the value of all property to which the qualifying income interest relates will be included in the transfer tax base of one of the two spouses. If a marital deduction were permitted for the entire value of property which could be appointed during the life of the surviving spouse to individuals other than the surviving spouse, then property subsequently transferred would escape transfer taxation in the absence of a provision specifically treating the exercise of the power as a constructive transfer by the surviving spouse. The rule of § 2056(b)(7)(B)(ii)(II) eliminates the need for such a provision.

B.   INCOME INTERESTS CONTINGENT ON ELECTION

Estate of Clack illustrates a more subtle application of the § 2056(b)(7)(B)(ii)(II) rule that no one can have power to appoint the property to anyone other than the surviving spouse. The Service consistently took the position that this rule is violated where the surviving spouse's income interest is contingent on the executor making a QTIP election. After initially prevailing on this point in the Tax Court in *Estate of Clayton* and *Estate of Robertson*, the Service lost in the Fifth Circuit and the Eighth Circuit. Nevertheless, the new QTIP regulations promulgated on March 1, 1994 reasserted the Service's position. Reg. § 20.2056(b)–7(d)(3) and–7(h) (Example 6). Subsequently, however, the Service's position as applied to decedents dying before the effective date of the new regulations was rejected by the Sixth Circuit in *Estate of Spencer*.

A divided Tax Court decided to throw in the towel in *Estate of Clack* with respect to decedents dying before March 1, 1994. Only eight judges joined Judge Wells' opinion for the court in *Estate of Clack*; eleven judges joined four separate concurring opinions, and five judges joined three separate dissenting opinions. In Action on Decision 1996–011, the Service conceded the issue as to these decedents:

> "Defense of the Service's position following rejection by the Courts of Appeals in three different circuits and by the Tax Court in *Estate of Clack* would be problematic and would also raise problems in the consistent administration of the QTIP provisions. Accordingly, in cases involving estates of decedents dying prior to the effective date of Reg. § 20.2056(b)–7(d)(3), we will no longer take the position that an income interest for life that is solely contingent upon the executor's selection is not a qualifying income interest for life, so long as the election is properly made."

In T.D. 8779, 63 Fed. Reg. 44391 (Aug. 19, 1998), the Service conceded the issue as to all decedents by amending Reg. § 20.2056(b)–7(d)(3) in accordance with the decisions of the three appellate courts and with the Tax Court's decision in *Estate of Clack*.

(c)   OTHER TECHNICAL REQUIREMENTS

There are a myriad of other technical requirements for obtaining QTIP treatment, some of which are discussed below.

ILLUSTRATIVE MATERIAL

A.   NONTRUST TRANSFERS

Most QTIP transfers are in trust. Indeed, a "QTIP Trust" in tax jargon has emerged as a valuable estate planning tool. See p. 643. The QTIP Trust is an attractive alternative for some transferors to the § 2056(b)(5) power of appointment trust because it does not require that the surviving spouse be given a general power of appointment over the property. As a result, the decedent can obtain the tax benefits of the marital deduction while retaining control over the ultimate disposition of the property following the death of the surviving spouse.

However, nontrust transfers also are eligible for QTIP treatment. For example, Reg. § 20.2056(b)–7(h) (Example 1) explains that a bequest of a personal residence to the surviving spouse for life, remainder to the children, qualifies for the marital deduction. § 2056(b)(7).

B.   THE QTIP ELECTION

The marital deduction is available for a qualified terminable interest transfer only if the executor elects to have the transfer so treated on the federal estate tax return. (In contrast, the marital deduction under § 2056(b)(5) applies automatically if the statutory requirements are satisfied.) Once made, the election is irrevocable. However, an executor's QTIP election does not bar a surviving spouse from timely disclaiming the QTIP interest. Rev.Rul. 83–26, 1983–1 C.B. 234.

As a matter of Federal tax law, it would appear that an executor may elect QTIP treatment without a specific direction in the will of the decedent. Nonetheless, to protect the executor and the estate from potential litigation, it is prudent for a decedent's will specifically to direct the executor to elect or give clear criteria for a decision not to elect. In any event, the will should contain exculpation language to protect the executor from liability for any action taken with respect to QTIP property. This language is especially important where the husband and wife have children from prior marriages.

Reg. § 20.2056(b)–7(b)(3) states that the election is to be made by the executor on the estate tax return, regardless of whether the executor is in possession of the qualified terminable interest property. If there is no executor appointed, the election is to be made by the person in possession of the QTIP property.

Reg. § 20.2056(b)–7(b)(2) permits an executor to elect to have a portion of a QTIP trust treated as deductible so long as the partial election relates to a fractional or percentile share of the property in the trust and the surviving spouse possesses a qualifying income interest for life in the entire trust. The latter requirement prohibits the severance of the non-elected portion of the trust into a trust in which a surviving spouse does not possess a life income interest. However, so long as the trust provides the requisite life income interest for the surviving spouse without regard to the executor's QTIP election, the fraction or percentage (even if defined by means of a formula) of the trust for which QTIP treatment has been elected may be divided into a separate trust to reflect the partial election. Moreover, the governing instrument may direct that any payments of principal to the surviving spouse shall be charged first to the elected portion, or, if the trust is severed, to the separate QTIP trust. The opportunity to elect marital deduction treatment for an amount determined by the executor is a significant post-mortem planning opportunity. This aspect of the QTIP election is discussed at p. 643.

Section 2056(b)(7) issues also arise in connection with post-mortem actions taken by the surviving spouse. Suppose, for example, a surviving spouse elects against the will and receives an interest in property which satisfies the statutory requirements of a qualified terminable interest. Presumably the executor may elect to treat this interest as a qualified terminable interest. But suppose the election of the surviving spouse is made after the decedent's estate tax return has been filed. If the executor has made a QTIP election on the previously filed estate tax return, no subsequent election may be made with respect to a property subject to the surviving spouse's election. If the executor did not make a QTIP election on the originally filed return, the executor may file a new return electing QTIP treatment for the property subject to the surviving spouse's election so long as the subsequent return is timely filed. If the due date for the return has passed, the executor cannot elect QTIP treatment. See Reg. § 20.2056(b)–(7)(b)(4).

In Rev.Proc. 2001–38, 2001–1 C.B. 1335, the Service stated that it will treat a § 2056(b)(7) election as null and void where the election was not necessary to reduce the estate tax to zero because no estate tax would have been imposed regardless of whether the election was made. Examples include where the executor made a QTIP election even though D's taxable estate was less than the exemption equivalent of the unified credit, and where the election was made with respect to property intended to soak up D's remaining amount available credit.

C. TAXATION OF SURVIVING SPOUSE

Two QTIP provisions ensure that the underlying policy of the marital deduction is served by taxing the property either when the surviving spouse gives it away during life or when the surviving spouse dies. Under §§ 2519 and 2044, the transfer or termination of the surviving spouse's income interest is treated as a transfer of the underlying property.

1. *Section 2519*

Section 2519(a) provides that the "disposition of all or part of a qualifying income interest for life in any property [as to which a deduction was allowed under §§ 2056(b)(7) or 2523(f)] shall be treated as a transfer of all interests in such property other than the qualifying interest."

Suppose A has a qualifying income interest in a trust with a corpus of $1,000,000, the remainder of which is payable to A's children. The value of the income interest is $400,000. A assigns an undivided one-half interest in A's income interest to B, an unrelated third party. A's assignment of one-half of the income interest is a gift of $200,000 under § 2511. The value of the remainder interest ($600,000) is treated as a transfer under § 2519(a).[12] At A's death, one-half of the value of the trust is included in A's estate under § 2036. This is so because A's transfer of one-half of the qualifying income interest results in a transfer by A of not only the portion of the corpus relating to the transferred income interest but also that portion of the corpus in which A has retained an income interest. See Reg. § 25.2519–1(a) and (g) (Examples (3) and (4)). If A were subsequently to transfer any portion of the retained income interest, A would presumably be treated as making a gift under § 2511 of the value of the transferred interest. The portion of the corpus attributable to the transferred interest would be removed from A's estate unless the gift occurred within three years of death. See § 2035(b).

---

12. This example ignores the application of § 2702, which would increase the amount of the § 2519 gift to $800,000 because A's 50% retained interest is valued at zero.

Suppose, instead of giving up an undivided portion of the income interest, A assigns all the income for two years to B. A has disposed of a portion of the qualifying income interest the value of which is a gift under § 2511. What is the amount of A's transfer under § 2519? Under the theory of the regulation, A has made a present transfer of the value of the remainder interest in the trust. When A dies the trust corpus (reduced by the value of B's interest if still in existence) would be included in A's estate under § 2036(a)(1).

2. *Section 2044*

Section 2044 includes in the gross estate the value of any property at the date of death of the surviving spouse in which the surviving spouse had a qualifying income interest that was not disposed of inter vivos. Thus, any increase in value with respect to the remainder interest that occurs between the death of the decedent spouse and that of the surviving spouse is included in the estate of the surviving spouse.

Section 2044(c) provides that property includible in the gross estate of a decedent under § 2044 shall be treated as property passing from the decedent. Thus, such property is treated as passing from the surviving spouse for purposes of determining the basis of the remainder interest under § 1014, as well as the availability of current use valuation under § 2032A, a charitable deduction under § 2055, a marital deduction under § 2056, and installment payment of estate tax attributable to interests in closely held businesses under § 6166.

For estate tax valuation purposes, property held by the QTIP trust is not aggregated with property owned outright by the surviving spouse at death. See Estate of Mellinger v. Commissioner, 112 T.C. 26 (1999). As noted earlier, p. 587, aggregation is applied in the case of § 2056(b)(5) trusts.

Revenue Ruling 98–8

1998–1 C.B. 541.

ISSUE

What are the gift tax consequences to the surviving spouse of the acquisition by the surviving spouse of the remainder interest in a trust subject to a qualified terminable interest property (QTIP) election under § 2056(b)(7) of the Internal Revenue Code?

FACTS

The decedent, D, died in 1993 survived by S, D's spouse. Under the terms of D's will, a trust (the QTIP Trust) was established under which S was to receive all of the trust income, payable at least annually, for S's life. On S's death, the remainder was to be distributed outright to C, D's adult child. S was not given a general power of appointment over the trust property.

On the federal estate tax return filed for D's estate, the executor made an election under § 2056(b)(7) to treat the trust property as QTIP, and a marital deduction was allowed to D's estate for the value of the property passing from D to the QTIP Trust.

Subsequently, S, C, and the trustee of the QTIP Trust entered into the following transaction: (1) S acquired C's remainder interest in the QTIP Trust; (2) S gave C a promissory note in the face amount of x dollars (the value of the remainder interest) for the remainder interest; (3) the trustee distributed all of the QTIP Trust assets (having a value of x + y dollars) to S; and (4) S thereupon paid x dollars from those assets to C in satisfaction of the promissory note.

At the conclusion of the transaction, the QTIP Trust was terminated; S held QTIP Trust assets having a value of y dollars (which was equal to the value of S's life interest in the trust); and C held assets having a value of x dollars (which was equal to the value of the remainder interest in the trust). S contended that the transaction was not subject to gift tax because S received full and adequate consideration (the x dollar remainder interest in the QTIP Trust) in exchange for the x dollar promissory note given by S to C.

LAW AND ANALYSIS

* * * The estate tax marital deduction provisions are intended to provide a special tax benefit that allows property to pass to the surviving spouse without the decedent's estate paying tax on its value. Tax is deferred on the transfer until the surviving spouse either dies or makes a lifetime disposition of the property. Under either circumstance, a transfer (estate or gift) tax is paid. * * *

The statutory scheme of the QTIP provisions is consistent with this congressional intent. Thus, a marital deduction is allowed under § 2056(b)(7) for property passing from a decedent to a QTIP trust in which the surviving spouse possesses a lifetime income interest. Sections 2519 and 2044 act to defer the taxable event on the marital deduction property only so long as the surviving spouse continues to hold the lifetime income interest.

Under § 2519, if a surviving spouse disposes of any part of the qualifying income interest, the spouse is treated as making a gift of the remainder interest in the underlying property (i.e., all interests in the property other than the income interest). Correspondingly, under § 2511, the disposition of the income interest by the spouse is treated as a gift, to the extent the income interest is transferred to another for less than adequate consideration.

The term "disposition," as used in § 2519, applies broadly to circumstances in which the surviving spouse's right to receive the income is relinquished or otherwise terminated, by whatever means. See H.R. Rep. No. 201, 97th Cong., 1st Sess. 161 (1981) that states:

The bill provides that property subject to a [QTIP election] will be subject to transfer taxes at the earlier of (1) the date on which the spouse disposes (either by gift, sale, or otherwise) of all or part of the qualifying income interest, or (2) upon the spouse's death.

A commutation, which is a proportionate division of trust property between the life beneficiary and remainderman based on the respective values of their interests is, in the context of a QTIP trust, a taxable disposition by the spouse of the qualifying income interest, resulting in a gift under § 2519 of the value of the remainder interest. The commutation of the spouse's income interest in the QTIP trust is essentially a sale of the income interest by the spouse to the trustee (or the remainderman) in exchange for an amount equal to the value of the income interest. Sales and commutations are expressly characterized as dispositions in the applicable legislative history and regulations. [See Reg. § 25.2519–1(f), –1(g) (Example 2).] * * * See also, Estate of Novotny v. Commissioner, 93 T.C. 12 (1989), in which the surviving spouse and remainderman divided the sale proceeds of QTIP property proportionately on the basis of the respective values of their interests; the court indicated that the commutation constituted a disposition by the spouse of the income interest for purposes of § 2519 and was thus subject to gift tax.

There is little distinction between the sale and commutation transactions treated as dispositions in the regulations and the transaction presented here, where S acquired the remainder interest. In both cases, after the transaction the spouse's income interest in the trust is terminated and the spouse receives outright ownership of property having a net value equal to the value of the spouse's income interest. Similarly, the remainderman receives ownership of property equal in value to the remainder interest. Thus, the transaction in the instant case essentially effectuates a commutation of S's income interest in the trust, a transaction that is a disposition of S's income interest under § 2519. Therefore, under § 2519, S is regarded as making a gift of x dollars, the value of the remainder interest in the QTIP Trust. * * *

This conclusion that S has made a gift is also supported by an additional analysis. S acquired an asset (the remainder interest in the QTIP Trust) that is already subject to inclusion in S's transfer tax base under § 2044. In analogous situations, the courts have recognized that the receipt of an asset that does not effectively increase the value of the recipient's gross estate does not constitute adequate consideration for purposes of the gift and estate tax. See Commissioner v. Wemyss, 324 U.S. 303, 307 (1945); * * * Merrill v. Fahs, 324 U.S. 308 (1945) * * *.

Likewise, in the present situation, property subject to the QTIP election was intended to be subject to either gift or estate tax. S's receipt of the remainder interest does not increase the value of S's taxable estate because that property is already subject to inclusion in S's taxable estate under § 2044. Rather, S's issuance of the note results in a depletion of S's taxable estate that is not offset by S's receipt of the remainder interest. Thus, for estate and gift tax purposes, S's receipt of the remainder interest cannot constitute adequate and full consideration under § 2512 for the promissory note transferred by S to C. * * * [A]ny other result would subvert the legislative intent and statutory scheme underlying § 2056(b)(7). Therefore, under § 2511, S has made a gift to C equal to the value of the promissory note S gave to C.

In addition, a gift tax would be imposed under the above alternative rationales even if S acquired only a portion of C's remainder interest; e.g., S acquired 60 percent of C's remainder interest. If, under applicable state law, such a transaction results in a partial termination of the trust, S would be treated as disposing of part of S's income interest in the trust, and the commutation analysis would apply. * * *

Further, the conclusion of this revenue ruling would be the same if S transferred to C property or cash rather than the promissory note. The economic effect of the transaction is identical, regardless whether S uses S's own funds to finance the transaction or gives a promissory note and discharges the note using some of the QTIP Trust assets received in the transaction. Thus, the result is the same for transfer tax purposes.

HOLDING

If a surviving spouse acquires the remainder interest in a trust subject to a QTIP election under § 2056(b)(7) in connection with the transfer by the surviving spouse of property or cash to the holder of the remainder interest, the surviving spouse makes a gift both under § 2519 and under §§ 2511 and 2512. The amount of the gift is equal to the greater of (i) the value of the remainder interest (pursuant to § 2519), or (ii) the value of the property or cash transferred to the holder of the remainder interest (pursuant to §§ 2511 and 2512).

ILLUSTRATIVE MATERIAL

A. OTHER TAX RULES AFFECTING THE SURVIVING SPOUSE

Reg. § 25.2519–1(b) provides that if a donee spouse has a qualifying income interest in any property, it is rebuttably presumed that a marital deduction was taken for the initial transfer. To avoid application of § 2519 upon a transfer of the qualifying income interest, the donee spouse must establish that a deduction was not taken for the initial transfer. Reg. § 20.2044–1(c) provides a similar presumption for property subject to § 2044. In the case of a QTIP interest created by an inter vivos transfer, the presumption can be rebutted by a gift tax return for the calendar year of the transfer which shows that no deduction was claimed for the transfer. In the case of a QTIP interest created by a testamentary transfer, the surviving spouse may rebut the presumption by providing a copy of the decedent's estate tax return showing that no QTIP election was made with respect to the qualifying income interest. However, problems will arise where the gift qualified for the annual exclusion, where the estate of the transferor was not large enough to require the filing of an estate tax return, or where a partial QTIP election was made.

Where a decedent has created a QTIP trust, its value will be included in the surviving spouse's estate, which may not have assets sufficient to pay the estate tax attributable to the value of the QTIP. In other circumstances, even though the estate of the surviving spouse has sufficient property to pay the estate tax, the surviving spouse may not want that property to bear the burden of the tax attributable to the QTIP. Section 2207A(a) provides the estate a statutory right of recovery against "the person receiving the property" for the estate tax attributable to inclusion of the QTIP, which is computed as the difference between the actual estate tax payable and the estate tax which would have been payable had the property not been included.

Section 2207A(a)(2) provides that the statutory right of recovery may be waived by specific direction in the surviving spouse's will. Absent a testamentary waiver, the estate's failure to exercise its right "is treated as a transfer for Federal gift tax purposes of the unrecovered amounts from the persons who would benefit from the recovery to the persons from whom the recovery could have been obtained. * * * The transfer is considered made when the right of recovery is no longer enforceable under applicable local law." Reg. § 20.2207A–1(a)(2). To avoid litigation, the will of the decedent should specifically provide the extent to which the executor is to exercise the right of recovery.

Section 2207A(b) grants to a spouse who disposes of a qualified income interest the right to recover "from the person receiving the property" the amount of the gift tax payable by reason of § 2519. The right of recovery is limited to the gift tax attributable to the value of the interest treated as transferred under § 2519. The failure of a spouse who disposes of a qualifying income interest to assert the right of recovery "is treated as a transfer for Federal gift tax purposes of the unrecovered amounts to the persons from whom such recovery could have been obtained," and is deemed made when the right of recovery is no longer enforceable. Moreover, any delay in the exercise of the right of recovery "may be treated as an interest-free loan with appropriate gift tax consequences." Reg. § 20.2207A–1(a)(2). The conclusion that waiver of the right of recovery constitutes an additional gift is presumably based on the general principle that the amount of a gift does not include the gift tax payable with respect to the gift. However, if the waiver of the right to recover gift tax constitutes an additional taxable gift, it follows that where the right is exercised the amount of the gift must be reduced by the gift tax attributable to that transfer. In other words, a "net gift" computation must be made.

(6) Charitable Remainder Trust with Life Estate in Surviving Spouse

Internal Revenue Code: § 2056(b)(8)

Regulations: § 20.2056(b)–8

ILLUSTRATIVE MATERIAL

A.   TECHNICAL ASPECTS OF § 2056(b)(8)

Prior to the enactment of § 2056(b)(8), the bequest of a life interest in a qualified charitable remainder trust did not qualify for the marital deduction because the interest of the surviving spouse was a nondeductible terminable interest. Therefore, the estate of the decedent received a deduction only for the value of the charitable remainder.

Because outright gifts to charity and to a surviving spouse are both exempt from the estate tax, Congress concluded that the estate tax also should not be imposed where outright ownership is split between these otherwise exempt beneficiaries through the charitable remainder trust vehicle. Congress thus enacted § 2058(b)(8) to exempt the terminable interest received by the surviving spouse in a charitable remainder trust from the definition of a nondeductible terminable interest. Accordingly, where the surviving spouse is the only individual non-charitable beneficiary of a qualified charitable remainder trust, the value of that spouse's interest in the trust is deductible under § 2056(a) and a charitable contribution deduction is allowed for the value of the remainder interest. Because the surviving spouse receives an interest which terminates at death, no portion of the charitable remainder trust is included in the estate of the surviving spouse.

If the decedent provides a qualifying terminable interest for the surviving spouse, but the trust does not meet the requirements of a qualified charitable remainder trust, a charitable deduction for the portion of the property included under § 2044 will be allowed to the estate of the surviving spouse. Pursuant to § 2044(c), property included in the gross estate of the surviving spouse under § 2044(a) is treated as property passing from the surviving spouse for purposes of satisfying the requirements of § 2055. In many cases, a QTIP trust may be a preferable alternative to a § 2056(b)(8) trust where the decedent wants to benefit both the surviving spouse and charity.

4. VALUATION OF INTEREST PASSING TO SURVIVING SPOUSE

Internal Revenue Code: § 2056(b)(4)

Regulations: § 20.2056(b)–4

United States v. Stapf

375 U.S. 118 (1963).

■ MR. JUSTICE GOLDBERG delivered the opinion of the Court. * * *

Lowell H. Stapf died testate on July 29, 1953, a resident and domiciliary of Texas, a community property jurisdiction. At the time of his death he owned, in addition to his separate estate, a substantial amount of property in community with his wife. His will required that his widow elect either to retain her one-half interest in the community or to take under the will and allow its terms to govern the disposition of her community interest. If Mrs. Stapf were to elect to take under the will, she would be given, after specific bequests to others, one-third of the community property and one-third of her husband's separate estate. By accepting this bequest she would allow her one-half interest in the community to pass, in accordance with the will, into a trust for the benefit of the children. It was further provided that if she chose to take under the will the executors were to pay "all and not merely one-half" of the community debts and administration expenses. * * *

In fact Mrs. Stapf elected to take under the will. She received, after specific bequests to others, one-third of the combined separate and community property, a devise valued at $106,268, which was $5,175 less than she would have received had she retained her community property and refused to take under the will.

In computing the net taxable estate, the executors claimed a marital deduction under [§ 2056(a)] for the full value of the one-third of decedent's separate estate ($22,367) which passed to his wife under the will. * * * The Commissioner of Internal Revenue disallowed the marital deduction * * *. Respondents then instituted this suit for a tax refund. The District Court allowed the full marital deduction * * *. 189 F.Supp. 830. On cross-appeals the Court of Appeals, with one judge dissenting on all issues, held that [the marital deduction] was allowable in full. 309 F.2d 592. For reasons stated below, we hold that the Commissioner was correct and that [the marital deduction is not] allowable.

I.   THE MARITAL DEDUCTION

By electing to take under the will, Mrs. Stapf, in effect, agreed to accept the property devised to her and, in turn, to surrender property of greater value to the trust for the benefit of the children. This raises the question of whether a decedent's estate is allowed a marital deduction under [§ 2056(b)(4)(B)] where the bequest to the surviving spouse is on the condition that she convey property of equivalent or greater value to her children. The Government contends that, for purposes of a marital deduction, "the value of the interest passing to the wife is the value of the property given her less the value of the property she is required to give another as a condition to receiving it." On this view, since the widow had no net benefit from the exercise of her election, the estate would be entitled to no marital deduction. Respondents reject this net benefit approach and argue that the plain meaning of the statute makes detriment to the surviving spouse immaterial.

[Section 2056(a)] provides that "in general" the marital deduction is for "the value of any interest in property which passes * * * from the decedent to his surviving spouse." [Section 2056(b)(4)] then deals specifically with the question of valuation:

"[(4)]   Valuation Of Interest Passing To Surviving Spouse.—In determining for the purposes of [subsection (a)] the value of any interest in property passing to the surviving spouse for which a deduction is allowed by this subsection—* * *

[(B)]   where such interest or property is encumbered in any manner, or where the surviving spouse incurs any obligation imposed by the decedent with respect to the passing of such interest, such encumbrance or obligation shall be taken into account in the same manner as if the amount of a gift to such spouse of such interest were being determined."

The disputed deduction turns upon the interpretation of (1) the introductory phrase "any obligation imposed by the decedent with respect to the passing of such interest," and (2) the concluding provision that "such * * * obligation shall be taken into account in the same manner as if the amount of a gift to such spouse of such interest were being determined."

The Court of Appeals, in allowing the claimed marital deduction, reasoned that since the valuation is to be "as if" a gift were being taxed, the legal analysis should be the same as if a husband had made an *inter vivos* gift to his wife on the condition that she give something to the children. In such a case, it was stated, the husband is taxable in the full amount for his gift. The detriment incurred by the wife would not ordinarily reduce the amount of the gift taxable to the husband, the original donor.[13] The court concluded:

> "Within gift tax confines the community property of the widow passing under the will of the husband to others may not be 'netted' against the devise to the widow, and thus testator, were the transfer inter vivos, would be liable for gift taxes on the full value of the devise." 309 F.2d 592, 598.

This conclusion, based on the alleged plain meaning of the final gift-amount clause of [§ 2056(b)(4)(B)],[14] is not supported by a reading of the entire statutory provision. First, [§ 2056] allows a marital deduction only for the decedent's gifts or bequests which pass "to his surviving spouse." In the present case the effect of the devise was not to distribute wealth to the surviving spouse, but instead to transmit, through the widow, a gift to the couple's children. The gift-to-the-surviving-spouse terminology reflects concern with the status of the actual recipient or donee of the gift. What the statute provides is a "marital deduction"—a deduction for gifts *to the surviving spouse*—not a deduction for gifts to the children or a deduction for gifts to privately selected beneficiaries. The appropriate reference, therefore, is not to the value of the gift moving from the deceased spouse but to the net value of the gift received by the surviving spouse.

Second, the introductory phrases of [§ 2056(b)(4)(B)] provide that the gift-amount determination is to be made "where such interest or property is encumbered in any manner, or where the surviving spouse incurs any obligation imposed by the decedent with respect to the passing of such interest * * *." The Government, drawing upon the broad import of this language, argues: "An undertaking by the wife to convey property to a third person, upon which her receipt of property under the decedent's will is conditioned, is plainly an 'obligation imposed by the decedent with

---

13. See, e.g., Commissioner v. Wemyss, 324 U.S. 303. There the Court stated that under the Revenue Act of 1932 mere detriment to the transferee did not constitute the requisite "consideration in money or money's worth" to the transferor so as to relieve him of gift tax liability. Respondents' reliance on this case ignores that it involved neither a determination of who was to be considered the beneficial donee nor a valuation of the gift received by such donee.

14. The portion of the language relied upon provides that the valuation be "in the same manner as if the amount of a gift to such spouse of such interest were being determined."

respect to the passing of such interest.' '' Respondents contend that "encumbrance or obligation" refers only to "a payment to be made *out of* property passing to the surviving spouse." Respondents' narrow construction certainly is not compelled by a literal interpretation of the statutory language. Their construction would embrace only, for example, an obligation *on* the property passing whereas the statute speaks of an obligation *"with respect* to the passing" gift. Finally, to arrive at the real value of the gift "such * * * obligation shall be taken into account * * *." In context we think this relates the gift-amount determination to the net economic interest received by the surviving spouse.

This interpretation is supported by authoritative declarations of congressional intent. The Senate Committee on Finance, in explaining the operation of the marital deduction, stated its understanding as follows:

> "If the decedent bequeaths certain property to his surviving spouse *subject*, however, *to her agreement*, or a charge on the property, for payment of $1,000 to X, the value of the bequest (and, accordingly, the value of the interest passing to the surviving spouse) is the value, reduced by $1,000, of such property." S. Rep. No. 1013, 80th Cong., 2d Sess., Pt. 2, p. 6. (Emphasis added.)

The relevant Treasury Regulation is directly based upon, if not literally taken from, such expressions of legislative intent. [Reg. § 20.2056(b)–4]. The Regulation specifically includes an example of the kind of testamentary disposition involved in this case:

> "A decedent bequeathed certain securities to his wife in lieu of her interest in property held by them as community property under the law of the State of their residence. The wife elected to relinquish her community property interest and to take the bequest. For the purpose of the marital deduction, the value of the bequest is to be reduced by the value of the community property interest relinquished by the wife."

We conclude, therefore, that the governing principle, approved by Congress and embodied in the Treasury Regulation, must be that a marital deduction is allowable only to the extent that the property bequeathed to the surviving spouse exceeds in value the property such spouse is required to relinquish.

Our conclusion concerning the congressionally intended result under [§ 2056] accords with the general purpose of Congress in creating the marital deduction. The 1948 tax amendments were intended to equalize the effect of the estate taxes in community property and common-law jurisdictions. Under a community property system, such as that in Texas, the spouse receives outright ownership of one-half of the community property and only the other one-half is included in the decedent's estate. To equalize the incidence of progressively scaled estate taxes and to adhere to the patterns of state law, the marital deduction [in effect at the time permitted] a deceased spouse, subject to certain requirements, to transfer free of taxes one-half of the non-community property to the surviving spouse. Although applicable to separately held property in a community property state, the primary thrust of this is to extend to taxpayers in common-law States the advantages of "estate splitting" otherwise available only in community property States. The purpose, however, is only to permit a married couple's property to be taxed in two stages and not to allow a tax-exempt transfer of wealth into succeeding generations. Thus the marital deduction is generally restricted to the transfer of property interests that will be includible in the surviving spouse's gross estate. Respondents' construction of [§ 2056] would, nevertheless, permit one-half of a spouse's wealth to pass from one generation to another without being subject either to gift or estate taxes. We do not believe that this result, squarely contrary to the concept of the marital deduction, can be justified by the language of [§ 2056]. Furthermore, since in a community property jurisdiction one-half of the community normally vests in the wife, approval of the claimed deduction would create an opportunity for tax reduction that, as a practical matter, would be more readily available to couples in community property jurisdictions than to couples in common-law jurisdictions. Such a result, again, would be unnecessarily inconsistent with a basic purpose of the statute.

Since in our opinion the plain meaning of [§ 2056] does not require the interpretation advanced by respondents, the statute must be construed to accord with the clearly expressed congressional purposes and the relevant Treasury Regulation. We conclude that, for estate tax purposes, the value of a conditional bequest to a widow should be the value of the property given to her less the value of the property she is required to give to another. In this case the value of the property transferred to Mrs. Stapf ($106,268) must be reduced by the value of the community property she was required to relinquish ($111,443). Since she received no net benefit, the estate is entitled to no marital deduction. * * *

ILLUSTRATIVE MATERIAL

A.   PROPERTY SUBJECT TO AN ENCUMBRANCE

Under § 2056(b)(4)(B), where an interest passing to a surviving spouse is encumbered in any manner, or the surviving spouse incurs an obligation imposed by the decedent in connection with the passing of such interest, the marital deduction is reduced by the amount of such encumbrance or obligation.

Commissioner v. Estate of Hubert

520 U.S. 93 (1997).

■ JUSTICE KENNEDY announced the judgment of the Court and delivered an opinion, in which the CHIEF JUSTICE, JUSTICE STEVENS, and JUSTICE GINSBURG join.

In consequence of life's two certainties a decedent's estate faced federal estate tax deficiencies, giving rise to this case. The issue is whether the amount of the estate tax deduction for marital or charitable bequests must be reduced to the extent administration expenses were paid from income generated during administration by assets allocated to those bequests.

I

The estate of Otis C. Hubert was substantial, valued at more than $30 million when he died. Considerable probate and civil litigation ensued soon after his death. * * *

* * * The settlement agreement divided the estate's residue principal between a marital and a charitable share, which we can assume for purposes of our discussion were a total of $26 million the day Hubert died. The settlement agreement divided the $26 million principal about half to the trusts for the surviving spouse and half to a trust for the charities. The Commissioner stipulated that the nature of the trusts did not prevent them from qualifying for the marital and charitable deductions. The stipulations streamlined the Tax Court litigation but did not resolve it.

* * * The estate's administration expenses, including attorney's fees, were on the order of $2 million. The estate paid about $500,000 in expenses from principal and the rest from income.

* * * The estate did not include in its marital and charitable deductions the amount of residue principal used to pay administration expenses. The parties here have agreed throughout that the marital or charitable deductions could not include those amounts. The estate, however, did not reduce its marital or charitable deductions by the amount of the income used to pay the balance of the administration expenses. The Commissioner disagreed and contended that use of income for this purpose required a dollar-for-dollar reduction of the amounts of the marital and charitable deductions.

In a reviewed opinion, the Tax Court, with two judges concurring in part and dissenting in part, rejected the Commissioner's position. * * * The Court of Appeals for the Eleventh Circuit affirmed the Tax Court. * * * [W]e now affirm the judgment. * * *

We begin with the language of the marital deduction statute. It allows an estate to deduct for federal estate tax purposes "an amount equal to the value of any interest in property which passes or has passed from the decedent to his surviving spouse, but only to the extent that such interest is included in determining the value of the gross estate." § 2056(a).

The statute allows a deduction for qualifying property only to the extent of the property's "value." So when the executors value the property for gross estate purposes as of the date of death, the value of the marital deduction will be limited by its date-of-death value. This is directed by the statutory language capping the deduction at "the value of any interest . . . included in determining the value of the gross estate." It is made explicit by Reg. § 20.2056(b)–4(a), which says "value, for the purpose of the marital deduction . . . is to be determined as of the date of the decedent's death [unless the estate uses the alternative valuation date]."

Reg. § 20.2056(b)–4(a) provides that "value" for marital deduction purposes is "net value," determined by applying "the same principles ... as if the amount of a gift to the spouse were being determined." Reg. § 25.2523(a)–1[(e)], * * * which parallels Reg. § 20.2056(b)–4(d)[,] * * * provides:

> "If the income from property is made payable to the donor or another individual for life or for a term of years, with remainder to the donor's spouse ... the marital deduction is computed ... with respect to the present value of the remainder, determined under [§ 7520]. * * * ''"

Section 7520, in turn, refers to present-value tables located in Reg. § 20.2031–7. The question presented here, involving date-of-death valuation of property or a principal amount, some of the income from which may be used to pay administration expenses, is not controlled by the exact terms of these provisions. For that reason, we do not attempt to force it into their detailed mold. It is natural, however, to apply the present-value principle to the question at hand, as we are directed to do by [Reg.] § 20.2056(b)–4(a). In other words, assuming it were necessary for valuation purposes to take into account that income, * * * this would be done by subtracting from the value of the bequest, computed as if the income were not subject to administration expense charges, the present value (as of the controlling valuation date) of the income expected to be used to pay administration expenses. * * *

The parties here agree that the marital and charitable deductions had to be reduced by the amount of marital and charitable residue principal used to pay administration expenses. The Commissioner contends that the estate must reduce its marital and charitable deductions by the amount of administration expenses paid not only from principal but also, and in all events, from income and by a dollar-for-dollar amount. The Commissioner cites the controlling regulation in support of her position. The regulation says:

> "The value, for the purpose of the marital deduction, of any deductible interest which passed from the decedent to his surviving spouse is to be determined as of the date of the decedent's death [unless the estate uses the alternative valuation date]. The marital deduction may be taken only with respect to the net value of any deductible interest which passed from the decedent to his surviving spouse, the same principles being applicable as if the amount of a gift to the spouse were being determined. In determining the value of the interest in property passing to the spouse account must be taken of the effect of any material limitations upon her right to income from the property. An example of a case in which this rule may be applied is a bequest of property in trust for the benefit of the decedent's spouse but the income from the property from the date of the decedent's death until distribution of the property to the trustee is to be used to pay expenses incurred in the administration of the estate." Reg. § 20.2056(b)–4(a).

The regulation does not help the Commissioner. It says a limitation providing that income "is to be used" throughout the administration period to pay administration expenses "may" be material in a given case and, if it is, account must be taken of it for valuation purposes as if it were a gift to the spouse, as we have discussed * * *. The Tax Court was quite accurate in its description of the regulation when it said:

> "That section is merely a valuation provision which requires material limitations on the right to receive income to be taken into account when valuing the property interest passing to the surviving spouse. The fact that income from property is to be used to pay expenses during the administration of the estate is not necessarily a material limitation on the right to receive income that would have a significant effect on the date-of-death value of the property of the estate." 101 T.C., at 324–325.

There is no indication in the case before us that the executor's power to charge administration expenses to income is equivalent to an express postponement of the spouse's right to income beyond a reasonable period of administration. By contrast, we have no difficulty conceiving of situations where a provision requiring or allowing administration expenses to be paid from income could be deemed a "material limitation" on the spouse's right to income. Suppose the decedent's other bequests account for most of the estate's property or that most of its assets are nonincome producing, so that the corpus of the surviving spouse's bequest, and the income she could expect to receive from it, would be quite small. In these circumstances, the amount of the estate's anticipated administration expenses chargeable to income may be material as compared with the anticipated income used to determine the assets' date-of-death value. If so, a provision requiring or allowing administration expenses to be charged to income would be a material limitation on the spouse's right to income, reducing the marital bequest's date-of-death value and the allowable marital deduction.

Whether a limitation is "material" will also depend in part on the nature of the spouse's interest in the assets generating income. This analysis finds strong support in the text of Reg. § 20.2056(b)–4(a). The regulation gives an example of where a limitation on the right to income "may" be material—bequests "in trust" for the benefit of a decedent's spouse. The example suggests a significant difference between a bequest of income and an outright gift of the fee interest in the income-producing property. A fee in the same interest will almost always be worth much more. Where the value of the trust to the beneficiaries is derived solely from income, an obligation to pay administration expenses from that income is more likely to be "material." In the case of a specific bequest of income, for example, valued only for its future income stream, a diversion of that income would be more significant. The marital property in this case, however, comprising trusts involving either a general power of appointment (the GPA trust) or an irrevocable election (the QTIP trust), was valued as being equivalent to a transfer of the fee. * * * As a result, the limitation on the right to income here is less likely to be material. The inquiry into the value of the estate's anticipated administration expenses should be just as administrable, if not more so, than valuing property interests like going-concern businesses, * * * involving much greater complexity and uncertainty.

The Tax Court concluded here: "On the facts before us, we find that the trustee's discretion to pay administration expenses out of income is not a material limitation on the right to receive income." 101 T.C., at 325. The Tax Court did not specify the facts it considered relevant to the materiality inquiry. As we have explained, however, the Commissioner does not contend the estate failed to give adequate consideration to expected future administration expenses as of the date-of-death in determining the amount of the marital deduction. We have no basis to reverse for the Tax Court's failure to elaborate. Here, given the size and complexity of the estate, one might have expected it to incur substantial litigation costs. But the anticipated expenses could nonetheless have been thought immaterial in light of the income the trust corpus could have been expected to generate. * * *

The Commissioner directs us to the language of § 2056(b)(4), which says:

> "In determining . . . the value of any interest in property passing to the surviving spouse for which a deduction is allowed by this section—
> * * *
>
> (B) where such interest or property is encumbered in any manner, or where the surviving spouse incurs any obligation imposed by the decedent with respect to the passing of such interest, such encumbrance or obligation shall be taken into account in the same manner as if the amount of a gift to such spouse of such interest were being determined."

We interpreted this language in United States v. Stapf, 375 U.S. 118 (1963). The husband's will there gave property to his wife, conditioned on her relinquishing other property she owned to the couple's children. We held that the husband's estate was entitled to a marital deduction only to the extent the value of the property the husband gave his wife exceeded the value of the property she relinquished to receive it. The marital deduction, we explained, should not exceed the "net economic interest received by the surviving spouse." Id., at 126. The statutory language, as we interpreted it in *Stapf*, is consistent with our analysis here. Where the will requires or allows the estate to pay administration expenses from income that would otherwise go to the surviving spouse, our analysis requires that the marital deduction reflect the date-of-death value of the expected future administration expenses chargeable to income if they are material as compared with the date-of-death value of the expected future income. Using this approach to valuation, the estate will arrive at the "net economic interest received by the surviving spouse." Id., at 126. The statutory language, as we interpreted it in *Stapf*, is consistent with our analysis here. Where the will requires or allows the estate to pay administration expenses from income that would otherwise go to the surviving spouse, our analysis requires that the marital deduction reflect the date-of-death value of the expected future administration expenses chargeable to income if they are material as compared with the date-of-death value of the expected future income. Using this approach to valuation, the estate will arrive at the "net economic interest received by the surviving spouse." Ibid. * * *

The Commissioner also invites our attention to the legislative history of the marital deduction statute. Assuming for the sake of argument it would have relevance here, it does not support her position. The Senate Report accompanying the statute says:

> "The interest passing to the surviving spouse from the decedent is only such interest as the decedent can give. If the decedent by his will leaves the residue of his estate to the surviving spouse and she pays, or if the estate income is used to pay, claims against the estate so as to increase the residue, such increase in the residue is acquired by purchase and not by bequest. Accordingly, the value of any additional part of the residue passing to the surviving spouse cannot be included in the amount of the marital deduction." S. Rep. No. 1013, 80th Cong., 2d Sess., Pt. 2, p. 6 (1948).

The Report supports our analysis. It underscores that valuation for marital deduction purposes occurs on the date of death.

The Commissioner's position is inconsistent with the controlling regulations. The Tax Court and the Court of Appeals were correct in finding for the taxpayer on these facts, and we affirm the judgment. * * *

■ JUSTICE O'CONNOR, with whom JUSTICE SOUTER and JUSTICE THOMAS join, concurring in the judgment.

"Logic and taxation are not always the best of friends." Sonneborn Brothers v. Cureton, 262 U.S. 506, 522 (1923) (McReynolds, J., concurring). In cases like the one before us today, they can be complete strangers. That our tax laws can at times be in such disarray is a discomforting thought. I can understand why the plurality attempts to extrapolate a generalized estate tax valuation theory from one regulation and then to apply that theory to resolve this case, perhaps with the hope of making sense out of the applicable law. But where the applicability—not to mention the validity—of that theory is far from clear, the temptation to make order out of chaos at any cost should be resisted, especially when the question presented can be resolved—albeit imperfectly—by reference to more directly applicable sources. While Justice SCALIA, Justice BREYER, and I agree on this point, we disagree on the result ultimately dictated by these sources. I therefore write separately to explain why in my view the plurality's result, though not its reasoning, is correct.

* * * Calculating the estate tax, however, takes time, as does marshaling the decedent's property and distributing it to the ultimate beneficiaries. During this process, the assets in the estate often earn income and the estate itself incurs administrative expenses. To deal with this eventuality, the Tax Code permits an estate administrator to choose between allocating these expenses to the assets in the estate at the time of death (the estate principal), or to the postmortem income earned by those assets. § 642(g). Everyone agrees that when these expenses are charged against a portion of [the] estate's principal devised to the spouse or charity, that portion of the

principal is diverted from the spouse or charity and the marital and charitable deductions are accordingly "reduced" by the actual amount of expenses incurred. * * * The question presented here is what becomes of these deductions when the estate chooses the second option under § 642(g) and allocates administrative expenses to the postmortem income generated by the property in the spousal or charitable devise. * * *

All that remains in this statutory vacuum are the Commissioner's regulations and revenue rulings, and it is on these sources that I would decide this issue. The key regulation is Reg. § 20.2056(b)–4(a). * * * The text of the regulation leaves no doubt that only the "net value" of the spousal gift may be deducted. There is also little doubt that, in assessing this "net value," one should examine how the spousal devise would have been treated if it were instead an inter vivos gift. * * *

The plurality latches onto Reg. § 25.2523(a)–1(e), and to the statutes and regulations to which it refers. * * * In the plurality's view, these regulations define how to "tak[e] [account] of the effect of any material limitations upon [a spouse's] right to income from the property." Reg. § 20.2056(b)–4(a). The plurality frankly admits that these regulations do not speak directly to the antecedent inquiry—when an executor's right to allocate administrative expenses to income constitutes a "material limitation." * * * The plurality nevertheless believes that these regulations bear indirectly on this inquiry by implying an underlying estate tax valuation theory. * * * It is on the basis of this valuation theory that the plurality is able to conclude that the Tax Court's analysis was wrong because that analysis did not, consistent with the plurality's theory, focus solely on anticipated administrative expenses and anticipated income. * * * Because [Reg.] § 25.2523(a)–1(e) and its accompanying provisions do no more than suggest an estate tax valuation theory that itself has questionable value in this context, these provisions do not in my view provide any meaningful guidance in this case. * * *

Fortunately, Reg. § 20.2056(b)–4(a) further directs the reader to consider a second method of determining the amount of the marital deduction:

> "In determining the value of the interest in property passing to the spouse account must be taken of the effect of any material limitations upon her right to income from the property."

From this we ask whether the executor's right to allocate administrative expenses to the postmortem income of the marital bequest is a material limitation upon the spouse's "right to income from the property," such that "account must be taken of the effect." Because the executor's power is undeniably a "limitation" on the spouse's right to income, the case hinges on whether that limitation is "material." * * *

We can quibble over which definition of "material"—"substantial" or "relevant"—precedes the other in the dictionary * * *, but this debate is beside the point. The Commissioner has already interpreted the language in Reg. § 20.2056(b)–4(a). In Revenue Ruling 93–48, the Commissioner ruled that the marital deduction is not "ordinarily" reduced when an executor allocates interest payments on deferred federal estate taxes to the postmortem income of the spousal bequest. Rev.Rul. 93–48, 1993–2 C.B. 270. * * *

It is, as an initial matter, difficult to reconcile the Commissioner's treatment of interest under Revenue Ruling 93–48 with her position in this case. For all intents and purposes, interest accruing on estate taxes is functionally indistinguishable from the administrative expenses at issue here. By definition, neither of these expenses can exist prior to the decedent's death; before that time, there is no estate to administer and no estate tax liability to defer. Yet both types of expenses are inevitable once the estate is open because it is virtually impossible to close an estate in a day so as to avoid the deferral of estate tax payments or the incursion of some administration expenses. Although both can theoretically be avoided if an executor donates his time or pays up front what he estimates the estate tax to be, this will not often occur. Both types of expenses are, moreover, of uncertain amount on the date of death. Because these two types of expenses are so similar in relevant ways, in my view they should be treated the same under § 20.2056(b)–4(a) and Ruling 93–48, despite the Commissioner's limitation on the applicability of Revenue Ruling 93–48 to interest on deferred estate taxes.

But more important, the Commissioner's treatment of interest on deferred estate taxes in Revenue Ruling 93–48 indicates her rejection of the notion that every financial burden on a marital bequest's postmortem income is a material limitation warranting a reduction in the marital deduction. That the Ruling purports to apply not only to income but also to principal, and may therefore deviate from the accepted rule regarding payment of expenses from principal * * *, does not undercut the relevance of the Ruling's implications as to income. * * * Thus, some financial burdens on the spouse's right to postmortem income will reduce the marital deduction; others will not. The line between the two does not, as Justice SCALIA contends, depend upon the relevance of the limitation on the spouse's right to income to the value of the marital bequest * * * since interest on deferred estate taxes surely reduces, and is therefore relevant to, "the value of what passes." * * * By virtue of Revenue Ruling 93–48, the Commissioner has instead created a quantitative rule for Reg. § 20.2056(b)–4(a). That a limitation affects the marital deduction only upon reaching a certain quantum of substantiality is not a concept alien to the law of taxation; such rules are quite common. * * *

[T]he proper measure of materiality has yet to be decided by the Commissioner. The Tax Court below compared the actual amount spent on administration expenses to its estimate of the income to be generated by the marital bequest during the spouse's lifetime. * * * One amicus suggests a comparison of the discounted present value of the projected income stream from the marital bequest when the actual administrative expenses are allocated to income with the projected income stream when the expenses are allocated to principal. App. to Brief American College of Trust and Estate Counsel as Amicus Curiae 1–2. The plurality, drawing upon its valuation theory, * * * looks to whether the "date-of-death value of the expected future administration expenses chargeable to income ... [is] material as compared with the date-of-death value of the expected future income." * * * None of these tests specifies with any particularity when the threshold of materiality is crossed. * * * The proliferation of possible tests only underscores the need for the Commissioner's guidance. In its absence, the Tax Court's approach is as consistent with the Code as any of the others, and provides no basis for reversal.

I share Justice SCALIA's reluctance to find a $1.5 million diminution in postmortem income immaterial under any standard. * * * Were this Court considering the question of quantitative materiality in the first instance, I would be hard pressed not to find this amount "material" given the size of Mr. Hubert's estate. But the Tax Court in this case was effectively preempted from making such a finding by the Commissioner's litigation strategy. It appears from the record that the Commissioner elected to marshal all her resources behind the proposition that any diversion of postmortem income was material, and never presented any evidence or argued that $1.5 million was quantitatively material. * * * Because she bore the burden of proving materiality (since her challenge to administrative expenses was omitted from the original Notice of Deficiency), Tax Court Rule 142(a), her failure of proof left the Tax Court with little choice but to reach its carefully crafted conclusion that $1.5 million was not quantitatively material on "the facts before [it]." 101 T.C., at 325. I would resist the temptation to correct the seemingly counterintuitive result in this case by protecting the Commissioner from her own litigation strategy, especially when she continues to adhere to that strategy and does not, even now, ask us to reconsider the Tax Court's finding on this issue.

This complex case has spawned four separate opinions from this Court. The question presented is simple and its answer should have been equally straightforward. Yet we are confronted with a maze of regulations and rulings that lead at times in opposite directions. There is no reason why this labyrinth should exist, especially when the Commissioner is empowered to promulgate new regulations and make the answer clear. Indeed, nothing prevents the Commissioner from announcing by regulation the very position she advances in this litigation. Until that time, however, the relevant sources point to a test of quantitative materiality, one that is not met by the unusual factual record in this case. I would, accordingly, affirm the judgment of the Tax Court.

■ JUSTICE SCALIA, with whom JUSTICE BREYER joins, dissenting.

The statute and regulation most applicable to the question presented in this case are discussed in today's opinion almost as an afterthought. Instead of relying on the text of § 2056(b)(4)(B) and its interpretive regulation, Reg. § 20.2056(b)–4(a), the plurality hinges its analysis on general principles of valuation which it mistakenly believes to inhere in the estate tax. It thereby creates a tax boondoggle never contemplated by Congress, and announces a test of deductibility virtually impossible for taxpayers and the IRS to apply. In my view, § 2056(b)(4)(B) and Reg.

§ 20.2056(b)–4(a) provide a straightforward disposition, namely that the marital (and charitable) deductions must be reduced whenever income from property comprising the residuary bequest to the spouse (or charity) is used to satisfy administration expenses. I therefore respectfully dissent. * * *

The Commissioner contends that Treasury Regulation § 20.2056(b)–4(a), which interprets § 2056(b)(4)(B), mandates the conclusion that payment of administration expenses from marital bequest income reduces the marital deduction. * * *

As the courts below recognized, the crucial term of the regulation for present purposes is "material limitations." Curiously enough, however, neither the Commissioner nor the respondents come forward with a definition of this term. * * *

In the context of Reg. § 20.2056(b)–4(a), which deals, as its first sentence recites, with "[t]he value, for the purpose of the marital deduction, of any deductible interest which passed from the decedent to his surviving spouse" (emphasis added), a "material limitation" is a limitation that is relevant or consequential to the value of what passes. Many limitations are not—for example, a requirement that the spouse not spend the income for five years, or that the spouse be present at the reading of the will, or that the spouse reconcile with an alienated relative.

That this is the more natural reading of the provision is amply demonstrated by the consequences of the alternative reading, which would leave it to the taxpayer, the Commissioner, and ultimately the courts, to guess whether a particular decrease in value is "material" enough to qualify—without any hint as to what might be a "ballpark" figure, or indeed any hint as to whether there is such a thing as "absolute materiality" (the two million dollars at issue here, for instance) or whether it is all relative to the size of the estate. One should not needlessly impute such a confusing meaning to a regulation which readily bears another interpretation that is more precise. Moreover, the Commissioner's interpretation of her own regulation, so long as it is consistent with the text, is entitled to considerable deference. * * *

The concurrence contends that the other (more unnatural) reading of "material" must be adopted—and that no deference is to be accorded the Commissioner's longstanding approach of reducing the marital deduction for any payment of administrative expenses out of marital-bequest income—because of a recent Revenue Ruling in which the Commissioner acquiesced in lower court holdings that the marital deduction is not reduced by the payment from the marital bequest of interest on deferred estate taxes. * * * The concurrence asserts that interest accruing on estate taxes "is functionally indistinguishable" from administrative expenses, so that Revenue Ruling 93–48 "created a quantitative rule" shielding some financial burdens from affecting the calculation of the marital deduction. * * * I think not. The Commissioner issued Revenue Ruling 93–48 only after her contention, that Reg. § 20.2056(b)–4(a) required the marital deduction to be reduced by payment of estate tax interest from the marital bequest, was repeatedly rejected by the Tax Court and the Courts of Appeals. * * *

My understanding of Reg. § 20.2056(b)–4(a) is the only approach consistent with the statutory requirement that the marital deduction be limited to the value of property which passes to the spouse. * * * As the plurality and the concurrence acknowledge, one component of an asset's value is its discounted future income. * * * The plurality and the concurrence also properly acknowledge that if residuary principal is used to pay administration expenses, then the marital deduction must be reduced commensurately because the property does not pass to the spouse. * * * The plurality and the concurrence decline, however, to follow this reasoning to its logical conclusion. Since the future stream of income is one part of the value of the assets at the date of death, use of the income to pay administration expenses (which were not included in calculating the assets' values) in effect reduces the value of the interest that passes to the spouse. As succinctly explained by a respected tax commentator:

> "Beneficiaries are compensated for the delay in receiving possession by giving them the right to the income that is earned during administration.... [I]t is only the combination of the two rights—that to the income and that to possess the property in the future—that gives the beneficiary rights at death that are equal to value of the property at death. If the beneficiary does not get the income, what the beneficiary gets is less than the deathtime value of the property." Davenport, A Street Through *Hubert's* Fog, [73] Tax Notes 1107, 1110 (1996).

If the beneficiary does not receive the income generated by the marital bequest principal, she in effect receives at the date of death less than the value of the property in the estate, in much the same way as she receives less than the value of the property in the estate when principal is used to pay expenses. * * *

■ JUSTICE BREYER, dissenting.

* * * Justice SCALIA explains why the Commissioner's interpretation is consistent with the regulation's language and the statute it interprets. I add a brief explanation as to why I believe that it is consistent with basic statutory and regulatory tax law objectives as well. * * *

The Commissioner's position also treats economic equals as equal. The time when the administrator writes the relevant checks, and not the account to which he debits them, determines economic impact. Thus $100,000 in administration expenses incurred by a $1 million estate open for one year, paid by check on the year's last day will (assuming 10% simple interest and assuming away here irrelevant complexities) leave $1 million for the spouse at year's end, whether the administrator pays the expenses out of estate principal or from income. On these same assumptions, a commitment to pay, say, $100,000 in administration expenses out of income will reduce the value of principal by an amount identical to the reduction in value that would flow from a commitment to pay a similar amount out of principal. This economic similarity argues for similar estate tax treatment.

I recognize that the statute permits estates to deduct administration and certain other expenses either from the estate tax or from the estate's income tax. * * * But I do not read that statute as allowing a spouse to escape payment both of the estate tax (through a greater marital deduction) and also of income tax (through the deduction of the administration expenses from income). One can easily read the provision's language as simply granting the estate the advantage of whichever of the two tax rates is the more favorable, while continuing to require the estate to pay at least one of the two potential taxes. To read the "election" provision in this way makes of it a less dramatic departure from a Tax Code that otherwise sees what passes to heirs not as the full value of what the testator left, but, rather, as that value minus a set of permitted deductions. § 2053(a) (specifying deductions). * * *

The Commissioner's insistence upon reducing the date-of-death value of the trust dollar-for-dollar poses a more serious problem. Payment of $100,000 in administration expenses from future income should reduce the date of death value of assets left to a wife in trust not by $100,000, but by $100,000 discounted to reflect the fact that the $100,000 will be paid in the future, earning interest in the meantime. (Assuming a 10% interest rate and payment one year after death, the reduction in value would be about $91,000, not $100,000.) Nonetheless, the Commissioner's practice of reducing the marital deduction dollar-for-dollar might reflect the simplifying assumption that discount calculations do not make a sufficiently large difference sufficiently often to warrant the administrative burden of authorizing them. Or it might reflect the fact that when administration expenses are taken as a deduction against the estate tax, their value is not discounted. Were the Commissioner to defend the dollar-for-dollar position in some such way, her approach might prove reasonable. And this Court will defer to longstanding interpretations of the Code and Treasury Regulations * * * that reasonably "implement the congressional mandate." United States v. Correll, 389 U.S. 299, 307 (1967); see National Muffler Dealers Assn., Inc. v. United States, 440 U.S. 472, 488 (1979). Regardless, I would not decide this matter now, for it has not been argued to us.

Finally, although I agree with much that Justice O'CONNOR has written, I cannot agree that the amount at issue—"almost $1.5 million of administration expenses deducted from income"—is insignificant and hence immaterial. * * *

ILLUSTRATIVE MATERIAL

A.   DETERMINATION OF THE SHARE OF DEATH TAXES TO BE BORNE BY THE MARITAL BEQUEST

Section 2056(b)(4)(A) provides that in determining "the value of any interest in property passing to the surviving spouse * * * there shall be taken into account the effect which" any estate or other death tax (state or federal) has "on the net value to the surviving spouse of such interest." The share of death taxes payable out of the spouse's bequest is determined under local law, which generally looks to the testator's intent. Riggs v. Del Drago, 317 U.S. 95 (1942). The marital deduction is reduced by any federal estate tax payable from the surviving spouse's bequest. This reduction in turn increases the taxable estate and the estate tax payable from the spouse's share, thereby pyramiding reduction of the deduction. The final deduction can be computed either by trial and error or by means of an algebraic formula involving simultaneous equations. See IRS Publication No. 904.

If the decedent's will or local law provides for "equitable apportionment" of death taxes among the beneficiaries according to their proportionate share of the tax burden, a surviving spouse who receives a deductible marital bequest is not charged with any share of the federal estate tax. See Robinson v. United States, 518 F.2d 1105 (9th Cir.1975); Estate of Penney v. Commissioner, 504 F.2d 37 (6th Cir.1974); Dodd v. United States, 345 F.2d 715 (3d Cir.1965). Where the decedent's will does not clearly apportion death taxes, courts often resolve ambiguities in favor of the surviving spouse where the decedent intended to maximize the available marital deduction.

B.   "MATERIAL LIMITATION" ON SURVIVING SPOUSE'S RIGHT TO INCOME

Under § 2056(b)(4)(B), where the property passing to the surviving spouse is encumbered, the encumbrance is taken into account in determining the amount of the marital deduction. Reg. § 20.2056(b)–4(a) implements § 2056(b)(4)(B) in providing that the marital deduction only may be taken for the net value of the interest passing to the surviving spouse.

Although seven of the Justices in *Estate of Hubert* agreed that the marital deduction did not have to be reduced under this rule to reflect the estate's payment of administration expenses from income generated by assets allocated to the surviving spouse, a majority could not agree on a definition of "material limitation." The plurality opinion of Justice Kennedy, joined by Chief Justice Rehnquist and Justices Stevens and Ginsburg, used a present-value materiality test, whether the "date-of-death value of the expected future administration expenses chargeable to income [is] material as compared with the date-of-death value of the expected future income." In contrast, the concurring opinion of Justice O'Connor, joined by Justices Souter and Thomas, used a rule of "quantitative" materiality—a limitation "affects the marital deduction only upon reaching a certain quantum of substantiality." In dissent, Justices Scalia and Breyer would find the $1.5 million of administration expenses paid out of income, representing 5% of the estate's value, as material under any standard.

The post-*Hubert* regulations eliminate the concept of materiality and provide that only administration expenses of a certain character that are charged to the marital property will reduce its value. A reduction is made to the date of death value of the property passing from the decedent to the surviving spouse for "estate transmission expenses" incurred during the administration of the estate and paid from the marital share. Reg. § 20.2056(b)–4(d)(2). No reduction is made for "estate management expenses" incurred with respect to the property and charged to it because the expenses would have been incurred in any event. Reg. § 20.2056(b)–4(d)(3). But the amount of the allowable marital deduction is reduced per § 2056(b)(9) by the amount of such management expenses that are deducted under § 2053. In addition, the value of the marital share is reduced by the amount of estate management expenses paid from the marital share but attributable to a property interest not included in the marital share. Reg. § 20.2056(b)–4(d)(4).

"Estate transmission expenses" are defined as all administration expenses that are not management expenses. "Estate transmission expenses are expenses that would not have been incurred but for the decedent's death and the consequent necessity of collecting the decedent's assets, paying the decedent's debts and death taxes, and distributing the decedent's property to those who are entitled to receive it." Reg. § 20.2056(b)–4(d)(1)(ii). Examples include executor commissions, attorney fees, probate fees, expenses incurred in will construction and will contest proceedings, and appraisal fees. In contrast, "estate management expenses are expenses that are incurred in connection with the investment of estate assets or with their preservation or maintenance during a reasonable period of administration." Reg. § 20.2056(b)–4(d)(1)(i). Examples include investment advisory fees, stock brokerage commissions, custodial fees, and interest.

5.   TYPES OF MARITAL DEDUCTION BEQUESTS

"All marital deduction planning can be broken down into three components—how much marital deduction to take (entire marital deduction, optimum marital deduction, or less than optimum marital deduction); what kind of marital deduction vehicle to employ (outright bequest, power of appointment trust, QTIP, * * *); and what funding mechanism to use to satisfy the bequest. Much is discussed and written on the first two components and many planners spend most (if not all) of the discussion time with clients explaining the options for how much and what kind. Often times very little thought is given to the third component—how to design the formula to express the marital or bypass shares and how to actually transfer assets in satisfaction thereof. Yet, out of the three marital deduction components, this is the least flexible because planners have numerous ways to take a second look at the first two components and make postmortem changes in the estate plan. * * * The only one of the three components where there is very limited flexibility to make post-mortem changes is the one given the least amount of attention when originally planned, and with the increased use of QTIP elections and GST exemption planning, the need for properly designed funding formulas is greater than ever before."

Detzel, The Heart of the Matter—Efficient Use of Formula Clauses in Estate Planning, 30 U. Miami Inst.Est.Plan. 16–1, 16–1 (1996).

a.   INTRODUCTION

It is relatively simple to draft a bequest to accomplish a testator's desire to convey either specific property or all the property included in that individual's estate outright to the surviving spouse. However, where the property to be conveyed to or for the benefit of the surviving spouse is to be equal to either (a) a specified portion of the decedent's estate or (b) the amount necessary to produce no tax at the decedent's death, the drafting task is more difficult. The testator must also decide whether the property is to go outright to the surviving spouse or in trust. If a trust is chosen, the form of the bequest must comply with the requirements of § 2056(b)(5), (7) or (8) or constitute an estate trust.

Where the amount of property passing to a surviving spouse is to vary according to the size of the decedent's estate, or is to be limited to the amount necessary to produce no estate tax at the decedent's death, the marital bequest is usually expressed by one of two basic types of formula clauses. A *"pecuniary"* formula grants to the surviving spouse a specific dollar amount usually described as *"an amount* (in cash or property) *equal to"* the amount of the marital deduction desired. Under a *"fractional"* formula bequest, the surviving spouse does not receive a specific dollar amount but rather that *"fractional share"* of the decedent's estate equal to the amount of the marital deduction desired.

The question of how to express the desired amount of the marital deduction, no matter which formula is chosen, may be extremely important. Careless expression of the marital deduction amount may result in the payment of more estate tax than desired. In other situations, it may be desirable to equalize the estates of the two spouses to produce the minimum aggregate transfer taxes on the spousal unit. In such a case, proper drafting of the marital deduction clause is crucial to insure that the appropriate amount of the decedent spouse's estate passes to the surviving spouse in a form that qualifies for the marital deduction and the balance passes in a form that will avoid taxation in the surviving spouse's estate (although the surviving spouse may be given interests in the non-marital bequest). Finally, if the objective is to provide maximum deferral of estate taxes, but it is desirable to use both a trust over which the surviving spouse will have a general power of appointment and a qualified terminable interest property trust, then the function of the marital deduction clause is to differentiate between two forms of marital deduction bequests. The following materials discuss considerations involved in selecting between the types of marital deduction clauses that have been developed. Additional estate planning aspects of the marital deduction are discussed at p. 640.

b.   CONSIDERATIONS IN SELECTING THE FORM OF A MARITAL BEQUEST

Polasky, Marital Deduction Formula Clauses in Estate Planning—Estate and Income Tax Considerations

63 Mich.L.Rev. 809 (1965).

[There are two basic types of formula marital deduction clauses.]

Pecuniary Formulas. The first basic type, often referred to as a "pecuniary bequest," provides for a dollar amount bequest. Its function is simply to measure the dollar amount or value of the gift * * *.

The pecuniary bequest, carved out of the estate before disposition of the residue, was a distinct departure from the prior practice of providing for primary objects of bounty through a division of the residuary estate. When drafted as a general legacy, the amount (once determined) is fixed and is satisfiable before division of the residue among the residuary legatees. Thus, though the dollar amount of the widow's share was fixed, the fractional portion of the total estate assets actually received by the widow would vary with fluctuations in estate assets between the time of valuation and distribution, a relatively larger share being received by her if assets declined in value during administration and the converse being true when a general appreciation in asset values occurred.

Fractional Share Formulas. Concern over a number of additional, potentially troublesome administrative problems foreseeable in connection with a pecuniary clause led to development of a second major species of formula—the "fractional share." This quite different clause measures the gift in terms of a fractional share of the decedent's estate * * *. Since the fraction, computed on the basis of federal estate tax values, remains constant in relation to the residuary estate (however defined) upon which it operates, the marital deduction gift shares ratably in any appreciation or depreciation of assets prior to distribution. Use of the fractional share clause does, however, require rather careful specification of the manner in which the fraction is to be determined. Moreover, problems of determining the appropriate shares of income and principal to be distributed become complicated where partial distributions occur during administration. * * *

V.   Advantages and Disadvantages of Types of
Formula Clauses—a Comparison * * *

B.   *Choice as Between Formula Clauses*

1.   *"True" Pecuniary and Fractional Share Clauses*

Marshalling the pros and cons in choosing between types of formula clauses is somewhat more difficult because of the proliferation of varieties of pecuniary and fractional share patterns and the emergence of clauses which can only be described as hybrids.

If discussion can be limited to the "true fractional share" clause (requiring a distribution of a fractional interest in each asset of the residuary estate, as described) and the "true pecuniary" clause (distribution date values being used to measure the quantum necessary to satisfy the gift), some observations are possible.

a.   *Advantages of Pecuniary Clauses*

Most commentators would probably agree that the pecuniary formula is easier to express than the fractional share; certainly it is easier to explain to the client. Others, however, have suggested that the fractional share provision is perfectly susceptible of lucid draftsmanship * * *.

The pecuniary formula also offers somewhat greater opportunities for post-mortem planning than does the true fractional share, though some of the imagined joys of the tax-value formula have been curtailed by Rev.Proc. 64–19 [see p. 634]. As an officer of a major corporate fiduciary puts it, "This type of formula clause permits a certain amount of post-mortem estate planning if the fiduciary is given authority to select and allocate assets. With such a grant of authority, municipal bonds may be allocated to the marital gift and stocks allocated to the residuary trust designed to bypass the wife's estate for estate tax purposes, or perhaps a balanced portfolio allocated to the marital gift and stock in a family business to the residuary trust. A clause of this type may be set up in a way which permits a good deal of flexibility in the allocation of assets."

Further, * * * the pecuniary formula allowing selection of assets permits a choice of timing and tax impact in recognition of gains and allocation of tax basis at distribution. In addition, it does freeze the widow's share, in terms of dollar value, upon determination of the "amount"; this is accompanied by a shifting of appreciation (and depreciation) during administration to the nonmarital share.

b. Advantages of Fractional Share Clauses

These latter features, which explain the appeal of the pecuniary to some counselors, are regarded by fractional-share enthusiasts as reasons for avoiding a pecuniary clause. The flexibility, as they see it, leads to administrative problems stemming from "the fundamental duty and responsibility of a fiduciary to be impartial and the inadvisability of employing any technique which might possibly sow the seeds of family discord by giving to the wife and children a different type or quality of interest in the estate." A true fractional share, deemed to require distribution of a fractional interest in each available asset, tends to forestall opportunity for preferential treatment stemming from asset selection and clearly avoids recognition of gain or loss on distribution (while passing the estate's basis to the distributee).

To some, it appears safer and would be preferable on this ground alone, although this assumption seems questionable. The fractional share does, nevertheless, present greater administrative problems for the fiduciary. Even when properly drawn, extreme care in trust accounting is required in applying the fraction to income and principal distributions, and the problem is compounded by the fact that the fraction cannot be definitely ascertained until federal estate tax values and the content of the gross estate have been finally determined. Meanwhile, non-pro-rata partial distributions alter both the pool and the fraction of the pool to which the marital share is entitled.

On final distribution, distribution of a fractional share of each asset does have the advantage of not requiring a second valuation of assets (a not inconsiderable burden where closely-held stock or other small business interests are involved); yet the distribution of fractional interests presents both a cumbersome procedure and seemingly undesirable fractional property interests. Even applying a relatively simple fraction like $^{4100}/_{7243}$ to 100 shares of stock indicates the problem, though it is common practice to sell the portion not apportionable in whole shares (with such expense as that involves). Distribution of a similar fractional interest in Greenacre is certainly possible (if not desirable), but it leaves a rather awkward fractional interest in the several devisees, particularly if later disagreement leads to a partition action. Disagreement has been expressed with the conclusion that a fractional share of each asset should be distributed absent specification to the contrary. Some have suggested that the clause could permit selection of assets equivalent to the distribution date value of the fractional share. Yet such selection of specific assets, equal in value, requires a second valuation as of distribution date * * *.

2. "Hybrid" Clauses

Departure from the true fractional share in favor of a ratable-sharing fraction [the share allocated to the surviving spouse is to be fairly representative of appreciation or depreciation in the value of property available for distribution] (satisfiable with selected assets) tends to ameliorate some of the true fractional share's disadvantages, but at the same time some of the orthodox fractional share's posited advantages are lost (thus incurring disadvantages similar to those posed by the pecuniary). Similarly, departure from the orthodox or true pecuniary in favor of one of the several tax-value pecuniary clauses [under which the quantum of assets to be selected to satisfy the marital bequest is determined on the basis of federal estate tax values] tends to pick up, in some measure, advantages associated with the fractional share while modifying or departing from advantageous features of the orthodox pecuniary clause. Neither of the exchanges, however, is even! The degree to which relative advantages and disadvantages are substituted varies with the type of clause used.

a. Minimum–Value Pecuniaries

The tax-value pecuniary employing a minimum-value clause [under which assets distributed in satisfaction of the marital bequest have a distribution date value of not less than the marital deduction allowable] represents a comparatively minor departure from the orthodox pecuniary. In many cases, it will yield quite similar results (except for possible differences in allocation of bases of assets received by the distributee). In other, less typical situations, such as a distribution comprised entirely of appreciated assets, the tax-value clause results in "over-funding" and no capital gain vis-à-vis minimum funding but recognition of capital gain under a true pecuniary. But, in either case, the widow is assured of at least a minimum actual value equal to the allowed marital deduction.

b. Ratable–Sharing Pecuniaries

The ratable-sharing pecuniary, that hybrid using tax values and requiring a sharing of appreciation or depreciation, results in a significantly greater deviation from the true pecuniary. One commentator has summarized its advantages as follows: (1) like the true pecuniary (and fractional-share) "it makes certain that the maximum marital deduction will be available," (2) it eliminates the "constructive sale" possibility and avoids recognition of gains on distribution, (3) the requirement of equitable sharing of appreciation or depreciation during administration avoids the administrative problems posed by a formula (like the true pecuniary) permitting the fiduciary to prefer one beneficiary over another, and (4) the "tax value formula clause requirement of sharing of appreciation or depreciation does not apply to each individual asset but only to the estate as a whole," as distinguished from the true fractional share.

In short, it has the same advantages and disadvantages as a fractional share formula, which permits distribution of selected assets equivalent to the distribution date value of the fractional interest in the residue. But, *in addition*, it presents the additional administrative problem, previously noted, of apparently requiring that at distribution date the assets distributed must have both a federal estate tax value equal to the marital deduction to be obtained and distribution date values representing a ratable sharing of appreciation and depreciation of the pool from which they are drawn. To the jaundiced eye, the acquired disadvantages seem to somewhat outweigh any additional advantages as compared to the true pecuniary, the tax-value minimum-value pecuniary, the true fractional share, and, last *and* least, the "pecuniary fractional share" (permitting distribution of selected assets equal in value to the fractional share of the pool to which the marital share is entitled).

3. *The Ultimate Choice*

* * * Where analysis suggests that it will probably be desirable both to avoid recognition of gain or loss at distribution and to minimize augmentation of the widow's potential estate by channeling appreciation to the residuary trust, the tax-value pecuniary with a minimum-value provision may be useful. In the larger number of estates, where possible recognition of gains is not deemed serious from an overall tax analysis or where the probable composition of estate assets suggests that careful selection of assets for distribution can largely avoid gain on satisfaction of a fixed amount due, the true pecuniary formula may appear best.

Both the minimum-value and the true pecuniary assure the widow of a minimum amount * * *, though a decline in values during administration may significantly reduce the share of assets allocable to the residuary legatees. If this latter point is of major concern to the testator, it might be well to provide pecuniary legacies in the minimum desired dollar amount for both the widow and other beneficiaries, these to be satisfied before application of the formula to the residue.

If, on the other hand, family relationships and circumstances suggest the desirability of ratable-sharing of appreciation and depreciation during administration, it may be suggested that the true, orthodox fractional-share formula should be employed in preference to any of the described hybrid clauses; and the inherent administrative obligations of careful fiduciary accounting and distribution of the available residue according to the determined fraction should be manfully shouldered.

* * * Further, though thoughtful and able commentators may rationally differ, this preliminary analysis suggests that the ratable-sharing tax-value pecuniary formula, regardless of local fiduciary law, may be an unhappy choice absent peculiar circumstances not here considered. Indeed, *should* state law be deemed to require ratable-sharing when a tax-value pecuniary provision is employed, use of the true pecuniary would be preferable to the minimum-value provision.

Revenue Procedure 64–19

1964–1 C.B. (Part 1) 682.

SECTION 1. PURPOSE

The purpose of this Revenue Procedure is to state the position of the Internal Revenue Service relative to allowance of the marital deduction in cases where there is some uncertainty as to the ultimate distribution to be made in payment of a pecuniary bequest or transfer in trust where the governing instrument provides that the executor or trustee may satisfy bequests in kind with assets at their value as finally determined for Federal estate tax purposes.

SECTION 2. BACKGROUND

01. The Internal Revenue Service has received inquiries concerning the amount of the marital deduction which should be allowed for a pecuniary bequest in a will or for a transfer in trust of a pecuniary amount where the governing instrument not only provides that the executor or trustee may, or is required to, select assets in kind to satisfy the bequest or transfer, but also provides that any assets distributed in kind shall be valued at their values as finally determined for Federal estate tax purposes. The question is the same whether the amount of the bequest or transfer is determined by a formula fixing it by reference to the adjusted gross estate of the decedent as finally determined for Federal estate tax purposes, or its amount is determined in some other fashion by which a fixed dollar amount distributable to the surviving spouse can be computed. Any bequest or transfer in trust described in subsection 2.01 is hereinafter referred to as a "pecuniary bequest or transfer" for purposes of this Revenue Procedure.

.02 Where, by virtue of the duties imposed on the fiduciary either by applicable state law or by the express or implied provisions of the instrument, it is clear that the fiduciary, in order to implement such a bequest or transfer, must distribute assets, including cash, having an aggregate fair market value at the date, or dates, of distribution amounting to no less than the amount of the pecuniary bequest or transfer, as finally determined for Federal estate tax purposes, the marital deduction may be allowed in the full amount of the pecuniary bequest or transfer in trust. Alternatively, where, by virtue of such duties, it is clear that the fiduciary must distribute assets including cash, fairly representative of appreciation or depreciation in the value of all property thus available for distribution in satisfaction of such pecuniary bequest or transfer, the marital deduction is equally determinable and may be allowed in the full amount of the pecuniary bequest or transfer in trust passing to the surviving spouse.

.03 In many instances, however, by virtue of the provisions of the will or trust, or by virtue of applicable state law (or because of an absence of applicable state decisions), it may not be clear that the discretion of the fiduciary would be limited in this respect, and it cannot be determined that he would be required to make distribution in conformance with one or the other of the above requirements or that one rather than the other is applicable. In such a case, the interest in property passing from the decedent to his surviving spouse would not be ascertainable as of the date of death, if the property available for distribution included assets which might fluctuate in value. * * *

SECTION 4. SCOPE

.01 The problem here considered is restricted to the situation involving bequests and transfers in trust described in sections 1 and 2.01. It does not arise in other cases, for example:

(1) In a bequest or transfer in trust of a fractional share of the estate, under which each beneficiary shares proportionately in the appreciation or depreciation in the value of assets to the date, or dates, of distribution.

(2) In a bequest or transfer in trust of specific assets.

(3) In a pecuniary bequest or transfer in trust, whether in a stated amount or an amount computed by the use of a formula, if:

(a) The fiduciary must satisfy the pecuniary bequest or transfer in trust solely in cash, or

(b) The fiduciary has no discretion in the selection of the assets to be distributed in kind, or

(c) Assets selected by the fiduciary to be distributed in kind in satisfaction of the bequest or transfer in trust are required to be valued at their respective values on the date, or dates, of their distribution. * * *

ILLUSTRATIVE MATERIAL

A.   FIDUCIARY DISCRETION IN SATISFYING MARITAL BEQUEST

Rev.Rul. 60–87, 1960–1 C.B. 286, held that the funding of a pecuniary bequest with property having a fair market value different from its basis may constitute a taxable exchange for income tax purposes because the surviving spouse's right to receive a specified dollar amount is satisfied in kind. In an attempt to avoid this income tax consequence of funding pecuniary marital bequests, draftsmen devised a pecuniary formula which required the assets comprising the marital share to be valued at the date the marital share was funded at their estate tax value and permitted the marital share to be funded with assets in kind to be selected by the executor. This type of pecuniary formula became widely used. It also raised two potential tax issues which may be illustrated by the following example.

Assume the decedent's will specified a marital bequest of an amount equal to one-half of the decedent's adjusted gross estate. Assume further that at date of death the adjusted gross estate was $2,000,000 and that, at the date of distribution, assets worth $1,000,000 at the date of death have depreciated in value to $750,000 whereas the balance of the assets have appreciated in value to $1,250,000. If the trustee satisfied the marital bequest by transferring to the spouse all the assets which depreciated in value, the estate avoided recognition of gain on the distribution and the surviving spouse received property less in value than the marital deduction claimed. If the surviving spouse then died without further change in the value of the property distributed pursuant to the marital bequest, the share of appreciation attributable to those assets which could have formed a portion of the pecuniary marital bequest but were not distributed escaped tax in the estate of both the decedent and the surviving spouse.

Rev.Proc. 64–19, which was the product of negotiations between the Internal Revenue Service and representatives of the American Bar Association, attempts to cure these problems. With regard to instruments executed prior to October 1, 1964, both the executor and the surviving spouse must execute agreements the effect of which is to require the pecuniary bequest to be satisfied by a fair mix of appreciated or depreciated property so that the distribution pursuant to the pecuniary bequest approximates that of a fractional share. However, the marital deduction will not be allowed as to this form of pecuniary formula bequest if contained in instruments executed after that date. After that date, the pecuniary formula bequest must either require the executor to distribute assets in a mix which approximates a fractional share or to satisfy the bequest by a distribution of assets the value of which is determined at the date of distribution.

The position stated in Rev.Proc. 64–19 is in accord with the Commissioner's argument in Estate of Hamelsky v. Commissioner, 58 T.C. 741 (1972), that a pecuniary bequest of the type found in Rev.Proc. 64–19, § 2.01, failed to qualify for the marital deduction because the power in the executor to diminish or defeat the marital bequest by distributing depreciated assets to the surviving spouse constituted a terminable interest. The court held that the bequest qualified for the marital deduction because under both local law and the decedent's will the executor was under a fiduciary duty analogous to that described in § 2.02 of Rev.Proc. 64–19 to distribute assets fairly representative of appreciation and depreciation.

In Rev.Rul. 90–3, 1990–1 C.B. 174, decedent's estate was valued at $900,000 on March 1, 1987, the date of death. The estate incurred $50,000 of deductible expenses. The will contained a pecuniary bequest of $600,000 to child, with the residue to surviving spouse. As a result of the stock market crash of October 1987, the value of the estate declined by $200,000 and remained at approximately that level until January 18, 1989, the date of distribution. Local law required that the assets used to satisfy the pecuniary bequest be valued at the date of payment. The surviving spouse received approximately $50,000, rather than the $250,000 value of the residue at the date of death. The Service noted that a marital deduction generally is allowed under Rev.Proc. 64–19 where a pecuniary bequest to the surviving spouse is satisfied with assets valued at the distribution date. The Service extended this principle in Rev.Rul. 90–3 where the surviving spouse does not receive the pecuniary bequest. The Service ruled that "[i]f a pecuniary bequest is required to be paid with assets valued at the time of payment, the possibility that post death fluctuations in the fair market value of estate assets may diminish the residuary bequest to the surviving spouse does not cause the residuary bequest to be a nondeductible terminable interest." As a result, the $900,000 value reported as the gross estate would be offset by the $250,000 marital deduction, even though the value of both had declined by $200,000.

In the case of a fractional formula bequest, the share of the decedent's estate ultimately received by the surviving spouse will, by definition, reflect any changes in the market value of the assets comprising that share between the valuation date and the date the marital bequest is actually funded. Thus the estate tax abuse to which Rev.Proc. 64–19 is directed does not occur. Furthermore, because the surviving spouse is not entitled to a specific dollar amount which is satisfied by the funding of the marital bequest, the distribution of assets to fund the marital share does not result in income recognition to the trust.

SECTION C. THE GIFT TAX MARITAL DEDUCTION

Internal Revenue Code: § 2523

Regulations: § 25.2523

The introduction of the marital deduction into the estate tax was necessarily accompanied by a correlative revision in the gift tax. Thus, for inter-spousal gifts of non-community property made before 1977, the gift tax marital deduction was one-half the value of the property transferred. For transfers made after 1976 and before 1982, § 2523 allowed a gift tax marital deduction to the extent of the full value of the first $100,000 of post–1976 gifts of non-community property to a spouse, no deduction for the next $100,000 of such gifts, and a deduction of 50% of the value of such gifts in excess of $200,000. The Economic Recovery Tax Act of 1981 removed all quantitative limitations on the amount of the gift tax marital deduction. Accordingly, the full value of any qualifying inter-spousal transfer occurring after 1981 in either a separate or community property state is eligible for the gift tax marital deduction.

The wording of the gift tax provisions closely parallels that of the estate tax in defining the type of interest which will qualify for the marital deduction and the provisions are interpreted in the same manner. However, there are important differences between the two.

First, the donor is the person who must elect the gift tax deduction for a transfer of qualified terminable interest property. The election is made on a gift tax return for the calendar year in which the interest was transferred. In contrast, the decedent's executor elects QTIP treatment on the estate tax return.

Second, the terminable interest rule has been broadened in the gift tax to reach the more divergent types of transfers possible through an inter vivos gift. Section 2523(b)(1) disallows a marital deduction for a transfer of property in which the donor-spouse has retained an interest which may ripen into possession or enjoyment at the termination of the donee-spouse's interest. Statutory exceptions are made to this rule for transfers of life estates with a power of appointment (§ 2523(e)), transfers of qualified terminable interest property (§ 2523(f)), transfers of income interests in charitable remainder trusts (§ 2523(g)), and for transfers where the only interest retained by the donor arises from a right of survivorship in a joint tenancy or tenancy by the entirety, but then only if the two spouses are the sole tenants (§ 2523(d)). Section 2523(b)(2) disallows the deduction if the donor retains a power, exercisable alone or together with any person at any time whatsoever or on the occurrence or non-occurrence of any contingency, to create another interest in such manner as to convert the donee spouse's interest into a terminable interest. Thus, no gift tax marital deduction is available for a transfer of property in which the donor retains the right to appoint the property at or after the death of the donee spouse.

Third, there is no provision in the gift tax parallel to § 2056(b)(6) of the estate tax, permitting the deduction with respect to the proceeds of life insurance, endowment and annuity policies held by an insurance company where the surviving spouse is given a power of appointment. However, an interest of this kind would appear to be within the ambit of § 2523(e).

Fourth, the gift tax has been decoupled from the estate tax since 2004, with a lower gift tax exemption ($1 million) compared to the estate tax exemption ($1.5 million in 2004–05; $2 million in 2006–08; and $3.5 million in 2009), followed by a one-year repeal of the estate tax (but not the gift tax) in 2010 until the gift tax and estate are recoupled in 2011 and thereafter with a common $1 million exemption.

SECTION D. SPLIT GIFTS

Internal Revenue Code: § 2513

Regulations: § 25.2513

As indicated previously, a gift of community property is considered a gift of one-half the property by each spouse. As an historical matter, in order to permit equivalent treatment with respect to non-community property § 2513 was enacted to provide that, if a husband and wife consent[15] to so treat all gifts made by either of them during a calendar

---

15. Each spouse must "signify" consent to gift splitting, which is done by signing the gift tax return. However, the failure of a spouse to sign a gift tax return in the space indicating consent will not bar gift splitting if such consent can otherwise be determined from the return. Jones v. Commissioner, 327 F.2d 98 (4th Cir.1964).

If only one spouse makes gifts during a reporting period, only that spouse is required to file a gift tax return (the other spouse consents to gift splitting on the return filed

year,[16] a gift to a third party shall be considered as a gift of one-half the property by each spouse.[17] The abandonment in 1981 of the community property model for marital transfers renders § 2513 conceptually unnecessary. Spouses may achieve the same result by two transfers: first, a transfer by one spouse to the other of one-half of the property followed by a transfer by the donee-spouse to the ultimate recipient of the property. Retention of § 2513 eliminates the need for the intervening transfer and precludes attributing the gift entirely to the transferor spouse on the ground of an agreement by the transferee spouse to make the transfer to the ultimate donee.

Each spouse must be either a citizen or resident of the United States in order to split gifts. Splitting is not available if, after the gift and during the calendar year, a spouse dies or a divorce occurs and either spouse remarries. Splitting is available only as to gifts made during marriage. Consequently gifts made during the calendar year in which marriage occurs, but before marriage, or by a surviving spouse during the calendar year in which the other spouse dies but after such death, may not be split. Rev.Rul. 55–506, 1955–2 C.B. 609.

A new consent is required for each calendar year. The consent must be given prior to the 15th day of April following the close of the calendar year for which a return is due or prior to the time a gift tax return is filed by either spouse, whichever is later,[18] and consent may not be given after a notice of deficiency has been sent to either spouse for the year in question. § 2513(b)(2); Reg. § 25.2513–2(a). A consent made by a timely filed return may only be revoked prior to the due date of the return for the calendar year in which the gift was made. § 2513(c); Reg. § 25.2513–3. The consent may be given by the executor of a deceased donor for gifts made prior to death. Reg. § 25.2513–2(c); Rev.Rul. 55–506. If no executor or administrator is appointed the surviving spouse may give consent. Rev.Rul. 67–55, 1967–1 C.B. 278. Consent may be given by one spouse for the other, if the latter is unable to consent because of illness, absence, or non-residence, provided the consent is ratified within a reasonable time after the spouse is able to do so. Rev.Rul. 54–6, 1954–1 C.B. 205.

Once consent is given, the liability of each spouse for the gift taxes of both spouses for the entire reporting period is joint and several. § 2513(d). Because each spouse is jointly and severally liable for the entire gift tax the

---

by the donor spouse) so long as the total gifts to each third party donee since the beginning of the calendar year do not exceed $20,000 and no portion of the property which is given constitutes a future interest. Reg. § 25.2513–1(c).

16. Splitting is not permitted if either spouse retains a general power of appointment over the property transferred. Reg. § 25.2513–1(b)(3).

17. Where a spouse transfers property in part to the other spouse and in part to third parties, gift splitting is available only insofar as the gift to third parties is ascertainable at the time of the gift. Reg. § 25.2513–1(b)(4).

18. If a gift tax return on which consent has not been signified is filed, an amended return on which consent is signified filed after the due date of the return for the reporting period in which the gift was made will not be effective to permit gift splitting. Clark v. Commissioner, 65 T.C. 126 (1975); Rev.Rul. 80–224, 1980–2 C.B. 281.

payment by a spouse of the other spouse's gift tax will not be treated as a gift by the spouse paying the tax. Reg. § 25.2511–(d). However, if a spouse dies within three years of the date of a gift to which such spouse has consented, the amount of gift tax, if any, paid by the consenting spouse will be included in that spouse's gross estate under § 2035(b) (because the consenting spouse's estate has been depleted by the amount of the tax paid). The amount of the gift deemed made by the consenting spouse is not a gift by that spouse for purposes of § 2035 (because the consenting spouse's estate has not been depleted by giving the consent). However, the consenting spouse will be treated as having made an adjusted taxable gift of one-half the value of the gift. Thus, the consenting spouse's cumulative transfer tax base will include the adjusted taxable gift, with a credit effectively granted under § 2001(b)(1)(B) for the gift tax paid on that gift. Where the consenting spouse dies within three years of the transfer, the transferor spouse subsequently dies within that time, and the transfer is included in full in the estate of the transferor, the consenting spouse's estate is entitled to a refund of the tax attributable to the adjusted taxable gift resulting from the consent to split gifts. § 2001(e); Rev.Rul. 81–85, 1981–1 C.B. 452. Similarly, no portion of a split gift is an adjusted taxable gift in the estate of a non-donor spouse where the donor spouse predeceased the consenting spouse, both spouses died within three years of the transfer, and the gift was included in the gross estate of the donor spouse under § 2035. Rev.Rul. 82–198, 1982–2 C.B. 206. The purpose of § 2001(e) is to prevent the inclusion of any part of a split gift in the transfer tax base of the consenting spouse when the full amount of the gift is includible in the gross estate of the transferor.

A guardian or personal representative may consent for an incompetent or deceased spouse, if they have authority under state law to give the consent. In many cases, the filing of the consent exposes the decedent's or incompetent's estate to the payment of a gift tax for which it would not otherwise be liable, such as where only the surviving spouse made gifts during the reporting period immediately preceding death or incompetence. A number of states have enacted statutes specifically authorizing a guardian of an incompetent spouse or the personal representative of a deceased spouse to give the consent required by § 2513, but only after receiving court approval of this action. However, a decedent by will can prohibit such an action. Furthermore, it would seem that where an executor arbitrarily refused to consent to gift splitting under § 2513, a court would intervene to compel the consent. In re Estate of Floyd, 76 D. & C. 597 (Orphans' Ct., Del. County, Pa. 1951).

SECTION E.   PLANNING CONSIDERATIONS

1.   OBJECTIVES OF ESTATE PLANNING

Estate planning for spouses is not a mechanical task. Its principal purpose is to satisfy the dispositive objectives of the parties. Psychological and financial security for the surviving spouse may be the paramount concern. Other potential major considerations may include preservation of spousal wealth for the benefit of younger generations. Control over the ultimate disposition of the separate property of each spouse also may be an important factor. The question of tax minimization does not arise until these objectives have been properly identified. At that point the estate planner will attempt to achieve these objectives at the least tax cost.

This is not to say that tax minimization techniques do not play an important role in estate planning. Indeed, when the potential tax savings of a particular alternative are discussed, the parties may well adjust their objectives. However, the conscientious advisor must be sensitive to the fact that tax minimization is frequently not the principal objective of the parties.

2.   THE ECONOMICS OF TAX MINIMIZATION

The graduated transfer tax rate structure applies to the transfer tax base of each spouse separately. Therefore, the lowest aggregate amount of transfer tax is paid when the marginal rate of tax on the last transfer of each spouse is the same. This result is often called "estate equalization." Implicit in "estate equalization" is the assumption that the estate of each spouse has utilized its exemption equivalent to the extent possible or necessary to avoid payment of any transfer tax. However, while estate equalization may result in the least amount of aggregate transfer tax, it may not maximize the wealth available for use by the spousal generation, because if no tax is paid when the first spouse dies, more is available for the benefit of the surviving spouse. Moreover, the saved taxes may be invested; and if invested profitably for long enough, the profits may exceed the increased estate tax their inclusion will cause in the estate of the second spouse. The concept of saving tax now, investing the saved taxes, and then paying tax on the saved tax plus its unconsumed growth is known as "deferral." "Maximum deferral" describes a bequest which passes to the surviving spouse all the property owned by the decedent in excess of the deductions and credits available to the estate.

Prior to the 2001 Act, commentators vigorously debated the relative advantages and disadvantages of the "estate equalization" and "maximum deferral" approaches. Compare Pennell & Williamson, The Economics of Prepaying Wealth Transfer Taxes, Tr. & Est., June 1997, at 49 (favoring "estate equalization" approach), with Christensen, The Wisdom of Deferring Estate Taxes, Tr. & Est., Aug. 1997 (favoring "maximum deferral" approach).[19]

Supporters of estate equalization argued that it could result in more property in the hands of the succeeding generation at the death of the surviving spouse. But the assumptions made in reaching that conclusion

---

19. For detailed numerical examples highlighting the pros and cons of the "estate equalization" and "maximum deferral" ap-proaches, see McDaniel, Repetti & Caron, Federal Wealth Transfer Taxation 687–89 (4th ed, 1999).

were critical and depended upon educated guesses as to the rate of growth of assets, their income yield, the income tax rate at which they will be taxed, the estate tax rate which will apply to the surviving spouse, and the rate of consumption of both income and principal by the surviving spouse and residuary beneficiaries. Of course, these factors could not be predicted precisely. Thus, the choice among maximum deferral, estate equalization, or something in between often turned on other considerations.

The advantages of maximum deferral included the psychological benefit that no tax is due upon the death of the first spouse, elimination of potential liquidity problems at that time, provision of a larger pool of assets specifically dedicated to the support of the surviving spouse, and the opportunity to receive a new income tax basis at the death of the recipient spouse. But maximum deferral also could produce its own problems. There could be liquidity difficulties at the death of the surviving spouse. Unless an estate trust is used, the income from the entire marital bequest must be distributed currently to the surviving spouse and thus taxable at rates higher than those which would have applied had a more flexible approach been used. Unconsumed appreciation and income will be subject to estate tax at the death of the surviving spouse. Only the amount of the exemption equivalent would be available for the decedent to pass to the next generation either outright or beneficially before the death of the surviving spouse. And, unless a qualified terminable interest property trust was used, the surviving spouse would have the right to control the ultimate disposition of all the property received from the decedent.

In practice, then, an assessment of the foregoing considerations, rather than pure mathematical analysis, in most cases controlled the form and amount of the marital bequest.

The 2001 Act, however, ended all debate. With the uncertainty surrounding the scheduled repeal of the estate tax in 2010, followed by its return in 2011, any potential tax savings from equalizing estates by enlarging the estate of the first spouse to die would be dwarfed by the additional tax incurred in the estate of the first spouse if the second spouse were to die in a year for which either the estate tax is not in effect or the estate tax exemption equivalent is reduced below the level in effect during the year of the first spouse's death.

3. TECHNIQUES TO ACHIEVE MARITAL DEDUCTION OBJECTIVES

The marital deduction objectives of the parties may be met in part by inter vivos transfers and in part by testamentary transfers. For example, because one principal objective is to assure that where the aggregate assets of the spouses exceed the exemption equivalent, each spouse should have assets sufficient to absorb the individual exemption equivalent no matter who dies first. The estate plans of the spouses must also provide for the disposition of this exemption equivalent amount in a manner which will not cause inclusion in the estate of the surviving spouse. Failure to so provide will lose the benefits of "estate splitting." This objective can be accomplished by testamentary gifts of the exemption equivalent amount outright or in trust for beneficiaries other than the surviving spouse, or even to a trust of which the surviving spouse is a beneficiary, so long as the trust is neither a QTIP trust for which deductible treatment has been elected nor a trust over which the surviving spouse is granted a general power of appointment.

Where maximum deferral is sought, inter vivos giving in excess of the amount needed to assure maximum use of both exemption equivalents is not necessary. However, income tax considerations may suggest larger inter vivos gifts. If the wealthier spouse has retained the property and is the first to die, the property will receive a new income tax basis in the hands of the surviving spouse. On the other hand, if it appears that the less wealthy spouse will likely be the first to die, lifetime gifts of appreciated property may achieve income tax basis step-up at no transfer tax cost.[20]

Some have suggested that separately owned property be put in joint names to augment the estate of the less wealthy spouse and assure that the property returns to the donor if he or she survives. There is no transfer tax disincentive to the creation of joint tenancies between spouses. However, joint interests are an inflexible planning tool. Upon the death of one joint tenant, the property will automatically pass to the survivor. Moreover, only one-half the income tax basis of the property in the hands of the surviving spouse will be determined by its estate tax value because only one-half the value of the property will be included in the estate of the first to die.

When planning for testamentary marital transfers the advisor must determine the appropriate form for the bequest. The transfer may be outright or in trust. If in trust, the trust may be a § 2056(b)(5) power of appointment trust, a § 2056(b)(7) QTIP trust, a § 2056(b)(8) "marital-charitable" trust, an estate trust, or some combination of the available forms. The appropriate form depends upon the parties' objectives. Power of appointment and estate trusts grant the surviving spouse the right to control disposition of the property. As between these two options, the estate trust offers a limited amount of post-mortem income tax planning flexibility because the income need not be distributed currently. The power of appointment trust, while requiring current income distribution, allows the decedent spouse to determine who will succeed to the property if the surviving spouse fails to appoint the property. But if ultimate control over the disposition of the property is an objective and current income distribution is not an obstacle, the QTIP trust is generally the appropriate vehicle.

Post-mortem flexibility to determine the appropriate marital deduction bequest may also be an objective. There are two basic planning tools. First, assuming an election is available to treat only a portion of a QTIP trust as deductible, the use of such trusts to fund all or a portion of the marital bequest leaves the executor with the power to determine the size of the marital bequest. Second, disclaimers provide the surviving spouse or other beneficiaries the opportunity to adjust the size of the marital share.

---

20. If the donee spouse dies within one year of the gift and the property returns to or for the benefit of the donor, § 1014(e) denies a basis change.

However, to assure maximum utility of the disclaimer as a post-mortem estate planning tool, the will of the decedent should provide direction as to where the disclaimed property will go. For example, if property disclaimed by the surviving spouse passes to a residuary trust in which the surviving spouse has an income interest and a special power of appointment, the disclaimer is not a "qualified disclaimer" unless the surviving spouse also disclaims the power of appointment over the residuary trust. This problem may be avoided by providing that property disclaimed by the surviving spouse shall pass to a trust in which the surviving spouse has only an income interest (and/or a corpus interest which is determined by trustees other than the surviving spouse).

Where the amount of the marital bequest is to be stated as a formula amount (e.g., x% of the decedent's gross estate or that amount which, when all deductions and credits available to the decedent's estate are taken into account, produces no tax on that estate), a further decision must be made as to whether the formula should be expressed as a pecuniary or fractional share bequest.

A complete marital deduction analysis must also include consideration of the effect of state death taxes. In jurisdictions which have not adopted the Federal marital deduction, a maximum deferral bequest may result in state taxes in an amount that significantly depletes or even eliminates the residuary bequest.

4.   THE TASK OF THE ESTATE PLANNER

It is appropriate to conclude a discussion on the estate planning aspects of the marital deduction as it began—with a warning. Tax considerations should not divert the advisor from the very human problems which undergird and may sometimes frustrate the most precise tax planning. For example, suppose that the tax advisor suggests that it would be appropriate for the wealthier spouse to transfer to the less wealthy spouse an amount equal to the exemption equivalent. This sound tax advice may be frustrated in the event of a subsequent divorce of the parties. How should the tax advisor communicate this possibility and its consequences to, and evaluate it for, the clients? As another matter, it cannot be safely assumed, of course, that the spouse whose death is presumed to occur first in the computations will in fact die first. In this instance, the tax planner must prepare an alternative set of calculations which show to the clients the transfer tax results if the proposed dispositive arrangements are undertaken and the order of deaths is reversed. Another obviously delicate problem for the tax advisor is to be sure that both spouses have contemplated the possibility of remarriage of the surviving spouse because an estate plan that appears attractive from a tax standpoint may lose its appeal to a spouse who envisions a significant amount of his or her property winding up in the hands of a new spouse rather than in the present family. No mathematical calculation can capture these intangible factors. But they are as important in planning marital deduction bequests as are the correct computations of the benefits of tax minimization or tax deferral.

SECTION F.   POLICY ISSUES

ILLUSTRATIVE MATERIAL

A.   THE TAXABLE UNIT

One of the structural decisions that is required to be made in the development of a normative transfer tax is the unit upon which the tax will be imposed. In the case of single persons, of course, the individual is the taxable unit and donative transfers from that unit are subject to transfer taxation. In the case of married couples, the issue is whether each spouse is to be regarded as a separate taxable unit, so that all transfers by either spouse should be subject to tax, or whether the spouses together constitute a single taxable unit and only transfers from that unit should be subject to tax.

Different countries may reach different conclusions about whether a marital couple constitutes one or two taxable units for transfer tax purposes. Generally, the decision appears to rest on the non-tax views that the country holds with respect to marital rights and relationships, the gender pattern of the holdings of wealth, and on marriage itself. Adoption of a transfer tax system as such does not compel as a structural matter the adoption of any particular view of the marital unit for transfer tax purposes. It is necessary that, once a decision has been made as to the appropriate unit, the implementing technical rules conform to that decision and do not create tax preferences or tax penalties through provisions that depart from or are internally inconsistent with the basic decision.

The Economic Recovery Tax Act of 1981 abandoned the community property model as the determinant of the taxable unit and moved in the direction of regarding a married couple as a single taxpaying unit for transfer tax purposes. If the marital unit is the appropriate taxable unit, only transfers out of that unit should be subjected to transfer taxation. Transfers between spouses would be disregarded because these all occur within the taxable unit. The 1981 Act stopped short of fully treating the marital unit as a single taxable unit because all transfers by either or both of the spouses out of the marital unit were not cumulated to determine the rate applicable to any given transfer. Instead, each spouse is regarded as a separate taxable unit as to transfers to persons other than the transferor's spouse. Moreover, continued applicability of the terminable interest rule means that transfers of non-qualifying interests in property between spouses remain subject to transfer tax. For a discussion of the issues involved in treating the spousal unit as a single taxable unit for purposes of the transfer tax and simplifying the terminable interest rule, see Gutman, Reforming Federal Wealth Transfer Taxation after ERTA, 69 Va.L.Rev. 1183, 1218–40, 1253–59 (1983).

*

PART VII

THE TAXATION OF TRANSFERS FROM GENERATION TO GENERATION

THE GENERATION–SKIPPING TAX AND THE CREDIT FOR TAX ON PRIOR TRANSFERS

SECTION A.   THE CONCEPT OF PERIODICITY IN A TRANSFER TAX

There are several policy reasons for imposing a transfer tax on every generation. First, the concept of horizontal equity in a normative transfer tax requires that two taxable units, each transferring the same amount of wealth, pay the same amount of transfer tax. To achieve this, a tax should be imposed on transfers of property at least once each generation. If a given amount of wealth is, under one family arrangement, subjected to the transfer tax on three occasions over a one-hundred year period and another family's wealth of equal amount is taxed only once every hundred years, the two family accumulations are treated inequitably as compared to one another. While complete equity in the frequency of imposition is not achievable in a transfer tax based in part on transfers at death, fairness requires some approximation of equivalence.

If transfers are not taxed each generation, it is also difficult to achieve progressivity, which is a form of vertical equity. Usually, only very large estates can make transfers that skip generations, i.e., that transfer wealth from grandparents to grandchildren. It is likely that the smaller estates generally cannot make such transfers because intervening generations will need the principal. Since the tax-saving possibility in generation-skipping transfers ("GSTs") increase as the estate becomes larger, such transfers may reduce or eliminate progressivity.

Finally, the opportunity to avoid transfer tax through GSTs creates an incentive to dispose of property in a tax-minimizing manner. The transfer tax system should intrude as little as possible on non-tax decisions with respect to the form chosen to transmit wealth. A tax preference for GSTs creates an incentive to use tax-minimizing forms of disposition even if the transferor's property would be transferred in a different way absent the tax benefits.

The generation-skipping tax is designed to redress these problems.

1.   THE SITUATION PRIOR TO THE TAX REFORM ACT OF 1976

Prior to the Tax Reform Act of 1976, wealthy transferors could easily avoid the imposition of the transfer tax for one or more generations. For example, if an individual had a taxable estate of $10,000,000 and left it outright to her two children equally, the estate tax under the rates then applicable would have been about $6,000,000 and her children would each have received $2,000,000. Assuming that the children then lived on the income from their inheritances without consuming principal, each of their estates would have paid an estate tax of about $750,000 when the property passed to their children, so that the latter would, in total, have inherited $2,500,000 of their grandparent's wealth. On the other hand, the grandparent could have left her estate in trust, the income going to the children with the remainder to the grandchildren. Under this arrangement, her estate would still have paid an estate tax of $6,000,000, the same as in the first case, but the estate tax on the death of the children would have been entirely avoided. The grandchildren would therefore have inherited $4,000,000 of that grandparent's wealth. The amount passing to the grandchildren would be over 50 percent greater in the second case than in the first, although the effect of the two transactions over the two generations was otherwise essentially the same. This effect could be enhanced by using transfers which kept property in trust for more than one generation and thereby avoided the transfer tax on more than one intervening death. But skipping one or more generations for estate tax purposes did not involve skipping generations as far as enjoyment of the assets was concerned. An intermediate beneficiary, while alive, could enjoy the income, control investments, obtain principal needed for her support, control the disposition of income and principal to persons other than herself, and even be able to withdraw the greater of $5,000 or 5 percent of the principal annually during her lifetime—all without incurring estate or gift taxes except as to the amount of principal she could have withdrawn for herself at the moment of death, i.e., the greater of $5,000 or 5 percent of the principal. (See p. 358 for a discussion of the treatment of powers to withdraw the greater of $5,000 or 5 percent of principal.)

Transfers that avoided the tax on intervening generations could be made in several forms. The simplest involved an outright transfer from grandparent to grandchild. No tax would be paid upon the death of the child even though normal devolution patterns would have passed the property from generation to generation. As a second variant, the grandparent could transfer property to a child for life, remainder to a grandchild. Again, no transfer tax would be imposed upon the death of the child even though he may have been given quite extensive powers over the property. This "life estate-remainder" technique could be used to avoid transfer tax for an even longer period by granting the grandchild a life estate upon the death of the child, the remainder to a great-grandchild (assuming the applicable rules against perpetuities were satisfied). Still greater flexibility could be obtained by using a trust with discretionary power in the trustee to benefit one or more intervening generations before ultimate disposition to a remote generation.

The techniques used by tax advisors to effect generation-skipping transfers—and the resulting effects on tax equity—were graphically described in Casner, ESTATE AND GIFT TAX CHANGES, 103 Trusts and Estates 932 (1964). This article, part of which is quoted below, also provides a useful summary of other estate planning devices we have discussed in prior chapters:

"In discussing a problem in connection with the drafting of wills which may lead to some consideration for change in the not too distant future, I would like to develop it by assuming a conversation that I might have had with a client who wanted to have his will made and said simply, 'I want a very simple will. I want the property to go to my son outright. I have complete confidence in him and in his ability to deal with it.'

"Let us assume that A is our client, aged 75, and S is his son, aged 50, and that the amount of the property that would reach S's hands after the tax debt has been paid would be $250,000. I pointed out to A that the income from this $250,000 will be taxed to S on top of whatever other income he may acquire, and that if S ever sells the property and it has appreciated in value, the capital gain will be taxed to S.

"I further pointed out to A that when his son dies, assuming that there has been no change in value and eliminating a number of other factors that might enter the picture, S would pay $65,700 in taxes to move this $250,000 to his child. Then if S's child on his death leaves the property outright to his child, the grandchild of S, there will be another $45,000 plus in taxes. As a result of following out this plan of outright giving, therefore, A's $250,000 would have decreased by somewhere around 45% by the time it reached S's grandchild.

"That realization shook A a bit and he asked, 'Is there any way we can arrange this to avoid this depreciation?'

"I said, 'Yes. It isn't necessary to pay that tax as the property passes from S to his child and then to the grandchild, if you don't want to. In your will we can transfer this $250,000 to a trustee to pay the income to your son for his lifetime. Then we can provide that on his death the trustee will pay the income to his child for life. We can further provide that on the death of the child the property will go outright to S's grandchild at whatever age we decide he should be able to get it into his hands.'

" 'Well,' A said, 'that is quite a different arrangement from what I had in mind. It is not at all similar to give my son just the income from the trust for life instead of the complete ownership.'

"I agreed with him but suggested we could modify this idea and still accomplish our goal. I said, 'First, suppose we put S in as the trustee. Now he has the property and he is managing it just as he would if he owned it outright. He would decide when to sell it and what to reinvest the proceeds in as he would if he owned it.'

"A said, 'That certainly helps, if it can be done and the result not changed. Is there any more you can do to get the plan a little bit more like what I had in mind when I came in?'

"I said, 'Yes. We can add a power in your son by his will to appoint the property in any way he wants, to anyone except himself, his estate, his creditors, and the creditors of his estate.'

"He said, 'You mean when he dies he can have practically the same control as to where the property would go on his death as if he owned it outright except that he just can't appoint it to his estate or creditors of his estate?'

" 'Yes, the law allows that.'

" 'Well,' A said, 'that is getting pretty close now to what I had in mind because I have a feeling that I would like my son to decide on his death where the property will go in the light of conditions that then exist, and he ought to be in a position to take it away from his children if they haven't shown him the proper parental affection, etc., just as he could if he owned it. Is there anything more you could do?'

" 'Yes,' I continued, 'We can give your son a power by deed, exercisable any time during his lifetime, to appoint this property to anyone but himself, his estate, his creditors, or the creditors of his estate. So that if, during his lifetime, he wants to give it to his children he can do so and not have to pay any gift tax. The *Self* case[1] held that this kind of power was a limited power to appoint and its exercise was not subject to gift tax. It is true that the Treasury Department does not agree with the case on one point and would contend that your son was at least making a gift of his life interest in the property that he has appointed.[2] However, this issue does not affect the saving of the tax on your son's death.'

" 'The only thing I see wrong with this now,' A remarked, 'is that you haven't provided for my son to get his hands on any of the money during his lifetime if he should need the principal, which he could do if I gave it to him outright.'

" 'Well,' I said, 'we can do something about that without changing our estate tax result. We can give your son a power to invade the corpus during his lifetime to any extent that may be necessary for his health, education, support, or general maintenance. The law says he can have that kind of power and, when he does what is left will pass on without any delay. So, if he doesn't need the principal as long as he lives, it will be there, and we will save this $65,000 which otherwise we would have to pay if we gave it outright as you first suggested.'

" 'Well,' A went on, 'that is amazing. Now, is there anything more we can do because I would like my son to be able to get his hands on the money if he wanted to without this standard that you have been talking about.'

---

1. [ED.: 142 F.Supp. 939 (Ct.Cl.1956). The *Self* case is discussed at p. 376.]

2. [ED.: The Tax Court adopted the Treasury's view in Regester v. Commissioner, 83 T.C. 1 (1984). The *Regester* case is discussed at p. 376.]

" 'Yes,' I answered. 'We can give your son a power to withdraw annually $5,000 or 5% of the corpus, whichever is greater, and the mere existence of this power will upset our plans only to the extent that in the year in which he dies we will have to include in his estate for estate tax purposes the amount that was still withdrawable in that year. It would not be a tax on $250,000, but only on the $5,000 or 5% figure. And he can have that non-cumulative power every year to draw down that amount.'

" 'Well,' he said, 'that just about does it. That is just about what I had in mind. Is there anything more that you might like to suggest to me?'

" 'Yes. It may be that your son will get into a position where he needs more than $5,000 or 5%, whichever is greater. So we can put in as another trustee, along with your son, a person who has no interest under the trust and we can give that trustee the power to pay him the whole principal any time he wants to, in his uncontrolled discretion.'

"He said, 'Can we pick who the trustee will be?'

" 'Yes, we can pick the trustee. The only thing is that he must approach his job honestly and not agree ahead of time what he is going to do and he must not have an interest under the trust. We are not involved here with the so-called related and subordinate trustee problem, which comes up only in connection with the taxation of income to the creator of a trust while such creator is alive.'

"So he said, 'I think that would be a good idea. We have confidence in So-and-So. We will put him in as a co-trustee and give him the power to pay the principal over and above the $5,000 or 5% without regard to the standard you mentioned if that trustee in his uncontrolled discretion decides that the principal should be paid to my son.'

"Virtual Ownership

"The purpose of going through this story is to show how close, under present law, you can come to what the client has in mind of giving the property outright to his son and yet save the $65,000 that otherwise would go in taxes on the son's death. In a situation of this sort it is difficult to justify spending the $65,000 when you can do all these things under present law and come that close to total ownership.

"We can provide, of course, that in default of the exercise of these powers by S the trust will go for his child and we can set up the same powers for his child, so that when he dies, the property can go on to the grandchild, thus saving the $45,000 that otherwise would be paid in taxes at that time. And we can keep on doing this, for the grandchild, for the grandchild's child, and on and on, if you are in Wisconsin, which has no rule against perpetuities as to certain kinds of arrangements.

"Even in any other state that is governed by the common law rule against perpetuities, we can have the arrangement continue until 21 years after the death of the survivor of ten healthy babies selected from families of good longevity, so that we can be fairly certain the trust will be operating, before the property falls into the hands of someone outright, for as much as 100 years or more, and even then the fund won't be subjected to an estate tax until the one into whose hands it finally falls dies, which may be 40 or 50 years later.

"In other words, the estate and gift tax law that we now have in effect says, 'You can pay the tax or not, as you please, for a period of 100 to 150 years.' Those who choose to pay it oftener are doing so by setting up arrangements that are not greatly different from the arrangement they can set up within the tax-exempt area that the law permits." (932–33)

As the materials in this chapter are considered, determine the extent to which the plan developed by Professor Casner can be utilized after the enactment of the tax on GSTs and in what ways it must be modified. As another matter, if you represented S in the above situation, would you have any reason to object to the form of disposition recommended?

2.   THE TAX REFORM ACTS OF 1976, 1986, AND 2001

Congress first adopted a GST tax in 1976. It was immediately the subject of withering criticism as special interest groups pressed for its repeal. The Treasury Department conceded that Chapter 13 was "overly complex from an administrative standpoint and may have an undue influence on estate planning in many common situations where skipping a generation for estate tax avoidance purposes is generally not a primary motivation."[3] However, Treasury adamantly opposed repeal of the generation-skipping tax without the enactment of a simplified substitute that also redressed the equity and neutrality defects of the 1976 legislation. After hearings held in 1981 and 1984, Congress responded in the Tax Reform Act of 1986 by repealing the 1976 legislation retroactively to its inception and enacting an entirely new tax on GSTs that simplified Chapter 13 and broadened its application.

The 2001 Act repealed the GST tax for GSTs occurring after December 31, 2009. To comply with the Congressional Budget Act of 1974, the GST tax is restored for decedents dying after December 31, 2010.

SECTION B.   TRANSFERS SUBJECT TO THE GST TAX

Internal Revenue Code: §§ 2601; 2611; 2612; 2613; 2651; 2652

Regulations: § 26.2612–1

It is important to remember that the tax on a GST is assessed in addition to the estate or gift tax. For example, as discussed in more detail

---

3.   Senate Finance Subcommittee on Estate and Gift Taxation, Hearings on the Generation–Skipping Transfer Tax, 97th Cong., 1st Sess. 62 (1981) (statement of Deputy Assistant Secretary of the Treasury David G. Glickman).

below, a taxable gift to a grandchild may generate not only a gift tax calculated using the applicable gift tax rate, but also a GST tax using the maximum transfer tax rate. Similarly, a bequest may be subject to both the estate tax and GST tax.

Section 2601 imposes a tax on a "generation-skipping transfer." Section 2611 defines a "generation-skipping transfer" by describing three forms of transfers that skip over a generation: (1) the "direct skip" (2) the "taxable termination" and (3) the "taxable distribution." In the examples throughout this Chapter, "D" refers to the transferor, "S" refers to the transferor's spouse, "C" refers to a child of the transferor, "GC" refers to a grandchild of the transferor, and "GGC" refers to a great-grandchild of the transferor.

1.   THE DIRECT SKIP

A direct skip is a transfer of an interest in property to a "skip person" that is subject to the gift tax or estate tax. § 2612(c)(1). A "skip person" is a person who is assigned to a generation that is two or more generations below that of the transferor pursuant to § 2651. § 2613(a)(1). The "transferor" is the donor in the case of an inter vivos gift of the decedent in the case of a testamentary transfer. § 2652(a). Thus, a transferor's gift or bequest to her GC is a direct skip because GC is a skip person. That is, GC is two generations below the transferor.

A skip person also includes a trust if the only persons with "interests" in the trust are skip persons. § 2613(a)(2)(A). For example, a transfer to a trust whose sole beneficiary is the transferor's GC is a direct skip because the only person with an "interest" in the trust is a skip person. In determining who has an "interest" in a trust, future interests are generally ignored. Section 2652(c)(1)(A) states that a "person has an interest in . . . a trust if . . . such person . . . has a right (*other than a future right*) to receive income or corpus from the trust." (emphasis added). This means that a trust that has only skip persons as present beneficiaries and non-skip persons as future beneficiaries will normally be treated as a skip person because the future interests held by non-skip persons are disregarded. For example, a direct skip is deemed to occur when D transfers property to a trust from which income will be paid to GC for ten years and the corpus will then be distributed to C. Since C's interest in the trust is ignored, the only person holding an interest in the trust is GC, a skip person.[4]

A trust is also a skip person if no person holds an interest in the trust and at no time after such transfer may a distribution be made from such a trust to a non-skip person. § 2613(a)(2)(B). Suppose that when GC is age 10, D creates a trust which will accumulate income until GC is age 21 and

---

4. One type of future interest that is not disregarded is a future interest held by a charity in a charitable remainder trust. § 2652(c)(1)(C). Thus, if D transfers property to a charitable remainder trust from which income will be paid to GC and the remainder to a qualifying charity, a direct skip has not occurred because the charity's remainder interest qualifies as an "interest" in the trust.

will then distribute the income and principal to GC, or to GC's estate if she dies before reaching age 21. The trust is treated as a skip person because neither GC nor anyone else is deemed to have an interest in the trust and no trust distribution may be made to a non-skip person. GC's right to receive income and principal when she reaches age 21 does not constitute an "interest" under § 2652(c)(1)(A) because most future rights to receive income or corpus from the trust are disregarded.[5].

2.   THE TAXABLE TERMINATION

Section 2612(a)(1) defines a "taxable termination" as the termination of an interest in property held in trust unless either:

(A) immediately after the termination, a non-skip person has an interest in the property, or

(B) at no time after such termination may a distribution be made from such trust to a skip person.

To see how this definition operates, consider a situation in which D transfers property in trust, income to C for life, remainder to GC. Since a non-skip person, C, has an interest in the trust, a direct skip has not occurred upon the creation of the trust. When C dies, however, and the trust distributes the corpus to GC, a taxable termination occurs. C possessed an "interest in property held in trust" as defined in § 2652(c)(1)(A), because she had an income interest. The termination of this interest upon her death is a taxable termination unless the exceptions described in subparagraphs (A) or (B) of § 2612(a)(1) apply. Since the only person having an interest in the property after the termination is GC, a skip person, the exception in subparagraph (A) does not apply. Moreover, the exception in subparagraph (B) does not apply. Since the trust has no additional property to distribute, it cannot make a distribution to a skip person after the termination.

Consider another example where D transfers property in trust, income payable jointly to D's children, C_1 and C_2, while both live, with all income then payable to the survivor, and upon the survivor's death, remainder to D's grandchild, GC. The creation of the trust is not a direct skip because the trust is not a skip person as a result of non-skip persons, C_1 and C_2, having an interest in the trust. The subsequent death of C_1 is not a taxable termination because C_2, a non-skip person, has an interest and, therefore, the exception in subparagraph (A) applies. Upon the death of C_2, however, a taxable termination will have occurred because neither subparagraph (A) nor (B) will apply.

3.   THE TAXABLE DISTRIBUTION

Section 2612(b) defines taxable distribution as "any distribution from a trust to a skip person (other than a taxable termination or a direct skip)." Suppose that D irrevocably transfers property in trust, income to C for life,

---

5. See note 4 for a type of future interest that is not disregarded.

remainder to GC and that D also gives the trustee discretion to distribute up to one-half the income to GC during C's life. The transfer to the trust is not a direct skip since C, a non-skip person, has an interest in the trust. What happens when the trustee distributes some income to GC? A direct skip has not occurred because the distribution of income to GC is not a transfer subject to the estate or gift tax as required by § 2612(c). (The irrevocable transfer of the property into the trust was the transfer subject to the gift tax. See Reg. § 25.2511–2(b), (c) and (d).) Moreover, a taxable termination has not occurred because C's interest in income has not been terminated.[6] However, a taxable distribution has occurred.

Frequently, there will be overlap between taxable distributions on the one hand and taxable terminations and direct skips on the other hand. In those situations, the rules applicable to direct skips or taxable terminations apply. § 2612(b). For example, suppose that D transfers property in trust, income to C for life, remainder to GC. D's transfer to the trust is not a direct skip because C, a non-skip person, has an interest in the trust. The distribution to GC upon C's death could be described as a taxable termination or a taxable distribution, but the language of § 2612(b) makes clear that classification as a taxable termination applies. Giving precedence to taxable terminations over taxable distributions is important because, as discussed in the next sections, different persons are liable for the GST tax depending on whether the transfer is a taxable distribution or termination (§§ 2603, 2662(a)(1)), different deductions are allowed in calculating the GST tax liability for taxable terminations and taxable distributions (§ 2621(a)(2) and § 2622(b)) and the alternate valuation date is available for a taxable termination occurring at an individual's death but not for taxable distributions (§ 2624(c)).

ILLUSTRATIVE MATERIAL

A.   WHO IS THE TRANSFEROR

To determine whether a GST has occurred, it is important to identify the transferor. In general, the donor, in the case of a gift subject to gift tax, and the decedent, in the case of a bequest of property subject to the estate tax, is treated as the transferor in a GST. § 2652(a)(1). If a married couple elects under § 2513 to split gifts, each spouse will be treated as a transferor of one half of the gift for purposes of the GST tax. § 2652(a)(2).

The donee or surviving spouse who receives qualified terminable interest property ("QTIP") (see p. 590 for a discussion of QTIPs) must include the fair market value of the QTIP in her estate under § 2044. Accordingly, under § 2652(a), the donee or surviving spouse becomes the transferor of the QTIP property at her death since the property is subject to the estate tax in her estate. Section 2652(a)(3), however, allows the spouse who created the QTIP to

---

6. It could be argued that the distribution of income to GC terminates C's interest in that income and, therefore, that a taxable termination has also occurred with respect to that income. But such an analysis would nullify the concept of taxable distributions and, therefore, has not been adopted by the Regulations. See Reg. § 26.2612–1(f) Ex. 10.

elect to be treated as the transferor for purposes of the GST tax after the surviving spouse's death. This election is often called the "reverse QTIP election". As discussed at p. 666, it is unlikely that transferors will make this election after 2003.

B.   GENERATION ASSIGNMENTS

Section 2613(a) defines a skip person as a person who is assigned to a generation that is two or more generations below that of the transferor. Section 2651 creates two categories of persons in order to determine the generation. The first category applies to lineal descendants. Section 2651(b)(1) assigns a generation to an individual who is a lineal descendant of a grandparent of the transferor by "comparing the number of generations between the grandparent and such individual with the number of generations between the grandparent and the transferor." Similarly, § 2651(b)(2) assigns a generation to a lineal descendant of a grandparent of a spouse (or former spouse) of the transferor by "comparing the number of generations between such grandparent and such individual with the number of generations between such grandparent and such spouse." For example, where D makes gifts to his GC, his spouse's GC from a previous marriage, and his grandnephew, all donees will be assigned to a generation two levels below D. Spouses and former spouses of the transferor are assigned to the transferor's generation. § 2651(c)(1).

The second category applies to persons who are not lineal descendants. Such persons are assigned to generations based on their age. An individual who is not more than 12 1/2 years younger than the transferor is assigned to the transferor's generation. § 2651(d)(1). An individual who is more than 12 1/2 years but not more than 37 1/2 years younger than the transferor is assigned to the first generation below the transferor. § 2651(d)(2). An individual who is more than 37 1/2 years but not more than 62 1/2 years younger than the transferor is assigned to the second generation below the transferor. § 2651(d)(3). An additional generation is assigned for each additional 25 year interval. Id.

Adopted children are included in the category of lineal descendants. § 2651(b)(3)(A). Thus, an adopted child will always be assigned to the generation immediately below the adopting parent regardless of the age difference. For example, if D adopts a child 40 years younger than she, the child will be assigned to the generation immediately below her although the age category would have assigned the child to the second generation below D.

C.   CONTINGENT REMAINDER INTERESTS AS SKIP PERSONS

Suppose that D creates a trust, income to A for life and on A's death to accumulate the income until D's child, C, reaches the age of 40, at which time the accumulated income and principal will be distributed to C. If C dies before reaching age 40, the trust's assets are to be distributed per stirpes to C's descendants. What happens if A dies while C is 35 years old? Has a taxable termination occurred?

A's interest has terminated, but we need to examine the two exceptions in § 2612(a)(1) to determine whether a taxable termination has occurred. See p. 655. If either exception applies, there is no taxable termination. The exception in § 2612(a)(1)(A) does not apply since a non-skip person, C, has an interest in the trust. Similarly, the exception in § 2612(a)(1)(B) appears not to apply since distributions could be made to C's descendants, who are skip persons, if C dies prior to reaching age 40. However, Reg. § 26.2612–1(b)(1)(iii) states that the possibility of a distribution to a skip person will be disregarded if it can be ascertained by actuarial standards that there is less than a 5 percent probability that the distribution will occur. Thus, if there is less than a 5 percent chance that distributions will be made to C's descendents, the exception in § 2612(a)(1)(B) will apply and A's death will not be a taxable termination.

Section C.   Exceptions to Generation-Skipping Transfers

There are some important exceptions to the general definition of direct skips, taxable terminations and taxable distributions.

1.   Direct Skips

Predeceased Ancestor Exception. A gift or bequest by D to GC that is subject to transfer tax at a time that C, who is the parent of GC, is dead, is excluded from classification as a direct skip. § 2651(e)(1). For example, if D makes a gift to GC at a time that GC's parent, C, is dead, the gift will not be a direct skip and, therefore, will not be subject to the GST tax. This exception also includes transfers to collateral heirs if the transferor has no living lineal descendants at the time of the transfer. For example, suppose that D's nephew is deceased and that D makes a gift of property to her deceased nephew's child. The gift is not subject to the GST tax so long as D has no living lineal descendants at the time of the transfer.

Skips Over More Than One Generation. Since § 2613 defines a skip person as a person assigned to a generation "which is two or more generations below" the transferor, a gift by D to his great grandchild is subject to only one GST tax. Reg. § 26.2612–1(a)(1). This result conflicts with the objective of the GST tax to assess a transfer tax on each generation.

Annual Exclusion Exception. An outright gift to an individual that qualifies as a direct skip is not subject to the GST tax if the gift qualifies for the gift tax exclusion under § 2503(b) or (e). § 2642(c).[7] Gifts in trust that are direct skips and which qualify for the gift tax exclusion are only excepted, however, if (1) the trust has only one beneficiary during that beneficiary's life and (2) the assets of the trust are includible in the beneficiary's estate if she dies before the trust terminates. § 2642(c)(2). For example, suppose D transfers $500 to an irrevocable trust for the benefit of GC, subject to GC holding a lapsing power of withdrawal (i.e., GC holds a Crummey power). The trust will pay income to GC for life and principal to

---

7. Section 2642(c) provides this exception by adjusting the formula for calculating the tax rate applicable to direct skips such that a zero rate is applied. The formula is discussed in Section D.

her estate upon her death. The entire transfer is not subject to the GST tax under § 2642(c)(2) since it is a direct skip that qualifies for the annual exclusion.[8]

2. TAXABLE TERMINATIONS

Terminations Subject to Estate or Gift Tax. The regulations state that a taxable termination will not occur if the termination is itself subject to the estate or gift tax. Reg. § 26.2612–1(b)(1)(i). In that situation, the transfer instead will normally be treated as a direct skip or as a taxable termination. For example, suppose D transfers property in trust, income to spouse S for life, remainder to GC, and a QTIP election is made for the trust. S's subsequent death might appear to result in a taxable termination because it terminates her interest in the trust, no non-skip person has an interest in the trust and the trust cannot after such termination make a distribution to a skip person (since the trust, itself, has terminated). See § 2612(a)(1). Reg. § 26.2612–1(b)(1)(i) dictates, however, that no taxable termination occurs because S's gross estate includes the QTIP principal under § 2044. See p. 590. S's death instead results in a direct skip because S is treated as the transferor, Reg. § 26.2652–1(a)(1), of the trust property to a skip person, GC, that is subject to the estate tax. § 2612(c)(1). Reg. § 26.2612–1(f) Ex. (5).

Partial Terminations. Section 2612(a)(2) treats certain distributions as terminations. Suppose that D creates a spray trust such that trustee has discretion to pay income to C_1 and C_2, and their descendants. On the death of the first child, one-half of the trust principal is to be distributed to that child's living descendants per stirpes and the other one-half of the trust principal stays in trust until the surviving child's death. If C_1 dies first and one-half of the trust principal is distributed to C's children, under § 2612(a)(1) no taxable termination has occurred because a non-skip person, C_2, has an interest in the trust. Instead, the distribution would be a taxable distribution under § 2612(b) but for § 2612(a)(2). Section 2612(a)(2) treats such a distribution as a taxable termination, which trumps classification as a taxable distribution. § 2612(b).

Simultaneous Terminations. Suppose that C and GC have an interest in the trust that terminates at the same time and the trust principal passes to GGC. Have two taxable terminations occurred? Reg. § 26.2612–1(b)(3) states no; only one taxable termination occurs. Similarly, suppose that D transfers property to a spray trust in which trustee has discretion to pay income to C or GC, and that on C's death, the trust principal goes to GGC. On C's death, Reg. § 26.2612–1(b)(3) holds that only one taxable termination occurs, although both C's and GC's interests have terminated. This creates an odd result that conflicts with the objective of assessing a transfer tax on each generation, but which is consistent with the treatment of skips

---

8. Arguably, GC could be treated as the transferee for GST purposes by virtue of the Crummey power. Section 2612(c)(3) makes clear that D, not the Crummey power holder, is the transferee. See Reg. § 26.2612–1(f) Ex. (3).

over more than one generation discussed immediately below. Note that if the trust had continued for GC's life, a taxable termination would have occurred on C's death, and another on GC's death.

Skips Over More Than One Generation. Similar to direct skips, a taxable termination that skips more than one generation is subject to only one GST tax. Suppose D transfers property to trust, income to C, remainder to GGC upon C's death. Only one GST tax is assessed on C's death, although C's death triggers a taxable termination that skips over two generations (C and GC).

3. TAXABLE DISTRIBUTIONS

Skips Over More Than One Generation. As is the case with direct skips and taxable terminations, a distribution that skips multiple generations is subject to only a single tax. For example, suppose D creates a spray trust in which the trustee has discretion to distribute income to C, GC or GGC, with remainder to GGC. A distribution of income to GGC is a single taxable distribution even though two generations have been skipped.

The Move–Down Rule. Suppose that D transfers property to a trust for the benefit of GC and GGC. During GC's life, the trust income may be distributed to GC and GGC in the trustee's absolute discretion. The transfer to the trust is a direct skip for which a GST tax is generally assessed. § 2611. Distributions of income to GC are not taxable distributions that are also subject to the GST tax because § 2653(a) causes D to be "moved down" a generation for purposes of determining whether a GST has occurred. As a result of the "move down," § 2653(a) treats D as being only one generation above GC. Distributions to GGC, however, are taxable distributions, since D is still two generations above GGC after the "move down." See Reg. § 26.2653–1(b) Ex. 1.

SECTION D.   CALCULATING THE GST TAX

Internal Revenue Code: §§ 2602; 2603; 2621; 2622; 2623; 2624; 2515

The amount of the GST tax is the product of the "applicable rate" and "taxable amount". § 2602. If no exemption is applied to a GST, the applicable rate is the maximum federal estate tax; there is no graduated rate structure for GSTs. The "taxable amount" varies, depending upon the type of GST that has occurred. This section discusses calculation of the GST tax assuming a 45% applicable rate, the maximum federal estate tax rate for 2009. Situations where the applicable rate is adjusted downward because of the GST exemption are discussed in Section E.

1. DIRECT SKIPS

In a direct skip the taxable amount is the value of property received by the transferee. § 2623. The tax is paid by the transferor or, in the case of a transfer from a trust, the trustee. § 2603(3).[9] The taxable amount in a direct skip does not include the GST tax, itself. Thus, the GST tax for direct skips is calculated on a GST tax exclusive basis. Section 2515, however, treats the amount of the GST tax as an additional taxable gift where the direct skip is a gift.

For example, suppose D gives $1 million to GC in 2009. The taxable amount is the $1 million received by GC. The GST tax, assuming an applicable rate of 45%, is therefore, $450,000 which D will be liable to pay. In addition, D will have to pay a gift tax on the transfer. Assuming that D is at the highest gift tax rate of 45% with no available exclusions or unified tax credit, D's gift tax liability will equal $652,500 (45% times $1 million gift plus 45% times the GST tax of $450,000). D has incurred a total tax liability of $1,102,500 as a result of the transfer. Thus, the total amount needed to transfer $1 million to GC in the form of an inter vivos gift is $2,102,500.[10]

Section 2515 attempts to equalize the effect of a direct skip by gift with one by bequest. This attempt is only partially successful. Since the estate tax is tax inclusive, the estate tax is computed on all estate assets, including those used to pay the estate tax and GST tax. Section 2515, in contrast, causes the gift tax to become tax inclusive only to the extent of the amount used to pay the GST tax.

In the above example involving an inter vivos gift, D needed to start with $2,102,500 in order for GC to have $1 million after paying the gift tax and GST tax. How large must D's taxable estate be for GC to receive $1 million after the federal estate tax and GST tax are paid, assuming that no unified credit is available and that the estate tax rate is 45 percent ? The answer is $2,636,363.63, as shown below.

Taxable estate	$2,636,363.63
less estate tax	−($1,186,363.63)
	$1,450,000.00
less GST tax	−($450,000.00)
Amount to GC	$1,000,000.00

The difference between the $2,636363.63 outlay for a GST bequest and the $2,102,500 outlay for a gift is attributable to the fact that the gift tax is tax exclusive. Although § 2515 requires the gift tax base to include the GST tax, the gift tax base does not include the amount used to pay the gift tax itself. In contrast, the estate tax base includes the entire amount used to pay the estate tax as well as the GST tax.

---

9. Direct skips that involve "trust arrangements", are subject to a special rule in Reg. § 26.2662–1(c)(2). If the direct skip involves less than $250,000, occurs at death and involves a trust arrangement, the executor of D's estate, not the trustee, must pay the GST tax. The executor is entitled to recover the tax from the trustee or the recipient of the property.

10. This is equal to the amount with which D would have started had D made a taxable gift to C and then C made a taxable gift to GC. If D had started with $2,102,500, he could have made a gift of $1,450,000 to C and paid a gift tax of $652,500. C would then have made a gift of $1,000,000 to GC and paid a gift tax of $450,000.

Although § 2515 applies only to gifts, bequests have their own anomaly. Section 2603(b) directs that the GST tax be charged directly to property comprising the GST unless the governing instrument (e.g., D's will) directs otherwise by specific reference to the GST tax. For example, suppose that D wishes to leave $1 million to GC, and that D's will is silent as to the source of payment of the GST tax. Assume that no unified credit remains, that the estate tax is paid from other bequests, and that the applicable rate for GST purposes is 45%. D's bequest to GC would have to be $1,450,000 in order for GC to have $1,000,000 after payment of the GST because § 2603(b) mandates payment of the tax from the bequest. Note that the amount of the bequest and the GST tax are interdependent in this example—the taxable amount (i.e., the amount received by GC) is dependent on the amount of the GST tax which is in turn dependent on the amount received by GC. The formula to calculate the GST tax in this situation is:

GST tax = .45 x (bequest − GST tax)

This in turn becomes:

GST tax = (.45/1.45) x (bequest)

In this example, the bequest of $1,450,000 multiplied by .45/1.45 results in a GST tax of $450,000.

If D's will had specifically required payment of the GST tax from other sources, the bequest need only be $1 million to GC. § 2603(b). Note, however, that regardless of the requirement in the will, the GST tax for a transfer of $1 million to GC is the same—$450,000. The reference in the will to payment of the GST tax only affects the source of the GST tax payment.

2.   TAXABLE TERMINATIONS

The taxable amount in a taxable termination is the value of all property with respect to which the taxable termination has occurred less deductions similar to those allowable under § 2053. § 2622(a). Note that this amount includes the GST tax liability itself and, therefore, the tax on taxable terminations is tax inclusive. The treatment of taxable terminations is thus similar to the treatment that would have occurred had the property been transferred outright to the skipped generation and then included in the skipped generation's taxable estate.

The GST tax in the case of a taxable termination is payable by the trustee. The alternate valuation date provided by § 2032 is available for purposes of determining the value of a taxable termination that occurs "at the same time as and as the result of the death of an individual." § 2624(c).

To illustrate the computation for taxable terminations, consider a situation where D transfers $1,818,181.81 inter vivos to a trust, income payable to C for life, remainder to GC. Assume that the unified credit and annual exclusion are not available and that D's gift tax rate and the applicable rate are both 45%.

Upon the transfer, D incurs a gift tax liability of $818,181.81 (45% x $1,818,181.81) which he pays from other sources. At C's death, a taxable termination occurs. Assuming that the trust res is $1,818,181.81, the trustee will pay a GST tax of $818,181.81 (45% x $1,818,181.81) out of the trust res leaving GC with $1 million. The total outlay by D required to transfer $1,000,000 in this format to GC is $2,636,363. This is the same outlay that was required for a direct skip in the form of a bequest illustrated on p. 662.

If D creates a testamentary trust with the same terms, the total outlay would increase to $3,305,785.11. The estate tax on $3,305,785.11 is $1,487,603.30, leaving $1,818,181.81 to pass to the trust. The taxable termination on C's death results in a GST tax of $818,181.81, leaving $1 million for GC. The total outlay for the testamentary trust is higher than the inter vivos trust because the gift tax is tax exclusive.

3. TAXABLE DISTRIBUTIONS

The taxable amount in a taxable distribution is the amount received by the transferee reduced by expenses she incurs in connection with the determination, collection or refund of the GST tax imposed on the taxable distribution. § 2621(a). It may appear that since the GST tax is imposed on the amount received by the transferee, the GST tax on taxable distributions is tax exclusive like the tax on direct skips. However, unlike direct skips, where the transferor is liable for the GST tax, the transferee is liable for the GST tax on taxable distributions. § 2603(a)(1). This means that the GST tax on taxable distributions is tax inclusive, i.e., the amount which will be used to pay the GST tax is included within the GST tax base.

To illustrate, suppose that D transfers $1,818,181.81 to a spray trust, income and principal payable to C and GC at the discretion of the trustee (T), remainder to GCC. D incurs a gift tax of $818,181.81 (45% x $1,818,181.81). If T distributes $1,000,000 to GC, GC will pay a GST tax of $450,000 leaving GC with $550,000.[11]

SECTION E. THE GST EXEMPTION AND THE APPLICABLE RATE

Internal Revenue Code: §§ 2631; 2632; 2641; 2642(a)–(d), (f)

Regulations: § 26.2632–1; § 26.2642–1

1. OVERVIEW

Every individual is allowed a GST exemption to allocate among inter vivos and deathtime GSTs and transfers to trusts that are not direct skips.

---

11. Note that if T had distributed the entire trust res of $1,818,181.81, both a taxable distribution and taxable termination will have occurred. See Reg. § 26.2612–1(f) Ex. (7). In that situation, the rules for taxable terminations apply. § 2612(b).

§ 2631(a) and (c). The GST exemption equals the exclusion amount for the estate tax unified credit. In 2009 this amount is $3.5 million. In 2010, the GST is repealed. In 2011, the GST is scheduled to reappear and the exclusion amount will drop back to $1 million, the exclusion in 2001, with adjustment for inflation.

As discussed below, the allocation of all or a portion of the exemption to a particular transfer determines the "applicable rate", i.e. the tax rate applicable to the generation skipping transfer. For example, if in 2009 D allocates her entire $3.5 million exemption to a $3.5 million gift to GC, the applicable rate is zero, and therefore the GST tax is zero. The effect of an allocation to a transfer to a trust that is not a direct skip is to exempt from tax the fractional share of the transferred property to which the exemption has been allocated. Thus, for example, if D transfers $1 million to a trust of which C is the income beneficiary and GC is the remainder person and D allocates $1 million of her GST exemption to that transfer, no GST tax will be paid upon the termination of the trust—even if the trust principal has grown to $50 million. The policy aspects of the exemption are discussed at p. 671, infra.

The applicable rate encompasses the GST exemption in an algebraic formulation. The applicable rate is the maximum federal estate tax rate in effect at the time of the transfer multiplied by the "inclusion ratio." § 2641(a). The inclusion ratio is equal to 1 minus the "applicable fraction." § 2642(a)(1). The applicable fraction is the amount of the GST exemption allocated to the transfer divided by the value of the property transferred.[12] § 2642(a)(2).

For example, suppose that in 2009 D transfers $1,500,000 to a trust, income to GC for life, then remainder to GGC. A GST has occurred at this moment because no non-skip person has an interest in the trust. If D allocates $1.5 million of his GST exemption, the applicable fraction is 1 ($1.5 million divided by $1.5 million). The inclusive ratio is zero (1 minus 1). The applicable rate is, therefore, zero (45% multiplied by zero). Thus, no GST tax will be due.

Alternatively, if D allocates $300,000 of his GST exemption to the transfer, the applicable fraction is 1/5 ($300,000 divided by $1.5 million). The inclusion ratio is 4/5 (1 minus 1/5). The applicable rate is therefore 36% (4/5 x 45%) and the GST tax is $540,000.

2.   ALLOCATION OF THE GST EXEMPTION

A transferor of property may allocate her GST exemption to transfers that are direct skips (to trusts or otherwise) or transfers to trusts that are not direct skips. See § 2631(a). In general, an individual may choose to which of these transfers the exemption will be allocated. An allocation to GSTs, other than direct skips that are inter vivos gifts, may be made by an

---

12. The value of the transferred property is reduced by any federal estate or state death taxes attributable to the property that is recovered from a trust and any charitable deductions allowed with respect to the property. § 2642(a)(2).

individual (or his executor) at any time on or before the due date of the transferor's estate tax return (regardless of whether a return is actually required). § 2632(a)(1). Once an allocation is made it is irrevocable. § 2631(b).

In some situations, a transferor is deemed to make an allocation unless she expressly elects otherwise. If the transfer is an inter vivos direct skip, any unused portion of the transferor's exemption (up to the amount of the transfer) will be deemed allocated to the direct skip unless the transferor elects otherwise in a filing on or before the date a gift tax return for the transfer would have to be filed. § 2632(b). Reg. § 26.2632–1(b)(1). The unused portion of the transferor's exemption is that portion of the exemption that has not been allocated by the transferor to prior transfers or deemed allocated by the transferor to a prior inter vivos direct skip. Also, if a transferor makes an inter vivos transfer that is not a direct skip into a trust and that trust may subsequently make a taxable distribution or experience a taxable termination, the transferor is deemed to have allocated any remaining portion of his exemption to the transfer unless he elects otherwise. § 2632(c). Any remaining exemption, which is not allocated on or before the estate tax return due date, is deemed allocated to direct skips occurring at death and all trusts with respect to which a taxable distribution or termination might occur at or after the transferor's death. § 2632(e)(1).

A married couple has two GST exemptions. The exemptions are not freely transferable between the spouses and the unused exemption of one spouse cannot be aggregated with the remaining exemption of the other. However, married individuals may elect § 2513 gift-splitting treatment for inter vivos generation skipping transfers and, therefore, in effect share their exemption. § 2652(a)(2). Also, in the case of QTIP transfers, the transferor spouse or her executor may elect to be the transferor of the property for purposes of the GST tax even though the property will be included in the tax base of the transferee spouse for the gift and estate taxes. § 2652(a)(3). This election is frequently called the "reverse QTIP election" and is made by the transferor to maximize use of her GST exemption. Prior to 2004, the reverse QTIP election was helpful because the GST exemption exceeded the unified credit exclusion amount. Most estate plans of the first spouse to die transfer to a QTIP trust (see p. 642) all the first spouse's assets other than an amount equal to the unified credit exclusion amount. An amount equal to the unified credit exclusion amount is transferred to a non-marital trust for the benefit of children or grandchildren. Without the reverse QTIP election, the first spouse would be unable to allocate to the QTIP trust the portion of the GST exemption that exceeded the unified credit exclusion amount. The election allows the first spouse to allocate her GST exemption to the QTIP trust to reduce the GST tax that might otherwise be due upon the death of the surviving spouse. For example, in 2002 the GST exemption amount was $1.1 million while the unified credit exclusion amount was $1 million. Suppose that upon D's death in 2002, she transferred $1,000,000 (the applicable unified credit exclusion amount) in trust, income to C for life, remainder to GC. D allocated $1,000,000 of her $1,1,00,000 GST exemption to this transfer. She transferred her remaining assets in a QTIP trust, income to her surviving spouse, remainder to GC. Without the reverse QTIP election, the remaining $100,000 of D's GST exemption would be unused. With a reverse QTIP election by D's executor, D's estate can allocate her remaining exemption to the QTIP trust so that the QTIP trust will benefit when the surviving spouse dies.

It is unlikely that the reverse QTIP election will be made for transfers occurring after 2003 because the GST exemption will equal the unified credit exclusion amount. This parity will allow the first spouse to allocate all her GST exemption to the non-marital disposition. For example, in 2009 D would likely transfer $3.5 million in trust for C and GC and allocate her entire $3.5 million GST exemption to the transfer. Since she has used her entire GST exemption, no "reverse QTIP election" is needed.

3. THE APPLICABLE RATE

As discussed above at p. 664 the applicable rate is equal to the maximum federal estate tax rate multiplied by the inclusion ratio. § 2641(a). To repeat the drill: the inclusion ratio is equal to 1 minus the applicable fraction. § 2642(a)(1). The applicable fraction is the amount of the GST exemption allocated to the transfer divided by the value of the property transferred. § 2642(a)(2).

The inclusion ratio is determined at the time some portion of the transferor's exemption is allocated to the transfer. § 2642(b). Thus, where the allocation is made on a timely filed gift tax return or is deemed allocated under § 2632(b) or (c), the gift tax value is used to determine the inclusion ratio. § 2642(b)(1). If, on the other hand, the allocation is not made on a timely filed gift tax return, the inclusion ratio will be determined by reference to the value of the property at the time the allocation is made. § 2642(b)(3). If property is transferred at or after the transferor's death, the estate tax value is usually the value to be used to determine the inclusion ratio.[13] § 2642(b)(2). If the beneficiary of a QTIP interest is treated as the transferor, the estate tax value of the property included under § 2044 is used to determine the inclusion ratio. § 2642(b)(4).

Once the inclusion ratio is determined for a trust, that ratio is used to calculate the applicable rate to be applied to all subsequent taxable distributions and terminations of the trust so long as no further transfers to the trust occur. See Reg. § 26.2642–1(b)–(c) and (d) Ex. (1) and (2). Since, as discussed at p. 590, D may allocate her exemption to transfers into trusts that are not direct skips and since the inclusion ratio is also determined at that time, an opportunity to save significant GST taxes arises.

---

13. On exception is that qualified real property for which the special use § 2032A election (see p. 786) is made is valued for GST tax purposes under § 2032A so long as the recapture agreement described in § 2032A(d)(2) provides that the signatories are personally liable for the recapture of GST tax. Reg. § 26.2642–2(b)(1). Another exception is for the payment of pecuniary bequests with property other than cash. Reg. § 26.2642–2(b)(2) and (3).

For example, suppose in 2009 D transfers $3.5 million into a trust, income to C for life, remainder to GC, and that she allocates her entire $3.5 million GST exemption to the transfer in a timely-filed gift tax return. Since the inclusion ratio calculated at that time is zero (1 minus $3.5 million/$3.5 million), the applicable rate applied to subsequent GSTs from the trust will be zero. If at the time of C's death, the trust principal is $10 million, that $10 million passes to GC with no concurrent GST tax liability (or, for that matter, estate tax liability). Where the applicable rate is zero, all appreciation occurring subsequent to the transfer to the trust is shielded from the GST tax.

The applicable fraction and inclusion ratio must be recomputed if additional property is transferred to a trust after some portion of the transferor's exemption has already been allocated to it. § 2642(d)(1). The numerator of the recomputed applicable fraction is the sum of the exemption allocated to the later transfer plus the "non-tax portion" of the trust immediately before the transfer. § 2642(d)(2). The "non-tax portion" of the trust is the product of the value of all the property in the trust immediately before the transfer and the applicable fraction in effect for the trust before the transfer. § 2642(d)(3). The denominator is the sum of the value of the property involved in the later transfer (reduced by federal estate and state death taxes paid by the trust with respect to such property and by any charitable deductions allowed with respect to the transfer) and the value of all the property in the trust immediately before the transfer. Id.

For example, assume that A transferred $1 million to a trust and allocated $500,000 of his GST exemption to the trust. The applicable fraction with respect to the trust is 1/2 (and the inclusion ratio is 1/2). When the trust corpus has a value of $4 million, A transfers $3.5 million more to it and allocates another $500,000 of GST exemption to the trust. The numerator of the new applicable fraction is $2.5 million (the $500,000 exemption allocated to the second transfer plus $2 million—the non-tax portion of the trust immediately before the transfer). The denominator of the new applicable fraction is $7.5 million (the value of the trust immediately before the transfer—$4 million—plus the amount of the subsequent transfer—$3.5 million). The new applicable fraction is 1/3. The inclusion ratio is 2/3 and, therefore, the applicable rate for subsequent generation-skipping transfers will be 2/3 of the maximum tax rate at the time of such transfers.

As discussed at p. 658, an outright gift to individuals and certain transfers to trusts that qualify for the annual exclusion and that are direct skips are not subject to the GST tax under § 2642(c). The mechanism by which this exclusion is achieved is through the inclusion ratio. Section 2642(c) assigns an inclusion ratio of zero for the qualifying transfers.

ILLUSTRATIVE MATERIAL

A.   ESTATE TAX INCLUSION PERIOD

Section 2642(f) provides that where D transfers property that is includible in his gross estate after the transfer (other than by § 2035), D's allocation of his GST exemption cannot become effective until after the estate tax inclusion period ("ETIP"). Section 2642(f)(3) generally defines the ETIP as the period for which the transferred property would be includible in the transferor's estate, except that the ETIP terminates either when a GST with respect to the property occurs or the transferor dies. Note that the ETIP rule will often result in GST taxation of any appreciation in the transferred property that occurs during the ETIP period. For example, suppose in 2009 D transfers $500,000 to a trust, income to D, remainder to GC. D allocates $500,000, which is the remaining amount of his $3.5 million GST exemption, to the transfer. On D's death the trust res is valued at $1,000,000 and a taxable termination occurs. D's inclusion ratio is 1/2 because his $500,000 allocation exemption only became effective on his death. The regulations provide that an allocation made at the time of the transfer cannot subsequently be revoked even though it is not effective until D's death. Reg. § 26.2632–1(c)(1). D's executor may allocate any unused exemption to the property at the time of D's death. Reg. § 26.2632–1(d)(1).

The regulations expand the scope of § 2642(f) to apply where the transferred property would be included in the estate of the transferor's spouse if such spouse died after the transfer. Reg. § 2632–1(c)(2). Two important exceptions exist. First, property is not considered to be includible in the gross estate of the transferor's spouse for the ETIP rule if the spouse possesses only the right to withdraw not more than the greater of $5,000 or 5% of the trust corpus, and such withdrawal right terminates no later than 60 days after the transfer of the property in trust. Reg. § 26.2632–1(c)(2)(ii)(B). This is, in effect, a de minimis exception. Second, a QTIP for which the transferor has made a "reverse QTIP election" (see p. 665), is not subject to the ETIP rule. Reg. § 26.2632–1(c)(2)(ii)(C). If this second exception did not exist, the benefit of making the "reverse QTIP election" would be greatly reduced (see p. 666).

B.   NONTAXABLE TRANSFERS AND THE INCLUSION RATIO

The regulations address the manner for calculating the inclusion ratio in the case of nontaxable transfers. Reg. § 26.2642–1(c)(2) states that the denominator is reduced by the value of nontaxable property in the case of a direct skip. For example, if D makes a $13,000 cash gift to GC that qualifies for the annual exclusion, the denominator of the applicable fraction is zero with the result that the inclusion ratio is zero.[14]

Reducing the denominator to zero works when the entire transfer is nontaxable but fails when the transfer is partly taxable and nontaxable. Example (3) of Reg. § 26.2642–1(d) solves the problem by dividing the transfer into two parts. Suppose that D transfers $14,000 in an irrevocable trust, income to GC for ten years, remainder on GC's death to GC's estate. GC is given a Crummey power with respect to $5,000 so that $5,000 of the transfer qualifies for the § 2503(b) annual exclusion. Example (3) states that solely for computing tax on the direct skip (the transfer to the trust), the transfer is divided into two portions. One portion equals the amount of the nontaxable

---

14.   Reg. § 26.2642–1(c)(2) states that if the denominator of the applicable fraction is zero, then the inclusion ratio is also zero.

$5,000 transfer and is assigned a zero inclusion ratio.[15] The other portion of $9,000 is assigned a value of $9,000 for the denominator of its applicable fraction. If D has adequate GST exemption, the numerator is also $9,000 (unless D elects not to have her exemption apply). The result is that the applicable fraction for the $9,000 portion is 1 ($9,000/$9,000) and the inclusion ratio is zero (1 minus 1). Although Example (3) states that the approach of using two portions applies "(s)olely for purposes of computing the tax on the direct skip," presumably the two inclusion ratios will also apply for the taxable termination that occurs on GC's death. See Reg. § 26.2632–1(a).

SECTION F.   INTERRELATIONSHIPS OF GST TAX WITH ESTATE, GIFT AND INCOME TAXES

Internal Revenue Code: §§ 2654; 2661

1.   IN GENERAL

The GST tax interacts with a number of provisions in the estate, gift and income taxes. The following discusses the more important of those interactions.

Disclaimers. A disclaimer that results in property passing to a person at least two generations below the original transferor results in imposition of the GST tax. Thus, if D's child makes a qualified disclaimer and the disclaimed property passes to D's grandchild, a GST tax is imposed on the transfer. On the other hand, a qualified disclaimer by D's GC may prevent a GST tax. For example, if GC disclaims D's bequest so that the property will pass to C, the disclaimer will eliminate the GST tax.

Administrative Rules. In addition to the provisions of the estate and gift tax that have been incorporated in the generation-skipping tax and discussed above, the administrative provisions of the Code, discussed in Chapter 38 are made generally applicable to the generation-skipping tax by § 2661. Section 2032(c)(2), discussed at p. 680, does not permit the use of the alternate valuation date unless its election would result in the reduction of the sum of the estate and generation-skipping taxes imposed on property included in the decedent's estate. Section 6166(i), discussed at p. 782, treats any generation-skipping tax paid on account of a direct skip occurring at the same time and as a result of D's death as additional estate tax for purposes of electing to defer the estate tax attributable to certain closely held business interests.

---

15. Section 2642(c)(2) states that a direct skip to a trust for the benefit of an individual which is nontaxable under § 2503 is assigned a zero inclusion ratio where (A) during the life of the individual, no portion of the corpus or income of the trust may be distributed to (or for the benefit of) any person other than such individual and (B) the trust's assets are included in such individual's gross estate if the trust does not terminate before the individual dies.

Income Tax Basis. Section 2654(a) provides basis adjustments for property transferred in a GST that are intended to be analogous to those provided by §§ 1014 and 1015 with respect to property received from a decedent and by inter vivos gift. The general rule is that the basis of property transferred in a GST is increased (not in excess of fair market value) by the portion of the GST tax attributable to the appreciation in value of the property immediately before the transfer.

If the GST is a taxable termination that occurs at the same time and as the result of the death of an individual, the assets receive a fair market value basis unless the inclusion ratio is less than one. § 2654(a)(2). In the latter case, the basis increase is limited to the product of the full basis increase and the inclusion ratio. Id.

Income Tax Deductions. Section 164(a)(4) provides an income tax deduction for the GST tax attributable to trust income distributions. For example, consider a trust for which the GST applicable rate is 45% and a beneficiary of the trust, GC, whose income is taxed at the marginal rate of 35%. If trust distributes $1,000 of income to GC in 2009, GC pays a GST tax of $450. She also recognizes $1,000 of gross income. Section 164(a)(5) allows her to deduct the $450 GST tax liability, resulting in taxable income of $550 and an income tax liability of $192.50 (35% x $550). The result is a total tax liability of $642.50 ($450 GST tax plus $192.50 income tax). The trust itself pays no income tax on the $1,000 of income because it is allowed a deduction for distributable net income. See §§ 651(a) and 661(a). The rationale for the § 164(a)(5) deduction is to achieve the same result as would have occurred had the trust paid the income tax on the $1,000. Had the trust paid income tax of $350 on the $1,000 income, $650 would have been distributed to GC, resulting in $292.50 of GST tax liability and an aggregate tax liability of $642.50. For similar reasons, § 691(c)(3) permits an income tax deduction for the GST tax paid on account of a direct skip or taxable termination occurring as a result of the death of the transferor attributable to "items of gross income of the trust which were not properly includible in the gross income of the trust for periods before the date of such termination."

Redemption to Pay Estate Tax. Finally, § 303(d) makes the special redemption rules of § 303, discussed at, p. 784, applicable to the GST tax attributable to transfers occurring on and as a result of the death of an individual.

2.   PLANNING CONSIDERATIONS

The structure of the GST tax and its interaction with the estate and gift tax create some important planning considerations. First, since the GST tax is tax exclusive for a direct skip while tax inclusive for taxable terminations or distributions, planners prefer to avoid taxable terminations and distributions where the $3.5 million GST exemption is not available. Second, since the gift tax is tax exclusive, planners prefer to structure GSTs, or the creation of trusts that will result in GSTs in the future, as inter vivos gifts, instead of as bequests. Third, maximum benefit is derived from the GST exemption by allocating it to property transferred into trust which is most likely to appreciate in value.

Estate planners will usually allocate an amount of the GST exemption to a transfer in trust such that the inclusion ratio is zero. This insures that all future appreciation of trust corpus will escape the GST tax. Moreover, planners prefer that the trust to which the exemption is allocated have only skip persons as beneficiaries to obtain the maximum benefit from the exemption. This will often result in transferors creating separate trusts for skip and non-skip persons or attempting to divide an existing trust into separate trusts. For further discussion, see Suter and Repetti, Trustee Authority To Divide Trusts, 6 ABA Probate & Property 54 (1992).

SECTION G.   EFFECTIVE DATE RULES

In general, the GST tax applies to generation-skipping transfers made after October 22, 1986. However, inter vivos transfers made after September 25, 1985 are subject to the tax and are treated as if made on October 23, 1986. A number of exceptions to this rule are set forth in Reg. § 26.2601–1 and §§ 1433(a)–(d) of the Tax Reform Act of 1986, Pub. L. No. 99–514, 99th Cong. 2d Sess. (1986), as amended by § 1014(h) of the Technical and Miscellaneous Revenue Act of 1988, Pub. L. No. 100–647, 100th Cong. 2d Sess. (1988).

SECTION H.   POLICY ISSUES

1.   EVALUATION OF THE GENERATION–SKIPPING TAX

The current GST tax represents a significant congressional commitment to achieve greater equity in the transfer tax system. Moreover, when the tax applies, its coverage is more comprehensive and rational than the structure it replaced. However, it is important to note the policy decisions reflected in the legislation and alternatives which, if adopted, could improve the statute.

In deciding the role and scope of a tax on GST, Congress must address four basic issues: the level of transfers at which the tax will begin to apply, the event or events that will trigger the tax, the tax base and the tax rate. The following discussion focuses on these issues.

a.   THE LEVEL OF TRANSFERS AT WHICH THE TAX SHOULD APPLY

Under Chapter 13, the generation skipping tax will generally apply to transfers in excess of the GST exemption. It is necessary to analyze the objectives underlying the exemption to determine whether its size and structure are appropriate.

Structure of the Exemption. One of the purposes of the revised generation-skipping tax was to eliminate for a significant body of taxpayers and their advisors the need to consider and plan for the imposition of the GST tax. The decision to use an exemption rather than some other mechanism to avoid imposing an undue burden on taxpayers and their advisors was apparently prompted by several other considerations. First, a trust containing only exempt property would never have to keep any records relating to the tax. Second, due to the limited application of the tax, its most vociferous opponents could no longer argue for its repeal on the ground that most practitioners are unable to cope with the law. Finally, the Treasury would be relieved of the burden of monitoring, and providing the information necessary for the administration of the tax in the vast majority of trusts.

While the use of an exemption reduces the administrative burden of record keeping and monitoring, the structure of the exemption removes from the reach of the tax, subject only to the limitations imposed by the applicable rule against perpetuities, not only the GST exemption amount but also any appreciation that occurs after the exemption is claimed with respect to the transferred property. Thus, to achieve simplicity, Chapter 13 abandons the notion of periodic imposition of tax with respect not only to the exempt amount, but also its growth. The latter result is not compelled by the use of an exemption. An exemption could be structured to include appreciation in the tax base once the trust reaches a size that exceeds the exemption amount. Moreover the simplification theoretically made possible by the exemption has been significantly reduced by the decision to reflect the exemption in the tax rate rather than associating it with particular assets. Significant complexity arises in calculating the applicable fraction for initial transfers to a trust, subsequent transfers to a trust, and after a multiple skip has occurred.

Finally, the simplification potential of the exemption carries a significant price tag. First, many lawyers will not be knowledgeable about the GST tax so the exemption's applicability and intricacies may not be recognized in many cases. Second, there will be a psychological push to use trusts to take advantage of any available exemption. The frequency of "grandchild exclusion" trusts in post–1976 wills indicates that individuals will create trusts to take advantage of "benefits," even though in pre-generation-skipping tax days, those same individuals did not take advantage of unlimited generation-skipping opportunities.

b. GENERATION–SKIPPING TAXABLE EVENTS

Chapter 13 represents a significant improvement over prior law in that direct skips are subject to the tax. However, there is a lack of symmetry in the treatment of multiple skips as compared to transfers that skip more than one generation.

The lack of symmetry is illustrated by the following examples. A trust for C for life, then for GC for life, remainder to GGC is subject to two GST taxes. Similarly, a trust for GC for life, then outright to GGC is subject to two GST taxes. But a trust for C for life, then outright to GGC is subject to only one GST tax. An outright transfer directly to GGC is likewise subject to just one GST tax. GGC is the ultimate recipient of the property in each case but the tax burden differs depending upon the form of the transfer. If multiple GST taxes are imposed on some trust dispositions, multiple taxes should also be imposed on an equivalent basis for dispositions in which a member of a higher generation does not possess an interest in the transferred property.

Both a 1969 Treasury study[16] and 1984 ALI Draft[17] proposed a single tax no matter how many generations were skipped by a transfer. This suggestion is inconsistent with the theoretical norm that a tax should be imposed in a manner that approximates the result that would have occurred had the property actually passed through the transfer tax base of each intervening generation. Moreover, the failure to impose an additional tax on multiple generation skips provides a tax preference for those with wealth sufficient to make such transfers. Several reasons, however, led the Treasury and the ALI Reporters to conclude that the structure necessary to impose symmetrical multiple taxation did not result in benefits sufficient to outweigh its complexity. First, multiple taxation results in additional statutory complexity. Second, as has been noted in the planning literature, careful drafters can blunt the effect of multiple taxation. For example, a sophisticated drafter could provide a savings clause to ensure that the property of any generation-skipping trust is passed through the estate of any grandchild who dies prematurely, thus avoiding a second generation-skipping tax while making available the deductions and credits that apply only to the estate tax. Third, it is the first generation skip that causes the greatest equity and neutrality problem.[18] Finally, existing empirical evidence indicates that very little property is transferred in a way that skips more than one generation.

The Chapter 13 solution, treating some generation-skipping transfers as subject to multiple taxation and others as subject to a single tax, is an

---

16. U.S. Treasury Dept., Tax Reform Studies and Proposals, House Ways and Means Committee and Senate Finance Committee, 91st Cong., 1st Sess. 389–92, 397 (Comm. Print 1969).

17. American Law Institute, Federal Estate and Gift Tax Project: Study On Generation–Skipping Transfers Under the Federal Estate Tax Discussion Draft No. 1, pp. 1–8, 11–20 (March 28, 1984).

18. The proposition is demonstrated by the following excerpt from Professor Shoup's classic study, Federal Estate and Gift Taxes, in which it is assumed "that the estate tax base is a circulating fund of constant size and that generations skipped are of constant duration. Then, if all decedents leave all their property in trusts that skip only one genera-

tion, 50 percent of the estate tax base is lost * * * If all decedents leave all their property in trusts that skip two generations instead of one generation, the estate tax base is one-third what it would be under no skipping, instead of one-half. The reduction in base, from what it would be under one-generation skipping, is from 50 to 33 1/3 (with 100 as the base under no skipping). This is a decrease of one-sixth (16 2/3 percent) of the base under no skipping. Three-generation skipping reduces the base from 33 1/3 to 25, or by one-twelfth of the base under no skipping. Thus, the big erosion occurs with one-generation skipping. Further skipping is proportionately much less serious." C. Shoup, Federal Estate and Gift Taxes 33 (1967).

unwarranted compromise. Because of the tax difference, transferors will be induced to utilize tax minimizing forms of disposition.

c.   TAX BASE AND TAX RATES

The purpose of the GST tax is to approximate the tax result that would have occurred had the property passed through the tax base of an individual in the intervening generation. Thus, one must decide whether a GST should be treated as a taxable gift or bequest by the intervening generation. One must also decide the tax rate to be applied to the transfer.

The prior version of Chapter 13 attempted to replicate the tax burden of a GST precisely by identifying a "deemed transferor" and calculating the tax due by reference to the transfer tax profile of that individual. This attempt to achieve precision caused significant administrative problems. Current Chapter 13 abandons the attempt at precision and instead imposes a flat-rate tax at the maximum marginal transfer tax rate. The use of a flat-rate tax at the maximum tax rate greatly simplifies the administration of the GST tax. However, the tax base for GSTs, in trust is calculated on a tax inclusive basis while the tax base for direct skips is calculated on a tax exclusive basis. As noted earlier (see p. 659), this imposes heavier tax burdens on taxable terminations or taxable distributions than direct skips. The lower rate on direct skips violates the neutrality principle.

PART VIII

VALUATION

CHAPTER 34

TIME OF VALUATION

Internal Revenue Code: §§ 2031; 2032; 2512; 2602(d)

Regulations: §§ 20.2031–1; 20.2032–1; 25.2512–1

To compute the estate tax owed under § 2001, it is necessary to determine the value of the gross estate. Similarly, the value of gifts determine gift tax liability and the value of property included in a taxable termination, taxable distribution or direct skip determines liability for the generation-skipping tax. At first glance, the meaning of so customary a word as "value" appears simple. An examination of the opinions of experts in various fields, however, soon destroys the illusion of simplicity. Value may mean one thing to economists, another to business executives, and still another to the Treasury Department and the courts. It is, therefore, not surprising to find a valuation dispute arising at some stage of many transfer tax proceedings.

Valuations of property for transfer tax purposes present at least as many problems as there are kinds of property or interests to be valued. The topics covered in this Part contain the fundamental valuation problems applicable to most situations, as well as special problems arising in transactions made important by their frequency of use and their relevance in estate planning.

SECTION A. THE VALUATION DATE

Since values fluctuate for many reasons, the value of any item of property must necessarily be fixed for transfer tax purposes as of a specific date. For the gift tax this date is the date on which the gift is made.[1] For the estate tax, value is fixed at the date of death unless the estate elects under § 2032 to value the estate at six months after the date of death, the alternate valuation date.[2] For purposes of the generation-skipping tax, property is valued at the date a generation-skipping transfer is made. The estate may elect the alternate valuation date for taxable terminations and direct skips occurring as a result of death. § 2624(b) and (c).

1. Where the subject of the gift is stock, the date of valuation is the earlier of the date the stock is transferred to the donee on the books of the corporation, Rev. Rul. 54–135, 1954–1 C.B. 205, or the date the certificate, properly endorsed, has been delivered to the donee. Rev. Rul. 54–554, 1954–2 C.B. 317.

2. Federal estate tax returns are due nine months after death.

676

1. ESTATE VALUATION OF PROPERTY TRANSFERRED INTER VIVOS

a. DISPOSITION OF DONATED PROPERTY

The broad language of the first paragraph of § 2031 suggests that when an inter vivos gift is includible in the donor's gross estate, the value to be included is the value of the transferred property at the date of the donor's death (or at the alternate valuation date under § 2032). See e.g. Commissioner v. Estate of Dwight, 205 F.2d 298 (2d Cir.), cert. denied, 346 U.S. 871 (1953). A problem arises, however, when the donee has disposed of the property prior to the valuation date. Is its value, for purposes of inclusion in the donor's estate, then to be traced to the property which the donee has received in exchange for the gift, or in which he has invested the proceeds of sale of the gift? Or is its value to be determined solely by reference to the specific property which was the subject of the gift? If the latter, should its value be fixed as of the decedent's death or as of the date the donee disposed of it?

If a donor transfers property in a transaction which results in includibility under § 2036 or § 2038, the value at donor's death of either the transferred property, if retained by the donee, or the replacement property, is the includible amount because the donor-decedent retained sufficient powers over the property so that the transfer was not complete for estate tax purposes until death. For example, where property which was the subject of a revocable transfer was sold and the proceeds reinvested in new property on behalf of the donee, the donor-decedent's estate included the value of the new property at his death. Howard v. United States, 125 F.2d 986 (5th Cir. 1942).

A different rule applies to property included under § 2035. The IRS and courts determined under the pre–1982 version of § 2035 that when property transferred by a decedent was includible in her estate under the predecessor of § 2035(a) and the property had been disposed of by the donee prior to decedent's ("D's") death, the property to be valued was the same property which D had transferred. Rev. Rul. 72–282, 1972–1 C.B. 306 (where D transferred 5000 shares of Y stock within 3 years of death to a donee who immediately sold the Y stock and reinvested the proceeds in X stock, D's gross estate included the value of the 5000 shares of Y stock at his date of death); Estate of Humphrey v. Commissioner, 162 F.2d 1 (5th Cir. 1947) (where donee squandered through imprudent investments a cash gift made within three years of death, the value included in donor's gross estate was the amount of the cash gift, not the remaining value of the assets). Any enhancement in value resulting from additions or improvements made by the transferee, or income received subsequent to the transfer (or property purchased with such income) was not part of the value included in the estate under old regulations. Reg. § 20.2035–1(e), withdrawn in, 61 Fed. Reg. 516 (Jan. 8, 1996). These principles should continue to apply when the current version of § 2035(a) requires inclusion of transfers in the gross estate.

2.   VALUE OF PROPERTY AFFECTED BY EVENT OF DEATH

The event of death may affect the value of property includible in D's gross estate. The most obvious example is insurance owned by D on his life. Immediately prior to death, the value of the policy is generally its replacement cost. Reg. § 20.2031–8(a)(1) and (a)(3) Exs. (2), (3) (see p. 413). The event of death causes the value of the policy to increase to the entire amount payable on death. Section 2042 specifically requires inclusion of the amount receivable by the executor or other beneficiary.

In other situations, where the statute does not specifically define the includible amount, the question has arisen as to the appropriate time to value the includible interest. The courts have uniformly held that the appropriate moment to measure the value of includible property is the moment of death because that value represents what the decedent ("D") is transferring. For example, where D's employment contract provided annual payments for fifteen years after the termination of his employment if he did not engage in a competing business for a defined period, the present value of the future payments at the date of death was included in his estate. Death was the appropriate moment to measure D's rights because the possibility of forfeiture was extinguished. Goodman v. Granger, 243 F.2d 264 (3d Cir. 1957). Similarly, in United States v. Land, 303 F.2d 170 (5th Cir. 1962), D owned a partnership interest subject to an agreement which permitted his partners to purchase that interest for two-thirds of its fair market value if D desired to sell the interest during his life. At death the other partners had the option to purchase the partnership interest at fair market value and, if they did not, the partnership would be dissolved. The partnership interest was included in D's estate at its full fair market value because the option to purchase at two-thirds fair market value expired at D's death. The event of death does not always increase the value of included assets. For example, if D owned a part of a business the success of which depended primarily upon her personal ability, the value of that interest for estate tax purposes will be reduced from its value immediately prior to her death. See Rev. Rul. 59–60, 1959–1 C.B. 237, and the discussion at p. 687.

Although the courts have agreed that the value at death is determinative, they have not always agreed which factors existing at the moment of death should be considered. In Estate of McClatchy v. Commissioner, 106 T.C. 206 (1996), securities laws restricted D's ability to transfer stock because D was considered an "affiliate" under Rule 144 of the Securities Act of 1933. D's estate, however, was not subject to the restrictions after D's death because the estate's executor was not an affiliate. The Tax Court ruled that the stock should be valued for inclusion in D's gross estate without the restrictions because, at the moment of D's death, D was transferring shares not encumbered by the restrictions. The court stated: "The valuation depressant occasioned by the securities law restrictions during decedent's lifetime became interesting history—nothing more—at the instant of his death, and unlike the usual case where death brings no change in value, the restricted value of the shares in decedent's hands while he was living does not serve to control the value transferred." (211). The Court of Appeals in Estate of McClatchy v. United States, 147 F.3d 1089 (9th Cir. 1998), reversed the Tax Court, however, stating:

"There is no question that the estate tax is on the transfer of property at death and that, therefore, the property to be valued is the interest transferred at death, 'rather than the interest held by the decedent before death or that held by the legatee after death.' Propstra v. United States, 680 F.2d 1248, 1250 (9th Cir. 1982) (citing Estate of Bright v. United States, 658 F.2d 999, 1001 (Former 5th Cir. 1981) (en banc). However, the Commissioner argues that, because the stock was transferred to a non-affiliate estate upon McClatchy's death, this is one of those rare cases in which death itself alters the value of the property. See *McClatchy*, 106 T.C. at 214 (reasoning that the stock transferred 'at the moment of death and passed to the decedent's estate,' causing the securities law restrictions to 'evaporate at the moment of death'). According to the Commissioner, then, the stock is to be valued at its higher value in the hands of the non-affiliate estate because the property was transformed prior to distribution to the estate. * * *

"In *Land*, a partnership interest was restricted to two-thirds of its value during the partner's lifetime, but upon death, the surviving partners had to pay full value in order to purchase the interest. Because death 'sealed the fact' that the interests would be purchased at full value, the court ruled that the full value controlled for estate tax purposes, 303 F.2d at 175. In Goodman v. Granger, another case on which the Commissioner relies, an employment contract provided for the payment of benefits after the termination of employment, dependent upon contingencies which could cause forfeiture of the payments. Upon the employee's death, however, the possibility of any of the contingencies was extinguished. The court reasoned that '[d]eath ripened the interest in the deferred payments into an absolute one;' consequently, the estate tax was measured by 'the value of that absolute interest in property.' 243 F.2d at 269.

"In these cases, death clearly is the precipitating event and is the only event required to fix the value of the property. Similarly, the death of a key partner can instantly decrease the value of a business. See *Ahramson*, 674 F.2d at 768. But in the instant case, death alone did not effect the transformation in the stock's value. The value of the stock was transformed only because the estate was a non-affiliate. Thus, contrary to the Commissioner's assertion, the property was not transformed prior to distribution to the estate. If the estate had been an affiliate, the securities law restrictions still would have applied. See 17 C.F.R § 230.144(c)(3)(v) (setting forth restrictions on sale of securities by an affiliate estate but providing no limitation for a non-affiliate estate). * * *

"Making the amount of estate tax dependent on the affiliate or non-affiliate status of the executor contradicts the principle that valuation should not depend on the status of the recipient. * * * *Bright*, 658 F.2d at 1006 (''It would be strange indeed if the estate tax value of a block of stock would vary depending upon the legatee to whom it was devised.'')

"The Commissioner's position would lead to the following anomaly described by the estate in its brief. Taxpayer A, an affiliate, and Taxpayer B, a non-affiliate, each own $1,000,000 worth of stock, but because of the securities laws restrictions Taxpayer A's shares are worth only $800,000. Taxpayer A's estate plan uses non-affiliate executors, while Taxpayer B's uses affiliate executors. Thus, when Taxpayer A dies, his $800,000 interest is worth $1,000,000 to his estate whereas taxpayer B's $1,000,000 interest is worth $800,000 to his. The result is that, by using affiliate executors a non-affiliate decedent who transfers a more valuable asset than an affiliate decedent, pays less estate tax than the affiliate decedent.

"The Tax Court's holding contravenes the general principle that '[t]he tax is measured by the value of assets transferred by reason of death, the critical value being that which is determined as of the time of death.' *Goodman*, 243 F.2d at 269, quoted in *McClatchy*, 106 T.C. at 214. At the time of death, the stock belonged to McClatchy, an affiliate of the corporation, depressing their value to that reported by the estate. The Tax Code itself defines the value of the estate for estate tax purposes to include 'the value of all property to the extent of the interest therein of the *decedent* at the time of his death.' 26 U.S.C. § 2033 (emphasis added) * * *.'' (1091–1094).

3. ALTERNATE VALUATION DATE

The provision for the alternate valuation date was enacted in the Revenue Act of 1935 as a direct result of the sharp drop in values after 1929. Congress declared that it was designed to prevent "the danger of complete confiscation of estates due to a sudden decline in market values." S.Rep. No.1240, 74th Cong., 1st Sess. 9 (1935). Without such a provision, the estate tax payable could exceed the liquidation value of the assets of an estate.

The alternate valuation method is available only if an estate tax return, based on date of death values, is required under § 6018. Moreover, an estate may only elect to use the alternate valuation date if it reduces both the value of the gross estate and the amount of estate (and generation-skipping) tax payable. § 2032(c). These requirements insure that an alternate valuation date election cannot be used to obtain a step-up in income tax basis at no additional estate tax cost. Absent this restriction, for example, if D died leaving all property in excess of his remaining estate tax exemption to a surviving spouse in a transfer that qualified for the marital deduction, the executor would be able to elect the alternate valuation date if the property increased in value, thus obtaining an increased income tax basis at no additional estate tax cost. Because it may not be possible to determine whether the alternate valuation election will reduce the estate and generation-skipping taxes, the regulations allow the estate to make a protective election. Treas. Reg. § 20.2032–1(b)(2).

The executor of an estate eligible for the alternate valuation date must elect its use on the first estate tax return filed.[3] An election on a late return will be effective so long as the return is not more than one year late. Treas. Reg. § 20.2032–1(b)(1). An estate's failure to make a timely election precludes use of alternate valuation date, even if there was reasonable cause for the failure. Estate of Eddy v. Commissioner, 115 T.C. 135, 141 (2000). An election to utilize the alternate valuation date may not be revoked unless the revocation is made in a subsequent estate tax return that is filed on or before the due date of the return. Treas. Reg. § 20.2032–1(b)(1).

In general, when the alternate valuation date is elected, all property included in the gross estate at decedent's death under §§ 2033–2044 is valued as of that date and is referred to in Reg. § 20.2032–1(d) as "included property". The Regulations define "excluded property" as property earned or accrued with respect to included property after the date of death and prior to the alternate valuation date. Excluded property is not included in valuing the gross estate at the alternate valuation date. Examples of excluded property are interest on bonds and rents on property included in the decedent's gross estate to the extent such income accrued subsequent to death and prior to the alternate valuation date.

There are two exceptions to valuing included property on the alternate valuation date. First, property distributed, sold, exchanged, or otherwise disposed of within six months following D's death is valued on the date of disposition. § 2032(a)(1). For example, if D dies on January 1 and D's estate sells an asset on March 1, the value of that asset on the date of sale will be included in D's gross estate. Second, changes in the value of property during the alternate valuation period that are attributable to the mere lapse of time are ignored and the value is determined as of the date of death. § 2032(a)(3). For example, the decrease in value of a term annuity attributable to the mere passage of time during the alternative valuation period is ignored and the value of the annuity at the date of death is included in the gross estate. The value of such property is adjusted, however, for changes in market conditions during the alternate valuation period, such as changes in prevailing interest rates. Prop. Reg. § 20.2032–1(f)(1) (2008).

The alternate valuation method may be used in connection with the valuation of property subject to the generation-skipping tax in the case of a direct skip or a taxable termination that occurs as the result of death. § 2624(b) and (c). In the case of a direct skip occurring as a result of death, the property is valued for generation-skipping tax purposes the same as for estate tax purposes. Accordingly, if the transferor's estate elects the alter-

---

3. The election is normally made by checking a box on the estate tax return. Where an executor failed to check the election box, but had shown values for includible assets in the schedules on the estate tax return under the column "Alternate Value" and had computed the taxable estate and tax liability based on the alternate value, the IRS permitted the use of the alternate valuation date. Rev. Rul. 61–128, 1961–2 C.B. 150.

nate valuation date, the same value is used in determining the generation-skipping tax. Where a taxable termination occurs as the result of an individual's death, the alternate valuation date may be used for generation-skipping tax purposes even if the estate does not elect its use under § 2032 for estate tax purposes. H.Rep. 99–426, 99th Cong., 1st Sess. 828 (1985).

ILLUSTRATIVE MATERIAL

A. DETERMINATION OF "INCLUDED PROPERTY"

1. General

When the alternate valuation date is used, income earned by the estate from the date of death to the alternate valuation date is not included property. However, income realized after death but accrued prior thereto is treated as included property. Reg. § 20.2032–1(d).

Disputes arise about whether income realized after death had accrued prior to death. The taxpayer in Estate of Johnston v. United States, 779 F.2d 1123 (5th Cir. 1986), attempted to exclude from the gross estate proceeds from the sale of oil and gas during the period between the date of death and the alternate valuation date. The court concluded that where the alternate valuation date is chosen, the estate should include the in-place value of the reserves remaining on the valuation date together with the in-place value of all oil and gas sold during the intervening six months valued as of the date of severance. Subsequently, in Estate of Holl v. Commissioner, 967 F.2d 1437 (10th Cir. 1992), the court made clear that the in-place value of oil and gas sold during the six-month alternate valuation period is not the actual sales price. Since the sales price represents the value of extracted oil, not in-place oil, the court required a discount from the sales price to reflect the lower value of the in-place oil.

2. Cash Dividends

Reg. § 20.2032–1(d)(4) provides that dividends declared before D's death, which are paid to D's estate because she was the stockholder of record on or before her death, are included property. This makes sense since D, as the stockholder of record, possessed the right to receive the future dividends at the time of her death. On the other hand, dividends declared before D's death which are payable to the stockholder of record after her death are normally excluded property since at the date of death, D did not have the right to receive her dividend. An exception to the rule that dividends payable to stockholders of record after D's death are excluded property exists for extraordinary dividends that alter the nature of the investment represented by the stock. For example, if a corporation declares a distribution that represents a partial liquidation (a distribution of one of its lines of business) the distribution will be treated as included property. Reg. § 20.2032–1(d)(4).

The treatment of dividends becomes more complex when stock is selling ex-dividend on a stock exchange at the alternate valuation date. Normally, stock traded on an exchange is valued as the mean between the highest and lowest selling price. Reg. § 20.2031–2(e). Suppose a cash dividend is declared after the date of D's death and is payable to shareholders of record after the alternate valuation date. Suppose further that the stock is trading ex-dividend on the alternate valuation date. When stock is sold ex-dividend, the seller is entitled to the dividend payment. The ex-dividend price quoted on the stock exchange will not reflect the true value of the shares because the selling price excludes the amount to be paid as a dividend. The dividend, itself, however, is not included property taxable to the estate because D possessed no right to receive the dividend at the date of his death. Rev. Rul. 54–399, 1954–2 C.B. 279. The IRS and courts have resolved this dilemma by ruling that the value of stock selling ex-dividend on the alternate valuation date should be the ex-dividend selling price increased by the amount of the declared dividend. Rev. Rul. 60–124, 1960–1 C.B. 368; Estate of Fleming v. Commissioner, 33 T.C.M. 1414 (1974). Note that this approach may create anomalous results. If the shareholder-of-record date is the day before the alternate valuation date, the dividend is excluded property and only the market value of the stock is included at the alternate valuation date. But if the shareholder-of-record date is one day after the alternate valuation date, the value of the dividend is now includible. Some have suggested that this problem could be eliminated by treating the date on which the dividend is declared as the date at which the dividend accrues.

3. Stock Dividends

Reg. § 20.2032–1(d)(4) states that stock dividends are to be treated in the same manner as cash dividends. The courts have disagreed, however, about application of this rule. On the one hand, it could be argued that any stock dividend paid after D's death and on or before the alternate valuation date should be included property because it is not "new property of the estate but rather is a further fractionalizing of existing shares." Estate of Schlosser v. Commissioner, 277 F.2d 268 (3d Cir. 1960). On the other hand, it could be asserted that a stock dividend is not included property to the extent its source is capitalized post-death earnings. Tuck v. United States, 282 F.2d 405 (9th Cir. 1960); McGehee v. Commissioner, 260 F.2d 818 (5th Cir. 1958). *Schlosser* is probably the correct view since a stock's value on the alternate valuation date where no stock dividend has occurred will include post-death earnings that are retained by a corporation. It seems that the occurrence of a stock dividend sourced in such earnings should not change the result.

B. MEANING OF "DISTRIBUTED, SOLD, EXCHANGED OR OTHERWISE DISPOSED OF"

Property that is "distributed, sold, exchanged or otherwise disposed of" by the estate before the alternate valuation date is valued at the date of such disposition § 2032(a)(1). Reg. § 20.2032–1(c)(1) states that "[t]he phrase 'distributed, sold, exchanged, or otherwise disposed of' comprehends all possible ways by which property ceases to form a part of the gross estate." The Regulations further provide that property is deemed distributed upon the first to occur of (1) entry of an order of distribution of a probate court having jurisdiction over the estate if the order subsequently becomes final; (2) segregation or separation of the property so that it becomes unqualifiedly subject to the demand or disposition of the distributee; or (3) actual payment or delivery to the distributee.

Although the Regulations refer to "actual payments or delivery," the courts have held that distribution occurs when the economic benefits of the property are transferred to a person other than the executor, not when the property itself, is actually transferred. Thus, where the economic benefits of property were transferred before actual delivery of the property, the courts have ruled that a distribution had occurred. See, e.g., Hertsche v. United States, 244 F.Supp. 347 (D.Ore. 1965), aff'd per curiam, 366 F.2d 93 (9th Cir. 1966). Similarly, the IRS and courts have held that a "distribution" does not occur where the property has been delivered but the economic benefits have not been shifted. See e.g. Rev. Rul. 78–378, 1978–2 C.B. 229 (although real estate passed directly to heir upon decedent's death, there was no shift of economic benefit and therefore no "distribution" where property remained subject to claims of the estate); Reardon v. United States, 429 F.Supp. 540 (W.D.La. 1977), aff'd per curiam, 565 F.2d 381 (5th Cir. 1978).

Where D's revocable trust provided that at his death the corpus was to be divided into separate trusts for the benefit of his children, the distribution took place at the time the corpus of the original trust was transferred to the trustees of the successor trusts. Rev. Rul. 73–97, 1973–1 C.B. 404. The Service reasoned that the transfer to the successor trustees constituted "an actual paying over" to the distributees within the meaning of Reg. § 20.2032–1(c)(2)(iii). Similarly, in Rev. Rul. 71–396, 1971–2 C.B. 328, D devised his entire estate to three separate trusts. Within the alternate valuation period the executor divided the assets of the estate into three accounts, each of which corresponded to a separate trust. However, no decree of distribution had been entered and the executor retained his dominion and control over the assets. The Ruling held there was no distribution because there had been no shifting of economic benefits as a result of the executor's allocation.

Reg. § 20.2032–1(c) states that the phrase "distributed, etc." does not apply to transactions which are mere changes in form, including exchange transactions in which no gain or loss is recognized to the transferor under §§ 351, 354 or 355. Hence, exchanges pursuant to one of the types of tax-free reorganizations described in § 368(a) are not deemed to be dispositions of the assets owned by the estate. But if property is received in the exchange which constitutes taxable income, a disposition of the stock owned by the estate does occur. Thus, where an estate exchanged stock for stock, warrants and cash in a reorganization, more than a mere change in form had occurred and the estate was held to have disposed of the amount of stock attributable to the value of the taxable warrants and cash received. Estate of Smith v. Commissioner, 63 T.C. 722 (1975). Rev. Rul. 77–221, 1977–1 C.B. 271, held that in such a situation the value of all the stock exchanged by the estate had been disposed of since the exception in the Regulations is applicable only to transactions that are wholly tax-free for income tax purposes.

The concession in the Regulations that certain income tax-free transfers are not exchanges for estate tax purposes raises difficult issues. For example, is it proper for estate tax purposes to say that an estate owning all the shares of stock in a corporation manufacturing shock absorbers for sale in a limited geographical area has not changed the form of its investment if it exchanges its stock for General Motors stock in a section 368 merger? Similarly, is it appropriate to characterize an estate's exchange of a warehouse for 10 percent of the stock of a corporation engaged in a manufacturing business as a mere change in form of investment simply because the exchange is not a taxable event for income tax purposes under section 351?

C. CHANGES IN VALUE DUE TO MERE LAPSE OF TIME

An interest in property which changes in value due to the mere passage of time is included in the gross estate under the alternate valuation method at its date of death value. § 2032(a)(3). Patents, estates for the life of persons other than the decedent, remainders and reversions are illustrations of the types of interests covered by § 2032(a)(3). However, changes in value attributable to a change in market conditions rather than the mere lapse of time are taken into account. This rule was illustrated in Rev. Rul. 69–341, 1969–1 C.B. 218, where the rate of monthly payments under a Civil Service joint and survivorship annuity was increased between D's date of death and the alternate valuation date to reflect an increase in the cost of living due to inflation. Since the increase in the monthly rate was not caused by mere lapse of time, but was caused by a change in market conditions (inflation), it was taken into account at the alternate valuation date.

D. POST–DEATH TRANSACTIONS AS AFFECTING ALTERNATE VALUE

The courts have not agreed about changes in value of property arising from restrictions imposed on D's assets after the date of death. In Estate of Hull v. Commissioner, 38 T.C. 512 (1962), rev'd on other issues, 325 F.2d 367 (3d Cir. 1963), a partnership agreement that entitled D's estate to a continuing share of partnership profits was amended after D's death but before the alternate valuation date to reduce the amount to which the estate was entitled. The estate accepted the amended agreement in an arm's-length transaction. The court held that the value of D's interest in the future profits of the partnership should be determined on the alternate valuation date using the new agreement. Similarly, in Kohler v. Commissioner, T.C. Memo. 2006–152 (2006), D's estate exchanged stock not subject to transfer restrictions in a tax-free reorganization for stock subject to transfer restrictions. The presence of the new stock restrictions substantially reduced the value of the stock. The court held that the value of the stock to be included in D's gross estate on the alternate valuation date should reflect the transfer restrictions. In contrast, in Flanders v. United States, 347 F.Supp. 95 (N.D.Cal. 1972), an estate entered into a post-death agreement with Marin County, California to use land only for agricultural purposes for ten years in exchange for a reduction in property taxes. The restriction reduced the value of the property by 88%. The court held that the value of the land at the date of death before the restrictions were imposed should be include in D's gross estate on the alternate valuation date: "The option to select the alternate valuation date is merely to allow an estate to pay a lesser tax if unfavorable market conditions (as distinguished from voluntary acts changing the character of the property) result in a lessening of its fair market value."(99). The court did not consider whether a similar result could have been reached by viewing the execution of the agreement as a disposition of an interest in the property equal in value to the amount by which the restriction reduced the unrestricted fair market value of the property.

The IRS proposed regulations in 2008 that appear to adopt the holding of *Flanders*. Prop. Reg. § 20.2032–1(f) states:

The election to use the alternate valuation method under section 2032 permits the property included in the gross estate to be valued as of the alternate valuation date to the extent that the change in value during the alternate valuation period is the result of market conditions. The term *market conditions* is defined as events outside of the control of the decedent (or the decedent's executor or trustee) * * * that affect the fair market value of the property being valued. Changes in value due to mere lapse of time or to other post-death events other than market conditions will be ignored in determining the value of decedent's gross estate * * *.

The first example in the proposed regulations considers facts identical to *Kohler* and rejects the *Kohler* court's holding. Prop. Reg. § 20.2032–1(f)(3) Ex. 1 (2008). The example concludes that imposition of the transfer restrictions on the stock was not a change in market conditions pertaining to the stock. Id.

Although death may be viewed as an inevitable consequence of the lapse of time, death is treated for purposes of § 2032(a)(3) as a change in market conditions distinct from the mere passage of time. For example, where D owned a life insurance policy on a person who died after D's death but before the alternate valuation date, the increase in value of the policy resulting from the insured's death was taken into account on the alternate valuation date. Rev. Rul. 63–52, 1963–1 C.B. 173. See also Estate of Hance v. Commissioner, 18 T.C. 499 (1952) (decrease in value of annuity due to annuitant's death was taken into account).

CHAPTER 35

VALUATION METHODS

The estate tax Regulations define "value" as "fair market value", or "the price at which the property would change hands between a willing buyer and a willing seller, neither being under any compulsion to buy or to sell, and both having reasonable knowledge of relevant facts." Reg. § 20.2031–1(b). The gift tax definition is the same. See Reg. § 25.2512–1. The test is an objective one. See, e.g., Estate of Kahn v. Commissioner, 125 T.C. 227, 231 (2005). At what price would the property change hands between a hypothetical buyer and seller who have reasonable knowledge of the facts? Any fact relevant to this question of value is admissible in a court proceeding even though the parties may not have had actual knowledge of that fact. Facts which occur after the valuation date, however, may not be considered unless they could have been reasonably anticipated on that date. *Gross v. Commissioner*, 272 F.3d 333, 341 (6th Cir. 2001).

SECTION A. VALUATION OF BUSINESS INTERESTS

Internal Revenue Code: §§ 2031; 2512

Regulations: §§ 20.2031–1, 2, 3, 4, 5, 6; 25.2512–1,2,3,4,6(b)

1. VALUATION OF STOCK IN GENERAL

Rev. Rul. 59–60

1959–1 C.B. 237.

SECTION 1. PURPOSE.

The purpose of this Revenue Ruling is to outline and review in general the approach, methods and factors to be considered in valuing shares of the capital stock of closely held corporations for estate tax and gift tax purposes. The methods discussed herein will apply likewise to the valuation of corporate stocks on which market quotations are either unavailable or are of such scarcity that they do not reflect the fair market value.

SEC. 2. BACKGROUND AND DEFINITIONS.

.01 All valuations must be made in accordance with the applicable provisions of the Internal Revenue Code. * * * Sections 2031(a), 2032 and 2512(a) * * * require that the property to be included in the gross estate, or made the subject of a gift, shall be taxed on the basis of the value of the property at the time of death of the decedent, the alternate date if so elected, or the date of gift.

.02 Section 20.2031–1(b) of the Estate Tax Regulations * * * and § 25.2512–1 of the Gift Tax Regulations * * * define fair market value, in effect, as the price at which the property would change hands between a willing buyer and a willing seller when the former is not under any compulsion to buy and the latter is not under any compulsion to sell, both parties having reasonable knowledge of relevant facts. Court decisions frequently state in addition that the hypothetical buyer and seller are assumed to be able, as well as willing, to trade and to be well informed about the property and concerning the market for such property.

.03 Closely held corporations are those corporations the shares of which are owned by a relatively limited number of stockholders. Often the entire stock issue is held by one family. The result of this situation is that little, if any, trading in the shares takes place. There is, therefore, no established market for the stock and such sales as occur at irregular intervals seldom reflect all of the elements of a representative transaction as defined by the term "fair market value."

SEC. 3. APPROACH TO VALUATION.

.01 A determination of fair market value, being a question of fact, will depend upon the circumstances in each case. No formula can be devised that will be generally applicable to the multitude of different valuation issues arising in estate and gift tax cases. Often, an appraiser will find wide differences of opinion as to the fair market value of a particular stock. In resolving such differences, he should maintain a reasonable attitude in recognition of the fact that valuation is not an exact science. * * *

.02 The fair market value of specific shares of stock will vary as general economic conditions change from "normal" to "boom" or "depression," that is, according to the degree of optimism or pessimism with which the investing public regards the future at the required date of appraisal. Uncertainty as to the stability or continuity of the future income from a property decreases its value by increasing the risk of loss of earnings and value in the future. The value of shares of stock of a company with very uncertain future prospects is highly speculative. The appraiser must exercise his judgment as to the degree of risk attaching to the business of the corporation which issued the stock, but that judgment must be related to all of the other factors affecting value.

.03 Valuation of securities is, in essence, a prophesy as to the future and must be based on facts available at the required date of appraisal. As a generalization, the prices of stocks which are traded in volume in a free and active market by informed persons best reflect the consensus of the investing public as to what the future holds for the corporations and industries represented. When a stock is closely held, is traded infrequently, or is traded in an erratic market, some other measure of value must be used. In many instances, the next best measure may be found in the prices at which the stocks of companies engaged in the same or a similar line of business are selling in a free and open market.

SEC. 4. FACTORS TO CONSIDER.

.01 It is advisable to emphasize that in the valuation of the stock of closely held corporations or the stock of corporations where market quotations are either lacking or too scarce to be recognized, all available financial data, as well as all relevant factors affecting the fair market value, should be considered. The following factors, although not all-inclusive are fundamental and require careful analysis in each case:

(a) The nature of the business and the history of the enterprise from its inception.

(b) The economic outlook in general and the condition and outlook of the specific industry in particular.

(c) The book value of the stock and the financial condition of the business.

(d) The earning capacity of the company.

(e) The dividend-paying capacity.

(f) Whether or not the enterprise has goodwill or other intangible value.

(g) Sales of the stock and the size of the block of stock to be valued.

(h) The market price of stocks of corporations engaged in the same or a similar line of business having their stocks actively traded in a free and open market, either on an exchange or over-the-counter.

.02 The following is a brief discussion of each of the foregoing factors:

(a) The history of a corporate enterprise will show its past stability or instability, its growth or lack of growth, the diversity or lack of diversity of its operations, and other facts needed to form an opinion of the degree of risk involved in the business. * * * The detail to be considered should increase with approach to the required date of appraisal, since recent events are of greatest help in predicting the future; but a study of gross and net income, and of dividends covering a long prior period, is highly desirable. * * *

(b) A sound appraisal of a closely held stock must consider current and prospective economic conditions as of the date of appraisal, both in the national economy and in the industry or industries with which the corporation is allied. It is important to know that the company is more or less successful than its competitors in the same industry, or that it is maintaining a stable position with respect to competitors. Equal or even greater significance may attach to the ability of the industry with which the company is allied to compete with other industries. Prospective competition which has not been a factor in prior years should be given careful attention. * * * The loss of the manager of a so-called "one-man" business may have a depressing effect upon the value of the stock of such business, particularly if there is a lack of trained personnel capable of succeeding to the management of the enterprise. In valuing the stock of this type of business, therefore, the effect of the loss of the manager on the future expectancy of the business, and the absence of management-succession potentialities are pertinent factors to be taken into consideration. On the other hand, there may be factors which offset, in whole or in part, the loss of the manager's services. For instance, the nature of the business and of its assets may be such that they will not be impaired by the loss of the manager. Furthermore, the loss may be adequately covered by life insurance, or competent management might be employed on the basis of the consideration paid for the former manager's services. These, or other offsetting factors, if found to exist, should be carefully weighed against the loss of the manager's services in valuing the stock of the enterprise.

(c) Balance sheets should be obtained, preferably in the form of comparative annual statements for two or more years immediately preceding the date of appraisal, together with a balance sheet at the end of the month preceding that date, if corporate accounting will permit. Any balance sheet descriptions that are not self-explanatory, and balance sheet items comprehending diverse assets or liabilities, should be clarified in essential detail by supporting supplemental schedules. * * * If the corporation has more than one class of stock outstanding, the charter or certificate of incorporation should be examined to ascertain the explicit rights and privileges of the various stock issues including: (1) voting powers, (2) preference as to dividends, and (3) preference as to assets in the event of liquidation.

(d) Detailed profit-and-loss statements should be obtained and considered for a representative period immediately prior to the required date of appraisal, preferably five or more years. * * * Potential future income is a major factor in many valuations of closely-held stocks, and all information concerning past income which will be helpful in predicting the future should be secured. Prior earnings records usually are the most reliable guide as to the future expectancy, but resort to arbitrary five-or-ten-year averages without regard to current trends or future prospects will not produce a realistic valuation. If, for instance, a record of progressively increasing or decreasing net income is found, then greater weight may be accorded the most recent years' profits in estimating earning power. * * *

(e) Primary consideration should be given to the dividend-paying capacity of the company rather than to dividends actually paid in the past. Recognition must be given to the necessity of retaining a reasonable portion of profits in a company to meet competition. Dividend-paying capacity is a factor that must be considered in an appraisal, but dividends actually paid in the past may not have any relation to dividend-paying capacity. Specifically, the dividends paid by a closely held family company may be measured by the income needs of the stockholders or by their desire to avoid taxes on dividend receipts, instead of by the ability of the company to pay dividends. Where an actual or effective controlling interest in a corporation is to be valued, the dividend factor is not a material element, since the payment of such dividends is discretionary with the controlling stockholders. The individual or group in control can substitute salaries and bonuses for dividends, thus reducing net income and understating the dividend-paying capacity of the company. It follows, therefore, that dividends are less reliable criteria of fair market value than other applicable factors.

(f) In the final analysis, goodwill is based upon earning capacity. The presence of goodwill and its value, therefore, rests upon the excess of net earnings over and above a fair return on the net tangible assets. While the element of goodwill may be based primarily on earnings, such factors as the prestige and renown of the business, the ownership of a trade or brand name, and a record of successful operation over a prolonged period in a particular locality, also may furnish support for the inclusion of intangible value. * * *

(g) Sales of stock of a closely held corporation should be carefully investigated to determine whether they represent transactions at arm's length. Forced or distress sales do not ordinarily reflect fair market value nor do isolated sales in small amounts necessarily control as the measure of value. This is especially true in the valuation of a controlling interest in a corporation. Since, in the case of closely held stocks, no prevailing market prices are available, there is no basis for making an adjustment for blockage. It follows, therefore, that such stocks should be valued upon a consideration of all the evidence affecting the fair market value. The size of the block of stock itself is a relevant factor to be considered. Although it is true that a minority interest in an unlisted corporation's stock is more difficult to sell than a similar block of listed stock, it is equally true that control of a corporation, either actual or in effect, representing as it does an added element of value, may justify a higher value for a specific block of stock.

(h) Section 2031(b) of the Code states, in effect, that in valuing unlisted securities the value of stock or securities of corporations engaged in the same or a similar line of business which are listed on an exchange should be taken into consideration along with all other factors. An important consideration is that the corporations to be used for comparisons have capital stocks which are actively traded by the public. In accordance with § 2031(b) of the Code, stocks listed on an exchange are to be considered first. However, if sufficient comparable companies whose stocks are listed on an exchange cannot be found, other comparable companies which have stocks actively traded in on the over-the-counter market also may be used. The essential factor is that whether the stocks are sold on an exchange or over-the-counter there is evidence of an active, free public market for the stock as of the valuation date. In selecting corporations for comparative purposes, care should be taken to use only comparable companies. * * *

SEC. 5. WEIGHT TO BE ACCORDED VARIOUS FACTORS.

The valuation of closely held corporate stock entails the consideration of all relevant factors as stated in section 4. Depending upon the circumstances in each case, certain factors may carry more weight than others because of the nature of the company's business. To illustrate:

(a) Earnings may be the most important criterion of value in some cases whereas asset value will receive primary consideration in others. In general, the appraiser will accord primary consideration to earnings when valuing stocks of companies which sell products or services to the public; conversely, in the investment or holding type of company, the appraiser may accord the greatest weight to the assets underlying the security to be valued.

(b) The value of the stock of a closely held investment or real estate holding company, whether or not family owned, is closely related to the value of the assets underlying the stock. For companies of this type the appraiser should determine the fair market values of the assets of the company. Operating expenses of such a company and the cost of liquidating it, if any, merit consideration when appraising the relative values of the stock and the underlying assets. The market values of the underlying assets give due weight to potential earnings and dividends of the particular items of property underlying the stock, capitalized at rates deemed proper by the investing public at the date of appraisal. A current appraisal by the investing public should be superior to the retrospective opinion of an individual. For these reasons, adjusted net worth should be accorded greater weight in valuing the stock of a closely held investment or real estate holding company, whether or not family owned, than any of the other customary yardsticks of appraisal, such as earnings and dividend-paying capacity.

Sec. 6. Capitalization Rates.

In the application of certain fundamental valuation factors, such as earnings and dividends, it is necessary to capitalize the average or current results at some appropriate rate. A determination of the proper capitalization rate presents one of the most difficult problems in valuation. That there is no ready or simple solution will become apparent by a cursory check of the rates of return and dividend yields in terms of the selling prices of corporate shares listed on the major exchanges of the country. Wide variations will be found even for companies in the same industry. Moreover, the ratio will fluctuate from year to year depending upon economic conditions. Thus, no standard tables of capitalization rates applicable to closely held corporations can be formulated. Among the more important factors to be taken into consideration in deciding upon a capitalization rate in a particular case are: (1) the nature of the business; (2) the risk involved; and (3) the stability or irregularity of earnings.

Sec. 7. Average of Factors.

Because valuations cannot be made on the basis of a prescribed formula, there is no means whereby the various applicable factors in a particular case can be assigned mathematical weights in deriving the fair market value. For this reason, no useful purpose is served by taking an average of several factors (for example, book value, capitalized earnings and capitalized dividends) and basing the valuation on the result. Such a process excludes active consideration of other pertinent factors, and the end result cannot be supported by a realistic application of the significant facts in the case except by mere chance. * * *

ILLUSTRATIVE MATERIAL

A.   UNLISTED SECURITIES

Disputes over the value of stock of unlisted corporations constitute a large portion of estate and gift tax litigation. It is difficult, however, to extract any settled principles of overriding precedential value from the cases. The courts often recite the factors they considered in determining value without stating the actual weight accorded each factor. Indeed, as the court in Estate of Godley v. Commissioner, 286 F.3d. 210, 214 (4th Cir. 2002): stated, "The weight to be given to these various factors depends upon the facts of each case."

Section 2031(b) values stock that is not listed on an exchange for the estate tax "by taking into consideration, in addition to all other factors, the value of stock or securities of corporations engaged in the same or a similar line of business which are listed on an exchange." There is no comparable provision in section 2512 for the gift tax. However, Reg. § 25.2512–2(f) determines the value of unlisted stock for the gift tax by considering, among other factors, the value of the stock of comparable corporations listed on a stock exchange. The comparison between an unlisted and listed company is in most cases rough at best; listed companies may well have different capital structures and it is rare that the operations, markets, sources of supply, etc., of a publicly traded corporation will be closely analogous to that of an unlisted corporation. See, e.g., The Northern Trust Company v. Commissioner, 87 T.C. 349 (1986).

In an attempt to provide administratively a legal framework within which the essentially factual and objective judgment of fair market value is to be made, the Service promulgated a series of Rulings culminating in Rev. Rul. 59–60. Although dated, Rev. Rul. 59–60 is the starting point for courts to determine value. The court in Estate of Jelke v. Commissioner, 507 F.3d 1317, 1321 (11th Cir. 2007), cert. den., 129 S.Ct. 168 (2008); observed, "Revenue Ruling 59–60 provides the foundation for undertaking an analysis of a closely-held stock's value. Although it has been modified and amplified over the years, Revenue Ruling 59–60 still remains the focal point for the proper method of valuing closely-held securities." As discussed in Rev. Rul. 59–60, section 7, p. 692, no formula can be applied mechanically to all valuation cases. Indeed, some courts have criticized the use of a formula in any case. See, e.g., Estate of Magnin v. Commissioner, 81 T.C.M. 1126 (2001).

The valuation of unlisted stock is usually a two-step process. The value of the underlying enterprise is determined first, usually by experts applying some combination of four methods of valuation: book value, asset value, capitalization of estimated future earnings and capitalization of estimated future dividends.

1. *Book Value*—Book value is determined by dividing the value of the net assets as shown on the corporate balance sheet by the number of shares of stock outstanding. This method is often unreliable because book values ordinarily represent original cost less depreciation and depletion. Allowance for appreciation or diminution in value caused by market fluctuations is seldom

made. Proper allowance on a corporation's balance sheet for the value of intangible assets is also uncommon. Although the courts will admit evidence of book value, it is a controlling factor only where no other accepted method of valuation is available.

2. *Asset or Liquidation Value*—Asset or liquidation value is also unreliable when used exclusively because it fails to take into account value which is attributable to the earning capacity of the assets as part of a going concern.

3. *Capitalization of Estimated Future Earnings*—The capitalization of estimated future earnings method is applied by taking the annual earnings record of the enterprise, the shares of which are to be valued, and estimating the future earnings. The capitalization rate is then selected on the basis of the earnings record, the future prospects, and the risks involved. For example, if the average annual earnings of a corporation are $10,000 and the capitalization rate selected is ten percent, the value of outstanding stock is $100,000. Application of this method gives rise to many difficult problems. Determination of the average past earnings and the anticipated earnings and especially selection of a capitalization rate involve important questions of judgment.

4. *Capitalization of Estimated Future Dividends*—The capitalization of estimated future dividends method is applied by taking the dividends paid record of the company and its anticipated dividend rates and applying a capitalization rate similar to that used in the case of capitalization of earnings. In addition to the problems inherent in capitalization of earnings, which apply as well to the dividend method, the tendency of corporations to pursue conservative dividends policies greatly weakens the evidential force of this method.

After the underlying enterprise value has been determined and allocated to the shares of stock in question, value may be further adjusted to account for lack of control, p. 712, for lack of marketability, p. 719, the size of the block of stock being valued, p. 697 and the presence of restrictions on transferability, p. 728.

The inherent problems with each valuation method mean that the objectivity sought by the Regulations is a chimara. Personal judgments, not science, determine the outcome.

For a comprehensive listing of factors considered by the courts in valuing closely held stock, see John A. Bogdanski, Federal Tax Valuation (2006).

B.   UNLISTED SECURITIES AND LIFE INSURANCE

As discussed in Chapter 23, a company may use the insurance proceeds it has received on the life of a stockholder to redeem D's stock. In Rev. Rul. 82–85, 1982–1 C.B. 137, the sole shareholder of a corporation caused it to obtain and pay the premiums on a life insurance policy on the shareholder's life. The corporation and the shareholder agreed that the insurance proceeds would be used by the corporation to redeem that portion of his stock equal in value to the insurance proceeds. The Ruling concluded that the insurance proceeds were not includible in D's gross estate under § 2042 because the corporation was the beneficiary of the policy. See Treas. Reg. Reg. § 20.2042–1(c)(6), The Ruling concluded that instead the proceeds of the life insurance policy would be reflected in the value of D's stock.

Rev. Rul. 82–85 did not provide detail about the manner in which the policy proceeds would be included in the calculation of the stock value. Usually, the corporation is contractually obligated to redeem D's stock for a specific price. Should this obligation offset the insurance proceeds in determining the value of the corporation and D's stock? Note that this would mean that the insurance proceeds would have no impact on the corporation's value if they were used to redeem D's stock. In Estate of Cartwright v. Commissioner, 183 F.3d 1034, 1038 (9th Cir. 1999) and Estate of Blount v. Commissioner, 428 F.3d 1338, 1345–46 (11th Cir. 2005), the courts held that a corporation's contractual obligation to redeem stock should offset the value of insurance proceeds that will fund the redemption.

C. LISTED SECURITIES

The value of securities selling on an established market is ordinarily fixed at the mean between the high and low prices on the date of valuation. Reg. §§ 20.2031–2(e)(1); 25.2512–2(b). In determining the value of such stock, amounts which might be expended as broker's commissions and stock transfer taxes if the stock were to be sold may not be deducted from the market price. Scott v. Hendricksen, 41–2 U.S.T.C. ¶ 10,098 (D. Wash. 1941); see Reg. § 20.2031–1(b). Such expenses, when actually incurred, are deductible, if at all, under section 2053. See p. 510.

Where a listed security is sold during the alternate valuation period in an arm's length business transaction, the actual selling price is used as the value rather than the mean between the high and low prices on the date of sale. Rev. Rul. 70–512, 1970–2 C.B. 192; Rev. Rul. 68–272, 1968–1 C.B. 394.

D. MUTUAL FUND SHARES

In elaborating upon the definition of fair market value, Reg. § 20.2031–1(b) provides that "in the case of an item of property * * * which is generally obtained by the public in the retail market, the fair market value of such an item of property is the price at which the item * * * would be sold at retail." How should this rule be applied if separate markets exist for buyers and sellers? A person wishing to buy shares in an open-end mutual fund can normally only purchase the mutual fund shares from the fund for a price that reflects the net asset value of the shares plus a sales charge. Also, the investor can normally only sell the shares by selling the shares back to the fund for their net asset value. Private trading in mutual fund shares does not occur. Which value of these shares should be used—the higher amount that a purchaser must pay or the lower amount that a seller would receive?

Initially, the IRS argued that the higher value should be used. After the Supreme Court rejected this argument in United States v. Cartwright, 411 U.S. 546 (1973), the IRS changed its position. Reg. §§ 20.2031–8(b) and 25.2512–6(b) now state that the value is what a shareholder will receive upon the sale of shares to the fund.

E. VALUATION OF UNINCORPORATED BUSINESS INTERESTS

Regs. §§ 20.2031–3 and 25.2512–3 contain rules for the determination of value of unincorporated business interests such as partnership interests. Both Regulations direct that the earning capacity of the business and the value of its assets be considered. As is the case in valuing stock, the courts weight earning capacity and asset value differently depending on the context. See e.g. Harwood v. Commissioner, 82 T.C. 239, 265 (1984) (court weighed asset value more heavily than earning capacity in valuing gifted partnership interests where partnership's earnings were very cyclical).

The Regulations specifically direct that good will be included among the assets considered in valuing unincorporated business interests. To determine whether good will exists, it is necessary to conclude that it would be purchased by a prospective purchaser. Estate of Bluestein v. Commissioner, 15 T.C. 770 (1950). Where the profitability of the business is primarily dependent upon the decedent's contribution, no value will be allocated to good will in valuing the decedent's interest in the business since the good will disappears at decedent's death. In Estate of Brandt v. Commissioner, 8 T.C.M. 820 (1949), the IRS attempted to assign a substantial value to the goodwill of a successful engineering partnership in which the decedent was a partner. The court held that because the success of the business was directly proportional to decedent's personal efforts and reputation, no good will survived and none was includible in decedent's estate. The court was careful to point out, however, that such a finding is dependent upon the facts of each case: "That this was a partnership does not, of course, negative the existence of good will." For similar analysis, see Estate of Maddock v. Commissioner, 16 T.C. 324 (1951).

The computation of the amount of good will presents difficult problems. In general, the principles outlined in Rev. Rul. 59–60, p. 687, are to be applied. However, where there is no better basis for determining the value of intangible assets, Rev. Rul. 68–609, 1968–2 C.B. 327, prescribes a formula approach to be used. See Philip Morris, Inc. v. Commissioner, 96 T.C. 606 (1991), for an illustration of the application of Rev. Rul. 68–609.

F.   ETHICAL PROBLEM

One factor to consider in valuing unlisted securities is the price offered for the stock in an arm's length transaction. In this context consider the following excerpt from CORNEEL, ETHICAL GUIDELINES FOR TAX PRACTICE, 28 Tax. L. Rev. 1 (1972):

"The Bostonians* were asked the following question:

"At the time of the audit of an estate tax return you are approached by a potential buyer who indicates an interest at $100 a share. You are certain that if the agent, who has indicated a willingness to settle for $50, were to hear of this offer he would insist on at least $80 for estate tax purposes. Assuming the estate tax rates are substantially in excess of the capital gains rates, would you:

"1. Settle as quickly as you can with the agent, then sell the stock.

"2. Inform the agent of the pending offer.

---

* [ED.: The author relies in part on responses to a questionnaire that he circulated among 100 Boston tax practitioners, both lawyers and accountants. Those tax practitioners are referred to as "the Bostonians".]

"Do you think it would be proper to make an agreement to sell the stock with a closing date postponed until after probable completion of the audit?

"Do you think it would be proper to sell the stock and not tell the agent about it?

"Most of the Bostonians were inclined to settle the tax audit quickly without disclosure to the agent of the pending offer. Many would be embarrassed to sign an agreement to sell the stock without disclosing the fact to the agent even though it is clear that the sale, particularly if it takes place a substantial time after the date of death, is really only limited evidence of value at the time of death. On the other hand, it must be admitted that if the offer was low, every lawyer would urge it as proof positive in support of his low estate tax valuation." (22–23)

2. SIZE OF HOLDING AS AFFECTING FAIR MARKET VALUE

a. THE BLOCKAGE DOCTRINE

Helvering v. Maytag

125 F.2d 55 (8th Cir. 1942).

■ WOODROUGH, CIRCUIT JUDGE.

* * * [T]he cases as submitted to the Board involved only two questions: (1) What was the fair market value on January 18, 1934, the date of death of Dena B. Maytag, of the 133,859 shares of common stock of the Maytag Company which were a part of her estate, and (2) what was the fair market value on December 15, 1934, of the 400,000 shares of the same stock which were on that date transferred (by way of gift) by E.H. Maytag in four trusts of 100,000 shares each? * * *

Dena B. Maytag died testate on January 18, 1934, and included in her estate on the date of her death were 133,859 shares of the common stock of the Maytag Company. E.H. Maytag (Elmer H. Maytag), on December 15, 1934, gave (by way of gift) and transferred in trust 400,000 shares of common stock of the Maytag Company, under four separate trusts of 100,000 shares each for the benefit of his four children, respectively * * *.

The amounts of the stocks outstanding on January 18 and on December 15, 1934, may be shown by the following tables:

January 18, 1934—

    59,263 shares of $6 first preferred stock.

    285,488 shares of $3 preference stock.

    1,617,922 1/2 shares of common stock.

December 15, 1934—

    59,263 shares of $6 first preferred stock.

    285,483 shares of $3 preference stock.

    1,617,922 1/2 shares of common stock. * * *

All three classes of stock of the Maytag Company were listed on the New York Stock Exchange. On January 17, 1934, 1,375,602 shares of the common, which were equivalent to 85% of the total of 1,617,922 1/2 shares of common then outstanding, were owned of record by F.L. Maytag (founder of the business, husband of Dena B. Maytag and father of E.H. Maytag) and members of his immediate family. Only the remaining 242,320 1/2 shares of common were in the hands of the public and thus the block of 133,859 shares of common to be valued as of January 18, 1934, was more than 50% of the then floating supply. On the other valuation date, December 15, 1934, the family holdings of common stock amounted to 1,363,627 shares, or 84% of the total outstanding. * * *

In the estate tax return which was filed for the estate of Dena B. Maytag, there was included in the gross estate therein reported 133,859 shares of the common stock of the Maytag Company at a value of $2.50 a share. In the gift tax return of E.H. Maytag for the year 1934, the value of the 400,000 shares of Maytag common stock transferred to the four trusts during that year was stated to be $2.50 a share.

In his respective audits of the estate tax return of the estate of Dena B. Maytag and of the gift tax return of E.H. Maytag for 1934, the Commissioner of Internal Revenue determined that the 133,859 shares had a value of $4.75 a share on January 19, 1934, and that the 400,000 shares had a value of $4.5625 a share as of December 15, 1934. As the Board observed in its opinion, the January 18, 1934, value of $4.75 per share determined by the Commissioner was the mean between the bid price of 4 5/8 and the asked price of 4 7/8 on the New York Stock Exchange, no sales having been recorded on that day; the December 15, 1934, value of $4.5625 a share determined by the Commissioner was the mean between the high of 5 and the low of 4 1/8 of sales recorded on that day on the New York Stock Exchange.

On their respective appeals to the Board of Tax Appeals, it was contended on behalf of the taxpayers, as further observed by the Board in its opinion, that the value on January 18th was between $1.50 and $2 a share and that the value on December 15th was not in excess of $2.50 a share. * * *

After commenting upon the other evidence in the case, including the testimony of the Commissioner's witnesses, the records of earnings, intrinsic value, the company's business, etc., the Board observed, just before reaching its conclusion as to the values, that upon the evidence it doubted "very much that the numbers of shares of stock here involved" could have been sold within a reasonable time after January 18th and December 15th, respectively, without affecting the prevailing market prices. The Board then stated its conclusion to the effect that upon all the evidence, it was its opinion that the 133,859 shares of Maytag common stock had a fair market value of $3.10 a share on January 18th and that the 400,000 shares had a fair market value of $3.80 a share on December 15, 1934. Those same conclusions as to value, namely, $3.10 a share and $3.80 a share, respectively, were also separately stated by the Board in its findings of fact. * * *

It is conceded that the question of value is a question of fact and the findings which the Board made upon the issue of value are not reviewable here if the values found are supported by substantial evidence. "But the question of what criterion should be employed for determining the 'value' of the gifts is a question of law." Powers v. Commissioner, 312 U.S. 259, 61 S.Ct. 509, 510, 85 L.Ed. 817. Likewise as to the value of the estate in question. If as a matter of law the Board did not value the property according to the best available criterion, and if the shares of stock should have been valued according to the New York Stock Exchange quotations as contended by the Commissioner, the decisions of the Board ought to be reversed.

In support of his position that the market quotations on the stock made available to the Board constituted "primary" or "best" evidence of the value, and that the production of such evidence rendered the opinion and other evidence considered by the Board inadmissible, the Commissioner has pointed out that the valuation of property for tax purposes ought to conform as nearly as possible to standard business practices (Maass v. Higgins, 312 U.S. 443) and it is said to be familiar knowledge that the business world of banks, trust companies, insurance companies, trusts, etc., in valuing its security portfolios makes no discounts because of the size of the security holdings (illustrative examples are instanced from the record). He also observes that the method followed by the Board resulting in reduction of the values below the stock market quotations would have the result of frustrating the intent of Congress to impose estate and gift taxes at rates graduated according to the size of the estate or gift. A person making a gift of a large number of shares of a particular stock would be taxed at a lower valuation than the person transferring a small lot of the same stock. Such differentiation, he says, offends against the fundamental principle of uniformity in taxation.

It is also argued that as a matter of reality the changes in ownership of the two blocks of stock involved, occasioned by the death and the transfers in trust, might make no change whatever in the supply of the stock on the stock market. There was no evidence that the blocks of stock to be valued were added or expected to be added to the supply in the market. Without assuming some increase in the supply on the market for which demand would be lacking, it is argued that there could be no reason for evaluators to go outside the market quotations of what was asked and bid and the prices at which the stock actually sold, and that no one's opinion of a stock value could be taken against the market figures. Compared with the stock market yardstick of valuation, any other is said to be speculative and vague and unconvincing.

The courts, including our own, have held in many cases that where the question arises in litigation as to the value of property regularly traded in on an established market, the question merely is as to the price it commanded in the market at the particular time and the reasoning and philosophy of such decisions have been developed in the brief of the Commissioner. He has also called attention to the long period in which the Treasury Regulations referred to have endured. The method prescribed in the Treasury Regulations for determining the value of listed stocks goes as far back as 1919 (R. 37, Art. 15(2) 1919 Ed.). The old provision of the regulations (last sentence (3) Art. 13 (1934) Art. 19 (1936)) to the effect that the size of estate holdings or gifts of securities would not be considered by the Commissioner for gift or estate tax purposes was dropped in 1939 after validity of the provision had been challenged in the courts.

On the other hand, while we are cited to no direct ruling of the Supreme Court or this court upon the precise contentions here presented for the Commissioner, they have been frequently considered by other federal courts and the decisions are unanimously against him. As well as any controverted question of administrative law may be settled without declaration by the Supreme Court, it is established that the size of a block of listed stock may be a factor to be considered in its valuation for gift or estate tax purposes. Where, as in this case, the taxpayer affirmatively shows that a block of listed stock to be valued is very great in comparison with the amounts of the stock which have been traded in on the exchange where it is listed, that the block of stock could not be sold on such market at its quoted prices within a reasonable time by skilled brokers following prudent practices for liquidation and that the true value of the block of stock is in fact different from the price quotations, then the taxpayer is entitled to have all other proper evidence of the value of the block of stock considered together with the market quotations. * * *

We conclude that there was substantial evidence before the Board of the values found by it and that the evidence was competent.

ILLUSTRATIVE MATERIAL

A. THE BLOCKAGE DOCTRINE

1. In General

The blockage doctrine is explicitly recognized in Reg. § 20.2031–2(e). The taxpayer has the burden of proving the existence of facts that justify a blockage discount. Helvering v. Safe Deposit and Trust Co. of Baltimore, 95 F.2d 806 (4th Cir. 1938); Estate of Van Horne v. Commissioner, 720 F.2d 1114 (9th Cir. 1983). The taxpayer must show that the market is too thin to absorb his shares at the market price within "a reasonable time by skilled brokers following prudent liquidation practices." Mott v. Commissioner, 139 F.2d 317 (6th Cir. 1943). In Estate of Auker v. Commissioner, 75 T.C.M. 2321 (1998), the court held that a "reasonable time" is six months or less for the sale of real estate. Alternatively, the taxpayer may attempt to discharge her burden of proof by showing that a buyer could not be found for so large a block unless a lesser price were accepted or that the cost of selling such a block in a manner which allowed the market price of the stock to remain stable would be exorbitant.

Reg. § 20.2031–2(e) states that where the taxpayer shows that sale of a large block would depress the stock price, "the price at which the block could be sold * * * outside the usual market, as through an underwriter, may be a more accurate indication of value * * *." Although the Regulations are silent, the Service and a court have ruled that the taxpayer may not subtract the underwriting expenses and other costs associated with selling the block outside the usual market in determining the block's value. Rev. Rul. 83–30, 1983–1 C.B. 224; Gillespie v. United States 23 F.3d 36 (2d Cir. 1994). They reasoned that since such expenses are deductible as costs of administration under § 2053(a)(2), consideration of the expenses in valuing the block would create a double benefit.

The size of a block of stock may increase the value of that block above the prevailing market quotations if the size gives the holder real or effective control of the corporation in question. See Helvering v. Safe Deposit and Trust Company of Baltimore, 95 F.2d 806 (4th Cir. 1938). See p. 712 for a discussion of control premiums.

2.   Works of Art

The courts often apply blockage doctrines in valuing works of art. See, e.g., Janis v. Commissioner, 461 F.3d 1080 (9th Cir. 2006); Estate of O'Keeffe v. Commissioner, 63 T.C.M. 2699 (1992); Estate of Smith v. Commissioner, 57 T.C. 650 (1972), aff'd, 510 F.2d 479 (2d Cir. 1975). In *Janis*, 461 F.3d at 1083–1084, the court explained the application of the blockage doctrine to works of art as follows:

> In general, a blockage discount is applied to property in an estate in an attempt to reflect the market's response to a large number of items. Traditionally ... a blockage discount is applicable in response to a large number of works by one artist, usually in an artist's estate. The Estate of Sidney Janis is not an artist's estate, and does not involve a large number of works by one particular artist, but rather works by different artists. However, since it is a valuation problem involving a gallery inventory, some of the general principles are applicable.

> A number of factors have been considered in determining whether a blockage discount is appropriate and to what extent it should be applied to the subject properties. Consideration was given to the prominence of the artists; the types of works in the estate; the distribution of the items (for example, the number and types, and their quality and sale ability); the number of similar items available in the marketplace; the market's response to such works around the valuation date; the number of sales and the prices at which sales were made during the period immediately preceding and following death; the annual sales of the gallery; length of time necessary to dispose of the items; the works that are saleable within a relatively short period of time; the works that can only be marketed over a long period; the demonstrated earning capacity of the business; the tangible and intangible assets, including goodwill; and, the reputation of the gallery and the provenance. (1083–1084)

B.   THE BLOCKAGE DOCTRINE IN THE GIFT TAX

Reg. § 25.2512–2(e) recognizes the existence of a blockage factor in valuing gifts. The valuation issue may be somewhat more complex where listed securities have been given to several donees on the same valuation date. In Rushton

v. Commissioner, 498 F.2d 88 (5th Cir. 1974), the court upheld Regulation's requirement that the blockage discount be measured on the basis of each separate gift rather than an aggregate of all the shares transferred by the donor on the valuation date. To illustrate the effect of this holding, consider a situation where a donor owns 200,000 shares of stock in a company. An appraiser has advised that although the stock is currently selling at $10 per share on an exchange, an attempt to sell all 200,000 shares within a reasonable period of time will depress the price to $7 per share. If the donor makes a single gift of the shares to a friend, the shares will be valued at $7 per shares for purposes of calculating her gift tax liability. On the other hand, if the donor gives 2000 shares to each of her one hundred friends, the shares will be valued at $10 per share.

In Calder v. Commissioner, 85 T.C. 713 (1985), the court subsequently applied the *Rushton* rule to gifts of works of art, concluding that both the separate gift rule and the blockage doctrine were applicable to gifts of art, as well as of stock.

b. MINORITY DISCOUNTS

Estate of Bright v. United States

658 F.2d 999 (5th Cir. 1981).

■ ANDERSON, III, CIRCUIT JUDGE: This case presents to the en banc court an important question involving the principles of federal estate tax valuation. Mary Frances Smith Bright died on April 3, 1971. During her lifetime, she and her husband, Mr. Bright, owned 55% of the common stock of East Texas Motor Freight Lines, Inc., 55% of the common stock of twenty-seven affiliated corporations, and 55% of the common and preferred stock of Southern Trust and Mortgage Company (the stock of all such corporations is hereinafter referred to collectively as the "stock").

During her lifetime, Mr. and Mrs. Bright held the 55% block of stock as their community property under the laws of the State of Texas. The remaining forty-five percent is owned by parties unrelated to the Brights; a thirty percent block of stock is owned by H. G. Schiff, and the remaining fifteen percent is owned by two or three other individuals. None of the stock was publicly traded and no market existed for any of the stock on the date of Mrs. Bright's death. Mr. Bright is executor under the will of his wife. The will devised Mrs. Bright's interest in the stock to Mr. Bright as trustee of a trust for the primary benefit of Mrs. Bright's four children.

After audit of the estate tax return, the government assessed a deficiency, which was paid by the estate, and the instant suit for a refund of over $3 million in federal estate taxes and assessed interest was brought in the district court. The sole issue before the district court was the value of the estate's stock. Before the bench trial on the fair market value issue, the district judge ruled as a matter of law that "no element of control can be attributed to the decedent in determining the value of the decedent's interest in the stock ... for estate tax purposes. The parties are hereby ordered to proceed with preparation for trial and trial of this case on that basis." At the trial the district court found that the value of the stock was consistent with the testimony of the estate's expert witnesses, and entered judgment for the estate. * * *

The only issue facing the en banc court is whether the district court erred in entering the above-quoted pretrial order relating to the element of control. We reject the heart of the government's arguments, and also reject a secondary government argument because it was raised for the first time on appeal.

Two principal arguments constitute the heart of the government's case, the first based on its description of the property transferred as an undivided one-half interest in the control block of 55% of the stock, and the second based on family attribution between the estate's stock interest and the stock interest held individually by Mr. Bright.[1]

First, the government argues that the property to be valued for estate tax purposes is an undivided one-half interest in the control block of 55% of the stock, and that the proper method of valuation would be to value the 55% control block, including a control premium, and then take one-half thereof. Both parties agree that the estate tax is an excise tax on the transfer of property at death, and that the property to be valued is the property which is actually transferred, as contrasted with the interest held by the decedent before death or the interest held by the legatee after death. United States v. Land, 303 F.2d 170 (5th Cir. 1962). See also Ithaca Trust Co. v. United States, 279 U.S. 151 (1929); Edwards v. Slocum, 264 U.S. 61 (1924) * * * Both also agree that state law, Texas in this case, determines precisely what property is transferred. Morgan v. Commissioner, 309 U.S. 78 (1940) * * *. Both parties agree that, under Texas law, the stock at issue was the community property of Mr. and Mrs. Bright during her life, that Mrs. Bright's death dissolved the community, that upon death the community is divided equally, that each spouse can exercise testamentary disposition over only his or her own half of the community, and that "only the decedent's half is includable in his gross estate for federal tax purposes." Commissioner v. Chase Manhattan Bank, 259 F.2d at 239. Under Texas law, upon the division of the community at death, each spouse owns an undivided one-half interest in each item of community property. Caddell v. Lufkin Land & Lumber Co., 255 S.W. 397 (Tex. Com. App., 1923).

In its brief the government argued that, because the interest to be valued was an undivided one-half interest in the full 55% control block, the

1. The government also argued in the court below, and argues on appeal, that the district court's pretrial order held as a matter of law that a minority discount should be applied. The government argues that a minority discount should be allowed only if evidence supporting a discount is adduced. We do not disagree with the government's statement of the law, but we reject the government's characterization of the district court's pretrial order. The order did not mandate a minority discount; it held only that the interest to be valued was in fact a 27 1/2% interest, which of course left open for proof at trial whether or not the taxpayer would in fact adduce proof to support a minority discount. Accordingly, there is no merit in the government's argument.

proper method would be to value the whole, including its control premium, and then take one-half thereof to establish the value of the estate's undivided one-half interest. The estate points out that the government's argument overlooks the fact that the block of stock is subject to the right of partition under Texas law at the instance of either the surviving spouse or the estate of the deceased's spouse. Tex. Prob. Code Ann. § 385 (Vernon 1980). The government has not argued that partition would not be freely granted in a case involving fungible shares, such as this case. Thus, the estate has no means to prevent the conversion of its interest into shares representing a 27 1/2% block, and we conclude that the estate's interest is the equivalent of a 27 1/2% block of the stock. Accordingly, we reject the government's approach of valuing the 55% control block, with its control premium, and then taking one-half thereof. Accord Estate of Lee v. Commissioner, 69 T.C. 860 (1978).

Having determined that the property which is to be valued for estate tax purposes is the 27 1/2% block of stock owned by the estate, we turn to the government's second argument, which is based on the doctrine of family attribution[2] between the successive holders of interest to be taxed, the decedent, the executor, and the legatee, on the one hand, and the related party, Mr. Bright, on the other. The government argues that the following facts are relevant and should have been considered by the district court in valuing the 27 1/2% block: the fact that Mr. and Mrs. Bright were husband and wife and held their stock during her lifetime as a control block of 55%; the fact that Mr. Bright held the estate's 27 1/2% block after her death as executor and subsequently as trustee of the testamentary trust for their children, while he simultaneously held another 27 1/2% block in his individual capacity, thus continuing the control block after death; and the fact that the government might be able to adduce evidence that Mr. Bright, as executor or trustee, would not be willing to sell the estate's 27 1/2% block as a minority interest, but would be willing to sell it only as part of the block of 55% including his individually-owned stock so that a substantial control premium could be realized.[3] Such facts and evidence, the government argues, would have formed the basis of expert testimony

---

2. At several points, the government's brief seems to disavow any attempt to import family attribution into this area. A close reading of the government's brief reveals, however, that the government shuns only the argument that family attribution *requires* or *mandates* that the stock of related parties be valued as a unit. The government's position is that the relationship between the decedent, executor or legatee, on the one hand, and another stockholder, on the other hand, is a fact relevant to value. When we refer in this opinion to family attribution, we refer to this non-mandatory version. Similarly, our opinion deals only with family attribution based on the identity of the decedent, the executor or the legatee. It is this identity which is irrelevant under the case law and reasoning which this opinion will develop.

3. This opinion will show that all three facts are irrelevant to the proper valuation formula because they depend upon the family relationship between the decedent, the executor or the legatee, on the one hand, and another stockholder, i.e., Mr. Bright in his capacity as an individual stockholder, on the other hand. The third factor is inadmissible also because it assumes an unwillingness to sell in direct contradiction to the established valuation formula which assumes a *willing* seller.

that the value of the estate's stock includes some control premium. For several reasons, we reject the government's attempt to import into this area of the estate tax law this kind of family attribution, and we hold that the foregoing evidence proffered by the government is not admissible to prove the value of the stock at issue.

First, we reject any family attribution to the estate's stock because established case law requires this result. A recent case directly in point is Estate of Lee v. Commissioner, supra. There Mr. and Mrs. Lee held as community property 4,000 of the 5,000 outstanding shares of the common stock of a closely held corporation. They also held all 50,000 shares of the preferred stock. Upon the death of Mrs. Lee, the community was dissolved, leaving Mr. Lee and the estate of Mrs. Lee each with an undivided one-half interest in each item of the community property. 69 T.C. at 873. The Tax Court held that this was the equivalent of 2,000 shares of common stock and 25,000 shares of preferred stock, and that the estate's interest was a minority interest. 69 T.C. at 874.

In United States v. Land, supra, this court held that a restrictive agreement, which depressed the value of a partnership interest but which by its terms expired at decedent's death, did not affect value for estate tax purposes because the estate tax is an excise tax on the transfer of property at death and accordingly valuation is to be made at the time of the transfer, i.e., at death, and the valuation is to be measured by the interest that actually passes. 303 F.2d at 172. It follows necessarily from our *Land* holding that the fact that Mr. and Mrs. Bright held their stock during her lifetime as a control block of 55% is an irrelevant fact. It is a fact which antedates her death, and no longer exists at the time of her death. Dictum in *Land* also suggests that the post-death fact—that the estate's 27 1/2% will pass to Mr. Bright as trustee of the testamentary trust—is also irrelevant:

> Brief as is the instant of death, the court must pinpoint its valuation at this instant—the moment of truth, when the ownership of the decedent ends and the ownership of the successors begins. It is a fallacy there, therefore, to argue value before—or—after death on the notion that valuation must be determined by the value either of the *interest that ceases or of the interest that begins*. Instead, the valuation is determined by the interest that passes, and the value of the interest before or after death is pertinent only as it serves to indicate the value at death.

303 F.2d at 172. (Emphasis added.)

Beginning at least as early as 1940, the Tax Court has uniformly valued a decedent's stock for estate tax purposes as a minority interest when the decedent himself owned less than 50%, and despite the fact that control of the corporation was within the decedent's family. Mathilde B. Hooper v. Commissioner, 41 B.T.A. 114 (1940) * * *. Similarly, many district courts have either expressly or impliedly rejected the application of family attribution to an estate's stock in the valuation process for estate tax purposes. Obermer v. United States, 238 F. Supp. 29 (D. Haw. 1964);

Sundquist v. United States, 74–2 U.S.T.C. ¶ 13,035 (E.D. Washington 1974). Our research has uncovered no cases, and the government has cited none, which have attributed family owned stock to the estate's stock in determining the value thereof for estate tax purposes.[4]

Although the cases in the analogous gift tax area do not unanimously support the taxpayer's position, the weight of authority seems to reject family attribution in this context. In Estate of Charles W. Heppenstall, 18 T.C.M. (P–H) ¶ 49,034 (1949), the donor owned 2310 shares, which represented more than 50% and, therefore, control of the stock of the family corporation. He made gifts of 300 shares each to his wife and three children. The government argued that the shares given should be valued as control stock. The Tax Court rejected this argument, saying, "In making the gifts, Charles W. Heppenstall, Sr. did lose, or surrender, his control over the Company, but he did not convey that control to any one of the donees or to all of them jointly." The court cited Mathilde B. Hooper v. Commissioner, supra, an estate tax valuation case which applied a minority discount in valuing the decedent's stock notwithstanding the fact that the decedent's stock together with that of his brother would have created a control block. In holding that each 300 share gift must be valued separately, the *Heppenstall* court relied on Lawrence C. Phipps, 43 B.T.A. 1010 (1940), affirmed 127 F.2d 214 (10th Cir. 1942), a blockage discount case where the government was making the argument on the other side of the fence. In *Phipps*, the government argued that gifts to several family members should *not* be aggregated, while the taxpayer argued for aggregation in order to create a block of stock large enough to obtain a blockage discount. The Board of Tax Appeals held that the gift to each donee should be valued separately and that there should be no aggregation. Accord Rushton v. Commissioner, 498 F.2d 88 (5th Cir. 1974).

4. The government relies on three district court cases which apply a "unity of ownership for disposal" theory in the context of undivided interests in real property. Cutbirth v. United States, 38 AFTR 2d 6271 (N.D.Tex.1976); Dattel v. United States, 37 AFTR 2d 1525 (N.D.Miss.1975); Blackburn v. United States, 6 AFTR 2d 6146 (S.D.Ind. 1960). Such cases are distinguished because real estate, unlike fungible shares of stock, is not freely subject to partition. For example, see Texas Probate Code § 381(a) and (b) which provides in pertinent part: "When, in the opinion of the court, the whole or any portion of an estate is not capable of a fair and equal partition and distribution * * * it shall order a sale of all property which it has found not to be capable of such division." This point was made by the *Dattel* court: "In other words, a person owning an undivided half interest in a property is not entitled to one-half of the acreage." 37 AFTR 2d at 76–1527. By contrast, in the instant case, the government has not disputed that a partition is freely available, and accordingly we have held that the estate's interest is the equivalent of a 27 1/2% block of stock. This being so, the only remaining factor in the instant case which might suggest a "unity of ownership for disposal" is the family relationship between the decedent, executor or legatee, on the one hand, and another stockholder, on the other hand. For the reasons set out in this opinion, we reject the application of family attribution in this context. Of the three cases cited by the government, only one, *Cutbirth*, 38 AFTR 2d at 76–6273, suggests that a family relationship can be a factor pointing to "unity of ownership for disposal purposes." The suggestion occurs in a jury charge, and does not discuss the case law or legal principles which, we believe, demonstrate the impropriety of family attribution in this context. Thus, we accord little weight to this suggestion in *Cutbirth*.

In Whittemore v. Fitzpatrick, 127 F. Supp. 710 (D. Conn. 1954), the donor owned all 820 shares of the family corporation. He made simultaneous gifts of 200 shares to each of three sons. The government argued that the entire 600 shares of stock given should be valued as a control block. Holding that the gift to each son must be valued separately, the court applied a minority discount. Although there was no discussion of whether the stock of the father and the three sons should be lumped together because of family attribution, the court implicitly rejected that concept.[5] * * *

We conclude that the case law reflects long established precedent that family attribution should not apply to lump a decedent's stock with that of related parties for estate tax valuation purposes. This constitutes our first reason for rejecting family attribution in the instant context.

Our second reason for rejecting this kind of family attribution is our conclusion that the doctrine is logically inconsistent with the willing buyer-seller rule set out in the regulations. Reg. § 20.2031–1(b) provides in pertinent part:

> The fair market value is the price at which the property would change hands between a willing buyer and a willing seller, neither being under any compulsion to buy or to sell and both having reasonable knowledge of relevant facts.

This cardinal rule for determining value has been universally applied, both by the Internal Revenue Service[6] and the courts.

It is apparent from the language of the regulation that the "willing seller" is not the estate itself, but is a hypothetical seller. In Revenue Ruling 59–60, the Internal Revenue Service has so held:

> Court decisions frequently state in addition that the *hypothetical* buyer and seller are assumed to be able, as well as willing, to trade and to be well informed about the property and concerning the market for such property.

1959–1 C.B. at 237 (emphasis added). Courts also have so held. In United States v. Simmons, 346 F.2d 213, 217 (5th Cir. 1965), this court said that "the 'willing buyer and seller' are a hypothetical buyer and seller having a reasonable knowledge of relevant facts." In Rothgery v. United States, 475 F.2d 591 (Ct. Cl. 1973), the Court of Claims said:

> [I]t is necessary to begin the resolution of any valuation problem by presupposing a "willing seller." In the present case, therefore, we must begin with the assumption that the decedent's 125 shares of stock in the corporation were not bequeathed by the decedent to his son, the

---

5. Other gift tax cases in which a minority discount was allowed for gifts of stock in a family controlled corporation are: Koffler v. Commissioner, 47 T.C.M. (P–H) ¶ 78,159 (1978); Meijer v. Commissioner, 48 T.C.M. (P–H) ¶ 79,344 (1979); W. G. Clark v. United States, 75–1 USTC ¶ 13,076, 36 AFTR 2d 65–6417 (E.D.N.C. 1975).

6. See Rev. Rul. 59–60, 1959–1 C.B. 237, modified by, Rev. Rul. 65–193, 1965–2 C.B. 370 and Rev. Rul. 77–287, 1977–2 C.B. 319.

plaintiff, and that such shares were available for sale by the decedent's estate as a "willing seller."

475 F.2d at 594.

The notion of the "willing seller" as being hypothetical is also supported by the theory that the estate tax is an excise tax on the transfer of property at death and accordingly that the valuation is to be made as of the moment of death and is to be measured by the interest that passes, as contrasted with the interest held by the decedent before death or the interest held by the legatee after death. Earlier in this opinion, we noticed that our United States v. Land, supra, decision logically requires a holding that the relationship between Mr. and Mrs. Bright and their stock is an irrelevant, before death fact. Thus, it is clear that the "willing seller" cannot be identified with Mrs. Bright, and therefore there can be no family attribution with respect to those related to Mrs. Bright. Similarly the dictum in *Land*—that valuation is not determined by the value of the interest in the hands of the legatee—means that the "willing seller" cannot be identified with Mr. Bright as executor or as trustee of the testamentary trust. Therefore, there can be no family attribution based on identity of the executor and trustee, Mr. Bright. The *Land* dictum is established law. Edwards v. Slocum, 264 U.S. at 62, 44 S.Ct. at 293 (Holmes, J. saying, "It [the tax] comes into existence before, and is independent of, the receipt of the property by the legatee."); Ithaca Trust Co. v. United States, 279 U.S. at 155, 49 S.Ct. at 292 (Holmes, J. saying, "The tax is on the act of the testator, not on the receipt of the property by the legatees."); Walter v. United States, 341 F.2d 182, 185 (6th Cir. 1965) ("[T]he estate tax is imposed upon the *transfer* of property by a decedent, and not the *receipt* of property by a beneficiary * * *." (emphasis in original)); See also Commissioner v. Chase Manhattan Bank, 259 F.2d 231, 255 (5th Cir. 1958); Connecticut Bank and Trust Company v. United States, 439 F.2d 931, 935 (2d Cir. 1971); Reg. 20.2033–1(a) ("[S]uch tax is an excise tax on the transfer of property at death and is not a tax on the property transferred."). The *Land* dictum also comports with common sense. It would be strange indeed if the estate tax value of a block of stock would vary depending upon the legatee to whom it was devised.

Our final reason for rejecting family attribution is based upon the important policy that the law should be stable and predictable. This policy is especially important in the tax laws, because there is widespread reliance by taxpayers upon established tax principles in planning their affairs. Estate of Hattie L. McNary v. Commissioner of Internal Revenue, 47 T.C. 467 (1967). Accordingly, we decline the government's invitation to depart from Estate of Lee v. Commissioner, supra, and the numerous other cases cited and discussed above.[7]

---

7. We note that the Internal Revenue Service has acquiesced in several of the Tax Court cases which have applied a minority discount for estate tax valuation purposes notwithstanding the family control of the corporation of issue. See Mathilde B. Hooper v. Commissioner, supra; * * *.

Accordingly, we affirm the district court's ruling to the extent that it defined the interest to be valued as equivalent to 27 1/2% of the stock, to the extent that it excluded as evidence of value the fact that the estate's stock had, prior to decedent's death, been held jointly with Mr. Bright's interest as community property, and the fact that, after death, the particular executor (Mr. Bright) and legatee (Mr. Bright as trustee) was related to another stock holder (Mr. Bright individually), and to the extent that it excluded any evidence that Mr. Bright, as executor or trustee, would have refused to sell the estate's 27 1/2% block except in conjunction with his own stock and as part of a 55% control block. We hold that family attribution cannot be applied to lump the estate's stock to that of any related party, but rather that the stock is deemed to be held by a hypothetical seller who is related to no one.

Having rejected the heart of the government's arguments, we turn finally to a secondary argument raised by the government for the first time on appeal. The district court ruled before trial that "no element of control can be attributed to the decedent in determining the value of the decedent's interest in the stock" and that the parties must try the case on that basis. (R. 115.) We have held that decedent's interest did not constitute control, and that there can be no family attribution to lump the estate's stock with that of related parties. However, the government complained at oral argument that the district court's order sweeps more broadly, and that the order prevented the introduction of evidence which would have been proper. For example, although the "willing buyer" is also hypothetical, both he and the "willing seller" would have "reasonable knowledge of relevant facts." Reg. § 20.2031–1(b). Thus, both the "willing seller" and the "willing buyer" would know that Mr. Bright individually owned, as of the date of death, 27 1/2% of the stock, that Mr. Schiff owned 30%, that the 27 1/2% being offered by the "willing seller" would provide the margin of control for either Mr. Bright or Mr. Schiff, and that the "willing buyer" might negotiate a resale to either Mr. Bright or Mr. Schiff. The government contends that the foregoing facts constitute admissible evidence, and that such facts might affect the value of the 27 1/2% minority interest which is to be valued. The relevance of such facts, the government argues, is contemplated by the willing buyer-seller rule, which presupposes that they both have "reasonable knowledge of relevant facts." Such facts are to be distinguished from the kind of facts which we have held to be irrelevant on account of their derivation from family attribution based on the identity of the decedent, the executor or the legatee. Family attribution facts are irrelevant because the valuation is based on a sale by a *hypothetical seller*—not Mrs. Bright, not Mr. Bright as Executor and not Mr. Bright as trustee—who is related to no one. The "willing buyer-seller" rule renders irrelevant only the real seller and buyer, not the other stockholders. Thus, while the identities of decedent, the decedent's estate and the decedent's legatee are irrelevant, the remaining stockholders in the corporation are in no sense hypothetical. Thus, the government argues that such facts are among the "relevant facts" of which the hypothetical seller and buyer have knowledge. Although this particular application of the willing buyer-seller rule has not been widely recognized, a few cases have acknowledged the relevance of such facts. Marian Otis Chandler, 10 T.C.M. (P–H) ¶ 41,193 at p. 41–392 (1941); Estate of Bernon Prentice, 25 T.C.M. (P–H) ¶ 56,003 (1956) ("There is evidence that a block of stock of Fulton Trust of the size owned by the decedent could not have been sold at one time on the over-the-counter market at prevailing prices, and that the holder of such a block would probably be forced to take the lower price in order to dispose of it. On the other hand, there is testimony that such a block might bring a higher price than market, if a buyer could be found who wanted to acquire control of the bank." At p. 16). * * *

Although we assume arguendo that such facts are admissible, as the government urges, we need not reach the issue of whether the district court's pretrial order in this case was too broad, *i.e.*, whether the order precluded the introduction of such facts. We have searched the record carefully, and have concluded that the government did not raise this issue in the court below. The issue was raised only vaguely, if at all, in the government's briefs to the panel and the en banc court. At oral argument, the issue was clearly raised for the first time. Because the government failed to raise this issue in the district court and because we find that no miscarriage of justice will result, we decline to entertain it on appeal. * * *

For the foregoing reasons, we

Affirm.

Revenue Ruling 93–12

1993–1 C.B. 202.

ISSUE

If a donor transfers shares in a corporation to each of the donor's children, is the factor of corporate control in the family to be considered in valuing each transferred interest, for purposes of section 2512 of the Internal Revenue Code?

FACTS

P owned all of the single outstanding class of stock of *X* corporation. *P* transferred all of *P*'s shares by making simultaneous gifts of 20 percent of the shares to each of *P*'s five children, *A*, *B*, *C*, *D*, and *E*.

LAW AND ANALYSIS

Section 2512(a) of the Code provides that the value of the property at the date of the gift shall be considered the amount of the gift.

Section 25.2512–1 of the Gift Tax Regulations provides that, if a gift is made in property, its value at the date of the gift shall be considered the amount of the gift. The value of the property is the price at which the property would change hands between a willing buyer and a willing seller, neither being under any compulsion to buy or to sell, and both having reasonable knowledge of relevant facts.

Section 25.2512–2(a) of the regulations provides that the value of stocks and bonds is the fair market value per share or bond on the date of the gift. Section 25.2512–2(f) provides that the degree of control of the business represented by the block of stock to be valued is among the factors to be considered in valuing stock where there are no sales prices or bona fide bid or asked prices.

Rev. Rul. 81–253, 1981–1 C.B. 187, holds that, ordinarily, no minority shareholder discount is allowed with respect to transfers of shares of stock between family members if, based upon a composite of the family members' interests at the time of the transfer, control (either majority voting control or de facto control through family relationships) of the corporation exists in the family unit. The ruling also states that the Service will not follow the decision of the Fifth Circuit in *Estate of Bright v. United States,* 658 F.2d 999 (5th Cir. 1981).

In *Bright*, the decedent's undivided community property interest in shares of stock, together with the corresponding undivided community property interest of the decedent's surviving spouse, constituted a control block of 55 percent of the shares of the corporation. The court held that, because the community-held shares were subject to a right of partition, the decedent's own interest was equivalent to 27.5 percent of the outstanding shares and, therefore, should be valued as a minority interest, even though the shares were to be held by the decedent's surviving spouse as trustee of a testamentary trust. *See also, Propstra v. United States,* 680 F.2d 1248 (9th Cir. 1982). In addition, *Estate of Andrews v. Commissioner,* 79 T.C. 938 (1982), and *Estate of Lee v. Commissioner,* 69 T.C. 860 (1978), *nonacq.,* 1980–2 C.B. 2, held that the corporation shares owned by other family members cannot be attributed to an individual family member for determining whether the individual family member's shares should be valued as the controlling interest of the corporation.

After further consideration of the position taken in Rev. Rul. 81–253, and in light of the cases noted above, the Service has concluded that, in the case of a corporation with a single class of stock, notwithstanding the family relationship of the donor, the donee, and other shareholders, the shares of other family members will not be aggregated with the transferred shares to determine whether the transferred shares should be valued as part of a controlling interest.

In the present case, the minority interest transferred to A, B, C, D, and E should be valued for gift tax purposes without regard to the family relationship of the parties.

HOLDING

If a donor transfers shares in a corporation to each of the donor's children, the factor of corporate control in the family is not considered in valuing each transferred interest for purposes of section 2512 of the Code. For estate and gift tax valuation purposes, the Service will follow *Bright, Propstra, Andrews,* and *Lee* in not assuming that all voting power held by family members may be aggregated for purposes of determining whether the transferred shares should be valued as part of a controlling interest. Consequently, a minority discount will be not be disallowed solely because a transferred interest, when aggregated with interests held by family members, would be a part of a controlling interest. This would be the case whether the donor held 100 percent of some lesser percentage of the stock immediately before the gift. * * *

ILLUSTRATIVE MATERIAL

A.   MINORITY DISCOUNTS AND CONTROL PREMIUMS—IN GENERAL

The courts have applied the regulation's rule that the "degree of control of the business represented by the block of stock to be valued" should be considered in valuing stock. See, e.g., Succession of McCord v. Commissioner, 461 F.3d 614, 631 (5th Cir. 2006). The ability of a block of stock to control corporate affairs can affect the value of the block in several ways. For example, the dividend paying capacity of a corporation might not be considered as significant by the owner of a minority block of stock because he would not control the board of directors which is responsible for declaring dividends, but would be considered important by a controlling stockholder. Similarly, the holder of a controlling block of stock might estimate the earning prospects of a company to be greater than a minority stockholder based on the changes in the company's business or management that only a controlling stockholder could implement.

Some courts have approached the role of control by valuing the company assuming control, dividing the number of shares into that value and then applying a discount (the "minority discount") to calculate the value of minority blocks of stock. See e.g. Estate of Frank v. Commissioner, 69 T.C.M. 2255, 2262–63 (1995). Other courts have valued the corporation as a whole assuming no control, and, therefore, have not discounted minority ownership further but have added premiums (the "control premium") to controlling blocks of stock. See e.g. Estate of Jung v. Commissioner, 101 T.C. 412, 423–446 (1993); Estate of Trenchard v. Commissioner, 69 T.C.M. 2164, 2171–74 (1995). A few confused courts have initially valued the corporation assuming control and then added a control premium to the controlling block, in effect counting the control premium twice. See United States v. Parker, 376 F.2d 402 (5th Cir. 1967); Driver v. United States, 76–2 U.S.T.C. ¶ 13,155 (W.D. Wis. 1976).

In Estate of Newhouse v. Commissioner, 94 T.C. 193, 247 (1990), the Tax Court stated that the sum of the values of all the blocks of stock ownership in a corporation need not equal the value of the entire corporation. This may occur, for example, where the corporation is valued as a whole assuming control, but none of the stockholders in fact owns a controlling block.

As *Estate of Bright* illustrates, in determining whether a minority interest discount is appropriate, courts have generally focused simply on the percentage of shares owned by a decedent or transferred by a donor. The relationship of the transferee to the other shareholders is considered irrelevant. The common practice of allowing discounts for minority interests in the family-controlled corporation context invites transfer tax avoidance. Tax advisers have devised corporate capital structures and gift programs which take full advantage of this invitation. See e.g. Novack, Cut Your Estate Tax in Half, Forbes 160–162 (Oct. 19, 1998).

B.   PLANNING WITH MINORITY DISCOUNTS

The use of minority discounts in estate planning is described in Repetti, Minority Discounts: The Alchemy in Estate and Gift Taxation, 50 Tax. L. Rev. 415 (1995):

"I. Introduction

"A pernicious force is stalking the American economic landscape. Individuals owning valuable properties have watched their value decrease by 30 to 40% with the stroke of a pen. This wholesale and wanton destruction of value has not created consternation, however. Indeed, it is often the result of careful planning for which the owners of the devalued property pay large fees to appraisers and lawyers. A common tool of estate planning involves the purposeful diminution in value of family property in order to reduce estate and gift taxes.

"[The] * * * basic strategy * * * involves dividing up control of an asset such as a business or real estate. Division of control reduces the value of the assets because it impairs the ability of the donees to direct the use of the assets to more profitable pursuits. Because donees will incur transactional costs in negotiating among themselves before implementing any new activity with respect to the asset, this strategy frequently results in the reduction in the value of the transferred property by up to 40%.

"This technique presents a major mystery. The maximum statutory tax rate applied to gifts or estates is 60%.[8] Although a donor may save transfer taxes by reducing the value of the transferred property, the tax savings will not equal the donee's economic harm if the diminution in value is real. For example, a reduction by $100 in the value of real estate transferred upon the taxpayer's death will reduce estate tax by up to $60, but the legatee will receive property that is worth $100 less. In most situations, a rational taxpayer would not engage in such a transaction. Thus, it is unlikely that the taxpayer has destroyed value by $100. Instead, the high marginal tax rate on estates and gifts makes it economically feasible on an after-tax basis for a donor to destroy some value so long as the remaining residual value has been transformed into something that will escape taxation. The estate planning devices transform a portion of the value formerly associated with control into an option or opportunity for the donees to recreate the 'value' attributable to control. So long as this option or opportunity escapes estate, gift and income taxation and has a value greater than any after-tax value in the asset that has been permanently destroyed, the donor and donee will benefit.

"For example, consider a parent who transfers a family business to two children, giving each child an equal right to control the business. The sum of the values of the children's interests in the business is less than the value that the business had when owned entirely by the parent. This reduction in value

---

8. IRC § 2001(c). Although § 2001(c)(1) refers to a maximum rate of 55%, § 2001(c)(2) increases the rate to 60% for amounts that exceed $10 million but are less than $21.04 million in order to phase out the benefits of the graduated tax rate and the unified credit.

reflects the fact that neither child can implement her plans for the business unilaterally. Thus, if one child wishes to sell the business but the other does not, the former will not maximize profit from the sale because a third party buyer will have to negotiate control with the latter. If the value of the business is discounted by $100, the donor saves $60 in gift tax because the gift tax applies to the value of the property transferred to each donee. Note that if this diminution in value is irreparable, the children have lost $100. Suppose, however, that they can restore $100 of value by incurring $10 of transaction costs to negotiate an agreement to sell the business together to a third party. If they do so, they will enjoy a net increase of $90 in value, while the donor will save $60 in gift tax. So long as the children incur transaction costs of less than $60 to restore the $100 value, there will be a net benefit to the family.[9]

"This phenomenon results from a fundamental discontinuity between the estate tax and the gift taxes. Although the gift tax is intended to serve as a backstop to prevent circumvention of the estate tax, the definition of the tax base for gift tax purposes differs significantly from the tax base for estate tax purposes. The gift tax base is the value of *each* gift measured using a purely hypothetical transferee and not considering the personal characteristics of the actual transferor or transferee. The estate tax base is the value of *all* property held by the decedent at the time of death regardless of whether the property will be divided among legatees, again using a hypothetical third party standard. * * *

II. An Overview of the Dichotomy Between Estate & Gift Taxation

" * * * This discontinuity allows a person owning a controlling interest in an asset to avoid paying a transfer tax on the control premium by making inter vivos gifts of the asset. For example, suppose a donor holding 60 shares of common stock in a closely held corporation that has 100 shares of issued and outstanding stock is able to sell all 60 shares to a third party for $1,000 per share. The donor probably would be able to sell one share of stock to a third party for a substantially lesser amount, say $700 per share,[10] because the share of stock, by itself, would not provide control of the corporation.[11] One method

9. The analysis in the text assumes no taxable capital gain upon the children's sale of the business. In fact, if the parent had a low tax basis in the business, the children would have taxable capital gain because they would receive the asset with a carryover basis under § 1015(a). If the children could have avoided the capital gains tax by receiving the asset at the parent's death and obtaining a stepped-up basis under § 1014(a), the tax payable in the inter vivos gift context is an additional cost that should be factored into the analysis. Therefore, so long as the children can avoid incurring transaction costs *and* capital gains tax expenses of $60 in restoring the $100 value, there will be a net benefit to the family.

10. One study that analyzed publicly announced mergers and acquisitions for the period 1968 to 1987 found that purchasers of controlling interests paid, on average, a premium of approximately 37 to 38% over the market price in order to obtain a controlling interest. Robert P. Lyons & Michael J. Wilczynski, Discounting Intrinsic Value, 128 Tr. & Est. 22, 22–24 (1989). In other words, the study found that minority interests in corporations trade on public exchanges on average at discount of approximately 27 to 28% of the intrinsic value of the corporation. Id. * * *

11. See Ward v. Commissioner, 87 T.C. 78, 106 (1986) ("The minority discount is recognized because the holder of a minority interest lacks control over corporate policy, cannot direct the payment of dividends, and cannot compel a liquidation of corporate assets.").

to reduce the gift tax is to divide the shares among several donees so that no donee would have control. The value of each gift would not reflect a control premium. Indeed, the donor need not give all her stock away during her lifetime. So long as she reduces her percentage ownership below 50%, she can reduce the value of stock for estate tax purposes that she retains as well as stock that she gives away. In the prior example, if she gave away 11 shares, she would reduce her ownership to 49%, eliminating a control premium for gift and estate tax purposes.

"Another method to reduce the value of gifts involves dividing up an asset but retaining control of the asset. This is accomplished by making gifts of interests in a partnership, into which valuable assets have been placed. For example, suppose that the donor owns valuable rental property. Rather than give individual interests in the real estate to his children and, as a result, lose control of the real estate, the donor can form a limited partnership to hold the real estate and give limited partnership interests to his children. The donor, or frequently, the donor's wholly owned corporation is the general partner, enabling the donor to continue to control the real estate. Because the limited partners lack control, a minority discount is permitted in valuing the limited partnership interests. * * *

"VI. ARGUMENTS AVAILABLE TO THE SERVICE TO CAPTURE LOST VALUE

"The Service has employed [various] * * * approaches that may accomplish roughly the same objective of trying to capture the transferred opportunity to participate in control. These approaches apply the substance-over-form or step transaction doctrine to combine a series of gifts and bequests that have the long-term effect of transferring control. * * * It is likely, however, that these approaches have only limited application and are not very effective in capturing all the value transferred to family members because they easily can be avoided with careful planning.

"A. Substance Over Form

"One method to capture the control premium where a series of gifts of minority interests is made to a single donee is to apply the substance-over-form doctrine. Disregarding an initial transfer permits a subsequent transfer to be treated as conveying control. For example, in *Estate of Murphy v. Commissioner*,[12] the taxpayer, who suffered from lung cancer, transferred 0.88% of the outstanding stock of a closely held corporation 18 days before her death to her two children, reducing her stock ownership to 49.65%. The taxpayer made the gifts after repeated written suggestions by her accountant that she would save significant amounts of estate tax if she held less than 50% of the company. At her death, she bequeathed the remaining 49.65% to her two children.

"The Tax Court denied a minority discount for the bequest because, in substance, the gifts never occurred. The court noted that, after making the gifts, the taxpayer continued to control the corporation and to serve as chairman. Finding that the sole purpose of the gift was to obtain a minority discount, the court concluded that transfers effected solely to reduce transfer

---

12.   60 T.C.M. 645 (1990).

tax, which have no impact on the transferor's beneficial interest, will be disregarded. * * *

"The paucity of cases applying the substance-over-form doctrine suggests that it is of limited usefulness to the Service in dealing with the transfer of an opportunity to participate in control. * * * A well-advised taxpayer could easily avoid the substance-over-form argument by insuring the existence of circumstances that indicate that a transfer of control in fact had occurred. For example, after the transfer the donees could call a new board of directors meeting. If they want the donor to continue as chairman of the board, they should vote to do so and set forth their reasons. At the directors' meeting, they also can discuss their future plans for the business and direct the officers to implement those plans.

"1. *Family Partnerships*

"Application of the substance-over-form doctrine to family limited partnerships merits special consideration. A donor may use a limited partnership to increase the size of a minority discount. For example, if a donor transfers an undivided interest in rental real estate, the courts normally permit only a 10 to 20% discount to reflect the estimated cost the donee would incur in obtaining a partition since an undivided interest in real estate gives the owner the right to the use and enjoyment of real estate. If, however, the real estate is contributed to a limited partnership, the gift of the limited partnership interest should qualify for a larger discount because the limited partner's rights in the real estate are more circumscribed. A limited partner probably has no right to the use and enjoyment of the land unless the partnership agreement so provides. Moreover, a limited partner normally is restricted from participating in the management of the real estate and also normally is not able to withdraw from the partnership and receive the value of his interest.

"The Service could use either of two arguments to challenge the use of a limited partnership. First, the Service could argue that the transfer of real estate to the partnership prior to the gift of the partnership interest served no business purpose. Second, the Service could argue that the partnership should be ignored because it is not a partnership for federal tax purposes.

"The courts ignore an entity's existence when it was not formed for a business purpose and has no business activity. Similarly, courts ignore the existence of an entity by treating it as a conduit even if it has a business purpose or activity, if the entity's role in a particular transaction serves no business purpose other than tax avoidance. Because the courts frequently have held that limiting liability is a valid business purpose, placing rental real estate into a limited partnership prior to giving the interest to a donee in order to shield the donee from tort or environmental liabilities should constitute a valid business purpose.[13] Similarly, placing securities in a limited partnership prior to making gifts in order to create a portfolio large enough to retain a sophisticated investment advisor and to reduce brokerage commissions should constitute a valid business purpose.

"Assuming that a valid business purpose exists for using a limited partnership, the courts nevertheless may refuse to respect the partnership for federal

---

13.   See, e.g., Bramblett v. Commissioner, 960 F.2d 526, 533 (5th Cir. 1992) * * *.

tax purposes if it engages in no profit seeking activity. Section 7701(a)(2) defines a partnership for purposes of the income, estate and gift taxes as an entity 'through or by means of which any business, financial operation, or venture is carried on ....' For example, if a partnership merely holds a personal residence or vacation property that is used only by family members who are partners, the courts may disregard the partnership.[14] A failure to rent it or to plan to sell it for gain probably would not satisfy the definitional requirement that it carry on 'a business, financial operation, or venture.'[15]
* * *

"B. Step Transaction Doctrine

"The courts also have used the step transaction doctrine to combine gifts made during a short period of time. While the substance-over-form doctrine disregards a transfer, the step transaction doctrine combines a series of transfers into one. Thus, where a majority owner has made a series of transfers to a single donee, the step transaction approach combines those transfers in order to deny a minority discount.

"In applying the step transaction doctrine, the courts have not provided detailed analysis comparable to the step transaction analysis in the corporate reorganization area. For example, in *Driver v. United States*,[16] the court refused to apply a minority discount where the taxpayer transferred a majority interest in a closely held corporation to her nephew by making two gifts on December 31, 1968 and January 2, 1969. The court characterized the gifts as 'an effort to convert a transfer of a majority interest into one of a minority interest by effecting it in two installments two days apart.' The court cited *Gregory v. Helvering*[17] but provided no additional analysis.

"The decision in *Driver* begs the question of how much time should elapse between gifts. * * * Analogy to the corporate reorganization area suggests that subsequent gifts should be combined with a previous gift only where, at the time of the current gift, the taxpayer already had decided to make the subsequent gifts and the time between gifts was so short that it was unlikely that the subsequent gift was motivated by nontax considerations. * * *

"The second context in which the step transaction doctrine has been used to deny a minority discount is where the actions of the donors indicate that they intended to act together to retain control or where the donees at the time of the gift already planned to sell control jointly. In *Blanchard v. United States*,[18] the court refused to apply a minority discount for the donor's gifts of minority interests in a family-owned corporation to her children where the

---

14. The Service adopted this position in § 1.701–2(d) (Ex. 6) of the regulations but subsequently revoked the example in Announcement 95–8, 1995–7 I.R.B. 56 (Feb. 13).

15. See Form Builders, Inc. v. Commissioner, 58 T.C.M. (CCH) 1415 (1990) (ignoring partnership for income tax purposes where there was no sharing of profits); Reg. § 1.761–1(a) (merely sharing expenses does not create partnership for federal income tax purposes); see also Bruce N. Lemons & Richard D. Blau, Significant Issues May Remain for S Corporation Partners Despite IRS's Newest Ruling, 81 J. Tax'n 132, 134 (1994) (arguing that partnership will not exist for income tax purposes when there is no joint profit motive).

16. 76–2 USTC ¶ 13,155 (W.D. Wis. 1976).

17. 293 U.S. 465 (1935).

18. 291 F.Supp. 348 (S.D. Iowa 1968).

family sold all the stock to a single buyer less than three weeks later. The court noted that the sale was being negotiated at the time the gifts were made. * * *

"In summary, the step transaction doctrine, like the substance-over-form doctrine, is not an effective tool to combat minority discounts. Planners may avoid the step transaction doctrine by providing sufficient time between transfers and by structuring the gifts in such a way that a joint sale of the gifts is not inevitable." (416–421, 450–462).

Professor Repetti concludes that legislative action is necessary to deal effectively with minority discounts. He suggests that Congress enact a statutory provision which would assign a portion of the control premium automatically to each transfer of a minority interest where the transferor and family members control the entity or asset both before and after the transfer.

C. FAMILY LIMITED PARTNERSHIPS, STEP TRANSACTIONS, AND BUSINESS PURPOSE

As described by Professor Repetti, above, a common device to reduce value involves placing an asset into a limited partnership or limited liability company and then making gifts of interests in that entity to donees. Any interests retained by the donor will also have a reduced value in the donor's gross estate since they will also represent a minority interest. Suppose, for example, that a taxpayer owns stock in a corporation that has a value of $1 million. A common strategy is to exchange that stock for an interest as a limited partner in a partnership that restricts the taxpayer's ability to withdraw the stock from the partnership and to participate in the management of the partnership. If the form of the transaction is respected, the value of the partnership interest will be included in the gross estate at a value much lower than $1 million value of the transferred stock.

The IRS had limited success challenging family partnerships employing traditional substance-over-form arguments, such as the step-transaction and business-purpose doctrines, discussed above. In Senda v. Commissioner, 433 F.3d 1044, 1048–1049 (8th Cir. 2006), the court held that transfers of stock to a family limited partnership followed by transfers of limited partnership interests to the taxpayer's children on the same day should be treated under the step-transaction doctrine as transfers of the stock to the children. As a result, the partnership was disregarded in valuing the taxpayer's gifts However, in Holman v. Commissioner, 130 T.C. No. 12 (2008), the court rejected application of the step-transaction doctrine and allowed a minority discount where the taxpayers transferred stock to a family limited partnership and six days later transferred limited partnership interests in that partnership to their children. The court concluded that the passage of six days was sufficient to preclude disregarding the partnership.

The courts have rejected the notion that a partnership needs a valid business purpose to be respected for transfer tax valuation purposes. In Strangi v. Commissioner, 115 T.C. 478 (2000), aff'd on this issue, 293 F.3d 279 (5th Cir. 2002), D transferred assets into a limited partnership in exchange for interests as a limited partner. At D's death, his estate valued his limited partnership interests at a discount of 33% below the value of the partnership's assets. The issue before the court was whether the interests as a limited partner should be disregarded so that D would be treated as owning his share of the partnership's assets directly. The court determined that the partnership lacked a business purpose, but that it nevertheless should be taken into account in valuing D's estate because it validly existed under state law. A third party buyer would pay a price for D's interests that reflected such interests were limited partnership interests. See also, Knight v. Commissioner, 115 T.C. 506 (2000) (reaching same conclusion).

This reasoning is incorrect. The issue is not whether a partnership validly exists for state law purposes, but whether it should be respected for tax law purposes. In the income tax, the courts long ago determined that they would disregard an entity that lacked a business purpose to determine the tax effect of a transaction involving the entity even though the entity validly existed for state law purposes. See, e.g., *Gregory v. Helvering*, 293 U.S. 465 (1935). In the estate and gift tax, the courts have also sought to identify the substance of a transaction. See, for example, p. 212 discussing the reciprocal trust doctrine. The courts in *Strangi* and *Knight* should have disregarded the partnership interests and valued D's share of the partnership's assets as though D owned them directly. Such treatment would have been consistent with the substance of what D had transferred since in most circumstances family partnerships can be easily dissolved with no adverse tax consequence.

The IRS has successfully challenged family limited partnerships using § 2036 where it has shown that D retained enjoyment of the assets that she transferred to the partnership. See Chapter 15 for a discussion of those cases. For the impact of §§ 2703 and 2704 on minority discounts, see Chapter 36.

D.   LACK OF MARKETABILITY DISCOUNT

A discount from the otherwise determined value of unlisted stock for lack of marketability may be allowed when the taxpayer can show that the stock to be sold lacks a ready market and the otherwise determined value was based upon publicly traded stock. The discount reflects the fact that a purchaser would pay less for an asset which could not be readily resold and is usually permitted by the courts without inquiry into whether the stock will be sold or held as an investment.

Courts generally determine the discount for lack of marketability by comparing the sales prices of registered stock of comparable companies to the sales price of nonregistered stock of those companies. See Estate of Jung v. Commissioner, 101 T.C. 412, 435–437 (1993). The marketability discount should not reflect the extra costs associated with selling nonregistered stock for the reasons discussed at p. 697 in connection with blockage discounts.

SECTION B.   VALUATION OF REAL PROPERTY

Revenue Procedure 79–24

1979–1 C.B. 565.

SECTION 1. PURPOSE.

The purpose of this Revenue Procedure is to provide the guidance necessary to properly utilize the market data approach in appraising unimproved real property for federal income, estate, and gift tax purposes.

SEC. 2. DEFINITION OF UNIMPROVED REAL PROPERTY.

Unimproved real property is defined as land without significant buildings, structures, or any other improvements that contribute to its value.

SEC. 3. PROCEDURE.

.01   The best indication of the value of property being appraised is the price paid for the property in an arm's-length transaction on or prior to the valuation date. When the property to be appraised has not recently been the subject of an arm's-length transaction, the best method of estimating the value of unimproved real property is by use of the market data or comparable sales approach. This approach uses arm's-length sales of properties that exhibit the most similar characteristics to the property being valued. The sales transactions used will adhere to the following definition of fair market value:

The fair market value as defined in section 1.170A–1(c)(2) of the Income Tax Regulations, section 20.2031–1(b) of the Estate Tax Regulations and section 25.2512–1 of the Gift Tax Regulations is the price at which the property would change hands between a willing buyer an a willing seller, neither being under any compulsion to buy or to sell and both having reasonable knowledge of relevant facts. Fair market value is a definite amount paid in cash or its equivalent for a given property and is the same regardless of the purpose for which it is appraised.

.02   Potentially comparable sales may be obtained from tax assessors, real estate brokers, appraisers, the recorder of deeds or other sources. The appraiser should first make a detailed inspection of the property being appraised and the potential comparable properties. During the inspection of the property to be appraised and each potential comparable property, the following factors or information should be considered:

(a) Location, including proximity to roads, schools, shopping, transportation, and other amenities;

(b) Configuration, topographic features, and total area;

(c) Restrictions as to land use or zoning;

(d) Road frontage and accessibility;

(e) Available utilities and water rights;

(f) Existing easements, rights of way, leases, etc.;

(g) Soil characteristics;

(h) Vegetative cover, such as: grass, brush, trees, or timber;

(i) Status of mineral rights;

(j) Riparian rights;

(k) Other factors affecting value.

Additional information necessary includes the name of the buyer, the name of the seller, the deed book and page number, the date of sale, sale price, property description, amount and terms of mortgages, property surveys, the assessed value, tax rate, and the assessor's appraised fair market value.

Detailed analyses of the comparable property sales should include considerations of similarity of highest and best use legally permissible, the time interval between sale date and valuation date, economic similarities and trends affecting the neighborhoods. If any sale is a distress sale, a forced sale, or one negotiated with unusual terms provided by the seller, it should be discarded. Probative value is added to the use of comparable property sale when each sale price has been confirmed by either the purchaser, seller, real estate broker involved in the sale, or lawyer or title company handling the transaction. At this time, it may be determined whether there was any compulsion exercised by either party to the sale or if there were any motives affecting the purchase price.

.03 Comparable property sales may be used only after the sales prices have been adjusted for differences between the properties. In making adjustments the appraiser should adjust to the property being appraised. Many property features are of equal value and require no adjustment of the sale price. Adjustments for time are necessary unless prices for real estate are static between the dates of sale and the valuation date. Adjustments are a judgmental conclusion of the appraiser and are usually shown as a percentage change.

The results determined from the market data or comparable property sales approach will generally be an array of indicated values for the unimproved property being appraised; such values should not be merely averaged. A review should be made of the comparable sales and only those sales having the least adjustment in items and/or the least total adjustments should be considered as comparable to the property being appraised. The adjustments should be reviewed to assure that adequate and meaningful data were used and that each adjustment was properly weighted. The appraiser should then conclude that two or three adjusted sales furnish the most reliable estimate of fair market value of unimproved real property by the market data or comparable sales approach.

ILLUSTRATIVE MATERIAL

A. IMPROVED REAL ESTATE

For improved real estate, the courts will often use the capitalization of income method in addition to the comparable property sales method to determine the property's value. See e.g., Shepherd v. Commissioner, 115 T.C. 376, 392 (2000), aff'd, 283 F.3d 1258 (11th Cir. 2002).

B. FRACTIONAL INTERESTS

The courts frequently permit ''minority discounts'' for fractional interests. A commentator explains:

''The term minority discount in the context of undivided interests in real estate, however, is a misnomer; an undivided fractional interest in land merely gives the possessor the right to the use and enjoyment of the land in a manner that does not conflict with the other owners.[19] Even where an individual owns a 90% undivided interest in real estate, the value of the interest would not equal 90% of the value of the entire parcel because the 90% owner would have to obtain a partition of the property in order to obtain the right to exclusive possession of 90% of the property. Thus, a purchaser would deduct the costs and uncertainties of obtaining a partition in determining the value of the 90% individual interest.[20] For example, in *Estate of Pillsbury v. Commissioner*[21] the Tax Court allowed a 15% discount for a 77% undivided interest in real estate to reflect the illiquidity of the interest and the fact that the owner of the interest would have to share control of the parcel with the other joint owners. Because the owner of an undivided interest in real estate has a right to partition and to gain total control of a portion of the real estate, the discounts tend to be lower than for minority blocks of stock, usually only about 10 to 20% below a pro rata portion of the value of the total parcel.[22] In contrast, minority discounts for closely held corporations usually average 20 to 30%.[23]"

Repetti, Minority Discounts: The Alchemy in Estate and Gift Taxation, 50 Tax L. Rev. 415, 428–429 (1995).

C.   VALUATION OF JOINT TENANCIES

Recall from Chapter 21 that § 2040 includes in a decedent's estate property he held as a joint tenant to the extent that the other joint tenants had not contributed to the acquisition of the tenancy. In Estate of Young v. Commissioner, 110 T.C. 297 (1998), the Tax Court held that no minority discount should be allowed for amounts included under § 2040(a):

19.   Anna C. Fowler, Valuation of Undivided Interests in Realty: When Do the Parts Sum to Less Than the Whole?, 13 J. Real Est. Tax'n 123, 125 (1986).

20.   *Id.* For an excellent discussion of the valuation of other types of interests in real estate, specifically remainder interests and conservation easements, see Kingsbury Browne, Jr. & Walter G. Van Dorn, Charitable Gifts of Partial Interests in Real Property for Conservation Purposes, 29 Tax Law. 69, 86–93 (1975).

21.   64 T.C.M. 284(1992).

22.   See, e.g., Propstra v. United States, 680 F.2d 1248 (9th Cir. 1982) (15% discount); Estate of Cervin v. Commissioner, 68 T.C.M. 1115 (1994) (20% discount); Estate of Pillsbury v. Commissioner, 64 T.C.M. 284 (1992) (15% discount); Zable v. Commissioner, 58 T.C.M. 1330 (1990) (10% discount); Estate of Youle v. Commissioner, 56 T.C.M. 1594 (1989) (12.5% discount); Estate of Van Loben Sels v. Commissioner, 52 T.C.M. 731 (1986) (combined minority discount and lack marketability discount of 60%); Estate of Quinn v. Commissioner, 43 T.C.M. 352 (1982) (11% discount).

23.   Most cases do not separately state the discount for a minority interest in a closely held corporation, but instead combine it with a discount for lack of marketability. Recent cases that have separately stated the minority discount for closely held corporations, however, show that the minority discount ranges from 20 to 30%. See, e.g., Northern Trust Co. v. Commissioner, 87 T.C. 349, 385 (1986) (25% discount); Estate of Frank v. Commissioner, 69 T.C.M. 2255, 2263 (1995) (20% discount); Estate of Luton, 68 T.C.M. 1044, 1050–55 (1994) (20% discount); Estate of Ford v. Commissioner, 66 T.C.M. 1507, 1518 (1993), aff'd, 53 F.3d 924 (8th Cir. 1995) (20% discount); Estate of Lenheim v. Commissioner, 60 T.C.M. 356, 371 (1990) (30% discount); Carr v. Commissioner, 49 T.C.M. 507, 514 (1985) (25% discount).

"Under the scheme of section 2040(a), the amount includable in a decedent's gross estate does not depend on a valuation of property rights actually transferred at death, or on a valuation of the actual interest held by the decedent (legal title); instead, decedent's gross estate includes the entire value of property held in a joint tenancy by him and any other person, except to the extent the consideration for the property was furnished by such other person. See Estate of Peters v. Commissioner, 386 F.2d 404, 407 (4th Cir. 1967), affg. 46 T.C. 407 (1966). Contrary to petitioner's argument, the statute does not inquire how much a willing buyer would pay to purchase the decedent's interest in the joint tenancy at the date of his death, because, at the moment of death, decedent no longer holds any interest in the property. The property passes by right of survivorship, unlike property governed by section 2033 which passes under a decedent's will or by intestate succession. Even if prior to death, decedent sold his interest in the joint tenancy (and by doing so severed the joint tenancy with right of survivorship), the value that a willing buyer would pay does not necessarily compare to the approach taken by Congress in section 2040. Section 2040(a) provides an artificial inclusion of the joint tenancy property: the entire value of the property less any contribution by the surviving joint tenant. Except for the statutory exclusions in section 2040(a), there is no further allowance to account for the fact that less than the entire interest is being included. * * *

"As a result of this artificial inclusion, we conclude that section 2040 is not concerned with quantifying the value of the fractional interest held by the decedent (as would be the case under section 2033). The fractional interest discount, as applied in section 2033, is based on the notion that the interest is worth less than its proportionate share, due in part to the problems of concurrent ownership. These problems are created by the unity of interest and unity of possession. However, at the moment of death, the co-ownership in joint tenancy is severed, thus alleviating the problems associated with co-ownership. We conclude that the Young Property is not entitled to a fractional interest discount."

D. VALUATION OF REAL PROPERTY USED IN FAMILY FARMS AND BUSINESSES

See p. 786 for the special rules applicable to the valuation of family farms and businesses.

Section C.   The Use of Mortality and Interest Tables in Valuation

Internal Revenue Code: § 7520

Regulations: §§ 20.2031–7; 25.2512–5; 20.7520–1, 3; 25.7520–1, 3

Special problems arise in connection with the valuation of life, remainder, and reversionary interests, as well as the valuation of annuities. The value of these interests depends upon the longevity of a person who is used as a measuring life and an appropriate rate of return or interest rate for such property. Section 7520(a) requires that the values be determined using tables prescribed by the IRS. The tables are published in two volumes. IRS Publication 1457, "Actuarial Values Book Aleph" (the Book Aleph) contains tables and examples for determining the values of annuities, life estates, terms of years, remainders and reversions, IRS Publication 1458, "Actuarial Values Book Beth" (the Book Beth) includes tables for calculating the values of remainder interests in charitable remainder unitrusts, as defined in Reg. § 1.642(c)–5. See p. 545. for a discussion of charitable remainder unitrusts. Some of the Tables are reproduced in Regs. §§ 20.2031–7(d)(6) and 25.2512–5(d).

The tables determine value for property interests measured by a life by making gender neutral actuarial assumptions about the longevity of the measuring life. These values are presented for various interest rates. The actual interest rate selected by a taxpayer to calculate a value must equal 120% of the federal midterm rate in effect under § 1274(d)(1) for the month in which the valuation date falls.[24] Congress opted for a "bright-line" determination of appropriate rates of return instead of trying to determine suitable rates based on the nature of the specific property.

Annuities—The IRS has issued tables to value annuities payable for a term certain or for a measuring life. The tables apply to an "ordinary annuity interest", i.e., the right to receive a fixed amount at the end of year for a fixed period of time or for a measuring life, Regs. §§ 20.7520–3(b)(1)(i); 25.7520–3(b)(1)(i); 20.2031–7(d)(2)(iv) and 25.2512–5(d)(2)(iv); which is not issued by a company regularly engaged in the sale of annuities.[25] Reg. § 20.2031–7(b).

If the annuity will pay a fixed sum for a period of years, Table B of the Book Aleph is used.[26] For example, assume that an annuity will pay $1,000 each year for 10 years and that 120% of the Federal midterm rate is 10%. Table B would require a factor of 6.1446 to be used. (The relevant portion of Table B is reproduced in Appendix A of this Casebook.) This factor, multiplied by the yearly $1,000 annuity payment, yields a value for the annuity of $6,144.60.

If the annuity will pay a sum at the end of each year for a measuring life, than Table S of the Book Aleph is used.[27] Suppose that A, age 40, will receive $1,000 per year for her life and that 120% of the Federal midterm rate equals 10%. (The relevant portion of Table S is reproduced in Appendix A of this Casebook.) Table S states a factor of 9.3589 which yields a value of $9358.90 for the annuity (9.3589 x $1,000).

Terms of Years and Life Interests—If the interest is the right of a person to receive the income of certain property or to use certain nonin-

---

24. If an income, estate or gift tax charitable contribution deduction is allowable for any part of the property transferred, the taxpayer may elect to use the Federal midterm rate for either of the two months preceding the month in which the valuation date falls.

25. Annuities issued by companies regularly engaged in the sale of annuities are valued by comparison to "comparable" contracts. Reg. § 20.2031–8.

26. Table B annuity factors are not included in Reg. § 20.2031–7. Reg. § 20.2031–7(d)(2)(iv).

27. Table S annuity factors are not included in Reg. § 20.2031–7. Reg. § 20.2031–7(d)(2)(iv).

come-producing property, for a term of years or for a measuring life, then Tables B and S in the Book Aleph are again used.[28] Regs. §§ 20.7502–3(b)(1)(i); 25.7502–3(b)(1)(i); 20.2031–7(d)(2)(iii) and 25.2512–5(d)(2)(iii). For example, assume that A has the right to receive all the income for 10 years from property which has a fair market value of $100,000. Table B would require a factor of .614457 to be used, assuming a 10% interest rate. This would result in a value of A's term interest equal to $61,445.72 (.614457 X $100,000).

Suppose instead that A, age 40, has the right to receive all the income from the same property for the rest of his life. Table S of the Book Aleph would require a factor of .93589 to be used, again assuming a 10% interest rate. Thus A's life interest would be valued at $93,589 (.93589 x $100,000).

Remainder or Reversionary Interest—If the interest is the right to receive property at the end of one or more measuring lives or defined period, Tables B and S again apply. Regs. §§ 20.7520–3(b)(1)(i); 25.7520–3(b)(1)(i); 20.2031–7(d)(2)(ii) and 25.2512–5(d)(2)(ii). For example, assume that A is given the right to receive a fee simple interest in property in 10 years and that the property has a current fair market value of $10,000. Table B would require a factor of .385543 assuming a 10% interest rate with the result that the value of the remainder interest is $3,855.43 (.385543 x $10,000). The Table B factors for term remainder interests are reproduced in Reg. § 20.2031–7(d)(6).

Alternatively, suppose that A is given the right to receive the property upon the death of B, who is currently 40. Table S would require a factor of .06411 assuming a 10% interest rate. The value of the remainder interest would therefore be $641.10 (.06411 x $10,000). The Table S factors for life remainder interests are reproduced in Reg. § 20.2031–7(d)(6).

Recall that § 2037 requires decedent's estate to determine whether her reversionary interest immediately before her death exceeds 5% of the property subject to the reversionary interest (see Chapter 16). For example, suppose D transferred property in trust, income payable to S for life and remainder payable to D, or if D is not living, remainder payable to C or C's estate. The value of D's reversionary interest equals the probability that she would survive S immediately before her death multiplied by the value of the remainder interest. The tables published by the IRS do not provide the information necessary to make this determination, but the IRS will perform the calculations upon request.

ILLUSTRATIVE MATERIAL

A. SPECIAL RULES FOR TRANSFERS TO FAMILY MEMBERS

Section 2702 applies special valuation rules where a donor makes a transfer of an interest in property to a family member while retaining an

---

28. Table B and Table S term-of-years and life-interest factors are not included in Reg. § 20.2031–7. Reg. § 20.2031–7(d)(2)(iii).

interest in the same property. For example, § 2702 may apply to a transfer from parent (P) to child (C) of a remainder interest where P retains a life estate in the underlying property. Rather than simply value the gift by reference to the transferred remainder interest, § 2702, if applicable, would disregard the interest retained by P and treat P as having transferred all value in the property to C. The interest retained by the transferor will not be disregarded if it is a "qualified interest," an interest that is required to pay a fixed amount to the transferor each year. Section 2702 is discussed in Chapter 37.

B.   MORE THAN ONE MEASURING LIFE

Table R(2) of Publication 1457 shows the factors to be used to value a remainder interest in property that vests upon the death of the last to die of two persons. Values of property interests dependent upon more than two lives may be obtained from the IRS. Regs. §§ 20.2031–7(d)(4) and 25.2512–5(d)(4).

C.   PROBABILITY OF OTHER EVENTS

The use of probabilities to determine values is not confined to actuarial estimates of life spans. In Rev. Rul. 71–67, 1971–1 C.B. 271, the IRS used the American Remarriage Table which compiles statistics about the rates of remarriage for persons of different demographic features to value a support obligation which would terminate upon the death of decedent's spouse.

The use of statistics will often be affected, however, by the fact that unlike death (in most instances), remarriage or procreation are usually voluntary acts. In Rev. Rul. 61–88, 1961–1 C.B. 417, the IRS addressed the appropriate method to value a remainder interest contingent upon the life beneficiary dying without issue. The IRS ruled that in the absence of facts tending to show that the birth of issue to the life beneficiary was impossible, actuarial formulas could not be used. But, the IRS further stated that the remainder interest could be valued by considering "all known circumstances relative to the particular life tenant, rather than women aged 44 in general." Similarly in Rev. Rul. 76–472, 1976–2 C.B. 264, the IRS ruled that D's vested remainder interest, which could be diminished if his 53–year–old mother had additional issue, could not use "actuarial formulas" but rather must consider "all known facts and circumstances."

Why is the IRS willing to determine contingent value in the circumstances of the rulings, but not the value of the grantor's reversionary interest in Robinette v. Williams, discussed at p. 317? Is a different standard applied where a donor attempts to reduce the value of his gift by assigning value to his contingent retained interest?

D.   INDIVIDUAL USED AS MEASURING LIFE TERMINALLY ILL

Use of the valuation tables is generally mandatory. Reg. §§ 20.7520–1(a)(1); 25.7520–1(a)(1). The Regulations prohibit the use of a person as a measuring life, however, if the person is terminally ill at the time of the transfer of the property interest. Regs. §§ 20.7520–1(a)(1); 25.7520–1(a)(1); Regs. §§ 20.7520–3(b)(3)(i) and 25.7520–3(b)(3). In general, a person is considered terminally ill if there is at least a 50% probability that the person will die within 1 year. However, if the person used as a measuring life survives 18 months or longer after the transfer date, that person will be presumed to have not been terminally ill at the transfer date unless clear and convincing evidence shows otherwise.

E. LOTTERIES

It is not clear whether the courts will allow departure from the tables in valuing annuities payable by a state to a lottery winner where the annuity is not transferable. Taxpayers have argued that a discount from the value determined by using the tables should be allowed where the annuity is not transferable. Reg. § 20.7520–3(b)(1)(i), which applies to the estates of decedents dying after December 3, 1995, does not list non-transferability as a circumstance that allows departure from the tables. The regulation does, however, state that the tables "may" not apply to a "restricted" annuity, although it fails to define what "restricted" means.

In cases that involved decedents dying prior to the effective date of the regulation, the courts have split. The Courts of Appeals for the Ninth Circuit and Second Circuit have concluded that values determined by the tables for lottery annuities may be reduced to reflect the fact that the annuities are not transferable. Shackleford v. United States, 262 F.3d 1028 (9th Cir. 2001); Estate of Gribauskas v. Commissioner, 342 F.3d 85 (2d Cir. 2003). The Court of Appeals for the Fifth Circuit has concluded otherwise. Estate of Cook v. Commissioner, 349 F.3d 850 (5th Cir. 2003).

Courts that have decided cases for decedents who died after December 3, 1995 have also split. In Estate of Donovan v. United States, 95 AFTR 2d 2005–2131 (D. Mass. 2005), the court ruled that lack of transferability did not cause a lottery annuity to be "restricted" within the meaning of the regulation and, therefore, that the value of the annuity determined by the tables could not be reduced to reflect the fact that it was not transferable. See also Anthony v. United States, 2005–2 USTC ¶ 60,504 (M.D. La. 2005) (value of annuity received in settlement of lawsuit could not be reduced to reflect non-transferability because non-transferability is not a "restriction" under Reg. § 20.7520–3(b)(1)(i)). In contrast, the court in Negron v. United States, 502 F. Supp. 2d 682 (N.D. Oh, 2007), ruled that the value of a lottery annuity could be reduced to reflect non-transferability. The *Negron* court's analysis is suspect, however, because it relied on *Shackleford* and *Gribauskas* without considering whether Reg. § 20.7520–3(b)(1)(i), which did not apply in those cases because the decedents had died before December 3, 1995, would have changed their holdings.

IMPACT OF BUY–SELL AGREEMENTS, LAPSING RIGHTS AND LIQUIDATION RESTRICTIONS ON VALUATION

Internal Revenue Code: §§ 2703, 2704

Regulations: §§ 20.2031–3(h); 25.2703–1; 25.2703–2; 25.2704–1; 25.2704–2

Often in a closely held business, the owners will wish to restrict ownership to persons they know and can work with. As a result, the owners will agree to restrict inter vivos and post mortem transfers of their stock or other proprietary interests to third parties. These agreements frequently give other owners the right to purchase a proprietary interest at a predetermined price when an owner dies or when an owner wishes to make an inter vivos transfer.

If the prices designated in such agreements establish the value of ownership interests for transfer tax purposes, the agreements can become very powerful planning devices. For example, if an agreement permits other owners to purchase stock at a fixed price upon the owner's death and this price establishes the stock value for estate tax purposes, the owner has "frozen" the value of his stock. This technique is a variant of the "estate freeze."

In other types of agreements, some owners are given valuable voting or liquidation rights in connection with their proprietary interests but these rights lapse in certain events. If these rights lapse at death, the issue is whether the value of the proprietary interests should be determined without considering the lapsed liquidation or voting right.

In still other situations, restrictions are imposed on an owner's ability to liquidate a corporation or partnership. The question is whether such restrictions will be disregarded in valuing the owner's interest.

This Chapter considers the rules that have been developed to consider the impact of the foregoing arrangements on transfer tax valuation.

SECTION A.   RESTRICTIVE TRANSFER AGREEMENTS

The tax effect of an agreement that gives owners the right to purchase the proprietary interest of another owner depends upon the type of agreement and whether the statutory requirements of § 2703 as well as judicially developed requirements are satisfied.

1. TYPES OF AGREEMENTS

a. FIRST OFFER AGREEMENTS

Under a "first offer agreement" an interest may not be sold to outsiders either inter vivos or at death unless it has first been offered to the other owners at an agreed price, or at a price to be computed according to a specified formula. No right to buy an interest arises until such time as the owner decides to sell it.

First offer agreements do not have the effect of limiting the value of the property interest for transfer tax purposes to the price specified in the agreement because the agreement price becomes material only when the owner decides to sell the interest. Until that time, the owner—or the estate and then the legatee—possesses the right to enjoy the income to be derived from the business interest. See Commissioner v. McCann, 146 F.2d 385 (2d Cir. 1944); Worcester County Trust Co. v. Commissioner, 134 F.2d 578 (1st Cir. 1943). However, subject to § 2703 and certain judicially created requirements which are discussed below, the existence of a first offer agreement may depress the value of the interest below that determined absent the agreement because the owner does not have the same powers of disposition as an unrestricted owner. See Mathews v. United States, 226 F.Supp. 1003 (E.D.N.Y. 1964); Estate of Reynolds v. Commissioner, 55 T.C. 172 (1970).

b. OPTION AGREEMENTS

An option agreement provides the option holder the right, but not the obligation, to purchase the property subject to the option. If the option holder decides to exercise this right, the property owner is required to sell the property to the option holder.

An option agreement for a closely held business frequently provides that, upon an owner's death, the other owners have the right to purchase his interest at a price determined by the agreement. For estate tax purposes, the value of the interest subject to such an option agreement that satisfies § 2703 and the judicial tests will usually not exceed the price at which the optionees may purchase it. See May v. McGowan, 194 F.2d 396 (2d Cir. 1952); Rev. Rul. 59–60, 1959–1 C.B. 237. The courts assume that if the value of the business interest is in excess of the option price, the optionee will exercise the option to buy the interest so that the maximum amount the estate can hope to realize from the business interest is the option price. See Wilson v. Bowers, 57 F.2d 682 (2d Cir. 1932).

The impact of option agreements on valuation for gift tax purposes differs from the impact for estate tax purposes. The purchase price in the option agreement does not fix the value of property subject to the option for gift tax purposes because the restrictions do not affect a donee until the donee desires to sell the interest. Rev. Rul. 189, 1953–2 C.B. 294. The option agreement may, however, have a depressing effect on value, if the requirements of § 2703 are satisfied. See e.g., Spitzer v. Commissioner, 153

F.2d 967, 970 (8th Cir. 1946); Ward v. Commissioner, 87 T.C. 78, 105 (1986).

c.   BINDING AGREEMENTS

"Binding agreements" or "mandatory buy-sell agreements" are similar to "option agreements" except that instead of merely having the right to purchase the optioned property, the buyer is obligated to purchase the interest at the death of the owner. The estate tax effect of such agreements are similar to that of option agreements. See e.g., Estate of Littick v. Commissioner, 31 T.C. 181 (1958); Estate of Seltzer v. Commissioner, 50 T.C.M. 1250 (1985).

As is the case with option agreements, the price designated in a mandatory buy-sell agreement will not define the value of the property subject to the agreement for gift tax purposes but will be considered as a factor in determining value if the requirements of § 2703 are satisfied. See Harwood v. Commissioner, 82 T.C. 239, 260–263 (1984), aff'd, 786 F.2d 1174 (9th Cir. 1986), cert. den., 479 U.S. 1007 (1986) (agreement requiring surviving partners to purchase deceased partner's interest for book value in the event they wished to continue the partnership did not establish value of interest for gift tax purposes). See Ward v. Commissioner, 87 T.C. 78 (1986).

2.   SECTION 2703

Estate of Lauder v. Commissioner

64 T.C.M. 1643 (1992).

■ HAMBLEN, CHIEF JUDGE: Respondent determined a deficiency of $42,702,597.67 in the Federal estate tax due from the Estate of Joseph H. Lauder (petitioner). * * *

FINDINGS OF FACT

Some of the facts have been stipulated and are so found. The stipulations of facts and attached exhibits are incorporated herein by this reference.

Joseph H. Lauder died testate at age 81 in the State of New York on January 16, 1983, survived by his wife, Estee Lauder (Estee), and his two sons, Leonard A. Lauder (Leonard) and Ronald S. Lauder (Ronald). (References to the Lauders are to Estee, Joseph, Leonard, and Ronald collectively.)

I.   *Background*

A.   *Estee Lauder, Inc.*

Estee Lauder became interested in skin care and cosmetics as a young girl while assisting her uncle, a chemist, with the preparation of skin creams in a laboratory behind her family's house. Estee and Joseph entered the cosmetics business just after World War II.

On May 20, 1958, Fragrance Products Corp. was incorporated under the laws of the State of New York. In 1963, the name of the company was changed to Estee Lauder, Inc. (ELI). At all times pertinent hereto, ELI and its subsidiaries and affiliates were engaged in the manufacture and distribution of cosmetics, fragrances, and related products.

In the beginning, ELI sold four basic skin care products through a few beauty salons in New York City. Estee and Joseph were ELI's sole employees and business was conducted in the rented basement of a building in New York City.

Saks Fifth Avenue was the first specialty store to carry ELI's products. Through the mid-seventies, the Lauders maintained a policy of distributing ELI's products exclusively through high-end specialty and department stores.

Leonard and Ronald began working part-time for the business during their early teenage years, delivering orders and doing odd jobs. Leonard, who is 11 years older than Ronald, joined the business on a full-time basis in 1958 after graduating from the University of Pennsylvania and serving in the United States Navy. At that time, ELI generated annual sales of $800,000 and its facilities were so small that Leonard shared an office with Estee, served as the only salesman, and was also responsible for public relations, product advertising, marketing, and package delivery. Leonard became president of ELI in 1973.

Ronald joined the business on a full-time basis in 1967. Prior to that time, Ronald attended the University of Pennsylvania, studied international business at the University of Brussels (while working in ELI's factory in Belgium), and served in the United States Coast Guard. Initially, Ronald serviced two major accounts and was coordinator of marketing groups. Ronald became ELI's vice president for marketing and sales in 1973.

Estee attributed the success of the business to the family's hard work. The Lauders shared the view that it was of utmost importance to keep the business in the family. As one of the few privately held cosmetics companies, the Lauders believed that ELI operated at a substantial advantage over its competitors. In their view, ELI was in a position to take more risks and move more aggressively than publicly held companies. Further, market share and sales could be built without concerns of showing an immediate profit.

* * *

D. *The ELI Agreement*

On May 28, 1974, ELI common stock (voting and non-voting) was owned as follows:

Shareholder	Voting	(%)	Nonvoting	(%)	Total
Estee	2,546	(67)	9,754	(32)	12,300
Joseph	684	(18)	7,452	(24)	8,136
Leonard	285	(7.5)	6,951	(22)	7,236
Ronald	285	(7.5)	6,951	(22)	7,236
Totals	3,800		31,108		34,908

On this date, the Lauders and ELI executed a document entitled "Shareholder Agreement" (the 1974 agreement). The 1974 agreement states in pertinent part:

Article 2. Voluntary Transfer

2.1 Notice

If any Shareholder during his lifetime (the "Offeror") intends to transfer any Shares which he owns, he shall give written notice to the Corporation and the other Shareholders of his intention to do so. The notice shall state the number of Voting Shares and the number of Nonvoting Shares to be transferred.

2.2 First Offer

Within 60 days after the receipt by the Corporation of the foregoing notice, each of the other Shareholders shall have the option to purchase for a purchase price determined in accordance with Article 6 hereof, such portion of the Voting Shares and such portion of the Nonvoting Shares set forth in such notice (the "Offered Shares") as the number of Voting Shares and the number of Nonvoting Shares owned by him on the date of receipt of such notice shall bear to the total number of Voting Shares and the total number of Nonvoting Shares owned by the Shareholders, provided, however, that if any Shareholder does not purchase his full proportionate share of the Offered Shares, the unaccepted Shares may be purchased by the other Shareholders proportionately.

2.3 Second Offer

If for any reason all the Offered Shares are not purchased by the Shareholders within 60 days after the Corporation's receipt of such notice, the Corporation shall have the option to purchase all of the Offered Shares not purchased by the Shareholders for a purchase price determined pursuant to Article 5 [6] hereof on a date to be mutually determined by the Shareholders, but not later than 90 days after the Corporation's receipt of such notice. Notwithstanding anything herein contained to the contrary, if the Offeror at the time of giving notice owns more than fifty percent (50%) of the Voting Shares, the Corporation shall be required to purchase all of the Offered Shares which are Voting Shares and which are not purchased by the Shareholders for a purchase price determined pursuant to Article 6 hereof on a date to be mutually determined by the Shareholders but not later than 90 days after the Corporation's receipt of such notice.

Article 3. Transfer Upon Death

Upon the death of any Shareholder, all of the Shares then held in the estate of the deceased Shareholder shall be offered for purchase according to the terms of Paragraphs 2.2 and 2.3 of Article 2 hereof * * *

Article 6. Purchase Price

6.1   Determination of Value

The purchase price of Shares to be purchased hereunder shall be the net per share book value of such shares (excluding any value for all intangible assets, such as goodwill . . ., etc.) as determined in the last audited annual statement of the Corporation preceding (a) the date the notice with respect to such shares is received by the Corporation; (b) in the event of a transfer pursuant to Article 3 hereof, the date of death of the deceased Shareholder; or (c) in the event of a transfer pursuant to Article 4 hereof, the date of termination of employment (the "last Audited Statement Date"). The determination in such last audited annual statement shall be final and binding upon all parties.

While the 1974 agreement generally applies to voluntary transfers and transfers after the death of a shareholder, the agreement also mandates that a shareholder's stock be offered for sale to the remaining shareholders upon: The shareholder's termination of employment with ELI, or an involuntary transfer by operation of law (e.g., bankruptcy).

Article 6.2 of the agreement states that in computing the purchase price for the shares, book value is to be reduced by the amount of any dividends paid subsequent to the date of the last financial statement and before the closing date of the stock sale and adjusted by the receipt of any unrecorded tax refund or prepayment of any tax deficiency. Article 6.3 states that the purchase price for the shares may be paid either in cash or by delivery of a 10–year debenture bearing interest at 4 percent.

The 1974 agreement was Leonard's idea. Leonard arrived at the book value formula after consulting with Arnold M. Ganz, a close family financial adviser now deceased. Leonard did not compare the stock prices of publicly traded cosmetics companies with their respective book value. No appraisal of ELI or its stock was obtained in connection with the 1974 agreement. In arriving at the formula price, Leonard considered that companies listed in the Standard & Poor's 400 Index were selling at approximately book value. An index within the Standard & Poor's 400 reflects an average price-to-book-value ratio of approximately 2 to 1 for cosmetics companies during 1974.

Estee had no specific recollection of the 1974 agreement. Ronald did not know who decided that the price per share under the 1974 agreement would be based on book value. Ronald recalled that Leonard explained the book value pricing formula to him. Ronald did not give much thought to the pricing formula before agreeing to join in the 1974 agreement.

The purchase price per share of ELI common stock on May 28, 1974, as determined in accordance with Article 6 of the 1974 agreement, was $614.70.

* * *

G. *The EJL Agreement*

* * *

EJL was formed as a holding company for ELI * * * on December 14, 1976.

On the same day, the Lauders and EJL executed a document entitled "EJL Shareholder Agreement" (the 1976 agreement). On that date, the common stock of EJL was owned as follows:

Shareholder	Voting	(%)	Nonvoting	(%)	Total
Estee	2,546	(67)	9,754	(32)	12,300
Joseph	760	(20)	7,376	(24)	8,136
Leonard	247	(6.5)	6,989	(22)	7,236
Ronald	24	(6.5)	6,989	(22)	7,236
Totals	3,800		31,108		34,908

The terms of the 1976 agreement are essentially identical to those of the 1974 agreement, except that: (1) The first option to purchase rests with EJL; (2) payment may be made in cash or in 20–year debentures bearing interest equal to the average industrial bond yield for "Aa" rated bonds for the 3 months preceding their issuance; (3) EJL's consent is required for any transfer of common stock to a nonshareholder and the prospective shareholder must agree to be bound by the terms of the 1976 agreement;[1] and (4) the formula for determining the purchase price of the shares is based on book value reduced by the amount of dividends payable, as well as dividends paid, during the period between the valuation date and the close of the stock sale.

Prior to executing the 1976 agreement, neither the Lauders nor EJL obtained an appraisal of EJL or its stock, nor did they compare the stock prices of publicly traded cosmetics companies with their respective book values. Leonard did not examine the Standard and Poor's 400 Index in determining the pricing formula used in the 1976 agreement. An index within the Standard & Poor's 400 reflects an average price to book value ratio of approximately 3 to 1 for cosmetics companies during 1976. Estee had no specific recollection of the 1976 agreement.

The purchase price per share of EJL common stock on December 14, 1976, as determined in accordance with Article 6 of the 1976 agreement, was $1,212.07.

* * *

---

1. The 1976 agreement states that in deciding whether to consent to a transfer to a nonshareholder, EJL should consider the Lauders' intention to maintain EJL as a family business and to prevent stock transfers to a competitor.

J. *Amendment of the EJL Agreement*

In February 1983, Ronald began serving as Deputy Assistant Secretary of Defense for European and NATO policy. At that time, Ronald resigned his position as an officer of EJL and its related companies. Ronald nonetheless continued to serve as an EJL director.

From April 1986 to November 1987, Ronald served as U.S. Ambassador to Austria. Pursuant to Federal law, Ronald was required to resign his positions with EJL, including his position as a director. On April 18, 1986, the Lauders agreed to amend the 1976 agreement to provide that the resignation of an employee, officer, or director of EJL required in connection with the acceptance of an elected Government office or appointment to a position in public service would not be deemed to be a termination of employment under the agreement. Consistent with this amendment to the 1976 agreement, Ronald was not obligated to offer his shares for sale to EJL or the remaining shareholders while serving as Ambassador to Austria. Ronald eventually returned to EJL in November 1987.

From June 1981 (when the shares held by the University of Pennsylvania were redeemed) through the time of trial, EJL common stock has been held solely by the Lauders or by trusts for the benefit of the children of Leonard and Ronald.

* * *

VI. *Federal Estate Tax Return, Deficiency Notice, and Petition*

On the date of Joseph's death, EJL common stock was owned as follows:

Owner	Voting	Nonvoting	Total
Estee	2,546	7,684	10,230
Joseph	760	5,996	6,756
Leonard	247	5,614	5,861
Ronald	247	5,614	5,861
Trusts for the children of Leonard and Ronald	0	4,100	4,100
Total	3,800	29,008	32,808

On April 30, 1983, petitioner sold decedent's 6,756 shares of EJL common stock to EJL at $4,111 per share, the price per share being determined pursuant to the terms of the 1976 agreement.

Petitioner reported decedent's shares of EJL common stock as having a date of death value of $29,050,800 (or $4,300 per share) on its Federal estate tax return. In the statutory notice of deficiency, respondent determined the date of death value of decedent's stock to be $89,517,000 (or $13,250 per share). In its petition, petitioner alleges that the correct date of death value of the stock is $27,773,916 (or $4,111 per share).[2]

---

2. The parties stipulated that as of June 30, 1982, and June 30, 1983, the purchase price per share of EJL common stock, determined in accordance with Article 6 of the 1976 agreement, were $4,300.32 and $4,971.83, respectively.

Opinion

The issue for decision is whether the formula price contained in restrictive shareholder agreements, to which decedent was a party, controls the valuation of stock in a closely held corporation for purposes of the Federal estate tax.

Sections 2031 and 2033 provide that the value of the gross estate includes the value of all property to the extent of the interest therein of the decedent at the time of his death. The relevant value is normally the fair market value, which is "the price at which the property would change hands between a willing buyer and a willing seller, neither being under any compulsion to buy or sell and both having reasonable knowledge of relevant facts." Sec. 20.2031–1(b), Estate Tax Regs.; United States v. Cartwright, 411 U.S. 546, 551 (1973). The determination of fair market value is a question of fact. Estate of Newhouse v. Commissioner, 94 T.C. 193, 217 (1990); Estate of Gilford v. Commissioner, 88 T.C. 38, 50 (1987).

If the property to be included in the gross estate is stock that is not listed on an exchange, and cannot be valued with reference to bid and asked prices or historical sales prices, the value of listed stock of corporations engaged in the same or a similar line of business should be considered. Sec. 2031(b).

The courts, particularly the Court of Appeals for the Second Circuit to which this case is appealable, have long recognized that the value of corporate stock may be limited for Federal estate tax purposes by an enforceable buy-sell agreement or option contract which fixes the price at which the stock may be offered for sale to the remaining stockholders. * * *

Several requirements have evolved for testing whether the formula price set forth in such restrictive agreements is binding for purposes of the Federal estate tax. It is axiomatic that the offering price must be fixed and determinable under the agreement. In addition, the agreement must be binding on the parties both during life and after death. * * * Finally, the restrictive agreement must have been entered into for a bona fide business reason and must not be a substitute for a testamentary disposition. See Reg. § 20.2031–2(h) * * *.

Petitioner contends that the formula price set forth in the shareholder agreements is controlling for purposes of determining the estate tax value of decedent's stock. Petitioner maintains that the shareholder agreements establish a fixed and determinable price for the stock, that the obligation to offer the stock to the remaining shareholders is binding both during life and at death, and that there is a bona fide business purpose for the agreements. Petitioner argues that the formula reflects a fair, objective measure of the value of the stock, which approximated fair market value on the dates that the shareholder agreements were executed.

Respondent concedes that the shareholder agreements establish a fixed and determinable selling price for decedent's stock. However, respondent contends that various transfers of EJL stock by the Lauders during the period in question reveal that the Lauders themselves did not consider the agreements binding. Respondent further contends that the formula price grossly undervalued the EJL stock on the dates the shareholder agreements were executed. Respondent argues that the formula price was derived without an appraisal of EJL, that the value of intangibles is not taken into account under the formula, that the parties to the agreements did not negotiate with respect to the formula, and that the agreements do not provide for a controlling interest premium with respect to the shares held by Estee.

We are convinced that the shareholder agreements created enforceable obligations against decedent both during his life and after his death. * * * Moreover, we conclude that the Lauders considered the agreements to be binding, notwithstanding that EJL stock was transferred to nonshareholders both contemporaneously with and subsequently to the execution of the agreements. In particular, the Lauders executed formal waivers, consistent with the agreements, with respect to: (1) The 1976 stock swap between decedent and Leonard and Ronald; (2) the transfers of stock in trust for the benefit of the children of Leonard and Ronald; and (3) the transfers of shares to the University of Pennsylvania. In addition, each transferee was explicitly bound by the terms of the agreements. On the whole, we cannot agree with respondent that these transfers were inconsistent with the Lauders' intent to maintain family control over EJL.[3]

Nor do we view the amendment of the agreement in 1986 allowing Ronald to continue to hold EJL common stock while serving as an ambassador to be particularly significant. In our view, the amendment reflects a reasonable reaction to an unforeseen contingency involving Ronald's desire to pursue public service.

The foregoing aside, we are left to decide whether: (1) the restrictive shareholder agreements served a bona fide business purpose; and (2) the agreements were intended as a testamentary device to transfer decedent's stock to the natural objects of his bounty for less than adequate and full consideration. Specifically, section 20.2031–2(h), Estate Tax Regs., provides in pertinent part:

> Even if the decedent is not free to dispose of the underlying securities at other than the option or contract price, such price will be disregarded in determining the value of the securities unless it is determined under the circumstances of the particular case that the agreement

---

3. Respondent contends that the transfer of stock to the University of Pennsylvania was inconsistent with the Lauders' desire to maintain family control. Specifically, respondent argues that the University could have held its shares until the death of each of the parties to the agreement, thereby gaining outright control of EJL. Although respondent's argument may apply in theory, we cannot agree that such a plan would have been in the University's best interest. Indeed, the University opted in 1981 to have its stock redeemed pursuant to the terms of the agreement in effect at that time.

represents a bona fide business arrangement and not a device to pass the decedent's shares to the natural objects of his bounty for less than an adequate and full consideration in money or money's worth. * * *

Section 20.2031–2(h), Estate Tax Regs., was first adopted over 34 years ago. See T.D. 6296, 23 Fed. Reg. 45299 (June 23, 1958). Contrary to petitioner's position, the regulation requires not only that the agreement meet the business purpose prong of the test but also that the agreement not be a testamentary device. See St. Louis County Bank v. United States, [674 F.2d 1207 (8th Cir. 1982)]. * * *

In discussing the issue presented in this case, one commentator has observed that legitimate business purposes are often "inextricably mixed" with testamentary objectives where, as here, the parties to a restrictive stock agreement are all members of the same immediate family. * * * More specifically, it has long been recognized that restrictions placed on the transfer of stock in order to maintain exclusive family ownership and control may serve a bona fide business purpose. Estate of Bischoff v. Commissioner, [69 T.C. 32, 39–40]; Estate of Littick v. Commissioner, 31 T.C. 181, 187 (1958); * * *. At the same time, however, the family may achieve testamentary objectives to the extent that the agreement allows for the possibility (and generally the probability) that stock held by members of a more senior generation will be sold to subsequent generations (children and grandchildren) at a bargain price. * * *

With these considerations in mind, it is evident that intrafamily agreements restricting the transfer of stock in a closely held corporation must be subjected to greater scrutiny than that afforded similar agreements between unrelated parties. * * * Hoffman v. Commissioner, 2 T.C. 1160, 1178–1179 (1943), affd. sub nom. Giannini v. Commissioner, 148 F.2d 285 (9th Cir. 1945) ("[T]he fact that the option is given to one who is the natural object of the bounty of the optionor requires substantial proof to show that it rested upon full and adequate consideration.").

Turning to the case at hand, there can be no question that the shareholder agreements, on their face, serve the legitimate business purpose of preserving family ownership and control of the various Lauder enterprises. We are persuaded that these concerns were a motivating factor in the Lauders' decision to enter into the agreements.

* * *

Notwithstanding the business purpose for the agreements, petitioner also bears the burden of proving that the agreements were not intended as a device to pass decedent's shares to the natural objects of his bounty for less than an adequate and full consideration in money or money's worth. Suffice it to say that Leonard's testimony that the agreements were not so intended is insufficient to satisfy petitioner's burden of proof on this most critical point. Davis v. Commissioner, 88 T.C. 122, 141, 144 (1987), affd. 866 F.2d 852 (6th Cir. 1989).

Petitioner asserts that the agreements are not testamentary in nature on the grounds that: (1) Decedent was not in poor health or apprehensive of imminent death at the time the agreements were executed; (2) there was an interval of several years between the execution of the agreements and decedent's death; (3) the parties adhered to the terms of the agreements; and (4) any one of the Lauders could have predeceased the others.

In contrast, there are compelling circumstances suggesting that decedent, who was in his seventies when the agreements were signed, entered into the agreements as a substitute for a testamentary disposition to pass on his interest in the business to the members of his family for less than adequate consideration. We are most concerned with the arbitrary manner in which Leonard, an experienced businessman, adopted the adjusted book value formula for determining the purchase price of the stock under the agreements. Leonard admitted that he arrived at the formula without a formal appraisal and without considering the specific trading prices of comparable companies. Nor does it appear that Leonard obtained any significant professional advice in selecting the formula price. Leonard settled on the book value formula himself after consulting with Arnold M. Ganz (a close family financial adviser now deceased). Notably, there is no mention of Mr. Ganz in Leonard's affidavit submitted along with petitioner's original motion for partial summary judgment. We further note that Schutzer, petitioner's expert, declined to evaluate decedent's stock on the basis of book value because he did not believe that "real world" investors would value the stock in this manner.

In arriving at the book value formula in 1974, Leonard testified that he considered that companies listed in the Standard & Poor's 400 generally traded for book value. Assuming that Leonard considered the Standard & Poor's 400, we find it somewhat incredible that Leonard, as president and director of EJL, was unaware or overlooked the fact that the Standard & Poor's 400 indicated that the average price to book value ratio of cosmetic companies ranged between 2 to 1 and 3 to 1 during the period in question.

We are also concerned by Leonard's testimony that he did not have EJL appraised out of anxiety over the confidentiality of EJL's financial statements. Such testimony seems contrived in light of the engagement of the Warburg investment banking group in 1975 for the purpose of investigating the feasibility of raising capital for the company through the private placement of $15 million in long-term notes. Although Leonard was evasive on the point, it is clear that in carrying out its "due diligence" investigation Warburg was privy to detailed financial information regarding EJL's operations and projected revenues. Further, Warburg was permitted to release a private placement memorandum to at least one insurance company before the Lauders withdrew from the transaction in 1976.

No less significant is the fact that the record is devoid of any persuasive evidence that the Lauders negotiated with respect to the formula price. To the contrary, the record indicates that Leonard unilaterally decided upon the formula price. Ronald could not remember who decided upon the formula and only recalled that Leonard had explained the formula to him. Estee had no specific recollection of either of the agreements. Given these circumstances, it appears that the parties never intended to negotiate the matter, fully recognizing that an artificially low price would provide estate tax benefits for all.[4]

As a final matter, we question the propriety of expressly excluding the value of all intangible assets from the book value formula. In our view, the cosmetics industry is somewhat unique in that intangible assets, such as trademarks and trade names, represent a significant component of the aggregate value of total assets. Moreover, there can be no doubt that much of the value in EJL is attributable to the name "Estee Lauder" and to the goodwill generated over the years by virtue of the Lauders' creative and novel marketing of EJL products. This point is supported in the record by the fact that Estee was compelled to transfer the "Estee Lauder" trademark to EJL to enable the latter to negotiate for loans and other credit in the public market. Thus, while we appreciate that an adjusted book value formula may provide a simple and inexpensive means for evaluating shares in a company, we cannot passively accept such a formula where, as here, it appears to have been adopted in order to minimize or mask the true value of the stock in question. See Estate of Trammell v. Commissioner, 18 T.C. 662 (1952).

Considering the foregoing factors in conjunction, an inference may fairly be drawn that the agreements were designed to serve a testamentary purpose. To finally resolve whether the agreements are binding for estate tax purposes, we turn to the question of whether the price to be paid for decedent's stock under the agreements reflected adequate and full consideration in money or money's worth.

With respect to the issue of the adequacy of the consideration, we begin with petitioner's alternative argument that:

> Mutual promises, made when any one of the shareholders could have predeceased the others, themselves provide full and adequate consideration for the Shareholder Agreement.

From petitioner's point of view, there is no need to demonstrate any nexus between the formula price and the fair market value of the subject stock.

* * * [W]e fully appreciate the utility and merit of shareholder agreements in maintaining family ownership and control of business organizations. We agree that the mutual promises of the parties to a restrictive shareholders agreement generally provide full and adequate consideration for the agreement where the parties deal at arm's length. See, e.g., Cartwright v. United States, 457 F.2d 567, 571 (2d Cir. 1972), affd. 411 U.S. 546 (1973); Fiorito v. Commissioner, 33 T.C. 440, 446 n.1 (1959). In particular, it can be assumed that unrelated parties will tend to negotiate a formula serving their best interests and reflecting a fair price. Where the

---

4. Presumably, if decedent and Estee were pursuing an identical agreement with unrelated parties in the place of Leonard and Ronald, they would have been motivated, by virtue of their advanced age, to negotiate a formula ensuring as high a price as possible for their shares balanced against their desire to maintain continuity of management and control.

parties to a restrictive shareholders agreement are truly unrelated and there is no indication that the agreement was intended as a testamentary device, there generally is no basis for respondent to seek to value the stock at a price higher than that paid under the agreement. See Estate of Seltzer v. Commissioner, T.C. Memo. 1985–519. In short, the gross estate will include the actual amount paid by the remaining shareholders to the deceased shareholder's estate.

In contrast, the assumption that the formula price reflects a fair price is not warranted where, as here, the shareholders are all members of the same immediate family and the circumstances show that testamentary considerations influenced the decision to enter into the agreement. In such cases, it cannot be said that the mere mutuality of covenants and promises is sufficient to satisfy the taxpayer's burden of establishing that the agreement is not a testamentary device. Rather, it is incumbent on the estate to demonstrate that the agreement establishes a fair price for the subject stock. Where the estate fails in its burden of proof and the Court finds that the restrictive agreement sets an artificially depressed price for the subject stock, it follows that the estate of the deceased shareholder will be required to pay additional Federal estate tax based on the fair market value of the stock as determined by the Court.

In light of the circumstances present in the instant case, we must consider the adequacy of the consideration in terms of the price to be paid for decedent's stock as of the dates the agreements were executed. As previously indicated, petitioner maintains that the adjusted book value formula reflects a fair, objective measure of the value of the stock, which approximated fair market value on the dates that the shareholder agreements were executed. Respondent argues to the contrary.

We have considered whether such formulas reflect full and adequate consideration in our prior cases. In particular, in Bensel v. Commissioner, 36 B.T.A. 246, 252–253 (1937), affd. 100 F.2d 639 (3d Cir. 1938), the Board of Tax Appeals (our predecessor) concluded that an option price, negotiated between a father and son who at the time were estranged, was controlling for estate tax purposes. The Board held that the option price was not lower than that which would have been agreed upon by persons with adverse interests dealing at arm's length. The Board concluded that the consideration was full and adequate in money or money's worth at the time the option contract was entered into.

We followed the Bensel analysis in Estate of Bischoff v. Commissioner, 69 T.C. 32, 41 n.9 (1977). In short, we rejected respondent's argument that the buy-sell agreement in question was merely a substitute for a testamentary disposition in part on the ground that the formula price to be paid for a partnership interest represented the fair market value of the assets of the partnership.

Notably, the phrase "adequate and full consideration" is not specifically defined in section 20.2031–2(h), Estate Tax Regs. In defining the phrase, we begin with the proposition that a formula price may reflect adequate and full consideration notwithstanding that the price falls below fair market value. See, e.g., Estate of Reynolds v. Commissioner, 55 T.C. 172, 194 (1970). In this light, the phrase is best interpreted as requiring a price that is not lower than that which would be agreed upon by persons with adverse interests dealing at arm's length. Bensel v. Commissioner, *supra*. Under this standard, the formula price generally must bear a reasonable relationship to the unrestricted fair market value of the stock in question.

With the foregoing in mind, we turn to the expert reports and the question of whether the book value formula price reflected adequate and full consideration for decedent's stock on the date the shareholders agreements were executed. The opinion of an expert is admissible if it will assist the trier of fact in determining a fact in issue. See Fed. R. Evid. 702. However, we are not bound by any expert opinion that is contrary to our judgment. * * * We add the oft-repeated caveat that a question of value, such as that presented herein, is an inherently imprecise exercise and capable of resolution only by a Solomon-like pronouncement. Messing v. Commissioner, 48 T.C. 502, 512 (1967).

* * *

We agree with [taxpayer's expert] that a comparative valuation approach, with an emphasis on the price/earnings ratios of industry competitors, is the most reliable basis for valuing the decedent's EJL stock on the dates the agreements were executed. Nonetheless, after considering EJL's relative position in the cosmetics industry, we are not convinced that [the expert's proposed] price/earnings multiples of 9 and 9.5 provide an accurate measure for valuing the EJL stock.

Market value is an implicit estimate of the growth and earnings prospects of the subject company. In our view, EJL's overall financial performance, with particular emphasis on its sales and income figures, generally compared favorably, during one or both of the valuation dates, with Faberge, Noxell, and to a lesser extent Mary Kay. In addition, EJL secured gains in market share of cosmetics sold during the period 1970 through 1976. There is no compelling evidence in the record that EJL's market share was expected to decline in the near future. To the contrary, Leonard declared in a 1975 interview that he expected EJL's sales and profits to "at least double in the next three to five years."

We disagree with [taxpayer's expert's] decision to treat the Lauders' selective distribution strategy as a negative factor in his evaluation. To the contrary, much of EJL's success during the period in question is attributable to the goodwill arising from the name "Estee Lauder" and the Lauders' uncanny sense for how to best market their products. As previously indicated, the Lauders were very selective when deciding which individual stores within a retail chain would be permitted to sell EJL products. Once a new door was established, the Lauders were both aggressive and creative in marketing EJL products, using targeted mailings, gift-with-purchase promotions, and free demonstrations. The Lauders were industry leaders in this particular end of the market. While there may have been some movement towards one-stop shopping during the period in question, we are in no way convinced that this detracted from EJL's prospects for continued profitability and success.

With the foregoing in mind, we conclude that EJL's operating performance and future earnings potential are best reflected in price/earnings multiples of 11 and 12.5 for May 1974 and December 1976, respectively.

Next, we consider the proper discount for lack of liquidity or marketability to apply in valuing the EJL stock. Both parties agree that such a discount is necessary.

We view [taxpayer's] 60–percent discount for lack of liquidity to be clearly excessive. At the same time, we cannot agree with [the IRS] that a 25–percent discount is appropriate. Based on all of the circumstances, we conclude that a discount of 40 percent is appropriate. Cf. Estate of Hall v. Commissioner, 92 T.C. 312, 326, 341 (1989); Estate of Gilford v. Commissioner, 88 T.C. 38, 61 (1987); Estate of Oman v. Commissioner, T.C. Memo. 1987–71; Estate of Gallo v. Commissioner, T.C. Memo. 1985–363.

Applying these multiples and discounts to the earnings * * *, we conclude that decedent's EJL common stock would have sold for $1,485.13 and $2,153.02 per share as of May 1974 and December 1976, respectively. In contrast, the prices for the stock as determined in accordance with Article 6 of the agreements were $614.70 and $1,212.07 per share, as of May 1974 and December 1976, respectively.

Comparing these two sets of figures, we are unable to conclude that the formula price reflects the price that would be negotiated between two unrelated parties. Consequently, we cannot agree with petitioner that the formula price reflects full and adequate consideration on the dates the agreements in question were executed. Considering all of the circumstances, particularly the arbitrary manner in which the formula price was selected, we conclude that the agreements were adopted for the principal purpose of achieving testamentary objectives. Thus, the formula price is not binding for purposes of valuing the EJL stock held by decedent on the date of his death.

* * *

As a consequence of our holding that the formula price is not binding for purposes of the Federal estate tax, further proceedings will be necessary to determine the fair market value of the EJL stock held by decedent on the date of his death. §§ 2031, 2033. While we do not here render the agreements invalid per se, we hold that for Federal estate tax purposes they have no viability and that the valuation provisions are, simply put, an artificial device to minimize such taxes.

To reflect the foregoing,

An appropriate order will be issued.

1990 Senate Report on Proposed Revision of Estate Freeze Rules[5]

136 Cong. Rec. S15,679–S15,683 (Oct. 18, 1990).

Present Law and Background

* * *

Options and buy-sell agreements

Description: Under * * * a common freeze device, a member of an older generation grants a member of a younger generation an option to purchase property at a fixed or formula price. Such an option may be part of a buy-sell agreement under which the survivor (or the corporation) has the right to purchase stock from the estate of the first to die. An option may freeze the value of property at the strike price which in turn may be below the fair market value of the property at the date of death.

Estate tax consequences: A restriction upon the sale or transfer of property may reduce its fair market value. Treasury regulations issued in 1958 acknowledge that the existence of an option or contract to purchase may affect the estate tax value of stock. Those regulations provide that the restriction is to be disregarded unless the agreement represents a bona fide business arrangement and not a device to pass the decedent's stock to natural objects of his bounty for less than full and adequate consideration.[6]

Some courts have gone beyond the Treasury regulations and held that the price contained in a buy-sell agreement will limit [a property's] fair market value for estate tax purposes if the price is fixed or determinable, the estate is obligated to sell, the agreement contains restrictions on lifetime transfers, and there is a valid business purpose for the agreement.[7]

In applying this standard, a number of courts have held that maintenance of family control and ownership is a business purpose that precludes the possibility that the agreement serves as a testamentary device.[8] Continuation of family ownership and control has been found sufficient even when the "control" being preserved is only the right to participate as a limited partner.[9] It also has been held sufficient when one party to the agreement has already contracted a terminal illness.[10]

---

5. The Senate brought the bill which contained §§ 2703 and 2704 to the floor before a formal report could be printed. Since the Senate bill was then substituted for the House bill, there is no formal House or Senate Report (other than a Conference Committee Report) on §§ 2703 and 2704. However, this informal Senate report was printed in the Congressional Record of October 18, 1990.

6. See Treas. Reg. § 20.2032–1(h).

7. See Seltzer v. Commissioner, * * * [50 T.C.M. 1250 (1985)]. See also Weil v. Commissioner, 22 T.C. 1267, 1273–74 (1954).

8. See, e.g., *Estate of Bischoff v. Commissioner*, 69 T.C. 32, 39–40 (1977).

9. *Id.*

10. In Littick v. Commissioner, 31 T.C. 181, 186 (1958), the decedent, who had contracted a terminal illness, entered into a fixed-price buy-sell agreement with his brothers one year prior to death. Finding "nothing in the record to indicate that the [fixed price]

In Saint Louis County Bank v. United States, 674 F.2d 1207 (8th Cir. 1982), the Eighth Circuit held that the maintenance of family ownership and control of the business standing alone to be an insufficient ground for giving effect to a buy-sell agreement. Conceding that such purpose established the existence of a business purpose, the court went on to consider whether the agreement was a tax avoidance device. In finding evidence that might establish a tax avoidance motive notwithstanding a business purpose, the court considered the health of the decedent when the agreement was made, the disparity of the sale price from fair market value, and the enforcement of the agreement against other parties.

* * *

Reasons for Change

Options and buy-sell agreements

The committee believes that buy-sell agreements are common business planning arrangements and that buy-sell agreements generally are entered into for legitimate business reasons that are not related to transfer tax consequences. Buy-sell agreements are commonly used to control the transfer of ownership in a closely held business, to avoid expensive appraisals in determining purchase price, to prevent the transfer to an unrelated party, to provide a market for the equity interest, and to allow owners to plan for future liquidity needs in advance. However, the committee is aware of the potential of buy-sell agreements for distorting transfer tax value. Therefore, the committee establishes rules that attempt to distinguish between agreements designed to avoid estate taxes and those with legitimate business [purposes]. These rules generally disregard a buy-sell agreement that would not have been entered into by unrelated parties acting at arm's length.

* * *

Explanation of Provisions
* * *

Buy-sell agreements

[Section 2703] provides that the value of property for transfer tax purposes is determined without regard to any option, agreement or other right to acquire or use the property at less than fair market value or any restriction on the right to sell or use such property, unless the option, agreement, right or restriction meets three requirements. These requirements apply to any restriction, however created. For example, they apply to restrictions implicit in the capital structure of the partnership or contained in a partnership agreement, articles of incorporation, corporate bylaws or a shareholder's agreement.

---

was not fairly arrived at by arm's-length negotiation or that any tax avoidance scheme was involved," the U.S. Tax Court valued the stock at its fixed price, rather than its stipulated fair market value, 31 T.C. at 187.

The first two requirements are that the option, agreement, right or restriction (1) be a bona fide business arrangement, and (2) not be a device to transfer such property to members of the decedent's family for less than full and adequate consideration in money or money's worth. These requirements are similar to those contained in the present Treasury regulations, except that the bill clarifies that the business arrangement and device requirements are independent tests. The mere showing that the agreement is a bona fide business arrangement would not give the agreement estate tax effect if other facts indicate that the agreement is a device to transfer property to members of the decedent's family for less than full and adequate consideration. In making this clarification, it adopts the reasoning of *Saint Louis County Bank* and rejects the suggestion of other cases that the maintenance of family control standing alone assures the absence of a device to transfer wealth.

In addition, [§ 2703] adds a third requirement, not found in [pre–1990] law, that the terms of the option, agreement, right or restrictions be comparable to similar arrangements entered into by persons in an arm's length transaction. This requires that the taxpayer show that the agreement was one that could have been obtained in an arm's length bargain. Such determination would entail consideration of such factors as the expected term of the agreement, the present value of the property, its expected value at the time of exercise, and consideration offered for the option. It is not met simply by showing isolated comparables but requires a demonstration of the general practice of unrelated parties. Expert testimony would be evidence of such practice. In unusual cases where comparables are difficult to find because the taxpayer owns a unique business, the taxpayer can use comparables from similar businesses.

The bill does not otherwise alter the requirements for giving weight to a buy-sell agreement. For example, it leaves intact [pre–1990] law rules requiring that an agreement have lifetime restrictions in order to be binding on death.

* * *

ILLUSTRATIVE MATERIAL

A. THE THREE REQUIREMENTS OF § 2703(b)

As discussed in the Senate Finance Committee Report, § 2703(b) imposes three requirements for a restrictive agreement's price to represent the value of an asset for transfer tax purposes. The first two requirements, that the agreement is a bona fide business arrangement and is not a device to transfer property to decedent's family for less than full consideration, generally codify the requirements contained in the penultimate sentence of Reg. § 20.2031–2(h).[11] Consequently, case law interpreting those requirements under Reg. § 20.2031–2(h) will generally be applicable to § 2703. As noted in the Senate Finance Committee Report, Congress intends that the two requirements serve

---

11. See above for a difference between § 2703(b) and prior law.

as independent tests. The existence of a bona fide business arrangement will not, by itself, suffice to conclude that the agreement fails to serve as a testamentary device.

1. Bona Fide Business Arrangement

The use of a restrictive agreement to maintain family control of a business satisfies the requirement for a bona fide business arrangement. See, e.g., St. Louis County Bank v. United States, 674 F.2d 1207, 1210 (8th Cir. 1982); Estate of Bischoff v. Commissioner, 69 T.C. 32, 39–42 (1977); Estate of Littick v. Commissioner, 31 T.C. 181, 187 (1958). Similarly, the use of an agreement to retain control within the current group of owners who are not family members also satisfies the business arrangement requirement. See Estate of Carpenter v. Commissioner, 64 T.C.M. 1274, 1280 (1992).

2. Testamentary Device

By asking whether the arrangement constitutes a device to transfer property to decedent's "family," § 2703(b)(2) applies a standard different from prior law which asked whether there was a device to transfer property to "the natural objects of his bounty," see Reg. § 20.2031–2(h). In applying the "natural objects" of the decedent's bounty test, courts have noted that it may encompass a group different from decedent's family. Gloeckner v. United States, 152 F.3d 208 (2d Cir. 1998) ("... an intended beneficiary need not be a 'relative', in the commonly-understood sense of the word to qualify as a natural object of a decedent's bounty.") Interestingly, the regulations under § 2703, do not use the word "family" in discussing the testamentary device standard, but instead refer to "the natural objects of the transferor's bounty," Reg. § 25.2703–1(b)(1)(ii). This reference may be beyond the scope of § 2703(b)(2).

The device standard in § 2703(b) is otherwise the same as employed under prior law. To determine whether the arrangement constitutes a testamentary device, the courts have examined the relationship of the owners, their health and the price designated in the agreement. In Commissioner v. Bensel, 100 F.2d 639 (3d Cir. 1938), the court determined that a buy-sell agreement was not a device where a father and son's relationship was hostile and protracted negotiations had occurred. In contrast, in Estate of Dorn v. United States, 828 F.2d 177, 181 (3d Cir. 1987), the court found that options granted by decedent to her children and grandchildren were devices because her executors had admitted that the sole reason for the options was to limit the amount includible in her estate.

In St. Louis County Bank v. United States, 674 F.2d 1207 (8th Cir. 1982), the court concluded that an agreement was a device in part because the decedent was in poor health at the time the agreement was executed and because the agreement had not been enforced. But see Estate of Littick v. Commissioner, 31 T.C. 181 (1958) (although decedent was terminally ill at time agreement was executed, the court determined that agreement was not a device because the purchase price under the agreement was, in the court's view, the result of the arm's-length negotiation).

As illustrated in *Estate of Lauder*, the courts will also scrutinize the price or formula designated in the agreement to determine whether it reflects adequate and full consideration as of the date the agreement was executed.

Where a formula price is used, the courts ask whether the formula considers the factors and yields a price that a formula negotiated at arm's length would. See, e.g. Estate of Hall v. Commissioner, 92 T.C. 312 (1989) and *Estate of Lauder*. Similarly, where a fixed price is established in the agreement, the courts will respect it if it is a price comparable to one that would have been negotiated at arm's-length. *Estate of Bensel.*

Estate of Lauder indicates that the reasonableness of the formulary price is determined at the time the agreement is executed. Is it necessary to revise the formula to reflect changed circumstances? In *Saint Louis County Bank*, the court suggested that decedent's failure to change the formula for pricing stock after the corporation changed the nature of its business could indicate an intent to use the agreement as a testamentary device. Where a fixed price is used in lieu of a formula, failure to review the fixed price to reflect changes in a company's value could similarly evidence a testamentary device. In Estate of True v. Commissioner, 390 F.3d 1210, 1223 (10th Cir. 2004), the court determined that the failure of a buy-sell agreement to require periodic review of the agreement's fixed price was evidence of testamentary intent. Similarly, in Estate of Godley v. Commissioner, 80 T.C.M. 158 (2000), the court held that a fixed price in an option agreement was evidence of a testamentary device where there was no mechanism to reflect changed circumstances. But see Estate of Amlie v. Commissioner, 91 T.C.M. 1017 (2006), where the court upheld a buy-sell agreement that used a fixed price with no adjustment mechanism. Although there was evidence that decedent's stock had increased in value in the three year period between the execution of the buy-sell and decedent's death, the court did not consider whether the parties' failure to amend the price was evidence of testamentary intent.

3. *Comparability to Similar Arrangements Entered in an Arm's Length Transaction*

Section 2703(b)(3) adds a third requirement that the restrictive agreement be comparable to the general practice of unrelated parties. The Regulations which describe the third condition merely repeat the Senate Finance Committee Report's discussion of this requirement.

The comparability requirement supplements the device standard. It requires the fact finder to examine an objective standard to confirm that there is no device. In Estate of Blount v. Commissioner, 428 F.3d 1338, 1344 (11th Cir. 2005), the court held that the estate did not satisfy this requirement of § 2703(b)(3) where its expert witness only testified at trial about the accuracy of the price in the agreement and failed to discuss whether the terms of the agreement were comparable to similar arrangements entered into at arms-length.

B.   AGREEMENTS TO WHICH § 2703(b) APPLIES

Section 2703(b) applies to options or agreements entered into or granted after October 8, 1990. Revenue Reconciliation Act of 1990, P.L. 101–508 § 11602(a). Agreements entered into on or before October 8, 1990 will be governed by prior law which only imposed the first two requirements now contained in § 2703(b)(1) and (2). An agreement entered into on or before

October 8, 1990 will become subject to § 2703(b), however, if it is "substantially modified" after that date. *Id.*

C. EXECUTION OF BUY–SELL AGREEMENT IS NOT A "TRANSFER"

In Estate of Littick v. Commissioner, 31 T.C. 181 (1958), the IRS argued that the execution of a buy-sell agreement among the decedent, a company he controlled, and his brothers constituted a transfer described in the predecessor of §§ 2035(a), 2036 and 2038. The Service asserted that since the agreement had been executed shortly before decedent's death for no consideration and decedent had retained the right to income from the stock, the stock should be includible in his estate at its full market value under the predecessors of § 2035(a) and § 2036. The Service also asserted that since the buy-sell agreement did not require the company to pay what it considered to be the fair market value of the stock, the estate could terminate the agreement and, therefore, that the predecessors of § 2035(a) and 2038 applied. The court rejected these arguments, finding that signing the buy-sell agreement did not qualify as a "transfer of property" within the meaning of the predecessor sections. See also Cobb v. Commissioner, 49 T.C.M. 1364 (1985) (grant of option is not a transfer of the underlying property for purposes of §§ 2035 and 2036).

D. SECURITIES ACT RESTRICTIONS

Under certain circumstances the Securities Act of 1933 may have the effect of restricting the transferability of stock.

Rev. Rul. 77–287, 1977–2 C.B. 319, provides the IRS view of the effect of securities law restrictions on the valuation of stock, including the factors to be taken into account and the weight to be assigned to the various factors.

E. INTERACTION OF § 2703 WITH FAMILY PARTNERSHIPS

As discussed in Chapter 35, taxpayers will frequently place assets in family limited partnerships in order to reduce the value that will be taken into account for transfer tax purposes. In Holman v. Commissioner, 130 T.C. No. 12 (2008), taxpayers transferred stock they held in Dell Computer Corp. to a limited partnership and then made gifts of limited partnership interests to their children. They valued the limited partnership interests for gift tax purposes at less than one half the value of the Dell stock. The low valuation was based on the restrictions on transfer of the partnership interests that were contained in the partnership agreement, the lack of marketability of the transferred partnership interests, and the lack of control that the donees had over partnership assets because they were limited partners. The court applied § 2703(a) to increase the value of the gifts by disregarding the restrictions on the transferability of the partnership interests. The court determined that the restrictions did not satisfy the requirement of § 2703(b)(1) that the restriction be a "bona fide business arrangement" because the partnership did not engage in a business, but instead merely held Dell stock. The court also viewed the restrictions as a device to transfer property for less than fair market value since all the partners in the partnership were members of the same family and the restrictions were designed to prevent the children of the family from dissipating the family's wealth.

In *Holman*, the Service employed § 2703(a)(2) to disregard the restrictions on transfer of the limited partnership interests. In other cases, the Service has sought to use § 2703(a)(2) to disregard the partnership, itself, in order to argue that the transfers were not of partnership interests, but rather of the assets held by the partnership. See, e.g., TAM 9842003 (July 2, 1998). If successful, this argument would increase the value of the transfers because all the restrictions normally contained in a partnership agreement that restrict a limited partner's access to and control over partnership assets would be ignored. The courts have rejected this application of § 2703(a)(2). In Strangi v. Commissioner, 115 T.C. 478 (2000), aff'd on this issue, 293 F.3d 279 (5th Cir. 2002) the court stated:

> Respondent . . . argues that the term "property" in section 2703(a)(2) means the underlying assets in the partnership and that the partnership form is the restriction that must be disregarded. Unfortunately for respondent's position, neither the language of the statute nor the language of the regulation supports respondent's interpretation. Absent application of some other provision, the property included the decedent's estate is the limited partnership interest and decedent's interest in Stranco.

> In *Kerr v. Commissioner*, 113 T.C. 449 (1999), the Court dealt with a similar issue with respect to interpretation of section 2704(b). Sections 2703 and 2704 were enacted as part of chapter 14, I.R.C., in 1990. See Omnibus Budget Reconciliation Act of 1990, Pub. L. 101–508, 104 Stat. 1388. However, as we indicated in *Kerr v. Commissioner, supra* at 470–471, and as respondent acknowledges . . ., the new statute was intended to be a targeted substitute for the complexity, breadth, and vagueness of prior section 2036(c); and Congress "wanted to value property interests more accurately when they were transferred, instead of including previously transferred property in the transferor's gross estate." Treating the partnership assets, rather than decedent's interest in the partnership, as the "property" to which section 2703(a) applies in this case would raise anew the difficulties that Congress sought to avoid by repealing section 2036(c) and replacing it with chapter 14. We conclude that Congress did not intend, by the enactment of section 2703, to treat partnership assets as if they were assets of the estate where the legal interest owned by the decedent at the time of death was a limited partnership or corporate interest. * * * Thus, we need not address whether the partnership agreement satisfies the safe harbor provisions of section 2703(b). Respondent did not argue separately that the Stranco shareholders' agreement should be disregarded for lack of economic substance or under section 2703(a).

See also, Church v. United States, 2000–1 U.S.T.C. ¶ 60, 369 (W.D. Tex. 2000) (reaching same conclusion).

3. JUDICIAL REQUIREMENTS

In addition to the three requirements of § 2703, the courts have imposed additional requirements before they will conclude that an agreement fixes value for transfer tax purposes.

a.   NECESSITY OF ENFORCEABLE AGREEMENT

The courts require that the agreement be enforceable. In Estate of Hammond v. Commissioner, 13 T.C.M. 903 (1954), the decedent granted to his son-in-law an option to buy certain securities for a price roughly equal to half their value at the decedent's death. The option was unenforceable, however, because decedent had failed to amend a revocable trust agreement under which the stock was held so as to bind the trustees to the option price. Nevertheless, the trustees made the sale at the option price under a provision giving them the right to sell the trust corpus. The court, declaring that the agreement must be enforceable in order for the option price to be used as value, held that the fair market value of the stock was to be included in the decedent's gross estate.

Compare Citizen's Fidelity Bank and Trust Co. v. United States, 209 F.Supp. 254 (W.D.Ky. 1962), where the decedent, at age 75, had entered into an agreement with her sons pursuant to which the sons agreed to work for no compensation for the remainder of the decedent's life. In exchange, the sons received the right to purchase at any time the stock of the corporation owned by the decedent or her estate. The decedent agreed not to alienate the stock and the agreement was binding upon the "heirs, legatees, executors and administrators" of the various parties. The Government's contention that the option was void under local law as an unreasonable restraint on alienation was rejected because the court interpreted the agreement to apply only to the executors of predeceased sons and to the decedent.

In some cases, the Commissioner has attacked restrictive agreements on the ground that they were not specifically enforceable. See, e.g., Wilson v. Bowers, 57 F.2d 682 (2d Cir. 1932). It is not clear, however, that specific enforceability is a requirement for restrictive agreements to have the effect of limiting value.

b.   NECESSITY THAT AGREEMENT BIND BOTH DURING LIFE AND AFTER DEATH

As discussed in *Estate of Lauder*, the courts also require that the agreement apply to the property both during life and after death. Reg. § 20.2031–2(h) states that "[l]ittle weight will be accorded a price contained in an option or contract under which the decedent is free to dispose of the underlying securities at any price he chooses during his lifetime." The rationale is that if the transferee had the unrestricted right to dispose of the property during life, the owner was free to realize full fair market value until death. See e.g. Hoffman v. Commissioner, 2 T.C. 1160 (1943), aff'd sub nom. Giannini v. Commissioner, 148 F.2d 285 (9th Cir.) cert. denied, 326 U.S. 730 (1945); Reg. § 20.2031–2(h) ("Little weight will be accorded a price contained in an option or contract under which the decedent is free to dispose of the underlying securities at any price he chooses during his lifetime.")

Suppose that the decedent ("D") can transfer the property, but that the agreement requires the transferee to take the property subject to the agreement. The courts should respect the value established by the agreement upon D's death for estate tax purposes since the property in the hands of the transferee would still have been subject to the agreement. D would not have been "free to dispose of the underlying securities at any price he chooses during his lifetime" as stated in Reg. § 20.2031–2(h) because a transferee would not pay more than the price established in the agreement. See generally Fiorito v. Commissioner, 33 T.C. 440, 446 (1959) (option agreement excisable upon partner's death determined value of partnership interest for estate tax purposes because partner could not transfer his interest while he was alive without his partners' consent).

Section B. Lapsing Rights and Restrictions on Liquidation: § 2704

1990 Senate Report on Proposed Revision of Estate Freeze Rules[12]

136 Cong. Rec. S15,679–S15,683 (Oct. 18, 1990).

[Pre–1990] Law and Background

* * *

Lapsing Rights

Estate freezes often involve the creation of a right that terminates over time or lapses at death. In *Estate of Harrison v. Commissioner*, [52 T.C.M. 1306 (1987)] * * *, a father retained both a limited and general partnership interest after forming a partnership in which his sons received limited partnership interests. Held in conjunction with the general partnership interest, the father's limited partnership interest was worth $59 million (because the general partnership interest carried with it the right to liquidate the partnership); held alone, the limited partnership interest was worth $33 million. [The partnership's assets were more valuable outside the partnership because the partnership agreement restricted limited partners' access to and control over partnership assets. As a result, the limited partnership interest was more valuable if it could be liquidated.] The father died owning both interests, but the general partnership interest was immediately sold to the sons for $700,000 pursuant to a buy-sell agreement taking effect at death. The United States Tax Court held that the limited partnership interest was includible in the father's gross estate at a value of

---

12. See note 5, above, for an explanation of the peculiar legislative history of § 2704.

$33 million [because the father's right to liquidate the limited partnership interest had lapsed at death.].

Reasons for Change

* * *

Lapsing Rights

The committee is concerned about the use of lapsing rights to transfer value free of transfer tax. Such rights are difficult to value when created and may not be exercised in an arm's length manner.

Accordingly, the committee does not believe it appropriate to give value to lapsing voting rights carried by preferred interests. In addition, it believes that property transferred at death is more accurately valued by disregarding lapsing restrictions and by adding back the value attributable to a lapsing right to the value of the transferor's interest in the business.

* * *

Conference Report on H.R. 5835, The Omnibus Budget Reconciliation Act of 1990

H.Rep. 964, 101st Cong., 2d Sess. 1130, 1137–1138 (1990).

* * *

Treatment of certain restrictions and lapsing rights

In general

The conference agreement [adopts rules] regarding the effect of certain restrictions and lapsing rights upon the value of an interest in a partnership or corporation. These rules are intended to prevent results similar to that of *Estate of Harrison v. Commissioner*, 52 T.C.M. 1306 (1987). These rules do not affect minority discounts or other discounts available under [pre–1990] law. The conferees intend that no inference be drawn regarding the transfer tax effect of restrictions and lapsing rights under [pre–1990] law.

Lapsing rights

[Section 2704] provides that the lapse of a voting or liquidation right in a family controlled corporation or partnership results in a transfer by gift or an inclusion in the gross estate. The amount of the transfer is the value of all interests in the entity held by the transferor immediately before the lapse (assuming the right was nonlapsing) over the value of the interests immediately after the lapse. The conference agreement grants the Secretary of the Treasury regulatory authority to apply these rules to rights similar to voting and liquidation rights.

Example 6.—Parent and Child control a corporation. Parent's stock has a voting right that lapses on Parent's death. Under [§ 2704], Parent's stock is valued for Federal estate tax purposes as if the voting right of the parent's stock were nonlapsing.

Example 7.—Father and Child each own general and limited interests in a partnership. The general partnership interest carries with it the right to liquidate the partnership; the limited partnership interest has no such right. The liquidation right associated with the general partnership interest lapses after ten years. Under [§ 2704], there is a gift at the time of the lapse equal to the excess of (1) the value of Father's partnership interests determined as if he held the right to liquidate over (2) the value of such interests determined as if he did not hold such right.

Restrictions

Under [§ 2704], any restriction that effectively limits the ability of a corporation or partnership to liquidate is ignored in valuing a transfer among family members if (1) the transferor and family members control the corporation or partnership, and (2) the restriction either lapses after the transfer or can be removed by the transferor or members of his family, either alone or collectively.

Example 8.—Mother and Son are partners in a two-person partnership. The partnership agreement provides that the partnership cannot be terminated. Mother dies and leaves her partnership interest to Daughter. As the sole partners, Daughter and Son acting together could remove the restriction on partnership termination. Under [§ 2704], the value of Mother's partnership interest in her estate is determined without regard to the restriction. Such value would be adjusted to reflect any appropriate fragmentation discount.

This rule does not apply to a commercially reasonable restriction which arises as part of a financing with an unrelated party or a restriction required under State or Federal law. [Section 2704] also grants to the Treasury Secretary regulatory authority to disregard other restrictions which reduce the value of the transferred interest for transfer tax purpose but which do not ultimately reduce the value of the interest to the transferee.

ILLUSTRATIVE MATERIAL

A. IN GENERAL

Section 2704 contains two distinct rules. First, lapses of voting rights or liquidation rights with respect to a corporation or partnership are treated as taxable transfers where the holder of the lapsed right and her family control the entity immediately before and after the lapse. § 2704(a)(1). Family is defined to include the (a) holder's spouse, (b) any ancestor or lineal descendant of the holder or her spouse, (c) the holder's brothers and sisters and (d) any spouse of any individual described in (b) or (c). § 2704(c)(2). Control is defined as holding 50 percent, by vote or value, of the stock of a corporation, holding 50 percent of the capital or profits interests in any partnership, or holding any interest as a general partner in a limited partnership. Reg. §§ 25.2704–1(a)(2); 25.2701–2(b)(5).

Second, where a transferor transfers an interest in a family-controlled corporation or partnership, restrictions on liquidating the entity are disregarded in valuing the transferred interest if either the restriction lapses after the transfer or the transferor or his family has the right to remove the restriction after the transfer.

B. TRANSFERS UPON LAPSE

Upon the lapse of a voting or liquidation right, the holder is deemed to make a transfer equal to the difference between the value of the holder's interest before the lapse and the value after the lapse. § 2704(a)(2). For example, in the *Harrison* case, the father's limited partnership interest was worth $33 million or $59 million depending on whether the partnership could be liquidated. The lapse of the father's ability to liquidate the partnership would be treated as a transfer of $26 million. See Reg. § 25.2704–1(f) Ex. 1.

Since the statute applies only where the holder and members of the holder's family control the entity both before and after the lapse, § 2704(a) in effect assumes that the holder has transferred the lapsed right to family members. However, § 2704 does not specifically identify the transferee. Thus, it is possible that the deemed transfer will not qualify for a marital deduction, charitable deduction or annual gift tax exclusion even where the identity of the transferee is obvious because, for example, there is only one other stockholder or partner.

C. INTERACTION OF § 2704(b) WITH MINORITY DISCOUNTS

The statement in the Conference Report that § 2704 does not affect minority discounts or other discounts available under present law is misleading. Part of a minority discount is attributable to the inability of a minority owner to compel liquidation of the entity. The language of § 2704(b) clearly eliminates the portion of the minority discount attributable to the inability to compel liquidation despite the Conference Report statement.

The IRS had also initially sought to apply § 2704 to deny or reduce minority discounts in the context of family partnerships by disregarding restrictions on a partner's ability to withdraw from the partnership and receive the value of her interest. See, e.g., TAM 9842003 (July 2, 1998). The courts, however, rejected the argument. In Kerr v. Commissioner, 113 T.C. 449, 472–473 (1999), aff'd, 292 F.3d 490 (5th Cir. 2002), the Tax Court stated:

"Section 2704(b)(2)(A) broadly defines an applicable restriction as 'any restriction which effectively limits the ability of the corporation or partnership to liquidate'. However, section 2704(b)(3)(B) excepts from the definition of an applicable restriction 'any restriction on liquidation imposed, or required to be imposed, by any Federal or State law'.

"In what we view as an expansion of the exception contained in section 2704(b)(3)(B), the Secretary promulgated section 25.2704–2(b), Gift Tax Regs., which states in pertinent part: 'An applicable restriction is a limitation on the ability to liquidate the entity (in whole or in part) that is more restrictive than the limitations that would apply under the State law generally applicable to the entity in the absence of the restriction.' Thus, the question arises whether the partnership agreements involved herein impose greater restrictions on the liquidation of KFLP and KILP [the family limited partnerships] than the limitations that generally would apply to the partnerships under State law.

"Section 10.01 of the partnership agreements states in pertinent part that the partnerships shall dissolve and liquidate upon the earlier of December 31, 2043, or by agreement of all the partners. Petitioners direct our attention to TRLPA section 8.01, which provides that a Texas limited partnership shall be dissolved on the earlier of: (1) The occurrence of events specified in the partnership agreement to cause dissolution; (2) the entry of a decree of judicial dissolution. TRLPA ['Texas Revised Limited Partnership Act'] section 8.04 provides that, following the dissolution of a limited partnership, the partnership's affairs shall be wound up (including the liquidation of partnership assets) as soon as reasonably practicable.

"On the basis of a comparison of section 10.01 of the partnership agreements and TRLPA section 8.01, we conclude that section 10.01 of the partnership agreements does not contain restrictions on liquidation that constitute applicable restrictions within the meaning of section 2704(b). We reach this conclusion because Texas law provides for the dissolution and liquidation of a limited partnership pursuant to the occurrence of events specified in the partnership agreement or upon the written consent of all the partners, and the restrictions contained in section 10.01 of the partnership agreements are no more restrictive than the limitations that generally would apply to the partnerships under Texas law. Consequently, these provisions are excepted from the definition of an applicable restriction pursuant to section 2704(b)(3)(B) and section 25.2704–2(b), Gift Tax Regs.

"Respondent counters that we should compare the restrictions contained in section 10.01 of the partnership agreements with TRLPA section 6.03, which provides:

> A limited partner may withdraw from a limited partnership at the time or on the occurrence of events specified in a written partnership agreement and in accordance with that written partnership agreement. If the partnership agreement does not specify such a time or event or a definite time for the dissolution and winding up of the limited partnership, a limited partner may withdraw on giving written notice no less than six months before the date of withdrawal to each general partner * * *.

"Respondent's reliance on TRLPA section 6.03 is misplaced. TRLPA section 6.03 governs the withdrawal of a limited partner from the partnership—not the liquidation of the partnership. TRLPA section 6.03 sets forth limitations on a limited partner's withdrawal from a partnership. However, a limited partner may withdraw from a partnership without requiring the dissolution and liquidation of the partnership. In this regard, we conclude that TRLPA section 6.03 is not a 'limitation on the ability to liquidate the entity' within the meaning of section 25.2704(b), Gift Tax Regs.

"Respondent's position herein is inconsistent with section 25.2704–2(d) (Example 1), Gift Tax Regs., which states in pertinent part:

D owns a 76 percent interest and each of D's children, A and B, owns a 12 percent interest in General Partnership X. The partnership agreement requires the consent of all the partners to liquidate the partnership. Under the State law that would apply in the absence of the restriction n the partnership agreement, the consent of partners owning 70 percent of the total partnership interests would be required to liquidate X. * * * The requirement that all the partners consent to the liquidation is an applicable restriction. * * *

"Significantly, the restriction on liquidation in the partnership agreement described in the example was not compared with a State law provision (such as TRLPA section 6.03) pertaining to withdrawal from a partnership. Rather, the terms of the partnership agreement are compared with a partnership liquidation provision similar to TRLPA section 8.01. With these points in mind, we reject respondent's argument regarding TRLPA section 6.03.

"We are mindful that the Secretary has been vested with broad regulatory authority under section 2704(b)(4). However, the regulations in place do not support a conclusion that the disputed provisions in the ... partnership agreements constitute applicable restrictions."

.   .   .

See also, Estate of Jones v. Commissioner, 116 T.C. 121 (2001) (same); Estate of Knight v. Commissioner, 115 T.C. 506 (2000) (same).

In response to these decisions, the IRS appears to have abandoned its efforts to apply § 2704 to disregard restrictions on a partner's ability to withdraw from the partnership and receive the value of her interest. See e.g. Peracchio v. Commissioner, 86 T.C.M. 412 (2003), where the IRS abandoned its § 2704 argument. We believe, however, that the judicial decisions are incorrect. Reg. § 25.2704–2(b) refers to the "limitation on the ability to liquidate the entity (in whole or in part)." The ability of a partner to withdraw from the partnership and receive the value of his interest is the ability to liquidate "in part" since the partner is liquidating his interest, i.e., converting his interest into cash. The language employed by the TRLPA in distinguishing between a "dissolution" and "withdrawal" is irrelevant. A partner's withdrawal for value is a liquidation "in part" in the same manner that a partnership dissolution is a liquidation "in whole." This principle is understood in the income tax area, where Reg. § 1.704–1(b)(2)(ii)(b)(2) applies the safe harbor requirements for tax allocations to "liquidation of the partnership (or any partner's interest in the partnership)."

CHAPTER 37

ESTATE FREEZES

Internal Revenue Code: §§ 2701, 2702

Regulations: §§ 25.2701–1, 2, 3, 4; 25.2702–1, 2, 3, 4, 5

Estate freezes involve an attempt by a transferor to shift future appreciation in an asset to transferees without incurring a transfer tax. To accomplish this, the transferor retains an interest in the asset equal to most of its current value and transfers to the donee the right to participate in future appreciation. Since the transferor has retained most of the current value, she incurs a minimal gift tax. Moreover, if the right to participate in future appreciation is a completed gift, the future appreciation will not be included in the transferor's estate unless one of the retained interest provisions in §§ 2036–2038 applies.

For example, in a classic estate freeze, older generation transfers common stock of a family corporation to younger generation and retains preferred stock with a fixed dividend and liquidation right that assertedly has a value equal to the corporation's total value. Even if the company becomes more profitable, the preferred stock will not appreciate because of its fixed dividend and liquidation rights. Moreover, the common stock will not be includible in older generation's estate unless she retained an interest in the common stock.[1] To the extent that the corporation fails to pay dividends on the preferred stock, more value is shifted to the younger generation.

In a similar arrangement, older generation may transfer property to a trust, retaining an income interest for a term of years, with remainder to younger generation. A gift tax would apply to the transfer of the remainder interest, but all future appreciation in the trust asset will have been shifted to the younger generation so long as transferor does not die during the term and does not retain an interest in the remainder. Since transferor selects the property and may indirectly control the income stream generated by the property (as in the case, for example, of dividends payable on stock of a family corporation), Treasury tables, which are based on rates of return for federal securities, may underestimate the value of the remainder interest.

In 1987, Congress first attempted to address some of the potential abuses by adopting § 2036(c) which would, for example, have included the transferred common stock in the transferor's estate. Because § 2036(c) was deemed too vague and broad, Congress repealed it and adopted Chapter 14.

---

1. The Tax Court rejected the argument that the common stock should be included in the transferor's gross estate because the retention of the preferred stock constituted the retention of the enjoyment of the corporation's income under § 2036(a)(1). Estate of Boykin v. Commissioner, 53 T.C.M. 345 (1987).

Sections 2701 and 2702 of Chapter 14 attempt to address the problems summarized above.

SECTION A. SPECIAL VALUATION RULES FOR CERTAIN INTERESTS IN CORPORATIONS AND PARTNERSHIPS: § 2701

1990 Senate Report on Proposed Revision of Estate Freeze Rules[2]

136 Congressional Record S15,679–S15,683 (Oct. 18, 1990).

[Pre–1990] Law and Background

Preferred Interests In Corporations And Partnerships.

Description: In one common estate freeze transaction, the "preferred interest freeze", a person owning preferred and residual interests in a corporation or partnership transfers the residual interest to a younger generation while retaining the preferred interest.

The preferred interest may enjoy preferred rights as to income or management. It also may carry discretionary rights regarding the amount, timing or fact of payment. Such discretionary rights include: (1) a right to "put" the frozen interest for an amount equal to the liquidation preference of the frozen interest; (2) a right to liquidate an entity and receive assets; or (3) a right to convert the nonappreciating retained interest into an appreciating interest.

Gift tax consequences: The transfer of a residual interest in a corporation or partnership for less than full and adequate consideration is a gift. The value of the residual interest is generally determined by subtracting the value of the preferred interest from the value of all interests in the corporation or partnership. The value of preferred stock then is determined by looking to comparable stocks. The Internal Revenue Service has ruled that the most important factors in determining the value of preferred stock generally are its yield, dividend coverage, and protection of its liquidation preference.[3] Voting, redemption, liquidation, and conversion rights also may add to the value of the preferred interest. Under the "willing buyer, willing seller" valuation standard, it is assumed that rights will be exercised so as to maximize the value of the owner's retained interests without regard to the actual likelihood of exercise.

---

2. The Senate brought the bill which contained §§ 2701 and 2702 to the floor before a formal report could be printed. Since the Senate bill was then substituted for the House bill, there is no formal House or Senate report (other than a Conference Committee Report) on §§ 2703 and 2704. However, this informal Senate report was printed in the Congressional Record of October 18, 1990.

3. See Rev. Rul. 83–120, 1983–2 C.B. 170.

For example, in *Snyder v. Commissioner*,[4] a grandmother transferred publicity traded shares of a growing corporation to a newly created holding company in exchange for preferred stock and common stock of the holding company. The preferred stock had a par value equal to the value of the holding company less $1,000, was callable at the election of the preferred shareholders, and, in effect, could be put to the company at par. The grandmother then transferred the common stock to a trust for the benefit of her grandchildren and valued the common stock at $1,000. Although finding that the grandmother did not expect to exercise the put option in the absence of unanticipated and extraordinary financial need, the U.S. Tax Court nonetheless held that the value of the common stock was $1,000, because a willing buyer would pay more only with some assurance that the option would not be exercised.

The failure to exercise rights in an arm's length manner after the initial transfer of common stock may give rise to a gift. The Internal Revenue Service has held in several private letter rulings that the failure to exercise rights with respect to an equity interest can give rise to a gift.[5]

Estate Tax Inclusion Relating to Estate Freezes: Section 2036(c)

In the Omnibus Budget Reconciliation Act of 1987, the Congress addressed the estate freeze transaction by including the value of the transferred appreciating interest in the decedent's gross estate and crediting any gift tax previously paid (Code § 2036(c)). Section 2036(c) generally provides that if a person in effect transfers property having a disproportionately large share of the potential appreciation in an enterprise while retaining an interest, or right in, the enterprise, then the transferred property is includible in his gross estate. Dispositions of either the transferred or retained property prior to the transferor's death result in a deemed gift equal to the amount that would have been includible had the transferor died at the time of the transfer.

* * *

Reasons for Change

Repeal of Section 2036(c)

The committee believes that an across-the-board inclusion rule is an inappropriate and unnecessary approach to the valuation problems associated with estate freezes. The committee believes that the amount of any tax on a gift should be determined at the time of the transfer and not upon the death of the transferor.

Moreover, the committee is concerned that the statute's complexity, breadth, and vagueness posed an unreasonable impediment to the transfer

---

4. 93 T.C. No. 43 (Nov. 2, 1989).

5. See LTR 8723007 (Feb. 18, 1987) (finding a gift on the failure to declare a noncumulative dividend); LTR 8726005 (March 13, 1987) (finding a gift on the failure to exercise conversion right); LTR 8610011 (Nov. 1, 1985) (finding a gift on the failure to redeem stock). See *Snyder* at 28–29 (finding a gift by reason of the failure to exercise a conversion right that would have permitted accumulation of unpaid dividends).

of family businesses. The committee also is concerned that many taxpayers have refrained from legitimate intrafamily transactions because of uncertainty about the scope of its rules. Moreover, the [pre–1990] rules are over inclusive because they apply if the transferor retains virtually any interest in the income from, or rights in, the enterprise.

Accordingly, the committee bill repeals § 2036(c) retroactive to the date of its enactment.

Replacement For Section 2036(c)

While the committee believes that section 2036(c) is not the appropriate method of taxing freeze transactions, the committee nonetheless is concerned about potential estate and gift tax valuation abuses. Accordingly, the committee bill generally substitutes for § 2036(c) a series of targeted rules generally designed to assure a more accurate determination of the value of the property subject to transfer tax.

In developing a replacement for current § 2036(c) the committee sought to accomplish several goals: (1) to provide a well defined and administrable set of rules; (2) to allow business owners who are not abusing the transfer tax system to freely engage in standard intrafamily transactions without being subject to severe transfer tax consequences; and (3) to deter abuse by making unfavorable assumptions regarding certain retained rights.

Preferred Interests in Corporations and Partnerships

The committee is concerned about the potential transfer of wealth through the use of discretionary rights in a partnership or corporation. For example, wealth may pass from a preferred shareholder to a common shareholder if the corporation fails to pay dividends to the preferred shareholder. Even if the preferred stock is cumulative, such failure results in a transfer equal to the value of the use of the money until the dividend is paid. Or, by exercising conversion, liquidation, put or call rights in other than an arm's-length fashion (or by not exercising such rights before they lapse), the transferor may transfer part or all of the value of such rights.

Accordingly, the committee adopts certain rules designed to eliminate the potential for transferring wealth through nonexercise of discretionary rights. [Section 2701] values at zero certain discretionary rights on the assumption that they will not be exercised in an arm's length manner. [Section 2701] also assures a full transfer tax from the failure to exercise cumulative distribution rights in a timely fashion by compounding unpaid distributions.

The committee believes that the residual interest in a corporation or partnership may have value in excess of current projected cash flows because it carries with it the right to future appreciation. The market often gives substantial value to this "option value." Accordingly, [§ 2701] provides for a minimal value for the residual interests in a corporation or partnership. This minimum value, in effect, sets a floor on the discount rate used in valuing the preferred interests in a corporation or partnership that is not dramatically below the market rate. This floor reflects the minimal coverage that a purchaser of the preferred stock might require in the market for traded securities.

Explanation of Provisions

In General

[Section 2701] repeals § 2036(c) retroactively and provides in its place rules generally intended to assure more accurate gift tax valuation of the initial transfer. These rules modify the valuation of specific retained rights in corporations and partnerships * * *.

Preferred Interests In Corporations And Partnerships

[Section 2701] provides rules for valuing certain rights retained immediately after the transfer of an interest in a corporation or partnership by the transferor or applicable family members. The rules rely on present law principles regarding the valuation of residual interests, with an adjustment to reflect the actual fragmented ownership. The rules apply to the transfer of a residual interest to (or for the benefit of) a family member. In applying the rules, an individual is treated as holding amounts held through a corporation, partnership, trust or other entity. [Section 2701] does not affect minority discounts or other discounts available under present law.

Retained Rights Affected By The Bill

A retained liquidation, put, call, or conversion right is valued at zero, unless such right must be exercised at a specific time and amount. For instance, a liquidation right that is required to be exercised at a fixed date for a sum certain is unaffected by the bill.

A retained distribution right that is noncumulative or lacks a preference upon liquidation is valued at zero if the transferor and applicable family members control the entity. For a corporation, control is defined as holding, before the transfer, at least 50 percent (by vote or value) of the stock of the corporation. For a partnership, control generally is defined as holding at least 50 percent of the capital or profits interest in the partnership. In addition, any general partner in a limited partnership is deemed to have control. In determining control, an individual is treated as holding any interest held by a brother, sister, or lineal descendent.

Example 1: A father who holds convertible debt and 50 percent of the stock gives the stock to his daughter. The corporation has only a single class of stock. In valuing the gift, the conversion feature of the debt is valued at zero. Assuming that this conversion feature otherwise would have been valued at $1,000, the bill increases the value of the gift of the stock to the daughter by $500. If the father had only given half of the stock to the daughter, the gift would be increased by $250.

A cumulative distribution right having a preference upon liquidation is valued under a special standard under which the determination as to whether the cumulative distribution can reasonably be expected to be timely paid is made without regard to whether the transferor retains control.

Exceptions

[Section 2701] contains five exceptions to the above rules. First, [§ 2701] does not apply to any right conferred by a retained interest for which market quotations are readily available on an established securities market. [Section 2701] also does not apply if the market quotations are readily available for the transferred interest.

The second exception is for a retained interest that is of the same class as the transferred interest. Under this exception, [§ 2701] does not affect the valuation of a gift of common stock if the transferor only retains rights of that class of common. Likewise, [§ 2701] does not affect the valuation of a gift of a partnership interest if all interests in the partnership share equally in all items of income, deduction, loss and gain in the same proportion (i.e., straight-up allocations).

The third exception excludes a retained interest that would be of the same class as the transferred interest but for nonlapsing differences in voting power (or, in the case of a partnership, nonlapsing differences with respect to management and limitations on liability). Nonlapsing limitations on liability are permitted only if the transferor or applicable family member does not have the right to alter the transferee's liability. Under this exception, [§ 2701] does not affect the valuation of a transfer of nonvoting stock in an S corporation, coupled with the retention of voting stock in such corporation.

Except as provided in Treasury regulations, a right that lapses by reason of state law would be treated as nonlapsing for these purposes. The committee intends that the regulations exempt lapses occurring by reason of state law that do not have the effect of transferring value not contemplated by state law, as when a lapsing right to management effectively extinguishes a right to be redeemed at fair market value.

Fourth, [§ 2701] provides an exception in situations where the rights in the retained interests in the business are proportionally the same as all of the rights in the transferred interests in the business, other than voting rights. This exception would apply, for instance, if the retained and transferred interests consisted of two classes of common stock, which shared in all distributions, liquidation and other rights in a two to one ratio.

Fifth, [§ 2701] does not apply to a right to convert into a fixed number (or a fixed percentage) of the shares of the same class as the transferred stock, if such rights are nonlapsing, subject to proportionate adjustments for splits, combinations, reclassifications and similar changes in the capital stock, and adjusted for accumulated dividends not paid on a timely basis. A similar exception applies to rights in partnerships. This exception is provided because the full appreciated value of such right will be subject to later transfer tax.

* * *

Example 4: F owns 25 shares of the 100 outstanding shares of noncumulative preferred stock in Company X. F's father, GF, owns the remaining 75 shares of the noncumulative preferred in Company X. F owns all of the 100 outstanding shares of the common stock in Company X. F gives 10 shares of common stock to his son. Under [§ 2701], the noncumulative preferred stock of both F and GF would be given a value of zero in determining the amount of the gift by F to his son. Thus, the amount of the gift would be the same amount as if F gave 10 shares of common to his son in a corporation that had only 100 shares of common stock outstanding.

Definitions

Liquidation, put, call or conversion right: A liquidation, put, call or conversion right is any liquidation, put, call or conversion or similar right the exercise or nonexercise of which affects the value of the transferred interest.

Distribution right: A distribution right generally is a right to distributions with respect to stock of a corporation or a partnership interest. A distribution right does not include any right in a junior equity interest.[6] Junior equity interests do not affect the value of the transferred preferred interests because the valuation of the preferred interests does not affect the value of the junior equity interests, i.e., the value of the preferred interests does not depend upon the value of the junior equity interests. In addition, a distribution right does not include any liquidation, put, call, or conversion right, or a guaranteed payment determined without regard to income.

Family: A "member of the family" is, with respect to any transferor, the transferor's spouse, a lineal descendent of the transferor or the transferor's spouse, and the spouse of any such descendant. An "applicable family member" is, with respect to any transferor, the transferor's spouse, ancestors of the transferor and the spouse, and spouses of such ancestors.

Transfer: Except as provided in Treasury regulations, any redemption, recapitalization, contribution to capital, or other change in the capital structure of a corporation or partnership is treated as a transfer of an interest in such entity if an individual or applicable family member thereby receives a retained right affected by [§ 2701]. Regulations also may provide that such an event results in a transfer if the individual or applicable family member thereafter holds such an interest.

Example 5: Mother and daughter together own all the common shares in a corporation. Mother redeems her shares for preferred stock. [Section 2701] applies in valuing the preferred stock received by mother for purposes of determining whether the redemption results in a gift to daughter.

---

6. In a case of a corporation with only one class of preferred stock and one class of common stock, the junior equity interest is the common stock.

Example 6: Father and son form a partnership to which each contributes capital and in which the father receives a preferred interest and the son receives a residual interest. [Section 2701] applies in determining whether, and the extent to which, the capital contributions result in a gift.

Transfer Tax Treatment Of Accumulated Distributions

[Section 2701] increases the taxable gifts or taxable estate of a transferor who retained cumulative preferred stock valued under the rule described above. The amount of the increase is the excess of (1) the value of the distributions payable during the period beginning on the date of transfer and ending on the date of the taxable event determined as if all such distributions were paid on the date payment was due and all such distributions were reinvested by the transferor as of the date of payment at a yield equal to the discount rate used in determining the value of the applicable retained interest over (2) the value of the distributions paid during such period computed on the basis of the time when such distributions were actually paid.

Where the retained preferred cumulative stock is transferred to the transferor's spouse in a transfer that qualifies for the gift or estate tax marital deduction no adjustment is made with respect to taxable gifts or the taxable estate of the original transferor, but the spouse is then treated as the transferor. Any payment of any distribution prior to the end of the 4–year period beginning on its due date would be treated as having been made on such due date. [Section 2701] provides that a taxpayer may elect to treat payment of a distribution after the 4–year period as a taxable gift for purpose of chapter 12.

The amount of unpaid accumulated dividends and interest thereon that is subject in the gift or estate tax is capped at an amount equal to the excess of the fair market value of the common interests in the business at date of death over the fair market value of the common interests in the business at the date of the transfer multiplied by a fraction equal to the value of the preferred interests in the business held by the transferor divided by the value of all the preferred interests in the business. The purpose of this cap is to limit the amount of increase under the provision to the benefit adhering to the donee from the failure to pay dividends.

[Section 2701] provides that Treasury Regulations would provide for appropriate transfer tax adjustments for rights previously valued under [§ 2701] in order to prevent the double taxation of rights that were given a zero value under [§ 2701].

Minimum Value of Residual Interest

[Section 2701] also establishes a minimum value for a junior equity interest in a corporation or partnership. This minimum is the value that would be determined if the total value of all the junior equity interests equaled 10 percent of the sum of the total equity in the corporation or partnership plus any debt which the corporation or partnership owes to the transferor or members of his family. This minimum value is intended to reflect the "option value" of the right of the residual interest to future appreciation.

Statute of Limitations

Under [§ 2701], the gift tax statute of limitations runs for transfers subject to the rules governing preferred interests in corporations and partnerships and to increases in taxable gifts with respect to cumulative preferred stock only if the transfer is disclosed on a gift tax return with sufficient detail to appraise the secretary of the nature of the transferred and retained interests. Thus, the statute would not run on an undisclosed or inadequately disclosed transfer, regardless of whether a gift tax return was filed for other transfers in the year in which the transfer occurred.

ILLUSTRATIVE MATERIAL

A. TRANSFERS SUBJECT TO § 2701

1. In General

The special valuation rules of § 2701 apply to transfers of an equity interest in a corporation or a partnership to a "family member" (transferor's spouse, spouse of lineal descendent, and lineal descendent of transferor or transferor's spouse) where the transferor or an "applicable family member" (transferor's spouse, ancestors of transferor and her spouse, and spouses of such ancestors) holds an "applicable retained interest." Reg. § 25.2701–1(a)(1) and 1(d)(1)–(2). The special valuation rules assign a zero value to the "applicable retained interest", thereby increasing the value of the transferred interest. Note that family members do not include brothers, sisters, nieces and nephews. Also, "family members" do not include persons in generations older than the transferor. Thus, a transfer of an equity interest to the transferor's parent, grandparent, nephew or niece is not within the scope of § 2701.

2. Indirect Transfers

Section 2701(e)(5) and the regulations thereunder treat certain changes in the capital structure of a corporation or partnership as transfers to which § 2701 applies. For example, the regulations state that a contribution of capital to a new or existing entity is a transfer. Reg. § 25.2701–1(b)(2)(i). Suppose P transfers his business worth $900 to a corporation for preferred stock and his child C transfers $100 cash for all the common stock. Section 2701 applies because P, who holds an applicable retained interest, the preferred stock, is treated as having transferred the common stock to C. If P's preferred stock is determined to have a value less than $900 after the application of § 2701, P will have made a taxable gift to C of that difference.

Similarly, a transfer may occur in a recapitalization. Suppose that P and C each holds 500 shares of the common stock of a family corporation and that each block of 500 shares has a value of $500,000. In a recapitalization, P exchanges all his common stock for preferred stock while C keeps his common. P is treated as having transferred his common stock to C. To the extent P's preferred stock after the application of § 2701 has a value less then $500,000 (the value of P's interest before the recapitalization), he will be treated as having made a gift of that amount to C. See Reg. § 25.2701–3(d) Ex. 4. See Reg. § 25.2701–1(b)(2)(i) for other situations when transfers may be deemed to have occurred.

B. APPLICABLE RETAINED INTERESTS

The term "applicable retained interest" is the lynch pin of § 2701 and has two categories. The first category, "extraordinary payment rights," is intended to address situations where the transferor has reduced the value of the transferred interest by retaining a valuable right which is discretionary. Extraordinary payment rights include the right of the transferor to put her retained interest back to the corporation or partnership or to compel liquidation of her interest. See Reg. § 25.2701–2(b)(1). Assigning a zero value to extraordinary payment rights reflects skepticism about whether the right will ever be exercised by the transferor.

The second category, "distribution rights," are rights to receive distributions with respect to an equity interest that is not subordinate to or of the same class as the transferred interest. Reg. § 25.2701–2(b)(3). Distribution rights retained by the transferor are assigned a zero value, if the transferor or transferor's family controls the entity, because of skepticism about whether distributions to the transferor will ever occur. For example, dividends payable on preferred stock are distribution rights to which a zero value is assigned (unless the requirements for "qualified payment rights", discussed below, are satisfied).

1. Qualified Payment Rights

Some economic rights are not treated as applicable retained interests. A "qualified payment right" is the right to receive fixed dividends payable at least annually on cumulative preferred stock. Reg. § 25.2701–1(a)(2)(ii) and § 25.2701–2(d)(6). Although a qualified payment right is technically a distribution right that would constitute an applicable retained interest, it is assigned its fair market value. Reg. § 25.2701–1(a)(2)(ii) and(iii). The fact that the dividend is cumulative makes it less likely that its owner has transferred hidden value.

To illustrate the application of this principle, consider the following overly simplified examples:

1. *Example One*—P, an individual, holds all the nonvoting preferred stock and voting common stock of X Corp. X Corp has a value of $1,500,000. The nonvoting preferred stock has a noncumulative preferential dividend right which entitles its holders to receive an annual dividend of $100 before a dividend may be paid on the common stock. Assume, for the sake of simplicity, that the preferred does not participate in liquidation. P transfers all her common stock to her child, C.

P has transferred an equity interest, the common stock, to a "family member," C. The preferred stock's right to noncumulative preferred dividends is an "applicable retained interest" which is a "distribution right" since the dividend right is not subordinate to or the same class as the common stock P transferred. Reg. § 25.2701–2(b)(3). Distribution rights retained by the transferor are assigned a zero value, if the transferor or transferor's family controls the entity. Reg. § 25.2701–2(b)(2). Since "applicable family members" control the corporation (§ 25.2701–2(b)(5)), the distribution right is assigned a value of zero for purposes of valuing P's gift to C. As a result, P is treated as having made a gift of $1,500,000 to C, the value of P's interest in X Corp ($1,500,000) less the value of her retained interest ($0).

2. *Example Two*—Assume the same facts as Example One, except that the annual dividends for the preferred are cumulative. P's right to receive cumulative dividends is a "qualified payment right" that will not be assigned a zero value. Regs. §§ 25.2701–2(b)(6), 25.2701–1(a)(2)(ii) and (iii). If the value of the qualified payment right is $1,000,000, P will be treated as having made a gift of $500,000, calculated as $1,500,000 (the value of all interests held by P) minus the value of the qualified payment right ($1,000,000). See Reg. § 25.2701–3.

As illustrated in *Example Two* above, § 2701 does not assign a zero value to qualified payment rights such as cumulative dividend rights. What happens if the cumulative dividends are never paid and P transfers the cumulative preferred stock? Section § 2701(d) generally increases the amount the transferor of a qualified payment right is deemed to transfer by an amount equal to the value of all qualified payments scheduled to be made over the value of the qualified payments actually made. § 2701(d)(2). The values are calculated by assuming that the qualified payments were invested at a yield equivalent to the interest rate used to calculate the value of the qualified payments at the time the § 2701(a) transfer occurred. Reg. Reg. § 25.2701–4(c). The amount may not, however, exceed the amount by which the other equity interests in the corporation subordinate to the preferred increased in value as a result of the failure to pay the qualified distributions. Reg. Reg. § 25.2701–4(c)

For example, suppose P (parent) transfers all the common stock to C (P's child) while retaining preferred stock with a cumulative dividend right of $100,000 per year. Assume that the appropriate interest rate to value the preferred is 10% compounded annually. If no dividends are paid, P dies three years after the transfer and the preferred stock is included in P's estate, § 2701(d) would in general increase P's gross estate by $331,000. This amount represents what P would have had if she received the dividend payments of $100,000 per year and invested them at 10% compounded annually. See Reg. § 25.2701–4(c). If the common stock has not appreciated in value, however, during the three year period, no amount would be added to P's gross estate. Reg. § 25.2701–4(c)(6).

2. *Liquidation Payment Rights*

A "liquidation payment right," the right to receive liquidating distributions if a liquidation occurs, is also generally assigned its fair market value subject to an exception. Reg. § 25.2701–2(b)(4)(ii). If the transferor, members of the transferor's family or applicable family members have the ability to compel liquidation, the liquidation participation right is valued either as though the ability to compel liquidation did not exist or as though it is subject to the lower of rule described below. Reg. § 25.2701–2(b)(4)(ii).

3. *The "Lower Of" Rule*

Consistent with the assumption that the transferor will act to minimize the value of his retained interests, § 2701(a)(3)(B) directs that if the transferor or applicable family member holds a qualified payment right and one or more extraordinary payment rights, then the value of all the rights must be determined as though the extraordinary payment right is exercised or not exercised to yield the lowest value. The regulations call this the "lower of" rule. Reg. § 25.2701–2(a)(3).

To illustrate the "lower of" rule, suppose P owns all 1,000 shares of X Corp's preferred stock which pays an annual cumulative dividend of $100 per share and also owns all 1,000 shares of X's voting common. X Corp has a value of $1,500,000. P also has the right to put all the preferred stock to X at any time for $900,000. P transfers all the common stock to C, P's child. P has retained both a qualified payment right (the right to receive cumulative dividends) and extraordinary payment right (the put right). Using a 10% interest rate (which we will assume is the appropriate valuation rate), the qualified payment right, by itself, would be valued at $1,000,000. However, because the "lower of" rule applies, the put right is assumed to be exercised or not exercised such that the lowest total value for the rights is obtained. Since the total value of the rights is $900,000 if the put right is exercised or 1,000,000 if not exercised, the value assigned to P's preferred stock would be $900,000. Thus the amount of P's gift under § 2701 is $600,000 (the $1,500,000 value of X Corp less $900,000).

C. THE SUBTRACTION METHOD OF VALUATION

The Regulations require the "subtraction method" to be used to value a gift when § 2701 applies. As illustrated in the foregoing examples, the subtraction method generally treats the transferor as having transferred an amount equal to the difference between the value of all interests in the entity after the transfer and the value of the retained interests where the transferor initially owned all the interests. If the transferor did not initially own all the interests in the entity, the calculation becomes more complex.

To insure that any reductions in value are treated as having been transferred as part of the transferor's gift, the Regulations direct that a four step method be used.

Step 1. Calculate the fair market value of all "family-held" equity interests in the entity immediately <u>after</u> the transfer as though all the interests were held by one individual. Reg. § 25.2701–3(b). For this purpose "family-held" means interests held by the transferor, applicable family members and any lineal descendants of the parents of the transferor or the transferor's spouse. Regs. §§ 25.2701–3(a)(2)(i), 25. 2701–2(b)(5)(i).

Step 2. Subtract the following items from the amount determined in Step 1:

(1) the fair market value of all family-held "senior equity interests"[7] *other than applicable retained interests* held by the transferor or applicable family members;

(2) the fair market value of any family-held equity interests of the same class or a subordinate class to the transferred interests held by

---

7. "Senior equity interests" are interests having a right to distributions of income or capital that is preferred to the rights of the transferred interests. Reg. § 25.2701–3(a)(2)(ii).

persons other than the transferor, members of the transferor's family, and applicable family members of the transferor;

(3) the § 2701 value of all applicable retained interests held by the transferor or applicable family members.

Note that Steps 1 and 2 determine the value of equity interests that are subordinate to the applicable retained interests and that are held by the transferor, members of the transferor's family and applicable family members.

Step 3: Allocate the difference calculated in Step 2 to the transferred interests (i.e. to the gift) and other subordinate equity interests[8] held by the transferor, applicable family members and members of the transferor's family.

Step 4: The amount allocated in Step 3 to the transferred interests is then reduced to reflect a minority discount or blockage discount to determine the value of the gift.

Examples of application of the four steps are provided in Examples 1 through 5 of Reg. § 25.2701–3(d).

D.   MINIMUM VALUE OF COMMON STOCK

If § 2701 applies to the transfer of an equity interest, the value of all "junior equity interests" in the corporation or partnership may not be less than 10% of (1) the total value of all equity interests in the entity plus (2) the total amount of any indebtedness of the entity owed to the transferor and applicable family members. § 2701(a)(4); Reg. § 25.2701–3(c)(1). "Junior equity interests" are defined as common stock or, for partnerships, a partnership interest whose rights to income and capital are junior to the rights of all other classes of partnership interests. Reg. § 25.2701–3(c)(2). As discussed in the 1990 Senate Report, Congress intends this minimum value to reflect the "option value", i.e. the right to participate in future appreciation of common stock and subordinate partnership interests.

SECTION B.   SPECIAL VALUATION RULES FOR TRUSTS AND TERM INTERESTS: § 2702

1990 Senate Report on Proposed Revision of Estate Freeze[9] Rules

136 Congressional Record S15,679–S15,683 (Oct. 18, 1990).

Present Law and Background

* * *

Trusts and Term Interests in Property

Description: Another common estate freeze transaction involves the retention of a term of years or life estate in a trust or property. For

---

8. "Subordinate equity interests" are equity interests which have rights to the distribution of income or capital which are subordinate to applicable retained interests. Reg. §§ 25.2701–3(a)(2)(ii) and (iii).

9. For a discussion of the peculiar legislative history of this Report, see note 2.

example, a parent may transfer property or money to an irrevocable trust for the ultimate benefit of a child in which the parent retains an income interest for a term of years. Or, an owner of property may sell a remainder interest in the property to a child. Or, older and younger generations may jointly purchase term and remainder interests in property from a third party. All these transactions effectively shift future appreciation in the property to the younger generation.

Gift tax consequences: The above transfers result in a taxable gift if the value of the remainder interest exceeds the value of any consideration paid for such interest. The value of the remainder interest is the value of the entire property less the value of rights in the property retained by the grantor. Rights retained by the grantor generally are valued pursuant to Treasury tables that assume a rate of return on the underlying property equal to 120 percent of the applicable Federal midterm rate (Code § 7520, Treas. Reg. § 20.2512–5(f)). Use of the Treasury tables is allowed even when they do not accurately predict the actual rate of return from the property. For example, in 1977, the Internal Revenue Service ruled that the application of tables based on an interest rate of 6 percent per year was appropriate in valuing a trust whose corpus consisted of stock that had paid an average dividend of 3 percent for the preceding ten years. According to the ruling, "departure from strict application of the tables is permissible in exceptional cases where use of the tables would violate reason and fact; for example, where transferred property may yield no income at all or the income is definitely determinable by other means."

Reasons for Change

Trusts And Term Interests In Property

In addition, the committee is concerned about the undervaluation of gifts valued pursuant to Treasury tables. Based on average rates of return and life expectancy, those tables are seldom accurate in a particular case, and therefore, may be the subject of adverse selection. Because the taxpayer decides what property to give, when to give it, and often controls the return on the property, use of Treasury tables undervalues the transferred interests in the aggregate, more often than not.

Therefore, the committee determines that the valuation problems inherent in trusts and term interests in property are best addressed by valuing retained interests at zero unless they take an easily valued form— as an annuity or unitrust interest. By doing so, the bill draws upon [pre– 1990] law rules valuing split interests in property for purposes of the charitable deduction.

Explanation of Provisions

Trusts and Term Interests in Property

[Section 2702] * * * provides rules for determining whether a transfer of an interest in trust to a member of the transferor's family is a gift, and the amount of the gift. These rules do not apply to the extent that the transfer is incomplete. Nor do they apply to a transfer of an interest in a personal residence inhabited by the holder of the term interest.

Valuation of Initial Transfer

[Section 2702] requires that the value of a remainder interest be determined by subtracting the value of the income interest from the value of the entire property. [Section 2702] provides that the value of an interest retained by the transferor or an applicable family member is zero unless such interest is a "qualified interest." A qualified interest is (1) a right to receive fixed amounts payable at least annually, (2) a right to receive amounts payable at least annually which are a fixed percentage of the trust's assets (determined annually), or (3) a non-contingent remainder interest if all the other interests in the trust are qualified payments. A qualified interest generally would be valued * * * by reference to § 7520.

Thus, a person who makes a completed transfer of nonresidential property in trust and retains (1) the right to the income of the trust for a term of years and (2) a reversionary right (or a testamentary general power of appointment) with respect to trust corpus is treated as making a transfer equal to the value of the whole property. The same result obtains if the transferor retains (1) the right to both income and appreciation for a term of years plus (2) a testamentary general power of appointment over trust corpus for that period. In contrast, the creation of a trust the only interests in which are an annuity for a term of years and a noncontingent remainder interest is valued under [pre–1990] law.

Sale of Remainder Interest and Joint Purchase of Interests in Property.

Under [§ 2702], the retention of a term interest (including a life estate) in property is treated like the retention of an interest in trust. Moreover, a joint purchase of property is treated as an acquisition of the entire property by the holder of the term interest, followed by a transfer of the remainder interest. Thus, for purposes of determining the amount of the gift, [§ 2702] effectively treats the purchaser of a life estate pursuant to a joint purchase as making a transfer of the entire property less the consideration paid by the remainderman.

A special rule applies to a term interest in tangible property where the non-exercise of the term-holder's rights does not substantially affect the value of the property passing to the remainderman. In that case, the value of the term interest is the amount for which the taxpayer establishes that the interest could be sold to an unrelated third party. Such amount is not determined under the Treasury tables, but by reference to market norms, taking into account the illiquidity of such interests.

For example, the rule could apply to the joint purchase of a painting or undeveloped real estate (the value of which primarily reflects future development potential). On the other hand, the rule would not apply to a joint purchase of depletable property. Treasury regulations would provide for the proper treatment of improvements or other changes in property governed by this special rule.

ILLUSTRATIVE MATERIAL

A.   IN GENERAL

Prior to the adoption of § 2702, transfer taxes could be reduced significantly by using a grantor retained interest trust (GRIT). For example, suppose that P, age 50, irrevocably transfers property worth $1,000,000 into trust, retaining an income interest for 20 years with remainder to C, P's child. Using the methodology described in Chapter 35 and assuming that 120% of the federal midterm rate (see § 7520(a)) equals 10%, the value of the retained interest would be $851,356. This amount is calculated by multiplying $1,000,000 by .85136, the factor obtained in Table B of the Book Aleph (Publication 1457) for a 20 year income interest. The remainder interest transferred to C would be valued at $148,644, calculated as $1,000,000 multiplied by .148644, the factor in Table B for remainder interests.[10] Thus, the value of P's gift to D would be $148,644.

The abuse that Congress was concerned about arises where the property transferred by P generates no income but instead merely appreciates in value. Suppose, for example, that the property is a growth stock that pays no dividends. Although Table B assumed that income would be generated at the rate of 10 percent and paid to P, no amounts will in fact be paid to P. In effect, P will have transferred most of the value in the growth stock, including its earning potential, to C without paying the associated transfer tax. For example, if the stock increases in value at a rate of 15% compounded semiannually, C would receive stock worth $16,366,537 at the end of 20 years.

Section 2702 will generally increase the amount of a gift by valuing a retained interest, other than a qualified interest, at zero where an individual transfers an interest in trust to or for the benefit of the individual's family and the individual or an applicable family member retains an interest. § 2702(a); Reg. § 25.2702–1(a). "Qualified interests" are discussed below. Members of the individual's family include the individual's spouse, any ancestor or lineal descendant of the individual's spouse, any brother or sister of the individual, and any spouse of the foregoing. Reg. § 25.2702–2(a)(1). The term applicable family member is defined in Reg. § 25.2702–1(a) by reference to Reg. § 25.2701–1(d)(2), discussed at p. 766.

For example, suppose P transfers property worth $1,000,000 into an irrevocable trust, retaining the right to receive trust income for 10 years, remainder to C, P's child. Since C is a member of P's family, and P has retained an interest in the trust which is not a qualified interest, P's retained interest is valued at zero and P is treated as having made a gift valued at $1,000,000. See Reg. § 25.2702–2 (d) Ex. 1.

---

10. The factors for remainder interests are also reproduced in Table B of Reg. § 20.2031–7(d)(6).

B.   QUALIFIED INTERESTS

1.   *General*

As discussed in the Senate Report, Congress adopted § 2702 to prevent disguised transfers of wealth from occurring where a transferor has retained an income interest in property knowing that the property would in fact generate no income. The potential for abuse is greatly reduced where a trust is required to make annual distributions to the transferor regardless of whether the trust property generates income. Because of this, § 2702(a)(2)(A) does not assign a zero value to "qualified interests."

There are three types of qualified interests. The first, a qualified annuity interest, is an irrevocable right to receive annually a payment of a fixed amount. § 2702(b)(1); Reg. § 25.2702–3(b)(1). For example, the right to receive $10,000 per year is a qualified annuity interest. Qualified annuity interest are valued using the rules discussed in Chapter 34 for valuing annuities under § 7520. Estate planners usually refer to grantor trusts with a qualified annuity interest as a GRAT (the acronym for grantor retained annuity trust).

The second type of qualified interest, a qualified unitrust interest, is an irrevocable right to receive annually a payment equal to a fixed percentage of the net fair market value of the trust's assets determined annually. § 2702(b)(2); Reg. § 25.2702–3(c). For example, the right to receive 10% of the value of the trust's assets, determined annually, would constitute a qualified unitrust interest. Qualified unitrust interests are also valued as if they were interests described in § 664. Reg. § 25.2702–2(b)(2). See p. 544 for a discussion of § 664. Planners call grantor trusts with qualified unitrust interests GRUTs.

The third type of qualified interest is a qualified remainder interest. A qualified remainder interest is a non-contingent remainder interest retained by the transferor where all other interests in the trust are qualified annuity or unitrust interests. Reg. § 25.2702–3(f). The logic is that where all the other interests are qualified annuity or unitrust interests, the value of the qualified remainder interest cannot be overstated since payments have to be made for the qualified annuity and unitrust interests. Qualified remainder interests are also valued as if they were interests described in § 664. Reg. § 25.2702–2(b)(2).

2.   *Contingent Qualified Interests*

Section 2702(b) requires that qualified payments be "fixed." Sometimes a grantor will establish a trust, income to herself for a term of years, but, if she dies during the term, income to her spouse for the rest of the term so long as her spouse is still living. The IRS has argued that the interest of the grantor's spouse is not a qualified interest because it is not "fixed", but rather is contingent upon surviving the grantor.

The argument has had mixed success. In Schott v. Commissioner, 319 F.3d 1203 (9th Cir. 2003), the grantor transferred property to a GRAT that provided that a percentage of the initial net fair market value was to be paid to the grantor for fifteen years unless she died. If the grantor died prior to the end of the fifteen-year term, the annuity was to be paid to her spouse for the balance of the term.[11] If the grantor died prior to the end of the fifteen-year term, and if the spouse did not survive the grantor, the annuity payments would cease, and the remaining GRAT property would be held in trust for the surviving spouse or for the descendants of the grantor. The court held that the interests of the grantor and her spouse were "fixed" because their value could be actuarially determined. The court said that the legislative purpose of section 2702 was to prevent undervalued gifts. Since the value of the grantor's and spouse's interests could be actuarially determined, the court concluded that the interests fell "within the class of easily valued rights that Congress meant to qualify." (1207) The court distinguished an earlier decision, Cook v. Commissioner, 269 F.3d 854 (7th Cir. 2001), which had found a similar interest to be not qualified because the interest of the grantor's spouse had an additional contingency, that the grantor and spouse be married at the time the spouse's annuity began, which could not be actuarially determined.

The Tax Court has refused to follow the *Schott* court, rejecting the notion that ease of valuation is the linchpin for determining that the interest is fixed. Estate of Focardi v. Commissioner, 91 T.C.M. 936 (2006). In addition, the IRS says that it will not follow *Schott*. T.D. 9181 (2005).

The IRS has been more generous, however, in finding that an interest is fixed, where the trust will pay the income to the grantor's estate in the event the grantor dies during the term. The IRS amended its regulations (Reg. 25.2702–3(e) Ex. 5.; T.D. 9181 (2006)) to hold that such an interest is qualified for the entire term after the Tax Court so ruled and invalidated an earlier regulation to the contrary. Walton v. Commissioner, 115 T.C. 589 (2000).,

3.   *Promissory Notes as "Payment"*

The IRS amended regulations in 2000 to forbid the use of promissory notes to pay income interests after September 20, 1999. Reg. § 25.2702–3(d)(5). To illustrate the concern, consider TAM 9717008 (April 25, 1997), where a donor owned 910,466 shares of stock valued at $22,266,584, which he expected to double in value over the next two years. Donor transferred the stock into a GRAT, which paid him an annuity of $12,212,914 per year for two years. At the end of two years, the trust corpus was payable to the remaindermen, donor's children. The trust instrument permitted the trust to make each annuity payment with a promissory note, which would bear adequate interest, and would be payable upon termination of the trust out of the trust principal (i.e., the shares of stock). The trust did not have sufficient cash to pay the annual annuity because the stock paid small dividends. The trust instrument stated that the donor's interest in the trust was intended to qualify as a qualified annuity interest under § 2702(b)(1) and that the trustee was authorized to amend the trust retroactively to insure compliance with § 2702(b)(1). Because

---

11. In *Schott*, the grantor had retained the power to revoke her spouse's interest. This power, however, did not affect the court's analysis because Reg. § 25.2702–2(b)(6) treats a qualified annuity or unitrust interest held by the grantor's spouse that may be revoked by the grantor as a valid qualified interest of the grantor. It states, "If a transferor retains a power to revoke a qualified annuity interest or qualified unitrust interest of the transferor's spouse, then the revocable qualified annuity interest or unified interest of the transferor's spouse is treated as a retained qualified interest of the transferor."

of donor's larger annuity interest, donor reported a taxable gift of only $120,907 upon the transfer in trust.

As expected, the shares approximately doubled in vale. Upon the trust's termination, the trust paid its promissory note to donor using 522,265 of the shares. The remaining 388,201 shares, valued at $20,186,452, were transferred to the donor's children. The GRAT and promissory note allowed the donor to transfer over $20 million of stock to his children while reporting a taxable gift of only $120,907. The amended regulations eliminate this strategy.

C. TRANSFERS OF AN INTEREST IN TRUST

Section § 2702 applies to "transfers of an interest in trust." Section 2702(c), however, expands the scope of § 2702 beyond trusts. Under § 2702(c)(1), a transfer of a property interest with respect to which there is one or more term interests is treated as the transfer of an interest in trust. Thus, where P transfers a remainder interest in land to C, retaining a 10 year term interest, P's transfer is treated as the "transfer of an interest in trust." Section 2702(c)(2) expands the reach of § 2702(c)(1) even further. It treats a joint purchase of property by family members where one member acquires a term interest[12] as though the person holding the term interest acquired the entire property and then transferred the nonterm interests to family members for an amount of consideration equal to any amounts paid by the other family members. By treating the term interest holder as having acquired the entire interest and then having conveyed interests to family members, § 2702(c)(2) triggers the applicability of § 2702(c)(1). The result is that the transaction is treated as a transfer of an interest in trust to which § 2702 applies.

D. QUALIFIED PERSONAL RESIDENCE TRUSTS

Section 2702 does not apply to the transfer of an interest in trust if all the trust property is to be used "as a personal residence by persons holding term interests in such trust." Section 2702(a)(3)(ii). "Personal residence" means the term holder's principal residence as defined in § 1034, one other residence of the term holder within the meaning of § 280A(d)(1) or an undivided fractional interest in either one. Regs. §§ 25.2702–5(b)(2)(i), 25.2702–5(c)(2)(i).

The regulations permit two types of trust to qualify under § 2702(a)(3)(ii)—the "personal residence trust" and the "qualified personal residence trust" (QPRT). Personal residence trusts are rarely used because the regulations impose strict requirements. The only asset the personal residence trust is permitted to hold is the personal residence and, in certain circumstances, proceeds paid to the trust as the result of the destruction or involuntary conversion of the personal residence. See Reg. §§ 25.2702–5(b)(1) and (2). Thus, the personal residence trust cannot hold cash to pay operating expenses. Moreover, the trust instrument must prohibit the sale or transfer of the residence during the original term of the trust. Id. In contrast, the regulations expressly permit a QPRT to hold cash that is reasonably anticipated to be needed to pay expenses, to sell the residence and reinvest the proceeds in a new

---

12. Section 2702(c)(2) defines term interest to include either a life interest or in   interest for a term of years.

residence and to receive or make improvements to the residence. Reg. § 25.2702–5(c)(5).

Because of the greater flexibility, the QPRT is often used as an estate planning device. See e.g. P.R. 200728018 (2007). Usually, the grantor transfers her home in trust, retaining the right to live in it for a term of years, with the remainder to her children. Since the regular valuation rules under § 7520 described in Chapter 34 apply and the personal residence will normally generate no income, the QPRT enables the transferor to shift all future appreciation to the remainder interest holders, while still living in the house. Note that this shift will only occur, however, if the transferor does not die during the term of the retained interest because under such circumstances, the full value of the house would be included in the transferor's gross estate under § 2036. See Chapter 14. Where do the transferor parents live after the QPRT term expires and the property vests with their children? In P.R. 9425028 (March 28, 1994) the IRS ruled that an agreement between the grantor and remainder beneficiaries entered into at the time the QPRT was created pursuant to which the remainder beneficiaries agreed to rent the residence to the grantor for a fair market price after the QPRT terminated did not disqualify the QPRT or affect the value of the remainder interest.

The prospect of paying rent to children does not appeal to many parents. The parents may, therefore, seek to purchase the home at the term end. Reg. § 25.2702–5(c)(9), however, requires the trust instrument to prohibit the trust from selling the residence to the grantor of the trust during the term of the grantor's interest or any subsequent time that the trust is a grantor trust under §§ 671–678.[13] Without this rule, parents could transfer cash to the trust in exchange for the home which would then be distributed to their children without incurring an additional transfer tax. Moreover, the children and the trust would also not incur a capital gains tax because for income tax purposes the parents would be treated as the home owner.

After the trust has distributed the home to the children, the parents may purchase the home directly from the children for its fair market value, but the children would then incur a capital gains tax to the extent the purchase price exceeds their tax basis. If parents instead decide to pay less than fair market value to the children, a taxable gift would occur.

---

13. A grantor trust is disregarded for income tax purposes and the grantor of the trust is treated as directly owning the trust assets.

*

PART IX

ADMINISTRATIVE ASPECTS OF WEALTH TRANSFER TAXES

CHAPTER 38

TAX RESPONSIBILITIES OF THE EXECUTOR

INTRODUCTORY MATERIAL

As explained in Chapter 5, the executor of an estate that exceeds a threshold amount ($3.5 million in 2009) generally must file an estate tax return, and pay any estate tax due, within nine months of the decedent's death. §§ 6075, 6151(a).[1] The executor, however, may request extensions of time for both filing and payment.

In addition to federal tax filing and payment responsibilities, the executor is confronted with a significant number of statutory elections and non-statutory optional courses of action during the period of estate administration.

Section 6036 requires the executor to notify the Service of his qualification as executor, but the filing of an estate tax return satisfies this requirement. Reg. § 20.6036–2. In any event, the executor should consider filing a notice of fiduciary relationship (Form 56) with the District Director for the district in which the executor will file tax returns.[2] Any subsequent communications regarding the decedent's income, gift, and generation-skipping tax liabilities will be sent to the executor.

The executor is responsible for filing the estate tax return, an income tax return for the decedent for the period prior to death, income tax returns for the estate, a gift tax return for the year in which the decedent died, and gift tax returns for any unreported gifts made prior to the year of death.

In filing returns, the executor must make certain elections which may affect the tax liability of the estate, the surviving spouse (if any), and the beneficiaries, as well as the executor's own personal liability for federal taxes. For example, the executor must decide whether to file a joint income tax return with the decedent's surviving spouse, whether to consent to gift splitting for gifts made prior to the decedent's death, and whether to elect the alternate valuation method. If given discretion, the executor may elect deductible treatment for qualified terminable interest bequests. In addition, during the period of administration, the executor must make decisions concerning the choice of fiscal year for the estate, when and how to distribute property, and when to terminate the estate. These elections and considerations relating to their exercise are outlined at p. 797.

---

1. In 2007, 49,924 estate tax returns were filed. Internal Revenue Service 2007 Data Book, Table 3.

2. Reg. § 301.6903–1. The executor is required to attach a copy of the decedent's will to Form 56.

Unless otherwise directed in the decedent's will or prohibited by local law, the executor may seek to recover from a beneficiary (other than the surviving spouse to the extent the property qualified for the marital deduction) who has received life insurance proceeds which were includible in the decedent's estate (§ 2206), property subject to an includible power of appointment (§ 2207), or property which was subject to a qualifying income interest (§ 2207A(a)), the estate tax attributable to such items.

Finally, in connection with the winding up of the affairs of the estate, the executor typically will want to be discharged from personal liability for any unpaid federal taxes of the estate or the decedent. The procedure for obtaining this discharge is discussed at p. 800.

Section A.   Liquidity Problems

Problems arise when the estate lacks sufficient liquid assets to pay the estate tax or when the estate would fail to realize the true worth of assets sold to raise the cash necessary to pay the tax. Congress has provided, in §§ 303, 2032A, 2057, 6161, 6163, and 6166, measures to ameliorate the liquidity problem.

1.   Extensions of Time to Pay the Tax

As noted in Chapter 5, an extension of time for filing the estate tax return is entirely separate and distinct from an extension of time for the payment of tax. Regardless of when the return is filed, the tax must be paid within nine months after the date of death, *unless* (1) an extension of time to pay is granted under § 6161, (2) the executor elects to defer payment of the tax attributable to an includible remainder or reversionary interest pursuant to § 6163, or (3) the executor elects to pay the tax in installments as permitted by § 6166.[3]

Section 6161(a)(1) authorizes the Service to extend the time for payment of estate tax for "a reasonable period," not to exceed 12 months, upon a showing of "reasonable cause." Successive annual extensions of up to ten years also may be granted pursuant to § 6161(a)(2) upon an identical showing.[4] Finally, in the case of an estate tax deficiency assessed after an audit, successive annual extensions of up to four years may be obtained under § 6161(b)(2), again upon a showing of "reasonable cause."[5] Reg. § 20.6161–1(a)(1) contains several examples of "reasonable cause" for an extension of time to file an estate tax return. An application for an

---

3. The statute of limitations is suspended for the period of any extension granted under §§ 6161(a)(2) and (b)(2), 6163, and 6166. § 6503(d).

4. Extensions under § 6161(a)(2) also are available for the payment of any installment due under § 6166. In such cases, how-

ever, the period of the extension cannot be longer than one year from the due date of the last installment.

5. An extension is not allowed if the deficiency is due to negligence or fraud. § 6161(b)(3).

extension must be filed on or before the due date for the payment of the tax or the deficiency. Reg. § 20.6161–1(b).

If a reversionary or remainder interest is included in the decedent's gross estate, § 6163(a) allows an executor to elect to postpone the payment of the tax attributable to that interest until six months after the termination of the preceding interest or interests in the property. This extension does not extend to future interests created by the decedent's own testamentary act. Reg. § 20.6163–1(a)(1). Thus, the six-month extension would not be available where the decedent devised a life estate to her child and the remainder to her grandchild. Additional extensions of up to three years are authorized by § 6163(b) upon a showing of "reasonable cause."

If payment is postponed under either §§ 6161 or 6163, the estate will accrue interest at the § 6621 rate until the tax is paid. § 6601(a). In addition, the Service is authorized to require the estate to post a bond to secure payment in accordance with the extension in an amount up to twice the deferred amount. § 6165.[6]

2. PAYMENT OF TAX IN INSTALLMENTS

Section 6166 permits an executor to pay the estate tax attributable to a qualifying closely held business interest in installments for up to fourteen years (annual interest payments for the first four years, followed by up to ten annual installments of principal and interest). To qualify for the election, the value of an included "interest in a closely held business" must exceed 35% of the decedent's "adjusted gross estate," a term defined as the decedent's gross estate less any deductions allowable under §§ 2053 (funeral expenses, administration expenses, claims, and mortgages) or 2054 (casualty losses).[7] The value of a closely held business interest is determined by the estate tax value. Thus, if special use valuation pursuant to § 2032A is elected, that value will govern for purposes of § 6166. In addition, if the closely held business is a farm, the residential buildings which are occupied by the owner, lessee, or employees are included in determining the value of the interest. § 6166(b)(3).

An interest in a closely held business includes (1) a proprietorship, (2) a partnership interest constituting at least 20% of partnership capital, and (3) stock constituting at least 20% in value of a corporation's voting stock. Even if the applicable 20% test is not met, a partnership or stock interest may still qualify if the partnership or corporation has 45 or fewer[8] partners

---

6. For an extension obtained under § 6163, the bond is conditioned on the principal or surety notifying the Service each year whether the precedent interest remains outstanding. Reg. § 20.6165–1(b).

7. The portion of the value of a closely held business attributable to passive assets is disregarded in determining (1) whether the estate is eligible for § 6166 deferral, and (2) the amount of estate tax that may be paid on a deferred basis. A special rule permits the shareholders of certain holding companies to utilize § 6166. § 6166(b)(9).

8. The 2001 Act increased the number of allowable partners and shareholders from 15 to 45, which is still less than the 75 partners or shareholders permitted under the subchapter S corporation rules. § 1361. As a result, the owner of an S corporation with 46–75 partners or shareholders is ineligible to

or shareholders.[9] The determinations required by the preceding sentences are to be made immediately prior to the decedent's death. § 6166(b)(2)(A). Two or more interests in closely held businesses are considered a single interest in applying the 35% test if more than 20% of the total value of each such business is included in the decedent's gross estate. § 6166(c).[10]

The maximum amount of estate tax that can be deferred under § 6166 is computed by multiplying the total estate tax, net of credits, by the ratio of the closely held business interest to the adjusted gross estate. § 6166(a)(2). Interest on the deferred estate tax is payable annually commencing the year following the decedent's death, until the first installment of the deferred estate tax is due on the date selected by the executor within five years of the usual due date (nine months after the date of death). § 6166(a)(3). A special 2% interest rate applies to the deferred estate tax attributable to the first $1 million in taxable value of a closely held business interest (i.e., the first $1 million above the exemption equivalent of the unified credit). § 6601(j)(2). Thus, in 2009, the 2% interest rate applies to the tax on a closely held business interest valued at between $3.5 million and $4.5 million. In addition, the interest rate on the deferred estate tax attributable to the taxable value of a closely held business interest in excess of $1 million is 45% of the rate applicable to underpayments of tax. § 6601(j)(1)(B). The interest paid is not deductible for estate (§ 2053(c)(1)(D)) or income (§ 163(k)) tax purposes.[11]

If funds or property aggregating one-half or more of the value of the business are withdrawn, or if there is a disposition by the estate of one-half or more of its interest in the closely held business, the postponed tax is accelerated and may no longer be paid on the installment basis.[12] In this

---

extend the time for payment of the estate tax attributable to the S corporation.

9. For purposes of the 20% and 45-person rules, stock or partnership interests owned by spouses as community property, joint property, tenants by the entirety, or tenants in common are treated as owned by one person. § 6166(b)(2)(B). Special attribution rules are provided to prevent avoidance of the 45 person rule. Shares of stock or partnership interests "owned, directly or indirectly, by or for a corporation, partnership, estate or trust [are] considered as being owned proportionally by and for its shareholders, partners or beneficiaries." § 6166(b)(2)(C). For these purposes, trust beneficiaries are those with present interests in the trust. Under § 6166(b)(2)(D), the attribution rules of § 267(c)(4) are applied to treat all stock and partnership interests held by the decedent or any member of his family as owned by the decedent for purposes of determining the number of shareholders or partners and, subject to the limitations of

§ 6166(b)(7), may be applied for purposes of determining whether the requisite 20% interest was owned by the decedent.

10. A surviving spouses interest in business property owned as community property, joint property, tenants by the entirety, or tenants in common is treated as having been included in determining the value of the decedent's gross estate. § 6166(c).

11. The Tax Court is authorized to issue declaratory judgments regarding an estates initial or continuing eligibility for deferral under § 6166. § 7479.

12. The acceleration provisions do not apply to exchanges of stock pursuant to certain tax-free reorganizations and corporate divisions (§ 6166(g)(1)(C)), to transfers to the decedent's devisees, legatees, or intestate takers (§ 6166(g)(1)(D)), or to certain redemptions of stock to pay death taxes and administration expenses pursuant to § 303 (§ 6166(g)(1)(B)). See Rev.Rul. 86–54, 1986–1 C.B. 356 (applying § 6166(g)(1)(B) to series of § 303 redemptions).

situation, deferral is no longer necessary because the withdrawal or disposition frees up funds with which to pay the estate tax liability. Any undistributed estate income in any taxable year ending on or before the due date of the first installment of taxes must be applied to any unpaid portion of the estate tax. § 6166(g)(2).

Section 6166 must be elected by the executor in writing prior to the due date of the decedent's estate tax return (including extensions). However, there are two safeguards that preserve the benefit of deferral in the face of any valuation uncertainties at that time that call into question the estate's eligibility for the § 6166 election. First, the executor may make a protective election, contingent on the possibility that the valuation as ultimately determined satisfy the § 6166 requirements. Reg. § 20.6166–1(b).[13] Second, if the executor does not initially make a § 6166 election but the Service on audit later increases the estate tax liability, § 6166(h) permits the executor to elect to pay the deficiency in installments.[14]

3.   Redemption of Stock to Pay Estate Taxes and Expenses

Section 303 permits certain stock that has been included in a decedent's gross estate to be redeemed and taxed at preferential capital gain rates, even though the proceeds otherwise would be treated as dividend income taxable at ordinary income rates under §§ 301 and 302. With the reduction of long term capital gain tax rates after 1997, § 303 has assumed greater importance in post-mortem planning.

As with § 6166, § 303 is designed to prevent the estate from having to sell or liquidate a closely held business in order to raise funds to pay the estate tax and related funeral and administration expenses. In contrast to § 6166, however, § 303 does not apply solely to closely held business interests. To qualify for § 303 treatment, the value of the stock of the redeeming corporation included in the gross estate must exceed 35% of the excess of the gross estate less the deductions allowable under §§ 2053 and 2054.[15] Thus, if a corporation is publicly held and the decedent's holdings satisfy the 35% test, a redemption of that stock from a qualified shareholder will result in capital gain rather than ordinary income, even if the corporation does not satisfy the § 6166(b)(1) tests—i.e., it has more than fifteen shareholders, or the decedent did not own 20% of the value of the voting stock of the corporation. However, where shares are publicly held and traded on a established securities market, there generally will not be a need to invoke § 303 because the shares can be sold on the open market.

---

13. A final notice of election must be filed within sixty days after the values are finally determined. Reg. § 20.6166–1(d).

14. The executor must make the election within sixty days after the Service determines the estate tax deficiency. § 6166(h)(2).

15. The stock of two or more corporations can be combined to satisfy the 35% requirement if the decedent's gross estate includes at least 20% or more of the stock of each corporation. For purposes of this test, stock representing the surviving spouses interest in property held by the decedent and the surviving spouse as community property or as joint tenants, tenants by the entirety, or tenants in common is treated as having been included in the decedent's estate. § 303(b)(2)(B).

Section 303 treatment is not restricted to shares redeemed from the decedent's estate.[16] Rather, the rules apply to any shares of stock included in the decedent's estate redeemed from any shareholder whose "interest" is "reduced directly (or through a binding obligation to contribute) by any payment of" death taxes or funeral and administration expenses. § 303(b)(3). Section 303(b)(3) eliminated a defect in prior law that permitted qualifying stock included in a decedent's estate to be redeemed from any holder of such stock at capital gain rates, regardless of whether the holder was obligated to pay the death taxes or funeral and administration expenses. The legislative history makes clear that § 303 applies "where the party whose shares are redeemed actually has the liability for estate taxes, State death taxes, or funeral and administration expenses in an amount at least equal to the amount of the redemption." H.R. Rep. No. 1380, 94th Cong., 2d Sess. 35 (1976). If the committee report is taken literally, § 303 applies only where the actual proceeds of the redemption (without reduction for any income tax liability) are used by the distributee to pay the qualified expenses. Thus, for example, if stock is redeemed from a marital deduction trust, § 303 will not apply because, in the usual case, the marital share bears no portion of the estate's tax liability or funeral and administration expenses. On the other hand, if the redemption is from the estate, § 303 applies even if the proceeds of the redemption are distributed to the marital deduction trust.

Where applicable, § 303 may be used to provide cash to those responsible for the payment of estate taxes and funeral and administration expenses. Because the redeemed stock is given a stepped-up basis under § 1014, the redemption will result in little, if any, gain and thus little, if any, income tax liability. However, if the redemption price exceeds the fair market value of the stock for estate tax purposes, and if the committee report's position is adopted in the regulations, the redeeming party will have to find an additional source of cash in the amount equal to the income tax payable on the redemption to satisfy the requirement that an amount equal to the redemption proceeds be used for the payment of taxes or expenses.

Distributions eligible for § 303 treatment must be made within three years and 90 days after the decedent's death (§ 303(b)(1)(A)), with extensions permitted for a Tax Court proceeding (§ 303(b)(1)(B)) and for installment payments under § 6166 (§ 303(b)(1)(C)).[17] Section 303 also applies for generation-skipping transfer tax purposes. § 303(d).

---

16. Where stock included in the gross estate could have been redeemed under § 303 but instead is exchanged for other stock with a basis determined with reference to the basis of the old stock, the new stock can be redeemed under § 303. § 303(c).

17. In any event, where a redemption takes place more than four years after the decedent's death, § 303 will apply only to the extent of the lesser of the unpaid taxes and expenses existing immediately prior to the distribution in redemption or the amount of taxes and expenses paid during the 12 months following the distribution. § 303(b)(4).

4. FAMILY FARMS AND SMALL BUSINESSES

Internal Revenue Code: § 2032A

Staff of the Joint Committee on Taxation, General Explanation of the Tax Reform Act of 1976

94th Cong., 2d Sess. (1976).

Prior law

Under the estate tax law, the value of property included in the gross estate of a decedent is the fair market value of the property interest at the date of the decedent's death (or at the alternate valuation date if elected). The fair market value is the price at which the property would change hands between a willing buyer and a willing seller, neither being under any compulsion to buy or to sell and both having reasonable knowledge of relevant facts. One of the most important factors used in determining fair market value is the highest and best use to which the property can be put.

* * * [I]n all cases, it is presumed that land would change hands between a willing buyer and a willing seller based on the "highest and best use" to which that land could be put, rather than the actual use of the land at the time it is transferred.

Reason for change

The Congress believed that, when land is actually used for farming purposes or in other closely held businesses (both before and after the decedent's death), it is inappropriate to value the land on the basis of its potential "highest and best use" especially since it is desirable to encourage the continued use of property for farming and other small business purposes. Valuation on the basis of highest and best use, rather than actual use, may result in the imposition of substantially higher estate taxes. In some cases, the greater estate tax burden makes continuation of farming, or the closely held business activities, not feasible because the income potential from these activities is insufficient to service extended tax payments or loans obtained to pay the tax. Thus, the heirs may be forced to sell the land for development purposes. Also, where the valuation of land reflects speculation to such a degree that the price of the land does not bear a reasonable relationship to its earning capacity, the Congress believed it unreasonable to require that this "speculative value" be included in an estate with respect to land devoted to farming or closely held businesses.

However, the Congress recognized that it would be a windfall to the beneficiaries of an estate to allow real property used for farming or closely held business purposes to be valued for estate tax purposes at its farm or business value unless the beneficiaries continue to use the property for farm or business purposes, at least for a reasonable period of time after the decedent's death. Also, the Congress believed that it would be inequitable to discount speculative values if the heirs of the decedent realize these speculative values by selling the property within a short time after the decedent's death.

For these reasons, the Act provides for special use valuation in situations involving real property used in farming or in certain other trades or businesses, but has further provided for recapture of the estate tax benefit where the land is prematurely sold or is converted to nonqualifying uses.

Gutman, Reforming Federal Wealth Transfer Taxes After ERTA

69 Va.L.Rev. 1183 (1983).

* * * I.R.C. § 2032A provides a preferential valuation method for certain farmland and real estate used in a closely held business. The Tax Reform Act of 1976 added § 2032A. After the 1976 Act, the executor of an estate, upon election, could value qualified real property for estate tax purposes on the basis of its current use rather than the value determined in accordance with generally applicable "willing buyer-willing seller" valuation principles. An executor could determine "use value" for farmland by one of two methods. First, where comparable farmland was rented for cash, the executor could value the included farmland by dividing the average annual gross cash rental for the comparable land by the average effective interest rate for all new Federal Land Bank loans. As an alternative, or where the information necessary to determine the numerator of the formula fraction was not available, the executor could determine value on the basis of a number of statutorily specified "facts and circumstances."[18] Special use valuation could not reduce the value of the gross estate by more than $500,000, and if property that had been specially valued was disposed of or ceased to be used for a qualifying use within ten years of the decedent's death the estate tax benefit attributable to the reduced value was recaptured without interest. The recapture tax phased out ratably over the following five years.

ERTA expanded the availability of special use valuation by relaxing a number of the qualification requirements and amending the formula valuation method to permit its use where comparable land was rented for crop shares as well as for cash. It also increased the maximum reduction in estate tax value in three increments from $500,000 to $750,000[19] and limited the estate tax recapture liability to ten years. * * *

The subsidy element in the special use valuation provision arises from the opportunity to report qualified real property at a value lower than that which would result from the application of generally accepted valuation principles. When the ERTA changes are fully effective the combination of a

---

18. § 2032A(e)(8). The section represented, in substance, a codification of standard real estate appraisal techniques as applied to farmland.

19. [ED.: The $750,000 ceiling on special use valuation is adjusted for inflation, in $10,000 increments, for decedents dying in 1999 and beyond. § 2032A(a)(3). In 2009, the inflation-adjusted ceiling is $1,000,000. Rev. Proc. 2008–66, § 3.29, 2008–45 I.R.B. 1.]

maximum marginal estate tax rate of fifty percent with a value reduction cap of $750,000 permits a maximum conditional tax reduction of $375,000. If the specially valued property continues to be used in a qualifying manner for ten years, the conditional estate tax reduction becomes permanent.
* * *

The legislative history of § 2032A indicates that Congress accepted without question the proposition that estate tax valuation of farmland and real estate used in a closely held business at fair market value would cause the forced disposition of such property.[20] Congress also assumed that the encouragement of "family farming" was sound economic policy and that the "family farm" was or should be encouraged as a significant component in domestic agriculture. Had the legislators sought expert guidance, they would have discovered that the majority of agricultural economists have concluded that farm efficiency tends to increase with size. Thus, if Congress intended to perpetuate "small" family farms, it has arguably chosen to subsidize inefficient farm production. Moreover, the premise that "family" farms historically pass from generation to generation and that such farms are or have been a significant component of agricultural land tenure is also suspect.[21]

Apart from the fact that the premises upon which Congress acted appear not to reflect reality, the question arises whether even if the premises were sound, the enacted legislation would accomplish the articulated objective at an acceptable cost. Reducing the transfer tax burden associated with the ownership of a particular asset makes it less expensive to pass that asset to an heir at death. That benefit, however, is bought at a cost. The cost includes farmland price increases resulting from the exploitation of the "estate tax shelter" created by special use valuation, the consequent additional entry barriers for younger farmers, the reduced availability of farmland as older farmers hold land to realize estate tax benefits, and possible structural changes in the agricultural market such as higher debt ratios and new pressures on the rental market. Although these effects are difficult to quantify, the consensus view of the agricultural economists who have studied the question indicates that such problems do exist.

Even if, in concept, a provision to limit estate tax value to "use" rather than fair market value resulted in minimal or acceptable efficiency losses, the current statutory valuation formula produces return values that are far below the price at which land is actually sold for use as farmland. The statutory formula determines value by capitalizing the earning stream of the farmland. The income from the property is multiplied by a capitaliza-

---

20. There is little empirical evidence to support this proposition. * * *

21. See N. Harl, Experiences and Problems with Use Valuation of Land (June 9–10, 1980) (paper presented at a meeting of the Commissioners Advisory Group, Internal Revenue Service, Washington, D.C.). Profes-

sor Harl's studies indicate that "very few farm and ranch businesses have continued as a going economic entity into the next generation" and that "traditionally" most farm and ranch businesses have begun and ended within one generation.

tion rate which is the reciprocal of a contemplated acceptable rate of return on the investment in the property. The rate of return utilized in the special use valuation formula is the average interest rate charged for all Federal Land Bank loans over the five years preceding the valuation date, which has ranged from approximately 8.5% to 11.8% depending upon the year of the decedent's death and the federal land bank district in which the decedent resided. Thus, the formula capitalization rate ranges from approximately 11.76 to 8.47. The annual rate of return, however, on equity from farm production, an empirically determinable amount representing actual farm yields, varied between 1.5% and 3.7% from 1976 through 1980.[22]

As a consequence of using an incorrect rate of return to determine the capitalization rate, estates eligible to use the formula on the average report qualifying farmland at discounts of between fifty and sixty percent.[23] Predictably, if the denominator of the valuation formula were based upon actual rates of return on invested equity, the values reported would correspond closely to the actual sale price of farmland. Thus, even if this provision is retained, Congress should at least amend it to insure that the formula method produces a realistic use value.

Finally, the current provision produces horizontal inequity among those who are eligible for special use valuation. Estates able to obtain the information required by the formula are, in general, able to report qualifying farmland at values that are significantly lower than the values produced by the "facts and circumstances" method. This occurs because the "facts and circumstances" method determines use value by taking actual market factors into account. The formula method, although intended to produce a realistic value, fails to achieve this result because of the variance between the assumed and actual rates of return on farm equity investments.

In summary, the entire concept of special use valuation is suspect. From an efficiency standpoint, it will raise farmland prices, elevate entry barriers, and encourage inefficient farm production. It may also hasten the trend toward larger farms, but as a matter of efficient farm production, this may be desirable. From an equity standpoint, the system rewards one taxpayer for putting his property to less than an optimal use while punishing a similar taxpayer for taking full advantage of his property. As a distributional matter, this scheme results in a lower effective rate of tax on the fair market value of tax-preferred assets transferred by wealthier decedents and thus reduces the progressivity of the system. When these problems are combined with the complexity of the system[24] and the costs of implementing and monitoring a special use valuation election, the provision emerges as a prime example of poor tax policy.

---

22.   U.S. Dept of Agriculture, Economic Indicators of the Farm Sector, Statistical Bull. No. 674, at 141 (1981).

23.   Miscellaneous Tax Bills V: Hearings Before the Subcomm. on Taxation and Debt Management Generally of the Senate Comm. on Finance, 96th Cong., 2d Sess. 474–75

(1980) (statement of Harry L. Gutman, Deputy Tax Legislative Counsel) * * *.

24.   Section 2032A may even be combined with § 6166 to achieve subsidies under both sections.

ILLUSTRATIVE MATERIAL

A. IN GENERAL

Section 2032A abounds with a host of difficulties of technical interpretation and practical application.[25] Most of these difficulties arise from the statutory language designed to ensure that (1) the property constituted a substantial part of the decedent's estate and was used for farming or other business purposes prior to and at the time of the decedent's death; and (2) the estate tax benefits resulting from the special use valuation are recaptured if the decedent's heirs dispose of the property or cease to use it for farming and other business purposes within the ten-year period following the decedent's death.

B. QUALIFIED REAL PROPERTY

To be eligible for special use valuation, the real property must satisfy four tests. First, the real property must be located in the United States. § 2032A(b)(1).[26]

Second, at the date of the decedent's death, the real property must have been used for a "qualified use" by the decedent or a member of the decedent's family. § 2032A(b)(1). The term "real property" includes roads, buildings, and other structures and improvements "functionally related to the qualified use," including residential buildings and related improvements if regularly used by the owner or lessees of the property or their employees in operating or maintaining the property. § 2032A(e)(3). The term "qualified use" means the devotion of the property to "use as a farm for farming purposes"[27] and use in any other trade or business.[28] § 2032A(b)(2). The term "member of the decedent's family" includes the decedent's ancestors and spouse, as well as lineal descendants (and their spouses) of the decedent's spouse and parents. § 2032A(e)(2). At least 50% of the adjusted value of the gross estate must consist of such real property. § 2032A(b)(1)(A).[29]

Third, the real property must have been "acquired from or passed from the decedent to a qualified heir." § 2032A(b)(1). The regulations contend that "[i]f successive interests (e.g. life estates and remainder interests) are created by a decedent in otherwise qualified property, an election under § 2032A is available

---

25. During 1992, § 2032A was elected by the estates of 305 decedents (1.1% of estates with tax liability), resulting in $172 million of valuation reduction. Eller, Federal Taxation of Wealth Transfers, 1992–1995, 16 Stat.Inc.Bull. 8, 15 (Winter 1996–97).

26. The decedent also must have been a United States citizen or resident at the time of death. § 2032A(a)(1)(A).

27. See § 2032A(e)(4) (definition of "farm") and (5) (definition of "farming purposes"). Rental of special use property on a "net cash basis" is a qualified use if the lessor is a surviving spouse or lineal descendent of the decedent and the lessee is a member of the spouses or descendent's family. § 2032A(c)(7)(E).

28. See Reg. § 20.2032A–3(b)(1) (term "trade or business" requires "active business," not mere "passive investment activities").

29. The "adjusted value" of the gross estate is computed with reference to the full fair market value of property, not its § 2032A special use value, as reduced by mortgages and other debts that are deductible under § 2053(a)(4). § 2032A(b)(3). Property transferred within three years of death is included in applying the 50% test even if it is not otherwise included in the estate. § 2035(c)(1)(B).

only with respect to that property (or portion thereof) in which qualified heirs of the decedent receive all of the successive interests.... Where successive interests in specially valued property are created, remainder interests are treated as being received by qualified heirs only if such remainder interests are not contingent upon surviving a nonfamily member or are not subject to divestment in favor of a nonfamily member." Reg. § 20.2032A–8(a)(2). However, the courts have disregarded the regulation and applied § 2032A where successive interests were not held by qualified heirs. See Estate of Davis v. Commissioner, 86 T.C. 1156 (1986) (remote contingent remainder to charity); Smoot v. United States, 892 F.2d 597 (7th Cir.1989) (power of appointment exercisable by qualified heirs in favor of nonqualified heirs).

Fourth, for at least five of the eight years prior to the decedent's death, the property was owned and used in a qualified use by the decedent or member of decedent's family, and the decedent or member of decedent's family materially participated in the operation of the farm or other business. § 2032A(b)(1)(C). Reg. § 20.2032A–3 explains that "[n]o single factor is determinative of the presence of material participation, but physical work and participation in management decisions are the principal factors to be considered." At least 25% of the adjusted value of the gross estate must consist of such real property. § 2032A(b)(1)(B).[30]

C.   RECAPTURE RULES

In order to give teeth to the recapture rules which apply if the decedent's heirs dispose of the property or cease to use it for farming and other business purposes within the ten-year post-death period, a notice of election and accompanying recapture agreement must be attached to the timely-filed estate tax return. § 2032A(a)(1)(B), (d). The election is irrevocable (§ 2032A(d)(1)) and the agreement must be signed by each person with an interest (whether or not possessory) in the property subject to the special use valuation (§ 2032A(d)(3)). Under the agreement, the qualified heirs agree to pay the "additional estate tax" if they dispose of the property[31] or cease to use it for farming and other business purposes within ten years.[32] § 2032A(c)(1). The amount of additional estate tax triggered by these recapture rules equals the estate tax saved by making the § 2032A election. § 2032A(c)(2).

Although the income tax basis of property bequeathed from a decedent generally equals the fair market value of the property at the time of the decedent's death (§ 1014(a)(1)), the basis of qualified real property is its special use value under § 2032A (§ 1014(a)(3)). If additional estate tax is imposed under the recapture rules, the qualified heir can elect to increase the basis of

---

30. The rules relating to "adjusted value" under the 50% test of § 2032A(b)(1)(A), see n.29, also apply for purposes of the 25% test of § 2032A(b)(1)(B).

31. Dispositions to a family member (§ 2032A(c)(1)(A)), tax-free involuntary conversions under § 1033 (§ 2032A(h)) and like-kind exchanges under § 1031 (§ 2032A(i)), and qualified conservation contributions under § 170(h) (§ 2032A(c)(8)) are not treated as a disposition for these purposes.

32. The recapture rules are triggered even if another family member continues to use the property for farming and other business purposes. See Williamson v. Commissioner, 974 F.2d 1525 (9th Cir.1992) (property leased to qualified heir). For detailed rules on the cessation of the qualified use of property, see § 2032A(c)(6).

the specially-valued property by the excess of the fair market value on the estate tax valuation date (date of death or alternate valuation date under § 2032) over the value of the property determined under § 2032A. § 1016(c)(1). This basis increase is deemed to occur immediately before the disposition or cessation of qualified use (§ 1016(c)(3)) and thus reduces any gain (on any disposition) or depreciation deductions (on any cessation of qualified use). The cost of this basis increase is that the qualified heir must pay interest on the additional estate tax attributable to the disposition or cessation of qualified use. § 1016(c)(5).

D.   CONSERVATION EASEMENTS

Section 2031(c)(8) provides an exclusion for a portion of the value of "land subject to a qualified conservation easement" where (1) the land is located in the United States (or in any U.S. possession);[33] (2) the land was owned by the decedent or a family member throughout the last three years of the decedent's life; and (3) a contribution of a "qualified conservation easement"[34] was made by the decedent, a member of the decedent's family, the decedent's executor, or the trustee of the trust owning the land. § 2031(c)(8)(A), (C).[35]

If the executor makes the § 2031(c)(6) election, the exclusion is allowed in the amount of the "applicable percentage" of the land, less any estate tax deduction for the easement if it is created at the decedent's death. § 2031(c)(1). The "applicable percentage" is 40% if the easement is worth at least 30% of the value of the land unencumbered by the easement; if the easement is worth less, the applicable percentage is reduced by 2 percentage points for each percentage point that the easement's value falls short of 30%. § 2031(c)(2).

The exclusion may not exceed a $500,000 "exclusion limitation." § 2031(c)(3). The exclusion does not apply to debt-financed property. § 2031(c)(4)(A). The exclusion also does not apply to the portion of the land value that is attributable to a "development right" retained by the decedent in the conveyance of the qualified conservation easement. § 2031(c)(5), (7).

The 1998 Act clarified that qualified conservation easements could be granted after the decedent's death by the executor and still qualify for the estate tax charitable deduction, but only if no income tax charitable deduction were allowed. § 2031(c)(9). The election to exclude the value of land subject to a qualified conservation easement from the estate must be made on the estate tax return on or before the due date (including extensions) for filing the return. § 2031(c)(6).

33. Prior to the 2001 Act, the exclusion was available only if the land was located within 25 miles of a metropolitan area, national park, or wilderness area, or within 10 miles of an Urban National Forest. The Senate Report explained that removing this geographical restriction would "further ease existing pressures to develop or sell environmentally significant land in order to raise funds to pay estate taxes and would, thereby, advance the preservation of such land." S. Rep. No. 30, 107th Cong., 1st Sess. (2001).

34. A "qualified conservation easement" is defined by reference to § 170(h) as an interest in land or a perpetual restriction on its use granted to a public charity or government "exclusively for conservation purposes." § 2031(c)(8)(B).

35. The charitable deduction for qualified conservation easements logically belongs in the estate tax charitable deduction, § 2055, rather than in the definition of the gross estate, § 2031.

5. PLANNING FOR ESTATES WITH ILLIQUID ASSETS

Planning for anticipated liquidity problems will in most cases involve attempting to ensure that an estate will meet the various value requirements of §§ 303, 2032A, or 6166.

The availability of § 6166 depends simply upon qualification through meeting the different value and ownership tests of that section. Thus, the planner will focus on advising which, and to whom, assets should be disposed of inter vivos by the client. In so doing, the planner should keep § 2035(c) in mind. For purposes of determining eligibility for §§ 303, 6166, and 2032A, the estate tax valuation date value of property transferred within three years of the decedent's death is included in the decedent's gross estate to the extent required by § 2035(a).

Where the property is potentially eligible for both § 6166 and § 2032A, the planner's task may be difficult because qualification for, and election of, the latter may remove eligibility for the former. To the extent possible, the tax advisor probably will try to ensure that the installment payment provisions will be available in the event § 2032A is not utilized and leave to the executor the choice whether to elect special use valuation where the result of that election will preclude the use of the installment payment provisions.

Where § 303 treatment is sought, the tax advisor must focus on more than simply the value tests. The decedent's will or other dispositive instrument should provide that the stock to be redeemed carry with it the burden to pay death taxes and funeral and administration expenses in an amount equal to the value of the stock to be redeemed. At a minimum, this means that stock which is anticipated to be redeemed should not be devised as part of a marital bequest where under local apportionment rules the marital share bears no portion of the estate's taxes and expenses. Moreover, because a post-death redemption under § 303 may result in some taxable income to the redeeming party, the decedent and the redeeming corporation should consider the execution of a redemption agreement which gives the redeeming shareholder an option to redeem the stock rather than requiring such stock to be redeemed.

Planning to use § 2032A may be a very difficult task. The tax advisor will have to monitor carefully the changes in value of both the client's special use property and the aggregate estate, advising where necessary the inter vivos disposition of property not subject to § 2032A. Finally, to the extent possible, it is important to provide that the special use property pass to a qualified heir who will not trigger a recapture event.

6. POLICY ISSUES

The first excerpt below argues that §§ 303, 2032A, and 6166 are inadequate to accommodate the special needs of farms and small business. The second excerpt takes a critical look at the liquidity rationale for relief provisions for farms and small businesses.

Chason & Danforth, The Proper Role of the Estate and Gift Taxation of Closely Held Businesses

32 Real Prop., Prob. & Tr. J. 103 (1997).

* * * The transfer taxes are particularly burdensome * * * for the recipients of interests in closely held businesses. These interests are often difficult to value, and their owners may face liquidity problems because a ready market for interests in closely held businesses does not exist. Congress has partially responded to the concerns of owners of closely held businesses with special provisions in the Internal Revenue Code * * *.

Members of Congress have proposed even more lenient treatment of closely held businesses under the estate tax because of its perceived harshness and its potential to force the liquidation of businesses. Leniency may be improvident, however, if the only problems facing closely held businesses under the estate tax are steep rates and illiquidity. The rates under § 2001 are no higher for closely held enterprises than they are for any other form of wealth, and the deferral allowances of the Code should solve true liquidity problems. * * *

This article argues that encouraging productive work by recipients of wealth may be the only goal of the estate and gift tax that is both achievable and economically sound. * * *

* * * The primary benefit of estate and gift taxation evaporates when it taxes the transfer of interests in closely held businesses in which the recipients will participate. Estate and gift taxation benefits society by encouraging productive work on the part of recipients. If a recipient receives an interest in a closely held business and intends to manage the business, then no benefit exists for taxing the transfer of the business. * * *

The special estate and gift provisions already in the Code do not properly address the problem of taxing the transfer of interests in closely held businesses. The special use valuation rule of § 2032A simply allows certain recipients of interests in closely held businesses to escape what would otherwise be the unfair taxation of their interests based on highest and best use. When § 2032A applies, the business has a reduced going concern value, though the underlying property may be economically more valuable in another use. Section 6166 provides relief from the illiquidity of closely held businesses when the recipients must pay estate tax. Section 303 allows the owner of a closely held corporation to pay the estate tax attributable to the corporation with corporate assets without recognizing ordinary income. Thus, none of these provisions provides the appropriate dispensation to recipients of closely held businesses from wealth transfer taxation.

Current transfer taxation of closely held businesses retains all of the costs of the larger system, but none of the benefits. Moreover, the special provisions in the Code related to closely held businesses do not solve this dilemma because they do not address its central issue: interests in closely held businesses are distinct from other wealth.

Congress should thus provide legislation that goes beyond the current treatment of interests in closely held businesses. Of course, any revisions of the Code should allow special treatment of closely held businesses only where the recipients of the interests plan actively to manage the business. Moreover, special treatment should apply to transfers under the estate and gift tax, whereas currently the special provisions for closely held businesses apply only to the estate tax. Preventing abuse by taxpayers may be difficult. But, helping the transfer of closely held businesses and promoting the growth of productive capital are worth the effort.

Gutman, Reforming Federal Wealth Transfer Taxes After ERTA

69 Va.L.Rev. 1183 (1983).

* * * [T]he provisions designed to relieve alleged estate liquidity problems have effects that go well beyond collecting the appropriate amount of tax on an even-handed basis. An alternate system is needed. Although § 6161, the discretionary deferral section, provides one solution to the liquidity problem, taxpayers object to its being the sole statutory liquidity relief provision precisely because its availability lies within the discretion of the Commissioner. They would prefer a provision available at their election.

Absent the need to budget for revenue receipts, there should be no objection in principle to allowing an estate electively to treat its transfer tax liability as a loan from the government to be repaid as funds become available. The deferred payments, however, must bear interest at a rate that equates the present value of the obligation with the amount due if the tax were timely paid. In order to avoid needless monitoring costs, such a system must also discourage estates from deferring payment even when sufficient liquid funds exist to discharge their tax obligation.

The forgoing observations permit two tentative proposals with respect to the appropriate form of a provision designed to relieve liquidity problems. First, relief should be available only when an estate contains illiquid assets in an amount sufficient to make current payment of all or some portion of the tax burdensome. Second, so long as the interest rate is appropriate, the length of time over which payment may be deferred should be determined principally by reference to the need to minimize the administrative burdens associated with the federal governments role as a creditor of the estate.[36] As the deferral privilege in these circumstances would not create an incentive to defer tax payment, one can assume that taxpayers would not elect deferral unless a liquidity problem actually existed. To the extent this assumption is correct, criteria for eligibility could be rather lenient.

---

36. These questions involve resolution of such issues as tax liens, liability for payment of tax, and transferee liability.

Deferral of tax liability could be available whenever net nonmarketable assets exceeded a specified percentage of a decedent's taxable estate. The maximum amount of tax to be deferred would be the ratio of the value of the net nonmarketable assets to the taxable estate multiplied by the tax due. An estate electing deferral would specify its payment schedule, which could be as long as twenty years.[37] Interest on the unpaid amount, at a rate determined in advance of each calendar quarter, would be payable quarterly in arrears.

This proposal addresses liquidity problems of all types. Illiquidity is not exclusively the problem of estates containing farmland or closely held business interests. It can arise when an estate contains vacant land held for investment, valuable artworks, coins, or other nonmarketable tangibles. Relief should be available without regard to the type of asset that causes the liquidity problem and the proposal achieves this goal without creating an incentive to elect deferral.

If the holders of illiquid income-producing property still argue that certain interests cannot generate the cash flow necessary to discharge the tax liability, one or both of two circumstances exist. Either the asset has been overvalued, or the asset is being employed for a use that the marketplace has dictated to be less than optimal. The former is difficult to rectify by statutory rules and must be dealt with administratively; the latter should not be subtlety rewarded through the tax system. If government policy is to encourage suboptimal use of property, the government should not hide the costs of encouraging that activity through reduced tax receipts and the vagaries of the tax legislative process. Rather, Congress should identify such costs and relegate them to their appropriate priority as part of a conscious decision to allocate and maximize the return on government spending.

Section B.   Post-Mortem Estate Planning

During the period of administration of an estate, the executor must make a number of statutory elections and nonstatutory decisions. In so doing, the executor will attempt, to the extent possible, to maximize the aggregate after-tax benefits (both in terms of income yield and preservation of the corpus of the estate) to the estate beneficiaries. This process, commonly known as postmortem estate planning, is frequently very complicated. The decisions involved must be made within the constraints imposed by the executor's fiduciary responsibilities to all the beneficiaries, which in some circumstances may conflict with the desire to maximize after-tax benefits.

37. The disposition of a nonmarketable asset could cause acceleration of the deferred tax attributable to that asset. Such a rule, however, would cause administrative difficulties and is unnecessary if the interest rate is adequate. The government should project receipts in accordance with the payment schedules of taxpayers electing deferral. If this is done, the failure to accelerate has no cash management impact.

An executor may be faced with over one hundred post-mortem elections,[38] and a detailed discussion of the advantages and disadvantages of each election is obviously beyond the scope of this book. Instead, the following excerpt summarizes the major post-mortem planning issues an executor must consider.

Browne, Effect of Elections by an Executor Upon the Estate and Upon the Beneficiaries

23 N.Y.U. Tax Inst. 1239 (1965).

A fiduciary should approach an election having in mind his duties to use reasonable care, to deal with all beneficiaries impartially and to be loyal. There is probably no duty, as such, to minimize taxes. Reasonable care, however, demands close attention to tax consequences, particularly by professional fiduciaries. A course of action conducive of the greatest tax saving is not foreclosed by a fiduciary's duty to act impartially as long as he has the power to make appropriate restitution among classes of beneficiaries. Finally, there is some reason to believe, if not conclude, that greater risk of breach of duty to exercise reasonable care in tax matters exists in the case of elections created entirely by the Code than in the case of non-Code elections which by their nature involve many considerations outside of the field of taxation. * * *

PARTIAL CATALOGUE OF FIDUCIARY ELECTIONS OF TAX CONSEQUENCES

Elections Originating in the Internal Revenue Code

1. Joint v. Separate Return

A joint return of the decedent and the surviving spouse permits aggregation of the decedent's income until the date of his death with the income of the surviving spouse for the full calendar year in which death occurred. There is a problem of the authority of an executor to consent to a joint return in view of joint liability aspects. (§ 6013(a)).

[la. Gift Tax Returns

The executor is required to file any federal gift tax return which the decedent would have been required to file. The executor must determine whether to take advantage of the gift splitting provisions of § 2513 with the surviving spouse. Factors to be taken into account in making the election include the relative gift tax brackets of the two spouses, the future gift program of the surviving spouse, the size of the surviving spouses estate, and the like.]

---

38. See Blattmachr & Slade, More than One Hundred Post–Mortem Tax Planning   Elections, 66 N.Y.St.B.J. 26 (1994).

[1b. Qualified Terminable Interest Property Election

When given the discretion, the executor may elect to treat as deductible under § 2056(a) the value of qualified terminable interest property as defined in § 2056(b)(7). For a discussion of the factors to be taken into account in making the election, see p. 642.

2.   Medical Expenses of Decedent

Medical expenses of the decedent paid by the executor within one year of death may be deducted on the income tax return of the decedent for the year in which the expenses were incurred; or, alternatively, on the estate tax return. The [7.5] percent portion of medical expenses that is nondeductible for income tax purposes [cannot] be deducted as a claim against the estate. [Rev.Rul. 77–357, 1977–2 C.B. 328.]

3.   Acceleration of Bond Income

The executor may elect to accrue in the estate income tax return or in the decedent's final income tax return the excess of the redemption price of Series E bonds over the decedent's cost in instances where the decedent was not reporting the annual increase in redemption price currently. (§ 454).

4.   Alternate Valuation

Assets of an estate [except possibly those valued pursuant to § 2032A] may be valued for estate tax purposes either at the date of death or [six months] later (or at some interim date in cases of disposition) [if the assets have declined in value]. The election may have direct bearing upon [the income tax basis of the assets under § 1014,] the size of the marital deduction and qualification for benefits of §§ 303 and 6166. (§ 2032).

[4a. Special Use Valuation

"Qualified real property" may be valued at actual use value as determined by application of statutory formulas rather than at highest and best use value. § 2032A. Election requires consideration of effect on qualification for §§ 303 and 6166, as well as analysis of present estate tax savings compared to future depreciation and depletion allowances and income taxes.]

5.   Administration Expenses

These are available as income tax or estate tax deductions in any proportion desired. The category includes executor's commissions, legal and accounting fees. (§§ 212, 642(g) and 2053(a)(2)).

These should be contrasted with certain expenses deductible both for income tax and for federal estate tax purposes, e.g., real estate taxes owed by the decedent at the date of death. (§ 691(b)). Note should be made of the relationship of this election to formula marital deduction bequests and residual gifts to charity. Administration expenses allocable to tax exempt income and accordingly not deductible for income tax purposes may be claimed on the estate tax return. Allocation of administration expenses permitted between income and estate tax returns. Method of making election and filing of waivers. Election can be irrevocable.

6. *Payment of Estate Tax in Installments*

[An] election [is] available depending upon [the] interest of the estate in a closely held business. Use of the election results in the imposition of certain restrictions and involves payment of * * * interest. Interplay of other elections (e.g., alternate valuation) upon qualification as an interest in a closely held business is important. (§ 6166).

7. *Request for Immediate Tax Audit*

A discretionary means of relieving the executor of personal liability. The election may be in conflict with interests of beneficiaries. (§§ 6501(d) and 2204).

Non–Code Elections Having Tax Consequences

1. *Distributions in Cash or in Kind*

Distributions in kind in satisfaction of pecuniary legacies result in realization of capital gain by the estate if the value of the property has appreciated. A problem of disallowance of the marital deduction is likely where a power to distribute in kind is coupled with the use of date of death values. (Rev.Proc. 64–19, [1964–1 C.B. (Part I) 682].)

2. *Choice of Fiscal Year*

The executor may elect to keep records and file tax returns on a fiscal as opposed to a calendar year basis. This permits the spreading of income through the employment of short fiscal years at the beginning and end of estate administration. There is a problem of added bookkeeping requirements. (§ 441).

3. *Accumulation or Distribution of Estate Income*

The general discretion of the executor in this respect offers opportunities to balance the ultimate income tax liability of the estate with that of income beneficiaries. (§§ 661 and 662). The problem arises of undue prolongation of estate administration. (Reg. § 1.641(b)–3(a)).

4. *Renunciation of Certain Powers*

A power to invade principal for the benefit of a life tenant may result in disallowance for federal estate tax purposes of a charitable remainder. An irrevocable disclaimer by the income beneficiary made [in accordance with § 2518] may preserve a charitable deduction. (§ 2055(a)). While not an election of the executor, strictly speaking, it may be his responsibility to review the problem with the income beneficiary. * * *

6. *Choice of Investments*

An obvious election having tax consequences. Sale of principal assets at a loss so as to enable purchase of tax exempt bonds for the benefit of the life tenant may result m surcharge of trustee to the extent of the loss.

7. *Charging Expenditure to Income or to Principal.*

Although the executor elects to charge administration expenses to income, thus enhancing the residue distribution to charity, the amount of the residue will be reduced for purposes of the charitable deductions.

8. *Allocation of Tax Payments*

An election to charge such payments to residue or to various legacies and bequests may have serious tax consequences particularly in the marital deduction areas.

9. *Termination of Administration*

Determining the final year of administration coupled with timing of income tax deductions of the estate may result in excess deductions which can be passed through, in the year of termination, to the beneficiaries. (§ 642(h)). The problem arises of the responsibility of an executor for wasted excess deductions due to realization in a year prior to the year of termination.

10. *Settlement of Claims*

Executor has some discretion as to the timing of settlement between one year and another. This, in turn, bears upon the timing of termination of administration. A tax refund controversy may be sufficient to prolong administration.

SECTION C. PERSONAL LIABILITY OF THE EXECUTOR

Singleton v. Commissioner

71 T.C.M. 3127 (1996).

■ JACOBS, JUDGE:

Respondent determined that petitioner in his capacity as a fiduciary of the Estate of Marguerite B. Greer (sometimes referred to as the Estate) was personally liable under 31 U.S.C. § 3713(b) for unpaid estate taxes owing by the Estate in the amount of $32,443, plus interest. Respondent reflected this determination in a notice of liability mailed to petitioner on December 21, 1993.

Petitioner acknowledges that he permitted Estate assets to be distributed before all estate taxes had been paid; however, he disputes personal liability for the unpaid estate taxes on the basis that * * * he did not have knowledge of the Governments claim for unpaid estate taxes prior to July 24, 1981 (when petitioner and the other co-executor agreed to a tax deficiency of $12,701 on behalf of the Estate and signed Form 890 and by that date the greatest amount of distributions by the Estate to others had been made). * * *

FINDINGS OF FACT

* * * Petitioner resided in Hot Springs, Virginia, at the time he filed his petition. He is an attorney engaged in the practice of law in Bath County, Virginia.[39]

Petitioner and Faith B. Gardiner were co-executors of the Estate of Marguerite B. Greer; petitioner was also the attorney of record for the Estate. Ms. Greer died on April 29, 1976; at the time of her death, Ms. Greer was a resident of Bath County.

Ms. Gardiner was an adopted child of Ms. Greer and was the sole beneficiary of Ms. Greer's estate. Ms. Gardiner resided in New Jersey at all relevant times.

During 1978, Ms. Gardiner took Estate assets to her residence in New Jersey to have them appraised. The property was stolen during a burglary of Ms. Gardiner's home. A $38,000 theft loss was claimed on the estate tax return.

The estate tax return was filed on June 4, 1979. The amount of tax shown on the return to be due ($7,972) was paid at the time the return was filed. * * *

Respondent examined the estate tax return in 1981 and disallowed the $38,000 theft loss, contending that at the time of the theft the assets stolen no longer were the property of the Estate but rather had been distributed to Ms. Gardiner as beneficiary. Petitioner and Ms. Gardiner agreed to the resulting tax assessment of $12,701 by signing Form 890 (Waiver of Restrictions on Assessment and Collection of Deficiency) on July 24, 1981. The assessment for the $12,701 deficiency occurred on December 7, 1981. * * *

Statutory interest of $31,275 had accrued on the deficiency through December 21, 1993 (the mailing date of the notice of liability to petitioner). Penalties assessed with respect to the deficiency through December 21, 1993, totaled $191. Payments on the deficiency were made as follows: $7,000 on April 22, 1982; $4,537 on December 27, 1990; and $186 on January 17, 1991.

The Estate made the following disbursements during the years 1976–1990:

Total Disbursements	Disbursements to Ms. Gardiner	Disbursements to Petitioner	Disbursements to Service
[$324,320	$36,681	$14,900	$20,713]

39. During most of the period of time relevant to this case, petitioner was the prosecuting attorney for Bath County, Virginia, an elected position. He had a private law practice on the side.

* * * Sometime after 1981, Ms. Gardiner suffered severe financial and physical difficulties; at the time of trial, she was comatose in a nursing home in North Carolina. The IRS made no attempt to collect the deficiency, interest, or penalty from Ms. Gardiner.

OPINION

The executor of an estate has the ultimate responsibility for payment of the Federal estate tax. § 2002. If the executor pays the debts of the estate, or distributes any portion of the estate to a beneficiary, before satisfying the estates obligation to the Government for estate taxes, then the executor is personally liable, to the extent of the payment to the estates creditors or the distribution to the beneficiary, for so much of the estate tax as remains unpaid. 31 U.S.C. § 3713(b).

In the instant case, the IRS determined that petitioner was personally liable for unpaid estate taxes due by the Estate of Marguerite B. Greer because he allowed the Estate to make payments to its creditors, as well as a distribution to Ms. Gardiner as sole beneficiary of the Estate, without first satisfying the estate tax claim of the Government. * * *

A representative of an estate paying a debt of the estate before paying a claim of the Government is liable to the extent of the payment for unpaid claims of the Government. 31 U.S.C. § 3713(b). Here, there is no question but that petitioner permitted the Estate to make payments to others and that at the time the notice of liability was mailed to petitioner there remained unpaid estate taxes.

The Estate made payments to Ms. Gardiner not only prior to the date the co-executors signed Form 890 (that is, prior to July 24, 1981) but also in 1982 and 1986 totaling approximately $15,500. These latter payments appear to be made to Ms. Gardiner as beneficiary, rather than as executor. In defending his making the latter payments, petitioner states in his post-trial brief:

> those payments were made at a time when Petitioner was attempting to communicate and resolve the tax liability with the Internal Revenue Service. As indicated by this Petitioner previously the State of Virginia inheritance tax division closed the estate and Petitioner never received any response to its [sic] communications to the Internal Revenue Service and while, with hindsight, the payments to Faith B. Gardiner were not advisable, at the time, she was in necessitous circumstances and Petitioner could get no response from the Internal Revenue Service.

Petitioners argument misses the point. As petitioner apparently recognizes, the distributions to Ms. Gardiner were inadvisable. No distributions should have been made to Ms. Gardiner before the Estate satisfied its tax obligation. Petitioner could have avoided the situation he now faces by making a written application for discharge of personal liability as provided for in § 2204(a).[40]

Petitioner made payments of approximately $70,000 to Ms. Gardiner even before the estate tax return was filed. Petitioner is an attorney. He knew or should have known that distributions to a beneficiary of an estate prior to satisfying the estate tax are made at the executors peril.

Petitioner states in his post-trial brief:

but for the disallowance of the 1978 theft from the estate, this case would not be in court as that deficiency assessment caused the estate to have insufficient funds to pay all claims including the claim of the Internal Revenue Service.

Again, petitioners argument misses the point. It was petitioners permitting the Estate to distribute funds to others which resulted in the plight petitioner now faces, rather than the disallowance of the claimed theft loss. Consequently, we hold petitioner liable under 31 U.S.C. § 3713(b).

When an executor incurs personal liability under 31 U.S.C. § 3713(b), his liability for unpaid estate tax and accrued interest thereon prior to the date the executors liability for the estate tax arose is limited to the amount of payments made to others. To our knowledge, there are no cases discussing whether an executor is liable for interest accruing after the notice of liability has been mailed. Respondent requests us to hold that interest accrues until the estate tax, and interest accrued thereon, is paid. In this regard, respondent argues that we should extend the rationale this Court adopted in Baptiste v. Commissioner, 100 T.C. 252 (1993), aff'd. 29 F.3d 1533 (11th Cir.1994), aff'd. in part and rev'd. in part 29 F.3d 433 (8th Cir.1994) to cover the situation involved herein. We decline to do so. *Baptiste* involved transferee liability. We held in that case that a transferees liability for interest accrued on unpaid estate tax owed by a transferee (that is, the interest accrued on the tax after the transferee liability arose) was not limited (under § 6324(a)(2)) to the value of the property transferred from the estate to the transferee. The Court of Appeals for the Eighth Circuit disagreed and held that the interest accrued is limited to the value of the property transferred. * * *

40. Section 2204(a) provides:

(a) General Rule. If the executor makes written application to the Secretary for determination of the amount of the tax and discharge from personal liability therefor, the Secretary (as soon as possible, and in any event within 9 months after the making of such application, or, if the application is made before the return is filed, then within 9 months after the return is filed, but not after the expiration of the period prescribed for the assessment of the tax in § 6501) shall notify the executor of the amount of the tax. The executor, on payment of the amount of which he is notified (other than any amount the time for payment of which is extended under §§ 6161, 6163, or 6166), and on furnishing any bond which may be required for any amount for which the time for payment is extended, shall be discharged from personal liability for any deficiency in tax thereafter found to be due and shall be entitled to a receipt or writing showing such discharge.

In our opinion, an executors liability under 31 U.S.C. § 3713(b) is different from that of a transferee. A transferee has the benefit of enjoying the transferred property; such is not the case with an executor. To require an executor (here, petitioner) to be subject to the interest on funds he did not have the benefit of enjoying would constitute a punitive act for which there is no legal authority.

To reflect the foregoing,

Decision will be entered under Rule 155.

ILLUSTRATIVE MATERIAL

1. SCOPE OF EXECUTOR'S LIABILITY

As the Tax Court explains in *Singleton*, "distributions to a beneficiary of an estate prior to satisfying the estate tax are made at the executor's peril." The liability rules of § 3713 apply even where the executor does not personally benefit from the distribution. These rules also apply to non-attorney executors as well. See United States v. Coppola, 85 F.3d 1015 (2d Cir.1996); Leigh v. Commissioner, 72 T.C. 1105 (1979).

Report of Committee on Tax Aspects of Decedents' Estates, Liability of Fiduciaries and Transferees for Federal Estate and Gift Taxes

2 Real Prop., Prob, & Tr. J. 250 (1967).

* * * [A] cautious lawyer will not * * * advise his personal representative * * * to make substantial distributions from the estate before becoming certain of the amount of taxes due the United States from the estate, or taking suitable indemnity.

While it has been said that before a fiduciary becomes liable for a payment to another than the government, the payment must have been voluntary and not under compulsion, the usual order of distribution by the probate court does not constitute compulsion and does not prevent the collection of the tax from the executor, personally, even though the estate has been closed and an order of discharge entered. The executor is liable, as fiduciary, to the extent of the value of the property coming into his hands, for the amount of the tax on the estate, whether or not it came into possession, but he will not be held liable, personally, for an amount greater than the value of the assets which came into his hands nor for an amount greater than the sum of the improper payments or the unpaid tax, whichever is smaller.

In order for personal liability to attach to the executor, he must have knowledge of the debt to the United States or have knowledge of facts which put him on inquiry, but if he seeks to avoid liability by reason of lack of knowledge, he must bear the burden of proof. As a practical matter, it will be difficult for an official executor to prove that he did not have knowledge of facts putting him on inquiry as to the amount of the estate tax due, since the questions asked on the estate tax return deal with all types of inter vivos transactions, and a bona fide attempt to give candid answers to them would be likely to elicit the facts with regard to liability in respect of nonprobate items. A personal representative has a duty to collect the probate estate for the benefit of creditors and failure to exercise diligence in locating and dealing with probate assets will doubtless make him liable to creditors, including the United States. * * *

Once the notice of fiduciary capacity has been given, the "executor" assumes the powers, rights, duties and privileges of the decedent's estate but becomes liable for the tax only in his fiduciary (unless he makes some improper payment or distribution) until such time as the fiduciary gives a notice of the termination of the fiduciary capacity, or until the statute of limitations (if any) has expired. If a notice of termination of fiduciary capacity is given, the Internal Revenue Service will send any communications thereafter, including deficiency notices, to the distributees or transferees, unless personal liability is asserted against the executor.

Since there is general agreement that it is in the public interest that estates be administered as expeditiously as possible, consistent with the protection of the interests of creditors, beneficiaries and tax collectors, § 2204 of the Code makes it possible for an executor to secure a discharge from his personal liability.[41] Upon receiving such a discharge, he will be free to distribute the assets and wind up the administration of the estate without fear of having a personal liability by reason of subsequent increases in the net estate, and any controversy over the amount of tax due will be between the beneficiaries or transferees and the government. The usual practice would be for the personal representative to remain in office until final determination and payment of all taxes; the convenience of the beneficiaries would be met by large distributions of assets pending the final determination of the amount of taxes due.

This provision in the Code permits the executor to apply, personally or by properly authorized agent, to the district director for the district in which the estate return was filed for determination of the amount of the tax as soon as possible and in any event within [nine months] after making the application or after the return is filed, whichever is the later. The application may not be filed after the statute of limitations has run on assessment of the tax. If the district director notifies the executor of the amount of tax due, and the executor pays it, or, if the district director fails to notify the executor of the amount of tax due within the year, he will be discharged automatically.[42] In practice, if the district director is not pre-

41. [ED.: In order to compute the estate tax liability, an executor must determine the amount of the decedent's post–1976 adjusted taxable gifts. Section 2204(d) provides that, if the executor in good faith relies on gift tax returns furnished by the Service under § 6103(e)(3) to determine the decedent's adjusted taxable gifts, the executor is entitled to be discharged from personal liability for gifts not shown on the gift tax returns (except for gifts made within three years of the decedent's death). Section 6905 permits an application by the executor for discharge from personal liability for the decedent's gift and income tax liability.]

42. [ED.: Where the time for payment of the estate tax has been extended under §§ 6161, 6163, or 6166, the executor may still

pared to state a sum which will satisfy the claim of the United States and he wishes to preserve his right against the executor personally, he will give the executor the option of withdrawing the application or being faced with a deficiency notice which will exceed any amount of tax which probably is due.

In order for the discharge provision to operate, a complete return must have been filed, and it is implicit that its provisions cannot be invoked if no return is filed. While there seem to be no cases on the point, it would appear logical that a notice of discharge secured as a result of filing a fraudulent estate tax return would not serve as a defense to personal liability for the correct amount of tax. * * *

The executor is entitled to written evidence of his discharge. * * *

When the executor is discharged by the state court, he should give notice of such discharge to the district director to whom he gave notice of qualification, together with satisfactory evidence of discharge and the name and address of the successor fiduciary, if any. If this is done, a deficiency notice served thereafter will not be effectual against the former executor as such, but of course the notice of termination will have no effect upon a deficiency notice addressed to the former executor personally, for the reason that the order of the state court discharging the executor can have no effect upon his personal responsibility to the United States. A deficiency notice directed to the executor personally, but served after such decree and even after the district director has received notice of termination of fiduciary capacity, is fully effective to establish personal liability.

When a personal representative, after discharge by the state court and notice of termination of fiduciary capacity to the district director, nevertheless participates in the tax dispute, he becomes liable as executor as though he never had been discharged and had not given notice to the district director. A discharged executor who fails to give the notice is estopped to deny that he was executor at the time of granting an extension. A discharged executor, upon being appointed administrator *de bonis non*, resumes the power to act for the estate.

SECTION D. ETHICAL PROBLEMS INVOLVED IN THE ADMINISTRATION OF ESTATES

The executor is faced with resolving conflicting interests during the period of estate administration. First, there are statutory obligations involving elections which may benefit one class of beneficiaries at the expense of others. The exercise of these elections, as well as the exercise of discretion generally, must be made in the context of the executor's fiducia-

be discharged from personal liability for estate tax upon the provision of a bond in such amount, not to exceed the amount of the unpaid tax, as the District Director determines. Reg. § 20.2204–1(b). Where § 6166 has been elected, the provision of an agreement consenting to the creation of a lien on designated property in accordance with § 6324A will be treated as the furnishing of such a bond. § 2204(c).]

ry relationship to all the beneficiaries. Finally, the executor will be aware of his personal liability and will desire to minimize his individual exposure to the extent consistent with the foregoing obligations.

Some of these issues have been discussed in connection with the areas of substantive law to which they relate. The following excerpt from Corneel, The Duty of Loyalty in Estate Planning and Administration (unpublished paper, June 7, 1976), illustrates an aspect of the lawyers duty in this context:

> "A lawyer has been retained by a widow-executrix as attorney for an estate. He knows that in the administration of the estate there are certain options beneficial to her but adverse to the interest of the other beneficiaries. Under the will it is not clear whether as executrix the widow can legally favor herself. The lawyer also knows that the other beneficiaries consider him the lawyer 'for the estate rather than lawyer for the widow only.' Indicate your views as to the lawyers course of action.[43]

	Most Likely	Ethically Preferable
1. He would explain the situation to the widow only and leave the choice to her.	T	
2. He would explain the situation to the widow and the other beneficiaries and urge them to work out the manner of dealing with the options, the lawyer confining himself to giving a fair explanation to all.	ATIL	ATIL
3. The lawyer would suggest to both sides that they hire their own counsel.		TL

> "*Comment.* While the question deals with the proper course of conduct for the lawyer, it is clear that it also involves a decision as to the proper course for the widow who is both executor and beneficiary. She, herself, is under the obligation to deal impartially as among all of the beneficiaries.

> "As far as the lawyer is concerned, while technically his sole clients may be the estate and the executrix that represents it, he cannot disregard the fact that all of the beneficiaries in effect regard him as their lawyer. Under these circumstances it would seem that he has a

---

43. [ED.: A questionnaire containing this question was sent to over 100 insurance agents, trust officers, lawyers, and accountants in the Boston area. "A" means the answer supplied by a majority of accountants, "I" insurance agents, "L" lawyers, and "T" trust officers. The letters "T" and "L" are shown in more than one place because the number of trust officers and lawyers who gave each of the answers indicated was either the same or only one apart.]

choice of two roles. He can either tell the beneficiaries of the problems that exist, that he will represent the estate as such and advise the widow as executrix accordingly and that if beneficiaries including the widow as beneficiary, wish to assert their own special interest, they should consult their own counsel.

"The other alternative is in effect to act as counselor and mediator. In that role the lawyer must fairly explain the situation to all and try to help them reach agreement. If the lawyer fails in this, then he will probably be required to resign from any further participation in the proceeding. The reason for this is that in his role as mediator he is likely to have received confidential communications from one or more of the persons concerned which he should not then be in a position to use against them."

In representing an estate, the lawyer is bound by the general rules governing advice that can be given with respect to positions taken on the tax return. Formal Opinion 85–352 provides the bars ethical rules applicable to tax lawyers, as explained in the accompanying task force report. Circular 230 provides the governments ethical rules applicable to lawyers who practice before the Service.

FORMAL OPINION 85–352[44]

A lawyer may advise reporting a position on a tax return so long as the lawyer believes in good faith that the position is warranted in existing law or can be supported by a good faith argument for an extension, modification or reversal of existing law and there is some realistic possibility of success if the matter is litigated.

The Committee has been requested by the Section of Taxation of the American Bar Association to reconsider the "reasonable basis" standard in the Committees Formal Opinion 314 governing the position a lawyer may advise a client to take on a tax return.

Opinion 314 (Apr. 27, 1965) was issued in response to a number of specific inquiries regarding the ethical relationship between the Internal Revenue Service and lawyers practicing before it. The opinion formulated general principles governing this relationship, including the following:

[A] lawyer who is asked to advise his client in the course of the preparation of the clients tax returns may freely urge the statement of positions most favorable to the client just as long as there is *a reasonable basis* for this position. (Emphasis supplied).

The Committee is informed that the standard of "reasonable basis" has been construed by many lawyers to support the use of any colorable

---

44. Formal Opinion 85–352 was issued on July 7, 1985 by the American Bar Association Standing Committee on Ethics and Professional Responsibility. This opinion is based on the Model Rules of Professional Conduct and to the extent indicated the former Model Code of Professional Responsibility of the American Bar Association. The laws, court rules, regulations, codes of professional responsibility, and opinions promulgated in the individual jurisdictions are controlling.

claim on a tax return to justify exploitation of the lottery of the tax return audit selection process. This view is not universally held, and the Committee does not believe that the reasonable basis standard, properly interpreted and applied, permits this construction.

However, the Committee is persuaded that as a result of serious controversy over this standard and its persistent criticism by distinguished members of the tax bar, IRS officials and members of Congress, sufficient doubt has been created regarding the validity of the standard so as to erode its effectiveness as an ethical guideline. For this reason, the Committee has concluded that it should be restated. Another reason for restating the standard is that since publication of Opinion 314, the ABA has adopted in succession the Model Code of Professional Responsibility (1969; revised 1980) and the Model Rules of Professional Conduct (1983). Both the Model Code and the Model Rules directly address the duty of a lawyer in presenting or arguing positions for a client in language that does not refer to "reasonable basis." It is therefore appropriate to conform the standard of Opinion 314 to the language of the new rules.

This position reconsiders and revises only that part of Opinion 314 that relates to the lawyers duty in advising a client of positions that can be taken on a tax return. It does not deal with a lawyers opinion on tax shelter investment offerings, which is specifically addressed by this Committees Formal Opinion 346 (Revised), and which involves very different considerations, including third party reliance.

The ethical standards governing the conduct of a lawyer in advising a client on positions that can be taken in a tax return are no different from those governing a lawyers conduct in advising or taking positions for a client in other civil matters. Although the Model Rules distinguish between the roles of advisor and advocate,[45] both roles are involved here, and the ethical standards applicable to them provide relevant guidance. In many cases a lawyer must realistically anticipate that the filing of the tax return may be the first step in a process that may result in an adversary relationship between the client and the IRS. This normally occurs in situations when a lawyer advises an aggressive position on a tax return, not when the position taken is a safe or conservative one that is unlikely to be challenged by the IRS.

Rule 3.1 of the Model Rules, which is in essence a restatement of DR 7–102(A)(2) of the Model Code,[46] states in pertinent part:

> A lawyer shall not bring or defend a proceeding, or assert or controvert an issue therein, unless there is a basis for doing so that is not frivolous, which includes a good faith argument for an extension, modification or reversal of existing law.

45. See, for example, Model Rules 2.1 and 3.1.

46. DR 7–102(A)(2) states:

In his representation of a client, a lawyer shall not:

(2) Knowingly advance a claim or defense that is unwarranted under existing law, except that he may advance such claim for an extension, modification or reversal of existing law.

Rule 1.2(d), which applies to representation generally, states:

> A lawyer shall not counsel a client to engage, or assist a client, in conduct that the lawyer knows is criminal or fraudulent, but a lawyer may discuss the legal consequences of any proposed course of conduct with a client and may counsel or assist a client to make a good faith effort to determine the validity, scope, meaning or application of the law.

On the basis of these rules and analogous provisions of the Model Code, a lawyer, in representing a client in the course of the preparation of the clients tax return, may advise the statement of positions most favorable to the client if the lawyer has a good faith belief that those positions are warranted in existing law or can be supported by a good faith argument for an extension, modification or reversal of existing law. A lawyer can have a good faith belief in this context even if the lawyer believes the clients position probably will not prevail.[47] However, good faith requires that there be some realistic possibility of success if the matter is litigated.

This formulation of the lawyers duty in the situation addressed by this opinion is consistent with the basic duty of the lawyer to a client, recognized in ethical standards since the ABA Canons of Professional Ethics, and in the opinions of this Committee: zealously and loyally to represent the interests of the client within the bounds of the law.

Thus, where a lawyer has a good faith belief in the validity of a position in accordance with the standard stated above that a particular transaction does not result in taxable income or that certain expenditures are properly deductible as expenses, the lawyer has no duty to require as a condition of his or her continued representation that riders be attached to the clients tax return explaining the circumstances surrounding the transaction or the expenditures.

In the role of advisor, the lawyer should counsel the client as to whether the position is likely to be sustained by a court if challenged by the IRS, as well as of the potential penalty consequences to the client if the position is taken on the tax return without disclosure. Section [6662(d)] of the Internal Revenue Code imposes a penalty for substantial understatement of tax liability which can be avoided if the facts are adequately disclosed or if there was substantial authority for the position taken by the taxpayer. Competent representation of the client would require the lawyer to advise the client fully as to whether there is or was substantial authority for the position taken in the tax return. If the lawyer is unable to conclude that the position is supported by substantial authority, the lawyer should advise the client of the penalty the client may suffer and of the opportunity to avoid such penalty by adequately disclosing the facts in the return or in a statement attached to the return. If after receiving such advice the client decides to risk the penalty by making no disclosure and to take the position initially advised by the lawyer in accordance with the standard stated

---

47. Comment to Rule 3.1; see also Model Code EC 7–4.

above, the lawyer has met his or her ethical responsibility with respect to the advice.

In all cases, however, with regard both to the preparation of returns and negotiating administrative settlements, the lawyer is under a duty not to mislead the Internal Revenue Service deliberately, either by misstatements or by silencing or by permitting the client to mislead. Rules 4.1 and 8.4(c); Drs 1–102(A)(4), 7–102(A)(3) and (5).

In summary, a lawyer may advise reporting a position on a return even where the lawyer believes the position probably will not prevail, there is no "substantial authority" in support of the position, and there will be no disclosure of the position in the return. However, the position to be asserted must be one which the lawyer in good faith believes is warranted in existing law or can be supported by a good faith argument for an extension, modification or reversal of existing law. This requires that there is some realistic possibility of success if the matter is litigated. In addition, in his role as advisor, the lawyer should refer to potential penalties and other legal consequences should the client take the position advised.

Report of the Special Task Force on Formal Opinion 85–352

39 Tax Law. 635 (1986).

On July 7, 1985, the American Bar Association Standing Committee on Ethics and Professional Responsibility (the "ABA Committee") issued Formal Opinion 85–352, which restates the ethical standard governing the lawyers duty in advising a client on positions that can be taken in a clients tax return. Formerly, the ethical obligations of lawyers engaged in tax practice were addressed generally in Formal Opinion 314, issued in 1965, which established "reasonable basis" as the minimum standard for advice with respect to a position in a tax return. Opinion 85–352 substitutes "some realistic possibility of success, if litigated" for "reasonable basis." This Report examines Opinion 85–352 and how it will apply to tax practice. It concludes that Opinion 85–352 properly rejects a low standard of tax reporting, reduces some of the potential for misuse of the governing ethical standard, and, properly interpreted and implemented, should work to improve the reliability of tax advice furnished by members of the bar. * * *

Reasons for Revision

Opinion 85–352 explains that as a result of serious controversy over the "reasonable basis" standard, and also as a result of persistent criticism by distinguished members of the tax bar, IRS officials, and members of Congress, sufficient doubt had been created regarding the validity of the "reasonable basis" standard as to erode its usefulness as an ethical guideline.

In addition to its determination that Opinion 314 should be restated because "reasonable basis" had become an ineffective ethical guideline, the

ABA Committee also noted that since publication of Opinion 314 in 1965 there have intervened in succession the Model Code of Professional Responsibility and the Model Rules of Professional Conduct, and that neither employs nor otherwise refers to "reasonable basis." Moreover, as explained below, the Model Code and Model Rules emphasize the role of good faith in determining whether counsel may advise the assertion of a position, and Opinion 314 includes no reference to good faith.

Scope of Opinion 85–352

Formal Opinion 85–352 restates the lawyers duty in advising a client as to positions that can be taken on a tax return. The same principles should apply to all aspects of tax practice to the extent tax return positions would be involved. For example, it should govern the lawyers duty as to tax advice in the course of structuring transactions that will involve tax return positions, including tax advice in the course of preparing legal documents such as employee benefit trusts, wills, and business buy-sell agreements. However, Opinion 85–352 does not address a lawyers duty and responsibilities in negotiation and settlement procedures with the Internal Revenue Service, which are the subject of discussion in Opinion 314, and which continue to be governed by Opinion 314. Nor does Opinion 85–352 address the lawyers duties and responsibilities in tax litigation. * * *

"Good Faith" as an Objective Standard

The Opinion restates relevant passages of applicable guidelines to the effect that the lawyer, in advising a client in the course of preparation of the clients tax return, may advise the statement of positions most favorable to the client if the lawyer has a good faith belief that those provisions are warranted in existing law, or can be supported by a good faith argument for an extension, modification, or reversal of existing law. It states expressly that a lawyer can have a good faith belief even if the lawyer believes the clients position probably will not prevail.

The Opinion does not, however, leave "good faith" open to subjective interpretation. It instead applies an objective standard to the determination of whether good faith is present. The Opinion explains:

> However, good faith requires that there be some realistic possibility of success if the matter is litigated.

The result is an objective standard which can be enforced. A lawyer cannot advise taking a tax return position unless there is a realistic possibility of success, if litigated. The Opinion makes clear that it derives this standard from the Model Code and DR 7–102(A)(2), as well as from Rule 3.1 of the Model Rules which is "in essence a restatement" of the Model Code and DR 7–102(A)(2). Because the Model Code and Disciplinary Rules have been adopted in many states, the Opinion in effect purports to be the ABA Committees restatement of what is in those jurisdictions a mandatory ethical requirement. Consequently, state disciplinary bodies should scrutinize lawyer conduct with respect to the new standard of Opinion 85–352 to the same extent as they should examine activities involving other standards of professional conduct.

The determination that good faith requires a realistic possibility of success if litigated also may have meaning for the tax preparer penalty. The regulations provide that the penalty is inapplicable if the preparer takes the position "in good faith and with reasonable basis." Reg. § 1.6694–1(a)(4). The regulations elsewhere describe "reasonable basis" to mean a position that is "arguable but fairly unlikely to prevail in court." Reg. § 1.6661–3(a)(2). It is possible that the Treasury will now conclude in its regulations that "good faith" requires a realistic possibility of success if litigated. The Treasury may urge the Congress to enact a new standard for defense to the tax preparer penalty. Similarly, it is possible that the new standard for asserting tax positions will be reflected by an appropriate amendment of Circular 230, which regulates practice before the Internal Revenue Service.

The courts also should apply the new standard in other relevant situations. For example, in an unreported decision, United States v. Yorke (D.Ind., July 19, 1976), the court dismissed a criminal tax prosecution of a taxpayer on the ground that counsel, in advising the position relied upon by the taxpayer, had a "reasonable basis," and "it would be unfair to judge the clients criminal liability on a stricter standard than his lawyers ethical obligation." Taxpayers no longer can rely upon such advice for protection against successful prosecution.

Role of the Audit Lottery

The standard adopted by Opinion 85–352 does not permit taking into account the likelihood of audit or detection in determining whether the ethical standard is met. Whether the return will be audited or not is simply of no consequence to the application of the new standard. The determination of whether there is a realistic possibility of success is made without regard to the reality of the audit lottery, and assumes that the issue is in court and to be decided.

Comparison of "Some Realistic Possibility of Success If Litigated" With "Reasonable Basis"

Doubtless there were some tax practitioners who intended "reasonable basis" to set a relatively high standard of tax reporting. Some have continued to apply such a standard. To more, however, if not most tax practitioners, the ethical standard set by "reasonable basis" had become a low one. To many it had come to permit any colorable claim to be put forth; to permit almost any words that could be strung together to be used to support a tax return position. Such a standard has now been rejected by the ABA Committee. The Opinion expressly states that to the extent "reasonable basis" had been construed to support the use of any colorable claim on a tax return or to justify exploitation of the lottery of the tax return audit selection process, the construction was an improper interpretation and application of what was meant by "reasonable basis."

More important to differentiating between "reasonable basis" and the standard articulated by Opinion 85–352 is that the new standard requires not only that there be some possibility of success, if litigated, rather than merely a construction that can be argued or that seems reasonable, but also that there be more than just any possibility of success. The possibility of success, if litigated, must be "realistic." A possibility of success cannot be "realistic" if it is only theoretical or impracticable. This clearly implies that there must be a substantial possibility of success, which when taken together with the assumption that the matter will be litigated, measurably elevates what had come to be widely accepted as the minimum ethical standard.

A position having only a 5% or 10% likelihood of success, if litigated, should not meet the new standard. A position having a likelihood of success closely approaching one-third should meet the standard. Ordinarily, there would be some realistic possibility of success where the position is supported by "substantial authority," as that term is used in § 6661 of the Code and applicable regulations. A position to be asserted in the return in the expectation that something could be obtained by way of concession in the bargaining process of settlement negotiations would not meet the new standard, unless accompanied by a realistic possibility of success, if litigated. If there is not a realistic possibility of success, if litigated, the new standard could not be met by disclosure or "flagging" of the position in the return.

If the Position Falls Below the Standard

If the standard is not met, the position may be advanced by payment of the tax and claim for refund, which necessarily sets forth in detail each ground upon which a refund is claimed. A position may be advanced in litigation if it is not frivolous. The lawyer may bring a proceeding, and assert an issue therein, if there is a basis for doing so that is not frivolous, which includes a good faith argument for an extension, modification, or reversal of existing law. In such a context good faith does not require that there be a possibility of success that is "realistic." Model Rule 3.1; DR 7–102(A)(2).

If the client determines to proceed to assert a position in a tax return that is not supported by a realistic possibility of success if litigated, the lawyer must withdraw from the engagement, at least to the extent it involves advice as to the position to be taken on the return, subject to usual rules governing withdrawal. Model Rule 1.16(a) provides that a lawyer shall not represent a client, or having done so shall withdraw from the representation of the client, if "the representation will result in violation of the Rules of Professional Conduct or other law. * * * " To avoid conflict with obligations imposed upon tax return preparers, the lawyer should first determine whether the position meets the ethical standard. If not, the lawyer must counsel the taxpayer not to assert the position, and, unless this advice is accepted by the client, the lawyer may not prepare the return, and pursuant to Rule 1.16(a) must withdraw from further representation involving advice as to the position taken on the return. Only if the position meets the standard may the lawyer prepare the return, sign it, and present it to the client.

Other Duties

Opinion 85–352 reiterates that in the role of advisor the lawyer has a duty to counsel the client whether the position is likely to be sustained in court if challenged. The lawyer should express a prediction of outcome, to the extent possible. No additional burden is imposed by the requirement that the lawyer conclude whether there is "some realistic possibility of success if litigated." The lawyers advice to the client should not be limited to whether there is a realistic possibility of success, or whether the position is or is not likely to be sustained, but should include the lawyers complete assessment of the prospects for success to the extent it is practicable to do so. * * *

Opinion 85–352 continues the position of Opinion 314 that if the applicable ethical standard is met, the lawyer has no duty to require as a condition of continued representation that riders be attached to the clients tax return. However, in all cases, and in all dealings with the Internal Revenue Service, "the lawyer is under a duty not to mislead the Internal Revenue Service deliberately, either by misstatements or by silence or by permitting the client to mislead." Thus, although a lawyer has no obligation under the opinion to flag doubtful positions of law as such if they meet the ethical standard, the lawyer has an obligation to counsel that the entries on a tax return must not be misleading. * * *

Tax Returns Are Not Adversarial Proceedings

Opinion 85–352 makes the new ethical standard applicable to return preparation in all cases. Although the Opinion recognizes that the taking of aggressive positions on tax returns may be the first step in development of an adversarial relationship between the client and the Internal Revenue Service, the lawyer, nevertheless, may not advise the taking of such positions in disregard of the new ethical standard. If the lawyer does not have the requisite good faith belief in the position, he may not ethically advise its being taken. If the client nevertheless takes the position, the lawyer must withdraw.

The Opinion does not state that the general ethical guidelines governing advocacy in litigation are determinative, or suggest that tax returns are adversarial proceedings. To the contrary, a tax return initially serves a disclosure, reporting, and self-assessment function. It is the citizens report to the government of his or her relevant activities for the year. The Opinion says that because some returns, particularly aggressive ones, may result in an adversary relationship, there is a place for consideration of the ethical considerations regarding advocacy. Thus, the Opinion blends the ethical guidelines governing advocacy with those applicable to advising, from which the new ethical standard is derived.

The Opinion recites that the ethical guidelines governing tax return positions are no different from those applicable to advising on civil matters generally. But the *standard* to be derived from the guidelines necessarily depends on the facts and circumstances relevant to the particular application of the guidelines. Good faith is the touchstone for derivation of the standard under both the Model Rules and the Model Code. Good faith, though to be employed and interpreted objectively, may produce different outcomes in different settings. Good faith in advising a client not to perform a contract, for example, if based upon conduct of the other party, may be quite different from good faith in advising that a position be taken on a tax return. In the context of a tax return, good faith requires an objective determination that there is "some realistic possibility of success, if litigated."

Regulations Governing Practice Before the Internal Revenue Service

Reg–138637–07.

Background and Explanation of Provisions

This document contains proposed amendments to § 10.34 of Circular 230. Section 330 of title 31 of the United States Code authorizes the Secretary of the Treasury to regulate the practice of representatives before the Treasury Department. Pursuant to section 330 of title 31, the Secretary has published the regulations in Circular 230 (31 CFR part 10).

On May 25, 2007, the President signed into law the Small Business and Work Opportunity Tax Act of 2007, Public Law 110–28 (121 Stat. 190), which amended several provisions of the Internal Revenue Code to extend the application of the income tax return preparer penalties to all tax return preparers, alter the standards of conduct that must be met to avoid imposition of the penalties for preparing a return that reflects an understatement of liability, and increase applicable penalties. On June 11, 2007, the IRS released Notice 2007–54, 2007–27 IRB 1 (see § 601.601(d)(2)(ii)(b)), providing guidance and transitional relief for the return preparer provisions under section 6694 of the Internal Revenue Code, as recently amended.

Final regulations are, simultaneously to these proposed regulations, being promulgated on September 26, 2007, modifying the general standards of practice before the IRS under Circular 230. Those final regulations finalize the standards with respect to documents, affidavits and other papers as proposed, with modifications. Those final regulations, however, do not finalize the standards with respect to tax returns under § 10.34(a) and the definitions under § 10.34(e) because of the amendments made by the Small Business and Work Opportunity Tax Act of 2007. Rather, the Treasury Department and the IRS are reserving § 10.34(a) and (e) in those final regulations and are simultaneously issuing this notice of proposed rulemaking proposing to amend this part to reflect these recent amendments to the Code.

The Treasury Department and the IRS have determined that the professional standards under § 10.34 of Circular 230 should conform with the civil penalty standards for return preparers. Previously, for example, on June 20, 1994 (59 FR 31523), the regulations were modified to reflect more closely the rules under section 6694 and professional guidelines. The standards with respect to tax returns in § 10.34(a) of these proposed regulations have been amended to reflect changes to section 6694(a) of the Internal Revenue Code made by the Small Business and Work Opportunity Tax Act of 2007.

Under § 10.34(a) of these proposed regulations, a practitioner may not sign a tax return as a preparer unless the practitioner has a reasonable belief that the tax treatment of each position on the return would more likely than not be sustained on its merits, or there is a reasonable basis for each position and each position is adequately disclosed to the Internal Revenue Service. A practitioner may not advise a client to take a position on a tax return, or prepare the portion of a tax return on which a position is taken, unless (1) the practitioner has a reasonable belief that the position satisfies the more likely than not standard; or (2) the position has a reasonable basis and is adequately disclosed to the Internal Revenue Service. The definitions of "more likely than not" and "reasonable basis" under § 10.34(e) also are proposed to be amended to reflect these changes in accordance with the well-established definitions of these terms under the section 6662 penalty regulations.

On June 11, 2007, the IRS released Notice 2007–54, 2007–27 IRB 1 (see § 601.601(d)(2)(ii)(b)), providing guidance and transitional relief for the return preparer provisions under section 6694 of the Code, as recently amended. In order to apply § 10.34 of these regulations consistently with the transitional relief under Notice 2007–54, § 10.34(a) and (e) are proposed to apply to returns filed or advice provided on or after the date that final regulations are published in the Federal Register, but no earlier than January 1, 2008. * * *

§ 10.34 Standards with respect to tax returns and documents, affidavits and other papers.

(a) *Tax returns.* A practitioner may not sign a tax return as a preparer unless the practitioner has a reasonable belief that the tax treatment of each position on the return would more likely than not be sustained on its merits (the more likely than not standard), or there is a reasonable basis for each position and each position is adequately disclosed to the Internal Revenue Service. A practitioner may not advise a client to take a position on a tax return, or prepare the portion of a tax return on which a position is taken, unless—

(1) The practitioner has a reasonable belief that the position satisfies the more likely than not standard; or

(2) The position has a reasonable basis and is adequately disclosed to the Internal Revenue Service.

(e) *Definitions.* For purposes of this section—

(1) *More likely than not.* A practitioner is considered to have a reasonable belief that the tax treatment of a position is more likely than not the proper tax treatment if the practitioner analyzes the pertinent facts and authorities, and based on that analysis reasonably concludes, in good faith, that there is a greater than fifty-percent likelihood that the tax treatment will be upheld if the IRS challenges it. The authorities described in 26 CFR 1.6662–4(d)(3)(iii), or any successor provision, of the substantial understatement penalty regulations may be taken into account for purposes of this analysis.

(2) *Reasonable basis.* A position is considered to have a reasonable basis if it is reasonably based on one or more of the authorities described in 26 CFR 1.6662–4(d)(3)(iii), or any successor provision, of the substantial understatement penalty regulations. Reasonable basis is a relatively high standard of tax reporting, that is, significantly higher than not frivolous or not patently improper. The reasonable basis standard is not satisfied by a return position that is merely arguable or that is merely a colorable claim. The possibility that a tax return will not be audited, that an issue will not be raised on audit, or that an issue will be settled may not be taken into account.

(3) *Frivolous.* A position is frivolous if it is patently improper.

(f) *Effective/applicability date.* Section 10.34(a) and (e) is applicable for returns filed or advice provided on or after the date that final regulations are published in the Federal Register, but no earlier than January 1, 2008.

Treasury Department Circular No. 230

(Rev. 4–2008).

§ 10.33   Best practices for tax advisors.

(a) *Best practices.* Tax advisors should provide clients with the highest quality representation concerning Federal tax issues by adhering to best practices in providing advice and in preparing or assisting in the preparation of a submission to the Internal Revenue Service. In addition to compliance with the standards of practice provided elsewhere in this part, best practices include the following:

(1) Communicating clearly with the client regarding the terms of the engagement. For example, the advisor should determine the client's expected purpose for and use of the advice and should have a clear understanding with the client regarding the form and scope of the advice or assistance to be rendered.

(2) Establishing the facts, determining which facts are relevant, evaluating the reasonableness of any assumptions or representations, relating the applicable law (including potentially applicable judicial doctrines) to the relevant facts, and arriving at a conclusion supported by the law and the facts.

(3) Advising the client regarding the import of the conclusions reached, including, for example, whether a taxpayer may avoid accuracy-related penalties under the Internal Revenue Code if a taxpayer acts in reliance on the advice.

(4) Acting fairly and with integrity in practice be fore the Internal Revenue Service.

(b) *Procedures to ensure best practices for tax advisors.* Tax advisors with responsibility for overseeing a firm's practice of providing advice concerning Federal tax issues or of preparing or assisting in the preparation of submissions to the Internal Revenue Service should take reasonable steps to ensure that the firm's procedures for all members, associates, and employees are consistent with the best practices set forth in paragraph (a) of this section.

(c) *Applicability date.* This section is effective after June 20, 2005.

§ 10.34 Standards with respect to tax returns and documents, affidavits and other papers.

(a) [Reserved]

(b) *Documents, affidavits and other papers*—

(1) A practitioner may not advise a client to take a position on a document, affidavit or other paper submitted to the Internal Revenue Service unless the position is not frivolous.

(2) A practitioner may not advise a client to submit a document, affidavit or other paper to the Internal Revenue Service—

(i) The purpose of which is to delay or impede the administration of the Federal tax laws;

(ii) That is frivolous; or

(iii) That contains or omits information in a manner that demonstrates an intentional disregard of a rule or regulation unless the practitioner also advises the client to submit a document that evidences a good faith challenge to the rule or regulation.

(c) *Advising clients on potential penalties*—

(1) A practitioner must inform a client of any penalties that are reasonably likely to apply to the client with respect to—

(i) A position taken on a tax return if—

(A) The practitioner advised the client with respect to the position; or

(B) The practitioner prepared or signed the tax return; and

(ii) Any document, affidavit or other paper submitted to the Internal Revenue Service.

(2) The practitioner also must inform the client of any opportunity to avoid any such penalties by disclosure, if relevant, and of the requirements for adequate disclosure.

(3) This paragraph (c) applies even if the practitioner is not subject to a penalty under the Internal Revenue Code with respect to the position or with respect to the document, affidavit or other paper submitted.

(d) *Relying on information furnished by clients.* A practitioner advising a client to take a position on a tax return, document, affidavit or other paper submitted to the Internal Revenue Service, or preparing or signing a tax return as a preparer, generally may rely in good faith without verification upon information furnished by the client. The practitioner may not, however, ignore the implications of information furnished to, or actually known by, the practitioner, and must make reasonable inquiries if the information as furnished appears to be incorrect, inconsistent with an important fact or another factual assumption, or incomplete.

(e) [Reserved]

(f) *Effective/applicability date.* Section 10.34 is applicable to tax returns, documents, affidavits, and other papers filed on or after September 26, 2007.

ILLUSTRATIVE MATERIAL

A. DUTY TO INFORM CLIENT ABOUT CHANGES IN TAX LAW

Formal Opinion 210 (Mar. 15, 1941) holds that "where the lawyer has no reason to believe that he has been supplanted by another lawyer, it is not only his right, *but it might even be his duty* to advise his client of any change of fact or law which might defeat the client's testamentary purpose as expressed in the will" (emphasis added). Courts have thus far refused to impose a duty on attorneys to keep clients informed about changes in the tax law. See Stangland v. Brock, 747 P.2d 464, 469 (Wash. 1987).

B. MALPRACTICE LIABILITY FOR NEGLIGENT TAX PLANNING ADVICE

In recent years, there have been a growing number of lawsuits against lawyers for failing to achieve desired estate and gift tax savings.[48] One hurdle

---

48. See Corneel, Guidelines to Tax Practice Second, 43 Tax Law. 297, 297 (1990) ("Malpractice claims arising out of tax work, which were virtually unheard of before the Seventies, have become an everyday occurrence."); Rule, What and When Can a Taxpayer Recover from a Negligent Tax Advisor?, 92 J.Tax'n 176, 176 (2000) ("The number of malpractice suits brought by taxpayer-clients against their tax preparers and advisors multiplied during the last decade."). See also Todres, Tax Malpractice Damages: A

that claimants must surmount is the lack of privity between a disappointed beneficiary and the lawyer. See, e.g., Blair v. Ing, 21 P.3d 452 (Hawaii 2001); Ferguson v. Cramer, 709 A.2d 1279 (Md. 1998); Trask v. Butler, 872 P.2d 1080 (Wash. 1994).[49] Compare Streber v. Hunter, 221 F.3d 701 (5th Cir.2000) (holding law firm and several attorneys liable for malpractice in connection with tax advice relating to potential transferee liability for gift tax, even though Fifth Circuit previously had held that attorneys' tax advice was supported by "substantial authority" for § 6661 penalty purposes), with Stevenson v. Severs, 158 F.3d 1332 (D.C. Cir.1998) (per curiam) (affirming dismissal of malpractice claim against estate planning attorney for failing to set up insurance trust where client, after retaining new counsel, transferred ownership of life insurance policies to trust; client's survival for three years after date of transfer negated potential application of § 2042). See also Camenisch v. Burns, 52 Cal.Rptr.2d 450 (1996) (dismissing $1 million claim for negligent infliction of emotional distress against estate planning attorney on similar facts; claim alleged knowledge that estate would be liable for $525,000 in estate tax under § 2042 if client died within three years caused him to "suffer severe alarm, anxiety, shock, loss of sleep, and other stress"); Cleveland v. United States, 2000 WL 1889640 (N.D.Ill. 2000) (refusing to hold tax attorney liable for alleged malpractice that precipitated audit by Service, caused severe financial and psychological harm to client, and ultimately led to client's suicide).

Comprehensive Review of the Elements and the Issues, 61 Tax Law. 705 (2008); Todres, Tax Malpractice Developments in the Estate and Gift Tax Area, 83 Taxes 33 (Oct. 2005); Todres, Tax Malpractice: Areas in Which It Occurs and the Measure of Damages—An Update, 78 St. John's L.Rev. 1011 (2004); Todres, Malpractice and the Tax Practitioner: An Analysis of the Areas in Which Malpractice Occurs, 48 Emory L.J. 547 (1999); Todres, Tax Malpractice in the Estate and Gift Tax Areas, 77 Taxes 13 (Nov. 1999).

49. See Begleiter, First Let's Sue All the Lawyers—What Will We Get: Damages for Estate Planning Malpractice, 51 Hastings L.J. 325 (2000); Begleiter, The Gambler Breaks Even: Legal Malpractice in Complicated Estate Planning Cases, 20 Ga.St.U.L.Rev. 277 (2003); Fogel, Attorney v. Client—Privity, Malpractice, and the Lack of Respect for the Primacy of the Attorney–Client Relationship in Estate Planning, 68 Tenn.L.Rev. 261 (2001).

*

PART X

INTERNATIONAL ASPECTS OF WEALTH TRANSFER TAXATION

CHAPTER 39

U.S. JURISDICTIONAL PRINCIPLES

The U.S. wealth transfer taxes are global in reach with respect to U.S. citizens and residents (domiciliaries). Thus, section 2031 imposes a tax on the value of property "wherever situated" and, with one exception, the gift tax applies to donative transfers of property regardless of where the property may be located. The generation-skipping tax is applied similarly.

Other countries also may impose a wealth transfer tax on property which is subject to U.S. tax because, for example, they may tax on the basis of residence, situs of the property, or some other criterion. In these situations (and others), the possibility of international double taxation is present. This possibility is alleviated by the U.S. through its foreign tax credit mechanism and/or through tax treaties.

Nonresident aliens may own property situated in the U.S. Special rules are provided to impose the U.S. wealth transfer taxes only on the value of property "situated within the United States."

The United States has entered into relatively few wealth transfer tax treaties with other countries. Generally, in such treaties, the U.S. seeks to mitigate the possibility of international double taxation by providing rules to establish the decedent's residence in one country or the other and to establish priorities of tax jurisdiction with respect to particular types of property.

In this Chapter, principles on which the U.S. asserts taxing jurisdiction are considered.

SECTION A.   CITIZENSHIP

International Revenue Code: §§ 2107; 2501(a)(3); 2661; 877(a),(b),(g)

Regulations: § 1.1–1(c)

ILLUSTRATIVE MATERIAL

A.   LOSS OF U.S. CITIZENSHIP

As noted above, the United States taxes its citizens on a world-wide basis regardless of where the property transferred is situated. If a U.S. citizen loses her citizenship, she becomes subject to a different tax regime. Under Reg. § 1.1–1(c), whether there has been a loss of nationality by a U.S. citizen is determined under the Immigration and Nationality Act. It is critical that an individual voluntarily renounce citizenship. Afroyim v. Rusk, 38, 387 U.S. 253 (1967). Accordingly, the expatriating act must be performed by an individual (a) voluntarily and (b) with the intent of relinquishing U.S. citizenship. In 8 U.S.C.

§ 1481, certain expatriating acts are designated which presumptively evidence voluntary loss of citizenship including, for example, obtaining naturalization in a foreign country, taking an oath or affirmation of allegiance to another country, and formally renouncing U.S. citizenship before a diplomatic or consular officer in a foreign country. For illustrative cases, see Breyer v. Meissner, 214 F. 3d 416 (3d.Cir. 2000); Rexach v. United States, 390 F.2d 631 (1st Cir. 1968); Nishikawa v. Dulles, 356 U.S. 129 (1958). There is no presumption created with respect to the intent test, but instead the requisite intent must be ascertained from the individual's words and conduct. Vance v. Terrazas, 444 U.S. 252 (1980).

SECTION B.   EXPATRIATION TO AVOID U.S. WEALTH TRANSFER TAXES

Section 2107(a), as amended by the 2004 Act, provides that if a decedent who is subject to § 877 dies in a year in which she is present in the U.S. for more than 30 days, the U.S. estate tax is imposed on all her property wherever situated. § 877(g).

The tax treatment of expatriates has been the subject of several recent statutory changes. The provisions in effect prior to 1996 were ineffective and were largely ignored by the IRS. Congress, in 1996, reacted to some highly publicized expatriation cases by substantially strengthening the statutory scheme. The 2004 Act further strengthened the provisions.

Section 877 generally applies to a former U.S citizen who loses her citizenship, for tax years ending within 10 years of the date citizenship is lost, if her average annual income tax for the five most recent taxable years before the loss of citizenship exceeded $124,000, her net worth as of the date she lost citizenship equaled or exceeded $2,000,000, or she fails to certify under penalties of perjury that she met the requirements of the Code for the 5 preceding taxable years.

Report of the House Ways and Means Committee

H.R. Rep. No. 108–548, pt. 1, 108th Cong. 2d Sess.254–257 (2004).

Explanation of Provision

In general

The bill provides: (1) objective standards for determining whether former citizens or former long-term residents are subject to the alternative tax regime; (2) tax-based (instead of immigration-based) rules for determining when an individual is no longer a U.S. citizen or long-term resident for U.S. Federal tax purposes; (3) the imposition of full U.S. taxation for individuals who are subject to the alternative tax regime [of section 877(b)] and who return to the United States for extended periods; (4) imposition of U.S. gift tax on gifts of stock of certain closely-held foreign corporations that hold U.S.-situated property; and (5) an annual return-filing requirement for individuals who are subject to the alternative tax regime, for each of the 10 years following citizenship relinquishment or residency termination.

Objective rules for the alternative tax regime

The bill replaces the subjective determination of tax avoidance as a principal purpose for citizenship relinquishment or residency termination under present law with objective rules. Under [section 877(a)(2)], a former citizen or former long-term resident would be subject to the alternative tax regime for a 10–year period following citizenship relinquishment or residency termination, unless the former citizen or former long-term resident: (1) establishes that his or her average annual net income tax liability for the five preceding years does not exceed $124,000 (adjusted for inflation after 2004) and his or her net worth does not exceed $2 million, or alternatively satisfies limited, objective exceptions for dual citizens and minors who have had no substantial contact with the United States; and (2) certifies under penalties of perjury that he or she has complied with all U.S. Federal tax obligations for the preceding five years and provides such evidence of compliance as the Secretary of the Treasury may require.

The monetary thresholds under the bill replace the present-law inquiry into the taxpayer's intent. In addition, the bill eliminates the present-law process of IRS ruling requests.

If a former citizen exceeds the monetary thresholds, that person is excluded from the alternative tax regime if he or she falls within the exceptions [in section 877(c)] for certain dual citizens and minors (provided that the requirement of certification and proof of compliance with Federal tax obligations is met). These exceptions provide relief to individuals who have never had substantial connections with the United States, as measured by certain objective criteria, and eliminate IRS inquiries as to the subjective intent of such taxpayers.

In order to be excepted from the application of the alternative tax regime under the bill, whether by reason of falling below the net worth and income tax liability thresholds or qualifying for the dual-citizen or minor exceptions, the former citizen or former long-term resident also is required to certify, under penalties of perjury, that he or she has complied with all U.S. Federal tax obligations for the five years preceding the relinquishment of citizenship or termination of residency and to provide such documentation as the Secretary of the Treasury may require evidencing such compliance (e.g., tax returns, proof of tax payments). Until such time, the individual remains subject to the alternative tax regime. It is intended that the IRS will continue to verify that the information submitted was accurate, and it is intended that the IRS will randomly audit such persons to assess compliance.

Termination of U.S. citizenship or long-term resident status for U.S. Federal income tax purposes

Under the bill, an individual continues to be treated as a U.S. citizen or long-term resident for U.S. Federal tax purposes, including for purposes of section 7701(b)(10), until the individual: (1) gives notice of an expatriating act or termination of residency (with the requisite intent to relinquish citizenship or terminate residency) to the Secretary of State or the Secretary of Homeland Security, respectively; and (2) provides a statement in accordance with section 6039G.

Sanction for individuals subject to the individual tax regime who return to the United States for extended periods

The alternative tax regime does not apply to any individual for any taxable year during the 10–year period following citizenship relinquishment or residency termination if such individual is present in the United States for more than 30 days in the calendar year ending in such taxable year. Such individual is treated as a U.S. citizen or resident for such taxable year and therefore is taxed on his or her worldwide income.

Similarly, if an individual subject to the alternative tax regime is present in the United States for more than 30 days in any calendar year ending during the 10–year period following citizenship relinquishment or residency termination, and the individual dies during that year, he or she is treated as a U.S. resident, and the individual's worldwide estate is subject to U.S. estate tax. Likewise, if an individual subject to the alternative tax regime is present in the United States for more than 30 days in any year during the 10–year period following citizenship relinquishment or residency termination, the individual is subject to U.S. gift tax on any transfer of his or her worldwide assets by gift during that taxable year.

For purposes of these rules, an individual is treated as present in the United States on any day if such individual is physically present in the United States at any time during that day. The present-law exceptions from being treated as present in the United States for residency purposes generally do not apply for this purpose. However, for individuals with certain ties to countries other than the United States and individuals with minimal prior physical presence in the United States,a day of physical presence in the United States is disregarded if the individual is performing services in the United States on such day for an unrelated employer (within the meaning of sections 267 and 707(b)), who meets the requirements the Secretary of the Treasury may prescribe in regulations. No more than 30 days may be disregarded during any calendar year under this rule.

Imposition of gift tax with respect to stock of certain closely held foreign corporations

Gifts of stock of certain closely-held foreign corporations by a former citizen or former long-term resident who is subject to the alternative tax regime are subject to gift tax under [section 2501(a)(5)], if the gift is made within the 10–year period after citizenship relinquishment or residency termination. The gift tax rule applies if: (1) the former citizen or former long-term resident, before making the gift, directly or indirectly owns 10 percent or more of the total combined voting power of all classes of stock entitled to vote of the foreign corporation; and (2) directly or indirectly, is considered to own more than 50 percent of (a) the total combined voting power of all classes of stock entitled to vote in the foreign corporation, or (b) the total value of the stock of such corporation. If this stock ownership test is met, then taxable gifts of the former citizen or former long-term resident include that proportion of the fair market value of the foreign stock transferred by the individual, at the time of the gift, which the fair market value of any assets owned by such foreign corporation and situated in the United States (at the time of the gift) bears to the total fair market value of all assets owned by such foreign corporation (at the time of the gift).

This gift tax rule applies to a former citizen or former long-term resident who is subject to the alternative tax regime and who owns stock in a foreign corporation at the time of the gift, regardless of how such stock was acquired (e.g., whether issued originally to the donor, purchased, or received as a gift or bequest).

Annual return

[Section 6039G] requires former citizens and former long-term residents to file an annual return for each year following citizenship relinquishment or residency termination in which they are subject to the alternative tax regime. The annual return is required even if no U.S. Federal income tax is due. The annual return requires certain information, including information on the permanent home of the individual, the individual's country of residence, the number of days the individual was present in the United States for the year, and detailed information about the individual's income and assets that are subject to the alternative tax regime. This requirement includes information relating to foreign stock potentially subject to the special estate tax rule of section 2107(b) and the gift tax rules of this bill.

If the individual fails to file the statement in a timely manner or fails correctly to include all the required information, the individual is required to pay a penalty of $5,000. The $5,000 penalty does not apply if it is shown that the failure is due to reasonable cause and not to willful neglect.

Effective Date

The provision applies to individuals who relinquish citizenship or terminate long-term residency after June 3, 2004.

ILLUSTRATIVE MATERIAL

A.   TECHNICAL ISSUES

1.   Estate Tax.

If a decedent who is subject to § 877, was not present in the U.S. for more than 30 days in the year in which she died, then the estate tax in general applies only to her U.S. situs property. A wealth transfer tax credit of $13,000 is allowed against the tax so computed (the equivalent of a $60,000 exemption). § 2107(a), (c)(1).

If the special rule dealing with ownership of stock in certain foreign corporations is applicable, a proportionate foreign tax credit is granted if another country also imposes a tax on the property included in the U.S. gross estate by reason of that rule. § 2107(b),(c)(2). In determining the value of the stock of the foreign corporation, no reduction is allowed for corporate liabilities. Treas. Reg. § 20.2107–1(b)(1)(iii)(*a*). The rules of § 957 are applied to determine if the requisite "voting power" exists.

2.   *Gift Tax.*

If a nonresident alien who is subject to § 877 makes a gift in a year in which she was in the U.S. for more than 30 days, the U.S. gift tax applies under § 877(g) regardless of where the transferred property is located and regardless of the nature of the property.

Special rules also apply to gifts by a nonresident alien who is subject to § 877 but was not in the U.S. for more than 30 days. The U.S. gift tax applies to transfers by such person of intangible property situated in the U.S., as well as transfers of tangible property in the U.S. Contrary to the normal U.S. rule, a foreign tax credit is allowed for any foreign taxes imposed on such gifts. § 2501(a)(3). The following property is considered situated in the U.S. and hence subject to gift tax:

    a) Shares of stock in a U.S. corporation;

    b) Debt obligations of a U.S. person, including bank deposits;

    c) Debt obligations of the U.S. or a state or local government;

    d) Intangible property of any type issued by or enforceable against a U.S. resident or corporation.

These special rules apply regardless of where the stock or written evidence of the property or obligation is located. § 2511(b); Treas. Reg. § 25.2511–3(b). A rule similar to that applicable to the estate tax with respect to transfers of stock in certain foreign corporations (12.6.1) is also applicable in the gift tax context. § 2501(a)(5).

B.   NON–TAX STATUTORY PROVISIONS

Congress back-stopped the expatriation tax provisions with a formidable rule in § 352 of the Illegal Immigration Reform and Immigrant Responsibility Act of 1996. Under that provision, any alien whom the Attorney General determines has renounced his U.S. citizenship for purposes of avoiding U.S. tax may be permanently denied entrance into the U.S. The tax planner obviously must assist a client contemplating expatriation to balance projected U.S. tax savings against what might prove to be a very adverse impact on his personal affairs.

SECTION C.   DOMICILE

Whether the U.S. will impose its wealth transfer taxes on a global or only on a situs basis in the case of a transferor who is not a U.S. citizen depends on whether the transferor is a "resident" of the U.S. The issue is also important where a tax treaty is involved. See p. 857. Reg. § 20.0–1(b)(1) provides that a person is a U.S. resident if her "domicile" is in the U.S. The issue is a factual one and the following Ruling sets forth the tests employed by the Internal Revenue Service to resolve the question.

Revenue Ruling 80–209

1980–2 C.B. 248.

ISSUE

For purposes of the federal estate tax imposed by section 2001 of the Internal Revenue Code, was a person who entered the United States illegally and who continued to live in the United States until death a resident of the United States at the date of death?

FACTS

The decedent entered the United States illegally in 1959. Two years later, the decedent's spouse also entered the United States illegally. Up to date of death in 1978, the decedent continued to remain in the United States. The decedent never secured a visa from the Government, nor did the decedent every apply for and receive official permission to reside in the United States. Therefore, the decedent was at all times after entering the United States subject to the laws regarding deportation of aliens.

In 1963, the decedent purchased a home in the United States and resided there until death. The decedent was, during the fifteen years prior to his death, a member of several local clubs and an active participant in community affairs.

In 1964 and in 1972, the decedent purchased real property in the decedent's native country through the services of an agent. After the purchases, the properties were leased to a succession of tenants.

The representatives of the decedent's estate have argued that the decedent was not a resident of the United States and that the real property located in the decedent's native country is not includible in the federal gross estate.

LAW AND ANALYSIS

Section 2001(a) of the Code imposes a tax on the transfer of the taxable estate of "every decedent who is a citizen or resident of the United States." The tax imposed by section 2001(a) applies, in general, to property owned by a resident of the United States regardless of where the property is located.

Section 2101 of the Code imposes a separate tax on the transfer of the taxable estate of "every decedent nonresident not a citizen of the United States." Under section 2103, the gross estate of a nonresident who is not a United States citizen includes, for purposes of the tax imposed by section 2101, only property situated in the United States.

Section 20.0–1(b)(1) of the Estate Tax Regulations defines the term "resident" as follows:

A 'resident' decedent is a decedent who, at the time of his death, had his domicile in the United States. . . . A person acquires a domicile in a place by living there, for even a brief period of time, with no definite present intention of later removing therefrom. Residence without the requisite intention to remain indefinitely will not suffice to constitute domicile, nor will intention to change domicile effect such a change unless accompanied by actual removal.The question of whether the taxable estate of a decedent who is not a United States citizen is subject to the federal estate tax under section 2001 of the Code depends upon where the decedent was domiciled at the date of death.

The requirements for acquiring a domicile are (1) legal capacity to do so; (2) physical presence; and (3) a current intention to make a home in the place. Restatement (Second) of Conflict of Laws s 15, Comment a (1971).

Legal capacity to acquire a domicile of choice has been found to exist even when people are subject to transfer to another domicile at the direction of others. See, e.g., Stifel v. Hopkins, 477 F.2d 1116, 1120 (6th Cir. 1973). Therefore, the fact that the decedent was subject to deportation does not render the decedent legally incapable of acquiring a domicile.

Because the decedent was physically present in this country at the date of death, the decedent would have been domiciled in the United States if the decedent had a current intention to make the United States a home. However, once a person has established a domicile in one place, it is presumed to continue in that place until it is shown to have been changed. Mitchell v. United States, 88 U.S. (21 Wall.) 350 (1874). The presumption can be rebutted upon facts showing an intention to remain in the United States for an indefinite period or on a permanent basis. See generally, Restatement (Second) of Conflict of Laws s 18, comment d (1971). Some of the factors used in determining such requisite intention are home ownership, local community ties and living with one's family in the claimed domicile. See Farmer's Loan & Trust Co. v. United States, 60 F.2d 618 (S.D.N.Y.1932).

In the present case, the fact that the decedent lived in the United States for a long time with the decedent's family and that the decedent established strong community ties indicates an absence of any fixed intention of returning to the native country.

The purchase of property located in a person's native country is not sufficient to conclude that the decedent was not domiciled in the United States, especially since the location of an investment is not indicative of domicile. See Rodiek v. Commissioner, 33 B.T.A. 1020, 1034 (1936), affirmed, 87 F.2d 328 (2d Cir. 1937), Ct. D. 1229, 1937–1 C.B. 290. The facts in the present case thus indicate that the decedent intended to remain in the United States indefinitely.

HOLDING

The decedent was domiciled in the United States at the date of death. Therefore, the taxable estate of the decedent is subject to the federal estate tax imposed by section 2001 of the Code. Further, the same conclusion would result, under the facts presented, if the decedent had entered the United States legally in 1959 as a nonimmigrant holding a visa and had remained in the United States after the visa expired. Even though such a decedent, at the time of entry, may not have had the intent to remain in the United States, nevertheless, that decedent may subsequently form the intent to remain in the United States indefinitely and establish domicile in the United States.

ILLUSTRATIVE MATERIAL

A.   OTHER EXAMPLES

In Estate of Nienhuys v. Commissioner, 17 T.C. 1149 (1952), the decedent in 1940 made a business trip abroad from his native country of Holland. Because of the German invasion of that country, he did not return to Holland but instead came to the U.S. He remained in the U.S. until his death in 1945. At all times after his arrival in the U.S., the decedent intended and desired to return to Holland. The court concluded that the presumption of domicile in Holland was not overcome. The fact that the decedent filed federal income tax returns as a resident was not relevant to the domicile issue. Accordingly, the estate tax return was properly filed as that of a nonresident alien decedent.

See also Rev. Rul. 80–363, 1980–2 C. B. 249, in which a nonresident alien who was an employee of an international organization entered the United States on a G–4 visa, a non-immigrant visa granted to employees of international organizations. After arrival, the decedent formed the intent to remain in the U.S. indefinitely and, in fact, remained in the U.S. until his death. Despite the nature of the visa on which the decedent entered the U.S., domicile was established in the U.S.

Section D.   Situs Rules

Internal Revenue Code: §§ 2104–2105

Regulations: §§ 20.2104–1; 20.2105–1

Sections 2104 and 2105 provide a set of "situs" rules to determine whether particular types of property are situated within the U.S. or in a foreign country. For estates of U.S. domiciliaries, the situs rules determine whether and the extent to which a foreign tax credit is available to offset U.S. tax liability for death taxes imposed by another country. § 2014(a) (last sentence). For estates of nonresident aliens, the situs rules determine whether the U.S. estate tax will apply at all. §§ 2101, 2103, 2106. As discussed at p. 857, the situs rules may be modified by a tax treaty.

Property Situated Within the U.S.: Under § 2104 and Reg. § 20.2104–1, the following property is considered situated within the U.S.:

(a) Real estate located in the U.S.;

(b) Tangible personal property located in the U.S. (except for certain works of art as noted below);

(c) Shares of stock issued by a corporation organized under the laws of the U.S.;

(d) Transfers of property described in §§ 2035–2038 if the property was situated in the U.S. either at the time of the original transfer or at the decedent's death;

(e) Debt obligations issued by a U.S. person (as defined in § 7701(a)(1)) or by the U.S. or a state or local government (except as noted below); and

(f) Certain deposits with a U.S. branch of a foreign corporation if the branch is engaged in the commercial banking business.

Property Situated Outside the U.S.: Under § 2105 and Reg. § 20.2105–1, the following property is considered situated without the U.S.:

(a) Real estate located outside the U.S.;

(b) Tangible personal property located outside the U.S.;

(c) Works of art owned by a nonresident alien that are at the time of death on loan or exhibition in the U.S.;

(d) Shares of stock in a corporation organized and incorporated under the laws of a foreign country (unless § 2107(b), p. 829 applies);

(e) Proceeds of insurance on the life of a nonresident alien;

(f) Debt obligations issued by a U.S. corporation and deposits with a U.S. bank if the interest on such deposits would not be subject to U.S. income tax by virtue of § 871(h) or (i); and(g) Deposits with a foreign branch of a U.S. commercial bank.

ILLUSTRATIVE MATERIAL

A. GENERAL

In Wodehouse v. Commissioner, 19 T.C. 487 (1952), the taxpayer, a well-known author, transferred one-half interests in manuscripts of novels and short stories to his wife. Both were British subjects and residing in France at the time of the transfers. At the time of the transfers, the manuscripts physically were present in France. Subsequently, the manuscripts were sent to the U.S., U.S. copyrights were obtained, and royalty payments were made on the books and stories after they were published in the U.S. The court concluded that the situs of the property at the time of the transfer was in France. Accordingly, the assignments constituted the transfer of property by a nonresident alien of property situated outside the U.S. and the U.S. gift tax was not applicable.

U.S. real estate is situated in the U.S. and a lifetime transfer by a nonresident alien is subject to U.S. gift tax. Davies v. Commissioner, 40 T.C. 525 (1963), involved a plan to avoid this result. A nonresident alien father sold U.S. real estate to his son for a cash down payment plus a note and mortgage. The father provided the funds for the down payment by making a cash gift to the son. In addition, each year the father would deposit funds in the son's bank account in England which were used by the son to make payments on the note. The court held that the father made a gift of the U.S. real estate to the extent of the difference between its fair market value and the note that the son gave to the father; the court ignored the gift of the funds which the son was obligated to use to make the down payment. However, subsequent gifts which were used to make payments on the notes were not subject to U.S. gift tax because they were not pursuant to any prearranged plan or commitment. While the father hoped and expected that the funds he deposited in his son's account would be used to pay the note, there was no obligation on the son to so use them and hence annual gifts of U.S. real estate did not result.

B. USE OF FOREIGN CORPORATIONS TO AVOID U.S. ESTATE TAX

Because of the situs rules for corporate and governmental securities, nonresident alien individuals usually create an offshore corporation which in turn invests in U.S. stocks and securities. At death, the individual owns only stock in a foreign corporation and thus his U.S. investments are not subject to U.S. estate tax. Individuals from countries which have no estate tax (such as Canada) who desire to own U.S. real estate (perhaps a second home) also may try to insulate themselves from U.S. estate tax by owning the property through a foreign corporation. The IRS on occasion has challenged the use of foreign corporations to avoid U.S. estate tax.

Fillman v. United States, 355 F.2d 632 (Ct. Cl. 1966), involved a Swiss decedent who in 1939 had formed two Argentinean corporations. Funds and securities were transferred to the new corporations because of concern that the German army might invade Switzerland. Both corporations engaged in the purchase and sale of securities in South America, New York and London. The corporations opened custodial accounts with a New York trust company. The trust company, at the time of the decedent's death, held securities consisting of stocks in U.S. corporations, Republic of Uruguay bonds and debentures of a U.S. corporation. Under the 1939 Code, all stocks and bonds of foreign or domestic corporations owned by a nonresident alien but physically present within the U.S. at the time of his death were includable in his estate for U.S. estate tax purposes. The issue was whether the decedent "owned" the securities at the time of his death or whether they were owned by the two Argentinean corporations. Based on evidence that the corporations acted only on behalf of the decedent, the court held that the corporations were merely custodians for the decedent, that he was the true owner of the shares held by the U.S. trust company, and that the value of the stocks and bonds held by the U.S. trust company were subject to U.S. estate taxation.

A different approach was adopted in Estate of Swan v. Commissioner, 247 F.2d 144 (2d Cir. 1957). In 1939, the decedent, a resident and citizen of the Netherlands, established two family foundations in Liechtenstein and Switzerland. Under the terms of the foundations' charters, the decedent had sole and unlimited management of and control over funds in the foundations. The decedent could withdraw funds and amend or terminate the foundations at any time. Funds of both foundations were deposited in New York banks. Because of the German invasion of Holland, the decedent in 1940 instructed the banks in New York to transfer funds and securities in his personal accounts to the foundations. The decedent died in 1943. The decedent's estate argued that the foundations should be classified as foreign corporations. The court, however, held that the securities were subject to U.S. estate tax under the predecessor of § 2104(b) and the exemption for cash deposits in the predecessor of § 2105(b) applied to the cash funds but not to the securities. The court reached this conclusion on the basis that the entities in question were more like revocable trusts; but regardless of whether the foundations were classified as corporations or as trusts, the predecessor of § 2104(b) applied because it reached revocable transfers in "trust or otherwise."

The foreign entity must be classified as a corporation for U.S. tax purposes under the tests set forth in Reg. § 301.7701–2 in order for a foreign investor successfully to use a foreign corporation holding U.S. assets to avoid U.S. estate tax. Reg. § 301.7701–2(b)(8) lists those foreign entities that always will be classified as corporations for U.S. tax purposes. For other types of foreign business entities, the "check-the-box" approach in general allows the foreign investor to choose whether the entity will be classified as a corporation or a partnership. Since the estate tax treatment of interests in foreign partnerships is less clear than that of foreign corporations, corporate classification generally is preferable.

Planning for the use of a foreign corporation as an investment vehicle also requires that U.S. income tax treatment of the corporation be carefully considered.

C. PARTNERSHIP INTERESTS AND OTHER INTANGIBLES

Despite the increasing use of partnerships and limited liability companies in cross-border business and investment transactions, there is very little authority on the proper situs rule to be employed with respect to interests in such entities. In part this dearth of authority results, for example, from the Service's position that it will not issue advance rulings on the issue whether a partnership interest is an "intangible" asset and hence free of U.S. gift tax if transferred by a nonresident alien. Rev. Proc. 2008–7, 2008–1 I.R.B. 229, § 4.01 (26). In one published ruling, the Service concluded that the situs of a partnership interest under the U.S.–U.K. estate tax treaty is where the "partnership business is carried on." Rev. Rul. 55–701, 1955–2 C.B. 836. The ruling noted that U.S. state court rules applicable to the situs of partnership assets were not controlling.

Under Reg. §§ 20.2104–1(a)(4) and 20.2105–1(e), intangibles not covered by any other rule are sited in the U.S. if the written evidence of the property is not "treated as the property itself" and the intangible "is issued by or enforceable against" a U.S. resident, corporation or government unit. The first requirement would be satisfied by bearer bonds but poorly matches assets such as copyrights and patents. Intangibles such as know-how and good will seem to fall totally outside the definitional requirements.

D. TRUSTS

Under § 7701 (a)(30), a trust is a U.S. resident if (a) a court in the U.S. can exercise primary jurisdiction over the administration of the trust (the "court" test) and (b) U.S. fiduciaries have the authority to control all "substantial decisions" concerning the trust (the "control" test). All other trusts are treated as foreign trusts. These tests are spelled out in detail in Reg. § 301. 7701–7. Suppose a trust is formed under U.S. law and has two trustees, one a U.S. person and one a foreign person. The trustees can act only upon a vote of a majority of the trustees. Although the "court" test is met, the "control" test is not and the trust would be classified as a foreign trust. See Reg. § 301.7701–7 (d) (1) (v), Ex.1.

E. U.S. BANK ACCOUNTS

Section 2105(b) provides that certain U.S. bank deposits and certain U.S. debt obligations are treated as situated outside the U.S. Section 2105(b)(1) applies to deposits described in § 871(i)(3) if any interest on the deposit would have been exempt from U.S. income tax under § 871(i)(1). The portfolio interest exemption in § 871(h)(1) includes most interest on bank deposits. The other rule situating interest on U.S. bank deposits outside the U.S. is for interest on "deposits with persons carrying on the banking business." The quoted phrase has been the subject of some litigation and administrative interpretation. The following authorities interpreted the identical phrase as it was contained in § 861(c) prior to the 1982 Revenue Act.

In order for the bank deposit situs rule to apply, the nonresident alien decedent must have had a direct and enforceable claim against the bank in which the funds were on deposit. Thus, in Estate of Ogarrio (Daguerre) v. Commissioner, 40 T.C. 242 (1963), aff'd per curiam, 337 F.2d 108 (D.C. Cir. 1964), a nonresident alien decedent had held an account with a U.S. brokerage firm, which owed the decedent money from a sale transaction which it had carried out for him prior to his death. Distribution of the sales proceeds had not been made as of the date of death. The court held that since the brokerage firm remitted the funds due to the decedent to his U.S. bank account after the time of his death, the funds could not be excluded from U.S. estate taxation on the basis that they constituted bank deposits under section 2105(b). While the brokerage firm was acting as the decedent's agent in selling stock, it was not acting as agent for him when the firm deposited these proceeds from sale in its own bank account prior to remitting them to the decedent's bank account. Accordingly, there were no funds on deposit "for" the decedent at the time of his death as a result of the sale transaction. See also, Rev. Rul. 65–245, 1965–2 C. B. 379 (same result as *Ogarrio*; there must be a direct and enforceable claim against a bank in order to qualify for the bank deposit exception in section 2105(b)). In Rev. Rul. 82–193, 1982–2 C. B. 219, a nonresident alien decedent created an irrevocable trust in the U.S. and retained a reversionary interest therein. A U.S. bank was the trustee and at the date of the decedent's death, the trust corpus consisted of a certificate of deposit issued by the bank. The Ruling concluded that interest income earned by a simple trust on deposit in a U.S. bank should be treated as if it had been received by a nonresident alien directly. Thus, under then section 861(c), the income from the trust bank deposit would not have been U.S. source income. Accordingly, the decedent nonresident alien's reversionary interest in the bank deposit was excludable from the estate. The Ruling "clarified the intent of" Rev. Rul. 69–596, below. See also Estate of Worthington v. Commissioner 18 T.C. 796 (1952) (decedent was a nonresident alien and at the date of her death funds were held on deposit in the bank accounts of an investment advisory firm in the U.S.; the court concluded that the decedent possessed a direct and enforceable claim against the bank deposits); Estate of de Guebriant v. Commissioner, 14 T.C. 611 (1950) (trustees held funds on deposit in a U.S. bank after termination of the trust pending final accounting to the decedent nonresident alien who held the remainder interest in the trust; the court held that the funds on deposit were held by or for the decedent for purposes of winding up the trust estate and the deposits were exempt from U.S. estate tax).

On the other hand, if there exists a relationship other than that of creditor and debtor between the bank and the depositor, the U.S. bank deposit will be held to be situated within the U.S. and subject to tax. See, e.g., Rev. Rul. 69–596, 1969–2 C. B. 179 (funds placed with a U.S. bank by a nonresident alien and held by the bank in a fiduciary capacity do not constitute deposits with persons carrying on a banking business); Rev. Rul. 55–143, 1955–1 C. B. 465 (a nonresident alien died with certain cash funds which he had placed in a safe deposits box rented from a U.S. bank; since the funds were not general deposits with the bank in the sense of creating debtor-creditor relationship, the cash was includable in the decedent's estate).

F.   ROLE OF FOREIGN LAW

Foreign law determines the nature of property interests held by a nonresident alien. In Rev. Rul. 72–443, 1972–2 C. B. 531, the decedent was a resident of Norway, a community property country. Using community funds, the decedent had purchased in his name alone U.S. real estate located in a noncommunity property state. The Ruling concluded that only one-half the value of the real property was included in the decedent's gross estate under § 2103. See also Estate of Zietz v. Commissioner, 34 T.C. 351 (1960) (under German law, decedent had only the equivalent of a life estate in property situated in the U.S.; the U.S. assets thus were not subject to U.S. estate tax).

CHAPTER 40

THE FOREIGN TAX CREDIT

Internal Revenue Code: § 2014(a), (b)

Regulation: § 20.2014–1

The United States, under § 2031, asserts estate tax liability on the value of all property "wherever situated". Thus, the gross estate includes, for decedents who were either citizens or residents of the United States at the time of death, the total value of all interests in property located in the United States and in other countries as well. Because many other countries also impose estate or inheritance taxes, the possibility of double taxation arises if a United States citizen or resident dies owning property located in another country. Section 2014 provides a foreign tax credit for the estates of U.S. citizens and residents (subject to limitations described below) if the U.S. imposes its estate tax with respect to property situated in a foreign country and that foreign country also imposes an estate tax on part or all of that same property. The foreign tax credit is limited in a manner which permits the offsetting of taxes paid to the foreign country with respect to property situated in that country only to the extent that the property is taxed by the United States. Thus, if a foreign country imposes an estate tax at a higher effective rate than that imposed by the U.S., a credit is to be allowed only to the extent of the effective rate of tax imposed by the U.S. Reg. § 20.2014–1(b).

The allowable credit is subject to two limitations. The first limitation restricts the credit to that amount of the foreign death tax which the value of the property in the gross estate "situated within" the country imposing the tax bears to the value of all property subject to the foreign death tax. § 2014(b)(1); Reg. § 20.2014–2. Under the second limitation, the credit cannot exceed that portion of the gross estate tax (reduced by the credits provided by §§ 2010, 2011 and 2012) which the property in the gross estate subject to the foreign death taxes (reduced to take into account any marital or charitable deductions with respect to that property) bears to the gross estate (reduced by any marital or charitable deductions). § 2014(b)(2); Reg. § 20.2014–3. The maximum credit is the smaller of the two limitations.

The United States has also entered into a few treaties with other countries to prevent double taxation of estates. In general, the treaties seek to prevent double taxation by prescribing specific rules for determining the situs of property and providing that one of the taxing countries (usually the country of domicile or the country of nationality) shall give a credit for estate taxes paid with respect to property situated in the other taxing country. Reg. § 20.2014–4(a) provides that in the case of a death tax convention with a foreign country, the estate is entitled either to the credit allowed under § 2014 or that allowed under the treaty, whichever is more beneficial to the estate. Gift tax conventions have been entered into with only a few countries.

Estate of Schwartz v. Commissioner

83 T.C. 943 (1984).

■ SWIFT, JUDGE: [Decedent was a U.S. citizen who was a resident of Spain at the time of his death. He had established two accounts in Spain with Spanish banks but was not engaged in a trade or business in Spain at the time of his death. The decedent's estate paid Spanish estate tax on the bank deposits and claimed a foreign tax credit on the U.S. estate tax return. The Service denied the foreign tax credit on the ground that the bank deposits were not "situated within" Spain under § 2014(a) and Reg. § 20.2014–1(a)(3).]

* * * Petitioner argues that the bank deposits were located within Spain in every practical and economic sense and that under the pertinent statutory provisions the bank deposits must be treated as located within Spain for Federal estate tax purposes. To the extent the applicable Treasury regulations require an opposite result, petitioner argues that the regulations are unreasonable and invalid. Regardless of where the deposits were located from an economic standpoint, respondent argues that under the controlling statutory and regulatory provisions decedent is deemed to have been a nonresident of Spain and decedent's bank deposits must be treated as if they were located outside of Spain. Respondent therefore concludes that petitioner is not entitled to a Federal estate tax credit for estate taxes paid to Spain with respect to those bank deposits. One court decision supports respondent's interpretation of the applicable law, namely, Borne v. United States, an unreported case (N.D. Ind. 1983, 52 AFTR 2d 83–6444, 83–2 USTC par. 13,536). For the reasons explained below we agree with petitioner.

One is tempted to reach a conclusion herein simply on the basis of the realities of the location of the bank deposits in question—namely, the deposits were made in a SPANISH branch of a SPANISH bank by decedent, a SPANISH resident; and respondent's argument that such property should be treated as located outside Spain could be rejected out-of-hand as nonsensical. However, a more judicious approach requires a detailed analysis of the applicable statutory and regulatory provisions. We will first discuss the relevant statutory provisions, followed by a discussion of the regulations and of the two decisions on which respondent relies.

With respect to estates of decedents who were either United States citizens or United States residents on the date of death, section 2014(a) (with certain limitations and subject to any treaty in effect between the United States and the foreign country[1]) allows a credit against Federal

---

1. There was no death tax treaty in effect between the United States and Spain at any relevant time herein.

estate taxes due for foreign estate, inheritance, legacy or succession taxes that are actually paid to any foreign country with respect to property that is both includible in the gross estate and situated within the foreign country. Section 2014(a) requires a determination, among other things, of whether property is "situated within (the) foreign country." Thus, in this case, we must determine whether the decedent's bank deposits with Spanish banks are to be treated as being located within Spain on the date of decedent's death. It is not enough if the deposits are only to be treated as being located outside of the United States or in some foreign country. Under the statute, they must be treated as having been located within Spain on the date of death.

Subchapter A of chapter 11 of the Internal Revenue Code of 1954, as amended, governs the estates of decedents who were either United States citizens or residents of the United States on the date of death. Subchapter B of chapter 11 of the Internal Revenue Code of 1954, as amended, governs the estates of decedents who were both non-residents of the United States and not citizens of the United States. Decedent herein was not a United States resident, but he was a United States citizen on the date of death, and therefore he is governed by the provisions of Subchapter A.

Thereunder, section 2014(a) addresses the question but provides no specific rules for the determination of the location of property of decedents who were either United States residents or United States citizens. Rather, section 2014(a) simply makes reference to and incorporates the rules applicable to decedents who were neither United States citizens nor United States residents (which rules are found in subchapter B of chapter 11 of the Internal Revenue Code of 1954, as amended—specifically in sections 2104 and 2105), and makes those rules applicable to a decedent who otherwise is governed by section 2014 (because of his status as either a United States citizen or a United States resident on the date of death).

The last sentence of section 2014(a) provides as follows:

> The determination of the country within which property is situated shall be made in accordance with the rules applicable under subchapter B (sec. 2101 and following) in determining whether property is situated within or without the United States.

An appreciation of the precise words used and not used in the above quoted statutory language is important. That language makes specific reference to and incorporates the "rules" of subchapter B, but does not state that the actual residence and citizenship of the particular decedent will be treated any differently than what they actually were on the date of death. In other words, the effect of the last sentence of section 2014(a), combined with the provisions of sections 2104 and 2105 of subchapter B, is that the determination of where property is located on the date of death for the estates of both United States residents or United States citizens, on the one hand, and nonresidents who also are not United States citizens, on the other, is to be based on the same general rules.

Accordingly, in the instant case, whether decedent's bank deposits are treated as having been located within Spain will be governed by the same rules that would be used to determine whether bank deposits would be treated as having been located within the United States under subchapter B. Those rules will be applied to decedent's particular situation herein, taking into account his actual citizenship and residency status on the date of death (namely, U.S. citizenship but Spanish residency).

It is appropriate to apply the applicable rules of subchapter B to decedent's situation in accordance with our understanding of those rules, as explained above (and to do so before proceeding further to explain why we disagree with respondent's argument that section 2014(a), in addition to incorporating the general rules of subchapter B, also requires that decedent's actual residency in Spain be ignored). In order to apply the rules of subchapter B to decedent herein, who is otherwise governed by subchapter A, generally when the words "the United States" appear in the statutory and regulatory provisions the word "Spain" must be substituted.

The first applicable section is 2104(c) which provides in relevant part as follows:

SEC. 2104. PROPERTY WITHIN (SPAIN)

(c) Debt Obligations.—For purposes of this subchapter, debt obligations of,

(1) a (Spanish) person, or

(2) (Spain), a State or any political subdivision thereof, owned and held by a nonresident not a citizen of (Spain) shall be deemed property within (Spain). With respect to estates of decedents dying after December 31, 1969, deposits with a domestic (Spanish) branch of a foreign corporation, if such branch is engaged in the commercial banking business, shall for purposes of this subchapter, be deemed property within (Spain). This subsection shall not apply to a debt obligation to which section 2105(b) applies or to a debt obligation of a domestic (Spanish) corporation if any interest on such obligation, were such interest received by the decedent at the time of his death, would be treated by reason of section 861(a)(1)(B), section 861(a)(1)(G), or section 861(a)(1)(H) as income from sources without (Spain).

The general rule reflected in section 2104(c) is that the location of debt obligations are governed by the location of the obligor, not by the location of the obligee. Therefore, under the general rule, obligations of a (Spanish) person or company are treated as property within (Spain). The statutory language speaks in terms of debt obligations held by a "nonresident not a citizen of (Spain)" only because those statutory provisions (namely, the provisions of section 2104(c)) in their own right only pertain to decedents who are neither citizens nor residents of (Spain). It is obvious to us that when that rule is applied to RESIDENTS of (Spain) (as the last sentence of section 2014(a) requires), the general rule must be the same—that is, the location of the obligor will control, and the location of debt obligations of

(Spanish) persons and (Spanish) companies owed to (Spanish) residents will be considered to be within (Spain).

Any interpretation of the general rule of section 2104 (c) other than that set forth in the prior paragraph, as it applies to United States citizens who are residents of Spain, would be absurd. Debt obligations of Spanish persons held by NONRESIDENTS of Spain would be treated as located WITHIN Spain, but such obligations held by RESIDENTS of Spain would be treated as located OUTSIDE Spain. Any such interpretation would also ignore the fact, previously explained, that the only reason the words "nonresident not a citizen" are used in section 2104 (and the associated sections 2101 through 2108 of subchapter B) is that those provisions in their own right only pertain to non-(Spanish) citizens who also are NOT residents of (Spain), and therefore there was no reason to refer expressly to "RESIDENTS" of (Spain) in those sections.

Based on our analysis of the general rule of section 2104(c), as set forth above, when that rule is applied to a debt obligation of a Spanish obligor which is held by a United States citizen who also is a resident of Spain, the Spanish identity of the obligor requires that the debt obligation be treated as Spanish property. Only if one of the exceptions found in section 2104(c) (2) to the general rule is applicable, or if the provisions of section 2105 are applicable, will the property in question be treated as located without Spain. * * *

[The court found that none of the then existing exceptions to § 2104 (c) (2) was applicable.]

We will now address respondent's specific arguments. As previously mentioned, respondent argues that the cross reference in section 2014(a) to subchapter B requires not only that the principles and rules of sections 2104 and 2105 apply, but also that the decedent's actual residence in Spain be ignored and that the decedent be treated as a nonresident of Spain. Respondent refers to certain language in section 20.2014–1(a)(3), Estate Tax Regs., and to two district court decisions in support of his argument. We acknowledge that the pertinent language in the regulation is ambiguous, and we surmise that that ambiguity may well be responsible for the result reached in at least one of the district court decisions. However, we are not bound by the district court decision, and we are obliged to resolve any ambiguities in the regulations in a manner which is reasonable and consistent with the statutory scheme.

It is a fundamental principle of statutory construction that a common sense, rather than a literal, interpretation of words should be adopted where adoption of the literal interpretation would lead to an absurd result. 1 Mertens, Law of Federal Income Taxation, Sec. 3.02, p. 4 (1981). Furthermore, a "common sense interpretation is the safest rule to follow in the administration of income tax laws. (Citation omitted.)" Keeble v. Commissioner, 2 T.C. 1249, 1252 (1943). It is also well established that where administrative regulations are ambiguous the rules of statutory construction will apply. 1A Sands, Statutes and Statutory Construction, sec. 31.06 (1872).

The ambiguous language in the regulations is found in the fourth sentence of section 20.2014–1(a)(3), Estate Tax Regs. For purposes of understanding that regulation it is not necessary to substitute "Spain" for "the United States." The fourth sentence of the regulation provides as follows:

> Whether or not particular property of a decedent is situated in the foreign country imposing the tax is determined in accordance with the same principles that would be applied in determining whether or not similar property of a non-resident decedent not a citizen of the United States is situated within the United States for Federal estate tax purposes.

* * *

We think the statutory rule is clear, and we emphasize that the statutory language simply states that the "rules" of sections 2104 and 2105 shall be utilized in determining the country in which property is located. The statutory language does not use the additional words found in the regulation thereunder that create the ambiguity (namely, "similar property of A NONRESIDENT DECEDENT not a citizen of the United States.") (Emphasis added.) The statutory language thus avoids and clarifies the ambiguity found in the regulation, and thereby obviates the need to invalidate the regulation.

* * *

Respondent's reliance on Borne v. United States, an unreported case (N.D. Ind. 1983, 52 AFTR 2d 83–6444, 83–2 USTC par. 13,536), is on point but is unpersuasive. That opinion simply adopts respondent's argument without any analytical explanation. In fact, the ambiguous language contained in the regulation is referred to as if it were a part of the statutory language of section 2014. Under our interpretation of the statute, due to the decedent's residence in Canada in that case, the bank accounts involved in Borne should have been treated as being located in Canada.

* * *

For the reasons set forth above, we find that the bank deposits which decedent owned in branches in Spain of Spanish banks were located within Spain for purposes of the Federal estate tax credit.

Decision will be entered for petitioner.

Reviewed by the Court.

■ DAWSON, SIMPSON, STERRETT, CHABOT, PARKER, KORNER, SHIELDS, HAMBLEN, COHEN, CLAPP, and JACOBS, JJ., agree with FAY and WILBUR, JJ., concur in the result. WHITAKER and GERBER, JJ., did not participate in the determination of this case.

■ NIMS, J., concurring: The majority by implication invalidates section 20.2014–1(a)(3), Estate Tax Regs., insofar as it applies to the facts of this case. I would do so expressly. The regulation lays down the blanket rule that the situs of a nonresident U.S. citizen's property is to be determined by the obverse of "similar property of a non-resident decedent not a citizen of the United States." But the situs of some property, including bank deposits in a U.S. bank, is determined differently in the case of a RESI-DENT decedent not a citizen of the United States. Since the regulation fails to take this distinction into account, it is invalid and we should clearly say so.

■ GOFFE and WRIGHT, JJ., agree with this concurring opinion.

ILLUSTRATIVE MATERIAL

A.   CREDITABLE TAXES

Reg. § 20.2014–1(a)(1) provides that the foreign tax credit is allowable only for foreign estate, inheritance, legacy or succession taxes. Thus, it was held that Canadian income taxes imposed on appreciated property transferred at death were not creditable under § 2014. Estate of Ballard v. Commissioner, 85 T.C. 300 (1985). Since Canada has no estate tax, this result meant that estates of U.S. citizens or residents could claim only a deduction under § 2053(a)(3) for the Canadian income taxes.

The Canadian government, after many years of effort, succeeded in changing these results in the 1995 Protocol to the U.S.–Canada Income Tax Treaty. Under Article 19 of the Protocol (Article XIXB, paragraph 6 of the Treaty as amended by the Protocol), the Canadian income tax imposed at death may be credited against the U.S. estate tax of a U.S. citizen or resident, subject to the limitations generally imposed on the amount of the allowable credit.

Unless changed by treaty, however, the general rule requiring that the foreign tax be a form of "transfer" tax is applicable.

B.   GOVERNMENT LEVEL AT WHICH TAX IS IMPOSED

Reg. § 20.2014–1(a)(1) provides that qualifying transfer taxes imposed by a political subdivision of a foreign country are creditable against U.S. estate tax. Typically, U.S. estate and gift tax treaties apply only to taxes imposed at the national level. But that does not preclude crediting of subnational taxes if the statutory tests for credibility are met. See Borne v. United States, 577 F.Supp. 115 (N.D. Ind. 1983) (treaty did not apply to Canadian provincial taxes; however, the requirements of § 2014 were met).

C.   LIMITATIONS ON THE ALLOWABLE CREDIT

As noted above, the U.S. allows a foreign tax credit only up to the U.S. tax on the foreign property. Foreign taxes in excess of the limit are not creditable. The U.S. imposes the limitation because it is unwilling to permit its tax on U.S. property of the decedent to be reduced by foreign taxes on foreign property.

The operation of the two limitations imposed by § 2014(b) is illustrated by the following example.

D was a U.S. citizen and resident at date of death. D's taxable estate consists of $10 million in U.S. property and $1 million of property situated in

Country X. Country X imposed an estate tax of $770,000 on D's property in Country X.

The computation of the first limitation is as follows:

$$\frac{1,000,000}{1,000,000} \times 770,000 = 770,000$$

The second limitation is as follows:

$$\frac{1,000,000}{11,000,000} \times 770,000 = 70,000$$

Thus, only $70,000 of the foreign death tax would be creditable by D's estate under § 2014.

The above example assumed that D's estate did not include any marital or charitable contribution deductions. If such items were included, the numerator and/or the denominator must be adjusted in the second limitation to the extent the amounts payable are attributable to U.S. and/or foreign country property.

The value of the decedent's foreign property is determined under the foreign country's rules and then converted to U.S. dollars. Reg. § 20.2014–2(a). Foreign estate taxes are converted to U.S. dollars using the exchange rate in effect on the date(s) of payment(s) of the taxes. Rev. Rul. 75–439, 1975–2 C.B. 359.

D. GIFT TAX

The U.S. does not allow a foreign credit against its gift tax for foreign gift taxes (except in cases covered by § 2501(a)(3), p. 829). The result may be changed by treaty. Special rules are applicable for gifts made to a spouse who is not a U.S. citizen. See p. 846.

E. GENERATION–SKIPPING TAX

The GST is applicable to transfers of property situated outside the U.S. and to transfers to non-U.S. persons by a U.S. citizen or resident. § 2652(a).

CHAPTER 41

TRANSFER TO A NON-CITIZEN SPOUSE

Internal Revenue Code: §§ 2056(a); 2056A(a),(b)(1)–(3),(10)–(12); 2523(i).

Regulations: §§ 20.2056A–2(b),(d); –5; –6(a),(b); –8

As discussed in Chapter 32, an unlimited marital deduction is available for property transferred to the transferor's spouse. The property remaining at the surviving spouse's death is then subject to transfer tax. But what if the surviving spouse is not a U.S. citizen and returns to live in her home country, taking all her inherited property with her? If she died, owning no U.S. situs property, there will be no U.S. transfer tax on the wealth accumulated by the marital unit. In such circumstances, since one premise of the unlimited marital deduction is taxation in the estate of the surviving spouse, it is arguable that the marital deduction should not be available to the estate of the first decedent spouse. This argument in turn opens the door to the larger issue of whether a U.S. citizen who expatriates should pay a transfer tax at the time of expatriation on wealth accumulated while a U.S. citizen or resident. See p. 825.

House Budget Committee Report on the Omnibus Reconciliation Act of 1989[1]

H.R. Rep. No. 101–247, 101st Cong., 1st Sess. 1429–1433 (1989).

[Pre–1989 Law]

In general

A deduction generally is allowed for Federal estate and gift tax purposes for the value of property passing to a spouse. Except in specified situations, no deduction is allowed if the interest passing to the spouse is terminable (i.e., the property cannot pass to another person on termination of the spouse's interest) (secs. 2056(b), 2523(b)).

Annual exclusion and marital deduction for property passing to noncitizen spouse

The marital deduction is generally disallowed for the value of property passing to a noncitizen spouse. The first $100,000 per year of gifts from a U.S. citizen or resident to a noncitizen spouse, however, is not subject to

---

1. The House Ways and Means Committee prepared the portions of the Report dealing with revenue measures. Text material in brackets reflects changes made by the Conference Committee on the 1989 Act. See H.R. Conf. Rep. No. 101–386, 101st Cong., 1st Sess. 668–670 (1989).

gift tax. In addition, property passing at death to a noncitizen spouse may qualify for the marital deduction so long as it satisfies the requirements of section 2056(b) and passes in a qualified domestic trust (QDT). Property passing to the spouse outside the probate estate is treated as passing in a QDT if it is transferred to such trust before the estate tax return is filed.

Definition of qualified domestic trust (QDT)

To be a QDT, a trust must meet four conditions. First, the trust instrument must require that all trustees be U.S. citizens or domestic corporations. Second, the surviving spouse must be entitled to all the income from the property in the trust, payable annually or at more frequent intervals. Third, the trust must meet the requirements of Treasury regulations prescribed to ensure collection of the estate tax imposed upon the trust. Finally, the executor must elect to treat the trust as a QDT.

Estate Tax on QDT

An estate tax is imposed upon distributions from a QDT made prior to the surviving spouse's death and upon the value of property remaining in a QDT upon that spouse's death. The tax, however, is not imposed on distributions of income, as defined under local law. The tax is also imposed upon the trust property if a person other than a U.S. citizen or domestic corporation becomes a trustee of the trust or if the trust ceases to meet the requirements of Treasury regulations prescribed to ensure collection of the estate tax.

The amount of the estate tax is the additional estate tax which would have been imposed had the property subject to the tax been included in the decedent's spouse's estate. If the estate tax for the decedent spouse's estate has not been finally determined, a tentative tax is imposed using the highest estate tax rate in effect as of the date of the decedent's death. When the decedent spouse's estate tax liability is finally determined, the excess of the tentative tax over the additional estate tax that would have been imposed had the property been included in the decedent's taxable estate is allowed as a credit or refund.

Credit for tax previously paid

If the marital deduction is denied solely because the spouse is a noncitizen at the time of the decedent's death, the estate of the surviving spouse who is a U.S. citizen or resident at death generally is entitled to a credit with respect to estate tax paid on property passing from the decedent. This credit is determined without regard to when the decedent spouse died. The credit is also allowed for the estate tax imposed against the QDT. For purposes of determining the amount of the credit, the net value of property treated as passing from the decedent's estate to the surviving spouse is reduced by the amount for which a marital deduction was allowed.

Explanations of Provisions

Gift tax on amounts passing to noncitizen spouse

The bill clarifies that the $100,000 annual exclusion for transfers by gift to a noncitizen spouse is allowed only for transfers that would qualify for the marital deduction if the donee were a U.S. citizen. For example, a gift in trust does not qualify for the $100,000 annual exclusion unless it is within one of the exceptions to the terminable interest rule.

The bill also provides that a nonresident noncitizen is entitled to a marital deduction or annual exclusion for gift tax purposes in the same circumstances as a U.S. citizen or resident. Thus, gifts from a nonresident noncitizen to a U.S. citizen spouse qualify for the marital deduction. In addition, each year the first $100,000 in gifts from a nonresident noncitizen to a noncitizen spouse is not taxed, so long as the gifts would qualify for the marital deduction if the donee were a U.S. citizen. The deduction and annual exclusion apply only if the property passing to the spouse is subject to U.S. gift tax.

Marital deduction for bequests to noncitizen spouse

Under [§ 2056A(b)(12)], the estate tax marital deduction is allowed for property passing to a noncitizen spouse if the spouse becomes a U.S. citizen before the estate tax return is filed, so long as the spouse was a U.S. resident at the date of the decedent's death and at all times before becoming a U.S. citizen. In addition, all property, probate and nonprobate, passing to a noncitizen spouse qualifies for the marital deduction if the property is transferred or irrevocably assigned to a QDT before the estate tax return is filed. * * *. The bill also confirms that property passing from a nonresident noncitizen to a noncitizen spouse qualifies for the estate tax marital deduction if it passes in a qualified domestic trust.

Definition of QDT

The bill retains the [pre–1989]–law requirement that property passing to a noncitizen spouse satisfy requirements generally applicable to the marital deduction such as section 2056(b) in order to qualify for the marital deduction. The bill modifies the independent requirements a trust must meet in order to qualify as a QDT. Under [§ 2056A(a)(1)(A)], only one trustee is required to be a U.S. citizen or domestic corporation, so long as no distribution may be made from the trust without the approval of that trustee. In addition, the bill eliminates the independent requirement that the surviving spouse have an income interest in a QDT.[2]

* * *

Estate tax on QDT

When imposed

Under [§ 2056A(b)(1)], lifetime distributions from a QDT and the property remaining in the trust on the surviving spouse's death remain

---

2. To qualify under the terminable interest rule, however, the spouse might be required to have an income interest. See I.R.C. sec. 2056 (b) (5), (7).

subject to an estate tax based on the decedent's rates and unified credit. The tax is imposed if the trust fails to meet the requirements regarding citizenship of trustees or the regulatory requirements designed to ensure collection. The tax ceases to be imposed if the surviving spouse subsequently becomes a U.S. citizen so long as either (1) the spouse was a U.S. resident at the date of the decedent's death and at all times thereafter, or (2) the spouse elects to treat any distributions upon which tax was imposed as a taxable gift made by (and any unified credit allowed against such a distribution as unified credit allowed to) the spouse for purposes of determining future estate and gift tax liability with respect to the spouse.

Amount subject to tax

Under [§ 2056A(b)(3)(A)], income distributions to the surviving spouse continue to be exempt from the estate tax on distributions. The Secretary of the Treasury is granted regulatory authority to modify the definition of income for purposes of determining the amount subject to the tax. The committee intends that such regulations define income so as to prevent avoidance of the estate tax. Thus, the characterization of income and corpus contained in the governing instrument would not control for purposes of the estate tax. For example, capital gain generally would not be treated as income for purposes of the estate tax on QDT's, regardless of the characterization contained in the trust instrument.

The committee understands that authority distinguishing income and corpus under section 643(b) would not necessarily be determinative for purposes of the estate tax. The committee also understands that these regulations may clarify the characterization of items that are presently unclear. The committee expects, for example, that the Secretary of the Treasury will provide rules for determining when payments under an annuity would be treated as income for purposes of the estate tax on distributions. The committee expects that payments under an annuity would be treated as corpus to the extent of the value of the annuity when acquired by the QDT.

[Under § 2056A(b)(3)(B), distributions from a QDT on account of hardship are exempt from tax.]

Finally, [§ 2056A(b)(11)] provides that payment of the estate tax on distributions is itself a distribution subject to the tax.

Availability of estate tax benefits

[Section 2056A(b)(10)(A)] allows charitable and marital deductions against the deathtime tax on QDT's so long as that property is includable in the surviving spouse's gross estate (or would have been includable had the surviving spouse been a U.S. citizen) and the requirements of those deductions are otherwise met. [Section 2056A(b)(10)] also allows the benefits of alternate valuation, special use valuation, capital gains treatment of redemptions of stock to pay estate tax, and extension of time to pay estate

with respect to the death time tax on QDTs if such benefits would be allowed to the surviving spouse's estate.

* * *

Recipient's basis in distributed property

Property distributed during the surviving spouse's life from a QDT receives a carryover basis. The basis of property is increased (but not above fair market value) by the amount of the estate tax allocable to the appreciation in the value of the property occurring after the decedent's death.[3]

* * *

Credit for previous estate tax

The credit for estate tax previously paid by the decedent spouse is allowed to a surviving spouse who is a nonresident noncitizen at the time of death. In determining the amount of the credit for estate tax imposed against a QDT, the value of property treated as having passed to the surviving spouse is not reduced by the amount that qualified for the marital deduction.

* * *

ILLUSTRATIVE MATERIAL

A.   QDOT RULES

1.   Security for Deferred Tax

Reg. § 20.2056A–2(d)(1)(i) provides that if more than $2 million in assets passes to the QDOT (in practice the acronym "QDOT" is used rather than "QDT" as in the foregoing excerpt), the trust instrument must require that either (a) a U.S. bank be at least one of the trustees or (b) the U.S. trustee must furnish a bond or security equal to 65% of the fair market value of the trust assets. Values are determined by reference to the date of the decedent's death.

If the QDOT assets are less than $2 million, the security requirements can be satisfied in one of two ways. First, the trust instrument must require that no more than 35% of the value of the QDOT assets, determined annually, can consist of foreign real estate. Alternatively, the security requirement can be met by satisfying one of the three tests in Reg. § 20.2056A–2(d)(1)(i), above. The assets of all QDOTs for the benefit of the surviving spouse must be aggregated in determining whether this $2 million threshold is met. If the QDOT owns stock or a partnership interest in which there are 15 or fewer shareholders or partners, the trust is treated as owning its pro rata share of the assets of the entity for purposes of establishing whether the $2 million threshold is met. The attribution rules of § 267(b) apply for purposes of

---

3. [ED.: See Reg.§ 1.1015–5(c)(5), Example 2.]

determining whether the 15 shareholder or partner requirement is satisfied. Reg. § 20.2056A–2(d)(1)(ii).

An anti-abuse rule is applicable. Even if one of the above tests is satisfied, the QDOT will be disqualified if it utilizes any device or arrangement a principal purpose of which is to avoid the collection of the deferred estate tax. Reg. § 20.2056A–2(d)(1)(v).

Annual reporting requirements are imposed on the U.S. trustee to help insure compliance with the above rules. Reg. § 20.2056A–2(d)(3).

2.   Computation of Deferred Tax

The following example, based on Reg. § 20.2056A–6(d), Example 1, illustrates the computation of the deferred estate tax under § 2056(d)(2) where a QDOT has been employed (as in the Regulations example, the rates and unified credit amount were those in effect in the 1995–1997 period). In 1995 the gross estate of the first decedent spouse (H) was $1,200,000. A bequest of $700,000 was made to a QDOT. The unified transfer tax credit then eliminates tax on the taxable estate of $500,000.

The surviving spouse died two years later at a time when the QDOT assets were worth $700,000. A gross tax was first computed on $1,200,000, the sum of the value of the QDOT assets at H's death ($700,000) and W's taxable estate ($500,000). A gross tax of $427,800 was computed with respect to the $1,200,000. A unified credit of $192,800 would have been allowed, leaving a net estate tax of $235,000. Under § 2056A(b)(2)(ii), there was then subtracted the tax that would have been imposed on W's actual taxable estate, i.e., zero. Hence H's deferred estate tax liability was $235,000.

B.   HARDSHIP EXEMPTION

Reg. § 20.2056A–5(c)(1) provides that a distribution from a QDOT to the surviving spouse qualifies for the hardship exemption only if it is made "in response to an immediate and substantial financial need relating to the spouse's health, maintenance, education, or support" (or that of any person whom the spouse is legally obligated to support). If the surviving spouse has other resources, e.g., publicly traded stock, from which the amount distributed could have been obtained, the hardship exemption is not available. Thus, if the surviving spouse owns $100,000 of publicly traded stock, a distribution of $50,000 would not qualify for the exemption. The Regulations do not specify the result had the QDOT made a $150,000 distribution.

C.   JOINTLY OWNED PROPERTY

Section 2056(d)(1)(B) extends the denial of the marital deduction for transfers to noncitizen spouses to jointly owned property that otherwise would be covered by § 2040(b), discussed at p. 347. Thus, if the surviving spouse is not a U.S. citizen, the rule that only one-half the value of jointly owned property is included in the estate of the first decedent spouse is not applicable. Instead, the full value of the jointly owned property is taxed in that spouse's estate (unless the surviving spouse can demonstrate that she provided part of the funds to acquire the property). For example, if H and W own jointly held property worth $100,000 at H's death, § 2040(b) would include only $50,000 in H's estate if W is a U.S. citizen; under § 2056(d)(1)(B), the full $100,000 is taxed in H's estate, if W is not a U.S. citizen. The noncitizen spouse can avoid this result by remaining a resident and becoming a citizen as specified in § 2056(d)(4). See Reg. § 20.2056A–1(b).

D.   TAX TREATIES

The impact of the enactment of the rules denying the marital deduction for transfers to non-citizen spouses on U.S. estate and gift tax treaties is discussed at p. 859.

CHAPTER 42

TRANSFERS BY NON-RESIDENT ALIENS

Internal Revenue Code: §§ 2101–2103; 2106

Regulations: §§ 21.2102–1(b)

ILLUSTRATIVE MATERIAL

A. ESTATE TAX

1. General

The U.S. imposes its estate tax on transfers of property by a nonresident alien (NRA) to the extent the property is situated within the U.S. under the situs rules discussed at p. 832. §§ 2101(a), 2106. Determination of the tax due begins, as in the case of a U.S. citizen or resident, with the valuation of the decedent's gross estate under §§ 2031 and following. § 2103.

From the gross estate situated within the U.S. is deducted the portion of § 2053 and § 2054 expenses that is allocable to the U.S. § 2106(a)(1). A charitable contribution deduction also is allowed for a transfer to a qualified domestic charitable organization. § 2106(a)(2).

A marital deduction is allowed in full under § 2106(a)(3) for the value of the U.S. property that passes to a surviving spouse if the requirements of § 2056 are met. But, as discussed at p. 846, special limitations are imposed if the surviving spouse is not a U.S. citizen.

The unified transfer tax rates under § 2001 are applied to the sum of the U.S. taxable estate as so determined plus adjusted taxable gifts of the decedent. The tentative tax is then computed in the same manner as for a U.S. decedent's estate. § 2101(b).

Three credits are allowed: the credit for state death taxes under § 2011 (which terminated after 2004 and was replaced by a deduction); the credit for gift taxes paid on pre–1977 gifts under § 2012; and the credit for estate taxes paid on prior transfers under § 2013. § 2102(a).

Finally, the NRA's estate is allowed a unified transfer tax credit of $13,000 (the equivalent of a $60,000 exemption).

As discussed at p. 856, tax treaties may modify the above rules.

2. Apportionment Issues

If the deceased NRA had property situated both within and without the U.S., the deductions allowable under §§ 2053 and 2054 are subject to apportionment. The allowable deductions are determined by a formula, the numerator of which is the U.S. gross estate and the denominator of which is the worldwide gross estate. It is immaterial whether the expenses involved were incurred or expended in the U.S. or in some other country. Reg. § 20.2106–2(a)(2).

If a tax treaty requires that the U.S. grant a full unified transfer tax credit, then the allowable credit is determined by multiplying the applicable credit amount under § 2010 by a fraction, the numerator of which is the U.S. gross estate and the denominator of which is the NRA's worldwide gross estate. § 2102(b)(3)(A).

Similar apportionment computations are required to determine the allowable state death tax credit. Reg. § 21.2102–1(b). After 2004, state death taxes are deductible and are subject to apportionment. § 2106(a)(4).

In making the above computations, foreign property values and expenditures first must be converted to U.S. dollars.

B.   GIFT TAX

The U.S. imposes its gift tax on transfers by an NRA if the gifted property is U.S. real estate or tangible personal property physically located in the U.S. Transfers of intangible personal property by an NRA therefore are not subject to U.S. gift tax regardless of where "located." § 2501(a)(2); Reg. § 25.2511–3(a),(b) (unless the special rule of § 2501(a)(3) with respect to expatriates is applicable).

Gifts which are subject to U.S. gift tax are taxed at the unified tax rates specified in § 2001. The unified transfer tax credit is not allowable, however. § 2505(a). The inflation-adjusted annual exclusion is available. Gifts by an NRA to her spouse may qualify for the marital deduction, but special limitations are imposed if the spouse is not a U.S. citizen. See p. 846. A charitable contribution deduction is allowed for gifts to a qualified U.S. charitable organization if the gifts are to be used in the U.S. § 2522(b).

The exclusion for gifts of intangible property in § 2501(a)(2) provides an important tax planning opportunity for an NRA who is planning to become a U.S. resident or citizen. The NRA can make unlimited gifts of intangible property, even if located in the U.S., to or for the benefit of family members just prior to entering the U.S. If properly structured, the transferred property will not be subject to U.S. estate tax either. However, the exclusion for gifts of intangibles by an NRA is not available if the NRA had expatriated.within the preceding 10 years and § 877(b) is applicable. § 2501(a)(3). Moreover, § 6039F requires that a U.S. donee or legatee report any gifts or bequests received in a taxable year in excess of the inflation-adjusted annual exclusion if the amount is received from a person who is not a "U.S. person." Failure to report such a gift or bequest can result in significant penalties.

C.   GENERATION–SKIPPING TAX

Section 2663(2) requires that Regulations be issued applying the GST to NRA transferors. Reg. § 26.2663–2 fulfills the statutory mandate.

In the case of property situated in the U.S., the GST applies fully to a transfer at death and, to the extent the transfer is subject to gift tax, to lifetime transfers. That is, a transfer by an NRA is subject to the GST only if and to the extent that the transfer is subject to U.S. estate or gift tax. Reg. § 26.2663–2(b)(1),(2). The determination of the situs of the transferred property is made at the time of the initial transfer to a skip person or to a trust that is not a skip person. Reg. § 26.2663–2(b). For example if an NRA transfers U.S. real property to GC, who is also an NRA, there is a direct skip transfer which is subject to U.S. gift tax and, therefore, the GST applies. Reg. § 26.2663–2(d), Example 1.

In general, the GST rules and planning approaches discussed in Chapter 33 are applicable also to transfers by NRAs.

CHAPTER 43

Wealth Transfer Tax Treaties

The U.S. has entered into relatively few bilateral tax treaties covering wealth transfer taxes. Nonetheless, it is possible for taxpayers to face international double taxation in this area as well as in income taxation. That result can occur, for example, when a decedent ("D") dies owning property in both the U.S. and another country and both countries treat D as a domiciliary under their own domestic rules. Similarly, the two countries may each tax the same property because of differing situs rules.

Wealth transfer tax treaties respond to these problems and seek to eliminate double taxation by, in general, establishing a single domicile, agreeing on which country may tax the transfers of particular types of property, and granting a credit for foreign taxes in some situations. As discussed at p. 838, the U.S. unilaterally grants a foreign tax credit to estates subject to worldwide taxation. For these taxpayers, the benefit of a treaty is to ensure that the credit mechanism functions as intended. A change in domiciliary or situs rules may benefit other taxpayers. In no event, however, can a tax treaty make a taxpayer worse off than under applicable Code rules. U.S. Model Estate, Gift and Generation–Skipping Tax Convention of 20 November 1980, Article 1. (All subsequent Article references are to the Model Treaty unless otherwise noted.)

In addition, U.S. treaties typically contain non-discrimination, exchange of information, and mutual agreement procedures. Arts. 10–12.

Relatively few U.S. treaties cover gift and generation-skipping taxes.

ILLUSTRATIVE MATERIAL

A. SAVINGS CLAUSE

The U.S. includes in all its treaties a "savings clause" under which it reserves the right to tax its citizens and domiciliaries as if the treaty had never come into effect. Art 1.3. Despite this general rule, specified Articles such as those on Deductions and Exemption (Art. 8), Relief From Double Taxation (Art. 9), Non–Discrimination (Art. 10) and Mutual Agreement Procedure (Art. 11), are not subject to the override in Art. 1.3. Art. 1.4. These exceptions to the general savings clause rule may be important in particular situations. For example, U.S. foreign tax credit rules might change and a U.S. taxpayer might then be able to claim the more favorable credit provided in Art. 9 of the Treaty. Perhaps more importantly, the tax treaty gives a tax credit for foreign gift taxes, which, as discussed at p. 845, typically is not available under the Code.

Generally, however, U.S. taxpayers derive the greatest benefit from treaty harmonization of domicile and situs rules.

B.   DOMICILE

Under Art. 4.1, domicile initially is determined under the domestic law of each country. Thus, an individual is a domiciliary of the U.S. if she is a "resident" of the U.S. Suppose, however, that D owns property in both treaty countries and the other country also treats her as a domiciliary under its domestic rules. Art. 4.2 establishes a "tie-breaker" procedure in such a case to establish domicile in one country or the other *for purposes of that treaty*, i.e., the tie-breaker is relevant only if resolution of the domicile issue is necessary to apply some provision in the treaty.

The tie-breaker looks to such factors as where D had a permanent home available; in which country were D's personal and economic relations closer ("center of vital interests"); in which country D has an "habitual abode;" and, finally, of which country was D a citizen. The tie-breaker rules give less certainty than might be thought since several of the terms employed have no content under U.S. tax law. Art. 4.3 provides an overarching tie breaker. If D had been a citizen of, e.g., the U.S. and during life was domiciled in both countries, but was domiciled in the other country for less than seven of the ten years preceding death, D is treated as a U.S. domiciliary regardless of the general tie-breaker rules.

C.   ESTABLISHING PRIORITIES OF TAXATION

U.S. bilateral treaties following the Model Treaty do not employ situs rules as a mechanism for establishing each treaty partner's right to levy tax.[1] Instead, treaty provisions establish which of the two countries has the prior right of taxation or the exclusive right of taxation with respect to specified types of property.

1.   *Real Property*

Suppose D, a U.S. citizen, dies owning real estate in a treaty partner country (referred to as "Country F"). Under Art. 5, Country F is given the first right of taxation. The U.S. also can impose its wealth transfer tax but it must provide a credit for the Country F tax. Art. 5.1, 9.

2.   *Business Property*

A transfer by D of assets located in Country F which form part of the business property of a "permanent establishment" of D's in Country F may be taxed in Country F. Art. 6.1. The term "permanent establishment" is defined in Art. 6.2 as a fixed place of business through which the business of an enterprise is carried on. Examples of permanent establishments include an office, warehouse, or workshop. Art. 6.3. Similar rules apply to a "fixed base" used for a service business. Art. 6.3. "Fixed base" is not defined.

While Country F is given priority of taxation, the U.S. also may tax the Country F business property and give the taxpayer a credit for the Country F taxes.

---

1.   In some older U.S. treaties, situs rules were employed. See e.g., U.S.–France Treaty Art. 3(2).

3. Other Property

All other types of property are subject to tax *only* in the country of domicile. Art. 7.1. This provision thus changes the U.S. situs rules for stock in a U.S. corporation held by a domiciliary in Country F, see p. 832.

Suppose the U.S. treats an interest in a partnership as personal property even if the partnership's only asset is real estate. Country F, however, treats the interest as real property. Under Art. 7.2, if D is a domiciliary of the U.S., the nature of the interest is determined by the law of Country F. Thus, Art. 6 would apply to the transfer, giving Country F prior taxing right. Similar rules apply to interests in trusts.

4. Deductions and Exemptions

Art. 8.1 of the Treaty provides that debt deductible according to the law of the treaty country entitled to tax shall be deducted pursuant to the ratio of D's property that may be taxed by that country to D's worldwide property. The U.S. views this provision as being coextensive with §§ 2053 and 2054 and thus applies that law in cases involving deductions claimed for the debts of D. See p. 491.

Art. 8.3 provides a deduction for transfers of property to qualified charitable organizations located in the other country. Compare the Code treatment at p. 536. By virtue of Art. 1.3, p. 856, this provision is relevant only in the older treaties in which the U.S. taxes on a situs basis.

Although Arts. 8.4 and 8.5 set forth rules for a U.S. marital deduction and a unified transfer tax credit, subsequent changes in the U.S. statutory rules have rendered the treaty provisions obsolete.

D.   RELIEF FROM DOUBLE TAXATION

The treaty partners accept reciprocal obligations to mitigate or eliminate international double taxation by providing a foreign tax credit in situations in which one country has a prior but not exclusive right of taxation (real property and business property). As in U.S. domestic law, Art. 9.6 limits the amount of the allowable foreign tax credit that a country must give to the part of the tax on the property in respect of which the credit is allowable. This allocation prevents the tax imposed by country F from offsetting the U.S. tax on property which the U.S. has the prior or exclusive right to taxation. Suppose that D, a U.S. citizen but a Country F domiciliary, transfers real estate located in the U.S. and business assets which are not part of a U.S. permanent establishment. The U.S. will tax all of D's worldwide assets but will give a credit only for the Country F taxes on the other business property; Country F in turn is required to give a credit for U.S. taxes attributable to the U.S. real estate.

If the credit allowable under a U.S. tax treaty is more favorable than the Code credit, a taxpayer may elect to apply the treaty credit. Reg. § 20.2014–4(a)(1).

E.   NON–DISCRIMINATION

U.S. tax treaties contain a non-discrimination article such as Art. 10. Under this provision citizens of one of the treaty countries "shall not be subjected in the other [country] to any taxation or any requirement connected therewith which is other or more burdensome than the taxation and connected requirements to which citizens of that other [country] in the same circumstances are or may be subjected." Art. 10.1. Contrary to the normal rule, the nondiscrimination article applies to state and local taxes. Art. 10.4.

The content of the non-discrimination article is less than clear. Thus, it can be argued that D who is a country F citizen and has property situated in the U.S. can never be in "the same circumstances" as a U.S. citizen owning identical property. Among other things, the U.S. citizen is subject to worldwide taxation and the Country F citizen is not. See Rev. Rul. 74–239, 1974–1 C.B. 372 (dual-status Canadian citizen not in similar circumstance because his worldwide income was not subject to U.S. tax); Watson v. Hoey, 59 F. Supp. 197 (S.D.N.Y. 1943) (estate of Irish decedent was not entitled to same exemption as resident and nonresident U.S. citizens; "by and large", U.S. rule did not discriminate unfairly). Is the U.S. citizen to whom comparison is being made a generic example or a hypothetical construct with the same specified business or property attributes as the foreign citizen—in which case the "comparison" is to the foreign citizen himself? (Art. 10.1 of the Model Treaty does state that a nonresident U.S. citizen is not in the same circumstances, thus limiting the comparison to a U.S. resident citizen.) Moreover, the "circumstances" to which one is to look are unclear. Are we to look at tax circumstances only? Or should differences occasioned by non-tax regulatory requirements or restrictions on ownership of particular types of property be considered? Despite these difficulties, the non-discrimination principle is deeply rooted in U.S. treaty policy.

Does § 2056A, denying a marital deduction for transfers to a surviving spouse who is not a U.S. citizen (see p. 846) violate a non-discrimination article such as Art. 10.1? As a technical matter it would appear not although an identical estate transferred to a U.S. citizen surviving spouse gets a full marital deduction. Technically, § 2056A applies to all *transferors,* whether they are U.S. citizens or non-resident aliens. Thus, the fact that the U.S. imposes an estate tax rather than an inheritance tax appears to preclude a discrimination claim.

F.   STATUS OF TREATIES AND TREATY OVERRIDES

Article VI, § 2 of the United States Constitution provides that international treaties and domestic legislation are of equal force. Thus, if a treaty provision and a Code provision are in conflict, the later in time prevails. In the international context, the unfortunate result of this approach is that Congress can override legislatively a prior conflicting treaty provision. While that procedure is constitutional, it also is a violation of international law. Fortunately, Congress has chosen to take this action only on a few occasions.

Given that treaties represent sovereign to sovereign obligations, courts are reluctant to find that treaty obligations have been abrogated by subsequent legislation. Thus, the courts require that there be a clear indication in the legislative history that Congress intended to override prior conflicting treaty provisions. Cook v. United States, 288 U.S. 102 (1933). See also Rev. Rul. 80–223, 1980–2 C.B. 217.

Apparently out of concern that § 2056A, discussed at p. 846, might conflict with some treaties, § 7815(d)(4) of the 1989 Act provided that § 2056A is inapplicable in the case of a transfer by a nonresident alien who was a treaty partner resident to the extent that § 2056A is inconsistent with the treaty.

*

APPENDIX A

	Table B					Section 3	

Annuity, Income, and Remainder Interests For a Term Certain

| | 9.8% | Interest Rates | | | 10.0% | | |
Years	Annuity	Income Interest	Remainder	Years	Annuity	Income Interest	Remainder
1	0.9107	.089253	.910747	1	0.9091	.090909	.909091
2	1.7402	.170540	.829460	2	1.7355	.173554	.826446
3	2.4956	.244572	.755428	3	2.4869	.248685	.751315
4	3.1836	.311997	.688003	4	3.1699	.316987	.683013
5	3.8102	.373403	.626597	5	3.7908	.379079	.620921
6	4.3809	.429329	.570671	6	4.3553	.435526	.564474
7	4.9006	.480263	.519737	7	4.8684	.486842	.513158
8	5.3740	.526651	.473349	8	5.3349	.533493	.466507
9	5.8051	.568899	.431101	9	5.7590	.575902	.424098
10	6.1977	.607376	.392624	10	6.1446	.614457	.385543
11	6.5553	.642419	.357581	11	6.4951	.649506	.350494
12	6.8810	.674334	.325666	12	6.8137	.681369	.318631
13	7.1776	.703401	.296599	13	7.1034	.710336	.289664
14	7.4477	.729873	.270127	14	7.3667	.736669	.263331
15	7.6937	.753983	.246017	15	7.6061	.760608	.239392
16	7.9178	.775941	.224059	16	7.8237	.782371	.217629
17	8.1218	.795939	.204061	17	8.0216	.802155	.197845
18	8.3077	.814152	.185848	18	8.2014	.820141	.179859
19	8.4769	.830740	.169260	19	8.3649	.836492	.163508
20	8.6311	.845847	.154153	20	8.5136	.851356	.148644
21	8.7715	.859605	.140395	21	8.6487	.864869	.135131
22	8.8993	.872136	.127864	22	8.7715	.877154	.122846
23	9.0158	.883548	.116452	23	8.8832	.888322	.111678
24	9.1219	.893942	.106058	24	8.9847	.898474	.101526
25	9.2184	.903408	.096592	25	9.0770	.907704	.092296
26	9.3064	.912029	.087971	26	9.1609	.916095	.083905
27	9.3865	.919881	.080119	27	9.2372	.923722	.076278
28	9.4595	.927032	.072968	28	9.3066	.930657	.069343
29	9.5260	.933544	.066456	29	9.3696	.936961	.063039
30	9.5865	.939476	.060524	30	9.4269	.942691	.057309
31	9.6416	.944878	.055122	31	9.4790	.947901	.052099
32	9.6918	.949798	.050202	32	9.5264	.952638	.047362
33	9.7375	.954278	.045722	33	9.5694	.956943	.043057
34	9.7792	.958359	.041641	34	9.6086	.960857	.039143
35	9.8171	.962076	.037924	35	9.6442	.964416	.035584
36	9.8516	.965461	.034539	36	9.6765	.967651	.032349
37	9.8831	.968543	.031457	37	9.7059	.970592	.029408
38	9.9117	.971351	.028649	38	9.7327	.973265	.026735
39	9.9378	.973908	.026092	39	9.7570	.975696	.024304
40	9.9616	.976237	.023763	40	9.7791	.977905	.022095
41	9.9832	.978358	.021642	41	9.7991	.979914	.020086
42	10.0030	.980289	.019711	42	9.8174	.981740	.018260
43	10.0209	.982049	.017951	43	9.8340	.983400	.016600
44	10.0373	.983651	.016349	44	9.8491	.984909	.015091
45	10.0521	.985110	.014890	45	9.8628	.986281	.013719
46	10.0657	.986439	.013561	46	9.8753	.987528	.012472
47	10.0781	.987649	.012351	47	9.8866	.988662	.011338
48	10.0893	.988752	.011248	48	9.8969	.989693	.010307
49	10.0995	.989756	.010244	49	9.9063	.990630	.009370
50	10.1089	.990670	.009330	50	9.9148	.991481	.008519
51	10.1174	.991503	.008497	51	9.9226	.992256	.007744
52	10.1251	.992261	.007739	52	9.9296	.992960	.007040
53	10.1322	.992952	.007048	53	9.9360	.993600	.006400
54	10.1386	.993581	.006419	54	9.9418	.994182	.005818
55	10.1444	.994154	.005846	55	9.9471	.994711	.005289
56	10.1498	.994676	.005324	56	9.9519	.995191	.004809
57	10.1546	.995151	.004849	57	9.9563	.995629	.004371
58	10.1590	.995584	.004416	58	9.9603	.996026	.003974
59	10.1630	.995978	.004022	59	9.9639	.996387	.003613
60	10.1667	.996337	.003663	60	9.9672	.996716	.003284

861

Section 1

Table S (10.0)
Single Life Factors Based on Life Table 90CM
Interest at 10.0 Percent

Age	Annuity	Life Estate	Remainder	Age	Annuity	Life Estate	Remainder
0	9.8484	.98484	.01516	55	8.3843	.83843	.16157
1	9.9309	.99309	.00691	56	8.2907	.82907	.17093
2	9.9316	.99316	.00684	57	8.1931	.81931	.18069
3	9.9298	.99298	.00702	58	8.0920	.80920	.19080
4	9.9267	.99267	.00733	59	7.9877	.79877	.20123
5	9.9225	.99225	.00775	60	7.8804	.78804	.21196
6	9.9176	99176	.00824	61	7.7696	77696	.22304
7	9.9119	.99119	.00881	62	7.6549	.76549	.23451
8	9.9055	.99055	.00945	63	7.5359	.75359	.24641
9	9.8981	.98981	.01019	64	7.4130	.74130	.25870
10	9.8897	.98897	.01103	65	7.2860	.72860	.27140
11	9.8804	.98804	.01196	66	7.1544	.71544	.28456
12	9.8701	98701	.01299	67	7.0177	70177	.29823
13	9.8593	.98593	.01407	68	6.8760	.68760	.31240
14	9.8486	.98486	.01514	69	6.7297	67297	.32703
15	9.8383	.98383	.01617	70	6.5796	.65796	.34204
16	9.8286	98286	.01714	71	6.4264	.64264	.35736
17	9.8194	.98194	.01806	72	6.2707	.62707	.37293
18	9.8106	.98106	.01894	73	6.1128	.61128	.38872
19	9.8016	98016	.01984	74	5.9521	59521	40479
20	9.7921	.97921	02079	75	5.7877	.57877	.42123
21	9.7820	.97820	.02180	76	5.6189	56189	.43811
22	9.7714	.97714	.02286	77	5.4457	54457	45543
23	9.7600	97600	.02400	78	5.2683	52683	47317
24	9.7478	.97478	.02522	79	5.0878	.50878	.49122
25	9.7344	.97344	.02656	80	4.9061	49061	.50939
26	9.7198	97198	.02802	81	4.7246	47246	.52754
27	9.7038	.97038	.02962	82	4.5443	45443	.54557
28	9.6867	.96867	.03133	83	4.3654	.43654	.56346
29	9.6682	.96682	.03318	84	4.1866	.41866	.58134
30	9.6485	.96485	.03515	85	4.0066	.40066	.59934
31	9.6275	.96275	.03725	86	3.8272	.38272	.61728
32	9.6052	.96052	.03948	87	3.6511	.36511	.63489
33	9.5812	.95812	.04188	88	3.4787	.34787	.65213
34	9.5556	.95556	.04444	89	3.3100	.33100	.66900
35	9.5282	.95282	.04718	90	3.1453	.31453	.68547
36	9.4988	.94988	.05012	91	2.9877	.29877	.70123
37	9.4675	.94675	.05325	92	2.8407	.28407	.71593
38	9.4338	.94338	.05662	93	2.7043	.27043	.72957
39	9.3977	.93977	.06023	94	2.5763	25763	.74237
40	9.3589	.93589	.06411	95	2.4540	.24540	.75460
41	9.3172	.93172	.06828	96	2.3383	23383	.76617
42	9.2723	.92723	.07277	97	2.2307	.22307	.77693
43	9.2242	.92242	.07758	98	2.1292	.21292	.78708
44	9.1728	.91728	.08272	99	2.0296	.20296	.79704
45	9.1183	.91183	.08817	100	1.9322	.19322	.80678
46	9.0605	.90605	.09395	101	1.8357	.18357	.81643
47	8.9996	.89996	.10004	102	1.7404	.17404	.82596
48	8.9354	.89354	.10646	103	1.6456	.16456	.83544
49	8.8678	.88678	.11322	104	1.5437	.15437	.84563
50	8.7963	.87963	.12037	105	1.4443	.14443	.85557
51	8.7211	.87211	.12789	106	1.3145	.13145	.86855
52	8.6423	.86423	.13577	107	1.1553	.11553	.88447
53	8.5600	.85600	.14400	108	.9016	.09016	.90984
54	8.4740	.84740	.15260	109	.4545	.04545	.95455

INDEX

References are to pages

†